D1241620

Social Deviance and Crime

An Organizational and Theoretical Approach

Charles R. Tittle
Washington State University

Raymond Paternoster
University of Maryland

Roxbury Publishing Company
Los Angeles, California

Library of Congress Cataloging-in-Publication Data

Tittle, Charles R.
Social deviance and crime: an organizational and theoretical approach / Charles R. Tittle
p. cm.
Includes bibliographical references and index.
ISBN 1-891487-37-X
1. Deviant behavior. 2. Criminal behavior. I. Paternoster, Raymond. II. Title.
HM811.T58 2000
302.5'42—dc21   99-34800
                                                                            CIP

Social Deviance and Crime: An Organizational and Theoretical Approach

Publisher: Claude Teweles
Supervising Editor: Dawn VanDercreek
Developmental Editor: Arlyne Lazerson
Production Editor: Carla Max-Ryan
Production Assistants: Renée Burkhammer, Josh Levine
Typography: Synergistic Data Systems
Cover Design: Marnie Kenney

Printed on acid-free paper in the United States of America. This paper meets the standards for recycling of the Environmental Protection Agency.

ISBN: 1-891487-37-X

Note to instructors: A comprehensive *Instructor's Manual/Testing Program* is available on disk or in bound format. There is also a dedicated *Student Website* accessible through Roxbury's website.

ROXBURY PUBLISHING COMPANY
P.O. Box 491044
Los Angeles, California 90049-9044
Tel.: (310) 473-3312 • Fax: (310) 473-4490
E-mail: roxbury@roxbury.net
Website: www.roxbury.net

*Dedicated with unlimited love to our spouses,
Debra Curren and Ronet Bachman: what poor
wretches we would be without them.*

Brief Contents

Detailed Contents

Part II
Explanations of Deviance and Crime

Preface

Deviant and criminal behaviors are fascinating to study—partly because the same behaviors are sometimes socially unacceptable or illegal and sometimes not, and partly because it is a puzzle why and how people differ in criminal or deviant behavior. In this book we give the reader an overview of scholarly thought about deviance and crime, but we do so in an unusual way that attempts to enhance inherent curiosity while preserving the intellectual integrity of the subject matter.

As our title, *Social Deviance and Crime*, suggests, we attempt to unite two scholarly topics—the study of deviance and the study of criminal behavior—that have typically been treated as separate phenomena. Traditionally, textbooks about social deviance have proceeded by introducing students to a series of specific deviant acts, such as mentally ill behaviors, alcohol abuse, prostitution, homosexuality, drug use, and so on. These deviant behaviors are usually portrayed as sharing little common conceptual ground, and they are treated as if they had separate, distinct causes. Books concerning crime have followed a similar path. Criminology textbooks typically describe a series of separate criminal acts, such as theft, white-collar crime, rape, homicide, auto theft, "victimless" crime, and so on. These behaviors are treated as if illegality is the only thing they have in common.

To some extent these standard textbook treatments correspond with practices among scholars. Although those who study deviance and those who study crime have sometimes argued that deviant/criminal acts share many essential features, and are subject to explanation by general theories, there have been few systematic attempts to link deviant and criminal categories. For the most part, deviant acts have been conceptualized as different from criminal acts, and treatments of the two have proceeded along two parallel tracks, with little or no convergence.

This book is built around an entirely different perspective. We view acts of social deviance and most acts of crime as conceptually similar. Both categories encompass behaviors that are socially disapproved. We differentiate specific acts, whether criminal or not, by the extent to which they are socially unacceptable. Further, we argue that socially disapproved conduct is potentially explicable by similar theories regardless of the legal status of particular acts. Therefore, this book differs from most others because it connects and unites criminal and deviant acts through common conceptual and explanatory schemes.

In addition, this book is meant to be conceptually distinct. Texts in the sociology of deviance and in criminology typically adopt either an "interactionist/constructionist" or a "substantive" orientation. Interactionist/constructionist books are mainly concerned with how some behaviors come to be criminal or deviant, and how some people come to be regarded as deviant persons or come to be ensnared in the criminal justice system. The focus is mainly on "the problematic nature of social reality" and on "negotiated" outcomes. A major theme of such books is how a person accused, or guilty, of some act acquires and manages a deviant identity or escapes stigma. Substantive textbooks, on the other hand, usually select a series of specific behaviors that are generally socially disapproved or that are the objects of official efforts at social control. Since each behavior is assumed to be a separate and distinct phenomenon, each is described, variations in it and among those who do it are outlined, and ad hoc explanations are presented.

We depart from both these approaches by treating deviance/crime as a unitary phenomenon, specific instances of which are differentiated mainly by how well organized their practitioners typically are. We build on a theme first developed by Joel Best and David Luckenbill in their book *Organizing Deviance*. We contend that organizational characteristics of a deviant behavior or a crime provide the key to whether extant theories provide adequate explanations for particular forms of crime or deviance. To differentiate degrees of organization, we spell out nine aspects, or indicators. On the basis of these indicators, we show that all deviant/criminal behaviors fall somewhere on a continuum from almost no organization to full organization. For simplicity, we divide this continuum into three distinct zones—individualistic, subcultural, and fully organized—and argue that it is useful to treat any type of deviant/criminal act as falling in one of these three zones. To illustrate this, we describe two specific forms of each general type of deviance and try to show that their positions on the continuum of deviance organization must be taken into account in order to explain and to understand them.

In addition to conceptualizing deviance/crime around degrees of practitioner organization, we focus mainly on trying to answer the questions of "why" and "how" deviant/criminal behavior occurs. We contend that there are similar causal explanations for deviant/criminal acts that have the same level of organization, and we explicate and apply general theories that pertain to those similarly organized forms of deviance or crime. These general theories are discussed within a fourfold classification scheme that derives from simultaneous consideration of the main location of the causal element of the theory (in the person or in the situation/context) along with the nature of the cause (motivational or constraint). We argue that many existing theories of deviance and crime contain some explanatory value, but all of them have gaps or weaknesses that limit their applicability and usefulness. Because of this, we contend that theoretical integration is necessary for a comprehensive explanation of deviance/crime, and we present one example of a contemporary integrated theory. The book also addresses questions about how and why some acts become deviant or illegal. In addition, it examines variations in rates of crime/deviance from place to place and time to time, and brings existing theories to bear in trying to explain such differences. Further, it describes and applies ad hoc explanations to general variations in deviance (such as age, sex, place of residence, and the like).

In sum, we offer a unique perspective for the study of deviance and crime. How the book conceptualizes its subject matter, the expectations it has for theory, and the comprehensiveness of its accounts for known variations in deviance/crime will be unfamiliar to most instructors who might use the book, and, of course, totally new to most students. We are challenging teachers to look at a familiar set of topics with a fresh new perspective, and we are challenging students to think about deviance and crime as an intellectually intriguing puzzle.

Although we have tried to focus on the inherent interest people have in the study of deviance and crime, we have also honored the complexity of the subject matter. Contrary to much popular opinion, deviant and criminal behaviors are not simple or easily understood. As difficult as some of the material is, we have tried to present it in an engaging way, relying on numerous examples. However, because we respect the teachers and students who will use this book, we refused to distort or "dumb down" the treatment. As a result, comprehension of some of the material requires careful study. We began with the premise that our readers, both students and fellow faculty, deserved a serious and comprehensive approach. The book is intended to be a work of scholarship as well as a teaching tool. We wanted to challenge and push students and teachers to think about crime and deviance in new ways, and to honor and pay homage to their intelligence and curiosity.

We owe many debts in the preparation of the book. First and foremost we acknowledge the patience, support, and advice of our spouses, Debra A. Curran and Ronet Bachman. In addition, we wish to thank the reviewers of the manuscript, who provided much useful feedback. They include: Patricia Adler, University of Colorado at Boulder; Peter Adler, University of Denver; Tom Bernard, Pennsylvania State University; Mitchell Chamlin, University of Cincinnati; David Curry, University of Missouri at St. Louis; Janet Hankin, Wayne State University; Alexis Piquero, Temple University; Frank Scarpitti, University of Delaware; and Richard A. Wright, Arkansas State University. Finally, we appreciate the excellent copyediting by Arlyne Lazerson.

Part I

Deviance and Crime as Social Phenomena

Misbehavior is a fact of life. In every society or social group some people, at least sometimes, do things that others find objectionable or that elicit punitive reactions of one type or another. This book is about those misbehaviors. It is divided into two parts. Part I, encompassing the first nine chapters, provides insight into the meaning of misbehavior, which is called deviance, and how it is manifested. It addresses the questions of why and how various kinds of conduct come to be regarded as inappropriate or wrong, and it describes the characteristics and patterns of various forms of deviant behavior.

Chapter 1

Deviance/Crime and Deviant/ Criminal Persons

This book is about deviance, or deviant behavior. These terms may be confusing to you at first because the word "deviance" is not one widely used by lay persons. Citizens often think of some behaviors as being illegal, weird, bizarre, or even immoral, but rarely do they regard them as being "deviant." "Deviance" is a term used by social scientists, mainly sociologists, to denote behaviors that are socially disapproved—regarded by most people in a given group as bad or immoral, illegal, or simply subject to social sanctions. To a sociologist, the term "deviance" has a special meaning. It conveys the idea that some particular behavior is in one way or another inconsistent with the standards of acceptable conduct prevailing in a given social group. Although most sociologists accept this general conceptualization, they disagree about a precise definition of deviance because they use different approaches in trying to determine exactly what the standards of conduct are in a given group (Gibbs, 1981). At least five ways of defining standards of conduct can be used. Let us consider each of these five and then decide which, if any, seems to be most helpful in understanding human behavior.

Conceptualizations of Deviance

In this discussion keep in mind that definitions are always arbitrary. A definition is not true or false; it is simply a guideline for identifying some phenomenon of interest to the scholar. Yet, definitions are extremely important. Communication requires that the reader know what he or she has in mind is the same thing the scholar has in mind when the word "deviant" is used. Definitions serve that denoting function. Moreover, in this context no definition is inherently better than another. The idea is to focus on behaviors whose study will broaden our understanding of society. Different approaches reflect the judgment of different scholars about what is most crucial for that purpose.

The Statistical Approach

In our quest for a conceptualization of deviance, we might consider standards of conduct as empirical expressions of the way people in a particular group actually behave (Wilkins, 1965). If most people smoke cigarettes, this could be taken as proof that cigarette smoking is "normal" in that group. Conversely, failure to smoke cigarettes in a social group in which most people do smoke would qualify as atypical, or deviant, behavior from the statistical point of view. From such a perspective, skydiving, eating snails, pledging oneself to celibacy, and murder are all deviant in the United States since they are all statistically unusual. On the other hand, smoking marijuana, speeding, "fudging" on one's income tax, and adultery would possibly all be conforming behaviors since they are (presumably) currently committed by a large proportion, if not a majority, of the population. And, of course, wearing clothes, marrying, and eating with a fork would unquestionably qualify as normal.

The statistical approach has the advantage of accurately reflecting an important aspect of contemporary social reality. There is a tendency for many people to assume that something that "everybody does" cannot be in violation of conduct standards. Indeed, a frequent justification for a person's action, particularly if that person is being sanctioned for the act, is to claim that everybody else, most others, or even lots of others do it. The following kinds of rationales are frequently heard: "Everybody speeds; how can it be wrong?" "Most people pilfer from their employers; it is the accepted thing." "All Presidents lie to the people or obstruct justice (even if not caught); why pick on Richard Nixon or Bill Clinton?" And it is surely the case that some people decide what to do primarily by watching what others are doing.

Furthermore, the statistical approach is relatively simple to apply, at least logically. We might simply collect information concerning the prevalence or frequency of a particular behavior, then array the data and calculate the mean (average) and standard deviation (dispersion around the mean). If the objective is to distinguish deviant from nondeviant categories of behavior, we would arbitrarily decide a cutting point; or if we wish to differentiate degrees of deviance, every act could be expressed in units of standard deviations from the mean (standard scores). One might decide that any behavior falling within two standard deviations of the mean (or one or three) is conforming, while any behavior outside that range is deviant. Or alternatively we might say that any behavior is as deviant as the magnitude of its standard score (meaning that the more it exceeds the mean in either direction, the greater its deviance). The main problem with such applications is that hard empirical evidence of the frequency or prevalence of a behavior can rarely be obtained.

Despite the simplicity of this approach, and the fact that it apparently corresponds with the everyday thinking of many people, there are good reasons why it is not the best method of identifying standards of conduct and defining deviance. For one thing, closer observation shows that statistical standards only superficially reflect how social groups, in fact, formulate standards of conduct. Most people in the United States, for example, would feel uncomfortable in classifying behaviors like church tithing, abstinence from cigarette smoking, and maintenance of premarital sexual virginity (all atypical behaviors) as inappropriate conduct. There is an underlying feeling by most that even though they are unusual, these behaviors are somehow "good" and acceptable, even desirable and to be encouraged. Similarly, most people feel some discomfort in defining behavior like adultery, lying to one's spouse or sweetheart, speeding, or pilfering from an employer as appropriate, even though they are frequently committed by a large proportion of the populace. On the other hand, most can easily accept the inappropriateness of acts that are atypical in the other direction—more evil, unacceptable, or undesirable than the average—as being beyond normal standards of conduct. These apparent inconsistencies expressed by ordinary citizens suggest that they are mainly concerned with evaluations of conduct, not just frequency. People judge rightness and wrongness, and they think of social norms in terms of what people "ought" to do. It is not difficult to recognize that the logical end point of statistical reasoning about norms would be a conclusion that rape, murder, and child abuse could all be appropriate conduct if enough people did them. This disturbs most people—even those who actually commit these acts. It appears, therefore, that common applications of statistical standards in judging the deviance of behavior are, in reality, more likely to be rationalizations for misconduct than real normative standards. It would be misleading to accept them as fundamental defining characteristics of deviance.

Moreover, there is little about atypicality of behavior that is sociologically interesting or that enlightens us about society. Consider again skydiving, celibacy, and murder. Skydiving is a recreational sport enjoyed by a few adventurers. The rest of society generally has little opinion about its appropriateness or its rightness or wrongness; it produces few consequences for society as a whole or for those who practice it; and its explanation is probably far more interesting to psychologists and psychiatrists than to sociologists. Celibacy, by contrast, usually grows out of a religious pledge made by a few who are highly honored for having done so, but beyond the psychological features of religious commitment and the sociological aspects of group influence, there is little of explanatory import or social significance. Moreover, it challenges one's intellect to grasp the similarity of celibacy and skydiving as forms of deviance. Finally, murder appears to be totally unlike either celibacy or skydiving, both in the psychology of the action and in the way the behavior is viewed by others. Unlike celibacy and skydiving, murder evokes much interest from social scientists and lay persons. But it is interesting, not for its rarity, but because most people believe murder is morally wrong or dangerous or threatening to the continuation of society. Thus, it appears that if we are to understand society we must use some method of identifying conduct standards (and thereby deviance) other than simple frequency of occurrence.

The Absolutist Approach

Another approach we might use to identify deviant behavior applies conduct standards set down by a social scientist (or group of social scientists) to all groups and individuals under study. With an absolutist orientation, we would decide what is good, useful, or just, and then measure deviations from those evaluative criteria. Two prominent lines of theoretical thinking in sociology often use this procedure. The first is functionalism.

Functional theorists view society as an interdependent mechanism much like a biological organism. All parts that work together are regarded as essential, and in that sense "good," or nondeviant. But just as a human body sometimes suffers disease, malformation, or self-destructive activities, a society sometimes contains dysfunctional (dangerous or destructive) elements (see Gross, 1959). For functionalists, any behavior that they regard as bad for society would be considered dysfunctional or deviant, regardless of the frequency of its occurrence or whether the people in that society disapprove of the behavior. Most of those who use this approach assume, however, that societies will usually condone those behaviors that are inherently good and will condemn those that are inherently bad. Indeed, it has been argued that the reason contemporary societies have survived throughout history is because they, in fact, practiced and condoned useful behavior while avoiding and disapproving dangerous behavior. Presumably, social groups that failed to do this sealed their fates and were eliminated in the historical evolutionary process (Parsons, 1951).

Functionalists assume that an investigator can, through logic and research, actually determine what is good for a society. For example, incest (sexual relations between relatives) is thought by functionalists to be dysfunctional for society (Davis, 1950; Murphy, 1980; Westermarck, 1922; Wilson, 1978). It is said that if widely practiced, incest could lead to biological deterioration of the population and that even if there were no biological danger, incest has the potential for destroying orderly social relations and disrupting the mechanisms for efficient child rearing. A father having sexual relations with a daughter, for example, jeopardizes his authority over her and places him in competition with suitors for her affections. The absence of authority makes effective socialization impossible, and sexual entanglement removes any incentive the father has for encouraging the daughter to mature and ultimately leave the family of origin to establish a family of her own. At the same time, the mother in such a family is cast as a competitor with the daughter for the father's affection and attention. This undermines the mother's relationship with the girl and inhibits her ability to train the child for adulthood. Under such circumstances the family may dissolve in conflict, but even if it does not, the daughter will not be successfully trained for a productive role in society. Therefore, to the extent that incest is widely practiced, it threatens the very fabric of society. According to some sociologists, therefore, it is obvious that incest is inherently deviant because it is socially dangerous. Moreover, they believe that most members of any existing society will disapprove of incest and will refrain from practicing it. This is because only those societies that in the past developed and enforced social rules prohibiting incest would have survived to be represented in the contemporary world. Similar arguments can be made for murder, rape, assault, homosexuality, child abuse, mental illness, and other behaviors.

Another set of absolutist thinkers employ a different rationale. Radical, Marxian, and humanist scholars often maintain that a sensitive and informed researcher can apply absolute moral standards to behavior in any given society or in any specific situation to decide whether various activities are unjust or evil (deviant) (Schwendinger and Schwendinger, 1974, 1983). Some believe that any behavior that results in exploitation of one person or a category of persons for the benefit of another or that threatens the dignity and quality of life for specific people and humanity as a whole is inherently evil, and thereby deviant (Simon and Eitzen, 1993). Others contend that any behavior causing people to suffer or violating any person's right to self-actualization and freedom is inherently immoral, or deviant (Platt, 1994). Marxists, for instance, point to the exploitative nature of economic relations in capitalistic societies and regard this inherent exploitation, along with the selfish and insensitive acts it breeds, as deviant or "criminal" because it corrupts human qualities (Bonger, 1916; Quinney, 1979, 1980). Similarly, humanists regard racial discrimination as deviant because it deprives a whole group of equal rights and human dignity.

Absolutist approaches have the virtue of making cross-cultural comparisons easier by providing an invariant (albeit subjective) standard of judgment. In addition, they tend to portray deviant behavior as a societal phenomenon, which gives broader sweep to the study of deviance. Absolutists do not bother with merely atypical behaviors or those disapproved by the people in a social group. Rather, they focus on behaviors that seem to have larger implications for society and the quality of life, regardless of their typicality or position on the continuum of public opinion. Hence, the main appeal of an absolutist approach to the study of deviance is that it forces adherents to wrestle with fundamental moral questions about social life.

Nevertheless, there are problems with an absolutist approach serious enough to render it inadequate for our purposes. It assumes that any trained (sensitized), careful observer can determine what is good or bad for society, what is contrary to human dignity, and what is fair or unfair. In practice, however, there is great disagreement among social scientists about these matters. What one observer believes to be functional for a society, another may find dysfunctional. Abortion, for instance, may be functional (it prevents overpopulation and promotes freedom of choice for women, thereby improving the quality of life and reducing exploitation) or dysfunctional (it undermines population maintenance and threatens the fundamental value of human life, which is presumably the basis for organized society). It has even been argued that a certain amount of deviance itself may benefit society because it serves as a safety valve to release pent-up frustrations; it helps define acceptable behavior; and it promotes group solidarity (Dentler and Erikson, 1959). Clearly, deciding what is "good" for society is largely arbitrary and subjective. Furthermore, concepts like "justice," "goodness," or "exploitation" depend completely on the definer's values. One person's justice is another person's exploitation, and good or evil are necessarily in the eyes of a beholder. There is no reason to believe that the values of social scientists are in any way superior, more desirable, or more defensible than those of anyone else, or that the values of any particular social scientist are any more justifiable than those of another social scientist. Consequently, using an absolutist approach in the study of deviance in any consistent and meaningful way is impossible.

The Legalistic Approach

A third way of identifying conduct standards that would help define deviant behavior is by reference to law. We could simply use illegality as the criterion of whether a given activity is in violation of behavioral norms. Accordingly, if the law prohibits an act, it would be deviant; and if the law requires an act, failure to perform it would be deviant. If the law is silent about or permits an act, that act would be considered consistent with conduct standards, or conforming.

The rationale for a legal criterion of deviance might differ depending on how we want to view the nature of law. We could imagine that the law expresses collective sentiments indicating that particular activities are regarded as dangerous or threatening enough to require efforts at control (see Tittle, 1994). Although recognizing that law-making is a political process that often reflects conflicting interests and the clash of power, we might nevertheless believe that, in the main, law reflects popular sentiment as well as efforts to promote the public good. We might assume this because power holders must, in the long run, accommodate to the opinions of their constituents and recognize public interests, or face revolt. Or we might assume collective sentiment because elites, acting in their own interests, not only make laws but also use their power to forge collective opinion favorable to those laws, thereby producing consistency between the law and public opinion. In any case, law could be regarded as the embodiment of the significant behavioral standards in a given society.

On the other hand, we might reject a consensual view of law but still accept illegality as a workable criterion of behavioral standards. From this perspective, law is almost totally an instrument by which the powerful maintain their elite positions and protect their privileges. Still, we could accept illegality as the appropriate criterion of behavioral standards because conformity and deviance are inherently whatever people powerful enough to impose their own views say they are. Norms, or conduct standards, are by their very nature products of "definitions of the situation" imposed upon a social group by power elites (McCaghy, 1976; Quinney, 1970).

Still another approach is to view law as a combination of popular sentiment and elite desires. We could contend that some law expresses consensus among the population (such as laws prohibiting assault, murder, child abuse) while other laws reflect the desires of special interests (such as laws prohibiting importation of competitive products, requiring licensing to provide certain services, or denying the right of laborers to strike). From this viewpoint, whether law is collectively or particularistically oriented is irrelevant. Whatever its character, law nevertheless expresses coercive potential—a key element of behavior norms. Thus, the conduct rules that matter are those that can be enforced. Since law reflects behavioral rules backed up by power of enforcement, it necessarily encompasses conduct norms—at least those worth social scientists' study.

A legalistic approach has the advantage of being straightforward and usually easily applied (since one need only examine the codification of laws), and it ties into an extremely important element of social life—the exercise of political power. Yet the legalistic conceptualization of deviance is not generally satisfactory. For one thing, not all societies have a clearly defined body of written statutes that can be identified as law. Primitive societies, for example, have what would be recognized as deviant behavior but no formally written law that defines it as such (Malinowski, 1926, 1927; Hoebel, 1960, 1968). A legalistic approach can be used effectively only in the study of modern, literate societies. To use it elsewhere requires decisions about what law is, thus assuming the resolution of a prior definitional problem. For instance, among the Cheyenne Indians who lived on the American plains, the ultimate wrong was to kill another Cheyenne, because it was believed that such an act bloodied the sacred arrows, thereby jeopardizing the ability of the entire tribe to survive and prosper (Llewellyn and Hoebel, 1941). Actual cases of such killings were managed through a routinized procedure and decisions were enforced by coercive power (Grinnell, 1972; Hoebel, 1960, 1968). Many would say this treatment indicates a legal process; therefore, killing of one Cheyenne by another was illegal and thereby deviant. But not all social scientists would agree, since there were no codified statutes among the Cheyenne.

What of the case of a Cheyenne woman who absconded with a lover? A Cheyenne woman's first husband was chosen for her by a brother, and marriages were usually arranged in consideration of a bride's price. Some women occasionally overcame a bad fraternal choice by running off with the man they really wanted to marry. In such cases the angered husband might do any number of things, but by the time the offending couple returned to camp several weeks later, he had usually cooled off and was willing to accept compensation. Observers report that the Cheyenne people regarded such behavior by a woman as inappropriate and bad, with great potential for causing disruption and problems for the tribe as a whole. But whether it was illegal and thereby deviant by a legalistic definition is debatable.

Second, many activities that are illegal are sociologically uninteresting, particularly since illegality may express antiquated sentiments of both the general population and the ruling elites. For instance, most states in the United States have laws prohibiting sale of tobacco products to minors. Yet such products are easily available in vending machines to all who care to purchase them; minors are officially accorded the right to smoke in designated areas by many schools; it is rare for the police to arrest anyone for selling tobacco to minors; and most people may not regard such sales as bad, dangerous, or abnormal (although public opinion about this appears to be undergoing a change). On what grounds, then, could one claim it to be deviant in a sociologically meaningful sense? The problem is that laws are rarely repealed, so when they become obsolete they simply fall into disuse.

Third, many activities are sociologically interesting because they seem to have important implications for society and because they appear to be inconsistent with general conduct standards, yet they are not illegal. For instance, it is not a crime to lie to one's spouse or sweetheart. Yet a three-state survey in 1972 showed that a large proportion of the people disapproved of it (Tittle, 1980b). Similarly, it is not illegal in many places to operate a topless bar, yet when such an establishment opens, it is frequently met with scorn, protests, and sometimes violent opposition by neighbors. Further, rarely do legal statutes prohibit eating human flesh, yet it is clearly outside the bounds of acceptable conduct in the United States.

Finally, although the legal process is an important one, it is not the only realm of human interaction. Conduct norms are ubiquitous at all levels of social organization from the interpersonal to the societal. Much can be learned about social organization and human behavior by studying violations of social rules that characterize nonpolitical entities. A legalistic approach, therefore, narrowly focuses attention on one tier of a multitiered system.

The Reactive Approach

A fourth way of defining conduct standards is by the social reaction to behavior. According to the advocates of this definition, when a social reaction to some behavior is condemnatory, punitive, or simply disapproving, it indicates that the behavior is in violation of behavioral standards in that group and is therefore deviant. Several variations of the reactive approach are possible. One is to emphasize the "typical" reaction to a class of behaviors. Another is to stress social reaction to particular instances of behavior while assuming that this particular reaction implies nothing about the deviance of the entire class of behaviors of which the particular case is an instance. Such basic differences are complicated by questions concerning which part of the social system must react negatively to qualify something as deviant. Some emphasize negative reactions by official agents and functionaries, but others accord more importance to informal reactions by a collective social audience.

Probably the best-known reactive approach to deviance is that embodied in the "labeling perspective." Labeling theorists are not all in agreement about what they are focusing on, and they are sometimes ambiguous in presentation. Nevertheless, most scholars agree that the predominant concern of the labeling perspective is legal reaction to *specific* acts, particularly the reaction of agents of the criminal justice system (such as police) to particular instances of behavior disapproved of by power holders, whose interests are embodied in the legal codes (Gove, 1980). Accordingly, some labeling proponents recognize no categories or classes of deviant behavior. To them, murder, rape, child abuse, or smoking marijuana are not necessarily deviant in the United States. Rather, specific acts of murder, rape, child abuse, or marijuana use may or may not be deviant depending upon whether officials arrest the perpetrator and label him/her as deviant. When labeling occurs, the particular act of murder, rape, child abuse, or marijuana use is deviant; otherwise, it isn't.

Some labeling theorists are more restrictive in what they define as deviant. They maintain that an act is not deviant unless and until a collective social audience has accepted the label of deviant for the act and/or the perpetrator. It is said that a label attached by officials must "stick"; that is, it must be recognized by the social audience and serve as the vehicle through which the group attributes bad character to the actor, or attributes badness to the act (Becker, 1963; Kitsuse, 1962).

Another way of applying a reactionist definition would be to accept the deviant nature of general categories of behavior, and use group attribution as the defining characteristic. Accordingly, if a social collectivity or its chief representatives *typically* react negatively to some behavior or *typically* attach a stigma to those who are caught, that kind of behavior would be deviant even if a particular perpetrator escapes being labeled; if people typically commit the behavior; if the conduct is unimportant for societal maintenance; or if the act is, in fact, legal. For instance, if a social group usually shows its condemnation of some class of behaviors by punishing specific acts of that class, or if it usually attributes bad character to those who commit such acts, then theorists would assume that in that social group those behaviors are deviant. Using this approach, we would treat apprehension and punishment, or group attribution of bad character, for a specific act as problematic—not as defining traits. For instance, if, in a given community, horse thieves are usually hanged by mobs when caught, using a reactionist's approach, we would consider horse theft to be deviant behavior in that community. And any particular act of horse thievery would be deviant even though the thief escaped, or if caught, managed to persuade the mob through bribery to let him get away.

A reactive definition has much to recommend. It identifies as deviant behavior acts that are clearly disapproved, either by officials or by group members. Moreover, these acts are at least considered important enough by key functionaries of the social system to warrant attention; that is, people think they need to "do something about" the behavior in question. This approach is conceptually clear, since it is relatively easy to think in terms of actual reaction to behavior. In addition, most things identified as being deviant by any other approach to deviant definition are usually also identified as deviant by a reactive approach—at least by the broader versions of that approach that recognize *categories* of deviant behavior.

There are problems, however, with a reactive definition of deviance that make it less useful for our purposes than might at first appear. The main one is that many sociologically interesting behaviors that appear to be in violation of conduct standards are not necessarily the focus of negative reaction. For instance, adultery in the United States is almost never dealt with by the police or the courts, and it rarely results in a deviant label for the actor. Even when there are citizen complaints, the police normally refuse to make arrests (LaFave, 1965). Yet surveys show that most people believe adultery to be wrong, bad, or inappropriate, and it is thought by many sociologists to have crucial implications for a major social institution—the family.

Second, the police frequently arrest people, and courts sometimes impose severe penalties, for behaviors that are not widely disapproved and do not seem to be sociologically important. An example is marijuana use, particularly during the 1970s when casual use of marijuana was widespread, not only among college students but among working adults as well (Goode, 1993).

Third, the narrower reactive definitions create unusual conceptual inconsistencies. If murder is regarded as deviant only when discovered and reacted against by official agents, then it must also be regarded as conformity if the perpetrator escapes punishment—regardless of the number of group members who may disapprove of it, how socially dangerous it might be, or how many people do it. Moreover, according to this kind of reactive definition, deviance can only be studied on a case-by-case basis after the fact, thereby making generalization or consideration and explanation of categories of deviance impossible. Common sense suggests that something is wrong with such a formulation.

Finally, the difficulty of ascertaining, empirically, when labeling has occurred (is an arrest a labeling act, or must one be convicted?) or when a label sticks (how do we know the boundaries of a social audience, how many must accept the label?) renders some versions of the reactive approach completely unworkable.

The Group Evaluation Approach

A fifth method of identifying conduct standards is by reference to the beliefs or opinions of group members. According to this approach, behavior regarded as unacceptable, inappropriate, or morally wrong *in the opinion of* the members of a group would be deviant. Quite simply, deviance is behavior held in disrepute by the people in a given group. Underlying this conception of deviance is a general approach that assumes consensus among group members about rightness or wrongness and about how people ought to behave. If this assumption is correct, social disapproval indicates that some behavior is outside acceptable standards of conduct. And such disapproval would suggest deviance regardless of the typicality or prevalence of the behavior, whether anything is actually done about the offense, or whether the shared concepts about rightness or wrongness grew out of common experiences or out of careful socialization by particular interest groups with an investment in promoting specific ideas. For example, if adultery is negatively evaluated by most people in a defined social context, it is classified as deviant behavior even if most people in that same context actually practice it. Moreover, adultery is still considered deviant even if it is fully tolerated by the members of that group without any form of sanction being imposed or there being any law against it.

A group evaluation definition is advantageous in several respects. First, the approach is conceptually clear. The idea of collective sentiments is straightforward and easily grasped. Moreover, it has intuitive meaning for most scholars and students alike. Second, this approach provokes sociologically interesting questions. Contemplation of how behavior is evaluated immediately evokes the traditional question of why some people do disapproved things; it also suggests investigation of the social processes by which opinions come to be shared and changed, or come to activate collective responses to behavior. The evaluational perspective invites explanation of why some behaviors generally thought to be wrong are not prohibited by law or why some are prohibited by law while not generally being considered inappropriate. Moreover, a group evaluation approach leads to queries about why a majority might consider some behaviors wrong, despite their being frequently committed, or why some acts that are considered wrong elicit sanctions or other social reactions while acts similarly inappropriate are ignored. Third, the group evaluational definition allows deviance to be treated meaningfully as a continuous variable. Some actions are considered wrong by almost everybody while others are regarded as wrong by only a small proportion. Thus, behaviors can be more or less deviant, depending upon the proportion of group members who believe them to be unacceptable, or upon the intensity of disapproval. From a scientific standpoint, this kind of precision is desirable.

But, like the other approaches, there are defects in this one as well. The major problem is that the evaluational definition treats all group members' opinions as equal. But clearly the opinions of some components of any social system are more important than the opinions of others because some people can implement their opinions with coercive action, and some are more influential in persuading other people to their points of view. Second, one can question the usefulness of a definition of deviance that treats as a violation of conduct standards some act about which nothing is ever done and for which no sanctions are brought to bear. Third, efficient application of this approach requires survey data, that is, public opinion information about perceptions of conduct. Such information is rarely available for all the acts that one might want to consider as potentially deviant, and in some societies no survey data about any behavior are available. Finally, this approach assumes that the boundaries of groups are clear enough to permit scholars to ascertain the thoughts of most people within those boundaries about the appropriateness of various behaviors. In reality, however, group boundaries are seldom unambiguous, particularly in a heterogeneous society with overlapping subcultures and diverse group identities. Where one group ends and another begins is often an arbitrary decision, and so are decisions about group opinion of behaviors.

A Synthetic Approach

Although each of the methods for defining deviance just discussed has some merit, none provides an unambiguous, sociologically meaningful, or completely desirable method for identifying violations of conduct standards. The reactive and the group evaluation approaches appear to be the most attractive because they have intuitive appeal; they evoke sociologically interesting questions, the answers to which reveal a great deal about society; and they are conceptually straightforward and clear—although not necessarily clear-cut in application. These two approaches are especially salient in getting right to the essence of group processes. In reference to the everyday world, two things about behavior make it interesting for discussion as deviance: most people believe it is wrong and/or there are usually negative sanctions associated with the behavior. Therefore, this book espouses a definition of deviance combining elements of a reactive and group evaluation approach.

Specifically, deviance is defined as *any type of behavior that the majority of a given group regards as unacceptable or that evokes a collective response of a negative type*. In this definition, "unacceptable" means the behavior is disapproved, wrong, inappropriate, bad, abnormal—in short, behavior that a group evaluates negatively. "Majority" means that over half of the people in a specified, bounded group regard the behavior as unacceptable. This is an arbitrary cutoff point, but the main objective is not to classify behavior as simply deviant or conforming but rather to array behavior on a continuum from very nondeviant (hardly anybody considers it unacceptable) to very deviant (almost everybody in the group considers it unacceptable), with any particular act falling somewhere on the continuum. Collective response of a negative type implies that the majority of the specified group typically does something to express its displeasure, or the officials who possess coercive power over the members of the group typically respond to the behavior in a way that expresses negative evaluation. The four key components to this definition of deviance, then, are as follows:

1. A demarcated group
2. Behavior (not an individual's thoughts or state of being) or a category of similar behaviors and either
3. Majority disapproval or
4. Negative action by
   a. The collectivity as a whole, or
   b. Components of the group with power or authority to coerce

In applying this definition, note that behavior is classified as deviant when the climate of opinion in a group reflects general disapproval of the behavior. If most people in Alabama think that photographing a nude person is a bad thing, then that act will be, by our definition, deviant in that state, regardless of anything else. Citizens of Alabama need not do anything about nude photography, nor do the police have to arrest anybody for it. The fact of attitudinal disapproval qualifies the behavior as deviant and worthy of our attention. Behavior will also be classified as deviant when officials typically respond in negative ways to it. For example, if the police in Kansas City usually arrest people when they discover them smoking marijuana, by our definition marijuana smoking is deviant in Kansas City, regardless of anything else. If Kansas City marijuana smokers are usually ostracized by most other people in Kansas City, then it can be concluded that marijuana smoking is deviant behavior in that place. Furthermore, some behavior may be deviant in speci-

Deviance in Everyday Life

In probably most of the United States it is not considered "deviant" to act like one who holds and practices the Jewish faith. Being a member of the Jewish faith is considered to be no different from being a Protestant or Catholic. In some areas, for example certain sections of New York City, Jews make up a majority of the local population, and acting non-Jewish may be considered "abnormal." In Troy, Alabama, however, those practicing the Jewish faith may be seen and treated as deviant. At least that's what the family of Sue and Wayne Willis probably feels. Their 14-year-old son Paul Herring was required by the public school's vice-principal to write an essay on "Why Jesus Loves Me." When his brother David did not bow his head for a Christian prayer during a school assembly, a teacher forcefully lowered it for him. It is also alleged by the boys' parents that a teacher asked Paul to remove a Star of David lapel pin he was wearing one day because she said it was a prohibited gang symbol. When Mrs. Willis complained about the treatment her children were receiving, one teacher allegedly replied, "If parents will not save souls, we have to." In the overwhelmingly Christian schools of Troy, Alabama, then, acting in accordance with the Jewish faith may constitute deviant behavior. (Pressley, 1997)

fied groups both because popular opinion disapproves of it and because there is a collective negative reaction. For instance, most people in Iowa believe that stealing something worth fifty dollars is wrong, and the police typically arrest the thieves they discover. Hence, in Iowa stealing something worth fifty dollars is deviant because it is disapproved, but it is also deviant because it is collectively reacted against.

From our definition, it is clear that an act may be deviant by either of two criteria, perhaps by both, but not necessarily by both. For instance, most citizens of a particular state may regard adultery as wrong but do nothing about its occurrence, and the police may rarely or never make an arrest for this offense. Still, adultery would be deviant in that state by our definition because people disapprove of it. On the other hand, police may routinely arrest people for selling alcoholic beverages in a particular state although most citizens of that state may not regard the sale of alcoholic beverages as bad or wrong. Nevertheless, that behavior would still fit the definition of deviance set forth because of the typical police reaction. In many cases, of course, group opinion will match collective response. This is generally true everywhere in the United States for murder, rape, burglary, incest, and cannibalism. But there are numerous instances where the two do not match—such as gambling, marijuana use, manufacturing dangerous products, and polluting the environment. To understand these divergences is part of the challenge of our study of deviance.

Legality and Deviance

In this same vein, it is important to recognize that mere illegality is not a reliable guide to whether some behavior is deviant. Law does not necessarily reflect public opinion. Indeed, it often, if not usually, expresses the desires and interests of special power groups who are able to mobilize legislative support, many times in direct opposition to majority views. Moreover, even when law does embody collective sentiment at the time it is enacted, it may not do so at some later point in time. As noted before, laws are seldom modified quickly in response to changing circumstances. As opinion changes, a particular law may become more and more inconsistent with the views of the majority, and sometimes its enforcement becomes lax or completely ignored. By our definition, if this occurs, the prohibited behavior would not be deviant although it would continue to be illegal. An illustration is marijuana use in many U.S. communities. Although illegal, it is nevertheless not disapproved and seldom is the object of police efforts at enforcement.

Finally, some laws may actually be consistent with public opinion but may not be enforced. Laws prohibiting prostitution in many communities in the United States do express collective disapproval, but only rarely are they enforced. This is true sometimes because the difficulty of controlling prostitution makes it a low priority for police; sometimes there are simply too few resources for enforcement; and sometimes the police are in corrupt collusion with the practitioners. In this case, then, prostitution would be deviant because it is generally disapproved, but its illegality would not be the key determinant. Illegality must be thought of as a variable that may or may not characterize deviance, but it cannot be regarded as a crucial characteristic on the basis of the definition proposed in this book.

What Is Crime?

Up to this point we have been speaking of crime and deviance as if deviance were the only problematic element. Actually, conceptualizations of crime are as varied as are conceptualizations of deviance. For our purposes, crimes are those acts that are subject to specified penalties imposed in routinized ways by institutionalized functionaries who are recognized by most members of a given social group as having the power or authority to do so. Criminal behavior has the potential of receiving a previously specified penalty in a standardized way imposed by somebody who occupies a position especially designated for that purpose. For a particular behavior to be criminal, the potential sanctions must be known ahead of time by most of those subject to them, and they must be imposed in a routinized way; that is, they must be of a nature consistent with social rules or expectations of the members of a given social group, implemented in ways that conform to patterns of expectations shared by the members of the given group, and if the system lasts long enough, passed on from generation to generation.

In modern societies most criminal behavior is easily recognized because specific acts are prohibited in written legal statutes; punishments for those designated acts are codified; and the punishments are imposed by a set of functionaries whose main, or sometimes only, job is imposing sanctions. Such functionaries include police, court officers, and prison or probation officials. Not all criminal behavior is easily recognized, however. Some behaviors pose challenges to legal authorities; in fact, one of the purposes of courts is to decide if a given instance of a behavior falls within one of the categories prohibited in the law. A good example is pornography.

Deviance in Everyday Life

Pornography is very difficult to define with any degree of precision. What one person might think is pornographic, another might think is artistic. In addition, is all art that is erotic pornographic? The difficulty of defining pornography is not limited to lay persons. As the following excerpt from the United States Supreme Court case of *Jacobellis v. Ohio* demonstrates, pornography is not easy to define even for Supreme Court Justices, although we may all recognize it when we see it. In that case, Justice Stewart concluded that:

> . . . under the First and Fourteenth Amendments criminal laws in this area are constitutionally limited to hard-core pornography. I shall not today attempt further to define the kinds of material I understand to be embraced within that shorthand description; and perhaps I could never succeed in intelligibly doing so. But I know it when I see it, and the motion picture involved in this case is not that.

For another example of the difficulty in defining pornography see the *Tin Drum* controversy in Deviance in Everyday Life on a following page.

U.S. law has never been effective in exactly defining pornography, although there have been many statutes to prohibit or restrict its production, distribution, and consumption. For instance, if pornography is defined in terms of lewd or vulgar depictions, one has to decide the meaning of "lewd" and "vulgar," two words whose meanings are as dim as the meaning of pornography itself. If pornography is defined in terms of nudity, the dividing line between artistic presentations of the human body and pornography cannot be made. If pornography is defined in terms of behavior or presentations that shock common sensibilities or defy local standards of decency, one must be able to determine the local standards of decency.

Moreover, no matter how pornography is defined, one cannot know for sure that some activity involves behavior or depictions that meet particular legal criteria until *after* the behavior has occurred and the judicial process has unfolded. For instance, in Palm Beach County, Florida, in the 1970s certain movies were confiscated by the police as being pornographic by prevailing community standards, and the projectionist and theater owner were prosecuted. After a trial, however, the jury decided the material was not pornographic, so the defendants were acquitted. Undaunted, the local prosecutor and law enforcement officials confiscated more films and had another trial, only to have a jury decide a second time that the material was not pornographic. On the third try, the prosecutor was able to get a jury to judge the film in question to be pornographic. Triumphantly, he proclaimed that community standards had been upheld. But it is clear that the person showing those films could not have known for sure ahead of time whether they were in violation of the law; after all, two of three juries did not see such violation. In addition, one could question whether a jury reflects community standards, since it is not chosen by random sample. The fact is, although crime is *apparently* easily identified, numerous instances demonstrate that it is often problematic. Nonetheless, in the main we can identify criminal behavior *relatively easily*.

Deviance in Everyday Life

How do we decide and who decides what is pornographic or not? In Oklahoma City, Oklahoma, who decides what is pornographic may be Bob Anderson. Bob Anderson is not a judge, he is not even the police chief or head prosecutor. In 1997, Mr. Anderson was the director of an organization called Oklahomans for Children and Families, a conservative religious group. It seems that Mr. Anderson was listening to a religious program on the radio when he heard the host state that he believed the movie *The Tin Drum* was pornographic. Mr. Anderson never saw the 1979 Academy-Award-winning movie that was based on the novel by German author Gunter Grass, nor did he know what the film is about. This did not prevent Mr. Anderson from taking it upon himself to rid Oklahoma City video stores of the film. He convinced local criminal justice officials that the movie was pornographic, and they acted, removing it from video store shelves. They even went to those who had checked out the movie to retrieve it, threatening criminal prosecution. The book and movie is set in Nazi Germany and portrays a little boy named Oskar who, seeing the horrors of adult life around him, refuses to grow up. The material that was objectionable to Mr. Anderson was a 30-second sequence of the movie that implied, but did not show, oral sex between 11-year-old Oskar and a teenage girl. While perfectly acceptable viewing in almost every other locale, watching *The Tin Drum* may constitute pornographic activity in Oklahoma City.

But what about nonmodern societies where there are no written codes? Interestingly enough, such societies often have law, and the identification of criminal acts is often no more problematic than in modern societies (Hoebel, 1960, 1968). Consider the Cheyenne Indians. Although these were not literate people, they had an elaborate system of institutionalized actors and processes for dealing with acts that the people recognized as deserving of punishment. The most important law was that prohibiting killing of another Cheyenne. The Cheyenne believed that relationships between the people and the Great Spirit would be undermined if the "sacred arrows" were tainted by killing within the group. The consequences would be disastrous, since the Cheyenne depended upon the natural environment to provide their means of subsistence. To anger the Great Spirit was to jeopardize the survival of the group as a whole.

Despite this belief, however, an occasional homicide did occur. When it did, any witness was expected to notify the nearest group of fraternally organized hunters/warriors whose job included acting as a police force. This fraternal group would then take the suspect into custody until the case could be adjudicated by the tribal chiefs. The chiefs would meet, hear the facts, take testimony, weigh extenuating circumstances, and decide what to do with the killer; that is, they would decide the length of time the killer was to be banished. Punishment was always enforced separation from the tribe for a period of years. But before sentence was imposed, a messenger was sent back among the people to communicate the sentence the chiefs had tentatively decided. The people would then discuss the case until some consensus was reached. Perhaps the people initially thought the sentence was too long. The messenger would go back to the chiefs and tell them what the people were thinking. Then the chiefs would reconsider. This process continued until a mutually agreeable sentence was worked out, that is, until the chiefs and the people achieved a high degree of consensus, or at least an acceptable compromise. At this point the fraternal group would take the perpetrator, along with things he or she needed for survival, some distance from the tribe and leave him or her to fend alone until the sentence was completed or until the individual was able to achieve redemption. Clearly, then, among the Cheyenne, killing was punishable in a routinized and socially recognized way by institutionalized functionaries. Hence it was a crime (Llewellyn and Hoebel, 1941).

Our definition of crime, however, may raise some questions. For instance, in a university there is a cadre of officials who stand in readiness to impose specified sanctions upon students who violate particular rules. The imposition of sanctions is routinized (spelled out in university handbooks), and the officials imposing them occupy positions that are acknowledged to embody the authority and power to so act. Are those university regulations laws? And are their violations instances of crime? Our answer would be yes. Violation of university regulations embodies all the essential features to make it a crime. However, in any legal system, there are hierarchies of law. Some legal mechanisms are subordinate to others, so that whenever there is conflict between the requirements of one level of legality and those of another, the imperatives of the higher-ranked system prevail. Moreover, hierarchy of law means that some levels of law are restricted, usually in terms of the kinds of sanctions that can be imposed.

In the case of university regulations, penalties are usually restricted to deprivation of privileges associated with university attendance, denial of a degree, blockage of access to university programs, or financial penalties. University officials cannot incarcerate violators or physically harm them; those sanctions are reserved to a higher level of legality, like criminal courts. In addition, the rules of higher legal levels, such as state or Federal laws, to some extent must prevail in the university. Before students can be barred from a university they must be provided with some semblance of "due process," such as a hearing and access to representation. In other words, if the university acts arbitrarily without regard for routinized procedures, the student can probably get reinstated by appeal to a state court of higher law.

The point is that law operates in many more circumstances than most people realize, although it is not always recognized as law or called by that name. But does law also incorporate rules imposed by force, such as those set forth by occupying armies or by more powerful surrounding communities against subcultural groups? Here the answer is "maybe." If the occupying army "sets up shop" and punishes people in an arbitrary way for violation of regulations set forth by the military commander, then it is not law (it is more likely brute force). In such cases, violations are not crimes but might more appropriately be called rule defiance. However, if the military commander formulates a set of rules, describes a routinized procedure by which they are to be enforced, specifies the range of penalties to which a violator is subject, and publicizes these plans so that all, or at least most, who are subject to the penalties know of them and understand the process to be used, then violation becomes a crime—provided, of course, that the commander has the power to coerce compliance in case the people do not recognize his right to enforce the rules.

The same is true of laws formulated by dominant groups and enforced against subcultural or minority groups. Even though the Amish have their own system of laws (Hostetler, 1980; Kephart and Zellner, 1994), they also must conform to laws of the larger society. And the principles of hierarchy apply. As long as Amish law does not usurp the laws of the states where the Amish live (or Federal law) or extend into domains prohibited by the larger legal domain, they can operate. But the larger legal domain can insist upon its mandates because it has the power to coerce compliance, a power that rests on the recognition by most people in the outside society of the right of the institutionalized functionaries to so act.

Criminal and Deviant Behavior

As our description of law and crime makes clear, criminal behavior is a special category of conduct; acts that fit in that category may or may not be deviant. Consider the case of marijuana smoking. It is a crime in many states to possess marijuana or to use it (using it implies possession, of course). But in many of those states, this law is rarely enforced, and public opinion does not find marijuana smoking unacceptable. In Florida during the 1970s, for instance, it was a crime to possess and use marijuana. But anybody who attended a rock concert could see that thousands of individuals possessed and smoked marijuana during the performance despite the fact that there were dozens of police officers in the stadium directly observing this behavior. Moreover, even though there were no firm poll data on the subject, it is likely that the majority of people in South Florida did not regard marijuana smoking as an especially bad thing. Marijuana smoking was a crime, but it probably was not deviant.

Similarly, one might think about gambling. Most forms of gambling are illegal in some states. But in many of those states the law is not typically enforced and public opinion is tolerant of gambling. In fact, churches, volunteer fire companies, and other service organizations may deliberately flout the law in providing public gambling activities for raising funds. Hence it is a crime to gamble, but it is not deviant. Moreover, in other states some forms of gambling are not even illegal. New Jersey has legalized casino gambling, Florida permits gambling on horse racing, and many states have lotteries.

Contrast these cases with the behaviors of chronic overeating or picking your nose in public. Both are probably regarded by most people in this country as unacceptable, or deviant, but neither is criminal. Negligence by the Exxon Corporation in permitting conditions that resulted in the huge oil spill at Valdez, Alaska, in 1989 was regarded by most Americans as a bad thing, unacceptable, deviant. Yet it was not illegal.

Finally, some acts are both deviant and criminal. Murder, of course, is publicly disapproved, and it is illegal. And so are rape, arson, thievery, assault, and many other acts. The important things to remember are that criminal and deviant behavior are not synonymous; that deviance is a far more inclusive concept than crime; and that the designation of acts as criminal depends on a political process that operates independently of the deviance or acceptability of the behavior.

Deviance and Prevalence

Another aspect of the definition being proposed here is that deviance is not determined by prevalence of occurrence. The majority of a given group may actually practice a particular act, or at least have committed it at one time or another, yet still believe that it is wrong, inappropriate, or despicable. Such a disapproved act would be deviant by our definition despite the fact that most people do it or have done it. An example is student cheating. If queried, most students will say they believe that cheating is wrong. Nevertheless, most students at some time or another during a college career cheat on exams, and some cheat often. Cheating, therefore, qualifies as deviant by our definition, even though it is typical behavior within the relevant group (students). Conversely, simply because something is unusual or atypical does not necessarily mean it is deviant. Eating snails is unusual behavior—not many people in the United States do it. Yet it is neither disapproved nor is there a negative reaction from society when individuals are caught doing it; therefore, snail consumption is not deviant. It is not how many are doing it that determines a behavior's deviance; rather, it is how the behavior is evaluated by group members and/or those in positions to use coercive power.

Deviance and Group Context

Further, and most important, the conceptualization of deviance underlying our definition is linked to particular group contexts. Accordingly, no behavior is universally or inherently deviant; it may be deviant in one group but not another; it may be deviant at one time in a particular group but not at another time in that same group; and it may be deviant for some within a given group but not others. Deviance is relative to time, place, person, and normative context. Therefore, almost any behavior may be deviant, and almost every behavior is simultaneously conforming and deviant. For instance, wearing clothes is conforming behavior in most communities in the United States, but it is deviant in nudist communities. Using marijuana is deviant in many communities in the United States, but it is not deviant in some college communities. Similarly, recreational sex is both conforming and deviant depending upon the normative context to which one is referring. In predominantly Catholic communities it is regarded as morally wrong and punishable, but in some modern urban communities "swinging" is quite acceptable. But even

within swinging communities, recreational sex is deviant for minors. Furthermore, some things are acceptable for men but not women and vice
versa.

Variation over time in deviance of behavior is illustrated by alcohol use in
the United States. During the prohibition era it was deviant, but now it isn't in
most of America. The same can be said of women wearing pants. One hundred years ago it was completely unacceptable; now it is not negatively evaluated in most, if not all, places in this country. Variation in deviance is also
shown by the history of marijuana use in the United States. Prior to the passage of the Marijuana Tax Act in 1937, smoking marijuana was legal and
nondeviant, and was practiced quite frequently in the southwestern United
States. There is also a good possibility that some things now regarded as
nondeviant will in the future be defined as deviant behavior. One is tobacco
smoking. With the publication of extensive and ever-growing evidence demonstrating the health hazards of tobacco smoke, even for nonusing bystanders, and with the growth of political action groups to combat tobacco use or
at least to confine it to designated areas, smoking may soon be disapproved
by the majority of the population. In like manner, if the "pro-life" political
movement is successful, abortion may once again become deviant. Along this
line, it is also instructive to remember that repressive actions by government
officials in the United States—such as relocating Japanese-Americans during
World War II—are deviant in times of political stability but are tolerated—
even applauded—during times of perceived governmental vulnerability
(Turk, 1982).

Clearly, a major component of the definition being proposed is its designation of deviance as an extremely relative phenomenon. From this perspective, it is misleading to portray specific actions like prostitution, bizarre behaviors usually regarded as mental illness, white-collar crime, or even homicide as inherently deviant. Each may or may not be deviant, depending upon
the normative context, historical period, and the particular factors operative
in that situation. Thus, homosexual conduct is nondeviant activity in San
Francisco in the 1990s but is probably thought of and treated as deviant in
Laredo, Texas. A few behaviors are deviant in such a large number of contexts
that initially they may appear to be universally deviant.

One illustration is incest. Every society has some form of incest taboo
prohibiting sexual relations between close kin. However, who is included in
the taboo varies from society to society, and not necessarily along biological
lines. Moreover, some societies exempt various categories of persons from
the taboo. For instance, brother-sister marriage in ancient Egypt was both
permitted and encouraged (Bagley, 1969). Hence incest prohibitions are
nearly universal but the exact behavior prohibited is not uniform, nor do the
norms apply invariantly within given societies. The same is true with respect
to homicide. Almost every society has some kind of rule prohibiting homicide, but the particular kinds of homicide prohibited or permitted vary
widely. In the United States, for instance, we permit soldiers to kill during
time of war or conflict, even force them to kill; police officers are sometimes
authorized to kill; and executioners are required to take the life of another. A
soldier can kill on the battlefield and be awarded a medal but can be prosecuted and treated like a criminal and deviant if he takes the life of a fellow soldier in his barracks. Moreover, homicide in self-defense is not deviant. Therefore, the act of killing another human being is often not deviant. Indeed, it is

probably impossible to identify any specific behavior that is deviant in all societies, for all categories of people, at all times.

Crime/Deviance and Social Stigma

Finally, deviant behavior is not the same thing as behavior by a deviant person. A deviant person is one who is believed by the majority of a group or by those in positions to coerce to be prone to deviance (which is, of course, behavior that fits the previously stated criteria). Deviant persons are those who have been attributed bad character by a social group or its coercive agents; deviant persons have reputations suggesting a propensity for deviant behavior. However, deviant persons perform many kinds of behavior, most of which are nondeviant. A deviant person may brush his or her teeth, wear clothes, drive a car, smoke cigarettes, stand in lunch counter lines, buy gasoline, and perform any number of other acts, all of which may be conforming in the particular normative context. Behavior by a person with a bad reputation is not necessarily deviant behavior.

It is true, however, that almost any behavior performed by a deviant person is more likely to be viewed as potentially deviant than would the same behavior by a nondeviant person. For instance, if an individual who is thought to be prone to deviant behavior is seen rapidly exiting from a bank, the probability that an observer will believe that this behavior indicates a deviant act is greater than if a nondeviant person is observed doing the same thing. Nevertheless, conceptually the behavior must be separated from the reputation of the person doing it. This is so, at least partly, because attribution of bad character is often an irrational process, at times bearing little relationship to actual behavior. For instance, a person may be defined by a social group as a deviant person even when he or she has not committed any of the acts presumably suggesting a propensity for deviance.

Individuals are sometimes attributed bad character in the absence of actual deviant behavior because of their physical characteristics. Extremely ugly people, midgets, deformed persons, or those mentally retarded are often objects of suspicion and assumed to be dangerous, that is, prone to deviance. They carry a stigma suggesting evil (Goffman, 1963). Such people are perceived as deviant even though they may be guiltless of the acts to which they are assumed to be prone. Similarly, persons of particular racial, ethnic, or religious identities are sometimes stereotyped as deviant persons (see Deviance in Everyday Life, p. 14). At times in the past, in the American South, almost any black person is automatically a deviant person, independent of his or her actual behavior. Similarly, in most places in the world a gypsy is automatically a deviant individual, and, as we have seen earlier, in some places in America Jews are thought of and treated as if they were deviant.

Further evidence of the irrationality of character attribution is the fact that even when a particular, potentially stigmatizing deviance is committed, the likelihood that the perpetrator will be labeled a deviant person depends on many factors, including the social status of the transgressor and of the offended party; the circumstances surrounding the act; the life style and physical characteristics of the perpetrator; this individual's response to being apprehended or punished; and the particular deviant act committed.

As labeling theorists have argued so convincingly, a person of high status who commits a criminal act is usually less likely to be labeled and eventually attributed a deviant character than is a low status person. If a physician is caught with an unpurchased watch in his or her pocket in a discount store, most people are willing to assume that it is "out of character"; that is, there must be some reason for the behavior other than bad character. It may be rationalized that the doctor probably forgot about the watch because there were more important things on his or her mind. Or if theft is acknowledged, the doctor may be excused for having been under stress, or be regarded as simply having made a mistake. "After all," people will reason, "doctors do not need to steal since they make a lot of money and could easily buy any watch they wanted." But a lower-status person caught with a watch in his or her pocket would not so easily be excused. Most people would tend to assume that this was, indeed, an act of theft and that it was consistent with the person's character. Since the lower-status person's inability to buy a watch is obvious to most, attribution of bad character is easy. The fact is, most people— upper, middle, and lower statuses—have trouble thinking of high-status individuals as deviant or criminal, no matter what they do. A good illustration is the comment by Ronald Reagan (then governor of California) concerning the criminal acts committed by President Richard Nixon and revealed as part of the famous Watergate scandal (bribery, obstruction of justice, defrauding the government of tax money, among others). He allowed as how Nixon may have broken the criminal law but was surely not a "criminal"—meaning that he did not have a bad character. Presumably, Reagan (and most others) would have no difficulty in labeling a lower-status person who defrauds the welfare system, hides evidence, or tries to bribe witnesses in a trial as a "criminal."

The advantages enjoyed by high-status people both in escaping the effects of the law and in avoiding stigma for many criminal acts (or for acts that, but for the power held by high-status persons, would be criminal) is widely recognized (Ermann and Lundman, 1996; Lofland, 1969; Schur, 1971; Simon and Eitzen, 1993). What is not so widely acknowledged, however, is the relative disadvantage of high-status people in being labeled for some other kinds of deviance. For instance, film actors are quickly labeled as prone to drug abuse, sexual indiscretions, or exploitation of others, often on the basis of inflammatory publicity concerning one deviant act. Professors are often quickly labeled as communists or homosexuals, sometimes on no more evidence than that the individual advocated freedom of speech or association for all. On the other hand, lower-status people may escape being labeled when they have committed assault or spouse-beating on the grounds that these are cultural mandates for them in the particular situation and not evidence of a character flaw. Social status is certainly one of the variables influencing attribution of bad character when actual deviant behavior occurs, but it does not always work to the advantage of those of high status.

Of the other variables influencing attribution of character in the case of actual deviance, perhaps the most critical is the life style of the transgressor. The sociologist John Lofland (1969) observed that people, places, and things can possess either a normal or deviant character. A school teacher or parent possesses normal character; a porno star and a sideshow freak possess deviant character; a church or a bowling alley possesses normal character; a prison or mental institution possesses deviant character; a car or business suit possesses normal character, while dramatic black eye makeup on a male or a hook on a blind person's cane possesses deviant character. If an individual hangs around with individuals already defined as deviant persons, or follows unconventional schedules or habitually goes to unconventional places (such as sleeping during the day and staying awake at night, and frequenting brothels), dresses in an unconventional manner (such as wearing tattered jeans or old army fatigues), has a strange occupation such as croupier at a casino, or occupies his or her time in unusual pastimes (such as raising pet snakes or tarantulas), and in addition commits a deviant act, that individual is much more likely to end up deemed a deviant person than would someone with a more ordinary life style (Lofland, 1969). Observers can easily imagine that a "night person" might be up to no good and are ready to receive any evidence confirming that preconception. It is harder for most people to think of a police officer or a person who wears a suit to work as "up to no good" than it is to think this of a tramp or a ticket taker for a porno movie house. The point is that an ascription of deviant character is more likely for individuals who go to deviant places that are surrounded by deviant hardware and populated by deviant others (Lofland, 1969).

Of course, just as physical characteristics sometimes lead to stigma in the absence of actual deviance, they also influence whether labeling will occur in the case of actual deviance. Black (African-American) people who steal are generally viewed by whites in many places as having confirmed their true character, whereas a white doing the same may be excused because the deviant act is "out of character." In addition, how people respond to being apprehended and punished may influence whether they are thought of as a deviant person. An individual caught with drugs may be defiant, insisting that the law is unjust, the police brutal, and the judge prejudiced. Such a person is more likely to be attributed bad character than is somebody who, upon being apprehended, is cooperative with the police, penitent, and remorseful.

The circumstances surrounding a deviant act can also make a difference about character attribution. Imagine two men who kill their wives with a dose of poison. One man does the deed because his elderly wife is suffering great pain from a terminal illness, and his love for her leads to a mercy killing. The other man kills his wife in order to collect insurance and run off with his secretary. The act in these two cases is the same, and both are instances of a category of acts deemed to be deviant—murder. Both may be prosecuted and punished, but the likelihood that the first man will be attributed a deviant identity is far less than that for the second. Similarly, a woman who steals from the rich and gives to the poor may escape the label imposed upon those who steal to gratify their own selfish needs or who steal from the poor. Or an FBI agent who illegally burgles a home looking for evidence to convict a felon may be admired, while a burglar who enters the same home for private gain is defined as a deviant person.

Finally, the deviant act itself affects the likelihood of someone being labeled a deviant person. Other things being equal, one who embezzles is viewed differently from one who robs another with a gun; those who defraud by violating antitrust laws are regarded in a different light than are con artists; and petty shoplifters are less likely to be labeled thieves than are pickpockets.

Applications

Deviance, then, is limited to those acts that are disapproved by the majority of a population or that are typically responded to negatively by the majority of a population or by those in positions to use coercive power on behalf of the collectivity. Empirical application of the definition requires: (1) data concerning group opinion about the morality or acceptability of a behavior, (2) information about the rate at which actual sanctions for various behaviors are imposed by authorities, and (3) data describing the actions of members of the social group regarding behaviors that occurred in the recent past. Sometimes all three kinds of data are required to make a judgment. In particular instances some behaviors may fail by one or another criterion but still qualify as deviance by at least one of the others. Often only one kind of information will suffice to demonstrate that the behavior is deviant. Unfortunately, none of the three kinds of information is easily available for most of the acts that a researcher might want to study as potential deviant behavior.

Data concerning majority opinion is difficult and expensive to collect. For one thing, collecting meaningful information presupposes identifiable group boundaries. It is easy enough to recognize political boundaries, but it is not always possible to locate precise "social boundaries" demarcating such entities as the "South" from the "North," Jews from gentiles, Mormons from others, inner-city neighborhoods from the rest of the city, or other cultural differentiations. For another thing, since general surveys can deal with only a limited number of behaviors, and regularly conducted surveys rarely include items that would be of interest to students of deviance, special surveys constructed for the purpose are necessary. Finally, surveys normally sample from large, politically defined populations with results that do not adequately represent small subunits. For instance, a national survey may accurately tell if the majority of the U.S. population disapproves of abortion, but it will not tell whether the people in Hope, Arkansas, or Mormons, or adopted people disapprove of it. This is because the sample may not include anybody from Hope, probably only a few Mormons, and no actually identified adoptees.

In the absence of special survey information (which can almost never be obtained), we must rely on indirect evidence of the beliefs of group members. Indirect evidence may consist of things like the results of elections where candidates have taken stands or been identified with specific kinds of behavior, or the results of local referendums such as that conducted in Dade County, Florida, in 1977 regarding homosexuality. In that county an ordinance guaranteeing equal employment rights for homosexuals was put to a popular vote. The election received national attention because Anita Bryant, a popular singer and major advertising figure for Florida orange juice, came out strongly against the ordinance. Since the measure was soundly defeated, one might conclude that most people in Dade County disapproved of homosexual behavior. Yet such a conclusion may not be justified because, first, everybody does not vote in elections, and, second, the vote was not a direct indicator of disapproval since other issues were intertwined in the referendum.

Other indirect evidence might be newspaper editorials, letters to editors, public speeches or statements by community leaders, or the action of jurors in particular cases. But all of these are also problematic as evidence of public opinion: newspaper editors and politicians may not have their hands on the pulse of the community; people who write letters to newspapers may be very unlike those who don't; and jurors certainly cannot be considered a representative segment of the population. Additional circumstantial evidence may help to build a general picture of public opinion. If the proportion of a given population who are in their 20s is high, one might reasonably assume greater likelihood of acceptability or nonacceptability of various behaviors because it is known that, in general, that age group holds a particular belief about the behaviors in question. Or if the population is made up mostly of Jews, Southerners, Republicans, females, or whatever, general knowledge about the group's typical beliefs may permit interpretation of the local situation.

Finally, common experience may suggest to an investigator that some things are or are not deviant in various locales. For example, few would quarrel with a judgment that interracial dating is deviant behavior in Biloxi, Mississippi, even if an investigator could not produce survey data. Our examination of the Willis children (Deviance in Everyday Life) in Troy, Alabama, who were ostracized because they were Jewish, convinces us that practicing the Jewish faith in that predominantly Christian community was probably considered deviant. Similarly, it is not too difficult to surmise that eating human flesh is disapproved by most people in any community in the United States, despite the absence of specific poll data. The judgment can be made because there are large numbers of ancillary indicators suggesting that most Americans would find this behavior unacceptable. Indeed, opinions of Americans about eating animals that have humanlike qualities are fairly clear. While poultry is readily consumed, hardly anyone would approve of eating cocker spaniels. Still, all in all, ascertaining public beliefs is easier said than done.

Similarly, applying the second part of the definition—collective negative reaction—is also difficult. Newspaper accounts or historical documents can establish whether a community has reacted in the past to instances of particular behaviors, but it cannot tell whether that reaction is "typical." Determining whether the reaction is "typical" requires knowledge of the frequency with which the behavior has occurred and how often it became known to the majority of the community or to the community's coercive agents. Such data would permit calculation of the proportion of actual instances that were reacted against. Usually, estimates have to be made from meager data. For instance, a community may be noted for once having driven a pornographer out of town, but this does not necessarily mean that they typically mobilized vigilante action against pornographers. Perhaps if a substantial number of people are arrested for a specific offense, one might conclude that arrest is a typical reaction to that behavior. But it would not be a certain judgment, since the actual known occurrence of the behavior may be so frequent that even the large number of arrests only scratches the surface. For example, if the police in a given locale arrest 30 people in a given year for illegal gambling, this might appear to be the usual response to gambling. Yet if the police know of 500 cases of illegal gambling where an arrest would have been justified, the 6 percent arrest rate (30/500) might suggest that arrest is not typical. But that judgment could only be made if both figures were available, a circumstance that would rarely obtain.

Further problems in using the proposed conceptualization occur in the case of subcultures within political entities or with subordinate political units within larger political arenas. Imagine that the coercive agents for an entire political entity do typically react negatively to instances of some specific behavior but that the majority of a subcultural group or the majority of a subordinate political group within the larger entity does not regard the behavior as objectionable. For example, while the United States government may have thought that segregation in public universities was deviant conduct, it certainly was not deviant to many if not most Alabamans and to

George Wallace, who, as governor of the state, tried to physically block African-American students from enrolling in the University of Alabama in the early 1960s. In applying the definition, we would conclude that segregating blacks is an instance of deviance if the coercive agents of the U.S. government are conceived as acting on behalf of, or with the coercive power of, the entire collectivity. But can coercive agents such as the U.S. Marshals, who are not members of a specific subcultural group, act on behalf of that group? Or can coercive agents who are members of a subculture, such as Alabama State Troopers, enforce alien rules (those inconsistent with local standards and formulated by others) and still be regarded as acting with collective authority? More pointedly, does a subculture have any coercive agents? This common problem is illustrated by enforcement of laws against gambling in inner-city, poor neighborhoods, where gambling is popular and not locally disapproved. When police arrest gamblers they act on behalf of a larger political entity (the city or state), but are they coercive agents for the poverty group? In short, is gambling deviant in those areas?

To resolve this definitional problem, we could propose a heuristic rule stating that coercive agents who operate in a group context without facing organized forceful opposition are exercising power on behalf of a group even if the agents are from an outside, alien, or oppositional group. By such a rule, gambling would be deviant in inner-city poverty areas despite favorable local opinion, and school segregation would be considered deviant even though at a particular time it mirrors the sentiments of many, if not most, of the white citizens. Similarly, even when a sectarian religious community within the United States believes in and practices polygamy, if law enforcement officers of the particular state where the sect resides arrest polygamists whenever possible, the behavior will still be deviant. That is because the ultimate coercive agents for that group are the state police. Definitionally, this would not be the case, of course, if the polygamists exhibit some form of organized resistance.

Although this example may make the definition seem strained, it points up a crucial aspect of deviance. As we have tried to emphasize, whether behavior is deviant or not is partly a matter of power. A given act is likely to be considered deviant when the behavior in question is committed by powerless persons against powerful persons who feel threatened by that behavior. Sometimes social rules are foisted upon people who are coerced into obedience—or at least an effort is made to coerce obedience. From the point of view of power holders, or the majority of a larger political entity, violations of such rules are deviations—subject to penalty. From our definitional point of view, such violations are subject to explanation. Thus, gamblers in inner-city neighborhoods are harassed and, if caught, punished and/or psychologically treated for "rehabilitation." Power holders may assume that gambling stems from evil motives or that sickness motivates violations of the rules against gambling. Yet the inner-city dwellers themselves may view the laws as unjust, illogical, and stupid. To them, violation may not be regarded as evidence of evil or sickness but may simply be indicative of doing what comes naturally. If a definition focuses only on local opinion, the crucial matter of conflicting viewpoints would be glossed over, and the critical consequences for those who follow local standards in defiance of the alien rules would have to be ignored. Therefore, what appears to be a strain in the definition is actually evidence that the definition reflects the nature of social reality—a reality that is itself often strained.

A final problem in application concerns situations where there is so much disagreement about behavioral standards and such great capriciousness in reaction to particular instances of behavior that it is meaningless to talk about deviance. Such circumstances exist during periods of social change when opinions are being transformed, or in periods characterized by political instability where coercive predominance has not been established. Whether marijuana use is deviant in some specific communities in the United States is impossible to determine because opinions are widely divided—often with some people holding no firm beliefs about acceptability or morality of the behavior. In these same communities laws may be in disuse—invoked and applied only capriciously in connection with other offenses. Under these conditions it could not be said that marijuana use is deviant, nor could it be said that it is conforming. Perhaps the best way to characterize this situation is as a case of social disorganization. That is, deviance is irrelevant; the norms are in the process of being formulated.

It is clear then that the proposed definition captures the most fruitful elements of the various previously existing definitions, that it is sociologically meaningful, and that it is straightforward. Nevertheless, actual application requires fairly concrete information—information usually impossible to obtain. Therefore, decisions about whether some behavior is or is not deviant will be somewhat tenuous, and the judgment will often be more speculative than scientific. Consider two examples.

Examples

Is *marijuana smoking* deviant behavior? To answer the question one would first have to specify a normative context. Marijuana smoking is deviant in some groups in the United States but not in others. Suppose the context is narrowed to the state of New Jersey. Although there are no up-to-date survey data to help answer this question, information collected in 1972 suggests that at that time 63 percent of the population of that state regarded marijuana use as morally wrong or very wrong. In addition, police data suggest that users were typically arrested. Hence, by our definition marijuana use was deviant in New Jersey as of 1972. Whether it is still deviant there is unknown. On the other hand, although there is no direct survey information, indirect evidence such as election results in city races for public office, newspaper accounts, and the population composition of Berkeley, California, suggests that the majority of people there do not regard marijuana use as wrong, bad, or inappropriate. And the police in Berkeley apparently do not typically arrest those who use it. Therefore, it would appear that marijuana smoking is not deviant in Berkeley, California.

By contrast, there is neither direct survey information nor good indirect data concerning the status of marijuana use in Miami, Florida. One would have to extrapolate to draw a conclusion. On the one hand, drug traffickers dealing marijuana are frequently arrested and prosecuted (especially if they are dealing large amounts), yet at rock concerts police officers practically have to wear gas masks to keep from breathing marijuana smoke but arrest hardly anybody. And public opinion in Miami is not noted for liberality, yet tolerance for this "vice" may be widespread. The truth is, we simply don't know if marijuana use is deviant behavior in Miami.

The second example is *public nose picking*. Is this behavior deviant? Again, the first step in answering is to specify where. Suppose we are interested in Dallas, Texas. There are no survey data concerning nose picking and there is no evidence that the community rises up in reaction against it or that the Dallas police typically do anything about it. Yet we somehow suspect that it is not acceptable. Our experience tells us that people in Dallas share common standards of courtesy with other Americans, and we know from past personal experience, perhaps extending all the way back to childhood, that reactions to public nose picking will be negative. Therefore, although the judgment is not well based in data, most of us would assume public nose picking to be deviant in Dallas, Texas, and perhaps everywhere else in the United States. But do we know?

Although it is difficult to apply the definition with certainty in most cases, this does not mean that the study of deviance is impossible or fruitless. Indeed, the very process of trying to ascertain whether a particular behavior is or is not deviant teaches us a great deal about social groups. ✦

Chapter 2

Photo: Mark C. Ide

Types of Deviance

It would be easier to study deviance if we could classify deviant behavior into categories that are homogeneous with respect to crucial characteristics. Classification brings order to seemingly disparate phenomena by grouping the individual instances into similar abstract types. Moreover, a typology might suggest underlying principles that could simplify the obvious complexities of this subject matter.

Difficulty of Classification

Unfortunately, classification by homogeneous traits is difficult because deviance has no inherent characteristics such as harmfulness, badness, or seriousness that would enable us to identify types. Whether some behavior is deviant or not depends upon social definitions that vary from place to place and from time to time. A given behavior may at one time be thought by a social group to be harmful or bad but in other historical eras not be so feared. Or behavior that one group or society thinks is important or serious may be considered quite innocuous by another. "Harmfulness" or "badness" cannot be objectively determined, and if it cannot be objectively determined then the placing of particular deviant acts into categories will necessarily be somewhat arbitrary.

Deviance is relative rather than absolute; its important features are not intrinsic but instead are products of the social contexts from which judgments of social acceptability or unacceptability emanate. Deviance makes sense only as a reflection of a particular normative system, and its classification must be intimately linked with a classification of the norms of that system at that historical moment, which are also emergent and relative. Thus, any typology of deviant behavior is necessarily bounded by time, place, status, and group. Moreover, because norms are seldom completely clear, any typology of deviation will incorporate ambiguities and redundancies, thereby inevitably violating one or another of the rules of good classification, particularly those requiring all instances to fit in the scheme and to fit in one place.

Not only does the relative, socially arbitrary nature of deviance make classification difficult, but the efforts of social groups themselves to classify the deviance they recognize often complicate attempts by scholars to develop workable typologies. When social groups try to classify behaviors, they do so unsystematically and piecemeal. As a result, indigenous typologies are usually even less coherent, comprehensive, and systematic than those constructed by scholars. Therefore, when scholars try to incorporate indigenous categories into their own typologies, it usually does not work. For example, modern societies collectively recognize a category of behaviors called crime, subject to management by official functionaries. At first, one might think that a classification scheme of deviance should include a distinct category for crime. We will now see that this is not so easily done.

The trouble with using crime as a distinct category in classifying deviance is that some criminal behavior is not deviant, and criminal acts are themselves extremely diverse. Indeed, since law making is political and arbitrary, any behavior whatsoever may be designated as crime, regardless of its characteristics. Contemporary legal codes prohibit such dissimilar acts as marijuana smoking, murder, and oral sex; in Hammurabi's ancient legal code, the diluting of drinks by tavern keepers, adultery, and blasphemy were all similarly designated as criminal (Hammurabi, 1904). Furthermore, any state legislature in the United States could at any time declare coffee drinking (or any other behavior) to be criminal so that it automatically would have to be included in the general category of crime, along with such acts as tax evasion, theft, murder, and rape. There is simply nothing about criminal behavior that makes it distinguishable as a category—other than the fact that all such acts have been designated as subject to official management by the lawmaking body of the particular society in question.

To some extent the law itself even recognizes this heterogeneity, and it attempts to subclassify criminal acts into at least two types: serious (felonies) and less serious (misdemeanors). But this distinction does not suffice because it fails to capture even a fraction of the diversity inherent in any legal code. In addition, the felony/misdemeanor distinction is arbitrary, inconsistent, and often contrary to collective perceptions about the behaviors in question. The point is this: a completely workable classification or taxonomy of deviant behavior is impossible, especially one that attempts to build upon "folk" or indigenous categories. Despite the seeming impossibility of the task, the attempt to develop typologies is nevertheless useful, and it is enlightening to study the classification schemes developed by others. Such exercises reveal the complexities of social life. For that reason we authors present a classification of deviance and invite your critical assessment.

Deviance In Everyday Life

To illustrate that any act, even the most innocuous behavior, may be made criminal, consider the following:

- In Alabama it is illegal to play Dominos on Sunday or wear a fake moustache that causes laughter in church.

- In Globe, Arizona, it is illegal to play cards in the street with a Native American.

- In California it is illegal to set a mousetrap without a hunting license.

- In New Britain, Connecticut, the speed limit for fire trucks is 25 m.p.h, even when going to a fire.

- In Sarasota, Florida, it is illegal to sing while wearing a bathing suit.

- In Chicago, Illinois, it is illegal to fish in one's pajamas.

- In South Bend, Indiana, it is illegal for monkeys to smoke cigarettes.

- In Lang, Kansas, it is illegal to ride a mule down Main Street in August, unless the animal is wearing a straw hat.

- In Waterville, Maine, it is illegal to blow one's nose in public.

- In Minnesota it is illegal to tease skunks.

- In St. Louis, Missouri, it is illegal for an on-duty fire fighter to rescue a woman who is wearing a nightgown; in order to be rescued she must first be fully dressed.

- In Newark, New Jersey, it is illegal to sell ice cream after 6 P.M., unless the customer has a note from his doctor.

- In North Dakota it is illegal to lie down and fall asleep with your shoes on.

- In Vermont it is illegal to whistle underwater.

A Typology Based on Middle-Class Norms

The scheme to be presented takes middle-class American (U.S.) norms as its reference base. It demonstrates the variety of deviant behaviors that can be recognized from just one normative perspective. After studying this typology you should be able to appreciate the volume and diversity of deviance that is possible when numerous normative contexts, over time and both within and across modern societies, are taken into account. In addition, this classification scheme illustrates why indigenously created categories, such as crime, cannot be incorporated into deviance typologies as separate and distinct categories, or types, of deviance. In considering the classification, you should be particularly alert to inclusiveness (does every deviant act from the middle-class point of view fit somewhere in the scheme?) as well as mutual exclusivity (does a given deviant act fit in one and only one category?). Moreover, you should critically assess how well the norms described in the typology actually reflect middle-class expectations. Although this scheme is more adequate than most, it too is defective in some important respects. Finding those defects will sharpen your understanding of the relativity and complexity of deviance.

The classification scheme is summarized in Table 2.1. Ten middle-class norms are identified and listed in Column l. Associated with each norm is a category of deviant behavior listed in Column 2. Column 3 lists specific examples of the various deviant acts within each category. The scheme ranks norms from most to least importance for middle-class people.

Although any such ranking is necessarily arbitrary, this one is based on three specific criteria. One is dominance. Where there are conflicts between the demands of two or more norms, the dominant norm takes precedence. For instance, the norm of *privacy* may sometimes conflict with the norm of *loyalty*. In most contests between the two, the norm of loyalty has prevailed; hence, it is probably perceived by most middle-class Americans to be more important. A second criterion has to do with the emotional investment most people have in the norm. The affect associated with the norm of *participation* usually turns out to be much less than that associated with the norm of *prudence*; therefore, it seems clear that prudence is regarded as more important than participation. Finally, the probability, severity, and institutionalization of sanctions for acts of deviance, as well as the chances of long-lasting stigma for violators, are taken to indicate the importance of the norm to middle-class people. For example, *intrusion* normally results in official, fairly severe sanction for offenders, and it usually carries a stigma lasting long after the official sanction ends. In contrast, *uncouth* conduct is rarely sanctioned officially, and any stigma that grows out of informal sanction is short-lived. Therefore, we conclude that the norm of *privacy* (violated by intrusion) is more important to middle-class citizens than the norm of *courtesy* (violated by *uncouthness*).

With these criteria in mind, let us turn to the typology itself and examine the various norms and associated deviance.

Loyalty/Apostasy

A primary, and possibly the most important, norm among middle-class Americans concerns the ultimate right of the group or collectivity to sustain itself through subordinating individual interests to group survival. Recogni-

Table 2.1 A Classification of U.S. Middle-Class Deviance

Norm	Deviance	Examples
Group Loyalty	Apostasy	Revolution, Betraying national secrets, Treason, Draft dodging, Flag defilement, Giving up citizenship, Advocating contrary government philosophy
Privacy	Intrusion	Theft, Burglary, Rape, Homicide, Voyeurism, Forgery, Record spying
Prudence	Indiscretion	Prostitution, Homosexual behavior, Incest, Bestiality, Adultery, Swinging, Gambling, Substance abuse
Conventionality	Bizarreness	"Mentally ill behavior" (handling excrement, nonsense talk, eating human flesh, fetishes), Separatist life styles
Responsibility	Irresponsibility	Family desertion, Reneging on debts, Unprofessional conduct, Improper role performance, Violations of trust, Pollution, Fraudulent business
Participation	Alienation	Non-participatory life styles (hermitry, street living), Perpetual unemployment, Receiving public assistance, Suicide
Moderation	Hedonism—Asceticism	Chiseling—Rate busting, Atheism—Fanaticism, Teetotaling—Alcoholism, Total honesty—Total deceit, Hoarding—Wasting, Ignoring children—Smothering them
Honesty	Deceitfulness	Selfish lying, Price-fixing, Exploitation of the weak and helpless, Bigamy, Welfare cheating
Peacefulness	Disruption	Noisy disorganizing behavior, Boisterous reveling, Quarreling, Fighting, Contentiousness
Courtesy	Uncouthness	Private behavior in public places (picking nose, burping), Rudeness (smoking in prohibited places, breaking in a line), Uncleanliness

tion of this right is expressed in the norm of loyalty. By middle-class standards, all people must commit themselves to the group or society as a whole and maintain that commitment against all challenges. Any behavior that seems to express disloyalty, weak commitment, or disrespect for the group is, therefore, unacceptable. Such behavior can be referred to as *apostasy*. Behaviors within the category of apostasy include revolutionary actions, betrayal of government secrets, cooperation with an enemy nation (treason), draft dodging, defiling the flag, surrendering one's citizenship, and advocating contrary government philosophies.

Revolutionary actions such as participation in a conspiracy to overthrow the government obviously display disloyalty, as do selling of military secrets to an enemy and gunrunning during war or helping an invader to establish

Deviance in Everyday Life

The United States Supreme Court in 1989 declared that the burning of the American flag was protected expression under the First Amendment. In this case, *Texas v. Johnson* 491 U.S. 397 (1989), the defendant, Gregory Lee Johnson, burned an American flag on the steps of Dallas City Hall to protest the policies of President Ronald Reagan. He was tried, convicted, and sentenced to one year in jail and fined $2,000 under a Texas statute that outlawed desecrating the flag. The Supreme Court argued that the fact that an audience may find a particular expression of speech offensive or disloyal does not justify it being prohibited.

control over an area. In a less obvious way, attempts to avoid the draft are taken to be indicative of disloyalty to the group, another way of saying that the person lacks the commitment to sacrifice for the interests of the group. And defiling the flag or advocating another governmental or economic philosophy (such as communism) is assumed to prove that the person holds the group in such low regard that he would be disloyal in a critical situation.

Clearly, most middle-class Americans endorse the norm of loyalty and consider it exceptionally important. No personal or other group obligation can excuse apostate behavior, and middle-class people usually display disgust and loathing for those who are guilty. Moreover, violations of the norm of loyalty almost always result in sanctions—often quite severe—and they usually evoke lifetime stigmatization whether or not there is official sanction.

Privacy/Intrusion

A second major middle-class American norm revolves around the concept of privacy. It holds that every person has the right to exclusive control over some things, especially private places and personal items. Sometimes there are disputes about the limits of exclusive control; for example, do parents or pet owners have a right to abuse their charges? Moreover, exclusive control over property is limited in view of potential consequences for others (you cannot burn your own house if it poses a fire hazard for other homes), and exclusivity is never absolute. In addition, the fact of ownership may be disputed. But, when exclusive control is recognized, the principle of privacy prevails; that is, only the owner may invade that domain. Hence the associated deviance is called *intrusion*, and it consists of acts that deny the controller or owner of some domain the exclusivity implied by ownership. Examples of intrusion include theft, burglary, rape, homicide, voyeurism, forgery, and record spying (unauthorized examination of bank accounts, hospital records, or other confidential information).

Deviance in Everyday Life

Video surveillance is rapidly becoming a tool of corporate management. Also, many city and town squares and streets are being monitored by video cameras, as are shopping centers and their parking lots, and convenience stores. Video cameras are being installed in many workplaces, enabling management to keep an eye on workers.

Theft constitutes intrusion because it deprives owners of exclusive control over their property. Burglary, of course, involves invasion of a private space, which usually provokes in the victim a sense of having been "violated." Rape is a deviant act in violation of the norm of privacy because most middle-class people believe that a person's body is a private domain to be entered only by request or permission. Forgery denies exclusive use of a signature and often implies usurpation of private funds, opinions, or duties.

The strength of emotion surrounding the norm of privacy is perhaps best grasped by considering the intrusion called voyeurism. Most people who discover that they have been under surveillance, without permission, while bathing, performing personal functions, engaging in sexual activities, or even working, feel an overwhelming sense of distress that they have been violated.

This is particularly interesting since such individuals have not actually been injured or harmed in a tangible sense. Yet they feel abused because their expectation of privacy was overridden, thus denying them the exclusive control that all expect.

Of course, most acts of intrusion are subject to sanction and, indeed, typically are sanctioned. In fact, most acts of intrusion are among the most feared of crimes, the so-called "index crimes" for which the FBI collects and publishes statistics. Yet the stigma and sanction are not as severe or long lasting as in the case of apostate behavior. It appears that recognition of the ultimate superiority of the group, reflected in the norm of loyalty, supersedes the rights of the individual, as it must for society to continue. In the final analysis, the only persons who may intrude into private domains with impunity are official representatives of the collectivity who act on authority of the group as a whole. Thus the government may confiscate property (with fair compensation, at least from the government's point of view) when it exercises the right of eminent domain, or where tax assessments are not paid and the property is offered for public sale. Government agents may enter private residences uninvited if authorized by court orders, and the state may even claim a citizen's life in the interest of group survival as when the individual is sent to die in combat or when the courts decide that the person must be executed. Similarly, the police and court officials may look at private records under authorized conditions, and the state is sometimes even authorized to forcefully invade a person's body to perform court-ordered sterilization, test for a driver's possible intoxication, or to search for evidence of illegal activity.

Deviance In Everyday Life

In a *New York Times* public opinion poll, 43 percent of respondents favored a Constitutional Amendment that would allow a woman to have an abortion only in order to save her life. A comparable poll in Ohio found that 47 percent of those asked would allow an abortion only when it was necessary to save the life of the mother.

Hence almost every domain of privacy may be set aside by the superior right of the group as a whole. This even extends to the question of rape. When law enforcement personnel search the inner cavities of human persons in search of illegally smuggled drugs, they are actually committing acts that would constitute criminal assault or rape were they not authorized by the state as an enforcement procedure. How far this would extend is unknown, of course, but it is conceivable that the government might even forcefully intrude into a woman's body for sexual or reproductive purposes should voluntary reproduction decline to the point where population maintenance were threatened. At present in the United States, many people would favor laws that force women to bear children once they are impregnated, even if that conception were the result of rape or incest, and even if the bearing of the child would cost the mother's life. Many believe it only a small step to requiring women to become pregnant.

Prudence/Indiscretion

The third most important normative area among middle-class Americans appears to be that concerning *prudence*. All people are expected to exercise selectivity in the practice of activities that are pleasurable. They are to use pleasure as a means to an end, not as an end in itself, and the expression of pleasure must be within specified limits or boundaries. The prescribed end is expected to be some contribution to the economic or social maintenance of society. A person is supposed to avoid activities that are frivolous or primarily oriented around self-gratification as well as activities that may involve nonproductive emotional involvements or that may disrupt productive emotional ties. Violation of the norm of prudence can be characterized as *indiscretion*. Indiscrete behavior would include prostitution, homosexual behavior, bestiality, adultery, incest, swinging, gambling, and abuse of drugs.

Prostitution (sexual activities as a commercial exchange), swinging (consensual exchange of sexual partners among married people), and bestiality (sexual activities with animals) all involve sexual interaction without emotion, thus challenging the usual linkage between emotional involvement and sexual expression that motivates the establishment and maintenance of stable, productive, and socially useful unions. Homosexual behavior (sexual relations with someone of one's own gender, incest (sexual relations with a relative), and adultery (sexual relations of a married person with someone other than his or her spouse) may involve emotional attachments that cannot be productive and that may provoke disruptive conflicts. Gambling and abusive recreational drug use convey images of obsession with self-gratification and frivolity. All of these indiscrete behaviors are sanctionable, but most of them usually do not receive official sanctions. They all do, however, ordinarily provoke substantial stigma from others, which expresses fairly long-lasting group disapproval.

Conventionality/Bizarreness

A fourth norm of middle-class America mandates that all must practice personal habits and lead lives that are similar to the conventions followed by most middle-class people. Violations of the norm of conventionality are called *bizarre* behavior; that is, relative to most middle-class people, the behavior in question is unusual or statistically atypical to such an extent that the sanity or "normality" of the individual is questioned. But not all statistically unusual behavior is deviant by middle-class standards. To qualify as bizarre, the behavior must be incomprehensible to the typical person. The average middle-class individual must be unable to imagine herself or anyone like her committing such an act; that is, the behavior must not have a good reason behind it. Some atypical behaviors are readily understandable to "normals." Clearly, religious celibacy is acceptable since it reflects devotion to an established faith and is believed to be good and useful. Likewise, skydiving, while unusual, is nevertheless comprehensible as a recreational search for adventure—fulfillment of the individualistic ideal of bravery—and is therefore not deviant. On the other hand, total sexual abstinence for no apparent good reason (such as among wedded people who fail to consummate the marriage) would be bizarre. And handling rattlesnakes as a part of religious ritual (La Barre, 1969) would seem to most middle-class people to be senseless and unacceptable, particularly if it were seen as an obligation that might endanger the young.

Other examples of unusual behavior that most middle-class people cannot imagine for sane people include consuming or playing with excrement, talking in nonsensical ways to others or to oneself—perhaps through unique sounds and words—or conversing with unseen creatures. Similarly, hiding from or attempting to counteract perceived threats or dangerous moves by individuals who "normals" do not believe are making such threats or dangerous moves, as well as eating the flesh of a human corpse, are acts so unthinkable that most middle-class people consider them indicative of "mental illness." Other bizarre acts may be considered deviant by middle-class standards but are not taken as evidence of total sickness. Strange sexual preferences like rubber fetishes (inability to experience orgasm unless wearing rubber garments), masochism (deriving sexual pleasure from personal physical pain), or desires to be diapered and powdered by a sexual partner are instances of unacceptable or bizarre behaviors qualifying as "perversions."

Another kind of unconventional behavior that is deviant by middle-class standards is that manifest in separatist life styles. One of the most dramatic and well-known groups that practice unusual living styles are the Amish, a sectarian religious group that resides in Pennsylvania, Ohio, Indiana, and other parts of the Midwest (Ammon, 1989; Hostetler, 1980, 1989). The Amish shun modern society and its conveniences, choosing instead to live in primitive farming communities. They plow their fields with horse-drawn implements, transport themselves in buggies, and refuse to use electricity or appliances in their homes. They dress in plain black "pilgrim" styles, eschewing any adornments such as jewelry or personal comforts like gloves. The Amish resist modern education and refuse on religious grounds to serve in the armed forces.

Other groups, like the Hare Krishna, separate themselves less completely but nevertheless are thought of as bizarre because of their unusual styles of dress (long flowing colorful robes, shaven heads except for a long pigtail at the back of the head, and sandals), and their evangelistic behavior on city streets and in airports, where they accost and attempt to convert passersby. And still other groups earn the deviant designation by periodically removing all clothes while performing ordinary tasks. Nudists who occasionally spend a weekend or a vacation at a "camp" are deviant enough, but those who live at nudist camps year round are considered to be especially perverted.

Deviance In Everyday Life

One example of behavior that is bizarre by middle-class standards was exhibited by a group of religious cult members referred to under the name of Heaven's Gate. The group was founded by Marshall Herff Applewhite and Bonnie Lu Nettles, who shared an interest in philosophy and metaphysics. The two founders of the group went by various aliases such as Bo and Peep, Guinea and Pig, and "The Two." Their religion consisted of a combination of Christian theology, folk wisdom, and a firm belief in UFOs. Bo and Peep believed that they were extraterrestrials who would lead their followers to a higher level of existence. They believed that their escape would come via a spaceship that hid in the tail of the comet Hale-Bopp. In order to reach the spaceship, however, followers had to shed their human skin. On March 28, 1997, authorities in San Diego, California, discovered the bodies of 39 members of this cult who had committed suicide.

Finally, a life style organized around night activity arouses suspicion, and if a person is unable to provide a reasonable excuse (such as a nighttime job), he or she is defined as probably doing bizarre behavior, although less reprehensible than the behaviors already mentioned. Since most middle-class folks work in the daytime and sleep at night (at least the late night), going out only in the early evening, they regard those who are up and about, especially if out on the streets, during the wee hours as somewhat bizarre and possibly up to no good. Few allowances are made for those who simply like to sleep during the day and visit, paint, or jog late in the night.

Some of the activities described here as bizarre behavior are subject to some form of official sanction; usually, however, sanctions are informal—ridicule, harassment, and rejection. Many of the more bizarre acts are formally sanctioned by incarceration in mental institutions, where therapists are employed to help their practitioners "recover," which means to begin to act in conventional ways. In all instances, however, there is a strong tendency toward stigmatization, which can be erased only with great difficulty. Probably the best example of stigmatization for "mental illness" is the case of Thomas Eagleton, a United States senator from Missouri who was the Democratic nominee for vice-president of the United States in 1972. When it became known that he had at one time been treated by a psychiatrist for emotional problems and had been given electroshock treatments, he was forced off the ticket, despite the fact that the treatment had taken place sometime in the past and had apparently been successful since the candidate was not then suffering from those emotional problems and gave no evidence of being prone to psychiatric difficulties. Stigmatization of those whose bizarre behaviors are not usually thought of as evidence of mental illness is common as well. It is unlikely that an Amish person could easily overcome the stigma of "ignorant" and "backward" should he or she choose to assimilate, or that even a "night person" could ever fully escape suspicion if his or her life were scrutinized in a police investigation.

Responsibility/Irresponsibility

Another norm of middle-class Americans prescribes responsible conduct. People, especially those on whom others depend, must be reliable. Violations of this norm constitute instances of *irresponsible* behavior. Examples include family desertion, refusal or failure to meet financial obligations, negligence in maintaining property or performing occupational roles, failure to fulfill professional standards, violations of trust, pollution of the environment, and selling defective, harmful, or useless products or services.

For instance, parents are expected to provide financial and emotional support for children, and spouses are required to fulfill marital obligations toward each other. Children and spouses, as well as members of the larger society, have a stake in faithful parental and marital role performance. When husbands or wives desert families, for whatever reason, they leave their dependants open to potential harm, and they may be helping to create burdens for the community should the children or deserted spouse need public assistance. This is thought by middle-class people to be irresponsible. Similarly, all individuals who participate in the world of commerce must be able to rely upon each other for basic financial dependability that justifies the trust on which contracts are based. Individuals, therefore, commit deviance when they renege on debts, delay payments, or evade contractual obligations.

Owners or managers of property are similarly expected to behave responsibly so that other property owners, innocent bystanders, or consumers of goods and services will not be harmed. Property owners must keep their buildings in good repair and cut the lawn so that property values in the area will not deteriorate. Moreover, owners are supposed to make sure their property does not pose a danger to others. For instance, a homeowner who leaves a swimming pool open and unattended entices neighborhood children to the dangerous possibility of drowning and is therefore guilty of irresponsibility.

Professionals such as physicians, lawyers, accountants, and police bear a special middle-class responsibility. Norms prescribe that they perform competent services for those who entrust themselves as clients, including in the case of the police, the entire community, and that the interests of the clients must take precedence over the self-interests of the practitioners. A physician who performs unnecessary surgery simply for the purpose of earning the fee for service is engaging in irresponsible behavior, as is one who prescribes medicine to be bought in a pharmacy the physician owns, or who reports to unrelated third parties about the illnesses of another. Similarly, a male physician who takes advantage of female patients who trust him to examine their unclothed bodies behaves irresponsibly and deviantly in violation of the role obligations of a physician. And it is deviant for a physician to keep people sick to guarantee income rather than to help them recover.

Other examples of professional irresponsibility include graft, theft, or burglary by police officers. Middle-class people regard as irresponsible, as well as intrusive, stealing by a police officer who is called to investigate a crime but ends up taking things. Similarly, police who fail to make an arrest in exchange for a payoff or sexual favors behave irresponsibly. And, of course, brutality or the use of force simply to gratify personal whims or to satisfy aggressive tendencies is unacceptable. Finally, police who use their positions, uniforms, or coercive power to enjoy privileges or to escape the law themselves garner the enmity of the middle class. This occurs at the level of police bribery or graft, and may be felt at a more minor level when citizens see police officers accepting "free" meals or drinks.

Deviant conduct of an irresponsible type also includes embezzlement or other forms of diverting organizational funds or equipment to private use. Within this category are fraudulent pyramid schemes, where entrepreneurs induce investors to put up money with the promise of a high rate of return but actually use the money put up by new investors as the "profit" for old investors (after taking their cut). These schemes are fraudulent because no actual product or service is produced. When new investors can no longer be found, the entire pyramid collapses.

Deviance in Everyday Life

Medical frauds, including anti-aging potions, arthritis remedies, diet gimmicks, and ineffective cancer treatments, cost Americans billions of dollars a year. Not only do medical frauds cost us money, they may also be costing us our health by luring us away from effective medical treatment. Why are we so enthralled by medical quackery? Because we want to believe in medical miracles and are convinced by the promises of easy treatments and cures made by unscrupulous medical quacks. Want to lose weight? Here are your options: (1) eat better, eat less, and stick to a regular exercise routine, or (2) sit on the couch with an electronic "muscle stimulator" attached to your flabby areas that effortlessly removes the unwanted pounds. Now, which option sounds more appealing?

Over the past several decades, the interdependency of human social life has become more fully recognized by middle-class people; as a result, the number and types of possibly irresponsible behaviors has expanded. Some of the newest, and to some extent still controversial, forms of deviance concern behavior that jeopardizes others through damage to the environment—even small incremental damages. Just as individuals may endanger public health and safety by spitting on the sidewalk, dumping garbage on the street, or putting carbon residues into the air through their automobile exhausts, now corporations are being held responsible for polluting the environment through discharge of toxic chemicals into rivers or the air, or by destruction of natural protective systems such as forests or sand dunes. Similarly, although swindlers have always been considered to be doing deviance by selling defective home siding (so-called "Tin Men") or roof painting jobs, now "respectable" businesses are being castigated for marketing defective or dangerous products, such as automobiles with improperly designed gasoline tanks that explode on rear-end impacts or children's pajamas that are excessively flammable (see Simon and Eitzen, 1993). The major forms of deviance involving useless products or services are medical frauds. Charlatans often sell ineffective or dangerous machines or drugs to desperate people who suffer continuous pain or incurable diseases.

The reason some of these newer forms of irresponsible behavior are controversial is the inherent conflict between the norm of responsibility and the norm of privacy. Although most middle-class people probably believe it is deviant behavior to sell a toy that has a high probability of injuring a child, some people would maintain that it is the responsibility of a parent to refuse to purchase such a toy or to teach the child how to use it safely. These people also probably believe that prohibiting a company from selling such an item is an invasion of the privacy of the owners and managers of the company. In like manner some would maintain that it is the individuals' responsibility to make wise choices and to protect themselves from market shenanigans; therefore, to them selling a useless or even harmful medical nostrum is not a deviant act.

Clearly, many potentially deviant acts are moving toward deviant status, and some that are now thought of as irresponsible could in the future sink back into acceptability with a slight turn of opinion. Nevertheless, it is likely that all those mentioned here as violating the norm of responsibility are deviant. Yet the ambivalence of these norms is reflected in the relative leniency of official sanctions. Even though the listed behaviors may be disapproved, usually they go unpunished or, if violations are punished, they are given only a "slap on the wrist." More often, these transgressions provoke private civil suits and some stigma, although usually not great or long lasting.

Participation/Alienation

Another middle-class norm specifies that everybody will take an active part in the social and economic life of the community or society and in the institutions it spawns. Those who fail to participate are guilty of *alienation*, unless they can provide an acceptable excuse. Deliberate defiance of the participation norm is illustrated by hermits, tramps, and bums, as well as by suicides. The perpetually unemployed, those receiving public assistance, the aged, and the handicapped all exhibit forms of involuntary alienation, but they are nevertheless held in contempt unless their inactivity is justified. It may be excused by visible physical defects but only if the symptoms are sufficiently debilitating to make participation impossible, or by an individual's reputation for perseverance that allows the middle-class audience to conclude that the nonparticipator has done all he or she could to fulfill expectations.

Almost every generation has its prominent examples of bohemians—those who reject middle-class standards of morality, work, or politics and withdraw into a world of their own. In the 1950s it was "beatniks"; the 1960s and 1970s had "hippies"; and the 1980s were the time of "punks." The hippies of the 1960s are probably best known because they were so numerous and had such an important impact on society. They became famous for "dropping out" of the middle-class system and "turning on." Many young people of that era came to regard traditional work ethics as dehumanizing; conventional nuclear families too confining; middle-class sexual mores as being "uptight"; and prohibitions on mind-altering drugs as fearful avoidance of self-actualization. They traded the "status seeking" of the establishment for subsistence living, communal sharing, sexual freedom, and drug-induced visions of what might be. Their very existence insulted middle-class standards, and so hippies came to symbolize deviant behavior in the minds of the middle class. Contempt is heaped upon any individual or group that denies the validity of the middle-class system by self-conscious refusal to play the game.

Denial of that validity is also evident among those who will not try, those who fail, those who live as parasites on the system, or those who escape completely, and they all earn a disreputable status. Hermits refuse to try, chronically unemployed street people fail, and loafers exploit public services—all forms of the deviance termed alienation. But alienation is more dramatically displayed by suicide. With the exception of altruistic acts of self-destruction, where somebody sacrifices his or her life to save others, suicide makes the ultimate statement of nonparticipation and so it is proportionally stigmatized—although the stigma ironically applies to the relatives of the deceased.

The importance of the norm of participation is shown by the suspiciousness with which the middle class regards any deviation. People receiving public assistance are assumed to be chiselers or "welfare cheats" unless they can individually redeem themselves, and middle-class people are ever alert to detect any evidence of immorality, deceit, or laziness by welfare mothers, the infirm, or the aged that would confirm their suspicions. If a person is inactive because of age, he or she must not be seen walking without a crutch or cane. An unemployed man must not laugh, drink beer, or be seen in recreation, no matter how long he has been unemployed or how hard he has searched for a job; nor must he refuse any kind of employment, no matter how degrading or dangerous it might be. And nonparticipating handicapped individuals must show their handicap so observers will know they have a right to be excused from the alienated status. Otherwise, such persons will be regarded as fakes and cheats, false claimants to special dispensation.

Although alienation is rarely dealt official punishment, it is the object of constant informal sanctions, and its practice carries a stigma that may endure into future generations, as when the police suspiciously keep a close watch on children from welfare families. Some bohemian behavior is illegal, and it is sometimes managed by arrest and prosecution or sometimes simply by police harassment, but usually bohemians suffer ostracism, criticism, and name calling. Likewise, the behavior of tramps, bums, street people, and welfare recipients is also sometimes a matter of official review but more often an object of informal scorn. The nonparticipation of the aged, handicapped, infirm, and suicides is almost completely a matter of informal criticism.

Moderation/Hedonism and Asceticism

Middle-class Americans subscribe to Emerson's golden mean. All things should be in moderation, and extremes of any kind—even for desirable activities—are unacceptable. This concern with moderation produces judgment of acts as deviant that fall on one end or another of a continuum from hedonism (too much of something) to asceticism (not enough of something). These rules of moderation apply to all realms of activity from work to play. Thus it is good to nurture a child but it is bad to practice "smother love" (hedonism) or to reject a child; one is expected to perform an honest day's work, but it is wrong to be a "workaholic" or "rate-buster" (Roethlisberger and Dickson, 1964 [1939]); it is good to drink socially but unacceptable to abuse alcohol or to teetotal.

The American middle-class ethic of moderation is really one of "sensible" compromise, well-roundedness, and adaptability. This can be seen most clearly in the apparent ambivalence that surrounds important issues like religion. While the middle class respects religion, regards itself as fundamentally religious, and promotes a religious outlook on life style and politics, it is clear that both atheists and fanatics are viewed with some measure of disgust. Although many religions teach that a believer should give up worldly goods to promote righteousness, and although members of the middle class believe in philanthropy, they would think actually giving away all one's property to charity a very foolish thing, just as they would regard hoarding one's possessions like a miser as inappropriate. Many religions also teach loving forgiveness of abuse (turn the other cheek), and the middle class does embrace patience and love, but it also regards too much pacifism as unacceptably "wimpish." In like manner, most religions endorse the virtue of modesty, which is embraced by the middle class, but the middle class rejects failure to "toot your own horn" as much as they do bravado.

The golden mean rules the middle-class psyche especially in matters of politics. Extreme conservatives as well as extreme liberals are anathema. The ideal politician is middle of the road, moderate, balanced. And while middle-class Americans ostensibly love freedom and hate totalitarianism, they tolerate "extremes in the defense of freedom" no better than extremes in the service of dictatorship. The history of American government has shown a repeated cyclical pattern as the pendulum swings from the "liberalism" of one generation of governmental policy to the "conservatism" of the next, each in its turn laying claim to having brought policy back to the middle ground.

Here, as with most deviance, violations are sometimes managed by formal sanctions but more often by informal reactions. While an administrator who cuts too many corners may be arrested, most simply find themselves on more and more precarious ground with their peers and coworkers. And administrators who slavishly adhere to the rules may find themselves formally dismissed because of an inability to get the job done, but more likely they will simply go nowhere in the organization, a type of informal reaction. Moreover, in most areas there are no formal sanctions to deal with hedonism or asceticism. Those who extravagantly waste their money are ridiculed and pitied as are those whose penuriousness deprives them of important comforts. But neither is formally dealt with unless the behavior is also so bizarre as to invoke the intervention of mental health personnel. And the "greasy grind," curve busting student along with the "space cadet" are subject to no more punishment than occasional scorn, ridicule, or social isolation.

Honesty/Deceitfulness

The middle-class normative system requires a certain degree of honesty, at least in important things. Everybody is expected to avoid lying, fraud, or misrepresentation, but this prohibition is subject to the restraint of the golden mean mentioned before. Persons who exceed the limit of tolerance for mendacity are exhibiting the deviance of *deceitfulness*. Examples include selfish lying, price-fixing by business people, fraudulent business activities, exploitation of the weak and helpless, bigamy, and welfare cheating.

Unfortunately, the limits within which honesty is to be practiced are not consistent across social contexts; the norm is situationally variable. For example, if you visit a sick male friend and are struck by his poor appearance, it is not good manners for you to tell him how bad he looks. Even if the man proclaims it himself, you are supposed to assure him that he will soon be well. Or if you are a male and your girlfriend buys a new dress and seeks your opinion, you mustn't tell her that you think it's ugly; middle-class norms call for diplomatic concealment in cases like this where the truth serves only to hurt someone. But when the sick person gets well and asks if you covered for him at work during the illness, you can't, according to the norm of honesty, say you did if, in fact, you didn't. Or if the girlfriend with the new dress asks her boyfriend what he did that day she was shopping, the fellow must not deny that he was with friends she does not like. There seems to be an understanding that selfish lying, which promotes one's personal interest, is unacceptable but that unselfish lying, which serves an altruistic purpose, is all right. Yet even this guideline is not infallible. An individual who lies in a court of law to protect a friend is no less guilty of perjury than one who lies to save his own skin; both will be condemned as disreputable, although the latter perhaps more thoroughly than the former.

Similar ambivalence prevails on the organizational level. Large businesses may peg their own prices at the level set by the dominant firm in an industry, all the time pretending that their pricing is a response to supply and demand market forces, without earning a characterization as deceitful. But companies actually meeting to discuss pricing is a form of conspiracy in violation of the law and of middle-class ethics. Another example is the case of a defense industry that persuades the Navy to buy its airplanes by general arguments suggesting the plane will be better and cheaper than those produced by its competitors. Such rhetoric is regarded as good business even if the company knows it has underestimated the cost and may not actually be able to fulfill the plane's performance requirements. But that same company will be deceitful if it actually falsifies test data, as the Goodrich corporation did in some of its brake operation tests for the A7D Light Attack Aircraft (Vandiver, 1996). Of course, knowing ahead of time just where the dishonesty of salesmanship stops and the deceitfulness of fraud begins is not easy.

Deceitfulness is also expressed when someone takes advantage of people unable to defend themselves, but here again a fuzzy line separates deviance and conformity. A storekeeper who charges exorbitant prices to migrant laborers who must trade in his store because they have no transportation to shop elsewhere is regarded as somewhat unsavory but still within the bounds of acceptable capitalism. But a storekeeper who shortchanges migrant laborers because they are unfamiliar with American money is deceitful.

Finally, those who receive services from governmental or private organizations through misrepresentation are regarded as disreputable if their deceit is blatant and technically in violation of written laws or regulations, but not if the deceit is subtle and merely in violation of the spirit of written laws or regulations. The welfare mother who claims her children have no father to support them when she, in fact, has an employed husband is condemned, whereas a person might be applauded for simply neglecting to reveal a disqualifying injury in order to obtain employment. A male senator who operates a farm at a loss in order to offset tax liabilities in other areas is regarded as a clever operator, but he is labeled disreputable when he conceals from tax officials the actual income he earns from speeches or other services rendered.

Peacefulness/Disruption

Quiet, tranquility, and order are the hallmarks of American middle-class communities and social life. Middle-class people dislike contentiousness and conflict; they seek agreement, cooperation, and harmony. Violations of these norms are called disruption. Examples include noisy or disruptive protests; boisterous revelry; quarrels, fights, or brawls, particularly in open or public places; and disagreeableness or contentiousness.

Contentiousness is disruptive because it disturbs the air of tolerance that middle-class people like to display. In conversation, one is supposed to avoid conflict-generating topics, and if they are broached, every point of view is to be granted respect if not equal validity. And if someone believes something passionately, he or she is to show restraint in its presentation and defense. In all things a person is expected to be reasonable. Those who have a "negative" attitude, who like to argue, who are loud and boisterous, or who don't want to go along with the group are regarded as disruptive and may be excluded from further group interaction, gossiped about, or ridiculed (although probably not face to face). The ultimate expression of this norm is evident in hospitals when people are dying. No matter how much pain the person is suffering or how dreadful the prospect of death, a dying individual is cajoled to restrain any groans, screams, or yells on the grounds that the noise disturbs others and is in bad taste as well (Sudnow, 1967). Hence one must even bear the agony of death in conformity with the peacefulness norm of the middle class, whose influence permeates hospitals and other social institutions dealing with sickness and death.

According to middle-class rules, one must express political anger, frustration, or chagrin through quiet, dignified methods, not loud, garish, or unrestrained protests. A quiet vigil in an unobtrusive place may be all right, although letters to political figures would be preferable. Marching in the streets, blocking access to buildings, and drowning out speakers with chants and catcalls are prohibited because they are clearly in violation of the norm of peacefulness. Thus, any form of political expression that inconveniences others or disturbs the peace and tranquility is deviant.

While the middle class tolerates ritualized occasions for bending the rules of peacefulness, they nevertheless require that parties and celebrations be restrained and restricted to particular places, times, and occasions, and within the bounds of proper decorum. The music should be confined to the host's home, the guests should not become intoxicated, and the entertainment should consist of quiet conversation on trivial subjects. Never should activities become raunchy or disorderly, wake up the neighbors, or involve indiscretion. Middle-class fun is peaceful and calm (and, remember, moderate).

Finally, when conflicts do occur, they are to be handled in a "mature," private manner. A husband and wife are not to yell at each other in public or in the presence of others; they are to maintain a facade of peaceful happiness or tolerance, at least until they are in a private place. Parents are prohibited from yelling at or disciplining children in company; family members must excuse themselves to private quarters. Adults who end up in angry conflict are never to employ fisticuffs or other forms of physical aggression or even to raise their voices to levels that might inconvenience others.

In short, any behavior that interferes with the orderly, peaceful flow of life must be avoided. Consideration for others is paramount, so disruption is regarded as unacceptable, to be managed mainly by avoidance or informal means, although sometimes by official sanctions, as when the police break up noisy parties, arrest participants in a fight, or disperse demonstrators who block traffic.

Courtesy/Uncouthness

Finally, there are a large number of middle-class rules concerning interpersonal interaction. The point of these middle-class norms is to ensure that an individual's behavior does not make the ordinary business of social intercourse too unpleasant and that necessary accommodation to other people be elevated to a civilized plane. Therefore, in almost every realm of activity there are middle-class norms requiring that the presence of others be taken into account so that they are not offended. Violations of those norms constitute a form of deviance called *uncouthness*.

Uncouth behavior includes any private behavior that is done in public—passing gas, scratching one's genitals, picking one's teeth or nose, spitting, performing bodily functions, vomiting, sleeping, burping, or having sex. Such behavior tends to offend others by introducing unpleasant smells, sounds, and sights. In the middle-class mind, it is enough that one endure these things when they are personally generated without having to share others' experience of them as well. Other rude acts are smoking in an elevator or a nonsmoking section of a restaurant, rushing ahead of someone to go through a door, interrupting a person who is speaking, breaking into a ticket line, or coughing and sneezing without covering one's mouth. Failing to keep one's body clean or to use deodorant is a form of uncouthness that offends others, as are crude table manners like making slurping noises while eating soup or drinking coffee.

The usual method of dealing with these transgressions is informal—a reaction of disgust or sometimes deliberate silence, followed by ostracism of the guilty party. Very rarely are there official sanctions for uncouthness, although sometimes arrests are made for sleeping or performing bodily functions in public places.

An instance in which formerly acceptable behavior is now becoming uncouth and for which formal sanctions are coming to replace informal sanctions is smoking behavior. Up until recently, smokers were relatively free to practice their habit just about anywhere. Although it was considered good manners to ask permission from those nearby, most smokers rarely bothered to ask and were seldom regarded as deviant. Within the past decade or so, however, smoking behavior has become much less tolerated. As medical evidence has accumulated showing that smoking damages not only the health of the smoker but also that of innocent bystanders, expectations have developed that smokers will confine their activities to designated areas and will honor the wishes of those who want to be protected. And in many places laws now require such segregation on airplanes, in restaurants, theaters, public buildings, and some places of employment. The full transition has not yet occurred, however. Although the airlines are held responsible for enforcing the smoking segregation under threat of the Civil Aeronautics Board, most other enforcement remains informal.

Summary

This typology of middle-class norms and deviance shows that there are enormous numbers and kinds of deviance—far more than usually come to mind when the subject of deviance is discussed. It is easy to imagine the large number and variety of deviant acts that would be evident if we built typologies based on the norms of all social classes, regions, ethnic groups, or subcultures. Yet if we were to construct such typologies, we would find substantial overlap with this one. That is because the middle class dominates U.S. society, both by imposing its standards through the schools, the mass media, and the law and by enjoying a degree of natural hegemony in behavior styles and thinking that flows from the admiration and emulation of those with higher status. For example, lower-class norms differ a little bit in a few of the categories, but, by and large, the lower class shares most norms with the middle class. And so it is for almost any normative reference we might choose. The fact is, there is considerable evidence of an overarching American culture exhibiting remarkable degrees of normative agreement. Nevertheless, we must be attuned to the many variations that do exist.

The Organization of Crime and Deviance

There are as many kinds of deviance as there are norms, and since norms are practically infinite, deviance at first appears to be hopelessly complex and conceptually disordered. Nevertheless, we have already seen that deviance can be categorized into types that reflect violation of different kinds of values embraced by people of particular social strata. Now we will see that deviance can be ordered in another way. Regardless of the normative system of which they are a part, deviant behaviors can be differentiated, classified, and understood by the manner in which they are typically expressed. A major distinguishing feature is how organized the deviance is in usual practice. Some is almost always expressed in unorganized form; other deviance is usually practiced in moderately organized form; and additional types are nearly always fully organized in their expression (see Best and Luckenbill, 1996).

Manifestations of Organization

What does organization mean? A fully organized deviance is one in which the participants can act in concert to accomplish explicit and clearly articulated goals because the practitioners are differentiated into coordinated roles and statuses. They behave in ways predictable to each other because of mutually shared norms, enforced by potential sanctions from other practitioners. Organization is both a product of and a cause of several features that are so inextricably bound together that it becomes difficult to distinguish organization per se from its causes, consequences, and byproducts. Therefore, to ascertain the degree of organization characterizing deviance, it is necessary to examine a collection of indicators that usually accompany organization. At least nine such criteria can be identified: (1) the extent to which the deviant behavior typically involves or requires cooperation of two or more people; (2) pervasiveness of the behavior—the amount of time and resources individual participants usually devote to the deviance or to deviance-related activities; (3) the frequency, depth, and effectiveness of communication among activists; (4) the extent to which there is a hierarchical distinction and coordination among roles and statuses of those practicing the deviance; (5) the degree to which the activity is characterized by a distinct internal culture of its own; (6) the extent to which the typical participant roots his or her personal self-identity in the deviant activity; (7) the comprehensiveness and integration of legitimations that practitioners use to justify their deviance; (8) the degree to which activists are subject to social control from inside a group; and (9) the amount, and systemization, of the effort that activists devote to recruiting new practitioners.

Each of these indicators is actually a continuous variable; any form of deviance expresses more or less of the quantity in question. The overall degree of organization of any deviance is a reflection of these nine criteria combined into a somewhat unique configuration. Although there is some consistency among them (a form of deviance high on one indicator will likely be high on most others as well), perfect congruence seldom occurs. That is why we need to consider each criterion as a separate aspect of social organization and to explain what it means.

Sociality

Some deviant behavior can be, and almost always is, performed alone; a person doesn't need to be taught how to do it; its practice does not require the cooperation of others; and its continuation does not depend upon emotional and social support from other practitioners (Best and Luckenbill, 1996). Since such behavior is ordinarily committed by isolated individuals, and since social organization always involves more than one person in coordinated activity, behaviors low on sociality are inherently unorganized. Completely unorganized deviance can include bizarre behaviors so unconventional that they are regarded as evidence of mental illness: eating feces, talking nonsense language, catatonic withdrawal, suicide (usually), and the like. These behaviors are often practiced by individuals who are unable to relate to others, much less join them in coordinated activities of a conventional or deviant nature. Other isolated acts of deviance may be more mundane or may involve someone who conducts an otherwise "normal" life, for example, singing in an elevator or the man who likes to wear women's clothing around the house.

Deviance in Everyday Life
An example of group suicide occurred on November 18, 1978, in the South American country of Guyana when over 900 members of a religious group led by the Reverend Jim Jones committed suicide. Most members of the religious cult, the People's Temple, killed themselves by drinking a poison concoction of cyanide and grape Kool-Aid; others killed themselves or were killed by guns. The Rev. Jim Jones' congregation was nomadic, settling in Indiana and California before moving to the remote jungle location in Guyana, which is on the border of Venezuela. Jones proclaimed himself messiah, and shortly before the mass suicide he had ordered the killing of U.S. Congressman Leo Ryan, who had visited the Jones camp (named Jonestown) to investigate alleged human rights abuses in the religious community.

This is not to say that such activities can never be organized or to deny that they ever are. It is not unheard of for several people to band together in planning and carrying out suicide pacts, and in at least one incident an entire group of several hundred cooperated in mass suicide (Hall, 1987; Layton, 1998). In addition, child or adolescent groups have on occasion organized themselves to use nonsense language, usually to aggravate adults. But these are unusual and obvious exceptions to the rule. Using nonsense language, commission of suicide, and the other bizarre behaviors mentioned are normally nonsocial activities. Consequently, they fall near the extreme on a continuum of sociality and usually on a continuum of organization as well.

On the other hand, some types of deviance are almost always practiced in the company of and in cooperation with others, often with many others. Perhaps the best examples are the activities of sectarian religious groups like the Hutterites (Kephart, 1976). The Hutterites are distinguished by unusual life styles and practices that have been disapproved by outsiders. For 400 years the Hutterites have lived in farming communities separated from the larger society. They enjoy a form of economic communism, mutually sharing the means of production as well as the fruits of their labors. Their communities are highly successful, based as they are on religious principles of self-sacrifice for group welfare. Yet their isolationism, their ever-expanding population and the accompanying need to buy more and more land, their religious principles requiring pacifism, and their unorthodox economic system have evoked enmity wherever they have settled (Kephart, 1976).

It is inherently contradictory to think of isolated individuals engaging in economic communism. Clearly some types of deviance require the presence and involvement of more than one individual, and because of this inherent sociality they are likely to be quite well organized. But the extent to which a given deviant activity is typically practiced in the company of or with the cooperation of others is not simply the matter of all or none implied by the example described. Between extreme instances such as catatonic withdrawal on one end of the continuum and economic communism on the other are many instances that fall somewhere in between. For instance, heroin or other illegal drug use involves much interaction with and cooperation of others. There has to be contact with a network to obtain a steady supply of the drug, some social relationships with trustworthy associates to avoid police and to learn the techniques, desire, and folklore of use, as well as relationships to manage problems that result from abuse. Yet, after enmeshment in these social networks, individuals often end up injecting the drug alone and experiencing the euphoria or the sickness of deprivation privately. Thus, drug usage is to some extent, but not totally, social.

Pervasiveness

The proportion of time, resources, and energy that typical participants devote to a deviant activity, relative to the other things they do, is a good predictor of the thoroughness of social organization. Since social organization is usually a product of sustained interaction among people, the more pervasive a deviant activity is for most of its participants, the greater the chances that individuals will find themselves in sustained interaction with others similarly occupied, and the greater the probability that norms, culture, social controls, and other organizational components will emerge. Some deviance ordinarily claims relatively little time and effort from those who do it. Murder, for instance, is seldom planned; usually it is a result of spontaneous anger or other emotion that leads to violence against friends, kin, or associates who happen to be present (Katz, 1988). The vast majority of killers spend little time thinking about their crime before they do it; the act is committed in a brief encounter, often no more than a few minutes; and the assailants rarely repeat the act. Hence murder and murder-related activities occupy only a minute part of anybody's life. Even among the few professional killers who repeatedly plan, execute, and reflect on the technicalities of murder, these activities take up a minor part of their lives compared with the other things they do, such as buying groceries, watching television, courting, or sightseeing. Murder is simply not a pervasive behavior; consequently, it is unorganized. Ironically, when killing does become pervasive and organized, it is no longer regarded as murder or as deviant; instead it is called war.

Although murder is extreme in its lack of pervasiveness, there are other types of deviance that are moderately demanding of time and resources. A good example is illegal gambling. Those who are "into" making bets on athletic contests or numbers or who like to play poker in private places for high stakes often spend some time every day or every few days investigating the games or events in question, perfecting their playing or handicapping techniques, calculating odds, and keeping up with outcomes. In addition, most gamblers talk frequently about their activities, ever in search of challengers. Yet for most participants, gambling is far from a full-time activity. Many work at regular jobs, maintain homes, raise children, go to the movies, and do most of the things everybody else does. Nevertheless, because investment of time and resources is proportionally much greater than for murder, the organizational level of illegal gambling is also higher. Of course, this does not mean that every gambler treats wagering as if it were an avocation or that all illegal gambling is reasonably well organized. No doubt some individuals sporadically gamble illegally and choose equally sporadic partners, and to that extent some gambling is less organized than it might be. But few would deny the pervasiveness of illegal gambling among some segments of the population, particularly those who live in inner city areas, nor would they deny that such gambling is moderately organized.

An example of highly pervasive deviance is that practiced by radical/revolutionary groups such as the Symbionese Liberation Army (SLA) that became famous during the late 1960s for their kidnapping of heiress Patricia Hearst and her subsequent involvement with them in a bank robbery and other holdups (Baker, 1974). Most members of the SLA lived in communes or gathered almost daily with other members. Their lives were consumed with discussions of politics, planning for revolutionary change or self-defense from the feared establishment, stockpiling arms and supplies for revolt, and recruitment. Such extreme expenditure of time, energy, and emotional commitments almost guarantees that a strong organization will emerge, which it did.

Communication

A third feature signifying the extent of deviant organization is communication among participants. Communication here refers not merely to the frequency or extent of message exchange, though that is important, but also to how effectively meaning is conveyed. Some people can talk to each other all the time but learn hardly anything about each other, while others manage to exchange ideas and develop mutual understanding with relatively little talking. The more organized the deviance, the more likely that practitioners will achieve mutual understanding of thought, attitudes, and intended actions, and the more they will be able to coordinate activity.

Sometimes communication is limited because practitioners are not known to each other. Indeed, much deviance is secretive and hidden, even from others holding similar preferences, and fear of revealing one's own secrets often inhibits efforts to find other activists. But even when fellow travelers can recognize each other, they may not be able to communicate—sometimes because of fear but occasionally because of physical or psychological barriers, like those preventing catatonics from talking to each other. On the other hand, some forms of deviance almost inherently require communication, so much so that activists make it easy for others to find them, sometimes openly declaring themselves or displaying symbols that everybody, including conventional people, can see.

Variations in the extent of communication among practitioners of different kinds of deviance can be seen in three examples. First, embezzlers exhibit almost no communication. They are usually bookkeepers working for legitimate businesses or other organizations such as banks, insurance companies, or charitable foundations. They take organizational assets and try to hide the losses through manipulative accounting. These criminals are typically conventional in outlook and life style, but they get involved in stealing because of some pressing financial problem, such as the need to pay off gambling debts. Once involved, they cannot call upon other thieves for emotional support or for training in better methods of embezzlement without jeopardizing themselves. In addition, they are usually too embarrassed to admit what they are doing or to disclose the reasons for their original financial problems, even to other embezzlers if they could find them (Cressey, 1953). Hence, embezzlers rarely communicate with anybody about their illegal activities, much less with a network of other embezzlers who might become organized for the mutual practice of their deviance.

In contrast are members of deviant sectarian religious groups. Their total lives are bound up in religious activities and in religiously inspired life styles necessitating constant, extensive communication with fellow believers. A good example are the Amish who live in Pennsylvania and parts of the Midwest (Kephart and Zellner, 1994). These primitive-living people spend all their time with each other in tight-knit agricultural enclaves. Contact with the outside world is discouraged and regulated; even access to the news media is denied. Children are educated in Amish schools; the community is almost completely self-sufficient economically; and all recreational, legal, and political matters are handled by the Amish themselves. As a result, all ideas, rationalizations, and opinions are totally forged through in-group interaction. Furthermore, the Amish meet regularly in congregations where spiritual leaders communicate with the rest. Thus, hardly anything of concern to an Amish person is not a matter of communication exclusively with other activists in this form of deviance.

A third example of deviance practitioners who communicate more than embezzlers but less than the Amish are nudists. Although some nudists go naked on hidden roofs or deserted beaches and never discuss their transgressions, many seek out others with whom they can share the experience, exchange ideas, or discuss problems. Locales have been established where nudity can be practiced in company with others. Advantages of such "camps" include greater safety from intrusion as well as the comfort of being surrounded by people who approve of the behavior, many of whom are also sympathetic and receptive conversationalists. But nudists do not stop at interpersonal communication. They have national facilities for publishing magazines and newsletters and they have many websites that are widely read by regular practitioners (and occasionally by those with prurient interests). Many nudists, therefore, are integrated into communication networks providing philosophies and opinions; information about events, locations, and facilities for nudity; and legal problems or other harassment. Yet nudists do not typically spend all their time with other nudists. Most are part-time participants, confining their deviance to weekends and vacations. The rest of the time most nudists act like conventional people, carrying on ordinary lives and participating in the ordinary activities of work, play, and politics of the clothed world. The depth of communication among nudists falls somewhere near the middle of the continuum of communication.

Differentiation and Coordination

Organization implies systematic, coordinated activity. To achieve that, any collectivity of individuals must differentiate themselves into separate roles and statuses, arranged so that some make decisions, receive information, and direct others, while other participants carry out tasks or engage in various activities at the behest or expectation of those in charge of coordination. Some deviance, as it is typically practiced, lacks any differentiation of roles and statuses and requires no coordination, while other deviance involves elaborate differentiation and systematic coordination. Those that lack differentiation and coordination fall near the unorganized end of the continuum of organization, while those more differentiated and coordinated fall near the fully organized end.

One illustration of deviance lacking differentiation and coordination is public nose-picking. Those who practice this form of unacceptable behavior have never been known to differentiate themselves by roles and obligations either among themselves or vis-à-vis those who are not nose-pickers. Nobody has ever identified nose-pickers who coordinate the activity of nose-picking among their peers or who coordinate the activity of nose-pickers in political activity, recruiting others, or in settling disputes among activists. Moreover, there is no evidence to suggest that some nose-pickers have higher status among nose-pickers than do others. As far as we know, there are no especially prestigious ways of picking noses, there is no honor in a long history of successful nose-picking, and there are no ways in which one nose-picker might become especially important as a representative of nose-pickers to the outside world. In other words, public nose-picking is almost completely unorganized in this respect.

A contrasting example is the Gypsies, a nomadic band of people believed to have descended from an ancient tribe in India (Kephart and Zellner, 1994). The Gypsy life style is inherently deviant from the point of view of dominant groups in most areas where the Gypsies roam. This judgment arises from the Gypsies' devotion to travel. They rarely have permanent homes, jobs, or roots in any community. Their style is to live off the land and the native populations, taking what they can from local residents through manipulations, scams, and theft, working only as a temporary means of survival, and moving on as necessary or as the mood strikes. The Gypsies, however, have an elaborate division of labor, with clear distinctions between men and women and between regular activists and leaders. Decisions about movement are made by designated leaders; marital arrangements are made by parents; and disputes are settled by indigenous courts. In matters of importance to the group as a whole, such as an arrest of an individual Gypsy or organized efforts of local authorities to run the caravan out of town, leaders negotiate on behalf of the whole group with the representatives of the outside world. In contrast to nose-pickers, the Gypsies are highly differentiated and coordinated.

Usage of illegal drugs falls somewhere between these two extremes. There is unquestionably role differentiation among drug users, including distinctions between suppliers and users, between novices and veterans, and between those who watch for intruders and those who enjoy drugs while the others stand guard. In addition, there is a status hierarchy among drug users. Veteran users, those who have many experiences and much knowledge of the drug world to share and who can discuss things effectively, have higher status than younger, less knowledgeable, and inexperienced users. But beyond the network of suppliers, there is little coordination of the differentiated activities of users. Nobody is recognized as being in charge; and concerted, goal-oriented activity of groups of users who pursue their own political or social interests is rare. In short, drug users have great difficulty acting in concert, and there is no designated segment of the drug world that can act on behalf of drug users. Hence drug use is only semi-organized in terms of differentiation and coordination.

Culture

Another key accouterment of organization is the extent of culture associated with the deviance. Culture refers to ideas, artifacts, language forms, rules of conduct, or any other thing passed on from one participant to another or from one generation of practitioners to another. Some deviant activists develop and share an elaborate culture while others lack any distinctive features that would provide temporal continuity for identification. For instance, Gypsies have unusual beliefs about cleanliness and filth, special ways of communicating and dressing, rules for appropriate behavior toward non-Gypsies, and distinct ideas about various aspects of life that are taught to Gypsy children the world over. They wear bright-colored clothing, marry young, and regard the upper body as clean and pure, while the lower body is seen as defiled. The two parts of the body must not mix, even indirectly. As a result, Gypsies do many things that make no sense to outsiders. They refuse to wash clothing for different parts of the body in the same container; they frequently and meticulously clean their hands with special soaps and towels; and they avoid contact with non-Gypsies lest the filth of the outsiders jeopardize their own attempts to remain pure. Gypsies live in extended families, and parents arrange marriages for their children, often at an age below legal limits in most American states. Individual Gypsies like to use various aliases, and they frequently misrepresent their real names to outsiders, partly to avoid identification by intruders seeking to collect debts or serve legal papers. Their special language includes reference to themselves as Rom rather than Gypsy and to non-Gypsies as Gadje. They regard all Gadje as legitimate objects of exploitation whose sole purpose is to be victimized through swindles and theft. All of these beliefs and practices are taught to children and constantly reinforced in everyday interaction. Such things distinguish Gypsies from all other groups and all individual Gypsies from other individuals, providing a focus for group solidarity and identity (Kephart and Zellner, 1994). Such is the essence of culturally supported deviance.

In contrast are those who organize their lives around delusions. Such individuals usually share no culture at all, partly because their delusions are idiosyncratic. Psychotics rarely develop any distinctive ideas about how best to deal with their visions of reality or why expressing them in one way rather than another is a good thing; nor do they normally employ tools or special implements in the practice of their deviance. Moreover, they have no mutual expectations about how people with delusions should relate to each other when together or when they see each other in public, nor do they have a peculiar shared language or even special shared words known only to practitioners. In short, there is nothing to be passed on from one delusional person to another or from veterans to novices—there is typically no culture. If there is any evidence at all of culture among psychotics, it is of a local and transitory type, perhaps growing out of common hospital experiences.

Thus, Gypsy behavior is an extreme instance of deviant activity supported and defined by culture; psychotic behavior is an extreme case of noncultural deviance. But there are many gradations of culture in between. For example, practitioners of public restroom homosexuality share a rudimentary culture, more extensive than that of nose-pickers but less encompassing than that of Gypsies (Humphreys, 1970). They recognize some norms of interaction—unspoken rules about how to initiate a sexual encounter in a public restroom and how to perform various roles from aggressor to guard. They use peculiar words to refer to various aspects of the deviant activity and the environment in which it takes place, such as "glory hole" to signify an opening cut in the wall of a toilet stall through which a man can stick his penis to be fellated by the occupant of the adjoining stall, or "tearoom" to designate a public restroom where sexual contacts might be made. And they share a folklore of previous experience. Yet the culture is limited; it does not include norms about such things as style of dress, occupation of the participants, ways of behaving outside the public restroom (except that participants are never to recognize other participants in other places). The tearoom activists make no use of unusual or distinctive artifacts, nor is the behavior characterized by peculiar symbols that allow practitioners and others to recognize regulars. Hence public restroom homosexuality falls about midway between public nose-picking and Gypsy life in the extent of its culture.

 ### Self-Identity

A sixth criterion of organization is how extensively practitioners form images of themselves in terms of the deviant activity (Best and Luckenbill, 1996). If a sample of militant feminists were asked to tell us how they think of themselves or to answer the question "who are you," and they answered truthfully, most would probably say they think of themselves primarily as political persons concerned with the rights and activities of women. Most would more than likely rank "feminist" very near the top of a list of nouns, such as "woman," "daughter," "writer," "American," "New Yorker," or "Catholic," that they might use to describe themselves. This would indicate that most conceive of themselves in a way heavily influenced by feminist activities and theory. In contrast, businesspeople who violate the laws against price fixing do not ordinarily think of themselves in terms of their illegal activities. If they truthfully answer the question "who are you," it would scarcely even occur to them to say they are "swindlers," "criminals," "price conspirators," or "thieves." Instead they would likely mention words like "businessman," "father," "husband," "Republican," or "Methodist," never mentioning anything at all about price fixing. In other words, their self-images would have little or nothing to do with their deviance.

The extent to which practitioners' self-images are built around deviance is also reflected in whether the typical activist is ashamed of his or her participation. Some deviant participants hide their activities, not wanting anybody to know except other activists with whom they participate directly. An example of this "hidden" deviant would be the "closet" homosexual, who keeps his sexual preference a virtual secret. Others are proud of their activities and hide them only when necessary for protection from intrusion or punishment. An example of someone on the extreme end of the homosexual continuum would be a member of the militant homosexual group ACT UP, who, among other things, attempts to expose prominent homosexuals who have been successful in hiding their identities as homosexuals. Feminists usually declare themselves openly; they feel pride in what they are doing, not shame or guilt. But price-fixing businesspeople try to remain hidden, even from other participants, and when exposed to public view, try to cover their shame with denials or rationalizations. Therefore, feminists are much further along the continuum of deviant self-concept than are business conspirators.

A type of deviance that falls somewhere between feminism and price fixing along the continuum of deviant self-concept is that of swinging (Bartell, 1971; Symonds, 1971). Many swingers draw some part of their psychic identities from open participation in recreational sex, but it is not a major identity for most of them, and most would feel some shame or embarrassment at public exposure. Yet many are willing to reveal themselves at least semipublicly by entering or exiting swinger clubs, running photo ads in swinger magazines (although usually with face covered) that are sold for wide distribution, and disclosing their activities in conversations with close friends. Replying honestly about themselves, most would report their occupational, parental, marital, and political identities first but would include "swinger" as one lesser identity. Of course, there are also some activists in recreational sex who have no sense of themselves as "swingers" but rather engage in it episodically, all the time feeling guilt and convincing themselves that these activities are temporary deviations that say nothing about the kinds of people they really are.

Hence, swinging would have to be somewhere near the middle of the self-concept continuum.

Philosophical Integration

One of the most important criteria of the extent of deviance organization is the coherence, comprehensiveness, and character of legitimations that the participants use to explain their activities to themselves and others (Buckner, 1971). Practitioners of some types of deviance have almost no intellectual rationale for what they do, indicating that the behavior falls on the lower end of a continuum of philosophical integration. When Americans burp in the presence of others, they usually apologize or excuse themselves but rarely try to justify the behavior. And if you ask them why they burped (or burp) in public, they probably won't have a ready answer. Some may spontaneously invent something like, "I had this gas and couldn't hold back." If pressed, many may try to justify their conduct, particularly if it appears that you are condemning or accusing them. They might say, "I've been ill lately," or "Well, why not, other people were wishing they had the courage to do the same thing." But such justifications would certainly be self-oriented and self-serving; they would not in the least suggest that the behavior was committed for altruistic purposes or that it sprang from larger philosophical concerns.

Other deviants have moderately well-built rationales for their behavior. Truckers frequently violate state or Federal laws designed to regulate load weights, hours of driving time during a given day, speed, truck maintenance schedules, and other aspects of hauling. Most drivers can readily recite their reasons for breaking the law. Some of these reasons, or legitimations, are narrow and self-serving: "I have to do it to make a living." "It is the nature of the business; if I didn't, the competition would wipe me out." "Company deadlines require it." At the same time, truckers also share some intellectual views that in their minds seem to legitimate systematic law violation. For one thing, they may tell you that the laws are silly, ill-conceived, impossibly complex, and inefficient in their intended purpose and that those laws are the products of an irrational and unfair legal process. Moreover, many truckers may argue that their deviance is actually a good thing because efficient transport of goods is essential to the vitality and productivity of the entire economy; some will point out that their crimes help to keep prices down by making the movement of goods less expensive; and a few will contend that their violations actually create jobs for other people. In short, truckers can present a more or less sophisticated, albeit fragmented, set of legitimations for their deviance. This is possible because those excuses have been developed, learned, and shared informally in numerous bull sessions at truck stops, cafes, and loading docks, as well as on the C.B. radio; on occasion, these legitimations have actually been used in self-defense by individual truckers.

Although trucker legitimations are of a higher order (more altruistic and more nearly reflective of a larger intellectual perspective) than those of the public burpers, they still fall far short of a comprehensive philosophy. The rationales truckers use are limited to trucking and its related activities; they draw on a limited range of moral or intellectual principles; and their justifications are somewhat isolated from each other, not really linked into a meaningful, coherent, or consistent world view. Therefore, trucking-related deviance is located more toward the middle of the continuum of philosophical integration than is public burping. Still, it does not come anywhere near the end of the continuum representative of full philosophical integration; that position is left to sectarian religious groups like the Amish, the Branch Davidians (whose compound in Waco, Texas, was assaulted by the FBI in 1993), or the Heaven's Gate group (who committed mass suicide in 1997 in the belief they could ride to the hereafter aboard a spaceship supposedly trailing the Hale-Bopp comet).

The Amish, for instance, are a deeply religious people who believe they are especially chosen and set apart by God. In order to maintain their purity and way of life, they refuse to mix with the outside world or to allow any changes that might disrupt their communities or life style. To further this goal, the Amish wear plain black garb, avoiding all jewelry or colors that might draw attention to them as individuals or reflect vanity. Most work as farmers or housewives, using primitive tools, equipment, and methods. They live simple lives in which modern conveniences like electricity and household appliances are rejected. The children are prohibited from attending public schools for fear they will be contaminated by worldly concerns.

In many respects Amish behavior is regarded as ignorant, ridiculous, and unacceptable by modern standards. But the rationale for this deviance is not self-oriented, nor is it self-serving, since the Amish way of life is hard and demanding, with few pleasures and no luxuries. Instead, each custom has a specific place in an elaborate theology/philosophy concerning the nature of the world, how one should relate to others, and the relationship between God and humans. An individual Amish farmer might not be able to articulate the full philosophy (because he is never required to do so), but it can easily be seen in the ideas, activities, meetings, and interactions among the Amish people. The philosophy is highly integrated (each part fits into a coherent whole), it is comprehensive (covering every conceivable aspect of human existence), and it is of a higher order, involving principles of behavior designed to serve a completely unselfish purpose.

Social Control From Within the Group

In general, the more organized a deviance is, the more its activists are subject to social control from within the collectivity of participants; that is, their behavior is regulated by sanctions. In the most organized forms of deviant behavior, participants are threatened with formal punishments administered under the authority of designated leaders. Social control, of course, presupposes the existence of shared expectations for behavior, so there are some forms of deviance where social control is completely absent simply because there are no group norms to be enforced. Some kinds of deviance are characterized by norms that are enforced informally, if at all. And the most organized forms of deviance have community norms enforced formally as well as informally.

An example of deviance where no norms or enforcement typically exist is purse snatching. Since purse snatchers are usually loners, they do not recognize any rules about how, when, and from whom to snatch purses (anybody can do it any way they want); how to interact with other purse snatchers (they rarely interact as purse snatchers per se); appropriate forms of dress while at work; or anything else. Even less so do purse snatchers have to worry about being formally sanctioned by representatives of a purse-snatching community should they violate some norms governing purse-snatching behavior. There is simply no formal social control among purse snatchers and probably very little informal control. Therefore, this form of deviance is located near the lower end of the continuum of organization.

❖ ❖ ❖ ❖

An example of deviance located near the middle of the continuum of control is swinging. Swingers do share mutual expectations about how they should behave toward each other, appropriate etiquette in contacting potential new partners, cleanliness, and discretion. For instance, it is expected that initial contact will be made by males to males rather than directly from one male to a female (Bartell, 1971; Symonds, 1971); if a person expresses no interest in a particular sexual activity, it will not be pursued; and it is understood that swingers will call the homes of their potential partners only at designated hours so that parental conversations can be safe from the ears of children. But these kinds of rules are usually enforced informally. There is no police force representing swinger groups that goes around punishing those who violate the rules, although there are bouncers in many swinging clubs who may eject rowdies or troublemakers. Instead, a couple who fails to respect the norms is likely to find itself isolated from further contact, yelled at, or belittled by those who are victimized by their misbehavior. Hence, swinging is partially subject to social control but is not fully controlled.

A form of deviance located near the upper, or fully organized, end of the control continuum is that practiced by Mafia families (Cressey, 1969; Ianni and Reuss-Ianni, 1972). These groups deal in deviance as a business. In order to make money and escape the law, they must arrange things so that employees perform their tasks dependably and efficiently and in a way that will not jeopardize the business operation or the safety of the Mafia leaders. Consequently, there is an elaborate set of norms governing the behavior of all kinds of personnel from narcotics distributors to bodyguards. And there is an efficient, formal procedure by which transgressors are handled, including official orders from leaders to kill disloyal or inefficient people. This is the ultimate formal control.

Recruitment

Finally, deviant organization is indicated by the nature of recruitment of new practitioners. In general, the greater the extent to which activists are committed to bringing in new participants, especially the more they use systematic means to recruit, the greater the degree of organization. Some deviance, such as that practiced by sectarian religious groups like the Mormons involves sustained, self-conscious, purposive efforts to persuade others to join. The Mormons require their young men to serve two years of missionary duty, during which they devote all their effort to evangelism (Kephart and Zellner, 1994). In addition, the Mormon group as a whole strongly encourages marriage and biological reproduction among the faithful (at one time even promoting a system of multiple wives), which enables these offspring to be inducted as new members through gradual socialization to share the precepts of the religion. But even though recruitment is extensive among the Mormons, it is not all-consuming, as it is among some radical/revolutionary political groups, where acquiring new followers is the main activity and prime reason for existence.

There are other forms of deviance, however, where the participants rarely if ever try to influence someone else to do it. Nonsense talkers, family deserters, and rapists rarely care whether others behave similarly, and the only recruitment is unintended: somebody observes or hears about the behavior and imitates it, sometimes simply in mockery or jest. Finally, some types of deviance, like prostitution, involve haphazard recruitment—sometimes systematic, sometimes irregular, and sometimes nonexistent (Davis, 1971; Hall, 1972; Sheehy, 1973).

While the extent of recruitment is usually indicative of the degree of social organization, it is not an invariant guide. Much recruitment to deviant activity of all types is a natural product of interaction, and some novices bring themselves in through curiosity and imitation, no matter what the intent of practitioners. Any time a number of people are in close enough contact with deviant participants to communicate extensively, some will be inspired to experiment personally with, or adopt, the practices of those who were previously regarded as weird or debased. Although most Mormon converts are products of evangelism or biological reproduction, some are brought into the church in unintended ways. Perhaps an individual gets acquainted with a Mormon co-worker and grows to admire that person's diligence and self-assurance. Because he wants to have those same qualities, he may try to learn more about the person. A friendly relationship may then lead to voluntary conversion with no special efforts having been expended by the admired Mormon. Or a few may read about Mormons and grow curious enough to contact church representatives, who will show the way to conversion.

Similarly, some females become prostitutes simply by being around other women who practice the trade. They learn through observation and conversation what is involved, the rewards and costs, and the rationalizations for participation. Through personal association they come to regard prostitution as an acceptable way of earning money and turn to it in a time of need without ever having been seduced, persuaded, or even encouraged—indeed, sometimes despite discouragement from participants. And some deviance relies upon simple curiosity to guarantee new activists. It is said that vice police must be rotated regularly to new duty to avoid being co-opted by those they are policing. Officers who patrol public restrooms to prevent homosexual acts sometimes end up as participants themselves, not because they were seduced but simply because observing and imagining what could motivate these men stimulated their curiosity to the point where it exceeded previous repugnance.

Obviously there is more to recruitment than organization. Whether people are drawn into deviance in the absence of systematic inducement depends upon the intrinsic appeal of the behavior, the number and distribution of practitioners, and the degree to which the activity is unacceptable. Other things being equal, behaviors that are fun or directly rewarding (like swinging) will benefit more from "natural" recruitment than will those that demand sacrifices (such as sectarian religious practice). When participants are numerous and widely dispersed (as are marijuana smokers), they are more likely to attract converts "naturally" than if the practitioners are isolated and secretive (as are enema freaks). And extremely deviant behaviors (such as necrophilia) are less likely to enjoy natural induction than are those closer to conventionality (like tax cheating). But these inherent advantages or disadvantages don't tell the whole story because activists in even the most unlikely forms of deviance sometimes manage to devote themselves to recruitment and to do it so effectively that they prosper. The key to successful recruitment, then, is commitment and systematization, although the kinds of things discussed above help or hinder.

It is also true that some fairly well-organized deviance is of such a nature that its activists engage in only limited recruitment. Sometimes this limitation is because exclusivity is one of the main attractions of the deviance. The greater the emphasis on exclusivity, the more problematic recruitment becomes. But there is an interesting tension between exclusivity and recruitment because in most such instances a modicum of growth must be guaranteed to ensure the continuity of the deviant activity, without which any claim to exclusivity would be meaningless. In other kinds of deviance, recruitment is necessary to keep the deviance going but it is potentially counterproductive since additional practitioners become competitors for scarce resources around which the deviance is built.

Cryonics exemplifies the exclusivity dilemma. Cryonics believers want their bodies frozen immediately after death (or in the case of the true believer even before death) on the assumption that some time in the future technology will have advanced to the point where all human life can be prolonged or the diseases from which the person suffered will have been conquered. Adherents plan for their bodies to be thawed and restored to life at that time. But such an outcome is possible only for a limited, exclusive clientele. For one thing, bodies must be frozen in special containers where a continuous flow of cooling chemical can be sustained for indeterminate periods of time. Preparations for freezing at the precise moment of death require unusual arrangements with medical institutions and personnel. Moreover, the maintenance of corpses in a frozen condition is legally questionable in most states in the United States, and freezing someone prior to death (in effect killing them) is a crime. Finally, the success of the cryonics effort depends upon the willingness of future generations to thaw and revive frozen bodies—a commitment supposedly to be cultivated and carried out by others in the movement long after their predecessors have entered the frozen state. The tremendous demands made on followers and the elaborateness of conditions necessary for success make it unlikely that large numbers can participate. The greater the population of cryonites, the less chance for success for any given one, and the greater the burdens for the unfrozen. Yet, at the same time, successful practice of cryonics requires that a sufficient number of new personnel be added regularly over many generations.

Prostitution is a form of deviance wherein some recruitment occurs but where too much is self-defeating. Pimps, operators of houses of prostitution, and managers of call-girl networks have a short-range interest in recruiting as many women into the business as possible. However, as the number of practitioners expands, so does the competition for clients; therefore, the less money each person makes, unless the number of patrons also increases, which is an unlikely possibility. The consequences of overrecruitment are of obvious immediate concern to those who directly serve the clients, but it eventually concerns their managers. When business finally becomes too slack to allow profit to outweigh risk, pimps and managers become more aware of destructive competition. Consequently, over time a form of equilibrium develops in which recruitment is balanced by restraint. Some pimps do continue to seduce new women who will be in their "stables," and some madams or call-girl managers continue to seek fresh employees to provide variety for their clients. In addition, an occasional practicing prostitute will herself informally induct one of her friends or associates into the business. All of this is made necessary by the fact that some prostitutes leave the life as they grow too old to compete successfully or simply tire of the hassle. Yet attempts to recruit are not excessive. Practitioners cannot afford really successful recruitment lest they put themselves out of business.

The Organizational Continuum

Clearly, different kinds of deviance reflect various degrees of each of these nine criteria of organization. But because the criteria are not always congruent, the nine indicators must be merged to reveal how organized any particular deviant behavior actually is. Imagine that one could accurately measure on a 100-point scale the degree to which any deviance possessed each of the nine characteristics discussed. We might find that a given type of deviance scores 42 on a scale of sociality, 68 on a scale of pervasiveness, 54 on a scale of communication, and so on. To derive the location of that deviance on a continuum of organization, one might then average scores across the nine criteria. If the average were 51, the deviance would be near the center of the continuum in the subcultural zone. By such a procedure, if a particular form of deviance scored quite differently on one or two of the criteria than it did on the rest, its overall organizational score would not be distorted. So, for example, if a specific form of deviance had scores in the 20–30 range on eight of the criteria but scored 80 on one criterion, it would end up in the individualized zone rather than close to the fully organized end, where it would have fallen had only the criterion showing a score of 80 been used to decide its degree of organization.

In thinking about amalgamation of the organizational criteria, remember that organization is itself a continuous rather than a discrete variable; some types of deviance have more of it than others. Therefore, strictly speaking, it is incorrect to isolate categories of organization, as some are prone to do when, for example, they talk about Mafia activities as "organized crime," presumably to contrast them with other crime that is not at all organized. Nevertheless, to discuss the subject effectively it is convenient to divide the organizational continuum into zones. Activities falling within given ranges can, for heuristic purposes, be regarded as "types" similar in degree of organization.

This is shown in Figure 2.1. It depicts two continuums. The first is an undifferentiated gradation of small increments from relatively less organization on one end through moderate organization in the middle to relatively more organization on the other end. The second continuum portrays the same gradations differentiated into zones representing thirds of the continuum. We can place deviant activities on the first continuum and end up with a full array from those with relatively little organization to those elaborately organized, and we could probably find some deviance that would fit on each step along the way, no matter how minute the increments, if we could measure the various components precisely enough. But this much detail tends to overwhelm, and information pertaining to the nine criteria may be too limited to permit as much precision as the graduated continuum implies. Therefore, it might be useful to categorize deviance into three "types"—individualized, subcultural, and fully organized.

In the next three chapters we will examine each of these types, beginning with "individualized deviance." It must be remembered, however, that dividing the continuum into thirds is arbitrary. It may be that some deviance near the upper end of the "individualized" range is actually more like another devi-

Figure 2.1   Continuum of Organization of Deviance

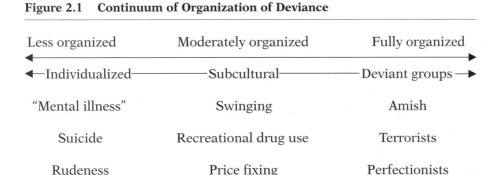

Less organized	Moderately organized	Fully organized
←Individualized—————Subcultural—————Deviant groups →		
"Mental illness"	Swinging	Amish
Suicide	Recreational drug use	Terrorists
Rudeness	Price fixing	Perfectionists

Criteria of Organization:
1. Sociality—involves more than one person in interaction.
2. Pervasiveness—proportion of time, resources, and energy devoted.
3. Communication—frequent and extensive message exchange with shared meanings.
4. Differentiation and Coordination—specialized roles and coordinated action.
5. Culture—collection of things passed on from one generation of practitioners to another via learning.
6. Identification—how extensively practitioners define self in terms of the deviant activity.
7. Philosophical Integration—coherence, comprehensiveness, and rationality of legitimations or rationalizations for the activity.
8. Internal Social Control—Degree of regulation via sanctions threatened or imposed by group members.
9. Recruitment—extent of systematic efforts to bring in new practitioners.

ance in the lower part of the "subcultural" zone than one near the lower end of its own range. Despite such potential distortions, identifying organization types permits us to conceptually order a disparate subject matter for clearer understanding. As we will see later, the extent to which a given deviance is organized bears on how well various theories explain it. Thus, organization is a crucial feature of deviance because it clusters and differentiates a plethora of behaviors, and it provides a key focus for explanatory schemes. ✦

Chapter 3

Individualized Deviance

In the previous chapter we authors suggested that deviance can be classified according to the degree of organization characterizing its typical expression. Since organization means orderly, predictable patterns of action among those who commit a given deviance and implies the ability to act in concert, it cannot be measured directly. Instead, to assess the degree of organization typical of various forms of deviance, we must examine a deviance for features that are ordinarily associated with organization. Nine such features were identified and discussed, and it was suggested that merging the nine would enable us to array different kinds of deviance on a continuum of organization. At one end of that continuum would be forms of deviance that typically show little or no organization and at the other end would be those forms of deviance that are usually highly organized. Other forms of deviance would be located on the continuum to indicate degrees of organization somewhere between the extreme anchor points. However, to simplify discussion, it was suggested that the continuum of organization could be roughly divided into thirds. The types of deviance in the lowest third could be called individualistic deviance because they generally show low degrees of organization, as reflected in the extent to which they fail to or only weakly manifest the nine features indicative of organization. In this chapter we will consider in detail two kinds of deviance that appear to be very individualistic—suicide and serial murder.

Suicide

At first blush it would seem easy to define suicide because to most of us it is simply killing oneself. The World Health Organization (WHO), an agency of the United Nations that compiles suicide statistics internationally, defines suicide as a suicidal act (further delimited as "self-injury with varying degrees of lethal intent") with a fatal outcome (O'Carroll, 1989). In reality, however, it is not easy to establish when a death is the result of suicide rather than an accident or foul play.

First, the definition provided by WHO does not specify any particular time frame. People who engage in behaviors that they know will kill them after a long period of time may actually intend to kill themselves, but the fact that death comes only after many years suggests to some that no suicide is involved. For instance, can people commit suicide by smoking if they do it specifically for that purpose? Some would contend that they cannot because suicide implies a relatively short time span between the actions and the resulting death. Thus, it is routine for coroners or medical examiners to investigate shootings and, finding no evidence to suggest an accident or foul play, rule that the victims committed suicide. But it is unheard of for coroners to search the histories of individuals dying of lung cancer to see if sometime in the past, perhaps many years ago, the smokers had declared that they were smoking in order to kill themselves. As a result, lung cancer victims are never classified as suicides, even when there is strong evidence that smoking caused their deaths.

A second complication concerns intent (cf. Shneidman, 1985). Does "intent" mean that people want to die or simply that they deliberately undertake acts (or neglect to do something) that they know or have strong reason to believe will result in death? For example, a person who leaps in front of a speeding train to rescue a child playing on the tracks may know that this action will result in death but nevertheless proceeds without actually wanting to die. It could be said that this person fully expected to die by choosing to run in front of the train—and that he or she expected to sacrifice his or her life for the child's safety. But at the same time, this person may not have desired or have intended death. Another, extreme, example would be the case of somebody threatening a woman's child in order to force the mother to shoot herself. Even though the mother intended to kill herself in order to save the child, could it be said that her death was really willful and therefore a suicide? Finally, what about a youth who takes his own life so a sick mother can receive his heart in a transplant operation. Though he willfully caused his own death, he did not really want to die. In all of these instances individuals undertake actions that they expect to result in their deaths. But are these cases of suicide? If they are not suicides, how would they be classified? Must people have as their sole purpose self-destruction? Is intent the same as wanting to die?

Third, the WHO definition concerns aggressive acts resulting in self-destruction. But some people who intentionally bring about their own deaths do so not by willfully acting, but by failing to act in certain circumstances. Consider a person diagnosed with a medical condition requiring a restricted diet who refuses to follow medical instructions, with full knowledge that death will result. This is not an instance of self-injury, but most of us would regard it as suicide by a failure to act. Or imagine the case of an individual who refuses to leave his home in the face of an erupting volcano or oncoming hurricane. Would his death, even if it could be established that he had resigned himself to death, be classifiable as suicide?

In view of these difficulties it would seem more sensible to define suicide as: death resulting from actions (or lack thereof) that an individual willfully takes (or neglects to take) with the desire and expectation that he or she be killed, regardless of the time elapsing between actions and death. Yet even with such a definition, it would be difficult to determine when acts of suicide occur. To classify a death as an instance of suicide, somebody (in our society it is usually a county coroner or a medical examiner) would have to determine what caused the death, whether the causal forces were set in motion deliberately by the victim, and whether the person wanted to die as a result of those actions. Making those determinations often requires much shaky inference. Unless somebody leaves a note (which is done in less than one-third of the cases actually ruled as suicide) it is often impossible to ascertain willfulness and desire to die. That is particularly true since victims of suicide, or their families, for financial reasons sometimes try to mislead others into thinking the act was an accident or the result of criminal actions. Suicide puts life insurance benefits in jeopardy, and a determination of suicide would disqualify the survivors from receiving benefits. Also, for many, suicide is socially stigmatizing. Thus, the lines between suicides, accidents, and criminal actions are often quite fuzzy.

How Much Suicide Is There?

Although many suicides are probably misclassified as something else and some other deaths are misclassified as suicides in every jurisdiction or country (Jobes et al., 1987; Phillips and Ruth, 1993), the overall quality of suicide data appears to vary from one jurisdiction to another (Moscicki, 1995).

In the states and counties of the United States, for instance, reporting officials range from elected coroners with no medical or forensic training at all to highly skilled medical examiners. This difference in ability and training affects how the cause of death is classified. And even medical examiners may differ tremendously in the criteria they use in deciding whether a suicide has occurred.

In one study 95 medical examiners considered a case in which a hunter challenged his companions to play Russian Roulette (a game in which someone places a single cartridge in a revolver and spins the chamber before putting the gun to his head and pulling the trigger). His companions refused to play but the hunter proceeded until he finally killed himself on the sixth try. Since the probability of a fatal spin after six tries is .67, and continuation of the game with no obvious intent other than death was indicated, it would seem that almost anybody would consider this hunter's death a suicide. Yet 28 percent of the sampled medical examiners said they would classify the death as "accidental" or "undetermined" (Jobes et al., 1987). In another study, 58 percent of 195 medical examiners surveyed either "agreed" or "strongly agreed" that the actual suicide rate is considerably greater than the reported rate (Jobes et al., 1987). And in a study of death certificates in California that examined variations in cause of death around symbolic ages (particularly important turning points in individuals' lives known to be associated with increased suicide), the researchers concluded there is much misclassification, with the greatest underreporting for those groups with historically lower suicide rates—such as blacks and females (Phillips and Ruth, 1993). Most experts agree, therefore, that suicide statistics are not especially accurate and that the source of error is most often undercounting (Douglas, 1967; O'Carroll, 1989).

Variations in Rates

Despite these problems official suicide data appear accurate enough for research and interpretation (see Gibbs, 1994a). One indication of their usefulness is the remarkable degree of regularity in suicide rates. One study reported that over a one hundred year period (1875–1975) the suicide rates in various countries were highly correlated (a correlation coefficient of .42). And the suicide rates of immigrant groups correlate more highly with those of the home country than with those of the host country (Lester, 1997b). Moreover, differences among demographic categories are large and generally stable both within a given country and among countries. Suicide usually varies directly with age, especially among males, with older people being far more prone to it than younger people; directly by Socioeconomic Status (SES) and dominant status, with minorities and lower-status people exhibiting lower rates than higher-status or dominant groups, and better-off societies exhibiting higher rates than poorer societies; directly by size of place, with rates much higher in large urban places than in rural places; and by sex, with males exhibiting much higher rates than females (Moscicki, 1995). In addition, nations and other political entities tend to show similar trends over time in suicide rates. For instance, states in the western United States tend to have higher rates than other states, and internationally Greece, Mexico, and the Netherlands consistently have the lowest rates among industrialized nations (Moscicki, 1995).

Yet there are anomalies (Gibbs, 1994a; Lester, 1997b). For one thing, rates seem to have been increasing all over the world in recent years, though more so among males than females (Diekstra and Garnefski, 1995). In addition, the suicide rate for males exceeds that for females in all countries in the world (that report data to the World Health Organization) except one. In the United States in 1991, for example, the rate for males was about 17.5 per hundred thousand but only about 4.3 among females. The exception is China, where for the period 1990–1994 the suicide rates for women were 33.5 per 100,000 and only 24.2 per 100,000 for men. Moreover, even though suicide is usually more common among older people, this age distribution is most characteristic of males. The age at which suicide is most likely among females appears to be contingent on the economic position of the country. In wealthier nations, the highest suicide rates among females are in the middle years; in the less wealthy nations, the highest female rates are among the aged; and in the poorest countries in the world, young adult females are more likely to kill themselves. Furthermore, even though suicide is generally more common among older people than younger ones, it is a more important cause of death among the young. In 1994 in the United States, suicide was the third leading cause of death among those aged 15–24 (Roberts et al., 1997), but it was not among the leading causes of death among older people (because other fatal conditions are so much more prevalent among the aged).

Even though racial and ethnic minorities usually have lower rates of suicide than majorities, evidence suggests that in large cities in the United States suicide rates among young (15–30) blacks of both sexes have been higher than among whites of the same age over the past 70 years (Hendin, 1987). As a final example, even though suicide rates show much stability, there are unusual disruptions in this pattern. For instance, California has been experiencing a dramatic decline (32 percent) in suicide during the past 20 years at the same time that rates in the United States have generally been increasing. It is the only state to show consistent reductions in teenage and young adult suicide (Males, 1994). And even though fifty years ago the U.S. suicide rates exceeded those in Canada, they no longer do. In 1960 the male suicide rate in Canada was 12 per hundred thousand (compared to 16.5 in the U.S.) and the female rate was 3 (U.S. rate: 4.8), but with steady increases the Canadian rates overtook the U.S. rates by about 1975. By 1988 the male suicide rate in Canada was 18.5 (17.5 in the U.S.) and the female rate was 5 (4.3 in the United States) (Sakinofsky and Leenears, 1997).

It appears, then, that despite errors of classification, suicide is one of the more predictable forms of deviance. Its stable patterns invite explanation, and the anomalies challenge our thinking. Among other things, suicide is fairly common in most societies. Despite substantial underreporting, rates in 1994 ranged from highs of 41.7 suicide deaths per 100,000 in Russia, 39.9 per 100,000 in Hungary, and 26.4 per 100,000 in Finland to a low of less than 1 suicide death per 100,000 in Egypt (see figures in Chapter 16). Moreover, over half of the 80 countries reporting to the World Health Organization had rates above 10 per 100,000. These rates have more meaning when one considers homicide rates seldom exceed 10 per 100,000 even in the most violent countries of the world; generally homicide rates are much lower than suicide rates. In the United States, for example, where there is much public discussion and fear of homicide, suicide rates are consistently higher than homicide rates. The death rate for suicide in 1994 was 12 per 100,000 while there were fewer than 10 homicide deaths per 100,000 (Statistical Abstract of the United States, 1998), and nearly 2 percent of all Americans eventually take their own lives (Phillips et al., 1994). The ratio of suicide to homicide deaths is even greater in other countries. For example, in Australia there are 5 suicides for each homicide, in Norway there are 10, in France there are 18 suicides for each homicide, and in Japan there are 252 suicides for each homicide (Zimring and Hawkins, 1997; Statistical Abstract of the United States, 1998). There is another important fact that should be brought out here. Although the high homicide rate in the United States is the source of a great deal of notoriety, the suicide rate in many other countries is substantially greater than our homicide rate. Also, official suicide rates both in the United States and elsewhere apparently do not even come close to reflecting the true extent to which people consider suicide.

Attempted Suicide and Suicide Ideation

Many more people attempt to kill themselves and fail (sometimes called "parasuicide") than the number who succeed. Many more think about committing suicide, even to the point of making plans but do not go through with it (Hughes and Neimeyer, 1990). There are no national population-based data about attempted suicide comparable to actual suicide data, but informed estimates about adult attempts, taking into account the whole life cycle, range from 1,100 to 4,300 per 100,000 (note that this is not directly comparable to annual suicide rates based on number of suicides in the specific year for every 100,000 people). For any given year, estimates of parasuicides range from 300 to 800 per 100,000. A large survey of over 18,000 adults in five communities found about 200 self-reported attempts per 100,000 adults per year. Overall, it appears that there are about 18 suicide attempts for every completed suicide (Moscicki, 1995).

Of course, suicide attempts are not always serious—people may not actually intend to kill themselves. Sometimes such attempts are clearly designed to fail, and at other times they fail because the means are not lethal enough. When people arrange it so that their attempts at suicide have a strong chance of being discovered before death or when they call for help themselves, it is likely that they do not really want to die but instead are seeking attention or trying to manipulate circumstances and other people. It is not so obvious in situations where a gun misfires or an overdose of medication makes the attempter sick enough to regurgitate. At any rate, females are much more likely to attempt suicide than males, although males are much more likely to succeed. In the United States this discrepancy appears to reflect the choice of method for suicide. Males are more likely to use guns to commit their suicide, and guns are almost always lethal, whereas females most frequently take poison or drugs.

Not only do many more people attempt suicide than actually succeed (especially females) but an even larger proportion think about committing suicide (referred to as suicide ideation). Estimates from surveys of different groups in different locales and covering different segments of the life cycle show overall ideation rates ranging from 2 percent to 60 percent. Ideation rates during the adolescent period of life usually range from 10 percent to 20 percent (Roberts et al., 1997). As with suicide attempts, ideation is more prevalent among females than males. However, much ideation may not be serious inasmuch as there is a long leap from thinking about suicide to performing actual behaviors that might bring about death. Nevertheless, various scales that measure the degree of "suicidal behavior" among individuals and array scores on a continuum from very low (those who have never thought about suicide) to very high (those who have actually attempted suicide) still find a substantial number of people near the upper end of such scales (Bonner and Rich, 1987).

Suicide as an Important Social Phenomenon

Overall, then, suicide rates in most countries in the world, particularly the more advanced ones, are surprisingly high—usually higher than homicide rates. In the United States annually there are approximately 30,000 recorded suicides, representing the eighth leading cause of death. In addition, many more people attempt suicide than actually succeed at it, and a still greater number contemplate it. This is all the more remarkable because of the common belief that human beings have an inherent instinct for survival and because of the fact that all societies discourage suicide except under relatively rare, designated circumstances (discussed later in this chapter). Later we will also examine various explanations of deviance that presumably apply to suicide. We authors contend that effectively explaining any deviance requires attention to the organizational characteristics through which it is typically expressed; hence it is important to assess whether suicide is typically an individualistic form of deviance and to examine some of its features.

Characteristics of Suicide

Although common features are frequently asserted (Shneidman, 1985), most scholars who study suicide do not think that all suicides are alike, either in motivation or characteristics. Though it is often stated that suicide is almost always associated with feelings of hopelessness, depression, cognitive rigidity, anxiety, and negative life stress (Dean et al., 1996), many experts deny that suicide necessarily stems from psychological deficiencies, contending instead that it may be a rational act. Such differences suggest that suicide can be classified into types.

Types

One type of classification might differentiate suicides by the extent to which they are "social," that is, whether more than one individual is active in the attempt. But there are other possibilities.

Classification by Cause

Perhaps the best-known classification is that by Emile Durkheim (1951 [1897]), the first scholar of note to deal with suicide. He identified four types according to the degree of social integration and social control involved. *Altruistic* suicide is that undertaken for the benefit of others or society as a whole; it reflects an excessively high degree of social integration. A soldier who attacks the enemy in the face of withering fire with certain knowledge that he will be killed, or the aged Eskimo person who wanders away to die in the cold to relieve his family of the burden of his care are committing suicide to further a higher cause and so are committing altruistic suicide. Recall the earlier discussion, however, in which it was noted that, according to some definitions, these are not suicides at all since the individuals do not necessarily want to die.

Egoistic suicides are stimulated by any number of things that affect most people, but they actually take place because individuals are poorly integrated into social groups whose expectations ordinarily regulate and restrain such tendencies. When depression, unusual stress, or heavy responsibilities strike unintegrated persons, they presumably feel free to end their own lives. Such would be the case of a divorced man who simply did not see any further reason for living. This is in contrast to *fatalistic* suicide, which presumably reflects an excess of regulation. The individual who commits fatalistic suicide is said to be oppressed by the restraints under which he is placed. An example might be that of corporate executives who are so overburdened with duties that they see no escape but death. Finally, *anomic* suicide occurs when there is an abrupt change in circumstances so that norms and regulations that previously governed people's lives are removed, which both disorients them and frees them to commit suicide. Examples would be those who kill themselves after suddenly becoming wealthy (perhaps after winning the lottery) as well as those who kill themselves after losing their wealth (perhaps as a result of gambling or a business reversal).

Classification by Distinguishing Features

Another type of classification hinges on the way in which suicide is committed (Phillips et al., 1994), and identifies seven types: overt, covert, acute, chronic, unassisted, assisted, and murder-suicide. *Overt* suicide occurs when the person kills himself or herself in such as way that it is easily noticed by others and attracts attention. Religious figures who immolate themselves in public to make a statement exemplify this class. *Covert* suicide, on the other hand, is hidden from view, often having been committed in such a way that it is mistaken for an accident. An example is the man who goes far into the woods to shoot himself and whose body may not be found for weeks, if ever.

Acute suicide is sudden and discrete, a direct and immediate result of overt actions or the absence of precautionary behavior. When people blow their brains out with guns it is acute. *Chronic* suicide, however, takes place over long periods of time, as when a diabetic individual neglects to regulate her blood sugar. As noted before, chronic suicides are probably never actually classified as such by the authorities who must determine cause of death. *Unassisted* suicide is that accomplished by lone individuals without social support or other aid, while in *assisted* suicide, people look to others for guidance or direct help. Assisted suicide may include two people carrying out a pact of mutual self-destruction; a physician or friend providing the means of death; or mass suicides, where large numbers of others, by their admonitions and examples, urge the individual on.

Deviance in Everyday Life

Dr. Jack Kevorkian is a Michigan pathologist who in his retirement assists the terminally ill to die with dignity. Kevorkian claims that he only assists in the suicide of those persons who are terminally ill or who have so lost the quality of their lives (such as through paralysis) that they would prefer to die. He also claims only to assist in the suicide of those persons who calmly and rationally make the choice to die. Kevorkian has assisted some persons to die through a dose of lethal drugs in a machine that he assembled. The state of Michigan revoked Dr. Kevorkian's medical license and the access to prescription drugs it provided. Kevorkian responded by assisting in the suicide of others by having them inhale carbon monoxide. He has assisted in the suicides of over 100 persons thus far. In an attempt to stop Dr. Kevorkian, the state of Michigan brought various charges against him on at least four occasions. He was finally convicted. Kevorkian takes no payment for his services, and aspires to open an assisted suicide clinic at some point in the future.

And, of course, *murder-suicides* are those in which individuals kill someone and then take their own lives. Sometimes murder-suicides accompany
other crimes, such as robberies or domestic assault; at times they involve
planned killings, as in euthanasia followed by suicide of the killer; and sometimes they resemble suicide pacts where one of the parties is unable to go
through with the suicide so the other kills the first and then ends his or her
own life.

Classification by Agency

Because some suicide appears to be passive acceptance of the inevitability of death while other suicide seems to reflect an attempt to use one's own
death to accomplish a purpose, suicide might be divided into two major
types: submissive and purposive.

Submissive suicides are characterized by a lack of psychological well-
being reflected in loneliness, low adaptive reasons for living, depression
(Bonner and Rich, 1987), withdrawal, apathy, indifference to the environment (Achte, 1988), hopelessness (Dean et al., 1996), or drug abuse (Moscicki,
1995). In such cases, the circumstances of life appear to close in on people to
the point where they feel helpless and unable to visualize acceptable alternatives to death. Their suicides seem to be expressions of surrender or escape;
they just give up and take (or neglect to take) actions that hasten what appears to be the inevitable, or they attempt to escape unbearable circumstances or shame. Submissive suicides seem to encompass Durkheim's fatalistic and anomic forms. Probably, most suicides by the aged, those physically
sick or disabled, and those who have lost loved ones or other important an-
chors in life (see Takahashi, 1989), as well as those who kill themselves to
avoid debt, dishonor, embarrassment, or responsibility are of this type.

Purposive suicides, on the other hand, are those in which the person uses
his or her own death as a device to influence others or to alter social circumstances. Unlike a passive suicide, the individual does not surrender or attempt to escape but instead actively employs death as a control maneuver. It
is clear that much suicide is an attempt to control; the evidence comes from
many suicide notes (Douglas, 1967) that suggest death was inflicted in order
to get others to do something, to get them to change their view of the victim,
to invoke sympathy or guilt, or to take revenge. One leading authority, drawing on such evidence, characterizes all suicide as a form of problem solving
(Shneidman, 1985).

The clearest examples of purposive suicide are those by females in societies where women are exceptionally subordinate (Counts, 1987). Indeed, in
various premodern societies, there were institutionalized procedures by
which powerless women could avenge themselves on men who abused the
power they held over the women. For instance, in several such societies, husbands were permitted to beat their wives as long as such beatings were within
prescribed limits and circumstances. But if a husband beat his wife excessively or in inappropriate circumstances (constituting abuse), the wife, who
had no power to retaliate directly, could expect social responses holding the
husband responsible for her death if she committed suicide and did it in prescribed ways to indicate her retaliatory purpose. In many instances, even
when the wife failed to follow prescribed norms, such as notifying somebody
of her purpose and wearing a ceremonial gown, the husband was nevertheless punished or otherwise held responsible for her death.

Among the Cheyenne, who regarded the death of any group member resulting from the actions of another Cheyenne as an exceptionally serious matter jeopardizing the welfare of the whole society, a husband who drove his wife to suicide would be held accountable as a murderer (Grinnell, 1972; Hoebel, 1968). Since brothers were responsible for arranging marriages for their sisters, the brothers were treated as murderers when their sisters committed suicide in protest of an arranged marriage that seriously contradicted their preferences. Apparently among the Cheyenne and in the societies examined by Counts (1987), women were aware of the consequences of their actions and were socialized to think of suicide as a control device.

Co-terminus suicide (two or more individuals committing suicide together) may involve submissive as well as purposive suicide. From an analysis of the audio tapes leading up to and during the Jonestown mass suicide in 1978, Black (1990) has concluded that the leaders, including Jim Jones and his close advisers and agents, committed suicide in the belief that it was a revolutionary, or controlling, act, which demonstrated freedom from outside forces and made a statement designed to influence the world. Most of the subordinate members of that group, however, apparently committed suicide fatalistically, or submissively, believing that they had nothing to live for or that they had no choice. And while the Heaven's Gate members, who killed themselves to join the spaceship supposedly trailing the Hale-Bopp comet, apparently viewed it as a purposive act facilitating their journey to a better existence, the seven members of the Friend of the Truth Church who committed suicide following the death of their leader seemed to have been submitting to the hopelessness bred by the belief that without their leader, there was no longer any reason to live (Takahashi, 1989). Suicide pacts between lovers also occasionally appear to be submissive responses to desperate beliefs that there is no hope (see Deviance in Everyday Life), but often they appear to be purposive acts to make others regret keeping them apart or actions designed to overcome the restrictions on their relationship by transporting themselves to another life where their love can flourish unhindered.

Deviance in Everyday Life

The Shakespearean tragedy *Romeo and Juliet* is a fictionalized account of lovers who commit suicide. This classic play is about two passionate lovers in fifteenth-century Verona, Italy, who have the misfortune of coming from two feuding families, the Capulets (Juliet's family) and Montagues (Romeo's family). In the play's climactic scene, Juliet, who has been forbidden by her parents from seeing Romeo and who has been promised in marriage to another, hopes to get out of her predicament by taking a powerful potion and feigning her death. Once revived, she plans to run off with Romeo. Romeo, upon hearing of Juliet's death rushes to her side in her tomb. Finding Juliet seemingly lifeless, Romeo is desperate in his grief. Unable to face life without her, he swallows a vial of poison and dies. When Juliet awakens from her stupor, she finds the dead Romeo. Pledging to be at her lover's side, she joins Romeo in death by plunging a dagger into her own heart.

As Forms of Aggression

Not only can suicides be classified as submissive or purposive, they can also be regarded as categories within a general classification of acts of aggression. From the classic theory by Henry and Short (1954) to contemporary work (Unnithan et al., 1994), various scholars have treated suicide and homicide as two manifestations of aggression stemming from a common source.

According to this argument, some people who experience frustration or other conditions stimulating aggressive impulses act outward by committing homicide (or, by implication, other forms of predatory violence), while others direct the aggressive impulses inward to commit suicide (Bachman, 1992). Different explanations point to the circumstances or conditions that direct aggression in one or the other direction, usually focusing on whether individuals are subject to strong or weak internal or external control.

Within this framework suicide might be regarded as a submissive response to one's aggressive impulses; homicide would reflect a more purposive response. Yet it is also possible that suicide, even if stemming from the same stream of aggressive impulses as homicide, could still reflect either submission or a purposive response. Some people experiencing aggressive impulses may be so controlled or regulated by either internal or external forces that they can only submit, killing themselves in hopeless surrender. Others may be constrained to the point where they cannot exhibit outward aggression directly against others; yet at the same time they may not be so controlled that they are prevented from aggressing indirectly by using self-inflicted death as a control maneuver meant to bring consequences for others. Finally, some may be relatively unconstrained, to the point where they can more openly express aggression outward through homicide or other predatory violence. And among the relatively unconstrained, there may be distinctions among individuals in the type and amount of control to which they are subject, so that some engage directly in predatory violence while others use external but indirect methods (cf. Tittle, 1995). Logically, the greater the use of external indirect methods for expressing aggression, the more likely are the practitioners to be organized. Thus although suicide may be thought of as an individualized form of deviance, expressing impulses from the same wellspring as other violence, satisfactory explanation may require comparisons with those other forms of violence that manifest greater degrees of organization.

How Well Organized Is It?

In Chapter 2 we identified nine features that must be taken into account in discussing degree of organization of deviance. The first, and most important, is the extent to which the behavior is typically performed in company with others and/or requires the cooperation of others in its performance. Although instances of suicide where two or more people take their lives at the same moment or one soon after the other attract a lot of attention, the evidence suggests that such behavior is relatively rare. Co-terminus suicide is of three types: dyadic, cluster, and mass.

Dyadic suicide involves two people who kill themselves together, usually having made some kind of pact ahead of time, as when two adolescent lovers decide to kill themselves because their parents forbid the relationship. Although there are no systematic statistics for dyadic suicide, various studies designed to estimate its frequency show the rate to be 1 percent or less of all suicides (Berman, 1996).

Cluster suicides are those that occur when a larger than normal number of suicides occurs in a restricted space and time frame (Coleman, 1987) such as when a spate of suicides among young people occur in a given year in a particular town. Two subtypes can be identified. The first, which we will call incidental cluster suicides, involves little or no direct communication among the perpetrators—simply a series of suicides within a fairly short period of time in a given geographic area. At other times there will be an outbreak of suicide in a larger area, such as the United States as a whole, for a relatively short period of time. An important element in these kinds of cluster suicides, especially among adolescents, appears to be suggestion or imitation (Phillips and Carstensen, 1988; Phillips, 1974; Stack, 1990). When one person commits suicide and the circumstances of that death are publicized, there is a tendency for others, who may have already been predisposed to suicide, to follow suit, often using the same methods. Moreover, after well-publicized suicides, there appears to be an unusual short-term increase in fatal accidents, suggesting that some of those who appear to have been accidentally killed were in fact committing suicide (Phillips, 1977, 1979). Yet, even for adolescents, incidental cluster suicides are rare, ranging from 1 percent to 13 percent of suicides in specific locales and for specific time periods (Moscicki, 1995).

Planned cluster suicides are those where a number of people, usually representing military or political groups, in order to accomplish some larger purpose, take their own lives in similar ways in specific kinds of locales and situations. Examples of this include (1) the Japanese kamikaze pilots who during World War II deliberately crashed their airplanes into Allied ships and other targets and (2) the members of Arab terrorist groups who periodically blow themselves up in public places congested with Israeli citizens. In these instances those who are to commit suicide are carefully recruited and indoctrinated to believe that their actions are heroic and essential to advance the political causes they embrace. While such forms of suicide attract much attention, they actually constitute a fraction of all suicides, and in any case may not represent deviant behavior.

Deviance in Everyday Life

An example of religiously inspired suicide occurred in ancient Roman times. In the Middle East, near the western shore of the Dead Sea in what is now the country of Israel, there was a natural fortress formed between two gorges. This Roman fortress, known as Masada, which rose some 1,200 feet on a cliff over the desert, was further fortified by King Herod around 37 B.C.E., who turned it into a mountain resort. In 66 C.E., during the Jewish revolt against the Romans, Masada was captured by a band of revolutionary Jews (Sicarii) led by Elazer ben Yair. The settlers held Masada for several years, converting it into a settlement complete with synagogue. In 72 C.E., the Roman general Silva was determined to stamp out all resistance to the empire, and laid siege to Masada with an army estimated to be between 10,000 and 15,000 strong. When it appeared to the revolutionaries inside that the Romans would soon breach their walls, all but a handful of the approximately 900 settlers took their own lives rather than being captured by the Romans and forced to live in slavery. (See, Maris, 1997)

Mass suicides also occasionally occur (Meerloo, 1962; Coleman, 1987). In these, fairly large numbers of people, usually members of a religious group, all commit suicide together. The most recent instance of mass suicide is that of the Heaven's Gate cult, several dozen of whose members drank poison in California in 1997 in the belief that they would be drawn up into heaven by a spaceship that was supposedly following the Hale-Bopp comet.

These suicides were inspired by the group's leader and were well planned in advance, as indicated by their video (prepared earlier) explaining to the world the reasons for the suicide. An even more dramatic case occurred in 1978 when over 900 members of a religious group called the People's Temple, who had earlier fled to Jonestown, Guyana, from the United States, drank poison (although evidence suggests that a few of them may have been murdered by gunshot when they refused to go through with the suicide) because a visit by U.S. Congressman Leo Ryan had convinced Jim Jones, the group's leader, that the group was in danger of being attacked or persecuted (Black, 1990; Hall, 1987; Layton, 1998). Another example is the 1986 suicides by seven female members of a religious cult in Japan, who killed themselves together the day after their leader died (Takahashi, 1989). Despite the fact that mass suicides seem to have occurred periodically in most societies at various times in history (Coleman, 1987) and the attention that mass suicides attract, they are extremely unusual compared to the number of suicides of lone individuals. Indeed, they are so unusual that most of the specific cases throughout recorded history can be listed, and they are dramatized because they depart from the normal pattern of suicide.

Hence even though suicide sometimes involves more than one person, the evidence suggests it is typically undertaken by lone individuals. Indeed, most suicidologists treat suicide as a private, individualistic act undertaken without consultation or social support (Berman, 1996; Maris, 1997). Although suicide occasionally takes place in concert with others in religious, political, or personal alliance; in response to social suggestion, with guiding instructions taken from "suicide manuals" (Humphrey, 1991) or political handbooks; or with an attending physician (see *Deviance in Everyday Life*, page 78; Won, 1991), clearly it does not require other people. Almost anybody with the desire to do so can take his or her own life without any help and with little technical knowledge.

Since incidental cluster suicides (where an unusual number of people in a given area commit suicide in a relatively short period of time) appear to be indirect consequences of modeling, only dyadic suicides, planned cluster suicides, and mass suicides express any degree of sociality. And many of those types qualify only as minimal expressions of organized deviance because their practitioners are not actually organized around, or for the purpose of, committing suicide. With only a few exceptions, "sociable suicides" are simply byproducts of organization for other activities or other purposes. Thus, those who make suicide pacts are already socially organized to do things other than suicide; they are often partners in marriage, business, or romantic relationships. Similarly, religious groups that end up committing mass suicide do not normally organize themselves originally for that mission. Ordinarily, the group forms around the practice of religious worship and life style; only later, in response to evolving circumstances, do the members use the pre-existing organizational structure to facilitate suicide.

Exceptions to the general rule that suicide involves little sociality include the Heaven's Gate group, although it is not entirely clear that even they originally had suicide in mind, and the planned cluster suicides of military or terrorist organizations, who obviously express a high degree of sociality. Another possible exception to the rule is the growing organization of people interested in physician-assisted suicide. Many of these individuals want to find a means for painless, efficient death because they are suffering much physical discomfort or a hopeless medical condition or because they anticipate

There is a Hemlock Society USA whose belief it is that terminally ill people should have the right to choose the terms of their own death and thereby die with dignity. It does not advocate suicide as a general solution to anyone's problems, just in the special case of terminal illness. It has an extensive education and service program, including publications, and provides leadership for state physician aid-in-dying legislation.

The Hemlock Society was founded by British journalist Derek Humphrey, who assisted his own wife's death in 1975. She had been suffering from bone cancer. In 1991 Humphrey wrote a "how-to" manual on assisting the terminally ill in dying, called *Final Exit: The Practicalities of Self-Deliverance and Assisted Suicide for the Dying*. The book is banned in some countries. In 1992, Humphrey founded another organization interested in assisting the death of the terminally ill—Euthanasia Research & Guidance Organization (ERGO).

The Hemlock Society USA (which also has organizations in many states) is not, however, the only organization in the United States devoted to the issue of assisted death. Among just a few others, there are the following organizations:

- Americans for Death with Dignity
- Choice in Dying
- Compassion in Dying
- Euthanasia Research & Guidance Organization—ERGO
- Compassionate Chaplaincy
- Dying Well Network
- Merian's Friends

they will confront such situations in the future. The magnitude of this organization (the formal manifestation is the Hemlock Society) is unknown, but it seems unlikely to encompass a very large number of people (Humphrey, 1991). Thus all forms of sociable suicide together appear to constitute only a small percentage of all suicides that occur.

Not only does suicide usually take place without the help or presence of others, but it is almost never a pervasive activity. Killing one's self normally takes little time, and the death itself is but a blink in the grand scheme of a lifetime. Moreover, though some people think often about suicide, and some plan their suicides carefully, devoting considerable time and preparation for the final event, most suicidal people spend but a fraction of their time in suicide activities. With the exception of those who search for medical help in committing suicide, or who pursue military or political objectives, the activities around and about suicide are minor compared to other things that people do, such as eating, bathing, studying, shopping, and occupational pursuits.

To the extent that other indicators of organization all depend on, or flow from, sociality and pervasiveness, suicide generally lacks those traits as well. For instance, with relatively few exceptions, people who plan for or actually commit suicide do not communicate with others who are also planning or thinking about suicide. Indeed, one of the main features of most suicide is loneliness; people feel isolated, downtrodden, and depressed to the point where they have so thoroughly turned their thoughts inward that irrational thinking and beliefs emerge (Achte, 1988; Dean et al., 1996). Although suicidal individuals sometimes make their feelings known to others—friends, family, or therapist—those people are not considered co-conspirators who might ally themselves with the individual in an organization for the promotion of suicide. Furthermore, suicidal people often have difficulty communicating their feelings, even to helpers, much less to others who might possibly be fellow travelers (Shneidman, 1985).

In addition, since suicidal people rarely act in concert, devote a comparatively small amount of time to the activity, and do not communicate with similar others, it is clear that role differentiation and coordination rarely occur among practitioners. The possibility of a shared culture emerging among suicidal people in interaction with each other applies only to a restricted range of suicides—probably only the mass suicides, where the intent for self-destruction was the rationale for the social alliance from the beginning, or the military/terrorist suicides, where units of suicidal bombers are formed and trained. However, in some societies there are generalized elements of a suicidal culture embedded in the larger cultural matrix (Lester, 1987). Sometimes such cultures take the form of social prescriptions saying that under specified conditions one is expected, or at least permitted, to commit suicide (Counts, 1990). In traditional Japan, conditions calling for suicide were those in which a person did a dishonorable thing, brought shame on those depending on him or her, or failed to fulfill a duty. Moreover, appropriate methods of suicide were well known, usually disembowelment with a sharp instrument such as a sword or knife (Meerloo, 1962). In traditional Eskimo society, as noted before, people learned from an early age that committing suicide by wandering off into the cold to freeze was permissible and expected when a person had become more of a burden than a producer. And in many nonmodern societies subordinate segments of the population learn that suicide is an option in seeking revenge on tormentors (Counts, 1987). Even in the United States, where suicide is contrary to cultural values, one can read books about how to commit suicide most efficiently (Humphrey, 1991), and there is considerable public debate in which rationales for suicide, especially among sufferers, are set forth (Blendon et al., 1992).

Suicide, then, is very rarely linked to an emergent culture among those who plan and interact with each other about it, although suicidal behavior is not absolutely devoid of culture since some, like suicide bombers, do share an emergent culture, and many others who commit suicide no doubt draw on general cultural themes in developing their own rationales and methods. Evidence for imitation in cluster suicides suggests as much. Influence of culture is particularly evident where a society's norms call for suicide in particular circumstances, but under such conditions self-killing is not deviant, so the issue of deviant organization is irrelevant.

Because most forms of suicide involve little sociality, require little pervasive attention, do not depend on communication among those who do it, do not exhibit socially differentiated roles and coordinated activity, and are devoid of culture, it follows that people who commit suicide also lack enough organization for their identities to be wrapped up in suicide activities, to possess a shared and well-integrated philosophy, to have group social control procedures, or to engage in systematic recruitment. Suicide bombers, of course, are a clear exception in that they obviously are well organized for the purpose of suicide. They do regard themselves with pride as people who commit suicide, they share a reasonably well-developed philosophy of life, religion, and politics, they are subject to social control from other members of their groups, and they engage in purposive systematic recruitment of other political bombers. But in the societies where these groups form, it is doubtful that such suicide is deviant behavior, so the fact that it is well organized is really irrelevant to our discussion of how well suicide, as a form of deviant behavior, is organized.

Those who commit suicide in societies like the United States, where suicide is deviant, rarely form their personalities around such a possibility, or ally with others to develop shared philosophies, collectively practice social control of each other, or recruit potential suicides. Given that suicide is not regarded as heroic and, in fact, is socially defined as sinful and cowardly, few embrace such concepts as parts of their own personalities or interact with others who might promote suicide or seek people for that purpose. A possible exception is the underground movement that is emerging among people who want to make physician-assisted suicide legal and available (Humphrey, 1991). Those in this crusade do regard suicide, at least under some conditions, as a noble act, or at least one deserving of dignity; they are proud to see themselves as potential suicides; and they shamelessly recruit others who share such views. Interestingly, the percent of people who endorse physician-assisted suicide in polls has grown large enough to suggest that such suicidal organization may be on the border of becoming nondeviant.

It seems clear enough, then, that suicide is typically an individualistic form of deviance. Because it shows little organization, effective explanation would seem to require special recognition of that fact. Later we will see whether this is so.

Summary

Suicide is difficult to define, and data concerning it are subject to much error. Nevertheless, it is a recurrent and widespread phenomenon with well defined patterns among societies and demographic categories that invite explanation, particularly in light of anomalies that seem to challenge our thinking. Suicide can be classified in a number of ways; some of the most interesting classifications regard it either as capitulation or as one of a number of different forms of aggression. Suicide is of particular interest because even though it sometimes exhibits organization, it is a form of deviance that is individualized in its typical manifestation.

Serial Murder

Most of us know of, if not about, serial murderers and their practice. The existence of serial killers has captured the modern American's attention and interest. We learn about them in the popular press and from every conceivable form of "expert" on TV talk shows. In the Introduction to Richard Tithecott's book (1997: ix), *Of Men and Monsters*, about one serial killer/cannibalist, Jeffrey Dahmer, James R. Kincaid wrote:

> Recent surveys of the store of general knowledge possessed by Americans reveal that 11 percent have a firm grasp of evaporation; 23 percent know pretty much where the equator is;. . .over 8 percent can do long division; Edgar Allan Poe is correctly linked to "writer" by 19 percent; as for the larynx, almost as many people regard it as a "body part" as feel it is "some kind of animal"; and one person (.002 percent) can locate Lake Huron on a map. Yet a

solid 100 percent, every single adult and child, knows Jeffrey Dahmer, identifies him as serial killer, homosexual, cannibal, ghoul . . .

Jeffrey Dahmer is only one of a long line of recent American serial murderers, which includes Richard Ramirez (the "Night Stalker"); Albert DeSalvo (the "Boston Strangler"); David Berkowitz (the "Son of Sam"); Ted Bundy, Danny Rollins, Kenneth Bianchi and Angelo Buono (the "Hillside Stranglers"); Richard Angelo (the "Angel of Death"); and Henry Lucas. While we all may know about these notorious killers, and something about their crimes, most of us do not know much about serial killing itself—its characteristics, types, alleged causes. In the remainder of this chapter, we hope to provide some background into this most individualistic of deviant acts.

What Is Serial Murder?

Scholars of serial murder often fail to agree as to exactly what is meant by the term. Some of this confusion arises from the fact that serial killing can refer to several very different types of murder. For example, is it serial murder when one person kills several people at a single moment in time, as when in 1984 James Oliver Huberty killed 20 people (and then himself) and wounded 19 when he opened fire with automatic weapons at the McDonald's in San Ysidro, California? Is it serial murder when one or more persons kill several victims over a relatively short period of time, as when Charles Starkweather and his girlfriend Caril Ann Fugate engaged in a one-week killing frenzy through three midwest states in 1958? Is it serial murder when one or more persons kill several others in a single location over a relatively long period of time, as when David Berkowitz killed six people in New York City between 1976 and 1977. And, is it serial murder when one or more persons kill others in several disparate locations over a relatively long period of time, as when Theodore Bundy killed at least 20 women between 1973 and 1978 in five different states? Is a serial killer anyone who kills more than one person? What exactly is meant by serial murder, and what does that term include and exclude?

One of the fundamental requirements of serial killing, to distinguish it from simple homicide, is that serial killing involves *multicide* or the killing of more than one person. Beyond this, scholars tend to agree on very little. For example, while many argue that there must be at least three deaths to qualify as serial murder (Holmes and DeBurger, 1985, 1988; Holmes and Holmes, 1998; Hickey, 1991; Lester, 1995), for others, two murders is sufficient (Egger, 1990, 1998), and for others, at least four killings are required (Hazelwood and Douglas, 1980). Recognizing that the decision is a somewhat arbitrary one, we will classify as a serial murder only those involving more than two victims. Even if we agree as to the requisite number of murders, we must deal with their timing: how far apart are the killings?

To better understand serial murder, it is useful to employ the distinction that several scholars make between three qualitatively different kinds of multicide: *mass murder, the killing spree*, and *serial murder*. Mass murder is killing more than two people at a single time and in a single place. It involves, therefore, one or more persons killing three or more persons in a single episode. One example of a mass killing occurred on July 13, 1966, when Richard Speck stabbed seven student nurses in a Chicago apartment. Another was the McDonald's mass murder by James Huberty mentioned earlier. A final example of a mass murder was when a heavily armed Charles Whitman climbed atop the campus tower at the University of Texas in Austin on August 1, 1966, and shot to death 16 persons.

Unlike the mass murder that takes place at a single time and usually in a single place, both the spree and serial killing involve longer periods of time over which the murders take place and usually a series of places.

Deviance in Everyday Life

In his song "Nebraska," singer-songwriter Bruce Springsteen writes of the life and death of spree killer Charles Starkweather. When asked in the song why he did what he did, Starkweather replies "Mister, I guess there's just a meanness in this world."

Charles Starkweather was an uneducated garbageman in Lincoln, Nebraska. On December 1, 1957, he robbed and then abducted a gas station attendant. In a struggle, Starkweather killed the 21-year-old attendant. Six weeks later, after a fight with the parents of his 14 year old girlfriend's (Caril Fugate), Starkweather killed them both and Caril's half-sister, two and a half years old. After remaining in the house for six days, Starkweather and Fugate hit the highways. By the time Starkweather and Fugate were captured, they had killed ten people. Starkweather was executed by the state of Nebraska; Fugate was given a life sentence.

Holmes and Holmes (1998) define a killing spree as the slaying of three or more people by one or more persons within 30 days. Charles Starkweather and his girlfriend Caril Ann Fugate were spree killers. Serial killing is distinguished from a killing spree by the pattern of killing—repeated acts of murder that occur over more than a 30-day time period. To qualify as serial killers, therefore, one or more persons must kill at least three victims, and the first and last homicides must have been committed at least a month apart. A serial killer does not have to commit the crimes within a particular jurisdiction; in fact, several different political/law enforcement jurisdictions may be involved or a single one. For example, John Wayne Gacy was convicted of killing 32 young men and boys, all at or near his Chicago residence. The killings occurred over a six-year period. Gacy, who was executed by the state of Illinois in 1994, was one of America's most notorious serial killers. Other serial killers who restricted their homicides to a limited geographic area were David Berkowitz, New York's "Son of Sam" killer, Juan Corona, who was convicted of killing 25 migrant workers in California, and Jeffrey Dahmer. Other serial killers commit their crimes over many jurisdictions, sometimes many states. We have already alluded to the fact that Ted Bundy killed women in at least five different states. Henry Lee Lucas and Ottis Toole traveled across the country in the early 1980s and are suspects in over a hundred homicides in more than 20 states (Levin and Fox, 1985).

This set of qualifications for a serial killer or serial killing is somewhat arbitrary, particularly the thirty-day time interval distinction between spree and serial killing. For example, by the definition of a serial killer established in the literature (and this chapter), Andrew Phillip Cunanan would be considered a serial killer because his murders took place over more than a 30-day time period even though the time pattern of killing more closely resembles a spree killing. Cunanan's first killing occurred on April 25, 1997, in San Diego, California. He then moved to Minneapolis and is thought to have been involved in two other killings before traveling to Chicago and murdering a wealthy businessman on May 4, 1997. Five days after this, Cunanan is believed to have moved to New Jersey where he allegedly killed a cemetery caretaker on May 9, 1997. Finally, on July 17, 1997, less than 90 days after the first murder, Cunanan presumably killed the internationally known fashion designer, Gianni Versace. The rapidity of the time interval for Cunanan's murders make him more like a spree killer than a serial killer, whose crimes generally span many months, if not years.

In sum, by our definition a serial killer is one or more persons who kill at least three people, with the first killing being at least 30 days earlier than the last killing. Serial killers do not have to commit their murders in one general area; David Berkowitz, Albert DeSalvo, Jeffrey Dahmer did; Ted Bundy and Danny Rollins did not. Nor do serial killers have to commit their murders alone; John Gacy and Ted Bundy did, Kenneth Bianchi and Angelo Buono did not. We further restrict our definition of serial killing to exclude acts of state-sponsored terrorism and the acts of political entities. This omits figures like Pol Pot, the one-time totalitarian ruler of Cambodia who was implicated in the murder of millions by the Khmer Rouge during the 1970s in the infamous "killing fields." For the same reason, we do not regard as serial killers the architects of the Nazi killing machine—Adolf Hitler, Adolf Eichmann, Joseph Mengele, and others. We do include as serial killing, however, the murders committed by organized crime members like Sammy "the Bull" Gravano, a modern gangster who admitted to many murders, and the multicides by medical personnel such as Richard Angelo, the "Angel of Death," a supervising nurse in the intensive care unit of a Long Island, New York, hospital. Angelo injected ill patients with drugs that put them in cardiac arrest. He is suspected of killing as many as 25 patients (Egger, 1998).

A Brief History of Serial Murder

Because stories about dramatic events make the national headlines, are the subject of numerous articles in magazines and newspapers, and become the focus of "cop" and "talk" shows on television, it may appear that serial murder is both a distinctively new and a unique American phenomenon. Neither, however, is the case.

Serial murder is as old as history itself. Lester (1995) relays the story of a serial murderer in fifteenth-century France, Gilles de Rais. Gilles was born in a tumultuous historical period. The black death had wiped out nearly one-third of the population of Europe, France was under the rule of an insane Charles VI, and two popes (one in Rome, one in Avignon, France) sat over the Catholic Church. Gilles's home life was no better than the state of affairs in the country; his parents, who were nobles, were distant cousins who had married to protect their personal wealth. They died when Gilles was only 10 years old. Like most children of the nobility, Gilles was trained in the military and served in several French armed campaigns against the English in the Hundred Years War. Apparently, it was in these military campaigns that Gilles developed a skill and taste for killing.

The conflict with the British ended in 1433, and Gilles returned to his estates with no outlet for his well-honed hostility. Soon after returning from his wars, Gilles began sexually abusing and murdering small children on his lands. It is not known how many children Gilles eventually killed, but the number is reputed to be anywhere from 140 to 800! In an effort to seize Gilles's land, the Duke of Brittany had him arrested and tried. Gilles was convicted of the murders of 140 children and was executed (Lester, 1995).

The case of Gilles de Rais is only one of a relatively large number of serial murders that occurred in the past. Henri Landru was a French "gigolo" who, in addition to swindling widows out of their money, killed them. Landru was responsible for the deaths of at least 10 widows (Lester, 1995). Others in the past include Vincent Verzeni, who killed and sucked the blood out of the bodies of several women in Italy in the mid-1860s; Peter Kurten, known as the "Vampire of Dusseldorf," was responsible for some 79 murders or attempted murders in Germany during the early 1900s; Vacher was a French serial killer of the 1890s who slashed and killed 11 women and had sex with their corpses; and Jack the Ripper, who terrorized London in the late nineteenth-century, killing and disemboweling at least five women (Ressler, 1997). Mary Ann Cotton was a female serial killer from England. Over a period of 20 years, she is thought to have killed approximately 15 family members and friends, usually by poisoning them with arsenic (Lester, 1995). In France in 1861, Martin Dumollard and his wife lured young females to their home with the ruse of their possibly being employed as servants. They killed at least 10 girls before being discovered by the police (Lester, 1995).

Many instances of serial killing in the past undoubtedly went unnoticed and unrecorded. Gilles' killings in France probably would not have been recorded had he not been arrested for economic reasons, which arose from the attempt by the Duke of Brittany to seize Gilles's land. Serial killing is a difficult crime to detect in today's world, and it was even more difficult to discover and record in the past, when communication was difficult.

Because our nation is relatively new, the history of serial killing in the United States is relatively well established. Holmes and Holmes (1998) have documented instances of serial killing in the United States in the mid- to late 1800s. One such killer was Joseph Briggen, an unsuccessful farmer in Northern California. Although his crops often failed, Briggen did have a pen of prize Berkshire hogs who were so robust and healthy that they were the envy of all around. Briggen claimed that his hogs prospered because of the special "feed" he prepared for them. However, he did not reveal the recipe. It was eventually discovered that Briggen frequently traveled to San Francisco, where he cruised the Embarcadero District and, under the ruse of employment, picked up homeless and transient men. Once at the farm, the men worked for room and board, and when they pressed Briggen for real wages, he simply killed them, ground the bodies up, and fed the mash to his hogs. Briggen was finally arrested and sent to San Quentin. Although the total number of victims is not fully known, there were at least 12 known homicides (Holmes and Holmes, 1998).

Then there was Johann Schmidt, a German immigrant who, between 1890 and 1905, married at least 55 women, took their cash, and then either left or killed them. He was known to have killed 15 women, but the body count may have been as high as 50 (Holmes and Holmes, 1998). Herman Mudgett turned a three-story row of connected buildings (a hotel called "The Castle") into a torture chamber, where he reputedly killed between 20 and 100 men, women, and children from 1893 through 1896 (Giannangelo, 1996). Sally "Black Widow" Skull married five men between 1834 and 1867. They either disappeared or met with unfortunate "accidents." Sally admitted to having shot one husband herself, claiming she thought he was an intruder (Holmes and Holmes, 1998). In the early 1900s Amy Archer-Gilligan operated a nursing home and was suspected of murdering nearly 50 of her elderly clients after bilking them of money (Holmes and Holmes, 1998). The "Hannibal Lecter" of his day was Albert Fish, an American serial killer who, in the 1920s, murdered and cannibalized between eight and fifteen children (Ressler, 1997). The list and descriptions could go on, but it is sufficient to say that serial killing is no recent phenomenon.

Deviance in Everyday Life

From the late 1970s until the early 1990s the world witnessed the activities of two of the most horrific and active serial killers known in history. These two killers worked in very comparable ways, though they were separated by thousands of miles. The two were Jeffrey Dahmer of Milwaukee and Andrei Chikatilo of the Ukraine.

Dahmer began his killings in June of 1978 with what would be for him a common *modus operandi*—he meets and has sex with a male stranger whom he then kills and dismembers. It was nine years before Dahmer killed again, in December of 1987. After that, Dahmer embarked on a killing rampage, mutilating his victims, having sex with their corpses, removing body parts, masturbating with them and storing them in his refrigerator, where they remained until he cooked and ate them. When he was finished, 15 boys and young men were dead.

Andrei Chikatilo's procedures and operations were very much the same as Dahmer's. He would lure unsuspecting children and women into a secluded area, where he would kill and dismember them. Like Dahmer, Chikatilo would have sex with his victim's body parts and corpse and cannibalize them. From 1978 to 1990, Chikatilo killed 22 boys, 14 girls, and 19 women before he was captured.

The serial killer is not a uniquely American phenomenon (though it certainly may seem so because we hear so much about the cases of John Wayne Gacy, Ted Bundy, Henry Lee Lucas, and Jeffrey Dahmer). There have been, and likely will continue to be, serial killers in many other countries. Take, for example, the case of the notorious "Jack the Ripper" in nineteenth-century London. "Jack" was only one of many British serial killers. Others in the more recent past include Dennis Nilsen, who killed 15 young male homosexuals in the early 1980s (Nilsen was eventually arrested after he complained to his landlord about the drains in his apartment, which, it turns out, were blocked by the chopped-up body parts of his victims). There were also Michael Lupo, who killed nine gay men in the late 1980s, and Colin Ireland, who killed five gay men in London in 1993 (Ressler, 1997). The eerie similarity among these three serial killings separated by a decade was that many of the victims had frequented the same gay bar, Coleherne's Pub, in west London. Frederick and Rosemary West were a married couple who killed 12 women in the town of Gloucester, England, in the early 1990s (Egger, 1998). One of England's best-known child killers was Robert Black, who kidnapped and murdered three young girls between 1982 and 1986 (Egger, 1998). Perhaps the most famous of England's serial killers was one who emulated "Jack the Ripper" by attacking prostitutes. Peter Sutcliffe, the "Yorkshire Ripper" (though Sutcliffe attacked his victims with a hammer rather than a knife or scalpel), is believed to be responsible for the murders of 13 women in Yorkshire, England, between 1975 and 1981 (seven other women were attacked but escaped with their lives).

The former Soviet Union, despite being an oppressive police state, was not free of serial killers. In fact, one of the most prolific serial killers on record was Ukrainian. Between 1978 and 1990, Andrei Chikatilo, known as "Citizen X" and the "Monster of Rostov" (and about whom a famous movie starring Donald Sutherland was made), mutilated and killed 55 women and children (Egger, 1998). Like many, but not all, serial killers, Chikatilo's killing was sexually driven. Unable to achieve an erection during normal sexual activity, Chikatilo discovered that he could obtain sexual release through the infliction of sadistic, horrendous pain. Like Jeffrey Dahmer, Chikatilo cannibalized his victims' excised sexual organs (Giannangelo, 1996).

Although the scene of much political violence, South Africa has had much less experience with criminal murder than many places in the world. Nonetheless, beginning in 1986, Capetown, South Africa, experienced the serial killings of young boys of mixed racial background, many of whose bodies were found near a train station. All of the boys had been strangled and sodomized. Because of these similarities, the killer became known as the "Station Strangler." From 1986 to 1994, between 12 and 21 murders of young boys were attributed to the "Strangler." After an extensive police investigation, Norman Afzal Simons was arrested and convicted of one of the slayings (Egger, 1998; Ressler, 1997).

In the early 1990s, Australia was the scene of multiple slayings that had a common characteristic—all of the victims were found in a forest. Seven bodies were discovered before Ivan Milat was arrested (Egger, 1998). In addition, several unsolved murders, possibly a series, occurred in South Yorkshire, England; several victims were killed in a similar manner, and four of the five were prostitutes or were believed to be prostitutes. In Canada, police think that the unsolved murders of six women in Ontario may be related. Most of the victims were abducted and dumped miles away from where they had last been seen; five of their bodies were found in rural "lovers' lanes," five were abducted or killed on a weekend, and in at least three of the five killings the victim's clothes were neatly folded and, with their shoes, placed beside the body (Egger, 1998). As Egger (1998:73) notes, there are few places on the planet that have completely avoided the appearance of the serial killer.

The Prevalence of Serial Murder

How much serial murder is there? That question, like most "how many" questions in the study of deviant behavior, cannot be answered with precision. The old saying that "if you ask five economists a question, you'll get six different answers" applies as well if you ask scholars researching serial murder how frequently it occurs. Unsatisfactory answers do not reflect scholars' disingenuousness or bad faith. Rather, the difficulty arises because good data are exceptionally hard to collect. It is difficult to get a good estimate of the number of serial killings in any given time period for a number of reasons, set out below.

First, as we have seen, there is *no real consensus* as to the meaning of "serial killing" or "serial killer." Some scholars reserve the term "serial killing" for those murders involving two or more victims attacked by the same assailant; others require three. Some exclude possible female offenders; some exclude killings with a financial motive; and others omit killings where there is a prior relationship between victim and offender. Since experts do not agree about the definition of serial killing, a reasonably accurate estimate of the actual number of such killings is elusive.

Second, as with many deviant acts, there are no official records concerning serial killing. When it counts the number of homicides known to police in the United States each year, the Federal Bureau of Investigation's Uniform Crime Reports does not keep a separate tally of murders committed by serial killers. Separate records of such homicides are not maintained by the Centers for Disease Control and Prevention, nor are they listed as a separate category in the Vital Statistics of the National Center for Health Statistics. Probably the only official public agency that attempts to keep a count of the number of serial killings in the United States is the F.B.I.'s Behavioral Sciences and Investigative Support Unit at the National Center of the Analysis of Violent Crime. This group's estimates, however, are based on reports from newspaper wire services. The unreliability of these data is shown by the fact that the F.B.I.'s Behavioral Science Unit first estimated that between 1977 and 1992 there were 331 serial murderers in the United States, with approximately 2,000 victims. After extensive investigations of those numbers, however, the estimates were revised to 191 serial killers and 1,007 serial victims (Egger, 1998:64).

Another hurdle obstructing an accurate count of serial murders in the United States is the *difficulty of identifying them*. Sometimes killers confess to their multiple murders, though such confessions are often misleading. For example, enjoying his notoriety, Henry Lee Lucas "confessed" to the murder of as many as 300 people, even though the actual number may be no greater than 10 (Lester, 1995); recent evidence suggests, in fact, that he may have committed only one murder. Unless the murderer provides compelling corroboration supporting his confessions, the police must depend on investigative work and forensic evidence. But discovering similarities in the way several murders were committed requires the police to overcome several impediments. One is that a given killing may not be suspected of showing similarity to another unless the killer leaves a distinctive signature at the crime scene, such as neatly folding the victim's clothes and placing them beside the body.

Furthermore, the conclusion that one unsolved murder is part of a pattern may be easier when it is committed within the same police jurisdiction; a conclusion is much harder when the slayings occur across several different jurisdictions. Egger (1998:180) uses the term "linkage blindness" to describe the fact that communication about unsolved murders or missing persons across law enforcement jurisdictions is so poor. Jurisdictional organization, in which officials think mainly about what transpires in their own territories, often impedes the flow of information among police units, preventing the identification of serial killings. In addition, law enforcement personnel tend to be somewhat secretive, which makes them reluctant to share information about cases, even with other law enforcement officials. Thus, it is difficult to estimate the number of serial killings because some are never identified as such. Experts contend that many of the thousands of children who are reported missing each year may be unrecognized victims of serial killers. Moreover, numerous homicide victims are discovered each year in graves, garbage dumps, and alongside roads in ditches; most are never even identified, and some of them may be victims of repeat killers.

A final obstacle in the identification of serial murders is the sheer *cost of establishing and implementing a long-term criminal investigation* of several murders, some of which may have occurred in different jurisdictions. The costs of labor, forensic analysis, experts, overtime, and travel can be onerous for already overburdened law enforcement budgets. This cost consideration suggests that some serial murders are not perceived as related to each other. Moreover, since some murders that may be serial grow "cold" (the investigation does not produce a suspect after a long period of time), the costs of keeping the case active may be prohibitive.

For example, in King County, Washington State, beginning approximately in July of 1982, a number of bodies of prostitutes and young teenagers were discovered and assumed to be the work of a serial killer—dubbed the "Green River Killer." A task force to investigate the crimes was established. At one time, this task force included nearly a hundred law enforcement officials, investigators, and experts. Although the killer has not yet been caught, the task force investigated some 200 suspects, at an approximate cost of $2 million a year. By 1998, the task force had been reduced to one investigator (Holmes and DeBurger, 1988; Holmes and Holmes, 1998; Lester, 1995). Similarly, in the case of British serial killer Peter Sutcliffe, the "Yorkshire Ripper," the initial list of suspects was approximately 268,000; 21,000 persons were interviewed, 31,000 statements from different people were taken, 250 detectives were involved in the case full-time for more than three years, approximately 5 million hours of police time were expended, and the total cost of the investigation was at least $7 million.

Because of all those obstacles, estimates of the number of serial murderers and victims of serial murder seem little more than informed guesses. Yet numerous scholars have offered such estimates. In their recent book on the subject, Holmes and Holmes (1998) note that some experts believe there are approximately 35 serial killers active at any time in the United States, though they regard that number as an underestimate. By their count (Holmes and Holmes, 1998:23–26), 37 serial killers operated in the 1970s, 59 in the 1980s, and 31 in the 1990s (up to 1997). This, too may be a substantial underestimate because it includes only known cases of serial murder, and it ignores altogether the number of victims. In an earlier work, Holmes and DeBerger (1988) estimated that there are at any one time approximately 360 active serial murderers in the United States and that there are between 3,500 and 5,000 serial murder victims annually. They arrived at the latter figure by summing the known serial murder victims, adding from one-fourth to two-thirds of the murder victims for whom there were no known offenders, and including a "probable proportion" of missing children, who might have been victims of a serial killer.

Norris (1989) estimates that there are approximately 500 active serial killers; *Newsweek* (1984) puts the number at 30; Levin and Fox (1985) peg it at 35; and Leyton (1986) projects 100. Overall, estimates of the number of active serial killers in the United States at any one time range from 30 to 500! The safest conclusion to be drawn about the prevalence of serial murder and the victims of serial murder in the United States is expressed by two of the leading scholars: ". . . the true number is unknown and probably will continue to be so" (Holmes and Holmes, 1998:19).

Is the Number of Serial Murders Increasing?

It is easy to imagine that serial murders are increasing. First, there is the intensive media attention given to them. From articles in news magazines to fictionalized accounts of serial murder in such popular movies as *Natural Born Killers* and *Silence of the Lambs*, most of us have an impression that serial murder is on the rise. Changes in rates of serial murder, however, are difficult to substantiate. For one thing, since there is no reliable baseline information about the number of serial homicides in any given year, determining change is practically impossible. In addition, the efficiency of the police may have changed over time so that what appears to be an increase in serial murder may simply reflect the greater probability of discovery and publicity about the cases.

As indicated before, detecting serial murder requires astute law enforcement investigation, and often there must be substantial communication by law enforcement officers in different jurisdictions. Until recently, homicide investigations were crude and each was usually conducted within a single jurisdiction. In the distant past, extensive homicide investigation was almost nonexistent, particularly since victims were frequently of little concern to society. Known victims of the serial killers have generally been poor, female, children, prostitutes, and homosexuals. Such victims did not generate much interest by officials. We like to believe that things are different today, and, if so, contemporary documentation of serial killing may be more accurate, which would give the impression of a rising rate. But preliminary, crude data suggest that the media attention given to serial killing is increasing faster than its actual occurrence. For example, despite extensive news coverage, Holmes and Holmes (1998) identified no upward trend in the number of serial killers operating in the United States over the past four decades.

Characteristics of Serial Murder

Personal Characteristics

Case study literature suggests that one of the most persistent characteristics of the serial killer is maleness. Approximately 90 percent of all persons arrested for homicide are male and so too are serial killers. Holmes and Holmes (1998:23–26) have identified 136 serial killers operating between 1960 and 1997. The researchers unambiguously determined (by name) the gender of 123 of them. Of these 123, 110, or 89 percent, were males. Other researchers have also found the serial killer to be overwhelmingly male (Leibman, 1989; Levin and Fox, 1985; Lunde, 1976).

Not all serial killers are male, however. For example, Aileen Wuornos killed seven men in Florida in less than one year. She lured these men to their deaths under the pretense of having sex with them. Velma Barfield, who was executed by the state of North Carolina in 1984, confessed to poisoning her fiance, her mother, and an elderly couple under her care (Egger, 1998). In his study of male and female serial killers, Hickey (1991) concluded that women are far less violent and brutal in their crimes than men, and they show far less evidence of sexual rage. In fact, his female serial killers were either "quiet" murderers (because many were either "black widows" who killed their spouses or partners), "angels of death" (nurses who killed the patients under their care), or women who killed for financial reasons. Dorethea Puente, for example, owned and operated a boardinghouse for the elderly in Sacramento, California. A state social worker noticed that checks issued to one of her clients were being cashed regularly even though the client had not been seen for several months. A police investigation found seven bodies buried in Puente's backyard, and she was eventually charged with killing nine residents and cashing their social security checks. Genene Jones, a nurse at a pediatric clinic in Kerrville, Texas, was convicted of injecting a drug into a 14-month-old girl, causing her death. Although Jones was charged and convicted of this one murder (and received a sentence of 99 years), she was suspected by authorities of having caused the deaths of at least 13 other children while she worked at the Bexar County Hospital during 1981–1982 (Egger, 1998).

In addition to being mainly male, serial killers also tend to be disproportionately white (Holmes and DeBurger, 1985; Levin and Fox, 1985; Lunde, 1976). This is contrary to the pattern for single-victim homicides, which reveals overrepresentation by African-Americans. One African-American serial killer was Wayne Williams, who was convicted of killing two young African-American boys in Atlanta, Georgia, in the late 1970s, and who was suspected in the deaths of at least 20 other missing young African-American males.

Finally, in addition to being primarily male and white, many serial killers are relatively young, generally between the ages of 25 and 35. For instance, the serial killer John Wayne Gacy, who was convicted of 33 murders in 1980, killed his first victim in 1970 when he was 28 years old. The murders continued until 1978, when Gacy was 36 years of age. Kenneth Bianchi, known along with Angelo Buono as the "Hillside Stranglers," killed at least 10 women in Los Angeles County and two more in the state of Washington between 1977 and 1979. Bianchi first killed when he was 26 years old. Finally, Theodore "Ted" Bundy was 23 years of age when the first woman he was suspected of murdering disappeared; he continued his killing until he was finally arrested in 1978. By that time, Bundy was implicated in the deaths of at least 17 women in five different states (Egger, 1998).

Besides these personal characteristics of serial killers, there are three other notable similarities in their crimes. One is that most serial killers work alone. While there are instances of pairs of serial killers working in tandem— Kenneth Bianchi and Angelo Buono (the cousins who comprised the "Hillside Stranglers"), Dean Corll and Wayne Henley, Henry Lucas and Ottis Toole, Ray and Faye Copeland, Cathy Wood and Gwen Graham—most serial killers act without help. The second is that most serial homicides involve victims who do not know one another—that is, they are stranger killings. There are, of course, exceptions to this. For example, the second of numerous suspected killings by Henry Lee Lucas was his mother. The score of other suspected victims, however, were strangers to him. Other serial killers such as Albert DeSalvo (the "Boston Strangler"), Ted Bundy, John Gacy, and Jeffrey Dahmer preyed on complete strangers or recent acquaintances. The third common characteristic of serial killing is that the killers generally have a history of trouble with the law before their killings began. They were not "model citizens" who led law abiding lives and then suddenly "snapped" and started killing. For example, John Gacy had been previously convicted of having sex with minor boys, and he was the object of several complaints regarding his homosexual conduct while he was on parole. Ted Bundy had a history of shoplifting and juvenile car theft. Kenneth Bianchi, one of the "Hillside

Stranglers," stole things from homes he was supposed to be protecting as a security guard.

Finally, there is one other possible common characteristic of serial killers, though there is some controversy about this. In an extensive study of serial murderers, the Federal Bureau of Investigation's Behavioral Science Unit concluded that most serial killers spent their childhoods in abusive, uncaring, and cruel homes. Among the problems noted were alcohol and drug abuse by parents, physical and sexual abuse at the hands of parents or other relatives, a parent's mental illness, and discipline that vacillated between brutal and neglectful. For example, Henry Lee Lucas's mother was an alcoholic prostitute who forced Henry to watch her sexual escapades with different men. His father was also an alcoholic, who lost both legs in a railroad accident. Lucas's mother then became the dominant influence in the home; she was brutal in her treatment of Henry. She choked him and one time struck him in the head with a 2 x 4 piece of wood that knocked him unconscious for 11 hours, fracturing his skull. Despite this treatment, Henry loved his mother and after her death was frequently seen lying on top of her grave. John Gacy's father was an alcoholic who frequently beat his wife and called John a "sissy" whenever he came to her defense. John's mother gave him frequent and unnecessary enemas when he was a child. Kenneth Bianchi's early life was spent in and out of foster homes, where he was placed by his teenage mother.

Since the early lives of many serial killers were awful, and their later acts were so brutal and egregious, it is tempting to quickly label the killers as "sick," psychotic, or distorted. Yet, there is disagreement about the import of early life events in the development of serial killers. Not all, or even a significant number of, children who grow up in dysfunctional families become adult serial killers. While there are many children whose parents are overbearing, or use erratic discipline, or who ignore or harshly punish them, very few go on to be serial killers. If a poor, even a physically abusive, early home life does not frequently lead to serial killing, it is difficult to claim that it is a primary causal factor. The fact is, most children are quite resilient in response to the things that their parents do to them, and the vast majority grow up to be fairly functional adults despite early mistreatment. While perhaps not always happy, those from dysfunctional families usually do not murder.

Furthermore, while many serial killers are indeed psychotic, most have come from fairly normal family backgrounds and despite their malignant acts, are psychologically unexceptional. For example, Ted Bundy, one of the most prolific of modern serial killers, does not appear to have had an unusually bad family life as a child. Although Bundy was an illegitimate child, he lived with several relatives before his mother married John C. Bundy, who adopted him at age four. The family, though poor, was not poverty stricken. In school, Ted was an average student, but his test IQ was 122. He was a loner, with few dates, and he expressed a lack of self-confidence around women (Egger, 1998)—but so do most adolescent boys. After graduating from high school in 1965, Bundy worked at a number of jobs and attended several different colleges before killing his first victim in 1974. When Bundy was examined by two court psychiatrists before his murder trial in 1979, neither found evidence of psychosis, and both determined that he had a pathological need to confront and try to dominate authority figures. They both concluded he had an "antisocial personality." (It is difficult to imagine anyone who has committed perhaps 20 or more murders not being considered "antisocial.")

Though not insane or psychotic, many serial killers fit the diagnostic category of being a psychopath or sociopath. These two terms generally describe the same set of symptoms. Such people lack emotional empathy and are concentrated on or obsessive about self. They are emotionally shallow and are unfeeling with respect to the pain, discomfort, or needs of others. They focus instead on their own selfish interests. Other attributes of psycho/sociopaths are tendencies toward impulsivity, unreliability, and dishonesty; they tend to manipulate others and (not surprisingly) show difficulties in forming emotional attachments to other persons (Cleckley, 1964; Hart and Hare, 1997). Because they show little remorse for their conduct, psycho/sociopaths have been described as lacking a sense of guilt or conscience. In the diagnostic literature, the term antisocial personality has replaced the earlier terms psychopath and sociopath.

Psychologist Robert D. Hare has devised a checklist for identifying antisocial personalities. There are 20 items in the list, and each item is given a score of 0,1, or 2, with higher scores indicating a stronger manifestation of the trait. The traits are: (1) glibness or superficial charm, (2) a grandiose sense of self-worth, (3) need for stimulation, (4) pathological lying, (5) conning or manipulation, (6) lack of remorse or guilt, (7) shallow affect, (8) callousness or lack of empathy, (9) parasitic life style, (10) poor behavioral controls, (11) promiscuous sexual behavior, (12) early behavioral problems, (13) lack of realistic long-term goals, (14) impulsivity, (15) irresponsibility, (16) failure to accept responsibility, (17) many short-term marital relationships, (18) a history of juvenile delinquency, (19) a court's revocation of early release and (20) criminal versatility. Total scores range from 0 to 40, and those with a score of 30 or higher are considered to be psychopaths or to have an antisocial personality (Hart and Hare, 1997). The following brief biographical synopses of recent serial killers will give you some impression of how well they "fit" the clinical designation of psychopath provided by Hart and Hare.

> Theodore Robert "Ted" Bundy was born out of wedlock and spent his early years with a series of relatives. Although possessing an above-average IQ (122), his high school grades were just average. Two of Bundy's ambitions were to go to law school and to become a politician. Bundy attended several universities for his undergraduate studies (University of Puget Sound, University of Washington, Temple University), and he often changed his major (Asian Studies, Urban Planning, and Sociology). During his college years, Bundy was involved in acts of shoplifting and burglary, and began to use alcohol heavily. After graduating from college with a degree in psychology, Bundy did attend several law schools but was not particularly successful at any of them. Friends of Bundy's commented that he was always charming and talkative, though he frequently boasted, lied, and tended to manipulate women for his own purposes (Leyton, 1986; Egger, 1998).

> John Wayne Gacy had, by all accounts, a normal childhood. He dropped out of high school and performed a series of odd jobs, one as manager of three fried-chicken restaurants owned by his father-in-law, who once described Gacy as "a braggart and a liar." Gacy frequently boasted of his sexual prowess, and his resume at the time included false information such as having a college degree and experience as a store manager. Gacy's first marriage failed, but he established his own construction business using money borrowed from his mother. His second marriage also faltered and eventually ended in divorce because he began a series of relationships with young men he knew and others he had picked up. Despite his interest in young men, Gacy insisted to others that he was also successful with women and was, in fact, bisexual. Gacy also inflated his business success, exaggerating how

much money he earned, how busy and important his construction firm was, and how politically connected he was to the local Democratic Party. Gacy always wanted to look like a celebrity. When he lived in Iowa, he instructed his friends to refer to him as "Colonel"; when incarcerated he asked the jail chaplain to send the archbishop of Chicago to visit him, and he often bragged of having connections to Chicago's mob (Egger, 1998).

David Berkowitz, the notorious "Son of Sam" killer, murdered six people during a killing rampage in New York City, between 1976 and 1977. At first blush, Berkowitz might appear to be a prime example of the psychotic, insane, or deranged killer because in his confession he claimed that a dog had ordered him to kill. The truth is more complex. Berkowitz, who was the adopted son of lower-middle-class Jewish parents, had an uneventful childhood. His parents doted on and perhaps spoiled him. Neighbors of the Berkowitzes commented that David was hyperactive, spoiled, and uncontrollable. During childhood there was no evidence of the "demons" that were later to plague him. He was known to be a bully, but Berkowitz had no official history of violence. He did set fires frequently, and his arsonist behavior continued into his twenties. Berkowitz joined the army, only later to rebel against it, becoming something of a radical who refused to carry his rifle while on guard duty in Korea. Eventually, he became an evangelical Christian. After returning to the United States upon completion of his stint in the army, Berkowitz had a succession of low-paying, dead-end jobs. He finally got work with the U.S. Postal Service as a letter sorter. His first killing, of two women, was on July 29, 1976; his last was in August of 1977. During his murder rampage, Berkowitz left notes for the police, at times taunting them. In one such note he revealed himself to be the "Son of Sam" (Sam Carr was one of Berkowitz's neighbors and it was Carr's dog that supposedly howled the death instructions). Berkowitz even corresponded with the famed *New York Daily News* columnist, Jimmy Breslin, to whom he denied responsibility for his deeds. After his arrest, Berkowitz was deemed, by a team of psychiatrists appointed by the court, to be too insane to stand trial. The prosecution, however, hired its own psychiatrist, the famous Dr. David Abrahamsen. Abrahamsen alluded to the possibility that Berkowitz's delusions and visions might have been exaggerated. Berkowitz pled guilty to six murders and was sentenced to 25 years to life for each. Just one year after he began serving his sentence, Berkowitz held a press conference to announce that his story of the talking dog and demons was a hoax, designed to get him off the hook.

In each of these short biographical sketches, we catch a glimpse of many of the characteristics of the psycho/sociopath, or of those with antisocial personalities. Those characteristics include early delinquency, lying, manipulation, showing emotional shallowness, and behaving as a self-interested "smooth-talker."

Types of Serial Murder

Serial killers can be typed in many ways. For example, Dietz (1986) argues for five different types of serial murderers: (1) the psychopathic sexual sadist, (2) the crime spree killer, (3) the organized crime killer, (4) the custodial poisoner and asphyxiator, and (5) supposed psychotics. Jenkins (1988) studied English serial killers who were active between 1940 and 1985 and devised a two-category typology: (1) the predictable killer (who had prior histories of violence), and (2) the respectable killer (had prior minor but not violent offending). Although there is substantial overlap among the different typological schemes, the one provided by Holmes and Holmes (1998) seems most useful. Using implicit or explicit motives of the offenders, they propose six types of serial killer.

The *visionary killer* is the least common type and is characterized by a severe break with reality. Such murderers are frequently driven by voices or images that command them to kill, and they may even be possessed by multiple personalities. This psychotic killer generally leaves a graphic, chaotic, and brutally vivid crime scene. An example is Joseph Kallinger. As an adolescent he experienced visions of a floating head, "Charlie," who demanded that Joseph kill everyone in the world, one at a time. Kallinger responded by slaying his own son, a youngster who lived in the neighborhood, and a nurse.

The *mission serial killer* does away with people because he is on a "mission"—he wants to destroy those persons or class of persons he has identified as being unfit to live. The mission serial killer, then, restricts his killing to those identified as belonging to the "inferior" group— such as prostitutes, homosexuals, or the sick. Peter Sutcliffe, the "Yorkshire Ripper," and his namesake, "Jack the Ripper," are examples of mission killers, both of whom targeted prostitutes. In the United States, Joel Rifkin was comparable. From 1980 through 1983, Rifkin murdered approximately 17 prostitutes in New York City.

The *hedonistic lust killer* is one of three subtypes of hedonistic serial killer. Hedonistic killers are distinguished by their effort to obtain pleasure from killing. The particular pleasure of the lust killer is sexual. The lust killer derives direct sexual satisfaction from murdering his victims, and/or satisfies his sexual desires by having sex with the corpse, or by mutilating or cutting off sex organs. The Ukrainian serial killer Andrei Chikatilo represents this type well. As observed earlier, he claimed to be able to achieve sexual satisfaction only by torturing and killing his victims (male and female). He also cannibalized his victims' body parts, particularly sexual organs. Jerry Brudos is an American example of the hedonistic lust killer; Brudos removed body parts from his victims, had sex with their corpses, and in one case removed the breasts from a victim and made an epoxy mold of them, which he kept as a "memento."

The *thrill killer* is the second subtype of hedonistic killer. These individuals are similar to lust killers in that they also derive sexual satisfaction from their murders. The thrill killer is different, however, in that he requires a live victim for sexual satisfaction. Thrill killers derive sexual pleasure from torturing, dominating, terrorizing, and humiliating victims, which death ends. The "Hillside Stranglers," Kenneth Bianchi and Angelo Buono, performed this type of serial murder. After abducting female victims, the two cousins would take them to Buono's house, where they were repeatedly tortured until unconscious, then revived. When the victims eventually died, the bodies were disposed of and new victims sought.

The *comfort killer* is the third and final subtype of hedonistic serial killer. As the name connotes, this killer murders for "creature comfort," such as financial gain. Examples include Faye and Ray Copeland, elderly Missouri ranchers. They asked their farmhands to purchase cattle on their own credit, with the promise of reimbursement from the ranch's later proceeds. Once the cattle were purchased, however, the ranch hands "disappeared," which nullified the Copeland's debt. The Copelands were linked with five such murders.

The final type of serial killer in the Holmes and Holmes scheme is the *power/control killer*. This type murders to obtain a sense of domination and total control over the victim. Sex may be involved, but the pleasure derived is not from the sex act itself (either with lust or with a thrill in mind), but in the complete control the offender has over the victim. Ted Bundy was a power/control killer. By his own admission, Bundy sought victims (usually young college girls) who he thought were particularly "vulnerable," trusting, and weak (Holmes and Holmes, 1998).

As you can imagine from the diverse types of serial killers, it is not easy to explain their sometimes bizarre conduct. In the next section, we will examine some explanations for serial killing.

Why Do They Do It?

When the malignant acts committed by serial killers are considered, it almost appears as if they defy explanation and understanding. However, many other acts discussed in this book, as well as many deviant acts we do not have the space to examine, appear strange, bizarre, or psychotic to many people. Despite difficulties, there are many possible explanations of serial killing. Unfortunately, there is meager evidence to support one explanation over another, so conclusions are often little more than conjecture.

Some argue that serial killing, as well as much other violence, has biological, or at least biosocial or biopsychological, causes. Sears (1991) has noted that because of constitutional defects (such as a dysfunctional autonomic nervous system) the serial killer has unusual need for stimulation, thrills, and excitement. He contends that because minor acts do not provide sufficient pleasure or excitement, such persons resort to major acts of brutality. Although Sears does not refer to it, there is a substantial body of thought in criminology that links violent behavior to low arousal states (see Raine, 1993, for a review of this extensive literature). Raine (1997), for example, maintains that antisocial persons are chronically underaroused, and empirical studies have consistently shown that violent offenders exhibit classic signs of underarousal, including low resting heart rates, abnormalities in their electroencephalograms, and poor skin conductance.

Two interpretations link low arousal levels and violent crime. One posits that the underaroused experience little fear of the consequences of a crime, which translates into an increased readiness to commit criminal acts. The second interpretation is compatible with that of Sears (1991) and links low arousal with crime directly via increased need for stimulation and excitement. The underaroused presumably seek stimulation to raise their depressed arousal levels to a "normal" state. No matter what the reason, low states of arousal are connected to the commission of crimes. Since we know that most serial killers do not really "specialize" in murder but have a prior history of other offenses, their low levels of arousal are predicted to dispose them to all sorts of crimes and deviant acts.

There are also sociological and psychological explanations of serial killing that trace its origins to childhood trauma and/or abuse. Storr (1972), for example, attributes acts of serial killers to the horrible things done to them—such as physical and sexual abuse by parents and other caretakers. The rage and violence directed at the killer's victims, it is argued, reflect the rage directed at him earlier in life. Although the link between a person's childhood and his adult hostile behavior is often intuitive, there are substantive reasons to support it. One possible theoretical process compatible with this explanation is that portrayed by social learning theory (Bandura, 1973; Akers, 1994), which is discussed in greater detail in Chapter 11. Within this general theory, one form of learning is imitative—a person learns by watching others and copying their behavior. Adult serial killers may be simply imitating the violence committed against them as children, or they may be imitating violent acts they witnessed.

There is some empirical confirmation of the influence of imitative learning in serial murder. For example, many serial murderers have experienced appalling instances of physical and sexual abuse as well as profound parental neglect as children. In addition, Widom (1989, 1997) has documented a strong correlation between experiencing and witnessing violence as a child and committing violent behavior as an adult. She suggests that this correlation results because those victimized as children learn destructive coping mechanisms, including skills in manipulation and denial as well as violent behavior.

Others (Dodge et al., 1990) have argued that those who were victimized as children develop information processing schemas that encourage them to interpret social cues as carrying hostile intent. Exposed to violence either directly as victims or indirectly, such persons sense hostility and attribute it even to benign or ambiguous cues from others. As a result, they employ violence first.

Still other learning-based theories of the serial killer find a connection between the violent models portrayed and a propensity to commit violent acts (Huesman et al., 1997). One possible reason is desensitization to violence brought about by constant exposure. Violence for some may be seen as both normal and acceptable, and as a result such persons may be more likely to resort to it.

Although there are numerous explanations of serial killing, little is actually known about it. Scholars do not know whether it is simply an extreme form of violent conduct encapsulated in general theories of deviance or if it is so unusual as to call for an entirely new and unique explanation. In any case, Huesman et al. (1997:183) are probably correct in concluding that it is doubtful if any one explanation will suffice to account for exceptionally hostile, repetitive, violent acts, like those committed by serial killers.

How Well Organized Is It?

Since we contend that the degree of organization of practitioners is a key characteristic of deviance, it is important to consider the organization of serial killing. Keep in mind that a highly organized form of deviance will have high levels of sociality (the deviance is committed in groups or at least practitioners depend in some way on others), is pervasive (the deviance or deviant life style consumes a large portion of participants' lives), has effective communication among its members, has differentiated roles and coordination among them, possesses a shared culture, serves as a major source of individuals' self-identities, has an integrated philosophy, has mechanisms of control among practitioners, and engages in systematic recruitment. As you can probably surmise from our discussion thus far, serial murder is toward the less organized, individualistic end of a continuum of organization.

First, serial killing is very low in sociality. For the most part, serial killers commit their acts alone, or with a single other individual, and they do not need support personnel to supply the means. David Berkowitz, Jeffrey Dahmer, John Gacy, and the Yorkshire Ripper (to name only a few) all acted completely alone. Though not all serial killers may have been discovered, those who have been revealed usually operated alone. There is, of course, the occasional serial killer who works with a single "partner"; Kenneth Bianchi and his cousin Angelo Buono, the "Hillside Stranglers," worked in tandem. They went on prowls together in search of a victim, abducted her, and usually returned her to Buono's home for the torture and ultimate killing. A few other serial killers who worked in pairs were the husband and wife "team" of Ray and Faye Copeland, and Dean Corll and Wayne Henley. Although they sometimes work in pairs, serial killers rarely include more than a dyad. Perhaps the most "social" of the serial killers were Henry Lee Lucas and Ottis Toole. Though they traveled the country with Toole's niece Becky Powell and her younger bother Frank, the two committed their murderous acts together, apart from their companions. It may be because the serial killers' behavior is highly criminal as well as deviant or because they possess so few redeeming qualities that they cannot form friendships with others, but the social network of serial killers is very narrow. Thus the sociality of serial killing is minimal.

Serial killing is not a pervasive activity; abducting and killing a human being, relatively speaking, is not time consuming. Serial killers therefore spend most of their time in other activities. However, some serial killers are so obsessed that they do spend a great deal of their time thinking about and searching for their next victim. For example, Ted Bundy stated that he slept little, preferring to drive around, sometimes all night, looking for the right victim (Egger, 1998). Before his killing rampage, Bundy engaged in a considerable amount of voyeurism; he reported spending many hours at night walking around the Seattle neighborhood where he lived (Leyton, 1986). Nonetheless, he managed a regular busy life during the daytime.

The "Son of Sam" killer, David Berkowitz, also frequently drove around at night looking for possible victims (Leyton, 1986), as did the "Hillside Stranglers" Kenneth Bianchi and Angelo Buono. Henry Lee Lucas and Ottis Toole spent many months on the roads of America on their killing binge. Yet, despite the sometimes protracted time serial killers spend stalking or searching for their victims, even the most active serial killers devote only a minority of their time to the deviant behavior. Even while they were in killing modes, Ted Bundy and David Berkowitz attended school and held jobs. The prolific killer John Gacy had a busy construction firm, and he was active in both local politics and charity work. In sum, serial killing is not a very pervasive activity.

Since serial killing generally involves only one or two persons, it follows that practitioners do not communicate much with each other. This deviance is mainly an isolated, solitary activity—so much so that even those close to the killer usually are not aware of what is going on. Those who later discover they had worked with or lived near an apprehended serial killer usually express surprise. The refrain "he was such a quiet person, I never would have known" is repeated many times. Thus, one of the women who at one time worked with Ted Bundy remarked that he was "the kind of guy a girl my age would look at and just say, Wow! Sort of Kennedy like" (Leyton, 1986:90). After Joel Rifkin confessed to murdering 17 prostitutes in New York, a high school classmate described him as "quiet, shy, not the kind of guy who would do something like this"; a friend of Juan Corona, convicted of killing 25 migrant workers in California, commented that "Juan kept to himself and never said much, for the most part"; and the one-time employer of the "Son of Sam" described David Berkowitz as "a nice quiet shy fellow" (Egger, 1998:251). The girlfriend of "Hillside Strangler" Kenneth Bianchi said that "The Ken I knew couldn't ever have hurt anybody or killed anybody; he wasn't the kind of person who could have killed anybody" (Egger 1998:132)—this despite Bianchi's having been accused of several murders involving abominable sexual torture. Rather than communicating with one another or other people, serial killers typically hide their malignant thoughts and acts from everybody.

Similarly, since serial killers rarely act with or in concert with more than one person, there is little role differentiation, and without role differentiation there is little need for coordination. Most serial killers act alone, and most of those who share the activity do so with only one other person. In the existing record of serial killers there is absolutely no evidence of any attempts to differentiate roles. What "role differentiation" that exists is usually due to each person's own unique predilection.

Because serial killers rarely act with others, spend little time committing their acts, and keep their thoughts and acts to themselves, there is no shared culture. A culture requires a social group; it would also seem to require a modest level of communication (how else would the culture be spread?). As a result of their generally solitary, secretive existences, serial killers have no developed culture; there is no "right" way to murder that is passed from one generation of serial killers to another, no typical artifacts, and no special language. Moreover, serial killers hardly have meaningful individual rationales for their behavior, much less an integrated philosophy of either life or death. Since there are no roles into which persons must be socialized, or culture or philosophy to learn, the practice of serial killing has no mechanisms for social control from a group of killers.

There is a sense in which some serial killers form their identities around their deviant role. For example, David Berkowitz went to great lengths to document and broadcast the fact that he was the "Son of Sam." He placed his signature in letters to the police and to *New York Daily News* columnist Jimmy Breslin (Leyton, 1986). Toward the end of his killing career, Berkowitz seems to have adopted the character and identity of the serial killer "Son of Sam." He wrote to New York City Police Captain Joseph Borelli: "I am deeply hurt by your calling me a wemon [sic] hater. I am not. But I am a monster. I am the 'Son of Sam'." Similarly, Ted Bundy's self-identity became enveloped in the being within himself he referred to as "the entity" (Leyton, 1986). Even in these cases, however, we cannot truly say that the person identified himself as a serial killer in the same way that a Mennonite or a Gypsy would have a self-identity built around unusual behavior patterns. The "self-identities" of serial killers are often distortions of reality.

Finally, serial killers engage in very little recruitment to fill the ranks of serial killers; they certainly do not have systematic recruitment procedures. While individual killers may enlist accomplices or companions, the companions are usually simply brought along for company rather than as novitiates.

Summary

In sum, serial killing is a solitary, secretive form of deviance that does not encompass the life of the killer, has no integrated philosophy or culture to impart, involves no role differentiation to speak of or mechanisms of internal control, and does not rely on the recruitment of new recruits. It is perhaps the quintessential form of individualized deviance. ✦

Chapter 4

Subcultural Deviance

Chapter 3 described two forms of deviance, suicide and serial killing, that show little organization among their practitioners. Although organization is really a matter of degree, ranging from none at all (an unlikely occurrence) to totally organized (also unusual), it is convenient to categorize the forms of deviance falling near the "no organization" end of the continuum as being individualized.

In the following pages we describe two forms of deviance, deviant drug use and gang delinquency, that show much greater organization among their practitioners than is evident for the individualized deviances. They fall somewhere in the middle of the continuum of organization, neither fully organized nor individualized. We call them "subcultural" deviances.

Deviant Drug Use

What is deviant drug use? This question is not easy to answer. As you have already learned, applying the definition of deviant behavior is often difficult. Although behavior is deviant when a majority of a given group regards it as unacceptable or when it typically evokes a negative response (either collectively or from designated authorities), group boundaries are not always clear, and there are rarely sufficient data to establish opinions about a given behavior or to assess the typicality of negative response. Assessing which drug use is deviant poses additional complications. For one thing, there is no generally agreed-upon understanding about what is or is not a drug; also, the extent and context of drug use bears heavily upon whether usage is regarded as acceptable or unacceptable. Finally, there is great inconsistency in the legal status of various substances, which affects the likelihood of collective negative responses, as well as the direction of public opinion.

A Common Conceptualization of Drugs

Drugs are commonly conceived as "substances" or chemicals that produce particular physical or psychic effects, such as mood or mind alterations (Stephens, 1987:15), relief of disease symptoms, or suppression of the causes of disease (such as antibiotics that kill the organisms producing respiratory ailments).

Issues

Many Substances Qualify. The problem with conceptualizing drugs in this way is that many "substances" not usually thought of as drugs can affect moods and thinking, relieve symptoms of disease, produce physiological reactions, and sometimes even attack the cause of a disease. For instance, eating chocolate puts a lot of people in a better mood, and inhaling perfume sometimes alters a person's thinking about the meaning of some kinds of social encounters. Among people with diabetes or with hypoglycemia anything naturally sweet will relieve the symptoms of low blood sugar, enabling them to think more clearly and manifest a more even-tempered approach to situations. Things with bad odors (such as excrement), if accidentally taken into one's mouth or even smelled, will produce a physiological response of gagging. And vitamin C, common in citrus fruit, is known to cure as well as prevent scurvy, a debilitating disease that once ravaged sailors who were on the seas for months without fresh fruit or vegetables. Despite fitting the common definition of drugs, however, chocolate, perfume, sweet foods, excrement, or vitamin C are rarely regarded as drugs.

❖ ❖ ❖ ❖

Effects Vary. To complicate the matter, various substances that are commonly called drugs do not always produce the same effects for everybody and in all circumstances. The effects of substances depend on (1) how they are used; (2) characteristics of the individual ingesting them; and (3) the social context in which they are used. Effects also vary depending on the peculiar interactions among these elements.

1. The behavioral response of a given individual to the use of a substance, as well as his or her physiological reactions, depends on the dosage, frequency of use, route of administration, and whether the substance is used by itself or in combination with other substances (see Goode, 1993). For example, small oral doses of alcohol, a popular legal drug (at least for those in the United States of appropriate ages who are not engaged in activities potentially dangerous for others, such as driving an automobile or flying an airplane) may produce hardly any effects, particularly for experienced users. Modest oral doses may produce pleasurable relaxation for many people. Very large doses may produce short-term undesirable consequences, such as loss of consciousness or of motor control and may cause death. Moreover, whether a dose is small or large depends on an individual's body size and rate of metabolism and whether the alcohol is consumed with or without food. In addition, the effects of even modest doses of alcohol are contingent on the frequency with which it is used. Finally, alcohol injected directly into the bloodstream produces different consequences than if it is taken orally (it is far more likely to cause death).

2. Effects that might be used to define substances as drugs depend not only on how the drugs are used but also on the characteristics of the different people who use them. Among such variables are biologically linked features like age, sex, body size, physical health and conditioning, and in some instances genetic structure (Stephens, 1987). For instance, there is reason to think that cocaine, especially in crack form, has a more intense physical effect on females than on males (Inciardi et al., 1993; but see Maher, 1996), and there is mounting evidence that genetic factors may predispose some individuals to alcohol addiction (Akers, 1992:98–99).

   In addition, diet, patterns of sleep and work, and use of medical treatment can influence the effects of drugs. Finally, the individual's attitude about use and his or her anticipation of what its effects might be are important influences on the person's reaction. For example, the feelings produced by marijuana use are not inherently pleasurable, and the first usage of heroin often makes people sick and nauseated (Stephens, 1991). Indeed, without a preconceived notion of what the effects will be and an interpretive framework defining those feelings as pleasant, many people will experience no effects at all from marijuana, or they will perceive the effects as unpleasant (Becker, 1953; Weil et al., 1968). If people believe they are receiving a drug that will have particular effects but in reality are ingesting a placebo, a good number of them will nevertheless experience the effects they expect to feel. That is why medical research to test new medicines relies on experimental methods in which the subjects do not know whether they are receiving the real drug or an inert substitute. Moreover, for some individuals, the knowledge that a substance is illegal, dangerous, or taboo apparently makes the high, and the appeal of it, more intense (Hanson et al., 1985:142; Waldorf, 1973:16).

3. The social context in which drugs are taken influences the taker's reaction. Given the import of the individual's state of mind concerning what drugs do or are perceived to do, it should be no surprise that the effects of substances that might be regarded as drugs are not uniform across social settings. For instance, hallucinogenic drugs like LSD (those that affect perceptual processes) are well known to produce "good trips" or "bad trips" (psychic experiences), depending partly on whether others more experienced are with the consumer. Visual distortions may be fun if others tell consumers what to expect and how to interpret the reactions, encourage them, and assure them that the experience is safe and that these others are there to help. By contrast, visual distortions experienced while alone or in company with people who disapprove may be frightening and psychologically damaging.

   Moreover, there are broad cultural understandings about some drugs that influence how individuals experience them. In some cultures people are taught that alcohol makes one gentle, quiet, kind, and loving, and intoxicated people in those cultures tend to follow that pattern (MacAndrew and Edgerton, 1969). Yet in other cultures, like that of the United States, where people learn that alcohol releases inhibitions, permitting one to be boisterous, aggressive, and even violent, intoxicated people tend to be rude, pushy, and violent.

Many drugs cannot even be used effectively without considerable knowledge provided by the social context. For instance, there are various techniques for using cocaine (both for powder and rock) that must be learned, and some methods of use apparently produce different degrees of intoxication (Inciardi et al., 1993; Williams, 1992). The same is true for heroin (Stephens, 1991:Chapter 4). And, people must learn, usually from other participants in the immediate social situation, how to use marijuana so as to produce any noticeable effect (Becker, 1953).

Since the consequences of ingesting different substances vary so much, it is difficult to apply usual definitions in deciding what is or is not a drug. Does a substance have to produce a given physical or mental effect every time it is used to be considered a drug? If not, then what proportion of the time and under what circumstances does the effect have to occur in order to qualify as a drug? One might even imagine that a substance could be called a drug if it ever produces particular physical or psychic effects. Clearly, identification of drugs as a distinct category of things different from nondrugs in a consistent and easily applied manner is impossible. Defining and identifying drugs, therefore, is imprecise, involving objective, subjective, and political ele-

ments. In light of these difficulties, a number of distinctions meant to simplify drug understandings have emerged.

Distinctions

In order to differentiate substances that can be identified unambiguously
as drugs from other drug-like substances, some authorities have focused on
whether a given substance is addictive or not. It was thought that addictive
substances would be a meaningful class, even though the problem of bifur-
cating other substances as drugs or nondrugs might remain.

At one point addiction was generally defined in terms of two elements:
dependence and tolerance (Akers, 1991). Dependence is the tendency of a
substance to produce measurable physiological changes during a period of
continuous usage such that cessation of the substance leads to uncomfortable physical reactions. These uncomfortable reactions, often called the
"withdrawal syndrome," may include such things as anxiety and irritability,
nervousness, chills and fever, tremors, cramps, nausea, inability to sleep, di-
arrhea, general physical sickness, and depression. Sometimes withdrawal responses are so severe that they require medical assistance. Severe reactions
are usually associated with long-term and extensive use of narcotics like heroin or morphine or of stimulants like methamphetamines. In other instances,
withdrawal symptoms are relatively mild, though persistent nonetheless.
Relatively mild withdrawal symptoms usually occur with cessation of nicotine, a substance present in tobacco products. Some reports contend that the
desire to avoid such adverse reactions constitutes the primary motive for substance use once a dependent person has made the cognitive link between the
substance and relief of withdrawal distress (Lindesmith, 1947, 1968).

Tolerance refers to the tendency of a substance to lose its potency for producing the effects the user has come to expect or associate with it. In other
words, one's body adapts, so that over time larger and larger doses are required to produce the same effects that a smaller dose previously brought
about. The tolerance phenomenon is most closely associated with narcotics
like heroin or morphine. Continuous heroin users will find that periodically
they have to increase their dosage in order to stave off withdrawal distress or
to achieve the purpose for which the substance was originally used, either
pain reduction in a medical context or usually some degree of euphoria (being "high") among nonmedical users. The development of tolerance is one
reason that illegal users of these substances have such a hard time in the
streets. Although some apparently can regulate and control their intake to
avoid the tolerance effect (Hanson et al., 1985), many find themselves drawn
into an upward-spiraling cycle of increased need at a growing cost. Another
factor that may contribute to the spiral is the drive to achieve the initial good
feelings associated with early use of the substance (the "rush"), which some
scholars contend is the primary motive for substance usage (McAuliffe and
Gordon, 1974; Waldorf, 1973).

A strict definition of addiction, and indirectly of a class of substances to
be regarded as drugs, then, is a substance that usually produces physical dependence and tolerance along with its other effects. The trouble is, some substances that have strong appeal to their users, even to the point of compulsive
craving (which some would like to call addiction) lack one or the other of
these characteristics. Nicotine usually produces withdrawal symptoms, but

there is no evidence that it leads to tolerance. Smokers do not continuously elevate their intake; fairly quickly, individuals tend to find a level of personal comfort and continue to smoke the number of cigarettes necessary to maintain that level. Partly for this reason, many authorities resisted for years the idea that nicotine was addictive. And apparently cocaine, one of the most potent substances for producing compulsive craving (Goode, 1993:30; Inciardi et al., 1993), has only minor, short-term withdrawal symptoms and little tendency toward tolerance build-up (Inciardi et al., 1993; Williams, 1992). Its appeal, a short-term euphoria, however, does lead many to binge (take another dose as soon as the high from a previous dose dissipates) for hours at a time or sometimes for days at a time, as long as the supply lasts (Inciardi et al., 1993; Williams, 1992).

There are, in fact, few substances that qualify as addictive using the strict criteria of dependence and tolerance, or even using a modified criterion that says a substance must be capable of producing either dependency or tolerance. Recognition of the shortcomings of this definition has led to a newer definition of addiction, apparently formulated, in part, to be able to classify as drugs those substances that produce compulsive behavior with destructive consequences or substances that some group of people, for political or other reasons, wants to restrict (Akers, 1992; Goode, 1993).

A number of authorities now define addiction in terms of "psychological dependence." By this criterion, a substance that has the capacity to produce craving or compulsive desire is addictive. But this definition creates even more problems because many substances seem to produce psychological dependence, at least in some people, even though few would call those substances drugs. In fact, anything pleasurable could be classified as a drug if the idea of intensified desire based on psychological or mental processes is employed broadly. Thus, chocolate and even eggs could be drugs because they have strong appeal, sometimes to the point of craving, for some individuals. Moreover, even the drugs that generate psychological craving can sometimes be discontinued, even by long-term users (see Granfield and Cloud, 1996; Johnson, 1978) and are often used in moderation (Cheung et al., 1991; Reinarman et al., 1997). Such imprecision has provoked still other authorities to make another kind of distinction.

Abuse

Since many substances that fit one or another of the criteria to be classified as drugs are socially and legally acceptable (alcohol, nicotine, caffeine, and in some places marijuana), are widely used, and are often used without much apparent harm to the users or society, some authorities have given up differentiating drugs from nondrugs, or of trying to separate addictive from nonaddictive substances. Instead, they focus on the degree to which drugs are used and/or on the extent to which their use has destructive consequences. Accordingly, abuse is defined as excessive use of a substance. Thus, alcohol use is one thing and alcohol abuse is another; also, theoretically, heroin use is different from heroin abuse. Under this conceptualization, alcohol or heroin abuse would exist when individuals' use begins to affect their ability to function effectively in society or to cause problems.

Any use of illegal substances has a high potential for causing a person some problems; that is, they may be arrested and incarcerated; they have to develop ties to unconventional networks for a supply; and the substances are likely to be expensive. Therefore, most scholars and practitioners who have tried to employ the abuse concept have modified it to accommodate this fact. In practice, substance abuse has come to mean: excessive use of a legal or legitimate substance (including prescription drugs) to the point where it has destructive consequences, or any use of an illegal substance.

The effort to bypass problems in defining drugs by shifting the focus to ways in which substances are used has not been very successful. Trying to decide when substance use is excessive has proven exceptionally difficult. For instance, some people, including medical personnel and blue-collar workers, can and do use narcotics for years while carrying on legitimate lives and performing important work (Winick, 1964; Hanson et al., 1985). Others seem to get in trouble with only minimal use. With the abuse approach, examination of the addiction process can only be post hoc. In addition, it is inconsistent to classify all uses of illegal substances as "abuse" even when that use does not actually cause problems for the person.

Moreover, differentiating abuse from use seems to imply that drug use, within limits, is not a bad thing. This flies in the face of political groups and law enforcement agencies who, for various reasons, regard the use of any artificial substances not required for the maintenance of life as socially undesirable, dangerous, or evil. Thus, the idea that some authorities might indirectly condone (by not condemning) substance usage, some of which might lead to costly and devastating consequences, struck many citizens as outrageous. Social, ideological, and political pressures on those who write about use soon led to corruption of the term "substance abuse" so that it came to mean any substance use that is disapproved (either by the general public or the person doing the defining). This, of course, made defining drugs or deviant drug use largely dependent on political rather than medical, psychological, or physiological concerns.

Legality

Another effort to make meaningful distinctions about substances that might be regarded as drugs is also politically linked, and for that reason it is not especially rational or useful. Some in the political arena simply differentiate between legal and illegal substances. Since many people assume that legal regulation is based on a scientific, reasonable, or rational foundation, this distinction implies separation of dangerous substances from relatively safe ones. Consequently, many citizens think of, or define, drugs as illegal substances. To them, legal substances such as alcohol, nicotine, or caffeine are not drugs, whereas illegal substances such as THC (the active ingredient in marijuana), heroin, and cocaine are drugs.

For some purposes, the legal/illegal differentiation is meaningful. It neatly defines when the police can be activated; consequently as criminal offenses, some types of substance use then become objects of study by criminologists. In most respects, however the legal/illegal distinction muddies the waters of definition. This is because, as you learned in Chapter 2, the process by which some activity comes to be included in the criminal code is political. Various interest groups, including law enforcement bureaucracies, vie to have their beliefs or economic interests written into law. In the political give-and-take, much misinformation is disseminated; there are often alarmist appeals to fear; efforts are made to tap into latent ideologies about the evil of "drugs" as a general category; and various contenders struggle to protect their domains. As a result, the legal regulations that emerge constitute a hodgepodge of inconsistencies that have little meaning outside of a law enforcement context.

Consider four substances well known in the United States: heroin, THC (in marijuana), alcohol, and nicotine (in tobacco products). The first of these (heroin) is completely illegal, and any possession or sale carries heavy penalties. The second (THC) is largely illegal except for small quantities in some jurisdictions, and its possession or sale, with the previously noted exception, generally carries moderate to heavy penalties. The third (alcohol) is illegal only if used excessively while operating machinery that might imperil the public safety or if the consumer is under legal age; penalties are calibrated to excessive use in situations jeopardizing public safety (most states specify .08 or .10 percent of blood alcohol concentration as unacceptable in those instances) or to the harm caused (for instance, penalties are different if an intoxicated driver kills somebody than if he or she merely smashes the auto into a tree). The final one (nicotine) is almost completely legal, the exceptions being for underage people (the laws for this are rarely enforced) or for use in specified places where smoking is prohibited; neither of these exceptions involves more than minor penalties. These four substances then vary in legality and seriousness, as reflected by potential penalty, in descending order: heroin (the most serious), THC, alcohol, and nicotine (the least serious). Yet, there is no underlying principle that would account for these differences in legal seriousness. We could posit that the rationale for illegality is physical harmfulness to the user, addictivity, or threat to public well being: these rationales are examined in the following paragraphs.

Health Consequences. Clearly the rationale for illegality is not physical harmfulness because the degree of damage caused by the drugs actually varies in exactly the opposite order to which the drugs are ranked in illegality. Most damaging to a person's health is long-term use of tobacco products, particularly smoking of cigarettes, which is associated with several dozen disease conditions, the best known of which is lung cancer (see Akers, 1992:237–238). Indeed, the negative connection between tobacco use and health has become so compelling that the tobacco industry, rather than face actual trials, agreed to a massive financial settlement with state governments for medical claims. Yet nicotine is the least illegal of these substances.

Deviance in Everyday Life

What are the health costs of smoking? They are pretty high according to a group of health care economists at the University of California at Berkeley. In 1998 they published a paper in which they estimated the smoking-related Medicaid health costs to be $12.9 billion per year or $322 billion over 25 years. The states with the highest expected smoking-related Medicaid costs were New York and California. It was estimated by the researchers that smoking-related diseases would demand approximately 15 percent of the total Medicaid budget of those states. (Miller et al., 1998)

By contrast, heroin, the most illegal of the substances, is actually the least harmful physically. Although people who use heroin often suffer general deterioration of health stemming from neglect of proper diet, exercise, and bodily care; are especially susceptible to contagious diseases like hepatitis and AIDS; and have a good chance of dying of an overdose, these consequences are apparently not due to the effects of the drug itself but rather to the life style associated with illegal use. In experimental conditions where regular, reliable doses of known strength are administered in clean conditions, using sterile needles, and where the subjects are shielded from weather and provided nutritious food, users apparently suffer no long-term bodily damage (short-term effects include reduced sexual capability and constipation) (Waldorf, 1973:66). Because the drug is illegal, all users, except those authorized by the government for experimental tests, must obtain their supplies on the black market. Drugs bought on the street are of unknown quality and quantity (since their purity is successively diluted by hierarchical networks of suppliers) and they are expensive. Moreover, equipment for mixing and injecting heroin is not legally available, which forces users to employ less sanitary, homemade devices or manufactured syringes that become contaminated from repeated use or from sharing among several users. Under such conditions, users live a life of desperate search for drugs or for the money to buy them. The search becomes a constant mission, leading to neglect of their health needs, and when they do have drugs, injection often poses a serious risk of infection or overdose (Waldorf, 1973; Hanson et al., 1985). Since the health consequences of heroin use seem to be a byproduct of the illegality of the drug, it is illogical to claim that serious legal consequences are in place to discourage or prevent unhealthy behavior.

Although marijuana use is the second most illegal of the four drugs under consideration, its consequences for health appear to be relatively benign (that is, compared to tobacco and alcohol). The main damage from marijuana use is to the lungs; just as heavy tobacco smoking can lead to respiratory difficulties, so can heavy marijuana smoking (Akers, 1992). But because marijuana use is rarely as continuous as cigarette smoking (marijuana is most often used for recreational purposes in occasional sociable situations), the chances of harm are much less. There is also some possible effect on memory and reproductive capability (but see Goode, 1993). So, although marijuana is not harmless, its health consequences do not match the seriousness of its legal status. Similarly, alcohol, the second least carefully regulated drug, is actually second only to tobacco in its potential for health damage. Heavy use over a period of time is known to cause liver problems, to affect other organs such as the kidneys, and to damage brain cells. In extreme cases it leads to death or organically caused mental illness (Akers, 1992:189).

Clearly, then, health consequences are not the underlying rationale for the illegality of drugs, and legal status does not provide a meaningful distinction for defining substances as drugs or for differentiating among substances that might be deviant because of their impact on health; neither does the underlying rationale concerning addictiveness.

Addictiveness. Some might imagine that the law attempts to regulate or prohibit drugs most carefully when the drugs hold the potential for addiction. To many, dependency on a substance deprives the person of autonomy and violates the human spirit. And to the extent that addiction is a surreptitious or unintended result of drug usage, it is all the more objectionable. Since some think the law is an instrument to promote the general welfare and uphold widely shared values, it is assumed that legal status is based on careful evaluation of the addictive potential of drugs. But is it?

As we have already seen, the concept of addiction is controversial. Even if one applies a broad definition—that a substance is addictive if it tends to produce physical dependence, psychologically compulsive craving, or physical tolerance—it is still not easy to assess addictiveness. For one thing, there are issues concerning how much use leads to how much addiction and how long it takes to produce different degrees of addiction. The most illegal of the substances, heroin, is indeed addictive by all three criteria. It produces physiological changes that signal withdrawal distress; it becomes tolerated by the body, leading to larger doses; and it generates a psychological reinforcement that induces most former users to return to its consumption even after they have physically withdrawn completely (O'Donnell, 1964; Tittle, 1972:28). Yet contrary to popular opinion, a good number of people experiment with heroin without becoming addicted. Those who do become addicted usually do so after a period of several months rather than immediately (Stephens, 1991), and some users control and regulate usage to be consistent with their financial and social means rather than plunge into a compulsive race to satisfy a dominant craving (Hanson et al., 1985).

Nicotine is on the other end of the continuum of legal regulation, but it, too, is addictive. Its addictiveness was finally acknowledged recently by tobacco executives, who had been the last holdouts, publicly denying tobacco's addictivity (although secret company documents reveal that they knew it all along and even deliberately manipulated the level of nicotine in cigarettes to increase the addictivity of the product). Nicotine produces physical and psychological dependence among most who try it, and within a fairly short period of use (though it does not seem to produce tolerance).

Deviance in Everyday Life

Smoking cigarettes is not the only way that tobacco products can harm you. One of the fastest-growing forms of tobacco use is smokeless tobacco—"snuff" and chewing tobacco. If you think there are no health risks from or any addiction due to smokeless tobacco, think again. Smokeless tobacco has been linked to gum disease and to cancers of the mouth, pharynx, and esophagus. People who stop using smokeless tobacco show the same withdrawal symptoms as those who smoke cigarettes—cravings, irritability, and hunger.

Those who try to quit smoking suffer considerable discomfort—so much that most fail in their efforts, at least the first few times they try. And the rate of relapse among those who have been off cigarettes for long periods of time testifies to the power of the psychological dependence, or craving.

The two middle substances would also be out of order if the rationale for legal regulation were addictive qualities. While marijuana is more illegal than alcohol, marijuana hardly manifests any of the criteria of addiction, while alcohol clearly does. Marijuana does not produce any signs of physical dependence, though it may show some tolerance (Akers, 1992:75), and its capacity to produce psychological dependence is limited to only a small proportion of users (Goode, 1993). Alcohol, on the other hand, produces bodily changes so serious that long-term alcoholics experience marked withdrawal symptoms characterized by the "shakes" or tremors (this degree of dependence develops only over a long period of time, often many years). Psychological dependence is so common that several million Americans suffer from "alcoholism" (Akers, 1992:195). And tolerance of alcohol is well established.

Although the four substances being considered do not show a perfect negative relationship between the degree of their legal regulation and addictiveness, as was shown with respect to health consequences, they are never-theless somewhat irrationally ordered. The most addictive, heroin, is the most severely regulated by law. But marijuana, the second most-regulated, appears to be the least addictive of the four, while nicotine, the least regu-lated, appears to be second in addictiveness, followed by alcohol. Thus, the rationale for illegality cannot be the addictive potential of substances.

Threat to Public Well-Being. Some might maintain that the law regu-lates or prohibits various substances in proportion to their potential effects on public order, safety, or essential institutions. A substance might increase the probability of crime, magnify the chances of accidents, contribute to the spread of disease, or undermine users' capacity for responsible work or fam-ily life. In evaluating these potentialities of the four substances, it is impor-tant to separate the inherent effect of the substances from the effects that emerge from the way they are used in specific social circumstances. We have already seen that the health consequences of heroin use are largely a result of the fact that it is illegal. Similarly, some of the consequences of alcohol use, such as highway accidents, stem from what some call "irresponsible" use rather than from alcohol per se or from the fact that in some places people have few alternatives for transportation besides their private automobiles. Traffic accidents caused by alcohol are much reduced in inner cities, where more people use public transport rather than private automobiles.

In addition, it is difficult to estimate accurately the degree of threat to public order, general social consequences, or cost of the use of various sub-stances. For instance, one huge public danger from cigarette smoking is fire (Goode, 1993). Countless homes, business buildings, and forests are acciden-tally burned each year because people are careless in disposing of still-lighted cigarette butts. Often, however, the causes of fires are never determined, so it is impossible to know how much damage is indirectly due to tobacco use. Moreover, one can legitimately wonder if this loss is inherent to the substance or if it is simply a byproduct of the way people use the substance. Certainly one can argue that if nobody smoked, this danger would be greatly reduced, but it could also be reduced if smokers were better educated about their so-cial responsibility and trained for safer use of tobacco. Similar problems oc-cur with the rest of the substances.

Despite these problems, it is not difficult to conclude that the four sub-stances we are considering do not reflect a potential threat to public well-be-ing corresponding to their rank of illegality. Heroin use has great potential to make users incapable of performing normal work, fulfilling familial respon-sibilities, or functioning as autonomous and effective members of society, and it is quite addictive. If it were legal, socially acceptable, and widely avail-able at a reasonable cost, there would likely be an increase in usage and in ac-cidents due to the reduced alertness users experience. Although crime would probably go down (because the price of heroin would decline and its avail-ability would increase, lowering the necessity of illegal behavior to obtain the resources for maintaining a habit), there is no question that heroin is inher-ently a potential public menace. But is it so much more of a threat than nico-tine or alcohol? And what of marijuana, which appears to carry less potential for public harm than any of the other substances, yet is near the top in legal regulation?

The estimated cost of medical care necessitated by long-term tobacco use is staggering—in the hundreds of billions, as is the cost of illness resulting from secondary smoke (Akers, 1992: 237–242; Goode, 1993:259–261). The amount of lost work time because of tobacco-associated illness is also astonishing to contemplate. And there are large consequences from the loss of life and physical debilitation from tobacco use, as well as the accidental fires associated with it. Given this, and the fact of addiction, it is hard to justify nicotine as a less societally damaging substance than heroin—certainly not the magnitude of difference implied by their legal statuses.

Similarly, the medical consequences of alcohol use are extremely costly as well as debilitating, and the impact on lives and families directly from alcohol use, or indirectly from accidents, is amazing. About half of the approximately 40,000 traffic fatalities per year in the United States are alcohol related. In addition alcohol has been implicated in a large proportion of crime and domestic violence—apparently because it releases inhibitions that might otherwise constrain criminal impulses (Akers, 1992:62–70). Thus, as threatening as heroin is to society, alcohol appears to be at least a close second—less addictive but with more direct consequences.

Deviance in Everyday Life

Although mainly used for recreation, marijuana may have some medical benefits. For cancer patients undergoing chemotherapy, marijuana's active ingredient, THC, is thought to reduce nausea and vomiting as well as to improve the patient's appetite. For those with multiple sclerosis, marijuana is alleged to reduce muscle pain, and for patients with glaucoma, marijuana is thought to reduce the pressure within the eye. In recognition of these possible medical benefits, some states have enacted laws that allow for the medical prescription of marijuana use. California is one such state, but in 1996 the state attorney general had the police bust the San Francisco Cannabis Buyer's Club, which had been selling marijuana to the ill. After a two-year investigation, police undercover officers discovered that the club was selling as much as several pounds of marijuana at a time, and was dispensing it with forged doctors' notes. In November of 1996, California voters approved Proposition 215, which legalized the medical use of marijuana. It should be noted, however, that in a recent study, researchers found that marijuana use (and cocaine smoking) comes with a risk of lung cancer. (Barsky et al., 1998)

Finally, marijuana, although the second-ranked of these four substances in illegality, appears to pose fewer threats to public well-being than the others. If legal, and thereby even more widely available than now, it would probably become associated with more medical consequences (after all, physiological damage from repeatedly filling one's lungs with smoke containing numerous chemicals is well established), more accidents (since it affects perception and impairs motor skills, (see Goode, 1993:195–196), and more fires due to careless use. And it might reduce work efficiency. But its lack of addictiveness, the fact that it is not smoked continuously, and its mellowing effects, which work against criminal impulses, suggest it is relatively benign.

Clearly, the law does not show its concern for public well-being in its treatment of various substances that might be called drugs. It is inconsistent and even to some extent irrational.

Trying to define drugs in terms of legality, then, or even using legality as a criterion for meaningful distinctions among substances, is simply not viable. It causes more confusion than clarification. If one were to try to use legal status, as reflected in the degree of regulation and extent of penalties for unlawful use, to judge potential health consequences, addictiveness, and threat to public well being, or as a meaningful distinction among substances, one would encounter a morass even more confusing than using the other distinctions discussed above.

Summary

Definitions of drugs are imprecise and impossible to apply in completely meaningful ways. Moreover, given the variety of ways that substances can and are used, and the myriad social responses to those conditions, it is extremely difficult to specify what is or is not acceptable or to establish typical reactive patterns characterizing authorities' behavior. Many substances are either drugs or they are druglike in their use and consequences. In addition, such substances are ubiquitous and many of them have been used for centuries. It appears that almost all societies are enticed by substances that will transform normal bodily and mental conditions. Some of these substances are regarded as boons, making life better by curing illness, relieving pain, enhancing performances of one kind or another, or generating desirable states of mind. But others come to be regarded as dangerous or unacceptable. How this happens and the ultimate rationale for the overall scheme of substance use, availability, regulation, and prohibition is rarely straightforward. That is why it is a mistake, especially in contemporary society, to speak of "drugs" as if they all fell into one undifferentiated category.

Nevertheless, despite considerable confusion and many illogical and unscientific conclusions about drugs, there is some degree of agreement about the substances that are at issue when deviant drug use is discussed. In fact, authorities have been able to classify deviantly used drugs into six or seven rather distinct categories (Akers, 1992:24; Goode, 1993:25; Stephens 1987: 21–33).

Classification of Deviantly Used Drugs

According to Goode (1993), drugs that have potential for deviant use include: depressants (general depressants and specific pain killers called analgesics), stimulants, antipsychotic agents, hallucinogens, marijuana, and inhalants. Most of these are classified on the basis of their effects on the central nervous system and on their kinship to each other, as indicated by "cross-tolerance" and "cross-dependence." The latter two terms refer to the likelihood that if tolerance or dependence for one drug exists, a similar drug substituted for the first will also show the same or a similar level of tolerance or dependence. However, to some scholars, marijuana appears to be in a special class, unlike other drugs, and the inhalants are classified as such because of the way they are ingested.

Depressants

Depressants block, abate, or inhibit electrical or chemical messages passing through the central nervous system. As a result, they produce a reaction of relaxation, decrease of inhibition, and reduced activity—or with high doses, they bring on drowsiness and sleep. The general depressants include barbiturates, such as Nembutal and phenobarbital, sedatives like Quaaludes, and miscellaneous hypnotics such as alcohol. These are usually in pill or capsule form (with the exception of alcohol) and are orally ingested. The pain killers encompass the narcotics, like heroin, morphine, and codeine, as well as synthetic narcotics like Methadone and Demerol. Though some of the pain killers are used orally, many of them are injected, either in muscle tissue or intravenously. The pain killers, in particular, are associated with relaxed feelings of well-being, competence, and not caring about anything else, and they are associated with an immediate "rush" of euphoria. Many of these depressants are physically addictive, and many can cause death at high dosages because they slow vital functions like heartbeat below the point necessary for keeping the body alive.

Stimulants

Stimulants produce effects on the central nervous system that are the opposite of depressants' effects. They enhance the movement of electrical and chemical messages in the central nervous system, leading to a "pick-up," excitement, alertness, or arousal. The stimulants include amphetamines like Benzedrine or Methedrine (frequently used by long-distance truckers to stay awake), antidepressants such as Prozac, as well as substances like cocaine and nicotine. Such drugs are often employed to energize the person for social interaction or to overcome fatigue. Cocaine, however, produces an immediate "rush" of intense good feelings that is temporary but powerfully reinforcing. In powder form it is usually inhaled through the nostrils, and in rock form (created by cooking powder cocaine mixed with water and sometimes other substances like baking soda) it is smoked in a special type of pipe with a glass stem (Inciardi et al., 1993; Sterk-Elifson and Elifson, 1993; Williams, 1992). Cocaine users often go on "binges," where they repeatedly readminister the drug as soon as the "high" begins to dissipate (usually after about fifteen or twenty minutes); the binge may last for hours or days, or usually until the supply is gone.

Anti-psychotic Agents

Better known as "tranquilizers," these drugs tend to suppress or reduce the symptoms often associated with mental illness or abnormal behavior—anxiety, for example. They include Thorazine, Valium, and Lithium. While such drugs are often medically prescribed (much less now than in the 1980s), they are also used deviantly by recreational users. Although useful for medical purposes, sustained use of large doses can produce marked physical addiction, which is shown by withdrawal symptoms similar to those of alcohol or narcotics.

Hallucinogens

Hallucinogens, like LSD and MDMA (known among recreational users as "ecstasy" or "Adam"), have complicated effects on the nervous system that involve more than simple stimulation or depression. The effects alter perception so that the person sees colors and images in unusual ways, mixes senses, comprehends the world in a continual movement, and feels a sense of timelessness. There is also an undermining of rational, logical order, and sometimes an experience of weird and distorted images (Goode, 1993:214–217). At

other times, and particularly for "ecstasy," users report experiencing an initial "rush," followed by a plateau involving insights about life and living, a
feeling of bonding with others, sensuality, and enhanced ability to communicate (Beck and Rosenbaum, 1994). All of the hallucinogens can produce psy-
chotic-like response patterns that last for several hours, and sometimes there
are "flashbacks" days later.

Marijuana

One of the most popular illegal drugs in the United States is marijuana.
Usually ingested as smoke from burning dried leaves and tops of *Cannabis
sativa* plants, marijuana is classified differently by different authorities.
Some include it as a hallucinogen (Akers, 1992; Stephens, 1987), while others
prefer to treat it in a category all to itself (Goode, 1993). The immediate physiological effects of marijuana are minimal, but it produces temporary deterioration of motor skills and elevated heartbeat. The subjective effects vary but
often include intensification of sensual experience (taste, sound, feel); mood
elevation to a carefree, whimsical level; and some distortion of time perspective.

Inhalants

Inhalants are gaseous substances that are sniffed or breathed. They include things like amyl nitrite ("poppers") or nitrous oxide as well as various
solvents, glues, propellants (such as used in aerosol cans), and fuels like gasoline. The effects are often dilation of blood vessels in the brain, leading to a
sense of intoxication, but some of them, particularly the solvents and glues,
also can produce delirium and unconsciousness (Akers, 1992:34). The ni-
trites are best known for use just before sexual intercourse to extend feelings
of orgasm. Although the inhalants do not produce physiological dependence,
they do hold a strong psychological appeal for many, particularly children.
Most of the inhalants are quite dangerous, even with moderately frequent
use, because they can adversely affect many vital organs in the body (Akers,
1992:34).

Variations in Drug Use

For various reasons, it is impossible to compile accurate data about the
extent and distribution of different kinds of drug use. Nevertheless, several
sources of information are used by experts for estimating drug use and distribution: (1) police-based data, including arrests for drug offenses and drug
testing of those arrested for crimes in 23 cities, the so-called Drug Use Forecasting information (DUF); (2) data from hospital emergency rooms in selected cities concerning treatment of people with drug-related problems such
as overdose (Drug Abuse Warning Network—DAWN); and (3) systematic surveys that have been conducted since the early 1970s.

Police data, of course, miss all drug users who are not arrested, and arrest
does not reflect the extent or frequency of use, or even all the drugs an
arrestee might be using. Indeed, ethnographic information (Adler, 1993; Waldorf, 1973; Williams, 1992; Sterk-Elifson and Elifson, 1993) suggests that arrest reflects only a tiny proportion of drug users. Also, the proportion of drug

episodes that involve problems serious enough to land a user in an emergency room is unknown, even if the DAWN reporting system included all cities in the United States. Finally, surveys suffer from problems of sampling, faulty recall, exaggeration, and deliberate deception or withholding. Many drug users are not in places where they would be subject to the nationwide sampling by the NIDA (National Institute of Drug Abuse) household surveys that are periodically taken. (Instead they live on the street, in communes, or in crack houses.) Youths who use drugs often drop out of school, so they are missed in the annual Monitoring the Future survey of drug use among high school seniors (also sponsored by NIDA but conducted by the Institute of Survey Research at the University of Michigan). Moreover, since most deviant drug use is illegal, some respondents to surveys, even with guarantees of anonymity, misrepresent (adults usually hide usage while youths sometimes report more than they actually use to appear grown-up or "in the know"). Some respondents, particularly heavy drug users, simply cannot recall accurately how much and how often they have used various drugs.

Despite these problems, the surveys are usually assumed to give a reasonable estimate of drug use patterns, particularly since they are the most comprehensive and comparable sources of information.

Extent and Trends

Table 4.1 reports 1996 estimates from NIDA concerning trends over the preceding few years in "illicit" drug usage.

Table 4.1 Percent Reporting Past Month Use of Illicit Drugs, Alcohol, and Tobacco in the U.S. Population Aged 12 and Older, 1979–1995[d]

Drug	Year								
	1979	1985	1988	1990	1991	1992	1993	1994	1995
Any	14.1	12.1	7.7	6.7	6.6	5.8	5.9	6.0	6.1
Any except marijuana		6.1	3.4	2.7	3.0	2.4	2.4	2.3	2.6
Marijuana	13.2	9.7	6.2	5.4	5.1	4.7	4.6	4.8	5.7
Cocaine	2.6	3.0	1.6	.9	1.0	.7	.7	.7	.7
Inhalants		.6	.4	.4	.4	.3	.3	.4	.4
Hallucinogens	1.9	1.2	.6	.4	.5	.4	.4	.5	.7
Heroin	.1	.1	.0[a]	.0[a]	.0[a]	.0[a]	.0[a]	.1	.1
Stimulants		1.8	1.2	.6	.4	.3	.5	.3	.4
Sedatives		.5	.2	.2	.2	.2	.2	.1	.2
Tranquilizers		2.2	1.3	.6	1.1	.8	.6	.5	.4
Analgesics		1.4	.7	.9	.8	.9	.8	.7	.6
Heavy alcohol[b]		8.3	5.8	6.3	6.8	6.2	6.7	6.2	5.5
Illicit Tobacco[c]		29.4	22.7	22.4	20.9	18.4	18.5	18.9	20.2

[a] Less than one-tenth of one percent.
[b] Defined as having consumed five or more drinks each day for five consecutive days during the last 30-day period.
[c] Use by those under age 18.
[d] Source: Adapted from Tables 5B, 6, and 12 of the NAADI 1995 National Household Survey on Drug Abuse.

The survey figures show several trends. First, most deviant drug use has declined since the late 1970s and early 1980s. This basic pattern is shown in the figures for "any" illicit drug use and repeated for most of the specific drug categories. In 1979, 14.1 percent of the population over age 12 had used some illicit drug during the previous month. By 1992 that figure had dropped to 5.8 percent. Note, however, that since 1992, with some fluctuations, there appears to have been a slight increase in some categories. Consider, for example, hallucinogens and illicit tobacco use. In 1992 four-tenths of one percent used hallucinogens in the month prior to the survey, while seven-tenths of one percent used them in 1995. Similarly, while 18.4 percent of youths under 18 used tobacco in 1992, a low point for the previous decade, 20.2 percent were using it in 1995.

Second, about half of the illicit drug use is accounted for by marijuana. If one excludes marijuana use, the overall figures for "any" illicit drug use drops to 3 percent or less since 1990. Moreover, the usage of drugs the public considers most dangerous, heroin and other analgesics as well as cocaine, is considerably below 1 percent. Still, given the base populations being considered, and the fact that surveys miss some of the most serious drug users, this amounts to as many as two million users of publicly feared drugs in a given month in the United States. Furthermore, even though overall illicit drug use is much less than it was in the late 1970s, it is still the case that in a given month over 12 million people engage in some type of deviant drug use. Clearly, then, this is a common form of deviant behavior.

Distribution

How is drug use distributed? Is deviant drug use mainly done by men or is it equally likely for women? Does drug use differ by age and race/ethnicity? Table 4.2 reports the relevant data for answering these questions.

Table 4.2 Percent Reporting Any Illicit Drug Use in the Past Month, by Age Group, Race/Ethnicity, and Sex, 1995

Sex		Age				Race			
M	F	12–17	18–25	26–34	over 35	WH	BK	HS	OTH
7.8	4.5	10.9	14.2	8.3	2.8	6.0	7.9	5.1	4.0

Source: Adapted from Table 12 of the NAADI National Household Survey on Drug Abuse.

As one can readily see, drug usage is more likely among males (about 40 percent more likely than for females), among young adults (about five times as likely as for middle-aged and over), and among blacks (but only a little more likely than whites). Trends in such figures for the period from 1979 until 1995 (not shown) show similar ratios across the whole time span, with a few exceptions. Deviations from the general pattern show the male-to-female ratio greater in 1979 (over twice as many males as females), and in several years (1979, 1988, 1992, 1993) overall drug use was greater among whites than among blacks. Thus, as with many types of deviance, drug usage is mainly an activity for males and young adults, though the extent to which that is true varies over time. Also, garnering data on variation in drug use by race or ethnicity is problematic.

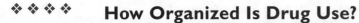

How Organized Is Drug Use?

In Chapter 2 we argued that a key feature of deviant behavior is the extent to which its practitioners are organized in typical situations where the deviance is exhibited. Since organization cannot be observed directly, it is best reflected in several indirect indicators of aspects of organization. Those indicators include sociality, pervasiveness, communication, differentiation and coordination, culture, self-identity, philosophical integration, social control, and recruitment. We contend that most deviant drug use is moderately well organized, though not fully organized. In other words, it falls in the middle of the continuum of organization, within a "subcultural zone." In the following discussion we will not assess the specific degree of organization of each of the dozens of deviantly used drugs: instead we will focus on a few typical ones, calling attention to exceptions where appropriate.

Sociality

Because drug use requires a good deal of knowledge about how to do it, how to obtain drugs (especially those that are illegal), how to avoid the potentially serious physical consequences (sometimes including possible immediate death), and how to keep from being arrested, it almost inevitably takes place within networks of people, at least in the initial stages; thus, it displays considerable sociality. It is a rare individual who, all on his or her own, decides to use drugs deviantly, sets out to obtain them, figures out how to use them safely and for maximum effect, and consumes them in isolation. In fact, almost all research concerning deviant drug use reveals a fairly extensive network of friends, associates, and suppliers surrounding the activity (Beck and Rosenbaum, 1994; Goode, 1970; Inciardi et al., 1993; Stephens, 1991). Most people learn to use drugs first in company with friends or others in a sociable situation where it is defined as fun, thrilling, or defiant, or where there is considerable peer influence (Akers, 1992; Duncan et al., 1995; Dusenberry et al., 1994; Ferguson et al., 1995). And if they continue to use, they have to become conversant with an elaborate structure of supply, involving numerous people, particularly other users (Adler, 1993). Furthermore, much drug use involves sharing among users, not necessarily for altruistic reasons but in order to establish a pattern of reciprocity, which helps to alleviate periodic short supplies (Hanson et al., 1985; Williams, 1992).

Some individuals do use drugs in isolation, at least occasionally. Heavily addicted heroin users (those who are "strung out") often inject themselves quickly after buying drugs (copping) wherever they can; those who regulate their use sometimes use drugs as one would take aspirin to help them get through the day (Hanson et al., 1985). Those who use barbiturates to sleep, and those who employ amphetamines to energize themselves for work or other tasks (such as students preparing for exams) may be thought of as lone users of drugs. And even some cocaine users apparently consume it alone in their own homes, in cars, on rooftops, or in alleys (Inciardi, et al., 1993; Sterk-Elifson, 1996). Nevertheless, all must learn this behavior, which is taught within a social network, and they must interact with others to obtain the drug. Moreover, many kinds of drugs, by their very natures, imply sociable contexts. Marijuana (Goode, 1970; Johnson, 1973), cocaine (Adler, 1993; Cheung et al., 1991), and the hallucinogens (Beck and Rosenbaum, 1994;

Dotson et al., 1995) are well known as "party" drugs, used for relaxation, stimulation of social interaction, or shared experiences.

❖ ❖ ❖ ❖

Because drug use usually involves other people (sociality), it is more organized than individualized deviant behaviors like suicide or serial killing. However, because it does not inevitably take place with others and may, in fact, take an isolationist turn after initial socialization or addiction, it cannot be regarded as fully organized with respect to this criterion.

Pervasiveness

Similarly, much drug use is pervasive; that is, it consumes almost all of the user's time. Users consume the drug or do things linked to it, continuously, with little else going on in their lives. Ethnographies, for instance, reveal that for some, using cocaine or hustling to obtain it goes on almost full time (Inciardi et al., 1993; Williams, 1992). Indeed, some people actually reside in "crackhouses," where they smoke rock cocaine (either "crack" or "base") almost continuously, often for hours or days at a time (Inciardi et al., 1993; Sterk-Elifson and Elifson, 1993; Williams, 1992). Residents usually work or hustle sporadically, buy drugs, and share with others in the house. House residents help provide a safe place for consumption, cook the drug into rocks, or exchange sex for the privilege of sharing the drug ("house girls") (Inciardi et al., 1993). Others, who try to maintain conventional life styles are tempted to use cocaine more and more regularly, often to the point of bankruptcy (Sterk-Elifson, 1996; Williams, 1992). And when there is a plentiful supply, users tend to stay high for longer and longer periods, to the point where important responsibilities, even those connected with smuggling and distribution, are jeopardized (Adler, 1993).

Heroin use is often even more "all encompassing" (Waldorf, 1973). Users frequently get caught up in a cycle of hustling (usually petty theft or drug running/selling) to obtain money for the drug; of searching for "connections" from whom to buy the drug; and of periodic retreat to inject and temporarily enjoy the high (Agar, 1973; Waldorf, 1973). Heavy heroin users tend to become drowsy and subdued for a period of time after consumption (called being "on the nod"), but soon after the effect of the drug begins to subside they must revert to hustling in order to obtain the means to stave off withdrawal symptoms or to provide for the next state of relaxation. In fact, heroin use becomes so pervasive that addicts come to neglect other aspects of living, such as eating regularly, bathing, caring for family responsibilities, or working at regular jobs (Stephens, 1991).

For several million people, alcohol use is quite pervasive. Some alcoholics stay intoxicated almost all the time, and others plan their daily activities around ways to use the drug without getting caught or having it interfere with other things. Many do little else but drink and sit or lie around in a stuporous state.

Not all cocaine, alcohol, or heroin use, however, is this pervasive (Akers, 1992:227–231; Cheung et al., 1991; Hanson et al., 1985; Reinarman et al., 1997; Sterk-Elifson, 1996), and many other deviantly used drugs are used only episodically or for occasional recreational purposes. Some use cocaine as a party drug a few times a year; some take heroin or cocaine occasionally or regulate their dosages to what they can manage; and most users of alcohol consume only a few drinks a week. In addition, although some marijuana smokers stay high most of their waking hours ("potheads"), most users are occasional consumers, just as users of hallucinogens like ecstacy or special K (ketamine) or barbiturates do it only sporadically (Goode, 1993).

Thus, drug use is typically far more pervasive in the lives of those who do it than is suicide (which is a one-time event) or serial killing, which is a short-term, sporadic activity. Sometimes drug use is totally pervasive, yet it is not always a completely pervasive activity, and sometimes practitioners do it only rarely.

Communication

Drug users can and do communicate well with each other (Agar, 1973). They share understandings about the drug experience and the drug scenes that permit messages to be sent and received without anything much being said. For instance, in crackhouses where sex is exchanged for a share of the drug (not all crackhouses allow shared sex or even drug purchases and sales), everybody knows the symbols indicating what is wanted and what is expected (Inciardi et al., 1993; Williams, 1992). Sometimes the symbolic behavior is simply public "flashing" by a female (spreading her legs to reveal she is not wearing underwear or lowering her jeans to tuck in a shirt, revealing her pubic hair in the process), and sometimes a male simply takes out his penis and points to it so that a "house girl" or any other female present will get the message that oral sex is wanted (with the implication that in exchange the woman can share the crack pipe, sometimes called the "devil's dick"). But there are far more subtle forms of communication, including special words, body language, and presentations of self that help identify users to each other and especially help to differentiate users from undercover law enforcement personnel who often try to pass themselves off as participants in the drug world (Jacobs, 1993, 1996).

In addition, most drug users learn a picturesque and rich slang (Hanson et al., 1985, Chapter 6; Inciardi et al., 1993:177–184; Maher, 1996) that facilitates drug interaction. The slang words denoting various kinds of drugs, equipment, feelings, law enforcement procedures and personnel, or roles within the drug community often change so that only those who are active in the deviant activity will know them. As a result of shared language and shared meanings attached to various experiences, drug users can interact effectively with each other, find drugs and conduct business transactions, evaluate the risks associated with situations and people, and carry on a life outside the mainstream of society.

Special languages include modes of expression and unique words for everything from the drugs themselves to the police. For example, heroin has been variously known as "smack," "H," "horse," "stuff," "tragic magic," and much more, while marijuana has been known variously as "pot," "reefer," "mary jane," "grass," etc. Police have been known as "narcs," "the man," "fuzz," "poh-lice," "heat," and many others (Agar, 1973; Jacobs, 1996). Among some cocaine users the argot centers around analogy with the popular TV series "Star Trek" (Williams, 1992). Within that context smoking the cocaine rocks is referred to as being "beamed up." Searching for cocaine to buy is to be on a "mission." To possess cocaine is to be "with Scotty." Others have different terms (see Incardi et al., 1993:177–184); some refer to roles within the drug-using community: "blueberries," "strawberries," "raspberries," and "skeezers" refer, respectively, to lesbians, young girls, gays, and heterosexual women who exchange sex for cocaine. "Skin poppers," "chippers," and "mainliners" denote, respectively, those who inject narcotics in muscle tissue, those who fool around occasionally with narcotics without actually being addicted, and those who use narcotics seriously by injecting directly into their veins. "Players," "chumps," and "lames" designate, in order, knowledgeable users who can successfully manipulate the world; those who claim to understand the world of hustles and aspire to be players but end up themselves being manipulated; and those who are complete objects of manipulation without understanding what is going on (Tittle, 1972).

Of course, not all drug users share the special language or learn effective communication patterns. People who become addicted to narcotics in a medical context—doctors, nurses, and patients—often are outside such communication channels. And some kinds of deviant drug users, such as barbiturate or inhalant consumers, are sometimes cut off from the larger communities of drug users and therefore lack the communication apparatus common to other drug users. Moreover, drug users rarely communicate in written form through newsletters, underground newspapers, or sacred documents, although some magazines such as *High Times* have been developed to appeal to higher-status drug users (Jonnes, 1996). But, in general, drug-using activists can be said to exhibit a fairly high degree of communication.

Differentiation and Coordination

Not only do deviant drug users communicate extensively, but their world is stratified and elaborately differentiated by roles. Those who import (smuggle) and distribute large volumes of drugs stand apart from lower-level distributors and sellers, who, in turn, have higher prestige and more power than those who sell small amounts of diluted drugs on the streets (Adler, 1993). At each higher level of the hierarchy, distributors make more money, have more flamboyant life styles and possessions, take fewer routine risks, and enjoy more respect. In addition, if the distributors are drug users, they have a ready, almost unlimited supply and do not have to engage in the more demeaning styles of behavior to support their habits.

Similarly, regular users fall into a pecking order. For example, at the top of the heroin world (see Waldorf, 1973) are those who use a lot of drugs in the most effective manner but manage their lives with skill and agility. Usually they know how to rap (carry on a line of interesting conversation); to make money without engaging in such low-level ripoffs as purse snatching or strong arming; and to avoid being exploited by others. They generally have sufficient finesse to avoid too much trouble with the police. Lesser figures engage in crude "rip-off" hustles to meet immediate drug needs, and they exhibit little honor in sharing or in respecting the needs of other drug users. At the bottom are those who have a very uncertain drug supply, have few skills and little knowledge, and survive by petty thefts from friends and family or by running errands and sometimes snitching for payoffs.

Despite the degree of stratification and role differentiation, the larger world of drug usage is not well coordinated. Although there are common misconceptions that a few giant drug cartels control drug distribution and thereby regulate the world of drugs, there is much evidence of competition among distributors, a lot of free enterprise, and variations among local networks (Adler, 1993). Moreover, in larger matters nobody speaks for the community of drug users as a whole; it is inconceivable that drug users could get themselves together to mount a political or social campaign to promote their activities; and there is no unified decision-making body.

Culture

We have already seen that deviant drug users generally share distinct and separate languages and modes of communication, which are passed on from one generation to the next. Because of this sharing, learning, and intergenerational transmission, language is part of the culture of drug use. But there is much more to the drug culture than mere language. Other cultural aspects include norms, values and attitudes, artifacts, and knowledge.

Many drug users behave selfishly, at least from time to time and especially in the latter stages of heavy addiction. They sometimes cheat each other, victimize families, businesses, and children, and show almost complete disregard for how their behavior might affect others. Most, nevertheless, are constrained by mutually shared expectations for behavior among drug users. A norm of sharing is common, and it manifests itself particularly among those in the early stages of use. In fact, most users are first introduced to drugs by friends, lovers, or associates who give them some of the substance that is being consumed (contrary to the popular assumption that people usually become hooked through the efforts of unscrupulous sellers out to make a buck). After fuller immersion in the networks of drug use, people learn that reciprocity is useful, especially for tiding one over in times of low supply. By embracing the norm of sharing, users temporarily low on resources can call on those with whom they have previously shared their own drugs or money. Moreover, some sharing seems to be based on genuine friendship and concern (Hanson et al., 1985; Williams, 1992).

For example, in crackhouses, which are usually private residences (such as apartments) where people can go to smoke cocaine out of the eyes of the public and the police, participants often share the cocaine they have purchased elsewhere and brought to the house. To be sure, most such sharing is based on quid pro quo. In exchange for somebody "cooking" the drug into rock form, sharing a pipe (and maybe sex), assuming the overhead of maintaining the house, and keeping order, the owner of the cocaine shares the resulting rocks. Members of the house, because of services as cooker, bouncer, sex partner, or lender of smoking apparatus also get a share—but only up to a point of equity (Inciardi et al., 1993; Sterk-Elifson and Elifson, 1993; Williams, 1992). There is even a form of reciprocity among smugglers and dealers, who extend credit, share information, and sometimes rely on competitors for temporary help (Adler, 1993).

Another marker of culture concerns the attitudes of drug users, which range from totally hedonistic to tolerant, but almost all share the notion that drug use is either a good thing or at least that it is not a bad thing. The extent to which such attitudes predate drug use is not known, but it is clear that association among drug users either leads to or enhances the idea that using substances to produce good feelings, euphoric experiences, relief of anxiety, new ways of perceiving reality, or escape from feelings of discomfort or inadequacy is a good thing. The effects produced by drugs are seen as having value in and of themselves, and these ends are seen as worth much risk taking

(Finestone, 1957). Furthermore, a common orientation is denigration of "conventional" attitudes or approaches to life, particularly those expressing the desirability of careful control of emotions; of responsibility; and of maintenance of natural modes of feeling and thought. In being able to transcend conventional limitations, drug users view themselves as superior to "squares" (Tittle, 1972).

The drug culture is also notable for the knowledge it develops and mutually shares about drugs. Because many drug users are hedonists, they push experimentation about the effects of drugs to their limits—far beyond what might be pursued in medical experimentation. In one sense, then, drug users know a lot more about the deviantly used drugs than do physicians. This knowledge is passed along in everyday conversation, in which experience is shared, and in tutelage of initiates. How to obtain drugs, how to use them, how much to use, and how to interpret the feelings are all essential pieces of knowledge that people must have if they are to use drugs without dire consequences. These are things that cannot be learned from books or films.

Finally, the drug culture includes many artifacts such as specialized equipment and locales. For instance, because equipment for injecting drugs is only available through medical channels, many users have to make their own syringes. It can be done by heating a test tube and stretching the end to a sharp point. The other end of the newly fashioned syringe is then fitted with a plunger extracted from a spray bottle and made more or less airtight by a cutoff end portion of a dollar bill wrapped around the test tube. Who would know how to do this without instruction? In addition, there are unique scenes for drug use that constitute artifacts. We have already mentioned crackhouses as unusual institutions, bearing only slight resemblance to the speakeasies popular during the alcohol prohibition era. Another example concerns "raves"—parties organized informally and announced by word of mouth, often held in large warehouses or unoccupied buildings, where hallucinogens like ketamine or ecstasy are freely used while people dance to special music (Beck and Rosenbaum, 1994; Dotson et al., 1995).

Thus, even though not all drug users participate in a culture of use, most do. Some medical users, kids who sniff glue or solvents, and some users of depressants and stimulants may be relatively immune from the influences of a drug culture, but most drug users find themselves enmeshed in a wideranging, diverse, rich set of meanings, norms, knowledge, and artifacts. Consequently, one would have to classify drug use toward the fully organized end of the continuum of organization with respect to the criterion of culture. However, because not all are exposed to that culture, the learning of aspects of drug culture are somewhat haphazard, and it is not a totally immersing experience for every drug user.

Self-Identity

There is great variation in the extent to which users of deviant drugs form their personalities around drug use or come to think of themselves primarily in those terms. To be sure, heavy users of heroin often embrace a self-concept of "dope fiend" or "junkie" (Stephens, 1991), just as some think of themselves as "potheads," "clunkers" (regular users of cocaine), "acid freaks," "speeders," or "alcoholics." And for this comparatively small proportion of drug users, such identities are points of pride that are readily projected to others—

except to law enforcement agents. But the vast majority of users regard drug use as simply an activity that they pursue, in no fundamental sense a defining characteristic of their beings. Indeed, for many, drug use, though it may be extensive, is rationalized as merely recreational. But because they recognize that such recreational activities may be illegal or socially unacceptable in some circles, they may conceal their usage, deny they are users, resist the entire concept of addiction, and feel shame or guilt when nonusers find out.

Philosophical Integration

Fully organized forms of deviance rest on a base of well-integrated intellectual interpretations and meanings that apply to all aspects of life and that mesh in systematic, coherent ways. Drug users do not share such a philosophy. The only interpretations and meanings that drug users have in common is a belief that it is a good thing, or at least not a bad thing, to seek pleasure, insight, or new experiences or to escape normal states with the use of chemicals. In addition, many drug users view outside intervention as oppressive, and they may extend this view to encompass generalized concepts about the nature of government as an instrument of the powerful or the unenlightened (Finestone, 1957; Goode, 1970; Stephens, 1991). But in no sense can the common elements of drug use philosophy be regarded as comprehensive (it is limited to a narrow zone of human existence) or well integrated (drug users themselves often find their stated reasons for doing what they do inconsistent and awkward). Ask a deviant drug user why he or she uses drugs, and you will get answers like: "It feels good," "I need it to overcome my inhibitions," "It makes me a mellower person," or, in rare instances, "To defy and contradict an oppressive set of laws" or "To gain insight." The answer will almost never be something like: "It is necessary to solidify the bonds of nature and create a better world" or "Drug use is a means of relating to God who controls all feelings and governs the universe."

In terms of the nine criteria of organization under consideration, drug users are less advanced on the criterion of philosophical integration than they are for any of the other criteria. They do share some meanings, and because there are many drug users with this minimal degree of shared understandings, drug use is definitely not completely unorganized by this trait. Yet, if this were the only criterion by which we judged organization, drug use would fall much closer to the individualized end of the continuum than to the fully organized end.

Social Control

Is there a system of sanctions employed by those involved in the drug world to keep other participants in line? Certainly this is so to some extent. There are, of course, no formal rules that drug users follow, and there are no collectively recognized functionaries who impose penalties in a systematic way. But there are many informal rules (see Johnson, 1973)—particularly about "snitching" and keeping confidences (Stephens, 1991; Tittle, 1972); etiquette of drug use in a group situation (Williams, 1992); not stealing from others in the drug world (especially not from dealers or distributors who are more successful) (Adler, 1993); or messing things up for other people (Inciardi et al., 1993). Some of these rules are sometimes enforced by regular henchmen in drug hierarchies, or by ordinary sellers and users, who may kill or injure the offending party (Bourgois, 1997) or set them up to be caught by the police. But contrary to popular assumptions, violations of drug world rules are often dealt with by informally withholding cooperation (Adler, 1993). Thus, users who come to be known as snitches cannot obtain drugs for their own use; they may be deprived of information available to others in good standing that would prevent arrest; or they might be denied credit on occasions when assets are not adequate. And a dealer who dips too far into the supply for personal use, fails to make good on a consignment, or otherwise proves unreliable will simply be deprived of the means to do business. Hence there is some internal social control, but it is not highly structured, formal, or systematic.

Recruitment

Finally, drug users do a lot of recruiting of new converts. For many years, partly as a result of propaganda by the Federal Narcotics Bureau (Lindesmith, 1965), the public perception of recruitment of new deviant drug users was a top-down vision. It was assumed that criminal organizations recruited and used dope pushers as Amway does door-to-door salespersons. The pushers were thought to engage in aggressive tactics, which they systematically pursued to entice nonusers, especially youth. The image was of drug pushers hanging around schoolyards, pulling select children aside to portray drug use as fun and status enhancing, and then giving away free drugs until the victim was hooked or had become a regular user. Much research has shown the falsity of that portrayal, at least for the illegal drugs.

Most new users of illegal drugs enter the drug world in an unsystematic hit-and-miss fashion, not recruited by dealers who set out to create new customers (Akers, 1992; Beck and Rosenbaum, 1994; Goode, 1970; Stephens, 1991; Waldorf, 1973). The recruitment process most often involves natural sharing among friends, associates, and family. The sharing of drugs stems sometimes from the user's belief that the drug is a good thing to share with cherished others—friends or family. At other times, sharing is based on status concerns in which one person attempts to gain or reinforce his prestige by providing another with a good experience, a forbidden fruit, or a hard to get substance. And often an associate observes drug use and its pleasurable effects and asks to participate, or even insists. Occasionally, a recruit will hear about a drug, usually by word of mouth but sometimes through the mass media, and seek out users in order to experience what he or she has heard about.

Ironically, the only systematic, organized recruitment to drug use is that which occurs for the partially legal drugs of alcohol and tobacco. Although initial use of these substances is similar to that of the illegal drugs—informally provoked, most often within social networks during the teen years (Duncan et al., 1995; Kandel, 1980)—there is something else going on that is not happening in the case of illegal drugs. Both alcohol and tobacco are heavily advertised on billboards, on television, and in newspapers and magazines. Television and movie characters smoke and drink (some authorities suspect payment to television and movie executives and actors by the tobacco and alcohol industry), and in years past company pushers would hang around athletic events and schools (at least colleges) giving away free samples.

There is a lot of recruitment to deviant drug use, as evidenced by the large volume of users and the induction of many young people from each generation. But with the exception of the partially legal drugs, it is not well organized, it is unsystematic, and it is not directed by a centrally structured institution.

Summary

Defining drugs is not easy, and deciding what is or is not deviant drug use is even more complicated. A large number of variables come into play to affect how drugs impinge on individuals, and common distinctions like addictiveness, abuse, or the components that supposedly affect legality may be inconsistent or even irrational. Moreover, though there are commonly employed classifications of substances, such schemes cannot be applied unambiguously. Nevertheless, enough agreement about these matters exists to speak in general about deviant drug use, and enough research exists to permit its classification according to the organizational continuum introduced earlier. Overall, deviant drug use appears to fall near the middle of that continuum, in the zone we call subcultural.

It moves fairly far away from the individualistic end of the organizational continuum because it is generally quite sociable, especially in early stages of use; it involves extensive communication, even a special language; there is much differentiation of roles and statuses; there is an extensive culture; and much recruitment, though unsystematic, takes place. However, this form of deviant behavior is not fully organized because none of the criteria mentioned above are present in complete form. Moreover, drug use is not entirely pervasive in the user's life unless that person is fully addicted; self-identity with the activity is limited; there is little overall coordination of activities; and the undergirding philosophy is narrow and somewhat incoherent.

Street Gangs

Another deviant activity, which is probably more organized than deviant drug use but which is still not completely organized, is that performed by gangs. We focus on street gangs rather than other kinds of gangs such as motorcycle gangs, prison gangs, gangs of skinheads, and gangs of English soccer hooligans, though all gangs have some organizational features in common. Street gangs are composed of youth who join together in neighborhoods for gang activity, much of which is deviant or illegal.

What Is Gang Delinquency?

Gang delinquency, like deviant drug use, is not easy to define. We can begin the process of understanding what gang delinquency is by breaking the concept into two constituent parts. Gang delinquency consists of: (1) delinquent acts that are (2) committed by members of gangs. The first element of this definition is easier than the second. Delinquent acts are violations of a state's code for regulating the conduct of youth. They include behaviors that would be crimes if done by an adult (murder, rape, armed robbery, theft, and the like), as well as acts that are considered crimes only if committed by those who are underage (as specified by each state)—so-called status offenses.

❖ ❖ ❖ ❖

> ### Deviance in Everyday Life
>
> Gangs are not a modern American invention, since they have existed at different times and in different cultures. Klein (1995:51) notes that the word "gang" in its modern usage goes back at least to the writings of Geoffrey Chaucer, the English author of the classic *Canterbury Tales* in 1390, and appears in Shakespeare's *The Merry Wives of Windsor*: "There's a knot, a gang, a pack, a conspiracy against me." Subsequent to this, there are records of youth gangs that existed in London during the 1600s. They committed a variety of criminal offenses, engaged in gang fights with other gangs, and had identifying names such as the Bugles, Dead Boys, and Hectors (Spergel, 1990; Pearson, 1983). Spergel (1990: 172) also notes that English gangs of the seventeenth and eighteenth centuries wore articles of clothing designed to distinguish the members from nonmembers. Urban historians in the United States have recorded the existence of gangs in New York City in the mid-1800s (Hyman, 1984). In the twentieth century, gangs have been found not only in the United States and Western Europe, but in Japan, China, Scandinavia, the former Soviet Union, Korea, Australia, New Zealand, and countries in both Africa and South America. (Klein, 1995; Oschlies, 1979; Spergel, 1990)

Thus, in addition to acts forbidden by a state's criminal code, delinquency also includes such behaviors as running away, truancy, smoking and drinking, and being beyond the control of a parent. Therefore, gang delinquency is any act of crime or a status offense that is committed by members of a juvenile gang. But for this to be meaningful, we must define exactly what a gang is; that is the tough part.

What Is a Gang?

One of the "facts" of criminology is that most acts of juvenile delinquency are committed in company with others rather than by a solitary offender (Erickson and Jensen, 1977; Reiss, 1988; Zimring, 1981). Does the mere fact that a number of youths commit delinquent acts together make them a gang and their acts gang delinquency? Sometimes kids come together and associate for benign reasons but end up doing mischief. For instance, a bunch of youths may be residents of the same neighborhood who happen to be crossing a park at the same time. They start talking with one another, someone obtains some beer, which is shared. They drink and their horseplay turns into vandalism and violence. Eventually they trash a closed concession stand in the park and harass and assault a passerby. Is this gang activity?

Klein (1995; Klein and Crawford, 1967) might argue that even though these youths were involved in criminal acts, this incident would not constitute gang activity because the boys were simply "contiguous individuals." They were physically proximate but they did not constitute a group; instead, they were simply a temporary collectivity of individuals with neither longevity nor group identity. From this perspective, then, gang delinquency implies something other than youthful offenders committing delinquent acts with one another. Thus, it is important to distinguish *group delinquency* from *gang delinquency*.

Group delinquency occurs when youths get together for convenience, to show courage, or for any short-lived reason and while together commit delinquent acts, disbanding afterward. Such youths do not identify themselves, nor are they identified by others, as being members of a "gang"—they simply "hang" together, and one of the many things they may do as a group of friends is occasionally to commit a delinquent offense. Gang delinquency, on the other hand, is a longer-term and more structured form of group delinquency. Gang delinquents often think of themselves, and are thought of by others, as members of a gang; there is, in other words, identification with a gang (though they probably would not use that term). They usually have different roles among themselves, and a hierarchy of power and authority is recognized by members. Gang delinquents typically share distinctive identifiers, such as an article or color of clothing, hand signals, characteristic graffiti, places where they hang out, and often a set of unique terms or slang for things that are important to them. Finally, gang delinquents normally claim an area, or "turf," as their own, which they are committed to defend. In other words, while all group delinquency possesses sociality, in a smaller subtype of that delinquency, groups show more of the features of organized deviance—pervasiveness, communication, internal social control, an integrated philosophy, and recruitment. These latter groups we will refer to as gangs and their activity as gang delinquency (see B. Cohen, 1969, and Spergel, 1984, who draw a similar distinction between gang and group delinquency).

It is important to emphasize that some gangs are well organized, while others are not. Some are so well organized that they can be considered close to the fully organized end of the continuum, while other gangs are much more transient, loosely organized, and characterized by shifting membership; the latter groups would be closer to the individualized end of the continuum of organization. Taken as a whole, however, gang delinquency is best understood as lying near the middle of a continuum from individualized to fully organized deviance, being best characterized as "subcultural" in nature.

While our conceptualization may seem somewhat ambiguous, it reflects the disagreement among scholars as to what constitutes a gang. In one recent collection of readings about gangs, three different articles had three different approaches to the definition of gangs (Huff, 1990). Beyond the fact that gang activity is group activity, and that the activity involved is delinquent or criminal behavior, there is little consensus in the criminological literature about what a gang really is (Knox, 1994).

Drawing on two helpful definitions of gangs that appear to capture their essential character without missing the fact that gangs come in different types with different structures, degrees of organization, and purpose (Curry and Spergel, 1988:382; Klein, 1971:111), we conceive of a gang as a collection of youths who reside in a limited area (that is, a neighborhood) and who regularly assemble so that they become recognized by others in the community as a coherent group. These youths are not only thought of by others as comprising a distinct group or entity, they think of themselves as belonging to a group—"I am one of them." To facilitate such identity, gangs frequently have symbols of membership that nonmembers do not; for example, a member's jacket or other article of clothing, a territory or meeting place (a clubhouse or a certain street corner), a handshake or set of unique signs for communicating. In order for a group to be considered a gang by our definition, it must also be involved in repetitive and serious acts of delinquency or deviance. This does not mean that the gang exists only for misbehavior. However, among the many things a gang may do, or among the many purposes it may serve for its members, it is frequently involved in criminal acts—sometimes serious criminal acts. The final requirement for our definition is that while a gang need not have a fixed set of members (that is, members may come and go and membership may be fleeting), it must have a set of core members who give the group some stability and structure.

Including the commission of deviant acts in the definition of a gang implies that criminal activity is a central and definitive behavior of gang members. Not all find this useful. Some scholars of gang activity have consciously avoided including the requirement that groups commit delinquent acts before they are considered gangs. In her study of "ganglike" youth groups in Boston, Morash (1983), for example, did not require that the gang members commit delinquent or criminal acts. Her definition does include many of the characteristics we have noted: members come from a defined or restricted geographical area, they have a regular place to meet, have identifying features, and have a core group. Bursik and Grasmick (1993) also prefer to define gangs without reference to criminal behavior, noting that the study of criminal activity ought to be independent of the study of gang membership. Still, an important factor that appears to distinguish gangs from other youth groups (sport or church groups) is that they are more than normally involved in criminal activity, and whatever inclination the members had for crime before entering the gang seems to get elevated by gang membership (Thornberry et al., 1993).

The Criminal Activity of Gangs

Paul Tracy (cited in Klein, 1995:112) analyzed arrests for gang and non-gang members in cohort data collected over many years in Philadelphia, beginning in 1945. He found that young gang members had three times the number of arrests as non-gang members, and older ones had five times the number of arrests as non-gang members. In their study of the offending rates of gangs in several inner-city areas, Fagan et al. (1986) found that gang members were more likely to have participated in both drug use and delinquency than non-gang members living in the same area. Thus, it appears that gang members are far more likely to engage in officially recorded delinquency.

Gang members do not seem to specialize in specific types of crime or deviance. There are few exclusively, or even predominately, drug gangs, violent gangs, or theft gangs. Rather, gang youths are quite versatile in their offending, committing the full range of criminal acts. Klein (1995:68) aptly describes this versatility as "cafeteria-style offending." The study by Fagan et al. (1986) also found that gang members do not seem to concentrate on one or a few offenses; rather, they spread their criminal activity across a variety of offenses.

According to Fagan et al. (1986), some gangs are extensively involved in drugs and alcohol, but most of this activity is personal usage rather than dealing, and seldom does it become heavy enough to be regarded as addictive. The most frequently used drugs are the relatively minor ones like alcohol and marijuana; use of serious drugs like cocaine and heroin is rare. Although drug selling does occur, it is not extensive, organized, or a financial enterprise of the gang as a unit. Most often it is done by individual gang members to earn money for themselves (Spergel, 1990). In fact, there is some evidence to indicate that gang members generally frown on extensive drug use among their members ("junkies" cannot be trusted by other gang members), and have ejected those who seemed to have a drug problem (Klein, 1995; Spergel, 1964). In further support of this, Hagedorn (1988) reports from his study of gangs in Milwaukee that while most gang members admit to drug use (60 percent), the majority of that use is of marijuana.

In a study of drug sales in two California cities, Maxson (1995) found that a minority (about 25 percent) of the drug sales involved gang members. She also cautions that even this figure might overstate gang involvement in drug selling since arrested gang members may have been selling drugs by and for themselves rather than as a sanctioned gang activity. Further, sales involving gang members are no more likely to be associated with firearms, violence, or large transactions (either in drug volume or amount of cash) than those involving non-gang persons. In several respects, gang and non-gang drug sales seem similar, a finding confirmed by Esbensen et al. (1993). Maxson further reports that drug selling is not characteristic of all or even very many gang members; rather, it seems to be concentrated among a few gang members. This is consistent with a conclusion that drug selling is characteristic of cliques within gangs, which has been suggested by Decker and Van Winkle (1996) from their study of St. Louis gangs. Fewer than 5 percent of the gang members they observed used drugs, and less than 15 percent sold them.

While common street gangs are not heavily involved in structured or organized drug sales, there are some gangs whose central activity is the selling of drugs and control of the local drug trade, especially the crack cocaine trade. These "drug gangs" have been the focus of media attention, and they are the targets of law enforcement agencies, which disseminate information about their prevalence. Such gangs, however, are not "street gangs," as the term is usually employed, although they may sometimes evolve from street gangs, and they are far less prevalent than street gangs. "Drug gangs" are more structured than ordinary street gangs, which are simply unsuited for conducting an organized and on-going financial enterprise like drug trafficking. Hagedorn (1990:150), from his study of Milwaukee gangs, tells us why this is so:

> It was too much of a hassle. This gang was not cut out to become an organized criminal venture. The police did not really bother their sales, but the organization necessary to pull off an on-going drug house was too much for this gang, whose members were concerned with "making it" day by day. While many of the adult members of this gang still sell cocaine and marijuana, it is done, as in most other gangs, individually and sporadically.

Drug gangs, being almost exclusively black, are also more racially homogeneous than street gangs, which may be composed of hispanics, blacks, or (though less frequently) whites (Klein, 1995). Other differences are summarized in Table 4.3.

Most gangs do not appear to specialize in specific types of crime, and the criminal acts they do commit are far more likely to be common, less serious offenses than major violent felonies. Gang members are more likely to commit minor acts of theft and vandalism, along with minor assaults, than armed robbery, kidnapping, murder, or rape. This does not mean that gang members are never involved in violence or homicide, but for the most part the kinds of criminal acts committed by gang members are not much different from those by non-gang members. Gang members, on the other hand, may commit criminal acts more frequently than nonmembers.

Table 4.3 Differences Between Street and Drug Gangs

Street Gangs	Drug Gangs
Versatile in offending	Offending specialists (drug crimes)
Larger structures	Smaller structures
Less organized	More organized
Diffuse leadership	More centralized leadership
Diffuse role obligations	Role defined by location in market
Loose code of loyalty	Strict code of loyalty
Territory defined by neighborhood	Territory defined by drug market
Members may sell drugs	Members do sell drugs
Intergang rivalries	Competition is controlled
Younger members	Older members
Racially Diverse	Racially more homogeneous

Adapted from Klein, Malcolm W., 1995. *The American Street Gangs*, p. 132. New York: Oxford University Press.

Gang Violence and Homicide

Issues about gang violence and homicide deserve separate discussion because most of the public attention given gangs today is related to their involvement in these crimes. Most citizens have read newspaper or magazine accounts of the increasing problem of homicides committed by gang members, and have heard accounts of what seem to be senseless "drive-by" shootings that kill gang members and innocent bystanders. Many people have the impression that these kinds of homicides are both prevalent and on the increase, but is this true?

Where gangs exist, gang violence is a serious problem, but gang activities account for a relatively small proportion of violent acts committed in the United States—even in urban areas. Miller (1975) estimates that in some cities crime by gang members constitutes one-third of the total number of violent crimes by juveniles. He also claims that in 65 U.S. cities, juvenile gang homicides make up about 25 percent of all juvenile homicides.

It is useful to compare Washington, D.C., and Los Angeles in terms of gangs and violence. For years, Washington, D.C., has been the "murder capital" of the country, with a typical year (1994) showing a homicide rate of 70 per 100,000. Yet it has virtually no gang problem. Los Angeles, on the other hand, has a much lower overall homicide rate than Washington, D.C.,—about 24 homicides per 100,000. It, however, has a very severe gang problem, and gang related homicides make up a substantial proportion of the total number of murders. Klein (1995) reports that not only are gang homicides prevalent in Los Angeles, but gang and non-gang homicides within the Los Angeles area show important differences.

First, Klein shows that gang homicides in Los Angeles County account for over one-third of all murders (between 35 and 40 percent), a proportion that has been growing. While rates of violent crime and homicide have been slowly declining in Los Angeles, gang-related homicides have been increasing. Figure 4.1 shows the gang and non-gang homicide rates in Los Angeles County over the years 1979–1991. Notice that until recently, the incidence of gang-related homicides was far less than the incidence of non-gang homicides. By 1991, however, the two were much closer. Moreover, while there was an overall declining trend for non-gang homicides over the 1979–1991 time period, there was an increasing trend for gang-related homicides. This increase in gang-related homicides can be seen even more clearly in Figure 4.2, which shows the absolute number of homicides in Los Angeles County that were gang related from 1979 to 1992. The number of gang-related homicides

Figure 4.1 Incidence (per 100,000) of Gang Homicides in Los Angeles County

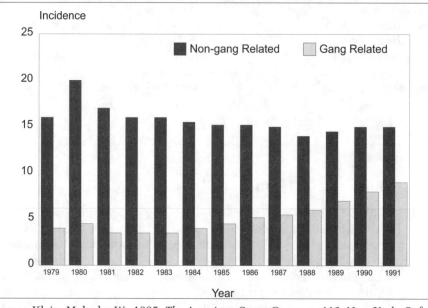

Source: Klein, Malcolm W., 1995. *The American Street Gangs*, p. 118. New York: Oxford University Press.

Figure 4.2 Number of Gang Homicides in Los Angeles County*

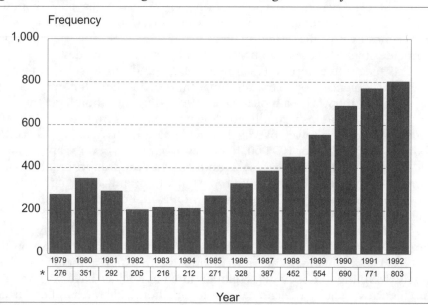

	1979	1980	1981	1982	1983	1984	1985	1986	1987	1988	1989	1990	1991	1992
*	276	351	292	205	216	212	271	328	387	452	554	690	771	803

Year

Source: Klein, Malcolm W., 1995. *The American Street Gangs*, p. 120. New York: Oxford University Press.

has increased by a factor of about four from 1982, when there were 205 recorded gang killings, to 1992, when there were 803 gang killings.

One type of gang violence that the public greatly fears is drive-by shooting. Drive-bys jeopardize innocent bystanders more than other forms of gang violence do because the accuracy of a shooter in a quickly moving vehicle is less than perfect. Table 4.4 reports the number of drive-by shootings and the number of deaths from drive-by shootings in Los Angeles County from 1989 to 1991. One can easily see from this table that: (1) the number of drive-by shootings is substantial, from 1,000 to 1,500 per year, an average of 3 to over 4 per day; (2) the number of drive-by killings is not trivial, from 78 to 141; (3) the number of both drive-by shootings and their resulting deaths increased over the short period from 1989 to 1991.

Table 4.4 Number of Drive-by Shootings and the Number of Drive-by Killings in Los Angeles County, 1989–1991

| Year | Number of Drive-by Shootings per: | | Number of Drive-by Deaths |
	Year	Day	
1989	1,112	3.0	78
1990	1,263	3.5	122
1991	1,543	4.2	141

Adapted from Klein, Malcolm W., 1995. *The American Street Gang*, p. 118. New York: Oxford University Press.

Second, Klein and his associates (1995: 114–115; Klein and Maxson, 1989; Maxson, 1990) found that gang killings differ from non-gang killings in a number of ways that make them more serious. For example, gang homicides: (1) more frequently occur in the street and less often take place in residences, (2) involve guns, (3) produce injury to other persons, (4) include more participants, (5) involve strangers, (6) victimize younger people, (7) involve more than one weapon, and (8) are associated with other violent offenses in addition to homicide. Hence, although violence generally, and homicide in particular, make up a small proportion of the total criminal activity of gangs (Klein, 1995), gang members are more often involved in violence, and their violence is generally more serious than that of non-gang juvenile offenders.

Although gang violence is getting more frequent and more lethal in some cities, for example, Los Angeles (see Figure 4.2), this is not true for all cities. Spergel (1990) notes that gang homicides fluctuate over long time spans, with periods of peaks and valleys. He observes (1990:189) that in Chicago there were about 63 gang homicides per year between 1969 and 1971; this declined to only 25 per year from 1973 to 1978, then increased again to approximately 70 per year from 1981 to 1986. While the number of gang homicides in Chicago is nowhere near the number in Los Angeles over the past two decades, both cities evidenced an increase in gang-related murders during the 1980s. This increase did not, however, occur in all or even most U.S. cities; in fact, gang homicides have declined in New York City and Philadelphia over the past twenty years (Spergel, 1990).

Current data do not indicate whether historical fluctuations in observed gang violence are due to changes in the behavior of youths or changes in police tactics or skills, which may sharpen or decline as gang units within police departments are created or disbanded. It is clear, however, that observed gang violence is greater in some cities than in others.

Do Gangs Select Young Criminals or Cause Crime?

We know from the preceding discussion that compared to non-gang youth, gang participants appear more likely to be heavily involved in delinquent and criminal behavior, and they seem more likely to commit serious violent crimes. Why is this? There are three contending explanations. One invokes "social selection." This explanation suggests that when gangs are recruiting new members, they do not randomly select possible candidates. Rather, since crime is an important activity to the gang, it selects those from among nonmembers who are already heavily involved in crime or who give evidence of "criminal potential." In this explanation, the gang attracts and invites criminals or potential criminals into the group—it does not really change people. If this account is correct, those who eventually end up in gangs would have had a high rate of criminal involvement even without their gang membership.

The second explanation for the supposed high levels of criminal/violent behavior within street gangs is that interaction among gang members stimulates criminal behavior. In this view, would-be gang members are no different from non-gang youth in either their pre-gang levels of involvement in crime or their propensity toward crime. Something intrinsic to gang life—the culture and dynamics of gang participation—is said to lead youth to commit criminal/violent acts at a high rate. Some contend that gang culture encourages expressions of masculinity, risk, and bravado, and that status systems within gangs in part reflect criminal expertise. According to this explanation, the gang does not attract "bad guys," it creates or causes them.

A third account sees the greater official rate of crime among gang members as an artifact of police bias and enforcement patterns (Chambliss, 1973). Because (1) gangs are perceived as bad, (2) the members of gangs are mostly children of low-status families, and (3) gang activities are more visible than equivalent activities by delinquents who are not so well organized, the police are more likely to monitor gang youth, observe their misbehavior, and arrest them—leading to their appearance in official statistics.

Of course, it is possible that all three explanations are true to some extent. Maybe the gang initially recruits members on the basis of their prior level of criminal involvement, thereby selecting "bad guys" or those with "bad guy" potential. Once in the gang, however, the initial "bad guys" could be made worse by the culture and status system of the gang. Hence the gang may both select and encourage criminal conduct among its members. At the same time, increased police attention and labeling may officially recognize more offenses.

Notice that these three explanations for the fact that gang members are more heavily involved than non-gang youth in officially recognized criminal/violent activity suggest different predictions about the level of criminal behavior expected for members and nonmembers before, during, and after gang membership. If the selection model is true (the gang attracts and recruits "bad guys"), gang members will exhibit more criminal behavior than nonmembers before, during, and after their membership in the gang. After all, these are already "bad guys," so when comparing them to non-gang youth ("good guys"), the bad apples should consistently show higher rates of criminal involvement. If, on the other hand, the gang causation model is true (the gang creates "bad guys"), then gang members will be no different from non-gang youth in their criminal behavior both before and after they belonged to a gang. If gang members are fundamentally similar to non-gang youth, the only time these two groups' criminal behavior should differ is during the period of gang membership. Finally, if the "police attention" argument is correct, then we should expect no differences in criminal behavior between non-gang and gang youth before gang membership. However, there should be much more crime among gang members while in a gang, as well as afterward because those youths will be known to the police as troublemakers.

Testing these different predictions should help determine why gang members have higher rates of crime. Thornberry and his colleagues (1993) report data from the Rochester Youth Development Study (RYDS) that are appropriate for examining the various possibilities. The RYDS researchers gathered data on a sample of youths from school districts in Rochester, New York, who were at high risk for serious crime. (They had characteristics similar to those of youths who previously had gotten into trouble.) The sample was followed over a long period of time, and information about involvement in crime and drug use was collected at different points in time. One of the questions asked of each Rochester boy was whether or not he was a member of a gang.

Thornberry and his group found that: (1) boys who were members of a gang at any time had substantially higher rates of crime and drug use (about four or five times higher) than non-gang boys; (2) boys who moved in and out of gangs reported rates of criminal behavior that were substantially higher than non-gang boys when they were gang members but not when they were outside gangs; and (3) boys who were in a gang for a long period of time had higher rates of crime than nonmembers at every point in time, but their criminal behavior while gang members was even higher than their criminal behavior before they were gang members. Collectively, these findings led Thornberry to conclude that gangs do not merely attract and select "bad guys." Their data are consistent with the explanation that gang affiliation does make things worse, at least for involvement in crime. And for those boys who were only transient members, the gang makes things a lot worse. Moreover, these results do not appear to be a mere function of increased police attention. A similar crime-escalation effect for gang affiliation has also been found using a nationally representative sample of youth (Esbensen and Huizinga, 1993). There is, therefore, something about the culture and dynamics of a gang that generates criminal behavior.

Extent of Street Gangs: The 'Gang Problem'

We know that gangs do a lot of crime and in some locations are heavily involved in violence and homicide. But how extensive is the "gang problem"? Here, as with most aspects of gangs, the data are thin. Nevertheless, we do know that there are a large number of gangs operating in the United States, and the number of cities having gangs has increased rapidly over the past decade.

In a comprehensive survey of police departments of 189 cities with a population of 100,000 or more (plus a few smaller-sized cities), Klein found gang activity in 176, or 94 percent, of them. In a second survey of cities with populations between 10,000 and 100,000 (approximately 2,250 of them), Klein found that 38 percent reported gang activity. Thus, there were approximately 800 to 900 smaller-sized cities with gang activity. Combining the two surveys led Klein to estimate that there are about 1,000 cities in the United States with gang activity. Since each city generally has more than one gang working, the actual number of gangs and gang members is much greater than 1,000. However, most cities contain only a few gangs, and the number of gang members in these cities is small relative to the total number of youths. Figures 4.3 and 4.4 show that most cities have fewer than five gangs and fewer than 500 gang members.

Figure 4.3 Number of Gangs in 766 Gang Cities

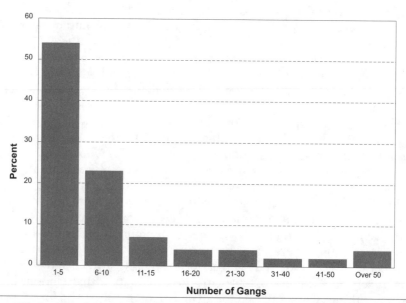

Source: Klein, Malcolm W., 1995. *The American Street Gangs*, p. 34. New York: Oxford University Press.

The gang problem becomes much greater in larger cities with populations of 100,000 or more. Figures 4.5 and 4.6 illustrate this. You can see that over 50 percent of them have more than 10 gangs, with almost one-half of the cities reporting more than 500 gang members. These findings are consistent with those of W. Miller (1982), who reported that 83 percent of the largest cities in the United States had a gang problem. Moreover, he noted that while gangs were more prevalent in larger cities, they could also be found in medium-sized (Weston, 1993) and small cities (with fewer than 10,000 population) as well as in suburban areas. Yet, gangs appear to be neither uniformly nor randomly distributed across the United States. Gang scholars (Klein, 1995; Miller, 1982; Spergel, 1990) have consistently observed that gangs are more likely to be found on the coasts, in southwestern states, and in some cities in the midwest (Chicago, St. Louis), and that they are very unlikely to be found in western mountain states or the northeast.

Figure 4.4 Number of Gang Members Reported in 739 Gang Cities

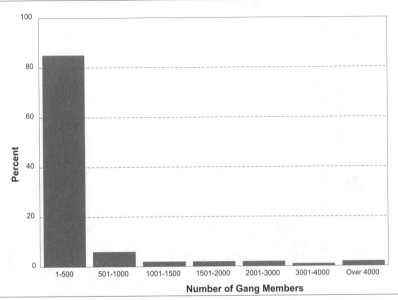

Source: Klein, Malcolm W., 1995. *The American Street Gangs*, p. 34. New York: Oxford University Press.

**Figure 4.5 Number of Gangs in 175 of the Largest Cities
            (over 100,000 population)**

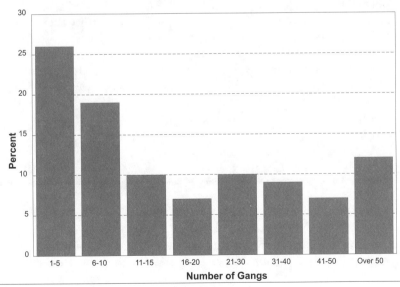

Source: Klein, Malcolm W., 1995. *The American Street Gangs*, p. 35. New York: Oxford University Press.

In documenting gang proliferation, Klein (1995: 90–91) observed that in 1990 there were just over 50 U.S. cities reporting gang behavior; by 1992 that number had doubled to more than 100, and by 1995 the number had increased to approximately 800, and may be as large as 1,100. He estimates that

Figure 4.6   Number of Gang Members Reported in 173 Gang Cities (over 100,000 population)

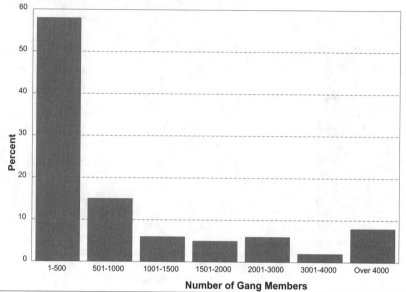

Source: Klein, Malcolm W., 1995. *The American Street Gangs*, p. 35. New York: Oxford University Press.

the number of cities reporting gang activity has increased by 345 percent over a thirty-year period. Spergel (1990: 183) notes that in Dade County, Florida, there were only 4 gangs operating in 1980, this increased to 25 in 1983, 47 in 1985, and by 1988 there were 80 gangs; in San Diego County there were only three gangs and fewer than 300 gang members in 1975, but by 1987 there were as many as 35 gangs and approximately 2,100 gang members. Moreover, since most large and many medium-sized cities already had gang problems, most of the growth in gang activity is in smaller cities. Klein (1995) reports that of the cities under 10,000 population that reported gang problems in the 1990s, 94 percent had no gang problem prior to 1984.

Composition of Gangs

Age

According to Klein (1995), in the past the average age for initial entry into a gang was quite young, around 11 years old. While there have been media reports about gang members as young as 5 and 6, this is the exception rather than the rule. In fact, there are probably very few gang members as young as eleven, though there may be young gang "wannabes"—what Klein refers to as the "unborns." They attempt to affiliate but are not really part of the gang itself. The lower age limit for most gangs is approximately 11 years, and it has not changed much over time.

The upper age limit of gang membership, however, has gotten higher over time as more older teens and some adults have continued to stay in gangs. The common assumption is that most gangs are composed of teenagers, with the peak age for gang membership in mid-to late-adolescence. Spergel (1990:217–218) estimates the average gang member in San Diego to be 19 years old and in Chicago approximately 18. Estimates of the average age of gang members from other cities are fairly close to these estimates. These ages nevertheless appear to be older than those in the past. Klein (1995) claims that in cities where gangs have existed for some time, the average age of members is in the range of 17 to 19; for those cities without a long tradition of gangs, however, the average age is much greater, in the early 20s. This increase in average age occurs not because youths enter a gang at a later age in these cities, but because they are staying in the gang longer. Some gangs even have members who are in their 30s.

Gender

One indisputable fact about gangs is that they are overwhelmingly male. Solid data about female gang members is sparse, but it is fairly certain that females are unlikely to be members of gangs, and they are particularly unlikely to be involved in violent gang crimes. Spergel (1983, 1986), for example, reported that between 1978 and 1981, 344 of 345 gang homicide offenders in Chicago were male, and between 1982 and 1984 in Chicago, well over 90 percent of the gang-related crimes involved male offenders. Bobrowski (1988) found that in Chicago over an 18-month period 98 percent of the gang members arrested for crimes were male.

Female membership in mixed-sex gangs is very rare, and autonomous female gangs are even more unusual (Campbell, 1990; Klein, 1995). Klein (1995) and Spergel (1990) contend that females are more likely to be "auxiliary" members of male gangs. That is, while they are semi-independent from the activities of the males, and the group of girls may have a name different from that of the gang (though a feminized version of the male gang name is more likely), they are nonetheless inextricably linked to the male gang. In such cases, the continuing existence of the female gang is linked to and dependent upon the connections the girls have with their male counterparts. Female gang members do have some similarities with male gang members: they, too, are likely to have higher rates of delinquency than non-gang girls, and their membership in gangs seems to increase their involvement in crime (Bjerregaard and Smith, 1993). Although female gang members commit more crime than do females not in gangs, female gang crime tends to be less serious (drinking, sex, running away, theft, joy riding, etc.) than that committed by males.

Ethnicity

Street gangs seem to be composed mostly of black, Hispanic, and, recently, Asian youths; very few gangs are predominately white. Klein (1995:105) estimates that of 800 "gang-involved" cities, fewer than 10 percent have predominately white gangs. Moreover, white gangs are more likely to be located in smaller urban areas. In fact, most scholars agree that the majority of street gangs in the United States are either black or Hispanic. Klein's own data from Los Angeles indicates that in 1990, 45 percent of the street gangs were Hispanic, 41 percent were black gangs, 9 percent were Asian gangs, and only 5 percent were white gangs. The predominance of Hispanic gangs, however, is only characteristic of Southern California and other southwestern states. In other parts of the country, street gangs are more likely to be black gangs. Asian gangs seem to be almost exclusively a west coast and New York City phenomenon.

In the preceding paragraph, we spoke of "Hispanic" gangs and "black" gangs as if they were racially homogeneous, and most gangs are. Research by Knox (1994) in Chicago shows that on average black gangs are 96 percent black, Hispanic gangs are 94 percent Hispanic, and white gangs are 88 percent white. When there is racial heterogeneity within a gang, it is usually because a white gang also has Hispanic members. Black gangs are almost exclusively black (see also Klein, 1995; Spergel, 1990). Apparently, however, cities differ with respect to the racial homogeneity of their gangs. In the St. Louis gangs studied by Decker and Van Winkle (1996), it was not uncommon for black gangs to have white members. This mixing usually arose when white youths lived in neighborhoods where black gangs existed. Even in St. Louis, however, the majority of black gang members are in gangs with only black members.

Perhaps the most racially/ethnically homogeneous type of gang is the Asian gang. Asian gangs are a very recent phenomenon in the United States, so little is known about them. Asian gangs are typically located in areas where there is no gang tradition and little history of gang research (Vancouver, British Columbia, and Garden Grove, California, for example). Also, it is more difficult for the police to infiltrate and obtain information about the activities of Asian gangs. Available information, however, suggests that Asian gangs are racially homogeneous internally, but not all Asian gangs are of the same ethnicity. In southern California, for instance, there are Korean, Vietnamese, Cambodian, Taipei, and Filipino gangs, as well as a much smaller number of Japanese gangs. In New York City, Asian gangs have extensive connections to organized crime syndicates in their home countries (Chin, 1990). The Chinese gangs are well organized and clearly structured, with a much more serious interest in financial pursuits than black or Hispanic gangs. Because they are organized for profit, Chinese gangs are less frequently involved in violence, and when they resort to violence, it is for instrumental purposes (to control markets).

Size

The problem with estimating gang size is that investigators do not know whom to count as a gang member. Not all gang "members" are equal participants; some are die-hard, core types while others are on the fringe of the group, shifting in and out of membership. Klein (1995) provides a vivid illustration of the problem. Near the University of Southern California there is a black gang called the Harpys. The Security Division of the university puts the size of the Harpys at approximately 150. The Los Angeles Police Department, however, lists the size of the Harpy gang at 800, more than five times the campus security estimate. There is, then, plenty of reason to be cautious about estimates of gang size.

Investigators do know that gang size varies tremendously. There are some exceptionally large gangs with members all over the country—such as Chicago's Blackstone Rangers and Vice Lords, with literally thousands of members. Klein (1995:104), however, estimates that the average gang has somewhere between a hundred (or less) and several hundred active members. Of course, what an investigator estimates as the size of gangs depends on what he or she defines as a gang member. Gang scholars (Klein, 1995; Spergel, 1990) have noted that in addition to the "core," there are regular members, peripheral or fringe members, and "wannabes" or "on-lookers." The more the count of a gang's members extends beyond the "core" members, the more diffuse and less cohesive the gang becomes.

How Organized Are Gangs?

Perhaps one of the most controversial questions in gang research is the extent to which gangs are organized. Traditionally, observers of gangs have tended to view them as very well structured, differentiated, and organized. It was thought that gangs were family substitutes for their members; there was a great deal of solidarity within the gang; there was a coherent gang ideology and code of conduct; there were formal roles that distinguished gang members; and there were special means of gang communication that included distinctive clothing and speech. Some, though, thought that the amount of organization and cohesion that gangs had been presumed to possess was exaggerated, and that gangs were in fact only very loosely knit groups whose members had minimal loyalty and permanence. For example, Yablonsky (1962) has characterized the violent gang as a loosely organized "near group" because of its weak structure, transient and partially committed members, and lack of consistent leadership. We believe that gangs can best be described as occupying the middle ground between completely unorganized types of deviance like suicide or serial murderers and very well-organized kinds of deviance like religious sects or organized crime. In some ways gangs are very well organized while in others they are not organized at all.

Sociality

One of the characteristics of organized deviance is that the deviant activity is a group behavior rather than actions of solitary individuals. On this dimension, gangs are fairly well organized. While it is true that gang members do things, such as commit crimes, by themselves, the literature indicates that most activity by gang members usually is done with other gang members, and if not with a gang member, with at least one or more other person. In other words, gang activity is a social activity. For example, in their study of St. Louis gangs, Decker and Van Winkle (1996) observed that the most common gang activities were: hanging out, fighting, selling drugs, drinking beer, playing in sports, going to dances, cruising, doing drugs, chasing girls, and going to parties. Other gang researchers have also found that a good portion of the time spent by gang members is in social activities, and usually with other gang members (Klein, 1971; Moore, 1978; Padilla, 1992; Jankowski, 1991; Short and Strodtbeck, 1974). Most, if not all, of these activities require the participation of others (hanging out, drinking, cruising, chasing girls). Since Decker and Van Winkle also had observed that gang members rarely socialized with other than gang members, we can surmise that most of what gang members do is in the company of other gang members.

In addition to gang members' socializing extensively with other gang members, the fact of membership requires other gang members. By definition there cannot be a gang of only one person. Although gang members do some things as solitary individuals (we have already alluded to the fact that much drug selling by gang members is for individual profit rather than a part of gang activity), their behavior as gang members takes place in a group context. Thus, gang activity scores high on the criterion of sociality.

Pervasiveness

We have seen that one of the features of deviant drug use that makes it more organized than fully individualized deviant behavior is the fact that it consumes a good deal of the person's time. This is also true of gang behavior, though it is not equally true for all gang members. Decker and Van Winkle describe the "exclusivity" of the gang for many of its members, and emphasize how the gang has constricted the social life and social relationships of its members. They found that nearly 80 percent of the St. Louis gang members they studied socialized solely with other gang members. The exclusivity of the gang for its members was not because gang members were social "wolves" with no outside group membership before entering the gang: many current gang members had been involved in religious, social, and athletic groups prior to joining the gang, but 75 percent of them had dropped out of these other groups after becoming affiliated with the gang. At least in St. Louis gang life is very pervasive, so much so that gang members have very little life outside the gang:

> The gang has become the primary reference and peer group for our subjects. Many, if not most, of the friends and relatives they would normally interact with are in the gang or in a gang. Their involvement in institutional activities—church, school, employment market, clubs—is constricted, with, of course, the major exception of the criminal justice system. For most of our subjects, then, their primary interpersonal interactions and activities are with other gang members (and/or hangers-on). (Decker and Van Winkle, 1996:142)

Klein's (1995) research among Los Angeles gangs and other extensive ethnographic work with gangs from other parts of the country (Moore, 1978, 1991; Padilla, 1992; Jankowski, 1991) indicates that not all gang members are as immersed in gang activities as the group Decker and Van Winkle studied. These lines of research indicate that there is pronounced individual variation in the extent of gang participation. Some youths, for example, are "core" members—they make key decisions within the gang, formulate plans, and map strategy. Klein (1995) estimates that they constitute about one-third to one-half of a gang's members. For these core members, the gang is pervasive. They are much more active in gang activities than fringe members are because the gang meets a dependency need that is not met in other social relationships. As a result, they are very involved in gang activities. In their interviews with members of St. Louis gangs, it is likely that Decker and Van Winkle interviewed mostly core members.

In sum, the gang is not necessarily a tight-knit social group. Some members are more committed to the gang, and for these core members the gang is their primary if not exclusive social group. Gang activity for them is pervasive. For about one-half of the members of a gang—those who are less committed (fringe members and recruits)—however, gang activity is simply something they drift in and out of. Overall, gang activity can be characterized as moderately pervasive.

Communication

One of the characteristics of organized deviance is that its practitioners communicate with one another extensively and share a common and distinctive argot or language. There are several ways that gang members communicate with each other and with the outside world that convey their identity and solidarity. One is through specialized slang. Gang members use words, phrases, and concepts that are understood only by other gang members and other gangs. For example, when one gang member wants to know the affiliation of another he asks, "Who do you ride?" or "What set you from?" Gang members have a rich slang that describes their world; crack cocaine is "rock" and PCP is "whack"; their territory or neighborhood is the "hood"; their power is expressed with the term "rifa" (to rule); someone who was killed got "zapped"; a stupid person is referred to by Chicano gangs as a "Tonto"; females used strictly for sex are "Toss Ups"; a timid person is a "Poo Butt"; and frequently the number 13 signifies that the particular gang is crazy or wild. Crip gang members frequently greet and refer to one another as "Cuzz" or "BK" (for Blood Killer since the Bloods are a rival gang of the Crips), and they disdain the use of the letter "B" in the written and spoken word. Members of Chicano gangs like to be "all choloed out" (looking good). (For a more complete discussion and a glossary of common gang terms, see Sachs, 1997).

Equally distinctive and expressive are nonverbal forms of communication. For instance, some gangs have distinctive "colors" (blue clothing for some gangs, red or black for others); some wear a particular type of sport clothing (there are Nike gangs, and Adidas gangs); some choose a particular manner of wearing clothing (pants that hang well below the waistline or shirts with the top button done up). Another prominent way to communicate within the gang and, more importantly, to define territory is with graffiti. Graffiti usually consists of well-known names (such as the names of streets or people) and special gang symbols, and it has several different functions. It is used to mark off a gang's territory or to issue challenges by marking the territory of another gang. It can be used to commemorate the death of a gang member, note important gang achievements, or even to announce news from the gang. Another form of gang expression and communication is with distinctive styles and locations for tattoos. Gang members will often decorate their bodies with their gang initials or logo to identify themselves. Finally, gang members symbolize and communicate their membership by "flashing" gang signs—finger gestures that reveal one's gang membership.

Each of these verbal and nonverbal forms of communication has several purposes. One of the most important is to provide an identification for gang members. Such group-identifying gestures strengthen internal solidarity. The second purpose is to communicate a threat to members of other gangs or to people living in a neighborhood that the gang is present and is establishing or has already established control. It should be remembered, however, that gang members differ in the extent to which they use special language, wear colors, flash signs, and get tattooed. Consistent with their position in the gang and its personal importance to them, core members are most likely to communicate in "gangese"; in fact, their entire expression may be in special gang symbols. As one moves away from the core toward the fringe or to new recruits, distinctive gang communication is likely to be employed less often, with less ease, and with less fluency.

Differentiation and Coordination

You already know that gang members are not equal participants, that for some ("core" members) the gang is a more central and extensive part of their lives than for others ("fringe" or "peripheral" members). The gang is perhaps best thought of as a loosely organized collection of smaller age-graded groups called cliques (Hagedorn, 1988; Klein, 1971, 1995; Moore, 1991). Think of a clique as a network of a few individuals of approximately the same age and same gender. While there is some communication across cliques, most of the behavior, communication, and interaction among gang members is within cliques. Moreover, each clique has its own leader or leaders and its own group of core and fringe members.

For example, in a typical gang there will be one or a small number of cliques of older gang members, in their early twenties (and sometimes early thirties). There will be core members within this group of "seniors" for whom the gang is still the primary social group, but most likely the members have jobs and families and retain affiliation only as fringe members. There may be a leader or a small number of leaders of this group, but since the gang affiliation is weak, it is possible that there is no recognized leader. The overall gang contains a larger collection of cliques where members are between the ages of 16 and 19. These cliques have a greater number of core members, and there is communication and interaction across the different cliques. But each clique usually has its own recognized leader, though some leaders may be more powerful than others. Not only are there more core members within this group of slightly older gang members [what Klein (1995:61) refers to as "Juniors"], there are also more fringe members, so the bulk of the gang's membership is between 16 and 20 years of age. Almost as numerous as the "juniors" is a collection of cliques where members are between 14 and 16 years of age; these comprise the newest members of the gang—the "babies." There are also a large number of core and fringe members among these new recruits, and they too will have their own leader, though this leader may also be integrated into one of the "junior" cliques. Finally, at the bottom of the gang age structure are those aspirants between 11 and 14 years who are not quite in but who want to become gang members.

Within any age-specific clique, role differentiation between core and fringe members is most important. Klein (1995:59–60) draws clear distinctions between the two primary types of gang members. Core members are more frequently involved in crime than fringe members, they are involved in a wider variety of gang activities, they are more likely to have personal "deficits" such as low IQ and higher impulsivity, and they have a greater psychological need for the gang. Core members tend to interact much more frequently with other core members (mostly of their own age) and less often with fringe members of the gang. Fringe members, on the other hand are as likely to be loners as they are to affiliate with gang members.

In addition to core members, fringe members, and wannabes, gang members can be grossly differentiated in terms of their location in an overall informal authority structure. There is one (or maybe a few) recognized leader of most gangs, sometimes with a formal title (President, King, Prince, Prime Minister, and the like), and many followers. Most gang researchers have argued that leadership in a gang is rarely fixed; it is more a functional position in which the leader varies by the type of task the gang is going to perform. The qualities that make one a good leader are usually age, in that time spent in the gang is an important criterion, and physical prowess, since the gang inevitably must defend itself. Other than leader and follower, core member or fringe, there is not much role differentiation within gangs. Although some gangs have specialized roles such as enforcer or "shooter" (one who kills others), this is the exception rather than the rule.

Culture

Culture consists of a body of knowledge, symbols, beliefs, and technology that is handed down from old members to new members. One component of gang culture is the system of communication consisting of specialized language and symbols, conventions of dress, graffiti, body decorations (tattoos), and signs. All of this must be learned, and older members teach newer gang members directly through instruction or indirectly as initiates imitate established participants. That is part of gang culture.

In addition, there is a shared set of values among gang members, although the specific values in the code may differ between gangs. For example, gang participants are expected to possess self-respect, a reputation for courage, virility, trustworthiness, loyalty, and physical prowess. Like most groups with a semblance of organization, gang members place a premium on loyalty to the gang, with a clear distinction between gang members and those who are not in the gang. Comrades are to be assisted and trusted while others are generally suspect.

Chicano gangs have a two-pronged support for the principles of respect and honor (Jankowski, 1991). Respect must be earned continually by each gang member through demonstration of courage and loyalty to the gang. Honor does not have to be earned; it is automatically bestowed on gang members when they join. But honor, like respect, is fragile, and one must be vigilant to make sure others do not take it away. For example, honor is threatened by an insult, and honor must be protected and defended; loose words may lead to violence, even death. Those who defend honor in the face of a challenge become even more respected, and their exploits and courageous acts become part of gang lore and the subject of graffiti art. In addition, Vigil (1988) and Vigil and Long (1990) found that friendship and interpersonal loyalty are prominent values in Chicano gangs. Other values that are frequently admired by gang members include wildness and *locura* (craziness), though when taken to an extreme such values become liabilities; an exceptionally crazy gang member can put the others in jeopardy (they unnecessarily kill a clerk during a robbery or disrespect a police officer making a routine traffic stop).

In their study of St. Louis gangs, Decker and Van Winkle (1996:100–103) report that the code of conduct among gang members consists of six rules: (1) don't disrespect your own colors, (2) don't run from a gang fight, (3) don't fight members of your own gang, (4) don't "snake" (turn in or inform on) a member of your own gang, (5) don't cooperate with police, (6) don't pretend to be a member of one gang while you are a member of another (that is, no perpetrating a fraud—don't "perp"). Similar rules may exist in other places. Fagan's (1989) research concerning four types of gangs in Chicago, Los Angeles, and San Diego suggests as much. However, Jankowski's (1991) study of gangs in Los Angeles, New York, and Boston, revealed an informal code of conduct in only two specific areas. Gang members could not do anything that constituted disrespecting a fellow member, and participants had to wear appropriate gang clothing.

An important part of gang culture centers around violence. This theme appears in initiation ceremonies and in such gang activities as fights, drive-by shootings, and murders. Padilla (1992:56) describes a ceremony known as the "violation" (the "V"). The violation is a severe beating given to one gang member by the others. The "V" was apparently an integral component of the Puerto Rican gangs he studied in Chicago, and was employed on three specific occasions: during the initiation of new members, when old members wished to leave the gang, and in order to discipline and sanction a gang member who had violated one of the gang's rules. Similar use of violence on newcomers has been documented by Moore (1978) in Los Angeles, Hagedorn (1988) in Milwaukee, Vigil (1988) in Los Angeles and San Diego, and by Decker and Van Winkle (1996) in St. Louis. Decker and Van Winkle note that the use of violence during the initiation ceremony has several important functions: it provides other gang members with information about the courage of a new member; it increases solidarity among gang members by providing a common, meaningful experience; it communicates gang rules and expectations to new members; and it provides the group with the material for its common stock of folklore. Violence against a gang's own members is, however, probably only a very small part of the violent world of gang members. Far more frequent are violent acts employed as a part of a gang's criminal activities (mugging and armed robberies, for example) and violence directed against other gangs.

Gang culture, therefore, is fairly well developed. It consists of language; nonverbal symbolic communication (graffiti, style of clothing, tattoos, signs, special colors and symbols); and collective rituals and ceremonies. Moreover, the culture of the gang is composed of a set of attitudes that portrays the gang in a positive light and paints a hostile picture of outsiders. Loyalty to the group is highly honored, as is courage, valor, and displays of self-respect and pride.

Self-Identity

We have argued that a given group is more organized to the extent that most members think of themselves primarily in terms of the group and develop self-concepts based on group membership and activities. By this criterion, street gang delinquency is more organized than is drug use. Members express their gang-related self-identities in numerous ways. They wear the clothes and colors of the gang, they use gang slang in their speech, they use gang signs and scribble gang graffiti, they associate primarily with other gang members, and they engage principally in gang activities. Clearly, gang members identify with the gang and a large part of their self-identity is linked to the gang. We have already noted the finding from Decker and Van Winkle's (1996) study of gang members in St. Louis that two-thirds of the youths they interviewed reported that all of their activities were with other gang members. They observe (1996:228–229) that once youths join a gang, they withdraw their commitment from other social institutions, and their lives become restricted to that of the gang:

> Gang involvement dramatically increases the social isolation of our subjects to a disturbing degree. . .Gang membership leads to isolation both as the gang assumes a more dominant role in the lives of its members and as institutions actively exclude such members from their activities . . . . Gang membership creates a world of peer-oriented, temporary, and unstable groups . . . which not only results in isolation from legitimate public organizations but also drives them away from non-gang peers. . . . Gang membership also distances our subjects from their families and relatives.

It would be a mistake, however, to overly romanticize the gang and what it means to its members. Although gang identification and activities form a substantial part of the identities of its members, gang members are not completely immersed in gang activity the way, say, a monk is totally immersed in the life style and philosophy of his religious order. While some core members totally submerge themselves in the gang, other core members and the vast majority of fringe members have lives and self-identities rooted elsewhere. Even among Decker and Van Winkle's gang members, about 60 percent had completed or were still attending high school. Gang life is even less a source of identity for fringe members of the gang. According to Klein (1995), fringe members are far less involved in a host of gang activities than are core members. Because fringe members often drift in and out of gang affiliation and participate sporadically in gang activities, their self-identities are clearly not fully tied to gang membership. In addition, conventional institutions hold some attraction even for core gang members. In his study of gangs in three cities, Fagan (1989) found that a majority of the gang members thought that getting a good education and job was important.

Philosophical Integration

As mentioned in our discussion of deviant drug use, fully organized forms of deviance provide their practitioners with a well-developed, synthesized philosophy that covers many aspects of life. While the gang provides its members with more of a "world view" than is characteristic of individualized deviant acts such as suicide and serial murder (and probably more than deviant drug use), it falls short of constituting a fully integrated philosophy. For some, mostly core members, the philosophy of the gang is wide, encompassing ideas about the superiority of gang life, the necessity of subordinating self to the group, and the corruption of police and other conventional institutions. Gang philosophy may also provide the gang member with a crude "world view," one that emphasizes the distance and conflict between the gang and the outside world (particularly individuals and gangs of minority races or ethnic groups) and the consequent value of gang cohesion (Jankowski, 1991). This philosophy is not likely to be completely shared by all, however.

Social Control

The literature indicates that gangs have well-developed systems of informal control to ensure that participants obey the rules and meet expectations. One way that gang members are disciplined for infractions of gang rules is to get signified by graffiti. A gang member's name may be placed on a wall with a gang insignia or logo, and the name will be crossed out or a question mark placed next to it, signifying that it is not clear whether the person is in good standing. As noted before, granting or withholding status and confirming honor are powerful informal mechanisms used by most gangs. Of course, sometimes gang members are actually expelled or refused the right of participation. They may also be socially censured by being ignored.

Perhaps the most common response to violations of gang rules is to physically and violently discipline the rule violator. Felix Padilla (1992:56–57) has reported that, at least within some Puerto Rican gangs in Chicago, the ritual of the "V" consists of gang members collectively hitting and kicking another member, and it may be brought about when a member has broken gang rules. In their study of St. Louis gangs, Decker and Van Winkle (1996) also observed that the most likely response to a violation of gang rules was a beating.

Overall, then, gangs appear to be quite well organized in their ability to exercise social control over their members. Those mechanisms appear to work most effectively when individuals are strongly drawn to gang activities and look to the gang for companionship and acceptance and as a source of pride and honor.

Recruitment

Gang membership is not fixed, since youths leave the group for any number of reasons: they "age out," find marriages or jobs, get arrested and imprisoned, get killed or injured, or simply quit the gang. One of the things that gangs must eventually face, therefore, is how to get new members. One reason that street gangs are not more fully organized is that, with few exceptions, there is little formal recruitment of new members. From research on gangs in several cities, Fagan (1989) reports that the gangs he observed have no formal system of recruitment; reflecting this, very few gang members reported that they had been actively recruited to join the gang. Gangs do not advertise the fact that they are interested in "expanding," nor do they actively pursue potential members in schools or on the street. Rather, for the most part, potential recruits go to the gang rather than the other way around. Quite simply, the gang is an attraction to many youths, and the gang itself merely has to sift through and informally screen potential members who seek it out.

One way the gang attracts new members is by making the incentives of gang membership obvious in the communities within which they operate. An obvious incentive is the gang's ability to provide a way for poor kids to get some of the material possessions they desire. Many youths want expensive footwear (sneakers frequently run $100 or more a pair), designer sports clothing, and gold jewelry. Gang members wearing these highly prized objects and flashing freely flowing cash look very enticing to those with weak cash flow and limited legitimate opportunities. While gang activity does not supply a steady source of income, there is the occasional score from drug dealing, robbery, burglary, or stealing cars that provides a financial windfall. In very poor neighborhoods, which offer their young people few decent-paying jobs, the possibility of having pocket money is especially alluring. Jankowski (1991:37–62) found that the most frequently given reason that youths joined a gang was the prospect of making some easy money.

Recruitment may at first be subtle and gradual. Younger youths may be initially enticed with financial incentives to provide some "services" for the gang—such as serving as a lookout or hiding drugs or guns. The money is usually easy and good. Before long, however, the unsuspecting youth finds that he is becoming more and more committed to the gang, perhaps finding himself needing the protection of the gang against rival gangs, and at some point he becomes a member.

Gang membership also provides a powerfully appealing system of protection in dangerous communities, areas where most potential gang members' lives are fraught with violence. There is the "normal" crime in such socially disorganized areas, and there is the violence brought on by the existence of rival gangs. Keep in mind that in areas with gang activity, any young person is a potential target or victim, and gang mentality says "if you are not a member of my gang, then you must be a member of another gang." Given this uncertainty about day-to-day safety, the lure of the gang for providing badly needed protection is understandable. From his study of Chicano street gangs in Southern California, Vigil (1988:154; 1993:99–100) concluded: "It was either get your ass kicked every day or join a gang and get your ass kicked occasionally by rival gangs."

Similarly, the need for protection from rival gangs and from general street violence was cited by Decker and Van Winkle's (1996:74) gang members as the most important reason for entering a gang. The response of one member of the Crips was typical: "It's like a comfortable feeling, you got somebody to back you up and protect you." The need for protection from street crime was also cited by the members of a black gang in Chicago (Johnstone, 1981). Clearly, then, given the prevalence of violence (both gang and non-gang) in certain communities, the gang does not have to recruit too hard to attract new members. In fact, of most concern is the selection of good members from a pool of eager potential recruits.

Another indirect recruiting route used by some gangs is to offer the gang as a social group that provides its members with a sense of belonging. One persistent finding in research is that gangs spring up in neighborhoods where there is a high prevalence of weak and broken families. It is possible that within this general social chaos the gang provides a second "family"—one that is intact, stable, and supportive. This social dimension of gangs may be particularly important to core members (Klein, 1995). In their study of St. Louis gangs, for example, Decker and Van Winkle (1996:63–64) found that youths referred to the "family" nature of their gang: "It's more like a family away from home. You with your friends, you all stick together. They ain't going to let nothing happen to you, you ain't going to let nothing happen to them," and "A gang is something you follow behind the leader. Do different things just like a family." Ironically, while the opportunity to join a "family" outside the home was an attraction of the gang to many, very few gang members reported that they would choose the gang over their biological families if forced to.

The informal, rather haphazard nature of gang "recruitment" is forcefully illustrated by current gang members' reporting that they essentially "floated" into the gang. Neighborhood youths become gang members simply by "hanging" and associating with members of a gang. In a process described as long ago as 1927 by Thrasher (1927), those who join gangs come from the same neighborhoods where they had initially formed informal play groups.

One, or a few, of the members of these play groups become fringe members of a gang while others are slowly, over time, brought into the orbit of the gang. Revealing illustrations of this informal "recruitment" process are found in the words reported by Moore (1991:48) of two of gang members who responded when asked reasons for joining the gang:

> I have no idea. I don't. I just fell into it . . . I just happened to live there in the environment. . . . Just from going to school, and knowing the guys, and living there, and talking with the guys every day in school.

The other youth answered:

> I guess by association, you know. I was in elementary school and the members of the White Fence gang that was in the school that they went to and we met there. . . In other words, you know we went to school together, and we played together and you know just become probably like being raised into the gang.

In fact, Moore (1991) reported that only 10 percent of the gang boys she studied had been actively recruited by the gang. This finding is corroborated by Fagan's (1989) research on gangs in Los Angeles and Chicago. He found no consistent attempts at recruitment in any gang. Like Moore's gang members, the youths in Fagan's gangs joined because they already had friends who were in the gang and they simply "hung out" with them. It would appear, therefore, that the street gang is not a fully organized deviant group in that it does not frequently engage in formal recruitment of new members.

Jankowski (1991:47–59) thinks that gang recruitment is more planned and active than do other scholars; in fact, he noted that all the gangs he studied had some type of recruitment system in place. He differentiated three strategies employed by the gangs he studied: (1) fraternity recruitment, (2) obligation recruitment, and (3) coercive recruitment. In the fraternity type of recruitment, the gang attracts members by emphasizing its social and fraternal functions. Usually this strategy involves a social function like a dance, where potential recruits are invited and initially selected. In the obligation type of recruitment, the gang appeals to the potential recruit's sense of duty and obligation to the community or neighborhood. In the coercive type of recruitment, which occurs when membership demands are especially urgent, such as during a gang war, "recruits" are reluctantly pressed into the service of the gang by threats and intimidation. It is not clear from Jankowski's description of these recruitment strategies how frequently each is employed.

Summary

The street gang is neither new nor uniquely American (though it is probably best developed in the United States). Being quite widespread and seemingly becoming more so, the gang is a social, financial, and protective device that serves the needs mainly of minority males living in larger cities. It consists of a loosely organized confederation of age-graded cliques with little role differentiation and little coordination in activities across cliques. Role differentiation within the street gang is generally limited to the core members, among whom the street gang rises almost to the level of fully organized deviance, and the fringe members who drift in and out of gang affiliation and behavior. When the nine criteria are considered together, the street gang is best understood as lying midway between completely individualistic deviance and fully organized deviance. While street gangs show considerable organizational capacity in some criteria (for example, they require a high level of sociality, there are unique and collectively understood forms of communication, there are established rules of conduct and a system of social control to enforce those rules, and for some members there is a high degree of self-identity), for several others (like pervasiveness, differentiation, philosophical integration, and recruitment) they are somewhat low on a continuum of organization. In the next chapter, we will examine new forms of deviance that are more organized than deviant drug use or gang delinquency—a religious movement known as Perfectionism and syndicated crime. ✦

Chapter 5

Fully Organized Deviance

In Chapter 3 you were exposed to two forms of deviance—suicide and serial killing—that fall near the "no organization" end of a continuum of organization; in Chapter 4 you read of two others—deviant drug usage and delinquent gang behavior—that are moderately organized. In this chapter we will consider two examples of well-organized deviance. One is Perfectionism, which gained a foothold in the Northeastern United States beginning in the 1830s, and the other is contemporary "organized crime."

Perfectionism

The early part of the nineteenth century was a time of great social and religious ferment in the United States. Various theological and philosophical movements emerged, and many found expression in new kinds of churches and communities that advocated radical forms of economic, familial, and religious organization and behavior. To carry out some of the ideologies being promulgated, several dozen utopian experiments in communal living were begun. Most of these movements and the communities they spawned lasted only a short time. Perfectionism, however, was one of the more successful of these movements, and its main community at Oneida, New York, lasted from 1848 until 1880, when it was dissolved in favor of a joint stock company that exists until this day and is well known as a manufacturer of silverware.

Beliefs

Perfectionists, under the guidance of their leader, John Humphrey Noyes, interpreted the Christian Bible to mean that once a person came to God through a conversion experience, he or she became spiritually perfect and was thereafter released from the bondage of sin. Although spiritual perfection did not necessarily imply actual physical perfection, the believers felt that they had transcended mundane and legal restraints and were free to pursue actual behavioral perfection based on their own inner feelings as guided by God. Furthermore, according to the dictates of this theology, the return of Christ promised in Biblical accounts actually had occurred about A.D. 60, so contemporary believers were, in fact, living in the Kingdom of God. Thus, they were mandated to live in this earthly existence under the conditions that the Bible taught prevailed in Heaven.

One of those conditions was that all thoughts and behaviors were to be unselfish, denying the importance of the individual in favor of glorifying God and advancing the collective interests of the religious community. This meant that all activities and properties were to be shared and relished. Therefore, they lived as socialists, practicing what they called "Bible Communism." Moreover, since worldly structures like legal marriage do not exist in Heaven, they were not to exist on earth. Hence, the Perfectionists condemned the selfishness of exclusive love ennobled in legal marriage and the traditional bonds between parents and children. Allan Estlake, a member of the community, described the appropriate attitude governing relations between the sexes in this way: "No matter what his other qualification may be, if a man cannot love a woman and be happy in seeing her loved by others, he is a selfish man, and his place is with the potsherds of the earth. There is no place for such in the " 'Kingdom of Heaven' " (Estlake, 1900:35). Thus, they embraced "complex marriage"—all members of the community were married to each other and shared sexual partners—and they separated parents from the children, who were reared by the community as a whole.

❖ ❖ ❖ ❖

Another theological principle that undergirded the Perfectionist style of life was a belief that in seeking to better one's spiritual condition, it was desirable to seek fellowship with those more spiritually developed and to avoid unnecessary association with those less advanced in spirituality. This principle of "ascending and descending fellowship" meant that everybody was encouraged to associate with and learn from older adults, particularly those who had been practicing Perfectionism the longest. And when adults needed to associate with children or with other adults less advanced spiritually, they were to counterbalance this exposure with more frequent interaction with those of higher spirituality. This principle of fellowship was carried over into the sexual domain, making the ideal relationships those involving younger with older people so that older ones could contribute to the spiritual development of the younger and teach them self-control. Hence, the most spiritual males (usually the older ones) were commissioned to introduce the young women into sexual activities, just as the older females were to introduce the young males. This occurred when the young person reached puberty and a particular level of spiritual growth was achieved. The appropriate timing was decided by a committee of leaders. And after that, in everyday practice, the older-younger combinations were encouraged, though not totally mandated. But all sexual encounters were voluntary, and anyone not wishing to honor a request from particular individuals was free to refuse. Moreover, despite critics' characterization of complex marriage as "free love," the Perfectionists conducted it under a system of careful regulation and attempted to infuse it with religious meaning. These theological principles were oriented toward four problems:

> The chain of evils which holds humanity in ruin has four links, viz—1st, a breach with God; (Gen. 3:8;) 2d, a disruption of the sexes, involving a special curse on woman, (Gen. 3;16;) 3d, the curse of oppressive labor, bearing specially on man; (Gen, 3:17–19) 4th, Death. (Gen. 3:22–24.) These are all inextricably complicated with each other. The true scheme of redemption begins with reconciliation with God, proceeds first to a restoration of true relations between the sexes, then to reform of the industrial system, and ends with victory over death. . . . Holiness, free love, association in labor, and immortality, constitute the chain of redemption, and must come together in their true order. (Quoted in Foster, 1981:90–91)

Practices

To avoid licentiousness and excess that might otherwise characterize group marriage, Noyes insisted that participants have achieved a high degree of holiness:

> From what precedes, it is evident that any attempt to revolutionize sexual morality before settlement with God, is out of order. Holiness must go before free love. Perfectionists are not responsible for the proceedings of those who meddle with the sexual question, before they have laid the foundation of true faith and union with God (quoted in Foster, 1981:91).

And further, to imbue the process with dignity and grace, and to reduce the awkwardness that might ensue from refusals or reluctance by objects of affection, members of the Perfectionist community did not speak publicly of sexual matters, and sexual encounters, referred to within the group as "interviews," were arranged through a third party—normally an older female (Fogarty, 1994:9). Though males and females were theoretically equally free to initiate a potential interview (Estlake, 1900:87–88), it was usually done by males.

Thus, if Sam Smith or Sally Jones were taken with each other, one or the other might engage in some degree of "courtship" or flirtation in the everyday activities where they worked side-by-side or were jointly engaged in other community activities. Indeed, it was said that life in the Perfectionist community was infused with a constant sense of excitement and exuberance stemming from the air of courtship that underlay all activities (Kephart and Zellner, 1994:76). Eventually Sam might ask Mary Thompson, an older, more spiritually developed member of the community, to see if Sally were interested in an "interview" with him. If Mary thought that was a good idea, based on her knowledge of the spiritual development of the two, she would speak with Sally, and if Sally were amenable, an encounter might be arranged for the next evening, during which Sally would come to Sam's private living quarters for a few hours. Sally would not spend the night, however, and neither of them was permitted to talk or gossip about the encounter later (Fogarty, 1994:9). Furthermore, Sam and Sally were not permitted to develop special, selfish attachments to each other. And if they were seen together too often or if attempts to arrange interviews were too frequent, they were likely to be denied sexual arrangements by the intermediaries or asked to undergo "criticism" before the whole community or, if all else failed, they might be separated, with one being sent away to another of the Perfectionist settlements (Fogarty, 1994). Hence sex and unselfish love were meshed through religious principles of sharing in the mutual pursuit of perfection with God. "Special," or exclusive, love was regarded as a violation of those principles and was therefore a form of sin to be discouraged.

John Humphrey Noyes, the founder and charismatic leader who made the Perfectionist community so successful, believed that love was of two types, each sanctioned by God, but for different purposes. Amative love was for the pleasure of humans in the glorification of God, while propagative love was strictly for reproductive purposes. But to practice amative love without regard for potential reproductive outcomes was irresponsible. Propagative love was to be undertaken only with specific intent to produce children, and only then with careful consideration for both biological and spiritual improvement. Hence during much of the history of the Perfectionist movement, members of the community were prohibited from reproducing (as we will see later, through a process referred to as "male continence"). Only later, after achieving what Noyes regarded as an appropriate level of collective spirituality, did they deliberately engage in propagative love, guided by the principles of eugenics and spiritual betterment, which Noyes called "stirpiculture." When stirpiculture was begun, participating couples were chosen by a committee of community leaders, following the usual rule of ascending or descending fellowship. As a result, many of the "stirpiculfs" were fathered by older men in the community, who were regarded as more spiritual, including especially Noyes himself, who fathered nine of the fifty-eight community children (Parker, [1935] 1973:257).

Not only did the Perfectionists differentiate amative from propagative love and discourage propagative love except under very select conditions, they also held women in much higher regard than did the outside world. As a result, they thought it unacceptable for women to be burdened with constant childbearing and childrearing or to be subject to the sexual whims of their husbands. Noyes's attitudes about the relationship between the sexes and the value of women stemmed partly from his interpretation of scripture and partly from his own personal experience. His legal wife, Harriet, whom he married before the experiments in community living were begun and with whom he had a conventional relationship until they both later entered into a mutually agreed-upon complex marriage arrangement with other Perfectionists, experienced six pregnancies while they were practicing conventional marriage. Five of those pregnancies ended in stillbirths, which convinced Noyes that ordinary sexual relationships were selfish and wasteful. As a result he determined that good men should find another way. Out of that conviction grew a system of birth control practiced quite effectively by the entire Oneida community for over twenty years.

How you might ask, did they manage to avoid pregnancy, given that there was a high degree of sexual activity, with most of the women having sexual intercourse with different men every two to four days and some every day (Carden, 1969:51)? After all, it was the middle of the nineteenth century and methods of contraception were not well advanced. Yet even though the Oneida community contained more than 200 adults for much of its existence, there were only 31 children accidentally conceived during the 25 years before the period in which there were deliberate attempts to propagate. It has been estimated that this degree of effectiveness is even greater than that achieved by modern oral contraceptives (Foster, 1981:95). This remarkable result was accomplished by "male continence," a practice founded on the responsibility of men and rooted in self-control. Men were taught that unselfishness, and thereby Godliness, required them to avoid ejaculation both during sexual activities and after withdrawal. Among the Perfectionists, sexual "interviews" would proceed from foreplay through copulation but without the male allowing himself to reach orgasm.

There is some indication that males were permitted to ejaculate during intercourse with females who were past menopause but not with women still capable of becoming pregnant (Kephart and Zellner, 1994:76). Hence the system of sexual exchange, while advantageous for older males who were granted greater access to younger females (but without the privilege of orgasm), was clearly more advantageous for females generally and for older females in particular. The practice of male continence made it more likely that females could achieve orgasmic pleasure and at the same time avoid pregnancy. Moreover, since emission was permitted only with older females, and the system of ascending fellowship favored it, older women were thereby more likely to find sexual partners than women of the same age in the outside world. Apparently the males, under the instruction of Noyes, developed the ability of continence to a fine art. They even came to endorse it as both easy and a more pleasurable form of sexual activity (DeMaria, 1978:169).

Concern for the status of women extended beyond the sexual realm. Although females were by no means equal to males in the Perfectionist community, they were accorded far more equality than women in the larger society had. For one thing, males and females were not automatically relegated to sex-differentiated roles. Although men were generally thought to be more spiritual, spoke most often at community gatherings, and more often occupied decision-making roles, each person, male and female, was allowed and encouraged to pursue the activities that interested him or her, and there was much emphasis on seeking variety in all things, including type of work. As a result, women often worked alongside men in the various economic and sustenance activities of the community. While women almost always did the mending and cooking, they also could be found in the foundry, on construction crews, and in agricultural endeavors, and men often contributed to the kitchen and clean-up chores.

One method used by the Perfectionists to accomplish tedious tasks, particularly those that needed to be done in a short period of time, was for large numbers to voluntarily pitch in. These work "bees" were not only efficient, they were also regarded as fun, sociable occasions where large numbers of the community members, even the children, participated in and enjoyed community endeavors that took away from individual selfishness and focused on group welfare.

Another way in which the Oneidans were ahead of their time with respect to female rights concerned dress and hair styles. Early on, in one of his writings, John Humphrey Noyes noted that traditional female dress, which at that time was floor-length dresses with full skirts, was degrading, implying that a woman was not "a two-legged animal, but something like a churn, standing on castors!" He suggested that when women and men achieved the proper relationship to each other, women's and men's clothing would be similar, both simple and beautiful, and he implied that then contemporary young girls' clothing, with frocks and pantalets, might serve as a model. From that hint, the women of the community cut their dresses to just below the knee and donned a type of pantaloon under them that went from mid-thigh to the ankle. Similarly, they cut their hair to neck length when the general fashion for women was to have long hair, often hanging below the waist (Robertson, 1970:297–298). They justified the haircuts by reference to the Bible, which stated that women's hair is to serve only as a covering (not as an adornment). But since long hair was usually worn braided atop the head, it did not actually cover much. So short hair hanging down was justified as more in keeping with Biblical injunction, and it was certainly more convenient, since brushing and maintaining long hair was a major investment of any woman's time.

Overall, then, the Perfectionists could be regarded as among the most progressive in elevating the status of women. Though at that time there were feminist groups agitating for some women's rights, particularly the right to vote, it was left to the Oneidans to free women from "effeminacy," to encourage them to undertake "manly" tasks and seek activities that suited their interests, and to dress in ways that were practical. In addition, the Perfectionists emphasized the right of women to enjoy sex, with a variety of partners of their choice, largely free of the fear of pregnancy. When children did result,

Deviance in Everyday Life

The Perfectionists were believers in "women's liberation" long before it became popular in the twentieth century. One example shows how progressive they were for the times with respect to the issue of equality for women: a woman, Mrs. Harriet Joslyn, was superintendent of the Oneida silk mill and a member of the Board of Directors of the Company. She therefore had direct control and supervision over numerous male employees—at a time when women rarely were involved in the management of any business.

the mothers were liberated from the necessity of constant child care since this was delegated to rotating shifts of care givers, who provided for the needs and education of the children on behalf of the whole community. In the Oneida community, the children were cared for in what was called the Children's House, which was a set of large apartments in the main building on the grounds (Mansion House). The children were raised from birth to age 12 by care givers referred to as the Mothers and Fathers of Children's House. As a result, women were "freed from" the burden of child care; this "benefit," however, was not always so highly regarded by the mothers, some of whom were prone toward selfish "special love" for their own children (Robertson, 1970:313). Nonetheless, it did seem to work well since all members of the community took an interest in the welfare of the children, and parents contributed through visiting, and by taking their turns as care givers for all of the youngsters. All accounts suggest that the children were healthier, better educated, and better adjusted than most children in the larger society.

The Perfectionists believed in and practiced unselfish sharing of all things, especially economic goods and property. When the Oneida community was begun in 1848, the initial plan was for the people to support themselves through agricultural pursuits. This proved to be difficult, so they moved into various kinds of manufacturing in order to be able to sell items to the outside world. The first such venture occurred when Sewall Newhouse was admitted to the community. He had invented a new type of trap for fur-bearing animals, which he brought with him when he joined the group. Under his tutelage, manufacturing the trap became an assembly-line type of operation (Robertson, 1970:228). Sales worldwide made the Oneida community an economic success (Edmonds, 1948). Later the Perfectionists manufactured and sold a variety of other items, such as silk thread and handbags, and they continued to produce and sell in the open market various kinds of agricultural products, especially strawberries. Eventually the group became so successful economically that they needed to hire outside workers to keep the various enterprises going and to perform some of the onerous work. Outsiders were paid top wage, and they were afforded the most favorable working conditions of the time, including a nine-hour work day at a time when businesses outside the community were requiring up to 12 hours of labor per day.

Historical Overview

The basic tenets of Perfectionism—that humans were not born depraved but were freed from the bonds of nature and legality to seek perfection through relationships with God—were well known in New England in the early 1800s because of revival movements with famous preachers like Charles G. Finney. As a theology, however, Perfectionism was not well articulated or systematically integrated. As a result, all manner of behavior came to be justified in the name of this particular form of religion. Indeed, some Perfectionists used its basic tenets to justify unfettered sexual license and other undisciplined behavior, and as a result Perfectionism came to have a bad reputation. It was left to John Humphrey Noyes to systematize Perfectionist thought and to implement it in organized community life, although it never really lost its taint; some said that under Noyes' leadership, behavior in the community even came to fulfill the worst expectations of its foes.

Noyes was born in 1811 in Brattleboro, Vermont, the son of a prominent family. His father, also named John, at one time was a Congressman, and his mother, an intensely religious woman, was a cousin of Rutherford Hayes, who became president of the United States. Although shy, self-conscious, and unsure of himself, especially with women, Noyes was a precocious intellectual. As a result he entered Dartmouth at the age of 15 and graduated in 1830, at the age of 19. At first he tried his hand at legal work but was not much of a success. Meanwhile he was having the same trouble most young men his age were experiencing in relating to members of the opposite sex (Thomas, 1977:5–6). After one disturbing episode he made his way back to Putney, Vermont, where his family then lived. At his mother's urging, he attended a religious revival under Charles Finney and was converted. Soon he felt the call to the ministry and entered the seminary at Andover.

Not finding Andover to his liking, he transferred to Yale in 1832, where he was attracted to the teachings of a particular professor whose ideas contained some of the germs of Perfectionism. He graduated in 1833 and was granted a license to preach. For a while he struggled, trying to achieve the holy life through adherence to legalistic strictures of the Bible. Eventually he came to the realization that this legalistic approach was incorrect because spiritual perfection was already present with conversion. When he publicly declared himself without sin in 1834, Yale revoked his license to preach. After a period of soul searching and aimless drifting and inchoate preaching, Noyes finally settled back in Putney, where he proceeded to convert family, friends, and others to his new way of thinking. At first his converts associated through Bible study classes, but gradually over a 10- or 12-year period they evolved a form of communal living (Parker, [1935] 1973).

In the meantime, Noyes continued to tour and preach and to write his views in a publication sponsored by the Putney Perfectionist community. During this period he experienced another failure in love, when the object of his affections, Abigail Merwin, married another man. And in a letter to a friend about the incident, he detailed some of his ideas about ideal marriage. To him, of course, such a marriage would not involve exclusive love or exclusive sexual access. Without his permission, however, parts of the letter were published in a religious magazine called *The Battle-Axe*. The views expressed in the letter, along with editorial comment by the magazine, provoked negative public reaction, and as a result Noyes became well known and reviled. Even so, the publicity seemed to attract some converts. One of these was Harriet Holton, the granddaughter of the lieutenant governor of Vermont. She became Noyes's legal wife in 1838, albeit under terms of a private kind of mutually agreed-upon contract along Perfectionist lines.

For the next few years the community at Putney grew, as more converts were made and as Noyes consolidated the strands of communal living and asserted his authority. By 1843, the Putney commune numbered 39; perhaps one-third of those who had become associated with the group left at some point, most apparently because of the heat of criticism, especially from Noyes (Thomas, 1977:164–165). Finally, in 1846 complex marriage was introduced at Putney, at first among two couples, the Noyeses and the Cragins (Thomas, 1977:104–107). It soon spread to include others, but it never came to include the whole group because internal dissension and reactions from the outside community led to the demise of the Putney commune. Word of the new arrangements leaked to the outside world and stirred animosity, but the immediate trouble grew out of an effort of the group to take in three young women from Putney who had been converted, one of whom was only 15 years old (Foster, 1981:102). Complaints led to the issuance of indictments and the arrest of Noyes, who, after posting a $2,000 bond, fled to New York City. Not long after, most of the other members at Putney dispersed as well. It was 1847.

Within a few months followers at Oneida, New York, invited Noyes to join them, which he did, perhaps because Oneida was close to the Canadian border in case he had other run-ins with the law. And in 1848 other former residents of the commune at Putney began to regroup at Oneida. By the next year there were 87 people at Oneida, within another year there were 172, and in 1851 the Oneida community numbered 205, with close to another hundred in the sister community at Wallingford, Connecticut (Foster, 1981:103). In 1849, in the midst of this growth, however, Noyes moved to another locale, Willow Place, near Brooklyn, New York, although he returned periodically to assist the community, which was technically led by one of Noyes's close associates, John Miller. In 1854, with the death of this associate, Noyes took up more or less permanent residence at Oneida. But during the time he was living at Willow Place, the Oneida community underwent several years of turmoil while they were trying to work out communal arrangements, satisfactory means of practicing complex marriage, and relationships with the outside world. There was internal dissension consisting of insubordination, disloyalty, and pleasure seeking. There were also grand jury complaints about the community. Some members left the group. At one point in 1852, the community temporarily suspended the practice of complex marriage for about six months because it was offending outsiders, which from his Putney experience Noyes had learned was not wise.

In making Oneida his permanent residence in 1854, Noyes began a consolidation movement to bring the members of five different communities of Perfectionists into two locales—Oneida and Wallingford. For the next three years the Oneida community continued to struggle economically, as it had from the beginning, but it overcame most of its problems of communal living. Finally in 1857 it showed its first profit and from then on, it prospered economically and socially, at least until internal dissension began to emerge again in the 1870s. Stirpiculture, the system of eugenics, was begun in 1868, which many believe was the beginning of the end of the group. Nevertheless, the Oneida commune continued until 1880, when it transformed itself into a joint stock company and officially disbanded, after having abandoned complex marriage for good in 1879. The few years prior to dissolution were not smooth, being marked by increasing internal dissension and even conflict generated by an organized movement to contest the group's leadership, which was by then in the hands of Theodore, John Humphrey Noyes's oldest son (Robertson, 1972). Despite the unhappiness of the later years, after the breakup most of the members continued to live in Oneida, to work in its industries, and to consider themselves Perfectionists. Even up to the 1960s, a good proportion of residents of the Oneida area were descendants of members of the community that practiced Bible communism (Carden, 1969; Edmonds, 1948).

Basis of Internal Order

To coordinate all the activities undertaken by Perfectionists and to keep community members working together in the suppression of selfish interests, several unusual mechanisms were brought into play.

Charismatic Leadership

Like many unconventional groups or movements, the Perfectionists depended heavily on a charismatic leader. John Noyes, though he was apparently somewhat shy by nature, had a weak speaking voice, was reluctant to commit himself totally to any one thing, and in later years developed a hearing problem that made it difficult for others to communicate with him, was an exceptionally magnetic figure. Most who came in contact with him were impressed with his persuasive nature and general bearing, and many became believers and disciples because they saw him as an extraordinary man, if not a God figure. He wrote constantly for various publications produced by the Perfectionists themselves, elaborating Perfectionist philosophy, addressing practical problems of the community, and countering misinformation promulgated by outsiders. Moreover, Noyes often took part in group discussions about community concerns and philosophical issues, usually persuading others to his point of view, even though all members, theoretically, had equal input to decision making. Through his example, teachings, and guidance, Noyes was able to inspire his followers to seek God, to put community concerns ahead of selfish interests, and to resolve potential conflicts in the collective interest. As later events proved, Noyes's leadership was the crucial component for the success of the Oneida experiment (Robertson, 1972:14–15), though other things were also important. When he became unable to continue his leadership, the group lost much of its cohesion, and within a fairly short period of time it broke up.

Collective Assembly

But charismatic leadership was not the only thing that made the Perfectionist organization workable; many utopian groups that failed had had good, charismatic leaders. It was part of Noyes's genius that he studied the other utopian communities that preceded his in order to discover the secrets to success. There appear to have been four things besides charismatic leadership that made the Oneida community work. One was the practice of gathering all members of the community together each evening in the assembly hall of the main building, the Mansion House. In these gatherings people discussed community issues; heard presentations, sometimes by Noyes himself; socialized; were entertained; debated philosophical and religious issues; and made collective decisions about matters of concern to the community. It was something like a daily town hall meeting in which there was the appearance, even if not the reality, of complete democracy. Such collective gatherings and collective decision making served to unite the community and keep people aware of the moral necessity of unselfishness. Indeed, the theme of self-sacrifice for the group was so prevalent that on one occasion a visitor touring the Mansion House inquired about the unusual but pleasant odor and was told that it was the smell of "crushed selfishness."

Mutual Criticism

A second practice that helped the Oneidans thrive as a community was something similar to present-day "group therapy." During a brief stay in the theology school at Andover, Noyes had become acquainted with a practice among some of the ministerial students of meeting regularly for the purpose of identifying each other's faults. He saw this as an especially useful procedure and dubbed it "mutual criticism" (Levine and Bunker, 1975). All members of the Perfectionist community, including the leaders, were urged and encouraged to submit regularly to criticism and to participate in criticism of others. In these sessions the person sat quietly before the assembled group or a smaller set of designated critics while different people in turn called attention to ways in which he or she might be failing as a person, a community member, or a religious adherent. If the individual were guilty of slothful work habits, this would be pointed out; if he or she were succumbing to special love, it would be noted; and if he or she were manifesting some selfish interest in items of property or certain foods or was not showing due regard for others or was being contentious, he or she would be admonished (Robertson, 1970:128–149). This constant public scrutiny and evaluation, particularly since it was done in the spirit of love and improvement rather than malice, apparently had a powerful corrective effect both on the individual being criticized and on the group as a whole. And sometimes when offending individuals did not offer themselves for criticism, it was urged upon them. Even illness was thought to be due to lack of holiness and the occasion for mutual criticism (Robertson, 1970). This practice, then, was both cathartic and unifying, as evidenced by the fact that when it fell into disuse in later years the integration of the community also suffered.

Religious Commitment

A third element that contributed to the success of the Oneida community was the religious commitment of the members, a commitment that was stoked by constant reminders of religious duty. Those who as adults became community participants were, for the most part, deeply religious people (DeMaria, 1978). They believed passionately in their principles and were willing to face persecution and ridicule to defend and practice them. And as the community grew, it made a serious effort to take in only those who demonstrated faith, commitment, and personal qualities of self-sacrifice. Many people, of course, tried to join the Perfectionists after the community succeeded and became known. Some were genuinely attracted to the life style, others were taken with the religious ideas; some were curious adventure seekers, and others thought the community offered easy personal advantages that could not be obtained in the outside world—"free sex," economic maintenance, and social support. Most applicants were screened and denied membership; some were taken in on a probationary basis but were denied full privileges, particularly of participating in complex marriage, until they proved themselves; and some became full participants only to be dismissed later or to leave on their own. This careful selectivity paid dividends in helping generate internal order.

However, there was one segment of the community that was not selectively chosen—the children. New members sometimes brought children with them. In addition, a few children were unintentionally produced during the years when only amative love was permitted. Also, there were children born as a result of the stirpicultural experiment. Although the community took collective pride in the children and tried to socialize them to the faith and to the communal system at Oneida, this effort was never as successful in producing committed members as was the method of religious conversion. As a result, in later years when dissension arose in the group, part of it stemmed from the unwillingness of the younger members who had grown up in the community to fully accept the system of self-denial and complex marriage. They had not become committed to it through religious devotion (Fogarty, 1994).

General Satisfaction

The final element contributing to internal order was the ability of the Perfectionist family to provide for the needs of its members. Most of those attracted to Perfectionism were intrigued because it promised spiritual security, but it later became attractive through its delivery of economic and social security. The early 1800s were a confusing time, marked by generally unstable economic conditions expressed in frequent recessions and by a plethora of new ideas and religious principles. Those who became Perfectionists found a solution to the chaos around them. A religious faith that guaranteed union with God—in the present rather than in the hereafter; an economic system that fed, clothed, and sheltered all equally regardless of personal success; and a social system built on collective social support and caring, unselfish love, and sexual satisfaction constituted a magnetic construction that bound the members in an alliance worth the cooperation it required. People generally tended to behave themselves and to conform to the expectations of others in the community because they did not wish to jeopardize the good things that the total experience offered.

Organized Deviance

We are discussing Perfectionism as a form of fully organized deviance, so it is instructive to consider systematically the kinds of deviance that were practiced and for which full organization became necessary. Remember that deviant behavior is that which a majority of some group regards as unacceptable or that typically evokes a collective response of a negative type, either action by authorities that reflects disapproval or some collective action by a larger social entity within which the offending party or parties is encompassed. Therefore, the issue is whether the Perfectionists regularly (so as to need organization) did things that most people in the nineteenth-century United States regarded as wrong or unacceptable or that inspired agents of social control to do things to prevent those behaviors or at least to show disapproval of them. Having read the description and history presented above, you can probably guess what were considered to be the deviant behaviors of the Oneida community, simply by applying contemporary standards.

Deviant Behavior

Heresy

One of the main deviant acts that members of the Perfectionist group continually committed was to challenge the tenets of conventional religion. By declaring themselves "perfect" and free of sin, as John Humphrey Noyes did early in his ministry, the Perfectionists were committing heresy, according to religious officials of most of the established churches, as well as many ordinary church believers. Such disapproval was indicated by overt actions of religious figures, as well as by rumor, talk, and written commentary in newspapers, letters, and books of the day (Robertson, 1970). Visitors to the community often made remarks suggesting that the Perfectionist heresy was even broader than it actually was. They attributed all manner of religious unorthodoxy to the Oneidans. To illustrate, the community had a reservoir of fresh water protected by a mound of dirt. On one occasion three different visitors asked what it was, and each was told by a different Perfectionist that it was a reservoir. The visitors were later overheard whispering that the community members were well schooled to tell the same cover story, for the visitors continued to believe that the mound of dirt was some kind of monument to a pagan deity.

Further evidence of the reaction against heresy was the fact that Noyes was stripped of his license to preach shortly after obtaining it because of the publication of his views on perfection, and later he was reviled after one of his private letters to a friend was published without his permission. In that letter he set forth his belief that legal marriage was selfish and that Godliness required the removal of restraints on the sexual freedom of a partner. This caused a storm of reaction in religious and other publications, where the Perfectionists were called licentious free lovers. And throughout the history of the Oneida community, there were periodic attacks attributing evil motives and ungodly character to those who were part of the Perfectionist family.

Adultery and Sexual Promiscuity

Not only did the Perfectionists practice heresy, but, according to the social norms of the time (and now as well), they were adulterers and sexually promiscuous. Since complex marriage involved sexual relationships among people who were not legally married to each other, it offended the consciences of ordinary people, who believed that married people should have exclusive sexual relations within the marriage, based on love between the marital partners, and that unwedded people should refrain from sex altogether until they were married. The Perfectionist philosophy of complex marriage, in which all are married to each other and all are equal participants in living out the Kingdom of God, even implied incest. Although the small group at Putney who first participated in complex marriage included Noyes's two sisters and their husbands, no firm evidence suggests that incestuous sexual contact was practiced (Thomas, 1977:109). But many outsiders assumed that life in the community was a continuous sexual orgy, openly pursued and without restraint. In any event, in the Oneida community, a given woman had numerous sexual encounters with different men over her lifetime—much different from the general society at the time.

The Perfectionists were often attacked in the press and in religious publications. In addition, on several occasions legal action against them was sought by people in the larger community. When the original community resided in Putney, Vermont, its practices, particularly the attempt to bring three young women into the group from the outside community, as well as the content of the lectures and writings of Noyes, caused such an uproar that a warrant for his arrest was issued. Noyes and other members of the community fled to different locales, leading to the breakup of the Putney community and ultimately to the establishment of the larger and longer-lasting community at Oneida. About four years after the establishment of the Oneida community, in 1852, attacks by a religious paper, *The Observer*, and other news sources were so intense that the Perfectionists suspended the practice of complex marriage for a period of time until there was "a change of public feeling" that would extend the "area of freedom" (Foster, 1981). The final dissolution of the community in 1880 was stimulated by petitions to the New York legislature for legislation to put the Perfectionists out of business.

Abuse of the Young

The principle of ascending and descending fellowship justified to the Perfectionists the introduction, by older people, of young people into complex marriage. However, to the outside world, this was a very bad thing. It was not just a form of sinful and illegal sexuality, it smacked of rape and exploitation. Since some of the girls were quite young when first brought into the complex marriage scheme, many outsiders assumed they were coerced, and in any case the disparities in the age of participants implied abuse of the young. Both rape and abuse were contrary to general norms, so the Perfectionists were thought to be continuously engaging in some of the most serious forms of deviance. Furthermore, because most people regarded child rearing as a responsibility of the parents, and believed that children required the special love that normally prevails between parents and children, they looked askance at the collective child rearing of the Perfectionists. Though there was no evidence of physical abuse or neglect, the separation of the children and the denial of special relationships between them and their parents were widely viewed as unacceptable.

Immodesty

The prevailing norms in the nineteenth-century northeastern United States required women to dress and behave modestly. They were to wear full-length dresses, to have long hair, to engage in "feminine" types of work, to be submissive and subordinate to men, and to be passive rather than aggressive in sexual matters. The fact that the Perfectionist women violated all of these norms made the group quite deviant in the eyes of many outsiders. Following the teachings of Noyes, women in the Oneida community were elevated from a submissive role to a plane almost equal to that of men. They seldom spoke in group gatherings, but they were at least theoretically equal decision makers. They took pride in pursuing "manly" activities and treated "effeminacy" as an evil to be overcome. And, of course, they dressed unconventionally and bobbed their hair. Moreover, while the women probably did not take the initiative in arranging sexual interviews, they certainly were aggressive in courtship. Furthermore, they were independent, at least theoretically, in being able to refuse sexual entreaties, even from higher-status males.

Sharing Property

Finally, the Oneidans pursued economic and sustenance goals in ways that did not meet the approval of the rest of society. Private ownership of property and pursuit of individual wealth were the larger society's dominant motifs at the time, just as they are now. The fact that Perfectionists personally gave up their own wealth to join the group and during the time they resided within the group did not own anything raised suspicions among non-Perfectionists. This common ownership even extended to toys, which were shared by all; individual children were denied even the right to possess a personal favorite, such as a doll (Robertson, 1970:311). Many outsiders assumed that Perfectionist leaders were charlatans and thieves, taking advantage of their followers, and that group members were dupes or that they were somehow coerced. It was recorded that visitors would often inquire about the location of the dungeon, on the suspicion that community members had to be punished to make them conform to the rules of work and sharing.

Fending Off External Agents of Social Control

Clearly, the Perfectionists were practitioners of terrible deviance by the standards of their time, and perhaps even by current social standards. It is important, therefore, to consider how they managed to survive for over 40 years, in several different locales, given their direct challenge to conventional social norms. Despite the fact that the original community at Putney was dissolved in face of legal threat and that in the early 1850s several members of the Oneida community were called to defend their practices before grand juries, not one community member was ever actually arrested and incarcerated; their communities were not overrun and burned by angry opponents; nobody was lynched; and, in fact, the community at Oneida was tolerated as a site for popular visits by interested citizens and curiosity seekers, sometimes as many as several hundred on a given day. The Perfectionists, therefore, did things that were considered bad, disgusting, loathsome, and evil, and they provoked much wrath, but very little actual collective response of a negative type was forthcoming. How did they manage to get away with it? They did it with the use of five techniques.

Relatively Few Complainers

During most of the history of the group the communist system of sharing seemed to work exceptionally well to ensure that almost all members were happy and satisfied (Robertson, 1970). It was a voluntary system rooted in religious faith and justified theologically. People participated because it was rewarding and satisfying. Consequently, not very many cooperated with outside authorities who were out to get the group, and there was no corroborating evidence for the wild rumors that existed. Moreover, there were few complaining parties from within the group that would have justified legal action or have inspired other methods of attack. There were instances of dissatisfaction and defection, especially at Putney, Vermont, and during the first few years at Oneida. But after the initial period of turbulence, remarkable stability in membership ensued, with only two or three departing per year, on average. Most of those who left on their own or with pressure from the group itself apparently felt little bitterness, perhaps because they were allowed to reclaim the wealth and property they had originally brought to the community. In one instance a civil suit was brought by a member wanting to leave the community who sought compensation for his labor during the time he had been with the family. Although the Oneida system provided for all of a person's needs in exchange for labor, the court nevertheless honored his claim. But the very fact that it reached the court made it an unusual case.

Exemplary Deportment

Under Noyes's leadership, the Perfectionists were careful to present themselves publicly with grace and good manners as hard working, well educated, well spoken, honest in business dealings, selfless, and with gentle natures. They did not flaunt their sexual activities, not even allowing public kissing of any kind (Estlake, 1900:63). They did not even speak of sexual activities in the open among themselves, much less with outsiders. They opened their community to visitors, who were accommodated with guides, entertainment, refreshments (usually strawberries and cream); later on they provided visitors a full meal. In the early years these accommodations, though disruptive and expensive, were made without charge, but later an admission fee to cover the cost of food was assessed. The purpose was to say to outsiders: "Come see for yourself. We are decent God-fearing people who conduct our lives in an orderly and sensible manner. The outrageous things you may have heard about us are not true, though we stand by our principles and are willing to provide justifications for them." Consequently, enemies could find no direct confirmation of the alleged evil that pervaded the Oneida community.

Good Relations With Neighbors

The Perfectionists made it a point to cultivate good relations with their neighbors. When they employed people from the outside, they treated them exceptionally well. The employees were afforded good working conditions, were paid top wage, and were not exploited, since members of the community worked alongside them performing similar jobs. The Perfectionists bought materials, foodstuffs, and finished products from outsiders, and in such transactions they proved themselves to be honest and of good character. In addition, the Perfectionists sold their own products in the open market, and, again, though careful to drive a good bargain, they became noted for providing high-quality products and for scrupulous business practices. They were quick to help neighbors in times of crisis, to pay their taxes, and to contribute to outside societal causes. One such cause was the War Between the States: the Perfectionists contributed extra money to the U.S. government. Because of a lucky mistake, however, no members were actually drafted (Robertson, 1970:111–112). Probably due to such relationships, when trouble arose, there always seemed to be defenders from the outside who would step forward to vouch for the economic contribution of the Perfectionists and for their good characters as individuals and employers.

Accommodation

Mindful of the near disastrous experience at Putney, and consistent with the effort to develop and maintain good relations with neighbors, the Perfectionists made it clear that they did not wish to offend others. They made no attempt to convert locals, and sometimes, whenever trouble began to brew, the community would temporarily suspend whatever activities seemed to be the focus of the outsiders' complaints. In 1852 they discontinued complex marriage for a period of time in response to outside pressure, and eventually they totally abandoned it a year before completely dissolving the community in 1880. Thus, though the Perfectionists were strongly committed to their beliefs and practices and defended them intellectually with dignity and strength, they were not arrogant enough to ignore sentiments or threats from outsiders, nor were they so fanatical that they persisted in the face of potentially overwhelming external pressure. Indeed, the final dissolution of the group, though a result of many things, was immediately in response to proposed state legislation that would shut them down and perhaps prosecute them.

Rapid Response to Attack

Finally, from the very beginning Noyes developed a habit of responding to criticism rapidly, usually in print, with well-developed counterarguments and theological rationales. He maintained this practice until his waning years, when leadership of the group was passed to his son, Theodore. As a result, most of the external attacks were fended off as based on false assumptions, and the attacks against actual beliefs and behaviors were usually diverted by well-argued contentions that these beliefs and behaviors were Biblically founded, at least as Noyes interpreted the Bible. Such "rapid response" served both to defend the group from enemies outside and to reinforce internal group solidarity, since the various publications in which such defenses appeared were widely read by the Perfectionists themselves. Knowledge of attacks from outside made the group aware of the need to stick together to protect itself, and the solid responses gave them personal reinforcement as well as assurance of the rightness of their mission.

Summary

It is clear, then, that the Perfectionists were organized to deal with a hostile environment, and through such organization Noyes was able to employ effective techniques of defense. But how well organized were they, according to the criteria set forth earlier? Remember that organization cannot be directly measured but must be inferred from indirect characteristics and processes. As we will show, they were exceptionally well organized.

How Organized Was Perfectionism?

Sociality

Organization is most likely to exist when some form of deviance requires more than one person in interaction, or at least when the deviance is typically manifest among sets of interacting people. If practitioners need others in order to perform the deviance, they will ordinarily establish the features of regular interaction that reflect organization. And sometimes, even when others are not needed directly, the fact that the behavior in question is under attack will mean that those who wish to do it will find association with others helpful. Since the Perfectionists constantly and repeatedly practiced at least five forms of deviant behavior that invited negative reactions from the outside world, it was more or less essential for them to associate with each other for protection and support, even if their religious ideals had not called for close association. Moreover, at least four of their characteristic deviances could not be performed alone: complex marriage (called adultery, "free love," or licentiousness by outsiders, and in modern terminology might be called "swinging"); collective child rearing, with prohibitions against strong parental involvement; sexual involvement of young people with older adults; and sharing all things in common. As a result, Perfectionism inherently involved a high degree of sociality on a regular basis, one mark of organization.

❖ ❖ ❖ ❖   ## Pervasiveness

The practice of Perfectionism was a full-time activity. People could not be Perfectionists only on Sundays, or at night, or when it might be convenient. Living, loving, and working were inextricably linked as ongoing and pervasive activities within a "family" context. Community life as a Perfectionist required constant study, self-sacrifice, and participation; and it involved total commitment of personal resources. Practically every thought and every deed, twenty-four hours per day, 365 days per year, were infused with the peculiar forms of deviance characteristic of the Perfectionists. They were literally consumed with the trappings of deviance; such pervasiveness signals a high degree of organization.

Communication

The Perfectionists not only shared property, mates, and values, but they talked about it extensively among themselves, on an abstract philosophical level. They met in collective assembly every evening, where theology, business, and practical problems of everyday living were discussed and where "home talks" by Noyes were given. In addition, almost all read the publications of the group, which were considered essential to maintain even in periods of economic difficulties. These publications contained statements and interpretations by Noyes, as well as other materials. Furthermore, the various Perfectionist communities, including ones at Wallingford, Connecticut, and Brooklyn, New York, as well as others, all shared correspondence and read the groups' publications. Although one could not say the Perfectionists had a separate and distinct language, they did share an understanding of unique meanings for ordinary words, and they did more or less invent new terms to refer to their own practices and beliefs. Words like "complex marriage," "special love," "stirpiculture," "interviews," "ascending fellowship," and "mutual criticism" had special meaning to Perfectionists, so explaining to outsiders what the terms really meant was difficult. Furthermore, the Perfectionists had a peculiar way of conveying meaning to each other by reference to Biblical contexts (Foster, 1981).

Differentiation and Coordination

One of the key hallmarks of organization is the degree to which roles and statuses are differentiated and diverse activities are coordinated in a systematic way. While the Perfectionists endorsed sharing in all things, elevated women above their usual status, and practiced a remarkable degree of democracy and voluntary cooperation, they did not completely enshrine the principle of equality; in fact, their theological scheme itself provided for considerable differentiation. First, all were ordered by the principle of ascending and descending fellowship. Some were, thereby, holier and of higher status than others. This difference in status underlay patterns of participation in decision making and in complex marriage, with the older, more spiritual members exercising more influence and power in debates about how to deal with various things and in having greater access and success in arranging sexual interviews.

The difference in status was reflected in who served on important committees, which supervised various community activities like industrial production and stirpiculture. Even though the group appeared to govern itself with much mutual discussion, debate, trial and error, and free reign, in the final analysis, all looked to Noyes for direction and ultimate instruction. In fact, Noyes himself described the Kingdom of God, of which the Oneida community was the prototype, as an absolute monarchy with authority coming from above but modulated by concern for the interests and feelings of those below (Foster, 1981:85). Thus, an ostensibly egalitarian community was actually stratified, and individuals who in theory were free spirits and free lovers were regulated by coordination of a fairly predictable form. And in this way, the group was able to act in concert, whether to collectively produce traps or travel bags, to entertain visitors, to defend itself from attack, or to suppress selfishness. Hence, as indicated by the group's degree of differentiation and coordination, the Oneidans were well organized.

Culture

Culture represents all those things shared by a group of continuously interacting people that are handed down from one generation to another through teaching and learning. In this, the Perfectionists were rich indeed. They shared a unique set of religious ideas and values, which they learned initially from John Humphrey Noyes and which they taught to newcomers to the family, whether children born to the group or people inducted through conversion. They shared, and passed on, a peculiar way of managing economic problems, of differentiating work by interest and talent rather than by gender or status, and, of course, their particular means of sharing marital partners and later use of planned reproduction. They had a peculiar style of dress, at least for women; an unusual manner of child rearing; uncommon ways of living, including eating only two meals a day, residing in private living quarters, meeting daily after work for community activities, sharing work collectively (frequent "bees"); and as already noted, a somewhat strange language or at least strange taxonomy. Perhaps one of the most distinct cultural traits—for other groups had practiced some type of free love and promoted eugenics—was the use of mutual criticism. In modern terms, we might say they engaged in frequent, if not constant, group therapy.

Self-Identity

A key indirect indicator of the degree of organization among practitioners of deviance is the extent to which the deviance serves as a source of psychological identity, that is, the degree to which the deviant activity helps define who the person is in his or her own mind and in his or her social relationships. By this criterion, the Perfectionists were extremely well organized. Simply by virtue of the fact that they withdrew into easily identified enclaves, braved the animosity of most people in the external world, and, when called upon, gave unstinting testimony to their beliefs and practices suggests that the Perfectionists used their deviance as a major source of personal identity. Furthermore, by participating in the Perfectionist communities and making no secret of it, individuals were setting themselves up for permanent stigma. A woman who might leave the group would be regarded in all future situations as an adulteress, or "loose woman." The stigma was even sharper for women who bore children without a particular father having been identified, much less having been designated as the legal parent of the child. Yet, Perfectionists gladly accepted this cost in proudly proclaiming their faith, at times even resisting strong attempts by outsiders to "rescue" them.

Philosophical Integration

Perfectionist philosophy was broad, covering all realms of nature from the relationship between humans and God to the relationships among humans. It provided a rationale for all the deviances practiced by the Perfectionists in trying to live as they believed people lived in heaven, and it provided for its own reward—heaven on earth. It clearly identified an ingroup (the believers) and an outgroup (the rest of the world), and it was systematic enough to cover all contingencies that might arise. Noyes was able to find Biblical support for anything he and the group decided to do. Of course, they did not make such decisions on a whim and then seek philosophical support. Rather, the religious and philosophical principles served as guides in discussions of action. Nevertheless, the philosophy was so well crafted and integrated that it could sanction everything from complete absence of propagation to eugenically guided reproduction; from group sharing of sex partners to complete separation from sexual activities; from seeking of interesting new experiences to self-sacrifice and denial; from prohibitions on "special" love to almost idolatrous adoration of Noyes. The sharing of such a philosophy was both an outgrowth of organization and an aid to its maintenance.

Social Control

The Perfectionists were able to succeed where other utopian groups failed partly because they had an effective system of internal social control to deal with everyday community problems, such as jealousy, laziness, greed, selfishness, or the violation of operative rules, such as talking openly of sexual matters. Recall that social control involves the application of positive and negative sanctions. The most effective of such sanctions are usually informal. Among the Perfectionists, "informal negative sanctions" were actually institutionalized in the form of regular sessions of mutual criticism. People were expected to volunteer to be criticized, but on occasion they might be asked to undergo it. Obviously, since they lived and worked in close alliance, all were subject to observation and evaluation by everybody else.

All indications are that it was an excruciating experience to face the whole community, or a select committee of critics, and have different individuals point out personal faults and misbehaviors; the object of the criticism just sat quietly and pondered what was being said (Carden, 1969:73–74). Yet mutual criticism was widely regarded as both corrective and cathartic (Levine and Bunker, 1975). Those who were criticized were often made aware of misdeeds of which they had not even been cognizant. Even though the objects of criticism may have disagreed in their hearts with what was said, the mutual interdependence of the group was such that a member being criticized thought it important to correct the defects that were perceived by others. Criticism was especially good at disturbing smug self-satisfaction; the one criticized usually hastened to make amends and to improve (Estlake,

1900:67–68). And it left the person with a sense of having been cleansed and purified because the criticisms were not malicious but were instead administered in the spirit of love and constructive anticipation, for all members could count on being subject to the same treatment sooner or later.

As important as mutual criticism was, it did not exhaust the methods of negative informal control. There was also some reliance on interpersonal persuasion for identifying misbehavior and getting it corrected. Thus, a spiritual elder might point out to a less spiritual person the error of her ways and remonstrate with her about why the offending behavior was wrong and what she should do about it. Such interpersonal intervention was especially effective when undertaken by Noyes, himself. This is illustrated by an occasion in the early days of the community at Putney before complex marriage was instituted. A couple of people not married to each other were involved in a secret liaison. When Noyes learned of it, he spoke with the two and rebuked them for their dishonesty and selfishness. This criticism led to confession and repentance. Later, however, Noyes was drawn to the same woman, and feeling guilty about an embrace, he insisted the two confess and discuss it with the other members of the group. Out of that discussion grew the first practice of complex marriage (Foster, 1981).

Interdependence served as an important underpinning for everyday informal control by way of positive sanctions. Apparently, the cooperation of other Perfectionists was somewhat contingent on an individual's conformity to group rules and adherence to the group's values. Since prestige was accorded to those viewed as being of higher spirituality, and since spirituality was the basis for association, especially for response to sexual overtures (the principle of ascending-descending fellowship), it is clear that the potential reactions of others served as a powerful force for inducing individuals to strive for behavioral perfection. Not only did conformity put a person in line to influence decisions by allowing her or him to serve on important committees, it generated favorable response from others in a variety of situations.

One area in which group approval was especially important was the system of sexual exchange, which was used as a central organizing focus and a method of social control. The use of intermediaries to arrange sexual encounters was done not just to avoid awkwardness and to permit females to refuse; it also served as a mechanism for monitoring, which is indicated by the fact that each sexual encounter was recorded (Carden, 1969:54). Hence a man was more advantaged in the scheme of complex marriage if he was known as a person of high spirituality, a reputation he acquired by conformity to the group's rules and endorsement of their values. An unspiritual man might rarely or never find a favorable response to his attempts to arrange "interviews," either because the woman would refuse the initiative or because the intermediary would advise against it (DeMaria, 1978:173–174). Similarly, a woman might benefit or suffer from the system of complex marriage depending on whether she was seeking the higher spiritual plane, especially if she were not physically attractive. Or a person who misbehaved might find himself somewhat isolated because others would wish to avoid an association of extreme "descending fellowship," either in work situations or in ordinary interaction, such as conversation around the dinner table or in the assembly hall during collective get-togethers in the evening.

In addition to informal control, the Perfectionists employed several techniques of formal control. The community prided itself on being democratic and encouraged full participation by all, but it was also organized into formal committees that oversaw various activities and made certain decisions. Such decisions flowed from open discussion and much communal agonizing with the affected parties, but the committees did accomplish a control purpose. For instance, a person might request a new job assignment, but if a committee, through debate and response with the person, came to the conclusion that the transfer was for selfish purposes, the request might be denied. And decision-making committees sometimes intervened without a request. If a person was manifesting too great a tendency toward special love for another person and was unable to overcome that weakness, he or she might be transferred from one community to another, at least for a time, until he or she could gain better control (Fogarty, 1994). And sometimes misbehavior would result in formal denial of the privilege of participating in complex marriage.

The ultimate formal sanction, however, was expulsion from the community. Those who could not, or would not, conform were required to leave. Whatever goods they brought with them when they joined were returned, though not always immediately. Apparently, such departures were usually smooth, although in one instance, a misbehaving man was literally thrown out of a second-story window of the Mansion House into a snow bank (Parker, [1935] 1973:223). Since community members depended totally on each other for survival, and benefitted in personal satisfaction from association with the family, the threat of rejection was potent.

The Perfectionists helped individuals internalize religious principles, and encouraged them to rely on those principles for guidance in seeking spiritual growth, which meant conformity to shared group standards. Moreover, they tried hard to select potential comrades who had the personal commitment and temperament for "family" living; they delayed full participation until such qualities were proven.

Recruitment

The Perfectionists were equipped for systematic recruitment. First, Noyes was a minister who, early in his career, toured the Northeast spreading his particular brand of the gospel. He continued to preach even after the Oneida community was thriving, sometimes delivering Perfectionist sermons to outside audiences. After a time, however, there was no longer any attempt to actively recruit new members for community life. In addition, the Perfectionists regularly published and distributed documents presenting their message. At first, such publications were a drain on the community's resources, but members considered it important to maintain them, even during times when finances were most scarce. Furthermore, individual Perfectionists, not all of whom lived in a community, no doubt witnessed to individuals on a regular basis. Finally, the steady stream of visitors to the community at Oneida provided an opportunity for the Perfectionists to make a statement about their beliefs and values. Such proselytizing was apparently quite successful in that there were many new converts, a large number of whom applied for membership in one of the various communities. Although only a few were permitted to enter the communist lifestyle, many nevertheless embraced the beliefs of Perfectionism and pursued its tenets as best they could while carrying on regular patterns of life apart from the community.

Another form of systematic recruitment involved biological reproduction and socialization of the young. Some of the adults who came into the Perfectionist fold brought their children with them. These children, of course, were not committed to the religious principles of Perfectionism, nor did they have identities linked to participation in Perfectionist activities. They had to be trained and taught, and in time most of them became full-fledged members with full rights. Children born to community members had to be trained as well. Although only a small number of children were conceived during the period the group was avoiding propagative love and practicing male continence, some were, and they had to be socialized just as were the children who came in with their parents. Later, of course, when the group turned to stirpiculture, several dozen children were born. Thus, even though proselytizing was the primary and most effective method of recruitment to Perfectionism, reproduction and socialization of the children by community members served as a secondary means of enlarging the group. This secondary method proved to be less effective, and as a result full commitment to the principles of Perfectionism was lacking in later years before the group dissolved. Most authorities attribute much of the dissension that contributed to the group's ultimate demise to these younger people, who chafed under an imposed system to which they had not voluntarily subscribed.

Summary

The Perfectionists exhibited an extremely high degree of organization. The very essence of their religion and life style involved practice and promotion of particular forms of deviance, as defined by the larger society of which they were a part. According to their enemies, they encouraged heresy from established religion; they were adulterers; they abused children; their women were uppity, immodest, and unladylike; and they shared property and economic resources rather than pursuing individual wealth. In order to engage in these forms of deviance and survive in the face of opposition, they had to be well organized.

Evidence of this organization is obvious from the collective, communal life style based on regular interaction among as many as 250 people who resided at the main community in Oneida, New York. This extended "family" network meant that there was a high degree of sociality and that the practice of Perfectionist deviance was a pervasive, all-consuming concern. The lines of communication, both spoken and written, were well oiled, based as they were on values and understandings common to all members of the group, and at least a partial set of unique words. Activities and roles were differentiated and coordinated along channels defined by the principle of ascending/descending fellowship; with the exception of the position held by the leader, John Humphrey Noyes, however, the group was not rigidly stratified. Internal order and conformity were guaranteed by effective systems of informal and formal social control, especially the collective practice of mutual criticism and the group's informal reaction to a member's behavior indicating his or her spiritual superiority or inferiority. All these features were embodied in a distinct and unusual culture reflecting the strong tendency of Perfectionists to develop their personal identities around involvement in the peculiar deviances of their group.

In addition, everything was justified and flowed from an intricately constructed, thoroughly integrated, religiously based philosophy rooted in specific interpretations of New Testament Biblical injunctions. These guiding values served as a basis for systematic recruitment of new members through proselytizing as well as for the socialization of children who came into the group with their parents or who were born to members.

It was almost impossible, then, to think of Perfectionism in terms of individual behaviors or to imagine it apart from its organizational context. It was what people did together that constituted deviance, and to explain and understand those behaviors, one has to pay attention to the group nature of what was going on. And even though it might be possible to explain each Perfectionist's behavior with one or another of the individualistically oriented theories you will encounter later in this book, such explanations would make no sense at all without an understanding of the organizational context of this behavior.

Organized Crime

Another example of a deviance whose practitioners presumably are extensively organized is that of "organized crime." However, there is dispute about the extent to which organized crime is "organized." In fact, some argue that the very notion of organized crime is a myth.

Most of us have an inkling of what is meant by organized crime because of the mass media. You are probably familiar with films such as *The Godfather* (and its sequels) or any number of others, like *Wiseguys*, or *Bugsy* (the story of the gangster Benjamin "Bugsy" Siegel). Moreover, some of you will probably have read one of the numerous books that describe organized crime. They include Peter Maas's *The Valachi Papers*, *King of the Gypsies*, and *Underboss*, Mario Puzo's *The Godfather* and *The Last Don*, and Gay Talese's *Honor Thy Father*. As you know from these sources, organized crime is crime committed by lawbreakers allied in businesslike entities dedicated to systematic, efficient criminal enterprise.

Beliefs and Practices

It is difficult to determine the beliefs and values of the practitioners of organized crime, or to ascertain if there is a distinct culture among them. That is because organized criminals are dedicated to secrecy. Unlike the Perfectionists who, for the most part, engaged in legal behaviors and were generally inclined to make their belief system known (if only to protect themselves against misunderstanding and to recruit new members), the activities of organized crime are illegal and the long-term existence of a syndicate depends on concealing itself from outsiders. The practitioners of organized crime do not maintain a newsletter to broadcast their activities or beliefs, nor do they maintain documents detailing their practices and views. The syndicate's "code of conduct" is unwritten, so there are no solid data about it. Our knowledge of their belief system is derived from government investigations of their activities, wiretaps of organized crime figures by law enforcement officials, and the testimony of a few informants.

Scholars of organized crime (Cressey, 1969) suggest that its practitioners share the belief that legitimate law has no moral force, that it is useful and desirable for "family" members to band together to promote and protect their own interests, which are often contrary to the interests of those who make and enforce the law. In these pursuits, practitioners are bound together by the principle of omerta—family members must stick together against all outside forces and maintain a complete shield of silence. Members of organized crime networks are supposed to do as they are instructed by their superiors in the family without question so that the illicit profits of the family can be maximized. They are never to speak of family business to outsiders; they are strictly forbidden from taking disputes outside the family; and they must not raise a hand against another family member. In other words, the organized crime "family" becomes the recruit's own family, and the most important principles of the code of conduct, or belief system, are to serve and protect the family at all costs and to maintain secrecy. If caught by the police, one must not snitch, even if it means long-term imprisonment. Those who violate these principles face almost certain death at the hands of other family members (Winslow, 1968:208).

The strength of this conduct code is expressed in the words of one of the top men in the Gambino crime family, the underboss Sammy "the Bull" Gravano. When Gravano and the elite of the Gambino crime family were about to be indicted, Sammy left town. He could tell no one of his whereabouts, not even his wife and children. As Sammy lamented, the code of the crime family was stronger than his loyalty to his own family: "Although my faith in John Gotti's Cosa Nostra was deteriorating, my basic loyalty to the true Cosa Nostra still came before loyalty to my own family" (quoted in Maas, 1997:268).

Keep in mind that this system of beliefs is an idealized set of behavioral guides, which are supposed to guarantee members' conduct. In reality, of course, members of organized crime families do not always follow the code. For example, they sometimes sleep with other members' wives; they pocket extra cash from criminal transactions rather than turn it all over to superiors; they frequently cheat one another; they sometimes "snitch" to avoid criminal prosecution or prison sentences; and they sometimes kill each other without authorization. In fact, much of what is known about organized crime comes from informants who turned against their crime families.

Deviant Activities

One of the easily overlooked truisms about organized crime is that above all else, it is about economics. The purpose of organizing criminal activity may have been something else originally, but now it is clearly to amass large amounts of money. It can do that because there is high demand for its services and products (narcotics, prostitution, loans, etc.) and low supply (many services are illegal, and others, like short-term loans, are not available legitimately because of scarce collateral or because the reasons for the loan are illegitimate). It has been estimated by the Wharton Econometrics Forecasting Associates (1986) that the Mafia earns approximately 50 billion dollars a year through its various criminal operations.

Because their primary activity is the pursuit of economic gain, other activities that characterize organized crime, such as violence and corruption of public authorities, can be viewed as ancillary—simply means to an economic end. Competitors must be vanquished, and within the outlaw realm "market share" is secured by sharing the total market with competitors or by literally eliminating the competition. In addition, business and its profits must be protected, often by bribing law enforcement and political officials.

Because the main purpose of syndicated crime is economic profit, it is important to consider more closely the kinds of money-making practices they exploit. They make money when laws forbid certain behaviors or products (prostitution, narcotics, "no-question" loans) for which there is a high demand; such prohibited activities or products then command an artificially high price (Packer, 1968). This situation virtually guarantees that somebody will become a supplier. For example, when there is high demand for the pleasures of narcotic use and laws deny access to narcotics, a tariff on narcotics is created. The effect is similar to that which would result if there were a $5,000 surcharge placed on all Japanese automobiles imported into the United States. This tariff of $5,000 would increase the price of the car and would reduce demand (the specific intention of the tariff). However, some demand would continue and some persons would pay the higher price for the Japanese car.

There are two differences between the Japanese car and narcotics, however. One is that the demand for now-expensive Japanese cars could be met legally (so long as the purchase of a Japanese car was not made illegal), and the demand for those cars (though reduced) could be met by legal automobile dealers. In the case of narcotics, however, which are illegal in addition to being tariffed, the demand cannot be met by legal distributors of the drug. Moreover, since narcotics are addictive, the demand for them is high despite exorbitant prices. There are, therefore, large profits to be made (high demand and high price for the product) by anyone willing to take the risk of supplying an illegal product. This is precisely what organized crime does: it attempts to capture inflated profits from illegal commodities, and in doing so it tries to minimize the risks involved.

One high-profit service that has always been a staple of organized crime is the chance to gamble, which is legally prohibited in many jurisdictions in the United States (Winslow, 1968; although for a contrary view, see Reuter, 1983); also, jurisdictions where gambling is legal are often difficult to reach. It has been estimated that over 60 million Americans engage in some form of illegal gambling, involving billions of dollars, each year (Winslow, 1968; Bequai, 1979). An illustration of the connection between organized crime and gambling concerns the history of Benjamin "Bugsy " Siegel. Siegel became famous in California during the 1930s and 1940s as a member of Meyer Lansky's crime family. He was known for having secured control over Hollywood unions. He then ventured to Las Vegas where his consuming passion, backed by organized crime money and a great deal of his own capital, became the building of the Flamingo Hotel and Casino. Siegel realized his dream of turning the desert town of Las Vegas into the gambling capital of America, and Las Vegas casinos became a major source of organized crime money from then on. Siegel's own personal success was short-lived, however, because he was murdered in his mistress's home by the mob in 1947 (Bequai, 1979). Yet the income from legal gambling in Las Vegas continues to line the pockets of organized crime figures who enjoy part ownership, or sometimes full but hidden ownership, of legitimate casinos. Casino ownership is only one source of gambling profit; there are also illegal lotteries (so-called "numbers" operations), illegal sports betting, illegal slot machines, and illegal card or dice games, often concealed in legitimate-appearing front organizations.

The second most lucrative source of revenue for organized crime is loansharking (Winslow, 1968), although lending money at unusually high interest rates (also known as usury or shylocking) is not the exclusive domain of organized crime families (Reuter and Rubinstein, 1978). Banking laws limit the rates that legitimate financial institutions can impose, but nothing restricts the interest charged by a loanshark. Most loanshark rates are many times higher than the prevailing legitimate rate (from 200 to 2,000 percent per year!) (Bequai, 1979), and charging any excess beyond the legally established rate is a crime. A normal loanshark rate is referred to as a "six for five," which means that if you borrow five dollars today, you owe six dollars in a week. This corresponds to a 20 percent per week interest rate. The actual interest depends on the relationship between the borrower and loanshark, the intended use of the money, the size of the loan, and the potential of the borrower to repay (Cressey, 1969). In most cases, the loanshark receives so much income from interest that he or she has little reason to want the loan repaid. In fact, some of the best profits occur when a debtor cannot pay and then has to do the loanshark's bidding. If the borrower is a politician, a judge or a law enforcement officer, it might be a favor; if the debtor is a businessperson, he or she might have to forfeit the business.

When people use loansharks, their "collateral" usually consists of the life and safety of themselves and their families. Loansharks employ "collectors" who "remind" borrowers that payment is due (and apply any necessary force). Despite these Draconian procedures, people resort to loansharks because they cannot get funds from banks: they have no property to serve as necessary collateral and no reputation that would justify a personal loan (ex-convicts, gamblers, and those without stable jobs are poor credit risks). People must avoid banks, of course, if they want to borrow money to fund criminal activities, to buy drugs, or to pay off other debts.

Selling illegal drugs is a third prominent business for organized crime. While some of the early crime bosses had reservations about distributing drugs, there is no such reluctance today. Even though the participation of traditional organized crime groups in international drug trade is less now than in the past—because of the intrusion of other groups such as South American and Mexican drug rings—it remains a multi-million dollar source of income. According to Maas (1997), one member of the Gotti family recently made $2 million every six months from his narcotics business.

Organized crime also infiltrates legitimate businesses, using capital secured from illegal activities. Sometimes these legitimate businesses are purchased outright with money from narcotics or gambling operations. At other times they are taken over when loans are not repaid, and on occasion they are simply confiscated through extortion. The number of businesses that organized crime has allegedly bought into is staggering. They include garment, food distribution, olive oil, baking, construction, and trucking businesses, to name only a few. One industry widely thought to be controlled by organized crime is waste disposal. Block and Scarpitti (1985) report that organized crime has ties to the largest waste management companies in the country.

In order to continue all their illegal or questionable activities, organized crime groups must get protection from public officials through bribery, extortion, and other illegal means. The 1967 President's Crime Commission Task Force on Organized Crime concluded that:

> All available data indicate that organized crime flourishes only where it has corrupted local officials. As the scope and variety of organized crime's activities have expanded, its need to involve public officials at every level of local government has grown. And as government regulation expands into more and more areas of private and business activity, the power to corrupt likewise affords the corrupter more control over matters affecting the everyday life of each citizen (Winslow, 1968:202).

Most experts agree that the history of organized crime is one based on corruption and bribery of public officials because syndicated illegality could not survive, at least not easily, without the active cooperation of public officials. Corruption presumably has occurred at all levels of government (local, state, and national) and has included persons in law enforcement, courts, corrections, and politics (Cressey, 1969).

Historical Overview

The historical roots of organized crime are hotly debated. Those who believe there are highly disciplined criminal cartels of Italians and Sicilian-Americans operating in large American cities trace the origins of such groups to the cultural heritage brought by immigrants from those two countries between approximately 1875 and 1920 (Cook, 1966; Gambino, 1974; Servadio, 1976; Abadinsky, 1985). That cultural heritage stemmed from the influence of the Camorra, which has its own origins in Naples, Italy, and the Mafia, whose birthplace was Sicily (Servadio, 1976; Bequai, 1979).

Unlike northern Italy, which rapidly urbanized and industrialized after the 1800s, southern Italy remained primarily rural and agrarian. Moreover, there was no strong centralized government in southern Italy, and local government was viewed as corrupt and ineffective in providing basic services. Extended families came to fill this vacuum. People started to develop intense loyalties to kin members, and together they cooperated in solving problems that could not be handled by the existing weak government, particularly the problem of protection from domestic enemies. This context gave birth to the Camorra, a secret society of criminals thought to have first appeared in the prisons of Naples (Bequai, 1979; Behan, 1996). Inside prisons, the Camorra extorted "protection" payments from other inmates and financial tributes from prison authorities to whom they guaranteed order (Behan, 1996).

Eventually the Camorra extended outside prisons in the form of a loosely organized federation of 12 families (each with its own boss) heavily involved in economic crimes. To protect their "business" interests, the Camorra used extortion and violence, and paid off corrupt local officials. It is alleged that the Camorra constituted an "organized" form of crime not only because of its internal structure, but because of collusion among the different families, who occasionally met to divide up territory and coordinate their activities (Bequai, 1979). After the unification of Italy, the Camorra became the most reliable source of public order (that is, for a sum of money, they acted as "police officers").

The Mafia was the Sicilian form of the Camorra, though it appeared much later. Like its counterpart in Naples, the Mafia was a secret criminal society that filled the vacuum left in the wake of a central government that was

Where did the term mafia come from? More than one writer claims that the term originated in Sicily during the late 1200s, when native Sicilians were attempting to drive the occupying French army off their land. In this story, a drunken French army officer allegedly assaults the girlfriend of a Sicilian lad who had gone to church to be married to the girl. She tries to flee but stumbles and hits her head against the church wall and dies. The young boy, returning to find his betrothed killed, cries, "Morte alla Francia"—"Death to all the French." News of the event spreads throughout the countryside, and it is claimed that the battle cry for the Sicilian freedom fighters then becomes, "Morte alla Francia Italia anela"—"death to the French is Italy's cry." After the French were driven out of Sicily, a secret society was allegedly formed to protect local citizens. This society took its name from the acronym for the battle cry—MAFIA (Gage, 1971; Albini, 1971). This, however, is simply one explanation of the origin of mafia, there are numerous others, and as is true with many matters dealing with organized crime, it is difficult to separate fact from fiction. (See Albini, 1971)

weak and a local one that was inefficient and corrupt. The predecessor of the Mafia was the gabellotto, which served as an enforcement arm for local landowners and nobles against peasant resistance. In disputes, the gabellotti ensured that landowners prevailed over peasants. Thus, extortion and intimidation were chief tools. Using extorted money from both parties, the gabellotti became the mafioso gabellotto—the one to whom one would go for a loan (Behan, 1996). Failure to repay loans evoked confiscation of property, injury, and perhaps death.

These early mafiosi, therefore, had a base of wealth, but they needed political protection, which they purchased from the weak government in Palermo, Sicily. It is argued that this culture was imported to the United States by Sicilian immigrants, who settled in major metropolitan areas on the east coast after the civil war and who are reputed to have first established their criminal cartels along New York's waterfront in the late 1890s and early 1900s (Gage, 1971; Bequai, 1979). Later, their influence was extended to other locales. According to this view, one of the first documented times that the Mafia flexed its muscles was in orchestrating the murder of New Orleans Chief of Police David Hennessey in 1890. Hennessey supposedly had discovered evidence of a major crime syndicate, called "the Mafia," that was attempting to form a national crime organization (Allen, 1996; Bequai, 1979).

Others dispute this history. Some argue that the Hennessey killing had nothing to do with a criminal group called "the Mafia" (Albini, 1971). Some scholars contend that the major immigration flow of the mafia from Sicily to the United States resulted from a fascist purge by Mussolini in the 1920s (Behan, 1996). According to another source (Maas, 1997), criminal cartels from Naples and Sicily came together some time after 1930 to form the criminal empire known as La Cosa Nostra.

While some doubt that a nationally organized crime syndicate existed in the United States in the early 1900s, there certainly were gangsters. For example, in the early 1900s Johnny Torrio was the head of an active band of criminals in New York called the Five Points Gang (Bequai, 1979). They committed robbery, extortion, and political fraud. Among the members of the Five Points Gang was the petty criminal Alphonse "Al" Capone. The ethnic make-up of the Five Points Gang was quite diverse, and it was not the only gang in town. Another one was headed by Frankie Yale. Torrio moved to Chicago around 1910 and joined the gang of his uncle, Jim Colosimo. Capone also went to Chicago in 1919, and that city became a hotbed of criminal gang activity. These early gangs could not be considered examples of "organized crime" because they were only loosely structured and there was virtually no cross-gang organization. The joining of these groups into a national crime syndicate needed some help. The Volstead Act of 1920 may have have supplied that help (Cressey, 1969; Albini, 1971; Gage, 1971; Bequai, 1979).

The Volstead Act prohibited the production and sale of alcoholic beverages, but it did nothing to reduce citizens' desire for spirits, thereby providing a catalyst for wider consolidation of criminal gangs. Prohibition invited entrepreneurs to provide illegal alcoholic beverages to Americans, and crime gangs quickly filled the void left by legitimate distillers. Bootlegging alcohol provided the urban gangs, which up to that point were splintered, with an incentive to coordinate their activities. The payoff from communication and cooperation on a national basis was potentially large enough to justify a businesslike organization with hierarchies of authority, accounting systems, and a complex, widespread network of distribution. And since success required protection from legal interdiction, politicians and law enforcement officials, including those who could operate across state lines and national boundaries, had to be bribed, intimidated, or eliminated.

Despite fertile ground for consolidation, competition among illegal suppliers worked against extensive criminal organization. According to one account, the professional gambler Arnold Rothstein was the first large-scale importer of illegal whiskey from England. His territory was New England and New York (Gage, 1971), but Rothstein (who was suspected of trying to fix the 1919 World Series) soon began to supplement his supply of illegal whiskey by hijacking the alcohol of his competitors. Soon, gang warfare broke out, and the subsequent years saw the rise of numerous gangsters (John T. Noland, known as "Legs Diamond"; Arthur Flegenheimer, known as Dutch Schultz; Al Capone) and countless gangland killings. Eventually it began to dawn on bootlegging gangs that the profits from illegal liquor were large enough to satisfy everybody, so gangsters within each city began to come together into crime syndicates. Examples include Detroit's Purple Gang, the Torrio-Capone syndicate in Chicago, and the Masseria syndicate in New York City. These syndicates slowly began to take the form of organized crime and consequently extended their activities to include other illegal but widely desired goods or services.

During the 1930s and 1940s, mergers of criminal gangs increased in many places. The work of these syndicates, and the extent of their organization and growing national focus, was revealed by New York District Attorney Thomas E. Dewey. Dewey successfully prosecuted "Lucky" Luciano, and his efforts brought organized criminal enterprises to light. Although Dewey's efforts won acclaim in New York, the idea of a national crime syndicate did not penetrate the rest of the country until the well-publicized hearings of the Senate Special Committee on Organized Crime chaired by Senator Estes Kefauver of Tennessee in 1951.

In its investigation, the Kefauver Committee called some 800 witnesses, from nearly every state in the country. It exposed the existence of organized crime as well as collusion between organized crime figures and corrupt local and state political figures. But discovering details about organized crime proved difficult because witnesses with direct knowledge about the activities of organized crime were frequently unwilling to talk. When asked if they were members of a criminal cartel known as the Mafia, all witnesses replied along the lines of, "What's the Mafia? I never heard of anything called the Mafia." The Committee nevertheless concluded that a national crime organization called "the Mafia" did exist in many large U.S. cities and that it was involved in numerous criminal enterprises.

The public and governmental officials became even more aware of the possible existence of a national crime syndicate when a large number of its members from all over the United States met at the estate of reputed New York mobster Joseph Barbara in Appalachin, New York, in 1957. Many believe that the Appalachin group was a national policy-making "board of directors" for the criminal syndicate (for opposing views, however, see Bell, 1962; Hawkins, 1973; and Reuter, 1983). Subsequent investigation of those captured in Appalachin revealed much telephone correspondence among them, although, once again, the suspects were tight-lipped about their activities (Cressey, 1969).

In 1963, under the administration of President John F. Kennedy, his attorney general and brother, Robert F. Kennedy, asked the United States Senate to again begin investigating the activities of organized crime. A Senate committee headed by John L. McClellan became interested in labor racketeering. During these investigations, the general counsel to the committee, Robert Kennedy, had a famous public confrontation with union boss James Hoffa. The McClellan Committee's investigation revealed a cozy relationship between union activities and organized crime. One of the star witnesses in the investigation was Joseph Valachi, a member of New York's Genovese crime family. He provided the committee with information about the national crime syndicate, called "La Cosa Nostra," in exchange for protection from the mob, which he believed intended to kill him. Although his veracity was called into question from the beginning, recent evidence has validated many of Valachi's claims (Maas, 1997).

All of what has been said in the preceding paragraphs was confirmed again in 1967, by a task force of President Lyndon Johnson's Commission on Law Enforcement and Administration of Justice. By the mid-1960s, most of the task force's evidence suggested that there were about 24 crime families operating in the United States. The most powerful of these were five whose operational center was New York City: the Gambino family, the Genovese family, the Bonanno family, the Profaci family, and the Lucchese family. There were, however, organized crime families in other American cities, like Philadelphia (the Annaloro family), Boston (the Patricia family), Chicago (the Accardo and DeLucia families), Miami (the Trafficante family), Kansas City (the Civella family), New Orleans (the Marcello family), and San Francisco (the Lima family). The activities of these crime families were understood to be loosely coordinated, each with some internal organization (a structure of roles and role behaviors, a "philosophy" or at least a code of conduct, and a way to recruit new members) and all sharing a loose collective organization [a National Commission made up of the heads of the most powerful families, which established strategies and policies and regulated disputes (Maas, 1997)].

These crime families all had colorful histories. The New York Gambino family can serve as an illustration of the pattern, although each of the families had its own peculiar details. Like most mafia families, it was established in bloodshed. The original heads of the family were Philip and Vincent Mangano, who were killed in 1951 (actually, Philip was murdered and Vincent simply disappeared) at the behest of Albert "the Mad Hatter" Anastasia, one of the most ruthless family bosses, who then assumed leadership over the Gambino family. Anastasia himself was ordered killed by his underling, Carlo Gambino, in 1957 (with the support of Vito Genovese, head of another New York crime family). Anastasia was murdered in typical mob fashion; he was shot by two gunmen while he was relaxing under a stack of hot towels in a Manhattan barbershop.

Deviance in Everyday Life

John Gotti is only the most recent of a long line of underworld or organized crime bosses. During the course of his rule of the Gambino family, Gotti had the distinction of earning two nicknames. One was the "Dandy Don." Don was the title given to the boss of each family, and "dandy" because he was such a snappy dresser, preferring very expensive and well-tailored double-breasted suits, $200 hand-painted ties, and a diamond pinkie ring (Maas, 1997). Gotti's other nickname was "the Teflon Don" because, despite the fact that he was the boss of the most powerful crime family in the United States and had ordered the murders of numerous foes, law enforcement officers had trouble getting charges to "stick"—prosecutions seemed to bounce off him. Gotti was no shrinking violet, however; he repeatedly "mugged" for TV cameras and seemed not to hide the fact that he was thought to be a crime boss. In fact, other than the infamous Al Capone, Gotti is the only organized crime figure to grace the cover of *Time* magazine, and the cover was done by the famous pop artist Andy Warhol. Gotti's luck would run out, however. After a federal investigation that included years of telephone wiretaps, Gotti was arrested and prosecuted for racketeering and murder and was given a life sentence in prison without parole.

When Gambino died in 1976, leadership of the family fell to Paul Castellano. Unlike the homespun, unassuming Gambino, who lived in a modest home in Brooklyn, Castellano had a love for the finer things in life and built a mansion for himself on Staten Island that cost over $3 million. During Gambino's reign as the boss of the family, there was tension between Castellano and another Gambino family member, Aniello (Neil) Dellacroce. Dellacroce ultimately served as Castellano's underboss, and himself had a captain, John Gotti, who was later to become famous in his own right. Castellano's practice of keeping his distance from the streets and the Italian social clubs frequented by family members proved costly. He had few allies in the family. After a short time, he was shot dead in a gangland killing, and John Gotti became the new boss of the Gambino family, until his conviction for racketeering and murder in 1991 (see Deviance in Everyday Life for a description of Gotti).

Basis for Success

As previously noted, the basic unit in organized crime is the family; there are about twenty-five families. The various families are allied through a Commission, which is composed of heads of the most powerful and wealthy families. The number of families represented on the Commission is small, usually between eight and twelve. The members of this body are not equally powerful; the wealthiest, the longest existing, and the most influential of the select few usually wield the most power (Cressey, 1969). The Commission has legislative, judicial, and executive powers, which it uses to make policy for organized crime generally, to resolve disputes between families, and to enforce its decisions. With the demise of an old boss for any given family, the Commission also installs a new boss.

Chain of Command

Although the Commission is the highest level, most of the activities of organized crime are conducted within each family, and loyalty to one's particular family (more specifically, with the boss of the family) is primary. Rather than identifying with organized crime or La Cosa Nostra in general, then, practitioners of organized crime identify with the family to which they belong. The size of each family varies from as few as 20 to as many as 700 (Cressey, 1969; Winslow, 1969). Family members need not be related by blood, as indicated by the fact that membership can change. For example, Sammy "the Bull" Gravano, who became the underboss to John Gotti in the Carlo Gambino family, started out in organized crime as a member of the Columbo family. Sammy had to change family membership because of a running feud he had with another member of the Columbo family (Maas, 1997). Although biological kinship is not required, recruits must have Italian fathers, and they must be nominated or recommended for membership by another member. Recruits must also undergo a formal initiation ceremony. After that, the newcomer is referred to as a "made guy," and until such a designation is granted, the person is not a member of the family.

At various times in the past, the "books" on family membership were closed so that new members could not be "made." This was the basis of a dispute involving the crime boss Albert Anastasia. In the 1950s he reputedly ignored the Commission's command to close the books on family membership. Anastasia not only defied the order, he sold membership in his family for $50,000 (Maas, 1997). When membership books are closed, potential recruits must wait until they are open again. No one part of an organized crime family is indispensable; when one family member, even the boss, is removed by death or incarceration, another one takes his place.

The head of each family is known as the boss or "Don" or capofamiglia. He decides the kind of rackets the family will pursue, distributes rewards to underlings, handles disputes within the family, authorizes the execution of outsiders and other family members, and forms or breaks alliances and agreements with the bosses of other families (Cressey, 1969). The functions of a boss are to amass and distribute profits for the family, and to keep internal and external order. Within each family the power and authority of the boss is absolute, even to the point where a killing requires his permission. For example, Sammy "the Bull" Gravano ordered the death of a wealthy drug dealer because during a wrangle over the sale of Sammy's nightclub, the dealer pulled a gun (an Uzi). Incensed, Sammy had the guy killed without first obtaining the approval of his boss, Paul Castellano. Although the penalty could have been Sammy's own life, Castellano forgave the break of protocol after hearing the full story (Maas, 1997).

When a boss dies or is sent to prison, the transfer of power to the next boss is usually done through the Commission. Unless a boss dies suddenly, he will have already prepared a successor or at least will have expressed a preference (usually his underboss). The potential replacement is then suggested to the Commission. They will formally approve (or not) and then install the choice as the new head of the family.

Beneath the boss is an "underboss." An underboss is usually appointed by the boss to be his primary "right-hand man." An underboss becomes the "acting" boss in the absence of the real boss, and is understood by other family members to be next in line as the new boss. An underboss typically exercises day-to-day control of illegal operations undertaken by the family. He also transmits information down the chain of command to those below him and up from below to the boss.

Next, but far less powerful and influential than the underboss, is the counselor or advisor, called the consigliere. A consigliere is often the boss's trusted companion, with extensive experience in the ways of the family. He may be a semiretired member of the family or may have been bypassed for promotion to underboss or boss. The consigliere's function is to advise the boss, act as the boss's spokesperson in dialog with other families, and at times to intervene in, and mediate, disputes within the family.

The third level of organization encompasses operations managers, referred to as captains or caporegime. The capos directly supervise the family crime business because the bosses and underbosses try to insulate themselves from the actual criminal operations of the family, in order to protect themselves from criminal prosecution. Thus, the capos serve as buffers between bosses and the actual working criminals who run the numbers game or distribute the narcotics. Rather than initiating orders, the capos translate orders from above and make sure that the orders are followed.

The lowest-level family functionaries are the "button men," soldiers, or soldati. They actually operate the illicit criminal activities, sending their profits up to the capos. Some soldiers are mere employees, while others are more like "subcontractors" who pay a proportion of their proceeds to the family. All soldiers are provided for economically by their superiors, and in return, soldiers must swear complete allegiance to the family, as well as silence about family business. They also enjoy other benefits, such as protection for their rackets, and help if that protection breaks down. Finally, below the soldati, are nonfamily members who do much of the "grunt" work of the criminal activities. Because they are not family members, they enjoy few of the benefits and protections discussed above.

Social Control

Given that people in organized crime are committed to antisocial activities and are accustomed to disobeying rules, it is important to consider how the Commission manages to maintain order among the various families, as well as how individual families maintain internal order. The Commission uses bribery and violence. It can prevent families from attacking each other through financial incentives. For example, after World War II, competition for control of the emerging international narcotics trade started heating up. Rather than allow a war among the families, the Commission held a series of meetings to discuss and distribute the "rights" to the drug trade. One such meeting, attended by members of both U.S. and Sicilian organized crime families, allegedly was held in Palermo, Sicily, in 1957. There the group agreed that the Bonanno family would coordinate the drug traffic between the United States and Sicily while the Luciano family would be in charge of the U.S. traffic (Bequai, 1979). The Commission has, on other occasions, prevented families from going to war against one another by partitioning crime territory among them, as for example in areas not under the direct control of one family, such as Las Vegas (Cressey, 1969).

Although the Commission tries to use persuasion and economic incentives to maintain order, it will resort to violence if necessary. It can have a given boss disciplined if he ignores its orders. For example, it is alleged that the Commission ordered the assassination of Albert Anastasia because of Anastasia's involvement (without the Commission's approval) in the disappearance of his own boss, Vincent Mangano (Bequai, 1979). The Commission is also suspected of being behind the shooting of Joseph Columbo. Columbo had organized the Italian-American Civil Rights League and was using it to picket FBI offices. Other members of the Commission thought that Columbo's activities were drawing too much attention to organized crime activities and were eliciting too much "heat" from the FBI. When Columbo refused to curtail his demonstrations, he was shot. Thus, a mixture of carrot (economic incentives) and stick (the threat and use of violence) enables the Commission to keep some semblance of order among the families.

Much the same carrot/stick combination allows bosses to maintain discipline and order within their own families. Bosses, it will be recalled, distribute the rights to conduct criminal activities within their jurisdictions. They elicit loyalty and conformity from their underlings by making sure all get a "slice of the action" and by ensuring that their workers are "taken care of" in other ways; for example, wives and children are supported if a family member is convicted and incarcerated. The process is shown in the case of Sammy "the Bull" Gravano.

Sammy was no more than a street thug in the early 1960s, doing stick-ups and break-ins. When he became a member of the Columbo family, however, he was given the right to own a club where illegal gambling took place, and to protect his interests by paying the police (Maas, 1997). From there, Sammy moved into loansharking and to control of a construction business. Sammy's success ensured his loyalty to the family. He himself said, "The better I did, the better it is for the borgata, the family" (Maas, 1997:106). He did well in the construction business because his family rigged the contracting process. A certain percent of the money he earned through rigged bidding went back to the family, so that when Sammy prospered, the family prospered. In this way family loyalty is maintained, and the largesse has a multiplier effect. Soldiers running criminal enterprises give a cut to their capos, who give a cut to their underbosses, who in turn give a cut to the bosses. So long as people are making money, internal order is assured.

The effect of economic incentives for ensuring discipline and order can be seen from the occasions where order breaks down. Trouble within the Joseph Profaci family started when a faction led by the Gallo brothers thought that Profaci was leaving them out of lucrative action made available to other members of the family (Cressey, 1969). When the expected economic incentives were not forthcoming, the Gallos "went to war" with other members of the Profaci family. Another example occurred when John Gotti's enforcer, Willie Boy Johnson, went to jail on a robbery charge. In keeping with family tradition, Johnson expected Gotti (more specifically, Johnson's capo, Carmine "Charley Wagons" Fatico) to take care of his wife and children while he was incarcerated. Fatico failed in that duty, so when Johnson was released from prison he became an FBI informant (Maas, 1997).

If economic incentives fail to secure the loyalty of family members, violence will. The recorded times that family members have been beaten or murdered are too numerous to count. One instance was the Joey Gallo shooting. After being released from prison in 1971, Gallo became well known among New York writers, artists, and theater people as a mobster. Among them he discussed writing books and making a movie about his life in organized crime. When Gallo's plans appeared in the newspapers, Joey's boss, Joseph Columbo, called Gallo in for a talk, but Gallo refused to meet with him. In a short time a "contract was put out" on Gallo. Another example is the killing of Louie Milito. Milito was a friend and partner of Sammy "the Bull" Gravano, who at that time was a *capo* in the Gotti family. Louie had a disagreement with another family member, Eddie Garafola, who also happened to be Gravano's brother-in-law. Milito wanted Eddie killed, but Gravano refused. Contrary to family rules, Milito went behind Sammy's back to get the killing approved, and he began a campaign of "bad-mouthing" other family members. He could not be brought back into line and was subsequently murdered (Maas, 1997).

There are, then, two primary ways that members of organized crime create conformity to the "rules of the game." The most important is the economic incentive; resort to violence is used only when economic persuasion fails. Economic incentives create a general sense of satisfaction and commitment among members of organized crime, especially since they would probably be among the deprived class were it not for their association with the syndicates. After all, they tend to have few legitimate skills, they are poorly educated, and most had records as petty criminals long before they became part of the mob. They obey because it is profitable. But all members know that misbehavior will jeopardize something even more valuable—their lives and safety. Still, violence is a two-edged sword; it is an effective control device but in the long run it may undermine the enterprise by attracting police and public attention.

Fending Off External Agents of Social Control

Members of organized crime have an ever-present problem: they face hostile outside agents of social control who want to destroy them or put them out of business. Despite this, organized crime has existed for a long time. It has been successful in resisting its enemies because (1) it provides services and products that are both in high demand and illegal, so their "customers" do not assist law enforcement; (2) members of organized crime families are well taken care of economically if they do their jobs and remain loyal, so they do not often complain or cooperate with legal officials; and (3) even if complaints are registered or assistance to law enforcement is rendered by customers or participants, organized crime has successfully protected itself by "buying off" corrupt criminal justice or political officials.

Satisfied Customers

Organized crime is in many ways similar to a noncriminal business. First, there is usually demand for the products or services. Customers are willing to pay for those commodities or services without coercion. No one forces customers to buy an automobile or a haircut, and nobody requires individuals to gamble, get a high-interest loan, or use the services of a prostitute. Illegitimate business differs in some respects in that it sometimes creates demand by extortion, as when the mob collects money from a "client" to protect him or her from the destructive potential of the mob itself. Second, businesses supply the product or service for a fee. Such transactions are usually satisfactory, but sometimes they are not. It is the nature of unsatisfactory transactions that most distinguishes legitimate from illegitimate business.

In the everyday world, when customers feel overcharged by a business, the product is shoddy, or contractual obligations are not being fulfilled, the customers have recourse. They can complain to the Chamber of Commerce or the Better Business Bureau, or in some instances they can seek redress in civil court. Organized crime, however, has an advantage. Their unsatisfied customers, who themselves are guilty of engaging in illegal behavior, ordinarily cannot complain to anyone. As a result, organized crime usually has two types of customers—those who are satisfied and those who are silently unhappy. Overall, then, there are few formal complaints to the police and few witnesses willing to testify at trials. Occasionally debtors might go to the police complaining that loansharks are extorting them or because they fear violence, but this is unusual. Most legal action against organized crime is instigated by governmental agencies, rather than being in response to citizen complaints and, as a result, is not very effective.

Satisfied 'Employees'

Organized criminals themselves are not likely to assist law enforcement officials or otherwise create problems. Most of the time, organized criminals make a lot of money and lead the "good life" (Maas, 1997:254). So long as they get a "piece of the action," organized criminals tend to maintain family solidarity and loyalty. But even if they become unhappy, dissatisfied employees have little recourse. They cannot, for example, appeal unfair labor practices to the National Labor Relations Board, nor can they take matters into their own hands (say, by setting up competitive loan businesses) without jeopardizing their own survival.

Political Protection

Another reason why organized crime has been so successful is that it has used its huge financial resources to corrupt law enforcement, judicial, and political figures who might otherwise pose a threat. Thus, even if customers or employees complain, not much happens because those who could act are paid off not to act. Organized crime simply could not exist, or at least not thrive as well as it does, without a vast system of protection afforded by political corruption (Cressey, 1969:249).

Exemplary Deportment

Organized criminals pride themselves on appearing as hard-working, normal citizens. In fact, they normally deny any Mafia connections. Many claim to be regular businesspersons, even if the business is a "front" (such as "importing olive oil," trucking, or running a nightclub) for more nefarious activities. Members of organized crime families are encouraged to establish "normal" identities. They are also expected to deport themselves so as to avoid calling attention to their activities. Ostentatious behavior is, therefore, strongly discouraged; living in "the neighborhood," driving an inexpensive car, and avoiding flashy clothing or jewelry are all preferred over conspicuous displays of wealth.

Good Relations With Neighbors

One way organized criminals avoid trouble is to act as "pillars of the community" by contributing money to community projects, being good neighbors, and displaying devotion as husbands and fathers. This behavior was shown by Sammy Gravano, as recorded by Maas (1997:225). At one point, Sammy set up his daughter, Karen, as the proprietor of a flower shop. One day a child went in to purchase a rose for Mother's Day. Upon learning that the rose cost more money than the girl had, she began to cry and started to leave. When Karen learned of the little girl's problem, she gave the child a carnation for her mother. Word soon spread among the children of the neighborhood, and they all descended on the flower shop. Karen described the situation to her father and noted that there were now 50 to 100 children coming into the shop. Touched by his daughter's generosity, Sammy offered to pay for a carnation to be given to each child. When neighborhood teachers came to thank Karen, she explained that it was her father's kindness. That generated a lot of good will for Sammy Gravano, which soon paid off. Later, several of the teachers came up to Sammy on the street and revealed that they had noticed he was being kept under surveillance with binoculars and cameras by people in cars. It was the FBI.

Accommodation

Organized criminals sometimes "lie low" to minimize difficulties. For example, when Thomas Dewey led an attack against organized crime in the 1930s and 1940s, many mobsters curtailed their more strident forms of crime, particularly murder. More recently, in 1970, after passage of Federal legislation threatening organized crime, Carlo Gambino, who was by then the head of the most powerful family, sought to move organized crime toward legitimate business (Maas, 1997:82). Among other things, he thought that trafficking in narcotics was getting "too hot" for organized crime. Reductions in activity, of course, are usually short-lived—until the "heat" passes.

Summary

Although it perpetrates much deviance, organized crime has flourished for many decades. It has been so successful because of a base of "satisfied" (and helpless) customers, "contented" (and helpless) employees, and a vast system of political protection; in addition, practitioners attempt to create normal identities for themselves, to generate good will within the communities where they live, and to accommodate to stepped-up law enforcement efforts by reducing the volume and visibility of crime.

We have used organized crime as one example of "fully organized deviance." Yet a major criticism leveled against students of organized crime is that they have exaggerated how well organized it really is. Therefore, let's consider whether organized crime is truly "fully organized."

How Organized Is 'Organized' Crime?

Sociality

We observed in Chapter 2 that deviance is more likely to become organized when lots of people do it together. Organized crime inherently involves numerous people. Beginning when bootleg whiskey was imported from Canada and Great Britain and distributed in illegal clubs ("speakeasies"), the coordinated action of many individuals has been necessary for syndicated criminal activity. Organized crime presumably represents a vast empire with many diverse activities, from loansharking to political corruption and including expansion into legitimate businesses. Success requires that people in different places work together and know what each of the other parties is doing and that the criminals associate with each other for protection from the law. None of the activities attributed to organized crime can be managed by any one person, or even by a few. In fact, the scholarly literature suggests that these criminal activities are undertaken by several families, each composed of dozens or even hundreds of people. Thus, sociality is high.

Pervasiveness

Although organized criminals do not commit crimes 24 hours a day, they nevertheless involve themselves in all-encompassing life styles that mandate repeated illegal behavior. Thus, even though mobsters have outside interests, such as spending time with wives and children or participating in religious and recreational events, their positions in the network of illegal enterprise take precedence and dominate their activities. If the bulk of the literature is to be believed, not only do members spend a good portion of time maintaining their criminal operations, but their commitments to the crime family and its work requires removal from interactions with "normal" people (except, of course, as businessmen to customers). Since their activities and orientations are so different from those of most people, interaction within conventional contexts is not only difficult, it is potentially dangerous. After all, outsiders may notify the police if they learn they are dealing with criminals, thugs, or even murderers. Because of this danger, the lives of organized criminals are circumscribed, with friends and associates limited mainly to other organized criminals, especially to members of the crime family itself, who constantly converse and share experiences about the business. Therefore, even though organized crime activity is not as all-consuming as Perfectionism was, it is still very pervasive for its practitioners. Since the most pervasive activity tends to be highly organized, we can conclude that organized crime is quite well "organized."

Communication

Organized crime figures share a far less developed system for exchanging information and transmitting messages than did the Perfectionists, but they do communicate verbally and effectively among themselves. Since their activities are subject to constant legal intervention, members of organized crime cannot risk written communication. (They are not known for their reading skills in any case.) And because they are not interested in justifying themselves to, or seeking new members from, the outside world, they do not publish newsletters, prepare video or audio tapes, or broadcast their philosophy and activities.

According to scholarly sources, there is, however, a routinized system through which information passes up and down. When a crime boss wants something done, he has little trouble making that known. And few mobsters are in the dark about what is going on around them in the organization, unless they happen to be marked as targets for murder. Moreover, all organized crime members share certain understandings, such as the meanings of a kiss, phrases like "put out a contract," and "going to the mattresses." These shared meanings are cultivated through constant usage and through informal interaction in Italian-American social clubs. These clubs, often located in the neighborhoods of organized crime families, are frequented almost daily. When crime figures congregate, they talk. They recount exploits and converse about the business. In fact, the conversations within these social clubs are so brisk and informative about family business that they are prime targets of FBI wiretaps. It was one such wiretap at the Ravenite Club in New York's Little Italy that led to the arrest and conviction of Gambino family boss John Gotti (Maas, 1997). Overall, then, organized crime scores fairly high on the organizational criterion of communication.

Differentiation and Coordination

A major indicator of the degree of organization among practitioners of deviance is the extent to which they play differentiated roles connected with, and coordinated through, particular status positions. Earlier we described how crime families allocate roles with distinct functions and expectations, some of which are specifically to coordinate the work of the rest. Recall that there is a hierarchy within each family. In order of descending power from the boss are underbosses, counselors, captains, and soldiers. Beneath all these are various nonfamily members who assist the family in criminal activities. Furthermore, there is differentiation across families. Some are larger, richer, and more powerful than others (the most powerful sit on the National Commission), and these families often dictate policy to the others. In sum, by all accounts, organized crime is based on highly differentiated roles, and it runs on elaborate schemes of coordination. Hence, by this criterion, organized crime is indeed organized.

Culture

Organized crime has a definite goal and a clear means to achieve it, along with a network of differentiated social roles and institutions. The nature of this network is taught to new members or aspiring members by precept and example. In addition, all participants share ideas about why their activities are good and why they are not bad, how to do business effectively, and the appropriate styles for carrying out their duties. All of this is handed down from one generation to the next through direct instruction and indirectly through folk tales about what has gone before, often through distinct linguistic symbols. Therefore, organized crime can be said to have an elaborate culture that must be, and is, passed on for the system to continue.

Self-Identity

One criterion reflecting degree of organization is the extent to which people identify with sets of practitioners or with the deviant activity itself. The Perfectionists were well organized according to this standard, and so are organized criminals. Once someone joins a crime family, his identity is inextricably linked with that family. He is no longer known to others as a unique person but instead is identified as a member of his particular crime family. In the initiation ceremony a new member swears total allegiance, and because his social and "professional" worlds then become constricted, he takes on an identity as a mobster, works with other gangsters, and severs ties with conventional society. The net effect is to link the person, in his own mind and the minds of others, to his life in organized crime.

Philosophical Integration

Although it cannot be said that organized crime has a well-integrated philosophy that includes interpretations of everything, it does have a set of values and beliefs shared by members in good standing. This "philosophy" includes a "world view." For example, one major crime figure once observed that Cosa Nostra considered itself a second government, more important than the United States government. The philosophy provides a rationale for criminal activities—providing people with what they want (Maas, 1997)—and it sets forth a broad guide to living, focused around reliability, respect, and duty. Yet the essence of these principles is self-serving, with little evidence of larger or more altruistic features. Consequently, organized crime would not score extremely high on this criterion of organization, though it would tend more toward the fully organized end of the continuum than toward the individualized end.

Social Control

The national crime Commission uses a combination of persuasion, economic incentive, and the threat or use of violence to ensure order in its ranks. Conflict among families usually arises for one of two reasons: (1) power struggles for dominance, or (2) control over criminal activity in neutral territory. Dominance on the Commission reflects the power and wealth of one's family, personal charisma, or successful intrigue and treachery. The Commission itself resolves disputes among families or family bosses in a patterned fashion. It normally meets and hears from all parties to a dispute, rendering its decision and attempting to persuade each party to accept it. Ordinarily the Commission provides some incentive for the disputing party to accept its decision. If decisions are not accepted, the Commission resorts to coercion, sometimes involving murder. Thus, the Commission uses a combination of carrot and stick to control the behavior of its constituent families.

At the next level down, the boss of a family also uses rewards and punishments to keep his family members in line. The boss is mainly responsible for providing criminal opportunities for his soldiers. When the soldiers are pursuing profitable enterprises, they generally behave themselves and conform to family rules. Sometimes, however, there are disputes over criminal operations and personal matters, and sometimes individuals fail to do what they are supposed to. These problems are most often handled by consultation and mediation. When they involve soldiers, the capos intervene, usually to negotiate a settlement (remember, the use of violence against another family member is forbidden, unless ordered by the boss). When problems involve capos, the underbosses or consigliere attempt to negotiate settlements. Only when these fail will the family try force. When family members do not abide by decisions arrived at in the manner described, more violent means are employed.

Together, these mechanisms of control help to maintain order within and among crime families. And because they are well developed, routinized, and effective, one would have to classify the "syndicate" as quite highly organized.

Recruitment

Because they thrive on illegal activities and are constantly being pursued by the law, organized crime families do very little open recruitment. Participants do not give lectures, publish tracts and brochures, or invite prospects for visits. Furthermore, though membership is apparently restricted to Italians or Sicilian-Americans (Bequai, 1979; Maas, 1997), many organized crime participants pointedly do not want their immediate relatives involved in the business, so recruitment by reproduction is rare (see Talese, 1971). Acquisition of new members is deliberate, focused, and circumspect.

Usually a family member will nominate a potential recruit who has shown special effectiveness or apparent loyalty (perhaps because he took the blame for a criminal act). The nominee is likely to be a lower-level criminal already working with, or for, the family. If the boss agrees with the recommendation by the nominator, and the books are not closed, the nominee will be approached about the matter. If he agrees to join the family, an initiation ceremony is planned, and during it the nominee will swear complete allegiance to the family. Of course, this recruitment rests on the nominee's having much familiarity with organized crime figures so that he has already developed some knowledge about the family and some desire to be more than a lower-level worker. And, depending on attrition or need for help in expanded businesses, mob participants may be on the lookout for appropriate recruits and may have been exploring this option with the person for some time.

Overall, then, there is no extensive recruitment—mainly because the syndicate does not need many new members—but that which does occur is systematic and planned. This activity, therefore, would score as moderately high on the criterion of recruitment.

Summary

In presenting material about the degree of organization among "organized" criminals, according to the criteria set forth in Chapter 2, we have so far followed the work of those scholars who contend that organized crime is real and is, indeed, well organized. Thus, it scores high on sociality because the activities require a number of participants, and it is pervasive activity for those who do it. In fact, it is like a calling, in that participants pledge total loyalty and they draw a great deal of their personal identities from their roles in the family. The participants communicate extensively and effectively with each other, especially in coordinated activity overlaid with a well-defined authority structure. There is an elaborate culture passed on from one generation to the next, and internal order is maintained by a routinized and effective system of formal and informal controls. Finally, although recruitment is limited, it is systematic and deliberate. The one criterion by which organized crime does not appear fully organized concerns its philosophy, which is narrow, self-serving, and poorly integrated. Nevertheless, given high scores on the other criteria, organized criminals appear to be quite well organized.

Not every scholar accepts the descriptions we have drawn on, however, so we turn to an alternative model.

Does Organized Crime Even Exist?

Since the publication of the 1967 President's Crime Commission Task Force Report on Organized Crime, which first systematically discussed the notion of a nationwide criminal cartel called the Cosa Nostra, its findings have been viewed with skepticism and subjected to criticism. In an article published in 1969, just two years after the Commission's report, Gordon Hawkins (1973) observed that belief in the existence of organized crime is a matter of faith rather than hard evidence. Hawkins (and he is not alone in this skepticism; see, for example, Turkus and Feder, 1952; Tyler, 1962; and Albini, 1971, 1997; Reuter and Rubinstein 1978; Reuter, 1983) contends that the factual evidence supporting the idea of organized crime is slim.

For one thing, during the government's several investigations into organized crime, virtually all the witnesses (who appeared before the committee because they were suspected members of organized crime) denied both knowledge of, and membership in, organized crime. Believers, however, maintain that these witnesses were merely following family codes of silence, violation of which would result in death.

Skeptics also note that much of what we presumably know about organized crime comes from only one key witness at Senator McClellan's hearings, Joseph Valachi, whose testimony, they claim, is of dubious validity. Valachi was one of the first alleged members of an organized crime family to tell authorities all that he knew of the operations of the syndicate. Yet, what he "knew" and told, critics contend, is often contradictory. Valachi himself provided no direct or corroborating proof regarding anything he claimed about organized crime. Moreover, Valachi is said to be an unreliable witness because he was out to destroy Vito Genovese in retaliation for Genovese's having tried to get him killed.

In addition, some regard the concept of organized crime as a myth, built up around minor acts that have generated fear and conspiratorial fantasies. Because people fear organized crime, they are subject to intimidation by minor hoodlums who draw on the myth to intensify their threats and make manipulation easier. These actions by minor criminals, in turn, further reinforce the image of a vast organized network, and when the victims describe those occurrences to others, the power of an imaginary syndicate seems to grow ever larger. Moreover, few people report being victimized directly by organized criminals. Although everybody seems to know somebody, or to have heard of somebody, who knows somebody else who allegedly was such a victim, not many businesses or individuals can provide first-hand data. Defenders, of course, attribute this lack of data to fear, contending that the legions of actual victims are afraid to reveal their experiences.

Because of the absence of hard data and the dubious evidence presented by a suspect witness, therefore, many scholars have questioned the existence of anything like organized crime or anything called the Mafia or the Cosa Nostra. In recent years, however, corroborating evidence has begun to appear to bolster Valachi's claims, as well as many of the early arguments supporting organized crime. This evidence comes from federal wiretaps of suspected organized criminals, particularly members of the Gambino family (whose boss, John Gotti, along with several upper-echelon members of his family, was convicted and imprisoned). Wiretaps were placed in the homes, places of business, and social clubs of suspected organized criminals. The content of these wiretaps seems to confirm the existence of, at the very least, a loose confederation of Italian-American crime families in major metropolitan areas of the United States. Although there is reason to doubt that this organization is all-powerful, as some would have it, there does seem to be a cartel in the United States that conducts extensive, coordinated criminal operations.

Other critics are more circumspect. While careful not to completely reject the notion of a national criminal syndicate, they do object to the depiction of organized crime as a bureaucratically organized formal structure (Albini, 1971; Smith, 1971; Reuter, 1983). Albini (1971, 1997) notes that the organization of "organized" crime is highly variable, that is, that it is not uniformly structured into hierarchial roles with different and coordinated obligations. In fact, organized crime consists of numerous groups, some poorly organized. Other critics have also noted that the portrayal of organized crime as structured into families with a national commission grossly exaggerates the amount of bureaucratic rationality among criminals (Kelly, 1997; Reuter, 1983). Haller (1997), for example, claims that criminal operations are carried out mainly by individuals, independent of families. The families' roles are limited to providing social interaction, mutual assistance, criminal opportunities, and foundations for predictable economic exchanges.

Multinational and International Organized Crime

Finally, it is important to remember that organized crime is not the exclusive domain of Italians or Sicilian-Americans. For example, in some parts of America, particularly in New York City and or the west coast, there are organized crime families composed of Chinese-Americans. Kleinknecht (1996) has noted that organized Chinese criminals have an extensive operation of gambling, extortion, and narcotics in nearly 20 North American cities. While Asian crime families do not appear to be as well structured as their Mafia counterparts, they have not been around nearly as long. In addition, there are Vietnamese, Cuban, and Colombian organized crime families in the United States.

There is also evidence of organized crime in other countries. Japan, for example, is the home of a well-developed criminal network often referred to as the Yakuza (Kaplan and Dubro, 1986). The Yakuza supply illegal products and services similar to those provided by the Mafia. In addition they invest vast sums of their criminal proceeds into legitimate businesses, such as construction, professional sports, and the entertainment industry. Finally, they protect their criminal enterprises by corrupting law enforcement and political officials. Russia has perhaps the most obvious example of organized crime. Along with the destruction of the old Soviet Union and the transformation of some member states into democratic, capitalistic entities, Russia has witnessed a rise in its own version of organized crime. Gangsters there are involved with the usual illegal enterprises, but they also supply legal goods and services—automobiles, housing, household appliances—which are scarce and overpriced in the legitimate market.

Summary

In sum, organized crime bears that name because it is a regimented, co-ordinated network of criminal activity. While experts may quibble about whether organized crime families in the United States or elsewhere have the rigid bureaucratic structure of the modern business, or whether the "boss" of a family is different from the CEO of a corporation, the conclusion is clear that organized crime bears the essential characteristics of fully organized deviant activity. Organized crime, in a nutshell, cannot be understood in isolation from its organizational context. Although the kinds of things that organized criminals do are all undertaken sometimes by individuals acting alone or within general subcultures of criminal activity, the coordination of criminal behavior into a successful long-term criminal/deviant enterprise serves as a good example of how deviance can be exercised within the context of full organization. ✦

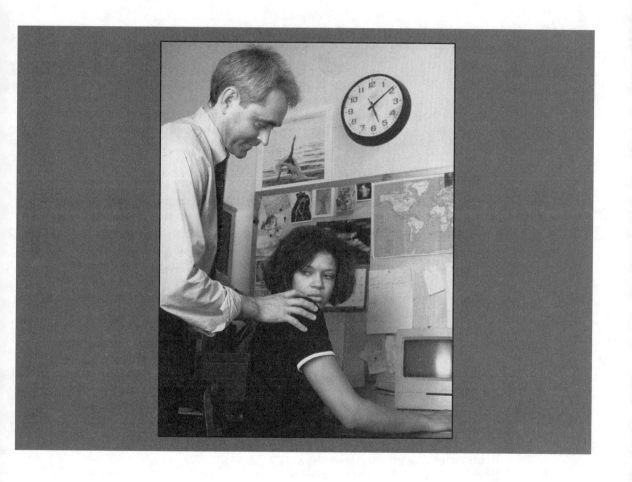

Chapter 6

Deviance/Crime and Society

Deviance of all types, from individualized to fully organized, is ubiquitous in modern times and has been a continuing concern in all societies, even though societies go to a lot of trouble to try to prevent it. This pervasiveness has led social thinkers to question whether deviance, even very serious forms, is as threatening to society as members of the society usually assume. Moreover, the persistence of deviance, even in communities dedicated to righteousness, raises the question of whether efforts to stamp it out entirely might be futile. Perhaps a certain amount of deviance is inevitable in any society—a society of saints as well as one of sinners.

The Inevitability of Deviance

Some theorists have come to the conclusion that the social processes identifying categories of acts as deviant and the processes of identifying and dealing with those who commit acts of deviance are an inherent, essential process in social life. In other words, some degree of deviance may be inevitable and may, in fact, be both necessary and healthy for social organization.

Possible Usefulness of Deviance

As noted in Chapter 1, there are ways that deviance can be useful for a social group (Dentler and Erikson, 1959). Even though deviance is often costly and destructive, there are at least seven consequences of its existence that may help groups. First, vicarious experiences garnered by observing and reacting to actual or imagined deviant acts may release pent-up frustrations associated with the constraints of regulated social life (Marx, 1981). Second, deviance may promote in-group solidarity as members unite in opposition to some threatening element from the outside (Durkheim, 1938 [1895]; see also 1997). Third, by denigrating deviant acts and those who do them, conforming members of society can enhance their own statuses and feelings of superiority, thereby providing rewards for conformity. Fourth, imagined and actual deviant behavior provides benchmarks for defining acceptable conduct that cannot be clearly demarcated in the abstract. Fifth, deviance activates the forces of social control, keeping them in good working order so that they can be mobilized quickly and work effectively in cases of genuine emergency. Sixth, identifying and managing deviance can effectively denote the moral boundaries of a group so that in-group members can be differentiated from those not part of the group in situations where there are competing social entities (Erikson, 1966). Finally, as will be discussed in Chapter 7, deviance is an important mechanism through which social change, often essential for social adaptation, occurs.

Some of these potential "functions" appear to some thinkers to be so important to the maintenance of a group (and possible to achieve only by dealing with deviance) that deviant behavior is regarded as a necessary evil for social groups—collectively and individually damaging but nevertheless absolutely crucial for the health and long-term well-being of the social group. An analogy might be made to an internal combustion engine. It burns (explodes) fuel to generate power for moving the pistons, which are ultimately connected to drive shafts that turn wheels. An explosion is a dangerous process that, if too large or not contained within the combustion chamber, can destroy an engine. Moreover, continuous explosions inside the engine produce wear and tear, necessitate constant infusions of new fuel, and require management of waste. It would be desirable, therefore, if internal combustion could occur without exploding fuel. But can anyone imagine such a thing? Certainly there are other kinds of engines, but the very nature of internal combustion is dependent on a process that is simultaneously useful and destructive. And so it is with social organization and deviance, according to some scholars. Social life without deviance is unimaginable because people in social groups always seem to find deviance of some type, and when they succeed in combating particular forms, they find other forms to replace them. So it seems that deviance may be inevitable in social organization, simultaneously necessary and undesirable.

To understand this argument, imagine a batch of people shipwrecked on an island with a harsh environment. To survive they need to organize themselves for building shelters, gathering or producing food, protecting themselves against wild animals, and avoiding the destructive consequences of selfishness. Such organization implies norms, or rules of conduct, by which the people approach each other in pursuing the tasks before them—because it is unlikely that people will automatically know when and what to do or that they will automatically share resources and respect the needs or rights of others. But to establish or imagine such rules is to imply violation. For people to comprehend rules, they must be able to imagine behavior contrary to the rules. Thus is born the concept of deviance. Once the idea of rules is operating, it is implied that without such guidelines people would behave in contrary ways; that is, rules emerge to control behaviors that are undesirable to rule makers or those they represent. But rules without enforcement do not automatically produce the desired behavior, so penalties for violation are invented to be imposed by the people collectively or by somebody in particular who is appointed or assumes the right to punish violators. But among our shipwrecked people, none of this is formally instituted, written down, or indoctrinated, so there is much room for disagreement about what is or is not acceptable or required and who may punish others for rule infractions.

The problem is that no rules are ever completely clear, even when legislated or handed down by powerful entities. Also, many norms are emergent; that is, they develop in the process of interaction as people observe a behavior and come to perceive it as wrong, even though they might not have realized they thought it was wrong until the actual episode. People learn social rules, many of which lie dormant most of the time, by confronting actual instances of behavior that may or may not qualify as deviance. When the processes of dealing with an actual instance have unfolded, observers then have a better understanding of what is or is not prohibited. Rule breaking, even when it was not known ahead of time to be such, and the response of a social network to that behavior, then, fashion and crystallize the system of norms.

The Elasticity of Evil

Sometimes social groups construct so many rules and engage so frequently in responding to real or imagined deviance that they cannot manage other aspects of living. And sometimes actual deviance is so extensive that it cannot be dealt with within the resources of the group. As a consequence, when deviance management becomes too time- and energy-consuming, social groups retrench; they either redefine some previously deviant behaviors as acceptable or they concentrate enforcement on the most egregious violations—usually violations reflecting the most serious forms of deviance—and tolerate the less egregious forms; they eventually come to see previously egregious forms of deviance as trivial. This process has been called the "elasticity of evil" (Cohen, 1974). Evil, or deviance, is greater or less, depending on the ability of a group to manage it.

In a society with many norms and many violations, such as America today, we now regard as minor many acts that previously were thought to be quite serious. For example, currently defined "soft pornography," which is widely accepted in movies and TV today, was once thought of as evil. Now there is partial nudity in TV programs and movies shown during "prime time" (the mid-evening hours). TV was not always this bold or risqué. The senior author can recall the public outcry in the 1950s when the movie *The Outlaw* pictured a man and a woman in the same bed (although completely covered) for the first time in public theaters. Up to that point it was merely implied that men and women actually slept together and had sex. Now it is routine for popular movies to feature sex acts, often of nude people in the same bed. The thought that people in contemporary America would get upset about the kind of scene that first appeared in *The Outlaw* is almost laughable. The point is that, given the amount of nakedness and sex that everybody in our society is now exposed to, few people have the time and emotional energy to be concerned with any but the most egregious violations of norms of etiquette. So, over time, we have come to tolerate more and more previously outrageous behavior to the point where it is no longer considered outrageous or deviant. Our concept of evil has changed, but we still have evil—now, however, the things that are regarded as evil are far more heinous than before. Hence, deviance is not fixed but is elastic—it "stretches" or contracts with the passage of time. What was once taken as completely unacceptable conduct begins to be taken for granted, and some behaviors that had been acceptable (smoking in buildings and airplanes, for example) become deviant.

This tendency to expand or constrict concepts of deviance can also be observed among individuals. If people are constantly exposed to behaviors that they regard as deviant, there is a tendency for them to lose sensitivity to the behavior's deviance so that after a while things previously regarded as deviant come to appear as routine. Those who think public nudity is wrong but for some reason go to visit or stay for a while in a nudist colony generally change their minds. If you are surrounded by naked people in a nonsexual setting, eating, playing tennis, swimming, conducting business, and conversing about politics, sports, and religion, before long it will seem natural. Indeed, if you are there and are the only one clothed, it is you who will begin to feel out of place and to believe you are doing something inappropriate. Tolerance often, though not inevitably, grows from direct exposure to a given behavior in a context in which it is regarded as morally or socially acceptable.

Demonstrating the elasticity of deviance, however, says nothing about its inevitability. What happens when societies actually succeed in eliminating (or reducing to minimal levels) the forms of deviance that they and other societies have found most heinous? It appears that such societies invent new deviance to replace the old. In groups of "saints," such as in monasteries and nunneries, and among religious communities like the Amish or Mennonites, there is no murder, mayhem, or rape, and there is very little theft. Yet those societies get mightily exercised about the evils of wearing bright clothing (which draws attention to self instead of God), failure to say prayers, or in the case of the Amish, using electricity or modern machinery for transportation, farming, or household chores.

In the United States as a whole—which, despite popular belief to the contrary and periodic upward swings, apparently has experienced substantial long-term reductions in violence (see for reviews of evidence: Gurr, 1981; Sutherland et al., 1992:59–61)—there has been a recurrent process of finding new forms of deviance. For instance, in this century Americans "discovered" and labeled as deviant, or as much more deviant than was previously the case, violence against children (Empey and Stafford, 1991; Pfohl, 1977), spousal battery (Tierney, 1982), stalking (Downey and Best, 1995), sexual harassment (see Benson and Thomson, 1982), hateful acts against groups (Jenness and Broad, 1997), sexual psychopathy (Ofshe and Watters, 1994; Sutherland, 1950a, 1950b), and hiding razor blades in Halloween candy given to trick-or-treaters (Best and Horiuchi, 1985). In addition, they rediscovered some forms of deviance, such as tobacco use (Markle and Troyer, 1979) and satanic cult worship (Goode and Ben-Yehuda, 1994; Ofshe and Watters, 1994) that had been of more concern at an earlier point in time. That is not to say that these forms of behavior did not exist before (although deviance may, in fact, often be imaginary rather than real—see especially Best and Horiuchi, 1985, and Ofshe and Watters, 1994) but rather that they were moved into the forefront of consciousness of the public and of the enforcers of conventional reality.

It seems, then, that social groups always have deviance, at least as much as they can socially and psychologically manage. And if they didn't, they would probably invent it. A more important issue than whether a society will have deviance, then, is the content of the normative systems at a given point in time. The norms, and consequently the forms of deviance, vary enormously among different social groups at the same time and also within the same group over time. The processes by which various behaviors come to be regarded as deviant in a given group at a particular time are often referred to as "the social construction of deviance," to indicate that no behavior is inherently deviant but instead is so designated by a set of social and political procedures. Is it possible to explain how and why normative systems take their peculiar forms? A number of theories have emerged to account for the puzzle of why some behaviors are deviant while others are not in a given society at a particular point in history. These accounts include three broad explanatory schemes and two more-limited explanations.

General Theories About Norms: Anomalies to Be Explained

From the preceding discussion we can conclude that deviance is highly relative; the behaviors that qualify as deviant vary from group to group, from time to time within the same group, and within a given group from one social status to another. Yet the rationale for particular behaviors being deviant is often obscure and illogical, posing a challenge of explanation for sociologists and other social scientists. Consider six examples from the United States.

Physical Violence

Street fighting is illegal in the United States, typically prompting police action to prevent it, and it is widely disapproved across different gender, racial/ethnic, and social class groups. In other words, it is deviant behavior according to the definition of deviance used in this book. Moreover, it is deviant behavior according to all the definitions of deviance considered in Chapter 1 (although, of course, it is not deviant behavior from the point of view of those who are integrated into the culture of the street gang). As a result, those who engage in this behavior are regarded as doing wrong; they are often stigmatized as bad people; they are frequently arrested and processed as delinquents or criminals; and injuries to participants are taken as evidence in courts of law to help convict perpetrators of criminal assault.

Although all this is true, prizefighting, which involves the same kind of behavior as assault—physical contact intended to inflict pain and injury on another—is not deviant. It is not illegal, not usually harassed by the police, and not disapproved by the majority of the population. Indeed, it is a popular form of entertainment in which participants are highly rewarded, sometimes even made into heroes. And injuries, rather than being used as evidence of criminal assault, are taken as signs of effective boxing talent—an ultimate manifestation of manhood. Professional wrestling, football, and hockey also involve intentional physical contact that often results in pain and injury, but these behaviors are not regarded as deviant.

What is the difference between street fighting and "contact sports" that would make one deviant and the other not? Both involve physical violence, and both frequently produce actual pain and injury, but one is unacceptable and the other isn't.

Sexual Expression

In the United States, as well as in most other societies in the world today, marital coitus (sexual intercourse) between a man and woman is regarded as acceptable behavior. Indeed, in some sense it is mandatory because denial of sexual access can be grounds for divorce in most states. Clearly, this type of behavior is usually thought of as normal—even laudatory or good. But the boundaries of what constitutes "normal" sex are fairly narrow, because sexual expression of almost any other kind by almost any other persons is more or less unacceptable, or deviant. While sex in the "missionary" position between married persons is acceptable, marital sex in other positions (or oral or anal sex) is often viewed with suspicion. In addition, almost any nonmarital form of sex is deemed unacceptable to a greater or lesser degree, such as when: one of the parties is not of age (statutory rape); not married to the other participant (adultery); or not human (bestiality); or sex is not done with a partner (masturbation), or is done with too many partners (promiscuity). Also unacceptable are consensual acts of sexual expression between same-sex partners (homosexuality). In fact, considering the views of the population as a whole, it is difficult to think of any sex act other than marital coitus that is not regarded as at least somewhat bad by most people.

Although acts of sexual expression are basically the same, involving some contact of one individual's body or part of his or her body with the sexual organs of another person or creature, the reaction by others to different sexual acts is not. As suggested above, if this contact is made between unmarried persons, between persons of widely divergent ages, between persons of the same gender, between people and animals, or among more than two people, it is regarded as bad or immoral. If the contact involves married (to each other) people of opposite gender, it is not deviant. What is the rationale for this? Can it be explained in a way that makes sense? Are there general principles that would permit us to understand these kinds of inconsistencies that occur in almost all societies?

Commercial Deception

To represent a product or service as something that it is not in order to realize personal gain from the deal is fraud. For example, if a person involves you in a phony investment scheme to steal your money, it is called a "confidence game" or a form of "bunko." Similarly, if a roof cleaner agrees to clean and paint your roof for a certain fee but only cleans the leading edges of the tile so that it looks entirely clean from the ground, such a person is usually regarded as a fraud or a "fly-by-night" operator. Both of these types of businesspersons are regarded as engaging in deviant behavior; they are stigmatized as criminals and are subject to arrest and prosecution, as well as being subject to civil action in a court of law.

Many standard "legitimate" business practices, however, use the same techniques without being either illegal or stigmatized. For instance, the very essence of advertising is often to make the product or service appear to be something it isn't. For years Listerine was advertised as a medicine for killing cold germs, thereby implying that it could prevent or cure colds, a claim that was patently false and misleading, as the Federal Trade Commission later declared. It is common also for products to be packaged in such a way as to deceive the consumer into thinking there is more of the product than there actually is. And guarantees on products are often written so that they are, in fact, useless. A good example is the guarantee on automobile tires that promises prorated replacement for the "life of the tread." Obviously, if the tire is defective, the tread will wear out quickly and the consumer will be owed nothing by the manufacturer.

Yet these business practices are not illegal; the police do not attempt to do anything about them; the companies or individuals who practice them are not labeled as crooks; and the acts themselves are not regarded by the majority of Americans as unacceptable but rather as routine aspects of competitive business. What, then, is the crucial difference (if any) between a confidence game and these business practices? Both involve deception of a consumer or a "mark" in order to enhance the economic standing of the deceiver—in short, fraud. This is yet another instance where the same behavior is deviant in one instance but not another. Why?

Gambling

Engaging in risky ventures in the hopes of winning a lucrative payoff is the essence of gambling. Some forms of gambling are acceptable and conforming while other forms are thought by most people to be bad, morally wrong, and deviant. Church bingo, life insurance, and stock investments represent acceptable, nondeviant, forms of gambling, whereas the numbers racket, betting on athletic contests, and alley craps are unacceptable and deviant. In church bingo the player pays a fee in the hopes that a low-probability event—getting the sequentially correct row of numbers on his card—will happen. If it does, the person gets a prize or a cash payoff, just as gamblers in a casino get a payoff if they guess the numbered slot where the roulette ball will fall.

In like manner, life insurance is a gamble. Using vital statistics for past years, the insurance company calculates the probability of death for various categories of individuals and then generates a premium schedule which, if paid by, say, 100,000 clients, will enable the company to pay all death claims among their policy holders that might reasonably occur and to have a profit left over. In essence, the company is betting you will not die within a given period of time. You, as the customer, are betting that you will. You, of course, hope they are right, but nevertheless you are betting your money that they are wrong. It is a gamble because you (actually your survivors) stand to gain a large sum of money if you are right and your life expires within the specified time. On the other hand, if you do not die in that time period, you will have lost the premium you paid, just as you would lose your money if you were to bet on a horse that did not finish in the money. (Actually, insurance is a bit more complex, since the insurance company invests some of the premium you paid in other business activities, enabling it to return some of your money even if you do not die in the specified time frame.)

Finally, when individuals (like day traders on the Internet) invest money in stocks in the hopes that the price will rise so that they can sell them at a profit, those individuals are engaging in a gamble. Clearly, the price of the stock might not rise; in fact, it might go down, as many investors painfully discovered on October 19, 1987, when the stock market crashed several hundred points in one day. Yet all these gambles are acceptable.

Not so with the "numbers" game. Suppose some entrepreneur sets up a business where he sells the right to make guesses on what the last five digits of the number of stocks sold on the New York Stock Exchange on a given day will be. He agrees to pay a bettor $500 if the bettor guesses the exact number, $100 if she guesses four of the numbers, and $10 if three of the numbers are guessed. The entrepreneur charges each individual two dollars to make a guess. This would be a numbers racket, and it would be illegal. It would attract the attention of the police; it would be regarded by most people (other than the players and the entrepreneur) as bad or wrong; and the entrepreneur and players would be subject to social stigma as lawbreakers and sleazy characters. The same would be true of a business where the bet concerned scores on athletic contests. And those who go into the alley behind a store or a house to shoot craps for money will be thought of as no-goods and their activity as dangerous; they will typically be arrested if discovered by the police.

Again, the activity is the same in each of these cases—gambling. But the social definition of its acceptability varies. Is there a general explanation to account for this apparently contradictory state of affairs?

Suicide

In the United States it is deviant to commit suicide. Those who attempt to do so and fail are subject to criminal prosecution in many states because suicide is illegal. And those who succeed bring shame and dishonor upon their families. Or at least it would seem so. In fact, however, when people knowingly sacrifice their lives to save somebody else or willingly give up their lives in the service of their country, such as when soldiers throw themselves into direct fire to attack an enemy machine gun nest, such instances of suicide are lauded, and the individuals are declared heroes.

It appears, then, that suicide is sometimes deviant and sometimes not. Are there general principles to account for these differences?

Cross-Sex Dressing

Finally, we can observe that women are allowed to dress like men (they can wear slacks and button-down shirts with ties or even heavy combat-type boots), while men are prohibited from dressing like women, and apparently this has been true in western civilization for a long time (Bullough, 1974). In other words, it is deviant behavior in the United States for a man to wear women's clothes (unless it is a special "time-out" occasion like a play or a spoof). Most people regard male cross-dressing as unacceptable, dangerous, and indicative of psychological or other problems. But it is not unacceptable for women to wear men's clothing. Indeed, it is now quite common.

You can demonstrate this contrast to yourself by imagining what would happen if your instructor in this class were a man and came to class tomorrow wearing a dress. Very likely he would be reported to the administration as a pervert, parents would be in touch with the Board of Regents to see if something could be done about this instructor, and students would giggle and ridicule him. But what would happen if your instructor is a woman and comes to class tomorrow wearing pants? Very likely nothing would happen. In fact, if your instructor is a woman, she has probably worn pants to class already this semester with no negative reaction. Is there some way to understand why cross-dressing is deviant for men but not for women?

General Theories About Norms: Explanations for the Anomalies

There are at least three general theories to explain these anomalies. The first is called consensus theory.

Consensus Theory

Consensus theorists begin with a view of society as a collection of people who are organized into a mutual benefit association (Davis, 1937; Hall, 1947; Parsons, 1951; for overviews see Bernard, 1983; Tittle, 1994). In any society, most members are thought to share a set of basic values and to recognize their common dependence upon each other for survival and the realization of those values. Thus, society is fundamentally a cooperative unit in which most people share common objectives. Their common goals and values are: survival and continuity of the society and preservation of the basic beliefs that are thought to be essential to that survival and continuity.

Hence behavior that most members of a society perceive as contributing to the survival and maintenance of the group as a whole, or that is perceived as promoting its basic values, will be encouraged and rewarded. Behavior that most believe contribute nothing to the survival and maintenance of society and may even contribute to its destruction and demise will be discouraged and discredited. Noncontributory behaviors that are thought to actually threaten the survival or continuity of society or that are believed by most to undermine its basic values will be regarded as dangerous and bad and will be prohibited and punished; that is, they will be socially defined as very deviant behavior. Behavior that neither promotes nor threatens the core interests of the group as a whole will be regarded as somewhat bad (or at least in bad taste) but not seriously deviant. Such behavior is likely to be tolerated but will certainly not be encouraged. Thus, whether a given behavior is deviant depends upon whether it is perceived by most members of society as contributing to the central goals and values of the group. How deviant a given behavior is considered to be will depend upon the seriousness of its perceived threat to the shared interests of the collectivity.

Every society is presumably concerned with regulation and control in order to channel behavior toward the survival of society and the realization of its goals, and survival is thought to be linked with basic institutions such as the family, the economy, the government, and religion. American society, for instance, is presumably based on a set of shared core values promoting controlled competition. That is, all aspects of our lives are oriented around competition, but not cut-throat competition. We are trained to compete but to do so *within rules*. We believe that competition, up to a certain point, is good for achieving personal and societal goals. But we recognize unrestrained competition as dangerous to the survival of all and a threat to the general welfare. Hence businesspeople are thought to contribute to productivity and overall societal welfare when they compete for customers. But this benefit is lost if the competition involves extortion, intimidation, or "dirty tricks" because productive participants are eliminated and the individual benefit of one player in the economic game rises above the general welfare that is supposedly promoted when all compete to provide the best product or service at the lowest price. Similarly, athletes are thought to reinforce basic societal values when they struggle to win a competitive game, but they are thought to undermine basic values when they break the rules to win.

Deviance in Everyday Life

An example of an athlete cheating occurred in July of 1996 when Chris Sabo, a professional baseball player with the Cincinnati Reds, was caught using a corked baseball bat. A corked bat, which makes the ball go farther when hit, is illegal, according to the rules of professional baseball. How did Sabo get caught? After hitting a pop-up to the shortstop in the second inning of a game against the Houston Astros, Sabo's bat literally exploded, sending pieces of cork onto the playing field. He was suspended for seven days. This is not the first time in recent baseball history that someone has tried to take an unfair advantage on the diamond. Albert Belle of the Cleveland Indians was suspended for six days in 1994 also for using a corked bat. Other players (pitchers) have been suspended for throwing "spitballs" and otherwise altering the ball to make it more difficult to hit.

Physical Violence

According to the consensus perspective, then, street fighting is deviant behavior while contact sports are not because street fighting is unregulated and uncontrolled violence that serves no societal interest and, in fact, threatens innocent bystanders as well as the participants. Organized contact sports, on the other hand, are regulated and controlled by rules and institutional procedures, thereby limiting their potential destructive consequences while at the same time epitomizing and reinforcing the basic competitive values of U.S. society.

Sexual Expression

Consensus theorists maintain that marital coitus between a man and a woman is approved behavior because it represents sexual expression controlled and regulated in the interest of society as a whole. Through marriage, the sex drive is linked to the institution of the family, where reproduction and socialization of the young can occur in an orderly and efficient manner, thereby contributing to the long-range survival of the society and the perpetuation of its core values. And confining sexual expression to the marital institution provides an incentive to strengthen the family so that individual members can sustain each other, giving and getting the economic and emotional support necessary for the larger community.

Any other form of sexual expression detracts from and undermines these goals. For instance, premarital sex is practiced in a social relationship that is inherently less stable than a marital unit, and to the extent that sexual expression is possible outside marriage, the motive to marry is reduced. Thus, premarital sex in a society like that of the United States will be disapproved and seen as somewhat deviant. But it will not be disapproved as much as other forms of nonmarital sex are because it at least holds the potential for leading to a stable family unit. And to the extent that premarital experience comes to be perceived as good training for successful marriage, it will become less disapproved.

By contrast, homosexual conduct is highly disapproved and is regarded as dangerous and evil; in short, it is very deviant. According to consensus theory it is loathed because it directly threatens the institution of marriage and family. To the extent that people develop interests in same-sex relationships and are allowed to express those interests, the less motivated will they be to pursue heterosexual relationships that might ultimately lead to marriage and reproduction. And there are few redeeming virtues of homosexuality that would contribute to societal goals or the preservation of societal values; indeed, its disease-producing potential has been realized in recent years in the development of the AIDS threat. While stable homosexual relationships certainly can provide emotional and economic sustenance for the partners, just as heterosexual ones can, they lack the community recognition that marital relationships enjoy and are therefore less stable.

To illustrate their argument, consensus theorists point out that society disapproves of male homosexuality more than it does female homosexuality. Although female homosexuality is deviant, it arouses a less negative response than does male homosexuality; this response occurs presumably because male homosexuality has greater potential to disqualify the individual for reproductive sexual activity. To the extent that a man is totally oriented toward other males, his capacity for sexual arousal with females is diminished. Since his *ability* to engage in sexual intercourse with a woman is completely dependent upon arousal capacity, a fully committed homosexual male is incapable of reproductive sex. A woman's *capability* for engaging in sex with a male, however, is independent of her arousal. Completely uninterested females may nevertheless be passive sexual partners, become pregnant, and produce children. Indeed, with the newly developed science of *in vitro* fertilization, homosexual women can easily bear children without sexual contact.

And although producing children outside the traditional family does not promote societal goals completely, it is more contributory than total absence of reproductive sex.

This same kind of reasoning can be applied to all other forms of nonmarital sex to explain why they are deviant, as well as differences in the degree of their deviance. Moreover, the consensus argument suggests that as societal needs change, so will the perceived deviance of the various kinds of sexual expression. For instance, in the contemporary world, where population survival rates are much greater than they were in the past, the perceived need for reproduction has declined, and so has the social disapproval of many forms of nonmarital sex. Indeed, one form of nonmarital sex, swinging (consensual sharing of sexual partners among married couples and singles), at one point became somewhat popular among middle-class segments of the population. The main rationale for swinging has been to provide controlled sexual variety in a context that will not threaten marriage. In the contemporary world this provision of variety is perceived as a necessity because the roles of males and females have changed so much that the possibility of sexual encounters outside marriage has begun to pose a threat to marriage itself. Hence swinging is justified as a method for preserving marriage and the family in the face of external eroding influences. According to the logic of the consensus perspective, if most people can be persuaded to recognize that justification, then swinging will become less disapproved. But, of course, the inherent disease-spreading potential of swinging will always make it less desirable for most people than monogamous sexual exclusivity.

Commercial Deception

Consensus theory explains why advertising with exaggerated claims is acceptable while other forms of fraud are deviant by reference to the values of controlled competition and the importance of high consumption in a capitalistic economy. Controlled competition in the economic world means that businesses are to compete but at the same time be accountable to rules of fair play and the consequences of inefficiency, incompetence, or injury they might perpetuate. Ideally, they must not gain an unfair advantage by being able to escape the social and legal consequences of their actions. Thus, "legitimate" business is that which has an established, identifiable place of operation, where a customer can go to complain if wronged. It is integrated into the community network through long-term contractual obligations that are legally enforceable, and by having a reputation that can be damaged by community stigma for bad business practices. And it is subject to taxation or other community obligations. Under these circumstances, exaggerated advertising, deceptive packaging, and meaningless guarantees are permitted as a means to stimulate consumption and vigorous economic activity, so essential to a capitalistic economy. Presumably, the competitive process will itself moderate such practices as consumers avoid businesses that violate the rules, stigmatize those that act irresponsibly, and bring lawsuits against those that fail to fulfill their contractual obligations.

But unacceptable fraud occurs when "illegitimate" businesses engage in deceptive practices. Such businesses have no established, identifiable place of operation (hence the term "fly-by-night"); they have no contractual ties; and they are not integrated into the community. Consequently, there is no place for the wronged consumer to complain; legal contracts are unenforceable; and community stigma means nothing. Moreover, illegitimate business contributes little to the overall economic vitality of the community, since it actually produces nothing, does not participate in the larger life of the community, and, perhaps most importantly, is not subject to taxation. Thus, deception by illegitimate business is deviant because it violates the values of controlled competition, and it threatens the vitality of a consumption-oriented economy by undermining the trust on which commercial transactions are based.

Gambling

Why are church bingo, life insurance, and stock investment acceptable forms of gambling, while the numbers racket, betting on athletic contests, and alley craps are not? The answer that consensus theory gives to the question is oriented around regulation and an activity's contribution to the goals of society. Each of the acceptable forms of gambling is regulated by rules enforceable by agents for the society as a whole, and each, in its own way, contributes to an important social goal or to the maintenance of an important social institution. Church bingo supports religion, which in turn helps to socialize children and to promote the values of the larger society. Life insurance protects families in the case of the early demise of breadwinners, thereby preserving and sustaining an important social institution. And, of course, stock investment is essential to the vitality of a capitalist economy.

But a numbers racket is totally private, without community input or regulation. It is free to wreak damage on its participants, to create conflict and disorder when losers complain and seek personal redress, and to promote the interests of the entrepreneur without accountability to the community. The same holds for betting on athletic contests, and for alley craps. Moreover, none of these activities contributes to the survival or continuity of society or to the sustenance of the values that support it. Hence, according to consensus theory, they will all be regarded as deviant.

To illustrate the argument, consensus theorists point out that numbers rackets, betting on athletic contests, and craps are sometimes transformed into acceptable activities by being brought under a regulatory umbrella and by being linked to important societal institutions. Several states, for instance, now have legalized state lotteries (a numbers racket); permit organized betting on horse races and jai alai under state regulation; and tolerate casinos for craps and other games of chance. In these instances, each activity is brought under some form of state regulation to guarantee fairness, to reduce conflicts arising out of disputes, and to recover some tax monies for useful social purposes, usually to support public education. The difference between deviance and conformity, then, is not in the nature of the activity but in its perceived relationship to larger societal goals and values, a relationship that is subject to change.

Suicide

In the United States, altruistic suicide (suicide that benefits the group or another person) is acceptable, but other kinds of suicide are not, according to the consensus perspective. A suicide that has the effect of saving another or that is done in order to carry out one's duty as a soldier or police officer is acceptable behavior because it helps to promote the goals of the society as a whole and to uphold its fundamental values. Suicide for nonaltruistic reasons represents a way of escaping social responsibility, a way of asserting individual rights over the interests of the group as a whole. Since group survival

❖ ❖ ❖ ❖

ultimately requires suppression of individual freedom in the group's interest, assertions of the precedence of individual rights, even the right to take one's own life, is regarded as dangerous.

Of course, what is regarded as altruistic suicide varies from society to society. While most forms of suicide are thought to be bad in the United States, in Japan it is acceptable for an individual who has shamed or dishonored his or her family or country to commit suicide. This point of view supposedly stems from the tradition in Japan, extending far into the past, where honor, especially family honor, is one of the most cherished values. Consensus theorists believe that one can make sense of such apparent anomalies in social definitions of deviance by reference to survival goals and fundamental values of a society.

Deviance in Everyday Life

The acceptability of taking one's life when faced with a terminal illness or debilitating disease is finding acceptance among physicians as well as the public. In a 1997 Gallup Poll of Canadian citizens, 75 percent of the respondents believed that doctors should be allowed to assist people to end their lives when they are suffering. In a random sample of practicing primary-care physicians in Monroe County, New York, it was found that 61 percent of the physicians believed that suicide can be rational under certain circumstances, and 31 percent supported the legalization of physician-assisted suicide under certain circumstances. (See Duberstein et al., 1995)

Furthermore, one can predict changes in those social definitions by monitoring changes in the perceived needs or values of a society. For example, public attitudes in the United States toward suicide by those with chronic, debilitating, and fatal diseases have softened in recent years. It is now possible for the totally disabled who are being sustained artificially by machines to end their own lives without social stigma for their survivors, and in Oregon it is legal for physicians to provide the means of suicide for extremely ill patients who request help in dying painlessly. Consensus theorists would contend that change is happening because the United States public is now coming to recognize that the cost of sustaining life under such circumstances, given current medical technology and the enormous number of people who are surviving to ages where such situations are likely, poses more of a threat to the survival of our society than does permitting such suicides, which presumably endangers collective control or basic values concerning the sacredness of human life. Moreover, it is significant that in many states there is now a legal procedure whereby such individuals may seek court approval for their suicide; in other words, while recognizing the permissibility of such suicide, the collectivity is nonetheless asserting its right to have the final word on this matter. In this way, an intensely individualistic act, suicide, is brought under social control and regulation—something you would expect if you believed that society is organized according to the consensus model.

Cross-Sex Dressing

Initially, the inconsistency of permitting female cross-dressing but treating male cross-dressing as deviant appears to be inexplicable. Yet there is an explanation consistent with the consensus perspective. Supposedly, one of the fundamental values of a competitive society revolves around individuals' struggle to be socially mobile, to be the best one can be, to strive to achieve the

highest status possible. Presumably, when such behavior is successfully promoted, it leads to improved productivity and a better life for everybody in the
society. Consequently, our society admires and rewards those who exhibit
such initiative, and it discredits those who fail to try, those who allow themselves to be downwardly mobile, and those who deliberately take on the characteristics of people lower in status than themselves. Therefore, it is conforming behavior to try to be like those of higher status, but it is deviant behavior
for an individual to try to be like those of lower status. Since in our society
males are generally of higher status than females, it is deviant for them to emulate females by cross-dressing. Such behavior would indicate a desire to be
like those of lower social status, which would represent a denial of the value
of struggling for higher status and would threaten the incentive system that
energizes a competitive social system. On the other hand, it is consistent with
the core values of American society for women to dress like males since wearing men's clothes suggests a desire to move into higher status positions
(Bullough, 1974). Hence female cross-dressing is tolerated while male cross-
dressing is prohibited, stigmatized, and thought to be a bad thing. This may
also help explain why female cigar smoking is more tolerated than a male's
use of lipstick.

Again, consensus theorists draw upon comparisons with other societies
at different times in history to show that disapproval of cross-dressing is a
function of the value system prevailing at the time. For instance, at most
times in the past in Western societies, it was deviant for females as well as
males to cross-dress. But prior to the democratic revolutions that occurred
within the past 200 years, there was no value system promoting social mobility. Indeed, the prevailing systems in the past were founded on the tenet that
high status was a matter of family heritage, based on biological superiority
transmitted through genetic linkages and sanctioned by divinity. Hence any
cross-dressing was prohibited because it denied the divine nature of social arrangements and was prohibited in the Bible (Bullough, 1974). Nevertheless,
since emulating someone of higher status is overt recognition of the person's
superiority and therefore indirect evidence of commitment to the values undergirding the system, cross-dressing by lower-status females was considered *less* deviant than cross-dressing by males, who were of higher status. In
the Middle Ages in Europe, it was common for women to disguise themselves
as males in order to be eligible for education and other opportunities otherwise denied women, particularly within the hierarchy of the Catholic church.
Upon discovery, they were punished, but the deviance was not treated as severely as it was when a male was caught cross-dressing. In fact, popular myth
suggests that at least one woman managed to work her way into the position
of Pope disguised as a male. Whether true or not, as the story goes, when she
was discovered, after having fainted in a parade in Rome as a result of pregnancy, the consequences were not as great as one might have imagined ahead
of time (Bullough, 1974). Her behavior was deviant, to be sure, but after all, it
did certify her recognition of the validity of the social structure as it revolved
around the theological order, something that an act of cross-dressing by a
male would not have done.

Conflict Theory

Conflict theorists view society in an entirely different light than do consensus theorists, and so their view leads to explanations that are quite diver-

gent from those of the consensus perspective. Rather than society being a mutual benefit association composed of individual members who share certain core values and recognize collective interests that are to be promoted by societal norms, conflict theorists believe it is more accurate to conceive of society as a collection of individuals and groups with separate and distinct interests who are struggling among themselves for the power to promote and protect activities that benefit themselves (Chambliss and Seidman, 1971; Liska, 1994; Quinney, 1970; for overviews see Bernard, 1983; Tittle, 1994).

At any point in time, those who are winning the struggle for power will be in a position to formulate and implement rules that promote their own interests and protect their powerful positions from competitors. Hence behaviors that are consistent with the interests of power holders, or that are neutral with respect to elite interests, will be acceptable, and behaviors that threaten the interests or positions of power holders will be deviant. Power holders use agents of social control, such as police and courts, to deal with acts that threaten their interests; in addition, they are able to influence the mass media, school curricula, and other sources of information to persuade most nonelite members of society to regard behaviors that are actually prohibited in the interests of elites as also threatening to the general population. Moreover, having control of the sources of information enables elites to create a moral sense in the general population concerning actions that are, in reality, dangerous mainly from the point of view of the power holders themselves.

There are basically two versions of the conflict perspective. One, called the dualistic version, is based on the ideas of Karl Marx. It asserts that societies, particularly capitalistic ones, are divided into two major classes. The elites, or bourgeoisie, constitute one class; the members of this class are more or less united in promoting the interests of those with wealth, land, or capital resources. The other major class is composed of nonelites, or the proletariat, who have little wealth, land, or capital resources but who work for and are dependent upon the bourgeoisie. Although different segments within the elite class may ostensibly hold overt power at different times, laws will be made and behaviors declared deviant on the basis of the interests of the elite class as a whole.

The second version of conflict theory views society as composed of multiple power groups, organized around many foci in addition to economic interests, who vie among themselves for influence about particular issues. The struggle for power concerning, say, religious questions in the schools will involve different participants than will the struggle for influence concerning immigration. And even those with mainly economic interests will be contending among themselves for power with respect to particular issues because their individual interests will not necessarily be the same. What is good for General Motors will not necessarily be good for the insurance industry. Resisting installation of safety devices in order to hold down manufacturing costs is regarded by the auto industry as useful and prudent (because it increases profits), but it is viewed by companies that sell insurance to motorists as detrimental to the companies' ability to maximize profit from collision and other insurance. And what is good for the financial industry, such as high interest rates, will often be devastating for the construction or real estate industries, which then have trouble selling houses. At any point in time, and concerning specific issues, any one of a multitude of contenders will temporarily dominate the scene, and when it does, it will set rules to promote its own interests.

Therefore, according to this pluralist conception of society, any complex society will have a changing system of norms, a hodgepodge representing the collective residue of rules that were instituted at one time or another by different power groups with divergent concerns. What is common to both the dualistic and pluralist views, however, is the belief that powerful groups determine what is deviant conduct and how to deal with deviant individuals. The specific characters in the power struggle may differ, but the deviance process is presumed to be a political one. For example, in the United States there were at one time laws, even a constitutional amendment, prohibiting the manufacture and sale of alcoholic beverages. These laws, the deviance that resulted from their enforcement, and the publicity used in the campaign to get the laws enacted were products of organized political activity by a group with moral and religious concerns—The Women's Christian Temperance League—in opposition to the desires and interests of other groups, such as the liquor and entertainment industries, which often are quite powerful, and in fact since that time have regained the upper hand (Gusfield, 1963).

Regardless of which version of conflict theory we focus on, the main implication is the same. What is deviant and what is not will be understandable only by comprehending (1) the focused interests of power holders at the time the rules were instituted and (2) the continuing power of various interest groups in the particular society in question. To explain the anomalies illustrated before, we must pose the question, "In what way does the deviant activity threaten the interests of a powerful elite or interest group?" Or "In what way does the acceptable behavior enhance the interests of a powerful elite or interest group?" Let us pose such questions for the specific illustrations described earlier and attempt to formulate an explanation for each of these anomalies.

Physical Violence

According to the conflict perspective, street fighting is deviant for two reasons: (1) elites fear that the hostility and aggression being expressed there will get out of hand and spill over into organized violence against the power holders, who are the real enemies of the class of people likely to be street fighters, and (2) street fighting threatens the health and strength of a segment of the labor force that many elites depend upon for their own economic welfare. This second factor is particularly important in a capitalist society like the United States because the most influential elites are generally economically oriented owners and managers of capital resources. Capitalists must have a readily available, plentiful, and easily exploited labor force; therefore, they will attempt to discourage any activities that might reduce the ability of parts of that labor force to work or that might reduce its overall size, as street fighting holds the potential for doing.

On the other hand, prizefighting and body contact sports are acceptable for two contrasting reasons: (1) they produce huge profits for certain powerful economic interests who promote and market them as mass entertainment, and (2) elites in general recognize that violent sports allow vicarious release of the hostility and aggression felt by exploited subordinates. Hence owners, advertisers, and the broadcast industry all share an economic interest in making sure that violent sports are promoted as being useful and good things and in guaranteeing that this view is adopted by the general population. And they share a common interest in cooperating to see that these contests escape the prohibitive power of restrictive legislation. Other elites without direct economic interests in these activities nevertheless cooperate because they know that the vast population of exploited workers (the main consumers of violent sports entertainment) need a vicarious outlet for the pent-up anger and hostility that they might otherwise direct against their exploiters. Therefore, all elites endorse the acceptability of contact sports and assist those who have a direct financial interest in violent sports in seeing that such sports are adopted as part of the American way of life.

Sexual Expression

The conflict perspective suggests that heterosexual coitus between men and women married to each other is seen as conforming behavior, while all other forms of sexual expression are seen as more or less deviant because elites have an interest in marital coitus as a means to guarantee a stable, plentiful, and easily exploited work force. A normative system that uses social expectations and legal coercion to confine sexual expression to marriage enhances the elite interest in the labor force in two ways. First, such a normative structure requires a man (or woman) to provide for the maintenance of spouse and children. Under such circumstances, a married person will be a more dependable worker. If necessary to support the family, a married individual will be more likely to seek work, even for low wages; married people, especially those with children, will be more willing to accept workplace indignities to ensure continued employment. This capitulation is especially likely if workers are numerous and jobs are scarce, a condition consciously promoted by elites. Thus, elites have a second interest in encouraging sexual expression only within the family context: to encourage orderly reproduction in a context where potential new workers can be produced and trained to have appropriate attitudes and habits that will make them useful to employers. Reproductive sex will, therefore, generate a plentiful work force, which will make workers compete for jobs, thereby keeping wages low. And if sex is confined within a family unit, it will make individuals more willing to compete for those lower wages.

Single people, on the other hand, have no such responsibilities. They are freer to choose not to work at all; they are more likely to leave a job if it is ungratifying or humiliating; and they are more likely to leave local areas to seek higher wages in a market with fewer available workers. Moreover, if single people can achieve sexual gratification outside marriage, they are less likely to lock themselves into the restrictive marital unit, and they are more likely to be careful to avoid reproduction, thereby reducing the supply of potential workers. From the conflict point of view, marriage and family are devices invented and used by elites to control and exploit subordinates. But since the elites can influence sources of communication and dominate local institutions, they are in positions to promote a normative system that defines marriage and family as wholesome, moral, ordained by God, and essential to the welfare of all of society, a litany that conceals their true purposes.

It follows that other forms of sexual expression will in one way or another threaten the positions and privileges of power holders. If individuals can gratify their sexual needs outside marriage, they will be less motivated to form a marital unit and therefore will be less constrained and less easily exploited. Moreover, nonmarital sexual activity is less likely to produce children (no possibility at all, of course, for homosexual relations, animal relations, or

❖ ❖ ❖ ❖

relations between people of widely divergent ages), and when children are produced they will be less likely to be socialized in an orderly and predictable way to accept the social arrangements that exist to benefit the elites.

Consideration of some situations where nonmarital sex is permitted can be cited as supporting the conflict approach. For example, in frontier areas with imbalanced sex ratios, such as in newly industrializing communities or where military outposts are stationed, prostitution is often allowed to exist, sometimes even promoted by elites themselves. Presumably this is to placate male workers or soldiers who are needed to serve the immediate interests of elites but who have no realistic opportunity for marriage. Under such circumstances nonmarital sex is more useful to elites as a pacifier of potential aggression than are social rules promoting marital sex; hence nonmarital sex in such situations is redefined as nondeviant.

Similarly, prostitution is sometimes used by business interests as a commercial inducement. In competition for customers, corporations have been known to entertain potential clients lavishly, even providing sexual services (Columbia Broadcasting System, 1969). The conflict argument suggests that these nonmarital sex practices are not defined as deviant because under those particular circumstances prostitution is more useful to vested interests than are the norms of marital sex. And premarital heterosexual activity is generally less threatening to the long-run interests of elites than is homosexual activity because premarital heterosexual contact may at least lead to reproduction or possibly to marriage, while homosexual conduct serves no elite purpose at all. Hence homosexual behavior will be seen as more deviant than premarital heterosexual behavior, although both will be somewhat deviant because they threaten the main vehicle used by elites to guarantee their own welfare.

Commercial Deception

If one follows the logic of the conflict perspective, the question of why advertising with exaggerated claims and other forms of business fraud are acceptable while frauds practiced by "illegitimate business" are deviant is easily answered. "Legitimate business" constitutes the most powerful and wealthy interest group in the United States. "Legitimate business" elites are therefore able to have their own devious activities viewed as acceptable while legally prohibiting other fraudulent activities and managing to influence public opinion to regard them as bad, wrong, or dangerous. Indeed, the very idea of "legitimate business" conveys the idea. Who is "legitimate"? Businesses with the power to control the law and social definitions are "legitimate," while those without such power are "illegitimate." Therefore, what "legitimate business" does in its own interest is part of the world of conformity and acceptability and what "illegitimate business" does in its own interest is deviant because powerful segments of the population have the ability to make it so— as well as the power to define themselves as "legitimate" and others as "illegitimate."

It is, then, easy enough to see that fraud by "legitimate" business is not deviant, but it is not so clear why fraud by "illegitimate" business is deviant. After all, the conflict perspective says that activities will be deviant only if they somehow threaten elite interests or if their prohibition serves elite interests. In what way does fraud by "illegitimate business" threaten elite ("legitimate") business, or, alternatively, in what way does prohibition of those activities serve the interests of "legitimate business"?

The answer is that fraud by "illegitimate" business undermines the market by destroying public confidence in business generally, thereby making commercial transactions on which "legitimate" business depends more difficult and costly. If consumers distrust all business activities, they will be more reluctant to buy products, and they will insist upon more credible evidence of the quality of the products or services before they agree to purchase them; both these demands will slow commercial activity and increase the cost of doing business. Con artists and fly-by-nighters presumably differ from "legitimate" business practitioners because they provide no actual service or product (only the illusion of doing so) and because they cannot be held legally accountable. When the Chrysler Corporation was caught committing fraud by selling, as new, automobiles that had been driven by Chrysler executives for several thousand miles with the odometers disconnected, the corporation was still able to maintain its position in the public eye by pointing out that, after all, they were still good automobiles, that they had merely been tested for reliability and quality assurance, and that the customers did, in fact, receive a workable automobile for the money paid. This outcome can be contrasted with the victim of a con game who pays for stocks that do not actually exist or who invests in the Brooklyn Bridge even though the bridge is not actually available for sale. Similarly, the legitimate roofer may use materials of lower quality than the contract states, but he justifies himself by noting that you nevertheless have a good roof that will last 15 years (instead of the 20 years you thought it would), while the roof you would get from the fly-by-night operator would not last until the end of the year.

The fraudulent activities of "illegitimate" business, then, actually threaten the market climate that is so useful to elite business. Also, it is in the interest of elites to clearly demarcate the fraud of "illegitimate" business from their own. By so doing, elite businesses can downplay their own fraud and win support of the public by appearing to be concerned with protecting the welfare of consumers. Thus, Chrysler is not only interested in making their own fraud seem trivial beside that of "illegitimate" business, but the corporation is also concerned with making the public believe it is the consumers' friend, as evidenced by its active opposition to "illegitimate" operatives such as the con artist. And "legitimate" roofers not only want to make their deviousness comparatively less heinous, but they also want to portray themselves as having the interest of the consuming public at heart, as indicated by their open and active opposition to the "fly-by-night" roofer.

Gambling

Clearly, church bingo, trading in life insurance, and stock investments represent activities beneficial to large, powerful interest groups in the United States: organized religions, the financial community, and corporate businesses, respectively. Therefore, according to the conflict perspective these forms of gambling will be regarded as acceptable activities because these interest groups will use their power to see that such behaviors are not declared illegal and to persuade less powerful segments of the population to view the behaviors as good and useful. On the other hand, it is much less obvious that numbers playing, betting on athletic contests, and alley craps are activities that threaten powerful elites. Rather, the conflict perspective would suggest that *prohibition* of these types of gambling actually serves the interest of a particular powerful elite—organized crime. Presumably, gambling is only profitable to gangsters when it is unavailable "legitimately." Under those conditions, demand is high and the profits great enough to justify involvement by criminal enterprise. Hence organized criminals supposedly exercise power and control over legislative representatives, and they finance public propaganda campaigns to see that certain activities are *illegal*, so that the gangsters can profit from selling the forbidden fruit.

Suicide

Elites, particularly the economic elites in a capitalist society like the United States, depend heavily upon being able to exploit subordinates as workers and consumers. Therefore, it is in their interest to socialize the members of our society to believe that life is worth living regardless of the quality of that life. If elites can successfully achieve that purpose, then workers will be willing to labor under miserable conditions for dismal wages, with no hope for the future. And no matter how bad life becomes, the properly socialized person will continue to engage in sacrificial labor, looking forward only to the afterlife, where comfort is guaranteed only for those who persevere in this life. Consequently, suicide represents the failure of elites to create a totally subservient labor force. Individuals who commit suicide are, in effect, saying that they do not have to do the bidding of power holders but are free to terminate their lives. Suicide therefore represents a long-range threat to the power and position of capitalist elites.

By contrast, altruistic suicide serves those same elite interests. To commit suicide in combat, to save others, or in the pursuit of dangerous duties helps to maintain the social system from which elites benefit and upon which their power is based. In effect, from a conflict point of view it appears as if elites are saying to their subordinates, "Your life is not your own; it is ours. We will tell you when you can or must sacrifice it. You must not terminate your life to escape." Selfish suicide is therefore deviant because it threatens the welfare of power holders, while altruistic suicide is conforming (even heroic) because it promotes the interests of elites.

Cross-Sex Dressing

Why are women allowed to cross-dress while it is deviant for men? A likely explanation in the conflict tradition begins with the recognition that males hold most of the power in our society (in fact in all societies). Emulation of elites represents tacit acknowledgment by the less powerful of superiority of those in power, thereby reinforcing the positions of power holders. Female cross-dressing is not deviant, therefore, because it is actually a compliment to males. But if elites emulate nonelites it is a rejection of the idea that their peers, other power holders, are superior. Cross-dressing by males is, in effect, an insult to other males. Moreover, it represents a break in ranks among elites, threatening their ability to stick together to maintain power and control over females. Consequently, it is regarded as unacceptable and is prohibited in custom, and sometimes in law.

Social Psychological Theory

A third general explanation of the content of norms, herein referred to as identity/fear theory (Tittle, 1994), contends that the collective emotions of those who dominate in a given society, as well as individual emotions of rule makers and the agents of social control, affect, if not determine, the content of a society's normative scheme. The theory predicts, first, that acts will be deviant when they have negative emotional significance for the dominant segments of a society. Second, acts will be regarded as deviant when their typical perpetrators represent categories of people, or a subculture, whose stereotypical characteristics evoke emotions of fear; such segments of a population are often said to pose a "symbolic threat." This perspective differs from conflict theory, which assumes that dominants are concerned only with promoting political or economic interests and protecting their positions of power, and it differs from consensus theory, which assumes that collective action enhances the general welfare and preserves essential community values. Instead, it points to emotional concerns that take precedence over economic interests or general societal welfare.

At the micro level, the everyday actions of rule makers, such as legislators, school officials, and religious figures, as well as control agents, such as the police, bureaucrats, or therapists, who deal with particular instances of troublesome behavior, may be influenced by numerous social psychological factors. In legislative action, for example, a law maker may act on his or her emotions in leading the charge for getting rid of an existing law or formulating a new one. This emotional motivation is illustrated by the work of a former governor of Florida, Bob Graham, in his campaign to repeal a state law requiring annual safety inspections of automobiles (that made it deviant behavior to drive a car with poor pollution control or faulty tires). He made no bones that his animosity was based on irritation at having been required, before he became governor, to sit in line for a long period of time on a hot summer day waiting to get his car inspected.

Similarly, a police officer or a school official may personally abhor homosexual behavior, so when suspects or unruly students who happen to be homosexuals, are involved in cases, the decisions are harsher than they might have been with other people. As a result, notions about the deviance of the original behaviors that brought these officials into action may be affected. Police brutality, for instance, is usually provoked when suspects fail to grant police officers the deference the officers think they deserve (Rubenstein, 1973; Skolnick, 1966; Westley, 1970). In other words, individual officers feel disrespected and respond accordingly against the source of their denigration. Because this reciprocal reaction process is so common in police work in the United States, disrespecting a police officer and police brutality have become familiar forms of deviance.

The expression of emotions in specific instances of social control, however, is less important than general emotions reflecting widespread psychological tendencies. When certain emotions are shared by almost everybody, they permeate all social institutions, especially those concerned with the making and enforcing of rules (Rachman, 1974; Tuan, 1979; Scruton, 1986). Two emotions—identification and fear—are particularly important because they are nearly universal.

Identity/fear theory assumes that individuals evaluate other people and behaviors by comparison with themselves. When confronting a problematic situation, they imagine whether they are capable of particular acts that might be deviant. They also contemplate whether the behavior would be pleasurable or in other ways beneficial to them personally, as well as whether such behavior involves social qualities they admire, like loyalty, or deviates from their own moral precepts. People also try to imagine how similar to themselves are those who do, or are likely to do, the behaviors at issue. "Identification" varies with the extent to which a person (1) can visualize himself or herself committing an act that might become deviant; (2) admires the personal characteristics of those performing the act; or (3) imagines herself or himself as similar to the person committing a given problematic act. In general, the stronger the identification, the less a person is inclined to regard an act as unacceptable, or deviant.

In addition to trying to imagine themselves doing a particular act, people judge whether the act is a personal threat. People experience fear when they perceive that particular persons, categories of persons, or situations/actions endanger their property, lives, social positions, or general welfare. Everybody is afraid of people or behaviors that represent direct or indirect competition in the contest to acquire and hold property, employment, lovers, prestige, or the like. Losing to a competitor may directly jeopardize one's property or physical welfare, but it also threatens one's public and self-images. Losing in competition is, therefore, humiliating (Katz, 1988). For instance, being mugged may deprive one of the money stolen, and being beaten may cause physical pain, but it is even more distressing to suffer the loss of autonomy when one is coerced into giving up one's money or forced to comply with another's command (Tittle, 1995). Moreover, being defeated in a real or a symbolic contest, regardless of the prize, is embarrassing in that it damages a person's sense of self and challenges his or her public image. Simply being reminded of one's possible weaknesses in such contests can produce those effects.

Fear, then, stimulates jealousy, resentment, and envy. Jealousy is rooted in the fear of losing an important relationship, and part of the pain of that potential loss is debasement implied by the challenge to one's worth as a friend, lover, or spouse. Similarly, it is common to resent or envy those with the things one desires or who succeed more often in the various kinds of contests that might be imagined. Although such emotions sometimes are directed toward actual persons, events, or conditions, they are most often broadly aimed at categories of people, conditions, or actions that symbolically call into question various competencies or that pose a menace to personally valued arrangements. Hence we all carry around generalized images of threatening people or situations; those generalized images (symbolic threats) become particularized dangers when the provocative acts, persons, groups, or conditions get close.

Emotions rooted in identification and fear heavily influence the way people individually and collectively react to behaviors they observe. The less the identification with the performer and the greater the fear, the more likely that the behavior will be regarded as unacceptable and liable for social control. But how do such individual emotions get translated into normative standards? To understand this, one must first recognize that it is mainly the emotions of members of the dominant strata that are incorporated into aggregate cultural patterns that are expressed in institutions and institutional processes. Because rule makers and enforcers give priority to the emotions of the dominant segments of a social group, processes influencing conceptions of deviance that occur in education, government, religion, organized recreation, the economy, and law will be consistent with patterns of identification and fear among dominant groups or categories.

The expectation that societal institutions will incorporate the patterns of identification and fear characteristic of dominant groups or categories is more complicated than it might at first seem. Few societies or subgroups have one dominant group or category in all areas of behavior. Patterns of dominance differ depending on the focus and image. A person or group can be influential in one context or in regard to some things while having no influence in other contexts or with respect to other types of behavior. Thus, adults usually prevail over youth, but white youth may sometimes dominate black adults. Females are often dominated by males, yet male children are subject to female adults. Furthermore, even when a given category of people generally dominates others, the extent to which they do so may vary with domains of concern. Hence, although males generally dominate females, this may not be true when the issue concerns children or other persons particularly relevant to females. Detecting patterns is fairly straightforward where dominance is monolithic, coercive, and obvious. However, when those conditions do not hold, which is most of the time, size of competing groups becomes important; norms will reflect the widest identification and the greatest overall fear. For example, in the United States whites are more numerous than blacks, Hispanics, and Native Americans. Because of this, the norms mostly reflect the patterns of identification and fear characteristic of whites.

The effect of emotions of identification and fear on norms is even more complex when social change is occurring. Arrangements of dominance can change without immediately altering the content of norms based on previous patterns. This disparity is possible because emotional propensities are transmitted from generation to generation through socialization. Although infants are genetically programmed to feel emotions, the specific objects, events, or categories of people that call forth identification and fear must be learned. The content of such learning reflects patterns of emotion by those who are socially dominant. However, because adults train their own children mainly to evaluate and respond as they themselves do, and then those children in turn teach their offspring much of what they learned as children, several generations usually go by before social structural modifications lead to alterations in institutional patterns of identification and fear.

Physical Violence

The social psychological account explains the fact that street fighting is deviant while prizefighting is not by reference to the emotions of identification and fear. Street fighting is usually done by younger people, people of lower socioeconomic standing, and often by minorities. Since the dominant segments of the United States population are adult, middle class, and white, they have trouble imagining themselves fighting in the street or deriving any pleasure from it. Moreover, they regard themselves as very unlike those who do fight in the streets, and their image of street fighting is not one that permits admiration of the qualities of those who do it. For dominant segments of the population, street fighting projects cowardice, not bravery, since fighters are reputed to use surprise tactics and to fight "dirty." Hence dominants cannot easily identify with street fighters.

In addition, dominant segments of the population fear the kind of people who do fight in the streets, and they fear the action itself. Although most adults, whites, and middle-class people rarely come into contact with street fighters or street fighting, they nevertheless associate it with the "out of control" violence that is perceived to grip our cities. Also, they feel threatened by the kind of "awesome chaos" that street fighters reportedly bring to bear. The willingness to employ unpredictable, unfeeling violence is presumably a mark of status among them (Katz, 1988).

As a result of such patterns of identification and fear felt by the dominant segments of our society, the general normative system has come to define street fighting as unacceptable, and it typically is subject to collective reaction of a negative type; that is, street fighting is deviant behavior. The situation with respect to prizefighting is different. Prizefighters, though often young and from lower-class and minority backgrounds, are nevertheless regarded as athletes who undergo rigorous and demanding training. They are admired for their skills and bravery and because they rely upon those qualities, rather than stealth and trickery, for victory. In addition, prize fighting is known to be a route for social mobility; it can bring fortune and fame to those who excel. Consequently, dominant group members can identify with prizefighters. They can imagine themselves in some sense like the boxers—hardworking, courageous, trying to be socially mobile—or at least they can imagine that they would like to have such qualities. Furthermore, prizefighting does not provoke much fear. It takes place in a controlled context; the fighters are not randomly perpetrating violence; and they are not vying for the possessions, positions, or relationships of the dominant members of society, who are mere spectators. Since prizefighting lends itself to identification and generates little fear among dominants, it becomes normatively acceptable. By contrast, because street fighting is not attractive to dominants and helps perpetrate images provoking fear, it is deviant.

Sexual Expression

Why, according to identity/fear theory, is it normatively acceptable to engage in marital coitus but unacceptable to varying degrees to practice other forms of sexual expression? Remember that in the United States, whites, males, adults, and middle-status people dominate. These segments of the population can easily imagine themselves having marital sex. It is done by people like themselves, it is pleasurable, and it involves sharing and possible procreation. Also, the fact that it is confined to a stable social unit formed around personal commitments makes marital sex an honorable and admirable activity. Moreover, for most people in dominant groups there is little to fear from marital sex; it does not hurt them; it does not jeopardize their social positions or property; there are no competitors; and the potential for humiliation is minimal (though not totally absent). Therefore, marital coitus is acceptable behavior.

Other forms of sex, however, pose varying degrees of difficulty for identification for whites, males, adults, and middle-class people. In fact, many nonmarital types of sexual activity generate fear. The extent to which they inspire fear determines how deviant they are. Of the various kinds of deviant sex, nonmarital coitus is the easiest for dominants to imagine themselves doing, and a large proportion in fact have. But extramarital and premarital sex do engender some fear. There is the danger of jeopardizing social statuses (including the loss of a marital partner for those practicing extramarital sex), of losing property, of facing competitors who might humiliate a loser, of contracting a disease, and of being brought into long-term commitments that are not desired. For these reasons nonmarital coitus is somewhat deviant.

Other forms of sexual expression evoke less identification and raise more fearful concerns and consequently are more deviant than nonmarital coitus. For example, most adult males cannot imagine themselves in a homosexual encounter, nor can they imagine themselves as having characteristics that they assume homosexual participants have—being wimpish and perverted. They find little to admire in homosexuals, and they do not think sexual contact with another man would be gratifying or pleasurable. Furthermore, they fear loss of social status and reputation, particularly as "masculine" beings; denigration in the eyes of women; and humiliation from other men should they engage in homosexual activity. Hence it is deviant behavior. And in similar fashion one could explain the varying degrees of deviance of nonmarital sex by reference to identification and fear among dominants.

Commercial Deception

According to identity/fear theory, the mystery of deception in "legitimate" business being acceptable while fraud in "illegitimate" business transactions is deviant is easily solved. Dominant segments of the population have more trouble identifying with "cheaters" whose sole purpose is fraud than they do with people mainly committed to supplying a product or service but who sometimes use fraud. Occasional slips can be justified as aberrations, not the fundamental nature of business. Moreover, "legitimate" business invokes admired qualities—hard work, careful management, disciplined investment—that make it easier for dominant persons to overlook instances of deception in order to imagine themselves being regular businesspeople. Furthermore, dominant individuals fear the consequences of "fly-by-night" operations. Such activity potentially jeopardizes one's property in ways that cannot be challenged in a court of law. In addition, it is humiliating to be duped; being duped leads to a loss of status and to damage to one's self-image as a competent, careful person. Finally, illegitimate business fraud poses a competitive threat to the economic livelihoods of many who directly depend on the activities of "legitimate" business.

Although a "legitimate" business—one with a location and legal status—may at times use unsavory tactics (Simon and Eitzen, 1993), may sometimes be represented by individuals of questionable character, and may often be moved from location to location, its fraudulent practices are less repulsive to most dominants than are those used by illegitimate business. In addition, it is far less feared. Ordinary business deception can lead to property loss; it can humiliate and undermine self-esteem; and it does at times carry serious competitive threats to many. Despite this, consumers have at their disposal many courses of action against the unscrupulous practices of legitimate businesses. In many cases the simple threat to take one's business elsewhere and to warn associates about the unethical business practices in question is effective; if not, one can use the civil courts to seek redress. And if all else fails, one can alert the mass media and organize a protest that can lead to a decline in business and a reduction in the profits of the offending company. Hence one reason that deception in legitimate business is only slightly deviant, while fraud in illegitimate business is seriously deviant, is that the two sources of fraud engender different degrees of identification and fear.

Gambling

From the perspective of identity/fear theory, deviant and nondeviant gambling differ in crucial ways. Deviant gamblers are reputed to have undesirable traits (which dominants do not admire)—personality problems of compulsiveness and weak self-control. In addition, deviant gambling is fear provoking because it can lead to loss of property, downward social mobility, and loss of self-esteem. Furthermore, such risk taking exposes one to competitors who are deliberately trying to "beat" you at the game; their success is directly denigrating and humiliating because it certifies your inferiority. Little wonder, then, that some gambling is deviant.

But, you might ask, doesn't nondeviant gambling potentially carry some of the same kinds of social psychological consequences? The answer is "yes, but," with the crucial difference being in the degree of identification and fear. It is much easier for dominants to see themselves risking money in the stock market (which over the past ten years has in fact returned handsome profits) or in life insurance than in alley craps. After all, investment and providing family security is different from simple chance; it usually requires careful planning, it is done prudently, and in most cases it is done rationally (there is a reasonable basis, other than sheer luck, for expecting a payoff or for taking the action). Furthermore, even though losing property, status, and self-esteem, as well as experiencing competitive humiliation, are possibilities in nondeviant gambling, the chances of experiencing them are usually much less. If a person loses money in a business deal, it may be painful, but it is not shameful because, after all, it does not reflect a human weakness or normally indicate an effort to get something for nothing. And the purveyors of church bingo and life insurance are rarely inclined to denigrate those who fail to win.

Suicide

Selfish suicide is deviant behavior in the United States, according to the identity/fear perspective, because most dominants think of people who kill themselves in unflattering terms. Most cannot identify with people they regard as weak, as cowards who do the deed to escape debts or because they cannot manage social relationships or the numerous problems of life. In addition, selfish suicide implies consequences that are feared by most. It carries unknown possibilities of a dreadful afterlife, and it means that everything valued in this life—statuses, relationships, and property—must be relinquished. Unselfish suicide, such as to rescue others or to spare a family the financial burdens of years of care, or suicide to relieve horrible physical pain, on the other hand, makes us think of integrity and concern for others—virtues that invite identification—or in the case of relieving suffering, of a humane action. And although death is inherently frightening, unselfish suicide is less likely to invoke public shame for relatives; in the case of suicide to relieve suffering, it is less frightening than the prospect of continued pain.

Cross-Sex Dressing

Can dominants (who are principally males, adults, whites, and those of middle-class status) identify with cross-dressing, that is, can they imagine themselves as cross dressers, find something to admire about cross-dressing, and contemplate some pleasure or gain from it? The answer is probably no, for cross-dressing implies a rejection of the male role and hints at homosexuality. Since white males generally regard the female role as highly undesirable, few think that emulation of it might be useful or that those who do it are to be admired. Furthermore, the same fears as those engendered by homosexuality come into play. On the other hand, since males enjoy their roles, they can easily imagine that if they were in the same position as women, they would try to be like men. Female cross-dressing generates some fear because it implies that women may become competitors for jobs, statuses, and property. Overall, then, female cross-dressing is somewhat deviant, but male cross-dressing is far more unacceptable because the ability to identify with the performers and the fear provoked by the behavior are much higher in degree.

Evaluation

The consensus, conflict, and social psychological perspectives offer different explanations for the deviance of various acts in a given society and are rooted in different assumptions about the nature of human social organization and behavior. Moreover, all three perspectives appear to offer plausible accounts for at least some of the situations considered here, and each theory has been supported by some empirical evidence. But which of them is the correct view?

There is really no way to know, on the basis of current research. Consensus advocates are impressed by research that shows a high degree of agreement about most things that are deviant as well as about the magnitude of punishment appropriate for various acts (Klockars, 1979:490–491; Rossi et al., 1974). Consensus proponents are also fond of the evidence showing a remarkable number of shared values among the members of a given population (Tittle, 1980b:46–53). But critics maintain that such consensus could itself be the product of the ability of power holders to control sources of communication and the ability of institutions of socialization to convince the population that things actually in the interest of elites are good for everybody. Thus, elites are said to have established "intellectual hegemony" over the population so that most people act on the basis of false consciousness: that is, they endorse and support things that they believe to be in their own interests but that, in fact, primarily promote the welfare of elites (Klockars, 1979). The ultimate form of power, according to conflict theorists, is to arrange things so that subordinates willingly support structural arrangements that benefit power holders because those subordinates believe it is right and just. After all, the "divine right of Kings" was a widely shared belief. Hence, conflict proponents maintain that rather than being evidence in favor of the consensus view of society as a cooperating, organic whole, widespread agreement about norms and values actually demonstrates the pervasive influence of powerful segments of the population.

Similarly, those with a conflict approach put great stock in historical and other research that shows the influence of powerful interest groups in the formulation of laws (Chambliss, 1975; Greenberg, 1981b; Quinney, 1970). Much research demonstrates that, by and large, the powerful win most struggles where their desires clash with the desires of others and that many laws ostensibly enacted to inhibit power holders in favor of the general public in fact work to the benefit of elites.

For example, when meat inspections were first legislated by the Federal government, they were hailed as a triumph of the public good over business interests. Prior to that time meat was often handled in an unsanitary way; tainted or spoiled products were sold to an unaware public; and there was no uniformity in grading. Government controls backed up by on-the-spot inspections were to guarantee that those practices would stop. Research, however, reveals that the impetus for government regulation, inspection, and grading came from the largest meat packers themselves (Chambliss, 1975:17–18; Quinney, 1970:77–82). They knew that such regulations would be expensive and that only the biggest and best-financed companies could afford to continue to do business; that is, they wanted to drive small operators out of the market, so the remaining big companies would have freer rein to charge higher prices and generate greater profits. Moreover, the public had become wary of meat purchases under the old system, and the large producers hoped to generate public confidence in their products by having the government certify them as safe and grade them reliably. Thus, as the conflict theorists note, the meat control laws were really created to benefit a particular economic elite although they were widely supported by the general public and believed to be in the public interest. In other words, selling unfit meat became deviant behavior because it came to threaten the interests of large producers and because prohibiting it served the welfare of elites.

But consensus defenders point out that even though control of meat production may have been inaugurated to serve the interests of elite meat producers, it also served the general public; they contend that had it not been perceived to be in the public interest, such legislation probably could not have been enacted, and if it had been enacted, the law would not have survived so long had it not been thought to be in the interest of the population as a whole. Indeed, the very fact that lobbyists and propagandists found it useful, even necessary, to advocate the meat control program as being in the public interest presumably demonstrates that the driving force of social organization is a shared concern for the maintenance and continuity of society as a whole. Thus, rather than demonstrating the truth of the conflict approach to society, the meat case actually shows the extent to which elites must fashion their agendas to collective concerns, thereby supporting the consensus approach.

As this illustration shows, it is impossible to decide the accuracy of the two approaches, because neither is precisely enough formulated to enable data to be unambiguously brought to bear and interpreted in a decisive way. Moreover, anomalies always seem to turn up that contradict both perspectives. For instance, neither theory seems to handle the issues of cross-dressing and suicide very well, and both seem strained in trying to account for the deviance of some types of gambling. It is in dilemmas like these that identity/fear theory shines. It has less often been the focus of debate and research and as a result there is as yet only scattered evidence supporting it (Tittle and Curran, 1988). Still, social psychology seems to provide plausible answers to many of the problematic instances where the other two accounts fail. Nevertheless, critics can easily point to possible reverse causation: Do men fear homosexuality (thereby providing the impetus for norms declaring it unacceptable) because of some inherent psychic aversion or because the pre-existing norms rendering it deviant guarantee social reactions that are fear provoking? Further, it is clear that psychological conditions generating norms are not universal; if they were, norms would not vary from society to society. Therefore, emerging norms to some extent must be responses to socialization, which is linked to already established norms.

It does appear, however, that all three theories reflect some reality. No doubt some laws, and some social rules, stem from the collective sentiments of the whole social group and represent embodiments of widely shared values, including protecting the group from what are generally perceived as dangerous acts. Rules like those prohibiting murder, incest, arson, and thievery would probably be formulated or widely shared socially, no matter whether elites or nonelites made the rules. Since laborers benefit from social rules prohibiting murder, wouldn't they enact homicide laws if they were in positions to do so and such laws did not already exist? Everybody fears being killed, robbed, burned out, and mutilated. One does not have to postulate that elites formulate norms and laws only for their own benefit.

But some social rules, such as those making it deviant to trespass or to surreptitiously paint murals on the walls of building in inner-city areas ("tagging"), do seem to benefit only, or at least mainly, elite property owners. Also, there are acts, such as cigarette manufacturing, that would be more deviant were it not for the actions of economic interest groups. And still other social rules, such as those prohibiting marijuana use for medical purposes, do not seem to make much sense except as somewhat "irrational" responses to social psychological factors. A better theory would be one that synthesizes the three theories and shows the conditions under which the principles underlying each come into play to produce specific outcomes.

Limited Perspectives

In addition to the three general theories described above, there are two additional perspectives concerning the content of norms that have more limited scope; that is, they do not purport to account for the entire content of the normative scheme for all societies, but instead each focuses on one or another domain within particular kinds of societies. A bureaucratic perspective explains norms (and accompanying deviant acts) that are enmeshed or institutionalized within formal systems of organization. And an account that we will call the "diffusion" perspective focuses specifically on the content of criminal law in the contemporary United States.

The Bureaucratic Perspective

Because most aspects of social life in modern society involve some connection with, or take place in, large formal organizations, conceptions of deviance often reflect the principles of bureaucratic organization. According to a bureaucratic perspective, any formal organization has three main objectives, each contingent on the success of the previous ones. They are: survival, meeting the organizations' needs as easily as possible, and growing. An organization, then, is an entity with an inherent dynamic. No matter what its original, ostensible goals at the time it is founded, it will "adapt and accommodate" to stay in business; it will do whatever it does in the easiest way possible consistent with its resources; and it will struggle to grow in size and to expand its domain. This may entail modifications in a bureaucracy's mission, as when the organization to fight polio accomplished its main goal and shifted to another cause. It may involve adjustment of an organization's internal definitions of clients or conditions. And it frequently includes expansion of organizational domains. All these can influence what is or is not regarded as deviance.

In struggling for survival and expansion, organizations focus on potential centers of financial and political help in the external environment; that is, they inevitably concern themselves with those within their social contexts who have potential power over them. In general, therefore, any organization will operate in a manner that promotes normative conceptions advantageous to its survival and expansion, and it will operate in ways contrary to conceptions that threaten its agenda. This means that organizations lend their support or opposition to movements affecting conceptions of deviance and sometimes engage in direct campaigns to promote conceptions that are favorable to themselves.

A couple of examples should make this clear. Even though the status of tobacco use is now shifting toward deviance in the United States (Connolly and Mintz, 1998), it was for several decades a fully acceptable, almost mandatory, behavior. It was not deviant despite its health-related consequences; its violation of religious injunctions to keep the human body—the "temple of God"—pure; and its earlier status as deviance (Markle and Troyer, 1979). How was this possible? Most authorities attribute it to the work of a giant bureaucracy set up by the tobacco industry. The American Tobacco Institute apparently propagandized for the use of tobacco; fought the publication of research documenting health hazards; aggressively advertised, especially among youth, to portray smoking as glamorous; contracted for actors and actresses to smoke in movies and in TV shows; suppressed damaging information; and bought political influence with campaign contributions and direct lobbying. The result was to overcome general conceptions of tobacco use as deviant and to stave off newer movements in that direction.

But is this the work of bureaucracy acting as an entity or is it simply an interest group's use of a particular instrument (the organization) to accomplish its economic purpose? The bureaucratic perspective suggests that the economic interest is only the initial impetus and that an organization itself sets in motion an inherent process for organizational survival, which operates independently of the original purpose. If so, this should become clear when the battle to make tobacco use deviant again begins to succeed. At that point, the American Tobacco Institute will probably change its focus (as well as its name) in order to preserve its organizational self, independent of the original economic motive. Thus, it might reorient to a new economic support group and mount a campaign to get marijuana use more fully accepted or legalized. It might become independent of the original support group and begin to collect funds from the public or private philanthropies to be dispensed to aid those previously damaged by tobacco use or to support medical research combating the health effects of smoking, thereby helping to reinforce conceptions of smoking as deviant. Or it could change its target population from the United States to foreign countries, where smoking is neither fully deviant nor fully acceptable.

The tobacco example suggests the adaptability of organizations for survival and the consequences of that for various concepts of deviance. Two other examples suggest that organizations will try to expand their operations or domains whenever possible. First, some contend that the Federal Bureau of Narcotics constantly struggles to bring more and more substances under its umbrella as "dangerous drugs" in order to claim larger budgets and to expand its operations (Becker, 1963; Dickson, 1968; Galliher and Walker, 1977). This tendency for narcotics bureaucracies to expand is especially evident since new, so called "designer drugs," are frequently being invented. Expanded organizations means, of course, that the field of deviant behavior is being expanded both by increasing chances of official reaction to instances of violation, and by changing public concepts, which often follow official designations of deviant status (Beck and Rosenbaum, 1994). Second, it has been argued that the American Psychological Association is constantly finding new uses for "talk" therapy as a way to expand organizational domains. Whereas at one time psychological services were reserved for seriously ill people with psychotic conditions, it is now touted as needed for everyday troubles like marital difficulties, anxieties about work or debt, minor compulsions, or unsuccessful personal relationships or accomplishments (Ofshe and Watters, 1994). Such domain expansion is both to satisfy the impulse toward growth and to avoid decline in the face of improved medical techniques and therapeutic drugs for dealing with major mental illnesses.

Not only do organizations struggle to survive and grow, but their actions reflect the conditions prevailing in their internal environments and consequently also affect conceptions of deviance. Bureaucracies conduct day-to-day operations in the easiest way possible within available resources. They will always try to get as many additional resources as they can, but if they fail to increase their assets, they adapt to whatever they have. Given fixed resources, therefore, an organization will tailor its operations to meet the workload. If the workload is large, an organization will try to restrict its reach by simplifying, categorizing, and routinizing, and in the process subtly change the definition of what is deviant. For example, in agencies of social control, such as prosecutors' offices, which are typically overloaded, individualized information will be ignored, cases will be stereotyped, and standard procedures for handling "normal" (typical, routine) cases will be implemented (Sudnow, 1965; Emerson, 1969; Cloyd, 1977). As a result, acts that were previously regarded as in great need of attention will now be ignored altogether, and some that were previously managed as particularly heinous will be engulfed within the "routine" category. Since deviance is, by definition, acts that violate public conceptions of acceptability or that typically elicit an official negative reaction, internal adjustments of this type alter the normative structure, particularly if enforcement agencies neglect some forms of deviance for a long period of time.

By contrast, an organization with fixed resources and a small or declining caseload will respond differently. Since the object is to use all the resources available to avoid losing them in future budget allocations, as well as to establish a need for more, the organization will expand its procedures to absorb all available resources. One way is to enlarge its reach by finding more and more instances that fall under the rubric of the organization's mandate. A medical bureaucracy, for instance, which normally confines itself to detection and treatment of physical ailments or disabilities, may find it useful to start detecting and treating psychological disturbances; uncovering spousal or child mistreatment; or ferreting out drug abuse. A similar interpretation, as it applies to medical radiologists, has been set forth by Pfohl (1977).

According to Pfohl's analysis, serious child abuse, where parents or other adults physically harmed children, leaving broken bones and other permanent injuries, had existed for some time but remained undetected or unpublicized by family physicians and pediatricians who treated the children. This was presumably because such practitioners were closely tied to the parents as clients (rather than to the children) and viewed parents as allies in promoting the health of children. It was left to radiologists, who examined the x-rays revealing physical injury, to raise the issue of child abuse. They were presumably motivated by a desire to enhance their own statuses by claiming concern and closeness to patients. And since the radiologists worked for physicians and hospitals rather than directly for patients, they were free to "blow the whistle" because their economic well-being was not linked to relationships with patients (or the parents in this case).

A bureaucratic perspective about norms, then, contends that the internal and external dynamics of organizations can have a great impact on the content of the normative scheme, particularly in modern societies where so many activities take place in and with organizations. Bureaucratic dynamics involve efforts to survive, to accomplish everyday operations as easily as possible, and to expand. Each of these dynamics can lead to modifications of conceptions of deviance in a society, to the invention of new forms of deviance, and to the demise of previous forms of deviance.

The Diffusion Argument

Recent research concerning hate crime laws in the United States has failed to find support for any of the theories reviewed in the preceding pages (Grattet et al., 1998). Instead, the researchers found a kind of contagion effect, in which the adoption of such laws spread rapidly regardless of the conditions the various theories postulated would be operative. This phenomenon suggests a different interpretation of normative content, at least in democratic societies. In such contexts, lawmakers are elected mainly by attracting and holding public attention. Since publicity about everyday legislative work is rare and enormously expensive, candidates and officeholders are constantly searching for positions that will impress voters. And individual politicians all over the country periodically send up trial balloons to try to win public approval. When one of those issues resonates with the public, or for other reasons is successfully enacted into law, it inspires politicians in other jurisdictions to "jump on the bandwagon." By so doing they can claim to be active, or at least to be vigilant in making sure that their jurisdictions are not behind others in legislative achievement. Consequently, a new law in one place is likely to be followed soon by similar laws in other places, regardless of public opinion, interest groups, or efforts to mobilize social movements. Wider diffusion of more-or-less random legislative initiatives that emerge from specific locales scattered throughout a larger context, then, may account for a substantial proportion of the legal code.

Processes of Deviance Creation

We have examined three broad and two more focused theories about why some behaviors are deviant and other, quite similar ones are not. While those theories help us understand why normative systems take different forms, they do not spell out the exact process by which norms get established or changed. In other words, those theories answer the "why" question, but they do not answer the "how" question. They explain why norms end up in a particular form but they do not explain or describe the procedures by which norms emerge or change. Various scholars, however, have tried to document and account for the processes by which behavior moves from being nondeviant to being deviant.

❖ ❖ ❖ ❖   ## Attributions of Evil

Since, by definition, deviance is behavior that is unacceptable to the majority of a group or that is typically reacted to in a negative fashion, any specific class of deviant behavior can be said to encompass some degree of "evil." Evil, in this sense, means that the behavior is perceived or portrayed as bad, harmful, dangerous, or loathsome, at least from the point of view of some members of society—sometimes most of the members of a society but sometimes only a minority who are able to coercively impose their definition on others. Sometimes "evilness" stems from the supposed effect of the behavior on some important institution, a vital value around which a social group coalesces, or the continuity of the group as a whole. At other times, the "evil" consequences of some behavior are conceived in terms of its effect on the interests of some particular segment of the population. Thus, a king may prohibit peasants from hunting on "his" land and back that prohibition with force. To him, peasant use of royal land is evil because it threatens his control, disrupts his recreation, and reduces his economic advantages.

A major source of attempts to attribute evil to specific behaviors are groups who stand to benefit in one way or another from getting some behavior defined as deviant. Such groups may be concerned with their own economic well-being (for instance, trying to get public use of some property defined as evil so that private owners may buy it to use for generation of private profit). Such groups may be devoted to perpetuating some moral code (say, a religious group tries to get others to regard card playing as evil because their concept of morality regards it that way). Sometimes interest groups are concerned with protecting some domain or category. This concern is illustrated by women's efforts to get unwanted sexual advances declared as evil rather than being instances of simple courtship, and by animal lovers trying to get commercial use of furs or laboratory use of animals for experiments to be thought of as evil. Groups may be interested in elevating their own statuses or in preserving a role for themselves, as when homosexuals try to get discriminatory actions against them to be thought of as evil.

Regardless of the eventual conception of evil that prevails, it is clear that "creating" deviance—bringing about a public conception of unacceptability or making sure that some behavior begins to elicit collective reactions of a negative type—is a political process in which some behavior that was not previously regarded as evil (sometimes because it was not in existence or had no connotation yet of being evil) comes to be so defined. And sometimes the demise of deviance—fading of public conceptions of it as evil or reduction in collective reactions of a negative type—implies a similar political process (although not always, since some deviance disappears because of neglect by opinion makers or rule enforcers). Central to these political processes are interested parties or groups who try to bring about redefinitions of behavior.

Sometimes interest groups can get their way through routine political action. In the United States this often involves little more than contributing money to political candidates who endorse desired positions or who are willing to do so in order to attract the contributions. But in other cases the process of deviance creation requires full-scale "social movements," wherein attributions of evil are made and elaborate campaigns to get those attributions accepted by the general population, or at least by rule makers, are mounted (Gusfield, 1967; Mauss, 1975; Schneider, 1978; Spector and Kitsuse, 1977).

Claims Making

Various scholars have documented sequential steps through which successful efforts to bring about public attribution of evil to a given behavior (or condition) usually go (Best, 1987; Jenness, 1995; Pfohl, 1977; Tierney, 1982). One of the most compelling is that by Best (1987, 1990), who analyzed how the problem of "missing children" came to evoke images of evil in the United States. He distinguished three elements in the process—grounds, warrants, and conclusions. In the beginning there were attempts by different interested parties to establish certain basic "facts" as a foundation for public claims that missing children were symbolic of a terrible evil. Extreme instances of well-publicized abductions were portrayed in emotionally gripping terms so as to imply that they were typical rather than unusual. This portrayal was followed by "estimates" of the magnitude of the problem as being far greater than anyone might have imagined, then projections of eye-popping growth or increase of missing children, usually with implications or direct statements that the problem was expanding to touch, in one way or another, just about everybody.

After these initial grounds were laid, the next step was to develop "warrants," or statements about why and how conclusions of evil about missing children ought to be drawn. The public campaign reminded people of the value of children as the hope for the future and portrayed them as inherently priceless, too valuable for the public not to be concerned. Emphases were placed on the blamelessness of children, and they were depicted as victims of kidnappers or seducers. Apparently this was to help counter reservations should people assume that many missing children were involved in their own disappearance (runaways). Warrants went on to associate many kinds of additional evil, such as pornography, drug selling, and Satanism, with the missing-child problem. Next, there was public indictment of governmental policies then in place to deal with the missing children, often grounded in well-recognized values like rights and freedoms that were being ignored or violated by current approaches, laws, or procedures for handling the issue of missing children.

Finally, in the concluding stage, specific efforts were directed toward creating public awareness and action by enlisting large numbers of people in searching for missing children (such as using pictures on milk cartons and passing around flyers with vital information about missing children). There was also much talk of prevention, again with extreme instances taken as the norm of everyday possibility. And the crowning achievement was the successful call for and implementation of new official control policies for keeping track of children, locating those out of place, and apprehending and punishing people who might have taken or harmed them. Once all of this had been achieved, there was an attempt to imply that other problems, including possible physical and sexual abuse by family members and incompetent teaching in preschools, were related to child abduction. Thus, over a period of a few months a form of behavior that had previously attracted little attention and was, according to many authorities, most often committed by a divorced parent trying to rescue children from the supposedly incompetent partner who ended up with custody, became an epidemic threatening huge numbers of children with death and degradation.

Best's analysis applies specifically to the missing-child problem, and it is clear that the movement was not a centrally directed or well-coordinated campaign but rather a collection of activities by more-or-less independent entities that nevertheless came together in a coherent process. Moreover, Best is careful to note that even in this specific instance, exact details, content of appeals, and sequences of events was contingent on unique or emergent circumstances. Still, we might expect that the process he laid out has general application to normative change. If so, we would expect that the first stage of movements to alter norms usually begins with publicity about a few real or imagined atrocities (dramatic, outrageous examples) concerning some behavior that heretofore was unknown or of little concern. Such dramatization will often be stimulated by "moral entrepreneurs," those with an intense belief or interest (Becker, 1963). This arousal will lead to perceptions and exaggerated claims that the atrocities are actually indicative of typical activities rather than unusual ones. From that, interested parties will project phenomenal growth and expansion of the behavior's importance to domains not immediately obvious. In other words, all manner of associated evil will be tied to the behavior in question.

The second stage will involve numerous attempts to show that the consequences of the behavior in question are morally and emotionally significant and that ignoring the behavior and its effects would be shameful, intolerable, and unthinkable. In particular there will be efforts to enlist recognized or proclaimed values in an indictment of current norms concerning this behavior or institutions for managing behaviors like it. Finally, if the movement succeeds up to this point, it will try to draw large segments of the population into participating in identifying, preventing, and responding to the behavior. In addition, it will pressure the institutional centers in society to promulgate new or improved means for apprehending and punishing perpetrators. Once those mechanisms are in place, there will be late-stage attempts to tie other behaviors to the newly dubbed deviance so that they too can be prevented or managed.

Summary

Deviance is present in all societies, and it appears to expand or shrink independently of actual success in controlling its volume. Such ubiquity suggests that deviance may be an inevitable feature of social groups, intimately tied to the processes of organization and interaction. However, variability from social group to social group in the exact behaviors that are regarded as deviant has spawned several theories about normative content. Three general theories—consensus, conflict, and identity/fear—suggest different bases for explaining and predicting what behaviors will or will not be deviant under various kinds of social conditions, and two specific accounts—a bureaucratic and a diffusion perspective—attempt to explain norms enforced by institutional agents or formulated by law-making bodies. Although each of these theories is plausible and enjoys some support, none is fully adequate. Moreover, each neglects the specific process by which its purported explanatory mechanisms play out to produce specific outcomes. Various scholars have emphasized the political nature of normative development and change and have tried to spell out the sequences or stages by which initial claims of evil eventually get expressed as conceptions of deviance. ✦

Chapter 7

Deviance/Crime and Social Change

We have already seen that deviance (and sometimes crime) consists of behavior that is negatively evaluated by a group or that evokes contrary collective responses, including actions by formal control agents. That is, deviant behavior is, in one way or another, regarded as bad or dangerous by most people in a specific group or by powerful people in that group who can back their opinions with organized force. Because there are so many forms of deviance, it is clear that a substantial part of social life must be devoted to doing something about it. All deviance, however, may not be especially detrimental for individuals or groups. Some categories of acts regarded by some social groups as deviant have few of the negative effects attributed to them (Best and Horiuchi, 1985; Goode, 1970; Goode and Ben-Yehuda, 1994). For example, among the Puritans witchcraft was highly deviant. As such, it was feared, and that fear provoked many responses that themselves had destructive consequences (Erikson, 1966). We now know that witchcraft, at least as the Puritans perceived it, did not even exist, much less endanger the group. On the other hand, social reactions to the supposed witchcraft ostracized many and sent innocent people to be burned at the stake. Also, the general distrust produced by the witch hunts undermined many social relationships.

Deviance and Everyday Life

The famous witchcraft trials in Salem, Massachusetts, may have had their origins in the home of the Reverend Samuel Parris. In the Parris home was a slave girl from Barbados named Tituba. Town gossip had it that Tituba was skilled in the magic arts. Tituba became the center of a small group of local girls, who assembled in the kitchen of the Parris home. The behavior of the group was very secretive until the winter of 1692, when several of the girls began to exhibit strange behavior, like uncontrolled screaming and scampering about the floor on all fours barking like dogs. Soon, the malady spread to other girls in the community. After unsuccessfully attempting to "treat" the girls, the town physician announced that the problem was not, in fact, a medical one—that the girls' behavior was the work of the devil. Town elders and ministers quickly agreed that the witches afflicting the girls had to be rooted out of the community. The girls eventually named three town women as witches—Tituba, Sarah Good, and Sarah Osburne. At a hearing for the accused witches, Tituba not only implicated the other two women but several other townspeople as well. Officials discovered, much to their horror, that the "problem" of witches and witchcraft was more widespread than they originally thought. The hysteria and hunt for the witches in Salem had begun. By the time it was over, some twenty-two people had died. (See Erikson, 1966)

Still, there are good reasons to think that making, breaking, and enforcing norms, even if the prohibited behavior is imaginary, is intricately meshed with, and perhaps essential to, other social processes that have great import for society. In Chapter 6, we saw that a certain amount of deviance may serve important purposes. In this chapter, we focus specifically on the way that deviance is intertwined with normal social processes—through its effect on social change.

Most social processes and institutions are geared to preserving societies' social norms, systems of stratification, social control procedures, social institutions, and cultural legitimations for their systems as they exist at any given time. Although this inherent conservatism is usually fairly effective at preventing much change, it has an ironic consequence: if a society is completely stable, it cannot maintain itself for very long. Social change is sometimes necessary to meet challenges, such as encounters with new or threatening groups, climatic changes, biological aberrations or mutations, technological innovations, unusual expressions of normal human impulses, or to placate groups of people in a social system who are not satisfied. Therefore, despite the bent of social processes toward maintaining structural arrangements, some degree of change often occurs in most societies, and in some social groups change is almost constant.

Types of Social Change

Social changes may occur in any of several ways.

Incremental

Some social change is brought about by incremental adjustments so slow that they are imperceptible to the collectivities experiencing them. Such change can be perceived only from the vantage of long stretches of history. For instance, the mid-seventeenth through the nineteenth centuries witnessed a slow decline in mortality rates in most of Europe, which led to an increase in family and population size (because fertility did not drop proportionately until long after the decline in mortality had begun) as well as to numerous adjustments in social arrangements. Later, fertility also fell and eventually, after a period of about 200 years, came into balance with the lower mortality (Thomlinson, 1965). This adjustment brought many social changes, such as alteration in the role of females (Weeks, 1981:35–40, 97–98) and an enhanced status for children (Empey and Stafford, 1991). This "demographic transition," however, was hardly noticed by those undergoing it. It became something of note only in multigenerational recollection. This slow, almost imperceptible, social change can be called "incremental."

Political

Other change, especially in modern democratic societies, is the result of organized political activity by various interest groups who actively promote their own agendas, such as making drug use (like marijuana, tobacco, or alcohol) or various medical practices (like abortion or assisted suicide) either more or less acceptable and widespread. As we saw in Chapter 6, focused social movements like these usually result from activities by interest groups with limited foci. For moral, ideological, or economic reasons they may try to influence public behavior, opinions, or the legislative process in order to accomplish one particular thing. Social changes stemming from broader-scale agendas identified with general political approaches like conservatism (emphasizing mainly private interests or individualistic solutions to problems) or liberalism (focusing mostly on collective well-being and community solutions to problems) also flow from ordinary political processes and produce changes, such as the way children are educated or criminals are punished, as one or the other approach comes to dominate (often being replaced in cyclical fashion later). These types of social change can be referred to as "political," and they encompass social movements that were discussed in Chapter 6.

Reactive

A third means of social transformation, and the one of interest to us here, is through deviance and responses to it. By definition, deviance represents different, unconventional, and unacceptable ways of behaving. And because deviant behavior is regarded as distasteful, dangerous, or threatening, organized social groups try to identify it (either pointing out things that are in fact dangerous or by inventing assumed danger in order to designate some acts as deviant) and then eliminate, or at least suppress it. Usually this works so that the vast majority of all forms of deviance are contained at the level where they have little effect on social arrangements. Sometimes, however, particular forms of deviance catch on and grow in popularity to the point where a society either has to split into two parts—those practicing or tolerating the deviance and those opposing it—or it has to change its normative system to make that behavior acceptable and no longer deviant. When the normative system makes an accommodation, social change has occurred. This type of social change can be called "reactive."

Reactive change has numerous facets and provokes many interesting questions. In this chapter, we will try to help you understand: (1) why or how "new" deviance gets started; (2) why some deviance thrives and grows while other deviance dies out, is killed, or is stymied at a particular stage of development; and (3) the process by which successful deviance leads to normative change. In considering these questions, you should bear in mind that unfamiliar forms of deviance are constantly emerging. You never hear about the vast majority of them because they do not succeed well enough to attract academic, media, or public attention; some that you do hear about never amount to much more than the short-lived flurry of media attention. The fact is that specific new or recycled forms of deviance rarely succeed; most of them fail—because of disadvantageous inherent characteristics or failure to organize effectively, or because the mechanisms of control in the larger society are too strong. Therefore, do not be misled into thinking that the processes to be described are common, or that social change due to deviance is an everyday thing. Nevertheless, production of social change through deviance is one of the most common ways change occurs and, as you will see, that process has been responsible for some of the most momentous changes in human history.

How Deviance Gets Started

We now know that categories of acts are not inherently deviant but are so designated by political and social processes. Those processes, however, begin after a specific behavior, real or imagined, comes into being. Theories we reviewed about norm making—including the designation of various types of acts as deviant or criminal—assume the existence or reality of particular human actions that might come to be defined socially as deviant (or at least they assume that such acts are perceived as real by some groups of people). But some behavior, when it is first manifest, is completely new, or at least is resurrected so that it appears to be new. Where does it come from?

Sources of New Behavior

There are essentially six sources from which behaviors unfamiliar to a group, but potentially deviant, may emerge: (1) chance or accident; (2) imitation of behaviors exhibited in another group or suggested by intellectual exchange; (3) intentional exploration by individuals or groups seeking new experiences or ways of doing things; (4) imposition, in which some person or group influences others, by persuasion or coercion, to take up a behavior that the imposer has invented or introduced; (5) accommodation, which occurs when a challenge or threat provokes an unplanned defensive maneuver that has not been used before; and (6) invention, where someone conceives in his or her mind an unfamiliar form of behavior, perceives (incorrectly) that it is occurring, and tells others of its "existence."

In illustrating these sources of new behavior, and in developing the themes in this chapter, the authors frequently use unrealistic, perhaps even silly examples. This is done to permit readers to focus on the ideas without experiencing the emotional reactions that often result when activities to which people are affectively committed are treated as objects of dispassionate analysis or are treated as instances of deviance.

Deviance in Everyday Life

You might think that toilet bowl caressing is too weird even for the subject of deviance and that "nobody does that." Well, you would be wrong. There is a fetish where people like to have their heads stuck in toilet bowls. There are other strange fetishes out there in the world too. Some fetishes are well known, like sadomasochists derive pleasure from being beaten, and "submissives" derive pleasure from being dominated and made subservient. Other fetishes are more unusual. One place where those with "different" tastes play is Pandora's Box, a palace of fetishism in New York City. In Pandora's Box you may find couples playing mistress and slave, doctor and nurse, wrestling in latex, and eating each other's shoes.

Random Events

Random or chance behaviors can happen in one of two ways: either the normal course of human activity generates inexplicable convergences of circumstances that produce the action, or chance actions may stem from biological atypicality. Convergence of circumstances is the more common source. All of us have probably at one time or another done things that were really unusual, perhaps even so bizarre as to be embarrassing, not because we intended them but just because they happened as a result of a number of weird circumstances coming about at once. Most of the time when this happens, people deny its significance, forget the episode, and move on. Sometimes, however, people hit upon new behaviors in this way, have a positive reaction, and want to repeat them.

Consider public toilet bowl caressing,[1] which to our knowledge does not yet exist, or at least it has not been done enough to attract public, media, or academic interest. Although some people touch public toilet bowls in the course of their occupations (such as plumbers who install them or custodial people who clean them), hardly anybody imagines caressing them, that is, feeling public toilet bowls lovingly and allowing one's hands to linger on the surface for longer than a moment. This nonbehavior could become actual behavior (which might then be socially defined as deviance) by a random convergence of events or because of a weird, internally driven impulse. Suppose, for instance, a woman is in a public toilet and drops her purse. Just as she is reaching to pick it up, somebody enters and distracts her attention, causing her hand to land on the toilet bowl. In trying to find the purse, she runs her hand around on the bottom of the bowl and experiences a pleasurable reaction of cool smoothness. The same could happen if a man inexplicably felt the urge to check the brand name of the toilet and in searching for the sticker ran his hand around the bottom of the bowl. They have each serendipitously invented a form of behavior that is potentially deviant; that is, if it is pursued, other people are likely to regard it as bad or unacceptable and react against it.

Random forces also operate when biological functioning leads some people down atypical behavioral paths, perhaps making them perform impulsive acts. Again, individuals may do it once and put it away as a bad dream, but they may also remember and for one reason or another wish to do that thing again. For instance, as a result of some neural misfiring in his brain, a man may get the urge to eat butterflies at about the time butterflies appear in the summer. Maybe he tries it and discovers that butterflies taste pretty bad, so does not pursue that particular type of potential deviance. On the other hand, he may find that butterflies satisfy him—perhaps because of some hidden psychological meaning, or maybe because others see him do it and express admiration of one who "does his own thing." Then he repeats the act and a pattern of behavior is born (since to our knowledge butterfly eating has never been practiced in the United States), which may come to be regarded as deviant.

Imitation

A second way new conduct may come to a group is through imitation of behavior that one or more individuals learn from other groups or that they learn about as possibilities through intellectual exchange. They may find out about the behavior in question by direct contact with practitioners—maybe they visit other groups or members of that group visit them—or indirectly through movies, TV, lectures, the Internet, or books. (In fact, if any of you take up public toilet bowl caressing, it may be because of imitation stimulated by reading the previous few paragraphs.) Imagine, for example, that you see a TV show about an esoteric group living in Pakistan who, among other things, collects navel lint; or suppose on a tour you actually come into contact with some of those Pakistani people, and they tell you about "navel lint collecting." You become intrigued and decide to try it yourself. By imitating others, you will have introduced a form of behavior that may become deviant in your own society or social group.

Exploration

New behavior can emerge when people deliberately set out to find new gratifications or to find new ways of doing things. Sometimes such exploration stems from boredom, sometimes from economic impulses to increase one's financial position, sometimes from curiosity, sometimes from deliberate efforts to find new gratifications, and sometimes to try to impress others with one's inventiveness. Whatever the motive, some people actually explore new behavioral options fairly often. Most of the time, what they discover is not new but is simply an independent discovery of behaviors already practiced by others in the group. Sometimes, however, new behaviors, some of which are candidates for definition as deviance, emerge. For example, hedonists are constantly searching for new drugs, foods, or sexual methods to enhance their sensory experiences. Every once in a while they actually find one. Similarly, entrepreneurs are constantly in search of new ways to make money. From time to time, they find them, too. And sometimes those new methods for producing sensory gratification or economic profit end up being deviant.

Imposition

Some initially imaginary forms of behavior are "imposed" on people by persuasion or coercion. Suppose a charismatic figure seeks followers, is successful in recruiting them, and wants to show the world that he is in command. One way to do that is by insisting that his disciples publicly commit outrageous, symbolic acts. He dreams up the idea of having them wear small bags of fresh dog excrement around their necks, and, because they believe he is God, they do it. Hence, a behavioral form, though born in the psyche of one person, has entered the social arena through imposition. A recent case of voluntary castration and, later, mass suicide in the expectation that followers would be brought up into a spaceship thought to be following the Hale-Bopp comet (Heaven's Gate group) reminds us that this example is not so far-fetched (*Newsweek*, 1997a, 1997b, 1997c).

As another example, suppose one country's military force defeats another country and sends in occupying troops. The occupiers' religious practices include ritualized daily prayer offered to house cats. They threaten to shoot anybody who does not join them in this practice, and by that means they introduce "cat prayer" as a new form of imposed behavior, which is likely to become labeled or defined as deviant in the conquered society.

Accommodation

Some new forms of potential deviance result from spontaneous efforts by individuals or groups to solve a problem or escape a threat. Suppose, for instance, that in a given society there is a catastrophic fire that temporarily destroys all normal sources of food. In desperation, someone begins to eat charred pieces of wood, a type of behavior that was previously unknown in that society. If eating charred wood starts to catch on, it may then activate processes of social definition that result in its becoming deviant when other foods are again available.

Deviance in Everyday Life

An example of the invention of delinquency is the McMartin Preschool sex abuse case. The McMartin Preschool was a very fashionable preschool in Manhattan Beach, California. In 1983, Judy Johnson reported to the police that her son had been sexually molested by Ray Buckey. Ray was an aide at the school and was the son of the owner of the school, Peggy Bucky. The police arrested Ray, but because there was no corroborating evidence, the local district attorney did not prosecute the case. The police chief of Manhattan Beach, however, sent a letter to some 200 parents of current and previous students of the McMartin School, suggesting that Ray may have had sexual relations with the students. Hundreds of children were interviewed by social workers (critics say the children were suggestively questioned), and by 1984 approximately 360 of them were diagnosed as having been abused. There was no convincing physical evidence that any abuse had occurred, however, and some of the children's confessions seemed bizarre: that they were forced into tunnels under the school (no evidence of tunnels was ever found), that they saw flying witches, and that they were taken by hot air balloons to another town where they were sexually abused. Judy Johnson, who made the initial claim, also charged that her husband had sodomized the family dog and that her son had been injured by an elephant and lion during a school trip. She was later diagnosed as suffering from paranoid schizophrenia. Nevertheless, 208 counts of child abuse were filed against seven adults who worked at the school. The trial lasted some six years, and cost the state approximately 15 million dollars. All the adults were eventually acquitted of all charges. (See Nathan and Snendeker, 1995)

Invention

Finally, some potential deviance does not actually exist except in the fertile minds of individuals who imagine that it does. In these instances, the initiators conceive of some new type of behavior and convince themselves that somebody is practicing it. They then publicize this "fact" and by so doing create the illusion of a behavior that may become defined as deviant even though nobody is actually engaging in that behavior (Ofshe and Watters, 1994). Suppose, for instance, that a woman with intense concerns for the safety of children literally dreams that a lot of youths are being mistreated by pediatricians, who inject them with alcohol. The dream is so powerful that she believes it is a message from God, so she commits herself to stopping this evil practice. She may then tell others of what is supposedly going on, begin to badger children to confirm the practice, and mount a campaign to alert the public to the dangers of the situation. If others start to believe her, or at least to become suspicious, and they accept the notion that this alleged behavior by pediatricians is bad or they begin a series of investigations or "witch hunts," then the woman has invented a form of deviant behavior that may not, in fact, exist at all.

Transforming Behavior Into Deviance[2]

There are many sources of new behavior, but when those new behaviors are first begun, they are not deviant. As we saw in Chapter 6, there are a number of ways that categories of acts get transformed into deviance but an essential ingredient in all cases is attribution of evil to the behavior.

Bad Habits

Most of the time performance of a single instance of a given behavior will not activate a deviance-defining process that leads people to perceive the behavior as evil. A lone instance of an unfamiliar behavior is unlikely to become known to anybody except the person who did it, or perhaps to a few who may have observed it. Moreover, most new behaviors are not inherently dangerous, so no one is likely to complain. If a novel behavior is repeated several times by an individual, it has a greater chance of becoming the object of efforts to define it as deviant. Still, as long as a socially unfamiliar behavior is confined to one person, the overall likelihood that it will get to be deviance in a larger group context is slight. It might be appropriate to call such behaviors "bad habits" (Buckner, 1971)—they are tolerated aberrations from typical patterns, but they are not deviant in the sense of being regarded as unacceptable, threatening, or dangerous.

Seeking Companions

Imagine, however, that the individual with a bad habit (a pattern of committing some type of behavior that is unfamiliar to others) decides that he or she would like to share the experience and attempts to locate others with the same kind of bad habit. The very act of searching for others is likely to arouse concern among observers and, as a result, increase the likelihood that a process of deviance defining will begin. This arousal of attention is even more likely if the search for other practitioners actually succeeds. In other words, if it turns out that this behavioral pattern (the bad habit) is not entirely unique to an individual but has independently come to characterize several randomly scattered people, and one or more of them has located others, then the chances are fairly good that someone will become concerned and begin the process of trying to get the behavior to be regarded as deviant.

For example, suppose the woman described above who discovered "toilet bowl caressing" starts doing it a lot. Those who see her caress bowls probably will not think too much of it. They may momentarily think she has a good reason to be feeling toilet bowls, or they may think she is disturbed; in any case, they are not likely to do anything about it. Similarly, if her family, friends, or associates find out about it, they may try to dissuade her from the habit, warning of health dangers or of possible loss of reputation or employment. Sometimes they may even try to get her to seek therapy. But regardless of the actual response of observers or family, the habit will be regarded by a small circle at most as "weirdness." That is, unless she takes the next step to start searching for other toilet bowl caressers, the social reaction process that might result in this behavior becoming a form of deviance is unlikely to unfold.

Often, even when a person with a bad habit begins to seek companions, nothing will come of it. There are many barriers that hamper one's ability to find people practicing a similar bad habit. People with bad habits usually try to conceal them, lest they be regarded as weird and suffer bad consequences. And approaching others to ask about unusual behaviors they might be practicing is inherently risky. To even raise the issue implies something about oneself as well as the person being approached. Our bowl caresser, therefore, has to be concerned about how others may respond to her overtures; some might try to rob her or otherwise take advantage because they figure she is not in a good position to complain to the police. Because of such considerations she cannot very well go around asking people if they like to caress toilet bowls. Nor can she drive through neighborhoods in a sound truck seeking fellow travelers or run an advertisement in a regular newspaper. Because of these difficulties bad habits are likely to be practiced alone. If this woman does find other bowl caressers, it will probably be by accident. If she lives in a city with an underground newspaper, she may be able to contact others through that medium.

Simply locating others, however, may still not result in a bad habit becoming deviant behavior, nor will it necessarily lead to companionship in the practice of the behavior. A major problem to be overcome is that of communication. Some practitioners of bad habits lack the necessary skills for effectively letting others know their intentions, and it is often clear that habits safely practiced alone may expose one to danger if practiced or talked about with others. How does that woman let others know she is interested in recreational bowl caressing without their suspecting ulterior motives? And while bowl caressing can be done alone quite stealthily, a group gathered in a public rest room for any reason, much less to caress toilet bowls, will pose unknown dangers.

Deviance in Everyday Life

Finding others and convincing them to join your group may be a little bit easier to do with the appearance of the Internet. Computer communication allows one to set up a web page that describes what one's activity is, what the group philosophy is, even how to join and contact others. For example, there is at least one website available for those with white supremacist views. The group is called the White Nationalists, and their website is called Stormfront. In it you can find views that are anti-Semitic, anti-black, anti-affirmative action, and anti-United Nations. In the first page of the website, the reader sees that "Stormfront is a resource for those courageous men and women fighting to preserve their White Western culture, ideals and freedom of speech and association—a forum for planning strategies and forming political and social groups to ensure victory." From the *Stormfront* website you can surf to the newsletter *(Stormwatch)*, a news distribution list, and conference bulletin boards.

Social Response

The greater the extent to which practitioners of new behavior seek others, locate them, and communicate, the greater the likelihood that they will begin to associate with each other. And it is the association that will probably attract attention and put into motion the people and groups who feel threatened by the behavior and who will try to "do something about" it. Action presupposes attribution of evil, which is the essence of social definitions of deviance. If these reactors are successful, a bad habit originally practiced by one

---

Deviance in Everyday Life

The drug is called Rohypnol, or "roofies," or "rib" or "rope" or the "Club Drug." The clinical name of the drug is Flunitrazepam, but it is known as the date-rape drug. When dissolved in a drink, it is colorless, odorless, and tasteless. It renders its victim helpless, and its effects include a drunk-like state, amnesia, and black-outs. It is reported to be ten times stronger than Valium. There have been numerous cases of men slipping a roofie into a woman's drink and having sex with her while she is blacked out. In fact, by 1998 the Drug Enforcement Administration had reported more than 2,300 documented cases of Rohypnol abuse, and the state of Florida was prosecuting approximately 100 cases where a sexual assault occurred with roofie use. Roofies are illegal in the United States. In order to better protect unsuspecting users, the manufacturer is planning to produce a new version of the drug that turns any liquid it is put into a deep blue to warn possible victims of the drug's presence.

or a few isolated individuals will become deviance—a category of behavior regarded as unacceptable to a majority or to those with the ability to coerce.

At this point, then, the protectors of society will have become active. Some will try to warn people of this emerging evil. Others will attempt to get laws enacted against it. Social control agents will try to prevent practitioners from getting together and they will try to isolate them from "normal" members of society lest they contaminate the innocent. Family, employers, and friends will be notified in the hopes that informal social control will be exercised to bring the deviants back into line. Efforts will be made to dissuade the practitioners from their evil ways, and, failing that, the innovators will be punished, incarcerated, or subjected to "therapy." All of these attempts at "social defense," of course, make life difficult for those who want to practice the deviance. As a result, many will give it up.

It is important to recognize that activation of a deviance-defining process does not necessarily require a large effort to transform people's thinking or to influence legislation. Social reaction declaring the behavior to be deviant may occur quickly and spontaneously. Some forms of new behavior, by their very natures, immediately offend social sentiments, tap into a reservoir of concern about obvious dangers to society, or threaten powerful interests. For instance, some men have recently begun to use a new odorless, tasteless drug, Rohypnol, dissolved in drinks to surreptitiously immobilize women for sexual abuse, a modern and improved version of the classic "Mickey Finn." This is the kind of thing that almost everybody (not everybody, of course, since some people will see all sorts of useful possibilities for themselves) in the United States automatically finds appalling and dangerous. Thus, launching a process to get it defined as deviant is no big deal; just publicizing it is enough.

How Deviance Succeeds

Despite being the objects of concerted attempts to dissuade or control their behavior, not all practitioners of new forms of deviance capitulate. Some begin to plot ways that they can practice their vice in the face of opposition. The route they take to that objective, and the effectiveness with which they confront the challenges it poses, will determine whether the particular form of deviance remains deviant or leads to social change, after which it becomes an acceptable form of behavior.

Deviant Group Organization

To be able to continue practicing a bad habit that has now become deviance, the committed will soon see that it would be advantageous to organize themselves. Organization permits practitioners to resist efforts at social control by outside society; it gives them a context for effective practice, especially if the activity is enhanced by cooperation or sharing; and it provides social and ideological supports to keep commitments strong (recall the discussion of organization in Chapter 2). Our toilet bowl caressers, for instance, will find that by hanging together they can warn each other of risks, they can bail each other out of jail, they can collect funds for legal defense, and they will always have a sympathetic ear when the going gets tough—none of which the individuals could do alone. Moreover, by getting together and talking of their experiences, they can share knowledge of the safest places to caress toilet bowls and the most unobtrusive methods for doing so. Finally, through association they will develop shared ideas about why toilet bowl caressing is a good thing, why it is not a bad thing, how to do it better, and the best kind of bowls to caress. They will also develop ideas of why they need to stick together, how dangerous the outside society is, and what is happening in the outside world that impinges on their lives.

Successful pursuit of toilet bowl caressing, and almost any other kind of deviance, therefore, requires organization; without it, the particular form of deviance will probably die out altogether or be practiced infrequently. Moreover, the degree to which this deviance is successful varies directly with the extent to which its practitioners form and sustain a tight-knit deviant group. In other words, a key to whether deviance has any chance of surviving to constitute social change depends on the effectiveness of its organization. The first problem for the individual practitioners of deviance committed to its perpetuation, then, is how to organize and sustain a group of practitioners.

Some degree of organization is likely to follow spontaneously from continual interaction. The more any batch of people interact, the more likely they are to evolve norms, a culture, stratification and coordination, and an integrating philosophy. And the more that group is under threat from the outside, the more likely it is to evolve social control processes within the group. Organization by itself may be effective or not. Success appears to depend on the nature of the deviance itself as well as on the configuration of organizational elements that emerges.

Crucial Characteristics of the Behavior

Not all deviance lends itself to organization among its practitioners. In fact, when practitioners are in competition with each other, organization is somewhat counterproductive unless the product or activity can be expanded. For instance, prostitutes compete with each other for a scarce supply of customers. As prostitutes become better organized, the less successful will any one of them be, because organization implies cooperation and regulation, which mandates more equitable distribution of benefits. And since it is unlikely that, by organizing, prostitutes can expand the market for their services, it is rare to find them effectively organized. At best they are able to achieve loose, unstable, extremely localized organizations or occasionally larger politically oriented organizations for the promotion of some goal common to them all (Jenness, 1993), such as legalization (which, ironically would make their services and products cheaper and open to numerous other providers who are now inhibited by the unacceptability or illegality of the activities).

Another feature of some deviance that inhibits organization is its tendency to become inherently more dangerous when several people practice it together. Illegally making bombs is one example. Terrorists and others who try to manufacture bombs in their basements or laboratories have to be extremely careful to avoid accidental explosions. Indeed, even with great care, bomb making (even legal production) often results in death and injury. The greater the number of people who gather together to make bombs, the more risk there is for any one person because he or she is not threatened just by personal mistakes but also by the mistakes of all the others. For that reason illegal bomb making is most often an individualized activity, or at best subcultural.

Configuration of Organizational Elements

Success in permitting practitioners of deviance to perpetuate their activities and protect themselves depends on the way organizational characteristics are configured. Proficiency in organizing for deviant activities, especially when the behavior is new and highly unacceptable, appears to involve four crucial elements: (1) efficient mechanisms for promoting commitment, (2) regulation of information, (3) developing dependency, and (4) effective internal social control.

Mechanisms Promoting Commitment

Clearly, the most important thing a group must do if it is to maintain itself and achieve its goals—particularly if the group is under attack from outside forces, as groups organized to practice deviance usually are—is to somehow get its members to want to be in the group and to commit themselves to remaining a part of it through thick and thin (Kanter, 1973). Four elements are useful in promoting commitment: (1) a sustaining philosophy, (2) charismatic leadership, (3) symbolic procedures, and (4) collective challenges.

Sustaining Philosophies

To generate and maintain commitment from its members, a group must have an overarching, shared account of its purposes and its rationale for being. Ideally, such a philosophy will spell out the benefits of group membership and of practice of the deviance around which the group is organized. For example, many religiously based deviant groups emphasize the rewards of the afterlife for followers who remain in the group and adhere to its principles. The Doomsday Cult studied by John Lofland (1967), which later became the Moonies, for instance, emphasized that after a period of time the earth as we know it would be destroyed and the faithful followers would be rulers in the new kingdom to be established. Other deviant groups emphasize that the style of life in the group or the deviance around which the group is focused are inherently rewarding (Kephart, 1976).

Successful philosophies also have "in-group/out-group" orientations. According to such accounts, those in the group are superior to those outside it and much better off for their group membership. Moreover, those not in the group are regarded as dangerous enemies out to destroy the group or individuals in it. Frequent assertions of in-group solidarity and out-group hostility abound, such as, "If you are not with us, you are against us." As a result, group members are encouraged to stick together in order to protect themselves from extinction and to preserve the good things they have. In the beginning, deviant groups thrive on their separation and differentness because it helps them forge an identity and a cohesive unit. Even groups that finally succeed in getting the outside world to accept or accommodate their particular type of deviance hardly ever begin that way. It is only later, as we will see, that circumstances change, and the focus of deviant philosophies shifts toward peaceful alliances with former enemies.

Finally, the philosophies that work best in keeping groups together are internally constructed to withstand evidential or logical challenge. Most are closed systems; that is, they provide answers to all questions such that it is inherently impossible to negate their claims. For instance, the Doomsdayers (Lofland, 1967) preached that the forces of good and evil were always struggling with each other but that ultimately the forces of good would win. Although there might appear to be day-by-day failures of God's overall plan, the outcome was sure to be favorable. Thus, if misfortune transpired, it was interpreted as a test of faith; if good things happened, it was taken as evidence that God's plan was unfolding. In essence, there was no way that the basic tenets of the faith could have turned out to be inconsistent with the facts. Similarly, revolutionary groups often contend that they are getting the upper hand over the establishments. If conventional forces resist, it is taken as evidence that the establishment sees the handwriting on the wall and is afraid. But if those in power offer concessions or negotiations, this is also interpreted as evidence of imminent success.

Effective philosophies, then, give participants good reasons to be in the group as well as good reasons not to be outside the group. More important, they portray the group as a necessary haven for protection from menacing forces who do not appreciate the things those in the group embrace and who are determined to destroy the group and any who venture outside its protective shield. Further, such philosophies are artfully structured to answer all questions by followers, thereby providing psychic and intellectual satisfaction, and to deflect any contrary evidence or arguments. Without such philosophies, deviant groups must rely on the inherent appeal of the deviance around which they are focused, or on coercion—neither of which can long sustain groups whose members are presented with attractive incentives for abandonment or threatened with costly consequences for continuing their affiliations.

Charismatic Leadership

Charisma is the quality possessed by a few select individuals that makes them unusually attractive to others, not necessarily physically, but in the sense that others look up to them, attribute almost magical qualities and abilities to them, and want to be around them (Weber, 1961). Charismatic figures attract followers and influence people by the sheer force of their being, in ways that are hardly describable, much less understandable. Sometimes malignant political figures have charisma—mystic auras—that compel attention. Many claim that Adolph Hitler was such a person; largely on the strength of his personality, he was able to rally an entire nation into a cohesive unit for making war and perpetrating unspeakable acts of terror (Grunberger, 1971; Heiden, 1944). Sometimes football coaches have charisma. Legend has it that Vince Lombardi, the former coach of the Green Bay Packers professional football team during the 1960s, was able to inspire his players beyond their natural abilities. Their exploits apparently stemmed to a large extent from their desire to please the coach (Dowling, 1970; O'Brien, 1987). Many religious figures, like Billy Graham (Frady, 1979; Pollock, 1979), Jim Jones (Hall, 1987; Layton, 1998), and Father Divine (Kephart and Zellner, 1994), possessed these magnetic qualities, as do nefarious individuals like Charles Manson (Bugliosi, 1974), and John Humphrey Noyes (Kephart and Zellner, 1994). In short, a few unusual human beings have charisma, which enables them to attract, hold, and influence followers.

Successful deviant groups—those that survive for long periods of time or that ultimately bring about reactive social change—usually form around charismatic leaders. Because of the appeal of such leaders, group members become more strongly committed to the group, often consenting to die for it or to perpetrate amazing acts in the name of the group or its leaders. Charles Manson's followers, for example, committed senseless murders on his command and later defied legal procedures, even though it meant almost certain conviction and imprisonment (Bugliosi, 1974). In the jungle of Guyana, South America, the Reverend Jim Jones's disciples drank poison in mass suicide (Hall, 1987; Layton, 1998), as did the compatriots of Do, the guru of the Heaven's Gate cult (*Newsweek*, 1997a, 1997b, 1997c). And the followers of Joseph Smith went on to found one of the world's leading religions (Church of Jesus Christ of Latter Day Saints) despite social ostracism and harsh physical circumstances (Mauss, 1994).

Deviance in Everyday Life

An example of symbolic procedures that build group identities are gang signs, clothing, colors, and distinctive graffiti. Signs are hand symbols that convey membership in a gang, and the flashing of a gang sign to another gang is frequently taken as a challenge. Some gangs are characterized by particular articles of clothing, sometimes a specific sports brand. In addition, the wearing of a distinct color signifies gang membership—blue for some, red for others. Graffiti is used to mark not only gang membership but also gang territory. Finally, it is not uncommon for gang members to have distinctive tattoos or self-inflicted body marks.

Symbolic Procedures

To keep a group cohesive, it is important to induce members to build their personal identities around the group. They must come to think of themselves as inseparable from the group. To achieve this, there should be special symbols that identify the members of the group to each other but that are unknown or uninterpretable to outsiders—perhaps emblems, handshakes, colors, styles of dress, or flags. A peculiar language, or argot, especially one that changes frequently, also helps to differentiate group members from others and to draw them together in common commitment. In addition, regular rituals serve to sanctify the group and the things for which it stands and to remind the participants of their unique place in the world. Finally, emotionally charged and rigorously challenging initiation ceremonies for new members create a psychological commitment.

Ceremonial induction into deviant groups (or even conventional groups like sororities and fraternities) often requires inductees to engage publicly in outrageous behavior or to make heavy sacrifices of time, resources, or things previously held dear. Once people have done these things, they have great difficulty changing their minds and leaving the group. The psychology of these initiations seems to be that portrayed in the theory of cognitive dissonance (Festinger, 1957). According to that theory, all people presumably strive to keep their cognitions about themselves, others, and the larger world consistent. Thus, if individuals perceive themselves as smart but encounter evidence (such as a bad test grade) contradicting that perception, they suffer psychological discomfort from the dissonance (dissimilarity) of two contradictory psychic messages. Because they are uncomfortable, they struggle to reduce the dissonance. They can work harder to get good grades, change their self-concepts, or discount the contradictory information. Usually they will choose the easiest method for reducing dissonance. Perhaps they will interpret the grade as unusual, not what they can really do because they were not feeling well that day, or maybe they will decide that the professor is no good or has it in for them, or the like.

Similarly, if a group can get new inductees to perform some dangerous or silly action that is inconsistent with their normal senses of self or their reputations, it creates potential dissonance, which the inductees can reduce by becoming more strongly committed to the group. Having made a public declaration, eaten raw liver, or killed somebody, an inductee must later, on reflection, either concede she or he is stupid or decide that membership in the group must be worth it. Since it is not easy to admit that one is stupid, most of the time initiates decide that membership is worth it, so they tout the virtues of the group despite any contrary evidence. Ironically, then, the harder it is to get into a group, the more likely it is that those who actually make it in will sustain their membership—despite many negative features of the group perceived by outsiders, who often cannot fathom why anybody would remain affiliated with it (Aronson and Mills, 1973; Gerard and Mathewson, 1973). In addition, it is awfully embarrassing (because it implies one is flaky) to later go back to observers and say, "I really didn't mean it last week when I declared I would never again eat meat (have sex, ride in a car, or whatever outrageous thing was required)."

Many deviant groups do not stop with initiation ceremonies but instead require continued sacrifice from their members. Ironically, the tightest knit groups are usually not those that provide the greatest physical comfort or well-being (see Kephart, 1976). The very practice of continuous sacrifice often unites group members and reminds them of their common cause and commitment. Thus, some deviant groups require celibacy (Father Divine group, Shakers); some require surrender of property (Oneida group, Mennonites); some require their members to work with primitive tools and forgo the advantages of modern technology (Amish); and some require relinquishment of exclusive sexual relations (swingers, Oneida group) or special relationships with children (Oneida group). Such hardship, of course, makes even more necessary a strong countering philosophy to set forth intangible rewards that membership in the group might provide.

Collective Challenges

To keep people in a group and unite them in cohesion, many groups identify collective challenges to be overcome or common goals to be achieved. By engaging all members in shared endeavors, the group diverts attention from personal doubts and provides each person with a sense of belonging and secure social support. They come to feel needed, and they find pleasure in meeting the challenges set forth, or at least in struggling to meet them.

One prominent challenge is always to resist the enemy from without. So even if the forces of conventional society are not very active in pursuing a particular deviant group, it is useful for the deviant group to imagine that they are. Indeed, it is important to remind the members constantly that they must not become complacent lest they be defeated or divided. Many deviant groups have regular training sessions to emphasize that point. It is particularly advantageous to have outstanding examples to reinforce the threat—instances where members have let their guards down and disaster struck. Particularly helpful are martyrs, those who have suffered because of their commitment to the group or their activities on its behalf. Martyrdom is so effective that many groups quickly martyrize those victimized by even the slightest abuse. Through telling, embellishment, and retelling, those episodes grow in magnitude and importance, and the individuals involved take on a sacred character so that they seem more virtuous and more holy than they really are. That is why martyrs become more iconoclastic when they have less actual contact with their followers. Indeed, the most useful martyrs are those who arose in the distant past and are not around to contradict, by their own telling or their own behavior, social processes of sanctification.

Deviance in Everyday Life

Many deviant groups try to get others to tolerate, if not approve of, their behavior. Even those who practice what is thought by common culture to be a despicable act try to convince those in the mainstream that they are not as bad as they are made out to be. One such organization is NAMBLA, the North American Man/Boy Love Association. As the title suggests, NAMBLA is the national organization for adult males who have an interest in intimate and loving relationships with young boys. NAMBLA is clear that it does not condone coercive or harmful acts between men and boys, only those that are both mutually desired and loving. The organization tries to portray intimate relationships between adult males and boys in a positive light, fighting the stereotype that such men are child molesters, perverts, or "sick." In addition to a national organization that promotes its philosophy, NAMBLA has a website, a newsletter, and a national board of directors. In 1998, membership in the group was available for a five-dollar fee.

While successful deviant groups often focus on the challenge posed by outside enemies, supposed or real, collective challenges are not limited to that. Some deviant groups take on large tasks, such as eking out a living in desolate circumstances, overthrowing entrenched governments, fighting legal restrictions on their activities, or developing better ways of practicing their deviance. Ultimately, the most successful deviant groups adopt the common goal of selling the world on their practice or at least of getting the outside world to tolerate them. But the selling comes much later, after some degree of success has already been achieved in creating and maintaining a deviant group. As was noted earlier in the discussion of sustaining philosophies, solving early problems requires, above all else, cohesion, which is enhanced by emphasis on differentness. In fact, deviant groups who have not been in existence for long seem to delight in accentuating distinctions between themselves and others.

Regulating Information

Successful deviant groups not only employ effective strategies for generating commitment and cohesion, but they also enhance the chances of survival when they develop mechanisms through which they can monitor and interpret information before it is consumed by members. Since the forces of conventional society usually take an active role in trying to do something about deviance, especially when it is repeated and shared among a number of practitioners, members of deviant groups are potentially bombarded with information contrary to the interests of the emerging deviant group. That information includes negative propaganda—about why the deviance is bad, why it cannot be good, the bad things that will happen to practitioners, and stories contradicting things the group stands for or showing that it is about to be crushed by conventionality. If the members receive those messages, they may be enticed to leave the group, to question its philosophy, or to lose confidence in its goals or leaders. Thus, it is advantageous if such information can be intercepted, transformed, and packaged in accordance with the philosophy of the group.

One way to accomplish that is to prohibit members from having contact with people on the outside, unless it takes place under controlled conditions, and to restrict their access to news sources or other "establishment" literature. They may be taught that outside people are manipulated, that establishment news is nothing more than biased propaganda, and that in any case group functionaries are in a better position to interpret events than are individual members. Many deviant groups, therefore, have regular "information" seminars, or meetings where events within and outside the group are discussed and interpreted. The more efficient groups designate special members as interpreters or "theoreticians" and give them the job of framing information in conformity with group goals, philosophy, and guiding literature. Often these interpreters are the group leaders themselves, but not always.

Techniques for regulating information, of course, are not normally presented to group members in that light, nor are they normally perceived that way. Outsiders tend to think that members of deviant groups are dupes of selfish leaders who are using their minions for personal power or gain. In fact, there is a tendency for outsiders to imagine the worst of deviant groups, especially believing that the members are coerced. Establishment media seem to delight in searching for, and sometimes finding, evidence consistent with the idea of coercion. However, deviants often participate with open eyes, recognizing they are controlled but personally perceiving that the way the group operates is not autocracy but an important way of improving things. Moreover, deviant group members usually think that whatever they are doing is voluntary.

Indeed, group functionaries may not themselves even realize that the procedures they institute actually have the purpose of restricting flow and interpretation of information, nor do they necessarily perceive or realize that they are autocratically controlling their charges. They often sincerely believe that outsiders distort information and that the only means to truth are those promoted by the deviant group. Moreover, they frequently view themselves as self-sacrificing and altruistic. This is not to say that coercion is foreign to deviant groups in trying to ensure that information is correctly interpreted. Later, we will see that discipline and social control are necessary for success, and they sometimes involve coercion.

One method of reducing the chances that group members will be exposed to damaging information is to encourage them to stick together at all times. This is usually easily accomplished by focusing on potential threats from the outside or by emphasizing the joys of in-group interaction. Natural ties that come from common identities and interests are usually strong. Nevertheless, there may be provisions to punish those who insist on too much personal isolation or who violate the rules of exclusive association. When members hang together, especially when confronting the outside world, they can keep an eye on each other. If something happens, or if there is the chance of exposure to contaminating information, one or the other deviant can report to the group as a whole and verify the events that are to be interpreted by the group "theorist" or leader. At worst, two or more members can view the event, at the time it is happening, more effectively through the lens of group philosophy than can one member alone.

Developing Dependency

Many of the techniques for generating commitment and regulating information have a dual effect. They also make individual group members more dependent on the group and thereby enhance group loyalty and cohesion. If group members give up all of their possessions to join, or if they commit outrageous acts in initiation and cut themselves off from contact with outsiders, including friends and associates, they must then rely on the deviant group for survival. Having isolated themselves from nonmembers, made themselves ignorant of outside events, declared themselves as deviants and followers of unacceptable social rules, and having surrendered the means of effective participation in conventional society, the committed will find it exceptionally hard to reintegrate should they at some point actually want to. Furthermore, when individuals adopt elements of a sustaining philosophy that support separation from conventional society, submit to regulations on information, and endorse the symbolic procedures of a deviant group, they are likely to alienate nonmembers, even those with whom they previously were closely associated. If people are too put off, they will be less receptive to deviant group members should they decide later to try to resume their former lives. Indeed, the admonition to "renounce your brother and your sister, give away your property, and come join me, otherwise you cannot enter such and such a promised state of being" is often acclaimed by charismatic leaders.

Hence, in the beginning, successful deviant groups usually make strong efforts to shut themselves off from the outside world, to encourage cooperative dependence on the group as a whole, and to undermine the means by which members might survive if they were to exit from the group. By renouncing the past, sharing all things, adopting roles relevant to the group but foreign to the conventional world, and encouraging members to view former friends or loved ones as potential enemies, deviant group members render themselves insularly dependent on each other. All needs and desires are met within the group, which becomes the exclusive source of gratifications. In the end, if deviant groups fail to create a deep-seated, positive desire to stay with the group, they may nevertheless succeed in creating cohesion by making it practically impossible for inductees to leave.

Effective Social Control

Social control is the process of rewarding people for conformity to expectations and punishing them for nonconformity. Despite the potential effectiveness of the previously described mechanisms in generating strong, cohesive groups, most deviant organizations also install social control procedures, at least as back-ups. We have already noted that encouraging or insisting that group members remain in contact with each other enables detection of violations of group rules. Usually, deviant groups prescribe punishments, most often informal ones, for departures from expectations. Thus, it is common for miscreants to be shamed in front of others for jeopardizing the group's rules; often the punishment comes with the possibility of repentance and redemption. It is also possible that rule breakers will be punished more severely, sometimes with banishment, for violating rules that jeopardize the survival of the group. The greater the extent to which practitioners are dependent on the group or committed to it and its philosophy, the more potent is the threat of shaming and rejection. Of course, sometimes deviant groups do not hesitate to torture or kill those who betray them.

The other half of the equation, of course, mandates reward for fulfilling the expectations of the group and promoting its survival and well-being. The most common type of reward available to conformists is the pleasure of association with the group and reaping the benefits it offers. If the group is organized to view pornography, being able to do it in the comfort of the group is its own reward. If the group promises that rewards for group members will come at some future time, as many religious groups do, then those eventual rewards represent positive incentives for group membership and compliance with group rules. And being able to interact and share experiences and ideas with people similar to oneself satisfies the social longing in the human spirit. In addition, deviant groups normally use prestige as a key positive reward. The most successful groups structure themselves into fine-grained hierarchies, with appropriate recognition and praise for each higher level of achievement (Mullen, 1966). Without conformity, those rewards do not accrue to members, so granting them is an important tool for keeping members on track.

Summary

Given the social control efforts by conventional society that are activated by processes which may result in a particular behavior being defined as deviant, the first task for the practitioners of that deviance, if their particular type of deviance is to succeed, then, is to organize effectively. This is not easy. Some deviance does not lend itself to organization, and not all methods of organizing are equally effective. There must be an advantageous convergence of techniques for generating and sustaining commitment. Such techniques involve, among other things, a shared, closed-system philosophy emphasizing the rewards of group membership and the necessity of members' differentiating themselves from outsiders.

Techniques also encompass a multitude of mechanisms to help link individuals' personalities and identities with the group—sacrificial inductions, symbols, rituals, and martyrs. And frequently, successful organization rests on the appeal of charismatic leaders and stems from collective challenges that draw members together in a common response. Furthermore, effective organization usually requires regulation of information exposure and generation of dependency for members, as well as efficient social control.

A particular effort at organization may falter with respect to any one or a combination of these elements. Some fledgling deviant groups never are able to evoke enough commitment from their members. Maybe the philosophy that develops is poorly constructed, or perhaps it does not sufficiently justify the group or the deviant activity. Some new groups don't bother with symbolic procedures and so fail to create the fusion between personalities and the group. Other groups lack the spiritual basis provided by a charismatic leader. Many beginning groups do not produce dependency in their members, nor do they manage to exercise effective social control of their members; as a result, they quickly fall apart from internal bickering or competition.

After all, the technology for effective group formation is not known to all, and it is not a matter of simple common sense. Since there are no manuals for those wishing to found new groups, the procedures employed are often trial and error—mostly error. It appears to be a lucky set of circumstances that enables some groups to hit upon the right combination of elements to achieve an effective and cohesive organization. And given that organization of deviant activities, unlike most organization of nondeviant activities, must be done hurriedly and in the face of much harassment, it is a wonder that such efforts ever succeed. But sometimes they do succeed, thereby planting the seeds of potential social change.

Social change, of course, does not automatically evolve from all successful deviant organization. Some deviance stops growing once the practitioners have located each other and formed a group, so the deviance never develops into a force for change. Sometimes that is because practitioners are few and the deviance has little inherent appeal to others who might be enticed to do it. At other times it is because the practitioners become self-satisfied with their accomplishments at having established a successful group and are happy to enjoy the fruits of their efforts, which is to practice the deviance in the relative safety of a group network. But most often a deviant group stops growing because the forces of conventional social control abandon efforts at repression and adopt a containment approach. This approach usually involves an unspoken truce in which the deviant group is allowed to exist and its members are permitted to do their thing as long as the deviant behavior is kept at the minimum level currently prevailing, remains confined to certain locales or areas, does not attract media attention, and the members do not attempt to contaminate the innocent or bring in new members. Often, deviant groups are glad to make such accommodations because they doubt their ability to go beyond what they have already done.

Recruitment

Some deviant groups are not satisfied with having successfully organized those who already practice the deviance. Instead, they begin to try to introduce nonpractitioners to the deviance and ultimately to recruit them to the deviant group. This may be because conventional society has kept up its pressure, refusing to back off to a level of simple containment. Sometimes it is because the terms of a containment truce are too restrictive for the deviant group. For some, such as religious cults or political revolutionaries, their sustaining philosophies mandate expansion. And some types of deviance require infusion of new members. For example, practitioners of public restroom homosexuality (Humphreys, 1970), who have never actually achieved full organization but who nevertheless try to recruit new participants, do so because the desire for anonymity makes new "trade" necessary. Similarly, swingers constantly seek new players because a basic tenet of the activity is to have sex without jeopardizing marital relationships (Bartell, 1971). Repeated sexual encounters with the same people increase the chances of romantic involvements, which would make swinging more dangerous to the marriages than contacts with strangers.

Recruitment of nonpractitioners to become participants in deviant activities or deviant groups is not easy, however. The processes defining some behavior as deviant result in negative attitudes about, and fear of, it among those not already involved, as well as provision for costly penalties in lost reputation and possible legal sanctions. Consequently, recruiters already face much resistance. In addition, because the behavior is deviant, its practitioners are under surveillance to prevent contact with nonpractitioners, especially ones that the larger society regards as particularly vulnerable. Hence deviant group recruiters cannot advertise openly, pass out leaflets inviting others, or go up and down streets with a sound truck announcing the openness of the group to new membership. In fact, they cannot easily approach people they meet on an individual basis. Imagine sitting by someone on a bus or airplane, striking up a conversation, and then having them suggest that you join a group of navel-lint collectors or at least try a little navel-lint collecting to see what it is like.

Despite such difficulties, some deviant groups and unorganized practitioners of deviance do manage to recruit others. In fact, it is striking how almost any behavior, no matter how bizarre or dangerous, can seemingly attract a following. Even jaded students of deviance, or agents of control, who think they have seen or heard everything, continually learn of unusual forms of deviance that substantial numbers of people get drawn into.

Much recruitment is not by design; some of it results from simple imitation. Observers may see somebody practicing a deviance, become curious about its appeal, and try it, sometimes finding it pleasing enough to continue. Evidence suggests that much drug use begins that way (Goode, 1970, 1993). Similarly, police departments have trouble keeping their vice officers clean because they are around deviant activities so much that their curiosity often gets the best of them. Imitative recruitment is sometimes actually stimulated by the mere fact that it is deviant. Those who like to "live on the edge" may be attracted even to deviance that has few or no inherently pleasing characteristics; the thrill of taking risks, of doing things that are socially unacceptable or dangerous, may be enough to send them looking for practitioners or other opportunities.

Other recruitment is also unsystematic, often occurring without any specific efforts on the part of deviant group members. Some takes place because individual practitioners on their own seek companions, partners, or victims. Deviant gamblers want others with whom to bet; very sick or despondent people sometimes need help in committing suicide; and those determined to satisfy homosexual desires require partners. Such people go looking for deviant opportunities. Thus, recruitment to deviant activities or groups is sometimes easy, and much of it happens without any deliberate campaigns or special efforts by practitioners. Some recruitment, however, is organized and systematic, with well-specified goals and procedures. Often these efforts fail miserably, but sometimes they succeed amazingly well. What influences their success or failure?

Lofland's Model

Lofland (1967) has set forth an ordered, sequential model describing the steps through which a person must go to be converted to deviant group activities (Lofland and Stark, 1965). Assuming that his model for individual conversion is correct, it implies that in order to succeed at recruitment, deviant groups must ensure that the largest possible number of potential recruits undergo those sequential steps.

The Individual's Experience

Tension. Lofland contends, first, that only particular types of individuals are susceptible to recruitment. They are individuals existing in a state of tension because their actual circumstances differ from an ideal state of affairs for themselves. We might say they are people with a problem, although they may not recognize that they have a problem until some activating event or circumstance creates a sense of awareness. For instance, a woman occupying a traditional wife and mother role may experience a vague sense of discomfort or unhappiness. She may not know exactly why she feels unhappy and may not even define her condition as unhappiness. Yet there is a tension, which is the initial circumstance predisposing her to potential later recruitment as a militant feminist. Or a factory worker may suffer from an unidentified malaise. He knows that despite continuous hard work, he still has financial problems, but his tension may not be recognized as a predisposition for later revolutionary action—not until subsequent events or conditions transpire.

Seeking. But according to Lofland, recruitment to deviant groups or activities requires more than being under tension, or having a problem. Individuals must have begun to seek solutions for their ill-defined condition. Since they are unable to articulate their problem, however, they cannot conceive its remedy. Typically, eventual deviants undertake a more-or-less random search for relief. Perhaps the traditional woman described above engages in religious pursuits to try to overcome her feelings of unhappiness, only to discover after a while that nothing has changed and that she still feels vaguely distraught. She may then turn to voluntary political or community activity, also without satisfaction. She may then involve herself in parapsychological pursuits, boning up on astrology and consulting fortune-tellers. Similarly, the factory worker may join a social group like the Masons, then having found no satisfaction, turn to hobbies, and finally attempt to resolve his difficulties with sexual exploits. No matter the specific activities pursued, the key step for future deviant recruits is to engage in a search for solutions through conventional, though perhaps marginally acceptable, means.

Desperation. The third requirement for eventual conversion, according to the Lofland model, is for the seeker to become desperate. That is, individuals under tension, who have unsuccessfully sought relief in multiple ways, finally reach the point where they think things are hopeless—that they will remain forever in the state of tension that seems to define their lives. This, of course, is an intangible, unmeasurable condition. Some reach a point of desperation long before others, and even when desperate, many continue to try conventional solutions. Perhaps if one could mark this turning point, it would be when the individual says to himself or herself, "I'm open to anything that will make me feel better about myself and my circumstances in life."

Opportunity. Many seekers who become desperate never take the next step into deviance. They may sink into depression or resign themselves to somehow going on—perhaps by continuing the quest for conventional answers. They may eventually find an actual solution, by luck or design. The housewife and worker may forever remain despondent, living miserable lives punctuated with sporadic futile searches for resolution. Or perhaps the woman finally divorces her husband, uses alimony to finance a return to college, and ends up pursuing a professional and satisfying career. The worker may take a night course in computer technology that opens up a new, more rewarding and satisfying life style.

The key factor that tips the pattern toward deviance appears to be the lucky (or unlucky?) happenstance in which a desperate, seeking individual is faced with an opportunity to become involved in deviance. But just any opportunity will not do; it has to be an opportunity in the form of a pleasing interpersonal contact between the seeker and a practitioner of deviance. For example, suppose the unhappy housewife happens to sit down on a city bus next to a militant member of a local feminist group. They strike up a conversation, enjoy the exchange, and decide they like each other. As a result they exchange phone numbers and vow to get together some time for lunch. Later they meet, develop a deeper acquaintanceship, and exchange views and ideas. Among the things talked about are the problems the housewife has. And she learns from her new acquaintance that the source of her problem is probably the oppressed position of women like her who sacrifice themselves for husbands and children. And she is told that feminism offers a way out of the situation.

Thus, according to the Lofland model, it is not enough to have become a seeker for a solution to one's problem; one must have become desperate in that search and while feeling the sense of desperation to have come in contact with, and established an interpersonal relationship with, a member of the deviant group. Clearly, the fortuitous convergence of these circumstances does not occur very often, so most potential converts to deviance never actually become real converts. Moreover, the intersection of desperation and opportunity does not always result in recruitment; there must follow a period of more and more extensive interpersonal interaction.

Sealing the Bonds. Over time, if the housewife continues to interact with the feminist and they become closely bonded, she will be exposed more and more to the feminist style of life and ideology. And at some point, she will be invited to hang out with other feminists in the organization. Through this contact she will conclude that feminists are not the way conventional society, her family, neighbors, and husband think they are. Instead of being rabid, irrational, bra-burning lesbians, she comes to perceive them as sensible, friendly women who faced the same problems she now does and have found a workable way to deal with them. As time goes on, she is likely to spend more and more time with these sympathetic companions and less and less time with her former associates, including her husband. Moreover, she is likely to be brought into group activities, become exposed to the philosophy, and learn of the efforts of conventional society (mostly males) to suppress the group and keep women subordinated. And she will find out about atrocities that have befallen women, learn to interpret everyday events through feminist "insight," and come to appreciate pioneers and martyrs who suffered because of their promotion of women's rights. In other words, her consciousness will be raised.

Induction. Meanwhile, those with whom she previously spent time will become concerned. They may try to dissuade her from associating with the evil, dangerous feminists who will lead her to neglect her children and reject her husband. If they do not succeed in this, they will begin to reject her and deliberately reduce their own contacts with her lest they suffer the bad repute that comes from associating with militant feminists or those who hang out with them. Thus, at the same time that the woman is being brought into closer alliance with the feminist group, she is being repelled by those in the conventional world.

Eventually most of this housewife's ties will be with the "deviants," and she will have been shut out by conventional people. Her parents may have rejected her, her husband may be seeking a divorce with custody of the children, her former church associates will have declared her a hopeless sinner, and neighbors will be gossiping about her neglect of the children (even if there is no actual neglect). At some point she will begin to think of herself as a militant feminist and may seek formal induction into the group. Once she undergoes the induction ceremony, which may require an outrageous declaration or action, she has completely alienated herself from the outside world and burned her bridges behind her.

Summary

The key point of recruitment, then, according to Lofland, is interpersonal contact and the development of social bonds between deviants and potential recruits. It is only through that process that initial fears and barriers can be overcome. Other methods of recruitment almost always fail. Impersonal communications through advertisements and other means are risky and unlikely to appear in the best format. Most nondeviants will not really listen to impersonal messages or appeals; everybody is bombarded with them all the time. Those who listen will not learn enough to make the deviance appealing because those messages will be countered by contrary discounting information from conventional sources. And through it all will be fear—of the unknown, of potential costs, and of the bad consequences that are assumed to accompany the deviance. For these reasons, impersonal recruitment does not work well. Many fledgling groups do not realize this and so fail in trying to expand; they assume that selling deviance is like selling soap, Madison Avenue style. Deviant groups who do succeed learn that they must send forth individual emissaries to identify susceptible candidates, establish close personal bonds with them, and slowly expose their new friends to practitioners and the benefits of the deviance.

A Successful Group's Strategy

To the extent that Lofland is correct, then, deviant groups who wish to mount a fruitful plan of recruiting must, in the early stages at least, try to find people who are under tension of some kind. Since regular, well-adjusted individuals are unlikely to find deviant groups or activities attractive (or if they do find them attractive, they are likely to be restrained in converting), groups who aim their campaigns toward "normals" will probably fail. Moreover, successful deviant groups must focus their recruitment attention on those who are already in the process of trying to solve their problems, and they must intervene at the precise point where desperation has come into play. Trying to recruit untroubled people will not work, and neither will approaching those who are troubled but have not yet become seekers. Furthermore, it will even be difficult to convert seekers who have not yet exhausted other potential remedies and come to the conclusion that things seem hopeless.

But having targeted the most fruitful population for recruitment, the deviant groups who are to succeed must approach their prey on an interpersonal level—one that involves gradually strengthening bonds and fuller exposure to other members of the deviant group as well as to their philosophies and ways of life. Eventually many of those so approached will become full-fledged group members as they are socialized by means of face-to-face interaction and finally undergo some induction ceremonies. Though many who reach this last stage in the sequence of steps to recruitment will convert, it is not a sure thing. An important element is how the members of the potential recruit's former social network respond. If the members of that social network give up efforts to rescue the recruit and cut off their socially supportive relationships, then conversion is highly likely. But if they continue to maintain their relationships with the potential recruit, the last push into deviance may be averted. That is why successful deviant groups must work especially hard to bring the recruit into full-time interaction with members of the group as early as possible and to undercut their ties with former friends, family, and associates. They may accomplish that by being especially attentive and by communicating a sustaining philosophy that emphasizes the rewards of group membership and the beauty of separation from conventionality.

Doing all of this is, of course, difficult, and most aspiring deviant groups make many mistakes in the process. Assuming that Lofland is right, organizational bungling may be one reason few forms of deviance ever produce social change. But is he correct about the recruitment process?

A Counter Model

While Lofland's account of the recruitment process makes a lot of sense, especially in its assertion that the key to proficiency is interpersonal contact, there are reasons to question parts of it (Snow and Phillips, 1980). For one thing, it does not appear that all converts to deviant activity have a problem or are experiencing tension prior to conversion. While many no doubt fit that pattern (Hamm, 1993; Knutson, 1981; Kressel, 1996), it appears that in many cases, *after coming into contact with deviant practitioners* and being exposed to their world view, people "reconstruct" their past lives to perceive that they were under tension. In other words, some evidence suggests that predisposition for deviance is less crucial than opportunity (cf. the notion of routine activities, Cohen and Felson, 1979; Felson, 1986). Many recruits to deviant groups begin as normals, but through interpersonal contact with practitioners, come to redefine normality as a problem state. Some come to embrace the deviance on its own merit.

For example, the case of Patty Hearst, daughter of a famous and wealthy tycoon, raises doubts about the Lofland model (Baker, 1974; Hearst, 1982).

Deviance in Everyday Life

The case of Patty Hearst is an excellent example of a phenomenon known as the "Stockholm Syndrome." In Stockholm, Sweden, during a bank robbery, a young woman was taken hostage and held at gunpoint for several days. The gunman could have killed his hostage but did not, instead keeping her alive over a period of days. The man was eventually captured by the police, tried, and sentenced to prison. Rather than turning against the man who had held her hostage at gunpoint and threatened her life, the young woman subsequently fell in love with her captor and married him while he was in prison. Psychologists explain the phenomenon as a fairly common response people have in life-threatening situations. Isolated from other sources of support, completely powerless and helpless, hostages frequently feel gratitude for any kindness shown by their captors. They soon develop a bond and sense of commitment to those who hold them.

Patty, who was the granddaughter of William Randolph Hearst, the newspaper owner who was the inspiration for the movie "Citizen Kane," was kidnaped in 1974 by a radical Maoist group calling itself the Symbionese Liberation Army (SLA). Patty was held blindfolded in a closet for 57 days, raped, and threatened with death. The objective of the SLA was the overthrow of the white-ruled establishment in the interest of racial justice; in pursuit of that goal they stockpiled weapons and robbed banks to finance their activities. After her kidnaping, Ms. Hearst apparently fell in love with one of her captors and then voluntarily adopted the group goals as her own. The "kidnaped heiress" became the "heiress-turned-revolutionary." She recorded a message to her father and other establishment figures denouncing capitalism and rejecting her heritage. She announced that she had changed her name to Tania and would "join the forces of the SLA." Many at the time thought that Patty had been brainwashed and was coerced into "joining" the group. This interpretation was later called into question when she was caught on camera using a machine gun to help rob the Hibernia Bank in Hibernia, California. During the robbery, the camera showed that no one in her group had a gun on her and that she seemed to be actively participating in the robbery. She was later convicted and sent to prison for the robbery. Later, after the group was attacked and decimated in a bloody gun battle with Los Angeles Police without her being present, she was "rescued." There then followed a period of "deprogramming," and finally a reintroduction to conventional society as the victim of coercion. Yet for a time, when her contacts were exclusively with members of the SLA, fostered by her interpersonal relationship with a specific member, she was apparently a full-fledged, dedicated member. If so, and Lofland's model is correct, we must conclude that prior to the kidnaping, she was a troubled person in search of a solution for her tension. Many people think that is a stretch because it appears that her "trouble" was an after-the-fact construction—one growing out of raised consciousness.

Similarly, many converts to recreational drug use (Akers, 1985; Goode, 1970), to white-collar business deviance (Calavita and Pontell, 1993; Schlegel and Weisburd, 1992), and to unorthodox religions (Kephart and Zellner, 1994) do not appear to have unusual problems or tensions prior to recruitment into the deviant activity. It seems more likely that they just happened to be in the wrong (right?) place at the wrong (right?) time so that circumstances threw them into close personal association with practitioners of deviance. Unfortunately, it is almost impossible to address this issue empirically. If the deviance induction process leads to reconstructions of the past, one can never take individuals' recollections as accurate guides to their states of mind prior to conversion to deviance. And since one cannot predict who will or will not ultimately be recruited to deviance, researchers cannot document states of mind for a large sample at some point and then later see who encountered and responded positively to opportunities for deviant induction.

Intensified Opposition

Regardless of how recruitment occurs, the fact is that some groups do it successfully but most don't. If a form of deviance is to succeed and eventually become legitimate behavior, thereby having brought about social change, it must catch on; that is, it must first grow until it encompasses a large enough proportion of the population to create a crisis of societal identity. And even if a group has mastered the art of recruitment, it will not necessarily succeed in converting the necessary numbers. One major reason is that success breeds intensified opposition; another is that growth activates a number of difficult organizational problems that most deviant groups cannot solve.

As a deviant group begins to branch out through interpersonal contacts, it attracts more societal attention; it activates more laws or other vehicles to stop or control it; and it stimulates creative actions by the agents of conventional social control. At this point, there will be an all-out campaign to isolate the deviants so they cannot reach potential recruits; to generate negative and fearful attitudes toward them so that people will avoid the deviants and be better able to resist recruitment efforts; to punish or entice away those who practice the deviance; and to disrupt deviant organizations. Two of these measures deserve special note.

Enticement of practitioners to become turncoats is often based on promises of leniency (to avoid punishment) as well as expectations for smooth paths of re-entry. Indeed, thriving careers await those who are willing to become professional "ex's" (Brown, 1996). If a woman allows herself to be "reclaimed" from devil worship, revolutionary activity, prostitution, assisted suicide cults, and the like, she can earn a good living making speeches to groups especially opposed to the specific deviance in question, writing articles or books, appearing on TV talk shows, or working as a counselor or adviser. Rewards for making discrediting statements about the deviance or its supporting group are also offered to disgruntled ex-members who may have left the group without prior enticement. It is important to recognize, however, that enticements are not usually offered in the early stages of organization; it is only when the deviance becomes popular enough to make being an "ex" interesting to large numbers of people and when societal agents of control need to create credible but unfavorable propaganda. If the people do not trust what the police or moral entrepreneurs say about deviance, they may be swayed by those who were on the inside and who have first-hand knowledge.

Deviance in Everyday Life

One way that majority groups try to disrupt the activities of minority groups is to portray them not merely as different but as dangerous. This is one explanation for what occurred at the Branch Davidian compound in Waco, Texas. The Branch Davidians were a splinter religious group from the Latter Day Saints who had established a religious community near Waco, Texas, in 1935 (Tabor, 1995). In 1993, the Federal Bureau of Alcohol, Tobacco, and Firearms (ATF) wanted to arrest David Koresh, the latest in a long line of the community's leaders, for weapons charges. ATF agents surrounded the Davidian compound and had planned to enter and arrest Koresh. The Davidians had been tipped about the planned assault, however, and ambushed the ATF agents, killing four agents and wounding 16, while suffering six fatalities of their own. After a prolonged standoff, the Davidian compound was stormed. During the siege, however, a fire broke out in the compound, which ignited weapons caches. When the conflagration finished, some 86 Davidians were left dead; some died in the fire, some were killed by gunfire thought to have originated from other group members. In preparing the siege, and justifying the events afterward, ATF and U.S. Justice Department officials reported that Koresh was messianic and "mad," that he was keeping people in the compound against their will, that he had children from several of the women, that the group was ready to commit mass suicide, and that many of the children were victims of both physical and sexual abuse. As a result, the Davidians became more than "religious nuts"; they were dangerous criminals.

The other noteworthy societal response to a deviant group showing success involves attempts to disrupt it. One method is to infiltrate the group with pretenders. Once in, and mistaken for true believers, they can monitor movements and identify members, raise disruptive questions, generate conflict among practitioners, and sow discord about the leaders. A particularly common and useful tactic is to develop damaging evidence that leaders are hypocrites who are duping the members of the group. The veracity of these accounts is less important, from the point of view of outside agents of control, than their effect in discrediting leaders in the eyes of members, or at least diverting leaders' time and energy to defending themselves, and creating unfavorable attitudes among outsiders who might be potential recruits. If all else fails, the ultimate tactic of disruption is to imprison or kill group leaders and sometimes ordinary members as well. Sometimes whole groups are simply crushed, often with excuses that it was a mistake or that the group in question really destroyed itself to avoid judgment in outside courts or public opinion.

Although successful recruitment stimulates extra efforts by agents of conventional society to destroy or arrest the growth of the group, and those efforts often accomplish their purpose, such counterattacks may actually aid the struggling deviant movement. Sometimes maneuvers to control deviant groups, at any point in the sequence from new deviance to social change, reinforce those individuals' or groups' determination; provide examples to support the philosophy and elevate martyrs; prove the necessity for vigilance; and create sympathy among outsiders. Thus, conventional society, through its efforts to prevent deviance and social change stemming from it, occasionally defeats its own purposes. The movement from individual deviance to legitimation, then, is a process of strategic moves and countermoves, much like a chess game. Either side can play wisely or foolishly, so the outcome is not entirely dependent on what either contingent itself does; rather, it is the interaction of good organizational responses by one side with poor organizational responses by the other side. Moreover, the process is dynamic in the sense that a response cannot be planned too far ahead but must come into play at the appropriate time following a move by the other contender.

Problems of Growth and Expansion

Despite the best efforts of society to stifle or eliminate growing deviant movements, some forms of deviance continue to succeed. Success, however, is not the usual outcome. Many groups that have managed to solve all the problems necessary for survival up to the point of needing growth and expansion find these new challenges too much. Not only must they contend with stepped-up efforts by agents of conventional society to put them out of business or to undermine them internally, but they must also confront unfamiliar challenges of organization that are created by the influx of new members. Those problems include: (1) how to effectively induct or socialize a constant stream of initiates, (2) how to communicate effectively from one localized group to another, (3) how to maintain a common unifying culture, and (4) how to contend with the weakening of "true belief."

Socialization

Recall that deviant groups who successfully recruit do so by means of interpersonal contact. This is necessarily a slow, step-by-step proccedure as each person is brought into closer alliance with the group and transformed through careful tutelage into a full member of the group. It is most effectively accomplished when there is a large pre-existing, cohesive body of members into which a few new recruits are brought. However, with a large number of new converts and with repeated and regular infusion, there is too little time for one batch of recruits to become assimilated before another batch is in line for induction. As a result, recruits at various stages of conversion may come to outnumber those who are fully integrated. This lag in assimilation inevitably weakens the cohesion of the group, in part because new recruits may find more in common with those experiencing their same problems than with fully inducted members. Hence, alliances among various levels of novices are liable to emerge, leading to subcultures within deviant groups. Ironically, then, the more success a group has, the more likely is it to sow the seeds of its own disintegration unless it is particularly adept at solving the problem of rapidly socializing large numbers of new members.

Communication

Communication among its members is a second problem for deviant groups who have managed to recruit widely. In localized groups, almost all things can be shared in common and all events can be interpreted through one lens—the official philosophy. Leaders can speak directly with followers, and practitioners can communicate with one another. Growth, however, usually leads the group to expand away from its local area into additional locales. Then, instead of integrating one localized group, the movement must try to integrate many groups in various locations. To accomplish this goal, there must be an overarching organization. But since all members can no longer interact interpersonally, direct verbal messages must give way to impersonal communication.

Impersonal devices include underground newspapers or newsletters, ordinary mail, phones, and e-mail. Hand-delivered newsletters are the most desirable because phones can be tapped, mail can be censored, and e-mail can be intercepted, enabling enemies to monitor activities or distort messages. To supplement impersonal communication, many successful deviant movements put leaders or "theorists" on the road, traveling from one locale to another to bring messages, offer encouragement, and interpret events. Traveling, however, exposes important group leaders to danger from outside enemies. Moreover, none of these means is as effective or as efficient as interpersonal contact on a minute-by-minute, day-by-day basis. In the absence of effective communication, local groups are left to their own devices. Inevitably, then, expansion means more diversity, less efficient solutions for problems of everyday living, and weaker overall cohesion.

Diverse Cultures

A particularly costly consequence of expansion into different locales is the group's decreased ability to forge a unified culture. When there is a small localized group, it experiences all things in common, or at least it can talk about all things, evolve a common interpretation, and develop unique solutions that are then passed on to the next generation. When a movement is fragmented and dispersed to different locales, it is no longer possible to maintain a completely common culture. Each local group will encounter somewhat different situations and environments. And since each group is not in direct, intimate contact with the others, each localized group will, to some extent, interpret and act on its own to deal with questions or circumstances. Hence, all will develop somewhat distinct cultures. Those distinct cultures help fragment the overall movement and undermine general cohesion. This effect of expansion means that it is a rare movement that can manage to keep its diverse parts on the same track to move toward legitimation.

Weakening of True Belief

In terms of its consequences for social change, the most important effect of growth and expansion is the resulting pressure on groups to de-emphasize their differentness. Remember that one of the features of early organization that enables practitioners of new deviance to survive is the tight cohesiveness that stems from separating group members from the larger society and getting them to embrace the idea that they are unique, different, superior, and vulnerable. Those who take the most pride in being deviant and in reveling in the deviance of the group are "true believers." Typically, they are rigid and dedicated, willing to sacrifice self for the group and unwilling to yield in their convictions. For them, the practice of the deviance itself is secondary to the survival of the group that emerges to protect those who practice the deviance and to perpetuate the philosophy undergirding that group.

However, as deviant movements recruit more and more people who were not previous practitioners, the less able they are to convert them to true belief and the less interest there is in maintaining a distinct deviant stance. The more people who are brought in, the greater the chances that some of them will be interested only in occasionally partaking of the pleasures or rewards of the deviance itself. They will want to do the deviance occasionally, at their convenience, but they will not want to do it all the time, nor will they want the supporting group surrounding the deviance to consume their entire lives. Thus, with wider recruitment, toilet bowl caressers will snare some who do not want to devote their entire lives to toilet bowl caressing or to the group that promotes it. Instead, they will want to caress toilet bowls only some of the time, say on Saturdays or vacations. Their objectives will mainly be to practice this deviance at their discretion, not to preserve the deviant group. Hence, they will want to try to get people outside the group to tolerate and perhaps accept toilet bowl caressing as legitimate activity. In short, with expansion will grow internal sentiments for accommodation, not separation, and for emphasizing the essential conventionality of toilet bowl caressers, not their distinctiveness. In other words, with increasing membership there will inevitably be a dilution in the overall group's cohesiveness.

Ironically, then, success produces failure—at least failure in maintaining a cohesive group. But at the same time, failure reroutes the path of the new deviance away from deviance toward acceptability—and into the mode of producing social change.

The Fruits of Success

As more new recruits are converted and as a given deviance grows, a number of processes begin to converge. The forces of conventional social control may come to perceive that the cause is lost. Indeed, so many people may now be practicing the deviance that a schism in society appears inevitable. Those who do the deviance may be almost as numerous as those who don't. Under such circumstances, the usual methods of control begin to seem counterproductive, because if they are conscientiously carried out, there will be more people imprisoned, killed, or ostracized than free, alive, and fully functioning in society. Society, then, can continue current trends and break into two parts, probably with bitter conflict, or it can come to some accommodation in which the deviance and its practitioners are made acceptable, or in which the deviance is redefined as never having existed and thereafter ignored. At this point most societies begin a slow process of accommodation with the deviance.

Seeking Tolerance

At the same time that conflict may appear inevitable in the larger society, processes within the deviant movement, described above, weaken it and generate internal pressures to seek accommodation with the outside world. Thus begins slow movement in both directions. Conventional society moves a little toward acceptance of the deviant activity and practitioners move a little toward being less deviant, seeking tolerance on the grounds that they are not as extreme as society imagines (and as the deviant practitioners in the past touted). At this point, deviant practitioners are probably not thinking about effecting social change, nor are they imagining that society will fully accept their behavior. They are simply making a plea that the rest of society will call a truce, become a little more tolerant, and leave them alone.

The main basis for claiming tolerance is the contention that the deviance in question is not really very different from many other things that are acceptable in conventional society, and that the practitioners of the deviance are pretty much like everybody else, with the exception of their fondness for the deviance. Furthermore, those who plead for tolerance are likely to invoke the values of the larger society in pursuit of those ends. For example, navel-lint collectors may try to get others to see that collecting navel lint is not much different from collecting stamps, salt and pepper shakers, or wine corks. They may contend that navel lint collectors are like everybody else. They fall in love, have families, hold jobs, vote, and take vacations. They are different from others only in that they happen to collect some unusual items. Finally, they may point out that it really is an issue of freedom. Since people in the United States brag about their personal freedoms and assert rights in political, religious, and other realms, then it is a logical extension of those beliefs to permit navel lint collectors the personal freedom to pursue their interests. In essence, the practitioners of the particular deviance are saying: "let us do our thing; it really isn't very different from what you do and we are a lot like other people; and besides it is a basic right we are being denied."

This is a far cry, of course, from earlier times when the practitioners were secretive and proud of their differences from others. This shift in character is usually accompanied by a more open exposure to the outside world, because

as the process unfolds, "coming out" can take place with less danger for practitioners. For instance, selected deviants may give interviews to magazine
writers, some may go on talk shows, and a few may be invited to give speeches
to specialized groups like college classes in deviance or seminars in law enforcement training.

Debate

Once the forces of conventional society are ready to back off from their
aggressive attempts to suppress the deviance and once the practitioners of
deviance are ready to retreat from their aggressive claims to differentness,
the two can meet somewhere in the middle. That middle ground may represent full acceptance of the deviance as a legitimate part of social life for all
who want to pursue it, or it may represent an uneasy tolerance, though not
full acceptance. Before any resolution can come about, however, a period of
widespread confrontation and "debate" must occur (Buckner, 1971).

This debate is not an official presenting of views as if there were two competing teams who meet in a giant hall with a moderator and timed responses.
Rather, it is an unsystematic, unplanned set of small confrontations that take
place in thousands of situations as practitioners of the deviance, or those who
might wish to argue their case, come into contact with nonpractitioners at
work, during commercial transactions, while engaged in recreation, and the
like. The debate involves discussion, contemplation, argument, and sometimes even open conflict. Over time, if the deviance has enough strength or
appeal, there may occur a slow shift toward legitimation.

Legitimation is not guaranteed, however, and some forms of deviance
stall at this point and never reach the point of full acceptability. Sometimes
they stall because of some credible new discovery about the deviance (such as
information that it really will injure you, can escalate to greater and more serious deviance, or lead to vicious outcomes) and at other times because opponents regroup to fight a rear-guard action that partially succeeds. It is impossible to predict exactly which deviant movements will finally succeed and
which ones will not, but there are some telling clues. Precursors of final success include statements by important conventional people who say things in
public like, "Well, I do not practice such and such myself, but my daughter
does, and I know that she is basically a good person and this behavior has not
harmed her in any way that I can see." Or perhaps an important public figure
will confess to having tried the deviance, though in a context where it was not
illegal (as William F. Buckley, the conservative columnist, once admitted having tried marijuana, but only on his boat outside the three-mile coastal limit
where it was not illegal).

Acceptance

Deviance has traversed the full route from new behavior to ultimate legitimation when it is finally regarded by the majority of people as not necessarily being bad, dangerous, or unacceptable and when it stops eliciting collective responses that are negative, including general gossip about practitioners,
informal ostracism or loss of status, enactment of new laws prohibiting the
behavior, or enforcement of the laws that already exist. There may actually be
repeal of coercive laws, but this is not necessary or even a normal outcome.

Usually, legal prohibition will remain on the books but simply fall into disuse. When all these things come about, clearly the behavior in question is no longer deviant—social change has occurred. Furthermore, ancillary behaviors and institutions connected with the practice of that deviance may then emerge and become part of the normal culture and social structure, thereby creating additional social change. For example, if assisted suicide ever becomes fully legitimate in the United States, it will alter many behavioral patterns and institutions. Among other things, it will probably lead to a decline of the industries that cater to the feeble and immobile, to a change in pension plans, and certainly to the way medical care is dispensed.

This final transformation of deviance into nondeviance, stemming from debate, may go on almost imperceptibly. Indeed, such change does not usually happen in discrete chunks, nor can it be pinned down to a specific time. It may not even be noticed until some time later when pollsters conduct a survey and find that the behavior in question is no longer deviant. Remember that becoming legitimate does not mean that a particular form of deviance comes to be practiced by all or most people, although that might occur. More often than not, the new normative behavior continues to be practiced only by a minority, though its new legitimacy is marked by the fact that the majority now view it as a possible thing to do.

An Overview of Reactive Change

The process by which reactive social change occurs starts with some new form of behavior or with the activation of some form of deviance already known but not practiced. If the initiators develop a pattern of behavior and seek others with whom to practice it, the behavior may stimulate social response resulting in its designation as deviance. Thereafter, practitioners may locate each other and form a tight-knit group to promote the practice of the deviance and protect themselves from forces of conventional social control. Developing such a group and solving organizational problems necessary for its maintenance are not easy, however, but are important if the deviance is to move toward legitimation. A critical element at this stage is the group's focus on complete separation from the outside society and emphasis on their differentness.

Eventually, successful deviant groups may decide to recruit others who do not at that time practice the deviance. This introduces a whole new set of problems for the deviant movement, and it spurs the forces of conventional society toward greater repressiveness. If the deviant movement manages to recruit heavily despite those efforts, however, it may move a step closer to legitimation. But successful recruitment inevitably threatens group unity and generates pressures toward accommodation. Further expansion causes a potential schism in society and leads to compromise. After first seeking tolerance, the deviant movement may move into full-scale debate with conventional society, and under some conditions may persuade a majority to accept the behavior as no longer unacceptable, thereby constituting social change. Former deviants then become conventional participants in society and warriors in opposing, designating as deviant, and attempting to repress other new forms of behavior.

While this model of legitimation is common, not all forms of new deviance that finally become acceptable follow it exactly. Some skip steps and others follow slightly different sequences.

Examples

A Success Story: Christianity

Practicing the Christian religion represents one example of a behavior that followed this model almost exactly and as a result, after a few hundred years, ended up fully legitimate. Jesus preached that he was the son of God and that those who believed him and followed him and his teachings could live everlasting lives. In so doing, he challenged the prevailing political and religious forces of his day. In response, he was declared to be a deviant, and the behavior of his followers became unacceptable as well as criminalized. Despite this, however, Christianity, as a way of life and religious practice, grew by leaps and bounds, ultimately succeeding to the point where conventional society had to accommodate it. It not only became nondeviant, it became the dominant religion in many parts of the world. So successful were the Christians that they ultimately became the leaders in trying to suppress or destroy other new religions that grew up, as well as old ones that had existed for a long time.

At first, of course, there were only a few practitioners of Christianity, and they organized themselves into exclusive enclaves for self-protection against the repressive forces of the Romans and local Jewish authorities. They certainly had a sustaining philosophy that promised eternal life and emphasized separation of Christians from the outside world; that theology, like many religious philosophies, was well constructed to deflect negative evidence. In addition, early Christian churches regulated information (a practice that was retained in full force until the Protestant reformation in the fourteenth century); practiced all the methods described earlier for stimulating commitment among its members (succeeding amazingly well); and solved the other problems of group maintenance.

Having managed to organize effectively, Christians very soon turned to outside recruitment, with the intent of converting the entire world. They were astonishingly victorious in that endeavor and did, in the end, convert most of the "civilized" world. Despite much persecution and many difficulties, Christian numbers continued to increase and churches spread far and wide. With clever solutions to problem of communication and weakening cohesion, their growth eventually created a crisis of societal organization and stimulated mutual movement toward compromise by the forces of then-existing society and the practitioners of Christianity. Many conventional people converted to Christianity or at least came to accept it as legitimate. Meanwhile Christians became less extreme separatists, far more willing to pursue conventional life styles instead of the stealthy patterns of early Christians, who hid in caves, met in secret, and identified each other by the sign of the fish. Moreover, Christians became adept at debate, finally persuading others to view Christianity as completely nondeviant. The triumph was complete when the church became the dominant institution in society, reaching into all domains with its admonitions and mandates. Of course, for reasons noted before, this ascendance was bought at the price of cohesion and purity of message. This loss of purity and cohesion was reflected in the later corruption that produced the Protestant reformation, a new form of behavior that became highly deviant (largely through the efforts of the established church). And through the same steps as the established church had earlier followed, Protestantism finally achieved legitimation as well.

A Stalled Ascent: Marijuana Usage

Marijuana has been used by many people in Caribbean society for centuries, but it was only introduced into the United States in the early part of the twentieth century (Goode, 1970, 1993). At first it was used by small groups of marginal people—prostitutes, musicians, criminals, or those, such as the Rastafarians, who employed it in religious rituals. Users' early organizations were weak because there was little initial opposition or concern about marijuana usage, and it remained an unknown practice to most Americans, though apparently growing slowly in popularity. During the 1930s, however, the public became inflamed about marijuana, perhaps because of propaganda efforts by the relatively young Bureau of Narcotics under the leadership of Harry Anslinger (Brecher, 1972). Anslinger was a moral entrepreneur who helped get marijuana classified as a narcotic by publishing magazine articles and making public speeches about the evils of the drug (Dickson, 1968). In one such article, he told a story about an entire family in Florida who were axe-murdered by their marijuana-using son. The not-so-subtle point was that although marijuana use may appear innocent on the surface, it can lead to mayhem and violence. As a result, marijuana usage became highly deviant; citizens feared and loathed it as debilitating and stimulative for crime and unrestrained sex. Laws were changed to incorporate marijuana into the dangerous drug category, and severe penalties were enacted for its possession, use, and distribution.

These efforts were apparently quite effective because for a time after that users became less visible and somewhat quiescent. Since they were not well organized in the first place, they were unable to protect themselves from the onslaught of conventional control. Moreover, they never attempted any systematic recruitment. Later, in the 1960s, marijuana usage and recruitment became more prominent, activating increased efforts at social control. The popularity of marijuana, however, was promoted not by deviant groups inter-

---

Deviance in Everyday Life

There is a national group whose purpose it is to decriminalize the use of marijuana. It is called the National Organization to Reform Marijuana Laws (NORML). NORML, which was founded in 1970, is not composed of ex-hippies and drug addicts, it is a respectable organization whose board of directors in 1998 included a Harvard Medical School professor and a Nobel Prize-winning chemist. NORML does not advocate the use of marijuana or other drugs; it simply believes that the decision to use marijuana is a personal one that should not be subject to criminal prosecution. In fact, it believes that much harm has been done to people who have been criminally prosecuted for marijuana use, and that law enforcement and judicial resources, which are limited, should be devoted to more serious crimes. In addition to being a clearing house for marijuana use information and a group lobbying for the decriminalization of marijuana use, NORML also advocates the medical use of marijuana.

ested specifically and exclusively in recreational drug use. Rather, by a historical accident, its usage came to represent a symbolic protest by young people against the forces of conventionality who were resisting racial justice and promoting an unpopular war in Vietnam. Recruiters for marijuana usage, then, represented organizations with political agendas who were engaged already in a social movement. To them, marijuana use was an ancillary concern, important for its symbolic import as protest and assertion of freedom, but not the primary reason for being. Even then, however, recruitment was not evangelical. It was the natural product of social interaction around common political and life style issues.

Nevertheless, very large numbers of people, at first youth and then later older adults, became at least occasional marijuana consumers. It looked for a time as if this form of recreational drug use might become fully legitimate. It was openly discussed in everyday interaction and in the public media, and the arguments its proponents set forth were powerful, especially in comparing marijuana with tobacco and alcohol. It was easy for proponents to show that the benefits of marijuana were at least as justifiable as for the other recreational drugs and that the harm to individuals and society was much less. Yet in the 1980s the trend stalled and began to reverse and has not recovered. Currently many people use marijuana, but it is not normatively acceptable. It still attracts police attention, and those caught are often imprisoned for long periods of time. Public figures suffer great damage if it is learned that they even used marijuana in the distant past, much less recently. And recent poll data indicate that marijuana is still regarded by the majority of the public as bad, dangerous, and unacceptable. Many people, and legal functionaries especially, are not even willing to permit marijuana use for medicinal purposes under a physician's direction and control (Morganthau, 1997a, 1997b), even though there is a strong possibility that it has important therapeutic uses (Cowley, 1997).

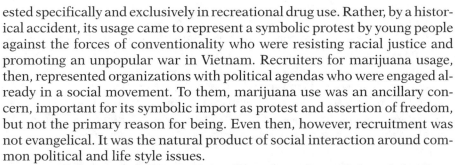

Deviance in Everyday Life

The case of Douglas H. Ginsburg is a perfect example of how public officials, even those with impeccable records of good behavior, can run into great difficulty if it is discovered that they were "deviants" and used drugs. Ginsburg was a Harvard Law School professor and former Assistant Attorney General for the U.S. Department of Justice who was nominated by President George Bush to fill a vacancy on the United States Supreme Court. A report that Ginsburg had used marijuana in the past created great turmoil and led President Bush to withdraw Ginsburg's nomination.

Why the marijuana movement deflated after reaching the next-to-the-last point on the upward slope toward legitimacy, and despite such apparent strength in debate, is not clear. Some think the conservative trend that overtook the country during the 1980s, partly in reaction to the liberalism of the 1960s and 1970s, was responsible. That political shift thrived on symbolic opposition to dependency, personal irresponsibility, and profligate life styles that many associated with the baby boomers. And the key icon used to evoke images of those undesirable characteristics was drug use, of which marijuana became the leading example. Thus, the debate shifted from marijuana per se to become a debate about total political philosophies. And the marijuana movement was the loser.

❖ ❖ ❖ ❖   ## An Aborted Trend: Communal Living

Our third example concerns a movement that had an auspicious start but did not progress very far up the ladder toward social change before stopping and then almost completely dying. During the 1960s a number of young people, especially at colleges and universities, began experiments in communal living. Communal living was not new to American life, having sprung up in various locales and in various times in history (see Kephart, 1976), but the scale on which it was practiced during the youth movement of the 1960s was unusual.

At first, communal living was undertaken in secret, usually by those most committed to the "Hippie" life style, which included much drug use, both recreational and exploratory, as well as open, nonexclusive sex (Reich, 1970). In addition, Hippies denigrated the work ethic and the acquisitive values of the larger society. Communal living was a way to share scarce resources and to live out the ideals of "self-actualization" while at the same time renouncing materialism and the "plastic" life patterns of conventional Americans. The Hippies contended that conventional people maintained wastefully large domiciles simply for housing symbols of their wealth and as arenas for selfishly controlling spouses and property. But conventional Americans generally regarded communal living as deviant; it was thought to be a dangerous and immoral threat to a basic institution (family) and an insult to general values. To most adults it suggested personal irresponsibility and dependency, and it contradicted widely held cultural themes emphasizing the importance of nuclear families and protective child rearing, exclusive sexuality, and achievement motivation marked by material symbols of success.

As Hippies became more organized, they recruited significant segments of American youth to their peculiar form of deviance, though their success did not extend to many adults, and it did not even encompass most youths. Moreover, the success of the communal living form of deviance did not last long. By the mid-1970s there were very few communes left in the United States.

Again, it is not certain why this form of deviance failed to go very far toward legitimacy. Nevertheless, the communal living movement did violate the provisions for success discussed in this chapter. First, communes were never well organized. The very emphasis on personal freedom on which communal living was based led to many problems. It is hard to acquire resources for survival and get the work of a household done when each individual is "doing his or her own thing" (which rarely involved much lucrative work) and spending a large part of the time under the influence of drugs. Hence, communal living in the 1960s, unlike some earlier successful efforts (e.g., Perfectionists and Mennonites), contained a philosophical flaw—the individual was exalted above the group. Personal freedom for one meant inconvenience and deprivation for others. Not only did conflicts about daily living emerge, but jealousy intervened, making open sexuality on a regular basis unworkable. Organization and personal freedom always hold each other at bay.

As a result, Hippies were ill organized for survival, and they were even less effectively organized for recruitment. Before long, most members of communes grew older and began to feel the pressures for adult responsibilities. Without strong organization to generate commitment and maintain the group, most ended up abandoning communes as youthful misadventures that simply did not fit with the social, cultural, and economic system of the

United States. Thus, this style of deviance hardly got off the ground as a producer of social change, and today there is little evidence in American culture of any long-range impact.

Summary and Conclusion

Deviant behavior is one source of social change. Sometimes new behavior emerges, stimulates a response from society making the behavior deviant, but fights for survival. If the deviance succeeds in overcoming repressive efforts by conventional society, it may spread to larger and larger numbers of the population. Eventually, such popularity will create a crisis for society in which it must stop or reverse the movement's growth, accommodate to the deviance, or split into factions. If society cannot stifle the deviant movement, it will usually accommodate it by altering its normative patterns to render the behavior no longer deviant; the society has thereby changed in reaction to the deviance.

The process of reactive change, however, is complicated and difficult, requiring adherents to solve numerous organizational problems. Not only are these solutions rarely achieved, but sometimes there are inherent characteristics of particular forms of deviance that undermine potential success. Nevertheless, occasionally some deviancies go through a full sequence of steps without committing fatal errors; sometimes they are even aided by strategic mistakes committed by agents of conventional society. These movements finally become legitimate and bring about social change. And sometimes those changes prove useful to society in the long run, thereby illustrating that deviance is not necessarily pejorative for social life.

Notes

1. The authors are grateful to Randy Grosch, a former student, for suggesting this and other examples.
2. Material in the next few sections is stimulated by the works of H. Taylor Buckner (1971) and Rosabeth Kanter (1973). ✦

Chapter 8

Extent of Deviance/Crime and Conformity

In order to understand deviance it is necessary to assess its prevalence, distribution, and causes. But to do those things, investigators need direct information about crime and deviance as well as indirect information in the form of data concerning conformity. As you will see, the sources of information about deviance are limited and are not fully adequate for providing detailed answers to the questions being posed. Yet, even if we could accurately document all criminal and deviant acts, it would not be very meaningful without a comparison to conformity. Therefore, it is useful to try to estimate the extent of conformity within a social unit and then extrapolate to deviance.

Knowledge that a thousand acts of a particular kind of deviance were committed in a given social unit is "free-floating" information. It takes on the most meaning when related to other information, such as the number of people in that social unit, the time period the data cover, or the total number of behavioral acts that occurred in that social unit in the specified time period. Usually, a thousand deviant acts have greater significance if those acts represent 10 percent of all behavior in a social unit than if they represent one-trillionth of all behavior. We say "usually" because sometimes social groups get quite excited about rare events, especially if those events provoke great fear or if they are thought to be especially outrageous. Such occasions are called "moral panics" (Goode and Ben-Yehuda, 1994). In ordinary social interaction, however, the frequency and distribution of deviance, not the moral heinousness of some particular deviant act, is relevant. Not only that, but some theories of deviance actually set themselves the goal of explaining conformity, in effect asking why everybody does not deviate rather than why some do. Therefore, the extent of conformity and the extent of deviance are intricately linked questions; one cannot reasonably consider one without considering the other.

How Much Conformity Is There?

At first it might appear easy to define conformity, since we have already defined deviance. Some might think that conformity is simply the opposite of deviance. If deviant behavior is behavior that is unacceptable to the majority of a group or that typically evokes a collective response of a negative type, including reaction by authorities, then presumably conformity would be behavior that is acceptable or that does not evoke a collective negative response. As you will soon see, it is not quite that simple. For one thing, such an approach does not recognize the difference between behavior that is *expected* by the members of a social group and behavior that is simply *permitted*. Yet in any social group some things "must" be done (or risk sanction) while other things "may" be done. You must obey traffic signals and you may go camping. Hence a person can commit normatively positive as well as normatively neutral behavior.

It is important to make clear that conformity is not simply "typical" patterns of behavior. Conformity and deviance hinge on social norms—collective, evaluational expectations about behavior. Seeking shelter from the cold is usually not conformity, even if almost everybody does it, nor is drinking water; members of a social group do not usually have a moral, or evaluational, sense about such things. Hence some behavior is neither deviant nor conforming; it is simply irrelevant to the normative scheme. But note that in many social groups, people do have a moral or evaluative interest in the kind of shelter people use, or in the kind of water they drink. In modern societies it would probably be required that people not live in houses with transparent walls; hence, residing in houses with opaque walls would be conformity. And it would probably be required that people not drink sewer water, making the drinking of other kinds of water conformity.

In considering the extent of conformity, it is also important to differentiate conformity to social norms from submission to power. Social norms are behavioral expectations shared by a group of people. An individual may fulfill those expectations, and thereby conform, without anybody directly or verbally requiring it. Many social groups are composed of only two individuals. Those two may share many norms, and conformity results when one or the other fulfills the obligations implied by the norms, regardless of how the conformer came to know of the expectations. In addition, however, numerous social situations involve power relationships, often between only two individuals. In such situations, one person may issue commands and expect the other to do what he or she is told. Following those orders is not necessarily conformity; we will call it obedience. For example, two people may be on a date when one demands something from the other. Submitting to that demand is an act of obedience, but it is not an act of conformity because it is performed in response to an immediate threat based on power rather than on a shared normative expectation.

Obedience sometimes does constitute conformity, however. It is conformity when the obedience is in response to commands issued by an authority figure or in response to shared expectations that certain actions by the authority figure should call forth particular behaviors by those subject to authority. An authority is someone who occupies a social position that is recognized by most members of the social group as implying the right to issue commands and have them obeyed. In American society police officers, parents of small children, judges, school teachers, military commanders, business executives, and many others have authority, or the recognized right to issue orders and expect to have them obeyed, at least to certain individuals within a designated zone of authority. If a police officer directs you to pull over at an intersection, your obedience is also conformity because the officer has legitimate authority. However, if a police officer commands you to submit to his or her sexual demands, your obedience would not qualify as conformity.

Finally, as noted in an earlier chapter, there are times and places where there are no norms at all, or where the norms are undergoing transition and people have no shared conceptions of what is right or wrong. Under those circumstances, sometimes called social disorganization or anomie, people simply do what they do without normative guidance, so it is not clear what is conformity or deviance.

Conformity, then, is not the same as obedience, although some obedience is conformity. Conformity is also not simply the opposite of deviance, for, as discussed in a preceding paragraph, a behavior can be conforming or neutral or normatively irrelevant. In our study, then, we will recognize positive conformity, which is behavior consistent with social norms (shared expectations), and conforming obedience to legitimate authority. We will not count as conformity behavior that is normatively neutral (simply permitted but not expected), normatively irrelevant (there are no norms), or behavior that represents obedience to illegitimate power.

Common Experience

The first, and most important, observation to make about conformity requires no hard data. Ordinary, everyday life teaches each of us that most people conform most of the time and that conformity is typical. In fact, a moment of reflection will convince you that conformity inevitably must far exceed deviance. Social life depends on orderly relationships, or the ability of social participants to predict the behaviors of others. Social norms help to ensure that predictability because they embody expectations, which in many instances become internalized imperatives linked to individual personalities and self-concepts, and they imply some probability of social sanctions, either positive or negative. As a result, all of us are enmeshed in multiple networks of norms that govern all domains of life. In effect, each person faces thousands of norms each day. They include expectations about when to awaken, what to eat, how to dress, how to speak, how to move about, control of emotions, and so on.

Most such norms are routinely obeyed, so routinely that we do not even think about them. Even the most heinously deviant person in the United States dresses pretty much like everybody else (though fashions vary, in modern society hardly anybody wears leaves or metal armor), eats similar foods (individual tastes vary, but hardly anybody eats feces or red ants), speaks in a systematic language that makes sense to others (usually English), walks (rather than crawls) or rides in motorized or wheeled vehicles (rather than on the backs of zebras), and refrains from killing people almost all of the time (even mass murderers end up killing only a few dozen people over a lifetime involving thousands of days and millions of interactions). You can imagine how difficult social life would be if this were not so. Would you have enough confidence even to go out of your house in the morning if you had no way of knowing whether people you will meet that day would be driving on the right side of the street, would be likely to kill you, would be speaking a different language, or were otherwise totally unpredictable in what they might do?

Contemplating the nature of social life will probably easily convince you that conformity is the rule. In fact, it is so much the rule that it is taken for granted. For most norms, only when there is a breach do people notice the rule at all. Since so many people so often drive on the right side of the road in the United States, we simply assume everybody will, and we gamble our lives on it. Occasionally, we see somebody driving on the wrong side of the road, and it dramatically attracts our attention. On those rare occasions we often hear people say something like, "Look at that fool; people are so unpredictable, you just don't know what they might do." However, it is the exception that proves the rule. If people were really unpredictable, it would be too risky to drive at all. From common experience, then, the answer to the question, "How much conformity is there?" is, "Incredible amounts; almost everybody conforms to most of the norms most of the time."

Evidence

Despite the obvious conclusion to be drawn from observations of everyday life, social scientists do not rely on such experiential evidence. They have compiled much data concerning conformity (Cialdini and Trost, 1998); some of the most compelling are from experiments.

Group Influence

❖ ❖ ❖ ❖

Although experimentation about conformity continues (see Cialdini and Trost, 1998, for a review of the research), the best-known laboratory work establishing the prevalence of conformity was conducted over fifty years ago (Sherif, 1936). Muzifer Sherif, a social psychologist, devised a clever setup, which he employed in a series of experiments to assess the extent to which people would follow group norms. He placed experimental subjects in a completely darkened room with his accomplices and on repeated trials asked each subject to judge how far a pinpoint of light moved. Actually, the light did not move at all, but without reference points it is difficult to ascertain whether or how far it moves. When in the room alone, subjects would judge the movement of the light one way, but in company with experimental confederates who, according to instructions from the experimenter, judged the light movement to be greater or less than the subjects' average when alone, the subjects would move their own judgment toward the mean established by the group.

A second famous set of experiments was devised to overcome a supposed structural defect in Sherif's apparatus. According to the psychologist Solomon Asch, the subjects in the Sherif experiments followed group standards because they had no objective way to determine the actual movement of the light (Asch, 1948). Asch assumed that with objective standards individuals would reject group influence and rely on their own abilities. To test this, Asch presented subjects with a line of set length to be compared with three lines of varying lengths (Asch, 1956). Again the test groups contained accomplices, who were instructed to select, in various sequences and degrees, the wrong comparison line. Subjects who were alone more accurately identified the correct comparison line than those in the groups, thus contradicting Asch's criticism and demonstrating the tendency of people to conform to group expectations.

Obedience

There have also been many experiments exploring conformity to the commands of legitimate authorities. Two classic experiments set the tone for others that followed (see Cialdini and Trost, 1998). In one setup, the experimenter placed subjects in a control booth with a line of 30 switches, each representing a 15-volt increment in electric shock up to 450 volts (Milgram, 1974). Switches were labelled from SLIGHT SHOCK TO DANGER— SEVERE SHOCK, with the last two switches marked XXX. The experiment purported to be a learning experiment. The subjects were to use electric shock to help another subject learn number sequences by increasing the voltage each time the "learner" made a mistake. The "learner," of course, was a confederate of the experimenter and experienced no shock, although the subject heard prerecorded expressions of pain. When subjects hesitated at increasing the voltage, they were told to "continue the experiment." As it turned out, a good proportion of the subjects (about 65 percent) administered what they thought were lethal doses in response to the expectations and commands of the experimenter, an authority figure.

Another famous experiment, designed to test the idea that people will not do things under hypnosis that they would not ordinarily do, had to be canceled because the experimenter could not find things that the subjects would not do under his command (Orne, 1962). Of course, the experimenter could not command people to do things like murder somebody, eat feces, or submit to sexual advances from ugly suitors, but he did try a large number of things that one would think experimental subjects would refuse to do. He had them perform nonsense tasks, do tedious work, and repeat procedures endlessly. In every case, almost all subjects did what they were asked. Eventually, the experimenter gave up and concluded that the idea he started with could not be tested ethically in the lab because subjects will do anything they think an authority figure wants them to do.

Summary

Common experience as well as experimental evidence shows that most people are influenced by group expectations most of the time and that they manifest this influence in conformity to social norms and obedience to legitimate authority. The degree of conformity does vary with a large number of conditions, such as characteristics of the person, the situation, and the norm in question. Yet, what is clear from a variety of different kinds of data (Cialdini and Trost, 1998), many of which are described below, is the pervasiveness of conformity.

How Much Deviance Is There? Sources of Information

Although there is much evidence suggesting that conformity is widespread, investigators cannot document the exact amount of conformity that occurs. There is simply too much behavior in too many domains for that kind of precision. And it is even harder to establish the facts about crime and deviance. At least three factors impede the search for knowledge about the occurrence, distribution, and causes of deviant or criminal behavior. First, as noted previously, there are bewildering numbers and types of norms that can be violated; counting all violations would be practically impossible. Second, norms reflect diverse group contexts; most deviance from one set of norms is simultaneously conformity to another set. This blurring of boundaries between conformity and deviance often makes categorization and enumeration meaningless as well as difficult. Third, deviant acts are hard to record and count because perpetrators often try to conceal their behavior from others, including those who want to count it. Since deviance is, by definition, conduct regarded by the majority of a group as socially unacceptable or likely to evoke sanctions from authorities, practitioners frequently fear disapproval or punishment and so are reluctant to be observed in the practice of the deviant behavior or to risk incrimination by discussing it with conformists or outsiders. Consequently, deviance is a complex, relative, and somewhat elusive phenomenon. Those who do it sometimes actually try to prevent others, including social scientists, from learning about it. Studying deviance is, therefore, both intellectually demanding and methodologically challenging.

In trying to understand deviant behavior in the face of these obstacles, social scientists have learned to rely upon multiple sources of information, triangulating them so that the weaknesses of some types of data can be compensated for by the strengths of other types (Bailey, 1987:263). In the study of deviance, seven distinct sources of information are used. They include: (1) police records and official statistics, (2) records of public regulatory agencies,

(3) private documents and records, (4) self-report surveys, (5) victimization surveys, (6) ethnographies and case studies, and (7) experiments. In considering these various kinds of information, it is important to keep in mind that each reveals something about deviance not shown by the other six. Moreover, each kind of data contains errors, many of which are inestimable, and each shows more about some kinds of deviance or crime than others. For these reasons, no single source of information can be relied upon to teach us about deviant or criminal behavior. Each of the seven types of data can be regarded as providing some evidence, defective in and of itself, but useful in generating estimates of the numbers we seek. The greater the number of sources of information, the more consistent the evidence across sources, and the stronger the evidence from each source, the more confidence we can place in our estimations, but we can never be absolutely sure of our conclusions.

Let us consider the strengths and weaknesses of each source of information.

Police Records and Official Statistics

The most systematic data about deviant behavior are kept by government law enforcement agencies. In the United States, the main data of this type are compiled by the Federal Bureau of Investigation from reports by local police agencies; these data are published annually in a volume entitled *Uniform Crime Reports*. These volumes contain figures on "crimes known to the police" as well as arrest figures. "Crimes known to the police" are (1) incidences reported to the police by citizens that, upon investigation, are judged by the police to fit their criteria of crime, or (2) incidences discovered by the police themselves that fit the definition of crime. "Crimes known to the police" obviously does not include criminal acts that go unreported or are undiscovered by the police. *Uniform Crime Reports* displays crimes known, and arrests made, for various geographic units (states, counties, and municipalities) and by size of place (population). In addition, the arrest figures are differentiated by age, sex, and race. Data collected by the FBI from local enforcement agencies are also sometimes made available in raw form to private scholars, who then analyze or break them down in ways different from the categories used in the published volumes.

Other useful official data available in the United States include government reports such as those showing the distribution and cause of death or disease (*Vital Statistics*); number of admissions to public hospitals for various conditions (such as drug overdoses); number of births that are illegitimate; traffic fatalities where victims were using alcohol; and numerous other matters. These various bodies of information can yield indirect estimates of some kinds of deviant behavior. For example, for different geographical areas, *Vital Statistics* reports the number of deaths each year attributable to various causes. Cause of death is decided by local medical examiners or coroners. From these we can estimate the number of murders and suicides committed, and such estimates will be independent of the statistics kept by police on crimes known and arrests made for homicide, thereby providing a corroborating tool. Similarly, figures compiled by the National Traffic Safety Council indicating the number of alcohol-related traffic fatalities can be used to estimate the extent and distribution of drunken driving, independently of police arrest statistics (Ross, 1982). And data from hospital emergency room admissions concerning drug overdoses permit estimates of drug abuse.

Of the official governmental data available for studying deviance, police statistics are probably the most useful. They reveal information about deviant acts of special significance—those that are subject to official management and that are routinely dealt with by government enforcement agencies. Moreover, police data include, although not exhaustively or inclusively, figures on criminal behavior that produces injury to others and that is regarded as especially bad by most people. And, most significantly, these data are collected at regular time intervals in the same way for reasonably comparable categories, thereby permitting analysis of temporal trends. Despite these great advantages, however, police data must be used cautiously and with full awareness of their limitations. Their defects are: (1) the deviant acts potentially covered in police statistics—criminal acts—represent only a tiny proportion of all deviant behaviors; (2) police data do not even contain information about all kinds of illegal behavior; (3) the accuracy of police data, even for the categories and legal offenses they are designed to include, is questionable (that is, the deviant acts reported to and recorded by the police constitute only the "tip of the iceberg"); and (4) using them, the relationship between crime and individual characteristics can be studied for only a small number of possibilities.

Restricted Coverage

The most severe limitation of police statistics for studying deviance is their restricted representation. Many acts of deviance are not criminal. If a deviant act is not criminal, it probably will not be reported to the police when someone notices it (betrayal of a friend, adultery, or overeating, for instance), and even if it is reported, the police will be unlikely to respond. Since such behaviors are not the business of police, the incidence of them is neither reported nor recorded in police data. For example, betraying a friend is deviant, but it is not a crime. When betrayal occurs, nobody calls the police, and even if they do, the police will not act. Ignoring the cries for help of a drowning child is deviant but not generally illegal. And sexual gratification with a corpse is quite deviant although not a crime unless graves are uncovered, corpses stolen, or other laws governing the sanctity of the dead are violated. In addition, there are many "everyday" deviant acts that are not prohibited in criminal law but that are unacceptable in the public's mind. These include refusal of physicians to treat seriously ill patients who can't pay, lying to one's spouse or sweetheart, passing gas in public, pushing ahead of someone on an elevator, reporting paranoid visions, pursuing unusual recreations like fire walking, fanatically practicing religious rituals, compulsively gambling, sexual abstinence in marriage, and thousands of other violations of "folk" norms.

In addition, there is an enormous amount of organizational or corporate misbehavior that is not technically illegal but that is regarded as wrong, even heinous, by the majority of the people (Simon and Eitzen, 1993). One outstanding example is the practice of exposing workers to dangerous conditions without informing them of the risk. For years asbestos workers breathed air filled with tiny asbestos particles even though there was a high risk of disability or fatality from a disease similar to emphysema (asbestosis). Officials of the asbestos companies and company physicians knew of the danger long before it became public knowledge, but they did not take steps to improve conditions or to warn their employees of the risk. Indeed, they often deliberately concealed the facts from workers, particularly those already afflicted, and later from courts of law when workers sued in civil court for damage compensation. Yet exposing employees to known hazards without warning is not a violation of criminal law, so its incidence, even if discovered, does not appear in police statistics.

Deviance in Everyday Life

One vivid example of an offensive action that was not deemed criminal was the behavior of asbestos makers. Asbestos can be a very valuable product; it has been used in insulation, roofing, cement boards and other construction products. It is also, however, a very deadly product to manufacture. When breathed, asbestos fibers can enter the lungs or, if swallowed, the digestive tract. Once in the body, asbestos fibers are related to such health problems as lung cancer, asbestosis (a noncancerous but serious respiratory disease), and mesothelioma (a rare form of cancer of the lining of the lung). Evidence of these diseases has appeared in thousands of workers in asbestos plants, shipyards, constructions sites, and practically everyplace where asbestos has been made and used. In addition, cases of mesothelioma have occurred in children of asbestos workers who were exposed to the fibers from the clothing of parents. The evidence seems to indicate that manufacturers of asbestos were aware that asbestos exposure was related to various diseases but did little about it. Civil suits filed against asbestos makers go back to 1929.

Similarly, manufacturing and selling dangerous products is not illegal unless a specific product has been tested by the Product Safety Division of the Federal Trade Commission, ruled to be unsafe, and banned (although selling a product that injures somebody may subject the manufacturer to legal liability for damages). Thus, when the Ford Motor Company sold Pintos with poorly designed fuel tanks so that rear-end collisions could easily result in fire, they were not behaving criminally. This designation of noncriminality occurs despite the fact that the management of Ford knew it was a serious hazard, even to the point of calculating the potential costs of liability suits lost to people injured or killed in fiery crashes relative to the $11 per car costs of correcting the design problems (Simon and Eitzen, 1993:222–224). Hence the company executives were not in violation of criminal law, and their offense, along with thousands of others like it that occur annually, could not be included in police statistics.

Several of these examples also illustrate that police statistics exclude much deviant behavior that is actually subject to legal regulation but which is not covered because the acts do not warrant criminal sanctions. For instance, failure to fulfill a contract is deviant but not criminal, although redress for such failure can be sought through civil law. A court may coerce the deficient parties to honor their obligations by threat or actual imposition of sanction, the implementation of which involves police force. But the contract default is not itself a crime; its victim would not call the police; and the case would not produce an incident of "crime known to the police" even if court-ordered police action were ultimately involved. Refusal to obey a court order to pay the plaintiff would be a crime, and it could potentially be so recorded in police statistics. But court-ordered actions are usually undertaken by special enforcement officers who do not report the results of their activity to the FBI. And even when handled by a sheriff or a segment of local police, the incident is not reported in *Uniform Crime Reports* because there is no category within which it could be encompassed.

Another example of deviance that is subject to regulation through civil law but that is not criminal or subject to recording in police statistics is negligence in maintaining one's property. Suppose a pair of homeowners leave a water well uncovered in their yard and a neighbor falls in, breaking a leg. Such carelessness would be considered deviant (at least by middle-class standards), and the person with the broken leg may sue for medical expenses and lost income during convalescence. Moreover, the court may regard the negligence as so gross that the property owners are required to pay additional "punitive" damages. Even though enforcement of the award may involve court-directed officers, no entry representing the incident will be made in published police statistics.

These examples only scratch the surface of the numerous acts of deviance that cannot be studied using official police data because the acts in question are outside the domain of police responsibility. Clearly it is an error to imagine that crime, especially that dealt with by uniformed police and recorded in *Uniform Crime Reports*, represents the bulk of deviant behavior in the United States or that one can get a reasonable estimate of deviance from police statistics.

Other Illegality

Police statistics are further limited because they do not include information about all crimes. Many criminal laws are enforced, if at all, by special regulatory agencies that do not keep systematic records of the violations they discover; nor do they report them to the FBI. The *Uniform Crime Reports* are about "ordinary" or "street" crimes; they exclude any consideration of most "white-collar," "organizational," "governmental," or "elite" crime. To learn about these criminal acts, one must rely upon other sources of information.

For example, many state laws are designed to regulate the preparation and sale of foodstuffs, drugs, and cosmetics; other laws regulate the conditions under which transportation, communication, weights and measures, advertising, business activities, and a host of other activities can be conducted. In addition, there are Federal laws covering some of these same domains and others. These regulations are administered by, and enforcement placed in the hands of, various state and Federal agencies. On the Federal level these include the Food and Drug Administration, the Agriculture Department, The Federal Aviation Administration, the Civil Aeronautics Board, and many others. Violations of regulatory laws render the perpetrators subject to fine and/or jail under either state or Federal jurisdiction; that is, they are crimes, often involving billions of dollars in losses and life-threatening conditions. But the procedures by which enforcement is undertaken almost never involves arrests by uniformed officers or the FBI. Instead, regulatory agencies usually notify violators of suspected illegality and request information or justification. The result is usually some form of "negotiation" between enforcer and violator producing an agreement that the practice will cease. Occasionally such negotiations fail and the violator is brought into court by subpoena. Even in those cases, however, no arrest is made and no crime is recorded as having become "known to the police."

This process is illustrated by the case of the Armour meat company, which continued to short-weight packages of bacon and frankfurters by as much as two and one-half ounces. The county Sealer of Weights and Measures in Sacramento, California, signed a complaint to get penalties imposed for this misdemeanor after he had warned the company to stop the practice and they had continued to do it anyway (*Consumer Reports*, 1963a). An example of a case where consent was not reached concerns the Quaker Oat Company, which pleaded "no contest" on six counts of short-weighting its packages of puffed rice and wheat. The company was fined $1,000 on each count (a total of $6,000) although their deviant practices saved the company $70,000 in six months (*Consumer Reports*, 1963b). Even though each short weight was an individual incidence of crime and the practice had been going on for a long time, *Uniform Crime Reports* did not reflect these crimes, and if we depended upon the police data, we would not know of them. Similarly, when Federal meat inspectors discover that packing houses illegally exceed the amount of water that can be injected into hams or sausages (see *Consumer Reports*, 1961), the companies are simply persuaded to stop, and if that fails they receive a small fine, like the twenty-five dollar fine that was assessed against the Kroger Company (*Consumer Reports*, 1968).

Thus, there are many crimes that are simply not subject to ordinary police management, and because they are not, police statistics will inevitably distort the picture of crime, not to mention the larger picture of deviance. Consider the multitude of laws and regulations concerning trucking. Each state in the United States has its own laws about licensing, load limits, taxes, and safety, which are enforced sometimes by state troopers, at other times by special officers in charge of weights and taxes, or on still other occasions by agents of the agriculture or health departments. In addition, the Interstate Commerce Commission, an agency of the Federal government, enforces Federal rules about hours and conditions of driving, licensing, and other matters concerning transport of goods across state lines. Violations of any of these laws can result in a penalty—usually fines or withholding of authorization to haul, but also the possibility of jail. Moreover, there are an astounding number of violations of these regulations as well as a few arrests. But none of them shows up in official statistics or in the *Uniform Crime Reports*.

As a young man, the senior author of this book worked the night shift at a truck stop adjoining a weigh station near the border of a southern state. He cannot recall a single night in which he did not witness, or know about, law violations. In fact, much of the culture of trucking was at that time oriented around illegal activities. Almost all truckers drove more hours in a twenty-four hour period than permitted by ICC regulations, and many of them drove for days without sleep, keeping awake with drugs (Benzedrine, or "Bennies") and falsifying their log books. Indeed, one reason for buying fuel at the truck stop in question was to find out if the ICC inspectors were at the weigh station next door; if so, the driver would take time to fabricate his log book before going on to the scale.

In addition, many of the trucks were overloaded, partly because load limits were not the same in all the states that had to be crossed, which forced the truckers either to load up only to the limit of the lowest state or to attempt to "beat" the officers at the weigh stations in the low-limit state or states. Since the overall profit from the larger load usually exceeded the penalty for overweight in the light-load state, there was a clear incentive to overload; and the greater the chances of eluding detection, the more advantageous it became. There were two ways to avoid penalty: a driver might bribe the officer on duty with money, a gift, or some of the cargo (such as beer in a dry state), or he might try to fool him into believing the load was within legal limits. One way of deceiving the duty officer was to take advantage of the fact that a truck has to be weighed half at a time. The load would appear lighter if it were shifted toward the rear when the front of the trailer was weighed but shifted forward when the rear wheels were on the scales. To accomplish this, the driver would couple the trailer at its frontmost point and then drive onto the scales. After the first measurement was taken, the officer would signal for the driver to pull up so his back wheels were on the scale for the second measurement. But before moving forward, the driver would set the brakes on his trailer and back the tractor up a little bit, slipping the coupling device backward under the trailer before locking it. The weight thus having been shifted forward, the driver would release his trailer brakes and drive the truck forward until the back wheels of the trailer rested on the scales. Successfully achieved, such a maneuver could make the load register several thousand pounds lighter than it really was.

Whether either of these tactics could be employed depended, of course, upon the particular officer on duty. Some officers could be bribed while others couldn't, and some were more aware of, and able to detect, the sliding tandem trick than others. Moreover, some officers were more tolerant of a failed attempt at trickery or persuasion than others were. Information about the duty roster of the weigh station was expected to be provided by the truck stop as a service to customers. Not only were the truckers systematically breaking the law, but the truck stop personnel were implicated in conspiracies to promote law violation.

In addition, the owner of the truck stop practiced his own scams, sometimes blatantly illegal, which required the tacit cooperation of truck drivers. For instance, all the fuel at the truck stop was overpriced by five cents per gallon, enabling the station to make a larger-than-normal profit from automobile drivers just entering the state who did not know they would encounter cheaper gas on down the road. However, a large sign in front of the station advertised "five cents per gallon discount to trucks." This was obviously a scheme to lure trucks by the false promise of a discount, but its significance went further. When drivers filled up, they were asked if they wanted the receipt to "show the discount" or not. Many preferred receipts for the full pump price even though they actually paid five cents per gallon less than that. They did this so they could charge their employers for a larger reimbursement than they were due, thereby cheating them; for independent truckers it provided proof for a larger tax deduction for business expenses than was actually true, thereby cheating the Federal government.

One might imagine that the symbiotic relationship of illegality binding the truckers and the owner of the station would promote insulation from mutual exploitation. But such was not the case since the owner used other means to "rip off" the truckers, and they in turn had their own methods for evening the score, such as stealing towels and furniture from the motel or vandalizing the station toilet for tissue or paper towels. For example, this truck stop offered only one grade of diesel fuel—an inferior grade—which was nowhere indicated. If drivers specifically requested #1 diesel, personnel were instructed to tell them to go to pump #1, which actually delivered #2 diesel, like all the other pumps. If truckers didn't ask for a particular grade, they would be serviced at whatever pump was nearest, including pump #1. Hence many drivers were misled into believing they were buying a better grade of fuel for the price than they actually were. Another form of deception concerned the brand of fuel being sold. All fuel, gasoline or diesel, sold in that part of the country came from one refinery operated by oil company "X." The station in question was a franchise of company "Y," which advertised the virtues of using brand "Y" fuel, although it in fact sold brand "X," as did all other oil product retailers in the area, no matter whether they were officially represented as brand "X," "Q," "R," or "Z."

Hence much of what the truckers, the owner, and the employees of the truck stop were doing was illegal or in violation of some regulatory mandates, but it was never "discovered" or became "known to the police." And even if these activities had been officially known to the police, their incidence would not have been reflected in *Uniform Crime Reports* because these offenses were subject to management only by specialized enforcement agents, not by ordinary street police.

Errors

Even for illegal acts within the domain of the uniformed police, there is much error in official data. For one thing, laws vary from place to place. What qualifies as a burglary in one jurisdiction may not be a burglary in another. As a result, police statistics are not strictly comparable; that is, the figures within a given category cannot be taken at face value as necessarily indicating the same behavior. But, more important, even if the laws were identical everywhere, the criteria used by local police to judge whether a given incident qualifies as a crime to be recorded differs from one police department to another and is subject to local administrative as well as political constraint. This disparity is possible because incidents reported to the police are not always unequivocally recognizable as crimes.

Suppose a young man returns home from college to find his parents away for the weekend. He breaks a window, enters the house, takes some food and the extra TV and goes on a trip with his buddies. His parents return, find the broken window, note the missing items, and call the police. The police must determine if a crime has been committed. Although it may appear to be a clearcut instance of crime from the evidence, the fact that nothing but the food and TV are missing raises suspicion. Whether this incident is recorded as a crime depends upon departmental and individual idiosyncrasies. It might, in fact, be recorded as a crime even though a crime did not occur (the young man had no criminal intent, provided that he had implicit permission from his parents to break in when he forgot his key).

Consider other cases. A man is found dead in the bathtub with a head injury that could have been caused by an accidental fall or by an assailant's attack. The police must decide which it is. Similarly, a woman reports she has been raped and accuses a particular man. The police question the man; he contends that there was a sexual encounter but by mutual consent. Upon further interrogation, the woman withdraws her earlier complaint. Did a crime of rape occur or not? It is possible she had second thoughts because of fear of retaliation or because she believed the police wouldn't do anything about it. But it is also possible that she concocted the story because she became angry with the man and wanted to punish him. How the police decide such cases depends upon local guidelines as well as on the proclivities of individual police officers.

Clearly, then, whether an incident is a crime or not is often uncertain, requiring police discretion. This discretion, however, opens the door for some individual officers and some departments to employ self-serving practices. What exact practices are self-serving, and how, will vary with local circumstances. Sometimes it is advantageous to a local police unit to present evidence of a rising, unmanageable crime rate; at other times it might be advantageous to show that their work has been so effective that the crime rate is dropping. When seeking additional funding for more personnel and equipment, a department needs to show a clear need; the most compelling evidence is a rising crime rate. But when faced with public criticism, with citizen demand for efficiency, or with threatened budget cuts, a department needs to show effectiveness; the most compelling evidence of this is a declining crime rate, although police often resort to the use of high arrest rates to convince funding bodies of efficiency. Depending upon these episodic needs, a department may develop strict or lenient guidelines for deciding ambiguous cases.

In addition, there are everyday considerations that come into play to influence whether given incidents are recorded as crime or not. Police know from experience that some kinds of cases will never unfold completely, so they are reluctant to record them as offenses or to go to the trouble of arresting somebody, only to have the complainant later refuse to testify or to have the charges ignored when a prosecutor refuses to go forward with the case. Disputes between family members or lovers often involve actual assaults, but most of them are reconceptualized later by the offended parties as minor quarrels of a private nature. For that reason, when the police are called to intervene in a "domestic dispute," they usually try to perform some on-the-spot social work until tempers cool, thereby forestalling later frustrations for themselves and, incidentally, also avoiding having to record an "assault" among the crimes known to the police.

The police can save themselves a lot of work if they follow restrictive guidelines in determining the criminality of reported acts. Such a restrictive approach is illustrated by a self-serving policy used by one large city police department a few years ago (*Newsweek*, 1983). It seems that for a long time the police had been handling robberies in a way that would let them avoid putting much effort into the cases. When a person reported a robbery, the police would make out a written report. Later they would call the victim's phone number once, and if the complainant did not answer the phone, the case would be thrown out of the files as a "false report," thereby relieving the police of any further investigative responsibility. Obviously, many victims didn't happen to be home at the time the call was made, so their cases were simply never recorded as real cases. The practice came to light because one construction worker who was robbed soon after getting his weekly pay complained to the Civil Rights Commission that the police did nothing to help recover his money, a failure that he attributed to his being a member of a minority group. Upon investigation, this police practice was discovered and stopped. As soon as this phony recording method was changed, the crime rate jumped substantially.

Finally, the practices used by local police in their everyday activities and the policies guiding them in ambiguous incidents are influenced by the political objectives of the local governing bodies who employ police (McCleary et al., 1982). Every city likes to look good to outsiders, and for cities that depend upon tourist trade, external image is crucial. Hence some cities systematically encourage conservative recording practices to preserve the reputation of the community by showing a low crime rate. The policy of other cities is more whimsical, depending upon the bent of the particular administration in office at a given time. It is often good politics for an incumbent mayor to be able to say the crime rate dropped while she or he was in office. One way to ensure showing a decrease is to influence the police to change their recording practices.

City policy about the kind of police force to be maintained is the most important contaminant of data. The more professional the police force, the more likely are cases to be treated uniformly and impersonally, with officers recording or not recording according to strict legal and bureaucratic rules. A less professionally oriented force may use a "service" or "watchman" style wherein officers decide to record cases through on-the-spot judgments that take into account the harm done, the will of the victim, the likelihood of apprehending and convicting the perpetrator, or the suspect's acquaintance with the victim. They record complaints, ferret out violations on their own, and sometimes bring charges against violators. But they do not issue periodic reports to the public on their activities (Wilson, 1968).

Not only do police data contain many errors stemming from recording practices of the local police departments and officers, but they contain large numbers of clerical errors as well (Sherman and Glick, 1984). Information is sometimes left out; what was originally one type of offense gets recorded as another; and sometimes additional false or misleading information is added. An illustration of this kind of inaccuracy concerns a misdemeanor committed during her college days by someone known to the authors. She and some friends went swimming on the Key West, Florida, public beach after sundown, unknowingly violating the local law concerning hours of beach usage. The woman and her friends were arrested and charged with "trespassing"; they spent a night in jail and ultimately each paid a fifty-two dollar fine. Years later she applied for a job as a researcher in a criminal justice agency and needed clearance to access confidential files. A security investigation revealed that her youthful offense had been mistakenly recorded in the computer files as "invasion of privacy," a much more serious offense than "trespassing," especially in her case since it suggested she had been guilty of illegally using confidential material. Fortunately, she had retained, as a memento, the receipt for her fine. It clearly showed a trespassing charge, so her supervisors were satisfied, despite the computer entry in the state criminal files. If this were an isolated incident, one could have more confidence in official statistics, but Sherman's research suggests such errors are common for all types of offense.

Hidden Street Crime

Criminal statistics compiled by the police reflect only a fraction of crimes that could potentially be included, because the police do not learn about a lot of the crime that takes place. Other sources of data, including records of private security police, victimization studies, investigations using self-reported admissions of criminal activity, and ethnographic data show that far more ordinary crime is committed than is known to the police—especially more than is officially recorded.

Why is this? The most important reason is that the police primarily depend upon citizens to inform them of criminal activities. Sometimes the police do assume an active approach in seeking out criminal behavior through undercover operations, surveillance, and patrol, but they find only a tiny proportion of all illegality by those methods. No matter how frequently the police patrol the streets, they will always fail to observe most assaults even though assaulters often take no steps to conceal their activity. Assaults usually take place inside buildings, shielded from police view, and even when they occur in the street, there is a low probability that the police will just happen to be in that area at the time. The police cannot be everywhere all the time. On even fewer occasions will the police observe theft, because thieves self-consciously hide their activities. Also, the chance that any given "victimless crime" such as gambling, narcotics sale, or prostitution will be observed is minuscule, because those activities are organized into self-protective networks to guard against police discovery.

Most crimes that come to the attention of police do so because citizens—usually victims—complain. Many fail to complain because they don't believe it will do any good or because it is simply more trouble to report than it is worth. If you don't expect your property to be recovered, and you aren't required to report for insurance purposes (most victims don't have insurance appropriate for covering their losses) there is little to be gained from police involvement and quite a bit to be lost. You lose your time, you are inconvenienced, and you may eventually be subpoenaed to testify in court, again suffering inconvenience and possible financial loss. If a woman is raped, she faces the embarrassment of a medical examination, the humiliation of detailed questioning, and, if the case goes to trial, the degradation of public exposure of her private life. And if people are buying illegal drugs, they are hardly going to report it even if they were cheated or robbed in dealing with drug merchants; it would jeopardize their drug supply and implicate them in wrongful activity. It is little wonder, then, that the police fail to learn of most ordinary criminal acts and that the accuracy with which police data reflect actual crimes varies with the type of offense, the recording policies of the various jurisdictions, and the clerical efficiency of the local department.

Limited Information

Even if police data were accurate and reflected all or most crime, and if crime and deviance were isomorphic, police statistics would still be an inadequate source of information about deviant behavior. They usually report characteristics of geographic/political areas but contain little information about perpetrators. With rare exceptions, police data do not permit scholars to examine the association between criminal behavior and characteristics of the *individuals* who actually do the crimes. Instead, police data ordinarily can reveal only how crime and other characteristics are related in whole population units. For example, a scholar can use *Uniform Crime Reports* to estimate crime rates in the states of the United States (or counties and municipalities) and can relate those rates to other aggregate characteristics of the populations, such as unemployment rates, income distributions, or density, for which appropriate data are available in other government publications. But a scholar cannot use these data to ascertain whether individuals who are unemployed, of low income, or who live in crowded households are more likely to commit crimes than those who are employed, of high income, or who live in spacious households. In other words, we might learn from police statistics that in political units where unemployment is high, the crime rate is also high, but we will not be able to conclude that unemployed people are actually committing those crimes. High rates of unemployment may characterize populations filled disproportionately with women and with young males on the streets seeking employment. These unemployed persons may be more vulnerable to victimization. Therefore, the high crime rates may indicate nothing about the criminality of unemployed people.

Although FBI statistics do report distributions of arrest by age, sex, and race, which (in conjunction with population figures obtainable from the Census) can yield estimates of the influence on criminal behavior of these demographic variables, such information only scratches the surface of what we need to know. Moreover, this limitation often leads to distortions. For example, some researchers have used racial differences as proxies for socioeconomic status distinctions, leading them to conclude that those of lower socioeconomic status are more likely to commit crime. They draw this conclusion from the reports that racial minorities have a higher aggregate rate of arrest than majorities. This, however, is a large leap in logic and could be quite wrong.

Overall, then, police data are an especially valuable source of information about deviance (particularly street crime), mainly because they are our only systematic data, but they are seriously deficient as the sole source of information. Indeed, taken at face value, they can paint a false picture of deviant behavior.

There are other official data concerning the work of courts and prisons. These materials are often useful for studying how agencies and agents of social control operate. It is instructive, for example, to see how the proportion of arrestees who are prosecuted varies from jurisdiction to jurisdiction or from one time period to another. Similarly, it is important to study such questions as whether prosecution was successful, whether cases were managed through trial or by plea bargaining, and whether defendants had private attorneys. But official court data are woefully inadequate for revealing much about deviant behavior.

Records of Public Regulatory Agencies

In addition to the police and court data, other information relevant to deviance comes from the records of various regulatory agencies. Some of this kind of information has already been described in showing that *Uniform Crime Reports* is limited as the sole source of data even about crime. But it is worth noting that there are literally hundreds of government regulatory agencies and law enforcement units other than the police. It is the job of these various units to keep tabs on business and other kinds of activity that affect the public or that are beneficiaries of particular kinds of governmental programs. They are charged with the responsibility of detecting and recording violations or irregularities and sometimes of taking action to stop those violations or to punish violators. A few examples of such agencies are: the Federal Department of Justice, which among other things enforces the antitrust laws, the laws against discrimination, and the laws governing interstate transportation of illegal substances; the Immigration and Naturalization Service, which administers the laws governing the movement of people across our national borders; the Treasury Department, which enforces laws concerning taxes, firearms, and illegal tobacco or alcohol; and the U.S. Postal Service, which deals with violations of postal regulations, theft of stamped material, illegal substances transmitted in the mail, and numerous other things.

All such agencies maintain files containing a great deal of information about deviance, some illegal and some not. But since these agencies do not compile and publish the information, those data become useful for understanding deviance only when individual scholars undertake the task of surveying the records and systematically organizing the evidence they contain. For example, the Justice Department is responsible for enforcing the laws that prohibit monopolies, price fixing, and other acts in restraint of trade. They record complaints, ferret out violations on their own, and sometimes bring charges against violators. But they do not issue periodic reports to the public on their activities. Yet private scholars can sometimes gain access to these files, as did Edwin Sutherland, who coined the term "white collar crime" (1949). Sutherland pulled together the information on antitrust activity and wrote a famous book demonstrating widespread and repetitive trust violations, and his conclusions have been confirmed by a more up-to-date study (Clinard and Yeager, 1980).

Similar types of studies could be done using the files of other departments of the Federal government. A recent example is a study of medical fraud, in which the investigators used records of the enforcement arm of the Social Security Administration, which handles Medicare and Medicaid matters (Jesilow et al., 1993; Rosoff et al., 1998). They found extensive evidence of fraud by practitioners who overbilled the government for care of aged patients. In many cases physicians would bill for tests not conducted, bill twice for the same test, and in some cases billed for more hours of work per day than there were actual hours in the day.

These various agency records are exceptionally rich as sources of information, but they are unlocked only by the efforts of individual scholars. Most such data remain dormant, and even when they come to light through the efforts of dedicated scholars, the evidence is limited to the time covered by the individual studies and it is uniquely reflective of the particular organizational schemes studied by the investigators. Also, of course, such studies expose only a minute proportion of the evidence. For all these reasons, data in agency records cannot stand alone in teaching us about deviance. Yet agency records allow insight about deviance not possible from any other source.

Private Records

Some scholars rely on records kept by private individuals, businesses, or organizations to provide information about deviance. For instance, virtually all retailers keep an eye out for shoplifters or employee theft. Often they hire

Deviance in Everyday Life

There are numerous governmental agencies that deal with crime but do not report it to official sources, such as the Uniform Crime Reporting Program. One such Federal agency is the National Park Police. Although we often think of national parks as places of recreation and fun, they are, unfortunately, also places of crime. The United States Park Police, part of the National Park Service within the Department of the Interior was started in 1791, and has jurisdiction over all National Parks and other federal/state lands. Virtually any kind of crime and/or deviant act that occurs in non-park areas has also occurred in a national park. For example, there have been homicides in Shenandoah National Park in Virginia and Lake Mead National Recreation Area in Nevada; satanic cult practices in Joshua Tree National Monument in California; and large quantities of marijuana found growing in Daniel Boone National Forest in Kentucky. In addition, there are more mundane acts of deviance in national parks, like peeping toms, domestic assaults, and assault.

private detective agencies to provide security. Most of them keep their own records of people they see or accost for shoplifting or theft, although they rarely report such incidents to the police. Sometimes, of course, when a thief is caught and the evidence is compelling, a retailer will call the local police and follow through with prosecution. More often, however, especially in the more "upscale" establishments, retailers prefer to handle the situation themselves (Cameron, 1964). They do not want to get a reputation for spying on the customers or distrusting the employees, and even when they spot someone stealing, they are often reluctant to do anything about it because those same people may be regular customers whom they do not want to alienate, or they may be otherwise good workers. And even when they do act, private security forces are likely to quietly stop the suspect, recover the concealed item, and issue a warning either not to do it again or not to return to the store. These private records, then, will contain much more information about particular kinds of deviance than will other sources, particularly police data. One study indicated that private detectives in one store in Chicago in a given year recorded two-thirds as many acts of theft as were reported to the police for the entire city (Cameron, 1964:123).

Similarly, private entities like insurance companies keep extensive records about claims made on policies they have issued. Some of those data, such as claims for theft loss, directly concern deviant activity, but others have indirect relevance. Since insurance companies want to protect their financial interests from fraud, they employ their own in-house investigators to ferret out information about the circumstances surrounding burglaries, auto thefts, and accidents. From time to time the investigators uncover suspicious circumstances that justify refusal to pay a claim, although those circumstances may not be compelling enough to warrant a complaint to the police.

Yet those suspicious circumstances are recorded in the files, which individual scholars can sometimes access to generate estimates of various kinds of deviance. For example, a common method of fraud is for someone to call the police from a shopping mall, reporting theft of their car, which in fact has been hidden somewhere in a garage by another member of the family. The plan is to file an insurance claim, be reimbursed, but later take the car out of hiding for continued use. Insurance companies are more likely to detect such scams than are the police because they have an incentive to check records to see if a state license is later issued to the owner of that automobile. The companies might put suspicious policyholders under surveillance, hoping they will reveal where the car is hidden. Another instance concerns self-inflicted injuries or fake auto accidents. Apparently, a good number of people each year cut off fingers or toes for the insurance payoff. Investigators become suspicious when such digits are the least useful or are on the nondominant hand or foot, or when such episodes are temporally or geographically concentrated. Of course, when fraud is detected, the company is more interested in getting its money back or in avoiding payout in the first place than in blowing the whistle to the police. That is why their files may be more revealing than police records.

The extent of private records that might be used for information about deviance is great, and new ones are being uncovered all the time. Private security forces or insurance companies are not the only sources of such data, although they are two of the more important. Consider the magnitude of possibilities in this so-called "information age" when so much is contained in all kinds of records—those of universities, credit bureaus, video rental stores, government-administered health programs, and on and on.

Surveys

Further information about crime and deviance comes from surveys in which a sample of people are asked to report, anonymously, the extent to which they themselves have engaged in conduct of a deviant or criminal nature or to project the likelihood that they will do such things under various circumstances.

Self-Report/Projection

A variant of the self-report approach is the "vignette" or "scenario" survey, in which respondents are asked to imagine themselves in the various situations described for them in stories and then to state what they think they would do or what they think the characters in the stories will do. Usually, surveys guarantee anonymity to the respondents; the questions are posed in neutral terminology to reduce respondents' fears about self-incrimination; and respondents are given checklists concerning frequency of commission of the various acts for specific time periods. For example, instead of asking, "How many times did you commit adultery last year?" or "What are the chances you will cheat on your sex partner during the next year?" a self-report survey would more likely phrase the question something like, "How many times during the past year did you have sex with someone to whom you were not married?" or "What are the chances on a continuum from 1 to 100 that within the next month you will have sex with someone to whom you are not married?" And since background information collected on each respondent includes marital status, the surveyor can extrapolate to estimate adultery. Moreover, the question would probably be preceded by a "neutralizing statement" that lets respondents know that what they are being asked to admit is a common behavior about which the surveyor will make no value judgments.

Such surveys were first begun in the late 1940s, became quite popular during the 1960s, and continue today as one of the most useful sources of information about deviant behavior. There are several ongoing projects that either survey the same population on a regular basis, such as the Monitoring the Future project, which annually estimates the amount of drug use among high school seniors (Johnston et al., 1991), or track the same respondents over a period of time, an example of which is the National Youth Survey that began in 1976 with youths aged 11 to 17, who have now been interviewed nine times (Elliott et al., 1985, 1989). In addition, there are many one-shot surveys, such as the three-state household survey by Tittle (1980b), the citywide survey by Evans et al. (1995), the national survey of sexual behavior by Laumann et al. (1994), and the school survey by Paternoster (1989a). Data from many of these surveys have been collected and stored in data banks (such as that maintained at the University of Michigan called the Inter-University Consortium for Political and Social Research) and are available to all scholars, not just the ones who were responsible for the original data collection.

There are four specific reasons that self-report/projection surveys are so widely used. First, they enable scholars to learn about deviant behavior that would otherwise remain hidden. As noted above, "official" data concern only those instances that come to the attention of authorities. Since most deviance is never discovered, it cannot appear in official records. Moreover, there are other sources of bias in official data, including personal prejudices of authorities, clerical errors, political considerations, and differential patterns of deployment of authorities. Second, surveys provide systematic information that overcomes problems in the data. Private records of companies or regulatory agencies are often not systematic, meaning that different information is collected for each instance in the records and the records are not themselves compiled for particular units of analysis. Hypothetically at least, survey researchers can ask about any form of behavior, collect responses to the same questions for all subjects in the survey, and contend only with errors that are response related or clerical, stemming from mistakes the investigator makes.

A more important advantage of self-report surveys, however, is their coverage. An investigator can ask about all manner of things that potentially could help specify the distribution of deviant behavior or serve as explanatory tools. For example, it is impossible to discover the distribution of criminal behavior by occupation or socioeconomic status using police or court data because, even though local police may collect information about occupation or income of arrestees, such information is not reported to, or compiled, by the FBI. And using official data about drug overdose cases admitted to hospital emergency rooms, researchers cannot learn whether IQ helps explain drug use because information about IQ is not collected or compiled or reported. A survey, however, can potentially yield evidence about crime and drug use as well as information about the socioeconomic status of those who commit crime relative to those who do not; similarly, data can be collected about the IQs of users and nonusers of drugs.

The fourth main reason for the popularity of self-report surveys is that they lend themselves to the use of sampling rather than requiring information about entire populations. Social scientists have learned that properly selected random samples (those in which selection of cases is determined solely by chance) of populations can yield results generalizable to the whole population with relatively little error. For instance, national pollsters regularly gauge the opinions and behaviors of over two hundred million American adults using samples of fewer than two thousand. Therefore, if researchers wish to estimate the amount of overeating in the United States, they can select a relatively small sample of the population and query the respondents about their eating habits. If properly done (note that there is a well-developed technology for this), the results will be accurate to within a few percentage points of what the researchers would have learned had they talked with every person in the United States.

This may seem astonishing to you, but it can easily be proven mathematically or, more practically, by comparing actual results from samples with those from full population coverage. Probably the best example is the U.S. Census. Before the advent of computers, it was impossible for the Bureau of the Census to compile and publish all the data it had already collected in the decennial counts of the population before it had to begin conducting the next census. To get results out sooner, The Bureau immediately took a 1-in-100,000 random sample of the census forms, compiled the data, and published the results. Later, it repeated the process with a 1-in-10,000 sample, and still later with a 1-in-1,000 sample. With the final count, one could compare published results of the full count with the various samples. The results showed little difference between the samples and the full count. This and other evidence has demonstrated the accuracy of sampling, so by now there is widespread agreement about the value of samples for efficient generalization, although, as will be seen later, there are some problems with sample surveys.

Despite the great advantage of self-report surveys for studying deviance, they suffer some defects that make it unwise to rely on them totally. Perhaps the most troublesome problem is the possibility that respondents will misreport the information being sought; you have probably already said to yourself, "Why would anybody admit deviant behavior to a surveyor?" And, in fact, even though the subjects are assured of anonymity and confidentiality, some do conceal their deviant acts, while others exaggerate their own misbehavior. People are most likely to withhold information when it is embarrassing or is something about which they are ashamed, and they are likely to inflate their reports of behavior that is status enhancing in their social milieu. Thus, a minister who has stolen may be hesitant to admit it because of the shame it implies, while an adolescent male with no sexual experience may say he is quite experienced because it conveys a more grown-up image. In addition, some survey respondents simply forget things, particularly correct time sequences; misinterpret the questions asked; or deliberately try to foul up the data (the latter maneuver is usually easily detected, so such cases are excluded).

Interestingly enough, however, much research demonstrates that self-report or projection data are far more accurate than the average person realizes (see, for example, Akers et al., 1983; Chaiken and Chaiken, 1984; Hindelang et al., 1981; Petersilia, 1978). In fact, most estimates place accuracy of professional surveys at more than 80 percent, and sometimes as much as 95 percent, depending on the type of respondent, the kind of deviance in question, and the professionalism of the surveyors. But you may wonder how social scientists can determine the accuracy of self-reports. Various methods have been used. One of the first and best-known tests of self-report accuracy was conducted by Clark and Tifft (1966), who asked college students to self-report their past delinquency and then later had them report again while hooked up to a polygraph machine (lie detector). Other studies compare self-reports with alternative sources of information about deviant behavior, such as arrest records (Hindelang et al., 1981); compare the consistency of self-reports with reports by peers about the person's misbehavior (Gold, 1966, 1970); or compare self-reports of some kinds of deviance, such as smoking among young adolescents, with independent chemical evidence (Akers et al., 1983).

Although evidence supports the conclusion that properly conducted self-report surveys can yield reasonably accurate data, it is important to note that this does not mean that anybody, under any circumstances, can obtain good data just by asking. It is essential that the investigator have an appropriate status that inspires confidence among respondents, that the questions be correctly phrased, and that the instrument be properly administered. But even under those circumstances one might wonder why subjects reveal potentially damaging information about themselves to surveyors, who are strangers. Actually, it appears that most people like to answer surveys. Among other things, it makes them feel important that their opinions or reports are being sought. Then, too, many people have a genuine interest in helping to promote scientific research about deviance. Even if they are ashamed or defensive about their own behavior, many will want to help scientists learn the causes and consequences of such behavior. And they often wish to know how much company they have, and realize that participation in surveys and later reading of the results is the only way to find out. In addition, confessing wrongdoing to a stranger seems to have a cathartic effect, much like confessing to a priest or a psychiatrist—as long as the person has confidence that the surveyor will go away and never be seen again. In fact, most scholars who have collected self-report data are impressed with the tendency of people to tell them "more than they wanted to know," often going into excruciating detail about the most private or heinous acts.

This tendency for people to reveal intimate details is also relevant to concerns that many social scientists themselves have expressed about self-report/projection surveys—the supposed tendency for such surveys to focus on less serious, or even trivial, forms of deviance, while neglecting the more serious ones (Nettler, 1978). While one advantage of surveys is the potential of learning about all kinds of deviance, many deviance scholars have not availed themselves of that advantage. Because the researchers began with an assumption (a false assumption, as it turns out) that respondents would be reluctant to report serious deviance, or because they feared antagonizing those who must approve access to some kinds of subjects of research (such as school boards or funding agencies), many of them, especially those studying school populations, have avoided questions about serious deviance and have overemphasized minor types of misbehavior. This, however, is not inherent to survey methodology. For example, many deviance surveys have asked, and received, good response to questions about serious crimes like assault (Tittle, 1980b), rape (Laumann et al., 1994), burglary (Elliott et al., 1985, 1989), extreme deviant sexuality (Laumann et al., 1994), and outrageous expressions of racial bigotry (Hamm, 1993).

A third problem with self-report or projection surveys stems from one of its strengths—sampling. Although sampling makes it possible to concentrate efforts on relatively few cases, and thereby improve the quality of data, most surveys deviate from the ideal of randomness. Many researchers even begin with a hand picked sample, usually one that is convenient. Many surveys, for example, are conducted on children in school. Unfortunately, there is a tendency to assume that the results from such surveys generalize to the whole population, or at least to the age categories covered. In fact, however, a certain number of youths do not attend school at all (dropouts) or they are absent on the day (or days) the survey is given; also, a certain number of the potential respondents refuse to cooperate. Similarly, general population surveys miss a substantial number of people who do not live in households (so called "street people," those in the military, those in prison or a hospital, and those in transit from one household to another), who happen to be away at the time of the survey and its follow-ups, or who refuse to cooperate. Such surveys attempt to sample on a geographic basis to identify people in households because there is no list of names of the general population from which to sample. Unfortunately, those missed in surveys may be the ones most likely to engage in deviant behavior.

Finally, surveys produce "regimented" information that may not reveal enough about the complexities of reality. For practical reasons of efficiency and comparability, surveyors try to arrange it so that respondents can answer in precoded categories. Even surveys in which questions are posed by interviewers are usually constricted, with only a few "open-ended" items, where respondents can elaborate their reports or thinking. Inevitably, then, use of surveys requires the investigator to know, or assume, quite a bit about some types of behavior ahead of time, and it leaves little room for discovery of new things or enrichment with qualitative detail. As critics have noted, this type of data collection focuses on incidents, events, or pieces of behavior, not the context and circumstances surrounding the behavior. You can easily appreciate this problem because you have no doubt filled out many forms in your life, including forms for application to college. Almost inevitably some answers you want to give will not fit in the allocated space, some questions will be irrelevant to your case, some of the precoded response categories will not include the answer that applies to you, and many of the questions will ask for the end products of strings of events and circumstances, making you want to explain and justify that end product but without space or time to do so. For example, an admissions questionnaire may ask if you ever failed a course. Maybe you did, but it was because you were ill for three weeks of the semester, lost your textbook and were afraid to ask for another one, and sat beside a student who constantly talked and distracted you. You will desperately want to explain your failure because you don't want whoever reads that application to think you are irresponsible and to deny you admission, but there is no space for you to provide the explanation. Under such circumstances some people skip the question, fail to provide the correct answer, or become suspicious of the entire form and fill it out carelessly. And even if all respondents answer honestly, interpreters of the information may not really learn what they hoped to find out about the issue at hand.

Victimization Surveys

Because of the problems and potential biases in official data and self-report surveys discussed in the preceding paragraphs, another kind of survey is regularly conducted to estimate the amount and geographic distribution of crime (the National Crime Victimization Survey). Instead of asking respondents about their own misbehavior, victimization surveys ask people about their own experience as a victim of crime. As in all surveys, the questions do not simply ask if people have been the objects of predatory crime; instead, they ask them how frequently they have experienced various described events, which in reality qualify as crime even if the person does not recognize it. When respondents report having been victims, questions are then posed to pinpoint the characteristics of the situations and perpetrators. Respondents are asked to describe when and where the incident occurred, who was involved, and the characteristics of the offenders, as observed or perceived by the respondent. In addition, they are asked if the incident was reported to the police; if so, what the outcome was; and if not reported, why not.

Such surveys permit an independent assessment of the amount and type of predatory crime, and they almost always indicate much more crime than shows up in police data, even in the data on "crimes known to the police." These surveys also allow estimates of the relative accuracy of police data for various kinds of crime. For example, it was from victimization surveys that criminologists were able to confirm that rape and assault are much less likely to be reported to the police than burglary or theft. Furthermore, such data permit an assessment of the accuracy of inferences about some characteristics of perpetrators garnered from arrest statistics. As suggested by police arrest data, perpetrators of predatory crime are most often observed by victims to be young males and members of minority groups.

Despite the obvious advantages of victimization surveys, they are extremely limited as sources of data about deviance in general. They focus on only one type of deviance—interpersonal crime that has a victim—thereby offering no insight about nonvictim crimes such as fraud or vice, about white collar or organizational crime, and certainly not about other forms of deviance that do not happen to be criminal or that are criminal but involve entities (such as the public in general in cases of price fixing) or organizations (such as the government or business as in the case of large scale fraud). Furthermore, the data are subject to their own errors, which may in some ways be as serious as the errors in police data that they are designed to overcome. In addition to the sampling and response errors characteristic of all surveys, the victimization surveys rely heavily on respondent observation and recall, both of which may at times be unreliable. For one thing, respondents sometimes remember an event that took place some time ago as having occurred more recently than it did, or vice versa. In addition, their remembrances of the characteristics of the perpetrators, assuming they actually saw them, are easily affected by their own selective perceptions, which are influenced by preconceived notions about the characteristics of criminals. Hence those who believe blacks are more criminally inclined may presume and report that a perpetrator not clearly seen was actually a black person. Finally, victimization surveys do not permit scholars to test many causal hypotheses, even about predatory crime, because the data center on events, with only limited information about the perpetrators.

Observation

The fifth kind of data relied upon by students of deviance is produced by observation. Scholarly observation, however, is not simply looking around to see what you might see, which all people do. Instead, observation as practiced by social scientists involves careful, systematic recording of activities and people's interpretation of those activities. Scientific observers are careful to seek input from multiple sources, to search for information that might contradict their hypotheses, and to pursue leads until they can be confirmed or negated. There are basically two kinds of scientific observation, sometimes called ethnography.

One type of observation (participant observation) requires the investigator to take on the identity and life style of those who are being studied; in effect, to become like the deviants in order to see the world from their points of view. Sometimes participant observers reveal that they are social scientists for the purpose of observing and learning, but at other times they are completely incognito. An example of participant observation of subjects who knew that the observer was a scholar is that by Patricia Adler, who studied drug smugglers who lived next door to her home in California (1993); an example of concealed observation is that by Festinger and his associates, who infiltrated a small cult who were getting ready for the end of the world that their leader had predicted (Festinger et al., 1956). In both cases, however, the investigators were doing what the subjects of the research were doing. In Adler's case, the smugglers were partying and using drugs, and in the Festinger case, they were hanging out, praying, and talking.

In contrast to the work done by Adler and by Festinger and his colleagues is that produced by scholars who observe deviant behavior without themselves being involved in it (nonparticipant observation). An example is the work of Bruce Jacobs (1993), who studied drug dealing on city streets in order to learn how dealers manage to identify and avoid drug agents ("narcs"). Such scholars sometimes enter the field with full disclosure of their status and intent (as scientists doing research), but at other times they assume ancillary roles that permit them to observe without participating. An example of the latter would be to pose as a taxi driver to justify being parked in areas where deviance is likely to occur or to overhear the conversations of people who hire the cab.

Observation is the only way to study some forms of deviance that are not subject to regulation by authorities and whose practitioners are not amenable to sampling in a survey (such as cult members). Moreover, observation permits preservation of the "context" and "qualitative flavor" of numerous deviant contexts (Polsky, 1967). Some of the richest literature in the deviance field is based on observation. There are, nevertheless, some inherent weaknesses with using observation as a tool for learning about the nature, extent, and distribution of deviance. The main problem is that observation is necessarily limited to a relatively small number of incidences or cases that are usually selected on a convenience basis, making generalization risky. Observation is therefore useful mainly for describing specific deviant behaviors in particular locales or for discovering things that might not have been known about before. It is weak as a tool for testing hypotheses from theories and even for describing the distribution and frequency of occurrence of the deviance in question.

A second problem in using observation is that the quality of the data depends on the skill and resourcefulness of the investigator. Some scholars are very skilled and some are not, so the comparability of different observational studies is questionable. Not many social scientists can successfully assume a deviant identity or an ancillary role enabling observation of deviance since most of them are middle-class college professors. They have little or no actual personal experience with deviants or deviance and look like, well, middle-class college professors. Moreover, even when social scientists do find themselves in possible vantages for observation, some cannot successfully carry off the interaction, and others are unable to see all that is going on, or put it together in a realistic way. Using observation as a tool of research is difficult, and few have the talent for it. Actually, most social scientists use observation most effectively when they enter situations as what they are and make it clear they are scholars with morally neutral positions who are there for one purpose—to conduct scientific research (see Inciardi et al., 1993; Tittle, 1972).

A third major defect with observational research is its subjectivity. What one investigator sees, another may ignore, and what one thinks is important, another may regard as trivial. As a result, observational research may be unreliable; certainly, it is rarely replicated. In at least some instances where replication has occurred, the results the second time around were different (Freeman, 1983; Jensen and Suryani, 1992). Moreover, since observational research is usually a one-time unique snapshot of deviant interaction, it is subject to deliberate manipulation by deviant practitioners. People engaged in deviant behavior don't usually want to be observed, and they are suspicious of those who try to do so. Consequently, they are prone to mislead, if possible. Almost all social scientific observers face this problem in the beginning, until their subjects become comfortable with their intrusion (if disguised as a new

deviant participant) or their presence as a nonparticipant observer. Some re-   ❖ ❖ ❖ ❖
searchers, however, may never overcome the subjects' trepidation, and neither the researchers nor their readers ever realize that the data are contaminated.

A final problem concerns practical difficulties in conducting observational research. Finding the appropriate milieus to observe and making effective and safe entry is just the beginning. For one thing, it is sometimes dangerous—terrorists, political revolutionaries, militia members, and criminals,
for example, may kill an observer perceived as a threat. An observer can be arrested, if not for the actual deviance, at least for having observed illegal activity without reporting it. In addition, courts may subpoena the investigator's
notes and compel testimony about what was observed, in effect requiring the
investigator to break his or her promise of confidentiality or face jail. Since
social scientists, unlike priests and doctors, have no legally recognized im-
munity, more than one of them has faced the dilemma of what to do in such
circumstances (Leo, 1995; Scarce, 1994). So far, all have chosen an honorable
way out (see Erikson, 1996, for a contrary view), but the possibility of such dilemmas deters much observational research and makes that which is undertaken more difficult, since the social scientist must convince the subjects of
his or her willingness to go to jail to protect their anonymity. It is usually a
hard sell. Furthermore, observational research sometimes requires observers to remain calm in the presence of behavior that they might find morally
despicable and in response to which they might in other circumstances take
action. For example, in his study of the underworld of crack houses, Inciardi
witnessed a rape of a young girl but was unable to do anything about it; even if
he could have done something, it would have jeopardized his life and his ability to continue the research (Inciardi et al., 1993:Appendix). Finally, observational researchers have to have good memories because they are not in positions to take notes without either "blowing their covers" or missing something that is happening while they are recording some previous action.

Thus, observational work is one of the more useful items in the social scientist's toolbox, but it is one that is limited in its applicability, relatively rarely
practiced, and often rife with problems. The results of such work, however,
are usually especially revealing and interesting to scholars and students alike.

Informant Research

In lieu of actual observation, many social scientists rely on informants to
tell them about different kinds of deviance. An informant is someone who is a
practitioner of some deviance or is in a position to observe practitioners but
who is not an actual social scientist. Nevertheless, using skillful interviewing,
scholars can often learn a great deal about deviance from such informants.
And if they establish good rapport, social scientists can sometimes transform
the informants into observers and interviewers. For example, Sutherland did
extensive interviews with a professional criminal named Chick Conwell, and
from that information wrote a fascinating book on the life of pickpockets
(Sutherland, 1937). Similar work has been done to learn about fences
(Klockars, 1974; Steffensmeier, 1986; Walsh, 1977), safecrackers (King and
Chambliss, 1972), various kinds of criminals (Akerstrom, 1993; Shover,
1996), addict inmates, using an incarcerated physician (Tittle, 1972), and nu-

merous other kinds of deviants. Sometimes there is just one informant, but often there are many informants.

Informant-based research is quite useful and far more practical than many other types of data collection, and for that reason is one of the more popular sources of information about deviance. However, it suffers many of the same defects as other types of research (Wright et al., 1992). One of the major problems is knowing how much credibility to give to the informants; they could be either uninformed or deliberately trying to mislead an investigator. Finding informants in the first place is often tricky; if an investigator chooses those who are brought into official institutions (such as people showing up at clinics for drug treatment, those arrested for some misdeeds, or actual program inmates), these may be the least informed or the least skilled of their types (since they got caught), so one does not know how well the information they provide generalizes. If informants are sought in natural habitats, there is always the problem of their being viewed as snitches. In addition, informants may not be good observers; after all, they are not trained as social scientists. Furthermore, they often have no real reason to act as informants unless they are paid, so their motivation for data collection may be limited. Even when they get paid, the money they receive may be a fraction of what they could get doing the deviant things they are supposedly reporting on.

Case Studies

In case studies, an investigator attempts to bring together and integrate data from several sources in order to understand the totality of some social phenomenon in a specific locale or with respect to a particular type of deviance. One example is a study of inmate organization in a Federal narcotics hospital, which was organized and operated like a prison at the time of the study in the late 1960s (Tittle, 1972). The investigator interviewed a random sample of the inmate population (survey), extracted data from hospital and police records (official data), observed life among the inmates and between inmates and staff members (nonparticipant observation), and engaged in lengthy discussions with the staff, including medical personnel (informant research). He then attempted to describe interactional patterns and organizational structure in the installation and among the inmates, as well as to test hypotheses derived from theories about subordinate groups; he took into account the unusual situation in the facility being studied (a hospital run like a prison, with some voluntary patients being free to leave and others under sentence), information about which was garnered from observation and discussion with hospital staff. The object was to paint a complete picture of the social structure within the hospital and to explain its features; in the process the investigator was able to uncover and describe various kinds of deviance from the official norms in the institution.

The crime/deviance literature contains many case studies of various kinds of deviance or deviance-generating circumstances. These case studies are especially helpful in uncovering and describing deviance that otherwise would be hidden, and they have the peculiar advantage of preserving the "gestalt" of the context or situation. In addition, they are stronger than many approaches because their authors use a variety of techniques for data gathering, which permit cross-confirmation of information. Since all kinds of data inevitably contain errors, it is useful, not just in case studies but in studies of crime or deviance generally, to bring different kinds of data to bear. If multiple sources of data point in the same direction, or show the same thing, then a social scientist can usually have more confidence in the conclusion. This convergence of different kinds of data is called "triangulation."

Despite these advantages, however, case studies alone are not adequate for describing amounts and distributions of various kinds of deviance or for testing explanatory hypotheses. For one thing, they are focused on narrow, specific domains that are often purposefully selected because they are so unusual, so the ability to generalize beyond the particular locale is limited. In addition, the results, especially those stemming from the overarching contextual structure perceived by the investigator, may not be reliable. Like most observational research, case studies are usually one-time affairs, never replicated, and depend on the skill and objectivity of the specific investigator. Finally, since various kinds of data are used, case studies incorporate all of the potential errors of the other specific sources of data.

Experiments

A final source of information about deviance comes from experiments. An experiment is a research design in which the investigator, or someone else (such as governmental authorities), manipulates some variable that may cause an outcome of interest and then attempts to ascertain if that manipulation actually brings about the effect. The strength of inferences from experiments depends on the ability of the investigator to control all potential contaminating conditions and variables so that the result can be attributed to changes in the variable that the experimenter manipulates. In an ideal experiment, an investigator begins with two groups that are exactly alike in every possible way, applies the supposed causal variable to one of the groups and a placebo (a treatment that is ostensibly like the experimental one but is actually neutral) to the other. The subjects do not know whether they received the placebo or the real thing. (In the best experiments even the investigator does not know which group received the treatment until after the experiment is completed.) After an appropriate interval of time, the outcome that is supposedly caused by the manipulated variable is then measured in the experimental and the control groups. During this whole process all other conditions are held constant. If the causal variable in fact produces an effect, the experimental group will have significantly more of the outcome variable than will the control group. It is important that the magnitude of the outcome in the two groups be compared, because even the placebo group will ordinarily experience some of the outcome, either because the subjects psychologically expect some change or because of naturally occurring changes in the outcome variable.

Of course, ideal experiments are difficult to conduct, especially for serious matters such as deviant behavior. While an experimenter can randomly assign subjects to experimental and control groups, thereby under some circumstances making them alike (within statistical error) it is often difficult to manipulate the variables of interest to students of deviance, at least while remaining ethical. Also, it is often difficult to maintain constant conditions for the length of time that it presumably takes for many of the social variables to have their effects, which in many instances is years. Furthermore, experiments are mainly useful for testing causal hypotheses about the effects of specific variables or conditions. They are of little value for learning about the extent and distribution of deviance, because they begin with a select sample of people, all of whom are presumably equal with respect to deviance. Nor can experiments lead to discoveries of new things, because in an experiment everything is held constant except the treatment variable, which has already been imagined by the experimenter and hypothesized as having a causal effect; in other words, there is little room for surprises in an experiment since all of the possibilities have been carefully planned.

Moreover, the results of experiments can seldom be generalized beyond the peculiar situations in which they are conducted. That is because of an inherent dilemma in research. The best experiment would be one in which all the subjects were clones. With clones, any initial differences between the two groups of subjects—including personal characteristics and behaviors—would be exactly the same. Then the experimenter could draw more correct inferences about the effect of treatment variables. The more homogeneous the subjects, the better for inferences, because only the experimental treatment would vary from the beginning to the end of the experiment. However, the more homogeneous the subjects, the less the ability to generalize to the larger population. Most experiments tilt toward stronger inferences, at the cost of generalizability. In fact, critics sometimes refer to experimental social science as "the science of sophomores" because so many experiments are conducted on college students, usually students in large sections of lower-level courses. Furthermore, because experimenters usually alter the natural world in order to create the control conditions necessary for inference, the causal effects they show may not apply to other kinds of contexts. Critics often speak of experiments, especially laboratory experiments, as "unnatural" and thereby inapplicable to the "real world."

It is much easier to conduct good experiments in contrived circumstances (laboratory) than in natural conditions (field) because in the natural environment it is rarely possible even to manipulate an independent variable, much less hold other conditions constant. Within limits, it is relatively easy to do these things in the laboratory. Students of deviance have used both types of experiments. An illustration of a laboratory experiment is one in which the investigators set out to determine the extent to which intoxication inhibits the ability of people to take into account potential costs and benefits of their actions (Meier et al., 1996). The objective was to test the hypothesis that deterrence, which requires rational calculation of potential punishments, is weakened by alcohol consumption. This hypothesis has been posed as an explanation for the high rate of drunk driving despite intense enforcement efforts.

Meier and his associates brought 10 students into the lab and on successive trials randomly assigned them to groups that would experience different degrees of intoxication and different degrees of punishment probability. The subjects then played a laboratory game in which they calculated the odds of winning or losing points that could, at the end of the experiment, be cashed in for money, and they were given the opportunity to take risks that could benefit them but that had different probabilities of resulting in costs. For a period of time prior to playing the game, however, the students drank a colored punch. The punch that was drunk by the various experimental groups contained different amounts of alcohol. After sufficient time for intoxication to occur, all were given Intoximeter tests to determine their blood alcohol levels. During and after the game, the subjects were monitored as to their ability to calculate odds and their willingness to take risks.

It is important to note that the proposal for this research had to be certified by the Internal Review Board for Research on Human Subjects ahead of time as safe and protective of the rights of the subjects. All of the students were at least 21 years old, knew that they might be consuming alcohol to intoxication, and volunteered for the experiment. In addition, all subjects were kept in the lab for a period of time after the experiment for "detoxification," and then they were safely escorted home. Incidentally, the experiment showed no significant difference between the intoxicated and nonintoxicated subjects in ability to play the risk game, which suggests that deterioration of rational thinking about costs and penalties may not explain why people drive while drunk.

An illustration of a field experiment is the well-known study of the effect of arrest on repeated domestic assault (Sherman and Berk, 1984). The experimenters arranged with the Minneapolis police department to randomly assign domestic assault complaints to one of three conditions. In the first condition, the investigating officers were to separate the combatants and order the assailant to stay away for eight hours. In the second condition, the officers separated the contending parties and counseled them, then, after a period of time, left. In the third condition, the assailant (usually a male) was arrested and jailed. Whether the victim reported further incidents within a six-month period was ascertained from police records; in addition, the victims were interviewed at the end of six months to see if they had experienced further problems without calling the police.

Like almost all field experiments, this one hit a snag. Sometimes the investigating officers did not follow the random assignment protocol, instead using their own judgments about what to do about the incident. They thereby upset the randomness essential for drawing a strong causal inference (Berk et al., 1989). Nevertheless, the investigators concluded that the most effective method for handling domestic assault cases was to arrest the assailant, because in that condition there were significantly fewer subsequent complaints or reports to the follow-up interviewers of further violence. Another problem, however, was that the experiment was unable to rule out the possibility that women whose assailants were arrested were inhibited from reporting subsequent assault by fear of antagonizing the men who were really angry about having been jailed. Furthermore, replications of the experiment in other cities generally failed to support the conclusion reached in Minneapolis (Dunford, 1992; Berk and Newman, 1985; Hirschel et al., 1992; Hirschel and Hutchinson, 1992; Huizinga and Elliott, 1990). It even appears that when arrest does deter further battery, it does so only for those men who are employed or married at the time. It has little or no effect on men who are unemployed or unmarried (Pate and Hamilton, 1992).

Summary

Scholars interested in deviance and crime, then, have a number of tools at their disposal for studying this phenomenon. All the sources of data have their unique advantages and can reveal a lot more about crime and deviance than is generally thought. None of them, however, is free of error, so no matter what information is relied upon, conclusions are always somewhat uncertain. Moreover, each of the data sources seems to be limited as to the aspects of deviance that it can best address. Some are especially useful for ascertaining the extent and distribution of deviance; others are adept at detailed description of specific expressions of deviance in particular contexts; and still others are designed to permit inferences about the causes of crime and deviance. Careful research requires that the most appropriate data for a particular question be used and that when more than one kind of data does apply, multiple sources of information be brought to bear before reaching firm conclusions.

In the rest of this chapter we will draw on some of the data sources described before to paint a brief picture of the prevalence of a few types of deviant behavior in the United States as well as historical trends in their incidence and frequency. Examining changes over time in deviance is especially difficult because most of the sources of data that are now routinely used by scholars were developed only within the past 60 years and were not perfected until much more recently. As a result, there is simply very little information about deviance prior to 1950, and what little data do exist are of questionable reliability and are not systematic. Furthermore, many behaviors that are now regarded as deviance, such as spouse or child abuse, computer fraud, and certain kinds of drug use, did not exist until recently, or if they did exist they were not recognized as instances of deviant behavior.

Generational Variations

Because there are thousands of different kinds of deviance, it is almost impossible to describe trends in their occurrence. Moreover, even for those deviances about which we have information, data are often not systematic enough to paint accurate pictures of intergenerational variation. For illustrative purposes, therefore, we focus on four common types of deviance in trying to show current prevalence and changes over time.

Violence

Although violence is abundant in the United States, contrary to popular opinion, rates of violence have not been on a continuous upward spiral. A compilation and review of the historical evidence suggests a great deal of irregularity but also an underlying general U-shaped pattern over the past 200 years, with periodic upward spurts about every 50 years—around 1850, 1900, and 1960 (Gurr, 1981). In other words, rates of violence were especially high 200 years ago, declined through most of the nineteenth century into the early part of this century, then began an upward trend. Whether that upward trend has begun to abate is a matter of controversy because it is not consistently confirmed by all sources of data and because the recent declines indicated by some sources of data may represent temporary variations that detract only slightly from the underlying upward trend.

We use three sources of data to illustrate current and long-range rates of violence. Figures 8.1 and 8.2 are based on two different data sources that are independent of the criminal justice system. The first figure uses homicide rates calculated from coroners' records and reported in vital statistics publications. The second figure is based on victimization reports gathered in na-

Figure 8.1 United States Homicide Trends[a]

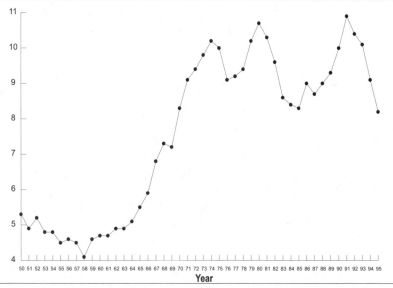

[a] Per 100,000 population as indicated in vital statistics.
Source: Compiled from the *Statistical Abstract of the United States*, 1951–1997, U.S. Census Bureau, Washington, D.C.

tional surveys. Other data are used for additional tables and figures to follow. Figure 8.3 is from police reports, and Table 8.1 uses self-report offense information from two national surveys of youth.

Table 8.1 United States Trends in Self-Reported Violence

	Year																
	79	80	83	84	85	86	87	88	89	90	91	92	93	94	95	96
Percentage of high school seniors who have ever gotten into a serious fight in school or at work[a]				17	18	17	18	18	20	19	18	19	18	16	15	17
Percentage of high school seniors who ever hurt someone badly enough to need bandages or a doctor[a]				11	12	11	12	10	12	13	13	13	13	13	12	14
Percentage of youth reporting having engaged in aggravated assault in the past year[b]	4	4	3			3			2			2				

[a]Source: Monitoring the Future Survey (Sourcebook of Criminal Justice Statistics, 1997, U.S. Department of Justice, Washington, D.C., p. 238).
[b]Source: National Youth Survey (Sourcebook of Criminal Justice Statistics, 1997, U.S. Department of Justice, Washington, D.C., pp. 238–288).

Vital statistics about cause of death show a distinct long-range upward trend in homicide over the past 45 years, with most of that upsurge having occurred in the 1960s (Figure 8.1). According to these data, as of 1995, the rate of homicide in the United States was 8.2 per 100,000 population. To make this meaningful, imagine the nearest city of about 100,000 population. If it were

Figure 8.2   United States Violent Crimes Victimization Trends[a]

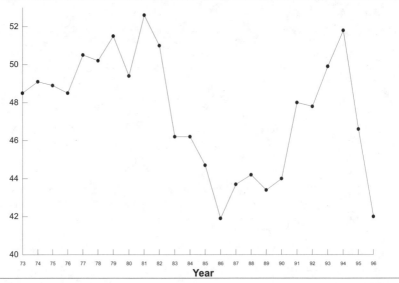

[a] Per 1,000 population age 12+.
Source: Michael Maltz and Marianne Zawitz, "Displaying Violent Crime Trends Using Estimates from the National Crime Victimization Survey." 1998. Bureau of Justice Statistics, Technical Report, NCJ 167881, U.S. Department of Justice, Washington, D.C.

average, that city would have had eight homicides in 1995, nine in the year before, 10 in 1993, and 11 in 1991. That same city, however, would have had only about 5 per year during the 1950s.

This kind of long-range upward trend, however, is not characteristic of other kinds of violence, at least as indicated by victim reports. As shown in Figure 8.2, the violent victimization rate (excluding homicide) has shown ups and downs over the 23-year period from 1973 to 1996. In comparing the two figures note that the rate for violent victimization is per 1,000 population, not per 100,000 as in the homicide data presented in Figure 8.1. This means that the rate of victimization is quite high and has been so for some time. Imagine again that city of 100,000 population, which had about 8 or 9 homicides per year. According to the victimization data, it would have experienced about 4,000 to 5,000 incidents of nonhomicide violence every year from 1973 to 1996.

The high rate of violence is confirmed by data shown in Figure 8.3, which is based on the violent offenses (rape, robbery, assault, and homicide) known to police (either reported by a citizen complaint or directly documented by a police officer) per 100,000 population. The figure shows a more dramatic upward trend over the past 35 years than either victimization data or coroners' reports about homicide. In addition, it more clearly documents a recent downturn, although the overall rates still remain much higher than in 1960. To put this in the context of that imaginary city of 100,000 population, these figures indicate that the city would have experienced about 750 violent incidents that came to the attention of the police during each year of the early 1990s. This rate, of course, is much less than the 4,000 to 5,000 uncovered in the victimization surveys. This disparity confirms what you would expect

Figure 8.3 United States Trends in Violent Offenses Known to the Police[a]

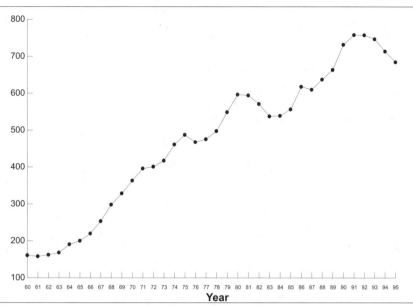

[a] Rape, robbery, assault, and homicide per 100,000 population.
Source: *Sourcebook of Criminal Justice Statistics, 1997*, U.S. Department of Justice, Washington, D.C., p. 306.

from our earlier discussion—that most acts of violence are not reported to the police.

Finally, the self-report data in Table 8.1 confirm that violence is common in the United States, although they do not show much variation over the period of time shown. It appears that about 18 percent of all high school seniors report having gotten into a serious fight during their lives up to that point, with about 12 percent of all seniors having hurt someone badly enough to need bandages or a doctor. In addition, the panel data from the National Youth Survey (in which the same youths are followed-up periodically) show that about 4 percent of the youth admit having committed aggravated assault in the past year, with the proportion going down to 2 percent as they enter adulthood.

In summary, then, a variety of data sources suggest that violence is relatively common in the United States, and some data sources suggest it has become more prevalent in recent decades but no more prevalent than it was 150 to 200 years ago. Two particular points should be noted about this. First, while violence is part of the American landscape, it is clear that violent behavior is not typical. All measures indicate that a distinct minority of people resort to violence, and most people most of the time manage human relationships without it. Second, reference to the past as a time when violence was not so prevalent ("the good old days") depends on exactly when in the past. Perhaps the 1950s were golden, relative to the present, but probably not the 1850s.

Deviant Sexual Activities

At least four sexual acts fulfill our definition of deviance; that is, the behaviors are disapproved by a majority of the population, or they typically invoke collective responses of a negative type, including negative reaction by authorities. They include homosexual behavior, extramarital sex, forced sex, and sex between adults and children (see Laumann et al., 1994).

Table 8.2 reports estimates of the extent of each of these behaviors in the United States as of the early 1990s, drawn from the National Health and Social Life Survey (NHSLS) (reported in Laumann et al., 1994).

Table 8.2 Percentage of Adults Reporting Various Forms of Sexually Deviant Conduct, 1992

	Male	Female
Homosexual behavior[a]	7.1	3.8
Extramarital sex[b]	24.5	15.0
Forced sex[c]		
a. Forcing	2.8	1.5
b. Being forced	3.2	21.9
Sexual Abuse[d]	12.0	17.0

[a]One or more sex partners of the same gender since puberty (p. 294).
[b]Sex with someone other than a spouse while married (pp. 590, 596).
[c]Being forced to do something sexual that the person did not want to do (pp. 335–336).
[d]Being sexually touched by an adolescent or adult before puberty (p. 340).
Compiled from data reported in Laumann et al., *The Social Organization of Sexuality: Sexual Practices in the United States*. 1994. The University of Chicago Press.

One can also estimate time trends in homosexual behavior and forced sex by examining data from the NHSLS that are reported by age of the respondent. In addition, we can observe temporal changes in premarital sex, which apparently has changed from being deviant to being nondeviant during this century (see attitude reports in Laumann et al., 1994). Table 8.3 shows the cohort data.

Homosexual Behavior

The first major sex survey in the United States included a large number of cases but was not based on a random sample (Kinsey et al., 1948). Kinsey and his associates used volunteers, who probably were more sexually active and more interested in different kinds of sexual activity than the general population. His data shocked the public because they revealed much higher levels of sexual deviance of various kinds than most people had imagined. Better data suggest that Kinsey's estimates were far too high, especially for homosexual behavior.

In considering same-gender sex, it is important to recognize that there are many facets to "homosexuality." To some people it means even one episode of same-gender sex; to others it implies repeated acts of same-gender sex (how many?). Some people focus on psychological preference for sex partners of the same gender, and still others think of homosexuality in terms of whether the person thinks of herself or himself as a homosexual. Although the Kinsey report showed different rates for these different aspects of homosexuality, the figure that has been best remembered is the estimate that 10 percent of males are more or less exclusively homosexual (see Laumann et al., 1994:288). Note that the figures reported in Table 8.2, based on a random sample and using the most liberal conception of homosexual behavior, are much lower than those reported by Kinsey and his associates (and they are consistent across good surveys—see Laumann et al., 1994:590).

Table 8.3 **Deviant Sexual Behavior by Age Cohorts, 1992**   ❖ ❖ ❖ ❖

Age	Male	Female
Homosexual behavior[a]		
18–29	4.4	4.2
30–39	6.6	5.3
40–49	3.9	3.6
50–59	4.2	2.2
Forced sex[b]		
18–24		25
25–29		22
30–34		24
35–39		26
40–44		22
45–49		18
50–54		17
55–59		18
Premarital sex[c]		
18–29	83.7	79.9
30–39	86.5	80.0
40–49	84.6	71.1
50–59	78.1	45.6

[a]One or more sex partners of the same gender since puberty (p. 303).
[b]Being forced to do something sexual that the person did not want to do (p. 337).
[c]Nonvirgins at marriage (p. 503).
Compiled from data reported in Laumann et al., *The Social Organization of Sexuality: Sexual Practices in the United States*. 1994. The University of Chicago Press.

Thus, it appears that even the minimum degree of homosexual behavior is relatively rare among the U.S. population (7.1 percent maximum), although even this may seem like a lot to some. Moreover, the prevalence of homosexual behavior appears to have remained relatively constant over time. As Table 8.3 shows, estimates for none of the age cohorts exceeds the current estimate, and there appears to be no upward trend. Remarkably, there is somewhat more same-gender contact (both males and females) for those who went through their teen years in the late 1960s and throughout the 1970s (those aged 30–39 in 1992) relative to other generations, including the present one. Those who witnessed the "youth revolution" of that time will testify that the theme of self-actualization and personal exploration characterizing that generation probably extended to same-gender sexual contacts.

Other Sexual Deviance

The figures reported in Table 8.2 concerning extramarital sex are also revealing in that they explode popular myths perpetrated in movies and novels that just about everybody is guilty of adultery. Although 25 percent of the males and 15 percent of the females admit infidelity, this is a far cry from a majority. On the other hand, the data concerning coercive sex may be shocking in the other direction—it is more prevalent than one might have imagined. Not only do a good number admit forcing someone to do something sexual (2.8 percent of males and 1.5 percent of females), but there is a relatively large number who perceive that they have been sexually abused as children or forced to do something sexual after their childhoods. Seventeen percent of females and 12 percent of males report having been victims of sexual touching by someone other than a child when they were children, and nearly 22 percent of the adult females report having been coerced sexually since reaching puberty.

Furthermore, there appears to have been some increase in coercive sex in recent decades, compared to the 1930s and 1940s. It is also interesting to note changes in premarital sex. Although those who grew up in recent decades show similar rates of sex before marriage, there was a rather dramatic shift in that direction for those who grew up in the late 1940s and during the 1950s (those 50 to 59 years old in 1992). This shift in behavior probably stimulated a rethinking of normative expectations that later resulted in premarital sex becoming nondeviant.

Drug Abuse

The term "drug abuse" usually refers to drug use that is illegal or that exceeds the bounds of social acceptability. Such a term is useful because not all drug use is deviant. In American society, using drugs prescribed by a physician is not deviant, unless the physician is bogus and the consumer is using the drugs for some purpose other than combatting a medical problem. Neither is it deviant to use over-the-counter nostrums, as long as the use is within socially acceptable bounds and for a medical purpose. Furthermore, a certain amount of alcohol use is normatively acceptable, but too much alcohol use qualifies as deviant behavior.

The acceptability of various kinds of drug use has had an interesting history (Goode, 1993; Lindesmith, 1965). Prior to Federal legislation early in this century, there were few legal restraints on the use of narcotic drugs. As a result, many popular products contained drugs that have since been banned or confined to medical usage by a licensed physician. It was common for people to use various preparations sold by traveling salesmen or in local stores that contained addictive drugs. Even Coca Cola at one time actually contained cocaine. Moreover, when narcotic drugs were administered by doctors, many patients, such as soldiers wounded in the War Between the States, became addicted but were able to continue to use the drug without legal constraint. As a result many people, especially women, even those who were "respectable" and of high status, were regular drug users, and a good number were addicted. When the Federal government intervened early in this century to regulate drugs, especially narcotic substances, the drug scene changed dramatically. Drugs then became available only through deviant subcultures; their use became disreputable; and the users became mainly lower-status, male, and minorities. Hence, there was a decline in overall use and a shift in the kind of people who used drugs. Later, in the 1960s many kinds of drug use, particularly use of marijuana and mind-altering drugs, became relatively popular, especially among younger people.

There were few hard data concerning the extent of drug use until fairly recently. Before the advent of surveys, scholars had to depend on police arrest data, which were highly inaccurate. Few users of drugs complained to the police and since the vast majority of instances of drug use do not result in arrest, scholars used indirect information like hospital admissions for drug overdoses. Now social scientists can look to the self-report surveys for regular updates on the extent of drug use. Table 8.4 reports trends in various kinds of deviant drug use since 1985, drawn from a household survey.

Table 8.4 Percentage Reporting Various Kinds of Drug Use in the Last Year

Type of Drug	85	88	90	91	Year 92	93	94	95	96
Any	16.3	12.4	11.7	11.1	9.7	10.3	10.8	10.7	10.8
Heroin	.2	.3	.2	.2	.1	.1	.1	.2	.2
Cocaine	5.1	3.6	2.7	2.6	2.1	1.9	1.7	1.7	1.9
Marijuana/hash	13.6	9.8	9.4	8.9	7.9	8.5	8.5	8.4	8.6

Source: *Sourcebook of Criminal Justice Statistics, 1997*, U.S. Department of Justice, Washington, D.C., p. 268.

Those data suggest a substantial amount of deviant drug use in the United States. Most of that is accounted for by marijuana use, which many people regard as a relatively harmless recreational drug, at least in comparison to other socially and legally acceptable drugs like alcohol and nicotine. In fact, marijuana use is not deviant in some groups or areas. About 8.6 percent of adults, or over 17 million people, reported marijuana use some time in 1996. But the most serious form of drug use, that of heroin, is characteristic of only a tiny proportion of the adult population, ranging from 0.1 to 0.3 percent. Even cocaine, which was fairly popular in the mid-1980s, is now used by less than 2 percent of the population. Although the percentage using heroin and cocaine is small, one should remember that the absolute numbers are still substantial. Thus, approximately 400,000 people use heroin at least once a year, and about four million individuals use cocaine at least once a year.

Recent trends show a U-shaped pattern. The 1980s were a time when many people used drugs—over 16 percent reported some type of use in 1985, including over 5 percent who used cocaine, nearly 14 percent who used marijuana, and 0.2 percent who used heroin. The popularity of drugs began to decline, however, and reached its low point in the early 1990s (a little later for cocaine) and then began a slight upward trend during the most recent years. For example, marijuana use declined from 13.6 percent in 1985 to 7.9 percent in 1992 and then rose to 8.6 percent in 1996.

Overall, then, Americans use a lot of unacceptable drugs. It is important to note, however, that drug users are a distinct minority and that the extent of use is apparently not a self-reinforcing cultural practice that leads to an ever-spiraling upward trend.

Suicide

As we saw in Chapter 3, suicide is socially disapproved in the United States, and it technically qualifies as a form of violence—but turned inward instead of outward. Interestingly, although ours is usually acknowledged to be a dangerous society with high rates of violence by people who attack others, lethal violence is actually more likely to be directed against oneself. While the coroners' data presented earlier suggest that a city of 100,000 population would have about 8 or 9 homicides in a year, similar data suggest that the same city would have about 12 suicides during that time (Figure 8.4). Suicide rates appear to be relatively constant, fluctuating a few tenths of a percent up

Figure 8.4 United States Suicide Trends (per 100,000 Population)

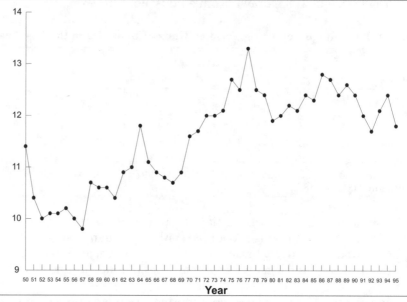

Source: Compiled from the *Statistical Abstract of the United States, 1951–1997*, U.S. Census Bureau, Washington D.C.

or down from year to year but within a narrow band from between 10 and 13 per 100,000 population (with 1977 showing the highest rate of 13.3 and 1957 showing the lowest rate of 9.8) for 50 years. This relative stability is what led the famous sociologist Emile Durkheim to declare suicide as a social fact in need of social explanation (1951 [1897]). However, although the range of variation is small, there does appear to be a trend, with a declining rate during the latter half of the 1940s to a low point in 1957 and since then an upward trend with a temporary peak in 1977. The good old days again seem to have been during the 1950s.

Summary

There are several sources of data about conformity and deviance used by social scientists, but all contain errors. To compensate for such inaccuracy, investigators often try to bring different kinds of data to bear on a given issue. When this is done, the evidence suggests that conformity rather than deviance is overwhelmingly the rule—most people conform most of the time. Nevertheless, much deviance characterizes the U.S. population. In addition, there appear to have been clear generational variations in violence, deviant sexual conduct, drug abuse, and suicide, but not necessarily in an ever-spiraling upward trajectory, as is often assumed. ◆

Who Does Deviance and Crime?

Chapter 8 discussed sources for estimating the extent of deviance and conformity and for plotting changes in its volume over the past century in the United States. One lesson from that exercise is that information about crime and deviance, especially noncriminal deviance, is quite limited. In fact, to estimate the volume of deviance it is often necessary to assume that data about crime can be extended to deviance generally, even though this assumption may be faulty and the data about crime are themselves insufficient. Information concerning the characteristics of people who commit either crime or other forms of deviance, and how frequently, is even more limited. And to make matters worse, there are almost no systematic data about the probability and types of deviance as they vary by *combinations* of roles and statuses. Indeed, the main "facts" about deviance that are reasonably agreed upon concern simple, one-variable demographic distributions of rates of crime or delinquency, which, as noted before, are quite restricted in their representation of deviance. This lack of data is particularly true of behaviors like those often thought of as arising from mental illness; forms of public uncouthness; body piercing; and hundreds of others for which no "official" data collections are attempted.

Despite this lack of systematic data, we can at least paint a rudimentary picture of the distribution of deviant behavior. In doing so, we will focus mainly on crime/delinquency, illegal drug use, deviant sexual activities, and suicide.

Demographic Variations in Deviance

Although the magnitude varies somewhat with the specific type of deviance in question, geographic location, historical period, and other demographic variables, one "fact" about deviance is unassailable—males generally do more of it than females. We will illustrate this first for crime and delinquency.

Gender

Except for a few relatively minor offenses, males seem far more likely to commit *criminal/delinquent acts* than females, and to do so more frequently (Elliott, 1994; Gottfredson and Hirschi, 1990:144–149; Nagel and Hagan, 1983; Smith and Visher, 1980; Steffensmeier et al., 1989a; Sutherland et al., 1992; Warren, 1991; Wilson and Herrnstein, 1985:104–115). However, the size of the male/female difference varies inversely with age (Farrington, 1986; Sutherland et al., 1992:161; Tittle, 1980b:81–86) and size of place (Sutherland et al., 1992:161; Tittle, 1980b:85), and is greater among whites than among disadvantaged minority groups (Sutherland et al., 1992:160; Tittle, 1980b:84). In addition, most evidence indicates that the magnitude of the difference is greater for serious and violent offenses than for more common and trivial criminal acts (Stark and McEvoy, 1970; Steffensmeier and Streifel, 1991; Sutherland et al., 1992) although some data contradict this conclusion (Tittle, 1980b:83).

To illustrate, Table 9.1 reports the number of arrests in 1996 for what are commonly thought to be the most serious criminal offenses—the Federal Bureau of Investigation's (FBI's) "index offenses." In addition to the raw number of arrests for each crime, the table shows the percentage of arrests for each crime that are males and females. The last column of the table shows the ratio of male arrests to female arrests. If there were no gender difference (that is, if males were as likely to be arrested as females), the reported gender ratio for any given offense should be equal to 1.0. If the ratio gets larger than 1.0 it means that males have more arrests than females, while a ratio smaller than 1.0 means that females exceed males in arrests.

Table 9.1 Number of Arrests for UCR Index Crimes by Gender, 1996

Offense	Male Arrests	Percent	Female Arrests	Percent	Male/Female Ratio
Murder	12,965	89.7	1,482	10.3	8.7
Forcible rape	24,066	98.8	281	1.2	82.3
Armed robbery	109,912	90.3	11,869	9.7	9.3
Aggravated assault	318,279	82.1	69,292	17.9	4.6
Burglary	234,208	88.7	29,985	11.3	7.8
Larceny-theft	726,006	66.2	370,482	33.8	2.0
Motor vehicle theft	114,125	86.4	17,898	13.6	6.4
Arson	11,703	85.1	2,052	14.9	5.7
Violent crime	465,222	84.9	82,924	15.1	5.6
Property crime	1,086,042	72.1	420,417	27.9	2.6
Total Index Crime	1,551,264	75.5	503,341	24.5	3.1

Source: *Crime in the United States, 1996.* U.S. Department of Justice, Federal Bureau of Investigation, Washington, D.C., p. 231.

No matter which offense we look at, males are arrested more than females. They are arrested almost nine times more than females for murder and over nine times more frequently for armed robbery, approximately eight times more often for burglary, six and one-half times for motor vehicle theft, five and one-half times for arson, and almost five times for aggravated assault. And with only a few exceptions, much the same picture prevails for less serious offending (*Crime in the United States,* 1996). For offenses involving violence, like simple assault and use of weapons, men are about four and twelve times, respectively, more likely to be arrested than women. Compared with women, men are also overrepresented in so-called "victimless" crimes, such as gambling, disorderly conduct, drunk driving, drunkenness, and vagrancy. Only for the two property offenses of fraud and embezzlement does the number of women being arrested come close to the number of men. Of all offenses only for the crime of prostitution are females more likely to be arrested. This consistently greater male to female ratio across both serious and less serious crimes is remarkable and clearly suggests that criminal offending is predominately a male phenomenon.

Official data on crime, however, may not give a true picture. In order for a crime to result in an arrest, it must be noticed by a victim, observer, or police officer. If observed by someone other than an officer, it must be reported to the police, who then investigate, and if they are satisfied they know who the perpetrator is, an arrest will be made. It may be that female offenders are more likely to escape this "filtering" process because their offenses more often go undetected or because the police are more lenient to females. To check on this possibility, scholars turn to other measures of crime, often self-reports by survey respondents.

Table 9.2 draws on a self-reported study of high school seniors. It shows the percentage of males and females who admitted participating in each of 11 criminal or deviant acts, as well as the male-to-female ratio of participation. Consistent with official records of arrest, males appear more likely to be involved in crime than females—far more so for violent acts (hitting a teacher, hurting someone in a fight, and using a knife or gun), but also for serious property crimes (major theft, vandalism, joyriding, breaking and entering, and arson). Only for the most minor offenses, like shoplifting and minor theft, do female participation rates come close to those for males.

Table 9.2 Percent of High School Seniors Reporting Involvement in Selected Delinquent Activities in Last Twelve Months, by Gender[a]

Offense	Male (Percent)	Female (Percent)	Ratio
Hit an instructor	5.0	0.7	7.1
Hurt someone badly in a fight	20.1	5.5	3.6
Used a knife or gun	7.5	1.7	4.1
Taken something worth $50	17.4	4.7	3.7
Joyriding	8.4	2.7	3.1
Breaking and entering	32.2	17.4	1.9
Setting fire to something	5.3	0.8	6.6
Gotten into trouble with police	13.2	4.5	2.9
Taken something worth less than $50	39.4	23.0	1.7
Shoplifting	36.1	25.2	1.4
Vandalizing school property	21.1	7.4	2.8

[a] Reported in 1994.
Source: Kathleen Maguire and Ann L. Pastore, *Sourcebook of Criminal Justice Statistics, 1994*. U.S. Department of Justice, Bureau of Justice Statistics, Washington, D.C.: USGPO, 1995.

These self-report results for youth are corroborated by data from 2,000 adults in three states (Tittle, 1980b). The acts about which respondents were queried included criminal acts such as petty and serious theft, violence (assault), and income tax violations, as well as non-criminal acts of deviance like overcharging a client (for business and professional people) or making personal use of an employer's equipment, sitting down during the national anthem, and lying to an intimate. The results in Table 9.3 show that although the gender ratios are smaller here than for the official data, there is still a clear pattern suggesting males are more likely to be deviant than females. And the difference between males and females seems to grow larger as the seriousness of the deviant act increases.

Table 9.3 Self-Reported Involvement in Deviant Acts by Adult Males and Females in Three States in 1972

Deviant Act	Male (Percent)	Female (Percent)	Ratio
Theft of $5	30	14	2.14
Theft of $50	10	4	2.50
Marijuana smoking	19	11	1.73
Illegal gambling	47	20	2.35
Assault	15	8	1.88
Lying to intimate	48	46	1.04
Income tax cheating	16	8	2.00
Sitting during anthem	16	12	1.33
Occupational deviance	37	38	.97

Adapted from Tittle, Charles R. *Sanctions and Social Deviance: The Question of Deterrence* Table 4.1, p. 83. New York: Praeger, 1980.

Although most data are fairly consistent in showing males to be more apt to commit crimes than females, there has been considerable controversy about whether these male-female differences have been changing in recent decades (Smart, 1979; Steffensmeier, 1978; Steffensmeier and Cobb, 1981; Steffensmeier et al., 1989a; Steffensmeier and Streifel, 1991). On one hand, feminist scholars claim that in response to modernization and female political organization (the women's movement), both the roles and freedoms of males and females are getting closer together. Not only does this role change create more opportunities for female crime; it also frees women from constant surveillance. Hence, one of the "rights" secured by the women's movement is the right to commit crime just as a male does. As a result, female rates of crime are said to be growing and are expected to eventually equal those of males (Adler, 1975; Simon, 1975). The evidence in support of this change includes a documented increase in absolute rates of female crime and delinquency (Merlo, 1995) but mainly rests on data showing relatively *higher rates of increase* in female than male crime.

Table 9.4 provides a little data on this point. It shows the percent change in arrests for index offenses between 1987 and 1996 for all males and females, and for males and females under the age of 18. Notice that for practically every comparison, female crime appears to be increasing far faster than male crime. For example, over the ten-year period from 1987 to 1996, there was a 12 percent increase in the number of arrests for all crimes among males, a 23 percent increase in violent index crimes, a 6 percent decrease in index property crimes, and a 1 percent increase in all index crimes. Females, however, evidenced larger increases in each of these categories over the same time period; a 36 percent increase in arrests for all crimes, a 76 percent increase in violent index crimes, a 14 percent increase in index property crimes, and a 21 percent increase in all index crimes. Most of this increase, especially for violence, is due to an increase in young (under 18) female arrests, especially for violent crimes. Females under the age of 18 showed a 53 percent increase in arrests for all crimes, 118 percent increase in violent index crimes, 40 percent increase in property index crimes, and a 45 percent increase in all index crimes. Although females continue to be arrested for fewer offenses than males, some evidence suggests the gap is narrowing.

Table 9.4 Percent Change in Arrests for Males and Females: 1987–1996

	Males		Females	
	Total	**Under 18**	**Total**	**Under18**
Offense				
All crimes	12.1	30.2	35.9	53.0
Index crimes:				
Murder	-1.5	53.3	-19.5	18.9
Rape	-12.4	-1.7	-17.4	-40.9
Robbery	8.6	52.9	31.6	117.0
Aggravated assault	35.4	60.4	94.3	124.1
Burglary	-20.8	-14.0	11.2	16.4
Larceny/Theft	-1.1	3.5	13.4	41.7
Motor vehicle theft	-1.9	3.5	43.4	53.5
Arson	2.8	33.8	16.0	54.0
Violent crime	23.2	52.7	76.4	118.1
Property crime	-6.1	-.7	14.3	40.3
All Index crime	1.1	6.2	21.2	45.3

Source: *Crime in the United States, 1996.* U.S. Department of Justice, Federal Bureau of Investigation, Washington, D.C., p. 219.

Not everyone agrees that females are becoming as criminal as males. The counterargument suggests that even though absolute rates of female crime have been growing, the increases are mainly due to very low levels in earlier years (Steffensmeier and Cobb, 1981; Steffensmeier and Steffensmeier, 1980). Thus, a group that commits 10 crimes in one year but commits 20 crimes the next (10 additional crimes) registers a 100 percent increase, while a group that commits 100 crimes in one year but 150 the next (50 additional crimes), registers only a 50 percent increase. On one hand it appears that the first group is gaining on the second group because the rate of increase is 50 percent greater (100 percent versus 50 percent), but the picture is different if the absolute number of crimes committed is considered. Hence, in the example, during the second year the first group commits only 20 percent as many additional crimes as group two (10 additional crimes versus 50 additional crimes).

While this debate cannot be definitively resolved, there are reasons to believe that both viewpoints have merit. Though the relative growth in female crime may be exaggerated, it is nonetheless clear that females are being arrested more frequently for crime than in the past, thereby contesting the dominance of males in this activity. Indeed, examination of trends in male-female rates of crime bring into sharp relief the import of several of the theories we will discuss in later chapters of this book.

The greater propensity of males for crime represents one of the "facts" of deviance, and this propensity also appears to extend to *deviant drug use*. For example, as shown in Table 9.5, men are more than three times more likely to have used marijuana than women, and approximately twice as likely to have used cocaine, inhalants, and stimulants. Generally, the gender ratio in favor of men is larger for drugs society regards as most dangerous. This pattern of male overrepresentation in serious drug use can also be gleaned from hospital emergency room data (National Institute on Drug Abuse, 1994).

Although the pattern is still clear, the male-female difference is much less pronounced among the young. A survey of high school seniors (Johnston et al., 1998) shows that females are as likely as males to report alcohol and marijuana use. The familiar pattern of excess deviance among males does appear when the more serious drugs of cocaine and heroin are examined, though even in this study the gender ratios favoring males are not as large as ratios for the general population. This difference between figures for high school students and those for the general population may indicate a change in trends for the future, or it may simply suggest that gender differences become more pronounced with age.

Table 9.5 **Estimated General Population Prevalence and Past Year Use of Drugs by Gender**

	Males	Females	Ratio
Alcohol			
Ever	88.4%	80.3%	1.1
Past year	71.8	62.4	1.2
Marijuana			
Ever	35.9%	11.3%	3.2
Past year	26.8	5.9	4.5
Cocaine			
Ever	12.9%	8.2%	1.6
Past year	2.4	1.1	2.2
Inhalants			
Ever	7.9%	3.9%	2.0
Past year	1.4	.7	2.0
Hallucinogens			
Ever	11.2%	1.9%	5.9
Past year	6.4	.7	9.1
Stimulants			
Ever	6.1%	3.2%	1.9
Past year	.9	.5	1.8
PCP			
Ever	3.6%	2.1%	1.9
Past year	.1	.1	1.0
LSD			
Ever	9.3%	1.1%	8.4
Past Year	4.9	.5	9.8
Heroin			
Ever	1.6%	.4%	4.0
Past year	.1	.1	1.0
Needle Use			
Ever	1.8%	.2%	9.0
Past Year	.7	.1	7.0

Source: *National Household Survey on Drug Abuse: Population Estimates 1994.* U.S. Department of Health and Human Services, 1995.

Deviant sexual activities are also differentiated by gender (Gosselin and Wilson, 1980; Janus and Janus, 1993; Laumann et al., 1994). According to the definition of deviance employed in this book, any sexual behavior that is generally disapproved in a social group or that evokes a collective response of a negative type is deviant. Since American society is complex and heterogeneous, not all forms of sexual expression are equally deviant or conforming in all parts of the country or in various segments of the population. Nevertheless, there is evidence that homosexual conduct, promiscuity, prostitution, adultery, bestiality (having sex with animals), various fetishisms (associating objects with sexual pleasure), sadomasochism (using physical abuse for sexual gratification), transvestism (pretending to be someone of the opposite sex), and molestation meet the criteria of deviance when the population of the United States as a whole is considered. In Chapter 8, in examining time trends in sexual deviance, we reported the percentage of adults who admitted homosexual behavior, extramarital sex, and forcing sex on someone else (Table 8.3). Those figures showed males exceeding females by almost two to one, but the differences in homosexual behavior appeared to be minimal for the most recent cohort.

Another component of what is generally thought to be "normal" sexual activity is having a limited number of sexual partners. When someone, either male or female (although the threshold is very likely different for the two genders), has a large number of sexual partners, he or she is to be regarded as promiscuous. Table 9.6 shows the reported number of sexual partners in the past year by respondents in the most recent and comprehensive sex survey. About 5 percent of the men reported having five or more sexual partners in the past year, while only 1.7 percent of the women reported that many. Men were, then, three times more likely than women to have five or more sexual partners in the past year. Furthermore, this difference cannot be a function of age or marital status, since among single persons between the ages of 18 and 25, 14.2 percent of the men reported five or more sexual partners while only 6.2 percent of the women did. Even among the most sexually active demographic group, then, men are over twice as likely as women to have a lot of sexual partners. The bottom panel of Table 9.6 also shows that the difference between men and women in the number of sexual partners is more general than their past year's behavior. When asked about the number of their sexual partners since age 18, 16.3 percent of the men reported 11 to 20 partners, and 16.6 percent reported having more than 21 sexual partners. The corresponding numbers for women were only 6 and 2.2 percent, respectively. The median number of sexual partners for men since age 18 was six, while it was only two for women. These gender differences prevail in other countries, such as Finland, the United Kingdom, and France (Laumann et al., 1994:191).

Table 9.6 Number of Reported Sexual Partners in Past Year

	0	1	2–4	5+		
Males	9.9%	66.7%	18.3%	5.1%		
Females	13.6%	74.7%	10.0%	1.7%		

Number of Reported Sexual Partners Since Age 18					
	0	1	2–4	5–10	11–20	21+
Males	3.4%	19.5%	20.9%	23.3%	16.3%	16.6%
Females	2.5%	31.5%	36.4%	20.4%	6.0%	3.2%

Adapted from Laumann et al., *The Social Organization of Sexuality: Sexual Practices in the United States*, Table 5.1A, p. 177, and Table 5.1C, p.179. The University of Chicago Press, 1994.

Men also differ from women in other dimensions of sexual activity that may be regarded as unacceptable by a majority. They are, for example, about three and one-half times more likely to masturbate once a week than women, are over twice as likely to use drugs before having sex or use adult movies to achieve sexual gratification, are over five times more likely to frequent nude clubs, and four times more likely than women to purchase erotic books and magazines (Laumann et al. 1994:82, 135). In addition, men are more likely than women to visualize sexual satisfaction in activities other than vaginal intercourse; that is, subjects were asked whether they thought they might enjoy the sexual practices listed in Table 9.7 (Laumann et al., 1994). The percentages of men and women who reported finding various sexual practices "very appealing" shows the standard pattern. Notice that as the sexual practice becomes more "different," or deviant, the greater the sex ratio becomes. Males, for example, are 12 times more likely to find group sex "very appealing." Since fantasies are not the same as reality, these figures may indicate nothing about actual sexual conduct. Nevertheless, since sex differences in these preferences track other gender differences, we might be safe in assuming that they indicate at least what men and women would do if given the opportunity, and perhaps what they have done.

Table 9.7 Percentage of Men and Women Who Found the Practice "Very Appealing"

Sexual Activity	Men	Women	Ratio
Vaginal intercourse	83.8	76.8	1.1
Watching partner undress	47.8	26.8	1.8
Getting oral sex	45.0	28.8	1.6
Giving oral sex	33.5	16.5	2.0
Group sex	13.3	1.1	12.1
Stimulating partner's anus	6.2	2.4	2.6
Using dildo	4.4	2.9	1.5
Watching sex	5.3	1.5	3.5
Sex with a stranger	4.1	0.9	4.5
Anal intercourse	2.8	1.1	2.5

Adapted from Laumann et al., *The Social Organization of Sexuality: Sexual Practices in the United States*, Table 4.2, pp. 152 and 154. The University of Chicago Press, 1994.

Moreover, actually reported homosexual behavior seems to be more prevalent among men than among women. Laumann et al. (1994:311) reported that men were over twice as likely as women to state that they identified themselves as homosexual (2 versus 0.9 percent), and over 50 percent more likely to identify themselves as bisexual (0.8 percent versus 0.5 percent). And men were almost twice as likely as women to report that they had actually had at least one homosexual experience at some time in the past (Laumann et al. 1994:295).

A final vantage on gender differences in deviance can be gained from official arrest statistics for sexual offenses. They indicate that, except for prostitution, males are arrested for sex crimes more often than females (*Crime in the United States*, 1996). And even for prostitution the disparity in favor of women arrested is not as great as one might expect—about 1.5 to 1. Approximately 60 percent of all prostitution arrests in 1996 involved the arrest of a woman, but 40 percent were arrests of males.

The evidence, then, suggests that with the exception of a few forms of sexual deviance, such as prostitution, males are more likely to engage in unacceptable sexual conduct than are females. This gender difference repeats that which exists for crime and deviant drug use, and it also extends to suicide. Recall (Chapter 3) that males have higher suicide rates than females. In the United States in 1995, for example, there were approximately 31,000 suicides, of which over 80 percent were committed by males. In fact, suicide was the ninth leading cause of death for males. The general age-adjusted suicide rate was 11.9 per 100,000 that year, while the male rate of suicide was nearly twice that at 19.8. Notice in Table 9.8 that the rate of suicide for men is far greater than that for women at every age, and is over six times greater between the ages of 15 and 24. The gender difference declines somewhat after age 25 but again increases in the 50s. By age 85, the male suicide rate is almost 12 times higher than for females. Clearly, suicide is more characteristic of males than females.

Table 9.8 Suicide Death Rate at Various Age Levels for Males and Females, 1995 (per 100,000 population)

| Ages | Death Rate | | Ratio |
	Males	Females	
5–14	1.3	0.4	3.25
15–24	22.5	3.7	6.08
25–34	25.6	5.2	4.92
35–44	24.1	6.5	3.71
45–54	22.8	6.7	3.40
55–64	22.0	5.3	4.15
65–74	28.7	5.4	5.31
75–84	44.8	5.5	8.14
85+	63.1	5.5	11.47

Source: National Center for Health Statistics, Centers for Disease Control and Prevention. *Report of Final Mortality Statistics, 1995.*

It is also true that males and females use different methods when they commit suicide. Vital statistics (Hoyert et al., 1997) show that males are far more likely than females to use firearms when they kill themselves; females, on the other hand, are more likely to use drugs. Since firearms are more lethal, this difference in suicide method may help explain why females attempt suicide more often while males are far more "successful" at it.

Summary

As suggested by the literature and as illustrated by the tables presented here, with few exceptions—probably those kinds of acts closely tied to the female role, such as prostitution—males are more likely to do deviance than are females. Why this is so is an interesting question. In subsequent chapters we will review various answers that have been proposed.

Age

The age distribution of deviance is not as consistent as the pattern for gender and deviance, since age variations seem to depend on the kind of deviance in question. For some kinds, youth are more likely to be offenders; for other kinds, middle-aged people seem more likely; and for still other types, the aged are most prevalent.

Such patterns can be seen in data for *crime and delinquency*. Youth apparently do more street crime, such as petty theft, burglary, and assault, than do older people, and middle-aged people commit more professional/occupational deviance and white-collar crime (Empey and Stafford, 1991; Hirschi and Gottfredson, 1983; Steffensmeier et al., 1989b; Sutherland et al., 1992: 152; Tittle and Ward, 1993). Table 9.9 shows the percent of each type of crime accounted for by arrests of young people of different ages. For the crimes that involve predation and strength, those under the age of 25 appear to be arrested more than those older. For example, nearly 65 percent of the arrests for robberies and burglaries are of those under the age of 25, and over one-half of all index crimes arrests are of persons 24 years of age or younger. For crimes involving more sophisticated opportunities, like forgery, fraud, and embezzlement, however, young persons make up a minority of arrestees.

Table 9.9 Percentage of Total Arrests Accounted for by Those of Various Ages, 1996

Offense	Under 15	Under 18	Under 21	Under 25
All crimes	6.1	19.0	32.2	45.2
Index crimes:				
Murder	1.8	15.0	36.3	56.2
Rape	5.8	17.0	30.0	43.5
Robbery	8.6	32.1	51.6	64.7
Aggravated assault	4.7	14.7	26.2	40.0
Burglary	14.0	37.0	53.6	64.2
Larceny/Theft	14.2	33.8	47.2	57.0
Motor vehicle theft	11.0	41.5	59.0	70.0
Arson	35.5	53.1	62.3	69.6
Violent crime	5.5	18.7	32.3	46.1
Property crime	14.0	35.2	49.5	59.5
All Index crime	11.8	30.8	44.9	55.9
Non-index crimes				
Stolen property	7.3	27.2	46.4	60.0
Weapons	7.3	24.4	42.0	57.3
Forgery	0.9	7.1	21.6	38.4
Fraud	1.7	5.8	16.1	32.4
Embezzlement	0.6	8.4	26.6	44.3
Drunkenness	0.5	3.3	11.2	23.5

Source: *Crime in the United States, 1996.* U.S. Department of Justice, Federal Bureau of Investigation, Washington, D.C., p. 230.

Self-reported studies of offending generally confirm the picture from official data—that street crime is predominately a pattern of behavior among the young. Table 9.10 shows the percentage of approximately 2,000 adult respondents (Tittle, 1980b) reporting their commission (or not) of nine deviant acts; the data are displayed for different age groupings. For seven of the acts there is a monotonically declining relationship with age. Those in the youngest age group (15–24 years) are the most likely to have committed each deviant act in the past five years, and those in the oldest age group (65 years and older) are the least likely. Two exceptions to this general age trend are illegal gambling and income tax cheating, for which the age group with the highest participation rate is 25–44.

Table 9.10 Respondents Admitting Having Committed Violations Within the Past Five Years (percentage)

Offense	Age			
	15–24	25–44	45–64	65+
$5 theft	46	23	10	2
$50 theft	16	7	3	2
Marijuana smoking	42	14	2	1
Illegal gambling	38	40	26	12
Assault	26	10	4	1
Lying to intimate	64	60	35	14
Income tax cheating	14	16	8	2
Sitting during anthem	36	12	6	3
Occupationally specific	59	47	24	9
Mean	38	25	13	5

Adapted from Tittle, Charles R., *Sanctions and Social Deviance: The Question of Deterrence*, Table 4.5, p. 90. New York: Praeger, 1980.

Even though age differences in criminal behavior seem to depend on the type of crime, there is a general tendency for involvement in most crime to be distributed by age in an inverted *j* pattern. Thus, most crime usually increases throughout the adolescent years, reaching a maximum in late adolescence or early adulthood. Thereafter it appears to decline steadily to the latest ages. The generality of this pattern, and its import for understanding deviance, however, has been the subject of much controversy.

Debate concerning age and crime has been stimulated mainly by Hirschi and Gottfredson (1983; and Gottfredson and Hirschi, 1990), who contend that the familiar inverted *j*-curve association between age and crime is invariant (the "invariance" contention) and inexplicable with social science variables (the "inexplicability" contention), and who further maintain that there is no interaction between age and any variable that explains or correlates with crime (the "noninteraction" contention); that is, the causes and correlates of crime are asserted to be the same at all ages.

These three contentions, or hypotheses, are important. If age and crime are related in constant ways across all conditions, and inexplicable except by the biology of aging itself (Gove, 1985), then the adequacy of numerous general social theories (examined later in this book) that imply an ability to account for age variations is in doubt and the importance of social, relative to biological, influences is potentially diminished.

An extensive review of the research evidence, by Tittle and Grasmick (1997), suggests that the shape of the curve representing the relationship between age and many kinds of crime for different populations is remarkably similar although the particular details of the relationships between age and crime for all offenses, social groups, points in history, and for all aspects of offending are not necessarily constant.

Whether relationships between age and various kinds of criminal behavior, can be explained with social scientific variables remains an open question. Although some studies are at least partially successful in accounting for age-crime relationships (see Greenberg, 1985; Warr, 1993), no attempt at empirical explanation has been fully satisfactory (see Kercher, 1987; Rowe and Tittle, 1977; Tittle and Grasmick, 1997). However, until more data concerning crime by those of various ages, as well as potential causes for it, are available, no conclusion can be drawn (Greenberg, 1981a; Steffensmeier and Allen, 1995).

The third Hirschi-Gottfredson age-related hypothesis, the one concerning noninteraction, has received the most attention (see for example, Shavit and Rattner, 1988; Tittle and Ward, 1993; Wolfgang et al., 1987). The evidence (see Tittle and Grasmick, 1997) suggests that while studies directly dealing with the noninteraction hypothesis are generally supportive, they are not strong enough to produce definitive conclusions, and studies with indirect evidence (e.g., Loeber et al., 1991; Nagin and Farrington, 1992a,b; Sampson and Laub, 1993; Smith, and Brame, 1994) show about equal amounts of support and contradiction.

More information is needed about the nature of age–crime relationships, whether they can be explained with social science variables, and whether the correlates and causes of crime interact with age. But for now one should note that patterns of age and crime—an inverted *j* for most crimes, particularly ordinary street crimes—are fairly stable; that they are of great theoretical importance and so will inform some of the later discussions in this book; but that they are only one aspect of age variations in deviance.

Drug use is also mainly a domain of the young, but it is not necessarily so for all drugs. Table 9.11 shows the percentage of each age category that reported using different drugs in the past year in the National Institute on Drug Abuse's National Household Survey (1997). About 19 percent of those between the ages of 12 and 17 and 25.3 percent of those between the ages of 18 and 25 reported some drug use in the previous year. These numbers declined to 14.3 percent for those between the ages of 26 and 34 and to 6.1 percent for those over the age of 35. And the greater prevalence of drug use among the young is not entirely due to marijuana, as some might think. When illicit drugs besides marijuana are examined as a whole, the age difference is still there. These data also show that members of the youngest age group (ages 12–17) are more likely to use the readily available but very dangerous inhalants. They are less likely to use both powder and crack cocaine than those between the ages of 26 and 34. Yet, even though those in the youngest age grouping are more likely to have used heroin than those much older, they are generally less likely than any other age category to have used alcohol and cigarettes.

Table 9.11 Percentage Using Different Drugs in Past Year, by Age

Drug	Age			
	12–17	18–25	26–34	35+
Any illicit drug	18.8	25.3	14.3	6.1
Any nonmarijuana	10.0	12.1	6.8	3.0
Marijuana	15.8	22.3	11.2	4.4
Cocaine	2.2	3.9	3.1	1.1
Crack	0.8	1.0	0.9	0.4
Inhalants	4.4	3.2	0.7	0.1
Hallucinogens	4.7	6.6	1.6	0.5
PCP	0.5	0.4	0.0	0.1
LSD	2.9	3.7	0.0	0.1
Heroin	0.3	0.5	0.2	0.2
Stimulants	1.7	1.5	0.7	0.5
Alcohol	34.0	75.1	74.6	64.1
Cigarettes	26.4	45.9	37.7	29.7

Source: National Institute on Drug Abuse, National Household Survey on Drug Abuse, 1997.

Overall, the data suggest that drug use is fairly low for those between the ages of 12 and 15; it generally rises until about age 20 and begins to decline steadily thereafter. The peak age for drug use differs, however, depending on the type of drug in question. For example, use of marijuana and cocaine peaks relatively early, by age 17. The peak years for cigarette smoking and binge drinking are a little later, between the ages of 18 and 20. But for all drug use, the peak period for use occurs before age 20.

Youth dominance in *sexual deviance* is also clear. We can get some clues about age and sexual deviance by considering the number of partners a person has had (Laumann et al., 1994). Having had five or more sex partners during the past year is a type of activity characteristic of younger persons. In fact, the difference between those between the ages of 18 and 29 and those 30 and older is quite striking (about 7 percent versus less than 1 percent). Other types of deviant sexual activities do not show such a stark pattern, though age differences are still clear. This is shown in Table 9.12, which reports the distribution of homosexual activity. Compared with older respondents, younger men are more likely to have had a homosexual experience, more likely to be attracted to people of the same sex, and more likely to find homosexuality appealing; also, they are more likely than older persons to identify themselves as homosexuals. Although this pattern is less pronounced among females, there is still a clear difference between women under and over the age of 50. A possible exception to this pattern, however, concerns fetishism, sadomasochism, and tranvestism, which are more likely to be practiced by those in middle age (Gosselin and Wilson, 1980).

Table 9.12 Homosexual Behavior and Attraction, by Age

Age	Any Homosexual Partner*		Same-Sex Attraction		Homosexual Identity	
	Men	Women	Men	Women	Men	Women
18–29	3.0	1.6	7.4	4.4	2.9	1.6
30–39	3.5	1.8	6.3	6.0	4.2	1.8
40–49	2.1	0.8	6.7	3.3	2.2	1.3
50–59	1.4	0.4	2.5	2.8	0.5	0.4

Adapted from Laumann et al. *The Social Organization of Sexuality: Sexual Practices in the United States*, Table 8.1, p. 303, and Table 8.2, p. 305. The University of Chicago Press, 1994.
*Within the past year.

We can also observe age differences in officially recorded acts of sexual deviance. Table 9.13 shows the number of arrests in 1996 for prostitution and for the category "sexual crimes" (which exclude rape and prostitution). The peak age category for arrests for sexual offenses is 15 to 19, and arrests decline steadily thereafter. Prostitution peaks later, between the ages of 30 and 34, but most arrests are for those under age 35.

Table 9.13 Total Arrests for Prostitution and Sexual Offenses by Age, 1996

Age	Arrest for	
	Prostitution	Sexual Offenses
Under 10	10	589
10–14	130	5,754
15–19	4,363	10,654
20–24	12,607	9,053
25–29	17,105	8,897
30–34	18,325	9,716
35–39	14,163	8,910
40–44	7,400	6,170
45–49	3,614	4,059
50–54	1,563	2,624
55–59	815	1,662
60–64	427	1,064
65+	514	1,467

Source:*Crime in the United States, 1996.* U.S. Department of Justice, Federal Bureau of Investigation, Washington, D.C.

Table 9.14 Suicide Death Rate by Age, 1995 (per 100,000)

	Age								
	5–14	15–24	25–34	35–44	45–54	55–64	65–74	75–84	85+
Rate	0.9	13.3	15.4	15.2	14.6	13.3	15.8	20.7	21.6

Source: Centers for Disease Control and Prevention, National Center for Health Statistics, *Report of Final Mortality Statistics, 1995.*

Though age patterns are fairly consistent for most forms of deviance, *suicide* is an exception. It appears to be fairly constant over most of the life cycle but with a marked upward trend in late age (Table 9.14).

Summary

Most deviance, then, is the province of the young, often those in late teens. A clear exception, however, is suicide, which shows little age differentiation until the later ages, and some forms of deviant sexual conduct, which are more likely for the middle-aged. These variations pose an interesting challenge for explanation and theory.

Minority Status

Although popular opinion suggests that those in minority positions, either racial or ethnic, are most likely to do deviance of all kinds, the evidence contradicts this generalization. Indeed, it appears that the relationship between minority status and deviance depends entirely on the type of deviance. While minorities are apparently more implicated in serious street crime, they are less implicated in occupational/professional or white-collar crime; while they are more likely to be users of opiates, they are less likely to consume barbiturates or cocaine. While minorities are more likely to engage in promiscuous heterosexual sex, they are no more likely to practice homosexuality and are less likely to try bestiality; and minorities are less likely to commit suicide than are members of majority groups.

If arrests are taken as indicative of actual *criminal behavior*, it appears that racial and ethnic minorities are substantially overrepresented in serious forms of street crime, less so for other forms of street crime, and underrepresented in arrests for drunk driving. Table 9.15 shows the racial composition of those arrested for serious and nonserious street crime. While blacks are less than 15 percent of the total United States population, with only two exceptions, they represent a far greater proportion of those arrested, and this overrepresentation is really quite large in the case of murder (54.9 percent), armed robbery (58.2 percent), and motor vehicle theft (40.2 percent). Only for drinking offenses does there appear to be no racial disparity. Thus, approximately one in three of those arrested for an index property crime is black, and 35 percent of those arrested for an index crime are black.

Table 9.15   Percentage of All Arrests for Various Crimes in 1996 Accounted for by Different Racial Categories

	Index Crimes				Non-Index Crimes		
	White	Black	Other		White	Black	Other
Murder	42.8	54.9	2.3	Simple assault	62.4	35.1	2.5
Forcible rape	56.1	41.6	2.3	Fraud	63.0	35.8	1.2
Armed robbery	39.8	58.2	2.0	Embezzlement	63.1	34.9	2.0
Aggravated assault	59.6	38.1	2.3	Prostitution	59.0	38.3	2.7
Burglary	67.9	29.8	2.3	Weapons	58.0	40.1	1.9
Larceny-theft	64.8	32.2	3.0	Drugs	60.4	38.4	1.2
Motor vehicle theft	56.6	40.2	3.2	Gambling	45.4	50.6	4.0
Arson	74.1	24.0	1.9	Drunkenness	81.1	16.2	2.7
Violent crime	54.6	43.2	2.2	Drunk driving	86.7	10.4	2.9
Property Crime	64.7	32.4	2.9	Disorderly	62.4	35.7	1.9
				Vagrancy	54.3	43.4	2.3
Total index crime	62.0	35.3	2.7				

Source: *Crime in the United States, 1996.* U.S. Department of Justice, Federal Bureau of Investigation, Washington, D.C., p. 232.

As noted in Chapter 8, arrest data are not necessarily good indicators of actual crime. This discrepancy occurs partly because of potential bias among individual police officers, partly because of deployment decisions by police departments, and partly because ordinary crime is more likely to be observed among those without much private space (such as would be the case for most minorities). Moreover, police data do not reflect most forms of white-collar and professional crime, which are recorded, if at all, in the files of regulatory agencies. As a result, researchers must rely on other kinds of information, such as that in Table 9.16, which shows the percent of each race admitting various crimes in a three-state survey. While nonwhites are more likely to have committed each of the offenses except occupational crime, the extent to which their numbers exceed those of whites is much less than in arrest data. And, of course, whites seem to commit a bit more occupational crime than the nonwhites.

Table 9.16 Percentage Admitting Having Committed an Offense in Past Five Years

Offense	White	Nonwhite
$5 theft	20	29
$50 theft	6	15
Marijuana use	14	22
Illegal gambling	31	35
Assault	10	13
Income tax cheating	11	15
Occupational crime	38	35

Adapted from Tittle, Charles R. *Sanctions and Social Deviance: The Question of Deterrence*, Table 4.3, p. 87. New York: Praeger, 1980.

These general patterns are confirmed in Table 9.17, which shows the percent of youth admitting various kinds of offenses, by race, from the National Youth Survey in 1983. Overall, racial disparities are greatest for the more serious kinds of crimes. For example, 1.6 times as many black youths as white youths admit at least one serious violent crime, and black youths on average, admitted over twice as many felony assaults as white youths. For index offending as a whole, black youths are more likely to have committed at least one offense, but the mean number of offenses is higher for whites (because their rate of property offending is so high). For less serious offenses, however, white youths generally have higher levels of participation and higher mean rates of offending.

There is also a greater propensity for minorities to use more dangerous drugs. One way to examine the relationship between minority racial status and *drug use* is to look at self-reports. Data from the National Institute of Drug Abuse Household Survey (1997) show that, with the exception of alcohol and cigarettes, participation in drug use is highest for black and Hispanic respondents and lower for whites. For example, 7.5 percent of black respondents admitted to using any illicit drug, while only 6.4 percent of white respondents did. Blacks were over twice as likely to use cocaine as whites, while Hispanic respondents were 1.3 times more likely. The disproportionate representation of blacks in serious drug use is vivid from the percent who report any use of heroin: 2.7 percent of black respondents reported that they had used heroin at some time in their lives; only 1.2 percent of the white respondents had ever used heroin; and only 0.8 percent of the Hispanic respondents had.

Table 9.17 Self-Reported Participation and Mean Level of Offending for White and Black Youth From the National Youth Survey, 1983

Offense	Percent White	Percent Black	Ratio[a]	Average White	Average Black	Ratio
Felony assault	6.1	9.9	1.62	107	236	2.21
Felony theft	7.6	9.4	1.24	470	176	0.37
Robbery	0.2	0.9	4.50	3	9	3.00
Index offenses	8.2	12.5	1.52	314	297	0.95
Minor assault	7.6	3.9	0.51	243	90	0.37
Minor theft	11.4	6.4	0.56	624	567	0.91
Vandalism	6.3	6.1	0.97	216	142	0.66
General delinquency	42.1	32.3	0.77	10,532	15,767	1.50

[a]Mean is rate per 1,000 and ratio is the ratio of black to white mean rate.
Adapted from Elliott et al., *Multiple Problem Youth: Delinquency, Substance Use, and Mental Health Problems,* Table 2.2, p. 33. New York: Springer-Verlag, 1989.

Another way to look at racial differences in serious drug use is to examine the death rates for drug-induced causes using records that are maintained by the U.S. National Center for Health Statistics. Consistent with what we have reported so far, these data show that both drug-induced and alcohol-induced deaths are more likely for racial minorities than for whites.

The racial minority pattern, however, is not upheld for most forms of sexual deviance. Table 9.18 shows the portion of each racial group that admitted having five or more sexual partners in the past twelve months, the past five years, and since age eighteen. Members of most minority groups were more likely than whites to have a large number of sexual partners. Blacks were more likely to have five or more sexual partners at each time window than either Hispanics or whites, and each of these three racial/ethnic groups is generally twice as likely as Asian Americans to have had five or more sexual partners.

Table 9.18 Percentage of Racial/Ethnic Groups Reporting Five or More Sexual Partners

	Past 12 Months	Past 5 Years	Since Age 18
White	2.7	12.4	42.0
Black	6.0	17.3	45.6
Hispanic	2.5	13.6	34.1
Asian	0.0	6.7	23.1

Adapted from Laumann et al., *The Social Organization of Sexuality: Sexual Practices in the United States,* Table 5.1A, p. 177, Table 5.1B, p. 178, and Table 5.1C, p. 179. pp. 177–178. The University of Chicago Press, 1994.

But the pattern is almost reversed for homosexual conduct. Table 9.19 shows that, compared with blacks and Asian Americans, whites and Hispanics are more likely to have experience with homosexual activity, be attracted to homosexual acts, and identify themselves as homosexual or bisexual. Perhaps the most telling piece of data is the fact that whites are twice as likely as blacks to identify themselves as being either homosexual or bisexual, and two and one-half times more likely than Hispanics.

Table 9.19 Sexual Experience With Same-Sex Partner and Appeal of Same-Gender (SG) Sex (percentage of all responses)

	SG Sex Since Puberty	Attraction of SG Sex	Identity as Homo-Bisexual
Males			
White	7.6	5.9	3.0
Black	5.8	5.3	1.5
Hispanic	8.8	13.3	3.7
Asian	0.0	14.3	0.0
Females			
White	4.0	5.1	1.7
Black	3.5	2.6	0.6
Hispanic	3.8	3.9	1.1
Asian	3.3	0.0	0.0

Adapted from Laumann et al., *The Social Organization of Sexuality: Sexual Practices in the United States*, Table 8.2, p. 305. The University of Chicago Press, 1994.

Similarly, *suicide* seems to be more characteristic of whites than of racial minorities. In 1995, suicide was the eighth leading cause of death among whites, and approximately 90 percent of all suicides were committed by whites. The death rates (per 100,000) of suicide for racial groups, by age levels, are reported in Table 9.20. First, notice that when age is ignored, the total death rate for suicide among whites (12.9) is almost double that for blacks (6.7) and others (6.9). In fact, in every age category the suicide death rate for whites is higher than the rates for blacks and other racial/ethnic groups. The suicide death rate for white males is the driving force behind the high overall white rate. Their suicide rates are substantially higher than all others. In fact, the overall suicide rate for white females (4.8) is lower than that for blacks or other groups (though slightly higher than that for females of other racial backgrounds).

Table 9.20 Suicide Death Rates (per 100,000) by Race/Ethnicity and Age, 1995

Age	White	White Males	Black	Other
5–14	1.0	1.4	0.5	0.6
15–24	14.0	23.5	10.1	10.7
25–34	16.2	26.8	11.7	11.6
35–44	16.5	25.8	9.3	8.8
45–54	15.9	24.6	6.9	6.8
55–64	14.4	23.6	5.7	6.3
65–74	16.7	30.3	7.3	8.3
75–84	22.1	47.5	6.8	7.8
85+	23.0	68.2	a	7.4
TOTAL	12.9	21.4	6.7	6.9

[a]Too few cases.
Source: National Center for Health Statistics, Centers for Disease Control and Prevention, *Report of Final Mortality Statistics, 1995.*

   ### Summary

The "facts" about minorities and deviance, then, are mixed. Minorities, especially blacks, appear more likely to be involved in ordinary crime but less involved in drunkenness or occupational white-collar deviance; they are more likely to use most, but not all, drugs; they are more likely to engage in sexual deviance of some kinds (unusual numbers of sex partners) but less likely to behave homosexually; and they are less likely to commit suicide. These patterns are especially interesting because they call into question various explanations that will be considered later. Since variations in deviance by race/ethnicity go in different directions, depending on the kind of deviance in question, they clearly challenge assumptions about biological causes and general racial inferiority (see Herrnstein and Murray, 1994), as well as those about the effects of economic deprivation.

Social Attachments

Unattached people appear to do more deviance than the socially attached. Social attachment refers to having strong social relationships or bonds with others. Such attachment can be with one person (married people are usually attached to their spouses), a few persons (parents are usually attached to children), or many people (active members of religious groups are attached to each other).

Table 9.21 Percentage of all Respondents Admitting Criminal/Deviant Acts, by Marital Status and Religious Activism

Offense	Marital Status			Religious Participation			
	Single	Separated or Divorced	Married	Never	Low	Med	High
$5 theft	41	28	17	27	23	21	15
$50 theft	13	13	5	10	7	6	5
Marijuana use	40	19	9	27	18	10	8
Illegal gambling	35	36	32	37	38	29	23
Assault	22	17	8	15	12	8	8
Lying to intimate	57	50	49	56	54	45	36
Tax cheating	11	19	12	13	13	10	9
Sitting/anthem	32	15	10	19	15	12	11
Occupational deviance	52	40	37	45	40	36	33
MEAN	34	26	20	28	24	20	16

Adapted from Tittle, Charles R., *Sanctions and Social Deviance: The Question of Deterrence*, Table 4.15, p. 120, and Table 5.8, p. 148. New York: Praeger, 1980.

This relationship between social attachment and deviance seems evident for *crime and delinquency*. It cannot be demonstrated easily, however, using official data, because most official records of crime do not include the suspect's marital status or other indicators of the strength of social relationships. Therefore, we must rely on survey data. Table 9.21 shows the percent of respondents in Tittle's 1972 three-state survey who reported committing each of nine different criminal/deviant acts, the data sorted by marital status and religious participation. Persons with weaker social attachments (the single and separated/divorced) are much more likely to report each of the acts than are those who are married. In addition, people less involved in religious activities are far more likely to do those acts than the more involved. When averaged across the offenses, those with no religious participation are almost twice as likely to be involved in some type of criminal/deviant act as those high in participation (28 versus 16 percent).

Not only are the less attached more likely to commit criminal acts, but they are also more likely to be *drug users*. In Table 9.21, 40 percent of the single but only 9 percent of the married respondents reported that they had smoked marijuana in the previous five years, and 27 percent of those with no religious participation admitted marijuana use relative to 8 percent of the high participants. Moreover, Tittle (1980b:162) reported that 26 percent of those who lived in communities whose spirit was rated as "low" (suggesting less cohesion and weak social bondedness) reported marijuana use in the previous five years, while only 9 percent of those in communities with "high" spirit had used marijuana.

Additional evidence about the relationship between social connections and drug use can be garnered from the National Household Survey (National Institute on Drug Abuse, 1997). Thirty-three percent of the youths who used marijuana at least once a week said that they did not get along with other kids, and 25 percent said that they were not liked by others. The corresponding percentages among the group of youths who had not used marijuana in the previous year was only 18.6 percent and 17.9 percent, respectively.

Finally, the rehabilitation literature suggests that treatment outcomes for people with drug problems are more favorable when there is marital stability and harmony (see the review by Caddy and Block, 1985).

Deviant sexual conduct is also more characteristic of the unattached. Perhaps it is obvious, but married people are less likely to be either homosexual or to have lots of sexual partners. Laumann et al.'s survey (1994:177), for instance, shows that those who have never married (but who have lived with a partner) are over six times more likely than the married to have had more than five sexual partners in the past twelve months.

Finally, *suicide* is most often done by socially isolated people. In his study of suicide rates in Europe in the nineteenth century, Durkheim (1951 [1897]) observed that in practically every age category, unmarried persons have higher suicide rates than the married. He attributed the higher rate for the unmarried to their being unconnected to social institutions, which meant that they had no one to rely on but themselves. Their unanchored, individualistic existence is both unhappy and freer from social constraints that might prevent suicide. Others have confirmed this. Gibbs and Martin (1964), for example, found that marriage insulates against suicide, though generally the insulation is greater for younger persons. Overall, their research indicated that the more integrated a person is occupationally, maritally, and socially, the lower the risk of suicide.

Maris's (1981) extensive research, too, found marriage providing a partial barrier to suicide; also, being integrated into any social network was a buffer. Table 9.22, from Maris (1981), shows that while only 33 percent of those who died of natural causes had no close friends, 49 percent of those who completed their suicides were friendless. Moreover, while 29 percent of those who died of natural causes had three or more persons they could designate as close friends, only 11 percent of those who completed suicide had three or more close friends. Those who died from natural causes and those who only attempted suicide were more socially integrated than those who completed their suicide.

Table 9.22 Percentage Having Close Friends in the Past Year by Type of Death

Number of Close Friends	Natural Death	Suicide Attempters	Suicide Completers
0	33	22	49
1	11	11	18
2	13	27	11
3 or more	29	35	11
Don't know	14	5	11

Adapted from Maris, Ronald W., 1981. *Pathways to Suicide*, p. 115. Baltimore: Johns Hopkins University Press.

Summary

The data are consistent in showing that socially bonded people, as indicated by such things as marriage, parenthood, and religious participation, are less likely to engage in a variety of deviant acts than are those less linked in social networks. Illustrations of this difference were pointed out using data for crime, drug use, deviant sexual activities, and suicide. A major exception to this general pattern, however, concerns deviance that reflects the normative standards of a social network itself. Individuals tightly knit with a set of people organized specifically for the practice of deviance, as were the Perfectionists and organized crime figures, are more, rather than less, likely to commit deviance—at least the kind associated with the group context itself. Later we will see that the relationships between social attachment and deviance have given rise to explanations and theories about social control as a major influence on behavior.

Place of Residence

In general, urban dwellers are more inclined toward crime and other forms of deviance than are residents of smaller places (Archer and Gartner, 1984; Clinard and Meier, 1992; Fischer, 1984; Sutherland et al., 1992:176–180; Tittle, 1989c). There are exceptions, however, and the relationship between size/type of settlement and deviance is complicated. Sometimes the relationship is not observed for specific types of deviance or in specific locales (Berman, 1973; Conklin, 1981; Krohn et al., 1984); at other times there is evidence of a reclining *j*-shaped relationship wherein rural areas show higher rates of particular forms of deviance than small towns or cities (Archer and Gartner, 1984; Tittle, 1989c). Some cross-cultural data actually show no association at all between violent crime and absolute size of place (Archer and Gartner, 1984), and some data call into question an association between growth or decline in population and changes in crime or deviance rates (Lodhi and Tilly, 1973).

For most *criminal acts*, especially serious ones, there appear to be higher levels in larger than in smaller places. Table 9.23 shows the distribution of criminal arrests by type of area (urban, suburban, and rural) in the United

States in 1996. It demonstrates that for all crimes, the arrest rate in urban areas (6,604 crimes per 100,000) is substantially greater than that in either suburban (4,135) or rural areas (4,431). Of particular note is the fact that the rate of arrest in urban areas is greater than suburban or rural areas for every serious (index) category.

Table 9.23 Rate (per 100,000) of Arrests for All Crimes and Index Crimes by Location, 1996

Offense	City Arrests	City Rate	Suburban Arrests	Suburban Rate	Rural Arrests	Rural Rate
All crimes	8,140,494	6,604.4	1,434,115	4,135.8	796,046	4,431.6
Index crimes:						
Murder	11,067	9.0	1,863	5.4	1,007	5.6
Rape	17,571	14.2	3,267	9.4	1,903	10.6
Robbery	104,995	85.2	9,777	28.2	2,112	11.8
Aggravated assault	293,681	238.3	53,353	153.9	21,768	121.2
Burglary	185,181	150.2	38,445	110.9	23,791	132.4
Larceny/theft	870,043	705.9	105,316	303.7	36,440	202.9
Motor vehicle theft	102,345	83.0	16,862	48.6	6,471	36.0
Arson	9,833	8.0	1,910	5.5	1,130	6.3
Index violent	427,314	346.7	68,260	196.5	26,790	149.1
Index property	1,167,402	947.1	162,533	468.7	67,832	377.6
Total index	1,594,716	1,293.8	230,793	665.6	94,622	526.8

Source: *Crime in the United States, 1995–1997.* Uniform Crime Reports, Federal Bureau of Investigation, pp. 235, 244, 253. U.S. Department of Justice, Washington, D.C.

These size-of-place variations may, of course, reflect the biases inherent in arrest data. Yet self-reports from The National Youth Survey conducted by Elliott (Elliott et al., 1989:Table 25), indicate that, in general, youth from urban areas admit more crime than do rural youths. Although the place variations are not as dramatic as in official data, this discrepancy may happen because self-reported offenses are not usually as serious as those in official police data. Nevertheless, type and size of place of residence represent important dimensions along which criminal conduct varies.

Deviant drug use is also more characteristic of urban than of nonurban residents. Uniform Crime Reports shows arrests for drug offenses and public drunkenness to be almost twice as high in urban areas as in nonurban areas (though this is not true for driving while intoxicated) (*Crime in the United States,* 1996, Tables 44, 50, and 56). This general pattern is confirmed by self-reports. According to survey data from the National Institute on Drug Abuse (1997), virtually every kind of drug use is more frequent in urban than in nonurban areas. Moreover, in Tittle's (1980b) three-state study of adults, those living in urban areas (19 percent) reported smoking marijuana in the past more than those in small towns (11 percent) or the "open country" (10 percent). And in their survey of a national sample of youth, Elliott et al. found higher levels of participation and frequency of drug use in urban than in rural areas (1989:Table 2.5).

In a similar fashion, acts of *sexual deviance* seem to be clustered in urban areas. The arrest rate for rape, prostitution, and other sexual crimes by location (*Crime in the United States,* 1996, Table 31) shows that rape arrests are about twice as likely to occur in larger metropolitan areas as in smaller areas. Other sexually deviant criminal acts follow a similar pattern, although the progression by each increment in size is not perfectly monotonic. For example, in 1996 the arrest rate for prostitution was 60.7 per 100,000 in urban areas, a figure almost seven times higher than the rate in suburban areas (9 per 100,000), and over sixty times higher than that in rural areas (1 per 100,000).

This trend is consistent for homosexual activity as well (Laumann et al., 1994:304). The greatest likelihood of having a same-sex partner is for current urban dwellers (in what Laumann et al. call the "top 12 central cities"), and the lowest rates are for rural dwellers. In fact, with few exceptions, there is a fairly consistent monotonically declining percent of respondents reporting homosexual activity from the most populated places of residence to the least, though the pattern is more marked for men than for women.

These differences might reflect migration to urban areas of those with homosexual interests, who are seeking greater tolerance. But those who lived in urban areas in early adolescence, before they could choose their own place of residence, were also about twice as likely to have had some previous experience with a homosexual partner as those who lived in rural areas. Thus, although part of the reason urban areas have higher rates of homosexual conduct than less populated ones may be migration of those with particular sexual preferences, that is not the only reason.

Interestingly, the usual pattern of deviance and size of place does not hold for at least one kind of deviance—*suicide*. Some studies show higher suicide rates in urban areas; others reveal higher rates in rural areas; and still others have found no urban-rural differences (see Lester, 1992, 1997a). These inconsistencies suggest a possible curvilinear relationship between suicide and size of place, wherein rates are elevated in very rural and very urban areas. But because most of the available data are for states, it is difficult to confirm such a relationship. It is true that some generally rural states like Montana and Wyoming have very high suicide rates, while more urban states like New Jersey and Ohio have very low rates, but this may represent some confounding with region. For example, rural states like Nebraska and Kansas have lower suicide rates than more urban states like Florida and Washington. When states within regions are examined, it appears as if suicide rates in urban areas are actually slightly lower than those in more rural states. For example, in the Northeast, suicide rates are lower in the urban states of Connecticut and Rhode Island than in the more rural states of Maine and New Hampshire. In the Midwest, suicide rates are higher in more rural states like North and South Dakota than they are in more urban states like Minnesota and Michigan. Overall, then, there seems to be no consistent relationship between size of place and suicide.

Summary

The relationship between larger size of place and deviance is frequently observed, but it is not as clearcut as many assume. While the general pattern is there, the association is not great; it does not hold for all kinds of deviance; and there are irregularities in the pattern. These data, then, present a challenge for theories to explain the overall size-deviance relationship but at the same time allow for exceptions and irregularities.

Socioeconomic Status

Variations in deviance by socioeconomic status appear to depend on the type and seriousness of deviance. The relationship between crime/delinquency and SES is somewhat controversial, but the pattern of deviant drug use seems fairly well established, with lower-status people being more likely to use opiates and higher-status people being more likely to use cocaine and alcohol. Deviant sexuality shows a mixed picture, with homosexuality being about equally distributed across the statuses, but "swinging" being more of a middle- and upper-status phenomenon. Finally, those in lower statuses are less likely to take their own lives than higher-status people.

One of the most controversial issues in the study of *crime and delinquency* is the extent to which there are social-class differences in offending (see Braithwaite, 1981; Clelland and Carter, 1980; Hagan, 1992; Kleck, 1982; Nettler, 1978, 1985; Stark, 1979; Thornberry and Farnworth, 1982; Tittle, 1985a; Tittle and Villemez, 1977; Tittle et al., 1978, 1979, 1982; Wright et al., 1999). We can only provide some data relevant to the debate, and suggest some tentative conclusions.

The most relevant research uses self-reported rather than official data, mainly because official data sources rarely include information about socioeconomic status. This deficiency has led some researchers to examine the connection between the average socioeconomic status in geographic areas (which can be determined from census data) and crime rates in those areas (which can be aggregated from police files), in order to infer the connection between individuals' socioeconomic status and crime. This approach, however, is methodologically suspect, partly because geographic areas are not socioeconomically homogeneous, but also because ecological correlations like this often provide inaccurate estimates of individual-level associations (Langbein and Lichtman, 1978).

Some self-reported data are presented in Table 9.24. It shows the percent of offenders and the mean rate of offending for youths from two social strata, middle and lower, in Elliott et al.'s (1989) National Survey of Youth (NYS). A tendency for those of lower social class to report more serious criminal and delinquent offending is evident, but the relationship does not hold for less serious violations. For example, while 9.6 percent of the lower-class respondents admitted engaging in felony assault, only 2.9 percent of the middle-class respondents self-reported any involvement in this crime. For the most serious offenses as a whole, lower-class youth (11.9 percent) were over twice as likely to report some involvement as middle-class youth (5.2 percent). The differences in the mean rates of offending for serious crimes are even more striking. For example, lower-class youths admit nearly four times more felony assaults than middle-class youths, and over one and one-half times more felony thefts.

However, for three common delinquent acts—minor assault, minor theft, and public order offenses—a greater percent of middle-class youths than lower-class youths report that they have committed at least one offense. Only for the offense of vandalism does the percent of lower-class youth exceed the percent of middle-class youth who admit committing at least one act. For General Delinquency, middle-class youths are more likely to have committed at least one minor type of delinquent act than are lower-class youths (45.7 versus 38.0 percent). But even for these less serious acts, lower-class youths committed 1.75 more offenses than did middle-class youths. Thus, the SES-crime connection appears strong among young people for serious offenses but much weaker, or nonexistent, for less serious offenses.

Table 9.24 Percentage of Offenders and Mean Level (per 1,000) of Offending for Youths in Middle and Lower Class in the NYS, 1983

	Middle Class (percent)	LowerClass (percent)	Ratio[a]	Middle Class (mean)	Lower Class (mean)	Ratio
Felony assault	2.9	9.6	3.31	54	206	3.81
Felony theft	6.3	9.3	1.48	246	391	1.59
Robbery	0.0	0.2	—	0	2	—
Index offenses	5.2	11.9	2.29	219	362	1.65
Minor assault	7.8	6.2	0.79	147	270	1.84
Minor theft	12.3	9.4	0.76	585	799	1.36
Public disorder	58.6	42.4	0.72	7,474	7,032	0.94
Vandalism	5.8	7.5	1.29	121	193	1.59
General delinquency	45.7	38.0	0.83	8,858	15,547	1.75

[a]The ratio of participation (mean) rates of lower-class to those of middle-class youth.
Adapted from Elliott, Delbert S. et al., *Multiple Problem Youth: Delinquency, Substance Use, and Mental Health Problems*, Table 2.3, pp. 38, 39. New York: Springer-Verlag, 1989.

Table 9.25 shows the relationship between social class and self-reported criminal offending for a sample of adults from Tittle's (1980b) three-state study. For these (most of which are less serious) criminal acts, there is no relationship between social class and offending since those at the highest socioeconomic level are as likely as those at the lowest level to have committed the acts in question at least once.

Table 9.25 Percentage of Adults Involved in Self-Reported Offending by Social Class

Offense	Socioeconomic Status Level				
	5 (High)	4	3	2	I (Low)
$5 theft	22	22	21	23	16
$50 theft	9	8	6	7	4
Illegal gambling	28	33	35	34	30
Assault	11	9	11	13	9
Income tax cheating	9	9	11	15	15
Occupational crime	32	36	40	46	40

Adapted from Tittle, Charles, R., *Sanctions and Social Deviance: The Question of Deterrence*, Table 4.8, p. 102. New York: Praeger, 1980.

In sum, the evidence seems to indicate a tendency for youths on the lower rungs of the socioeconomic ladder to commit more serious criminal and delinquent offenses than youths on the middle and upper rungs of that ladder but not necessarily more of the less serious offenses. And if crime/delinquency overall is examined, there appears to be only a small relationship between SES and offending (see Tittle et al., 1978; Tittle and Villemez, 1977; Tittle and Meier, 1990), with no relationship between SES and criminal behavior among adults. In addition, though there are few systematic data, research suggests that white-collar and professional crime is almost exclusively a middle- or upper-status phenomenon (Coleman, 1994; Friedrichs, 1996; Simon, 1999), no doubt because lower-status people have no opportunity for this type of crime.

Inconsistencies in the SES/deviance relationship are also apparent with respect to *deviant drug use*. Table 9.26 shows the association between drug-related offenses and social class in Elliott et al.'s nationally representative sample of youth. While the percent of youths from each of the two social classes involved in drug use and in driving while intoxicated are comparable (in fact, the preponderance of one social class over the other changes from offense to offense), the frequency of involvement favors youths from the lower rather than the middle class (for four of five offense categories the ratio of lower- to middle-status youth exceeds one).

Table 9.26 Percentage of Youths Using Drugs and Mean Frequency (per 1,000) of Drug Use for Youths in Middle and Lower Class in the NYS, 1983

	Middle Class (percent)	Lower Class (percent)	Ratio[a]	Middle Class (mean)	Lower Class (mean)	Ratio
Alcohol use	92.6	85.2	0.92	63,289	52,994	0.84
Marijuana use	39.0	43.9	1.13	17,040	40,536	2.38
Polydrug use	24.6	19.1	0.78	5,593	9,767	1.75
Drug abuse	5.7	9.3	1.63	9.01	8.98	1.00
DUI/DWI	52.1	40.4	0.77	11,856	24,773	2.09

[a]The ratio of participation (mean) rates of lower-class to those of middle-class youth
Adapted from Elliott, Delbert, S. et al., *Multiple Problem Youth: Delinquency, Substance Use, and Mental Health Problems*, Table 2.3, pp. 38, 39. New York: Springer-Verlag, 1989.

Table 9.27 Sexual Preferences by Education and Gender

Education	Attraction for Group Sex M	F	Actual 5+ Sexual Partners M & F	Actual Homosexual Contact M	F
Less than High School	13.2	0.8	2.5	4.5	4.9
High School grad or equivalent	11.4	1.2	2.5	2.7	2.7
Some coll/voc.	15.2	0.9	4.0	5.3	3.8
Finished coll	15.5	1.4	3.5	6.9	5.8
Masters/adv deg	8.3	1.8	3.0	4.9	4.1

Compiled from Laumann, Edward O. et al., *The Social Organization of Sexuality: Sexual Practices in the United States*, Table 4.2, p. 153, Table 5.1A, p. 177, and Table 8.1, p. 303. The University of Chicago Press, 1994.

This problematic relationship appears to characterize deviant *sexual conduct*, as well, although general information about class distributions of deviant sexual activities is rare. Some studies of unconventional sexual behavior such as "swinging" (mate swapping), fetishism, sadomasochism, and transvestism are of middle- or upper-class populations (Bartell, 1971;

Breedlove and Breedlove, 1964; Gosselin and Wilson, 1980; Walshok, 1971).
Homosexuality (Bell and Weinberg, 1978; Warren, 1974) may be more evenly
distributed over the class spectrum. The Laumann et al. study (1994) of human sexuality does not report specific sexual practices by general measures
of social class, although it does report various activities by education, which
some regard as a good proxy for SES. Table 9.27 shows preference for group
sex, having had five or more sex partners in the past twelve months, and same
gender sexual contact since age 18, by education. That table suggests no consistent class differences, although there does seem to be a general tendency
for the more highly educated to be more likely to have larger numbers of sex
partners and to have had homosexual contacts.

Indeterminacy also appears to apply to *suicide*. The relationship between
individuals' social status and suicide generally shows that those of higher status are more prone to suicide than those of lower status (Moscicki, 1995),
though there is some contrary evidence (Kitagawa and Hauser, 1973;
Labovitz and Hagedorn, 1971; Maris, 1969; Platt, 1984, 1986; Stack, 1982).
This micro-level relationship, however, does not necessarily generalize to the
macro level. Comparison of suicide rates between rich and poor states of the
United States does not show a clear pattern. For example, the suicide rate in
poor states like Mississippi (11.8 per 100,000 in 1994) and Arkansas (14.8) is
higher than in more affluent states like New York (8.2) and Connecticut (9.9).
But there are important regional, cultural, and perhaps religious differences
among these states in addition to differences in general wealth. Moreover,
other relatively affluent states have suicide rates more like those in Mississippi and Arkansas, such as Wisconsin (11.6) and California (11.8). In addition, some relatively poor countries have some of the lowest suicide rates in
the world, such as Italy (7.1 in 1992), Spain (6.6 in 1992), and Portugal (7.1),
while others have very high rates, such as Bulgaria (15.9), Hungary (33.5),
and Russia (41.7). Again, a comparison of rich and poor nations in order to
draw conclusions about individual SES level and suicide is hazardous because many of the relatively poor countries are also predominately Roman
Catholic. Yet other poor Roman Catholic countries, such as Poland (14.8),
have somewhat high suicide rates. Furthermore, many of the countries that
in the 1990s had high suicide rates were experiencing much economic, political, and cultural transformation (former Eastern-bloc countries and those of
the old Soviet Union). This suggests that suicide rates are high whenever lives
are in turmoil and anomie prevails (Durkheim, 1951 [1897])—conditions
that may have indirect connections with SES.

Summary

The relationship between socioeconomic status and deviant behavior is
not consistent and appears to depend on the kind of deviance in question.
While lower-class youths appear to commit more serious crime, they are not
necessarily more likely to commit less serious crime. There does not appear
to be a relationship between SES and crime among adults, perhaps because
higher-status people are more likely to commit white-collar and professional
crime, while those of lower status are more likely to do serious street crime.
The connection between lower status and drug use may be clearer, at least for
the less expensive or more addictive drugs. However, the evidence tips in the
other direction for sexual deviance and suicide. These varied patterns, then,
pose a challenge to theories about deviance, many of which assume it to be almost exclusively a lower-class phenomenon.

Geographic Location

People often assume great variations in deviance among different regions of the United States and among different countries of the world. Some of those assumed variations are real and substantial, particularly rates of violence, but the differences are mostly among geographic regions that are very diverse culturally and economically. Where geographic areas are similar in level of modernization and economic development, surprisingly few variations in deviance can be found. This applies to the states of the United States, where the main regional variations concern crime, especially violence.

Regional Variations

Contrary to popular belief, New England states have the lowest rate of serious *crime*, with southern and western states having substantially higher overall rates. Rates of all crimes are highest in the South; the violence rate is about 30 percent higher there than that in the Midwest, and property crime is about 50 percent greater than in New England (*Crime in the United States,* 1996).

Table 9.28 Crime Rates (per 100,000) by Region of the Country, 1996

Region[a]		Index	Violent	Property
Northeastern				
	New England	3,777.9	447.1	3,330.9
	Middle Atlantic	3,940.9	593.3	3,347.6
Midwest				
	East North Central	4,765.6	592.1	4,173.5
	West North Central	4,424.1	405.5	4,018.6
South				
	South Atlantic	6,081.8	777.8	5,304.0
	East South Central	4,580.3	562.2	4,018.1
	West South Central	5,783.9	671.1	5,112.8
West				
	Mountain	5,863.9	516.6	5,347.3
	Pacific	5,400.8	758.0	4,642.9

[a]New England: CT, ME, MA, NH, RI, VT; Middle Atlantic: NJ, NY, PA; East North Central: IL, IN, MI, OH, WI; West North Central: IA, KS, MN, MO, NE, ND, SD; South Atlantic: DE, DC, FL, GA, MD, NC, SC, VA, WV; East South Central: AL, KY, MS, TN; West South Central: AR, LA, OK, TX; Mountain: AZ, CO, ID, MT, NV, NM, UT, WY; Pacific: AK, CA, HI, OR, WA. Source: *Crime in the United States, 1996,* Table 4. Uniform Crime Reports. Federal Bureau of Investigation, U.S. Department of Justice. Washington, D.C.

Table 9.28 shows a detailed regional breakdown. For general index offenses, the highest rates are found in the South Atlantic states (Delaware, Washington, D.C., Florida, Georgia, Maryland, North Carolina, South Carolina, Virginia, and West Virginia) and the lowest, in the New England states (Connecticut, Maine, Massachusetts, New Hampshire, Rhode Island, and Vermont). Rates of violent crime are also highest in the South Atlantic states, with the Pacific states (Alaska, California, Hawaii, Oregon, and Washington) not far behind. Violent crime rates are lowest in the West North Central states (Iowa, Kansas, Minnesota, Missouri, Nebraska, North Dakota, and South Dakota). Within the Pacific region, rates of violent crime vary considerably, being particularly high in the coastal states but low in the mountain states (Arizona, Colorado, Idaho, Montana, Nevada, New Mexico, Utah, and Wyoming). Property crime rates are highest in both the Mountain states and the South Atlantic states and low in the New England and Middle Atlantic states (New Jersey, New York, and Pennsylvania).

Unlike crime, according to the national survey conducted by the National Institute on Drug Abuse (1997), adults in the South have the lowest reported rates of *drug use* (except for binge drinking). There is, however, no particular clustering of drug use in one region of the country. For example, while cocaine use is highest in the western United States, marijuana and alcohol use are highest in the North Central states. Marijuana use and binge drinking are lowest in the Northeast. Another national study of drug use, the Monitoring the Youth Survey conducted by a team of social scientists at the University of Michigan (Johnston et al., 1998), also shows minimal regional variation.

There do appear to be substantial regional variations in *sexual deviance*, with rapes known to the police ranging from a low of 13.2 in the Northeast to a high of 38.6 in the South (*Crime in the United States*, 1995:59). However, the clustering apparently depends on the kind of sexual deviance, because the South, which has the highest rape rate, shows the lowest rate of arrest for prostitution and for sex offenses other than rape and prostitution (*Crime in the United States*, 1995:209).

Regional differences also show up for *suicide*. Rates are very high in a few Western states, such as Nevada and Wyoming, where they are 23.4 and 22.5 (per 100,000), respectively; low in New Jersey (7.3) and Illinois (9.1); and consistently low in the District of Columbia (5.1) (*Statistical Abstract of the United States*, 1997). Suicide rates generally are higher in rural states, which, in addition to Nevada and Wyoming, include Alaska (20.0), Arizona (18.8), and Montana (18.5), and lower in more urban states like New Jersey, Illinois, Ohio (7.1), and Connecticut (9.9). Moreover, it appears that suicide rates overall are higher in the Western and Pacific Coast states, and lower in the Midwest and New England.

Mobility

Interest in a potential connection between geographic mobility and various behaviors has a long history in the social sciences. The predominant assumption has been that individual mobility, particularly movement from one society, or culture, to another, leads to deviant or criminal behavior (Cowgill, 1961), and numerous explanations have been developed to account for this putative association. Yet the empirical evidence is weak and contradictory (see Tittle and Paternoster, 1988). Some studies find such a relationship and others do not.

Illustrative of studies finding a general association is that by Tittle, whose three-state survey yielded the data presented in Table 9.29. There, mobility is measured by the number of counties the person has lived in within the preceding 10 years. Those who had lived in the same county for the whole time were, of course, classified as having low mobility. Those who had lived in two or three counties were classified as having moderate mobility, and those having lived in more than three counties were categorized as having high mobility. Note that those with low mobility report less deviance of all types than those with medium or higher mobility. Highly mobile respondents were twice as likely to report theft and almost three times as likely to report marijuana smoking as those with low mobility.

Table 9.29 Geographic Mobility and Percentage Admitting Having Committed Various Deviant Acts Within the Past Five Years

	Mobility		
	Low	**Medium**	**High**
$5 theft	16	30	32
$50 theft	5	10	10
Marijuana smoking	10	21	28
Illegal gambling	28	38	34
Assault	8	15	17
Lying to intimate	40	56	66
Income tax cheating	9	15	13
Sitting during anthem	10	18	27
Occupational deviance	32	46	54
Average	18	28	31

Adapted from Tittle, Charles, R., *Sanctions and Social Deviance: The Question of Deterrence*, Table 5.5, p. 138. New York: Praeger, 1980.

Data about geographic mobility related to other unacceptable conduct, such as sexual deviance and suicide, are sparse, but indirect evidence concerning associations between those acts of deviance and other variables usually connected with mobility, such as being socially unattached, suggest the likelihood that they too are connected with mobility, at least under some conditions (see Stack, 1980).

Summary

While there are some substantial regional variations in deviance, those variations are not consistent across kinds of deviance. Crime seems higher in the South and West and suicide somewhat more prevalent in parts of the West, while the South has low rates of drug use and some sexual deviance but high rates of other deviant behavior. In addition, the West and rural areas have higher suicide rates than other regions. Geographic mobility, too, is somewhat uncertainly related to deviance, although it seems to be positively associated with most forms of deviance under some conditions.

Personal Variations

Intelligence

The association between IQ (measured intelligence) and deviant behavior is variable and uncertain, depending on the type of deviance in question. For example, it appears to be present and negative for crime, weak and curvilinear for drug use, positive but limited to only some kinds of sexual deviance, and quite uncertain for suicide.

Many early criminologists, including Lombroso (1876), Goddard (1914), Healy (1915), and Hooton (1939), hypothesized or asserted a relationship between intelligence and *criminal behavior* (see Jacoby, 1994). This claim, however, has been exceptionally controversial because measures of intelligence may be biased, especially in that the tests may tap elements that are part of the cultural stock of white, middle-class people (the same class as the inventors of the tests). Certainly the idea that IQ measures something innate has been challenged by evidence that IQ changes over the life cycle and by the fact that average scores are rising too quickly to reflect genetic change. Moreover, many believe that IQ tests reflect learned rather than innate characteristics, thereby serving as a mere proxy for education (see Devlin et al., 1997; Fischer et al., 1996; Gardner, 1999; Gould, 1995; Kamin, 1995; Wahlsten, 1997).

Regardless of what it actually measures, IQ does seem to be linked to the probability of criminal behavior. For example, from an extensive review of the literature and some analysis, Hirschi and Hindelang (1977) concluded that while "normals" have an average IQ of 100, the average for delinquents is about 92. In one analysis of a sample of youths from Contra Costa County, California, they found that about 23 percent of the white youths in the lowest 20 percent of the IQ distribution were arrested two or more times, compared with only 6 percent of those in the upper 20 percent of the distribution. For black youths, those at the lower end of the distribution were about twice as likely to have two or more arrests. In their reanalysis of the Wolfgang Philadelphia cohort data (Wolfgang et al., 1972:62, 93), Hirschi and Hindelang found that differences in IQ scores between repeat offenders and nondelinquents ranged from nine to fourteen points. In West and Farrington's Cambridge Study in Delinquency Development (1973:84–85), approximately half of the boys with low IQ scores (IQs of 90 or less) had a police record; only 25 percent of those with high IQ scores (scores of 110 or higher) did. Overall, Hirschi and Hindelang (1977:574) estimate that the difference in IQ scores between nondelinquents and repeat offenders is approximately 12 points.

Such data on this question are somewhat suspect, however, because actual lower intelligence as well as lower measured IQ could lead to more arrests rather than indicate a greater propensity for misbehavior. The less intelligent may be less clever in avoiding the police (see Cullen et al., 1997), and those with lower IQ scores may be relegated to vocational tracks in school, leading to expectations for misbehavior (Menard and Morse, 1984). Yet self-report data generally show the same relationship with IQ (Hirschi and Hindelang, 1977:577; Lynam et al., 1993; Ward and Tittle, 1994). Therefore, the evidence, both for adults and youths, and using a variety of measures of IQ, indicates that the relationship between crime and delinquency and IQ is persistent (Henry and Moffitt, 1997; Quay, 1987; West and Farrington, 1973; Wilson and Herrnstein, 1985), though not large.

Table 9.30 Percentage of Drug Use in Past Month by Level of Education

Education Level	Any Drug	Marijuana	Cocaine	Alcohol	Binge Drinking
Less than HS	6.8	5.2	0.8	38.0	14.4
High school	6.0	4.8	0.7	54.0	16.4
Some college	6.9	5.5	0.8	58.2	17.9
College	3.8	3.0	0.7	66.6	15.2

Source: *National Household Survey on Drug Abuse: Main Findings, 1996*. National Institute on Drug Abuse, 1997.

Information about a possible relationship between IQ and other forms of deviance such as *drug use* is more difficult to obtain. The two large national surveys discussed thus far, the USIDA's National Household Survey and the Monitoring the Future Study, do not provide direct information about IQ. However, if we assume education to be a reasonable proxy for IQ, we can bring some indirect information to bear. The National Household Survey data concerning education and drug use are reported in Table 9.30.

The data show neither a strong nor a consistent relationship. In fact, there appears to be a weak curvilinear relationship. Those with less than high school have high levels of cocaine, "any drug," and marijuana use, while those with some college also have high levels of "any drug," marijuana, and cocaine use, as well as binge drinking. With some exceptions, drug use among those who have completed high school is generally lower than that in most groups.

The dearth of information is also evident with respect to IQ and *deviant sexual activities*, but attained education can be used as an indirect proxy for IQ. Recall that previously, in Table 9.27, we examined data concerning deviant sexual activities and education, taking education as a proxy for socioeconomic status. We concluded that there are no consistent class differences, although there is some tendency for the more highly educated to have larger numbers of sex partners. Thus, if having an education implies higher IQ (as well as higher SES), then we can draw a similar conclusion here—those with higher IQs may have more sex partners, but otherwise there does not appear to be a connection between IQ and deviant sexuality.

The relationship between intelligence and *suicide* is also somewhat uncertain. One study by White (1974) found that among adolescents, those who attempted suicide had low scores on IQ tests compared with the general population. However, an overall conclusion is not clear because research by Shaffer (1974) suggests that youths who committed suicide were above average in IQ. Further, in a study of attitudes toward suicide, Stillion et al. (1984) found that females who scored high on their IQ tests were less likely to agree with expressed reasons for suicide than those with lower IQ scores. This might suggest that suicide committers are of lower IQ, but there is no direct evidence on this point. At the macro level, Lester (1996) found a positive relationship between attained education and suicide. He reported that nations whose populaces have higher levels of education also tend to have higher levels of suicide, holding other variables, such as economic, cultural, and political characteristics of the country, constant. But as noted before, ecological correlations are not very revealing about individual behaviors, because in countries with generally higher education, those who actually commit suicide may be those with lower educations. This is clearly an area where more research is needed.

Summary

IQ is sometimes related to deviant behavior and sometimes not; and when it is related, the form or direction is not consistent. The clearest and most persistent pattern is that for crime and delinquency, for which there is a negative relationship.

Personality

The personalities of those who do deviant behavior are popularly thought to be different from those who do not. The evidence, however, suggests a mixed picture. It is uncertain whether criminals have unusual personalities, although users of illegal drugs, especially the most dangerous drugs, do seem to be differentiated. Data about sexual deviance and suicide are inconsistent or contradictory. Some data show personality differences for perpetrators of some kinds of unacceptable sex acts but not for others, and research on suicide fails to clearly identify recurrent personality characteristics of those who take their own lives.

Consider *crime and delinquency*. In a study of 500 delinquents and nondelinquents, the Gluecks (1950) reported several personality differences between the two sets of subjects. The delinquents were more anxious, assertive, extroverted, and impulsive. Other research has also identified some so-called personality differences between offenders and nonoffenders, such as poor socialization and self-control, though generally only on subscales of overall personality instruments (Arbuthnot et al., 1987; Wilson, and Herrnstein, 1985). For example, Megargee and Bohn (1979) found that adult offenders had elevated scores on a Psychopathic Deviate subscale of the Minnesota Multiphasic Personality Inventory. However, the MMPI was constructed on the basis of such distinctions in the first place, so the results are not very meaningful.

Impulsivity is the personality characteristic that has received the most attention. Since the 1930s when S. D. Porteus developed the Maze Test for impulsive behavior, adult and juvenile criminal offenders have often been found to have higher levels of impulsivity and poor self-control (West and Farrington, 1977; White et al., 1994; Wilson and Herrnstein, 1985). Yet, even impulsivity has not been shown to consistently predict criminal behavior (Arbuthnot et al., 1987). For example, in the White et al. (1994) research cited earlier, a measure of cognitive impulsivity was only weakly related to delinquency.

Confirmation of the inconclusive relationship between personality and crime is provided by general summaries (meta-analyses), at different historical points, of the entire body of research on personality and crime. Three such studies have failed to reveal any consistent differences between offenders and nonoffenders in personality (Schuessler and Cressey, 1950; Tennenbaum, 1977; Waldo and Dinitz, 1967).

Despite this, some recent, very credible research has shown a connection between some personality characteristics and criminal/delinquent offending. Caspi and his colleagues (1994; Moffitt et al., 1995) found negative emotionality and weak constraint to be related to delinquent offending, across genders, ages, and countries. Negative emotionality involves alienation, anger and aggression, and stress. Weak constraint is essentially low impulse control. However, while consistent, the reported correlations between the two personality dimensions and delinquent offending were only weak to moderate.

Other recent data concern emotional makeup and crime. In addition to self-reported offending, Elliott and his colleagues (1989) obtained information about youths' perceptions that family and friends thought of them as having emotional problems. These youths with ascribed emotional problems more frequently reported they had committed a delinquent/criminal offense than those without such problems, and this was particularly true for more se-rious forms of offending (pp. 64–65). Still, the issue of causal order is unre-solved, and it is unclear whether the offenses led to emotional problems or vice versa.

Overall, then, the connection between personality and crime or delin-quency is uncertain. Some very strong data suggest such an association, at least for two characteristics, but general summaries of the literature do not permit a strong conclusion.

The situation is clearer for *drug use*. A substantial body of literature shows some personality attributes to have a consistent and strong relation-ship with drug use (Cox, 1985; Gerstein and Green, 1993; Lang, 1983). They include "antisocial personality," sensation seeking, rebelliousness, self-ab-sorption, and personal competence (Cloninger et al., 1997; Cox, 1985; Smith and Fogg, 1978). Viewed collectively, the deviant drug user appears to be self-concerned, with a limited time horizon, and with an interest in immediate and easy gratification—traits that bring to mind someone with an impulsive personality. Recall that impulsivity is one of the few traits that are also impli-cated in crime and delinquency. In addition, research by Zuckerman (1979) and Huba et al. (1981) shows that those with disinhibitions, attraction to new experiences or thrilling events, and who are easily bored are more likely to use alcohol and drugs. However, it is not clear whether those characteristics resulted from drug use or produced it in the first place. In addition, while sen-sation seeking and impulsivity have been implicated in drug use, the evidence about other personality attributes such as depression, emotional distress, or alienation are inconsistent (see Cox, 1985, and Gerstein and Green, 1993, for reviews of this literature).

A rich clinical literature (based on reports of therapists treating people who are referred or seek help) (Dorr, 1998; Langevin et al., 1978; Stone, 1993; von Krafft-Ebing, 1965) links particular personality or emotional attributes and particular kinds of *deviant sexual activities*, though there is probably no such thing as a sexually deviant personality. "Mild" forms of sexually deviant activities (for example, sexual promiscuity) probably involve no real psycho-logical aberration, but the probability of psychological problems increases as the activity becomes more deviant (child molestation or sexual fixations, for example).

Clinicians have generally concluded that serious sexual deviance is symptomatic of an underlying personality disorder (Caprio, 1955). Freud, for example, thought that sexual deviance reflects the person's failure to success-fully maneuver through one or another of the stages of psychological devel-opment. A person who is frustrated during one or another of the developmen-tal stages may suppress conflicts into the subconscious. Such fixations may later cause sexual and other problems (Hall, 1954). Alfred Adler observed that women, having learned from cultural expectations that they are the weaker sex, may become promiscuous, using sex to manipulate men, and the psychiatrist Karen Horney believed that parental hostility may generate an intense feeling of anxiety and powerlessness, which later manifests itself in neurotic sexual symptoms (Oliver, 1967).

Others have suggested that specific forms of sexual deviance are the product of particular psychological abnormalities (Howitt, 1995). Wilson and Cox (1983), for example, argue that pedophiles (those who are sexually attracted to children), transvestites (those who identify with members of the opposite sex), and masochists (those who derive sexual pleasure from pain) are characterized by extreme introversion. Child molesters have been diagnosed as emotionally immature, with passive-aggressive personalities that produce sociopathic tendencies. Sexual disinterest and inability to enjoy sex has been linked to masochistic and narcissistic feelings; and homosexuality is often attributed to a passive/submissive personality (Oliver, 1967).

Unfortunately, there are few nonclinical data (from surveys or reliability-checked diagnoses of large, random samples of a population) linking personality types or attributes to specific types of sexual deviance. This lack of nonclinical data is especially noteworthy because psychiatric diagnosis is notoriously subjective and unreliable. Research by Hooker (1957), for example, showed that a group of psychologists and psychiatrists could not distinguish between the personality profiles of heterosexuals and homosexuals.

And despite extensive research, few personality traits have been shown consistently associated with either completed or attempted *suicides* (Lester, 1983). Three traits often appear among suicidal people—impulsivity, depression/hopelessness, and "anti-social" (Moscicki, 1995). But it is not clear whether depression and hopelessness are personality traits or simply risk factors. It is true, however, that those who think about, attempt, and complete suicide usually feel despair and self-doubt (Maris, 1981; Stillion and McDowell, 1996). In a study of suicides among patients in New York State Hospitals, Maris (1981) found mental disorders with the highest rates to be involutional melancholy and manic-depression. About 30 percent of the suicidal patients suffered from severe depression, and over half had moderate or severe bouts with depression. Feelings of hopelessness and desperation were even more strongly correlated with suicide attempts and completions.

Recent research by Plutchik and Van Praag (1997) shows impulsivity to be strongly correlated with suicide; this relationship coincides with findings by Stillion and McDowell (1996) linking suicide with antisocial personality disorder. It appears that impulsive persons—because they are self-centered, seek easy and immediate gratification, and are risk seeking—have a greater chance of suicide than the less impulsive. Moreover, the relationship between impulsivity and suicide is roughly of the same magnitude as that between impulsivity and violence. This conclusion fits with information presented earlier, and together such data suggest that impulsivity, or sensation seeking, is implicated in a rather wide sweep of deviant behaviors.

Summary

Despite popular belief, associations between personality and deviant behavior are generally uncertain, weak, or dependent on the specific kind of deviance in question. There is no one personality trait or attribute that is implicated in diverse types of deviant acts. Of the four forms of deviance we are using as illustrations, only users of the most dangerous drugs and those who engage in the most extreme forms of sexual deviance seem to have remarkable personalities.

Religiosity

Unlike IQ and personality, which show complicated and erratic relationships with various kinds of deviance, low religiosity consistently predicts most forms of deviance; that is, the greater the religiosity, the less the deviance.

This is certainly true for *crime and delinquency*. In a review of research existing in the early 1980s, Tittle and Welch (1983) found that of 65 published studies concerning the association between a measure of religiosity and some indicator of rule breaking, 85 percent showed that the greater the religiosity, the less the misbehavior, at least under some conditions. Although many of these studies lack scientific rigor, Tittle and Welch nevertheless concluded that they show the relationship between religion and crime to be one of the strongest in the field of criminology.

In his three-state study, Tittle (1980b) examined the association between religiosity and several different kinds of self-reported misbehavior among adults. His measures of religiosity included both the denomination and the amount of involvement in religious activities. Protestants, especially evangelicals, were less likely to report criminal and other deviant behavior in the past than either Catholics or those of "Other" faiths (non-Christian and undifferentiated Christian religions). Table 9.31 indicates that an even more important factor than type of religion is participation in religious activities. Those who "never" participated in religious events were generally almost twice as likely to have committed a deviant act as those who were highly involved. Tittle (1980b) found that the influence of religious denomination was eliminated when the extent of involvement was controlled, suggesting that the crucial factor in conformity is how extensively a person participates in religion. And recent research (Evans et al., 1995) confirms the importance of religious participation.

Table 9.31 Percentage Admitting Involvement in Various Deviant Acts in Past Five Years, by Degree of Religious Participation

Offense	Never	Low	Medium	High
$ 5 theft	27	23	21	15
$ 50 theft	10	7	6	5
Marijuana smoking	27	18	10	8
Illegal gambling	37	38	29	23
Assault	15	12	8	8
Tax cheating	13	13	10	9
Lying to intimate	56	54	45	36

Adapted from Tittle, Charles, R., *Sanctions and Social Deviance: The Question of Deterrence*, Table 5.8, p. 148. New York: Praeger, 1980.

The research evidence also indicates that *drug use* is more likely among those not involved in religion. In fact, the relationship between religion and drug use is probably even stronger than that for crime and delinquency (see Albrecht et al., 1977; Evans et al., 1995; Grasmick et al., 1991; Hadaway et al. 1984; Tittle and Welch, 1983, for reviews). For example, Tittle (1980b:148) found that those who never attended church were about four times more likely to have smoked marijuana in the past five years than those whose religious participation was "high." In addition, in their study Elifson et al. (1983) used six different measures of religion: (1) parent's church attendance, (2) the youth's own attendance, (3) importance of religion, (4) a belief in life after death, (5) a belief that God answers personal prayers, and (6) a measure of religious orthodoxy. They found a negative correlation between each indicator of religion and several different measures of delinquent offending and drug use. For each of the six religion indicators, the (negative) correlations with alcohol and marijuana use were higher than for any other measure of delinquent offending.

Table 9.32 Percentage Likely to Do Sexual Deviance, by Religious Denomination

	Group Sex Appealing		Had Same-Sex Partner*		5+ Sexual Partners**
	M	F	M	F	
Denomination					
None	17.0	2.0	10.7	9.7	5.8
Liberal Protestant	11.8	1.0	5.3	4.0	2.4
Conservative Protestant	10.0	0.8	3.3	3.5	3.0
Catholic	15.7	1.1	2.8	2.5	2.7
Jewish	—[a]	—[a]	5.0	6.7	3.6

[a] Too few cases.
* Since age 18.
** In past 12 months.
Adapted from Laumann, et al., *The Social Organization of Sexuality: Sexual Practices in the United States*, Table 4.2, p. 153, Table 8.1, p. 302, Table 5.1A, p. 177. The University of Chicago Press, 1994.

The general trend is also evident for *deviant sexual activities*. Table 9.32 shows the percent of different religious groups that probably do deviance, from Laumann et al. (1994). For most kinds of deviant sexuality the highest prevalence rates are for those who admit to no religious affiliation. For example, the proportion of respondents who reported a same-sex encounter is about twice as high for those who had no religious affiliation as for others. Indeed, for both men and women, the agnostic is substantially more likely to be in the "deviant" category than are the members of any organized religion. And the type of religion does not appear to be as strongly related to deviant sexual practices as the frequency of participation in religion (p. 305). Those who never attended religious events (even if they admit to a religion) were substantially more likely than attenders to identify themselves as homosexual or bisexual, and to have engaged in sexual activity with someone of the same sex.

The same pattern characterizes *suicide*. The first systematic student of suicide and religion examined suicide rates by geographic area and concluded that Protestantism is less effective than Catholicism in preventing suicide (Durkheim, 1951 [1897]). Durkheim found (p. 152), for example, that the average suicide rate in several Protestant countries was 190 per million inhabitants, but in Catholic countries it was only 58. In countries where neither religion predominated, the suicide rate was 96 per million. Durkheim interpreted this to imply that religious beliefs and social ties constrain individuals from suicide when they encounter difficulties. But because Protestant faiths are more centered around the individual, with fewer beliefs in common, people are freer to follow their personal inclinations.

Both individual and ecological research conducted since Durkheim has confirmed his suspected link between Catholicism and low suicide rates. For example, Dublin (1963) found that foreign-born American citizens who came from predominately Catholic countries (such as Ireland and Poland) had generally lower suicide rates than those who were born in predominately Protestant countries (such as Germany and Sweden). And in the 1990s, suicide rates in Catholic countries like Spain and Portugal were lower (6.6 and 7.1 per 100,000, respectively) than those in Protestant countries like Sweden (14.7) and Germany (13.8); also, suicide is less likely in both Roman Catholic and Muslim countries than in Protestant countries (Lester, 1996). But one should be careful using aggregate comparisons because some Catholic countries (such as Poland) have much higher rates of suicide than some Protestant countries (such as the Netherlands).

Nevertheless, individual-level data support the general relationship. In Chicago and New York, Maris (1969, 1981:248) found that suicide rates for white Protestant males and females were at least twice those for Catholics. Rates of suicide for Jewish men were comparable to those for Protestant men at young ages and to Catholic men at older ages, while rates for Jewish women were more comparable to the low rates of Catholic women at all ages.

From data collected in Chicago and from a representative sample of the U.S. population, Maris (1981:251–252) also found a relationship between church attendance and suicide, although it is curvilinear. Those who commit suicide are more likely to have attended church sometimes, but less likely to have attended regularly than are those who die a natural death.

Summary

Although low religiosity (religious belief, practice, and association with other believers/practitioners) is not always connected with deviance, it is highly likely to be. Indeed, this relationship represents one of the most consistent in the field of crime/deviance.

Family Structure and Process

Consistent with popular opinion, aspects of childhood family life also show fairly consistent, though not very large, associations with later deviant behavior. However, the relevant family features are not necessarily consistent from study to study or from one form of deviance to another.

Inconsistency is the case, first, for *crime and delinquency*. The Gluecks (Glueck and Glueck, 1950) concluded that family factors are among the most important determinants of juvenile delinquency. However, "family factors" can include many different things; families can be "broken" by divorce or death, they can include criminal parents, they can fail to supervise, they can be the context for abuse, or they can simply fail to prepare children for successful lives. To say only that family factors are related to crime and delinquency is not very revealing—it is important to specify the particular aspects of families that are associated with illegal conduct.

One family factor is "completeness"—whether there was a single parent for some or all of the period of childhood (in popular terminology, was the home "broken"?). There is some intuitive appeal to the idea that delinquents, and ultimately criminals, are more likely to come from homes where there are fewer than two biological parents. And the results of numerous studies have tended to confirm the notion, even though they are somewhat inconsistent and provide less support than the layperson would expect (see reviews in Wells and Rankin, 1986, 1991; and Loeber and Stouthamer-Loeber, 1986). Loeber and Stouthamer-Loeber's (1986) review of the research showed that in 40 of 50 studies (83 percent), evidence linked broken families and delinquency. Similarly, in their review of approximately 50 studies, Wells and Rankin (1991) concluded that delinquency in broken families was somewhere between 10 and 15 percent higher than in intact families. Many of the studies have concluded that broken families tend to produce delinquents more often than intact families because the families fail to supervise or to adequately socialize children.

One reason the relationship between broken homes and delinquency is not stronger may be because of inattention to how the home is broken. A home with a father absent because of divorce may have a different effect than one where the father has died. A key factor may be parental discord and conflict rather than the mere absence of one or both parents. Research tends to support this speculation. Nye (1958), for example, found that boys who lived in broken homes were less delinquent than those who lived in unhappy but intact homes, as did McCord (1982).

Lack of supervision of the child seems to be one of the most consistent and strongest predictors of delinquency (Rankin and Wells, 1990). The work of Glueck and Glueck (1950) was instrumental in bringing the importance of supervision to the attention of social scientists. In their original work and in the reanalysis of their data by Laub and Sampson (1988), closely supervised youth were far less likely to be delinquent in subsequent years. When official contact (with justice personnel, such as police officers) was used as the measure of delinquency, Patterson and Stouthamer-Loeber (1984) found that 21 percent of the nondelinquents in their sample were poorly monitored by their parents; 50 percent of those who offended once or twice were poorly supervised; and 73 percent of the multiple offenders were poorly supervised by their parents. When the measure of delinquency was based on self-reports, the relationship persisted, with the percent of poorly supervised children at 10, 30 and 76 percent, respectively. Hirschi (1969) also found parental supervision to be strongly related to crime. While 55 percent of the least-supervised youths had committed two or more delinquent acts, only 12 percent of those at the strictest level of supervision had committed that much delinquency. Further evidence of the importance of parental supervision in delinquency can be found in the review by Loeber and Stouthamer-Loeber (1986). Out of 11 studies of the relationship between parental supervision and delinquency, 10 found a significant association.

Finally, families may produce delinquents by neglecting to socialize their children or by failing to provide good role models. A number of specific family factors can be subsumed under these designations. Research has shown, for example, that an important element in the delinquency of children is the criminality of parents (Glueck and Glueck, 1950; Loeber and Stouthamer-Loeber, 1986). Emotionally cold parents or those who reject their children are also more likely to have delinquent children than are accepting, emotionally connected parents (Hirschi, 1969; McCord et al., 1961; Patterson and Stouthamer-Loeber, 1984). Other child-rearing practices that have been shown to be related to delinquency include overly strict or inconsistent parental discipline (Glueck and Glueck, 1950; McCord et al., 1961; Nye, 1958) and childhood abuse or neglect (Widom, 1989).

Family factors may also be related to adult deviance. Among the most delinquent individuals, an emotionally satisfying and stable marriage that occurs later in life is related to desistance from crime (West, 1982; Sampson and

Laub, 1993). Those with fewer criminal propensities, however, may be better able to pick good marriage partners.

The modest but persistent association of family factors with crime and delinquency is repeated for *deviant drug use*, mainly because researchers often employ general measures of offending that include drug use. Though it is sometimes difficult to cull out specific relationships between family factors and drug use, it is clear enough that the stronger the family, the less likely and the less frequent is drug use (Bachman et al., 1978; Elliott et al., 1989; Kandel et al., 1978).

Connections between family factors and *deviant sexual behavior* are less certain. Studies generally emphasize that very unusual sexual behavior is associated with deep-seated family conflict or aberration early in life, such as overbearing, rigid, or neglectful parents, or the use of excessively strict or lax discipline (Caprio, 1955). Bieber (1962), for example, links homosexuality with an assertive and overbearing mother and a passive father, and lesbianism has been attributed to "penis envy" brought about by an absent or neglectful father. Widom (1989) has connected deviant sexual behavior as an adult with the experience of sexual victimization in the family. But since most of the evidence is clinical in nature, it is difficult to draw solid conclusions about family life and deviant sexual practices. For example, Bell et al.'s (1981) survey research using snowball sampling (one respondent identifies the next and so on) found few family-related factors in the backgrounds of the homosexuals studied, and Gosselin and Wilson's (1980) study of members of deviant organizations found mixed results. Thus, even though there may be some linkage of disrupted families with sexual deviancy, there are probably just as many individuals who experience interrupted, conflicted family lives without becoming sexual deviants.

Research is clearer in the case of *suicide*. Having a suicide in one's family significantly increases the risk of one's own suicide. Maris (1981:76), for example, reported that 11 percent of the suicides he studied came from families where someone had committed suicide, compared with none for those whose death was by natural causes. As an illustration, he related the story of the Nobel-prize-winning novelist, Ernest Hemingway, who committed suicide in 1961 and whose physician-father also committed suicide. Maris (1981:165-166) notes that Hemingway's mother sent his father's suicide gun to him as a Christmas present. Moreover, three of the elder Hemingway's children killed themselves, and one of the granddaughters of Ernest Hemingway also killed herself. Maris's research in general revealed that suffering early childhood trauma (for example, losing a parent by death or divorce, alcoholism, mental illness, or foster care placement) and experiencing multiple family problems (adultery and sexual problems) increased one's risk of suicide. Other research confirms that trauma and disruptions of family and marital life are related to suicide (Dorpat et al., 1965; Jacobs, 1971; Orbach et al., 1981; Wright, 1985; Zilboorg, 1937; for a review of this literature, see Lester, 1997a:39–46).

Summary

As one might imagine, most of the research shows an association between some aspect of childhood family life and later deviant behavior. In the case of crime/delinquency and drug use, the most important such factor seems to be lack of supervision, while sexual deviance and suicide seem more closely related to family conflict and poor child rearing.

Peer Involvement

Group influence on some kinds of deviance is well established, as the examples reviewed in Chapters 4 and 5 suggest, but not all forms of deviance show such influence, which is why we refer to those forms as individualized forms of deviance. Moreover, peer influences may come into play even when there is little social organization among practitioners of particular kinds of deviance, as when adolescents smoke cigarettes in order to acquire prestige among other adolescents generally. In more intimate contexts, the import of "peer pressure" is well known, and we will discuss it in later chapters. For now, we are concerned with the extent to which there is a relationship between the deviance of individuals and deviance among their peers. Evidence suggests that such a relationship is strong for some forms of deviance like crime, delinquency, and drug use, is less strong for other forms like sexual deviance, and is almost nonexistent for still others like suicide.

One of the most robust "facts" in criminology is the association between having peers or close associates who commit *crime or delinquency* and one's own offending (see Akers, 1994; Reiss, 1986, 1988; Warr, 1993; Warr and Stafford, 1991). Virtually every study addressing this relationship has found a strong positive association between peer misbehavior and personal misbehavior. Elliott's National Survey of Youth (Elliott et al., 1989) demonstrates this general association. Table 9.33 shows the percentage of youths who had committed specific offenses at least once in the past year arrayed according to whether they had friends who also committed the act in question. While 33 percent of the youths with friends who committed petty theft also reported committing petty theft in the past year, only 5.5 percent of those without delinquent friends did so. Those with friends who stole, therefore, were six times more likely to have stolen themselves than those without thieving friends. And this relationship holds for all the items in the NYS study, and is also present among adults (Tittle, 1980b:96).

Table 9.33 Percentage of Youths Who Report That They Committed the Act at Least Once, by Whether They Had Delinquent Friends

Offense	With Delinquent Friends	Without Delinquent Friends	Ratio
Petty theft	33	5.5	6.0
Theft over $50	25	0.8	35.2
Assault	25	3.5	7.1
Vandalism	24	2.6	9.3

Compiled from Wave 1 data of the National Youth Survey, Elliott et al., 1989. *Multiple Problem Youth: Delinquency, Substance Abuse, and Mental Health Problems*. New York: Springer-Verlag.

This persistent finding has raised important questions about whether peers help produce misbehavior or whether misbehaving people select friends and associates who also misbehave (Elliott and Menard, 1996; Warr and Stafford, 1991). Those same questions pertain to drug use (Britt and Campbell, 1977; Ginsberg and Greenley, 1978; Kandel, 1978, 1980) because an abundant literature suggests that peers' *drug use* and one's own use are linked (see Jessor and Jessor, 1977; Kandel, 1978; Jessor et al., 1991). Table

9.34, from Elliott and his colleagues' (1989) National Youth Survey, provides some evidence. Those with friends who smoke marijuana are almost five times more likely to use the drug than those without marijuana-using friends. Those with drinking friends are twice as likely to drink and over nine times more likely to get drunk than youths whose friends do not drink. Although some part of these relationships for delinquency and drug use appear due to deviance-prone people selecting like-minded companions, there is also considerable evidence that peers also help produce misbehavior. Why this is so is explored in subsequent chapters.

The peer connection is less clear for deviant sexual conduct, partly because the evidence is scarce. It does appear, however, that some kinds of deviant sexuality are related to peer behavior. Sanday (1990), for example, argues that date rape and sexual manipulation on college campuses are due primarily to a supportive culture existing within the male student body generally, but more specifically, within the fraternity community. She contends that college men encourage sexual dominance by perpetuating rape myths and by actively participating in sexual games of domination and sexual manipulation. Cowling (1998:35) also notes that some rape is group linked. Further, group support and learning are a likely requirement for other deviant sexual activity, such as various kinds of "perversions," swinging, prostitution, and homosexual behavior, so one could expect a general relationship between a person's own engagement in those activities and such acts by peers. The peer relationship appears less often for deviant acts that are almost universally condemned, such as rape and pedophilia (Harrison and Gilbert, 1996).

Table 9.34 Percentage of Youths Who Report That They Committed the Act at Least Once, by Whether They Had Delinquent Friends

Offense	With Delinquent Friends	Without Delinquent Friends	Ratio
Marijuana use	69.9	14.9	4.7
Drinking beer	96.1	45.8	2.1
Getting drunk	54.6	5.8	9.4
Selling drugs	24.9	1	24.9

Compiled from Wave 1 data of the National Youth Survey, Elliott et al., 1989. *Multiple Problem Youth: Delinquency, Substance Abuse, and Mental Health Problems.* New York: Springer-Verlag.

There is little evidence of a general relationship between *suicide* and peer influence, since suicide is most often an individualistic act (see Chapter 3). There are, however, some outstanding exceptions, including several well-documented instances of mass suicides where a group of people, often led by a charismatic leader, have *en masse* committed suicide. There are also cases of group-influenced or contagious suicide.

Summary

Deviance among individuals and deviance among their peers appears to be strongly linked for crime, delinquency, and drug use, but less strongly so for sexual deviance. Such an association does not exist for suicide.

General Summary

Scholars search for regularities in phenomena of interest and then attempt to explain them (answer questions of why and how), either in ad hoc fashion or within larger, more abstract theories that apply to the phenomena of interest as well as to other phenomena. The patterns that cry out most loudly for explanation are those showing a clear difference among individuals or other units of analysis. Such differences are usually observed as associations, or relationships. Thus, if tall people are more likely than short people to be rude in a grocery line, we would say there is a patterned difference in rudeness, which then needs explanation. However, it is more meaningful to determine whether such differences occur in increments all along the continuum of height rather than occurring just for two categories, tall and short. If there are incremental differences, we would say that height and rudeness are related, and how closely they are related can be expressed statistically. In this chapter, we have examined a number of potential associations between various social variables and deviant behavior of different kinds. The relationships that have been established by researchers, then, are the main things that must be explained by the accounts and theories we will examine later.

Three variables in particular are strongly and consistently related to deviant behavior of many types—gender, social attachment, and religiosity. Therefore, we would expect social scientists to have been heavily concerned with those relationships. In addition, another variable, aspects of childhood family life, is usually, though not always, related to deviance. The challenge for students of deviance is even more pressing for variables that are inconsistently associated with deviance. Some variables are associated sometimes with deviance, but they may be associated in one direction for some forms of deviance and the opposite direction for other forms, or they may be related strongly to a given form of deviance in some studies but not related at all in other studies. In this connection, age is of particular interest because peak ages for deviance depend on the kind of deviance in question—whether street crime (late teens), white-collar crime (middle age), or suicide (aged).

There are also interesting variations for minority/majority status. Sometimes majorities are more likely to do deviance (such as suicide and homosexual conduct in the United States) and sometimes less likely (such as sexual promiscuity and addictive drugs). In a similar way, those who dwell in larger urban places are sometimes more likely to do deviance (such as crime) and sometimes they aren't (such as suicide). And variations by socioeconomic status and peer behavior are even more complicated, often showing negative associations for some deviance (serious street crime) and positive associations for other deviance (suicide). Furthermore, variables like geographic location, IQ, and personality show some selective relationships with particular forms of deviance but are not generally and consistently associated with deviance.

Therefore, the answer to the question, "What must students of crime and deviance explain?" is: "An awful lot." The explanatory agenda is far more complicated than one might initially imagine, so the challenge is clear. In the remaining chapters of this book we will describe those explanatory efforts and then leave it to you to decide if scholars have successfully met that challenge. ✦

Part II

Explanations of Deviance and Crime

No matter how deviance and crime are defined, and no matter what particular acts are deemed to be deviant or criminal, it is clear that some people commit specific acts of deviance or crime while others don't, that people differ in the frequency with which they commit various prohibited acts, and that individuals differ in the variety of offenses that they commit. The obvious question, then, is: "Why do people differ with respect to deviant or criminal behavior?" The search for an explanation—an answer to the question of why—is almost universal because human beings are interpretive animals— they seek to understand the world about them and to bring meaning to their experiences. Hardly anybody just observes or describes a bank robber, for example. Most people want to know why the robber did it, and many want to know why robbers in general do it. The answer is not as obvious as "in order to get money"; if it were, we would all be robbers. Similarly, an act of murder rarely escapes efforts to understand why it occurred. The urge to explain is illustrated in popular accounts of deviant or criminal behavior: "he just wanted something for nothing"; "she's crazy"; "he came by it honestly since his father was a crook too"; "the devil made her do it"; "he was under a lot of stress"; "the temptation was just too great"; and a host of others.

The social scientist also seeks to explain deviant and criminal behavior. Explanations formulated by scholars, however, differ in several ways from those set forth by laypersons. First, scholarly explanations are more disciplined; that is, the serious student of deviance is forced to think through the implications of his or her explanation while the layperson is free to express opinions about cause "off the top of his or her head" without fear of later being held accountable to the facts. Second, scientific explanations are designed to be general rather than ad hoc. The layperson can dismiss a particular bank robber as "crazy," but the scholar must wonder whether "craziness" is an adequate explanation for all bank robbery and if not, under what conditions it does apply. Finally, the scientist strives to understand acts of deviance within a logically organized system of explanatory principles called a theory. If "craziness" is offered as an explanation for bank robbery, it should be couched in a theory that accounts for "craziness" itself, spelling out why some people have it and some don't. In addition, the theory is expected to show how and when "craziness" eventuates in bank robbery rather than some other form of behavior. The successful theory not only provides an explanation for a particular bank robbery but it does so by treating this instance as a case of a more general pattern of behavior of which robbery is an instance. Furthermore, a theory gives rise to predictions about instances (perhaps not now encountered) where "craziness" is likely to be manifest and produce various kinds of behavior, including bank robbery.

Social scientists, then, are interested in, and attempt to formulate, explanations of deviance and crime that are disciplined, general, and encompassed within theories. Nevertheless, as will become clear, many of the "scientific theories" of crime or deviance are really nothing more than elaborations of common, everyday notions like the examples set out earlier; often the theories are not even very sophisticated elaborations, and in many cases they barely qualify as theories. Yet, it is necessary to consider the range of possibilities. There are dozens of "theories" of crime and deviance, but since many of these theories are similar, only the most representative will be discussed. Moreover, they will be presented within a classification scheme based on the predominant focus and assumption of the theory.

Some theories locate the primary causative component of deviance or crime within the individual person. They try to identify a relatively enduring characteristic of the individual that is responsible for the violation(s). Other theories maintain that the causative element lies outside the person in the social environment or situation. Therefore, we can distinguish two basic types of theory depending upon where the primary causative component is located—internal theories and external theories. Within each of these major types we can also find basic differences in assumptions about human nature. Some theories assume that human beings "naturally" conform to rules and are, therefore, rarely motivated to commit deviance or crime. With this assumption, deviance can only be understood as a response to some unusual motivation or extraordinarily strong impulse to deviate. To be classified as motivational, a theory must, therefore, attempt to spell out the process or processes that produce unusual impulses to offend. Other theories assume just the opposite about human nature—they assume that all people have the desire and motivation to break rules. According to these theories, the thing that differentiates those who break rules from those who don't is not motivation but rather the absence of constraints on behavior. Presumably, all are motivated to deviate but most are prevented from doing so. Those who commit crime or who deviate are simply individuals who escape the constraints that bind conformers. Following these themes, theories can be classified as either predominantly motivational or predominantly failure of constraint (control) types.

Combining these four elements—person or situational locale and motivational or control assumptions—one can characterize each theory of deviance as being one of four types. *External/motivation* theories explain deviant or criminal behavior in terms of elements external to individuals that provide them with an unusual stimulus or motivation to deviate. *Internal/motivation* theories find the cause of deviance in some characteristics inside the person that generate extraordinary motivations to deviate or offend. *Internal/constraint* theories explain deviance as the failure or absence of some internal constraint that normally prohibits people from acting out their deviant impulses. *External/constraint* theories interpret deviant or criminal behavior as a product of the failure or absence of external controls that would ordinarily inhibit expression of deviant impulses.

We will discuss a number of theories of why individuals do deviance or crime, classifying them into one of these four types. The accompanying table depicts the various classes of theories we will discuss, showing how they are placed in the cells of a fourfold table cross-classifying the location of the primary causal element with the main assumption about human nature.

Table II.1 Classification of Theories of Individual Deviance by Location and Nature of the Cause

Nature of Cause	Location of Cause	
	External	**Internal**
Motivation	Learning	Self
	Structural inducement	Reactance
	Situational inducement	Psychodynamic
	Interaction process	
Constraint	Deterrence	Self-control
	Social control	Morality

It should be kept in mind, however, that few theories exclusively emphasize either internal or external elements or exclusively employ a motivational or constraint assumption. Most theories pay some attention to combinations of variables, but all tend to have a prevailing theme that overshadows eclectic elements. Indeed, as we will see later, the tendency of theories to overemphasize one combination of components to the neglect of others constitutes their major defect.

While the objective of scientists is to develop theories within which explanations for the phenomena of interest are embedded, theory development is the ultimate goal, and the process of developing a theory is ongoing. Science normally begins with observation to establish regularities in the domains of interest. In the case of crime/deviance studies, early work was devoted mainly to describing various aspects of deviant behavior, the people who do it, and the situations under which it seemed to occur. After some empirical regularities have been identified, scientists then try to explain each of them. These explanations are not theories, because they apply to only one phenomenon or situation, and because their explanatory principles are concrete and ad hoc rather than being general and abstract. Eventually, scientists attempt to tie together these ad hoc explanations into more general theories that account for a number of specific empirical regularities. These overarching explanatory systems are called theories, or sometimes theory fragments if their scope and causal accounts are narrow. As science progresses, limited theories or theory fragments are also tied together with more general, abstract explanatory schemes called general theories.

At each step along this progression from description to general theory, scientists try to check out their explanations with data from the empirical world. To be useful, such data must be collected according to scientific principles, that is, gathered with care to see that biases are minimized, measurements are valid, and samples are adequate, and gathered according to a plan (or research design) that will permit inferences about cause.

This scientific mode for building knowledge advances at different speeds with respect to different objects of interest. Thus, for some phenomena, students of deviance are still in the descriptive stage, where they are establishing regularities, or facts, while for other things they have progressed to the general theory level. Since this book is designed to acquaint you with the field of deviance/crime studies, we have tried to show you how far our knowledge about various issues has gone. For that reason, Chapter 9 was devoted to describing empirical regularities (or lack thereof) that have been established by scholars, and Chapter 10 presents the ad hoc explanations that have been developed to account for those facts. After that, we will turn our attention to the theory fragments that have emerged and eventually to general theories. ✦

Chapter 10

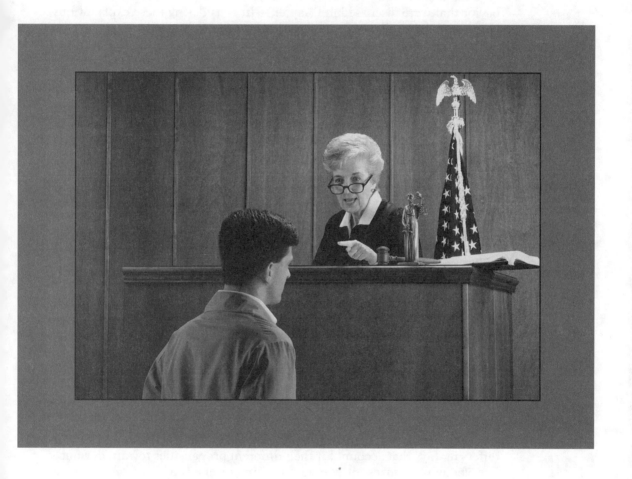

Ad Hoc
Explanations

In the introduction to this section, you were told that scholars first describe the phenomena of interest to them, at least as well as they can in the absence of theory directing them to the important features to be described. Once enough description has occurred to provide a pattern of behavior in need of explanation, scholars then try to make sense of it. This "making sense" involves the development of intellectual explanations that try to satisfy the questions of "why" and "how." Usually the first step in explanation is to try to account for the observed phenomenon as an isolated, self-contained entity. These accounts are called ad hoc explanations. In this chapter we will examine a number of such accounts of the empirical regularities about deviant behavior that were discussed in Chapter 9. In considering these explanations, bear in mind that all the "facts" described in Chapter 9 are also explicable using more general theories that portray them as specific manifestations of larger processes. Later we will consider those more general theories, and when we do you will see that the specific explanations to be presented below are often encapsulated within more general theories. Indeed, that is the way the scientific process would have it. The work of science is guided by the principle of inclusivity; that is, a comprehensive theory that encompasses many different phenomena is preferable to a collection of explanations of each phenomenon separately. But inclusive theories should be as simple as possible (Braithwaite, 1960). Despite these principles, many scholars still prefer to focus on specific empirical regularities as the ultimate object of explanation, and they prefer ad hoc explanations to explanations derivable from more abstract theories.

Gender

The facts about gender and deviance are fairly clear; with few exceptions, males do more deviance of all kinds than do females. While these differences are consistent with a number of general theories that will be presented later, three ad hoc explanations are often employed.

Biology

Physicality

Some scholars contend that the biological makeup of males and females differs in ways that account for their different propensities toward deviance. Everybody recognizes, of course, that human males and females differ in physical structure and features, including different genitalia, body shape, musculature, and possibly brain functioning (Broverman et al., 1980). Some contend that these differences alone are enough to explain much deviance, particularly that requiring great strength. But since most deviance is not strength related, a more compelling biological argument concerns the effect of hormones, particularly testosterone and serotonin.

The hormone testosterone is not exclusive to males, but males have higher concentrations of it and other gonadal steroids than females. Furthermore, it is not concentrated in equal amounts in all males but shows great variation. Neither is it fixed in any given person but instead varies across different situations—that is, some situations may lead a person to produce higher than usual levels of testosterone. In addition to producing the characteristic secondary sexual characteristics, such as chest hair and deep voices, testosterone influences aggressiveness (Svare and Kinsley, 1987), which is the tendency to be active, take risks, compete, and overcome fear. Since, by their very natures, almost all deviant acts involve risk taking (at least the risk of getting caught and suffering some bad consequences), it is plausible to imagine that male-female differences in deviance are due to differences in testosterone or other hormonal variations, such as levels of cortisol or serotonin.

There is evidence supporting this point of view (Brain and Susman, 1997; Olweus, 1979; Olweus et al., 1980). Research has linked testosterone levels to various kinds of deviance, and a number of documented male-female biological differences are consistent with the differences in deviant behavior (Olweus et al., 1980, 1988). In addition to testosterone, low levels of cortisol (a stress steroid) and serotonin (Bernhardt, 1997; Moffitt et al., 1998) have been found in empirical research to be related to male antisocial behavior. Hence, few scholars deny that biology has some effect in causing males to resort to deviance more often than females do. The linkage between testosterone and deviance, however, while persistent, is not strong (particularly among children and younger adolescents (Susman et al., 1989, 1991), and some research suggests that testosterone's effects are tempered and channeled by social variables (Booth and Osgood, 1993). Moreover, variations in the patterns of male-female differences, such as that showing urban females to be more deviant than rural males, young females to be more deviant than older males, and the gap between males and females to be much greater in some contexts than in others, suggests that biology can play only a partial role. The key question for most scholars now is how biology and social factors interact in producing gender differences in deviant behavior.

Evolutionary Drives

A second type of biological argument interprets male-female differences in deviance as an outgrowth of sociobiological impulses linked to evolutionary histories in which genetic impulses for effective reproduction have compelled different strategies (Ellis and Walsh, 1997). According to this explanation, human beings (as well as all other life forms) have evolved to their present state through a process of natural selection. Features of early forms of all species that were advantageous in reproductive competition were passed on to later generations, while those that were disadvantageous died out.

Since a female's genes can only be passed on through offspring that she bears and helps to survive long enough to also reproduce, it is in her interest to choose carefully partners who will not only provide good genetic stock but will also assist in the protection and rearing of children. In other words, females have a genetic predisposition for conservatism and against risk taking. Males, on the other hand, can experience an advantage in the reproductive struggle either by impregnating as many females as possible or by establishing an aura of having the stability and reliability that females need to enlist for successful child rearing. Either of these strategies puts a premium on success in economic and social competition. Hence, the evolutionary process has provided a genetic impulse for males to be risk takers and competitive (to succeed and thereby be attractive to females) as well as to be deceitful (to fool females into thinking they are successful). The net result is that males have inherited genetically programmed propensities for deviance while females have been genetically equipped for less deviance.

This evolutionary argument is plausible but can be directly verified only for microbes that evolve rapidly enough to be observed for multiple generations. It is indirectly verifiable by logical inference from observed facts about human behavior, but alternative social explanations fit as well or better. Therefore, whether one is satisfied with such explanations depends more on personal taste than on scientific evidence.

Socialization

Probably the most popular ad hoc explanation among social scientists for male-female differences in antisocial or deviant behavior is that of socialization. The basis of the socialization argument is that from the earliest ages, males and females are taught very different things about appropriate and inappropriate behavior (Anderson, 1988; Lorber, 1994). While there are exceptions, and such differences are less evident today than just a few decades ago, females are generally taught that conformity to social rules is always expected of them, that aggressiveness is not feminine, that security is better than risk taking, that violence is unacceptable, and that success in life for females depends on their being viewed as embodying these traits. Males, on the other hand, are taught that independence and assertiveness are admirable, that violation of some social rules is a mark of masculine autonomy, that courage and fearlessness are necessary for success, that tolerance or use of violence is manly, and that the males' progress in life will be somewhat dependent on acquiring these behaviors and frames of mind (Schlegel and Barry, 1991; Tavris and Offir, 1977).

Moreover, these lessons are reinforced by the response of others to actual behaviors as the child grows up, and they are emphasized by cultural patterns of prestige and social reward assigned to those who embody these learned components. Hence, the typical female develops attitudes, values, cognitive modes, and habits of behavior that are more conforming or that are likely to produce conforming behavior, while the typical male develops "deviogenic" (likely to produce deviant behavior) characteristics. And these learned traits are played out in actual behavioral probabilities of deviance that differentiate males generally from females.

For example, in U.S. society, most parents think fighting among children is wrong, but their tolerance for fighting by male children is much greater than for female children. If a female child comes home from school with a tale of having been in a fight, male and female parents alike tend to view this as inappropriate, even if the circumstances seem to justify the fight. More likely than not, a parent will advise a female child to "learn to get along with people," to avoid conflict-oriented situations or people, and to seek help from teachers and parents. This is done with an admonition that girls "don't fight." The same situation involving a male child may result in his being admonished to avoid bad situations or to seek the help of adults but with a countermessage that in the end he should not "let anybody push him around." Indeed, the father is likely to inquire as to whether the opponent's injuries exceed those of his son, and he is likely to brag to his associates that his son is "all boy" and well on his way to becoming a "man."

While there is much evidence consistent with the social learning explanation of male-female differences in deviance (Hagan et al., 1985, 1987; Shover et al., 1979; Simons et al., 1980), the issue cannot be settled, because little of the research actually takes biological factors into account, just as biological research fails to take social learning into account. Indeed, even if it were possible to identify and measure all relevant biological variables, separating social from biological influences would be a formidable task, because they may be closely intertwined and interconnected. Nevertheless, most social scientists, while recognizing that humans are not totally malleable, still regard social influences as more relevant than biological ones for sex differences in behavior. This position is based on the wide variability of male-female differences in deviance that correspond to the variations in social circumstances noted before.

Social Control

A third ad hoc explanation contends that males commit more deviance than females because they are less subject to surveillance, apprehension, or sanction, and because sanctioning for deviance committed by females is more costly to their reputations and social roles. Since adults, especially parents, are more fearful that harm will come to females than to males, or that the consequences of deviance are greater for females than for males, females are more closely watched and supervised during the formative years when deviance is most likely to occur. Then, in adulthood, social roles dictate less autonomy, less freedom of movement, and more accountability for females than for males. The net result of all of this is that females simply have fewer opportunities for deviance. Moreover, even with opportunities, they are subject to greater chances of getting caught, and punishments are more likely to be socially damaging, even though males are often punished in ways that are ostensibly more severe (for example, with longer prison sentences). Unlike the preceding two ad hoc explanations, this one assumes few gender differences in motivation for deviance. Instead it contends that females conform because they have little alternative—their positions in society imply constraints on their freedom to express deviant motivations in action. In other words, females offend less frequently than males not because the motivation for deviance among males is stronger but because the controls or constraints on male behavior are weaker (Hagan et al., 1985, 1987; Tittle, 1995).

This explanation also enjoys a good deal of support (Tittle, 1980b; Richards and Tittle, 1981), but it too cannot be accepted unequivocally, because there is contradictory evidence showing that female rates of deviance do not correspond very closely to changes in freedom associated with female roles (Steffensmeier, 1978; Steffensmeier and Cobb, 1981; Steffensmeier and Steffensmeier, 1980; Steffensmeier et al., 1989a). Also, it is impossible to separate learned or biological components from those that imply constraint or control. Nevertheless, the popularity of control explanations has risen among social scientists in recent years, and as a result such explanations have come to assume more prominence in accounts of male-female differences (Messerschmidt, 1986; Ogle et al., 1995).

The Power-Control Argument

A recently developed ad hoc explanation of male-female differences in deviant behavior combines socialization and social control arguments and tries to show how they come together because of the positions of parents in the workforce (Hagan, 1989a). Hagan contends that in modern industrial societies, males are more likely to be employed outside the home and thereby to be more autonomous. And even when both parents are in the workforce, males are more likely to have positions with greater authority. This workplace superiority is said to be translated into dominance in the home, where women are relegated to the task of child rearing and are given the responsibility for "reproducing" the authority relations on which the industrial and family systems are based. Because of this, mothers control girls more than boys, and as a result boys do more delinquency and become more risk oriented, which, by logical extension, pushes them into more deviance throughout the life course. However, when females attain equality in the workforce, as many have in modern societies, they are less likely to be delegated all of the child rearing. Consequently, female children in such families are less likely to be excessively controlled, and they are more likely to develop risk orientations equivalent to those of boys. In modern families, therefore, females are as likely to be delinquent as males and, by extension, to continue to deviate with more or less equal probabilities throughout life.

The immediate causes of male-female differences in some forms of deviance, according to the power-control argument, then, are differences in control exercised by the mother over the male and female children, which allows males to be more delinquent during childhood and adolescence and instills in them a risk orientation that portends a lifetime of greater deviance. But these immediate causes grow out of the power relations of the sexes in the workplace. Hence, differences in male and female propensities toward deviance should have been declining over the past few decades, and they should continue to decline with further equalization of work opportunities.

Though this too is a plausible argument, it cannot be confirmed. Whether male-female differences in deviance have been declining with greater equalization of workforce opportunities is controversial, as noted before, and specific tests linking workplace authority, family authority, and children's control and risk orientations are rare and not convincing (see Jensen and Thompson, 1990).

Age

The facts about age and deviance are not quite as consistent as are those about gender and deviance, but they still paint a stable pattern. For whole population groups there is a tendency for most forms of deviance to increase through the first fourth to third of the life cycle and then to decline steadily thereafter, with the major exception to that pattern being suicide. However, there appear to be segments of any population that do not follow the typical pattern, represented mainly by a small minority that achieves a high rate of deviance early and sustains it throughout most of the life course.

Biology

The biological arguments accounting for the age-deviance relationship focus mainly on the impact of puberty in accelerating the upward trend of deviance in the teen years and on the later effect of aging in reducing physical strength, energy, and sensual ability (Gove, 1985). Presumably, the biological changes that occur when youths begin to develop physically as adults throw them into confusion and motivate all manner of apparently nonsensical, deviant behavior that produces the rise in deviance characteristic of the teen years (Erikson, 1950; Hall, 1904). Later, the consequences of aging lead to a drop in deviance.

According to the biological explanation, the adult decline in deviance is due to decreasing interest as well as decreasing ability. Not only does aging typically erode a person's physical capability, making many kinds of deviance difficult or more dangerous, but it affects the nervous system by decreasing its capacity for being stimulated. Things that are exciting for young people often produce little thrill for adults, and the sensual stimulus of drugs, food, and sex becomes muted. Many argue that a decline with age is inevitable for forms of deviance that depend on activism or produce sensual satisfaction. Moreover, some have even contended that physical deterioration contributes to the rise in suicide among the aged as they become less and less capable of realizing physical gratification.

Some scholars also implicate biology in explaining the exception to the age effect represented by those who quickly become problem children and sustain that nature throughout most of the life course. They contend that life-long deviance is the result of neurological deficits. Such deficits may be attributable to traumas of birth, poor nutrition, and early experiences of infancy such as lead poisoning, but they are mostly the result of biologically inherited deficiencies that affect cognitive functioning or emotional control (Moffitt, 1990; Moffitt et al., 1994).

Despite the plausibility of the biological explanation for the general age and deviance relationship, it falters in face of the reality that deviance begins to decline for most people long before physical strength and neural sensitivity do, and in view of the fact that some individuals apparently continue to offend late into life despite erosion of strength and sensitivity (Blumstein et al., 1986, 1988a). Moreover, not all problem children become problem adults, and the shift from a troubled trajectory to a more conventional one that sometimes occurs in early adulthood appears to be linked with social relationships (Sampson and Laub, 1993).

Social Control

An alternative to the biological explanation is one that sees age patterns of deviance as a reflection of changes in the experience of social control as one proceeds through the life cycle (Sampson and Laub, 1993; Tittle, 1988). Since their freedom is restricted and they are extensively supervised by adult parents, teachers, coaches, and counselors, younger children are prevented from excessive amounts of deviance. However, as they move into the adolescent years and form alliances with peers, they gradually break supervisory bonds with adults, particularly parents, though they continue to enjoy dependent material support and leniency for misbehavior. This increased freedom of movement and escape from surveillance that goes with adolescence permits youths to avoid controls and leads to an increasing rate of deviance. However, after the teen years, when young people exhaust their dependency and must move into self-sustaining productive roles, they once again become subject to social controls that come from employment, property ownership, and parental responsibilities of their own. In addition, they become liable for full criminal sanctions as adults. This systematic reestablishment of constraining social relationships in the early adult years presumably produces a steady decline of deviance.

Thus, cyclical changes in social control during the typical life cycle correspond with the patterns of change in deviance. Further, it is possible to account for deviations from this pattern, as expressed by those who begin deviance early and continue it throughout life, in the same terms. According to this account, they are simply individuals who lacked the guiding hand of adults in the early years, responded as most adolescents do to their situations, and failed to become enmeshed in constraining social bonds as adults.

The validity of this explanation, particularly in comparison with the biological argument, has not been established, though it is more plausible. Attempts to use measured social control at various points in the life cycle to account for the age-deviance association have not proven satisfying (see Tittle and Grasmick, 1997).

Social Status

A third ad hoc explanation of age variations in deviance begins by noting that adolescence is a social status found mostly in modern societies (Sebald, 1992). In simple societies the status of child is well defined in terms of rights, responsibilities, and gratifications, and childhood's length is unambiguously specified as ending at the appearance of some biological marker (such as menstruation or a specific age) or at the achievement of a particular goal (such as killing an animal or an enemy). Similarly, adulthood is a well-defined status with designated rights, responsibilities, and gratifications that accrue to all who have moved out of the childhood status. Given these clearcut social standards, individuals can adapt their lives and achieve whatever goals are appropriate to their status. Further, preparation for adulthood takes place during childhood as youths learn by observation how to fulfill adult roles. And once the demarcation is passed, children instantly stop being children and become adults entitled to all the accouterments thereof. In other words, in simple societies people experience little anxiety about their social roles (but see Schlegel and Barry, 1991).

Beginning with industrialization, and increasing with modernization, however, children could not prepare for adulthood in the family or village context but instead had to undergo preparation in specialized institutions such as schools. While in preparation for adulthood, they are no longer children but not yet adults—they are something in between, called adolescents. In some situations they are regarded as children and the expectations associated with childhood are invoked, but in other situations adult expectations are imposed. Furthermore, it is not clear when adolescence begins or ends. There is no ceremony as in simple societies, and the only way individuals can know whether they are a child or an adult is when almost all other people in all situations treat them as occupying that status. This ambiguity is said to produce anxiety about one's self-identity, which in turn produces a plethora of "typically" adolescent behaviors that proliferate at an increasing rate until the individual finally achieves unambiguous designation as an adult.

Typical adolescent behaviors involve attempts to obtain recognition as adults by exaggerated emphasis on symbols of adulthood, to establish masculine or feminine identities through sexuality, to acquire prestige by pandering to peer approval, and paradoxically to retreat from the responsibilities of adulthood. Trying to be recognized as adults often takes the form of embracing, in an exaggerated way, the symbols of adulthood, such as engaging in "adult" pleasures (smoking, using alcohol and drugs, and having sexual intercourse), establishing personal autonomy (such as disobeying parents and officials and defying curfews), and flaunting personal property (such as cars, clothes, and recreational equipment), which, since legitimate sources of income are limited, often requires acquisition through theft (Greenberg, 1981).

Staking claims to sexual identities often produces deviant behavior in the form of violence and risky activities, as well as irresponsible sexual conquest among males, and of indiscreet sex and/or premarital pregnancy among females. Since prestige stemming from family, community, and employee roles that adults enjoy is denied to adolescents, they often turn to peers for approval. This can lead to such forms of deviance as vandalism, gang fighting, or criminal enterprise. Finally, because adult status is distant and often seemingly unattainable, youths are prone to shrink from its pursuit and commit so thoroughly to the adolescent life style that "immaturity" extends beyond the late teen years and manifests itself in reversion to the child's plea of "it's not my fault" when caught in misdeeds.

The average length of adolescence, and the accompanying ambiguity of its status, grew as the economic systems of technologically advanced societies required more and more specialized training and as the complexity of modern societies demanded greater education for effective living. As a result, the period during which teens are prone to deviance came to extend into the early twenties. Status anxiety thus explains the progression of deviance from childhood through about the first third of the life cycle and its subsequent dropoff as people finally settle into unambiguous adult roles.

Imitation

A final ad hoc explanation of the age pattern has been developed by Moffitt (1993). She contends that there are two distinct types of deviants, and two correspondingly distinct causal pathways. One type of deviant is what she calls the "life-course-persistent" offender. As the name implies, this type of offender begins committing antisocial and deviant acts at an early age and continues offending throughout life (that is, he or she persists in deviance). The second type of deviant is the adolescent-limited offender. Such deviants do not begin offending until mid or late adolescence, and they typically cease their offending when they begin to assume adult responsibilities and roles.

In addition to these two distinct offending "careers," Moffitt argues that there are different explanations for each type of offender. The life-course-persistent offender has various neurological deficits, many already present at birth, which cause dysfunctions in a child's cognitive and executive skills. These children are unruly at a very early age and are difficult to discipline. Parents are frequently overwhelmed with the child's behavioral difficulties and often respond destructively rather than constructively. As a result of the combination of a behaviorally difficult child and an overwhelmed or deficient parent, socialization breaks down and the child's self controls remain undeveloped. With initially weak social controls and self-control, it is difficult for the child to "catch up," according to Moffitt. Hence the child with early behavior problems also misses out on opportunities for socialization later in life. As a result, the unruly child becomes a rebellious teenager who

eventually becomes a deviant, antisocial adult. The life-course-persistent offender makes up a relatively small proportion (about 5 to 10 percent) of any
birth cohort.

The origins of the much more prevalent adolescent-limited offender are
quite different. Moffitt contends that most children are effectively socialized
and exhibit little in the way of conduct problems at an early age. Unfortunately, when such generally "normal" kids enter adolescence, two things happen: (1) they experience a maturity gap between the adult roles they wish to
occupy and their adolescent status, and (2) they come into greater contact
with, and are inspired to imitate, the life-course-persistent offenders. The
maturity gap and consequent desire to act "adult-like" provide the motivation
for the adolescent-limited offender to experiment with rebellious and frequently antisocial acts. Exposure to the life-course-persistent offender provides opportunity for mimicry. Since persistent offenders are already enjoying the rewards of maturity because of their deviance—such as possession of
items otherwise not accessible to adolescents, sexual experience, and greater
freedom and autonomy—they "assume social influence over youths who admire and emulate their style during adolescence" (Moffitt, 1993:687). As a result, in mid to late adolescence, a large majority of youths experiment with
deviant behaviors that allow them to symbolically claim maturity (smoking,
drinking, keeping late hours, having sex, and sometimes engaging in various
forms of crime). Eventually, these experimenters realize that the costs of adolescent deviance may be quite high. Also, by early adulthood they are assuming roles and statuses that legitimately provide the rewards of maturity,
which they acquired only illegitimately while adolescents. For most, rebellion and deviance cease in early adulthood, and these youths' antisocial "careers" are limited to a short span of adolescence.

Hence the age-deviance relationship of an upward trend until the late
teens or early twenties but with some individual deviations by those who continue to offend throughout the life course is explicable by the convergence of
two causal forces: the one resulting from neuropsychological deficits as they
interact with deviogenic environments to produce the aberrant pattern of
long-term, frequent deviance, and the other resulting from the merger of a
maturity gap experienced by "normal" adolescents and " 'social mimicry' of
the antisocial style of the life-course-persistent youth" (Moffitt, 1993:686).

Socioeconomic Status

In Chapter 9 you learned that the relationship between socioeconomic
status and deviance is somewhat problematic. In some instances there appears to be a positive relationship between some kinds of deviance and socioeconomic status (malfeasance/white-collar crime; abuse of prescription and
expensive drugs such as cocaine; and suicide); in other instances there appears to be a negative relationship (serious violence and abuse of opiates and
alcohol); and in still other instances there appears to be little or no relationship at all (vandalism, petty theft, and use of mild recreational drugs). Despite this mixed evidence, many scholars, and most laypersons, assume that
socioeconomic status is negatively related to all kinds of deviance, particularly all forms of ordinary (non-white-collar) crime, drug usage, and deviant
sexual activities. And to address this supposed general relationship between

socioeconomic status and deviance, a number of ad hoc explanations have
been put forth.

Biology

Some scholars contend that intelligence, achievement motivation, and
numerous psychological traits such as impulse control and positive emotionality, all of which affect success in a competitive world and thereby portend
socioeconomic status, are heavily influenced—if not entirely determined—
by genetic inheritance and/or biological functioning (Ellis and Walsh, 1997;
Herrnstein and Murray, 1994; Wilson and Herrnstein, 1985). Since these
same traits are also assumed by many to affect the likelihood of criminal/de-
viant behavior, it follows that the presumed association between socioeconomic status and deviance is a product of pre-existing biological factors.
Moreover, since there is evidence that deviance is stable across generations,
these same scholars contend that there is a natural causal cycle in which biologically linked deficiencies lead to lower socioeconomic status and deviance, which are in turn passed on from one generation to the next through the
reproductive process.

Deviance in Everyday Life

Why are children in poorer areas more likely to be antisocial? Part of the reason
may be environmental toxins. Scientists have found that environmental pollution
is not randomly distributed among geographical areas but seems far more likely to
be near poor neighborhoods. The term *environmental racism* has been coined to
describe this situation. For example, sewage waste from much of affluent
Manhattan is not treated there but is piped to West Harlem. Due to budget cutbacks
in the construction of the waste water treatment plant, the North River Waste
Treatment Plant is accused by community residents of fouling the air of West Harlem. In fact, on some days the air smells so bad that residents stay in with closed
windows. To make up for the plant's odor, New York City built a recreation center
for the community, complete with basketball courts, softball fields, and picnic
area. The park was built on the roof of the sewage plant.

Intergenerational transfer is thought to involve both direct and indirect
linkages. Directly, the genes prescribing low intelligence, weak impulse control, and other disadvantageous traits are presumably passed on through the
biological reproductive process. Indirectly, however, lower socioeconomic
status affects the biological functioning of successive generations because it
prescribes the conditions in which children live. Much evidence suggests that
poor nutrition during the formative years, exposure to lead in aging paint and
water pipes, and consumption of various toxins prevalent in the areas where
people with lower status reside all affect the brain (see Regulus, 1995), leading to inferior intellectual functioning and various emotional problems,
which then affect the likelihood of deviance.

While the biological account seems plausible to many, there is much evidence suggesting that socioeconomic status achievement is highly sensitive
to learnable inputs and opportunities for mobility (Duncan et al., 1972;
Fischer et al., 1996; Jencks et al., 1972, 1979). Hence, even though there is
much intergenerational stability in socioeconomic standing, the relatively
high degree of mobility, both upward and downward (Blau and Duncan,

1967; Cohen and Tyree, 1986; Lipset and Bendix, 1959; Pineo, 1976) suggests that the biological explanation of social status is limited. Moreover, there is considerable evidence suggesting that intelligence, at least measured intelligence (Fischer et al., 1996; Wahlsten, 1997; Winship and Korenman, 1997), achievement motivation, and various psychological traits like self-control are heavily influenced by culture and social learning (Gottfredson and Hirschi, 1990). Finally, the linkage between deviance and the characteristics supposedly determined or influenced by biology is tenuous (Neisser et al., 1996; Walters, 1992; Walters and White, 1989).

The biological argument is most challenged by the evidence that shows the relationship between socioeconomic status to be problematic or to be reversed. For example, if biological defects of lower status people account for low intelligence and high impulsivity, and these characteristics in turn influence or cause criminal deviance like theft, drug usage, and deviant sexuality, then one cannot reconcile the fact that disproportionate, almost exclusive, amounts of theft of a fraudulent type, abuse of expensive drugs like cocaine and prescription sleeping medications, and homosexuality or swinging occur among high status people.

Thus, even though some scientists embrace a biological explanation of associations between socioeconomic status and deviance, and even though this kind of explanation has grown in popularity in recent years (Herrnstein and Murray, 1994; Wilson and Herrnstein, 1985), the vast majority of scientists, both natural and social, interpret the contribution of biology to social status as minimal and to deviance as being only modest at best. The prevailing view, consistent with the bulk of evidence, sees social status as largely a social product, and, to the extent that socioeconomic status predicts deviance, the connection is seen as due to a whole host of social and cultural linkages (Cullen et al., 1997; Fischer et al., 1996). Indeed, most of the social theories that we examine later in this book provide plausible, and often reasonably well-supported, explanations of the supposed socioeconomic status/deviance association; in fact, many of them grew out of attempts to explain this particular phenomenon (Tittle, 1983).

Deprivation

Probably the most popular ad hoc explanation of a putative association between socioeconomic status and deviance concerns the direct and indirect effects of deprivation. It says that those with fewer resources, lower education, and less power will naturally have a harder time in life than those with advantages.

Economic Disadvantage

Since everybody presumably wants the things that higher status brings, far beyond necessities, it is assumed that lower-status people are highly motivated to obtain them through various forms of deviance. In fact, it is assumed they are likely to use whatever opportunities arise to try to overcome their deprivations, particularly in societies where people of all statuses can compare themselves and where they are encouraged to aspire highly. Moreover, in the face of failure, many disadvantaged people presumably become frustrated, which leads to blind aggression expressed in high rates of violence, often for no apparent reason, or to escapist behaviors resulting in alcoholism and drug addiction or even suicide.

Even though this account is easy to appreciate and resonates well with popular culture, the evidence favoring it is quite mixed. First, many lower-status people do not want the accouterments of high status (Kluegel and Smith, 1986; Vanneman and Cannon, 1987), and even those who are absolutely deprived to the point of bare subsistence often manifest honesty "to a fault." Indeed, the willingness of deprived people to accept their lot in life without deviation or revolt sometimes amazes revolutionaries and other social observers. Second, the prevalence of deviance among those of high status (Clinard and Yeager, 1980; Ermann and Lundman, 1996; Simon and Eitzen, 1993; Vaughn, 1983), suggests that if deprivation is a cause of deviance, relative and/or perceived deprivation are as important as absolute deprivation. However, everybody is deprived relative to some others (except, perhaps, Bill Gates, the richest man on earth at the present time), and many who are not absolutely deprived nevertheless perceive themselves to be. Hence the explanation of deviance as due to deprivation does not ring true. The frustration-aggression aspect of the argument (the contention that failure by lower-class people leads to blind aggression) is particularly suspect. That aspect of the argument is suspect partly because it has been shown empirically to have little validity (Berkowitz, 1969), and partly because frustration is as likely to stem from relative as absolute deprivation, making it common to those of all socio-economic statuses. Finally, since suicide, the ultimate form of withdrawal, seems to be positively related to social status (see Chapters 3 and 9), the idea that frustration stemming from deprivation leads to escape is illogical.

Deprivation of Law

One kind of deprivation experienced by people with few economic resources is restricted access to the machinery of law or other formal mechanisms to help resolve disputes (Black, 1976, 1989). Everybody, at one time or another, has conflicts with others. These can range from petty slights like discourtesy to serious issues about property ownership or love triangles. And disputes always have the potential to escalate to the point of violence or retaliatory theft. One thing that prevents such escalation is the availability of impartial third-party interveners such as police officers and judicial officials, or even community or religious arbitrators like marriage counselors, who can mediate.

For example, if neighbors disagree about a barking dog, the offended party might complain to the police about peace disturbance, and such a complaint might inspire the police to speak to the dog's owner and threaten arrest if the situation is not corrected. If all else fails, the offended party might sue the offending neighbor and have a judge decide the merits of the complaint. Since the police and courts have the authority to make and enforce judgments, disputants can get their complaints heard and perhaps answered, and if judgments go against them there is room for face saving. But without such mechanisms, disputes are more likely to fester and escalate, with potentially disastrous results. Hence, in the example of the barking dog, the offended party might complain directly to the dog's owner and in the process aggravate or offend him. The newly offended party might then respond with threats that insult the original complainant and so on until both are backed into corners where they feel they must defend their honor. Such disputes could eventuate in fights or even murder. Thus, conflict-resolving institutions help reduce some types of deviance among those who use them.

However, access to "law" or other third-party peace keepers is much more limited for those of lower socioeconomic status than for others (Black, 1980). The police are less likely to respond rapidly to calls from lower-class respondents, and they are less likely to take complaints made by lower-status people seriously, particularly if the complaints involve what the police regard as trivial or minor problems (Bachman, 1996; Black, 1980). Furthermore, since lawyers are expensive, the possibility of civil suits by lower-status people to resolve conflicts is greatly reduced, particularly since courts usually limit their attention to cases involving substantial amounts of money. Consequently, disputes among lower-status people are more likely to evoke "self-help," and as a result they are likely to have more deviance-generating effects (Black, 1983; Cooney, 1997).

Socialization

Family

Those who believe that lower-status people commit more deviance than others often explain that purported relationship as a consequence of poor child rearing, which produces individuals with defective personalities, weak self-control, and low morals. Faulty child rearing is thought to stem from an interrelated set of conditions. First, those of lower SES are more likely to grow up in incomplete or broken homes because of unemployment, financial deprivation, incarceration, and youthful marriages. This deficit of adults in the household makes supervision and training of children more difficult, especially since fertility (the number of children people have) varies inversely with socioeconomic status; that is, the lower the SES, the larger the family size (Sweet and Bumpass, 1987). In addition, those of lower socioeconomic status, because of their own backgrounds and the absence of education, generally possess less skill in dealing with the problems of children, in imparting commitments to conformity, or in inspiring youth to pursue educational or training programs that would make it possible for them to achieve their goals legitimately.

Much evidence documents the importance of the family both in training children for effective, nondeviant living and in controlling potential misbehavior either indirectly through social attachments or directly through supervision (Larzelere and Patterson, 1990; Loeber and Stouthamer-Loeber, 1986; Patterson, 1982; Tygart, 1991). Moreover, family instability and incompleteness do seem to be linked to socioeconomic status, though family instability is far from exclusive to the lower class (Collins, 1988; Garfinkel and McLanahan, 1986; Rapp, 1982). Thus, if lower socioeconomic status is predictive of deviance, which you will recall is actually somewhat problematic, it may be due to family deficiencies. However, it seems unlikely that families among the lower classes are so ineffective that their deviogenic effects greatly exceed the countereffects of religious beliefs, which are stronger among the lower classes (Demerath, 1965) and which appear to inhibit deviance (Evans et al., 1995; Tittle and Welch, 1983). And it seems questionable whether the deficiencies of lower-status families outweigh potentially deterring formal and informal sanctions that fall more heavily on the disadvantaged (see Sutherland et al., 1992, for a review of the evidence): Clearly, those with lower status are more closely monitored by the police and other social control

agents, such as welfare officials and employers, and they are given more severe punishments in the case of criminal behavior (Bridges and Myers, 1994).

❖ ❖ ❖ ❖

Subcultures of Poverty

Some contend that economic deprivation shared by a collectivity of people residing near each other leads to an adaptive subculture that emphasizes
values and orientations likely to produce deviant behavior by those within
the cultural milieu (Anderson, 1978, 1990; Lewis, 1961, 1966; Miller, 1958;
Wolfgang and Ferracuti, 1967). Some orientations of poverty subcultures include exaggerated emphasis on gender-differentiated peer groups; requirements that males be "tough" by showing physical prowess and courage; an
expectation that both males and females will cherish and pursue "autonomy"
(the ability to escape control by other people and situations); admiration for
individuals who show they are "smart" by manipulating or outwitting others
or the system, such as by "conning" someone out of money or being able to
make a living without working; putting a high premium on "excitement" (relief from the boredom of humdrum lives and repetitive, uninteresting work);
and sharing a belief that life is governed by "fate" (random events over which
one has little control), which often implies impending trouble or unforeseen
misfortune.

These subcultural orientations and standards are passed on from one
generation to the next through precept and example in familial, peer, and
neighborhood interaction, and they are enforced by means of informal social
control involving rewards of prestige for those who display the appropriate
traits and denigration for those who fall short. As a result, each person born
to a family of lower socioeconomic status is likely to learn a number of self-
defeating attitudes and values and is likely to face a set of social pressures for
conformity to such standards. Thus, subcultures of poverty presumably promote deviance in a variety of ways.

A subculture built around same-sex associations may encourage stereotypes of males as irresponsible rogues who have to be "trapped" into marriage and personal commitments, often by means of premarital pregnancies
(Anderson, 1990, 1999; McCall, 1994). This attitude leads males to exploit females, and it encourages females to use sexual enticements at an early age in
order to attract and "hold" males. The theme of male toughness, which may
represent a reaction to the humiliation of being economically helpless, signifies a readiness to engage in risky and dangerous activities and to discount
potential costs of misbehavior, and a willingness to resort to violence. Concern with autonomy causes people to avoid steady work, school, marriage, or
long-range commitments, which might otherwise constrain deviant impulses. The high status accorded those who can get something for nothing or
who are smart enough to have a scam both encourages unethical behavior
and discourages conventional activities that might lead to conformity. The
search for excitement frequently puts people in situations fraught with danger and opportunity for deviance. Finally, believing one's future cannot be
controlled and that potential disaster (in the form of becoming ill, being victimized, or losing one's source of livelihood) is just around the corner promotes instant gratification and works against planning and sacrifice for the
future. Consequently, individuals deeply engulfed in a subculture of poverty
will learn values and orientations that make it more likely they will end up engaging in various kinds of deviance such as theft, assault, deviant sexual activities, and shady dealings.

As Chapter 11 will show however, subcultural differences among socio-economic classes have not been firmly established—at least not in the sense of showing that there are distinct subcultures of poverty promoting deviance (Leacock, 1971; Ryan, 1971).

Community Contexts

Another explanation for putative socioeconomic status differences in deviance has to do with the extent to which the communities where people of various statuses reside are organized (Anderson, 1990; Bursik and Grasmick, 1993; W. Wilson, 1987). Typically, people who are less well off live where they can find cheap housing for rent; with economic success, they seek better housing, which is usually in another area, unless they are tied to the local area by employment opportunities. This movement produces two effects that undermine community organization (Shaw and McKay, 1969; see Tittle, 1989b). First, population instability, reflected by in- and out-migration but in contemporary advanced societies mostly by out-migration, makes purposive community organization unlikely. Since many people view their residence as temporary, they are disinclined to involve themselves in community affairs or invest their time and resources in a community from which they will not benefit. Also, organization is difficult because instability makes widespread patterns of acquaintanceship, the basis of effective community organization, difficult to achieve (Sampson and Groves, 1989).

When communities/neighborhoods are organized only in an informal sense, they cannot collectively monitor youth and deal with miscreants, promote neighborhood watches, or provide for educational, recreational, and civic needs. They cannot exercise the kind of community response that discourages undesirable activities and unsavory role models from locating themselves within the geographic boundaries of the community. And they cannot mobilize political responses that would permit them to demand and receive police services, efficient street lighting, or enforcement of city housing ordinances (Bursik and Grasmick, 1993).

Another set of conditions associated with changing demographic and economic circumstances also undermines the potential for effective community organization that might counter deviant behavior. As noted earlier, in-migrants to lower-status areas tend to be the less well off in search of affordable housing, while those who remain in the area do so mainly because they have no alternative or because of employment opportunities. In the past, industry, particularly that requiring labor-intensive but low-skill workers, chose to locate near lower-status residential enclaves in order to take advantage of the labor pool. In recent years, with increasingly advanced technology of production and the flight of better-educated people to the suburbs, industries have moved to the periphery of cities, where they have greater access to more-skilled workers and lower overhead. People who have moved toward the periphery along with industry are the more competent and better educated, who previously represented potential community leaders and conforming role models in lower-status inner-city areas. This out-migration has left many lower-status neighborhoods with even less possibility for organizing to deal with their own problems (Krivo and Peterson, 1996; Shihadeh and Ousey, 1996; W. Wilson, 1987).

The weak community organization characterizing many lower-status neighborhoods, which is largely the result of impersonal demographic and economic forces, is likely to lead to physically deteriorated surroundings. These conditions attract drug dealers, prostitutes, pornographers, loan sharks, and others who draw consumers of deviant services into the neighborhood and who serve as unconventional but "successful" models for youth to emulate. In addition, unsupervised, bored youth are thrown into company with peers and left free to roam the streets, while criminals are permitted to do misdeeds without fear of apprehension and punishment. However, this is not an inevitable process. Numerous studies have shown that some poor areas, particularly those bound together with religious, ethnic, or other background cultural ties manage to overcome handicaps and as a result have rates of deviance that are no greater than other neighborhoods and often much less (Bursik and Grasmick, 1993).

Minority Status

The relationship between minority status and deviance varies with the type of deviance in question. The evidence suggests that blacks, the main minority group in the United States, as well as Hispanics, are more likely to be involved in serious violence, certain kinds of illegal drug usage (particularly the opiates) and distribution, and some kinds of deviant sexual activities, such as early experimentation and prostitution. They are less likely, however, to be involved in white-collar crimes, prescription drug abuse, swinging, and suicide.

Socioeconomics

Since racial variations in deviance follow the same pattern as those for socioeconomic status, and since both blacks and Hispanics are disproportionately concentrated in the lower status categories, many of the explanations for the minority-deviance relationships are the same as for socioeconomic status. In fact, many contend that low socioeconomic status and all the things discussed in the previous section of this chapter denoted to explaining socioeconomic status differences in deviance that presumably go with it—biological deficiencies, economic and legal deprivation, poor or devio-genic socialization stemming from unstable families and subcultures of poverty, and unorganized communities—account for any minority-deviance relationship. In other words, if socioeconomic status were controlled, some contend, there would be no minority effect at all because race/ethnicity is essentially a proxy for social class. Nevertheless, there are some ad hoc explanations that go beyond mere socioeconomic status and its accompanying characteristics.

Biology

The same arguments about biology used to account for distributions of deviance over the socioeconomic status continuum have also been applied to minority-deviance relationships. Some argue, however, that minorities, particularly blacks, suffer from unique biological handicaps in the form of lower inherited intelligence (Herrnstein and Murray, 1994) and enhanced propensities toward violence (Ellis and Walsh, 1997). These claims are very controversial and are widely disputed, and much evidence suggests that any apparent differences in intelligence between blacks and whites is due to methodological weaknesses of the research supposedly showing that relationship (Devlin et al., 1997; Fischer et al., 1996; Fraser, 1995; Jacoby and Glauberman, 1995). Others claim that any apparent race-deviance relationship is due to influences from social contexts that affect learning opportunities (Sowell, 1995). If so, apparent differences in violence by race should largely disappear when demographic and social variables are controlled. That they do not completely disappear may be because it is impossible to statistically control for all relevant social conditions affecting blacks and whites so that they are completely equal. Apparently, the worst environmental conditions affecting the poorest whites in the United States are still better than the conditions affecting blacks (Sampson and Wilson, 1995).

Demographics

One explanation for greater amounts of deviance among minorities, at least as reflected in differing rates for population groups, is that minority populations are more likely to have the demographic characteristics that are indicative of higher rates of deviance in all racial or ethnic groups. In other words, there is a cluster of characteristics that is related to higher-than-average levels of deviance, and members of minority groups are more likely to possess these characteristics. Thus, blacks and Hispanics are much younger than whites, and they are more likely to live in cities. The median age for blacks in 1990 was 28.1, and it was 25.5 for Hispanics, compared to 34.4 for whites. And 51 percent of blacks and 61 percent of Hispanics live in cities over one million population, while only 34 percent of whites were residents of such large urban places (U.S. Census Bureau, 1990).

Another demographic characteristic indicative of greater likelihood of deviance is maleness. While Hispanics are more likely to be male than are whites, especially during the crime-prone younger ages, blacks are less likely to be male than either whites or Hispanics. Table 10.1 shows the ratio of males to females for various age segments of the U.S. population by race. Notice that in the late teens and early twenties, Hispanics have a higher male-to-female ratio than whites and much higher than blacks. Thus, Hispanics are mainly young, male, and urban dwellers. Blacks are mostly young and urban, though they are less likely to be male. Since youth, particularly youthful males, and urban dwellers are more prone to deviance, it would be surprising if blacks and Hispanics did not show higher rates of certain kinds of deviance. If deviance rates were standardized by age, sex, and place of residence, there would probably be few, if any, differences by race or ethnic characteristics. Thus, deviance among minorities is not likely to be something intrinsic to racial or ethnic characteristics (such as their biology). Still, if we are to explain these apparent racial/ethnic differences, it is important to explain why these groups have demographic features favorable to deviance.

Notice in Table 10.1 that the number of females comes to dominate the number of males much earlier in the black population than either the white or Hispanic population. By age 20, black females are more prevalent in the population than black males, but this does not occur until age 45 for whites and age 50 for Hispanics. These data suggest that something is happening to young black males. What? One possibility is that young black males are far more likely to die than whites. In 1990, the life expectancy for a white male was 73 years, for a black male it was only 64.5 years. The overall mortality rate for young black males is over twice that for whites, and death by homicide is almost eight times more likely for blacks than for whites.

Table 10.1 Ratio of Males to Females in the Population by Age and Race

Age	Whites	Blacks	Hispanics
Under 5	1.05	1.02	1.05
5–9	1.06	1.03	1.04
10–14	1.05	1.02	1.04
15–19	1.06	1.02	1.07
20–24	1.03	.96	1.19
25–29	1.01	.90	1.16
30–34	1.01	.87	1.10
35–39	1.00	.87	1.05
40–44	1.00	.85	1.00
45–49	.98	.83	1.00
50–54	.97	.81	.93
55–59	.94	.79	.86
60–64	.90	.75	.86
65–74	.79	.70	.78
75–84	.61	.56	.63
85+	.38	.42	.53
Overall	.95	.89	1.03

Compiled from Census of Population, General Population Characteristics. Washington, D.C.: U.S. Census Bureau, 1990.

The answer to this question involves both demographic and historical accounts. Consider, first, the question of why blacks and Hispanics are concentrated in cities, particularly large cities. This phenomenon is actually fairly recent. Originally, blacks and Hispanics were mostly rural because they came to this country to be farm laborers—Hispanics voluntarily and blacks involuntarily. With advancing technology and the accompanying decline in agricultural jobs, minorities were forced into cities in search of employment, and the larger the city, the greater the opportunities. Moreover, because of the disadvantages from discrimination, poor education, and deficient job skills, individuals most often migrated to cities already containing a number of their own cultural group who could help provide shelter, work, and a supportive and comfortable environment. Sometimes such minority communities even became more or less self-contained. Thus, the more minorities there were in large cities, the more attractive those cities became for other members of the same minority group. Over several decades, therefore, there was a spiralling increase in migration to cities, particularly large cities, by formerly rural minorities.

This trend was accelerated for blacks by the advent of the two world wars, particularly World War I. With white males away in service during the early part of this century, Northeastern and Midwestern factories, which were located mainly in large cities, sent recruiters to the South to entice blacks to come north and take manufacturing jobs, sometimes offering them bonuses and bus fare. The prospects of escaping discrimination in the South and fleeing with a promise of employment was enough to lure thousands of blacks to industrial cities, where they formed racial enclaves that served as beckoning safety nets for future migrations of their relatives, neighbors, and friends back in the South.

Hence because of the decline of agriculture and the lure of urban employment opportunities, along with the helping hand of urban minority enclaves, most minorities in this country are now urbanites, and the majority of them are residents of large cities. As we will see later, there is good reason to think that the conditions of life in cities is conducive to many forms of deviance. Thus, minorities have higher rates of some kinds of deviance at least partly because of an artifact of their history and migration patterns.

Minorities tend to be younger, and, in the case of Hispanics, more likely male during the periods of the life cycle when most deviance occurs, because of their subordinate economic positions and the accompanying deficits of education that go with lower socioeconomic status. Sex ratios and age compositions are linked to fertility (the actual reproductive behavior of women), which varies inversely with social class (Peterson, 1969:496–505). The inverse relationship between social class and fertility is easy to understand—it is partly because those with fewer resources and education have less access to contraceptives and are less skilled in their use. But it is also partly because children are more desired by lower status people, perhaps to enhance sexual identities among those who lack the means to establish such claims otherwise. In addition, those of lower socioeconomic status are more likely to uncritically fulfill religious injunctions.

The sex ratio at birth in almost all populations is unbalanced in favor of males. In fact, the sex ratio at conception is heavily unbalanced, with estimates ranging as high as 140 male conceptions to 100 females. But the mortality of males is higher than that of females at every age level from conception on. Because of higher prenatal mortality for males, the initially very high sex ratio is reduced to about 105 at the time of birth; that is, there are about 105 male babies born for every 100 female babies. This favorable sex ratio, however, continues to decline as the higher male mortality during the early part of the life cycle takes its toll. Eventually, usually in the mid-twenties, the sex ratio evens out and then begins to become unbalanced in favor of females. By age 65, the sex ratio is down to about 79. A quick glance around any retirement community would convince you that males are in a minority relative to females. Therefore, it follows that the overall sex ratio of most populations will vary inversely with the average age. The younger a population, the greater the chances that males will outnumber females; the older a population, the greater the chances that females will outnumber males. This principle, however, is sometimes upset by unusual mortality at young ages; this is apparently what happens with blacks in the United States. They have unusually high mortality from conception on, so that even though the black population has high fertility, it is not high enough to counterbalance the extraordinary mortality of the young.

As noted, the age structure of a population is partly a product of the fertility rate. The greater the fertility, the more children there are, and the younger the overall population. Hence, in general, the greater the fertility and the younger the population, the more likely that the population will have an excess of males. Further, since fertility is inversely related to socioeconomic status, the population segments that are least well off will have the greatest proportion of their numbers being young and male. Since minority populations are usually the poorest segments of an overall population—and certainly this is true of the U.S. population—they also have the highest fertility rate, which results in their median age being lower and, in the case of Hispanics, the number of males being larger. In fact, in 1992 the fertility rate for blacks was 1.25 times greater than that for whites, while the Hispanic fertility rate was almost 1.5 times greater than that for whites. And since deviance generally is most characteristic of youth and of males, minority populations are more likely to have higher rates of deviance.

In summary, then, minorities are likely to have high rates of certain forms of deviance because their demographic characteristics favor such outcomes. Any group whose members possess two or more of the characteristics most related to crime—live in cities, are young, and mostly male—will have higher rates of many kinds of deviance, regardless of anything else. Therefore, it follows that minorities will have high rates of deviance. This is because their histories of migration to cities and their lower socioeconomic status, which predicts high fertility with resulting predominance of young males, leads to deviance-favorable demographic characteristics.

Social Attachment

You learned in Chapter 9 that people who are married; have steady jobs or are involved in educational activities; participate in civic, religious, or other community organizations; own property; and are raising children are less likely than others to engage in most kinds of deviant activities. Since this is common knowledge among laypeople, they often advise youths to become socially enmeshed in order to avoid the temptations of deviance. But laypersons do not usually spell out why attachment has the effect that it is assumed to have. Students of deviance, however, do provide explanations, some ad hoc and some incorporated within more general theories, to account for why social attachment seems to be connected with conformity. In this case, the ad hoc explanations closely track a body of theoretical work concerning "social control." But because social control theory mainly summarizes and generalizes ad hoc accounts without embedding them systematically within a larger, more abstract explanatory system, our later discussion of it will recall many of the ideas discussed in the following sections of this chapter.

Restraint

One of the main reasons that social attachments and involvement in conventional institutions produce conformity is because they imply greater surveillance and, thereby, increased chances of getting caught in deviance. For example, unless the spouse is also engaged in deviant activities, a married person is frequently under the watchful eye of at least one other person who disapproves of deviance. Moreover, if an individual cares about his or her spousal relationship, the chances that deviance will jeopardize it constitutes a potent potential cost associated with deviance. Similarly, people dependent on steady jobs or heavily engaged in educational pursuits are subject to censure by associates who disapprove of deviance and whose good opinion might be jeopardized by such discovery; people with connections to other conventional organizations are similarly threatened. In addition, discovery carries with it the possibility of job loss, separation from the educational endeavor, and denial of the social prestige and support inherent in organizational participation. Loss of these connections, of course, is painful only for those who already have them, so social attachments not only make discovery of deviance more likely but they create the possibility of meaningful sanctions. Property ownership and parenting contribute to the constraining effects of social attachments because they constitute valuable assets, the loss of which would be costly.

Opportunity

Another way in which social attachments and involvements in conventional institutions affect conformity is through their restrictions on opportunities for deviance. Most forms of deviance require some attention and time, and they require situations where the deviance is possible. That is, the folk wisdom that "idle hands are the devil's workshop" has a kernel of truth to it. For example, an individual is not likely to use illegal drugs without spending some time thinking about it, being exposed to others who use them, having access to drugs, being where they can be used, and having the equipment and knowledge for their use. Students adhering to a demanding schedule of study, examinations, paper writing, and possibly part-time work have little time for the demands that opiate use requires. And married people cannot usually commit adultery without devoting some time to getting acquainted with potential co-conspirators in a flirtatious atmosphere, finding times and places for liaisons, and actually carrying forth a courtship of some kind. In other words, deviance requires time, attention, and energy that is simply not available to those conventionally involved. Being accountable for time, location, and social obligations to spouses, workmates, organizational comembers, children, and the institutions associated with property ownership and maintenance leaves little idleness to be filled with deviance, and it saps people of the strength necessary for pursuing deviance even if there were time.

Commitments

Social attachments are often accompanied by psychic or moral investments that some have called "stakes in conformity" (Briar and Piliavin, 1965; Toby, 1957). Those who devote time and effort to relationships or institutions usually care about them and have an incentive to maintain them. Most married people want their marriages to work and they are committed to trying to make them succeed. Most people value their jobs and their occupational activities, and as a result try to maintain them. Similarly, organizational participants, property owners, and parents normally exhibit a good deal of commitment to their organizations, their property, and their children.

❖ ❖ ❖ ❖

Commitment, in turn, reduces the motivation for forms of deviance that are not consistent with the welfare of the social groups to which one is committed. Indeed, commitment itself usually means that a person shares the ideas, beliefs, and values of those who constitute the social groups with which they are involved. For example, if a man is employed as a physician, he is likely to believe in certain moral and professional standards about patient welfare, the value of hospital standards for cleanliness, and the worthwhileness of the enterprise. Given these commitments, he is less likely to take sexual advantage of female patients, to use drugs, or to bring contraband materials into surgery than would someone, such as a temporary nursing aide, with similar opportunities but fewer commitments.

Summary

The relationships between social attachments and deviance, then, are explained in terms of three forces (cf. Hirschi, 1969). First, the relationship is seen as partly a product of the constraints emanating from socially enmeshing relationships that enhance the chances of being caught for deviance as well as the potential costs of sanctions that might ensue from apprehension. Second, the diversion of time and energy to potential deviance from conventional activities and responsibilities is generally more than attached people care to do. Finally, deviance is less likely for the socially bonded because involvement implies commitment to the welfare of the social networks of which one is a part and whose moral and normative standards one shares. Both commitment to social networks and belief in their principles reduce the motivation to commit deviance that might undermine them, thereby increasing the chances of conformity.

Spuriousness

One explanation of the association between social attachments and deviance is that prior antecedent variables cause both social attachment and deviance, thereby producing a spurious relationship between them. In effect, this explanation claims that social attachments only incidentally predict deviance because they are the effects of a common prior cause. Two potential prior causes have been identified.

Neuropsychological Deficits

Some contend that neuropsychological deficiencies such as low intelligence, weak impulsivity control, and negative emotionality are biologically determined or heavily influenced by biological factors and that these characteristics have two important effects: (1) they prevent people from forming social bonds, and (2) they have the direct potential for producing deviance. Hence, they are thought to create a spurious relationship between attachment and deviance (Moffitt, 1990; Moffitt et al., 1994). For example, those unable to control their impulses are likely to have difficulty forming long-term emotional relationships with other people or becoming involved in a concerted line of conventional activity that provides them with a stake in conformity. They are, in other words, unlikely to develop social attachments or commitments. Independent of this, because of their low impulse control they find themselves unable to resist the short-run temptations of crime and other de- viant acts. As a result, any observed correlation between social attachments, commitments, and crime/deviance may be spurious, due to the fact that both are products of low impulse control.

Since only a small minority of people suffer from neuropsychological de- ficiencies, and since the effects of such deficiencies would only turn up on the negative end of an association between social attachment and deviance, it is unlikely that these could account for the general relationship at issue here. Therefore, the neuropsychological account seems to assume that there is a natural, inherent tendency for normal people to form social attachments as well as to conform. Perhaps such a tendency stems from the fact that nurturance of human infants requires cooperative interaction with other people so that social relationships built on conformity to mutual expecta- tions come to be associated psychically with comfort and sustenance. This assumption cannot be demonstrated empirically, however, and, indeed, it flies in the face of assumptions on which most theories of social integration are based: that humans have a natural tendency toward selfishness and devi- ance, which is checked only by social constraints or socially induced self-con- straints.

Self-Control

A second variable thought to account for the social attachment-conformity relationship is self-control. Self-control is essentially the capacity to resist the short-run temptations of behaviors that provide immediate and easy gratifi- cation. Gottfredson and Hirschi (1990) contend that those with high self-con- trol are less likely to be attracted to a broad range of deviant acts than are those with less self-control. Since all are presumably naturally oriented to- ward self-gratification, when people with weak self-control confront an op- portunity for deviance (which is assumed to be naturally gratifying), they are likely to take it. Moreover, people with high self-control are also capable of making the personal sacrifices necessary to form and sustain social relation- ships, and they are likely to attach themselves socially because they see the advantages of such "social capital." Therefore, self-control affects deviance and social attachments separately, producing a spurious association between the two.

Overlaps and Contradictions

One major overlap between the self-control and the neuropsychological spuriousness arguments concerns impulsivity control, which in each argu- ment is regarded as a key condition that emerges in childhood and continues throughout the life course to produce a spurious social attachment-conformity connection. Those who embrace the neuropsychological position contend that impulsivity is largely determined by constitutional factors or biology— either genetic inheritance or some biological defect like brain damage or ex- cess hormones—while those who embrace the general theory of self-control argue that self-control is established early in life by effective child rearing. Ac- cording to Gottfredson and Hirschi (1990) and others (Larzelere and Patterson, 1990; Patterson, 1980, 1982) from whose work they draw, children who develop strong self-control are exposed to caregivers who care enough about them to monitor their behavior, actually do supervise them, recognize misbehavior when it occurs, and do something about it.

Another difference in these accounts concerns their basic assumptions about human nature. The biologically oriented scholars think that conformity is normal, that in the absence of some unusual problem like neuropsychological deficiencies or situational stress, people will naturally form social bonds and they will naturally conform. The self-control scholars, on the other hand, view deviance as normal and conformity as problematic. In the absence of special efforts by society to produce controlling elements, all would presumably deviate.

Both of these "spuriousness" accounts are contradicted by some evidence consistent with the idea that social capital is an intervening variable between impulsivity control and deviance (Nagin and Paternoster, 1994). Rather than seeing deviance and social relationships as independently caused by antecedent variables affecting each, some recognize that social attachments have inherently constraining effects, as discussed in the first part of this section, but that social attachments are themselves products of antecedent conditions such as neuropsychological deficits and learned self-control. Hence according to this argument, conformity is directly affected by social bonds, and social bonds themselves are the product of antecedent variables, which do not, however, directly affect conformity.

Size of Settlement

Although the relationship between size of place and deviance is not as straightforward as many scholars assume (see Tittle, 1989a), there is a persistent pattern by which larger size predicts greater chances of deviant behavior (Fischer, 1984; Tittle, 1989c). This phenomenon has attracted much attention by students of deviance (see Clinard, 1957; Clinard and Meier, 1992) and was the stimulus for a tradition of studies called "the Chicago School," which emerged in the early part of this century at the University of Chicago in the department of sociology. And because of its popularity, the apparent association between size of settlement and deviance has given rise to a number of ad hoc explanations as well as some more general theories.

Demographics

One of those explanations concerns movement of populations. Since larger places usually provide employment opportunities and exciting lifestyles not characteristic of smaller places, they attract migrants. This magnetic pull of hinterland residents to cities has two consequences that presumably increase the rates of deviance. First, since migrants are more likely to be risk takers, energetic, relatively deprived economically, and unencumbered—young, less well off, already deviant, mostly males without families or social ties—the populations of cities end up with an excess of individuals more willing and able to commit deviance (Gans, 1962). Second, the movement of large numbers of people into cities, either as permanent residents or as temporary sojourners who commute daily from surrounding suburbs, exacerbates problems of social integration that are central to the urbanism argument to be presented next.

While rates of deviance have been shown to vary with the demographic characteristics of populations, it is becoming less true that cities overall have distinctive demographic features, although inner-city areas continue to stand out. In modern societies, cities are as likely to grow from natural increase as from migration, and in any case, migrants are now less likely to be underprivileged or male. Further, the ubiquity of cities has led to demographic homogenization as cities have become the typical arenas for all of social life. Moreover, considerable evidence suggests that composition alone does not account for the relationship between size of place and deviance (Tittle, 1989a).

Urbanism

According to this explanation, which owes much to the ideas of Ferdinand Toennies (1957 [1887]), Georg Simmel (1971 [1903]), Louis Wirth (1969 [1938], and Robert Redfield (1969 [1947]), large, heterogeneous, densely concentrated populations find it difficult to achieve a sense of overall cohesion or to link themselves into interpersonal networks that make effective social control and healthy personality development possible. This difficulty arises because living in large concentrations forces everybody to interact frequently with strangers; it puts a premium on expedience and self-interest; and it promotes tolerance of misbehavior. Moreover, the pace of city life causes much stress for residents and it overloads their psyches with multiple stimuli. The result, sometimes called urbanism, causes many city dwellers to become pathologically motivated toward deviance, even suicide, and makes them feel they can get away with deviant behavior because of tolerance stemming from indifference and selfish interests and because of weak social control.

While some evidence supports this explanation (see Tittle, 1989a), particularly the notion that city populations are not well bonded in an overall sense and therefore can exercise less effective informal social control, other evidence suggests that urban dwellers are not as socially disconnected as the traditional urbanism account implies (Fischer, 1984), nor do they suffer more psychological problems than people in smaller places, at least not in contemporary societies. Moreover, variables from alternative explanations, including the compositional/demographic one described earlier have been shown to contribute to the urban variation in deviance, so that at best one can say that urbanism is only one of the conditions of city life that affect deviance.

Subcultures

A third explanation for the connection between size of place and deviance focuses on the features of urban living that give rise to subcultures, which promote deviant behavior (Fischer, 1975, 1995). According to it, natural interest in unconventional behavior is so rare that in small populations curious people are more or less isolated. As a result, they must forgo acting on their interests because of lack of opportunity, or they must risk sanction and social stigma. However, the larger, the denser, and the more heterogeneous a population is, the greater the chances that people with deviant interests can find each other and interact. Out of such interaction grows a subculture with its own norms encouraging this deviance, justifications for the behavior, and networks of people who accept the behavior as normal. Thus, large urban environments are more likely than rural or suburban ones to create a plethora of deviant subcultures, each promoting its own brand of deviance, because size makes more likely the "critical mass" for a given subculture to develop.

And because all subcultures must exist in the same context and each has an interest in tolerance, the overall urban environment provides many opportunities for learning about and committing deviance, and it sustains an atmosphere of tolerance that permits deviant practitioners to operate with impunity.

Although this explanation has not been fully tested, some evidence suggests that it is at least partly correct (Fischer, 1995; Tittle, 1989c). Although all forms of deviance are not subculturally linked, and subcultures are not limited to large cities, much deviance is promoted by subcultures, and many of those subcultures are more likely to develop in larger places. Moreover, whenever there is a subcultural organization built around a particular kind of deviance (such as illegal gambling) the rates of the deviance in question for members of the subculture appear to increase (Esbensen and Huizinga, 1993; Thornberry et al., 1983). So, even though the subcultural argument is not the full story, it appears that it at least helps explain why cities usually have higher rates of deviance.

Geographic Location

Regional Variations

As indicated in the last chapter, regional variations in deviance depend on the particular kind of deviance in question. While most kinds of criminal deviance, particularly violence, appear to be more characteristic of the South and West than of the Midwest and East, the South seems to have lower rates of drug use, most deviant sexual activities, and suicide.

Cultural Traditions

Some contend that different regions of the country have different values and orientations toward various aspects of life, religion, and personal responsibilities and that these values are passed on from one generation to the next and contribute to differences in rates of deviance. The South, for example, is often said to have a culture that encourages the use of violence. Such a culture prizes guns, promotes the belief that fear is the chief motivator of behavior, nurtures supersensitivity for personal affronts to honor, particularly among males, and cultivates the idea of self-help and personal responsibility. Presumably, these cultural traditions are rooted in a rural heritage that lasted longer in the South than in other regions. It includes the prevalence of fundamentalist religion; an aristocratic devotion to honor growing out of the plantation economy; the practice of slavery that required threats of violence to control involuntary laborers; huge socioeconomic discrepancies that generate masculine insecurities among a large proportion of its male residents; and the ever-present racial conflicts stemming from a large concentration of minorities.

Some observers argue that the same cultural traits that increase the chances of violence actually decrease the likelihood of other forms of deviance, which is why the South tends to rank low in deviant sexual activities, drug usage, and suicide. Religious devotion and fear of divine retribution, along with belief in personal responsibility and self-help, make it more likely that drugs and unconventional sex will be viewed as degradation, while suicide will be interpreted as cowardly and contrary to divine prerogative.

In their brilliant 1996 book, *Culture of Honor*, the psychologists Richard E. Nisbett and Dov Cohen argue that the Southern United States has a consistently high rate of violence because of the distinctive economic history of the South. This economic history, in turn, produced a unique culture that fosters the defense of honor and, ultimately, violence. Nisbett and Cohen argue that the South was originally a lawless frontier whose economy was based primarily on herding. Herding cultures, they observe, are typically characterized by a "culture of honor" where even minor personal affronts must be dealt with severely—frequently through acts of violence. Southern societies were settled by the Scotch-Irish, a people, Nisbett and Cohen argue, who have traditionally been herders and have a cultural tendency to respond to threats against person and property with violence. This historical tradition of violence carries over to today, Nisbett and Cohen argue. In their book they present experimental evidence which suggests that Southerners are more likely to see insult, become more physiologically upset by an insult, and show more readiness to respond in a physically aggressive manner.

While the cultural argument is plausible and considerable evidence seems to be consistent with it (see the evidence presented in Nisbett and Cohen, 1996), a good test has not yet been conducted. Many of the tests have compounded culture with social structure, particularly socioeconomic characteristics (see Loftin and Hill, 1974), and others have no measure at all of culture but take any regional indicators as proxies for cultures that presumably characterize the different regions of the United States. Moreover, there is good reason to question whether Southerners generally hold different values (Borg, 1997), particularly given the vast amount of migration from other regions of the country into the South.

Demographics

Another explanation for regional differences concerns demographic characteristics of the various populations. As we noted earlier, when a population has a large proportion of its people in lower socioeconomic statuses, its fertility will be higher than average, producing a disproportionate number of young people, a majority of whom will be male. Since young males are especially prone to deviance, a region like the South, which has a large proportion of its people in poverty, should tend to have high rates of deviance. Mitigating this demographic effect, however, is the fact that the South still is not as urban as other parts of the country. In 1990 only 26 percent of the population in the South lived in places of one million or more; the comparable figure for the Northeast is 49 percent, the Midwest, 33 percent, and the West, 52 percent (U.S. Census Bureau, 1990). Further, there is a high out-migration rate of young people from the South to urban centers elsewhere, the effect of which is boosted by a high in-migration rate of mid- to older-age people from other regions to the South.

Demographics play a different kind of role in the West. The West is closer to the frontier tradition than other regions, and in many parts of it, such as Montana, Wyoming, and the Dakotas, life is harsher. Therefore, it tends to have a younger, more male population because of out-migration of females and older folks.

Mobility

Although there is widespread belief that geographic mobility, particularly between countries and from rural to urban areas, is associated with deviance, the evidence is actually contradictory. Nevertheless, there have been many attempts to explain that putative association. We will review them here because many of them tap into fundamental social processes that are incorporated into the theories that we will consider later.

Demographics

Residential mobility, particularly from one society to another and from rural to urban areas, is usually undertaken in pursuit of economic opportunities, but because it is a disruptive experience, it is most likely to involve those who are unencumbered by social responsibility. Therefore, migrants who flooded this country during the first two decades of the century, who constituted the main movement of minorities from the South to the North and Midwest prior to the 1950s, and who in recent years made up the bulk of migrants from Mexico and Asia, were mostly young males, and those in lower socioeconomic categories. As we have already seen, they possess the characteristics likely to produce high rates of most forms of deviance.

However, there is a countertrend in modern societies with high rates of internal mobility. In the United States, people from all walks of life are on the move—to better houses, better jobs, better educations, and better climates, as well as to escape embarrassing backgrounds, disruptive marital experiences, and unpleasant environments. Moreover, much of this movement is from one city to another, from one small town to another, and from a good job to an equivalent or slightly better one elsewhere. It includes families as well as young males without social responsibility. Indeed, rates of mobility tend to be highest among those with moderate to high incomes and educations whose resources permit them to move with less uncertainty (Shumaker and Stokels, 1982). Hence it is no surprise that the evidence about the effects of mobility on deviance is mixed.

Culture Conflict

A prominent explanation for the supposed mobility effect that emerged early in this century, when so many people were crossing international borders to find new homes in the United States, concerned a clash between the norms and cultural values of the society from which people came and the standards of the new society (Sellin, 1938). These "cultural conflicts" produce confusion in the minds of the migrants about appropriate behavior and may lead to one of two kinds of deviance.

First, some migrants bring with them cultural practices that are directly in conflict with new standards. The classic illustration concerns an Italian immigrant who murdered his unmarried daughter's lover because upholding family honor in this way was required in the old country even though it clearly violated social expectations as well as the criminal law of his adopted society. A more contemporary example concerns the Rastafarians, immigrants to the south Florida area from the Caribbean, who use marijuana as a religious sacrament in their native land but who are regularly arrested and prosecuted for it in Florida.

Second, during the period of assimilation, many migrants know that they must adjust to new behavioral standards, but they are not sure to whom they should look for guidance. Moreover, since they initially settle in "disorganized" areas, open themselves to whatever employment is possible, and naively make themselves vulnerable to exploitation, they are likely to be exposed to many of the most unconventional normative environments (Clinard, 1957). Hence many of the normative standards adopted by international and rural-to-urban migrants presumably are actually deviant from the perspective of the whole society to which they have migrated.

Regardless of how valid the normative conflict account was in earlier decades, it now has much less force because of cultural homogenization through the mass media and because of the high rate of internal mobility. While heterogeneity and the conditions with which some migrants must contend still promote learning of unconventional standards in the new society, and still bring the transported behavioral standards of some migrants into conflict with local expectations, new migrants now can easily learn what is expected of them from television. And, of course, internal migrants already know what awaits them. It is easy, then, to understand why the relationship between migration and deviance may have declined in recent decades.

Social Integration/Control

The most prevalent explanation of the assumed mobility-deviance relationship contends that movement, or change, disrupts individual networks of social attachment that normally act to constrain deviant behavior and that normally prescribe conforming behavior. Thus, mobility is thought to set the individual free to deviate, at least for the period of time until new constraining relationships are developed (see Tittle and Paternoster, 1988, for a review of these arguments). The image of the migrant, then, is one of a socially isolated, anonymous individual with no friends, with family far away, and with no involvement in local community institutions like churches or voluntary organizations. Under these conditions there is little cost associated with deviance because nobody about whom the individual cares will find out.

However, like the other explanations already reviewed, this one has become muted in a time when large numbers of people move but sustain social relationships with their families, former neighbors, and friends by telephone, mail, or frequent visits and who maintain organizational identities through the exchange of information from one work or educational context to the other. So even though moving still disrupts social bonds to some extent, it is not nearly as dramatic as in the past. Moreover, most middle-class, family-oriented movers quickly establish new networks among residential and work associates.

Stress

Many scholars have tried to explain the effects of mobility on deviance as a product of the psychological problems associated with moving (Glueck and Glueck, 1950; McHugh, 1966; Lauer, 1974; Toffler, 1970). The presumed psychological problems include the stress of having to deal with new situations, uncertainty about oneself, sensory or cognitive overload, anxiety about how things will turn out, and disorientation. These psychological problems, in turn, lead migrants to seek solutions in deviance or to behave irrationally and in bizarre ways.

While there is no question that moving is burdensome and likely to produce stress, there is little evidence that such stress is more severe than that frequently encountered by most people in the rapid pace of modern life. In fact, residential mobility is often viewed positively and as an exhilarating experience. Thus, the reason for and the conditions under which a residential change occurs may be more important than the simple fact of migration. Moreover, there is no compelling evidence to show that short-term stress of this type produces deviance, since most people can cope with it reasonably well (Agnew, 1992).

IQ

Although the Intelligence Quotient, which is a score from a paper-and-pencil test designed to measure innate intelligence, is consistently linked in a negative way with many forms of deviance, particularly criminal and delinquent activities and certain kinds of drug use (Herrnstein and Murray, 1994; Hirschi and Hindelang 1977; Ward and Tittle, 1994), that linkage is not strong and for some forms of deviance, like suicide and white-collar crime, the association appears to be positive rather than negative. It is important also to remember that IQ may not actually measure innate intelligence (Fischer et al., 1996). Some contend that IQ tests measure what a person has learned, which may be, at least in part, a product of the educational advantages or opportunities for learning that a person has enjoyed. Others point out that the scores also reflect motivation to do well on such tests—an element that may vary by socioeconomic and minority status. Moreover, the content of IQ tests, which are constructed by middle-class, mainly white people, may be culturally biased against certain groups. Nevertheless, even if such tests do not measure intelligence, they at least measure something that allows prediction of the probability of various forms of deviance. The question is "why."

Success

One explanation for the association between IQ score and deviance is that whatever it measures—either intelligence or cultural learning of skills and knowledge—enables people to make their way in life without resorting to deviance. For example, youths with higher IQ scores typically do better in school, like educational activities more, remain in school instead of dropping out, and acquire academic credentials more readily than youths with lower scores (Hirschi and Hindelang, 1977). And adults with higher IQ scores are more likely to obtain and hold good jobs and achieve other forms of economic and social success (Herrnstein and Murray, 1994; Jencks et al., 1972; Jencks, 1979). Thus, whatever the tests measure, that characteristic is useful for involving individuals in conventional institutions, where they are subject to social control, and for enhancing success that, according to some arguments, reduces the motivation for deviance.

Social Control

Another explanation focusing on IQ and success contends that those with higher IQs are better able to assess the importance of conformity for achieving life's goals, and they are better able to grasp the possibilities of sanction and anticipate the potential costs associated with deviance (Wilson and Herrnstein, 1985). There is a counterargument, however, suggesting that higher intelligence permits one to deviate in ways that are less likely to provoke sanctions, thereby actually increasing some forms of deviance. Thus, white-collar criminals, most of whom are not caught or punished, can escape because of the clever way in which they manage their fraud or violence.

Labeling

A third explanation centering on the connection between IQ and success contends that early testing in the schools creates biases among school officials and teachers about the abilities of students (see Ward and Tittle, 1994, for a review of these arguments; see also Menard and Morse, 1984, 1986). These biases then are translated into "self-fulfilling prophecies" by the actions of school functionaries. Students with low IQ scores are often placed into vocational curriculum tracks instead of into college preparatory programs and as a result end up with few ambitions and with little success. Under these circumstances, many such youths drop out of school, get involved in street gangs, and end up committing crimes, using drugs, and engaging in deviant sexual activities (but see Jarjoura, 1993; Elliott and Voss, 1974). Labeling of low-IQ students can also produce negative outcomes when teachers and parents respond to these students as failures or neglect to give them the attention needed for effective learning (Harvey and Slatin, 1975; Rosenthal and Jacobson, 1969; but see Nash, 1976). Finally, when students begin to perceive that they have low intelligence, either because of teacher reaction, tracking, or direct knowledge of the results of the IQ tests, they may develop a negative self-image and feel doomed to failure. Poor self-attitudes are thought by many to be implicated in deviance because the person either capitulates to society's judgment and helps it along through deviant behavior, or because the individual uses deviance as a device to help restore self-esteem (Kaplan, 1980).

Associated Variables

A final explanation for IQ-deviance associations sees IQ as indicative of neuropsychological deficits that either lead directly to deviant behavior or handicap individuals in normal social interaction so that they fail to acquire the social capital necessary for success or for them to become subject to social control (Moffitt, 1990; Henry and Moffitt, 1997). Thus, low measured intelligence is often thought to indicate attention deficit disorders, impulsivity, and insensitivity to perceptual cues, all of which disadvantage a person in social exchange and may directly stimulate deviance.

Personality

Much of the evidence linking personality to deviance is questionable because measures of personality often incorporate indicators of deviance itself, creating a tautology, and because characteristics that have been identified as personality traits are often not distinguishable from each other. Traits also seem to change as the person moves through different stages of the life cycle and from one social role to another, rather than remaining constant as they should if they actually were indicative of personality (Caspi et al., 1994). However, the best research suggests at least two stable personality characteristics that seem to predict deviance. They are weak impulsivity control (or constraint) and negative emotionality. Here we consider the main ad hoc explanation of why these traits are associated with deviance.

With negative emotionality, a person tends to feel anger, anxiety, and irritability more readily than do most people. Such tendencies will cause people to have trouble managing everyday events and life course patterns in ways that will allow them to succeed economically and socially; failure to succeed thereby provides an incentive for deviance. People with negative emotionality are more likely to be suspicious of other people and to see the challenges of life as particularly onerous and unfair. Moreover, when these debilitating emotions are paired with weak impulse control, those people are more likely to resort to deviance as a means for overcoming the perceived problems, or they are simply more likely to lash out irrationally in fits of anger and violence.

Weak impulse control may be linked to deviant behavior because individuals are unable to restrain themselves from immediately seizing opportunities to gratify their desires. Everybody encounters situations where they could commit deviance that would be profitable and satisfying. However, most people realize that such opportunities are fraught with long-range danger, and since they have the ability to control themselves, they do not deviate. For example, most married people occasionally find themselves in company with willing potential extramarital sex partners. Such situations may appear appealing at the time, but if acted on, they could lead to sexually transmitted disease, difficult emotional entanglements, uncomfortable feelings of guilt, or loss of spouse. For those reasons, individuals with good self-control may decline to avail themselves of the opportunity. Those with weak self-control, however, do not, and perhaps cannot, stop to take into account the potential consequences of their actions. They are likely to act first and think later. This tendency can get them into a lot of trouble, as the data connecting impulsivity and deviance suggest (Gottfredson and Hirschi, 1990; Wilson and Herrnstein, 1985).

Family Structure and Process

Arguments about a link between deviance and family structure and/or process have waned and waxed with changes in the social and political climate, and even the accumulated evidence has varied in strength at different times during the past few decades (Wilkinson, 1974; see Sutherland et al., 1992 for a review of the evidence). It appears that, in general, incomplete families—those with fewer than two parents for some part of the child's developmental period—are slightly more likely to produce children with a greater possibility of deviance of various kinds, independent of other things (Rosen, 1985; Rosen and Neilson, 1982). However, the evidence also suggests that good child rearing by a caregiver can sometimes overcome the disadvantages of an incomplete family, and some family processes, such as parental conflict and spousal abuse, inconsistent discipline, totalitarian dominance or abuse of children by parents, weak attachment between parents and children, or poor supervision are likely to lead to deviance by children regardless of the family structure (Canter, 1982; Cernkovich and Giordano, 1987; Hirschi, 1969; Van Voorhis et al., 1988; Wells and Rankin, 1988). Furthermore, the number of caregivers relative to the number of children seems to be relevant (Broidy, 1995; Gottfredson and Hirschi, 1990; Tygart, 1991).

Socialization

The main explanation for the effects of family structure and/or process concerns the things that a child learns (Akers, 1985; Gottfredson and Hirschi, 1990). According to this argument, conformity requires one to know the social rules, to believe that they are legitimate, to have some moral commitment to the values underlying them, to understand the consequences of violation, and to have the ability to manage one's own behavior in view of conventional social expectations. All these things are accomplished when caregivers are willing and able to devote considerable time to instructing children in proper behavior, giving them a moral rationale for conformity, helping them to appreciate and contemplate the potential consequences of deviance, correcting them when they misbehave, and setting a good example by their own behavior (Larzelere and Patterson, 1990; Wilson, 1987).

The time and ability to engage in such child rearing is partly structural—two parents or other caregivers can do it better than one, and no matter how many parents or other caregivers there are, the greater the ratio of caregivers to children, the more likely it is that they can socialize children effectively. The more caregivers there are, generally, the more likely that one of them will be on hand at teaching moments, although this is not always true since sometimes both parents are employed outside the home. But effectiveness is not entirely determined by structure. Some parents love their children more than other parents, some are more skilled in child rearing, and some are better role models. But whatever the particular mechanisms, according to this explanation, the family matters mainly because of what and how it teaches children. This effect is likely to take hold early and continue throughout the life course.

Social Control

Not all scholars accept the idea that family structure and process have their main effects through socialization. Some contend that family relationships produce conformity mainly through their social control functions. Such functions are of two types—indirect, based on the effects of attachment (reviewed earlier in this chapter)—and direct, stemming from family members keeping an eye on children to ensure that opportunities for misbehavior are minimal and that misdeeds are punished. These effects are thought to have the most direct impact during childhood and adolescence, the years individuals are most prone to deviance. Later effects are indirect, as the individual continues to conform out of habit or moves into new roles where he or she must assume the job of loving or watchful parent and becomes constrained by a new set of social attachments and responsibilities in another family context.

Social Attachment

According to this argument, neither the size of families, the relative numbers of caregivers, the content of instructions to children, or the nature of child rearing matters as much as the social bonds between family members (Hirschi, 1969). If parents and children love each other and spend a lot of time together, then children will likely avoid deviance because they will not want to risk displeasing or embarrassing the parents; they will naturally share the parents' belief in the necessity and value of conformity; and they will be too heavily involved in family matters to find opportunities for devi-

ance or to become affiliated with peers who might provoke deviant actions.
This explanation assumes that all parents and other caregivers, even if they
themselves are involved in deviance, want their children to conform to conventional standards and that knowledge of appropriate behavior is obvious.
Hence, the explanatory mechanism is the quality of the relationship between
parents and children, and it is this explanation that leads some to discount
the importance of family structure, the nature of discipline, and other things
that some social scientists regard as so important.

Direct Supervision

Another way in which family structure/process can affect deviant behavior, particularly for young people, is when it promotes surveillance by parents
and other responsible adults. According to one ad hoc explanation, when parents or other caregivers spend a lot of time with children, keep up with their
whereabouts when they are away from home, and involve them in activities
that are supervised by adults—in other words, when families make sure it is
difficult for youths to encounter opportunities for deviance or increase the
chances they will be caught in case of deviation, the children are less likely to
do deviant behavior, and they are more likely to grow up with habits of conformity (Broidy, 1995; Wells and Rankin, 1988). Such surveillance, of course,
is more likely when there are two parents rather than one, when parents outnumber children, and when one or both parents or caregivers are not pulled
away from the children for extensive periods of time by employment, recreation, illness, or incarceration. And even with favorable structural circumstances, parents must care enough to follow through.

Peer Association

One of the best-established facts in the study of deviance is the relationship between deviant behavior of individuals and their association with deviant peers (Akers, 1985; Matsueda, 1988; Matsueda and Heimer, 1987; Warr,
1993, 1996). For almost all kinds of deviance, occurrence is likely to take
place in company with others, particularly the first time. For many kinds of
deviance, group support is essential for learning how to do the deviance and
for sustaining its practice. Furthermore, while peer association is particularly important for youthful deviance, it continues to affect the probabilities
of deviance throughout the life course (Tittle, 1980b; Tunnell, 1993). Therefore, with few exceptions, such as suicide (most of the time) and serial killing,
deviance is a group phenomenon. But why is this so?

Deviance in Everyday Life

The idea that people tend to behave as their friends and associates do is much
older than the study of deviance. For centuries social observers have noted that our
behavior is heavily influenced by the behavior of those with whom we associate.
Here is a sample of those observations:

Every man is like the company he is wont to keep. *EURIPIDES*

Can a man take fire in his bosom, and his clothes not be burned? *BIBLE*,
    Proverbs 6:27

He that lies down with dogs shall rise up with fleas. *LATIN PROVERB*

If you live with a cripple, you will learn to limp. *PLUTARCH*

A man is known by the company he organizes. *AMBROSE BIERCE*

Deviance in Everyday Life

In 1963, the sociologist Howard S. Becker wrote a classic book, *Outsiders*, that contained a chapter entitled "Becoming a Marijuana User." In this chapter, Becker described the learning and tutelage process that marijuana users go through. That is, users do not instantly appreciate the drug and its effects; rather, Becker argued, becoming a marijuana user required a group context. He came to these conclusions after conducting interviews with dance band musicians. (In addition to being an internationally known sociologist, Becker was an accomplished and practicing musician.) According to Becker, persons fall into marijuana use out of little more than idle curiosity, what he calls "vague impulses and desires." Idle experimenters cannot appreciate the drug and cannot become users until they have learned how to use the drug properly. That is, marijuana smoking is not like smoking cigarettes or a cigar, and novices must be taught how to inhale and "hold" the smoke. Once the proper technique is learned, initiates must learn how to interpret the effects of marijuana; this they do with the help of more experienced users. They, in a sense, tell the novices that the feelings they are experiencing are the effects of the drugs. Moreover, these experiences must be interpreted in a positive light before a user is created. All of this requires mentoring by experienced marijuana users.

Group Necessity

One reason often given for the peer association-deviance connection is simply that much deviance requires other people, often even organized groups. For example, for people to use illegal drugs, they must be able to obtain them, learn how to use them effectively, and have safe opportunities for use (that is, be able to find situations with low probability that somebody who disapproves or is authorized to sanction drug use will intrude and where there is someone who can help in case of bad consequences, such as overdose or contamination). Producing and distributing illegal drugs implies a network of people with whom potential users must associate, and since there is a technology of drug usage (how much to use, how to use, how to store, how to interpret effects, how to obtain and use equipment, and the like), new users must be trained by others (see Chapter 4). Finally, opportunities for safe usage are provided by associates, some of whom can watch for intruders. Hence it is extremely unlikely that a person could use illegal drugs without being affiliated with others involved in drug use or in other activities linked with drug use. In similar ways, much criminal/delinquent behavior, such as shoplifting, illegal gambling, and burglary, depends on group support, as do deviant sexual practices, particularly homosexual activities and swinging. In addition, groups provide social support, a body of supporting beliefs for deviant activity, and stimulation of courage (Matza, 1964).

Not only does much deviance require fellow travelers, but, as we learned in earlier chapters, deviants are sometimes fully organized for long-range survival. One of the features of such groups is that they often have well-developed procedures for recruiting new members. Further, many forms of deviance are at least partially organized in subcultures that feature some recruitment. Hence, deviance is frequently undertaken in a group context because those who already practice the deviance try to make it attractive to potential new practitioners and because those who want to engage in deviance, for whatever reason, often find it necessary to participate with others if they are to satisfy their desires.

Group Social Control

A second, and probably the most popular, ad hoc explanation of the peer association-deviance linkage is "group pressure." Laypersons and scholars alike note that it is hard for most people to resist collective expectations for behavior when they are with a group of peers. As a result, when the possibility of deviance arises, individuals often find themselves doing things they would avoid if alone. But what is the nature of this pressure, and how does it work?

Acceptability

Most people want to be part of, or integrated with, at least some groups of friends or peers; that is, they want people to like them, to spend time with them, and to permit them to participate in group activities. Therefore, they are sensitive to how others react to them. When it appears that others in a group expect certain behavior, failure to conform to those expectations carries the possibility of being rejected by the group. Therefore, one component of group pressure is the perceived effect of a person's behavior on the chances that others in the group will accept or reject the individual as a participant.

The more important the group is to the person, the more sensitive he or she is to potential rejection and the greater the influence of the group on the individual's behavior. In general, groups are important to people to the extent that they uniquely fulfill important needs. Thus, a person who has many groups that meet a particular need, such as companionship, is less dependent on any given one and is therefore less likely to fear rejection. Such a person is less subject to group pressure. Similarly, a group that does not meet a particular need at all, no matter what the competition, will be of little importance to the person and consequently will be able to exercise little control over him or her.

Since one's needs, and the means for fulfilling them, vary with situations and over the life course, the influence of peers on deviant behavior also varies. Peer influence is very powerful during the adolescent years, because adolescence is a transition period between childhood—when one's needs are met in close, intimate kinship groups—and adulthood, where with appropriate maturity those needs again come to be met in new familial arrangements. In the meantime, however, youths are breaking free of childhood familial bonds and have not yet established new adult familial relationships. This hiatus forces them to fall back on peer groups to meet many of their social needs, especially the need for social acceptance. Hence peer groups come to have great influence on adolescents, and some of that influence gets translated into "pressure" for deviance.

Status and Prestige

Another component of group pressure stems from the ability of a group to grant recognition, prestige, or status ranking to its participants (Kiesler and Kiesler, 1969). Though some group participants may not fear rejection from the group, they are nevertheless responsive to group expectations because of their desire for the rewards of ranking within peer contexts. Prestige and status elevation usually reflect conformity to group norms—the greater the conformity, the higher is one's status in the group. There is an important exception to this pattern, however, and that concerns deviance undertaken in the interest of the group as a whole. For example, if a group norm calls for sharing of financial resources, individuals who can and do share will be highly regarded. But in a crisis where failure to share protects the group from dissolution or attack from outside forces, those who are autonomous enough to defy the group norm—those who refuse to share—end up with advancements in prestige. But such crises are rare, and so the normal mode is for groups to control the behavior of participants by granting or withholding prestige rankings to those who meet the group's normative expectations. For individuals, this is translated into pressure to conform when they perceive that others will approve or disapprove of what they might do.

And just as the importance of acceptability in a given group, and therefore the group's ability to demand conformity, varies with the value of the group to the individual, so does individuals' competition for status depend on the value of the group and the social rank of specific individuals outside the group in question. Individuals with generally high social rank in many groups are less likely to be sensitive to the expectations for conformity in any given group. Since adolescents generally suffer from subordinate status in the larger society, they are especially attuned to peer groups who can provide recognition and prestige.

Why Deviance?

The social control argument reviewed above accounts for the general deviance-peer association linkage only to the extent that group processes produce deviance instead of conformity. Group manipulation of peer acceptability and recognition can generate conformity with the norms of the larger community or society when those norms coincide with the norms of the peer groups. Some peer groups, such as religious sects or swinging groups, have overarching normative schemes that conflict with the norms of the communities or the larger society of which they are a part, and through the group processes described above they are especially likely to produce deviant behavior. And while such groups account for some of the association between deviance and peer affiliation, they do not account for all of it. Of equal import are groups that do not have deviant norms but whose internal workings nevertheless generate deviance. In many contexts peers may not share recurrent mutual expectations for deviant behavior, but the dynamics of their interaction nevertheless occasionally leads to it. Three explanations have been offered for this phenomenon.

Mutual Suggestibility

When same-status peers (such as those of similar age and gender) interact without outside intervention, they usually do so in the context of leisure time. They are looking for something to do. Without specific goals, and open to anything interesting, such groups are sensitive to new experiences (Short and Strodtbeck, 1965; Whyte, 1955). New experiences, by definition, are not previously tested for normative acceptability and require on-the-spot evaluation. Moreover, in the context of idleness, the rewards of acceptability and high status go to those who are innovative. Consequently, even the members of generally conforming groups may stimulate each other to occasional deviance through mutual suggestibility. For instance, a group of adolescent boys who normally conform may be goofing off on a particular occasion. Wandering under a bridge, they find an old man sleeping, which prompts one of the boys to suggest they tease him for fun. None objects under the circumstances, and so they proceed. But the victim resists, things escalate, and the boys end up assaulting the oldster. Thus, group interaction sometimes leads to deviant opportunities that otherwise would not have emerged.

❖ ❖ ❖ ❖

Testing

In addition to the suggestibility that sometimes leads to deviance, some normatively conforming groups occasionally generate deviance because occasions of group interaction lead to tests of participants' claims to various statuses relevant to the community or larger society.

This testing is particularly the case for male adolescent groups, whose members are often engaged in masculinity testing to overcome anxiety about sexual identities; such anxiety is particularly acute among those denied adult opportunities to demonstrate such claims. Thus, a lot of what males do in the company of other males, particularly if not disciplined by specific goals or supervisors, is to challenge each other to prove manhood. These challenges take the form of insults to see how the victim will respond, dares to engage in risky behavior, and direct attempts to physically intimidate the other. The result is an increased chance of deviance.

Undermining External Control

Finally, group contexts, even if there is no system of deviant norms, tend to produce deviance because the dynamics of interaction tend to undermine the effect of external social control. For social control to be effective, individuals must recognize that a potential behavior is wrong and likely to provoke formal or informal sanctions; they must perceive that the sanctions will be applied to them personally with a reasonable degree of certainty and will have costly consequences; and they must not have available to them alternative motivations that outweigh such concerns. Group interaction, however, sometimes undermines these possibilities. If others in a given situation do not view a particular act as wrong, then it is difficult for an individual to sustain a belief that it is wrong. And if any in a group context discount the likelihood or probability of sanctions, others will look like cowards if they express their fears. Further, within a group, one's sense of individuality is subordinated to the whole, and a discrediting of personal responsibility takes over. Finally, what the group is about often tends to supersede personal concerns. Collectively, these processes mute those forces normally restraining individual deviance.

One description of the processes undermining social control and self-control calls them "techniques of neutralization" (Minor, 1980; Sykes and Matza, 1957). They are said to include: (1) denial of responsibility ("I didn't do it" or "It isn't my fault"); (2) denial of the victim ("He was a bum and deserved it anyway" or "That company is ripping people off and won't miss the money"); (3) denial of injury ("Nobody was hurt very much" or "It was just a rickety old car anyway and not worth much"); (4) higher loyalty ("I couldn't let my friends down" or "I had to defend my mother's honor"); (5) metaphor of the ledger ("This is not typical of me (or us); look at all of the good things I (we) have done" or "I'm a good person who works, goes to church, and pays taxes; I just lost my head"); and (6) condemning the condemners ("Who are you to blame me, you are cheating on your taxes" or "Everybody else is doing it"). These cognitive mechanisms presumably emerge situationally and prior to deviance and serve the function of releasing deviants from constraints. They are to be distinguished from psychological defense mechanisms that come into play to rescue a person's self and reputation after he or she is caught for deviance.

Spuriousness

A final ad hoc explanation for the deviance-peer association relationship asserts that the relationship is spurious because it is attributable to prior variables that account for both factors (Glueck and Glueck, 1950; Hirschi, 1969). Thus, the same variables that cause deviance are said to also cause people to seek out and associate with other deviants. According to this account, group interaction itself contributes little or nothing because what appears to be a connection between deviance and peer association is really a manifestation of the deviant propensities of the individuals involved. For example, self-control advocates contend that those who have not learned self-control at an early age, primarily in the family, will leap at later opportunities for self-gratification. Such self-gratification will include deviant acts as well as association with other deviants who will provide a pleasurable forum for bragging and mutual justification. This notion is expressed in the adage, "Birds of a feather flock together."

Prior Deviance

One of the best-established facts in the field of deviance is that deviance is associated with more deviance (Nagin and Paternoster, 1991a). And this association is no respecter of type of deviance. The best predictor of any given deviance, besides an instance of that same deviance, is prior commission of some other form of deviance. People do not specialize but instead seem very versatile in the deviance they commit (Gottfredson and Hirschi, 1990). Those who engage in theft are also likely to commit violent crime at a subsequent time. And those who commit any form of crime are also likely to use illegal drugs and to practice deviant sexuality. Thus, while some deviance, like unconventional sectarian religious practices, is focused, and some, like white-collar crime, is episodic, most of it appears to reflect a general propensity toward deviance of all types (Rowe et al., 1990). Although there are numerous general theories that account for this, there are also a number of ad hoc explanations.

Habitual Success

One account of why deviance leads to more deviance is that early manifestations pay off and therefore inspire the person to repeat that and other acts. For example, if temper tantrums "work" for a child—produce the desired results, say, getting a parent to allow some privilege, and result in few costly consequences like having to stay in one's room for a period of time— then that child will use them again. Moreover, since people tend to learn by generalizing from one situation to another, successful temper tantrums are likely to lead ultimately to defiance of parents, violation of laws, and general "out-of-control" behavior. Similarly, if people steal some desired item and get away with it, they are likely to steal again, and they are likely to undertake other deviant activities that promise some gratification. Hence success at deviance breeds more deviance until a habit of deviant behavior is created.

Association

Another explanation is based on the notion that deviance attracts others who share an interest in risky or unconventional behavior. When deviants are so attracted and hang together, they stimulate each other to further deviance. This occurs by means of group processes. But there is another thing that many researchers think is at work. People who practice any particular kind of deviance are subject to negative reaction from the larger society; consequently, they are likely to build resentment against conventionality and grow tolerant of all forms of deviance. As a result, deviants of all kinds share a kinship in their opposition to conventionality and their mutual interest in escaping the forces of outside social control. These common interests lead to association, which in turn leads to cross-fertilization. For example, thieves who hang out in particular bars known for harboring deviants are likely to become acquainted with prostitutes, drug dealers, and terrorists. And while they may initially have little interest in those activities, they will tolerate others who are "outside the law," and by talking with prostitutes or drug dealers they may come to regard those behaviors as appropriate for themselves.

Labeling

A third explanation for the fact that deviance leads to deviance is incorporated into a larger, more general scheme—called interactionist/labeling theory—that is discussed in detail later. For now, the point is that people who do deviance get reputations, and others come to think of them as deviants. Because others think of them as deviants, they treat them as deviants. Such treatment affects the individuals' self-images, throws them into company with others so labeled, and makes it difficult for them to follow conventional paths (Gove, 1975; Lofland, 1969). The result is more deviance. For example, a woman who neglects her children will not be well thought of by members of conventional society, and they will avoid social interaction with her. To meet her needs, say for employment and companionship, she then has to seek out others who are not well regarded by the community. This puts her in association with prostitutes or drug dealers who accept her and teach her their ways. At the same time, the community's response has caused her to question her own self-image, which prior to labeling was as a conforming person, and perhaps begin to change it. All this leads to additional deviance so that one who started out misbehaving in a limited way comes to misbehave in lots of ways.

Weakened Constraints

A final explanation for the fact that prior deviant behavior predicts future deviant behavior so well is that the commission of deviant acts may have consequences that weaken constraint against committing additional acts of deviance. In other words, no matter the causes of initial deviance, actually committing such acts can weaken subsequent social and personal controls, leading to additional deviance. For example, excessive drug and alcohol use as well as prostitution destroys conventional relationships and risks conventional careers, both of which weaken the capacity of informal controls to restrain conduct. Deviant behavior, therefore, frequently entails collateral consequences (soured relationships with spouses and children, lost jobs, and re-duced respect of others) that make deviant acts more likely in the future.

Spuriousness

Finally, as with so many of the associations between deviance and other characteristics we have examined, some researchers explain the association between prior and subsequent deviance as spurious because it is attributable to some antecedent variable that accounts for the early and the later devi-ance. Thus, some contend that neuropsychological deficits precede and cause initial deviance and continue to cause deviance throughout the life course, producing a spurious association between early and late deviance (Moffitt, 1997; Moffitt et al., 1994). Others contend that socioeconomic or mi-nority status, weak self-control, various personality traits, or even gender af-fect deviance independently at all points throughout any time span. In effect, these accounts deny that one act of deviance has any causal connection with subsequent acts of deviance.

Conclusion

In this chapter we have reviewed various explanations for the established patterns of deviance described in Chapter 9. These explanations are focused accounts aimed at answering questions of "why" or "how" for specific phe-nomena of interest, and are to be distinguished from explanations stemming from general, abstract theories that encompass accounts of many different phenomena but whose explanatory principles can be narrowly channeled to explain a given phenomenon of interest.

While there are numerous ad hoc explanations for a multitude of regular-ities, some common themes emerge. The most important have to do with things inherited genetically or due to biological functioning, things learned either in early childhood or upon entry to new situations that motivate or constrain deviance, deprivations of one kind or another that stimulate de-sires or needs that might be satisfied by deviance, group structures and pro-cesses, and social control involving positive and negative sanctions of a for-mal or informal nature, but mostly informal. As you will see, these themes are also the main ones reflected in the general theories set out in subsequent chapters. ✦

Chapter 11

External Motivation Theories

In this chapter, we will discuss four separate theories, or theoretical approaches, as examples of situational motivation theories current in the deviance/crime literature. These theories have in common the tendency to locate the main cause of offending in the situation external to the individual, and they all postulate that the particular situational factors identified by the theory lead to deviant behavior by creating or intensifying an individual's motivation to commit the acts in question.

Learning

Sutherland

Learning theory as an explanation for deviant or criminal behavior was first formulated and made popular by Edwin Sutherland (1939). Sutherland believed that people commit crimes for the same reasons they conform, that is, because they are exposed to social messages that favor the particular behavior performed. In other words, Sutherland viewed human behavior as a product of learning and of responding to behavioral cues and examples, particularly those encountered in interaction with primary groups. In attributing crime to a process of social learning, Sutherland's theory of differential association was a critical response to two competing explanations of crime/deviance that were popular at the time. One attributed crime/deviance to a multitude of individual factors while another attributed it to pathological factors. To Sutherland, crime was neither individual nor pathological, it was produced by "normal" processes (learning) that occurred through social interaction.

Although Sutherland set forth his theory in nine general statements, it has been succinctly summarized by DeFleur and Quinney (1966): "Overt

---

Deviance in Everyday Life

Edwin Sutherland's theory of differential association is one of the most prominent theories of crime and deviance. Sutherland stated his theory formally with nine principles. These principles are summarized below:

1. Criminal behavior is learned.
2. Criminal behavior is learned in social interaction with other persons through a process of symbolic communication.
3. Most of the learning occurs within the context of intimate, personal groups like family and peers.
4. The content of the learning includes specific skills or techniques of committing the act, and learning motives, rationalizations, and attitudes about the act.
5. People are exposed both to definitions and attitudes favorable to the violation of the law and unfavorable to the violation of law.
6. A person becomes deviant when the definitions favorable to the violation of law are more numerous than those unfavorable to the violation of law.
7. Favorable or unfavorable definitions are not equally powerful, but vary in frequency, duration, priority, and intensity.
8. Learning criminal or deviant behavior is no different from learning any other kind of behavior.
9. Criminal and deviant acts cannot be explained by any special need or motivation, because what motivates crime and deviance motivates noncriminal and nondeviant action.

criminal behavior has as its necessary and sufficient conditions a set of criminal motivations, attitudes, and techniques, the learning of which takes place
when there is exposure to criminal norms in excess of exposure to corresponding anti-criminal norms during symbolic interaction in primary
groups." The major point is that everybody is exposed to some criminal messages and some conforming messages (as well as many neutral messages),
and individual behavior patterns reflect the relative balance of the number,
source, and importance of those messages. That is, the key for understanding
crime is the ratio of antisocial to prosocial messages and definitions.

To illustrate the argument, consider three boys. The first lives in an inner-
city neighborhood where crime is prevalent and is accepted as an appropriate
way of life. In addition, the boy's father is fraudulently collecting unemployment compensation while his mother occasionally shoplifts to help overcome the family's economic deprivation. The second boy lives in the same
neighborhood, but his father has a legitimate job, and his mother believes
that honesty always pays. Moreover, these parents spend a lot of time with
their son, teaching him by precept and example that crime is unacceptable.
The third boy resides in a suburban neighborhood where little crime is seen
and where most people ostensibly disapprove of illegal behavior. In addition,
this third boy is heavily involved with his family, the members of which are
scrupulous law abiders.

According to Sutherland's theory, the first boy is the most likely of the
three to commit crime because he is exposed to an excess of definitions (messages), or examples, favoring crime. He sees crime occurring around him,
and he sees that those who commit crime are often rewarded with material
goods and prestige. In addition, members of his own family commit crimes.
Thus, he is probably exposed to more crime-favorable messages than to social messages unfavorable to crime. The second boy has a somewhat lower
probability than the first boy of committing crime, because the examples and
messages favoring crime to which he is exposed in the neighborhood are balanced somewhat by countermessages and examples in the family. Although
there is a mixture of norms favoring law violation and counternorms favoring
compliance with rules, the ratio of the mixture favors conformity. The third
boy, however, has the least probability of criminal behavior, because he is exposed to a large excess of conforming examples and messages.

This is not to say that the first boy will necessarily commit crime or that
the third boy will never do illegal things. The first boy, as a large part of his life
style, may read books that portray noncriminal heroes, he may spend much
of his spare time conversing with a local minister, and he may admire and
keep up with the career of a professional athlete who makes speeches about
the importance of conformity to the law. Despite the prevalence in his immediate environment of social definitions favorable to crime, the boy's own exposure to criminalistic examples may be minimal compared to these other
conformity-favoring influences. As a result, the net ratio and strength of
criminal to noncriminal examples may favor law obedience. Similarly, the
third boy may hang out with juveniles who are "into" illegal behavior; he may
have a girlfriend who has no respect for the law; and he may watch a lot of
television that portrays outlaws in a romantic way. Overall, then, the third
boy's repertoire of criminal examples may exceed the law-abiding influences
of his family and neighborhood environment. Such exceptions would, of
course, be rare since the social experiences of most people reflect the prevail-

ing messages within their neighborhoods, groups, and families. According to Sutherland, messages begun at an early age, continued over a long period of time, imparted by significant others, and portrayed intensely will have more impact than those encountered later in life, those that are of short duration and low intensity, and those conveyed by impersonal sources like TV, movies, or books.

It should be clear from the detailed description of the three boys that Sutherland's theory of differential associations could not be reduced to a simple theory asserting that we are deviant because we hang around with deviant people. After all, police officers, judges, psychiatrists, and drug abuse counselors hang around deviant people all the time. The theory of differential association asserts that the important explanatory factors in accounting for crime/deviance are pro-deviant and conventional *definitions* about behavior. Definitions are not limited to behaviors but would include verbal statements and exposure to television, magazines, and films.

Elaboration and Extension

Critique. Sutherland's theory was originally developed to explain criminal behavior, particularly criminal career patterns. He called his theory "differential association" because it focuses on differences among individuals in the extent to which they associate with groups or situations that present definitions (messages) favorable to crime. His scheme seems logical enough, and it does have inherent appeal because it seems to fit with common observations ("He who lies down with dogs shall rise up with fleas.") and to make sense out of many of the facts about crime. Nevertheless, it suffers from ambiguous terminology; it is difficult to use in a precise way; it fails to account for certain types of crime; and, for our purposes, it is too narrowly focused.

First, it is not entirely clear what Sutherland meant by "definitions favorable to violations of law." Such definitions could mean the same as reinforcements (rewarding or punishing responses) in psychological theories of learning or behavioral conditioning (see Akers, 1985), they could simply be behavioral examples or verbal messages, or they might refer to social norms (patterns of behavioral expectations). In addition, "favorableness" or "unfavorableness" is difficult to translate into concrete observation. Such words could imply that the definitions (reinforcements, examples, messages, or normative expectations) are directly criminal; they could mean that they are simply consistent with characteristics that are likely to lead to crime; or they could imply that the definitions are expressions of social approval for criminal behavior.

Second, even if exact referents for the concepts in the theory could be clarified, it would be difficult to measure the intensity, duration, and priority of the various definitions to which an individual is exposed in order to accurately measure the favorable/unfavorable ratio of definitions. It is usually easy enough to identify obvious social definitions such as those implied by criminal neighborhoods, peers, and families, but it is much harder to pinpoint the more particularistic influences, which, according to the theory, would tell us why some people in criminal neighborhoods and families do not become criminals while some people without obvious criminal influences do engage in crime. The ratio of all messages favorable or unfavorable to crime, weighted by Sutherland's specified modalities—priority (how early experienced), intensity, frequency, and source—that a person has experienced in a lifetime is at this point of the theory's development simply impossible to compile.

Third, it is hard to locate social definitions in Western societies that are favorable to criminal acts like sadistic rape of a nun, noninstrumental arson, or eating of human flesh, so instances of these acts and other unusual ones like them would be inexplicable by the theory of differential association. The task is particularly difficult if "definitions favorable to" refer to norms or behavioral examples, because there are simply no social contexts in which nun raping is normative, and the very idea of normative or exemplary cannibalism in modern societies is ludicrous. Consequently, the theory of differential association would seem to be most applicable to criminal acts that are common within at least some normative frameworks or that have cultural or group support. Conversely, differential association would seem to fail completely as a theory to explain acts that are very rare and individualistic in character (see Chapters 2 and 3).

Finally, since we are interested in the general phenomenon of deviance as well as crime, the theory of differential association, at least in the form in which Sutherland expressed it, will not suffice. He intended for his theory to refer only to crime. Nevertheless, it is not too difficult to think of the principles of differential association as general principles of human behavior, and it is possible to extend the theory to apply to deviance or conformity generally. One way to extend his formulation is to conceptualize it in terms of the general principles of learning established by behavioral psychologists.

Social Learning. Akers called his original reformulation of differential association theory "differential reinforcement" theory (Burgess and Akers, 1966; see also Akers, 1985), but his later elaborations came to be known as "social learning" theory. According to his argument, most human behavior, including deviant behavior, is a product of past "reinforcement," or rewards and punishments. The more effectively a behavior has been rewarded, the more likely it is to be repeated, and the more effectively it has been punished, the less likely it is to be repeated. In other words, people, like animals, can be conditioned, or habituated, to behavior by patterns of rewards and punishments—reinforcement schedules.

In discussing the theory, Akers focused on four elements of learning:

1. Differential association: the pattern of prosocial and antisocial groups and the norms of the groups to which one is exposed.

2. Definitions: one's own evaluation of conduct as right or wrong.

3. Differential reinforcement: anticipated costs and benefits of a behavior, both material and social.

4. Imitation: repeating a given behavior that was performed by others.

Deviance in Everyday Life

The idea that people learn by watching and mimicking others was not discovered first by Edwin Sutherland. The French criminologist, Gabriel Tarde, created a theory of crime in the 1880s that was highly critical of the popular biological/anthropological theory of the great Italian criminologist, Ceasare Lombroso. In 1890, Tarde published "Les Lois de l'Imitation," in which he discussed his theory of imitation as an explanation of crime/deviance. According to this theory, social behavior occurs because we imitate the actions of others. Thus, Tarde noted, one who takes part in the slaughtering of a pig is more likely to take the knife and attack a man.

Deviance is more likely, therefore, if people associate with others who commit deviant acts, if they see nothing wrong with committing deviant acts, if they see more to gain than to lose from deviance, and if they see others committing deviant acts.

If we consider a behavior and examine the influences immediately prior to it, it is plausible to see the behavior as a product of learning or past conditioning. The potential problem is how to explain initial acts of deviance, since they have not been reinforced. One answer from social learning theory is vicarious reinforcement. Human beings have the capacity to observe others being punished or rewarded for various acts and to incorporate those reinforced acts into their own behavior patterns without directly being punished or rewarded themselves. This is one characteristic that differentiates higher life forms from lower ones. Rats, pigeons, chickens, and other creatures can be trained, or conditioned, to do various things such as run a maze, peck a target, or run an obstacle course. The process by which they learn is called "operant conditioning." That is, the trainer punishes incorrect behavior (perhaps by electric shock) and rewards correct behavior (perhaps by providing some food) repeatedly until the subject has formed a correct pattern of behavior that can be performed on cue. But lower life forms cannot learn to run mazes, peck targets, or the like by watching others do it, or by being told how and why to do it. They must be directly reinforced repeatedly in order to learn.

Human beings, on the other hand, and to some extent other advanced species such as chimpanzees, can observe someone else performing a behavior and experiencing a reward or a cost, and can psychically place themselves in the position of that person and be themselves reinforced (Bandura, 1977, 1986). This is an example of imitative behavior. In addition, human beings can be told verbally that certain behaviors will produce unpleasant or desirable consequences, and on the basis of those verbal messages psychically experience the reinforcement process themselves, as if they had personally been rewarded or punished. As a result of vicarious reinforcement, people can become conditioned to perform behaviors that they have not previously performed and for which they have not been reinforced. This is one way to use the principles of learning to account for initial acts of deviance.

Another way is to recognize that much behavior is initially more or less random as people strive to satisfy fundamental needs. Since all people need food, they are physiologically motivated to seek it. Therefore, before they have been trained, or when the effects of training begin to fade, they are likely to seek food in the most direct fashion, regardless of social rules about etiquette or property ownership. If these "unsocialized" acts are ignored, the person will experience the reward of getting the food without any costs; that is, the individual will be positively reinforced, and will be motivated to repeat the act. If, on the other hand, the person is scolded and/or spanked and prevented from getting the food, he or she will be reinforced to not repeat the act unless the aversive stimulus of an empty stomach overcomes the effect of conditioning. But at this point the process of social reinforcement comes into play to explain repeat acts of deviance.

The point is that social learning accounts for some initial acts of deviance by the principles of both vicarious reinforcement and imitation, and it accounts for repeat acts of deviance through the principle of direct reinforcement, particularly direct reinforcement of social response. Other initial acts of deviance can be understood as random responses, or as due to inherent physiological drives.

Up to this point, the Akers formulation is nothing more than a more precise statement of the Sutherland idea, spelling out *how* learning of criminal or deviant ideas, attitudes, techniques, and the like occur, using the principles of learning elaborated by the work of psychologists. And like Sutherland's theory, it suffers from an inability to spell out ahead of time who, and under what circumstances, one individual rather than another will be exposed to a reinforcement schedule that will result in deviant or criminal behavior. Related to that problem is the inability to account for variations in subjective taste. Some people are reinforced in one direction by one thing, while others are reinforced in the opposite direction by that same thing. M & M's can be used successfully to condition some children in behavior modification programs, but there are always some children who don't like chocolate. Imprisonment may be a strong reinforcement for some people, but not for everybody. Some individuals get along quite well in prison; indeed, a few prefer it to life in free society. Social learning theory can only account for some individual tastes. It achieves that partial explanation using the principles of paired conditioning. Some reinforcers become rewarding or punishing because at some point in the past those factors were present, or shortly followed, when another, desirable reinforcer was used, so that the individual develops a coordinate "taste" (some drug addicts learn to like the feel of needles in their arms to the extent that they will inject themselves even when there are no drugs in the syringe). But many other tastes are simply accepted as given.

The Wilson-Herrnstein Elaboration. Two other social scientists have also applied the reinforcement model to criminal/deviant behavior (Wilson and Herrnstein, 1985). Their argument is similar to Akers's, but they extend the formulation by bringing in other variables that help account for individual taste and for initial, unreinforced acts of crime or deviance, and they identify circumstances in the social environment that influence the reinforcement process. They contend that many individual tastes (potential reinforcers) are biologically or genetically determined and that the motivation to engage in initial acts of deviance is also biologically or genetically influenced. For instance, individuals will vary in impulsiveness and learning ability as a consequence of biological inheritance (inheriting a difficult-to-condition autonomic nervous system). Impulsiveness will, in turn, influence initial criminal or deviant actions of individuals even before, and without, reinforcement. Because impulsiveness leads individuals to discount potential future negative consequences of behavior, it also affects how well reinforcement occurs. Similarly, innate intelligence, or learning ability (see Eysenck, 1977, 1982, and Eysenck and Gudjonsson, 1989), will influence the degree to which a given behavior can be learned vicariously, as well as the degree of reinforcement necessary to produce a repetition of it.

Wilson and Herrnstein also note that the value of different things as reinforcers is not inherent but is influenced by how those things are regarded in different social environments. Two such variations are (1) concepts of equity and justice and (2) the actual distribution of rewards and costs within a given social context. People do not evaluate potential rewards in absolute terms but rather take into account how much others are getting for similar efforts. For example, a woman in the United States may be glad to take a job at a pay rate of ten dollars per hour and feel that she is well paid until she learns that a man has taken a similar job with the same company for fifteen dollars per hour. Then she becomes dissatisfied, not because she found the pay rate insufficient to reinforce her work performance but because she regards the rate difference as unfair. In the United States currently there are cultural values prescribing equal pay for equal work that make it wrong to reward a male simply because he is a male. The reinforcement potential of the pay, then, is dependent on an external factor—concepts of fairness that are current in the social environment. If this woman lived in another society where cultural values made males more privileged, such as in India or Pakistan, she would not regard the difference as unfair, and the reinforcement value of the ten dollars per hour would be unaffected. Or if the American woman believed that this particular man deserved more than she for some reason (perhaps he is more experienced at the work or works harder), his pay would be consistent with standards of justice, and her reward would be unaffected.

Similarly, the reinforcement value of a particular thing depends on how plentiful or scarce it is in the environment, which is partly a function of the social structure that determines the values and distributions of commodities and services. For example, eight dollars per hour pay is not very reinforcing for those who have independent fortunes; it is very attractive for those who are in poverty. And the reinforcement value of a particular thing depends on how many other reinforcers are operative. Thus, those whose jobs provide them with psychic satisfactions, power, personal transportation, and job security are less concerned with the rate of pay than those whose work performance is totally dependent on the pay rate.

Therefore, although Wilson and Herrnstein contend that all human behavior can be understood in terms of differential reinforcement, they show that there may be wide variations in the learning patterns and in the resulting outcomes. Moreover, they contend that numerous social variables influence the degree to which any given individual is exposed to an effective reinforcement schedule for any given behavior. Thus, even though the essential process of behavioral production is simple and straightforward, the details are quite complex because they vary with a multitude of biological, social, and social structural conditions.

Application of Learning Theory

Narrow Application

The three versions of learning theory described above can be applied either narrowly to account for individuals' deviance or broadly to account for variations in deviance among categories of individuals. Narrow application to explain why one individual commits deviance and another doesn't requires tracking the exact sets of social definitions, or reinforcements, to which individuals have been exposed, particularly at early ages. And this type of application focuses mainly on the effects of those reinforcements in producing general cognitive states within the individuals—attitudes, values, commitments, habits, and the like—that come into play in a variety of circumstances. Hence the narrow application of learning theory is most appropriate to explain the personal variations in deviance described in Chapter 9. But, as noted, although the narrow application provides a satisfying intellectual account, it is impossible to identify actual reinforcement schedules and the attendant values of the potential reinforcers that specific individuals have experienced in order to predict their behaviors or confirm the theory empirically. Moreover, the fact that individuals' behaviors vary with social factors that do not remain constant from situation to situation and over the life course suggests that the narrow focus of learning theory on more-or-less fixed internal cognitive components resulting from early learning is limiting.

Broad Application

The broader approach of applying learning theory to predictions about categories of persons is more practical, useful, and accurate. It is more practical because information from which inferences about general reinforcement schedules for categorical memberships can be drawn is available. It is more useful because most of the facts about deviance, as described in Chapter 9, are rate or categorical variations. And it is likely to be more accurate because predictions can be made and confirmed.

In making a general application, one must assume that the definitions "favorable or unfavorable to crime," of which Sutherland wrote, and most of the reinforcers about which Akers and Wilson and Herrnstein write, are simply normative expectations. They represent ideas about appropriate, right, or correct conduct that are shared by the members of particular groups to which a person might belong and that are invoked as behavioral obligations, or guidelines. Moreover, these normative expectations can be thought of as organized primarily around roles and statuses, and they can be regarded as potentially "deviogenic" (consistent with or likely to lead to deviance) rather than directly deviant or criminal. With such conceptualizations, we can think of deviant behavior as mainly a product of learned normative behavior or as a consequence of efforts to meet normative expectations. Therefore, according to learning theory, deviant behavior will be mainly an expression of a person's roles, statuses, and group memberships, which, of course, are not fixed in all situations or throughout the life course. Everybody plays more than one role, occupies multiple statuses, and moves among various groups and cultural environments; hence to understand and predict deviance requires knowledge of the individual's frequency and intensity of exposure to various normative settings. Knowledge of the predominant normative context, however, permits considerable prediction of the probability of deviant behavior.

For example, in the United States, traditional role expectations for males imply that their behaviors should reflect independence, assertiveness, and courage. Females, on the other hand, are traditionally expected to behave in compliant, passive, and cautious ways. The role expectations for males, therefore, are consistent with much deviant behavior, since deviance usually

---

Deviance in Everyday Life

In American society, it is traditional for men to be involved in contact sports (football, rugby, hockey) and for women to be involved in sports where bodies don't collide (tennis, field hockey). What is "traditional" is not fixed but changes over time. For example, in 1998 there was for the first time a female ice hockey competition at the Olympic games. Although the rules were only slightly modified (no cross checking or body blocks), by all accounts the women's game was as rugged as the men's. The first gold medal for women's ice hockey was awarded to the U.S. team after an upset victory over the favored Canadians.

requires courage, risk taking, or aggressiveness. Role expectations for females, on the other hand, are consistent with conforming behavior. Generally, then, males should engage in more deviant behavior than females, and the evidence confirms that they do (see Chapter 9). But role definitions are not always clearcut in every context, and in addition they vary from place to place and over time. Individuals also differ in the intensity of the role-playing lessons to which they are exposed, and some persons may almost totally escape exposure to traditional gender role expectations. Consequently, not all males feel compelled to be masculine, nor do all females experience the expectations for femininity. Hence, some males conform and some females deviate, but overall the variety and amount of deviance should be greater for males. And where the role expectations vary, so should the behavior of males and females.

To illustrate: traditional role expectations for the genders are more likely to prevail among older people than they are among younger people; also, they are likely to be stronger among the higher socioeconomic classes and weaker among the lower classes, where females have greater necessity for participating in the labor force and engaging in "male-like" behavior. In addition, conventional roles are more likely to characterize white females than non-white females, although they are more likely to characterize non-white males than white males. Furthermore, traditional role expectations are more compelling among rural and small town dwellers than among city residents. According to learning theory, then, deviance should generally be more prevalent among males than females, but the extent to which male deviance exceeds female deviance should vary by age (greater among the young), race (greater among whites), socioeconomic status (greater among the higher classes), and place of residence (greater among rural and small town residents than among city dwellers). Moreover, when women of any age, race, place of residence, or socioeconomic status achieve autonomy and independence in the labor force and experience less emphasis on traditional role distinctions, their rates of deviance should move closer to that of males in the same statuses.

These predicted patterns can be confirmed with survey data collected in Iowa, Oregon, and New Jersey in 1972 (Tittle, 1980b). A random sample of residents aged 15 and over were asked to report how many times they had committed each of nine deviant acts (five of which were criminal offenses) within the past five years, and to express the probability that they would commit those acts if in the near future they were in a situation where they felt a strong need to do so. The nine offenses included theft (of a large and a small amount), marijuana smoking, illegal gambling, assault, lying to one's spouse or sweetheart, income tax cheating, remaining seated during the National Anthem, and a deviance that was specifically tailored to the main occupation of the respondent. Table 11.1 reports the relevant average percentages (across the nine offenses) of males and females with various social characteristics who had done each of the deviant acts or had expressed a high probability that they would do so if the appropriate situation presented itself. The last column of Table 11.1 reports the ratio of male to female percentages. If there were no gender difference, these ratios should be 1.0; if males are more likely to participate in a given act the ratio should be greater than 1.0; and it is less than 1.0 when females predominate.

Table 11.1 Self-Reported Deviance and Deviance Propensity by Gender and Other Social Characteristics (percentage)

Characteristics		Male	Female	Male/Female Ratio
Race:	White	28	19	1.47
	Non-white	32	24	1.33
Age:	15–24	45	36	1.25
	25–44	34	23	1.48
	45–64	19	12	1.58
	65+	10	5	2.00
SES:	High	33	22	1.50
	Medium	30	21	1.43
	Low	24	19	1.26
Autonomy:	Low	29	20	1.45
	Medium	30	21	1.43
	High	27	22	1.23

Adapted from Tittle, Charles R. 1980. *Sanctions and Social Deviance: The Question of Deterrence*, Table 4.2, pp. 84–85. New York: Praeger.

The first thing to note about the data in Table 11.1 is that the ratio of male to female deviance rate is always greater than one. This shows, as predicted by cultural learning theory, that every category of males represented in the table is more prone to deviance than the corresponding category of females. In other words, no matter what the offense type, males are more likely to have committed the act than females. However, the deviance rate for females (as well as for males) varies substantially from category to category. For instance, the deviance rate (percent reporting propensity toward deviance) for young women is 36, but the rates for women aged 55 to 64 is only 12, and it is as small as 5 for women 65 years old and over. A similar pattern for males is consistent with the argument that gender role obligations are stronger among the older categories. Yet, the deviance rate for some categories of females is greater than that for some noncorresponding categories of males, suggesting that gender differences in deviant propensity are linked to roles and not simply an expression of gender biology. Thus, females 15 to 24 report a deviance rate of 36, while men in the slightly older category of 25 to 44 have a similar rate of 34, and aged men (65 years and older) have a rate of only 10.

Finally, as predicted by the logic of the theory, the *ratio* of male to female rates is greater among whites than nonwhites (1.47 versus 1.33). This means that the deviance rate of non-white males is 30 percent greater than that for non-white females, while the deviance rate of white males is 50 percent greater than that for white females. Similarly, the male/female deviance ratio varies directly with age, going from 1.25 for the young age category to 2.00 for the oldest, meaning that the deviance of young males as a whole is 25 percent greater than that of young women, while the percentage of aged men who are deviant is twice that of aged women. Further, the ratio in favor of men is least among those of lower socioeconomic status (1.26) and greatest among those of higher status (1.50). Also, it is lower among those who scored high on a role autonomy scale (combination of occupation, labor force status, and household status) than among those who scored low (1.23 versus 1.45).

As these data show, the broad application of learning theory appears consistent with the "facts" about gender differences in crime/deviance. There is much evidence that the theory is consistent with other patterns as well (see Akers, 1985). For example, age variations can be understood as responses to learned normative expectations that vary with age-linked roles and statuses, and variations by socioeconomic status, minority status, size of settlement, and region can be likewise linked with related expectations about roles and statuses. Moreover, the theory accommodates aberrations from predicted patterns by acknowledging individual variations in perceptions, tastes, and intensity of exposure to normative expectations, and because it allows the impact of social norms to reflect social standards of justice and distributions of rewards/punishments.

Subcultural Applications

Despite the strength of learning theory, particularly in its broad application, it is limited because it does not attempt to explain variations in normative expectations or why individuals differ in their exposure to differing normative demands; rather, it takes these variations as "givens." Some offshoots from learning theory, however, attempt to correct this deficiency.

Several formulations, referred to here as subcultural theories, assume learning to be a key process that leads to deviance. However, they go a step further to try to account for variations in the *content* of learning and to show how specific pervasive learning contexts affect particular patterns of behavior. The basic argument is that deviant or criminal subcultures arise in response to environmental challenges, particularly the conditions of subordination or deprivation. Once they exist, however, their standards and values are then passed on from one generation to the next, constituting a set of messages to be learned by those exposed to them. Fulfilling those standards, then, comes to have criminogenic or deviogenic effects, because the individuals who spend most of their time within that cultural context come to identify with it and embrace the standards it represents, therefore becoming compelled by internalized attitudes and values, as well as by obligations to meet the collective expectations of those around them.

Cohen's Theory. The best-formulated account of why subcultures arise to overcome problems of subordination and deprivation is that by Cohen (1955), who began with an interest in explaining delinquent gang behavior. He observed that gang delinquency was mainly an activity of lower-class males who lived in inner-city areas. In addition, the evidence seemed to indicate that much of their delinquent activity centered around nonutilitarian property crime, and that the norms and values of gang delinquents appeared to be direct contradictions of middle-class norms and values. In other words, Cohen's observations of gangs led him to believe that, rather than taking things that they need or fighting solely to defend themselves from aggression, gang members steal needless and useless things simply to destroy them, or they derive satisfaction from tormenting and threatening other people.

Cohen theorized that the root cause of gang delinquency was the adverse experience of lower-class youth in public schools. He observed that lower-class youths suffer a huge disadvantage in the schools. Public schools are basically middle-class institutions. They are established by middle-class people to promote middle-class behaviors and values; they are supervised by middle-class administrators, and they are staffed by middle-class-oriented teachers. As a result, public schools are prepared to deal with middle-class children, and the expectations they have for students are built along middle-class lines. Lower-class youth, however, do not share these middle-class orientations. They come from deprived families that emphasize physical skills rather than the skills that would make them good pupils (use of language and the avoidance of conflict). As a result of lower-class child-rearing practices, lower-class youth arrive at school already behind middle-class children. They usually do not yet know the alphabet; they may not know how to hold a pencil or crayon; they have not been taught to sit quietly in a classroom; and they show more interest and skill in physical than in mental activity. Moreover, the lower-class child has not learned the niceties of middle-class etiquette involving deference to authority figures, polite language, or courtesy. Hence, lower-class youths are likely to be judged as inferior when measured by middle-class standards, and they are not likely to perform effectively in the academic arena. In short, lower-class youths are apt to fail in school, and they are likely to feel out of place, denigrated, and inadequate.

At this point, Cohen's argument suggests that almost all lower-class youths are likely to have bad school experiences. But since it is mainly inner-city lower-class youths who form gangs, clearly school failure is not an adequate explanation for gang participation. The crucial difference between inner-city and other lower-class youths, according to Cohen, is the proximity of residence. Inner city youths live close together in confined areas of the city, and their limited individual family space forces them into interaction with other youths similarly situated. This means that lower-class youths, each of whom has a personal problem of bad school experiences, come together often in non-school contexts. In such interactions, they share their personal problems, which become common problems of all.

In interacting and sharing their common problem, they develop a common or collective solution. The solution is to form a new social system that has goals and behavioral standards that lower-class youth can live up to. Thus, a subculture of gang delinquency arises to solve the problem of school failure and the consequent bad feeling the youths have as a result of those school experiences. In order to accomplish that purpose, according to Cohen, such a subculture must have several key features. First, it must provide goals that are achievable with the skills that the lower-class youths possess. Second, the goals, and the skills required to meet them, must be very different from those of the middle-class system that is being challenged. And the subculture must provide the means by which the middle-class system within which they could not succeed can be devalued, so that failure in that system will not appear to be failure at all, but rather a virtue.

The delinquent gang serves all three of those functions. First, it replaces school achievement with the goal of successful gang participation. Successful gang participation requires courage, loyalty, physical prowess, and a time commitment, all of which the lower-class boys amply possess. Second, the goals of the delinquent gang—to protect turf, to be tough in physical contact, to successfully steal property, to be rebellious—are almost the opposite of goals set out in the middle-class system. Third, many of the activities of the delinquent gang are designed as overt symbols of contempt for the middle-class value system. Whereas the middle-class world values property, the delinquent gang often steals property (usually from middle-class people or institutions) and throws it away. Whereas the middle class values peacefulness and compromise, the delinquent gang values conflict and confrontation.

Cohen's argument, then, contends that the delinquent gang emerges as a reaction to the unrealistic demands of the middle-class world as it is expressed in the school system. Participation in such gangs restores the lower-class boy's sense of self-esteem and accomplishment by permitting him to achieve goals on his own terms, and to demonstrate that the middle-class system within which he failed was contemptible anyway. The delinquent gang as a criminogenic subculture, then, is a functional response to a situation in which subordinates are deprived of the means of achieving; its formulation is made possible by the proximity of residence among the subordinates so affected.

Deviance in Everyday Life

By his own admission, Cohen's subcultural theory was limited in scope. It did not, for example, provide an adequate explanation for middle-class and female delinquency. Cohen had different theories of delinquency to account for these two different types. With respect to middle-class delinquency, Cohen suggests that middle-class male youths are confused about their sexual identity because their fathers' jobs removed them from the home for a significant portion of the day. In addition to keeping a father remote, a father's job is, according to Cohen, unintelligible to his son. Furthermore, when at home, middle-class fathers are less likely to behave in a "manly" fashion than lower- or working-class fathers. As a result, middle-class boys are confused as to what it means to act in a masculine way. To compensate for this sexual anxiety, middle-class young males act in an aggressive masculine way—they drink, smoke, and act violently.

Female delinquency is much more specialized for Cohen. It is primarily sexual, because young females' central problem of adjustment concerns their attractiveness to males. Females, he observes, walk a thin line between just sexual enough to attract attention and not so sexual as to be considered "loose." Some females cross over that line.

After gangs develop in particular areas, however, the original reasons for their formation do not necessarily drive other youth into affiliation with the delinquent subculture. In other words, each generation of youths does not have to experience failure and discomfort in school, interact outside school with other boys similarly situated, and then form a new subculture. Rather, subcultures continue in perpetuity in specific neighborhoods, often dominating the social scene and spending a lot of time protecting their turf from invasion by rival gangs. As a result, each generation of youths in those neighborhoods comes in contact with the delinquent gang/subculture long before they begin school. By constant exposure, these children learn that their reputations, statuses, even their survival depend on adherence to the standards of the gang. And over time they adopt the values of the gang and bid for acceptance by it. Of course, the school experience may reinforce the attractiveness of gang activity, just as gang participation may affect how well the youth does in school.

Cohen's account of how the delinquent gang, or subculture, arises and why its cultural messages are the way they are is but an example of the larger processes that his theory implies. In general language, his argument implies that subordination, wherever it exists, produces problems for those who experience it. Those problems include blockage of the ability to achieve the goals set forth by superordinates, discomfort in participating in the social environment dominated by superordinate values, and feelings of failure and low self-esteem. Further, according to the theory, if subordinates are thrown into constant interaction, they will talk about these common problems. Out of this interaction will emerge a collective solution in the form of a subculture with a distinct set of norms and standards that subordinates can live up to and that involve denigration of the norms and standards of the dominant culture, which the subordinates could not live up to.

Thus, the conditions for the development of a subculture are: (1) enduring subordination, (2) proximity, usually residential, of subordinates and (3) conditions permitting regular interaction around collectively shared problems stemming from subordination. The nature of the subcultural standards that will emerge are: (1) norms and values contrary to those of the superordinates but (2) that represent standards achievable by the subordinates and (3) that emphasize derogation of the standards of the superordinates. And although Cohen does not emphasize this, the conditions for the perpetuation of a deviant subculture is massive exposure of new generations, whether themselves subordinate or not, to members of a pre-existing subculture.

If this argument is valid, one should find deviant subcultures developing not only among urban lower-class boys but also among prison and mental hospital inmates, minority groups confined to ghettos, and unconventional religious groups residing within localized areas of intolerant countries. Prisoners and incarcerated patients are deprived of opportunities for successful achievement in their respective systems; they are in proximity; and they can usually find ways to interact and communicate despite efforts by their keepers to prevent it. Thus, if Cohen is right, prisoners should generally organize and exhibit a culture contrary to that prescribed by authorities. There is an extensive literature (Thomas and Peterson, 1977; Tittle, 1972) documenting this very process and showing inmate subcultures to be stronger where deprivation is greatest. Similarly, minorities, such as blacks in the United States who are segregated in inner-city areas, should have a subculture stressing norms that members of the white majority find incomprehensible. They apparently do (Anderson, 1978, 1990; Liebow, 1967; McCall, 1994). Finally, there is ample evidence to suggest that sectarian religious groups like the Amish, as well as unconventional groups like the Gypsies, got their starts as oppressed minorities in European countries (Kephart and Zellner, 1994).

Poverty Subcultures. As noted in Chapter 10, arguments about subcultures of poverty, since they are concerned exclusively with deviance among the poor, do not constitute theories but are instead ad hoc explanations. Nevertheless, it is important to recall them here because their authors implicitly (though they do not say so and probably do not realize it) focus the ideas contained in Cohen's theory on people who are economically subordinated. The contention is that the conditions of poverty lead to an adaptive subculture among the poor that emphasizes attitudes, values, and behavior standards contrary to those of the larger culture.

The most representative of the subculture-of-poverty arguments is the one by Walter B. Miller (1958; but see also Lewis, 1961, 1966), who attributes criminogenic traits to lower-class people. Misbehavior is supposedly motivated by efforts to "achieve status, conditions, or qualities valued within the actor's most significant cultural milieu." The lower class, he claims, embraces and passes on from one generation to the next a set of particular values or "focal concerns" growing out of a distinctive tradition many centuries old with an integrity of its own. Lower-class focal concerns are said to orient around trouble, toughness, smartness, excitement, fate, and autonomy. Presumably, anyone exposed to such a culture, especially during the formative years, would almost inevitably find himself or herself engaging in behavior that would cause conflict with the law.

For example, according to this argument, a boy who grows up in an inner-city area where most people are economically deprived will learn that people expect men to be tough. Males are supposed to prepare themselves to fight to prove their masculinity, and they are conditioned to expect trouble that may call for physical aggression. Moreover, they learn to admire and emulate "street smarts," which allow someone to achieve status or acquire material goods by the use of wit, or "rap," or manipulation rather than work. Such boys come to resent authority and control, and they see success or failure as a product of fate or luck rather than self-direction or planning. In addition, lower-class culture teaches people to orient themselves toward a life of boredom and drudgery; a lifestyle that provokes a search for, and places a premium on, excitement—to be sought through drinking, sexual flirtation, and physical combat. Under such influences a male will sooner or later find himself in fights or engaging in illegal or semilegal transactions to project a "smart" image.

Summary and Critique of Subcultural Applications. Subcultural arguments can be conceived of as applications of learning theory to situations where people are overwhelmingly exposed to a peculiar set of social messages that lead to the learning of deviogenic internal cognitive states, including a desire for acceptance. The central notion conceives of deviant behavior as a product of acquiescence to the normative demands of the groups one belongs to or comes in contact with. But whereas learning theory as expressed by Sutherland, Akers, and Wilson and Herrnstein emphasizes learning from a variety of influences, subcultural applications focus more narrowly on one pervasive learning context. Cohen, however, sets forth a theory to explain why subcultures develop and have the form and content that they do.

The major problem with subcultural theories is that their assumptions that members remain apart from the greater culture and that subcultural themes totally dominate their members' lives have been difficult to sustain in research. Although some groups, such as terrorists, sectarian religious groups, and organized criminals are heavily devoted to deviance, their members share a lot in common with conventional people—devotion to family, loyalty to friends, trustworthiness, faith in God, and the like (Ianni and Reuss-Ianni, 1972; Kephart and Zellner, 1994; Turk, 1982:71–98). Moreover, delinquent gangs have not been found to be nearly as cohesive or approving of criminal-delinquent behavior as subcultural theories imply (Klein, 1995; Miller, 1980; Yablonsky, 1959). Consideration of the supposed unique standards of the poverty culture particularly calls into question the subcultural argument. Evidence suggests that all people in the United States, regardless of social class, share an overarching set of values (McClosky and Zaller, 1984; Reinarman, 1987; Rossi et al., 1974; Tittle, 1980b). Indeed, if Miller is to be believed, middle- and high-status people would value weakness (rather than toughness), naïveté (instead of smartness), boredom (instead of excitement), and subordination (instead of autonomy), and they would show marked arrogance (instead of concern with fate). This seems absurd. Thus, subcultural standards would appear at best to show differences in degree rather than kind. If so, then their power to evoke deviance is much reduced. Others have even challenged the whole idea of a subculture of poverty (Leacock, 1971; Ryan, 1971). For example, Liebow's study of street corner men (1967) convinced him that the behavior patterns characterizing such men are nothing more than individual responses to similar experiences of deprivation and discrimination.

Other points of debate concerning subcultures have to do with their supposed origin in deprivation and with the processes by which they supposedly produce deviance. Remember Fischer's explanation for why larger settlements have higher rates of deviance, which was described in Chapter 10. According to him, subcultures arise spontaneously and naturally when people with mutual but unusual interests, which presumably are either inherent or learned from a variety of potential sources but are not necessarily indicative of subordination, come into contact. Such subcultures become cohesive if forced into competition with other subcultures, as they are in heterogeneous cities, not when they are under attack from larger forces of social control. Cohesion, in turn, activates processes of social control to generate conformity to the behavioral standards of the subculture while at the same time cultivating tolerance for behaviors performed by other subcultures. Hence subcultures promote specific as well as "spill-over" deviance from other subcultures occupying the same general physical space. This account, of course, portrays subcultures in ways that largely move them out of the realm of learning theory applications, and it avoids the insularity assumption that has been the basis of so much criticism.

Summary and Critique of Learning Theories

Learning theory, in its various forms as applied to deviant behavior, embraces the idea that deviance results from individuals having stored into their psychic systems attitudes, values, motivations, skills, knowledge about expected behaviors, ways of thinking, and characteristic responses consistent with, or favorable to deviant behavior. The process by which this occurs is usually thought to involve two elements. First, a pattern of behavior is established by repetitive reward and cost for behaviors performed: directly (the person experiences it); vicariously (the person sees others experience it or is told about it and imagines himself or herself in that position); or associatively (ancillary experiences come to be identified with direct or vicarious experiences and thereby come to have reinforcing effects). Second, attitudes and values undergirding such patterns are established by pairing moral or social admonitions with other reinforcements when the behavior or similar behavior occurs. The various learning theories differ from each other in the precision with which they spell out the learning process, in the accommodation to conditional factors that affect learning, and in their focus on the content of what is learned as it is linked with various social circumstances.

Learning theories are categorized here as situational motivation theories because the emphasis is on inputs to the learning process from the environment surrounding the individual as well as on the environmental activators, such as normative expectations, that call forth responses. Most, but not all, the things learned constitute motivators of behavior. However, since the things learned are stored in the psyche of an individual and since some of them represent constraints on behavioral impulses, learning theories cannot be regarded as entirely based on situational variables or entirely concerned with motivation. Such complexities should be a reminder that the classification scheme suggested here is oriented around major foci in theories and that no theory is narrowly enough constructed to be considered a pure type.

Learning theories can be applied fairly broadly, are eminently plausible, and enjoy considerable empirical support, particularly when used therapeutically to create or extinguish behavioral patterns in people (Bandura, 1969) or experimentally to train animals (Akers, 1985). However, they suffer from four major defects. First, they do not easily explain individualized deviance like stalking, child abuse, suicide, public nose picking, or forms of bizarre behavior usually called mental illness that enjoy no normative supports and for which there are few social messages or inherent characteristics that might constitute rewards or reinforcements. Moreover, the theories have trouble explaining single or initial acts of deviance. Learning theories are most effective in accounting for deviance that is at least subculturally organized; in which there are shared values, norms, and supporting rationalizations, as in homosexual conduct, unconventional religious practices, and organized criminal activities; and the theories are secondarily applicable to deviances that have inherent, self-reinforcing qualities, including things like sexual fetishes, recreational drug use, and theft. Further, learning theories apply best to deviance that is frequently committed by a given individual; they do not work well for one time or infrequent acts.

Second, the explanations offered by learning theory have difficulty avoiding tautology. This is partly because some of the important concepts are imprecise and partly because it is impossible to measure all of the potential learning moments in a person's life. The main mechanism by which learning presumably occurs is "reinforcement." However, reinforcement is often *defined* as some consequence of a behavior that leads to its repetition. So defined, there is no way to identify rewards or punishments independent of their outcomes. Thus, giving a child money to get good grades may or may not produce good academic work. By definition, however, it reinforces academic performance whenever good work follows the payment; in other words, the main reason to infer that money is rewarding to the child is if it produces the desired behavior. Therefore, to say that good academic work results from reinforcement is true by definition and is a tautology. Similarly, adherents sometimes "explain" deviance by looking into the backgrounds of perpetrators until they find something that plausibly could have reinforced the deviant behavior, and that is taken as evidence that the deviance was the result of reinforcement. Deviance, then, becomes the evidence that reinforcement has taken place as well as being the outcome that reinforcement supposedly produces. Such tautology is encouraged by the impossibility of identifying all the rewarding and/or punishing things a person has been exposed to up to the point where the act of deviance occurs.

Third, learning theory leaves many things relevant to deviant behavior unexplained, and in most applications it fails to take into account conditional variables in the social environment that affect reinforcement schedules. The theory does not explain why one individual experiences one set of reinforcements while another individual experiences a different set (the issue of different tastes raised earlier in this chapter). It simply takes the reinforcements to which a person has been exposed as its starting point. Moreover, it does not take into account things in the social environment that intervene between learned characteristics and their manifestation in actual deviance. For example, a young man may believe the law is corrupt, have no moral compunctions against theft, and know how to hot-wire an automobile (all learned) yet not steal any automobiles because none is available in his environment, because the cops are so prevalent that the person fears getting caught, or because he hangs with companions who occupy his time doing other things. In other words, learning theory cuts into a causal chain in the middle, ignoring what went before to produce learning inputs as well as what comes afterward to channel the things learned into conforming or deviant behavior.

Finally, the theory cannot easily deal with contrary cases, where people seem to have learned things but act contrary to the learning. There are many instances of "good" people who supposedly have been exposed to proper training with conforming attitudes, conventional values, and respectable habits who unexpectedly go berserk and kill their parents or go on crime sprees. There are numerous cases of people who are seemingly deeply involved in subcultures who nevertheless defy subcultural norms, such as Amish men who get drunk and have fights or terrorists who become informers against their comrades. And there are multiple instances of people who violate their own internalized moral standards out of rage, impulsive response to overwhelming opportunity, or intense group pressure.

Structural Inducements

Another type of situational motivation theory emphasizes events or structural regularities in the social environment that generate problems for individuals of particular statuses or with specific roles. Since people are coping animals, they try to overcome the problems, sometimes turning to deviant behavior as a solution. These theories portray deviance as a motivated response to conditions in the external environment that induce individuals to resort to deviant behavior. Because the conditions identified by the structural inducement theories are usually portrayed as trapping individuals between forces pulling or pushing in opposite directions, those theories are often called "strain" theories.

Anomie

Preliminary Considerations: Durkheim

Robert K. Merton borrowed the name of his theory from a term used in Durkheim's theory of suicide (1951 [1897]), but Merton's theory (Merton, 1938, 1949, 1968; see Tittle, 1995:71–87, for discussion of various modifications in the theory from 1938 to 1968) departs so far from Durkheim's original ideas that it is confusing to try to compare the two. We authors mention the linkage, as subtle as it is, because you will run across the term "anomie" often in the crime-deviance literature, and you need to be aware that it means one thing in Durkheim's work and another thing in Merton's work. To Durkheim, anomie refers to a relatively transient condition characterizing an entire social group or individuals therein in which there are no norms to govern their behavior. Without norms to guide them, Durkheim assumed that human beings would be unable to regulate their appetites—hence they would be miserable and prone to self-destruction. Usually this "normlessness," or social disorganization, occurs during periods of rapid change, when old norms are upset or called into question and new norms have not yet been established. An example illustrating how anomie affects individuals would be when a man loses his wife through divorce or death (Durkheim, 1951 [1897]:270–272). Now single, he can see no obvious norms (like social expectations for fidelity) that would regulate his behavior. Without socially defined limits, the single man's sexual appetite would be voracious and insatiable. Unable to be satisfied, the single man would find himself in a state of misery and would be more likely to commit suicide than if he had remained married. According to Durkheim, therefore, without normative and structural constraints, individuals become disoriented and unguided—in essence they are likely to try to move in several directions at once and are prone to excesses. Without guidance, they become subject to all manner of pathological behavior, including, particularly, suicide. In Durkheim's version of the theory, then, a state of strain (sudden divorce or financial ruin) produces anomie (a state wherein there are no limits on one's needs or desires), which in turn increases the likelihood of deviance.

Merton's Contribution

For Merton, anomie is not a relatively temporary state; rather, it is a characteristic feature of some societies. Instead of being concerned with the absence or disruption of norms, as was Durkheim, Merton is concerned with cultural and social mal-integration, where the means and goals promoted in a society are inconsistent and/or where consistent values and goals are incongruent with actual distributions and emphases on the means to realize those values and goals. According to Merton, societies are characterized by two structural features: (1) a commonly defined set of goals for its members to try to achieve and (2) a generally approved set of means to achieve those goals. A well-integrated society is one that places more-or-less equal value on both goal achievement and the use of approved means to obtain the goals. A society that lives and abides by these two rules—"winning is good, but it's important how you play the game"—would be well integrated. Such societies have low anomie and as a result place few strains on their members.

Other societies, however, are mal-integrated, or imbalanced, in that they place unequal stress on the goals or on the appropriate means for achieving those goals. The case that Merton was most interested in was the society that places far more cultural emphasis on goal attainment and deemphasizes the use of socially acceptable means. An example of this would be the society that says, "Winning isn't everything, it's the only thing." Merton regarded the United States as a prime example of a society like this.

Merton characterized the United States as being obsessed with the goal of financial success. According to him, everybody in the country is encouraged (exhorted) by schooling, example, advertising, and talk to believe that they must achieve at least a comfortable financial position, if not actual wealth. And the worth of individuals is judged primarily by those standards. Those who acquire wealth are accorded prestige, relied upon for advice about all things, exercise political power, and are attributed virtue. Those who fail in the economic realm are held in low esteem, denigrated, ignored, and held to be immoral or lazy. Those who fail to play the game are treated even worse. According to Merton, the American cultural system rewards success, with little regard for the methods by which people succeed. Although there are socially approved ways to achieve wealth—through schooling, hard work, investment, luck, or marriage—and people are expected to follow such cultural standards, there is relatively less emphasis on the means by which success is to be achieved than on the achievement of success itself. That is, what is important in our culture is that you become successful, not how you do it.

This unevenness is expressed in two ways. First, evaluations of people are based more on outcome than on process. Hence a person who becomes wealthy by devious means is more honored than a person who remains honest and poor. Second, the society devotes more effort to promoting the goals than it does to making sure everybody has the opportunity to achieve the goals. This disproportionate emphasis on each of two essential elements of the culture—goals and means—Merton called anomie, and he argued that it created strain for everybody in the United States, but it particularly caused strain for some segments of the population—those who, because they confront structural barriers to their success, cannot succeed, and those who, for a variety of reasons, do not think they can succeed. As a result of putting so much emphasis on getting ahead and so little emphasis on the use of acceptable means, Merton thought, American society was anomic and bred crime and deviance. In his words (1968:200), "a cardinal American virtue, 'ambition', promotes a cardinal American vice, 'deviant behavior'. "

Individual Adaptations. In a later chapter where we examine theories designed to explain why societies differ in rates of crime and deviance, we will revisit the cultural mal-integration aspect of Merton's theory. For now, we are interested in the effect of living in an anomic society on individuals, or categories of individuals. According to Merton's scheme, all citizens in the United States are strained by anomie and so all have to figure out some way to adapt to the dual demands of pressures for financial success and the reality of less emphasis on the use or availability of approved means. One mode of adaptation is, of course, psychological acceptance of the culturally approved goals and conformity to the approved means. Those who have the means to achieve success, or believe they have such means, follow this acceptance mode. But others make deviant adaptations of one kind or another, of which Merton identified four.

First, some employ unapproved means to try to achieve success goals; this he called *innovation*. In this response to anomie, individuals who anticipate failure, mainly because they do not have access to the culturally approved means for success or because they believe they do not have them seek some other route to success, and if they are unrestrained by moral considerations, they will resort to deviance. In other words, one response to anomie and strain is to use what Merton himself referred to as technically efficient but illegal means to reach culturally approved goals. For example, people who grow up in poverty in the United States are exposed to the idea that poverty is disgraceful and wealth is honorable, and they are encouraged to get out of poverty at almost any cost. But such people are disadvantaged in access to effective schooling or training. They may lack appropriate skills or financial resources for higher education, they have no investable resources to permit capitalist advancement. Also, they are not likely to be in situations where they can meet and marry successful people, even if they were attractive to such potential mates. The strain of expectations for success in the face of reality, according to Merton, is likely to lead such individuals—provided they lack moral inhibitions that would prevent it—to steal, to engage in fraud, and possibly to use violence to advance their agendas. In the academic context, this adaptation would characterize students with limited intelligence, little self-discipline, or inadequate academic preparation who want to graduate so desperately that they resort to cheating.

A second deviant way that people in an anomic society can adapt is through *ritualism*. This adaptation involves going through the motions of using the culturally approved means but without a corresponding psychological commitment to the goal of success. It is like the individual who no longer believes in the theology of his or her religion but who nevertheless continues to attend religious services. The best example would be of a businessperson who refuses to expand the business to become wealthier but who slavishly goes to work every day and simply keeps the enterprise alive. Ritualists, like innovators, are those who anticipate failure, either because they lack the means to succeed or perceive that they lack the means. However, ritualists differ from innovators in that they have moral inhibitions that prevent them from seeking to achieve success goals through culturally disapproved or illegal means. Wishing to succeed financially but believing they cannot, and being blocked by conscience, they adjust by denigrating the goal. It is a lot like the fox in Aesop's fables who, after numerous failed attempts to reach the grapes high up on the vine, finally gives up and declares that they were probably sour anyway. In American society, most people frown on somebody's challenging or ignoring goals of financial success, so even though the ritualist is not violating any rules, he or she is nevertheless deviant. In the academic context, it is again the student who initially desperately wants to graduate but lacks the skill or intelligence, so comes to anticipate failure. But this student, unlike the innovator, has moral compunctions that inhibit cheating. Consequently, such students psychologically redefine the goal of graduation as one of little import. They continue to go to class, to do their best, but without any hope or desire for ultimately earning a degree.

A third deviant adaptation that people can make if they are part of an anomic society, which places more emphasis on goals than means, is to reject, psychologically, both the goals of financial success and the usual socially approved means for getting to the goal. *Retreatists* are those who, for whatever reason, have repeatedly failed and in response finally give up and withdraw from active participation. Perhaps they did not have the necessary resources but only came to realize that after the reality of failure finally dawned, or perhaps they had the means but did not use them well or were unlucky. These could be people who were morally unable to innovate or perhaps tried to innovate but even failed at that. In any case, such individuals are likely to become alcoholics, drug addicts, skid row bums, or chronically unemployed welfare recipients. In the academic context, it is the students who, no matter how hard they try, are just not making it, so they give up. They decide that graduation is not worth the effort and that the process of studying, reading, and attending classes itself is of no value. Hence they either drop out of school or they hang around the university, frequently stoned or drunk, mooching off friends, perhaps still registering half-heartedly for a few classes but making no real effort to succeed until they are made to leave.

Finally, some people who actually fail or anticipate failure come to believe that their failures or potential failures are not their own fault but instead stem from an unfair or faulty social system. In response, they psychologically reject the societally prescribed goals of financial success as well as the socially approved means to achieve those goals, and they set out to replace society's goals and means with new ones. Thus, the fourth deviant adaptation is called *rebellion*. It is exemplified by political revolutionaries, evangelical religious adherents who want to transform the world, or student radicals who want to get rid of grades, course credits, degrees, and regimented patterns of instruction. Merton did not specify why some who fail, or who anticipate failure, come to blame their failure on the social system rather than on themselves, though he hinted that it was more likely when there was a pre-existing subculture of rebellion to which a person might become exposed.

By providing symbols reflecting cell location in a two-by-two table, Merton made it easy to remember these various adaptations. Note that in Table 11.2, column one, symbolized with a plus, represents possession of, or psychological acceptance of, the culturally defined goals, which in the United States is primarily financial success. Column two, symbolized by a minus, represents the absence of, or psychological rejection of, the goals. Row one, symbolized by a plus, indicates possession of, or psychic acceptance of, the socially approved means for achieving society's goals. Row two, with a minus designation, reflects absence of, or psychic rejection of, the socially approved means. By locating the cells relative to the goals and means, we can easily grasp the meaning of the various adaptations. The upper left-hand cell reflects conformity—presence of the goals and the means (+ +). The upper right-hand cell displays ritualism—absence of the goals but presence of the means (– +). The lower left hand cell shows innovation—the presence of the goals but the absence of the means (+ –). The lower right-hand cell symbolizes retreatism—absence of the goals and absence of the means (– –). Finally, the residual category, shown below the cells of the table is that of rebellion—the absence of goals and means but an effort to replace them with new goals and new means (– – + +).

Table 11.2 Adaptations to Anomie

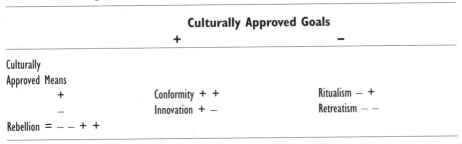

| | **Culturally Approved Goals** | |
	+	–
Culturally Approved Means		
+	Conformity + +	Ritualism – +
–	Innovation + –	Retreatism – –
Rebellion = – – + +		

Elaborations and Extensions

Critique. Merton's anomie theory has had enormous appeal to generations of students and scholars partly because it keys into something that everybody can appreciate—the frustration of trying to compete without the tools to win. It has also been popular because of its sweep; it potentially explains many kinds of deviance within one general scheme.

Unfortunately, the evidence has not been kind to the theory. There are a number of possible reasons for this. Probably the main problem is the narrowness of the explanatory focus, which is reflected in how easily it fits into our classification as a situational motivation theory. Almost exclusively it emphasizes how strain engendered by the social context compels, or motivates, the person to adapt, sometimes deviantly. To be sure, the theory does mention moral constraints that prevent some strained people from innovating, but the theory paints deviance mainly as a product of motivation. It ignores other things that often come into play—things like opportunity for deviance, the potential costs of deviance in the form of social or legal sanctions, personality variations that might influence how an individual responds to strain, or the influence of social groups with which the person might be affiliated. Furthermore, the theory has a hard time with reality because a lot of people with the means for achieving financial goals nevertheless perceive themselves as relatively bad off—relative to wealthier people—and some poor people perceive themselves as relatively well off—relative to poorer people. As a result, the premises of the theory that predict innovation among the poor but not the wealthy prove to be wrong when the "poor but honest" conform and "white-collar criminals" innovate. Thus, the weakest part of the theory is its failure to specify when objective rather than perceived conditions come into play and when an individual is likely to make one adaptation rather than another. Various theorists have suggested ways to overcome these problems, but others have simply tried to expand the typology to show more combinations of conditions.

Cloward and Ohlin. Richard Cloward (1959) noted that it is not enough for a person to be strained by social structural pressures and to possess the attributes that Merton prescribed for the various deviant adaptations. Before the strained individual can innovate and adapt to anomie with criminal or deviant activity, he or she has to first learn the skills or life styles associated with a particular pattern of response and encounter an opportunity to exercise them. Later Cloward and Lloyd Ohlin (1960) tried to specify how organizational and opportunity structures of various neighborhoods made it more or less likely that an individual living there would resort to one or another style of adaptation with specific features. For example, even if a deprived youth embraces the goals of financial success and wishes to innovate, he is more likely to do so if he lives in a neighborhood where there is a pre-existing criminal organization with which he can become affiliated to pursue a life of innovative crime. And youths with blocked goals who live in disorganized neighborhoods without well-defined criminal opportunities may resort to gang fighting or to drug use. Thus, there is more to deviance than simply being strained and lacking moral inhibitions against innovating. These things must converge with learning contexts and opportunities for various kinds of behavioral response. Unfortunately, Merton did not take the initiative from Cloward and Ohlin by bringing those additional variables into his theory in a systematic way (see Tittle, 1995:71–85). That was left to others.

Agnew. Robert Agnew (1992) took up the challenge articulated by Cloward and Ohlin and has gone far beyond it in extending and expanding Merton's basic idea that structural inducements provide the motivation for deviance. Agnew refers to his theory as General Strain Theory, suggesting that his version is far broader in scope than the original. One way in which Agnew's theory is more general than Merton's is in its identification of the sources of strain. Merton essentially suggested only one source of strain—the discrepancy between aspiration to fulfill a structural mandate and potential or actual achievement. Agnew postulates three sources of strain: (1) the failure to achieve positively valued goals, (2) the removal of positively valued stimuli from the individual, and (3) the introduction of negatively valued stimuli to the individual. Moreover, there are three subtypes of traditional strain: (a) a disjunction between aspirations and expectations, (b) a disjunction between aspirations and one's actual achievements, and (c) a discrepancy between an actual outcome and what one thinks to be a fair outcome. For Agnew, then, there are many sources of strain. Strain can arise not only when aspirations do not meet expectations but when something the individual values is taken away (say, the loss of a close friend or parent), and when something painful occurs to the individual (say, being the victim of a crime or living in a stressful environment). The point is that one reason Agnew's theory is general strain theory is because the sources of strain are far more diverse than under Merton's scheme.

Some examples of these various kinds of strain-inducing situations will help you appreciate Agnew's contribution. An individual can feel strain when a teacher assigns a poor grade (it blocks the student's goal of getting credit for the course). A young woman can feel strain when her parents try to prevent her from continuing to see a young man to whom she is attracted and has been dating (the parents may remove something that is positively valued). A businessperson will experience strain when a government inspector issues a directive requiring safety equipment to be installed at the owner's expense (imposition of an undesirable stimulus). We all feel stressed when it is hot and muggy and the auto air conditioning stops working as we are caught in traffic (there are unpleasant stimuli from the physical environment). Finally, it is stressful to wake up with a headache, to have an excess of intestinal gas, to have a bad day, or to grow tired when we have a lot of things to do (unpleasant responses from our bodies). In other words, all people face strains of various kinds, but some face more severe and more frequent strains. Strains in turn may affect our behavior.

Agnew argues that the first, and most important, thing that strain does is to generate negative emotions such as anger, distress, frustration, or despair. These negative emotions, in turn, stimulate the individual to try to eliminate the source of the strain or to do something about the negative emotions. In other words, Agnew, like Merton, assumes that human beings are coping animals and when they are faced with a problem—negative emotions in this case—they seek solutions. If the coping solutions successfully eliminate or at least reduce the strain to a manageable level, motivation for deviance is forestalled. Agnew suggests that persons may cope with strain in one of three ways—cognitive, behavioral, or emotional. With cognitive responses the individual mentally redefines the situation; with behavioral responses the person tries to avoid the adversity or accommodates to it; and in emotional coping the person resorts to various maneuvers to relieve internal discomfort. Although each of these accommodations can take conventional or deviant forms, most of the time people who face strain and its accompanying negative emotions cope in nondeviant ways. Agnew suggests that under some conditions, people adjust to strain and consequent negative emotions with deviant or unconventional responses, and the major strength of his theory is its identification of conditions that enhance the chances that coping will be deviant.

Among other things, he contends that strain that continually accumulates without periodic resolution is more likely to lead to deviant adaptations, and he suggests that heavy, more recent, long-lasting stress as well as clustering of different kinds of stress enhance the chances of deviance. In addition, he notes that many situational and other variables affect the likelihood of deviant coping. The variables include personality and other individual characteristics, social supports available to the person, costs of deviance, ability to adapt, learning histories that produce predispositions toward particular types of coping, and peer influences. The main theme of the theory, then, is that strain leads to negative emotion, which in turn leads to coping. When individuals can cope conventionally, they usually do. It is only when conditions preclude cognitive or emotional adjustments or encourage deviant adjustments that strain leads to misbehavior.

The second sense in which Agnew's General Strain Theory is more general than Merton's original formulation is in the scope of what it can explain. If strain is generated only when people's material aspirations are blocked or thwarted, then Merton's account might provide an adequate explanation of instrumental acts of deviance (acts that get people the things that they are otherwise prevented from getting). However, Merton's explanation for individuals resorting to violent rather than more expressive acts of deviance (sexual fetishes or drug use, for example) is less adequate. There is no compelling reason why even repeated economic failure would result in something like retreatist drug use rather than, say, pursuing sexual fetishes (perhaps another form of retreatism). In articulating several very different avenues through which individuals can experience strain, Agnew's theory can potentially explain a wide sweep of deviant acts. If you are feeling strain because noxious persons are hassling you, for example, and you can't cope through any other means, you can respond to the strain by slugging the annoying party (violence); by getting revenge—stealing or destroying some of the party's property (theft and vandalism); or reducing the strain to a more manageable level by drinking or using drugs. Agnew's theory is stronger, then, because the sources of strain are more numerous and because the constellation of deviant solutions are wider.

This is a theory that ought to make sense to all of us. You have no doubt been in many situations where things seem to close in on you. You have a lot of class work, your car breaks down, you lose your part-time job, and your girlfriend or boyfriend decides to seek more freedom. As a result, you feel a lot of anger, which cries out for you to do something. What can you do? Of course, you might redefine these things as unimportant, convincing yourself that "life goes on" and there will be better days. You might seek solace in religion or yoga, learning to relax and take things as they come. You might go to the gym and spend an hour punching the bobo doll to relieve the stress. Or you might go to work to catch up in class, call your father to help get the car fixed, look for another job, and begin to make new friends. None of these things is deviant. But suppose you were unable to do any of those things. You simply cannot redefine the problems as unimportant, you cannot dissipate your anger, and you cannot seem to do anything to correct the actual situation. The anger is locked inside and continually boils. According to Agnew's argument, you are then likely to yell at people, steal things, punch somebody out, or "diss" a date—all forms of deviance. But even then, whether you do any of these things depends on many factors, such as your moral feelings, how closely linked you are to those around you, and the opportunities to do these things and get away with them.

Agnew's theory, then, is a considerable improvement over Merton's formulation, though both center on the idea that stress or strain, under particular circumstances, accounts for deviant behavior. Agnew sees this possibility in a number of different kinds of strain while Merton limits his argument to one particular type. Agnew observes that features of the stress, such as its strength, cumulativity, and duration can affect outcomes, while Merton focuses on perceptions or actual experience of failure in goal achievement. In addition, the Agnew account specifies a causal chain with negative emotion being the intervening mechanism between stress and some response, and it treats deviance as a highly conditional outcome most likely to occur under a set of circumstances that prevent or make conventional coping more difficult. Thus, according to Agnew's account, strain *can* produce deviance, given a complicated set of circumstances; according to Merton's account, structural conflicts will produce deviance, given a simple set of circumstances: absence of means to achieve or the ability to perceive success and absence of moral constraints. Finally, Agnew's general theory of strain is able to account for a wider sweep of criminal/deviant behaviors than Merton's original formulation.

Marxian Conflict Theory

Preliminary Considerations

Another type of structural inducement, or situational motivation, theory is concerned with the mandates of particular types of economic or social systems. Although there are many versions of these Marxian, or conflict, theories (Bohm, 1982; Bonger, 1916; Quinney, 1970; Taylor et al., 1973), and most seemingly explain only why societies differ in their rates of crime or deviance, they can also be construed to imply explanations for individual behavior. However, it is important to note that Marxian conflict theories have rarely been thought of as general theories for explaining either societal or individual variations in deviance, and most of their adherents will be offended that they are discussed here in the same context as anomie and general strain theories. The theories are usually regarded as "radical," or "critical," politically oriented manifestos, though often rooted in careful case studies and historical analysis, designed to expose the evils of capitalist societies and to reorient scholars and lay persons alike away from dispassionate analysis (which their authors think is impossible) toward changing capitalist systems to be more socialistic or at least more just and humane. However, the objectives of this book are to expose you to systems of ideas that permit answers to questions of "why" and "how" with respect to behaviors that particular social groups regard as unacceptable and subject to negative sanction; it is not to tell you what is inherently good or bad from a moral or some other philosophical stance, nor to direct you to any action. We believe that behind the ideological veil of conflict writings there is a core of genuine theory that is subject to specification and test. Moreover, despite the theme of Marxian work as counter to, and oppositional with, traditional theories in the crime/deviance area, its core explanatory focus on strain and deprivation appears similar in many ways to that of Merton. It is that content that we wish to identify and elaborate.

Bongerian Interpretation

Perhaps the best version of conflict theory for deriving individual explanations is that by William Bonger (1916), a Dutch criminologist. He maintained that deviance is more likely in societies with capitalist economic systems than in those that are more socialistic because the profit motive that underlies capitalism forces most, if not all, people within those systems to become "de-moralized," that is, to become devoid of moral feelings and sympathy toward other people. The main intervening variables between capitalism and de-moralization are competition and deprivation. When people must compete with others, be it for economic survival or for differential rewards, they have to suppress their sympathies for the plight of their competitors in order to succeed. Insensitivity to the plight of others combined with a struggle for success or survival produces selfish behavior as competitors try to use whatever resources they can muster to promote their own goals at the expense of others. The result, according to Bonger, is that some people are inevitably deprived, and that, too, leads to selfishness in the struggle for survival. Thus, both competition and deprivation motivate self-gratifying, exploitative acts, and they undermine moral sentiments that might restrain deviance. In other words, capitalist economic systems produce a mental attitude of egoism and erode socially constructive sentiments of altruism (looking out for others). Consequently, in social systems promoting competition there will be much deprivation, selfishness, and deviance, tied together by "de-moralization."

It is not only the working class who are affected by enhanced feelings of egoism and diminished altruism, even the wealthy and powerful are affected by the emotional mood of capitalism. If the wealthy become egoistic, you may well ask, why don't they deviate? Well, they do, according to Bonger, but they do not commit "crimes." Long before labeling theorists developed the idea, Bonger argued that because of their economic and political positions, the acts of the powerful are not likely to be treated as criminal, harmful, or deviant. Instead of being called criminals, those in privileged economic positions are more apt to be called "shrewd businessmen."

Not all people within competitive systems, however, resort to deviance. By identifying the underlying logic of Bonger's argument, we can surmise that those most likely to deviate are the ones most committed to the competitive process and facing the stiffest competition; those who are losing in the competitive struggle; or those who are deprived as a result of the actions of competitors trying to advance their own goals. These same processes affect people who are not engulfed in competitive systems, however. Even though larger numbers of people in capitalist societies are committed to competition and larger numbers of them are victims of that process, almost all societies incorporate some forms of competition, even if only competition to promote the welfare of the society. Moreover, in any society some individuals are more competitive than others, and some individuals will be more deprived than others. Hence the Marxian analysis explains individual deviance, no matter what kind of society in which it occurs, as motivated by the desire to succeed

Deviance in Everyday Life

Tonya Harding and Nancy Kerrigan were skaters vying for a place on the 1994 United States Olympic team. At the Olympic trials in January of 1994, Jeff Gilooly, Harding's ex-husband, Sean Eckert, her former bodyguard, and two others attempted to keep Kerrigan out of the competition by hitting her in the leg with an iron bar. Kerrigan was severely injured in the attack and could not perform at the trials. Harding, who claimed to have no prior knowledge of the offense, pled guilty to charges of conspiring to hinder the prosecution of the case. She was banned for life from the U.S. Figure Skating Association. Nancy Kerrigan survived the attack, was invited to join the U.S. Olympic skating team, and won a Silver Medal in the 1994 games.

in competition or by the deprivation of actually losing or of being exploited by those who are winning.

You can appreciate the argument if you think of its application to contexts with which you are familiar. Academics in the United States is one of those contexts. Since most college classes are organized competitively, as reflected by grading standards built around the normal curve, it is inevitable that some students will win by getting good grades and some will lose by getting poor grades. And, as you know, this system is characterized by much cheating. But who cheats? According to the premises of the theory, it will be those who most want to get ahead but who face the greatest competition, those who are falling behind, and those who are at the greatest disadvantage (that is, who lack intelligence or have the poorest academic skills). Does this describe the students you know who cheat? Sports is another of those competitive contexts to which conflict theory applies. In any contest, some will win at the expense of others who lose. Therefore, we expect much cheating, which is why athletic contests always have officials and provide for penalties. But who is most likely to cheat, according to the theory? It is those who are driven to win but face strong competition and face the greatest possibilities of losing or those who lack the necessary skills to compete effectively. Does this remind you of Tonya Harding, the ice skater whose boyfriend and an accomplice tried to cripple her opponent, Nancy Kerrigan, at the 1994 U.S. Olympic trials?

This theory supplies a plausible account of deviance and potentially has great explanatory breadth because it can explain almost all kinds of deviance. Its weakness is that it does not satisfactorily explain why some competitive individuals, or those deprived by competition, do not resort to deviance, nor does it explain why those who do resort to deviance choose one form rather than another. Thus, it is not clear why a competitor who is losing turns to suicide rather than to underhanded business practices, or why someone who is deprived chooses theft while another becomes mentally ill or addicted to drugs. In application to the preceding examples, it does not tell us why some students who are doing poorly in school never cheat, while others with few competitors nevertheless do cheat. Furthermore, the theory takes no account of social structural features with rules of competition that restrain selfishness and exploitation or that aim to soften the effects of competition by redistributing wealth or institutionalizing the principles of justice. Moreover, it overlooks individual level variables like personality and moral commitments as well as processes of social control that restrain what people can do.

Summary and Critique of Structural Inducement Theories

Structural inducement theories contend that human problems often lead to attempted solutions that involve deviant behavior. The theories differ mainly in their identification of the structural conditions leading to stress or strain; their attempts to specify the process by which problems lead to deviance; and the conditions that affect the form and likelihood of deviance. The main appeal of these theories is that they set forth plausible explanations to which we can all relate. Everybody knows from experience that stress and strain sometimes cause people to misbehave. Moreover, these theories have broad scope in that they can presumably explain individualized as well as fully organized deviance. They are weak, however, in that they have not yet fully articulated the processes by which adaptations are made so that one can predict who will or will not resort to deviance or to particular types of deviance. Clearly, a lot more is involved than mere structural conditions that generate strain. The neglected variables include many learned characteristics about how to perceive situations and how to deal with stress, as well as the distributions of opportunities for conventional and deviant stress management responses. While Cloward and Ohlin note the importance of some of these things, only Agnew's formulation systematically identifies them. Yet his account does not permit one to understand when they will or will not be operative. The failure to reckon with additional variables has made the structural inducement theories vulnerable to empirical challenge. Moreover, these theories do not explain why some people are exposed to the conditions producing motivations toward deviance more than others. The theories take for granted the strain-producing conditions or start with strain itself, and then go from there. They are most valuable, therefore, in calling attention to one type of causal force in the production of deviance, but they provide an incomplete account.

Situational Inducements

Whereas learning and structural inducement theories are concerned mainly with larger, more-or-less stable features of social situations to which individuals are exposed over fairly long periods of time, a third set of theories that we classify as situational motivation theories deal with transitory elements that come into play in immediate social contexts through which individuals pass. The effect of these circumstantial or episodic factors or processes is to stimulate, or motivate, short-term deviant responses.

Routine Activities

Focus

Since routine activities theory (Cohen and Felson, 1979; Felson, 1986, 1994) was developed to account for long-range trends in particular kinds of crime and primarily addresses variations in predatory crime rates among ecological contexts such as cities or countries, we will consider it in more detail in Chapter 16, which is devoted to macro-level explanations. However, because the theory does feature things in the behavioral field that affect individuals' behaviors, its principles can be extended to the micro-level. Deviant behavior, particularly predatory types such as robbery, theft, burglary, and rape, is theorized to occur when three conditions converge or come together in time and space. The three are motivated offenders, suitable targets, and the absence of capable guardianship. The central proposition of the theory is that the probability of crime increases when there is a motivated offender at a scene where there is a potential target or suitable victim and where there is no credible guardian to deter or prevent the act from occurring. Convergence of the three elements is thought to be promoted by particular life styles linked to normal or routine patterns of employment, shopping, child rearing, and recreation—hence the name "routine activities." Suitability of targets and the absence of effective guardianship can be regarded as two aspects of opportunity, a situational characteristic, that help transform individuals' predispositions toward self-gratification into motivations for deviance.

Although routine activity theorists set forth few explanatory principles to account for motivation, they seem to assume that all people have an inherent urge to gratify themselves, an urge that apparently can be enhanced by various forms of deprivation (in some of their tests they use prevalence of poverty and the proportion of a population that is of minority status as proxies for the presence of motivated offenders—see, for example, Cohen et al., 1980). The theory plays up the idea that situational factors—target attractiveness and absence of effective guardianship—stimulate inherent self-gratifying impulses, thereby transforming them into actual motivations for deviance. In the macro-level formulation, target attractiveness refers to characteristics of potential victims or objects that make them suitable for gratifying a potential deviant's desires or needs. Absence of effective or capable guardianship implies, in part, reduced chances of apprehension and punishment, but there is also the implication that this feature of a "target"—having nobody around who can or will do anything about deviance—by converging with the basic urge for self-gratification by potential deviants, helps to stimulate motivation for misbehavior. That is why we classify routine activities as a situational motivation theory rather than as a control theory. The essence of the argument is that particular features of situations bring about motivation for deviance by keying into innate self-gratifying impulses; motivation in turn produces deviant behavior.

Application to Individuals

In applying the principles of routine activities theory at the micro-level, one must begin with the assumption incorporated in the macro-level account that all people can potentially become motivated for deviance. This potential is realized when individuals encounter situations where they perceive that deviant behavior can gratify their inherent needs and in which it appears possible to exploit the circumstances to achieve the desired result. Hence, deviance stems from a favorable juncture of need and potential gratifying circumstances. Potential gratifying circumstances include the basic features of situations that make them eligible to fulfill a potential deviant's need—such as the availability of a car to steal when the person wants to go someplace or wants to impress peers—as well as the absence of others near the automobile who might object, get in the way, resist, or call for help to prevent the act or impose sanctions after the act has occurred, or the presence of "the Club" (inanimate objects can be very capable guardians too).

Deviance in Everyday Life

Do theories of crime have anything to do with the real world? According to routine activities theory, crime is unlikely to occur if there are guardians around. As suggested, guardians that can thwart a crime can be people or inanimate objects. There is an entire industry of inanimate guardians that protect against car theft. LoJack, for example, hardens a car against theft by making it easy to retrieve when stolen. The LoJack unit is no larger than a chalkboard eraser and can be hidden in many places all over a car. When the car is stolen, a beacon in the LoJack device is activated, informing police of the car's location. The company claims that 90 percent of the stolen cars that contain a LoJack are retrieved, and 75 percent of those, within one day. Researchers have found that the presence of LoJack in some cars deters thieves from taking other cars. Other guardians include the product Failsafe, which is an electronic key with an encoded computer chip. In order for a car to be started, the Failsafe key must be inserted first. No Failsafe key, no start.

For example, drug use could be explained with these principles by noting, first, that most drugs have inherent or social features that make their use pleasurable. They stimulate the pleasure zones of the brain. Hence drugs are physiologically "attractive," though people might not know that unless they encounter a social situation that reveals it. Moreover, even when the physical attractiveness of drugs is known, they are likely to become socially attractive as well when a person is with others who are enjoying the drug; these others imply that they expect similar behavior from the potential deviant and that in this social context, they stand ready to prescribe methods and doses for "safe" consumption. Second, an individual may accidentally or purposively encounter situations in which drug use can occur without interference; that is, the drug is available at a cost the person can afford and there are no disapprovers to get in the way or prevent it—in other words these situations involve no effective or capable guardians. Third, these circumstances converge. The person, naturally equipped with a desire for self-gratification, or pleasure, encounters circumstances that let him or her know that use of a particular drug would produce pleasure and that such use is feasible in the immediate circumstances. Drug use, according to the theoretical principles of routine activities, then, results from motivation produced by the episodic joining of pleasurable urges, situations portraying the drug as capable of fulfilling those urges, and circumstances where usage is feasible.

As another example, one might explain non-marital sex as the result of the juncture of three conditions. An individual who is naturally inclined to seek pleasure meets a potential sex partner whose responses and attributes make the possibility of a sexual encounter seem highly desirable (target attractiveness) and the two are in circumstances where parents, mates, or other disapprovers cannot intervene (absence of effective guardians). This situation both provokes the motivation for deviant sex and permits its expression in actual behavior.

Evaluation

This theory has much inherent appeal, particularly in its emphasis on the episodic, situationally provoked nature of deviance, which contrasts with other theories that portray deviance as expressions of more or less permanent features of individuals, and in its implication that anybody is liable to do deviance, given the right circumstances. Moreover, routine activity's theoretical principles focus on general features of situations that make sense as provocateurs of deviance—attractiveness and feasibility. But the theory has a number of defects that prevent it from providing full explanations of deviance, the most important of which is its extreme simplicity. It is not clear, for instance, exactly what it is about situations that would make various kinds of deviance more or less attractive or feasible for different people. Some people may perceive that using drugs at a party is highly attractive, while someone else would view that same situation as disgusting. And while some individuals would view a convention in a city far from home as a situation making extra-marital sex feasible, others would regard it as dangerous because of the possibility of getting a sexually transmitted disease. Thus, different individuals respond in different ways to the same situation, and the same individual might respond the same way to different situations. But the theory does not enable us to predict the combinations that will evoke deviant behavior, because too many unspecified things are packed into each of the three concepts of the theory. Not only does the theory neglect to specify the features of situations that make them deviogenic, it ignores individual characteristics that make various kinds of deviance potentially more gratifying for some than others or that affect how they perceive and interpret circumstances. In other words, the theory has not produced a very detailed account of how offenders get to be "motivated."

Rational Choice

Another line of theory focusing on inputs from immediate situations is called variously "rational choice" (Cornish and Clarke, 1986), "economic" (Becker, 1968), or "utilitarian" (Caroll, 1978) theory. The basic idea is that all human behavior involves mental calculation of possible costs and benefits as they occur in immediate contexts. When the calculation shows benefits exceeding costs, the behavior in question is performed, but when it shows costs exceeding benefits, the behavior is curtailed and an alternative, more profitable, behavior is selected. An underlying implication is that the probability of deviance in a particular set of circumstances increases as the magnitude of the ratio of benefits from the deviance exceeds the costs associated with it (the ratio increases from one upward) and its probability decreases as the magnitude of the ratio of benefits declines (the ratio decreases from one downward). Although some versions of this argument, particularly deterrence theory, emphasize the cost side of the equation and fall under our rubric of external constraint theories (Chapter 14), we classify the rational choice scheme generally as a situational motivation theory because in the active mode of trying to explain why deviance occurs (rather than why it does not occur), excessive benefits can be thought of as the motivator of deviance.

The image of human beings projected by rational choice thinking is one of cold, unemotional, computerlike mathematical manipulations of probabilities and quantitative inputs that take place with lightning speed thousands of times a day as the person moves from one situation to another. The person is presumably constantly saying to himself or herself, "What is in it for me?" and then acting on the answer. In one situation, the answer might be that a particular form of deviance will pay off big and in another situation it might be that a specific type of deviance is not a good deal because the cost is too great or the benefit too small. And what the individual actually ends up doing will reflect those answers.

For example, a delivery man brings a package to a door and knocks in order to present it to the addressee. When nobody answers, he considers trying to open the door to leave it inside. He quickly reasons that if he returns it to the station, he will have to come back another time. Returning it would be inconvenient, and, given his workload, it would entail many units of cost to him and very few benefits. He thinks about leaving the package outside on the porch, and this would imply so many units of benefit because he could save time and move on to the next job. On the other hand, the package might get stolen or rained on, causing the addressee to complain and perhaps costing the delivery man money, a promotion, or at least a scolding—all of which imply so many units of cost. The benefit does not outweigh the cost in his mind. If he tries to open the door, somebody might think he is a burglar and call the police. This could result in lost time, translatable into so many units of cost to him. But trying to open the door might produce success, allowing him to save time, which in this case appears more beneficial than costly. So, he tries the knob, finds the door unlocked, and opens it to leave the package. Having opened the door, he now sees that he could steal something; stealing implies some probability of getting caught and punished but with a commensurate benefit, depending on the item he might steal. He then decides to look around to see if something can be stolen that will not be missed—this would provide a benefit with little potential cost. However, in looking around, he discovers the addressee, a woman, in the shower. Now he contemplates whether to leave quickly, spy on her for a while and then leave, or perhaps rape her. Each course of action carries a cost and a potential benefit for him. What he decides to do, according to the theory, will depend on the results of those calculations of cost and benefit. If he resorts to deviance, it will be because the deviant behavior was brought forth, or motivated, by something in the situation that made it profitable.

Clearly, this theory makes a lot of sense and it is useful as an interpretive device. It makes sense because we all know that much of what we do involves calculation of cost and benefit. We very frequently find ourselves doing the things that directly benefit us and are disinclined to do things that do not. We contemplate buying a new vehicle. In considering it, we weigh its cost relative to our need and decide accordingly. Similarly, we risk rejection (a cost) in favor of the potential benefit of a relationship when we engage in overtures to new friends or lovers; sometimes we forgo those overtures because the calculations are not favorable, and sometimes we follow through. Yet we also know that much of what we do is out of habit, with no calculation whatsoever; much behavior is impulsive and/or emotion driven with little evidence of calculation; and even when we calculate, we often do so inefficiently and with incomplete information—in other words, we act irrationally and take risks. In addition, many of the things we do (care for our children or elderly parents, make anonymous charitable donations) do not seem to be motivated by pure self-interest but by altruism or other non-utilitarian sentiments (Etzioni, 1988). Moreover, the theory is weak because it does not give us a basis for understanding what is valuable or costly to a specific person or for predicting when a person will misperceive costs and benefits.

This deficiency is illustrated by the childhood story of Br'er Rabbit, who, when caught by his enemy the fox, pleaded to be thrown into the briars as punishment. Since getting stuck by briars is painful and dreaded by foxes, this appeared to be a good thing to do. However, when released, the rabbit mocked the fox for letting him escape into his natural habitat. Briars are not painful to rabbits, whose coats are equipped for them, but without realizing this the fox assumed that what was costly to him was also costly to rabbits. Similarly, all things are not equally rewarding to everybody. One person likes chocolate and is often motivated to eat it despite the cost in weight gain; another person doesn't care for it at all. One individual regards overthrowing the government as highly desirable and worth much cost to achieve; another is satisfied with the government. Some women have high sex drives and are willing to risk much cost in lost reputation and possible disease to gratify that urge; other women have so little interest in sex that they don't participate even when there are almost no potential costs.

Without being able to explain these variations in "taste," rational choice theory is of limited value. That is why some social scientists have tried to expand the theory and to merge it with psychological and learning theories to fill in missing elements (Akers, 1990; Felson, 1986; Wilson and Herrnstein,

1985). Others, however, have used the rational choice argument in a tautological way to interpret events after the fact, much like some writers have misused the learning/reinforcement principles discussed in the beginning of this chapter. In this procedure, the analyst, who uncritically believes the argument, takes whatever behavior that is performed as evidence that it provides more reward than cost, and if some behavior does not follow from something that previously was assumed to be rewarding, then the analyst concludes that the particular thing is not, in fact, rewarding to the person. By this means, any behavior can be "explained" as a product of relative costs and benefits, but such explanations are delusional and add little to our base of knowledge.

❖ ❖ ❖ ❖

Interaction Process

A final theoretical approach emphasizing situational variables that generate motivation for deviance, which in turn produces actual deviant behavior, deals with sequential processes in interaction that lead to deviant outcomes (Birkbeck and LaFree, 1993). The theories of this type collectively grow out of a tradition in social psychology called symbolic interactionism (Cohen, 1966; Heimer and Matsueda, 1994; Matsueda, 1992). According to this argument, although actors in any situation start with a set of learned response patterns, role definitions, and some knowledge of normative expectations, no situation has completely predetermined rules or totally predictable outcomes. Instead, behavioral responses are negotiated as one party emits some behavior, another person responds to that behavior, then the original actor responds to the response and to other things in the situation that might have changed since the first response was emitted. This back-and-forth adjustment to others, to their reactions, and to features of the context produces unique sequences of events, sometimes leading to deviant behavior but not always to the outcomes that the actors intended when the interaction sequence began. Thus, to understand or explain a deviant outcome, one has to reconstruct the interaction process that occurred, learn the meanings and interpretations people employed when they responded, and come to see the developmental stages as the participants saw them. The explanation of deviance, then, is in the history of the interaction, and it is never wholly predictable.

For example, imagine that a couple are on a date with intent simply to have dinner, see a movie, engage in pleasant conversation, and part as friends. During the evening, the female inadvertently allows her skirt to rise, revealing her underwear. The male sees this and interprets it as a sign of sexual interest by the female. He then makes a suggestive remark, which the female takes as an insult. She responds by calling him a sexist pig. This makes him angry, so he calls her a tease. She slaps him, and he grabs her hand and they wrestle. In the scuffle the male proceeds to pin the woman's arms. About that time someone comes along and, thinking a fight is occurring, calls the police. Because she is embarrassed, the woman complains to the bystander that the male attempted to physically assault her. The police arrive, and the male is arrested for aggravated assault.

Several deviant acts have occurred: the male's suggestive remark, the female's slap, the male's pinning of her arms (which is a form of simple assault, though not aggravated assault), the woman's lie about the aggravated assault (or perhaps it is not a lie but a misinterpretation). According to interaction process theory, these deviant acts are the result of a unique sequence of events, each of which represented a response to a previous event and all of which together spiraled to an unintended end. The outcome was not predetermined, nor could it be predicted; it was a product of a particular interaction sequence. Even though some of the moves in the sequence were influenced by pre-existing attitudes, statuses, and role definitions, the exact direction they took was quite uncertain and even until the very end could not be foreseen. That the female was wearing a skirt rather than pants reflects role definitions and normative expectations for the respective genders. That the revealing of her underpants was interpreted by the male as having sexual implications reflects cultural patterns by which motives are imputed to various kinds of behaviors. And the male's suggestive remark stems from his own learned attitudes toward females and his interpretation of appropriate male behavior in certain kinds of situations. And so on, including the response of the woman to the appearance of the onlooker, which was conditioned by the woman's understanding of appropriate female conduct as nonaggressive and of how perceptions by others that she violated those norms might affect her future. Yet, even if one knew all of that, it would have been impossible to explain the outcome without reconstructing the set of circumstances that converged to produce the ultimate outcomes or acts of deviance. In that sense, then, deviance is not a product of fixed quantities but emerges as a product of on-going interactions, sometimes of a symbolic nature (like the male's suggestive verbal remark).

The importance of on-going interactions can be illustrated by imagining how the interaction between the male and female in this situation might have been different at each point in the sequence. Suppose the male, upon seeing the female's underwear, pretended not to notice, thereby impressing the female with his "sensitivity." In response, she makes a sexual overture, which is accepted by the male. They begin a sexual encounter in the automobile parked in the driveway of her parents' home, where they are observed by someone going by. The bypasser conceals himself to watch but is detected by the female who screams for her lover to do something. The embarrassed couple flees the scene, but the woman's father hears the commotion and reports to the police that a prowler is lurking in the neighborhood.

Now the deviant acts that have occurred are entirely different. Non-marital sex may be deviant in this neighborhood, and certainly sex in a semipublic place is a deviant act, but these are misbehaviors shared by the male and female. The bypasser may have engaged in deviance by watching a private act without announcing his presence, and he may be arrested for being in the wrong place at the wrong time. But the learned characteristics of the participants in this situation have not changed, nor have the structural features that might generate motivation for deviance from strain or stress; what has changed is the interaction sequence.

While this theoretical approach centers on the uniqueness of interaction sequences, it does not deny regularities that make for similar outcomes in common situations. Indeed, despite the differences among interaction sequences revealed by microscopic examination, scholars have found larger patterns in macro-level comparisons of situations with some ostensible commonalities, such as similar actors in typical contexts trying to accomplish analogous goals. It is like the forest-and-tree phenomenon. If people stand back from a bunch of trees they can see a forest, which has its own collective

features, but if they examine each tree closely, they will find minute varia-   ❖ ❖ ❖ ❖
tions suggesting that each tree is unique. This duality is shown particularly by
the work of Jack Katz (1988) and David Luckenbill (1977).

Katz

Jack Katz (1988) tries to answer the question of what domestic killers,
shoplifters, those who adopt roles as "badasses" in the street culture, those
who fight in gangs, rob, pursue "sneaky thrills," and commit "cold-blooded"
murder are trying to do, and he traces typical interaction sequences that lead
to those outcomes. Katz concludes that all forms of deviance have their own
uniquely seductive appeal as ultimately allowing the deviant to achieve autonomy or exhibit moral dominance in response to the mandates of specific
situations. But each form of deviance, as enacted by different individuals, has
a unique, contextually relevant purpose and history.

The typical spontaneous homicide involves friends, relatives, acquaintances, and lovers. The interaction sequence that ends in death for one of the
participants usually begins with a challenge to the killer's status, rights, or
dignity. That challenge, however, may take many forms. Regardless of form,
the challenge involves potential humiliation, which leads to rage that is expressed in murder when the person comes to perceive that his or her commission of homicide can serve a larger moral mandate. This type of "righteous
slaughter" is motivated by the killer's debasement stemming from situational
insults, but its enactment is undertaken in the guise of guarding abstract
goodness. Thus, a man happens upon his wife with a lover. He is offended, especially if the lover or wife tries to justify the situation at his expense. Perhaps
the wife says that this would not have happened had he been a better lover,
more attentive to her, or not have left her alone so often. Maybe one of the
things the lover says reminds the cuckolded husband of the children who are
supposedly being neglected. He then begins to think of the offending couple
as degrading the whole moral order that sanctifies marriage and sexual fidelity rather than as simply insulting him. Then he may begin to conceive of
himself as a potential instrument of the community who can act to remove
this affront to its integrity. Finally, if the sequence develops to this point, his
rage can be vented in a dramatic act of transcendence and moral triumph
(murdering both parties to this malignant act), allowing him to feel like a cru-
sader, at least temporarily. Yet, each development of the interaction depends
on responses of the parties, responses to the responses, and other things that
change in the dynamics of the interaction.

Katz describes acts of vandalism, burglary, shoplifting, and joyriding as
instances of sneaky thrills, each involving a peculiar technique for defying
convention and permitting young people to demonstrate competence and expand the boundaries of their concepts of self. By hiding their motives and
thoughts from adults, engaging in secret deviance, and transforming the prohibited acts into sexual metaphors, all in unique response to the specific circumstances that emerge, youthful deviants can overcome their vulnerability
to total intrusion and control by the adult world, and thereby experience lib-
erating personal triumphs. For instance, a girl who tries on clothes in a shop
and walks out with them under her coat can feel that she has broken free of
control, and she can revel in the ecstasy of putting something over on adults.
This is even more the case when she responds cleverly to inquiries, manages
to barely escape detection by adjusting to the entrance of a customer into the
area, and puts forth a bold front. All of these moves, of course, reflect some-

what unique sequences of action, response, and reaction as things change and develop, and as she adjusts to those dynamics.

"Badasses" create what Katz refers to as "awesomely deviant presences" that are rooted in unpredictable responses to whatever develops. A reputation for being out of control or capable of inflicting unanticipated harm on others gives those who otherwise would not be taken seriously a potent claim for the attention of others, and it permits control of people and situations without doing anything at all, once the reputation is established. But in any given circumstance the sequence of events is in response to previous actions and reactions and therefore has a unique character. Hence, a badass might enter a bar and ask someone why they are staring at him. The person might say that he isn't staring, which is disputed by the badass who, in an apparent fit of rage, pulls out a knife and slashes the chair next to the person. The victim, who by now is frightened and confused, might then say that he was staring because he admires the badass. The badass, in turn, calls him a liar and demands that he apologize. The apology is declared to be insincere, leading the badass to punch the guy out. And so it goes on like this in numerous situations, none unfolding in exactly the same way; thus, the badass establishes a reputation for violence, evil, and unpredictability.

Katz's work, then, illustrates a fundamental principle of interactionist theory. The explanation of deviance is in the situational progression of interaction, and in that sense is unique to every deviant act. Yet uniqueness does not preclude identification of overarching macro-level patterns of similarity.

Luckenbill

A second illustration of interactionist principles is in David Luckenbill's (1977) analysis of interaction sequences in homicide. In reviewing the natural history of the interactions that led to killings in 71 instances drawn from the files of one California county over a ten-year period, he discovered that despite the individuality of every case, there is a "typical" sequence of moves that eventuate in death. In all instances, murder represented a culmination of a set of mutual moves best characterized as a "character contest," in which the participants tried either to save "face" (a reputational image of autonomy or bravery) or to undermine the "face" of the opponent. Usually there were similar stages in the transaction. First, the person who eventually was the victim made a gesture that was interpreted by the offender as offensive in that it insulted, challenged, humiliated, or degraded him or her. Second, the challenged person typically responded in turn with a verbal or physical retaliation. Third, the two parties came to a tacit agreement that violence would be appropriate in the situation. Fourth, there was a resulting struggle that left the victim dead or dying. Finally, depending on the relationship of the offender to the victim and the behavior of observers, there was a situation-appropriate exiting of the scene by the offender.

In this way, what appears as nonsensical killings to distant observers— that is, they occur over seemingly trivial matters—makes sense within the immediate context. None of the participants in the cases examined by Luckenbill entered the situation with intent to kill; that is, they were not killers programmed by previously learned messages or compelled by structurally induced strain, although these things may have created some predispositions on which the demands of the situation could play. Instead, the killing emerged out of the interaction in which each party felt that he or she had to act in the manner called for. This is the message of interactionist theory.

Summary and Conclusion

In this chapter we have reviewed three general categories of theory that emphasize how external environments in which individuals find themselves affect their chances of deviant behavior by stimulating or enhancing their motivations toward deviance. Learning theories focus on how the social environments of individuals teach them things that come to be stored in their psyches to drive or predispose toward deviance. Structural inducement theories deal with characteristics of external environments that create psychic strains for the person and that stimulate deviant efforts to cope. Situational inducements are concerned with immediate interaction contexts that call forth, often in dynamic sequences, responses that eventuate in deviant behavior.

A major weakness of all these theories is their limited foci, which take for granted things that produce various kinds of learning, strains, or situational features. A second problem is that they do not provide the theoretical tools to completely explain or predict the process by which motivation is stimulated, produces action, or is channeled by various contingencies. Third, their causal sequences assume one-way effects. Learning and structural inducement theories portray their variables as having linear effects immediately and temporally, when in reality there is much feedback among them and from them to deviance and back, both reciprocally at a single point in time and sequentially over a span of time. Situational inducement theories see their variables as linked sequentially over time but ignore reciprocity at any given point. Therefore, some of the most interesting intellectual challenges concern methods for creating models that use the variables specified by these various theories in ways that would take into account mutual causality at any point in time as well as temporal interaction sequences in explaining specific forms of deviance (Thornberry, 1987). ✦

Chapter 12

Internal Motivation Theories

Internal motivation theories emphasize variation in the strength of individuals' impulses toward, or desires for, committing deviant acts, and they locate the sources of those motivations within the individuals' psyches. Unlike some theories that assume all people are more or less equally gratified by deviant acts, the theories to be described in this chapter contend that some individuals are far more interested in deviance than are others and that this variation in strength of motivation is the key to explaining why some are more likely than others to deviate. Therefore, internal motivation theories attempt to account for the variation among individuals in the attractiveness of deviance, and they place primary emphasis on that variation in explaining the likelihood of deviant behavior. These theories are further distinguished by their focus on internal states as the mainsprings of motivational variation.

Thus, if Jim vandalizes the school, steals watermelons from a local farmer, and forces girls to have sex, while Andy behaves himself, internal motivation theories contend that this is mainly because Jim is much more attracted to vandalizing, stealing, and raping than is Andy, or because Jim is generally more interested than Andy in deviance. The problem for such theories, then, is to account for Jim's enhanced interest in deviance or in specific deviant activities. They look first at the mental or internal characteristics of the two boys to discover why Jim needs to misbehave, or at least why he finds it more fun, satisfying, or useful to misbehave than Andy does. Internal motivation theories try to explain why differences between the two boys in internal mental characteristics exist or how they come about.

Of course, not all of the theories we classify as internal motivation theories entirely ignore the effects of potential control from external sources (such as the chances of getting arrested or of losing stature in the eyes of teachers or peers), or from other aspects of an individual's psychic structure (such as moral considerations). Nor do they completely deny the importance of motivational elements in the external social environment (such as normative expectations from peers). Rather, these theories emphasize that the most important causal factors are the internally based compulsions or urges for the particular gratifications that various kinds of deviance promise.

We will discuss three types of internal motivation theory, one of which has been most prominent among sociologists interested in deviance and two of which have been of more concern to psychologists. The best-known sociologically based internal motivation theories orient around the self; one version is called "labeling" theory, and the other version is called "self-esteem" theory. Unfortunately, the title, "labeling," and the history of that version of self theory encourages an unbalanced focus on late-life social processes while ignoring the implications of the larger social psychological tradition of symbolic interactionism (explained later in this chapter) from which it grows (see Heimer and Matsueda, 1994; Matsueda, 1992; Matsueda and Heimer, 1997). Drawing on the work of Matsueda, and hoping to help restore that balance, we refer to identity/labeling theory rather than simply labeling theory. The second version of self theory, focusing as it does on struggles to maintain self-esteem, is much more faithful to the symbolic interaction tradition.

A second type of internal motivation theory to be discussed, called reactance theory, is hardly known among those who usually study crime and deviance, but it is highly relevant and promises to become more popular. Finally, we will describe psychoanalytic theories that grew out of the writings of Sigmund Freud and are still popular, at least among clinical psychologists who are often involved in efforts to "treat" or "correct" deviant behavior.

Self Theories

There are a variety of theories in the field of deviance that deal with the self as a central component. Some of these theories are classified as control theories (Matsueda, 1992) because they emphasize how concerns about the self-image or self-evaluation act as checks on a person's impulses to commit deviant acts. According to such theories, deviance results when the checks associated with the maintenance of a self-image or self-esteem are weak or absent. Those theories are discussed in another chapter. The self theories to be discussed here emphasize processes by which concerns about the self provide the push, or motive, for committing acts of deviance.

Identity/Labeling Theory

Identity/labeling theory holds that human behavior is largely a process through which individuals seek to establish and confirm workable self-images. Infants are not born with any knowledge. Everything people think or know is acquired through association with other human beings, who convey ideas to them about who or what they are, appropriate behaviors, and aspects of the larger culture. The learning process, however, is not necessarily a one-way street in which the pre-existing social group feeds directives to the infant or child. Rather, according to this perspective, learning is a sequentially negotiated process in which information, largely based on language and mental symbols, is conveyed, provoking individuals to contemplate its meaning, putting themselves vicariously in the position of others (called role taking) to assess how reactions will appear to them, and then performing behaviors. Observers of that behavior, in turn, contemplate its meaning and consequences and then respond to it on the basis of their interpretations of its intent and significance. The individual then mentally processes the messages conveyed by the responses of others and reacts behaviorally to them. This mental processing of information and subsequent reaction produce complex patterns of interaction built around cognitive interpretations and meanings. Some of those patterns of behavior become routinized, or habitual, so that the sequence of action, interpretation, and reaction is more or less non-reflective. However, unusual challenges sometimes lead to new interpretations. This entire process of behavior, social response, adaptation, and behavioral reaction to the social response, and then further social response to the new behavior, all enacted with the aid of linguistic symbols, is called symbolic interactionism (Blumer, 1969; Cooley, 1902; Mead, 1934; Stryker, 1980).

Among the most important things learned, or negotiated, through symbolic interaction, according to this theory, is a sense of self. Just as infants are born without knowledge of the world about them, they have no consciousness of who and what they are. In fact, newborns do not even have awareness of the domain of their own bodies, much less a mental image of themselves as social entities. For example, it is common for infants to bite their own toes or fingers and cry out in surprise to learn that their appendages are attached and can produce feelings. The process of developing a sense of one's own body is partly one of direct exploration—because the physical entity exists—but developing a sense of physical boundaries is also indirect—because the symbols and meanings by which ideas of the physical person are shaped reflect the surrounding social environment. For example, people in one social context may come to regard extra-long fingernails as an essential part of their bodies, while people in other contexts may come to think of long fingernails as something foreign, to be eliminated.

However, developing a sense of self—a mental image of one's emotional structure as a separate and distinct being—is entirely indirect because it has no existence other than that which is developed through social interaction. One comes to know oneself through symbolic interaction in which ideas about what one is or might be are transmitted to one by occupants of the social context. The ideas suggesting the nature of the self are then contemplated by the person and responded to with specific behaviors. Those in the surrounding social environment, in turn, react in ways that confirm or deny the self implied by the individual's behavior. By this means the person comes to know himself or herself, and the self that comes to be known is made up of the social reactions of others. Theoretically, then, self-images are simply the reflected images that others have of us. We all possess, as Charles Horton Cooley (1902) called it, a "looking glass self."

Processes of Self-Concept Formation

The reflected appraisals of others are incorporated into one's psychic structure of self by either of two avenues. First, initial ideas of self are negotiated with adults and peers as children cognitively contemplate who or what they might be and emit trial behaviors consistent with those assumptions. Such trial behaviors can be thought of as claims made about oneself. Having made a claim of being the kind of person implied by a particular behavior that is performed, the individual then waits for a social response to confirm or deny that claim. If others, through their reactions, affirm that the person is what the behavior implies, then a tiny part of the self is formed. If the response of the social audience says that the person is not, or cannot be, what is claimed, then this disconfirming evidence undermines the portion of the self

---

Deviance in Everyday Life

In the spring of 1999, the North Atlantic Treaty Organization (NATO) began a bombing campaign to try to force Yugoslavian President Slobodan Milosevic to withdraw troops and paramilitary police from the province of Kosovo. Kosovo is one of the republics of the Yugoslav federation, and a majority of its residents are ethnic Albanians. Many, if not most, of the Albanian population wish to be independent of the federation. The independence movement took military form in the KLA, the Kosovo Liberation Army. Milosevic began a campaign to strike and rid Kosovo of the KLA. During the course of his campaign against the KLA, however, over a million Albanian Kosovars were run out of the country.

Hundreds, perhaps thousands, were killed. Exactly what Milosevic did, however, is the subject of symbolic negotiation. He and the residents of his federation, Serbia, claimed that he was only trying to create peace in Kosovo by confronting the "terrorist" group, the KLA. In the process, they claimed, citizens who assisted the KLA were injured. Milosevic, therefore, puts forward the identity of a Serbian patriot. NATO is arguing for a different self-image. According to them, Milosevic is a despot and murderer who engaged in a campaign of "ethnic cleansing" and who is ultimately responsible for the murders and rapes committed by his troops. Strengthening the NATO definition of what Milosevic is, the International War Crimes tribunal in the Hague, Netherlands, indicted President Milosevic as a war criminal.

implied by the behavior that evoked the response. Over time, through trial and error, by emitting behaviors that reflect tentative selves and observing responses to them, the young person forms a concept of himself or herself that is personally reassuring and that is rooted in social confirmation.

Self-concepts, however, by their very natures, are always somewhat tentative. Though they may be more or less stable, they are never concrete. Because of that, individuals always have potential anxiety about themselves, and, as a result, must continuously get confirmation of the selves they have at any given time. Thus, having developed a reasonably well-crystallized self-concept through trial and error, the individual continues to behave in ways that say to the social world: "This is who and what I am; tell me I am right." Having posed the question by their behavior, individuals then prepare to receive messages about themselves that those in the social world will send back. It is as if the individual extends little antennae to listen for the reaction of other individuals. If others send back messages that the person is what the behavior implies, she or he will be comforted by such confirmation. However, if others respond in ways that say to the person that the behavior is not reflective of the person behind them, the self is disconfirmed, and that individual will experience some emotional distress.

When a person's self is well crystallized, disconfirming evidence can usually be "managed" in ways that preserve the original self-concept. For instance, the individual might cognitively deny the response, discount the source of the reaction, ignore the reaction as aberrant, or the like. However, if the self is not fully formed, or if the disconfirming responses are massive and continuous, individuals must then rework their self-images. They do that by trying out new ways of viewing themselves, performing behaviors consistent with those new ideas, and waiting to see if others will accept them. Thus, the search for a stable, satisfying, and socially acceptable self motivates behavior of various kinds—either to form a self-concept through trial and error or to confirm a self-concept already formed.

A second avenue through which self-concepts are shaped involves social attribution. Sometimes social audiences decide that an individual is one or another kind of person and they collectively define the individual in those terms. Sometimes this attribution is consistent with the person's prior self-concept and simply reinforces it. Other times, however, the attribution may be contrary to the person's own self-definition. If it is, then the individual is likely to face a crisis of self. He or she may at first try to resist the attribution, or label, but social stigmas often arise from the insistence of social audiences that attributions are true. In fact, labeling frequently involves a process called "social construction," which encourages social audiences to reconstruct an individual's past in light of a more recent attribution that serves as an organizing principle. If attributions persist, or in the language of some, "if a label sticks," the person must reevaluate his or her own self-image. And since self-concepts are ultimately rooted in the reflected judgments of others, the person is likely to become what the social group has labeled her or him to be.

The Self and Deviant Behavior

Processes of self formation and confirmation ordinarily produce conforming people who regard themselves as conventional and who have incorporated the social controls in their environments into self-controls around their identities as nondeviant individuals. Those processes sometimes, however, produce people with deviant self-concepts, who then behave in deviant ways in congruence with those self-images. Either of the two routes to identity—exploration/reinforcement or attribution—may lead to deviant identities and deviant behavior. During the exploratory stage, children may try out all kinds of acts and all kinds of roles. Some of them may involve behaviors that are unacceptable generally to the social group. For example, a young boy may imagine himself to be a tough guy like those he sees on television. So, in conformity with that image, he slugs his sister with a toy. His parents, or other caregivers, may respond by calling him a "bad boy." Even though they may punish him for hitting his sister, their definition of him as "bad" helps reinforce the initial image of himself with which he was experimenting. As a result of this sequence of acts, his self-concept as tough or a bad boy begins to be solidified (see Matsueda, 1992).

Of course, according to the theory, he must seek further confirmation because the self, especially in the early years, is always tentative. Seeking confirmation requires further behavior of a "tough" or "bad" type in order to ascertain if the social audience will continue to accept the definition of himself that is implied by the behavior. If, over a period of time in which a series of such tests is performed, the social audience confirms the youngster's claim to being a tough guy, he comes to regard himself that way. And in order to sustain the self-concept he must periodically perform behaviors consistent with it, which means that he is motivated to commit deviant acts throughout his lifetime. Therefore, the exploration/reinforcement process provokes deviant behavior more or less randomly as part of initial self-formation experiments. Later, when a deviant self is solidified, that self-image leads to continuous deviant behavior for the purpose of gaining confirmation.

One can perhaps better appreciate the theoretical argument by examining how it explains conforming behavior. Consider again the boy who tries out the identity of himself as a "tough guy." He hits his little sister with a toy, but instead of his mother calling him a "bad boy," she chides him by saying that she is disappointed because this behavior is so uncharacteristic of the kind of boy she knows him to be. She then adds that she knows he is actually a good person, sweet, gentle, loving, and protective of his sister, and that she cannot understand what got into him that he would behave so inconsistently with his true self. She may also punish him, but in so doing she notes that the punishment is to remind him that the acts he committed are wrong. In other words, she clearly distinguishes between punishing the wrongful acts and giving feedback about the boy's character, or self.

Since this mother's response to the bad-boy behavior disconfirms the self implied by it, that line of development for the emerging self-concept is hampered. The boy then must contemplate that he is not a tough guy after all—that, in fact, he must be a good or caring boy. While entertaining this new idea of self, he must, according to the theory, try out some good-boy behavior to find out if there will be consistent response affirming it. He therefore performs such behavior, and his mother responds with praise. Eventually, if the same pattern is followed in numerous trials, the boy comes to form a concept of himself as good, conforming, and the like. He then fashions his behavior to test that idea, thereby establishing long-range patterns of conformity.

It is important to note in this regard that what some caregivers intend as negative feedback for deviant behavior actually is received by children as positive feedback. Punishment meant to send a message that some behavior is unacceptable may actually say to the child that the behavior he or she intended as a way of expressing a potential concept of self as bad is indeed confirming of that badness. The punishment itself helps crystallize a negative self-concept. Without other reactions from caregivers that alter the boy's "bad" self-concept (Conger and Simons, 1997), punishment may simply condition him to avoid situations where it is likely to be immediately forthcoming, while strengthening his motivation to emit deviant behaviors when it is possible to do so without immediate pain. In some cases deviant behavior is expressed carelessly, specifically to elicit punishment that confirms the motivating self. This is one explanation for masochism (a psychological disorder in which a person comes to enjoy pain). Hence, according to identity/labeling theory, the old adage, "spare the rod and spoil the child," is subject to considerable misuse. The theory's proponents might argue for a better adage: "Apply the rod and ruin the child's conforming self-concept, unless the rod is accompanied with feedback disconfirming a deviant self."

Not only may patterns of deviant behavior be encouraged by social reactions to exploration, but such patterns of deviance may also grow from "labeling" (attachment of an identity to an individual by a collection of people) in both the beginning and later stages of an attribution process, although it is not essential at either stage (Becker, 1963; Schur, 1971; Tannenbaum, 1938). Social groups can "label" a boy with a conforming definition, and even though that individual may not previously have defined himself in those terms, he might come to fulfill the social expectation. However, most theoretical attention has focused on attributions of deviance. Often such attribution accorded to an individual by the members of a social group is in response to a specific act of misbehavior, but at other times it may be based on erroneous assumptions of deviance.

Deviance in Everyday Life

Social audiences can sometimes try to force someone into a deviant role that the person might not be willing to accept. A very vivid example of this is Robert Scott's (1969) study of how people treat the blind. In his book, *The Making of Blind Men*, Scott describes how sighted people treat the blind as if they were completely incapable of carrying on a normal life. In fact, the sighted often actively resist those without sight who do try to make normal lives for themselves. The basis of this is the stereotypes of the blind that sighted people have. Scott argues that the sighted think that people without sight have a cluster of other characteristics in addition to the inability to see—helplessness, dependency, and melancholy. Based on this stereotype, sighted people treat the unsighted as if they were dependent and helpless—thus, Scott argues (1969:9), "making" blind men: "[w]hen, for example, sighted people continually insist that a blind man is helpless because he is blind, their subsequent treatment of him may preclude his even exercising the kind of skills that would enable him to be independent." Treating the unsighted as if they were helpless and dependent actually helps make them dependent.

For example, the police might mistakenly suspect a girl of prostitution because she is caught in the wrong company. And because she comes from a dysfunctional family, they may arrest her and refer her to the juvenile court for processing, on the assumption that she needs guidance that her family cannot or will not provide. As a result of having been picked up by the police and dealt with by the juvenile court, she may acquire a reputation among adults and other young people in her community as a "loose woman," even though she was innocent and it was happenstance that brought her into the arms of the law. If the social audience continuously and adamantly responds to her as promiscuous, according to the theory she is likely to begin to question in her own mind whether she is what others assume she is. To find out, she must, of course, behave promiscuously, which evokes confirming reactions from others who "knew all along" that was the kind of person she was. Hence she may come to be, through redefinition of self in response to a false social attribution, something she was not originally. And in the process she may come to commit the very acts of deviance of which she was originally falsely accused.

More often, however, people actually perform the original deviant behaviors that activate a labeling process. According to most theorists, initial acts of deviance, called primary deviance, may occur for many reasons. Some of these acts are the result of simple exploration in search of a meaningful self-concept; others are accidental and unintended. Moreover, primary deviance may be the result of episodic acts of impulse, expressions of temporary anger, or reactions to misinterpreted messages from peers or others, or they may be deliberate acts for seeking gratification in various situational contexts. But according to the theory, initial acts of deviance are of little import; they need not be explained since everybody at one time or another does them, and they have few long-range effects unless they are discovered and the person is labeled because of them. If primary acts of deviance lead to labeling, then the labeled individual is likely to repeat them and move on to other deviance as well—as a consequence of the labeling itself. Deviant acts that flow from stigma are called secondary deviance (Lemert, 1951, 1967).

Everybody at one time or another does silly, irrational, or bizarre things. Who among us has not gotten angry over an incident that others regarded as trivial? What individuals have not, at least a few times, said things that just did not "add up" to others, or even to themselves after they thought about it for a while? And can anybody claim not to have done at least a few really stupid things, most of which are the source of much embarrassment when later recalled? For most of us, such acts are fairly rare, and they really do not mean anything since they are episodic and unconnected to any systematic causal structures. Furthermore, usually such acts either go unnoticed by others, are noticed but discounted by them as simply aberrant and uncharacteristic, or are noticed by people who interpret them as evidence of weirdness but who do not do anything about it. The point is that we have all emitted behaviors that might have activated a process of social attribution that could have led to our being labeled as neurotic or even seriously mentally ill. Luckily for us, even though they could have resulted in an attribution process, those bizarre acts had no consequences for our lives.

According to labeling theory, some individuals are not so lucky because their primary acts of deviance are discovered by a person who tries to do something about them. In trying to do something about the original deviant act, discoverers put in motion a process with a whole series of consequences that eventuate in transformation of self and the production of secondary deviance. For instance, a teacher may see and take note of a young woman's unusual actions and conclude that she has a psychological problem. The teacher may call the woman in and suggest she see the school psychologist. Other students may observe the resulting visits to the counselor and conclude that the individual is psychologically disordered. Then in conversation among themselves, students will recall other things about the person that previously were of no import but that are now seen to fit the pattern of one who is psychologically troubled or disturbed. Perhaps one student will recall that several months ago the person in question said something to him that did not make any sense at the time. But now that he "knows about the individual's psychological problem," what she said at the time does make sense. Another student may note that previous encounters with the person in which she seemed to be irritated were overlooked at the time, but now he sees that it fits with the new knowledge of that person as psychologically unbalanced. And so on, in many conversations and in many contexts, the social audience "reconstructs" the biography of the individual to make it consistent with what is now "known" about her.

As members of the social audience reinterpret the past of this individual and convince themselves of the accuracy or possible accuracy of the label suggesting mental disturbance, they will also begin to interpret contemporary encounters in light of the person's personality or characteristics as they now "know" them to be. Perhaps some will avoid contact for fear they will not know how to handle the reactions of a sick person. Maybe others will decide to humor this girl and accept without challenge whatever she says or does in order to "help" her. Still others may become confrontational and say directly to the individual that her problems are known to others but that such problems do not excuse this or that, which the accuser finds objectionable. Males may become reluctant to ask the young woman out because they anticipate emotional outbursts that will be difficult to handle. Social audiences adjust to the person's new identity in dozens of different ways that convey the message, either subtly or directly, that she is "psychologically unbalanced." In other words, a process of social construction now comes to define the person as emotionally disturbed.

Theoretically, once this redefinition begins, the individual may try to resist it (Rogers and Buffalo, 1974). She may explain that the initial episode was unusual, that it was not like her, that the teacher misinterpreted it, or that the psychologist confirmed that it meant nothing. She may try to excuse it by saying that she was not feeling well that day, that she was upset because her boyfriend had confessed he was seeing someone else or because her parents announced they were divorcing, or that she had a hangover from having drunk too much the night before. She might explain the apparently irrational behavior as actually making some sense because she was doing such and such or trying to accomplish one thing or another. Often, of course, people do resist being labeled. Those around them accept their explanations, or they know the person well enough to realize that the present situation is "not like her." They assume that whatever caused it will go away, or they may dismiss rumors that the person actually was visiting the psychologist.

Although some individuals successfully ward off a disadvantageous label, others cannot maintain their previous public images. Their attempts to explain are rejected, their protestations are ignored ("the lady doth protest too much, methinks"), and they find themselves having to adapt to a social world that assumes they have a psychological problem. If this stigma is pervasive, the hypothetical young woman we are considering will eventually face an identity crisis. She will begin to wonder if maybe she is mentally unbalanced. After all, if everybody thinks she is weird and everybody behaves toward her as if she were weird, she may reason that she may actually be what the social audience defines her as. According to the theory, she is then motivated to perform behaviors to test that possibility. She behaves in ways according to her image of a disturbed person, and the social audience eagerly responds in ways that confirm that claim. This confirmation, in turn, helps lay a foundation for the internal reconstruction of her self-concept. "Reconstruction of the self" implies more deviant behavior, more receipt of confirmation, solidification of the new self, and so on. In other words, labeling by the teacher that resulted in stigma imposed by this girl's peers initiated a process that generated a pattern of deviant behavior motivated by the internal urge to find and maintain a workable self-image. The original attribution by the teacher, then, came to be a self-fulfilling prophecy.

Many theorists say that the labeling process is especially potent when it involves some kind of public ceremony and when the label is attached by some official functionary (Garfinkel, 1956). In the example of the girl labeled as psychologically disturbed, development of the stigma was entirely an informal process. Neither the teacher's actions nor the psychologist's diagnosis or conclusion were announced at a public gathering, and no actions to alert the public to her "condition" were made. For some kinds of misbehavior, however, the process of labeling is well structured, highly publicized, and is enforced by institutional action. The most dramatic illustrations of this process are seen in the handling of those who commit criminal acts or who are suspected of committing criminal acts. Usually there is an arrest that takes place in the presence of others besides the suspect, and it is effected by people in uniforms with guns and sticks who normally arrive in marked automobiles with flashing lights on top. Next there is a court hearing of one kind or another—an arraignment, at least, and perhaps a trial—that is open to observers and may be described in the newspaper. Ultimately, there is a public proclamation by a judge or a jury that may announce guilt—in other words, a statement that this person is a criminal. Under such circumstances, the person is liable to become stigmatized (Goffman, 1963) in the community or the larger society as a criminal. And this is likely even if he or she does not go through the entire legal process but is instead released after arrest, or released by court judgment. Having been arrested or prosecuted is often sufficient to convince most others that the individual is a criminal, despite acquittal or release.

According to labeling theory, the difference between the individual defined as a criminal by legal processing and others not so defined is not usually in the initial acts of crime since everybody at one time or another engages in "primary deviance." Rather, the difference is that the labeled person has been discovered in her or his misdeeds by someone who is in a position to make something of it and is inclined to do so, even though the individual activating the labeling process may have pure motives and think she or he is doing a good thing. Those who are most likely to end up being officially processed and ultimately labeled are usually the people who are both unlucky enough to be caught and who lack the personal and social resources to resist labeling and stigma. Thus, the poor, minorities, the unintelligent, and those who are already disliked are most often labeled (Schur, 1971).

Deviance in Everyday Life

There are critics who think labeling theory is a bunch of nonsense. One clear test to determine if hypothesized labeling effects make any intuitive sense is to ask yourself, "if I were arrested and taken down to the police station, and there were reporters and TV cameras there, would I try to hide my face like so many other criminal suspects do?" If you would, why?

Once a person has been officially stamped as a criminal, a number of consequences follow (Payne, 1973; Schur, 1971; Trice and Roman, 1970; Wilkins, 1964). That individual will then have trouble participating fully in society. People will be reluctant to employ him or her; the police will thereafter suspect the person of other crimes; and conventional folks will not want to associate with the stigmatized individual. In response, the labeled person will likely seek the company of others who have also been labeled, provided they can be found. The chances of finding other labelees is, of course, enhanced when there is a subculture of such people, which, in turn, is more likely in areas or societies where legal processes usually end in stigma (Braithwaite, 1989). Associating with other labeled people often inspires the commission of more crimes, the reaction to which helps solidify the individual's new identity as a criminal.

Summary and Critique of Identity/Labeling Theory

Thus, a person may develop a deviant identity through a trial-and-error process in early childhood or as a result of some audience attribution at a later time. In either instance, however, once a deviant identity has been initiated or fully crystallized, it then motivates deviant behavior consistent with that image. According to this theory, then, deviant behavior can be explained by reference to processes connected with the formation and confirmation of self-images. Ironically, by reacting toward deviance in stigmatizing ways, members of a social audience or its officials may produce the very deviance they wish to prevent. In the words of the criminologist Frank Tannenbaum (1938:19):

> The process of making the criminal, therefore, is a process of tagging, identifying, segregating, describing, emphasizing, making conscious and self-conscious; it becomes a way of stimulating, suggesting, emphasizing, and evoking the very traits that are complained of. . . . [t]he person becomes the thing he is described as being.

Since the theory places such stress on official processing as a procedure for attaching labels, it has been widely assumed that one can explain categorical patterns of deviance indirectly by examining biases in systems of social control. Differential labeling of the powerless presumably activates processes shaping identities that produce actual deviant behavior, even when no initial deviance has taken place.

We authors classify the identity/labeling theory as asserting internal causes because it implies that the need for a sense of self is rooted in a universal, inherent psychic characteristic of all humans. In addition, even though the self is fashioned from the reactions of others, the struggle to achieve a workable and stable self-image is an active, compelling force that leads individuals to make claims through behavior and to "negotiate" an outcome. Hence this theory is basically a motivation theory. As a type, then, it fits into our scheme as an internal motivation theory.

This theory, particularly the part about labeling by official actions of institutional functionaries, became very popular during the 1960s. It captured the imagination of the academic community, and many books and articles were written exploring the conditions under which labels were likely to be applied and "stick" and laying out the processes by which deviant identities were formed and "managed" (examples include: Dalph, 1979; Duff and Hong, 1996; Herman, 1997; Lofland, 1969; Pfuhl, 1986; Warren, 1974). Indeed, the bulk of attention was focused on physical conditions, such as blindness, dwarfism, obesity, or stuttering, that evoked disadvantageous, stigmatizing labels rather than on behavior that violated behavior norms (examples include: Davis, 1961; Goode, 1996; Levitin, 1975; Petrunik and Shearing, 1983; Weinberg, 1999). Many people thus came to associate the study of deviance exclusively with arguments revolving around labeling theory and the processes of social constructionism (Pfuhl, 1986).

Moreover, the labeling argument was accepted by many scholars on the basis of its plausibility and intellectually pleasing characteristics even before research was undertaken to test its validity (Hagan, 1973). Labeling principles even found their way into public policy recommendations, particularly in the form of diversionary programs for misbehaving juveniles (President's Commission, 1967; Schur, 1973). Some interpreted the theory to suggest that efforts at social control, such as penalizing criminals, punishing unruly children, or hospitalizing people for treatment of mental illness are counterproductive because they increase the probability of deviance rather than reduce it. And since ideas and evidence concerning deterrence were reawakening during the same historical period, labeling and theories of specific deterrence (discussed in Chapter 14) became rivals posing opposite effects for sanctions (Tittle, 1975).

A number of critiques (Akers, 1968, 1997; Bordua, 1967; Gibbs, 1966; Gove, 1980, 1982a; Mankoff, 1971; Wellford, 1975) found ambiguity in the formulations, or too much emphasis on the individual subject's passivity at being labeled, or failure to explain primary deviance, or exoneration of serious rule breakers whose misbehavior was blamed on social control agents. These criticisms, along with weak evidence, led to a decline of confidence in identity/labeling theory, especially the labeling part of it. However, there is still interest in the theory (Triplett and Jarjoura, 1994), and the research evidence continues to be mixed. Some research suggests that labeling usually occurs after a pattern of deviance is established rather than prior to it, that labels are not nearly so potent as the theory implies, and that sanctioning often prevents deviance rather than encouraging it (Akers, 1968; Gove, 1980). Also, a number of specific tests of labeling ideas failed to find confirming evidence (Gove, 1980; Gove, 1982a, 1982b; Smith and Paternoster, 1990). On the other hand, some research supports the argument (Farrington, 1977; Hagan and Palloni, 1990; Link, 1987; Link et al., 1989; Palamara et al., 1986), and much of the contrary evidence may not be relevant (see Paternoster and Iovanni, 1989).

Currently, scholars typically regard identity/labeling theory as suggesting an important process affecting deviance but a process subject to many contingencies and less powerful than initially thought. As a result, theoretical efforts have shifted toward specifying the conditions under which the self develops in one direction rather than another and the conditions under which sanctions or other official actions lead to more or to less subsequent deviance.

Self-Esteem Theory

A second self theory is more concerned with self-attitudes, or self-esteem, than with self-concept. Whereas identity/labeling theory postulates that people are motivated by a desire to fashion and confirm a stable sense of who they are—a workable self-image, which may be normatively deviant or conforming—which is validated by reinforcing responses from others, self-esteem theories contend that people seek to enhance positive evaluations of themselves. The focus of self-esteem theories is not so much on whether a social audience responds consistently to a person's outward expression of a more-or-less crystallized self-image but on whether the individual feels good about himself or herself (Kaplan, 1975; Rosenberg, 1979; Rosenberg and Rosenberg, 1978). Good feelings, or positive self-evaluations, may rest heavily on approving social responses, but they are not entirely dependent on them.

Self-Derogation

According to the most fully developed statement of this theory (Kaplan, 1980, 1995), all human beings possess a basic self-esteem motive that propels them to struggle to maximize positive self-attitudes and avoid negative self-attitudes. Three things mainly influence self-attitudes. The first is performance of behaviors or possession of attributes that the individual personally values. Second are the responses of other people whose opinions the individual cares about. Finally, there are internal psychological self-protective mechanisms that permit an individual to interpret inputs as positive for self-esteem and to deflect or reinterpret negative inputs. These three influences are themselves functions of: (1) inherent characteristics, such as physical attractiveness or intelligence, (2) socialization whereby the person comes to attach value to different behaviors and attributes and acquires internal psychological defense mechanisms, and (3) the person's placement in the social system, which influences whether she or he has the opportunity to do socially valued things or possesses the symbols of success.

According to this theory, when these influences impinge in such a way as to produce a negative self-evaluation, the individual both loses commitment to the normative system in which he or she is embedded and at the same time becomes motivated to deviate from its norms. Deviant motivation is, therefore, partly the result of absence of positive motivation to conform to the norms of an aversive context, and partly a search for alternative inputs that might enhance self-esteem.

Certain types of deviance, such as behaviors indicative of mental illness or interpersonal contentiousness, become attractive to those with poor self-attitudes because they permit the individual to avoid situations, people, and circumstances that might further those bad self-attitudes (*avoidance*). Other types of deviance, like violence, vandalism, or theft, have appeal to those with poor self-esteem because they represent direct *attacks* on the sources of negative messages and express the deviants' rejection of the normative structure that has served them so badly. Finally, some forms of deviance, such as gang delinquency, stem from involvement with others whose normative systems are contrary to the one in which the person's negative self-attitudes are rooted. Such involvement represents an effort to find new groups and interpersonal networks that will provide self-enhancing feedback. Some of these group *substitutions* are inherently deviant, such as being part of a revolutionary cell, while others lead to deviant behavior because the individual tries to conform to the substitute group's expectations. An example of this second situation might involve a girl who hangs out with male athletes to bolster her self-esteem by enjoying their suggestions that she is attractive; in trying to please them, however, she becomes sexually promiscuous, a form of behavior that is deviant by the standards of her usual interaction network.

❖ ❖ ❖ ❖

This theory, then, argues that deviance is useful for the person undertaking it because such behavior potentially enhances his or her self-esteem. For individuals with positive self-attitudes, deviance holds little appeal because conformity to the normative expectations in their environments has proven satisfying in fulfilling the need for positive self-attitudes. Those with poor self-attitudes, on the other hand, may find in deviance an avenue for overcoming low self-esteem. Whether they resort to deviance, however, is influenced by other conditions, including opportunity (Kaplan, 1995). Moreover, actual deviant behavior does not always produce the desired or expected effect on self-esteem, and it may even exacerbate the original negative self-attitudes. If a deviance relieves feelings of self-derogation, then the individual is likely to continue that specific form of deviance. If the net effect of deviance does not solve the person's problem, however, she or he will likely seek other forms of deviance. Whether a deviant response pattern "works" in solving the self-esteem problem is said to depend on a number of variables, such as the severity and certainty of punishment, the nature of the deviant act itself, and various characteristics of the person.

Deviance in Everyday Life

How can deviance enhance self-esteem? Eric Harris and Dylan Klebold were two teenagers attending Columbine High School in the Denver suburb of Littleton, Colorado. Eric and Dylan, and several of their classmates, seemed to be outsiders within their own school. The school social culture was dominated by a group of athletes, who by some accounts terrorized those who did not fit in. Eric and Dylan were not athletes, nor did they participate in any extracurricular activities. They, and their small group of friends, were really outsiders to the main student body. Scorned by classmates, Eric, Dylan, and their friends formed their own social group within the school. They seemed united by opposition to the "jocks." This group appears to have developed a negative and pessimistic culture, which emphasized violent music and video games. To define and set themselves apart, the group started to wear long black leather trench coats to school. They were dubbed "the trench coat mafia" by the other students. By all accounts, Eric and Dylan were successful members of this group. None of this would have been exceptional. There are outsiders in every high school who adapt by forming their own group, within which they find belonging and self-esteem. The difference here is that the rage inside Eric and Dylan exploded one day in violence against those they thought were persecuting them. On April 20, 1999, Eric and Dylan entered Columbine High School fully armed with guns and explosive devices. They went on a shooting rampage. By the time they fatally shot themselves, they had killed 13 students (6 of whom were athletes) and faculty and wounded 21 others.

An illustration may help. Suppose a boy has grown up in an environment where attracting attention from other people is important, and as a result that ability has become one he likes to think he has. He thinks this because in his home other family members granted him this attention. In other words, to feel good about himself this boy needs to attract and hold the attention of others. However, imagine that he is not physically attractive, that he is not very intelligent or well read and so is not interesting to be around, and that he has no athletic ability. As a result he is largely ignored by other people outside his family and so develops denigrating thoughts about himself that he is a failure; that is, he suffers poor self-esteem. According to the theory, this boy will be looking for some way to overcome those bad attitudes about himself. On a particular occasion, he accidentally burps at the lunch table and finds that other students stop eating, look at him, and laugh. Consequently, he realizes that to get the attention of others he will need to violate ordinary social rules. He then begins to take every opportunity to burp at the dinner table, to pick his nose in public, to pass gas when others are around, and in other ways to become a "gross" person. Because others pay attention and because he personally values such attention, his self-esteem grows as his deviant behavior increases. Or perhaps this boy comes in contact with a juvenile gang in his neighborhood. Falling in with them, he discovers that gang fighting and stealing attract attention not only from other gang members but also from such non-gang members as the police, neighborhood youth, and parents. By participating in the gang, he is working to enhance his own self-esteem, and so he continues to misbehave.

Sometimes, of course, these deviant activities backfire. By grossing others out, he may later find himself socially isolated so that his antics cannot attract much attention from anybody. Or his gang activities may result in arrest and incarceration with peers who do not find such behaviors worthy of much attention. These conditions may lead to a search for other ways of attracting attention, some of which will be deviant. The particular forms of deviance that result will depend partly on opportunity, on the relative costs of pursuing those activities, on whether the person can bring them off, and on the social audiences' reactions to the behaviors.

Summary and Critique of Self-Esteem Theory

These theories assume that people need and want to think well of themselves and that the extent to which they do so depends on their own ability to do and be what they value. Those personal values, incorporated in the self-concept, grow out of symbolic interaction and come to have a considerable degree of stability. However, when people are unable to do or be what they want, their resulting self-derogation leads them to seek alternative means, some of which may be deviant. This whole process, however, is directed by a number of conditions and contingencies so that it is not as simple as noting a person's self-attitudes and then easily predicting specific deviant outcomes.

This theory offers a plausible account of why people behave the way they do, and it is one to which we can all relate. Moreover, it enjoys some research support. Studies focusing on specific aspects of the self-concept have been favorable although research about self-esteem globally conceived is not generally supportive (Bynner et al., 1981; Heimer and Matsueda, 1994; Matsueda, 1992; McCarthy and Hoge, 1984; Rosenberg and Rosenberg, 1978; Rosenberg et al., 1989; Wells and Rankin, 1983), and there is some research indicating that deviant conduct actually improves the self-esteem of some people (Kaplan, 1980, 1995; Kaplan et al., 1982; Kaplan et al., 1986; Kaplan et al., 1987; Wells, 1989; but see Jang and Thornberry, 1998). Certainly, much evidence indicates that various kinds of deviance are interpreted by some of their practitioners as reflections of admirable traits (Akerstrom, 1993; Katz, 1988; McCall, 1994; Scully and Marolla, 1984; Shover, 1996; Tittle, 1972). Thieves brag about their exploits, murderers adopt self-righteous poses, adulterers exhibit smugness about their conquests or ability to elude detection, drug users become self-satisfied with their own coolness, and rapists fantasize about their supposed abilities at seduction. All this might suggest that those deviant behaviors enhanced the self-esteem of their practitioners, but it is often the case that practitioners select some implications of their behaviors and ignore others. If self-enhancing aspects of behavior that most others find loathsome can be perceptually selected, it is hard to understand why those with poor self-attitudes do not simply embellish their self-attitudes out of the material present in their original circumstances instead of turning to deviance. For example, why couldn't a person of poverty simply take pride in being able to manage on very little instead of stealing? Furthermore, a lot of deviant behavior does not later appear to be admirable to those who have done it. Quite often, deviants deny the traits implied by the deviance, make excuses for themselves, and suffer considerable loss of self-esteem (Bandura, 1977; Scully and Marolla, 1984), suggesting either that they are not driven by the struggle to enhance self-attitudes or that they seriously miscalculate. Finally, it is difficult to separate what people do to enhance their self-esteem from what they do in response to the expectations of others, out of fear of punishment, or as a reaction to the demands of the situation.

Summary of Self Theories

Self theories start with the basic idea that people need and want a workable, personally acceptable sense of who they are, and that self-concepts are linked to responses from social audiences. Sometimes those in a social context, including parents, respond in ways that lead to deviant self-identities. Those identities then motivate the person to seek confirmation, thereby leading to more deviance, sometimes even a deviant career. Poor self-attitudes can also motivate people to engage in deviant behavior in an effort to increase good feelings about self.

Reactance Theory

A second internal motivation theory relevant to deviant behavior was developed by Jack Brehm (Brehm, 1966; Brehm and Brehm, 1981). The theory contends that when people are deprived of some freedom, they will experience a psychological reaction that makes the thing they were deprived of more desirable, and it will stimulate a desire to recover the lost freedom. Reactance consists of a feeling of increased self-direction "that he can do what he wants, that he does not have to do what he doesn't want, and that at least in regard to the freedom in question, he is the sole director of his own behavior" (1966:9). For example, suppose that you were accustomed to sitting in the back row in your classes but that in a particular course the instructor told you that nobody would be allowed to sit in the back. According to the theory, you will suddenly have a much stronger desire to sit in the back than you did before the instructor's statement, you will resent the intrusion on your freedom, and you will want to recover that lost freedom. As a result, you might defy the teacher and insist on sitting in the rear anyway; you might move part of the way to the front, refusing by your actions to capitulate completely to the loss of freedom; you might try to organize a protest among other students; or you might seek indirect ways to restore the lost freedom, such as coming late or leaving early from class. All of these behavioral responses represent mild forms of deviant behavior.

The theory, however, also applies to more serious types of deviance. Consider the case of adolescents who are physically adults but who in modern societies are not granted the full status of adults. As you know, young people in the United States can do many things that adults do; they can drive cars, own personal property such as stereos, hold jobs, and be with members of the op-posite sex without adult supervision. Yet society, often through parents, says to them that they cannot drink alcohol, use drugs, have sex, drop out of school, and any number of other things. Because they have some of the free-doms that adults have, they are likely to feel that they deserve them all. Since many such freedoms are blocked, they experience psychological reactance in which using alcohol and drugs and having sex, going places that are prohib-ited, and dropping out of school come to have special appeal. Moreover, they are likely to seek ways to restore those blocked freedoms. They will often drink alcohol on the sly, use drugs, engage in sex, go where they are not sup-posed to, and the like. In other words, teenage "rebellion," or defiance— which if sustained and especially serious is called "delinquency"—is quite common. According to reactance theory, it is easily understood and ex-plained. Those who think they have certain freedoms will become especially motivated to do certain things if they are deprived of the freedom to do them, and if they cannot do the prohibited things, they will look for alternatives that indirectly represent regained freedom, sometimes even resorting to things like burglary, gang fighting, or vandalism. Because adolescents' freedoms are restricted, they behave deviantly (contrary to social norms of acceptability) to try to assert their autonomy.

But, you might wonder, if reactance theory explains adolescent deviance, how does it explain excessive adult use of alcohol and drugs, extramarital sex, or criminal behavior, since adults are presumably free of the constraints that apply to adolescents? The answer is twofold. First, some of those behaviors, such as excessive alcohol use, are simply the continuation of pleasurable ac-tivities begun in adolescence; that is, alcohol and drug use are inherently at-tractive things because they act on pleasure centers of the brain. Once they are begun, it is hard for many people to stop. Second, while adults are freer than adolescents, they are not entirely free. The demands of spouses, chil-dren, employers, and the law often impinge heavily on adults to prevent them from doing things they feel they are or should be free to do. The theoretical re-sult is the same as among adolescents—the adults develop a stronger desire to do them, they are motivated to do them despite constraints, or they try to overcome blocked freedoms through alternative, sometimes deviant, behav-ior.

A final example should make the argument clear. From time to time cases of "stalking" come to light (in fact, there are numerous cases each year that are not publicized). In such instances, people (usually males) become ob-sessed with love objects who have rejected them. They follow the love objects around, call constantly, and sometimes try to restrict the movements and ac-tivity of their victims, even occasionally ending up hurting or killing them. How do we explain such behavior? According to reactance theory, the spurned lovers perceived that they had the freedom to associate with and en-joy the company of the love object. However, the love objects did not cooper-ate, thereby removing or restricting the stalkers' perceived freedom. In re-sponse, the stalkers experienced an even more intense desire for the company of the love object and a motive to restore the lost freedom by intruding them-selves into the lives of the victims. They seem to be saying by their actions: "I will have you anyway and if I cannot have you as a lover I will assert my free-dom symbolically by controlling your life." Occasionally they go beyond try-ing to control the lives of the spurning lovers, resorting to ancillary actions that seem to declare personal freedom or at least to get the attention of the lost love object.

Reactance theory, then, poses an inherent internal mechanism that motivates deviance under certain conditions. That mechanism is the desire to retain freedom. It is clear, however, that one cannot explain most deviant behavior by simple application of the freedom principle. After all, (1) organized society places great restraint on the freedoms of everybody, (2) all who have their freedoms blocked do not resort to deviance, and (3) the simple principle of freedom does not account for why some do minor deviance while others engage in serious acts such as murder or suicide. Thus, almost everybody has at one time or another been spurned by a desired love object. Yet the vast majority of people do not stalk their would-be sweethearts, and they certainly do not end up killing them or somebody else. We may all experience psychological reactance, an increased desire for the lost freedom, but we do not all behave in deviant ways in response. To be applied effectively, therefore, the reactance principle must be understood as operating with greater or less force, and producing different kinds of outcomes, depending on a number of conditions. Brehm has specified some of those contingencies.

Contingencies for Reactance

First, reactance theory concerns concrete behavioral freedoms; it is not about freedom in the abstract. It is incorrect to assume that any loss or absence of freedom produces reactance. Only freedoms to do, or choose, specific things are relevant. One would not, for instance, contend that because they have less freedom, peasants in general are more likely to experience reactance than are landowners. Instead, the theory applies to particular freedoms that a peasant or a landowner might realistically have. The peasant may have, or reasonably assume he has, the freedom to plow the north field on Tuesday instead of the south field, and the landowner may have, or reasonably assume he has, the freedom to send money to support the king's army. If the landowner rides up one day and tells the peasant he must plow the south field today, the peasant will experience psychological reactance. He will develop a desire to plow the north (or east or west) field instead, and he will be

---

Deviance in Everyday Life

An example of "unrequited" love gone astray is the case of John Hinkley and the actress Jodie Foster. Hinkley was obsessed with the movie *Taxi Driver*, which starred Foster as a 12-year-old prostitute. In the movie, a loner, Travis Bickel, is rejected by Foster. To attract her attention and earn her love, Bickel stalks the President of the United States and engages in a shootout. Hinckley reportedly saw the movie 15 times, and reenacted the shootout scene. Whether the movie was influential or not, it is clear that Hinkley was madly in love with Foster and manically sent her love letters and repeatedly tried to reach her by telephone. She rejected him just as her character rejected Travis Bickel. To gain the attention and admiration of Ms. Foster, Hinkley stalked the President of the United States at the time, Ronald Reagan. On March 30, 1981, Hinkley attempted to kill President Reagan in Washington, D.C., firing several shots at the President. Reagan was only slightly wounded. A District of Columbia police officer was also injured. Reagan's press secretary, James Brady, was shot in the head and more seriously wounded. Brady is now confined to a wheelchair and has substantial brain impairment. At his trial, Hinkley was determined to be not guilty by reason of insanity and was remanded to St. Elizabeth's Hospital in Washington, D.C.

motivated to regain the lost freedom to decide for himself which one to plow.
Note that he probably will not contemplate being free to plow no fields at all,
and his behavioral reactions usually concern ways to defy the landowner
about field choice, not to revolt against the feudal system itself. Similarly, if
the king sends troops to demand tribute, which the landowner thought he
had a choice about, the landowner will experience psychological reactance in
which more than ever he wants to decide about tribute and will be motivated
to figure out how to avoid paying taxes. Only under extraordinary circumstances would the peasant become motivated to attack the landowner or the
landowner to overthrow the king.

Still, the theory concerns more than specific freedoms—it applies to sets
of similar freedoms. If a particular freedom is blocked or threatened, it is often perceived as implying a threat to other freedoms as well, so that reactance
to them is generated also. If students are routinely free to choose their
courses, eat lunch where they want, and stay out as late as they desire on
weekends, they are likely to perceive a restriction on weekend hours as
threatening to their other freedoms too. Even if the lost freedom is not particularly important in and of itself, it may assume importance because of what
deprivation implies for other freedoms. So, while the theory does not apply to
freedom in general and in an abstract sense, it does apply to a range of freedoms that people actually have at any given time.

Second, according to the theory, the person must know that he or she is
able to do the specific behavior or make the choice in question. The average
male citizen does not experience reactance upon becoming aware that he will
not be selected to make a trip to the moon, to play in the NFL, or run for President as a major party candidate. Those are not realistic freedoms for most of
us, though they are for some people. Air force pilots who apply for the space
program, star college athletes, and prominent senators or governors will experience reactance if they are blocked in their efforts to go into space, play
professional football, or run for President, and it is they who are likely to react deviantly to accomplish those goals. Moreover, for most of us, serious
criminal behavior is not a freedom that realistically exists. We know we do
not have the right to rob, burgle, or rape; we know we are likely to get caught,
and that the punishments are very costly. Hence, if we are walking down the
street and a police officer shows up, we do not feel resentment that our freedom to rob the jewelry store has been infringed, leading us to come back later
to do the robbery or to steal something else as a substitute. For some individuals, however, some criminal acts are realistic freedoms. Businesspeople
who operate in a dog-eat-dog world of competition, where people expect corner cutting, where price fixing is rampant, and where few are ever caught, are
likely to regard violations of the antitrust laws as freedoms that are realistically theirs to claim. Being blocked by a government investigation or an injunction, therefore, is likely to arouse feelings of reactance among them, and
they are likely to struggle to regain those lost freedoms. Sometimes they do
this by subterfuge in courts of law (perjury), sometimes by bribing judges,
and sometimes by financing the campaigns of politicians who oppose antitrust legislation.

Third, the degree of reactance aroused, and the range and seriousness of
behavioral responses, depends on the strength with which the threatened
freedom is held. Some of our freedoms are fundamental; we are sure we have
them. Others we are not so sure about; we have them sometimes and some-

times we don't. As adults in a free and affluent society, most of us are pretty sure we get to choose when and what we eat. That choice is much more problematic for children. Theoretically, then, being deprived by someone (or circumstances) of a steak we wanted to eat and being forced to consume crackers and cheese is more reactance generating than for a child to be told to eat his veggies. We adults know we have a freedom of choice; a child is not yet sure. Similarly, some freedoms are absolute, and others are conditional. Married people have an absolute right to sleep in their domiciles; their freedom to have sex with their partners, however, is conditional on the other's mood, health, and the like—in other words, it is problematic. Presumably, strongly felt and absolute freedoms generate more reactance when blocked than do less strongly held or conditional freedoms. And, of course, what is strongly felt or conditional varies from person to person, depending on background, learning, personality, and social circumstances, including a person's position in the social structure.

Fourth, personal judgments about, and reactions to, the loss of specific freedoms depend on the other freedoms that the person has. Suppose Mary has the freedom to pursue a career, own property, travel whenever she wants, and marry her fiancé, all of which are quite important to her. If her fiancé cancels the marriage, her reactance will be less than if she had none of the other freedoms. Thus, a person with few freedoms will value them more than a person with a lot of freedoms, and losing any one will have a greater reactance effect—unless the person with many freedoms perceives the loss of any given one as indicative of the possibility of the loss of others. Similarly, if Mary is about to lose half her freedoms, her reactance will be greater than if she is threatened with the loss of only one-fourth of her freedoms. Therefore, we could expect a person who is threatened with losing a large proportion of freedoms to be more likely to resort to deviance than one who is losing only one of many freedoms—again, unless the threat to that one freedom implies a threat to all or most freedoms.

Fifth, threats to, or potential losses of, freedoms are as important as actual losses, particularly if threats are perceived as generalizable to a range of freedoms. The likelihood of perceived generalizability depends on how the threat is issued and on where the threatened freedom lies in an ordered class of freedoms. A sharp command carries a wider threat and to a greater extent than does a soft command. In addition, being threatened with the possible loss of job privileges such as insurance coverage or parking, could easily lead to fear of job loss. Further, the reactance process can operate vicariously. When people see someone like themselves being threatened with the loss of a freedom, or actually losing a freedom, they are likely to feel reactance themselves because they empathize with the victim, imagining themselves in his or her place. And when someone like us reacts to a lost freedom with deviant behavior to regain it, we also feel that our freedom has been expanded. Imagine a bunch of young people hanging out in a mall. A security guard approaches and tells them they have to go home or at least break up into groups of two. The youths break up, but after going into the next corridor, some of them regroup. Those afraid to regroup nevertheless feel empowered by the actions of the few, just as some individuals who were not in the original bunch felt that their freedom was threatened by the guard's actions against those who were bunched.

Sixth, the magnitude of reactance generated by a threat, or action, depends somewhat upon whether there is a reasonable justification or legitimacy for the restriction. A teacher who insists on strict punctuality, explaining that since the desks are arranged inconveniently, latecomers will have to crawl over others already seated, will stimulate less reactance than a teacher who offers no good reason. A police officer can direct traffic without much negative reaction from motorists although another motorist trying to direct traffic would have trouble. The police officer is accorded legitimate authority; the other motorist is not.

This principle also applies to people of different statuses. A high-status person giving orders, even to those not under his or her jurisdiction, provokes less reactance than a low-status person under the same circumstances. Imagine that there is a highway accident. Two men, one in a suit and another in dirty jeans, get out of their respective cars and begin to tell onlookers to step back. All onlookers, regardless of their personal stations in life, feel more reactance to the commands of the man in dirty jeans than in response to the man in the suit—because their respective modes of dress imply differing social statuses. Moreover, high-status people exhibit more reactance when one of their freedoms is threatened by a low-status person than do low-status people whose freedom is in jeopardy from a high-status person. A doctor can more easily (that is, without generating reactance) tell a nurse what to do than a nurse can tell a doctor what to do, even outside the medical context.

Despite the qualifications implied by good reasons, legitimate authority, and varying social statuses, which reduce the magnitude of reactance, all restrictions on freedom create some psychological resentment and enhanced desire to reestablish the lost autonomy. This even extends to barriers to freedom that come from physical conditions. Earthquakes, floods, and economic depressions stimulate reactance because they limit the freedoms that people had, just the same as if the restrictions had been the result of orders by government officials. And so does aging or illness. A sick person who can no longer feed and bathe himself is likely to feel psychological discomfort and as a result insist on substitute behaviors to assert that at least he can control the TV channel, swallow or not swallow the water, and call the nurses at will.

Contingencies for Deviant Behavior in Response to Reactance

There are a number of conditions, besides those mentioned earlier, that affect an individual's behavioral response to reactance. The first is the intensity of the reactance. The greater the intensity of reactance, the greater the probability that the person will try to do something to retain or regain a threatened freedom. Since efforts to redress a loss of freedom often entail some potential costs, it is logical that the magnitude of the arousal would be important. All of us, almost daily, encounter situations or circumstances that threaten some of the freedoms we think we have. Most of the time, however, we do not do anything about it. At best, we simply suffer an intensified desire for the thing jeopardized by the freedom lost. For instance, we may get stuck in traffic, which increases our desire to get where we are going, but most of the time it is a minor annoyance. We simply do not experience enough reactance to lead us to express "road rage" by cutting somebody off, giving other motorists the finger, or shooting somebody. Occasionally, however, reactance is strong enough to generate action.

Even with intense reactance, we may not act. One reason is an absence of opportunity to engage in behaviors that would directly restore lost freedom. Opportunity consists of several components: action to directly restore lost autonomy must be possible, it must be realistic, and it must not entail costs that are too high. A prisoner whose right of family visitation is removed, for example, cannot change that policy by any immediate behavior, even if that blow to his autonomy is extremely intense. He might, over a long period of time, establish his good reputation and thereby win back the visitation right, but otherwise he is helpless. The inmate might contemplate some direct short-range action, such as starting a riot, the end result of which might be for the prison officials to concede to inmate demands by granting freer visitation, even to those to whom it was previously denied. Such a plan, however, has a low probability of succeeding, and most inmates know it. That is one reason there are relatively few inmate strikes or riots.

Moreover, some direct acts to restore lost freedoms involve costs that exceed the benefits of regaining a particular lost freedom or combating a threat to a freedom. Recall the discussion of the Perfectionists in Chapter 5. Because of their "immoral" life styles, they were at various times under threat from outside law officers. Under such conditions, they chose to cease the "immorality" rather than defy the authorities because they realized that the possibilities of being wiped out were real. Sometimes people suffering reactance miscalculate the odds of negative consequences, and they undertake actions to restore lost autonomy despite actual overwhelming costs. Such miscalculations, or recklessness, can have a dear price. The Symbionese Liberation Army, a revolutionary group you read about in Chapter 7, refused to accept the edicts of the law in conducting their affairs. They continued to rob banks, stockpile weapons, and recruit members. The police annihilated them.

Opportunity to behave in response to losses of freedom, therefore, is an important contingency determining whether any behavioral response occurs, especially any action of a deviant nature. Without opportunity, not much happens. It may not be physically possible to do anything; some of the things that are possible may have few realistic chances of succeeding; and some that are possible and realistic are eschewed because of the chances of even greater losses of freedom. To some extent, of course, whether any or all of these conditions of opportunity hold depends on how the aggrieved party perceives the situation. Irrational action to express reactance sometimes happens, particularly if the reactance is especially intense. At other times, people perceive the possibilities to be so hopeless that they capitulate completely to those who would control their freedoms and adopt an attitude of helplessness. Most of the time, however, people facing weak opportunities do nothing directly.

Even if direct restoration of lost freedom is not possible, people experiencing reactance often turn to indirect means. A boy denied the freedom to come and go as he pleases at school may not be able to change that situation, but he can let the air out of the principal's tires, show contempt for school lessons, or vandalize the building late some night. A soldier ordered into combat when he wants to be somewhere else cannot get the orders changed, but he can run away, feign mental illness (as Corporal Klinger on *M*A*S*H* did), or refuse to fire his weapon. A wife deprived of career opportunities may not be able to change her husband's ways, but she can have an affair, get a divorce, or spit in the food she is preparing for him. And a child told that she must go to bed is unable to dissuade her parents, but she can dally in the bathtub, prolong her prayers, and beg for another reading of a story. All of these are indirect ways that people can help regain lost autonomy. Whether any are chosen or whether one rather than another is chosen depends on opportunity, which involves the same three elements described above—Is it possible? Can it realistically succeed? Is the cost too great? There are some additional conditions, to be discussed shortly.

There are three other indirect ways that individuals can deal with reactance. One is to substitute for the deprived freedom a similar one that has not been restricted. People cut off from a sexual outlet may masturbate; those who lose their driving licenses may ride horses or bicycles; those deprived of legal avenues for gambling may turn to alley craps; and those who cannot get ice cream may substitute popsicles. A second indirect method for relieving reactance is to revel vicariously in the defiant behavior of others. Husbands acutely cognizant of the loss of their sexual freedom may watch a lot of pornography, mentally identifying with the sexual freedoms of the pornographic actors; parents who lose custody of their children may watch the *Jerry Springer* show, hoping to see an aggrieved parent slug the estranged mate who got custody of their child; and all those who have been victims of crime may relish watching movies like *Dirty Harry*, whose hero takes the law into his own hands. Finally, people may indirectly adapt to losses or threats to freedom by adapting cognitively. They may convince themselves that the lost freedom did not amount to much anyway, or they may deny that any freedom was lost.

Summary and Critique of Reactance Theory

Overall, then, reactance theory posits a basic desire to maintain the freedom that a person perceives she or he has. When such freedom is taken away or threatened, the person experiences a stronger desire for it and becomes motivated to regain what was lost. The magnitude of reactance depends on the importance of the particular freedom, the number of freedoms a person has, and the extent to which a particular freedom or a set of similar freedoms is lost or threatened. Expression of reactance may involve deviant behavior directly designed to overcome or restore the lost freedom, or it may take the form of indirect attempts to assert autonomy when direct response is impossible, unrealistic, or too costly. Often, however, people adjust to reactance by substituting one freedom for another or by cognitive adaptation. What a person does about reactance depends on its strength, opportunities for behavior to regain lost freedom, and probably (though Brehm does not discuss this) individual characteristics, such as habits, moral commitments, background, perception, group membership, and audience reaction.

Various parts of reactance theory, particularly those concerning reactance itself, have been supported by a large number of laboratory experiments (Brehm, 1966; Brehm and Brehm, 1981), but not by much nonlaboratory work. Despite the dearth of evidence directly relevant to deviant behavior, the argument is plausible and is one with which we can all identify. We know from personal experience that we experience reactance when our freedoms are threatened (we especially want to do the things we are prohibited from doing) and that we often contemplate actions to defy those threats, sometimes involving deviant behavior. It makes a lot of sense to interpret various kinds of deviance as mechanisms by which a person is trying to assert control, especially when that individual's autonomy has been jeopardized.

One problem is that the theory may not apply to most deviance. According to Brehm (1966), reactance occurs only when specific freedoms that people think they have are blocked. Much deviant behavior, however, violates social rules well known to the deviants, so it is hard to imagine that most of them feel they have the freedoms implied by the deviant behavior. For example, unless mentally unstable, all people know they are not "socially" free to break a ticket line, inject addictive drugs, abandon their families, embezzle company funds, pick their noses in public, or rape somebody. Yet, those behaviors happen all the time. More than likely, Brehm's assumption—that reactance flows only from blockage of freedoms people believe they have—is wrong. People probably feel reactance any time their autonomy is threatened, whether or not they perceive they have specific freedoms that are the objects of such threats. Therefore, deviant behavior can be interpreted as a maneuver to assert autonomy in the face of threats, even when people do not feel that they originally had the freedom to do the deviant things that they end up doing in response to reactance.

The problem, then, of course, is to account for why some people resort to deviant behavior while others do not, or why some employ serious forms of deviance while others use mild forms. Brehm's list of contingencies for behavioral response seems to work well here. Whether deviance at all, or of particular types, occurs, depends on intensity of reactance, opportunity, and personal characteristics. It remains, however, for theorists to specify more precisely how, when, and to what relative degree those three sets of variables converge. An "integrated" theory (one merging parts of previously existing theories) using an idea similar to reactance, which we consider in Chapter 15, attempts to do that.

Psychodynamic Theory

A third theory focusing on internal motivation for deviance is variously called psychoanalytic theory, the theory of the unconscious (Fine, 1962:35), or psychodynamic theory. Its originator is Sigmund Freud, an Austrian physician, whose works are contained in more than 26 volumes published during the early part of the twentieth century. Over the course of his career Freud's thinking changed, and even at a given time it is not entirely clear what he meant. As a result, numerous scholars have interpreted the theory somewhat differently (Klein, 1976). We draw on discussions by Hall (1954), Klein (1976), Brill (1921), and Fine (1962), as well as original statements (Freud, 1943 [1920]). Here we are concerned specifically with the part of his theory that focuses on elements in the human psyche that can motivate deviant behavior. In Chapter 13 we will return to other aspects of Freud's theory that concern internal constraints against deviant impulses. Although the theory to be discussed here and the one in the next chapter are somewhat linked, like much of Freud's thinking, they can also be seen as distinct accounts.

The psychodynamic theory of motivation contends that human beings possess various inherent, but somewhat contradictory, energy sources that press for fulfillment (Klein, 1976:32). These energy forces operate somewhat like instincts in that they represent impelling or pushing forces, or needs. They can be categorized into two broad categories, the life forces and the death forces. The various forces are often antagonistic to each other, and expression of either one inevitably comes up against a regulatory social system, the first agents of which are a child's parents. Human personality emerges from accommodations to conflicts. The infant adapts first to the conflicts between natural impulses and what the outside world demands or will permit, and from those adaptations develops internal psychic constraints that then become sources of more conflict.

For instance, an infant wants to eat anytime it is hungry, but a mother has her own interests so that sometimes the infant must wait. Eventually, because of the mother's reactions, a child comes to understand that one eats on a schedule, eats what is appropriate, and eats in the ways that society specifies. Once those things are learned, the personality then has three elements— the original needs (id), a rational thinking apparatus about appropriate methods of meeting the needs (ego), and a set of moral standards about right and wrong that would prohibit, for instance, eating other human beings (superego). In developing the various components of the personality, and after they are developed, new sources of conflict emerge in the psyche. Thus, early in life a child confronts conflicts between natural needs and the demands of society, and fairly soon thereafter begins to contend with inner conflicts among the developed parts of the psyche, such as contradictions between rational thought and conscience. Conflicts and attempts to resolve them lead to fears and anxieties, and a number of psychic and behavioral adaptations, some of which stem from having avoided resolution by forcing conflicts into the unconscious mind. After a while the person has to deal with three kinds of anxiety: reality anxiety (fear of actual things happening in the world), neurotic anxiety (the person is overwhelmed by an urge to commit some act or think some thought that may harm him), and moral anxiety (fear of being punished by one's conscience) (Hall, 1954:61).

Deviant behavior results sometimes from a playing out of the person's natural urges, because, as will be seen in Chapter 13, the person does not develop appropriate inner controls; it can also stem from patterned ways of adapting psychically, which become part of the personality. According to Brill (1921:15), "An occurrence in one's life, at the age of fifty, for instance, may be traced back to some childhood repression; there is always some subtle and intimate connection in our present emotional experience with something that occurred in the past." Some personality characteristics, therefore, predispose (or motivate) a person toward deviant behavior, which is then manifest when there is opportunity or provocation. For instance, an overactive conscience can lead people to commit crimes because they feel guilty and want to be punished. Deviant behavior can also result from regressing to an earlier stage of development or from expressing in overt behavior things that were earlier repressed into the unconscious. How these things can lead to deviant conduct will become clearer when you understand the various methods people use to manage conflicts. Freud identified four kinds of processes of conflict management—identification, displacement, using defense mechanisms, and transformation (Hall, 1954:74).

Identification

Identification involves reaching outward and incorporating the qualities of an external object into one's own personality. The external objects are usually other people, especially parents. Some identification has nothing to do with anxiety or conflict but is simply an expression of self-love in which the person seeks connection with others like himself. Other identification, however, does grow from frustration, feelings of inadequacy, and anxiety. Consider an inner-city boy who wants to be taken seriously but is not markedly intelligent, strong, or handsome (his natural urges conflict with the real world). He is likely to identify with drug dealers in his neighborhood who are successful and proceed to imitate them. He ends up using and selling drugs.

Displacement

Displacement is a psychic process through which a person seeks substitute ways to satisfy needs. A good example is the urge for oral gratification. A baby not only obtains sustenance through sucking but also acquires a need for the pleasurable sensations associated with the mouth. The urge for oral gratification, therefore, is established early and continues throughout life. At first it is acceptable to suck pacifiers, thumbs, or the corners of blankets, but later the child may be discouraged or punished for those things. In adulthood, the person may take up smoking, chew gum, or spit as substitute accommodations; substitutes may also include excessive or compulsive oral sex. This kind of substitution is sometimes said by psychoanalysts to be associated with homosexuality or prostitution.

The kinds of substitutes selected depend on the responses of people in the social environment and on opportunity. Thus, one person may go from sucking thumbs to lollipops to playing a trumpet because adults provided the lollipops and encouraged musical activity. Another person, however, may have no lollipops or musical opportunity but encounter a fortuitous chance to smoke cigarettes, or even later for a homosexual experience. Adaptations, then, are fueled by the original needs but channeled by environmental constraints and internal mechanisms.

According to Freud most adult interests and attachments are compensations for frustrated infantile and childish wishes. A weak person may compensate by getting a gun and ordering other people around. A person deprived of love may compensate by overeating. Displaced need satisfaction becomes habitual because it never provides complete satiation. Partial relief of a recurring need, however, has a powerful draw. Some deviant behavior is tried and some becomes habitual because it is a form of symbolic expression for deep-seated needs that cannot be met in socially approved ways.

Ego Defense

A third method of managing inner conflicts is the use of techniques of ego defense, which take the form of distortion, concealment, or denial. These procedures allow a person to escape dangers and threats that arouse anxiety. There are five such mechanisms, repression, projection, reaction formation, fixation, and regression, which are used to some extent by everybody. Without them many people would have no way of coping and would experience nervous breakdowns, leading to deviant, bizarre behavior. Therefore, most of the time the use of defense mechanisms prevents deviant behavior, but sometimes the mechanisms can lead to deviant behavior.

Repression

Sometimes painful or threatening conflicts are avoided by psychologically forcing them out of consciousness—in effect, denying that they exist. By repressing, the person may not see things that are plain to others. Sometimes unpleasant memories are repressed lest they bring up the circumstances of the original trauma that provoked fear or anxiety. The trouble is that things in the unconscious may nevertheless affect behavior, although people are unaware of them and cannot understand their own behavior. For example, a young boy may have been spanked and while being disciplined noticed a spider. He then associated spiders with being disciplined, which was an unpleasant event. To avoid anxiety, he repressed the memory, but retains an irrational fear of spiders. Thereafter, anytime the man sees or thinks about spiders, he experiences revulsive fear and withdraws in a fit of crying. If this occurs in public, it is likely to invite negative responses from others, and thereby qualify as deviant behavior.

Probably the best-known illustration concerns repressed feelings associated with the Oedipus complex. Freud contended that one of the most powerful of the innate urges was that of sensuality (not strictly sexuality, as many believe—see Klein, 1976:91–92). It is especially important because prohibitions coming from the outside world extend to what you can think as well as what you can do and therefore require anticipatory control (Klein, 1976: 89). Freud mapped sensual development into three major stages: infantile (up to age 5, which is further subdivided into oral, anal, and phallic phases that culminate in conflict about sensual feelings toward the parent of the opposite sex), latency, and puberty (Fine, 1962:64). Obviously the oral phase concerns sensuality around the mouth and its activities while the anal phase focuses on feelings centering on the anus. During the phallic phase the person begins to associate sensuality with the genitals, and it is during this time that vague feelings of attraction to the parents occur.

Sensual attraction to a parent, of course, poses a conflict, partly because society does not permit sexual contact between a parent and a child, and partly because the child fears antagonizing the same-sex parent. In fact, Freud thought that young boys are afraid that their fathers will castrate them if their feelings toward their mothers become known, and observing the genitals of girls helps confirm that fear. Girls, who feel sensually attracted to their mothers, also resent their fathers, but because they experience "penis envy," which is blamed on the mother, they switch affect toward the father. As a result, boys experiencing the Oedipus conflict are likely to develop hostile feelings toward their fathers, while the girls develop ambivalent feelings about their fathers and mothers. To adapt, a boy may displace that hostility onto other male authority figures, or he may practice identification, trying to take on the characteristics of the father, who is in the advantageous position.

In any case, young boys must learn to deal with the conflict, which sometimes involves repressing it and the hostile feelings associated with it into the unconscious. But lying in the unconscious, where the person is not aware of its presence, it may later pop out unexpectedly and cause problems leading to deviant behavior. Such a person, for example, is likely to have a lot of trouble dealing with male authority figures such as police officers, coaches, and bosses. His hostile reactions themselves may be regarded as deviant behavior, or they may lead to deviant behavior, such as mouthing off to an officer or refusing to follow directives of a job supervisor.

Projection

This defense mechanism entails attributing the causes of anxiety to other things or other people. Even though the individual's own psyche may be the source of some fear, he or she is able to manage it by perceiving that outside elements are responsible. For example, a man who is afraid of his own homosexual tendencies may project them onto others and begin to see others as homosexually aggressive against him. That is one reason why some men rail so strongly against homosexuals, or any semblance of male tenderness, and why some even attack or kill suspected homosexuals. They are trying to beat down those feelings inside themselves rather than dealing with them in some other way. And people who are anxious about their own abilities to achieve will sometimes project evil intent onto others, saying, in effect, "I am not getting ahead in life because other people are holding me back." This can sometimes become a rationale for striking out against perceived injustice and in the process engaging in various kinds of deviant behavior such as drug use, vandalism, or revolution.

Reaction Formation

Since inherent urges and their derivatives are contradictory and opposing, such as love and hate, or dominance and submission, when one urge produces fear or anxiety, a person can sometimes manage the conflict by concentrating on the opposite. For example, a person with strong sexual urges that cause internal problems may cope by becoming excessively chaste, and a selfish person may overcome internal disgust by displaying much altruism. Neither of these reaction formations represents deviant behavior, and indeed many lead to noble outcomes. However, other reaction formations call for socially unacceptable behavior: People who fear submission may concentrate on controlling others, thereby becoming overbearing in interpersonal relationships, and women who want love but are afraid of it sometimes become promiscuous.

Fixation

Psychological growth presumably proceeds continuously through infancy, through childhood and adolescence, and on to adulthood. At each stage in development, there are stage-related problems and conflicts. When a person has figured out how to manage the anxieties associated with one stage, it is often time to move on to a later stage. However, for some people the fears and uncertainties of that next stage, combined with the comfort of having figured out the present stage, may lead them to stop developing. They become "stuck," or fixated, at the lower level. Thus, a girl may fear reaching out to others outside the family because she anticipates that her parents will feel slighted and withdraw their love. This does not mean she will not grow older; it simply means she will continue to react as a child even when she is an adult. Such an individual may never be able to go on job searches, attend college, or forage for herself. Such dependence is clearly a form of deviant behavior in our society. People may also become fixated around a particular way of handling conflicts or around a particular trauma (Freud, 1943 [1920]:242–252). A person fixated on projection, for example, will constantly attribute bad motives to other people to the point of obsession and exclusion of other behaviors.

Regression

Finally, people may handle conflicts and insecurities at a given stage of development by returning temporarily to the solutions of an earlier stage. An adult who in general has learned to handle selfishness may, under conflict, revert to selfish behaviors that were practiced early in life. As Hall (1954:99) notes, it is common for healthy, well-adjusted people to regress from time to time to reduce anxiety. But sometimes it gets them in trouble. Thus, people may "eat too much, lose their tempers, bite their nails, pick their noses, break laws, talk baby talk, destroy property, . . . engage in unusual sex practices, . . . dress up as children, . . . and do a thousand and one other childish things." Those childish things are often defined as deviant when done by adults.

Transformation

The final way to handle conflict in psychodynamic theory is to compromise among contradictory elements and activities, thereby dissipating the energy in many directions. This is one way adults are more developed than children. Children tend to be focused and to have a narrow range of responses and interests. Adults, on the other hand, have generally expanded their interests, behaviors, and responses. Any given activity, such as playing tennis, participating in a political campaign, or doing productive work gratifies many instincts and their derivatives simultaneously, and it dissipates conflicts. Most of the time the activity does not lead to deviance, but there are people for whom constant activity is a fixation. They have to always seek new experience and excitement and be engulfed in physical movement. Sometimes the persistent search for ways to dissipate energy and avoid inner conflicts leads to experimentation with deviant activities that are energizing and exciting.

Summary and Critique of Psychodynamic Theory

According to Freud, all human behavior is a response to the pushes of innate energy forces in the human mind, or it reflects adaptations to the various psychic and social conflicts that instinctual drives bring about. Some of the driving forces behind behavior are in the unconscious, and few of the causes of behavior are obvious from the behavior itself or are known to the actor. Deviant as well as conforming behavior, then, results from a direct expression of an instinct or a combination of instincts; it is a compromise between impelling and restraining forces in the psyche; or it reflects some form of ego defense (Hall, 1954). The causes of deviance, therefore, are inside people's heads, and those causes are such that people do not understand the reasons for their own behavior. Indeed, the accounts people give for their deviant behavior, along with ostensible explanations, are often quite misleading.

Much psychodynamic thinking has an intuitive appeal, and a lot of the language and its mode of thought has been transferred to popular culture. Everybody uses terms like "Freudian slip" to refer to the hidden (usually sexual) meanings of inappropriate words that people use on occasion, and id, ego, and superego are well known. We see everyday behavior that doesn't make any sense except as reflections of inner turmoil. And we all recognize in ourselves the occasional use of internal conflict management techniques like identification, displacement, and projection. Moreover, much deviant behavior, such as the work of serial killers, obsessive hand washers, and those who eat feces appears too bizarre to be explained except by the principles of psychoanalysis.

But there are also many logical difficulties with the argument. For one thing it seems that almost any behavior can be interpreted in a variety of ways, with the interpretation depending heavily on how the observer wants to interpret it. Thus, one might explain an overbearing boss's behavior as due to identification he made with an authoritarian father, to displacement of his feelings of aggression toward his mother for her rejecting attitude, to some repressed memory he had of being mistreated by his first employer, to fixation at an early stage of anal development, which makes him afraid to let go of, and express, supportive emotions, to his projecting his own hostility onto his workers and thereby responding to his perception of their aggressiveness, or maybe to the fact that the boss has diabetes, which makes him grouchy. Similarly, an accident may be the result of a secret desire to hurt oneself; but it may also be due to recklessness, bad road conditions, an effort to show off by going too fast, or the convergence of a set of random factors over which nobody has control. There is nothing in the theory that would enable one to select among these possibilities. As the popular saying goes, "sometimes a cigar is just a cigar."

In fact, psychoanalysts contend that only by long-term association between patient and doctor in a therapeutic relationship can the true causes of the individual's behavior be known. This is called "clinical evidence." Because most of the causes of their behavior are presumably unknown to actors and are, in fact, supposedly disguised or totally unconscious, most kinds of scientific evidence cannot be brought to bear. One cannot, for example, experimentally manipulate the degree of a mother's love for her child and then measure the effect on later adult psyches or behavior. Ethical considerations preclude such things. In addition, the theory permits a multitude of possible consequences that depend on how various conflicts are managed by specific individuals, all of which precludes really relevant randomized studies using experimental and control groups. In like manner, one cannot accurately survey people about their relationships with their mothers, even using written psychological tests, because perceptions and memories are presumably distorted by ego defense mechanisms such as repression and reaction formation. Nor can one learn relevant information through observing how people behave.

Even though various scholars have tried to use experimental or survey techniques for testing Freud (Eysenck and Wilson, 1973a; Fisher and Greenberg, 1977a; Kline, 1981; Rachman, 1971), the studies are suspect and, at best, their results are mixed (see Eysenck and Wilson, 1973b; Fisher and Greenberg, 1977b). The validity of psychoanalytic theory actually boils down to subjective interpretations by individual therapists. Often with preconceived notions, they sift through information revealed in "talk sessions," dreams, or hypnosis, until they find something in the past that seems to provide a rationale for the condition that brought the patient to the therapist in the first place. However all children experience disturbing events, fear males more than females, (Hall, 1973 [1963]), undergo some conflict with parents, and do things that they are later ashamed of. A therapist can easily find things in all our backgrounds that could produce deviant behavior. But whether those things lead to deviance is highly problematic, and finding a psychodynamic reason to account for actual deviant behavior is at best a later construction of plausible scenarios from past events or memories. While such accounts may be useful for therapy, even if false, they do not constitute good evidence for evaluating the accuracy of a theory of deviance.

Therefore, because only "clinical" findings are truly relevant, it is hard to judge the overall validity of psychodynamic theory. Therapists are often very wrong, as became obvious when the "repressed memory" cases of child abuse became so common. Most of the "recalled memories" were shown to be created by the suggestive actions of the therapists themselves (Ofshe and Watters, 1994). Various studies also show great unreliability in psychiatric diagnosis (that is, therapists disagree among themselves about their diagnosis of the same case). A clear illustration is the famous experiment by Rosenhan (1973), who had normal people fake symptoms of mental illness to get admitted to psychiatric hospitals. Once admitted, they behaved normally, yet their deception was never detected. Moreover, the success of therapy is often poor (see Eysenck, 1973 [1952]), apparently no better than would occur without therapy.

Even if clinical evidence were impeccable and consistent, it would suffer from the fact that the samples are highly biased, being composed of people who are especially sick, those convicted of crimes, or those who can afford psychotherapy. Furthermore, some psychodynamic rationales appear far-fetched to most sensible scholars. "Castration anxiety" and "penis envy," for example, just do not ring true to most people. Although young male children below age five may fear their fathers' discipline, it is hard to imagine that little boys attribute enough cruelty to their fathers to think they would cut off their penises. In addition, this idea supposedly comes from the little boy's observing little girls without penises. But most little boys probably never see little girls nude.

A further illustration of "overreaching" in this theory is its attempt to explain so-called psychosomatic illnesses (Hall, 1954: 89). Modern medical research has shown that arthritis, asthma, and ulcers have organic causes that can be treated with medication. Psychoanalysts in an earlier period attributed arthritis to hostility, which was bottled up inside and ultimately spread to the muscles where it produced painful tension. Actually, arthritis stems from inflammation of joints. The psychoanalysts saw asthma, which is now known to be a form of allergy, as due to repression, which is translated into restrained breathing. And ulcers supposedly developed because of fear, which gets in the way of digestion. It is now known that ulcers are due to infection, which is easily treatable with antibiotics, or to irritation from foreign substances such as overuse of certain medicines. At this point, it seems ludicrous to have subjected people to psychotherapy to discover the inner causes of these physical illnesses. And it may in the future appear equally arcane to have attributed many forms of deviant behavior solely to the individualistic operation of psychoanalytic mechanisms. This outcome seems particularly likely since psychic processes are portrayed by the theory as operating largely independently of the post-childhood social context. Thus, Freud's account paid almost no attention to peer influences, group processes, or social control, which we now know at least interact with psychic processes in the production of deviant behavior.

Overall, then, although psychodynamic theory appears to offer some plausible explanations for some kinds of deviant behavior, it does not contain enough detail about when and how its theorized mechanisms operate in one direction rather than another to provide good explanations of most forms of deviance. Furthermore, it is difficult even to establish its validity in application to the kinds of deviance that do not yield to other explanations. At best, it applies to individualized misbehaviors, which were discussed in Chapter 3, but it seems to have little relevance for subcultural or fully organized forms of deviance, which were described in Chapters 4 and 5, respectively.

Summary and Conclusion

One major category of theories attempts to explain deviant behavior by looking inside the person for more-or-less stable motivations. Some of those theories focus on a struggle to develop and maintain self-concepts (labeling) and to acquire and sustain good self-esteem (self-derogation). Another theory traces deviant behavior back to a basic urge to preserve the freedom that a person thinks she has at any given point in time (reactance). And a final theory focuses on psychic development and functioning in which much of the motivation for human behavior becomes unconscious or disguised, as the person attempts to resolve conflicts between internal drives and external social realities and between various internal mechanisms themselves (psychoanalytic). Each of these theories begins with internal motivation, but all recognize that other things, such as opportunity, provocation, and potential cost of behavior, come into play to translate those motivations into actual deviant behavior. The theories differ, however, in the detail with which they spell out those contingencies and show how they intersect with motivation to produce deviant conduct. All of them need further articulation to spell out more precisely the conditions and combinations of conditions under which the motive elements they identify develop and get expressed in deviant behavior. ✦

Chapter 13

Internal Constraint Theories

Constraint theories, including the ones described here and in Chapter 14, generally pay little attention to the strength of motivation for deviance. Instead, they assume that sufficient motivation to disobey rules or expectations is always present because deviance is inherently gratifying. Internal constraint theories, therefore, aim to explain why people conform. Although most internal constraint theories recognize that other things, such as opportunity or external constraining forces, may interact with internal mechanisms in the production of deviance, they identify the primary causal element as the absence, in the minds and personalities of individuals, of cognitions or emotions that would *restrain* their impulses toward self-gratification. Thus, according to these theories, the main difference between people who do deviance and those who do not is that conformists are equipped with internal controls that make it difficult or impossible for naturally occurring impulses toward deviance to be manifested in actual behavior. Deviants, on the other hand, either have no internal constraints, or their constraints are permanently or temporarily too weak to prevent deviance.

There are two main lines of theory of this type, self-control and morality. While different, these two modes of thought share important conceptual ground. Self-control theories concern internal characteristics of persons that affect their *ability* to control their impulses. Morality theories deal with aspects of people's psyches or personalities that influence their *inclination toward*, or desire to, control their impulses for gratification or for engaging in behaviors that have deviogenic consequences.

Self-Control

Conditional Theories

Variations in the ability of individuals to control themselves has long been recognized as a personality characteristic (Caspi et al., 1994; Wilson and Herrnstein, 1985) linked empirically with deviant behavior. However, most general theories incorporate self-control only as a modulator or adjunct to some more-encompassing explanatory element. For example, there is "containment theory" (Reckless, 1967), which emphasizes dual constraints, some of which are inside the individual (inner containment) and some of which are external to the person (outer containment), in making it possible for a person to resist forces pushing toward deviance. The theory contends that a "good" self-concept is one of the main internal mechanisms of containment. Though Reckless does not spell out exactly why or how good self-concepts might have this effect, they are theorized to help people resist deviance because they aid them in controlling behavior that might stem from deviant impulses.

A second theory using self-control as a conditional element is that by Wilson and Herrnstein (1985). Although their formulation is based on the principles of reinforcement/conditioning discussed in Chapter 11, they contend that the reinforcement process is affected by the variations among individuals in tendencies to discount negative consequences, which they call impulsivity. Those whose personalities make it difficult to appreciate and act on the possible long-range costs of their actions are less likely to learn from experience, and they are less likely to respond to negative reinforcers such as potential punishment. Thus, when situational opportunities for immediate gratification emerge, some people respond to those opportunities despite potential long-range costs that would inhibit others. They respond because their personalities prevent them from acting rationally. Hence the social learning paradigm of Wilson and Herrnstein takes account of impulsivity in order to provide more effective explanations.

Self-Control as a Central Element

The Argument

A recent theory, however, uses self-control as its primary variable rather than as an adjunct (Gottfredson and Hirschi, 1990). This theory is not meant to explain all kinds of deviance but instead is addressed to acts of force or fraud undertaken in pursuit of self-interest, which the theorists call "crime." Yet, the theory is also said to explain "analogous" acts such as smoking, drug use, and promiscuous sex, so presumably it can explain most forms of deviance. Since, by definition, deviance is socially disapproved behavior likely to provoke a penalty, most such acts probably involve short-range thinking and therefore come under the explanatory umbrella of self-control theory.

According to Gottfredson and Hirschi's formulation, self-control is learned. The extent to which it is acquired is determined by the actions of those responsible for children during their formative years. Once established, usually prior to age 10, the level of an individual's self-control is said to remain relatively constant throughout the life course. Because all people are interested in gratification and because force and fraud are often useful in realizing one's desires, those with weak self-control are more likely than those with greater self-control to use force and fraud whenever the opportunity presents itself. Since opportunity is defined as a situation wherein a person's needs can be gratified without much chance of immediate costly consequences, deviance can be understood as an outcome of the convergence of a weakly controlled individual with an opportunity for committing self-gratifying force or fraud. The main implication of this is that those with weak self-control have a high probability of deviant behavior because opportunities are abundant, while those with strong self-control are unlikely to resort to deviance even when opportunity beckons.

But why is this? Since the practice of force and fraud is inconvenient for those who are its objects, the victims or potential victims of crime (or deviance) make it costly for perpetrators; in addition, much crime and analogous behavior has its own inherent penalty. As a result, sooner or later crime/deviance will lead to bad consequences. The behavior of people with weak self-control will be relatively unaffected by those potential consequences unless the costs are immediate. By contrast, the strongly controlled will anticipate long-range disadvantages stemming from deviant behavior and will curb their impulses accordingly. This theory, then, explains deviance as an expression of a naturally occurring motivation for self-gratification by those who lack the internal means to restrain themselves in their own long-term interests.

For example, all of us at one time or another are in situations where it appears we could steal something without much chance of getting caught. Maybe we see an unattended automobile with the keys in it. Perhaps we pass an open cash register. Or possibly we are left alone in somebody's house. According to Gottfredson and Hirschi's theory, we will all be tempted to take the automobile, steal the cash, or make off with some of the items in the house because such fraud would be profitable, or gratifying, to us. However, most of us refrain because we have high self-control, which enables us to hold our own impulses in check while we project beyond the immediate situation and come to realize that, in the long run, we probably cannot get away with it.

According to self-control theory you probably won't leap into the car and speed away; instead, you will first think about it. Even brief contemplation will make you realize that if you drive the car around very long, somebody will probably see you and connect you with the theft. And you will likely conclude that the chances of arrest and all that it implies are too great. Similarly, you probably won't grab the cash out of the register the instant the thought crosses your mind. Instead, you will hesitate while imagining that somebody might come into the room just as you are reaching in. Or you might rehearse in your mind how people will later put two and two together and suspect you because somebody might have seen you enter the room. Because the thought of having to explain what you were doing, or otherwise account for yourself, is embarrassing, and the cost of others not believing you is substantial, you will likely pass up the opportunity. And taking things from a house you happen to be alone in implies even more long-range risk.

Deviance in Everyday Life

In their book *A General Theory of Crime*, Gottfredson and Hirschi (1990) claim that those low in self-control are at risk for self-destructive behaviors other than crime, such as accidents. There has in the past been a substantial amount of research about the distribution of accidents. Since the beginning of the 1900s, statisticians have been studying accident distributions. For example, in a study of industrial accidents in a British munitions factory, Greenwood and Wood (1919) discovered that the distribution of accidents in the factory was not random. In other words, it was not entirely due to chance that someone had an accident. There was a small group of workers who experienced repeated accidents. Gottfredson and Hirschi would argue that these "accident-prone" workers had low self-control. Other research has confirmed the presence of accident- and even disease-prone persons.(Greenwood, 1950; Greenwood and Yule, 1920)

In a similar way, all of us have many opportunities to use force to get the things we want. Almost all males are at one time or another in situations where they ostensibly could coerce females to have sex without immediate bad consequences, and both males and females on many occasions find themselves angry and tempted to use force to get even with somebody. But according to self-control theory, we hold back, think about it, and conclude that we had better not follow through. Consequently, even with opportunity, there is little chance you will rape someone or punch somebody out.

In presenting this example, we are assuming you have strong self-control. Our assumption stems from the likelihood that you are a college student or a professor. Occupying either of those statuses suggests that you have already demonstrated your self-control in many previous instances in order to get where you are today. But maybe you don't have good self-control; certainly, many people suffer from impulsivity. If somebody with weak self-control were in the hypothetical situations described above, they likely would steal the car, take the cash, remove property from the house, rape somebody, or take revenge without thinking about the consequences until those consequences begin to unfold. At that point, of course, it is too late.

The emphasis in this theory is on the ability to control natural desires for gratification, an ability that some have as a result of their upbringing. Thus, deviant behavior is like a lot of other behavior in that it is normal or natural and reflects the same forces. For example, two individuals differing in self-control can be placed in a room with a dish of ice cream. One of them will pick it up and eat it because it looks good, while the other will hesitate and ask himself various questions, such as whether it was meant for him, whether it will add too many calories to his diet, and the like. However, even when a weakly controlled individual does hesitate, he is incapable of sustaining the delay for long or ultimately of subordinating desire to cost. The impulse for gratification is simply uncontrollable. Therefore, those who engage in deviance are also likely to be irresponsible in other things as well. They have more accidents, are more irregularly employed, accomplish fewer goals in life, get sick more often, have more children than they can afford, drop out of school more often, renege on their debts, and are more likely to smoke, abuse alcohol, and produce out-of-wedlock children. As a result, Gottfredson and Hirschi contend that one can predict the likelihood of criminal behavior by observing prior manifestations of other irresponsible behaviors.

Of course, not everybody encounters the same number or goodness of opportunities for particular kinds of deviance. Self-control theory recognizes this and grants that opportunity is a necessary condition for deviance, and it implies that the extent of opportunity may affect the probability of deviance. However, the theorists also contend that opportunity is so common that weakly controlled people will generally deviate more than strongly controlled people. For that reason, differences in self-control are said to account for all but one of the known variations in crime and deviance discussed in Chapter 9. Males are more deviant than females mainly because females have stronger self-control and only secondarily because they have fewer opportunities for deviance. And if lower-status people do more deviance than higher-status people, it is mainly because of their lower levels of self-control. Moreover, many of the variables, like social attachment and peer association, that predict deviance, are assumed to be themselves products of self-control.

The one exception to the central effect of self-control in explaining variations in deviance, according to Gottfredson and Hirschi, concerns age. They contend that changes in the probability of deviance over the life course, which are reflected in higher rates in the late teens with steady declines thereafter, are basically inexplicable. This pattern is presumably an inherent, natural phenomenon, not due to any social process or variable. Moreover, since the age effect cannot be explained and is invariant, the theorists contend that social scientists should simply accept it as fact and relieve theories of any obligation to account for it. According to Gottfredson and Hirschi, social theory is supposed to account only for differences among individuals that are impervious to age changes. Since all differences, such as those among people with various socioeconomic statuses, various minority/majority categorizations, or places of residence, are supposedly similar at all ages—and according to the theory, due mainly to variations in self-control—the theory does all it should with respect to age.

For example, even though the probability and rate of deviance declines after the late teens for both males and females, the magnitude of the male-female difference presumably remains relatively constant throughout the life cycle. If 15-year-old males engage in deviance twice as much as 15-year-old females, then 25-year-old males should show about twice as much deviance as 25-year-old females, even though the absolute amount of deviance among 15-year-olds may itself be twice as great as among 25-year-olds. It is this presumed *relative difference* between males and females at all ages that is what self-control theory aims to explain, not the decline exhibited by both males and females after the late teens.

The Nature of Self-Control

Gottfredson and Hirschi conceive of low self-control as a multidimensional construct rather than simply a manifestation of impulsiveness. They identify six different elements that go together to produce low self-control: (1) orientation toward the present rather than the future (or short-sightedness); (2) lack of perseverance in following courses of action; (3) being drawn more to the physical than to the mental and being outgoing rather than introspective; (4) insensitivity to the needs or suffering of others (self-centeredness); (5) intolerance for frustration; and (6) inclinations toward risk taking and opportunism.

The poorly controlled individual presumably thinks mainly about concrete things in the immediate situation, with little concern for the future, which is distant and out of mind. Those with high self-control, on the other hand, tend to anticipate future events and to calculate the relationship between present circumstances and future scenarios. Those with low self-control have difficulty maintaining their effort to complete tasks they set out to do. They lose interest, grow tired, become distracted, or simply give up. For that reason they have trouble holding jobs, staying married, paying debts, earning degrees, or saving money. By contrast, those with high self-control keep up their effort and sacrifice present comfort or gratification to achieve the goal or accomplish the tasks they begin.

Individuals with weak self-control are usually not thinkers but are often doers and are more often active than passive; they would rather engage the outside world than imagine what it would be like. The strongly controlled, in contrast, contemplate more than they act, and they prefer cogitation to physical action. Poorly controlled people don't think much about how their actions will affect others, nor do they care; strongly controlled individuals, however, empathize with the plight of other people, vicariously placing themselves in the others' shoes. Those who lack self-control also have quick tempers and "short fuses" and easily become irritated if things do not go their way. Their more-controlled counterparts are slow to anger, tolerant of adversity, and eager to conceal emotions that might suggest immaturity. Finally, the poorly controlled are said to be willing to take large risks for small gains because it is thrilling or exciting to do so and they are attracted by a hint of quick gain with little sacrifice.

All these characteristics presumably go together with more or less equal influence to form a gestalt, so, for example, those who are present-oriented also tend to be insensitive to the feelings of others, and those who are unable to handle frustration are also physically rather than mentally oriented. And despite some aberrations, measures of the various elements do seem to behave largely as predicted (Grasmick et al., 1993b; Longshore et al., 1996; Piquero and Rosey, 1998; Polakowski, 1994). The aberrations are of two types. First, there are people, such as successful athletes, who are physically

oriented but nevertheless persevere with much personal sacrifice to achieve
the goal of winning a competition. Second, some research has shown that
measures of risk-taking do not predict deviant behavior in the same way as
measures of the other dimensions of self-control specified by Gottfredson
and Hirschi (Grasmick et al., 1993b).

❖ ❖ ❖ ❖

The Source of Self-Control

Since the key variable in explaining deviance in this theory is self-control,
it is important to understand why some people have more of it than others.
The theory, therefore, tries to answer the key question of where self-control
comes from. Unlike most other theorists stressing impulsivity (see Caspi et
al., 1994; Wilson and Herrnstein, 1985), Gottfredson and Hirschi reject the
possibility of biological inheritance. Though recognizing that biological factors may affect the socialization process somewhat, they theorize that self-
control is nevertheless learned, mainly in the family context. The theory postulates that low self-control is the natural condition of humans. Presumably,
we are all born with an inherent urge to gratify our desires in the easiest way
possible. To become otherwise, we must be trained to rein in those impulses.
As a result, many remain weakly controlled, while only a few develop strong
enough self-control to avoid deviance altogether. This is why most people engage in at least some deviance during their lives.

Drawing on the research of Patterson and his associates at the Oregon
Learning Center (Patterson, 1980; Patterson et al., 1982), Gottfredson and
Hirschi theorize about the conditions that lead to strong self-control. According to their account, self-control can be acquired only when parents or other
caregivers do four things: (1) They have to love the child enough to monitor
its behavior. (2) They have to actually monitor the child's behavior. (3) They
must recognize misbehavior when it occurs. (4) They have to correct or punish the child for doing wrong. If even one of these steps is neglected, a child
will fail to develop self-control—no matter how well the other tasks are performed. In other words, the four things must all go together.

Some caregivers, of course, fail on the first count. They do not love their
charges enough to spend the necessary time and energy to keep watch over
them. Love of children cannot be taken for granted. Although some people
think that a biological connection like that between a natural parent and
child automatically produces emotional bonds, much evidence shows that
parents are capable of horrible abuse and neglect (Loeber and Stouthamer-
Loeber, 1986; Lutzker, 1998; Malinosky-Rummell and Hansen, 1993;
Maxfield and Widom, 1996) and that many children are not wanted, before or
after birth (Kitzman et al., 1997; Olds et al., 1997; Olds et al., 1998). This absence of concern for the welfare of children is even greater among those who
are not their biological parents but who end up as the socially designated
caregivers (Ellis and Walsh, 1997). Thus, the presence of enough love among
caregivers to motivate them to monitor their child's behavior is a variable;
those children lucky enough to have such caregivers are a point ahead of
those who don't.

Some parents or guardians care enough about their children to do what
is necessary but for one reason or another do not actually monitor them. Economic conditions may separate children from parents for large parts of the
day, as happens when both parents are working in jobs outside the home.
Caregivers may be sick or lack the necessary energy for supervision. Family
instability may reduce the ratio of caregivers to children, making it more dif-

ficult for one parent to keep an eye on all the youngsters. Similarly, in large families, the direct supervisory ability of parents is reduced. And caregivers themselves may lack the self-control necessary for studious oversight.

Although some caregivers may care about their children and supervise them closely, they may not succeed in instilling strong self-control because they do not recognize misbehavior when it occurs. Many caring parents are simply blind to wrongdoing by their own children. All of us have seen parents excusing their children's temper tantrums, aggression against other children or adults, theft or other forms of selfishness, and unruliness. They might do so with the excuse that the behavior is unimportant, cute, or simply a temporary lapse. Or they might simply make no excuse because they do not think what their child is doing is wrong or that it will have lifelong consequences. For example, suppose a child runs up to a guest in the home and kicks that person in the shin. A parent who cares about the child's development and is perceptive will probably react quickly to do something about it. A nonperceptive parent might laugh and declare that the kid is going to be really tough.

Finally, some parents who care about their children supervise them carefully and recognize misbehavior but fail to act in ways that complete the lessons of self-control. According to Gottfredson and Hirschi, the parent must punish the child, but they do not specify how harsh the punishment must be or its nature. Indeed, they sometimes imply that all that is needed is mild rebuke, expression of disapproval, or correction. The point of parental action is to let the child know that there is a cost associated with misbehavior. Although the theorists do not specify exactly how learning occurs (and in fact pointedly reject the idea of reinforcement/conditioning as it bears on motivation to commit various deviant acts), their statements imply that repeated pairing of misbehavior with penalty produces a permanent cognitive linkage in the mind of the child that later permits him or her to control impulses toward deviance.

Because the four-step sequence outlined above is not carried out fully for all children, many of them end up with weak self-control and subject to impulsive actions in response to whatever opportunities arise. However, even when caregivers perform poorly, all may not be lost because other social institutions occasionally make up for those failures. One of them is the school. Although it is secondary and usually not successful in completely overcoming defective family practices, Gottfredson and Hirschi grant that schooling may at least strengthen self-control. However, they contend that if the family and other social institutions fail to produce the personality trait of self-control by late childhood, usually by age 10, there is little hope that it will ever be produced. Correspondingly, once strong self-control has been developed, it is unlikely to weaken.

Summary and Critique of Self-Control Theory

Self-control theory focuses on the effect of a personality characteristic—the ability to defer gratification—established early in life. Weak self-control permits inherent impulses toward selfish actions to be expressed whenever opportunities are presented. Deviance is explained as the simple manifestation of an inherent urge for self-pleasing actions of force or fraud whenever a person with weak self-control encounters a situation where such actions can produce gratification without much obvious or immediate chance of costly consequences.

This theory has attracted a lot of attention and captivated the imaginations of many scholars. Not only is it simple and straightforward and capable of explaining a wide range of deviant acts, but it seems to make sense of most of the patterns of deviant behavior. For example, given that parents devote more time to supervising female children than to supervising male children, it follows logically that females will generally develop stronger self-control than males and as a result show lower rates of deviance. This is consistent with the evidence. Similarly, since the conditions of urban living make it more difficult for parents and children to be close to each other most of the time, urban children are more likely to escape parental monitoring and correction than are rural children. Theoretically, the result is that rural people have stronger self-control than urban people and consequent lower rates of deviance, which is again consistent with the data. And the well-known connection between deviance and size of family of origin (the more siblings a person has, the greater the chances that he or she will engage in deviant behavior) and between family intactness and deviance fits well with the idea that parent-child ratios affect the likelihood that the four steps to strong self-control will be followed to produce conforming individuals.

The theory also seems to ring true in its reflection of "common sense." Even laypersons recognize the importance of child rearing in producing useful personality characteristics, and it is not hard for most people to interpret deviance as unrestrained acts of selfishness. Hence this account of deviant behavior has become very popular and, many think, is self-evidently true.

Despite its popular appeal, however, there have been few direct tests of the validity of self-control theory, and collective evidence is somewhat mixed. The direct tests that have been conducted are generally favorable (Arneklev et al., 1993; Evans et al., 1997; Grasmick et al., 1993b; Keane et al., 1993; Longshore, 1998; Paternoster and Brame, 1998; Wood et al., 1993). In addition, the theory is supported by large bodies of ancillary evidence. One line of work consistent with the main tenets of the theory is that establishing a linkage between impulsivity and deviance (Caspi et al., 1994; Plutchik and Van Praag, 1995; Robins, 1978; Wilson and Herrnstein, 1985:173–174, 204–205). Another collection of evidence shows that deviant behavior by individuals is usually not focused on one type of deviance but rather includes a variety of different kinds of behavior (Blumstein et al., 1988b; Bursik, 1980; Farrington et al., 1988; Gottfredson and Hirschi, 1990:91–94; Horney et al., 1995; Osgood et al., 1988; Paternoster et al., 1997; Stander et al., 1989). This is congruent with the expectation of the theory that people will respond deviantly to a variety of opportunities. A third set of findings encompassed by the theory shows that people who are especially troublesome early in life tend to continue to have problems throughout the life course (Moffitt, 1993, 1997; Nagin and Farrington, 1992a, 1992b; Nagin and Paternoster, 1991a; Olweus, 1979; Robins, 1966; Rutter and Rutter, 1993). Finally, many studies demonstrate the impact of child-rearing practices on the development of pro-social personalities (McCord, 1991; Patterson, 1980; Smith and Thornberry, 1995; Wilson and Herrnstein, 1985:213–244).

Not all the evidence is favorable, however. For example, although Grasmick et al. (1993) found that their measure of self-control was related to self-reported deviance (both past and projected) and that there was an interaction between self-control and opportunity in producing deviance, their evidence showed opportunity to be more important than self-control. This imbalance suggests that situational as well as structural conditions may overshadow traits or motivations inside the person. In addition, research on life cycle changes in deviance suggests that some people with long-term patterns of misbehavior, who are presumably afflicted with weak self-control, may nevertheless shift to conforming patterns in response to changing social alliances (Sampson and Laub, 1993). Such evidence challenges either the idea that weak self-control is stable over the life course or that weak self-control produces deviance despite other conditions. Indeed, one recent study (Tittle and Grasmick, 1997) shows that measured self-control varies across age cohorts in a manner consistent with an interpretation that self-control is not age stable.

In view of various theoretical weaknesses, failure of the theory to enjoy full empirical support is not surprising. There are at least five deficiencies in the self-control formulation that render it less effective as a theory of deviance than it might be. First, like all control theories, its assumption that everybody is motivated toward deviance in more or less equal amounts at all times is a flaw. By failing to take strength of motivation into account it almost inevitably introduces errors into its explanatory scheme. For instance, rape is simply not attractive to men who gain sexual pleasure mainly from giving pleasure and who shrink from dominance or violence. Some other men, who might find rape gratifying, have alternative means for obtaining sexual satisfaction and for dominating, and those alternatives may be more or less available depending on the situation. For such men, rape is generally unlikely, regardless of self-control or opportunity, but its actual probability will depend partly on the availability of the alternatives. And even though self-control theory is less concerned with predicting or explaining specific forms of deviance than in accounting for patterns involving various kinds of deviance, it is still true that some individuals find all forms of deviance less gratifying than do other individuals.

On the other hand, some self-controlled people are so strongly motivated toward various forms of deviance that they are likely to deviate despite their favorable personality dispositions. In fact, it is quite plausible that strong self-control is often employed in the service of deviance. Thus, white-collar deviants who carefully plan and calculate in order to defraud clients; organized criminals who plot the takeover of vice operations or the execution of rivals; seducers who carry out well-planned campaigns to entice married people to become their lovers; and terrorists who organize massive uprisings through detailed fieldwork over long periods of time all contradict the premise of the theory that deviance is spontaneous, uncontrollable, and undertaken in response to random opportunities.

Second, even though the theory incorporates opportunity as a contingency for the expression of weak self-control in deviance, it does not give enough weight to variations in it. Although Gottfredson and Hirschi assume that deviant opportunities are so widespread that they cannot make much difference in who does or does not engage in deviance, it seems clear enough that there are great differences in the extent to which people encounter situations where they might ostensibly gratify their needs without immediate and obvious chances of detection. And there are also great differences in the quality of the opportunities that individuals have for deviance. This is partly because some opportunities are tied to a person's social position. Parents have more opportunities for child abuse than do those who aren't parents; employers and teachers have more opportunities for sexual harassment than do employees and students; and accountants have more opportunities for embezzlement than do mechanics. Hence, even if weak self-control is strongly implicated in deviance, the nature of the social structure within which various individuals operate will channel the way in which weak self-control is expressed.

Third, there is good reason to think that things besides self-control and opportunity are operative. One is morality, which we will discuss later in this chapter, and another is the actual probability of bad consequences. The theory of self-control stresses one's ability to inhibit impulses; it secondarily mentions willingness to control one's desires for self-gratification. It does not, however, explicitly allow for the possibility and likelihood that some people want to control their destructive impulses while others do not. Even if people have strong self-control—they are contemplative, cognizant of the feelings of others, tolerant of frustration, mentally oriented, capable of restraining present urges in favor of long-range goals, and can accurately calculate the chances of long-range cost—they may still commit acts of force or fraud because it pays off and they see no reason not to. Thus, a particular self-controlled husband may nevertheless abuse his wife because it feels good to him and he knows there is little chance of his getting caught; and he is not restrained by a conscience that defines the act as morally wrong. Others who have the ability to refrain from deviance will in fact do so because most deviant acts are loathsome in their minds. Hence, given opportunity, the inhibition of deviance may involve both ability and desire to curb one's impulses.

Fourth, there is reason to question the assertion that self-control or the desire to exercise restraint is a stable trait, once established. All manner of things, like depression, economic hardship, and stress, may temporarily disable one's self-controlling capabilities or inclinations, while new social affiliations may strengthen them. Furthermore, there is reason to imagine that people continue to learn from the consequences of their behavior even beyond childhood (see Tittle and Grasmick, 1997). If bad consequences inevitably accompany deviance, as Gottfredson and Hirschi contend, then weakly controlled people should continually gain in self-control as the punishments provoked by their impulsive behaviors feed back to their psyches. And since situations connected to statuses or various life events provide for more or less feedback, self-control should be somewhat dynamic—stronger in some conditions, weaker in others, regardless of where it began. A more complete theory would attempt to spell out those conditions so that the level of self-control after childhood would not have to be taken for granted but could be predicted from circumstances.

Finally, as a theory of deviance, the self-control formulation suffers because of its focus on acts of force and fraud undertaken for self-gratification rather than on deviance generally. Some acts of force undertaken for self-gratification, such as parents coercing children to stop making annoying noises, police officers handcuffing suspects, athletes punching or tackling opponents, and employers firing workers, do not fit any definitions of deviance, particularly not the one used in this book. In fact, they don't even seem to make much sense as "crime," although they clearly are instances that ought to qualify by Gottfredson and Hirschi's definition. Similarly, frauds like concealing a woman's fatal health condition from her, telling a husband or friend that the poem he wrote is better than you actually think, and promises of having given at the office to avoid solicitors may be "crime" by the theorists' definition, but they probably do not qualify as deviance. On the other hand, there are many forms of deviance, such as drug usage, suicide, consensual sexual exchanges among married partners, and sectarian religious practices, that involve no force or fraud. Thus, while some of these acts (though not all) may be explicable as manifestations of weak self-control, using the theory in that fashion would seem to violate its original intent.

In summary, then, the theory of self-control focuses on a form of internal constraint that, if absent, permits deviance to occur. Such deviance is an unrestrained expression of desires for self-gratification in the presence of appropriate opportunities. The argument has substantial face validity and much empirical support. However, there is some contrary evidence, and it has a number of theoretical flaws that stem mainly from too narrow a focus on one variable and too many untenable assumptions.

Morality

Morality theories contend that people differ in their propensities or probabilities for committing deviant acts because of variation in an internal psychological restraint that is based on considerations of right and wrong. This source of restraint is sometimes called "conscience." The conscience consists of moral precepts that are so deeply embedded in a person's psyche that she or he is reluctant to violate them out of fear of feeling guilty. Presumably, when a person is possessed of "internalized" values, she wants to avoid deviant behavior that is contrary to those values, and assuming that she is capable of self-control, she will, under most circumstances, though not all, refrain from misbehavior.

It is important to note the difference between behaviors that are habitual and those that are morally based. Violations of habitual patterns produce feelings of awkwardness—because the behavior is unfamiliar. Violations of moral standards, however, generate emotional responses of remorse or self-loathing. And it is the anticipation of those self-punishing feelings that serves to inhibit potential deviance. For example, people in the United States are habituated to driving on the right-hand side of the road. When they visit a foreign country, like England, where people drive on the left, motorists have trouble adjusting—both to driving on the "wrong" side of the highway and to manipulating the steering wheel on the right side of the automobile. The feeling they have is not punishing or guilt laden, though it may involve some degree of frustration. More likely they just feel awkward, as if they don't know how to do things that everybody else can do with ease. By contrast, some people (not many) have moral feelings about exceeding the speed limit. When they go too fast, even if inadvertently, they experience internal discomfort, or feelings of having done something for which they should be punished. Because those emotional responses of guilt are uncomfortable, even painful, individuals with internalized values against speeding are less likely to speed than others without such inhibitions.

This is not to say that morally inclined people never do deviance. Whether they do or not depends on the strength of the moral feelings, opportunities, the intensity of the motivation for deviance, and other situational

conditions, such as the presence of peers urging the deviant conduct. However, to the extent that morality theories are correct, the main factor in deviant behavior is the absence of internalized restraining moral values.

Shared Values and Social Order

As you learned in Chapter 6, social thinkers have generally attributed social order (society) either to coercion (conflict theory) or to shared interests
and values (consensus theory). In this chapter we examine theoretical issues
about the absence of morality as an explanation for deviant behavior, so it is
useful to remind ourselves that many theorists and social philosophers contend that collectively held moral values are central to social organization because they induce individuals to obey social rules. This position is laid out
most clearly by the British philosopher Thomas Hobbes (1957) in his book
Leviathan. Hobbes posed the timeless question, "What keeps society from deteriorating into a war of all against all?" That is, given self-interest and limited resources, why don't all people try to maximize their own gain at the expense of others? His answer was morality. To him, social order is possible because people are moral beings and have moral constraints against committing deviant acts.

Discovering the basis of social order was also the central problem for
Emile Durkheim (1933 [1895], 1961 [1903]), the famous French sociologist.
He posited that nonindustrialized, primitive societies are held together by
shared beliefs called the collective conscience. This common set of beliefs
emerges because primitive society is undifferentiated; individuals work and
live under similar circumstances so there is little specialization or diversity.
Shared experience leads to shared thoughts about right and wrong. Common
ideas about morality presumably connect individuals in simple societies to
one another, as well as link individuals across time.

Collective sentiments, or shared morality, of primitive societies, however,
begin to unravel as the societies evolve and progress. Population growth, enhanced communication, industrialization, and a growing division of labor
lead persons in the same society to have different tasks, problems, and a non-
uniform existence. If primitive societies are characterized by uniformity,
modern societies are characterized by diversity. The growth of modernity (reflected in the growth of the division of labor), therefore, erodes the collective
conscience, though it expands individual rights and freedoms (Jones, 1986).
But if individualism expands at the same time the collective conscience is diminishing, what holds modern societies together?

Durkheim reasoned that the glue for contemporary heterogeneous societies is the interdependence that individual specialization requires. That is,
although the division of labor destroys the uniformity of existence (people no
longer perform the same tasks), it also makes them rely more on others. For
example, what good is it to me if I can make only the front end of a car? I must
depend on others to make the back, top, and middle. Functional interdependence, therefore, presumably binds people together, but it is not enough to
ensure social order—because the division of labor could, under a philosophy
of individual utilitarianism, lead to egoism and social conflict. Functional interdependence has to be backed by a set of normative beliefs, values, or
norms. This "new" moral authority is supposedly incorporated in rules of
contract and mutual obligation embedded in corporate or guild-like associa-

tions (Gouldner, 1970). Those rules and corporate entities presumably provide the necessary restraints on individualism. But what about personal morality in modern societies? Although it no longer serves as the basis for collective order, as it did in primitive societies, personal morality nevertheless remains important in guiding individual conduct.

Talcott Parsons (1937:879–894), the famous American social theorist, also solved the Hobbesian problem of social order within a framework of instilled morality. To him, human action, both conforming and deviant, is influenced by "value-orientations," which consist of normative prescriptions for behavior (Blake and Davis, 1964:462). And these forces were said to operate independently of external sanctions (Wrong, 1994). Parsons (1951:3–67) held that in order for any social system to survive, it must ensure that rule-breaking be kept at a minimum. The "problem of order," therefore, requires that the actions of individuals converge with the demands of the social system, and this integration is ensured when there is an internalization of values and norms by the individuals in the social system. He goes on to note that the "binding" of the individual occurs when self-interest is replaced by the normative standards of the social system (that is, when persons adopt group-oriented behavior rather than behaviors that are immediately best for them).

Similarly, the contemporary sociologist Amitai Etzioni (1988, 1993, 1996) emphasizes the notion that compliance with social rules stems from moral or normative considerations. Much of his argument is designed to counter extreme rational choice contentions discussed in Chapter 14, which portray human conformity as a product of hedonistic self-interest. While not denying the importance of rational concerns about cost and benefits in making behavioral decisions, Etzioni contends that human conduct is also guided by moral and emotional considerations. For example, in deciding whether to be honest on their income tax returns, people take into account the possibility of a tax audit, but they also act on a belief in the legitimacy of the taxing authority of the government, and they take seriously their obligations as citizens of a legitimate government. People leave tips even when not planning to return to a restaurant because they think tipping is the appropriate, or right, thing to do. Therefore, people not only choose the most efficient and profitable line of action, but also the one dictated by their sense of duty and morality.

In sum, many important theorists have answered the Hobbesian question—"What makes society possible?"—by positing a general sense of morality, or internalization of normative sentiments. These theorists, however, have not specified crucial conditions necessary to explain individual deviant behavior as a function of morality. Before internalized moral standards can be used as efficient explanatory tools, scholars must establish how values or moral standards come to be internalized; why or if they remain constant over a lifetime; why some people are more moral than others; and why moral people nevertheless sometimes violate the norms. There is much disagreement about each of these issues.

How Internalization Happens

Natural Condition

There are two broad arguments about internalization. One, long associated with the idealist tradition in philosophy, contends that a moral awareness is inherent in humans (see Scott, 1971). According to these thinkers, even without training or instruction, people naturally come to have a sense of right and wrong, sometimes called natural law, which is embedded in their psyches. This contention is often associated with the philosopher Jean-Jacques Rousseau (1968 [1743]; see also Crocker, 1968), whose conception of the "noble savage" as having inherent goodness, or at least the possibility of developing it, contrasts with Hobbs's notion that human beings in their natural state are selfish and dangerous. However, there are many modern thinkers who espouse similar ideas. The best-known contemporary theorist who embraces the idea of inherent morality is the well-known political scientist James Q. Wilson (1993). Wilson contends that evolution has resulted in present human societies in which most individuals have an innate, natural moral *sense*. Although these natural inclinations are sometimes frustrated by constitutional or biological blockages or contrary effects of poor child rearing, Wilson suggests that "we are almost always able, in our calm and disinterested moments, to feel the tug of our better nature" (1993:11) and "we have a moral sense, most people instinctively rely on it even if intellectuals deny it" (1993:12).

Stages of Moral Development. Following in this tradition, two models of the development of higher-level moral reasoning have been set forth. Both emphasize that under the proper conditions, basic human rationality emerges to guide human conduct along moral paths (Scott, 1971:162–163). Both models imply that moral development potentially lies within the psyche of every person and that morality does not have to be specifically or directly taught.

According to Jean Piaget (1926, 1952), a Swiss psychologist, intelligence improves with the age of a child because a child's capacity for processing information develops. As children become more sophisticated in the way they process information, they are able to make more complex judgments about the world, including moral ones. Development occurs when someone experiences a test of his or her current ways of thinking and making decisions. The more intellectually developed people are, the more complex moral judgments and decisions they are able to make. Hence, intellectual and moral development are inextricably linked and are intertwined with age because experience must be cumulative.

In Piaget's theory, most children advance from a primitive to a complex stage of moral reasoning somewhere between the ages of 8 and 10. To demonstrate this, he related two stories to children of different ages. In one story a boy opening the door after being called to dinner accidently knocks over a chair with 15 cups on it; all of the cups fall and break. In the second story, a boy who has been told by his mother not to eat the jam nevertheless tries to reach a jar of jam on a high shelf while the mother is away. In the process he breaks one cup. The children were then asked which of the two boys is the naughtier and why. Younger children usually judge the first one to be naughtier because he broke 15 cups, while the second one broke only a single cup. They are apparently guided by concern with the immediate consequences of the action, paying no attention to the offender's intent, since breaking 15 cups is objectively worse than breaking a single cup. Older children, however, usually conclude that the second boy is naughtier because the first one had good intentions—he was merely coming to dinner and accidentally broke the cups. The second child is seen by older children to have been performing a forbidden act—trying to get to the prohibited jam—hence his conduct was more blameworthy, even though the objective outcome (one broken cup) was less serious. Older children, therefore, are guided by subjective considerations of intent, a more sophisticated form of reasoning.

Younger children are also likely to view behavior strictly in terms of its potential negative consequences for the actor. To them, a behavior is deemed bad if it results in punishment, regardless of the context or the circumstances. For example, children can be told the story of a man with a sick wife who will die unless she has a particular drug. The druggist grossly overprices the drug because it is to be used only by the very sick, who have no alternative courses of treatment. Because the husband cannot pay the exorbitant price, he later breaks into the store and steals the drug. He is caught and arrested. Very young children will regard this man as bad because he was caught and punished, focusing solely on the outcome of the case and not the context. They reason that "because the man was punished, he must be bad." By contrast, older children, who have had more exposure to complex, demanding situations, more often take into account the entire context of the event. The older, "morally independent," child considers notions such as intent, harm done, blameworthiness, and other more subjective characteristics of the situation. Thus, viewing the man's dire straits—his sick wife, his financial stress, the altruistic motive, the malignant overcharging by the druggist—the older child usually does not judge the man to be morally wrong.

Because of their undeveloped intellectual skills and lack of experience, younger children possess a very primitive sense of morality, which is associated with other distinctive, age-graded characteristics. They are, for instance, egocentric, which is manifest most importantly in the inability to empathize, or vicariously imagine themselves in the position (and mind set) of, another. Instead, those in the early stage of moral development think that everyone experiences and reacts to the world exactly as they do. Since young children have limited practice in role playing, they are seldom forced to see things as others do and react as others might. Older children, however, are more likely to have been forced by their interaction with others to rethink their views and perceptions as well as to alter their notions of how others think. In Piaget's terminology, older, more developed children are able to "decenter"—they look at the world from another's point of view. They develop this capacity through more complex play activities.

The two stages of moral development also manifest themselves in different types of punishment demands. The young child expresses belief in expiatory punishment in which transgressors are made to suffer some discomfort for their wrongful acts, and in which the amount of punishment is in direct proportion to the degree of objective harm produced. For example, younger children believe that a boy who vandalizes a neighbor's house, breaking two windows, should be spanked harder or should be deprived of more TV time than a boy who only breaks one window. Older children, who reason with greater moral independence, are more inclined to apply reciprocal punishment to teach the transgressor about the errors of his ways. For instance, a vandal may be required to restore the damaged property with his own money or work for the injured party.

Finally, in Piaget's schema, the shift in moral development coincides with changes in the prevailing authority structure. Younger children are under the unrelenting supervision and governance of powerful parental figures who

❖ ❖ ❖ ❖

authoritatively define good and bad conduct and determine how transgressions are to be punished. Since young children are powerless to change these parental rules, they acquiesce. With age, intellectual development, and experience with peers and with the larger social world, the child begins to question parental authority and to fashion personal moral rules and sanctions. As a result, parental authority is weakened and two new rules of justice in groups emerge. One is based on an equality principle, where the child believes that rewards should be distributed equally among all group members. Later an equity principle emerges in which rewards are expected in accordance with effort and contributions toward the group's goals. Piaget argued that development proceeds from the parental principle through equality and ultimately to the equity principle. The major components of Piaget's theory of moral development are shown in the top part of Table 13.1.

Table 13.1 Structure of Two Theories of Moral Development

Piaget

Stage	Characteristics				
Stage 1	Objective orientation	Egocentric	Moral realism	Expiatory punishment	Parental authority
Stage 2	Subjective orientation	Decentered	Moral independence	Reciprocity punishment	Equality and equity

Kohlberg

Level	Stage	Characteristics
Preconventional	1: Punishment and obedience 2: Instrumental relativistic	Avoidance of punishment and deference to authority. What's in it for me?
Conventional	3: Interpersonal concordance 4: Law and order	Loyalty. Concern about approval from others. Commitment to established order. Doing duty.
Postconventional	5: Social contract legalistic 6: Universal ethical principles	Respect for law, but mindful of dissent. Moral principles in accordance with one's conscience.

Adapted from material in Piaget (1952) and Kohlberg (1963).

The second theory of developmental stages in morality is really an elaboration of Piaget's account. According to Lawrence Kohlberg (1963, 1984), conscience is based on a dominant principle at each stage of development, and there are numerous stages (not just two as Piaget hypothesized) arranged in a hierarchy such that the early stages of moral reasoning are more primitive (less developed) than the later stages. Altogether, three levels and six stages are sequentially arranged such that each person who progresses must do so through the sequence of stages, with no "skipping." Everybody presumably begins at the first level, but only some advance to the highest step of moral reasoning. Many individuals become "stuck," or fixated, at particular levels or stages, so that people of all ages can be characterized by their advancement in moral reasoning. The bottom part of Table 13.1 depicts those stages.

Failure to progress through all the stages is said to reflect a dearth of challenges, or tests, for the person's moral schema. Developmental periods or stages reflect maturation, experience, and cognitive resources, but they do not coincide exactly with age. Three factors contribute to the level of one's moral development: (1) the degree of experience one has in resolving conflicts and empathizing with others of different capacities, (2) intelligence, and (3) the extent to which one is aware of self and other people.

The most primitive general level of moral development in Kohlberg's scheme is called "preconventional." It is characterized by two substages, the lowest being the "punishment/obedience" stage. In this phase, individuals make distinctions about right and wrong by reference to the physical dominance of those making the rules, which is reflected in their capacity to reward for compliance or punish for noncompliance. Morality is strictly instrumental; behavior is regarded as "morally right" because it has particular consequences for the actor, or, alternatively, compliance occurs simply because those in authority require it. This preconventional level is the most pragmatic, with the operative principle being "might makes right." An example of preconventional moral reasoning is that put forth by Nazi officers who justified putting Jews to death during World War II because "they were only following orders."

The second stage of the preconventional level is based on an "instrumental relativist orientation." It involves elements of empathy and fairness, but only to the extent that they directly benefit the actor. For instance, the individual employing this kind of moral reasoning implies that he or she will do something for you, not out of any sense of duty or loyalty, but solely with the expectation that you will soon do something for him or her in return. The person is saying in effect, "I will scratch your back if you scratch mine," not "I will scratch your back because you have a great need, or because you are my friend, or because humans should help each other." An example of someone at this level of moral reasoning would be a student who finds it morally acceptable to help another student cheat on a biology test as long as the person agrees to help him cheat on an economics test.

Those who successfully pass through the preconventional level advance to the "conventional level" of moral reasoning. This level is more sophisticated than the preconventional level in that it requires more cognitive competence. At the conventional level, compliance with rules is regulated less by immediate instrumental and pragmatic concerns and more by abstract notions such as loyalty, honor, and a concern with the approval of others. Here persons begin to think of the requirements of fidelity to the expectations of others, and to feel the need for compliance out of a sense of duty and "rightness," even if it is disadvantageous to self or involves no obvious benefits. At the initial stage of the conventional level (stage 3), moral reasoning consists of trying to determine what will please and be approved by others. For those at this stage, moral acts are those that meet with approval and social acceptance, and morality is judged more in terms of intentions than consequences. Stage 3 moralists are conventional in the sense that they comply with existing rules rather than question the basis of those rules. A stage 3 person, for example, will presumably feel morally justified in loyally denying a minority person a job if those around him believe minority persons are inferior and approve of his action.

In stage 4, still at the conventional level of moral reasoning, there is the beginning of a legalistic view of authority and authority-subject relations. Right behavior consists of doing one's duty and honoring one's commitments to authority or to social order and stability. When President Nixon referred to antiwar protesters during the Vietnam era as traitors and hooligans, and praised the obedience of "the silent majority," he was appealing to stage 4 morality.

Deviance in Everday Life

Sometimes behavior that is "moral" within a given group of individuals runs afoul of the law. Over the past several years, several large business interests have been brought to court over their use of racial stereotypes and discriminatory practices. In the early 1990s, the Denny's Restaurant chain was accused of refusing service and providing poor service to minority customers at several of its restaurants. In fact, in settling two class-action discrimination suits, Denny's paid nearly $54 million to approximately 300,000 customers who said that they had been subjected to discriminatory treatment. In another case, AVIS car-rental franchise owner John Dalton was accused of refusing to rent his cars to minority customers. Dalton ran five AVIS franchises in both North and South Carolina. Apparently, African-American customers who came to Dalton's car rental counters were told that no cars were available. As a final example, in 1996, top officials of Texaco Oil Company were caught on tape using racial slurs in discussing a racial discrimination suit against the company. The original suit was filed by six African-American employees who alleged that Texaco failed to promote minority employees. In 1996, Texaco agreed to pay $176.1 million to settle the suit.

Those who successfully pass through the conventional level, then enter the "postconventional" level of moral reasoning. At this highest level of moral reasoning, a person steps outside the immediate context of his or her life and develops moral principles of his or her own making, not relying on what is beneficial or what is required by existing authorities. There is an awareness that morality is somewhat relative rather than absolute, and one understands notions of moral diversity and compromise. In the first stage at this level (stage 5), individuals understand the legal underpinnings of morality and respect the duty of compliance that the law may command, but recognize that sometimes unjust laws are created and deserve to be violated in the interests of improving the lives of people. They understand the diversity of a democratic society, and recognize the importance of democratic institutions in solving problems and resolving disputes. A person at this level might believe stealing to be wrong and be willing to accept punishment for theft but nevertheless find it morally acceptable to steal something to feed a starving child.

Stage 6, in the postconventional level, is the highest plane of moral reasoning. The person operating on this level employs abstract universal principles of human dignity and justice, which may be in conflict with existing laws and prevailing currents of morality. Rosa Parks, an African-American woman and secretary in the NAACP, who refused to give up her bus seat to a white man in Montgomery, Alabama, in 1955, thus violating a city ordinance, applied Stage 6 moral reasoning. Her act of legal defiance in the name of a universal principle (human rights) was a major event in the Civil Rights Movement, leading to the boycott of the Montgomery bus line organized by Martin Luther King, Jr. and ultimately to Federal civil rights legislation.

Summary. One line of theorizing, illustrated here by two different theorists, sees moral development as a more-or-less natural process that is within the capacity of all people, provided that circumstances do not prevent them from undergoing it. For these theories, rules are not internalized, but ways of thinking develop that bear on the rules. Some people, however, are prevented from developing normal moral facilities, and as a result they are presumably free to commit acts of deviance that others find abhorrent. An important issue, however, is whether moral thinking corresponds with moral behavior. The theorists seem to assume that it does, but critics note that abstract thought does not always guide behavior (Bandura, 1977; Scott, 1971). Even if moral reasoning develops as the naturalists imply, it may not have much to do with deviant behavior. Moreover, the stages of moral development that the theorists have set forth are somewhat arbitrary, because in the final analysis whether one way of viewing moral issues is superior to another is a matter of judgment. People who embrace fundamentalist religious beliefs, for instance, regard absolute moral standards to be higher on the scale of goodness than the situational ethics reflected in Kohlberg's upper stages. The evidence that those in stage 6 previously, at an earlier age, reasoned preconventionally in no way proves that stage 6 is somehow superior.

Socialization

An opposing position contends that morality must be learned. Durkheim (1933 [1895]) felt that our moral consciences are fundamentally social—"society speaking within us"—and that they are produced through education and socialization (1961 [1903]). In other words, he believed that society must carefully cultivate conceptions of right and wrong in individuals if it is to hold deviant behavior in check. This contention is also endorsed by Parsons, who theorized that "value orientations" are the products of effective socialization. And it is implied by Etzioni, who contends that as members of groups and collectivities, individuals in societies come to share interests and values with others. That is, they internalize the moral standards of the group and develop a sense of duty and obligation to them.

Perhaps the best-known theorist who saw moral commitments as products of learning is Sigmund Freud (1943 [1920], 1961 [1930]). He conceived of human personality in three parts: the id, the ego, and the superego. The id, according to Freud, is primitive, infantile, unregulated, pleasure-loving, and impulsive. Left to its own, it knows no limitation. As a result of the id, social order is problematic because, as Freud observed (1961 [1930]:65) *"homo homini lupus"*—man is a wolf to man. Without restraint, the id would plunge social organization into chaos, into the Hobbesian war of all against all.

Limitation on the id is provided by the ego and the superego. Unlike the id, the ego is governed by the reality principle. The function of the ego is to channel the tension and need fulfillment of the id until it is able to be satisfied. In order to do this, the ego must be capable of tolerating frustration and tension. For example, the id may say "I need sexual release—NOW"—and will search for any way to accomplish that goal, perhaps contemplating rape. The ego, however, must be able to restrain the id and withstand the tension of unfulfilled sexual energy by finding an acceptable outlet for sexual release (consensual sexual activity, masturbation) or divert and sublimate that energy (dreams). The ego is able to perform these functions, according to Freud, because of training and education (Hall, 1954:30–31). In other words, through socialization an external authority provides a rational basis in the human personality for need fulfillment and conformity.

The part played by socialization in internalization of the norms and values of society, which generates morality and socially conforming behavior, is even more clear in the case of the second limitation on the id, the superego. According to Freud (Hall, 1954:31–35), the superego is the person's sense of morality. Unlike the ego, which operates with a sense of situational ethics— "this is not a good thing to do at this moment in this context"—the superego represents a more general code of honor or behavior. The superego has two components, (1) the ego-ideal, which represents children's understanding of what their parents consider to be morally good conduct, and (2) the conscience, which represents individual children's own understanding of morally inappropriate conduct.

The child's understanding of parental normative evaluations of good and bad is necessarily learned, and those understandings are internalized in order to secure parental acceptance and approval. After becoming part of the child's personality, parental expectations are used to guide the child's conduct. If children comply with parental expectations, they are praised, and if they deviate, they are chastised. Children's moral codes are not, therefore, of their own creation or handed down as an inherent part of human nature but are assimilated from the parents. The process by which this occurs is similar to contemporary notions of reinforcement and conditioning, discussed in Chapter 11. Children are first directly rewarded by parents and other authority figures when they comply with parental demands ("good girl") and are punished for failure to comply ("bad girl"). Later, after they have internalized the moral code of the parent, children are able to reinforce and sanction their own conduct by self-congratulation or condemnation. In sum, children do what parents and other authority figures demand in order to earn their approval and avoid their disapproval, and this eventually leads them to conform in order to escape feelings of shame and guilt. Hence the superego originates in culture, which is transmitted through socialization (Hall, 1954:34).

Social Learning. The idea that morality is learned is now embodied mainly in reinforcement/conditioning learning principles (Scott, 1971), especially in versions called social learning theory (Bandura, 1977). Chapter 11 discussed learning theories as explanations for externally generated motivations toward deviance. Here, we are interested in the extent to which inhibitions against deviant behavior become stored in the psyches of individuals through reinforcement.

Classical learning theories emphasized direct reinforcement; it was thought necessary for a child to commit specific acts and then experience rewarding or punishing responses to them in order to learn correct behavior (Scott, 1971). However, social learning theory takes account of the ability and tendency of humans to cognitively manipulate symbols and receive verbal and nonverbal messages about right or wrong and cost or benefit; to empathize with others and model their behavior according to whether the other's behavior was punished or rewarded; to reinforce oneself through personal feelings of satisfaction or condemnation; and to weigh costs and rewards relative to alternatives and to costs and rewards experienced by others (Akers, 1985; Bandura, 1977; Wilson and Herrnstein, 1985). From this point of view, moral lessons stem either from direct teaching, in which parents tell children what to do and why, or from abstract modeling. In modeling, children cognitively extract common attributes present in a wide range of modeled behavior in order to formulate personal rules, which they can then apply to situations with similar structural characteristics (Bandura, 1977:41).

For example, children notice what parents and other models, even those seen on television, do and say in a large number of situations, and they piece together sets of principles that appear to underlie the behavior seen or discussed. They are interested in learning from instruction and modeling because parents can approve or disapprove in the first instance and because the child vicariously experiences rewards or punishments imposed on models in the second instance. Once behaviors have been reinforced and cognitively associated with word symbols, they become part of the psychic organization of the individual and are expressed as moral standards and enforced by self-evaluations. The individual's own behavior, then, is partly maintained by anticipated external consequences but most often by self-reinforcement. That is, through social learning—direct and indirect reinforcement for behavior and associated word messages—people embrace standards of personal behavior and respond to their own actions with internal rewards or costs (Bandura, 1977:129). In the words of Bandura (1977:133), "As a result [of adult reactions] children eventually come to respond to their own behavior in self-approving and self-critical ways, depending on how it compares with the evaluative standards set by others."

Summary. In contrast to the natural-law theorists, who see morality as an inherent human quality, socialization theorists regard it as a product of teaching and training. According to the socialization orientation, without specific tutoring, individuals will not develop moral commitments and will be free to commit acts of deviance according to their own needs for gratification. And, of course, the degree of moral commitment to rules or to ways of evaluating situations will vary with the learning environment to which individuals are exposed. Again, however, even if morality is learned, there is still a question about the extent to which it guides behavior. Also, exactly how all the potential reinforcements fit together and mix is not yet clear.

The Life Course Stability of Moral Standards

The two approaches to morality just reviewed do agree in their implications for moral stability. Both regard morality as being largely established in childhood, but the theoretical reasoning of each nevertheless suggests that morality is subject to modification throughout the life course. From the naturalist point of view, people's personalities include their stage of moral development, which is more or less constant after childhood. However, if morality can naturally develop from social experience and interactional challenges, as both Piaget and Kohlberg contend, then it is conceivable that most people can continue to move up the scale of morality if their circumstances change. Thus, even if a person is fixated at a lower level of moral development, that person might attain a higher level by confronting new realities and gaining more self-awareness—provided, of course, that he or she is not constrained by some inherent intellectual barriers. It is not clear, however, whether the developmental theories provide for devolution in morality, a sliding back to a lower level.

Socialization theories, particularly those based on reinforcement/conditioning, imply that moral thinking as well as specific norms can become well established in a person's psyche during childhood. However, the theories note that any behavioral pattern due to reinforcement will weaken if there is not additional reinforcement later. Since the "real world" does not contain the same set of reinforcements as the childhood environment, and indeed, in complex societies confronts one with a diverse, inconsistent set of reinforcements, one might well wonder how, if morality is learned, it remains more or less stable.

The issue is especially salient in view of cases where people undergo great disadvantages for moral reasons, sometimes even sacrificing their own lives and forgoing great benefits that would accrue to immoral conduct. In religious terminology, temptation is all around us, and a pact with the devil has many immediate benefits. Therefore, if external reward and punishment were all that operated, one would expect the cost and forgone benefits of righteousness to reinforce immoral behavior. Why doesn't it? The answer given by social learning theory has to do with self and indirect reinforcement. As children, we not only internalize external moral standards, we also construct standards for ourselves, which become criteria for self-evaluation. Thus, individuals with an internalized belief about the wrongness of stealing will reward themselves with good feelings for passing up an opportunity to steal and will punish themselves with bad feelings (guilt) for contemplating or actually stealing. An individual, then, continually reinforces his or her own moral standards, producing long-term stability. Further, some individuals look to remote circumstances for reinforcement, and sometimes they pattern their behavior after distant models. Devout religious people, for instance, overlook this world's rewards and punishments with a view to rewards or punishments in the afterlife. And some people follow the examples of models whom they admire, such as cultural heroes, taking more seriously the vicarious reinforcement cues from what happens to them than they take the immediate potential reinforcements for their own behaviors.

Still, given the theoretical premises of learning theory, it is possible that over time the same processes that produced particular levels of morality in childhood could lead to a change in morality. Some may become more moral and some less if reinforcements in the external environment conspire to produce those outcomes, and if contrary reinforcements are strong or dominant enough to counter the self-reinforcements. If for some reason we begin to neglect self-reinforcement of moral precepts established in childhood, a spiral of deteriorating morality can be set in motion. Indeed, such changes are not unheard of, as suggested on one hand by religious conversions where the person takes on a new morality that was previously lacking, and on the other hand by some who sour on the good life and turn to a life of immorality.

Morality and Explanation of Deviant Behavior

Regardless of how internal moral standards are formed and whether they are completely stable or not, they have great theoretical bearing on behavior. Presumably, many of the differences among individuals in deviant behavior can be explained by the restraining force of morality, as it exists at specific times for individuals. Explanations of such differences involve two aspects of morality. First, people vary in the extent to which their psyches contain moral restraints concerning particular behaviors. Either because their social circumstances prevented the experience and challenges that lead to moral development, as Kohlberg would have it, or because the array of reinforcements they faced in childhood were unfavorable for internalization of moral standards, some people do not regard certain behaviors as morally wrong that most people find unacceptable (deviant).

For example, most religious people, especially Catholics, believe that suicide is morally wrong. To them, it is a mortal sin; which is to say, they have internalized the belief that it is contrary to God's laws. Therefore, even when such people are suffering great pain with no hope for relief, they refuse to contemplate taking their own lives. This is presumably because of anticipation of feelings of guilt or self-contempt, as well as fear of punishment in the hereafter. Others in similar circumstances feel no such moral restraints and, therefore, given the opportunity and other conditions, will freely take their own lives. One explanation for variations in suicide, then, is differences among individuals in their internalized inhibitions toward it.

In a similar way, some people are highly unlikely to use recreational drugs, engage in extramarital or homosexual sex, or commit a crime. They believe these things to be morally unacceptable, and actually doing them would violate their very sense of being, generating unpleasant emotions of self-loathing, even if on occasion they might be tempted to do one of those things. A few are even more restrained: they refuse to use drugs of any kind, even prescription drugs; they practice complete sexual abstinence; and they will not even take a paper clip home from the office. Others, however, have no such moral objections. When they feel the need, encounter an opportunity, and perceive that the chances of getting caught and punished are small, they act because there is no internal conscience that prevents it.

To employ theories of morality, one must recognize that individuals not only differ in how thoroughly they have internalized particular norms, or norms in general, but also that internalization of any social norm by a given person is rarely total. Also, internalization of some norms is more complete than for other norms. Thus, it is rare for anybody to have absolute moral objections to specific acts so that the behavior is impossible under any circumstances. For example, even the most conscience-ridden individual, who would feel absolutely awful contemplating a crime, might still do so to feed his starving child, and a conscientious objector to suicide might still do it if his or her life were standing in the way of the survival of others. And, of course, many people have only modest objections to specific norms so that their consciences are not much of a barrier should the right circumstances arise. In addition, some who have strong moral constraints against some acts have relatively weak morality as far as other acts are concerned. A person who is morally restrained from stealing may nevertheless have few internal objections to drug use or unconventional sex.

All of this suggests that, theoretically, deviant behavior may be explained by the extent of moral objections to it. Thus, the variations among individuals and from place to place that were discussed in Chapter 9 may be attributable to differences in morality. According to morality theory, females do less deviance than males because, in general, their consciences are more highly developed (perhaps because parents take more pains to instruct them) and because female role models are more often reinforced for moral behavior. Those who are socially attached presumably also embrace higher moral standards, which may be one of the reasons they are willing to make the personal commitments to families, communities, and churches in the first place. Similarly, those who reside in smaller places or in certain regions of the country, those who have higher IQs, those who are religious, those who come from more complete homes, and those who are less involved with deviant peers are theoretically more conforming because those characteristics also signify more internalization of the social norms. Finally, according to the theories, minorities and those with lower socioeconomic status are more likely to do some kinds of deviance because their internal commitments to the norms are less intense. This is assumed to be because the normative system is less rewarding for them. When the rules seriously disadvantage certain categories of individuals, it is more difficult for parents and other caregivers to teach those norms as moral imperatives. Moreover, positive reinforcement for models saying and doing the normative thing appears to be less likely for subordinates in a social system whose members are often judged by external appearances rather than by character. Such conditions make it more difficult for minority and lower-status children to internalize moral standards corresponding to the prevailing normative system.

Morality theories, however, have trouble explaining some of the facts of deviance, such as age variations, why some variables predict greater probabilities for some kinds of deviance and lower possibilities for other kinds, and some of the personality variations. Consider, first, that most forms of deviance peak in late adolescence or early adulthood. Since morality is presumably more or less crystallized in childhood and is fairly stable thereafter, it should not permit the adolescent rise in deviance. Even if morality were changing in adolescence, due to flagging self-reinforcement or changes in the behavioral rewards for role models, it is hard to then account for the declines in deviance that accompany adulthood. Clearly, if morality is a key factor in behavior, other things must come into play to offset or supplement it during adolescence. In addition, morality does not easily account for such facts as blacks having lower rates of suicide and homosexuality but higher rates of street drug use and promiscuity. Finally, since deviance seems to vary by the personality traits of impulsivity and negative emotionality, it is not easy to attribute such variations to moral commitments. Apparently, there are contingencies in the operation of morality that have not been well articulated in the theories.

Consider Kohlberg's theory of moral development. It does not necessarily follow that a person at the postconventional level is more likely to conform to social norms than one at a lower level of morality. A person who is primarily concerned with seeking approval from others (stage 3) or is committed to duty and to maintaining established order (stage 4) might be expected to avoid deviance to a much greater extent than one who follows abstract principles of conscience (stage 6), because deviance is, after all, a violation of social expectations. For instance, a stage 6 person might reason that suicide is the best course of action because it spares others a burden, while a stage 4 individual might refuse to consider it a reasonable possibility because of duty to religious principles. On the other hand, a stage 3 person, who is guided by concern for the approval of others, might succumb to peer pressure to use drugs, while a stage 6 person might refuse because of strong conscience about the social and personal damage of drugs. Thus, a higher stage of morality is not necessarily a predictor of less deviance, and the general relationship between stage of moral development and probability of deviance is complex.

Similarly, predictions from social learning theory are not straightforward or simple. The theory suggests that internalized moral standards may contain conflicting elements and that they are subject to many social contingencies, including the number of moral dimensions operative in a situation, types and numbers of alternatives that are available, personal variations such as impulsivity, the strength of motivation in a given circumstance, opportunities, and a variety of other conditions (Bandura, 1977:46). In other words, since behavior, according to the theory, responds to social and internal reinforcements, considerable variation from situation to situation can be expected. Moreover, people not only learn moral principles, they also learn exonerative moral reasoning, which can be brought into play to weaken internal restraints. As Bandura (1977:47) notes, "Because almost any conduct can be morally justified, the same moral principles can support different actions, and the same actions can be championed on the basis of different moral principles." Hence the same conscience that opposes murder on the grounds of the sanctity of life can be brought to justify capital punishment (perhaps for deterrence to preserve life in the long run); to oppose safety measures that have been proven to save lives (because of moral objections to government interventions, which is a higher, conflicting value); or to support abortion rights (to preserve personal freedom of choice or to avoid the hardship that would befall an unwanted child). Indeed, since exonerative moral reasoning is so often invoked, a major perspective called "neutralization theory" has emerged.

Theory and Techniques of Neutralization

David Matza (1964) and his associate Gresham Sykes (Sykes and Matza, 1957) contend that almost all people have conventional moral inhibitions against deviant behavior. Variation in commission of deviant acts, however, occurs because some people have more effectively acquired cognitive skills that may release them from moral obligations from time to time. No person constantly violates social rules, and when people do, the theory builders say they "drift" from conventional values—because they have the tools to escape from morality by self-justifications of their actions prior to a deviant act. Sykes and Matza (1957) identified five techniques for self-justification, and William Minor (1981) has added a sixth.

One technique of neutralization is called *denial of responsibility*. Potential offenders convince themselves that deviance is not their fault; that the actions are out of their control—the actions cannot be helped. Basically, the person is saying that circumstances conspire to make the behavior necessary, almost inevitable, despite its moral wrongness. For example, a woman having an extramarital affair might claim that she is overcome with passion, she is falling in love, the situation is provocative, her husband is a bad or unloving person, and she is under so much stress that her normal moral constraints cannot operate. In other words, if people have acquired the appropriate cognitive skills, in given circumstances where motivation for deviance is strong, they will release themselves from the tugs of conscience by declaring themselves helpless to do anything else.

The second relief from conscience comes from a *denial of injury*. The person is persuaded that the wrongdoing will not actually hurt anybody or anything, or that it is an entirely private matter. A thief might regard stealing as temporary borrowing, intending to repay, and a speeder might reason that nobody will be harmed by his or her misdeed. A drug user will think that any potential injury is personal, with no consequences for others, and even a rapist will imagine that no harm will be done since the victim has no doubt engaged in sexual intercourse many times before without pain, illness, or pregnancy. A president may justify marital infidelity as a private matter with limited consequences for those who might find it wrong. An especially clear example is a person defrauding somebody and conceiving that any losses will be covered by insurance anyway or that the person can take a tax deduction for the liability. If one can readily make a psychic adjustment so that a morally objectional act is rendered harmless, that person can then behave in ways that otherwise would be impossible.

Deviance in Everyday Life

Students of crime and deviance use a concept called "victimless crime." A victimless crime is an example of the denial of injury. Essentially, the position of those who advocate using the term "victimless crimes" is that some acts and behaviors harm no one, and if there is no injury there should not be a criminal offense. Victimless crimes include prostitution, abortion, drug use, and homosexuality. There is a question in some people's minds, however, about whether these or any acts are truly "victimless." For example, those who are "pro-life" would argue that abortion has a definite victim—the aborted fetus. The family of a drug addict and the spouse of the one who visits a prostitute may vocally argue that there are real victims of drug use and prostitution. Some members of the public may object to the large medical costs of AIDS they shoulder as customers of medical insurance companies and would argue that they are victims of drug use and homosexuality. Are there really "victimless crimes"? (see Meier and Geis, 1997)

A third technique allows the individual to escape the pangs of conscience by redefining the victim as blameworthy or less than human, or by denying that there is a victim at all. Victims of assault, rudeness, or economic exploitation can be seen as having deserved it for various reasons, such as overcharging a welfare recipient for a service because "she is living off the government anyway." Men who desert their wives sometimes reason that the woman was so difficult to live with that she brought it on herself. This *denial of victim* can also extend to blaming others for allowing the deviance to occur. A vandal might view an unguarded house as a suitable target because the owner did not show enough concern to watch over it.

Fourth is the device of *condemning the condemners*. Instead of viewing one's own misbehavior in a morally unacceptable light, the individual assumes an intellectually aggressive policy of finding fault with those who might blame her or him. A student cheater contends that the system of grades is corrupt and the teachers lazy; those who fail to read assignments claim the reading is too difficult or too uninteresting. Drug users point out that disapprovers often smoke cigarettes, consume alcohol, and use prescription medicines excessively, so are in no position to cast stones. Child abusers note that authorities often psychologically damage their own children or neglect to discipline them at all. And revelers call attention to the noisiness of the complainers' lawnmowers or televisions.

Wrongdoers can also sometimes *appeal to higher loyalties*. We observed this earlier in discussing how, because of the complexity of personal moral codes, an individual can condemn one kind of violation of the sanctity of life but not another by invoking a moral counterclaim. Terrorists murder and maim in the service of political freedom that presumably will reduce casualties later. Military strikes that kill civilians are morally justified as necessary byproducts of a larger program to ensure civilian safety. Hunters who kill game out of season often claim a necessity to feed their families, or a service to wildlife survival by thinning the habitat. Fraternity members sometimes facilitate rape out of loyalty to peers. Germans who shielded Jews during the holocaust in violation of the law did so because of commitments to moral principles beyond the law. And prostitutes often justify their activities by claiming they are helping protect the community from sexual predators.

Deviance in Everyday Life

An example of how an appeal to higher loyalties allows one to do deviance is provided by David Berkowitz, the "Son of Sam" serial killer. Berkowitz was an out-of-work postal employee in New York City who for over a one-year period, from 1976 to 1977, terrorized the streets of New York. Berkowitz roamed the streets at night selecting victims. He would then pull a .44 revolver out of a paper bag and shoot them. At the end of his spree, Berkowitz had murdered six people and maimed seven. He was tagged the "Son of Sam" killer because he claimed that he was only following the orders of a 6,000-year-old demon who spoke to him through "Sam," a neighbor's black labrador retriever.

Finally, as Minor (1981) explains, people are inclined to invoke a *metaphor of the ledger*. Here potential wrongdoers see their transgressions in the larger framework of their records of good deeds, saying in effect, "I have done so many good things that this one bad thing will not count much." We can see this in operation among delinquent gang members who dismiss complaints against their selling drugs or engaging in street fights by claiming to protect the community from invaders, providing employment to economically deprived local residents, and having given more blood to the blood bank than anybody else. Swingers pride themselves on marital stability, honesty, and being good parents. Killers often assume a form of righteousness in which they see themselves acting to uphold the community's values (Katz, 1988). And in courts of law defense attorneys always try to show that, apart from the crime in question, their clients have good moral character and records of dedication to their families and communities.

Overall, then, some people apparently can defy their own moral standards with an internal conversation that says, "I can't help it," "Nobody will be harmed." "It is a private matter." "Any potential victims deserve what they get." "Everybody else is doing equally bad or worse things." "It is to help somebody else." "I am acting as God's agent." "How can anybody think I am a bad person after all of the good things I have done in my life?" Note that these techniques of neutralization represent cognitive constructs that are learned just as moral standards are; they are stored in the individual's mind to be brought out with more or less facility as needed. Neutralizations are not the same thing as rationalizations, although they have the same content. Rationalizations are essentially excuses offered to others after a misdeed has been discovered by somebody who might disapprove. Neutralizations, on the other hand, come before the deviant act; they are offered by the potential violator to himself or herself, and they serve to loosen the hold of moral constraint that would otherwise inhibit the deviant impulse.

Therefore, the operation of morality in restraining deviance is full of contingencies. It is not as simple as saying that some are moral and therefore do no deviance. Although morality may affect deviance, apparently how much of an effect it has depends on its strength, the cognitive availability of techniques of neutralization, other characteristics of individuals, and the operation of a number of situational mitigations. Because people sometimes violate their own moral standards, the effort to explain and predict deviance using morality is exceptionally difficult and requires a good deal more articulation of behavioral dynamics than the theorists have so far set forth.

Summary and Critique of Theories of Morality

Theories of morality contend that a major cause of deviance is an absence of internalized moral standards that might inhibit deviant impulses. They assume that almost all people are sufficiently motivated by the gratifications inherent in deviant conduct that they will violate the norms if given the opportunity, and there is no moral restraint. Various theories set forth different accounts of why people have moral feelings, how those feelings might change over time, and how they work to inhibit deviant behavior. The major problems concern disagreements about how moral principles are developed; a potential gap between moral reasoning, which happens on the cognitive level, and behavior, which is sometimes divorced from rational mental processes; the fact that many conditions influence whether internalized moral standards are exercized; and uncertainty about how morality meshes with such personality characteristics as impulsivity.

It is still not entirely clear why some people have strong moral feelings and others do not. While social learning theory presents a persuasive case (Akers, 1994), it consists mainly of identifying a large number of variables that can affect moral learning. Until it is shown how those conditions actually converge (rather, how they might come together) and how morality is linked with specific social structural conditions, the theory will not provide good explanations. The developmental theories, along with the idealist philosophical underpinnings, seem to make sense when applied to whole populations but are of much less help in trying to explain individual behavior. It is one thing to say that everybody would be moral if something had not gotten in the way, but it is another to detail and bring together in a coherent fashion the things that actually get in the way.

Morality theories can also be criticized for assuming that moral thinking necessarily affects how people behave. Attitudes, in general, are not particularly good predictors of behavior (Eagly and Chaiken, 1998), and moral feelings can be thought of as deeply embedded attitudes. Much conduct is impulsive, in response to immediate situational requirements, or is the result of a group process, and it is often associated with variables that do not seem to reflect moral standards. Many people act and only later feel a burden of guilt, if at all. The morality theories assume that people contemplate the consequences of their behaviors prior to acting. But if self-control theory, reviewed in the first part of this chapter, is correct, many people act impulsively. Unless morality theories are modified to distinguish between ability to act morally and desire to do so and therefore use self-control as a contingency for moral conduct, they will not provide full accounting.

Despite this, there is evidence indicating that strong moral beliefs, defined as sentiments supporting the legitimacy either of the law in general or specific acts, inhibit to some extent acts of crime and delinquency (see Hirschi, 1969, and reviews in Akers, 1994, and Shoemaker, 1996), and are, as well, good predictors of drug use, sexual offenses, and violence (Bachman et al., 1992; Grasmick and Bursik, 1990; Nagin and Paternoster, 1991b; Paternoster and Simpson, 1996; Tittle, 1980b). In one study, Grasmick and Bursik (1990; see also Bachman et al., 1992; Grasmick and Green, 1980; Grasmick et al., 1993a; Meier and Johnson, (1977) examined the independent effect of punishment for deviance imposed by self (shame) and social censure (embarrassment) on three different kinds of deviant acts. They found that feelings of shame had the most pronounced effect on committing deviant acts. Persons who thought they would feel guilt and shame (the disapproval of one's self) if they were to commit the act in question were far less likely to do it. Feelings of possible social censure (the disapproval of others) had no effect, suggesting that when moral restraint is strong, there is little use for other inhibitions. Similarly, Paternoster and Simpson (1996) found that for intentions to commit corporate crime, considerations of cost and benefit (both formal and informal) were superfluous for those restrained by a strong sense of moral condemnation. But in these studies morality did not fully explain individuals' behavior. Moreover, in their study of sexual assault, Bachman et al. (1992) found that social censure, in contrast to self-censure, had a more pronounced restraining effect when moral beliefs were high, contradicting the part supposedly played by morality.

Finally, none of the morality theories is very clear about the exact conditions where morality will have more or less effect. The connections between stages of moral reasoning and deviant behavior are not straightforward, and how the conditions mentioned by social learning theory collectively converge to upset or support moral standards is not yet detailed. For example, if techniques of neutralization can come into play, it is hard to see why everybody does not deviate since we all learn those techniques—at least to use as rationalizations after the fact. The morality theories provide a plausible retroactive account of what might have been operative in deviant behavior, but they are weak as prospective instruments.

Summary and Conclusions

This chapter discussed what we authors call "internal constraint" theories. The theories posit that something inside the psyches of individuals acts to inhibit some individuals' natural impulses toward deviant behavior, even though deviant behavior is assumed to be inherently gratifying. Those who have no such constraints are theorized as being likely to behave deviantly, while those with the restraints are more likely to be conforming. Two such constraining mechanisms have served as the focus for theorizing—self-control and internalized moral standards. Learning, particularly in early childhood in the family context, is posited as important for both theories. Some morality theories, however, contend that a moral sense naturally emerges from greater and more diverse interactional experience, while other theories assert that moral standards must be taught. Both mechanisms have been shown to affect deviant behavior, but there are many contingencies that can affect the extent to which they operate. At the present time none of the theories concerning these two constraining traits has sufficiently articulated the conditions under which they affect behavior in order to provide full explanation and accurate prediction. In particular, the connection between the two mechanisms of internal control remain unexplored. It appears that theories of self-control and theories of morality need each other because some people have the ability to control their impulses in conformity with social rules (high self-control) but do not want to (weak morality). Others may want to conform (high morality) but lack the self-discipline necessary to do so. ✦

Chapter 14

External Constraint Theories

The theories discussed here contend that the main causal force in deviance is the absence of factors that might otherwise restrain deviant impulses. These theories assume either that motivation for deviance is ubiquitous and universal or that motivation is less important than constraining elements. Moreover, the theories in this chapter are concerned with the milieu within which the individual resides or moves, more so than with things that operate within the person's psyche. Hence the theories to be described look at the social or physical environment surrounding a person, and they interpret deviance as a more or less natural response to the absence of structures, relationships, or procedures in those environments that would otherwise control, restrain, or curtail deviant behavior.

Deterrence Theory: The Basic Idea

In Chapter 11 we discussed a line of thought variously called rational choice, economic, or utilitarian theory. It maintains that people calculate costs and benefits of various potential actions and decide how to act according to how well the deviant act produces benefits in excess of costs. However, some scholars have developed a theoretical approach—called deterrence theory, or sometimes the deterrence doctrine—by narrowing their attention to one part of the cost-benefit calculation (Andenaes, 1974; Gibbs, 1975; Zimring and Hawkins, 1973).

The basic premise of the deterrence argument is that *human behavior is mainly a reflection of fear of bad consequences*. When this fear is high, the individual refrains from deviant behavior; when it is very low or nonexistent, individuals commit any deviance that gratifies their desires at the moment. More specifically, degrees of fear (of bad consequences) are connected proportionately to probabilities of various kinds of deviance. Hence this theory is an elaboration of the utilitarian idea that people calculate costs, but it departs from utilitarian theory because it largely ignores benefits, or rewards, which in that formulation are balanced against costs. The deterrence theory in essence assumes the rewards of particular acts to be constant, and more or less equal, for all people, and it examines how costs vary from situation to situation, explaining actual deviant behavior as a response to the relative absence of costs.

Although this theory seems simple and straightforward, it has turned out to be quite complicated. It is partly for that reason that the following discussion is so lengthy. Another, more important, reason that we authors devote so much attention to deterrence theory is because of its popularity among U.S. laypersons. It stands out among all the theories of deviance presented in this book as the one that most nonacademics believe. Indeed, the principles of deterrence theory pervade all parts of American culture, reside in the minds of most authorities and subordinates, and are infused into every institutional domain. When citizens are asked to explain any form of deviant behavior, particularly criminal behavior, they typically assert that the reason for the behavior is that the consequences are not bad enough. And whenever Americans seek a solution to problems, particularly those stemming from deviant behavior, or when they propose ways of getting others to do things, they readily prescribe increased punishment, cost, or bad consequences. In short, Americans overwhelmingly seem to believe that fear is the prime motivator of behavior and that fear is the most efficient and effective thing to manipulate in trying to achieve individual or social goals. As you will see later, this apparent belief is hardly justified by logic, facts, or the behavior of most people.

Deterrence Theory: Details

Though based on a simple idea, deterrence thinking goes beyond the assertion that people respond out of fear or that behavior is a simple reflection of the possible bad consequences inhering in various circumstances (Lattimore and Witte, 1986). Though they are not well melded, there is a collection of ideas or postulates about why and how various circumstances provoke different degrees of fear for different individuals. This medley of propositions about the effects of bad consequences can be called a "theory," although this aggregation of principles lacks many of the features one might expect of a coherent, integrated explanatory system. It is because deterrence propositions are not precise and organized into a coherent framework that it has been referred to as a "doctrine" rather than a theory (Gibbs, 1975).

In trying to specify potential fear-generating aspects of situations as they bear on individuals, theorists have focused on four main categories of variables: characteristics of potential consequences, individuals' psychic structures that affect ideas about what is or is not to be feared, characteristics of situations, and attributes of individuals.

Characteristics of Potential Consequences

Objective Versus Subjective

The chance of bad consequences from deviance is an objective phenomenon, but subjective interpretation influences behavior. Probabilities are realistic, concrete features of specific situations or contexts, but most people do not know those probabilities. Instead, they have a notion about chances of bad consequences for themselves. For instance, there is a calculable chance that a driver who exceeds the speed limit by a specific amount for a given stretch of highway will be involved in an accident and killed. Given appropriate information, such as the number of autos during a particular period of time that exceed the speed limit by various amounts under specified conditions, and the number of fatal accidents, an engineer or scientist can establish that objective probability. However, most drivers do not know what that exact probability is, and even if they did, they would not take it into account in deciding whether to speed. Instead, if their actions are influenced by fear of a fatal accident, it is fear stemming from the perceptions they have about their own chances of being in a crash (Tuck and Riley, 1986). That is, people are affected by their *subjective* assessments of the potentially bad consequences of their behavior.

Thus, some drivers traversing the hypothetical stretch of highway mentioned above believe, or perceive, that the chances of a fatal accident while speeding are very low while others believe them to be very high. Moreover, some imagine that the chances of a fatal accident for other drivers are very high but are actually quite low for themselves. Others think the chances of a fatal accident in general are low, but they regard the chances as quite high for themselves. Clearly there is a difference between objective circumstances and perceived or subjective circumstances, and the relationship between the two is not always close. One reason for the discrepancy between the two is simple lack of information (Assembly Committee, 1975). People rarely have accurate information, but frequently they must act in the absence of this objective information. As a result, most of the time, people are forced to use their perceptions. But this is not the only reason that objective and perceptual domains differ. Even when people have access to accurate information, they may manipulate it incorrectly, they may ignore it for one reason or another, or they may misinterpret it or selectively perceive it (Bar-Hillel, 1980; Cherniak, 1986; Kahneman and Tversky, 1973; Kahneman et al., 1982; Nisbett and Ross, 1980; Plous, 1993).

Considerable experimental evidence shows that most people are poor processors of data, particularly probability information (Bar-Hillel, 1980; Kahneman et al., 1982; Nisbett and Ross, 1980; Simon, 1957; but see Koehler, 1996). Thus, when some people are told that the chance of a particular event is .5 under circumstance X, .6 under circumstance Y, and .7 under circumstance Z and that the chance of circumstance X for a person like themselves is .6, the chance of circumstance Y is .4, and the chance of circumstance Z is .75, they cannot calculate the probability of the event for themselves, and they cannot even make good guesses (Jungermann, 1983). And in real situations, where information is often almost totally lacking or is in imprecise form, people have trouble sorting out when bad consequences are likely and unlikely.

Evidence also shows that people do not always take information into account even when the information is available and even when they could process it correctly if they tried (Bar-Hillel and Fischhoff, 1981; Lyon and Slovic, 1975; Nisbett and Borgida, 1975; Wells and Harvey, 1977). Some people, for instance, consider themselves lucky, while others regard themselves as unlucky; some regard themselves as highly skilled at avoiding bad consequences, while others underestimate what they can do (Zimring and Hawkins, 1973). Individuals who think they are lucky or highly skilled at avoiding bad consequences are not really interested in information, because it is irrelevant to them, so they ignore it. Those who believe they are unlucky also have no use for information, because they figure bad consequences will happen anyway, no matter what the reality is for others. Some young people, for example, have not altered their life styles in response to the AIDS crisis (Horwitz, 1990:235–236). They believe they are lucky enough to escape infection, or they imagine that they can figure out when potential sex partners are more or less dangerous. Some incorrectly think they can discern infected individuals by looking in their eyes or by gauging their sincerity.

Deviance in Everyday Life

One of the most prevalent problems in estimating risk is the problem of overconfidence. Most of us have a tendency to be overconfident in the things that we do not know about. In a classic experiment, Fischhoff et al. (1977) and his colleagues asked subjects to answer questions that they probably would not know the answer to (ex: "What is the capital of Equador?"), and estimate how confident they were in their judgment. They found that subjects who gave wrong answers to 15 percent of the questions reported that they were 100 percent sure of their answers (they should have only been 85 percent confident). Moreover, for some of their wrong answers the subjects rated the probability that they were wrong as low as one in a million! There may be practical consequences of such overconfidence. For example, some single people claim that they can accurately determine, by physical appearance and other cues, who might be carrying the HIV virus. With this phenomenon known as "radar in the bars," they claim that they can reduce their risk of HIV infection in casual sexual encounters (Daum, 1996). Don't count on it!

And some people misinterpret information or simply misperceive what is out there. It is well known, for instance, that several witnesses to the same criminal event will not necessarily recall the same things from it. One witness will perceive that the bandit was young, wielding a gun, and agitated; another will report a middle-aged man with a knife, quite calm. And so it is in perceptions of bad consequences for oneself. Moreover, information is often selectively recognized and used. If a person's relative was recently killed in an accident, that individual is likely to be especially sensitive to information about accidents and to see the probabilities of accidents as greater than they are (Kahneman and Tversky, 1973; Slovic et al., 1982). Similarly, persons who have escaped apprehension for drug use many times are likely to become complacent and think that the probabilities are not really against them (Minor and Harry, 1982; Nagin and Paternoster, 1991a; Paternoster, 1989b; Saltzman et al., 1982).

When deterrence theory was first developing, it paid little attention to the distinction between objective and perceived risk. When such a distinction was recognized, there was an assumption that objective reality was closely enough linked to perceptions about it that propositions concerning objective conditions applied as well to perceived conditions. Now, however, most thinkers recognize that perceived reality is more important than objective reality in its effect on fear and ultimately on the extent to which bad consequences will affect the chances of deviant behavior (Teevan, 1976). Although the theory is not yet developed enough to specify the connection between objective reality and perceptions of that reality, much research is being devoted to discovering possible connections. Some of those connections can never be discovered, of course, because many of the features of bad consequences, such as how much pain or distress they produce, are almost entirely subjective. In the meantime, most theoretical work on deterrence is being devoted to the effects on fear of perceived or subjective reality, and it is mainly concerned with how reality impinges on the actor rather than how reality applies to the general case.

Certainty, Severity, and Celerity

In addition to the objective or perceptual features of bad consequences, fear is theorized to be influenced by other aspects of potential consequences. One of those is the perceived probability (certainty) of bad consequences (Andenaes, 1974; Zimring and Hawkins, 1973). Behavior is presumably more influenced when bad consequences are thought to be more likely. For example, there is good reason to imagine that if the chances, or perceived chances, of dying of a drug overdose, getting AIDS from a single sexual encounter, or being arrested for speeding were as high as 90 percent, there would be much less drug use, nonexclusive and unprotected sex, and exceeding of the speed limit. Moreover, even if the cost of the bad consequences were small, very large chances of experiencing them would still presumably have a deterrent effect (Logan, 1972). Hence, if drug overdoses simply made one sick, AIDS did no more than cause one to have headaches periodically, or speeding carried a fine of only five dollars, and the chances of those consequences were 99 percent, fewer people would take drugs, have risky sexual encounters, or speed than now—because the outcome would be so certain that even the minor costs would be aggravating. On the other hand, if the probability, or perceived probability, of bad consequences is small, many people presumably will do whatever deviance is possible. Thus, if the chances of getting caught for extramarital sex, robbing a bank, or cheating on an exam were one out of 10,000, a lot more people would engage in extramarital sex, rob banks, and cheat on exams. Indeed, some contend that the rates of these deviant acts are high precisely because the chances of bad consequences are relatively small.

Another feature of bad consequences that deterrence theory identifies as influencing their effects is magnitude, or severity (Gibbs, 1975). Presumably, large perceived consequences deter deviance more than small consequences. The rationale is that more severe costs bring greater discomfort to the would-be offender. Deterrence theory suggests, for instance, that threats of capital punishment prevent more crime than mere threats of imprisonment and that large fines prevent more misdemeanors than small fines (Becker, 1968). Moreover, some contend that large negative consequences operate almost in-dependently of anything else. Hence, it is argued, if members of religious groups prohibiting suicide are aware that they will be eternally damned for taking their own lives, presumably they will not commit suicide no matter how depressed or motivated they are. And legislatively imposed threats of death for crime supposedly deter even when the chances of arrest and convic-tion are small, just as the consequences of getting AIDS presumably prevents risky sexual behavior even though the probabilities of contracting the disease from one risky sexual encounter is small.

Magnitude of consequences is now recognized by deterrence theorists as being almost entirely a subjective phenomenon. One year of prison time is not equally severe for everybody, even though the law acts as if it were. Disad-vantaged people sometimes find that prison is better than freedom because they are fed, clothed, sheltered, medically treated, and required to work less and at easier jobs when incarcerated than when on the outside. And with ex-perience, they can often get along better in prison than when they are on the streets, so when released they mess up deliberately in order to return to a comfortable environment. Loss of reputation is worse for those with valuable reputations than for those with poor reputations. Getting a poor grade on an exam may mean a lot more to a student with a very high average than for one with a lower average. Failing a course may be more costly to one who is about to graduate than to one who has more time to make it up. Being beaten is not a penalty at all to a masochist, although it would be for most people. Because of the subjective nature of judging the magnitude of costs, those who employ the principles of deterrence to channel behavior often make mistakes. Sending a child to her room may not be much of a punishment if that room is equipped with a TV, stereo, magazines, and books, as many parents have learned by experience. And depriving a misbehaving youth of the right to at-tend school may help his classmates, but it may not be unpleasant for the youth himself.

Finally, deterrence theory originally took account of the swiftness with which bad consequences come about (Beccaria, 1963 [1764]; Bentham, 1948 [1780]; Gibbs, 1975). This feature is called celerity. Presumably, there is more deterrence when the time span between the act and the likely result is shorter. Potential deviants can more easily see the connection between the threat and the consequence. The further an event and its consequences are separated in time, the more likely is a person to "discount" the risk (Wilson and Herrnstein, 1985). Furthermore, celerity is important because it affects how well lessons from past experience are learned. When the consequences of people's past behavior are separated from deviant acts by long periods of time, by the time they actually suffer the consequences they are likely to have forgotten the reasons. Hence they will form weak mental associations between acts and their undesirable outcomes. Interestingly, even though utilitarian philosophers (Beccaria, 1963 [1764]; Bentham, 1948 [1780]) were concerned with celerity, contemporary researchers and theorists, with the exception of experimental psychologists who employ punishment to influence the behavior of rodents, fowl, and other animals, have largely ignored it.

Contemporary thinkers have been more concerned with the interactions among certainty and severity than with the isolated influences of either (Grasmick and Bryjak, 1980; Logan, 1972; Ross, 1986; Ross et al., 1990; Tittle, 1980b). At this point, deterrence theory suggests that in isolation, certainty is more important than severity, but that the two in combination are more effective than either alone. Moreover, within moderate ranges, certainty or severity can presumably compensate for each other. Thus, if there is low certainty, large negative consequences may produce more deterrence than if there were modest certainty and small negative consequences. But once certainty reaches a very high level, additional increments of severity would presumably have diminishing returns (Tittle and Rowe, 1974). Consider classroom cheating. If there is little chance of the teacher finding out about cheating, according to the theory, some deterrence can still be produced by specifying a very severe penalty, like dismissal from school. But if there is reasonably high certainty of apprehension, a low penalty, like a poor grade on a specific exam, will deter even better than the previous situation (Tittle and Rowe, 1973).

Source of the Bad Consequences

Bad consequences may be built into particular behaviors by deliberate design; they may grow spontaneously out of situations; or they may be inherent to certain acts. When bad consequences are systematically planned for a group of people by their representatives, they are usually called formal sanctions. This includes things like legal penalties for criminal acts, dismissal from religious groups for violations of their moral standards, or loss of job for occupational misbehavior—all of which are institutionalized consequences; that is, they are specified ahead of time, and a procedure for implementing them is in place.

When bad consequences emerge spontaneously from the reactions of other people, they are commonly referred to as informal sanctions. This includes things like losing prestige among one's friends, being divorced by a spouse, being shunned by professional associates, being ridiculed by peers, being denigrated by an opponent, or being denied privileges by one's parents. These consequences are informal because they are not systematically planned; they are not implemented through routine procedures spelled out ahead of time; and they are not predictable except in the sense that one might anticipate that something like them might happen if a deviant behavior is committed.

Bad consequences are also sometimes inherent to the activity. Some kinds of drugs can make one sick, produce psychotic episodes, and lead to death; some sexual contacts carry the possibility of diseases like herpes, gonorrhea, and AIDS, some of which are deadly and all of which promise misery; and speeding, gang fighting, terrorism, and climbing water towers to paint a class symbol may produce injury—not because any of this is planned or because somebody spontaneously reacts, but because the activities themselves are dangerous. Sensible people usually avoid such activities, and if they do so because they fear the bad consequences, then it is the result of what we will call "natural" deterrence.

It is easy to appreciate how inherent sanctions might curtail deviance. For example, suicide inevitably entails loss of something of potential value—one's life—and it may involve physical pain. These consequences are there regardless of whether loved ones find out, the law prohibits it, or anything else. And there is good reason to believe that many people who otherwise might resort to suicide refrain for those reasons. Indeed, the frequency with which suicide is attempted but not quite completed suggests the potency of inherent bad consequences (see Chapter 3).

In this connection, it is important to distinguish between bad consequences that are the result of human actions in response to an act (or an anticipated act) and those that are unintended or natural. Intentional consequences due to human agency are called sanctions. There is a clear difference between losing one's freedom through incarceration and losing it because of poor health resulting from a lascivious life style.

Deterrence theory has neglected the effects of bad consequences that are natural to particular behaviors (although its cousins, rational choice and conditioning-reinforcement theories have not). Instead, thinking about deterrence has been devoted almost exclusively to formal and informal sanctions. Recent statements of the theory have specified that informal sanctions are likely to be more effective than formal ones (Tittle, 1980b; Toby, 1981; Williams and Hawkins, 1986). The greater effectiveness of informal sanctions occurs mainly because they generally flow from people with whom one is personally involved and about whom one cares (Horwitz, 1990). Hence, informal sanctions are more certain than formal sanctions because individuals we know and often interact with know more about what we are doing on a day-by-day basis. If you slug your girlfriend or boyfriend, your friends are more likely to find out about it, and learn of it more quickly, than are school officials or the police. Your associates are much more likely to know whether you are using drugs than are the authorities. In other words, it is more difficult to conceal deviant behavior from those we know and like. But there is more to it than that. The potential sanctions from close associates are more severe in that they are potentially more painful and costly. Losing the respect of your parents, peers, or friends is a heavy penalty if you love them and care about their opinion. Going to jail implies temporary loss of freedom, but alienating your professional associates or loved ones implies permanent damage. Moreover, the response of family, associates, and friends occurs quickly (greater celerity), while legal or organizational sanctions take time. Therefore, informal sanctions are expected to have more effect than formal sanctions because they enhance the three elements of deterrence discussed above—certainty, severity, and celerity. Moreover, for those who are integrated into informal networks, formal sanctions deter, at least in part, because formal sanctions also activate informal sanctions (Andenaes, 1974; Tittle, 1980b; Williams and Hawkins, 1986; Zimring and Hawkins, 1973).

Of the three sources of bad consequences—formal, informal, and natural—deterrence theory suggests the most potent are informal social sanctions, probably because they are most certain, severe, and swift (Grasmick and Bursik, 1990; Grasmick et al., 1993a; Paternoster et al., 1983b, 1985; Tittle, 1980b). The second most important are formal sanctions, mainly because they imply informal sanctions as well for many people. Though neglected, the logic of the theory suggests that inherent bad consequences are of some importance but less important than social consequences, because most of the inherent consequences are perceived, often mistakenly, to be less certain and severe than the social consequences—and even less certain and severe than they, in fact, are. The theory, of course, also suggests that the three in combination are more effective than any one alone but that the degree of their combined effect is contingent on the social integration of the individual.

Sequences and Types of Effects

Deterrence theory has always distinguished among types of effects, which are partially linked to the frequency of bad consequences. One differentiation is that between specific and general deterrence. Specific deterrence concerns the effect on future behavior of bad consequences, or potential bad consequences, for people who have already directly experienced them. Specific deterrence, then, reflects the effect of bad consequences for a behavior on the one committing the act. In application to criminal behavior, specific deterrence bears on the issue of recidivism, or the probability that a person who has been punished for a criminal act will repeat the act. For example, the threat of going to jail presumably has a different effect on those who have been to jail before than it does on those who haven't, and it supposedly has a different effect for those who committed crimes before but escaped jail than for those who committed crimes but went to jail (Minor and Harry, 1982; Saltzman et al., 1982). Theoretically, the effect of the sanction loses its potency in proportion to the number of times it has failed to deter before, and it gains in potency in proportion to its previous success. So the first time a sanction is imposed or threatened, the more effect it should have. If it fails to deter, each successive time it is imposed it should have less effect, but if it succeeds its future success should be enhanced. That is because failure undermines perceptions of certainty, severity, or swiftness while success strengthens perceptions of those features.

A second common distinction in deterrence theory is that of specific deterrence versus general deterrence. General deterrence refers to the effect of a threat of bad consequences, either because someone is seen to have experienced those consequences or because the situation promises such consequences, on the behaviors of those who are exposed to the threats. Note that the effects of general deterrence may be registered by those who have previously been sanctioned as well as by those who have not been sanctioned (Paternoster and Piquero, 1995; Piquero and Paternoster, 1998; Stafford and Warr, 1993). Consider again the case of academic cheating. Suppose a teacher apprehends a girl cheating and makes a public example of her, and, as a result, the other students in the class refrain from cheating. This would be an example of general deterrence. If the punished student learned from this experience and as a result avoided subsequent cheating, it would be called specific deterrence.

It is important to recognize that the same sanction can produce both specific and general deterrence; it may produce neither; or it may produce one but not the other. Returning to the hypothetical cheating situation just described, where general deterrence was achieved, we can imagine that the future cheating behavior of the particular student who was caught and publicly punished might be unaffected or even that she might become embittered by the experience and deliberately increase her future cheating. This would mean that sanctions failed to achieve specific deterrence at the same time that they succeeded in producing general deterrence. Or, one could imagine the opposite situation in which the student who is punished decides never to cheat again, but because she was humiliated in front of the class, the other students decide that the academic system prohibiting cheating is corrupt and they set out to cheat more than they otherwise would have. This would be an instance in which specific deterrence was achieved but general deterrence failed. In applying the principles of deterrence theory, and particularly in evaluating evidence concerning the effects of bad consequences, therefore, it is essential to identify the level at which the sanctions are to have an effect. Data concerning recidivism (usually considered as the proportion of people suffering bad consequences, such as imprisonment or arrest, who repeat the offense), for instance, is applicable only to the issue of specific deterrence. And rise and fall in rates of crime indicate nothing about specific deterrence unless it can be shown that those fluctuations are linked to the career patterns of specific offenders.

Theoretically, then, general deterrence may involve no actual sanctions—only persuasive communications that create the impression in the minds of potential offenders in a population that severe consequences will be quickly forthcoming with an extremely high degree of probability. In effect, general deterrence is more a matter of propaganda than anything else because the facts about bad consequences are usually not favorable toward deterrence. The truth is, the chance of getting caught and punished for most kinds of criminal acts is not very high, and the chance that one will be in a fatal accident driving home intoxicated is actually quite small (Ross, 1982, 1993; National Highway Traffic Safety Administration, 1997). Most people far overestimate those chances, and perhaps as a result of the fear implied by the overestimations, they refrain from the activities (Tittle, 1980a). Deterrence, then, may be largely an illusion. But propaganda seldom stands alone, and messages are always "corrupted" by real facts. To what degree truth actually matters is a key issue for contemporary deterrence theorists, though people who try to use deterrence theory in shaping public policy don't seem to know this is a problem.

Psychic Organization

Deterrence is not only more or less likely depending on the characteristics of potential negative consequences, but it is contingent on the psychic organization that individuals bring to situations. People differ with respect to the things they fear, making some consequences very severe for some individuals but not at all costly for others. They differ in their cognitive abilities, which make them more or less sensitive to threats and potential bad consequences. They differ in their access to information and in their abilities to process it effectively, making threats more or less effective. They differ in their abilities to restrain their behaviors, making some more deterrable than others. Finally, they differ in moral beliefs that make deterrence less relevant.

What People Fear

The original utilitarian philosophy out of which deterrence theory grew assumed that all people fear the same things—particularly loss of liberty—or at least that most people feared the same things. We now theorize that what people fear varies greatly. Even though there are central tendencies indicating that most people fear things like death, being mutilated, and physical pain, there is reason to believe that even those fears are not universal. Many religious people believe that the afterlife is preferable to the present life, so death is a precursor to great rewards. For such people, possible death as a consequence of some action makes it more, not less, attractive, and it invites martyrdom rather than conformity. The possibility of martyrdom is one reason that laws prescribing death penalties for airplane hijackers, revolutionary terrorists, and religious fanatics often do not work (Chauncey, 1975). Moreover, as indicated in Chapter 3, quite a few people seek death because they find life so unpleasant. In addition, evidence suggests that many deaths presumably from accidents are really suicides (Phillips, 1977, 1979). Similarly, there are people who mutilate themselves and inflict pain on their own bodies—some apparently enjoying it immensely (called masochists). Finally, although most people are afraid of serpents, there are some who hardly fear them at all. Indeed, professional handlers and religious cults using snakes to test faith (La Barre, 1969) could hardly be deterred from misbehavior by a fear of snakes. Therefore, modern deterrence theory contends that deviance occurs when consequences that would be *subjectively* undesirable are absent, and it recognizes that what is subjectively undesirable must be established and explained independently of the deterrence process.

Perceptual Ability

As we noted earlier, the accuracy with which people perceive the chances of experiencing undesirable consequences varies greatly from one person to the next, and it strongly influences whether deterrence occurs. The effects of misperception are not always in the same direction, however, because accurate perception of low-probability outcomes or inaccurate perceptions of high-probability outcomes can upset deterrence, just as inaccurate perception of low-probability outcomes and accurate perception of high-probability events can enhance it. Since there is nothing about deterrence theory itself that would permit one to explain or predict perceptual ability, the best the theory can do is recognize that whether fear of bad consequences determines conformity is highly conditional. In effect, the operative postulate really is that deviance occurs when an individual's perceptual processes merge with the realities of situations to create subjective perceptions that the certainty, severity, and celerity of negative consequences are low.

Since the actual probabilities and magnitudes of unpleasant consequences are usually, though not always, low, the fact that most people conform most of the time suggests much misperception, at least if fear of consequences is the key to human behavior, as deterrence theory assumes. Indeed, one interesting application of deterrence thinking suggests that social order depends on almost all people mutually sharing a misperception that bad consequences are likely. Nobody knows for sure what others are thinking at any given time (people are collectively afflicted with "pluralistic ignorance"), and theoretically we are afraid to act in ways that will provoke negative responses. Yet in many, perhaps most, situations the assumptions on which we base our actions are false. Imagine four couples playing bridge, and all are bored. Each one, however, thinks the others are enjoying the game and fears that if he or she suggests that they do something else, the others will be offended or will react negatively. So even though all eight people want to do something else, they keep playing bridge.

They are all deterred, but the basis of deterrence is subjective inaccuracy, or "a shell of illusion." Sometimes an individual will break through that shell and discover that the consequences are not as imagined. Theoretically, that person is more likely to risk deviance again, hence the earlier stated proposition that the failure of deterrence reinforces itself. On the other hand, a shell-breaker sometimes finds that what he or she expected might happen, indeed, did happen, but it is too late, and the consequences help restrain others who might doubt that the shell of expectations surrounding them is an illusion. However, an interesting possibility is that in modern society massive exposure to the entertainment media undermines the effects of those realistic shell-breaking episodes.

In TV, movies, and plays many potentially bad consequences are "normalized" and made to appear of no consequence. In effect, the shell of modern illusion is heavily perforated. Yet, breaking through that perforated shell often has consequences that seem "unreal" to violators who have come to imagine that the unreal is real. For example, in mass media portrayals, characters seem to share the idea that if one person pulls a gun on another, the victim is obligated to do whatever the gun wielder says—even if the two are close friends. There is an implicit assumption that the gun handler will shoot, which supposedly enables him or her to control others without in fact intending to shoot them. But what if there is resistance? Indeed, when gun toters encounter resistance, which is in reality quite often, they then *have* to do something (the dynamics of the situation seem to demand it), usually something destructive because the shell of illusion has been penetrated. As a result, much killing evolves from situations where no killing was originally intended.

Information Processing

Another aspect of individuals' psychic organization that affects the deterrence process is information processing, which varies in style and accuracy from one person to another. We have already mentioned that most people do not know how to handle probabilities, and that they judge the chances of events on somewhat irrational bases such as a recent personal experience with some event, knowledge of some catastrophic outcome, or unknown fears (Piattelli-Palmarini, 1994; Plous, 1993). For example, some people are terrified of flying even though they will ride for long distances in automobiles. Yet the probability of being killed in an airplane accident per mile traveled is far less than the probability of a fatal automobile crash. One might imagine that the ability to process information would be directly linked with IQ and/or education, and to some extent it is. However, neither intelligence nor education guarantees objectivity. Indeed, some of the most intelligent and highly educated people, particularly those educated in the humanities, embrace "nonlinear," humanistic modes of reasoning that detract from effective manipulation of probability information. Thus, the deterrence principle again is subject to a number of different conditions.

Commitments

As you learned in Chapter 13, some people are restrained from much deviance by their beliefs that certain acts are immoral. Because they think it is wrong to do those acts, they rarely even contemplate them, and when they do consider committing them, they are restrained by fear of internal censure. For such people, deterrence is largely irrelevant (Burkett and Ward, 1993; Lanza-Kaduce, 1988; Tittle, 1980b). For example, it is not really necessary to provide criminal penalties for eating human flesh. Very few people would do it, even without such sanctions. Therefore, deterrence may be contingent on a person's degree of moral feelings about a particular act—the greater the morality, the lower the chances of deterrence, regardless of the characteristics of sanctions. Despite the effects of morality, many deterrence advocates, particularly economists (Becker, 1968), see behavior as if it were a mechanistic response to tangible costs. Other deterrence theorists, however, are coming to appreciate the interaction between morality and fear of sanctions (Tittle, 1977).

Individual's Attributes

Since modern deterrence theory recognizes that not all people regard consequences as equally likely, costly, or as quickly to occur, it also tries to take account of individual characteristics that affect the deterrent process. Two categories of such circumstances are especially important—personality and demographic features.

Personality

Three personality traits are particularly important in their conditioning effects on deterrence. The first of them is a characteristic sometimes called impulsivity (Wilson and Herrnstein, 1985; Zuckerman, 1994), sometimes weak self-control (Gottfredson and Hirschi, 1990), and sometimes inability to defer gratification. Some people, either because of biological inheritance or early childhood training (see Chapter 13), simply have less ability to restrain their own impulses, even when they want to. Consider two chocolate lovers faced with a dish of chocolate ice cream. Both may know that they should not eat it in order to avoid the bad consequences of weight gain, but one literally has more trouble letting it go than the other. Similarly, some individuals leap at any opportunity for deviant behavior to gratify a momentary desire without thinking about the consequences until later, whereas others are contemplative, reserved, and careful. Obviously, the threat of bad consequences will have different effects on these two individuals, for one will not be as capable as the other of restraining action in the interest of long-range interests while imagining what its costs will be.

A second important difference among people is in their general orientations to life. Some, again perhaps because of early childhood training or of biological inheritance or functioning, are generally optimistic about the future and themselves (Zimring and Hawkins, 1973). They believe that things will work in their favor, that they are lucky. Because they imagine themselves lucky, they discount the risk involved in deviance, and they mentally reduce the magnitude of the potential cost, telling themselves it would not be so bad, they could adjust, or the like. These individuals stand in contrast to the pessimists, who imagine that anything bad that can happen to them will happen. As a result they magnify risks and inflate costs and thus are more deterred by the same set of circumstances that fail to faze the optimist. The optimist, then, is likely to be a gambler who expects to win, while the pessimist is afraid to gamble for fear he or she will surely lose. A good example concerns risky sexual conduct. Optimists imagine that they can have multiple sex partners without using condoms and get away with it, because they are lucky. Pessimists fear even one indiscretion will give them the HIV virus. According to the deterrence theory, even though equal amounts of fear may produce equal conformity, the same circumstances will necessarily produce different amounts of fear for these two individuals, and their behaviors will therefore be different.

Finally, people vary with respect to their sense of mastery over the world and events; some have greater senses of self-efficacy (Bandura, 1997; Gecas, 1989). For whatever reason, some individuals believe they can control their own destinies and so they set out to alter conditions that might constrain them. They have less fear of drug overdoses, getting arrested, losing respect of their families, or getting diseases—because they believe they can control those things through their own efforts. Drug dealers, for instance, generally believe they have skills, a repertoire of tipoff clues and a "sixth" sense that enables them to identify and avoid narcotics officers who would arrest them (Jacobs, 1993, 1996). Many of them are wrong, of course, but their belief encourages them to ignore risk. On the other end of the continuum are individuals with low self-efficacy who think they are powerless in the face of the forces that control their lives. They do not believe they can do anything about risk factors, so they avoid doing things that might result in bad consequences. Some of these individuals are highly deterrable because they overestimate risk, seeing fate everywhere. Others with low self-efficacy proceed to gratify themselves despite risk because they figure the dark forces of nature will get them anyway, no matter what they do. Clearly, then, the operation of fear is not straightforward; it depends on whether people think they can be efficacious in controlling a situation. But even then, the effects are not the same for all who lack efficacy.

Demographic Traits

While individual personality characteristics intervene to make some individuals more deterrable than others, some characteristics of individuals are so common among those who share demographic status that there is good reason to theorize that whole categories of individuals are more or less deterrable. Although the evidence on this point is contradictory, there is reason to imagine that females as a group are more likely to perceive high risk of bad consequences, especially social consequences; to be more fearful of those outcomes; and thereby to be more deterred (Hagan et al., 1985; Richards and Tittle, 1981; Tittle, 1980b). It is likely that the female role makes it more costly to transgress social convention and/or because females are trained to be observant of social nuances that males ignore.

There is also evidence to suggest that young people are less influenced by some threats of bad consequences than are adults (Grasmick and Milligan, 1976; Sigelman and Sigelman, 1976; but see Tittle, 1980b:296–299). It is often said by adults, particularly in speaking of their children, that young people, especially adolescents, think they can "dodge bullets" (Claster, 1967). For whatever reason, young folks either do not perceive the risks of death, disease, or physical injury as intensely as adults, or they discount those risks as they apply to themselves. However, it is also probably true that youths are more sensitive to negative social reactions from their peers than are adults. So the interactions of age with fear are not all in one direction.

Situational Variations

Deterrence theorists also recognize that fear will probably be more or less operative depending on social circumstances. Among the things that might make a difference are (1) how various kinds of deviance are viewed in the situation by the participants, as well as by the members of the surrounding social environment, (2) the extent to which others share one's perceptions of the likelihood and severity of potential bad consequences, (3) whether those who are looked up to as role models ignore or act in conformity with shared ideas about consequences, and (4) the extent to which the participants in social interaction are bonded strongly or weakly to each other.

Type of Deviance

Fear is not always a factor when a person is contemplating deviance. Some deviance may be regarded as very wrong by one person contemplating it but not so wrong by others. It is possible that individuals' own moral feelings about some act color their perception of the consequences of doing it, independently of what others in fact might do (Etzioni, 1988; Tittle, 1980b; Warr, 1989). And if most people think some act is very wrong, an individual contemplating that act might well be more fearful of the consequences than if others regard it as trivial, independent of actual probabilities of response. Hence serious acts, so regarded either objectively or subjectively, may be more deterrable than trivial ones, even if they actually carry equal consequences, because the psychological sense of wrongness may itself generate fear.

On the other hand, some theorists, even the original utilitarians, have argued that deterrence depends on the correspondence between the seriousness of an act and the associated bad consequences (Zimring and Hawkins, 1973). When the two are out of sync, in either direction, it presumably upsets the deterrent equation because the human psyche seeks balance, or reasonableness. If a teacher were to prescribe imprisonment for one instance of academic cheating or if the cost of robbing a bank were a hundred-dollar fine, deterrence presumably would not work well, even if the chances of the penalty being imposed were equal and very high in both cases. A sense of "injustice" would supposedly intervene to cause mass protest, possibly in the form of increased violation.

Shared Perceptions

Sociologists and social psychologists have amassed much evidence concerning "group" effects that supersede individual inclinations (Kiesler and Kiesler, 1969; Nisbett and Ross, 1980). In many instances, shared group expectations, attitudes, or inclinations come to have more effect than individual personality, perceptual ability, morality, or demographic traits. And so it is with fear. A man may be much afraid of bad consequences, but in a group where others are not afraid, he will undertake the behavior anyway (Parker and Grasmick, 1979). Sometimes this undertaking occurs because of group "pressure" that persuades the man to act against his own best judgment, but often it is because his own judgments about reality become colored by perceptions of how others view it (Cialdini and Trost, 1998; Latane and Wolf, 1981). A woman may think that using cocaine is dangerous, but if her friends say and act as if it isn't, that woman may come to doubt her own fear. The opposite situation is also likely—fear shared within a group may create fear in an individual that did not exist before. Hence, although much deterrent thinking concerns individual phenomena, contemporary theorists note the powerful influence of group context. The operative principles are that fear of certain, severe, and quick bad consequences produce conformity, and that effect is enhanced when individuals' fears match those of their peer group.

Role Models

Potential bad consequences are thought to have more effect when people in high-status, respected, admired positions act according to the norms and act as if the potential bad consequences matter (Akers, 1985; Bandura, 1973, 1977; Bandura and Walters, 1963). Since human beings can learn from watching others or from imagining what the others are thinking, it is clear that the deterrence process is not always self-contained within individuals. If important people in a social group are not affected by potential bad consequences, many will observe them and take a lesson from them. The dangers of smoking, for example, which are well established, are ignored when successful, attractive, admired people such as baseball stars, famous actors, or political leaders smoke. The action of these admired people both mitigates the fear of bad consequences and makes the perceived payoff seem to override the risk. Deterrence, then, theoretically is cumulative; the greater its prevalence, particularly among role models, the greater its power. And the principle works in reverse as well; the less effective threatened fear is, especially among role models, the less its power becomes.

Social Bonding

Finally, outcomes may be influenced by the social integration of groups to which the individual belongs (Petee et al., 1994). Clearly, some kind of sanctions—informal social sanctions—and shared perceptions about various other kinds of consequences are directly linked to the strength of social bonds in groups (Horwitz, 1990). The more closely linked people are, the more they fear how others will react to their behavior—even how others will react if they disagree with them about the chances of various outcomes. Not only that, but whether sanctions have any effect at all, even when perceptions about them are favorable toward deterrence, probably depends on group support or influence (Cialdini and Trost, 1998).

Most deterrence theorists now acknowledge that most behavior is group linked. Individuals rarely act as isolated entities. And behavior that occurs in groups is not the same as behavior by an individual acting and thinking alone. Hence, all the principles of deterrence must be modified in light of whether the individual is functioning in isolation or as a member of a group, especially a tight-knit group. Interestingly, most people who want to use the principles of deterrence to control deviant behavior fail to recognize this tenet of contemporary deterrence theory. The law, for example, prescribes penalties directed toward individuals even though most criminal acts (indeed most deviant acts) are undertaken in groups (Reiss, 1986). According to lawmakers, terrorists and hijackers, for instance, are supposedly stopped by penalties oriented toward individuals, as are white-collar deviants. Yet we know that the demands placed on individual members of terrorist groups and on operatives for business organizations override individual concerns. Many criminal laws, therefore, do not work, at least partly because deterrence is misdirected.

Summary and Critique

Deterrence theory contends that since people are naturally inclined toward self-gratification, and since most deviance is gratifying, deviance results whenever there is little fear of bad consequences. The major assumption of the theory is that fear is the primary force in human behavior. Contemporary versions of the argument, however, attempt to take into account a large number of things that influence the processes by which fear is generated and acted upon. Indeed, what at first glance appears to be an unadulterated, ever-ready principle, and what many laypersons who want to use that principle think is self-evidently simple, is in reality quite complicated. Rather than setting forth a straightforward, universal, all-purpose principle about the effects of bad consequences, contemporary deterrence theory sets forth a highly conditionalized set of explanatory principles. The conditions concern characteristics of potential consequences, such as certainty and severity and objective and subjective features; mental functioning of the individual who is supposedly affected by the absence of bad consequences; other attributes of individuals, such as their personalities; and features of situations such as the extent to which ideas about costs are shared by participants. The best summary of the theory now is that fear of consequences sometimes, under some conditions, has some effects for some people.

After escaping research attention for many decades, hypotheses from deterrence theory began to be systematically investigated in the 1960s, and deterrence has been the focus of much empirical work during the past thirty years (for reviews, see Nagin, 1998; Paternoster, 1987). Indeed, reviewing the volume and complexity of that research would require a book in and of itself. Suffice it here to say that this extensive research can be interpreted in different ways. On one hand it has confirmed the credibility of the deterrent explanation by showing that it at least has to be taken seriously. This was an important achievement because prior to the mid-1960s scholars generally disputed the effects of threats of bad consequences despite the popularity of that belief among the lay public, who seemed to have total faith in fear as an explanation for behavior. However, as a result of the credibility of deterrence having been established by research, a contingent of scholars fell in love with the deterrence principle and joined political figures in promoting and extending its application for the solution of many kinds of public and social problems. As a result, serious proposals are now entertained to prevent juvenile delinquency by incarcerating, and even executing, younger and younger offenders (Moore and Wakeling, 1997; Singer, 1996); to stop teen pregnancy by forcing young mothers to forego schooling to care for their babies (Horowitz, 1995); to reduce welfare rolls by making everybody, including children, work at whatever jobs are offered, no matter how dangerous, difficult, or unpleasant (Rose, 1995; Shragge, 1997; Wilson, 1993); and to deal with adult crime by ever harsher sentences, including longer periods of incarceration with fewer amenities, humiliation through publicly visible work on chain gangs, and death (Durham, 1994; Gorman, 1997; Tonry and Hatlestad, 1997). And, of course, U.S. foreign policy has almost always been founded on the principle of deterrence, which is to try to force other nations to do what the U.S. government wants by threats of bad consequences—particularly the threat of total annihilation for those nations regarded as complete enemies.

The collage of research over the past thirty years has, however, challenged the generality and potency of deterrence (Blumstein et al., 1978; for contrary views, see Cook, 1980, and Nagin, 1998). In particular, it has undermined the notion that fear is the main mover of human behavior, and it has shown that bad consequences can have contradictory effects. Sometimes anticipated bad consequences deter deviance, sometimes they are irrelevant to deviance, and sometimes they actually generate more deviance (Sherman,

Deviance in Everyday Life

The chain gang returns. Very few Americans are old enough to have witnessed the appearance of chain gangs on state and local highways, but many of us have seen what they were like in movies. Chain gangs were popular forms of punishment, generally in Southern states, in which convicted defendants were literally chained together with leg irons and forced to work in groups. At first, chain gangs were used for road building at the beginning of the automobile age; then they were used for cutting grass and picking up trash along highways and county roads. They were watched over sometimes by armed authorities in motor vehicles or on horseback, other times by inmate "trustees." Although chain gangs were last used by the state of Alabama in the early 1960s, they are making a comeback in today's "get tough" on crime political world. In May of 1995, Alabama became the first state to reinstate the use of chain gangs. Then governor of Alabama, Fob James, first suggested the idea of bringing back chain gangs on a radio talk show during his political campaign for the state house. Alabama has over 300 inmates in a special chain gang prison dorm. Five inmates are chained together with leg irons and work on Alabama highways for twelve hours a day. They wear white uniforms with the words "Chain Gang" written in black. Other states have followed Alabama's lead and have implemented their own chain gangs (Florida, Arizona), and several others are considering it (Michigan, Colorado).

1993; Tittle, 1975). In fact, inconsistent results have been so powerful that separate theories to explain varied effects have emerged (they are reviewed in other chapters). Such results are the basis of the observation at the beginning of this discussion of deterrence theory that there is a wide gap between confidence in the effects of fear and the facts. We also noted that the pervasiveness of unrefined deterrent principles in the cultural and institutional structures of U.S. life also defies logic, and that ostensible commitment to them is inconsistent with the way in which people so committed conduct their own affairs. Let's consider, first, the logic.

A major assumption of the unmitigated deterrence argument seems to be that everybody is strongly motivated toward deviant behavior, so it is necessary to make deviance costly lest we all do it. Yet it is probably obvious to you that motivation for any specific form of deviance is highly variable from individual to individual and situation to situation. Clearly, most people have no interest at all in suicide, rape, or bizarre behaviors indicative of mental illness. For behaviors like theft, drug usage, and swinging, which seemingly have inherent rewards, individuals differ in their motivations to do them. And even when an individual is sometimes motivated toward one or another form of deviance, the strength of that motivation is not constant. You, for instance, might be tempted to use marijuana or abuse alcohol at a party even though those activities might not be very attractive most of the time. Hence it is not reasonable to imagine that deviance of all types would flourish in all circumstances if bad consequences were not in place.

On the other hand, gross deterrence thinking is illogical in an opposite way. It overlooks the possibility that motivation for deviance is sometimes so strong that potential bad consequences are no barrier. Hence terrorists are often so bent on achieving their goals that threats of death or other costs are irrelevant; religious adherents sometimes gladly sacrifice their lives and fortunes in affirming faith; and the needs of teenage males to assert their masculine claims through daring acts are usually so powerful that danger and risk are minor concerns. In other words, much human behavior is regulated by

Deviance in Everyday Life

Cutting down on your risks? Many people want to cut down on behaviors that result in bad side effects. In doing so, however, they often unknowingly create other risks. For example, air bags are in cars to protect people in collisions, and they do. But a deployed air bag can cause serious, even fatal injury to a child in a backward-looking car seat placed in the front seat of the car. Love those non-fat potato chips and cookies? Health researchers have found that people eat more of those no-fat products, thinking that they are safe, forgetting that they contain a lot of calories and salt, they often cause stomach distress, and can prevent you from eating healthier snacks like fruit. To protect teenagers, many educators suggest providing them with education about safe sex and condoms. Some argue that such a policy will only encourage sexual activity, under the belief that it is "safe," leading to unwanted pregnancies (since condoms are not 100 percent effective). Some research has shown that people who use sunscreen have a higher risk of skin cancer than those who do not. Does sunscreen cause cancer? Probably not. But perhaps those who use sunscreen think that it is safe for them to be out in the sun, and they stay exposed to the sun's rays longer than they should.

active impulses, not restraining fears. If it were not true, soldiers would not rush enemy machine gun emplacements where death and injury, both surely among the worst of consequences, are highly likely with great celerity; parents would not face mad dogs to protect their children; family members would not, out of a sense of love and duty, care for chronically sick relatives at great personal inconvenience and cost (Etzioni, 1988); and lovers would not climb mountains in search of edelweiss.

Third, even if cost were the premier element in human conduct, the deterrence notion that external costs are the most salient would not withstand examination. As noted before, some, perhaps most, people have an internalized sense of morality, so the wrongness of some behaviors is firmly entrenched in their psychic structures (Warr, 1989). Individuals with such morality cannot bring themselves to violate internalized rules even when they have strong desires to do so and there are virtually no chances of being caught and punished (Burkett and Ward, 1993; Decker et al., 1993; Silberman, 1976). They chose to refrain from performing the behavior because their emotional systems would inflict a heavy cost in feelings of guilt and loss of self-esteem. Does anyone seriously worry that people in modern, Western societies would start eating each other if there were no external penalties for that act? Actually, most people in such societies cannot even eat animals like cocker spaniels or Dalmatians that have human-like qualities, such as the ability to return love. They literally become physically ill from the thought. And if conscience is not real, how can we explain why many soldiers in combat fail to fire their weapons and juries fail to convict on convincing evidence when capital punishment is a possibility? Apparently, internal constraints against killing outweigh the demands of the situation. Or, how do we account for the fact that some drivers come to a complete halt at stop signs marking intersections of west Texas highways where they can see for miles in every direction?

Fourth, the deterrence notion more or less assumes that opportunities for deviance are constant from individual to individual and from situation to situation. Actually, opportunity is variable and, even when potentially present, it often shows itself only when the individual actively seeks it. Some people yearn a whole lifetime for the chance to pursue an extramarital encounter or to steal a million dollars, but they never meet a willing sexual co-conspirator or find themselves in a position to purloin that much money. Moreover, some people who are not integrated into the street life but want to use drugs have to go to a lot of trouble to find the drugs. The fact is, many people conform because they simply do not have the opportunity to do otherwise. The likelihood of experiencing bad consequences is irrelevant to them, so we would not explain the absence of deviance entirely in terms of the absence of potential bad consequences even if the theory of deterrence were generally accurate.

Finally, a fatal flaw of most deterrence thinking is the assumption that people act rationally most of the time. Actually, common sense and scientific evidence suggest that human beings have to work at being rational; it does not come easily. In many circumstances, emotion rules, and when emotion prevails, it clouds out thoughts of bad consequences on which deterrence is based. Everybody behaves stupidly from time to time; all people act on impulse sometimes; everybody occasionally becomes embarrassed, ashamed, humiliated, or angry; and everybody experiences pain, hunger, disappointment, intoxication (from drugs, alcohol, or various physical sicknesses), sleepiness, stress, or tiredness, all of which can lead to behaviors that are poorly thought out. Most of you can probably recall being so angry or so overcome with passion that you basically did not care what the consequences of your acts were; certainly, many people who have been in fights or who have been guilty of sexual indiscretions can relate to this.

Thus, deterrence theory, particularly as applied in vulgar, unmitigated ways, is plagued by its assumptions about motivation for deviance, by its neglect of internal constraints, and by its overestimation of the rationality of human behavior. And ironically, despite the apparent belief in deterrence, most people do not employ it for things that matter in their own lives. Parents, for instance, know they cannot effectively raise their children with punishment alone. Indeed, good parents develop relationships with their children based on love and respect, not fear. Teachers know that students behave better and learn more when they are enticed by the joy of learning than when they are threatened with punishment. Employers know that workers do more and better work when they feel good about what they are doing, when they are consulted about operations, and when they are well paid and appreciated than when they are under constant threats of being fired or suffering other bad consequences. Why, then, when asked, do people say they believe that fear of bad consequences is the best way to achieve social goals?

Social Control and Its Mechanisms

Social control theory, sometimes called social bonds theory, was previewed in Chapter 10 where we described various ad hoc explanations for the general negative relationship between deviance and social attachment. This theory, like most others we examine, does not exist in one coherent, systematic statement, but instead is expressed in a variety of "fragments" by numerous scholars (Briar and Piliavin, 1965; Nye, 1958; Reckless, 1967; Reiss, 1951; Toby, 1957). Nevertheless, by considering these fragments simultaneously, we can grasp a general theoretical account with distinguishing features. First, all the partial statements share common conceptual ground in their central notion that social relationships bind the person and restrain deviant impulses to such an extent that misbehavior can be explained as a failure of constraint, or as an absence of such binding social relationships.

Second, in one way or another each version or fragment of social control theory downplays the strength of motivation for deviance in favor of constraints. Some versions assume that most people find deviance inherently desirable or gratifying and because of that they are naturally motivated to engage in it. Other versions make some attempt to explain variations among individuals in motivation for deviance, but they assume control to be more important than deviant impulse in accounting for actual misbehavior.

Social control theory contends that social relationships represent conduits through which participants in those relationships can influence the behavior of each other. Moreover, whenever the participants in a social relationship or a network of social relationships share norms of behavior, they are likely to use the inherent mechanisms of control collectively to ensure conformity. Those mechanisms of control may also come into play automatically, without direct intent by network members. Hence the basic postulate is that individuals' likelihood of deviance from a norm varies inversely with their integration with the group embracing that norm. Or alternatively stated, individuals' probability of conformity to a group's norms varies directly with their social integration.

Clearly, whether social control results in conformity or deviance from the norms of a larger social group, such as a society, in which some smaller network of relationships might be embedded, depends on whether the norms of the smaller network are conforming or deviant relative to those of the larger society. Consequently, social control theory explains both conformity and deviance. If a sub-network (such as a delinquent gang) embraces deviant norms (deviant from the point of view of a larger, overarching network), such as expectations that members will on occasion steal or vandalize, then integration in that network will produce conformity to its internal norms (gang members will likely steal or vandalize), but it will produce deviance from the norms of the larger network (which prohibits stealing and vandalism). However, if a person is integrated into the larger network, then that integration will produce conformity to its norms (a youth bonded to a conventional family, school, church, and neighborhood will not likely steal or vandalize). To apply social control theory, then, one must specify what group's norms are at issue. One cannot simply assert that social integration produces conformity and expect to derive meaningful explanations.

The absence of integration into any group, on the other hand, is likely to lead to deviance from the norms of all groups. The effect of social isolation on deviance, however, will be less than the effect that social integration into a deviant group has on the production of deviance from the norms of the larger society. For example, youths who are not involved with conventional institutions will be subject to temptations of the moment, so they might steal or vandalize even though not affiliated with a gang that approves or expects it. At the same time, they will not be bound by the rules of the gang, so their behavior will generally be deviant from gang norms as well. Yet, they are less likely to vandalize, steal, or fight than if they were tightly knit with a gang that expected them to do those things and used the mechanisms of social control to induce them to follow the group's expectations.

Hence the nature of the normative system characteristic of any group with which one might be integrated, as well as the degree of integration into either overarching or sub-networks, is crucial in applying the theory of social control. Scholars usually simplify this situation by stating the main proposition of control theory as implying that social bonding with, or integration into, *conventional* networks produces conformity (meaning conformity to conventional or society-wide norms), and lack of integration into conventional networks (either because integrated into an unconventional network or not integrated at all) leads to deviance (from conventionality).

Accounts of exactly why and how such conformity (or absence of deviance) comes about, or inheres in social cohesion, vary from theorist to theorist, but there are six distinct themes. Most of these themes imply that deviance by an integrated person is avoided because it is potentially costly in one way or another. These six mechanisms by which social integration produces conformity can be divided into indirect and direct categories, and some of them, under various conditions, can operate either directly or indirectly.

Indirect Mechanisms

Self-Concept

Beginning with Emile Durkheim (1951 [1897]), the famous French sociologist who is generally regarded as the father of control theory, various theorists (Briar and Piliavin, 1965; Matsueda, 1992; Reckless, 1967; Reckless et al., 1957; Reiss, 1951) have contended that socially bonded individuals draw their main sense of meaning in life and their sense of self from social groups. Since for such individuals, violating the rules of their group jeopardizes a fundamental source of meaning, deviance potentially threatens their psychic organization and sense of well-being (see Heimer and Matsueda, 1994; Matsueda, 1992; Matsueda and Heimer, 1997). For instance, if a woman thinks of herself as a good person, honest, thoughtful, respectful of the rights of others, dependable, and trustworthy, she runs a great risk of psychic damage by doing things that others regard as bad, dishonest, insensitive, disrespectful, or unreliable. The risk is said to emerge because self-concepts grow out of, and are dependent on, the reactions of others (see Chapter 12). If a man regards himself as intelligent, but other people with whom he interacts react to him as if he were stupid, he experiences pain and, in the face of continuing social response suggesting his stupidity, he finds it difficult to sustain the notion that he is intelligent.

An integrated person, then, is, in Durkheim's sense, one with society, both unlikely to commit suicide for selfish or desperate reasons (which he called egoistic suicide), and more likely to commit suicide in the interest of the group (which he called altruistic suicide). Everything that a person is, or wants to be, is bound up with that social identity, so it is unusual for such people to even contemplate deviance. Even when deviance is contemplated by an integrated person, he or she is likely to refrain from acting on those thoughts, because the potential reaction of others will be perceived as very punishing or costly to his or her sense of self. Since the process involving contemplation of deviance, anticipation of a self-jeopardizing response from others, and decision to avoid deviance takes place in the mind of the potential deviant, the effects can be regarded as indirect.

One might wonder, however, how such a psychic process could be an instance of external causal influence, and how it could be regarded as social rather than individualistic. It is external and social because the activator of, or stimulus for, the process is outside the person, in the social context, which is composed of people whose reactions would constitute negative sanctions. Thus, members of the group within which the individual in question is integrated hold power over him or her in that their potential reaction controls his or her behavior. Later we will see that this indirect control potential can be transformed into actual direct control when individuals actively remind the person of aspects of self that they know or assume he or she cares about and about which their response will be relevant.

Social Approval

A second mechanism through which social integration theoretically brings about conformity rests on the concern that integrated individuals have to preserve their place in the group (Braithwaite, 1989; Briar and Piliavin, 1965; Felson, 1986; Henry and Short, 1954; Horwitz, 1990; Nye, 1958; Reckless, 1967; Toby, 1957). When individuals are tightly fitted into social networks, particularly if those social networks are effective in meeting the person's needs for acceptance, support, prestige, and human response, those individuals come to depend on the group. Under such circumstances, the person has a strong incentive to seek the approval of others. And since group acceptance and confirmation is largely contingent on conformity to group expectations, those who contemplate violations of group norms face the prospect of losing something important. This anticipation of potential disapproval by other members of a group then serves as a constraint on deviance. And as before, since curtailment of deviance occurs through a process by which the individual psychically anticipates potential social disapproval, it can be thought of as an indirect effect of an element residing in the social environment external to the individual. On occasion, of course, this indirect effect can become a direct effect if group members consciously manipulate a person's behavior by threatening disapproval.

Consider one example of how this process works. You have a set of friends with whom you hang out. You like them and they like you. Together you have a lot of fun and you depend on each other. That group is important to you because within it you feel good, you have a good reputation, and others look up to you and accept you as a worthy person. What do you think would happen if you were to steal some money from one of the group members, and the rest were to find out about it? Very likely it would jeopardize your position in that group and undermine your relationship with those friends. They would thereafter be less willing to hang out with you for fear you might steal again; they would likely lose some respect for you; and they would not want you around because others outside the group might think that all of them are thieves like you. Your thievery would, therefore, completely destroy your place in the group. Since you like that group, you do not want to risk its disapproval. Of course, you probably know or sense this, so if you happen to be tempted to steal from another group member, you will probably curb the impulse. That is the essence of indirect social control.

Investments

A third mechanism of constraint linked to social bonds and group integration has to do with the sacrifices a person makes for future payoffs (Briar and Piliavin, 1965; Felson, 1986; Hirschi, 1969; Reckless, 1967; Toby, 1957). Most people have long-range goals they wish to attain. If they are highly integrated within conventional society, their goals might include stable and enjoyable employment, material possessions, loving mates, children, or influence over others. Usually people's goals emerge out of the cultural patterns of particular groups of which they are a part, and achievement of the goals is linked to the prescribed norms of those groups. At any given time, then, people will have invested more or less effort, time, and resources in the achievement of goals acceptable within the group. If these people violate the rules of the group, they run the risk of losing the payoff. And the anticipation of that possibility is one of the things that keeps integrated people straight.

Think of a woman who has graduated from college and is an accountant in a business where she expects ultimately to earn promotion to a top position. This woman is married, with two children, and with her husband owns a house and two automobiles. To get to this place in life, she has studied hard, deferred her material gratification to save money for buying property, endured the pain of childbirth, and sacrificed her freedom by marrying. What would happen to her if she were to embezzle funds from the company where she works? Certainly, there is a chance of arrest and incarceration—formal sanctions that might deter her. But, even without arrest and incarceration, she might get caught by company officials, and as a result lose her job, imperil the chances of acquiring another similar job (because other employers will find out about her unreliability), and possibly lose her property as well (as part of a financial settlement to repay the company). Her ability to affect events in her community will be greatly diminished because she will no longer be in a position of influence. Furthermore, her husband may be embarrassed by the incident and decide to end the marriage, vying to gain custody of the children since the wife appears to be an unfit parent. Because of these possibilities, such a woman is likely to refrain from embezzlement and most other kinds of deviance. In effect, the greater her investments in the institutions of conventional society, the more she has to lose by deviant behavior; and since time, energy, and resources expended following the institutional paths prescribed by the group reflect the degree of integration with the group, one can say that one mechanism by which integration produces conformity is the chance of losing out on one's investment of social and material capital (Nagin and Paternoster, 1994).

Caring

When individuals are deeply affiliated with others in social networks, they usually grow to have affection for the people with whom they are linked and to care about the welfare of the collectivity they populate. Since deviant behavior potentially brings sadness, harm, disappointment, or material cost to loved ones, or to groups about which one cares, an integrated person usually tries to avoid such behavior in order to prevent the bad effects for others. Hence, the potential cost to others that an individual's behavior might bring about can serve as a potent indirect control device. It is indirect because restraint comes from the imagination of the potential deviant—of how his behavior will affect others. His consideration of such consequences is usually unknown to, and not directly intended by, those whose well-being is at the center of the process. For instance, young people who conform in the face of enormous pressure from peers often do so because they do not want to behave in ways they imagine will disappoint their parents or religious associates, they do not want to bring shame on their families, or they do not want to behave in ways they imagine will hurt significant others who might be distressed, saddened, or grieved. This kind of affection and concern is rooted in strong social ties.

Although this mechanism might appear similar to those discussed before—jeopardizing the sources of one's self-concept, fearing social disapproval, or endangering one's position in the group—there is a crucial difference. The mechanisms discussed previously are selfishly oriented. When integrated people conform to avoid negative reactions from others that might upset their psychic organization or to avoid responses from others that would undermine their positions in the group, they are behaving to benefit themselves. But when conformity is based on caring, the person conforms because he or she genuinely is concerned about others and does not want her or his behavior to be a burden to them, psychically, emotionally, or materially. Indeed, even when there is little possibility of personal cost, a person who cares about others is nevertheless likely to refrain from acts that might harm them.

Beliefs

A final indirect means by which social alliances control a person's potential deviant behavior turns on the tendency for people who are integrated in social networks to incorporate the norms or the values of those groups into their own internal moral systems (Braithwaite, 1989; Felson, 1986; Hirschi, 1969; Nye, 1958; Reckless, 1967; Reiss, 1951). The process by which this incorporation occurs, usually called "internalization," is discussed in Chapter 13, but here it is sufficient to note that an internalized norm or value is one that is so strongly instilled in the psychic structure of an individual that he or she feels emotional pain when the rule or principle is breached. These feelings of guilt, or emotional distress at having done wrong, can be invoked directly by others who remind the individual of the harm or badness of his or her act, or they can be indirectly generated when the offender observes the harmful consequences of his act or cognitively imagines how his acts would, or might, have caused harm. Strongly internalized beliefs, or moral values, may also affect deviance by minimizing the chances that one will contemplate deviant acts. But at the moment we are concerned with the restraining effect of potential guilt, particularly when invoked indirectly.

One of the most astute analyses of the processes of indirect social control keyed to guilt is that by John Braithwaite (1989), who emphasizes the usefulness of gossip for shaming. Gossip is talk among a group of people concerning wrong done, or presumed to have been done, by an individual who is not present. Knowledge of such talk, or believing that such talk is going on, invokes remorse in the object of the gossip—provided he or she is integrated in the group and has internalized their values. Feeling emotional distress at having done wrong or having been responsible for a bad outcome, in response to the provocation or actions of others, is called shame. In the case of gossip, the gossipers do not necessarily intend to influence the feelings of the wrongdoer since they speak of the alleged evil behind his or her back. Nevertheless, gossip has that effect because the objects of gossip know—from their own experience of having observed or having personally participated in gossip about previous cases of misbehavior—that talk about their wrongdoing will occur if they do wrong. And because the members of tight-knit groups can anticipate that gossip will provoke painful emotions of guilt, they are less likely to engage in deviance in the first place. Thus, gossip is a key tool of social control in integrated groups.

Deviance in Everyday Life

The use of gossip and then direct manipulation of social control is vividly seen in an example Malinowski (1926) provides for the Trobriand Island culture. It seems a youth had violated clan custom by engaging in sexual relations with his maternal cousin. While there apparently had been considerable gossip about the couple, most villagers did little about it—that is, until the girl's jilted ex-lover went public with the accusation against the couple. The accused boy thereupon got dressed in ceremonial clothing, climbed a sixty-foot coconut tree, and publicly explained the rationale of his actions before plunging to his death. In this case, and apparently in many other instances of clan incest among the Trobriand people, gossip does not necessarily bring about public condemnation and punishment, despite the cultural taboo against incest. Only when an aggrieved takes direct action is there any substantial consequence to the deviant act.

Imagine a member of a cohesive group in which the belief that people are morally obligated to pay their debts is widely shared. Because of closeness with the group, this man deeply believes in paying his debts—so deeply that failing to do so would cause much emotional distress. More than likely this man has on many occasions heard others in the group talk about how bad such and such a person is or what an awful thing it was when someone did not pay debts. And probably this individual has personally participated in such talk. By hearing and doing gossip, he has developed a sense of what happens to those who renege—they are shamed indirectly. As a result, this man will probably vow never to be the object of such talk and so will strive to pay his debts. People like this are conformists because of social control based on anticipated shame.

Now, imagine that an integrated person like this, who has heard and participated in gossip, inadvertently forgets a debt. Later realization of the error will produce shame because he knows from previous personal experience that others are gossiping about him. Realization of the violation, even though unintentional, nevertheless invokes feelings of remorse that are painful. An actual experience of shame like this, though indirect, will likely lead to quick correction of the oversight and to strengthening of resolve to avoid it in the future.

Summary

Each of the mechanisms of social control, rooted respectively in self-concepts, group approval, investments, caring, and beliefs, is dependent on an internal state or process but is responsive to what happens in the external social environment. The constraint stemming from each is an instance of indirect social control, and it is a product of closeness between the individual and other members of a social network. The resulting blockage of deviance is social because the ultimate source of constraint is what happens, or is anticipated might happen, in the external environment, and it is indirect because the activating agents in the external environment do not necessarily intend the outcome, nor are they necessarily proximately involved in bringing about constraint. Some of these elements may be implicated in direct social control, as we will see shortly. In addition, there are other mechanisms by which social cohesion directly affects conformity.

Direct Mechanisms

Manipulations

As noted above, some of the mechanisms of indirect social control may be involved directly whenever others intentionally "tweak" them. Such manipulation is often in response to actual deviance and is undertaken to serve as a warning to others (a form of general deterrence) or to stave off future misbehavior by the offender (a form of specific deterrence), but manipulation also helps prevent initial acts of deviance. Manipulation occurs when one or more individuals actually respond in ways that erode potential (or actual) deviants' self-concepts, undermine their positions in the group, jeopardize benefits to be derived from the deviants' investments, shame the people, or provoke their actual or potential concern for somebody about whom they care.

Thus, if you think of yourself as an honest person and others know that, they may, on occasion, invoke that concern in order to get you to do something they want, which in this case is to refrain from deviant behavior. Your mother, for instance, might warn you that it would be dishonest to show a fake ID, or if she knew you had done it, she might declare it to be "so dishonest!" Her purpose would be to stimulate your internal concern for maintaining a meaningful sense of self in the hopes that you would feel psychic strain and decide not to engage in the deviance, or not to engage in it again if the manipulation is in response to an actual misdeed (and possibly as an indirect tweak for your brother who overhears). Or your associates, upon discovering you betrayed a friend, struck your mother, or stole a fellow group member's wallet, might say to your face that they have lost respect for you or that they are not sure they want to hang out with you anymore. Even without your having done any of those things, other group members might inform you directly that they would lose respect for you if you do. And the same direct processes might involve each of the mechanisms discussed before.

Direct manipulation is possible because of the presence and strength of concerns for self, group approval, and caring, and its success is dependent partly on investments in group-linked things and partly on beliefs. Those mechanisms are, in turn, related to the depth of a person's integration into social networks. Moreover, manipulation is most likely to be successful when undertaken by members of the social networks within which one is integrated. Attempted manipulation by members of interpersonal networks is more successful than such efforts by others for several reasons. (1) Network members contribute to the mechanisms that make manipulation possible—they serve as entities about whom the potential deviant cares; they give more meaningful feedback for the potential deviant's self-concept or self-esteem, as well as social approval or disapproval; and they may be allies in the development of the potential deviant's investments and beliefs. (2) They are in better positions to know about the mechanisms and their strengths. (3) They are in close enough proximity to convey face-to-face messages.

A good analogy for this process has been put forth by Felson (1986). He refers to the mechanisms of control as collectively constituting "handles" and potential manipulators as being "handlers" who can grasp the handles in order to control the individual's behavior. Some people have large, visible handles; others have smaller, less visible ones; and still others have no handles (they lack the mechanisms that would make social control possible). And some people are capable of grasping even a small, invisible handle because they know intimately the individual with that unobtrusive handle and are good at manipulations. Others have little ability to grasp and use even large handles. Some mothers can invoke guilt or shame more effectively than others, even when a child has all the necessary prerequisites for being manipulated, and some children have few handles to grasp, even by effective handlers. In addition, circumstances that throw intimately linked people together (such as common residence) or separate them widely in time and space in ongoing fashion (such as members of a family having jobs and other social obligations in different parts of a city) affect the size and visibility of handles as well as the ability of potential handlers to grasp them. As a result, social control is more or less effective in preventing deviance depending on the degree of individuals' integration in groups, the presence and strength of mechanisms of control, and interactional life patterns (what Felson calls routine activities) of individuals and those with whom they are integrated.

Opportunity

Another mechanism by which social integration affects deviance has been identified by Hirschi (1969) and Felson (1986), who both note that individuals who are involved in conventional activities, especially with others like family or church members to whom they are tightly bonded, encounter fewer opportunities for deviance—partly because greater involvement leaves little time for deviance and partly because participation with others in conventional activities exposes one to constant surveillance by those who might prevent deviance. For example, a married man who is working on a construction crew five days a week and piling up lots of overtime, goes camping with his children, goes to PTA meetings, scouts, little league, and church functions nights and weekends, and who is involved in a civic club in which he is frequently attending public meetings and helping in community projects has little time to pursue an affair with another woman, even if he and his wife are not getting along very well. Moreover, he is almost never out of sight and sound of people who would get in the way of such an affair—friends of his wife, his children, church members, and others.

Deviance in Everyday Life

Making sound public policy can be difficult because one does not always know what to do, and what one intends to do may backfire. For example, sometimes trying to reduce deviance by one strategy may be in conflict with another strategy. According to the theory of social bonds, the idea of midnight basketball is a sound idea. It gets high-risk kids involved in a conventional activity for a period of time and is physically draining. According to the social control notion of "involvement," therefore, midnight basketball will reduce delinquent/criminal offending. Midnight basketball leagues were started in 1986 in a community just east of Washington, D.C. According to routine activities theory (see Chapter 11), deviance and crime are more likely when offenders and unguarded targets converge in time and space. Having kids out on the street going to and from basketball courts at midnight will put groups of high-risk kids in interaction with one another at a time of the day when potential targets are vulnerable (vandalizing, stealing cars, mugging). A routine activities theorist, therefore, might discourage the idea of midnight basketball leagues in urban areas as a good strategy to reduce youth crime.

Summary

Social control theory, then, pays little attention to motivation for deviance, assuming that because deviance is gratifying, motivation to do it is equal for everybody, or that it exists with sufficient strength in almost everybody that in the absence of constraint the individual will violate social rules. The central tenet of the theory is that deviance varies inversely with the degree to which an individual is integrated tightly with others in conventional social networks. The mechanisms of such constraint are direct and indirect. They include concerns about maintaining self-concepts, receiving social approval and prestige, protecting investments, caring about others, and avoiding discomforting feelings of guilt. These mechanisms operate indirectly when the person curbs his or her deviant impulses in anticipation of how deviance will affect one of these elements, and they function as direct controls when other people specifically remind the individual of those mechanisms, or when they actually "tweak" one of them. In addition, social bonds help produce conformity because of their effects in reducing opportunities for deviance. This restriction of opportunity comes about because of the time and place obligations of social involvement and because social integration subjects the person to surveillance by others who might disapprove of deviance and act to prevent it.

Source of the Control Mechanisms

Most control advocates begin their explanations of deviance with the condition of social integration (or its absence), taking it as a given. Rarely do they raise and try to answer the further question of why some individuals are more integrated than others. However, a few theorists have raised this question, and some recent developments provide promising leads that may one day be used to elaborate social control theory to provide a more complete theoretical account.

Theoretical answers to the etiology of social integration have encompassed three elements. The first concerns the structure and function of social groups to which the individual is introduced in the formative years. Some argue that a child born into a cohesive, loving primary unit that provides for her or his needs, exercises firm but balanced discipline, and socializes the individual to internalize the rules of the larger society and to feel a sense of alliance with and responsibility for others will have a high probability of becoming strongly integrated (Braithwaite, 1989; Nye, 1958; Reckless, 1967; Reiss, 1951; Toby, 1957). The essential elements for integration, according to these accounts, are (1) a pre-existing socializing agency (such as a family) that is internally cohesive and whose members are integrated with the larger social group, (2) effectiveness of the early socializing unit in providing for the needs of the person so that the individual bonds with the unit and the social group of which it is a part, and (3) effective training of the child to develop a socially useful self-concept, moral standards, socially approved investments, and social responsibility.

A second important factor for producing social integration is the nature of the community in which the primary socializing agency is located. Some societies, or communities, are tight-knit and interdependent (Kephart and Zellner, 1994) while others are not very cohesive. Because the community as a whole helps meet their needs, members of cohesive communities learn early that others care about them. In addition, the institutions of the whole social group link with, and reinforce, the efforts of effective primary socializing units (Braithwaite, 1989). For example, education in Amish society (Hostetler, 1980), an exemplar of community solidarity, not only produces

Deviance in Everyday Life

Is it possible to teach women to become good mothers? Perhaps yes. David Olds and his colleagues (Olds et al., 1997) conducted a randomized experiment in a rural community in New York state in which nurses visited the homes of potential "at-risk" children to provide prenatal care and maternal instruction. In a fifteen-year follow-up, the home visitation project seems to have had a positive impact. Compared with the control group, women who had at-home nursing visitation had fewer subsequent births, fewer months on welfare, fewer incidences of child abuse, fewer drug abuse problems, and fewer arrests.

skills for effective living but it is also designed to shape moral values and commitment to the group as a whole. Such lessons are easier to convey when the individual actually receives the support of the group and feels a sense of caring and acceptance by others. Social cohesion of communities is, in turn, influenced by the conditions of living; whether in large populous aggregates or smaller units, whether there is high geographic mobility, whether the population is homogeneous or heterogeneous, and whether there is a level of technology that influences where and how people work, play, procreate, and fulfill the functions of everyday living (Felson, 1986).

Finally, social integration is influenced by the sequences of choices individuals make, which are somewhat unsystematic and dependent on genetic inheritance, early socialization, and episodic opportunities that emerge (Nagin and Paternoster, 1994). No matter how well a socializing agency, or the larger society of which it is a part, fulfills the conditions usually producing social integration, some individuals exposed to them do not develop strong social bonds. Others, even when exposed to dysfunctional familial and community environments, nevertheless become well integrated in some conventional networks (Sampson and Laub, 1993). For instance, individuals with psychoneurological deficits stemming from brain damage or hormonal deficiencies may be incapable of social bonding (Moffitt, 1990; Moffitt et al., 1994; Raine, 1993). Individuals who fail to make early connections with others may see their alienation accumulate over time as it becomes harder and harder to build social capital. Yet even those who are not well integrated during a large part of their lives may later become so as a result of marriage, employment, or parenthood (Sampson and Laub, 1993) or possibly from religious conversion and affiliation with a community of believers.

Even though control theorists have identified some of the processes that affect the degree of social integration an individual might have, theory about those conditions is not well developed or articulated. For instance, it is not clear why or how some individuals can overcome early conditions unfavorable for integration, nor is it clear when the institutions of a community can make up for, or counteract, the work of early socializing agencies. One task for control theorists, then, is to fill out the theoretical terrain by accounting for the theory's primary causal elements—the social bonds that people have or lack.

Conditions for the Exercise of Social Control

Although the extent to which an individual is integrated into conventional social networks theoretically predicts the absence of deviance for the reasons detailed above, the accuracy of that prediction varies with a number

of conditions that affect how well the mechanisms of social control can operate. The most important of those conditions is the extent to which the groups
within which the individual is integrated are themselves cohesive and interdependent (Horwitz, 1990). This condition is important because social control, even of an integrated individual, requires awareness on his or her part of
potential reactions, a realistic expectation that the anticipated reactions will
be forthcoming, and an absence of conflicting responses, some of which are
controlling in one direction and others in another direction. Such conditions
are most likely to prevail when other people know an individual well, can
keep an eye on him or her, and have an incentive to do so. In other words, social control is most effective for integrated individuals in small homogeneous
groups that serve as exclusive sources for meeting the individual's needs.
(That is, the individual is dependent on the group because of an absence of alternative contexts in which to satisfy socially rooted gratifications.)

The second condition affecting how well social control can be exercised is
the extent to which social life unfolds through close encounters among those
cohesive with each other (Braithwaite, 1989; Felson, 1986). When closely
bonded people are nevertheless separated for large periods of each day or for
long spans of time, during which they are exposed to others with whom they
have few social linkages, social control loses some of its effectiveness. In
modern urban societies, for example, fathers work in one place, mothers another, and children attend school in special locales away from home. Adult
children are usually separated in geographic space from their families of origin (though they may be linked through electronic means). People travel a lot,
and they move over fairly long distances in various modes of transport
throughout a day. All of this produces a certain degree of anonymity, which
allows people to escape surveillance by those who know them. Modern people, especially urban dwellers, interact with relative strangers a good part of
the time. Those relative strangers do not know which handles to manipulate
for control, nor do they want to grasp those handles except to use them for
their own personal expedience. Thus, the greater the extent to which "routine
activities" make it impossible for others to know a great deal about an individual or to invoke the mechanisms of control, the less effective will social
control be.

Social control, then, maximally restrains deviance only: (1) if the individual is bonded sufficiently with conventional social networks to make the
mechanisms of control centering around self, social approval, caring, invest-

---

Deviance in Everyday Life

A group that in the past had very tight control over its members because their
lives were completely integrated into the group was the Shakers. The group originated in Manchester, England, and was a radical branch of the Quakers. The
Shakers were known for their dancing, shouting, and shaking during normally
staid Quaker religious ceremonies (hence the name "Shakers"). They were joined
by one Ann Lees (who shortened her last name to Lee), who added the practice of
celibacy to the group (all four of Ann's children had died in childbirth or soon after
infancy). Persecuted in England, the Shaker sect fled to New York State, where they
established a colony. A complete separation of the genders existed, and all property
was shared by the group. Celibacy meant that the group could not expand its membership by natural fertility. It therefore required expansion by conversion. By the
1840s there were some 6,000 Shakers in the United States. Today there are fewer
than 10.

ments, and conscience potent; (2) the individual is enmeshed in conventional social networks that are cohesive; and (3) the conditions of social life make surveillance and accurate feedback possible.

Summary and Critique

The theory of social control explains deviance as a failure of social restraint. It assumes that everybody is drawn to deviance because deviance is gratifying or rewarding but that only some people act on those desires. Those who express their deviant impulses in actual misdeeds do so because they are more free to do so than are those who conform. Freedom to deviate varies with the weakness or absence of social bonds. When individuals are unconnected with conventional social networks, they have little concern for whether their deviance might threaten their self-concepts or esteem, generate guilt or shame, elicit social disapproval or loss of status in the group, or hurt others about whom they care. In addition, they have few investments that might be jeopardized. Furthermore, they are likely to encounter numerous opportunities for deviance that could take place out of sight and sound of people who might prevent it. This freedom from social bonds that might constrain behavior is thought to be a product of poor childhood socialization or of early enmeshment in a disorganized or weakly integrated community. Lack of social bonds is also influenced by genetic and chance factors. Freedom to deviate also comes about when the potential effects of social bonds are eroded by conditions of life that disperse integrated people in time and space.

Control theory enjoys much popularity and considerable empirical support (examples include: Bellair, 1997; Kempf, 1993; Petee et al., 1994; Sampson, 1991; Sampson and Groves, 1989). It is especially strong because it explains both conformity and deviance, though using the theory effectively requires knowledge of the normative valence of the specific social networks within which an individual is embedded. Despite their strengths, however, control theories do not make full explanation or prediction possible. They are especially challenged by apparent aberrant cases where seemingly well-integrated individuals nevertheless deviate or where relatively unintegrated individuals conform. A major problem is that the theory does not recognize the possibility that motivations for deviance may vary in strength, and that such variation influences both how well the mechanisms of social control operate as well as whether they operate at all. As Braithwaite (1989) notes, various forms of deviance are simply unthinkable for some people, so they refrain out of moral principle (see Etzioni, 1988), regardless of social control. And other forms of deviance are thinkable but not gratifying enough for most people to do them, even without much social control.

The theory also suffers because its various components are not well articulated into a coherent whole. Some mechanisms of control may be more important than others, some may compensate for the absence of others, and some may work in conjunction. The exact relationship among the elements of control is not yet theoretically established, nor is their linkage with the external social environment. Furthermore, theory about why some people are more integrated than others is underdeveloped. Finally, many of the conditions discussed earlier that influence deterrence, such as the individual's perceptual ability, how she or he cognitively processes information, and his or her personality, as well as the characteristics of potential social reactions like certainty, severity, and celerity, also apply to social control mechanisms, but they have largely been ignored by control theorists.

Summary of External Constraint Theories

In this chapter we have discussed two theories that explain deviance as a failure of conditions or mechanisms in the environment external to the individual to restrain the expression of his or her deviant impulses. Deterrence and social control theories both assume that motivation for deviance requires little explanation, that it is omnipresent and capable of being taken for granted, and that it is of sufficient magnitude in almost all people to produce deviance when control is weak. Both theories portray control largely in terms of avoiding potential costs of deviance; neither is well developed, each consisting instead of loosely connected fragments; and both downplay the direct importance of moral concerns and opportunity. Finally, both theories largely ignore the sources of their primary variables.

Deterrence theory deals with potential costs that are thought to be universally painful—physical suffering, financial loss, social rejection, and incarceration—though it recognizes that perceptions about those universals depend on many factors. It focuses heavily on formal sanctions and on the characteristics of sanctions and their cognitive processing, emphasizing the probability or perceived probability, painfulness, and swiftness of sanctions. Social control theory, on the other hand, deals with costs that are highly variable from individual to individual because they are rooted in the nature of the person's relationships with other people. Indeed, the essence of social control theory is to explain variations in costliness, for it is those variations that dictate whether constraint will or will not occur. In addition, social control theory is mainly focused on costs stemming from informal processes, and it emphasizes how the reactions of others to which one is bonded might affect self-concepts, social approval and status, guilt feelings, or how behavior might harm those about whom one cares, or jeopardize investments linked to group involvement. However, control theory also notes that social bonding affects opportunities for deviance. These elements of control are usually indirect but many of them can be deliberately manipulated in acts of direct control.

Although deterrence and social control theories are usually regarded as separate explanatory schemes, and have been described in this chapter in those terms, it is clear that they actually could be conceived as one theory. In its more recent focus on informal sanctions and the conditions under which potential bad consequences have greater or less force, deterrence theory already incorporates much of the essence of social control theory. If deterrence theorists were to extend their thinking to take account of opportunity for deviance as social control theory does, particularly with the addition of the ideas of routine activity, it could easily engulf all the main concepts of social control theory. On the other hand, if social control theorists were to turn their attention to the characteristics of social reactions and individuals' cognitive processing, it could annex deterrence theory and be more complete because of it. And, clearly, both formulations could benefit from greater attention to variations in motivation for deviance. ✦

Integrated Theory

Each of the theories discussed in the preceding few chapters is plausible, at least as it applies to some deviance or crime, but all are limited since no one of them provides a general explanation for all types of deviance. Moreover, even when theories apply to a specific deviant behavior, their explanatory power is usually limited; that is, there are always many instances that do not fit the pattern. Hence, none of the theories can predict correct outcomes more often than not.

Requirements for Successful Theory

Theoretical inadequacy is mainly due to the fact that theories of deviance/crime are usually narrowly focused on a few causal processes or variables. As implied by the authors' scheme of classification, each theory tends to stress either motivation or the absence of constraint, and each tends to see the causal element as located mainly either within the person or in the social situation. In reality, however, every deviant act probably involves both motivation and absence of constraint, and every deviant act probably arises from some internal and some external elements.

Essential Elements

It is most fruitful, therefore, to think of criminal or deviant behavior as the product of the interaction or convergence of a number of variables or processes—not the result of only one, or perhaps only a few, such forces. Indeed, at least five things seem to be operative in any given act of deviance (Sheley, 1983).

Motivation

Some theorists (Gottfredson and Hirschi, 1990; Hirschi, 1969; Kornhauser, 1978) contend that deviant motivation is universally present, but there is much evidence suggesting that impulses to violate particular rules or laws are actually quite variable (see Tittle, 1980b). There is also good reason to believe that the strength of motivation is implicated in whether or not deviant behavior occurs. For instance, although everybody needs money, the intensity of that perceived need will not be the same for all individuals in all circumstances. Thus, the motivation to acquire money is not equal, and

---

Deviance in Everyday Life

Motivation for many if not most kinds of behaviors is probably not equally strong across persons. For example, people may have different motivations for sexual behavior. There is a phenomenon known as sexual addiction or sexaholicism, where the drive to have sexual activity is so strong and so compelling that persons afflicted with the malady find their entire lives consumed with it. Much like any other addiction, sex addicts seek sexual activity, sexual pleasure, and sexual stimulation, to the point that other components of their lives suffer. Persons with a sexual motivation disorder are driven to have promiscuous and compulsive sex and have a strong appetite for pornography, strip clubs, masturbation, or deviant fetishes. Some people, therefore, may have a stronger motivation for sexual behavior, and for sexually deviant behavior, than others. To assist those who wish to reduce their sexual motivation, there are numerous help groups similar to Alcoholics Anonymous, such as Sexual Compulsives Anonymous and Sexual Recovery Anonymous.

neither is the likelihood that a person will be motivated to get it by assaulting somebody or committing fraud. Similarly, some people perceive themselves as needing more sexual gratification than do others. Therefore, they may be more strongly motivated toward premarital or extramarital sex.

Although individuals may deviate because they are unaware of the rules forbidding the behavior, or because the behavior is accidental, most behavior is motivated. When we act, we often, if not usually, do so to accomplish some purpose, to respond to some immediate mandate, or because we have a habit of behaving that way. When an individual exceeds the speed limit, he or she may not realize it, or the violation may be inadvertent, and in that sense it may be unmotivated. But usually speeders break the law in order to get someplace on time, or perhaps to impress peers, or maybe out of habit. The desire to arrive quickly, to achieve status in a peer group, or to behave as one's habits dictate constitute forms of motivation. And, the greater the individual's perceived need to hurry, or to garner the admiration of peers, or the more firmly ingrained is a speeding habit, the more likely is speeding to occur, all other things being equal. Consequently, even though deviance in some instances may not involve motivation, most of the time it does. And most of the time the strength of motivation is a factor influencing whether deviance occurs. Therefore, any complete or successful theory of deviant or criminal behavior must account for the variation in the strength of the impulse to do or neglect to do the things that are to be explained by the theory.

Opportunity

A second factor is opportunity. Regardless of anything else, a person cannot steal cars if there are no cars to be stolen; a person cannot smoke marijuana if he or she cannot obtain it; and a married individual will not commit adultery if there are no willing partners with whom to conspire. People differ in the frequency of opportunities for crime or deviance, and opportunities vary from situation to situation for any given individual; this is one reason even the most deviance-prone people misbehave only episodically. Therefore, an adequate theory must incorporate opportunity to violate the norms as a key element.

Ability

Third, criminal or deviant behavior is contingent on the individual's ability to commit various acts. No matter how strongly motivated a person might be to steal an airplane, and no matter how many airplanes are available in the area, that individual is unlikely to attempt the theft if he or she doesn't know how to fly an airplane (although the person might hijack an airplane and a pilot). Similarly, a person without knowledge of how to obtain marijuana or how to smoke it for pleasure is less likely to use it than one who has those skills, even when other conditions that might otherwise lead to marijuana use are favorable.

Competing Motivation

Fourth, deviance is partly a function of the strength of competing motivations, generally or in specific situations. An individual might be motivated to commit adultery and know of a potentially willing partner but be more highly motivated at the time to attend a professional football game than to seek out the adulterous situation. Or a man might desire to rob a bank, have an opportunity to do so, and know how to do it but refrain from committing the act because at the time he had a stronger motivation to spend time with his girlfriend. Logically, then, the alternative motivations operating for individuals in various situations constitute important elements in the probability of actual deviance occurring, and therefore must be part of an adequate theory.

Constraint

Finally, the amount and nature of constraint on the individual's behavior is important. Constraint comes from potential costs, or unpleasant consequences should the behavior be performed or from physical, psychological, or social barriers to performance of the deviant act. Some of these costs are more or less constant, while others vary from situation to situation. Many people have internalized moral beliefs about particular behaviors, so they feel internal discomfort, often called guilt, that constrains them when they contemplate committing the acts about which they have moral beliefs (see Chapter 13). For example, some people have been taught that nonmarital sex is evil, so they refrain from doing it because of feelings about its wrongness—they anticipate that they will experience internal psychic discomfort, or feel guilty, if they do it. And some individuals believe it is wrong to underreport their incomes for Federal tax purposes, or overdeduct such things as charitable contributions. Even when it is extremely unlikely that these acts would be discovered, such individuals conform because of moral duty rooted in internalized values.

Other constraints involve more tangible costs that may vary from situation to situation. Those who are motivated toward nonmarital sex but who refrain from expressing those desires in actual behavior may refrain because they fear disease or the potential negative reactions of their spouses or families should they indulge and be caught, or perhaps because they fear rejection from potential partners. And, of course, the extent to which disease is feared, negative reactions from others dreaded, or possible rejection by potential sexual partners is perceived as painful will vary from individual to individual and for any given individual from situation to situation. Perceptions of the chances of getting a sexually transmitted disease are likely to vary from person to person because of a number of factors, including the known sexual history of the potential partner, and perceptions of the chances of spouses finding out will be different under different circumstances. Similarly, the degree to which people speed while driving is often determined by their perceptions of the chances that a state trooper is in the vicinity at that time. The potential perceived cost involved in delayed travel, possible fine, or "points" on one's driving record can deter speeding, but those perceived costs are rarely constant across time and situations.

Convergence

It should be obvious that these five forces (motivation, opportunity, ability, competing motivation, and constraint) converge/interact in the production of crime/deviance. Imagine an individual with a strong desire or motivation to commit criminal act X. If a social scientist were trying to predict the likelihood of act X, and applied a theory, such as differential association, anomie, or identity/labeling, that emphasizes motivation, she or he would predict a high probability of the crime by this individual. However, imagine further that in the particular circumstances surrounding this individual, constraint (such as a high probability of being arrested, of being rejected by peers, or of feeling guilt) was even stronger than the motivation to do it. Convergence of the two variables would produce no X act despite high motiva-tion. Failure of the theory would result because it dealt with only one element of an interactive or converging set. This illustration is symbolized in figure (a), where the length of the forward arrow represents the strength of motiva-tion to do act X while the length of the backward arrow represents the strength of constraint against doing act X:

(a)   ················▶ ◀·····················   (relatively low chance of X)

Now consider a second example involving act Y, where the strength of the individual's motivation is quite small—much less than it was in the example for act X. Again, if we only take into account the strength of motivation, as some theories suggest, we will predict little likelihood of the individual's com-mitting act Y. But imagine that in this case the constraint against act Y in the individual's circumstances is almost nonexistent. The probability of the act occurring is actually quite high. By considering only the motivational factors, we would again make an error in prediction, which would appear to chal-lenge the theory that gave rise to the prediction. But the incorrect prediction would be the result of not considering motivational and constraint variables simultaneously. This second example is symbolized in figure (b), where the forward arrow represents motivation and the backward arrow represents constraint:

(b)   ···········▶ ◀····   (relatively high chance of Y)

This same type of consideration also demonstrates the inadequacy of constraint theories (such as Hirschi's social bonds, or deterrence) used alone. Imagine that a woman is highly constrained from act Z—she is strongly bonded to conventional groups and society, and in her life pattern the chances of getting caught and punished by the law are high. Drawing on con-straint theories, we would predict little likelihood of Z. But imagine that in this instance the woman has an extremely strong desire or motivation to commit Z—so strong that the constraint is overshadowed. There is a high probability of Z despite high constraint. Thus, looking only at constraint would be misleading and produce an inaccurate prediction. This case is sym-bolized in figure (c).

(c)   ····················▶ ◀··········   (relatively high chance of Z)

Consider the opposite situation. An individual has little constraint against committing act Q, so theories focusing only on constraint would lead us to predict large chances of Q occurring. But suppose the individual in this instance has almost no motivation toward Q. The result would probably be that Q does not happen despite the prediction of constraint theories that it would. Here again empirical results would appear to challenge constraint theory. Yet the real problem would not be constraint theories per se but rather the failure to consider constraint in conjunction with motivation. This case is portrayed in figure (d).

(d)   ·····▶ ◀················   (relatively low chance of Q)

The same difficulties inhere in failure to take account of the other forces mentioned before—alternative motivation, ability, and opportunity. Con-sider the example of Z described above, where there is strong constraint but even stronger motivation, resulting in a prediction of act Z when both sets of factors are considered simultaneously. But imagine that the individual never has an opportunity to commit Z; potential Z victims, cooperators, or objects are not available. Even though motivation and constraint would lead us to expect Z, simultaneous operation of motivation, constraint, and opportunity would produce no Z. Once again the problem is the failure to consider the interaction of all key variables.

Since there are at least five forces that interact/converge to influence the likelihood of crime/deviance, it is clear that a general theory must be more inclusive than most of the theories considered earlier if it is to provide good explanatory and predictive power. But it is not enough simply to say that deviance is caused by a multitude of elements and to throw those elements together in a haphazard or undisciplined way. Good general theories specify the relative importance of these forces under various conditions and spell out in detail how they are linked to produce the effects that are to be explained or predicted.

Contingencies

A second major reason why theory is often unsuccessful is that most theories portray a process that operates the same way in all circumstances. For instance, Sutherland's theory of differential association recognizes no differences in individuals' capacity to learn, whether it be science, language, or definitions favorable or unfavorable to criminal or deviant behavior. Instead, Sutherland assumed that specific degrees (weighted by the modalities) of excessive exposure to crime-favorable definitions will produce the same degree of criminal behavior in all individuals. Similarly, his theory takes no account of the possibility that homicide might require far more exposure to excessive favorable definitions than does marijuana use, or that differential association might have little or no relevance for some forms of deviance such as necrophilia.

But even if differential association is a key force in producing deviance or crime, it probably operates differently for different individuals. For instance, since some people learn better or quicker than others (Eysenck, 1977), the theory would be better if it showed how learning modes modify the impact of differential association. And, it would be more complete if it specified the kinds of deviant acts that are most likely to be affected by differential association.

A second example is Hirschi's theory of social bonds. His formulation ignores individual perceptual accuracy about how specific behaviors might be viewed by conventional others or how such behaviors could alter patterns of involvement or attachment. As a result, it predicts that specific degrees of social bonding will produce the same amount of deviance in all individuals. Yet some people are probably objectively bonded to conventional society but cannot perceive or recognize the elements that would make those bonds constraining. And it is likely that the constraints of social bonds are more effective for some kinds of crime/deviance than for others.

Similarly, each of the theories discussed so far suffers from inadequate specification of the circumstances under which the postulated causal process operates with differing degrees of effect. Unless theories identify their contingencies and show how various conditions intertwine with and modify their causal process, they cannot be very effective in explaining deviance.

Integration

To overcome such problems, a number of scholars have begun to develop theoretical structures that combine parts of the various theories described, with the intention of producing general, integrated, coherent bodies of thought, usually referred to as "integrated theory" (Agnew, 1992; Colvin and Pauly, 1983; Conger, 1976; Conger and Simons, 1997; Elliott et al., 1979, 1985, 1989; Hagan et al., 1985; Kaplan, 1995; Matsueda and Heimer, 1997; Miethe and Meier, 1994; Pearson and Weiner, 1985; Sampson and Laub, 1997; Thornberry, 1987). The objective of such theories is to provide more comprehensive and precise explanations by recognizing the convergence, or interactive operation, of motivation, constraint, alternative motivation, opportunity, and ability and to take into account any conditions that might affect the causal process. Although a number of methods for achieving improved theories through integration have been set forth (Elliott, 1985; Meier, 1985; Messner et al., 1989; Tittle, 1995), the most promising appears to involve the merger of different causal arguments into some abstract process that expresses the essence of the combined causal arguments of several extant theories or, more precisely, theory fragments. This approach also takes advantage of the contribution of existing theories by using them to explain the inputs to the central causal process of the integrated theory. One illustration of integrated theory using this approach is called "control balance" (Tittle, 1995).

Control Balance Theory

Because the theory presented in the following pages tries to bring together a large number of earlier theories into one coherent account, it is necessarily complex. We authors will try to simplify and make it as clear as possible, using frequent examples and periodic summaries. However, you must pay close attention, asking yourself at various junctures, "Do I understand what I have read so far?" If not, then you should go back and reread what was presented before until you have a good comprehension of the material. Each part of the presentation builds on discussions that preceded it, so the account of the whole theory rests on a progression of steps. Hence, this theory, unlike many of the others we have discussed in this book, cannot be succinctly summarized and easily grasped. We are, therefore, asking you to concentrate especially hard in studying the following material. We will help as much as we can, but you must be an especially active partner in this intellectual pursuit.

The Basic Idea

Control balance theory starts with the idea that constraint, or control, is the main force in explaining deviance and crime, but it uses control in conjunction with strength of motivation in accounting for deviance. It also, however, conceives of motivation as itself being generated by various degrees of control. The phrase "being controlled" in this theory means that a person's behaviors are limited because: (1) others, either individually or collectively, can deny or grant things of value or can impose or withhold unpleasant things for the individual in question, or (2) the arrangement of physical or social "structural" phenomena affects behavioral discretion. For example, you are somewhat controlled by the person who is your teacher. He or she can award you a good grade or a poor one, and the more you want a good grade, the more controlled you are likely to be. In addition, you are controlled by the weather, a physical condition. If it is snowing, you cannot play tennis outside, even though you might want to.

This concept of control does not imply complete prevention of behavior but instead conveys the notion that a full expression of your impulses is curtailed or limited. The *extent* to which impulses are curtailed by social and physical arrangements varies from one person to the next and from one situation to the next. Thus, control is a continuous variable (going from very low to very high, with many gradations between) expressing the degree to which a person's desires or impulses are *limited* by others' abilities to reward or punish or by physical and social arrangements.

This theory contends that: a desire (1) to avoid control, or (2) to exercise more control than one is subject to, constitutes the major compelling force for humans and is implicated especially in criminal or deviant behavior. According to the theory, absolute variations in the strength of motivation to behave are of little import alone. Being strongly motivated to slug your professor, for instance, is not enough to explain what you actually do; the probable response to such slugging behavior is also crucial, and motivation itself hinges on the relative amount of control with which you begin. In actual practice, what counts is the degree of motivation relative to that of control. A person with 100 units of behavioral motivation who experiences 70 comparable units of constraint is equivalent to an individual with 10 units of behavioral motivation who is subject to 7 comparable units of constraint. They are both 70 percent controlled.

Although the theory recognizes many things that might incline a person toward a specific behavior (to be detailed later), it maintains that the most important factor is the degree of control to which the person is exposed relative to the control that he or she can exercise—or the *control ratio*. The fundamental argument of this integrated theory is that a control imbalance, either a deficit (having less control than that to which you are subject) or a surplus (having more control than that to which you are subject), is implicated in producing both the probability of deviant behavior and the type of behavior that a person is likely to commit.

The theory deals with three major types of behavior—conformity, submission, and deviance. The deviance category includes five types: predation, exploitation, defiance, plunder, and decadence. The five types of deviance are differentiated from each other mainly by their *seriousness*. Seriousness is defined as the degree to which a deviant act will, in general, *actually* activate countercontrolling responses, including: (1) manipulation by others of things of value to the individual who commits it (if you slug your professor, you probably will not get credit for the course), (2) manipulation by others of things unpleasant to the deviant (you will also be arrested and maybe go to jail if you slug your professor), and/or (3) emergence of physical or social barriers to the achievement of the deviant's goals (you may be barred from the campus and lose all your money paying lawyers' fees).

The theory contends that a person motivated toward deviance (where motivation comes from is explained later) will balance the advantages of deviance (measured mainly by gains in control) against the potential countercontrolling responses that particular kinds of deviance would stimulate. If this balancing is favorable, that form of deviance will occur; if it is unfavorable, a different form of deviance with less potential countercontrol connected with it will be used. But there is more to it, which we will discuss after telling you about the things the theory is trying to explain.

Categories of Deviance Explained by Control Balance Theory

Although control balance theory focuses on types of deviance differentiated by seriousness, it is interesting to try to characterize those types in more descriptive terms that imply the reasons why they are regarded as more or less serious.

Predation

One of the most serious forms of behavior involves *direct physical violence, manipulation, or property extraction by an individual or group for the benefit of a predator.* Such behavior is usually called predation, and it includes things like theft, rape, homicide, robbery, assault, fraud, price gouging by individual entrepreneurs, coercive pimping, and sexual harassment, as well as acts like parental use of guilt to elicit a child's attention (when done for the benefit of the parent). Some predatory acts may not actually be deviant or serious, but as a category of behavior, predation is widely regarded as very immoral, and most people, particularly those with the capacity for countercontrol, think of it as threatening even if they are not victims. Of course, when victims can, they will usually use countermeasures that produce unpleasantness for perpetrators. Victims may counterattack, seek indirect revenge, attempt to get others to intervene, make efforts to humiliate the perpetrators publicly, use gossip to destroy the reputations of their predators, or the like.

Exploitation

Exploitation involves acts of indirect predation. An exploitative individual or group *uses others as intermediaries or uses structural/organizational arrangements to coerce or to manipulate others, or to extract property from individuals or groups to benefit the exploiter.* Such acts include corporate fixing of prices, profiteering from activities that endanger workers or bystanders, influence peddling by politicians or bureaucrats, contract killings, and evangelists' using religious injunctions to elicit donations.

In almost all contemporary societies, acts of indirect predation are regarded by most people as wrong or bad. However, exploitative acts are probably not as disapproved as are direct predatory acts. Certainly, exploitation is less likely to be against the law or, if included in the criminal statutes, is less likely to bring about enforcement. Moreover, clues about the chances that exploitation will invite countercontrolling responses indicative of seriousness suggest that it is less serious than some other forms of deviance, including predation. Social audiences usually attribute evil and culpability proportionate to the direct involvement of an individual in a disapproved act, which is one reason exploitation is less serious than it might otherwise be (it involves indirect manipulation). Also, individuals or groups who are in positions where they can exploit are also able to influence public opinion, legal functionaries, and legislation to make their acts seem less despicable and to forestall legal reactions.

A controversial example of exploitation concerns television evangelists, known as televangelists. These are ministers who preach religion on television, make financial demands on their listeners, and who may be guilty of numerous deviant acts, including misusing donations for their own personal needs. A well-known example was the television ministry of Jim and Tammy Bakker in the 1980s. The Bakkers were TV preachers who had their own television ministry called Praise the Lord (PTL). It was a financially lucrative enterprise, so much so that the Bakkers planned and built their own religious theme park, Heritage USA. Jim Bakker fell from grace after news of financial misdealings and of an extramarital affair with a church worker came to light. Bakker bilked millions of dollars from his viewers to fund his and Tammy's lavish life style, which included six homes, large bonuses, luxury cars, and even an air-conditioned dog house for their pooch. Critics claimed that PTL did not stand for Praise The Lord as much as it did Pass The Loot. In 1989, Jim Bakker was convicted of twenty-four counts of defrauding the public; he was defrocked by the Assemblies of God Church; and later he was divorced by Tammy.

Defiance

The third general category of deviance dealt with by control balance theory is defiance. *Defiant acts are those expressing contempt for, or hostility toward, a norm, or a set of norms or to the individual, group, or organization with which that norm is associated.* Although defiant acts go against norms, they avoid harming the object of hostility to any great extent, and they do not produce any obvious benefit to perpetrators. Such acts include curfew violations, vandalism, and transgressions of status restrictions (underage drinking, for instance), mockery of supervisors by striking workers, sullenness by a marital partner, exaggerated demonstrations of compliance engaged in by employees or students, and political protests. These behaviors are viewed as "wrong" by most people because they challenge authority, or because they make life inconvenient for others. Thus, defiance of authority is deviant (it will probably generate reactions by people with countercontrolling abilities), but it is less serious than predation and exploitation.

Another common type of defiance epitomizes escape or withdrawal from a network of social relationships or normative obligations. Such defiance is evident in drug or alcohol abuse; various kinds of bohemianism (living unconventional life styles); "mentally ill" behavior like using nonsense language or talking loudly to oneself, or not responding to people or things in the environment; engaging in bizarre behaviors (like public nose picking); and committing suicide (at least in the American culture). Defiance, or showing distaste for a normative system through escape or withdrawal, can take many forms, and most such behaviors are somewhat "unacceptable," according to public opinion polls. Moreover, they often elicit response from social control agents, such as the police.

Plunder

The theory also explains an especially heinous and disreputable category of acts called plunder. In plundering, *individuals or organizations pursue their own ends with disregard for how their behaviors might affect others.* Those who plunder are so selfish and aloof that they create victims as a byproduct of their actions rather than from a conscious effort. Plunder is different from predation or exploitation in that its practitioners have such weak social consciousness, or consciences, that they do not perceive the damage caused by their acts. Exploiters and predators are aware that their actions are victimizing, and they know that their benefits come at the expense of other people, but they do them anyway. Plunderers, on the other hand, do not even comprehend the consequences of their actions.

Among the plunderous behaviors explained by control balance theory are the actions of decadent landowners whose fox hunts ravaged peasant fields in medieval times, contemporary corporate maneuvers resulting in massive pollution, attempts by powerful segments of populations to commit genocide against racial or ethnic groups, burdensome taxing of native populations by occupying armies, insensitive work requirements imposed by slave holders, and arrogant decimation of the natural environment by early entrepreneurs.

Deviance in Everyday Life

One of the best-known and catastrophic examples of corporate plundering is the Love Canal pollution case. Love Canal was originally intended to be a waterway between Lake Ontario and Lake Erie. It was started in 1896 by William Love, who wanted to use the canal to provide electric power. Because of a financial depression, however, the canal was never finished, and it remained a ditch that served as little more than a local swimming hole for neighborhood kids. In the 1940s, the Hooker Chemical Company began dumping chemical wastes into the canal that ran through its property. It dumped chemicals into the canal for approximately ten years. Before sealing it with a clay soil cap in the early 1950s, the company had dumped over 20,000 tons of chemical byproducts into the canal. Hooker eventually sold the land to the Niagara Falls School Board for $1. They built a school virtually right above the old canal. In the late 1970s, chemicals were detected seeping out from the canal. There were strange odors and pain-causing substances coming from the ground; children playing in the area were getting skin irritations; and people had toxic waste bubbling into their basements during heavy rains. The community suffered health problems too: women were having miscarriages at an alarming rate, and rare forms of cancers began appearing with regularity in the community. Eventually, the neighborhood closest to the old Hooker Chemical Company was evacuated, and homes were purchased by the state and Federal government and boarded up. It is a ghost town today. (See Colten, 1996)

Decadence

The theory also accounts for decadence, which is a collection of *impulsive acts guided only by the whim of the moment, with no consistent or rational organization*. Decadence is jaded, undisciplined excess, usually without meaning. Decadent people do not contemplate why they do things, nor do they have long-range goals other than decadence itself; hence, they are erratic, irrational, and unpredictable. The behavior of decadents encompasses excessive and bizarre sexual acts such as group sex with children, debauchery, humiliating human beings and other creatures for amusement, sadistic torture, and other forms of destructive pleasure. Most people everywhere regard decadence as loathsome. It is usually illegal, and efforts to enforce prohibitive laws are common; hence, decadent acts are very serious—the most serious of the deviant acts explained by control balancing.

Submission

One of the three main types of behavior explained by control balance theory consists of *passive, unthinking, slavish obedience to the expectations, commands, or anticipated desires of others*. Some examples are: eating excrement or drinking urine on command; assisting in the repression of peers in obedience to power holders; submitting to physical abuse, humiliation, or sexual degradation; or merely following lives of routinized behavior without thinking about whether there is an alternative or without contemplating challenge. Specific documented cases include: incarcerated inmates obedient to covert as well as overt orders, even to the extent of assisting guards in abusing inmates, including themselves; children abused by parents to the point where their interest in life evaporates; submissive sex partners or abused spouses who allow themselves to be degraded or mutilated; and slaves or sharecroppers who passively subordinate themselves to owners or other authorities. Submission is essentially complete obedience marked by *an inability to imagine alternatives.*

Deviance in Everyday Life

How can people just submit to authorities, you may wonder. Isn't there something wrong with them, you may ask, implying that "normal" people would resist inappropriate demands? Some insight into just how common submission to authorities may be was revealed in a classic series of experiments by Stanley Milgram (Milgram, 1974). Milgram, a psychologist at Yale University, was interested in the issue of conflict between obedience to authority and personal conscience. In the experiment, subjects were assigned the role of "teachers," who were instructed to administer an electric shock of increasing intensity to "learners" for each mistake the learner made. The "learners" were actually confederates of Milgram who were not actually shocked, but the "teachers" did not know this. The intensity of the purported shock ranged up to a painful 450 volts. As the scale of intensity increased, the "teachers" heard the subjects shout and scream for the shocking to stop. At times, the "teachers" were worried that they were causing great pain to the "learners," but they were told by the experimenters to continue. The subjects did! Milgram found that 65 percent of the "teachers" obeyed the commands of the experimenter (in spite of their personal objections) and punished the learner up to the 450-volt limit, and no "teacher" stopped shocking before hitting the 300-volt level. This experiment vividly showed that "normal" people can fairly easily submit their own will and conscience to that of an authority.

In some societies (probably the United States is one), submissive behaviors are deviant, but in other societies they may not be. In American society, most people think submissive behaviors are pitiful, tragic, or disgusting because they suggest suppression of the particularly valued human qualities of freedom, self-efficacy, and individualism. However, even though the original formulation of control balance theory treated submission as the least serious form of deviant behavior, it does not actually require that submission be deviant. Indeed, submission is now portrayed as a residual category—a style of behavior adopted when conditions make it impossible to conform or to employ deviant behavior to alter a control imbalance.

Conformity

Within control balance theory, conformity refers to a situation in which, fully aware of and able to contemplate alternative, nondeviant behavior, an individual or organization behaves according to normative expectations. Submission and conformity differ in that a conforming individual has the ability to visualize some other behavior, even if such visualization happens only some of the time. A submissive person, on the other hand, no longer has the capacity for imagining alternatives, having become so resigned that anything other than submission is inconceivable.

The Theoretical Argument

Control balance theory contends that the total likelihood of some kind of deviance and the probability of specific types of deviance are both produced mainly by the convergence of deviant motivation with constraint, although other variables also come into play. It also contends that deviant motivation and constraint are themselves mainly products of: (1) individuals' control ratios (the amount of control that a person can exercise relative to the amount that can be marshalled against the person), and (2) the likelihood that potential countercontrol actually will be exercised, which is linked to the seriousness of the potential deviant act. The process underlying the convergence of these and other variables in producing deviance, however, is complicated. Figure 15.1 depicts that process. Several things should be noted about the figure: (1) the heavy solid arrows portray powerful or dominant influences, the narrow solid arrows show secondary or lesser effects, and the broken lines reflect minor influences; (2) each bracketed number symbolizes a convergence of variables; and (3) the pluses and minuses portray positive and negative effects, while the combinations of plus and minus indicate that the effect may be either positive or negative, depending on the circumstances.

To understand the diagram, you should observe that it portrays five main variables, each signified by brackets. Each of those variables is produced by other variables, shown as arrows going into the brackets. It looks complicated but is much easier to understand by following the flow from the upper left-hand corner down and across the chart. Overall, it says that predisposition sometimes flowers into motivation for deviance. When that happens, if there is opportunity, deviance will occur, and if constraint is not too great, some specific forms of deviance will result. Exactly how and why this happens will become clearer as you go along, but for now it is important to familiarize yourself with the overall process.

Start from the upper left-hand corner and observe that the figure shows a variable called Basic Human Impulses going directly to Deviance via a broken arrow. In addition, it shows a skinny solid arrow leading from Basic Human Impulses to nexus #1. This is to suggest that Basic Human Impulses, which include social desires and human biological drives, are the primary movers of human action, especially when they are blocked. Though many of these impulses, like the need for food and water, are universal, they nevertheless vary enough in strength and form to qualify as "tastes." The variable of Basic Human Impulses includes *whatever an individual recurrently finds important to acquire*. Although primary desires or needs have only small direct effects on deviance (shown as a broken arrow), they "interact" with other variables in bringing about Motivation, which, as we will see, is a person's perception that deviant behavior can overcome a control deficit or extend a control surplus.

The left-hand corner of the figure also shows a concept, Desire for Autonomy, defined as a basic urge to escape control that can be exercised against oneself and to extend one's own control. The theory assumes that all human beings, because of dependency in childhood, harbor an underlying desire to

Figure 15.1 Casual Linkages of Control Balance Theory

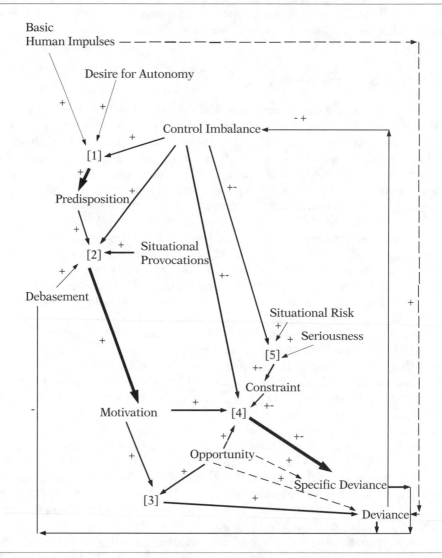

Adapted from Tittle, Charles R. 1995. *Control Balance: Toward a General Theory of Deviance,* pg. 172. Boulder, CO: Westview.

exercise more control than the have, and it assumes that this desire is closer to being a constant than a variable since its strength varies from individual to individual only within a narrow range. In other words, this theory assumes that you have a deep-seated need both to exercise control and to escape control exercised against you, whether you realize it or not. This concept is included in the diagram along with the variables in order to show that it is a necessary condition undergirding the deviance production process. Desire for Autonomy converges with a Control Imbalance and with Basic Human Impulses to produce a Predisposition to become motivated for deviant behavior, as shown by the arrow to the first bracket.

The cornerstone of the theoretical scheme is Control Imbalance, either a person's excess or deficiency, which is situated in the diagram in the upper center. Various Control Imbalances come together with particular Basic Human Impulses, along with a Desire for Autonomy to generate a Predisposition for deviant motivation. The heavy solid arrow going to bracket #1 symbolizes this convergence. The primacy of a Control Imbalance is also evident by its intrusion into the overall causal scheme (note the arrows going from it to three of the nexi): (1) by interacting with Situational Provocations and feelings of Debasement, or humiliation, in convergence #2 to provoke actual deviant Motivation, (2) through its conjunction with Motivation, Constraint, and Opportunity (nexus #4) to bring about forms of Specific Deviance, and (3) through alliance with Situational Risk and Seriousness (nexus #5) to produce Constraint. The importance of Control Imbalances in these different outcomes is portrayed by the thick solid arrows showing it running to the bracketed intersections.

The underlying theme of the theory is that: *deviance can be understood as a maneuver to alter control imbalances and thereby to overcome feelings of humiliation provoked by being reminded of one's unbalanced control ratio.* In other words, deviance serves a purpose for the individual. It helps overcome a control imbalance or the bad feelings that sometimes stem from it. This underlying reciprocity (from deviance back to the causes of the deviance) is depicted in the thin, solid, negatively valenced arrows from Deviance back to Control Imbalance and to Debasement. (Note that deviance can sometimes increase a control imbalance, which is indicated by the + on the arrow from deviance back to Control Imbalance.) However, they are thin to signify that Deviance, though undertaken to deal with problems associated with a Control Imbalance, usually has only a minor effect on one's overall Control Ratio, and normally the effect of deviance in relieving humiliation is temporary. Yet deviance can sometimes permanently alter a control ratio, in either of two ways. Deviance can cause an individual to be stigmatized or incarcerated, which affects the amount of control that the person can exercise as well as the amount that is experienced, or it can succeed so well that an individual ends up being able to exercise a lot more permanent control and being subject to a lot less control (for instance, if a person perpetrates fraud and becomes wealthy and powerful as a result). These alternative possibilities are indicated by the positive and negative sign attached to the return arrow from Deviance to Control Imbalance.

The convergence shown by the bracketed #1 is composed of interactions among Basic Human Impulses, Desire for Autonomy, and a Control Imbalance. Typically, it is activated by a blockage of some Basic Human Impulse that is linked with the Desire for Autonomy and that is influenced by an unbalanced control ratio. In essence, three conditions have to converge for Predisposition to emerge. Basic Human Impulses can occasionally lead directly to deviance, such as when a starving person steals bread, but by themselves such impulses are usually insufficient. Normally, Basic Human Impulses must be blocked, or become subject to denial—a circumstance closely linked with Control Imbalance.

The convergence of Basic Human impulse blockage, Desire for Autonomy, and a Control Imbalance in Figure 15.1 is signified as the bracketed nexus #1, which is distinct from, but is an essential contributor to, Predisposition. Predisposition toward deviant behavior cannot be thought of as a simple linear product of those three variables, but instead the three variables, or conditions, must combine to form a particular "interaction." This interaction is not necessarily of a linear multiplicative form (where the effect of the three variables is equal to their combined product), nor is it even of the form where the effect of one or the other of the variables depends on the value of another. "Interaction" of the three variables simply means that all of them, at least to a minimal degree, must exist simultaneously for Predisposition to emerge. For instance, you want a good grade in this class (a primary impulse for gratification), you have an intrinsic desire to escape from and to exercise control, and more than likely you have a control imbalance, being a student, young, and probably not very wealthy. Therefore, whether you realize it or not, you are predisposed toward deviance in the classroom.

But Predisposition toward deviant motivation is not enough to produce deviant behavior. For deviant behavior to occur, a number of links in a chain must be forged. The first of those necessary links is materialization of deviant Motivation. Like Predisposition before it, Motivation is produced by convergence of several variables, including Predisposition, but also involving Situational Provocations, and feelings of Debasement. In the usual case, Motivation arises when somebody with a Predisposition toward deviant motivation is confronted with a situation (1) that generates emotions associated with disgrace or humiliation linked to a realization that the person's control, relative to that of others, is less than it might be, and (2) that creates an awareness that deviant behavior can alter the subordination, the Control Imbalance, or the unpleasant emotions stirred by having been reminded of one's Control Imbalance.

For example, suppose you ask a question in this class and the professor responds by saying, "That is an exceptionally stupid question; how did you get into college anyway?" You are probably going to feel demeaned and humiliated, and you are going to become acutely aware that you have less control than that to which you are subject. And more than likely, you are going to quickly contemplate things you might do to overcome those feelings of humiliation and subordination. One possibility is, of course, to slug the professor. That would make you feel a lot better, and at least temporarily it would put you in control. In effect, by becoming conscious of the potential of overcoming your control imbalance and the feelings associated with it by slugging the professor, you have become motivated toward deviance.

Unlike the variables converging to produce Predisposition, the variables leading to Motivation are linearly interactive. Predisposition can be thought of as a necessary condition regardless of its strength; it simply exists or it doesn't. Motivation, however, is a matter of degree. Stronger motivation is more likely to lead to deviant behavior than is weaker motivation. The strength of Motivation is influenced by the intensity of Situational Provocations and Debasement, which are both ultimately rooted in the individual's control ratio. You are likely to become more strongly motivated toward deviance if the professor called you stupid than if he merely implied your stupidity by asking that particular question, assuming you would reveal that you had not read the assignment. And you are more likely to be demeaned by your subordination if your status is closer to that of the professor's than if the two of you are far apart in your respective control ratios. For example, a middle-class successful businessperson who has come back to college to finish a degree is more likely to be humiliated by a professor's putdown than is a financially struggling young person freshly out of high school.

Although Motivation toward deviance is necessary—and the stronger it is, the more likely it is to lead to deviance (other things being equal)—it is not sufficient for deviant behavior; there must also be Opportunity. No matter how motivated, a person cannot act deviantly without appropriate social and physical conditions to make deviance possible. Thus, the third bracketed convergence shows an intersection of Motivation with Opportunity. Control balance theory asserts that this convergence is causal—it is both necessary and sufficient for the display of Deviance, of some unspecified form.

Let's return to our hypothetical case of you, as a student, having become motivated toward deviance because of your public humiliation at the hands of your teacher. Because you are aroused, and conscious of weak relative control, you contemplate various forms of deviance—slugging the professor (predation), becoming sullen and unresponsive to questions (defiance), hiring someone to find "dirt" on the professor (exploitation), buying the university and closing it down (plunder). Even though you think about how those acts would relieve your situation, you are not likely to do most of them. One reason you probably will not respond with exploitation or plunder is an absence of opportunity to do so. If you are like most students, you cannot realistically plan on buying a university, and you probably do not know anybody you could hire for dirty work, even if you could afford it. There is almost always opportunity for some kinds of deviance, however, so if you are motivated, some, unspecified, type of deviance is likely to result.

Convergence of Motivation and Opportunity by itself will not necessarily lead to deviance in a specific category. Specific forms of deviance occur when these two variables converge with particular degrees of Constraint. It is important to emphasize that in the theory the explanation and prediction of some *deviance* is not the same as explanation and prediction of a specific *category of deviance*. The probability of Deviance of some unspecified type is unaffected by Constraint because, with Opportunity, Motivation can potentially lead to any kind of Deviance. And Constraint always permits some form of Deviance, even if only submission. Hence, Figure 15.1 shows convergence #3 leading only to Deviance. In the case of the humiliated student, we would expect him or her to do some kind of deviance, but we would not predict what kind without additional information.

Deviant Motivation produces specific categories of deviance by intersecting with Opportunity, Control Imbalance, and Constraint; this is portrayed in convergence #4. Remember that Motivation involves an individual's perception that deviant behavior will enhance his or her control ratio. Such perception, according to the theory, stimulates the person to want to use the *most effective means* to achieve that goal. The most effective means would call up the most serious deviant behaviors. When Motivation and Opportunity are present, some form of deviant behavior is likely, but the chances of particular kinds of deviant behavior reflecting various degrees of seriousness depends on the degree of Constraint and the person's Control Imbalance. If you are humiliated by a professor, you will want to do some of the more serious forms of deviance—you will want to slug him or her, or buy the university and shut it down. But you more than likely will not do either. A second reason, apart from opportunity, is that both of those forms of deviance will elicit countercontrolling responses that will be too costly for you. In short, you will balance the gain in control you would get from slugging the professor against the loss in control that will occur when the police arrest you, you are dismissed from the university, and you fail the course. Instead, you will probably slide down the continuum of seriousness to commit a deviant act that carries less potential constraint. Rather than slugging the professor, you are more likely to try defiance (refusing to laugh at jokes, pretending not to care about the lecture, or the like).

This Constraint, which affects the kind of deviance you are most likely to do, encompasses three cumulative components—the Control Imbalance, Seriousness of the potential act, and Situational Risk—signified by convergence #5. If there is Motivation and an Opportunity, the degree of Constraint, along with the direction of a Control Imbalance, will predict the Specific Deviance (a category) that is likely to occur. Constraint and the seriousness of the likely deviance will bear a negative relationship with each other—the higher the constraint, the less serious the likely deviance is to be. This negative relationship, however, is not linear across the full range of seriousness of potential deviant acts; rather, seriousness links with Control Imbalance. Imbalance on the deficit side portends types called "repressive deviance" (predation, defiance, submission), while Imbalance on the surplus side augurs deviance of an "autonomous" type (exploitation, plunder, decadence).

It is important to note that control balance is a probabilistic theory portraying a causal chain based on a number of variables that must converge in particular ways to maximize the predicted outcome. None of the variables in this theory is thought to act alone to produce deviance, and no outcome is absolutely determined. For example, even if a person has an opportunity for a particular deviance and is favorably disposed to commit it, that act may not happen because no provocation raises the person's consciousness or because the risk of countercontrols is prohibitive. Deviance-generating situations involve numerous conditions coming together simultaneously, but even then deviant behavior may not occur. This uncertainty is partly because of contingencies that may affect the operation of the causal process (variables that affect how the control balancing process is played out, which we will elaborate later). But before considering how contingencies might work, we need to understand why and how the convergences that we have been considering come into play to produce high probabilities of various outcomes.

Probabilities of Deviance

Since the opportunity to commit *some* kind of deviance is ubiquitous, control balance theory implies that a person's probability of engaging in some (unspecified) type of deviance is largely an expression of the motivation for deviance. And because deviant motivation is heavily influenced by a person's control ratio, the likelihood of deviance, of some type, reflects the person's control ratio. These probabilities, however, are not linearly related to the magnitude of the control ratio but instead are related in a U-shaped manner. Probabilities of deviance generally are least for those whose control ratios are balanced, and they are greatest for those whose control ratios are the most unbalanced, either in a negative or a positive direction. Hence, deviance of some unspecified kind is most likely for those with great deficits of control as well as for those with great surpluses.

This theory, therefore, denies that the commission of deviance is a simple reflection of prior background variables, although it identifies several more-or-less stable variables that often come into play, the most important of which is a person's control ratio. Instead, control balance theory depicts deviant behavior as a relatively infrequent outcome of a causal process centered around impermanent situational conditions. The theory contends that an actor must become motivated for deviance, which happens when a person with a predisposition for deviance confronts a situation that stimulates his or her acute awareness of a personal control imbalance and the realization that deviant behavior may alter the balance of control. Second, motivation, so stimulated, must be accompanied by opportunity for deviance, a situational phenomenon. Finally, for all forms of deviance except submission, motivation and opportunity must not be overwhelmingly countered by potential constraining responses. Possible countercontrol is both pre-influenced and situational; it is affected by the individual's control ratio and the seriousness of various forms of potential deviance and also by risk, which is situational.

Repressive Deviance

According to the argument of this theory, an individual with a control deficit is predisposed toward becoming motivated to perform predatory, defiant, or submissive behavior, and the larger the control deficit, the greater is the likelihood of one or another of these behaviors. This is so for several reasons. Above all, the larger one's deficit of control, the more likely it is that predation or defiance (rather than submission) will help overcome it. In addition, the influences that ultimately lead to deviant behavior begin with desires for autonomy or attempts to achieve ordinary goals of life, and they are mostly encompassed within, and expressed by, one's control ratio. Third, even though the provocations that might stimulate deviant motivation are situational, and therefore variable, and even though perceptions of the potential of deviance for overcoming a control deficit are influenced by highly variable individual characteristics, control ratios are so important that they can predict at least gross probabilities of outcomes. Finally, constraints that might prevent deviance usually influence motivated people to choose less serious deviance instead of choosing to forego deviant behavior totally.

The causal processes for repressive deviance can be illustrated by hungry people. The larger their control deficits, the less their ability to solicit, purchase, or demand food, so they will feel disadvantaged. Moreover, if food that is readily available to others is denied to them, they will feel even more deprived. And if they are directly informed that the food can only be consumed by those who already have it, they will experience disadvantage, as well as hunger, and in addition they will feel humiliated. Most people in such situations have a flash of insight that stealing can solve their problems. They will perceive that stealing may relieve their hunger as well as assist them to overcome feelings of being debased or ridiculed, which in the situation may well be more important than the original problem of hunger. Hence such people will not only become motivated to steal, they may also want to punch out any person who denies them food or verbally humiliates them. Attacking the immediate source of their problems, perhaps a grocer or restaurant manager, would help overcome the individuals' control deficit by putting the attacker in charge, at least for the moment. And even if the humiliated individual cannot retaliate against the grocer or restaurant owner, punching out somebody else will help. An assault or a theft would shift the terms of control and would temporarily relieve feelings of humiliation. Thus, hungry individuals are often "doubly" motivated to steal; theft would permit them to achieve an initial *and* a situationally generated goal.

Though much repressive deviance involves such double motivation, humiliation inherent in low control ratios often generates deviant motivation all by itself. On occasion, you have probably been made acutely aware of your relative control deficit. As an adolescent you may have been sitting in a shopping mall minding your own business, only to have a security guard tell you in a demeaning tone to leave. You probably felt a powerful urge to do some things you had not previously contemplated. You may have felt an impulse to get back at the security officer so that he would know that you cannot be pushed around. In other words, you probably experienced a need to balance the scales of control. It may have occurred to you to steal something just to show the officer and those he represents that you cannot be demeaned with impunity. Or you may have contemplated, at least momentarily, an assault. You may have wanted to sass the guard, call him bad names, challenge his authority, or perhaps pretend to obey but actually move slowly as a way of signifying that you are not completely powerless. Thinking about similar situations will make you appreciate the argument that motivation for some forms of deviance stems mainly from a poignant realization that others have more control than the actor does. In explaining the motivation for repressive forms of deviance, therefore, the theory focuses mainly on the *deprivation of control* and the humiliation that emerges from situational blockage of impulses.

The theory, however, as we noted before, recognizes that motivation is not the only thing operative. Those with control deficits who resort to deviance may activate controlling responses from other people—those potentially affected by the actor's attempts to overcome her or his control deficit by means of deviant behavior. And the more serious the deviant act (the greater the likelihood that it would be a problem for those affected by it), the more likely it is to stimulate counterresponses. Those with control deficits, therefore, are simultaneously likely to become motivated toward deviance and to be constrained. But since constraint is keyed to specific acts, motivation can be expressed in commission of acts that are less likely to activate countercontrol. The theory contends that motivation is compelling; those highly motivated but facing strong countercontrol will retreat to milder forms of deviance. This process produces an overall positive association between the degree of one's control deficit and the likelihood of some form of predation, defiance, or submission.

Autonomous Deviance

Control balance theory also predicts that those with control "surpluses" (those who can exercise more control than they are subject to) are likely to commit exploitation, plunder, or decadence, and the greater the surplus, the greater the chances of one or another of these. The explanatory process is the same as for repressive deviance, discussed earlier. The individual with a control surplus first encounters situations that bring about motivation to use deviance to extend that surplus. As with the individuals with deficits of control, the autonomous person wants to use the most effective means to extend his or her control; the most effective deviance is also the most serious, that is, the most likely to generate countercontrol. But the potential of countercontrol depends on how troublesome other people deem the act and the degree of the individual's control surplus. Nevertheless, since motivation is compelling, it likely will result in some form of autonomous deviance, depending mainly on opportunity, as the individual seeks less dangerous options for expressing his or her deviant motivation. The net result is an association between the degree of surplus and the probability of some form of deviance.

The process can be appreciated by considering an autonomous individual (one with a control surplus) who is hungry. Of course, the chances of this situation are extremely small because such people can get food easily if it is available, and they seldom face humiliating or demeaning responses. Moreover, even if resistance occurs, autonomous people can usually use their surplus control to overcome it. Potential controlling abilities, however, rarely have to be used by people with a surplus of control, because other people usually go to a lot of trouble to accommodate their needs voluntarily. However, these very accommodative acts on the part of subordinates, by stimulating the superior's awareness that deviance will extend his or her control advantage, actually motivate deviance among those with superior control.

Try to think of yourself as a well-known, rich, or politically connected person who enters a restaurant only to find that nobody notices you or does anything out of the ordinary. You will probably feel offended and start wondering why you are not getting the deference you think you deserve and have become accustomed to. According to the theory, at that point you will be provoked to bring to bear some of the control at your disposal. You may offer a bribe (advance tip), demand to confer with the manager, or verbally chastise the restaurant personnel. If they resist, you will then be stimulated to resort to deviance to extend your control. You might think about threatening to get them fired (exploitation) or you might contemplate storming to your preferred table and demanding that anybody obstructing you leave (plunder).

Imagine, on the other hand, the more usual situation. Restaurant workers immediately notice who you are and they hasten to take your coat and show you to a desirable table. You will not be motivated toward deviance because this is normal, consistent with your control ratio. However, if the restaurant host leads you into the dining room by pushing someone else aside, which is unusual, it probably will remind you of your superior control, and it likely will motivate you to employ deviant behavior to expand your control surplus. You may then think about ordering the host to clear all other customers from the room (exploitation) or require the chef to prepare your special meal immediately, regardless of what else he or she might be doing (plunder).

This is again an instance of "double motivation"—from blockage of the goal of obtaining food (hunger) and from realization that your dominance can be extended. Of the two, humiliation associated with failure to get deference is usually the more potent in creating deviant motivation. Once created, deviant motivation stimulates a desire to extend control as far as possible. Such extension is limited by the possibility of countercontrol that reflects the seriousness of the potential deviance. But those motivated to extend their control surpluses through deviance will not usually be absolutely deterred but instead will retreat to less serious types of autonomous deviance.

Summary

Control balance theory suggests that the main determinant of the *probability* of deviance of an unspecified type is the degree of *motivation* to alter a control imbalance, either a deficit or a surplus. Because the strength of motivation closely tracks individual control ratios (control that can be exercised relative to control experienced), those ratios predict the likelihood of some form of deviance. The more the control ratio deviates from unity in either a negative or a positive direction, the more probable is deviance.

Types of Deviance

Basic Assumptions

By bringing in an additional variable not implicated in explaining the general probability of deviance, control balance theory also explains the categorical type of deviance likely to be committed. The main variable explaining the likelihood of some form of deviance is the strength of motivation, which is partly determined by one's control ratio. The probability of specific types of deviance depends additionally on the likelihood that potential counter-control implied by a given control ratio, and implied by the particular act of deviance, will be activated. Whether potential control is expressed in actual countermeasures depends on the seriousness of a potential deviant act. The specific type of deviant act likely to be committed reflects a process by which the individual "balances" motivation with constraint. The theoretical explanation of this process begins with three assumptions: (1) all people are motivated to do some things; (2) some of the things that a person wants to do are rendered difficult by physical or social conditions or they pose problems for other people; (3) if an individual's potential behavior poses a problem for others, and those aggrieved parties can obstruct the behavior in question, they will. Alternatively, the individual's options may be controlled by "social structural" and physical arrangements. Because all people are constrained by their inability to totally prevent others from limiting their options, and because all, at one time or another, want to do impossible or difficult things, everyone is controlled.

Yet everyone also possesses some ability to control others and circumstances. Even babies exercise control, especially over their caregivers. Crying babies provoke those around them, whether caregivers or not, to adjust. Adjustments may include attending to the infant's needs, departing the scene, inserting ear plugs, getting someone else to attend to the baby, or hurting it. The fact that others have to respond in some way means that a screaming infant can control them. In a similar way, a slave can control (limit the options of) his or her master as well as other slaves by lagging or showing insolence, or ultimately, by self-destruction, all of which require some response. An owner might be provoked to sanction a lagging female slave, to attempt to persuade her verbally, to try to get other slaves to intervene, to accept the behavior and adjust to the loss of income it entails, and so on. Any of these adjustments requires some effort by the owner; even if the slave kills herself, the owner will have to deal with financial loss, get another slave, or manage the details surrounding the slave's death—disposing of the body and personal effects.

Thus, everybody has the capacity for potential control and to be controlled, but individuals differ in the relative amount of those two potentialities. Such differences are reflected in control ratios, which, as explained in the preceding paragraphs, are implicated in the *general* probability of deviance. The chances of *specific* categories of deviance occurring depends on the likelihood that particular deviant acts will stimulate potential counter-control. While potential countercontrol depends on the individual's control ratio, the likelihood that potential control will, in fact, be used depends on constraint. Constraint is heavily influenced by how much the deviance causes problems for others, but it also rests partly on the risk of apprehension and reaction, which are mainly situational. People must weigh the potential of countercontrol against the potential gratification connected with a deviant act, once they are motivated toward deviance.

Whether potential counter control is activated is linked to the kind of deviant act a person might employ to alter a control imbalance. Some acts almost certainly provoke countercontrol by other social entities, whereas other deviant acts rarely activate those capacities. Acts regarded as most dangerous, intolerable, or inconvenient to those who can exercise countercontrol will more likely provoke countercontrolling responses than behaviors regarded as less dangerous, intolerable,or inconvenient to others.

Hence, the exact deviant acts that motivated individuals are likely to commit depends to a great extent on the probability, or perceived probability, that a given act will bring about countercontrolling responses. Potential offenders, those who are motivated toward deviance, will want to use the most effective acts to alter their control imbalances. Those acts are usually the most serious—the ones most likely to stimulate potential countercontrols implied by the control ratio. The specific category of deviance chosen by an individual, then, is the most serious that he or she *can* do with the greatest likelihood of impunity—it is a result of "balancing" the advantages of gained control against the dangers of countercontrol. In practical terms, the actual likelihood of a specific form of deviance is a function of the relative strengths of the individual's motivation and the constraints he or she faces in the situation.

Control balance theory, then, portrays individual deviance as an outcome influenced by the strength of motivation in interaction with the magnitude and probability of potential controls that a person's actions might stimulate. Though they sometimes lead the individual to commit the most serious deviance, desires to use serious deviant acts to alter a control imbalance are typically squelched, partially curtailed, or channeled into alternative forms by the person's anticipation that they will result in controlling reactions from others. In the face of potential countercontrols, the individual does not normally give up but instead falls back to a less serious form of deviance as a device to solve the control problem. By taking the dynamics of control balancing into account, the theory permits prediction of the categorical form that deviance will take.

Manifestations

The results of these processes are portrayed in Figure 15.2, which shows a continuum (really two overlapping continuums), the left side of which is called the repression zone and the right side of which is called the autonomy zone. Each side of the continuum is divided into three segments representing greater degrees of control imbalance as one moves outward from the middle, balanced segment. The top row of that figure contains labels for the individuals with their respective control ratios, while the bottom row shows the labels for the kind of deviance that is likely to result from people in the respective segments.

Conformity. The middle of the continuum portrayed in Figure 15.2 is occupied by people who have control ratios near one, with nearly equal amounts of control exercised and experienced. The theory predicts Confor-

❖ ❖ ❖ ❖   **Figure 15.2 Continuums Representing Variations in Control Ratio and Predicted Forms of Deviance Associated With Positions on Those Continuums**

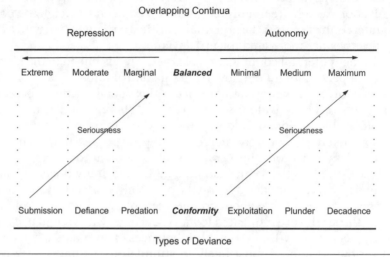

Adapted from Tittle, Charles R. 1995. *Control Balance: Toward a General Theory of Deviance*, pg. 189. Boulder, CO: Westview.

mity (deliberate obedience to rules with full consciousness) most of the time for such individuals. It does not predict conformity all the time, nor does it predict absolutely that people in particular circumstances will conform. This is partly because control ratios are not absolutely stable. Remember that autonomy can be thought of as a general condition covering all realms of human activity as well as being specific to realms or situations. Therefore, a person might generally conform but employ deviant behavior within a particular situation or with respect to a particular domain of activity.

Repressive Deviance. There are three categories of deviance associated with control deficits (the left, or repressive, side of the continuum). Starting from the middle and moving outward to the left, the first portion of the repressive side of the continuum is designated a Marginal zone. Marginal individuals experience somewhat more control against themselves than they can exercise back. Therefore, they do have a control deficit, but they are not totally controlled. With this small deficit, they may become motivated to correct that shortfall by stealing or directly coercing others. Recall that they are predisposed to deviant motivation because of the universal, latent discomfort of being subject to control. That latent disgust intertwines with episodic circumstances that provoke awareness of the control deficit. But since stealing or direct coercion of others, which would probably most effectively amend this control deficit, is also the kind of behavior that has the greatest chance of activating countercontrolling responses, it is realistically possible only for some people. Only individuals with small control deficits can contemplate escaping countercontrol—because they can exercise nearly as much control as is exercised against them. Thus, they have a generally low probability of deviant behavior, but when they do deviate, it is likely to involve Predation.

In thinking about the greater likelihood of predation by those with small control deficits, remember that the theory assumes that the Predation category is the most serious of the repressive deviances, and the theory assumes that the most serious forms of deviance are also the ones that will be most effective in altering a control imbalance. Therefore, all people with a control deficit who become motivated for deviance will want to use the most serious form of deviance—in this case predation. However, only those with small deficits can realistically contemplate doing such acts, so those with small deficits are more likely to choose predation than any of the other repressive acts. In addition to theft, predation encompasses behaviors like assault, rape, or homicide, as well as acts in which an individual directly preys upon another person or entity.

The next repressive segment of the continuum is called the Moderate zone because it characterizes those with modest control deficits. Those in this zone are likely to exhibit defiant behavior. Even though they are more strongly predisposed for action to overcome their control situations than are Marginal individuals, they can anticipate greater countercontrol in the case of more serious deviance. Hence, moderately repressed people are quite likely to commit some deviance, but Predation will not often be used. Rather, they more likely will do things to protest the sources of their control deficits, or to record their frustration by withdrawal from participation. Defiance enables people to overcome a deficit, at least temporarily, without activating massive countercontrol. This form of deviance includes such things as contravening curfews, engaging in adult pleasures and other status offenses by teenagers, protest actions by student rebels or striking workers, sulking, or hyperbolic overconformity among subordinates. Moderate control deficits are also predictive of escapist behavior patterns exemplified by alcohol and drug abuse, suicide, family desertion, mental illness, or countercultural participation.

The third, leftmost, segment of the repressive continuum is called an Extreme zone, and those with control imbalances placing them in this category are liable to Submission. These people have overwhelming control deficits, which generate powerful predispositions for deviance. But they are also so control disadvantaged that strong counterresponses to almost any deviance is inevitable. Despite strong motivation for predatory and defiant acts that would effectively overcome their deficits, such individuals will rarely do these things. Indeed, repeated and continuous subjugation dulls their spirits and erases cognitive creativity and the capacity for imagining alternatives. The result is slavish obedience to the demands of the situation and to others with more control.

Autonomous Deviance. The autonomous, or control surplus, end of the continuum is also broken into three segments. Starting in the middle of the whole continuum and moving toward the right, the first zone contains those with minimal surpluses. They exercise slightly more control than they experience. For them, motivation to use deviance grows out of an urge to extend their control, motivation that is produced when there is goal blockage and/or situational provocations. Circumstantial conditions that generate motivation for people with a surplus include those in which their control is successfully employed as well as when it is denied. However, despite having some surplus of control, such individuals cannot totally escape countercontrol, so they are cautious in committing direct acts of deviance that might stimulate controlling responses against themselves. Rather, they are likely to turn to exploitation, a form of indirect predation, which is possible because their control surpluses enable them to use other persons or organizational units to achieve things that enhance their own control.

Minimally surplused people, such as corporate executives, might direct their employees to engage in price-fixing, or gang leaders might lead their charges in neighborhood shakedown schemes. Politicians, who generally have a minimum of surplus control, might peddle their influence; famous actors might bribe or try to get their accusers fired in order to escape noxious publicity; and professional athletes might employ someone to incapacitate competitors. Furthermore, people with minimal surpluses, such as estranged husbands, might use intermediaries to create compromising situations for their wives hoping to produce more favorable divorce settlements; pimps might subsist from the earnings of their prostitutes. Finally, organized crime figures might hire operatives to punish or kill an uncooperative judge or juror or even a troublesome business associate.

The second segment of the autonomy end of the continuum portrayed in Figure 15.2 is called Medium autonomy. Individuals with control ratios relegating them to this segment have more surplus control than do those in the Minimal zone, and so they are fairly free of potential countercontrol, though they are not entirely autonomous. Because they see others generally conceding to, or serving, their needs and wants, medium autonomous people become convinced that little can stop them. Moreover, repeatedly controlling others causes them to grow insensitive to the plight of subordinates. The less controlled people are, the harder it is for them to appreciate the condition of others. Control, therefore, corrupts its wielders. They cannot empathize with subordinates, because they have had little personal experience with restraint.

Medium autonomy produces selfish or indifferent acts of plunder, including uncaring environmental pollution created by leaders of imperialistic nations or businesses extracting scarce resources from third-world countries; massive devastation of natural habitats by greedy corporate owners or executives; confiscatory taxation or enslaving work programs inflicted by autocrats or invading forces; pogroms, such as the holocaust or the campaigns of the last century against Native Americans, designed by political or military leaders to eliminate whole groups of people; and tyrannical acts like those of Jim Jones, leader of a religious group who ordered the suicide of hundreds of his followers (Layton, 1998).

The Maximum zone, the last segment of the autonomy end of the continuum on the far right, encompasses people with huge control surpluses—those who have almost complete license for exercising control and acting without worry about countercontrol. Such people are provoked by the slightest stimulus and by past successes in extending their already substantial control; moreover, they have little to fear, so they have a high probability of bizarre and jaded behavior, which reflects a search for meaning in the face of boredom with the mundane. The resulting deviance is called decadence, and those who practice it include autocrats like Nero whose excesses extended to fiddling while Rome burned. A few contemporary billionaires can be called decadent; they include Howard Hughes and perhaps Michael Jackson, both of whom apparently pursued kinky life styles and satisfied macabre tastes. These illustrations suggest that people with maximum control surpluses are totally oblivious to the possibility of countercontrol or the consequences that their actions have for others. Obviously, such individuals are rare.

Summary of the Control Balancing Process   ❖ ❖ ❖ ❖

This integrated theory is built around a central causal process that interprets deviant behavior as a mechanism employed to alter a person's control imbalance, either permanently or temporarily. Deviance is regarded as specifically functional, or useful, for those who do it—although this purpose is not necessarily evident to the individual or others, nor is it directly implicated in the specific form deviance takes. The autobiographical account of criminal behavior by Nathan McCall (1994) illustrates this. Having broken into a residence for the first time, he was exhilarated with a sense of control: "As I rifled through those people's most private possessions, I felt a peculiar power over them, even though we'd never met" (p. 46). Later, when he tried stick-ups, he felt even more in control, and it is clear from his description, remembered vividly years afterward, that the satisfaction of robbery was not from the money stolen or the ease of the life style. Instead, the gratification lay in the feelings connected with a perceived increase in control:

> Sticking up gave me a rush that I never got from B&Es. There was an almost magical transformation in my relationship with the rest of the world when I drew that gun on folks. I always marveled at how the toughest cats whimpered and begged for their lives when I stuck the barrel into their faces. Adults who ordinarily would have commanded my respect were forced to follow my orders like obedient kids. (p. 47)

When McCall ended up actually shooting someone, he felt even more control:

> I walked toward Plaz, looked into his eyes and saw something I had never seen in him before. Gone was the fierceness that made him so intimidating all those years. In its place was shock. And fear. It was more like terror. In that moment, I felt like God. I felt so good and powerful that I wanted to do it again. (p. 49)

Starting with the notion that deviance is undertaken to change relative distributions of control, control balance theory argues that motivation for deviance varies with individuals' control ratios, the amount of control they can exercise relative to that they are subject to. Moreover, the probability of deviance of some unspecified kind varies directly with the magnitude of a control imbalance in either direction from a balanced, middle position outward. Manifestation of deviant motivations in specific behaviors, however, is influenced by potential countercontrol in combination with the likelihood that it will be activated by a given behavior. Hence the theory explains the general probability of some form of deviance as well as the likely categorical type of deviance. The explanatory mechanism is a balancing of the potential

---

Deviance in Everyday Life

If true, perhaps a good example of plundering by one with medium autonomy is the business practices of Microsoft chairman Bill Gates. Gates is a billionaire, and perhaps the richest man in the world. He has been accused by many of his competitors, however, of being an unscrupulous businessman who threatens to destroy those who stand in his way and will resort to any tactic to secure a monopoly of the computer software market. For example, Microsoft is alleged to have tried to drive other web-based software packages off the market by shipping its own Internet browser with its popular Windows 98 operating system. In the late 1990s, the U.S. Department of Justice and the attorneys general of twenty states filed antitrust suits or complaints against Microsoft.

gain in control implied by deviance with the likely consequences of activating countercontrol. The theory, however, recognizes the importance of other convergent variables such as situational provocation of deviant motivation, opportunity for deviance, and various conditional variables (to be explained later). When a control ratio is near one, people generally conform. When it is unbalanced, the probability of deviance increases directly with the degree of imbalance. As control deficits increase, so does the *probability* of deviance generally, although the *seriousness* of likely deviance *decreases*. On the other hand, as a surplus increases, the *probability* and the *seriousness* of deviance both *increase*.

Although opportunity and situational provocations are necessary conditions, the theory contends that the likelihood of some form of deviant behavior mainly reflects motivation, which itself varies directly with a control imbalance. The specific form that deviance is likely to take, however, reflects both strength of motivation and potential controlling responses that particular deviant acts might stimulate. Both motivation and constraint are linked with a person's control ratio, but they are not determined by it. Those who become motivated toward deviance by situational provocation initially contemplate committing the deviance that would be most effective in altering a control imbalance, but they end up doing that which is possible given the constraint of the situation. Hence, actual behaviors grow out of a hydraulic relationship between motivation and constraint, given the presence of favorable opportunity.

Application to Societies and Other Organizations

While control balance theory's primary aim is to explain individual behavior, it also explains rates of deviance in social groups of various kinds (see Braithwaite, 1997). Societies, for example, can be distinguished from each other in terms of the *average* control ratio of their members. Most members of some societies, as well as other social entities, have control ratios that are near one. These "balanced" societies, according to the logic of control balancing, should have low rates of deviance.

Similarly, societies that are "marginally repressive," with members on average having slight control deficits, should exhibit low overall rates of crime and deviance, but when deviance does occur it should usually be of a predatory nature. The reason for a low probability of deviance but a greater probability of predation for individuals is aggregated here to make a prediction about whole societies. Remember that individuals with small deficits are less frequently motivated for deviance. However, when they do become motivated, they presumably want to use the most effective response in order to correct their control imbalance. The most effective is also the one most likely to generate countercontrol. By this general logic, societies whose members, on average, have moderate control deficits ("moderately repressive" societies) will have rather high rates of deviance, but most of it will be defiance. And those whose members are overwhelmingly suppressed will have a pattern of submissiveness.

By extending the reasoning about individual level causes of deviance, predictions about "minimally autonomous" societies, those whose average members have a slight surplus of control, can also be devised: they should be characterized by low rates of deviance, but exploitation should predominate among the deviant acts that do occur. Societies in which the average level of control is a considerable surplus will exhibit moderately high rates of deviance, mostly plunder. Finally, if there were to exist a society in which members' average control ratios showed a maximum surplus ("maximally autonomous" societies), it would be predicted to have a very high rate of deviance and much decadence.

This application of the theory assumes, of course, that other variables in the causal chain depicted in Figure 15.1, such as opportunity, show average values corresponding to the average control ratios. Such correspondence is actually unlikely to be the case, and because control ratios imply reciprocity (for some people to have control surpluses, others must have control deficits), it is even unlikely that many of the hypothetical societies identified above could exist. One would have trouble finding a society, for instance, where the average control exercised by individuals or other social entities is much greater than the average control experienced. "Average" can be conceived in different ways, however, making it possible to differentiate various types of societies. This is particularly true if one remembers that control balance theory concerns all forms of control, not just social control, and that some control exercised by people in one society may focus on people in other societies. For example, the citizens in a technologically advanced society probably have an average surplus of control because of their capability of controlling the physical world around them or because of the society's ability to dominate those in less developed societies.

The logic of the theory also permits one to explain relative rates of deviance among rulers and subjects in various kinds of political units. If rulers are far over on the autonomy end of the control ratio continuum, those who are ruled should be somewhere on the deficit side. In political units where rulers are constrained and the citizens relatively free, both should generally conform. If citizens have slight control deficits and rulers have slight control surpluses, citizens should commit a lot of predation, and rulers should do a lot of exploiting—although the overall rates of deviance in such units should be relatively low. By contrast, when rulers have a medium control surplus, and their control is much greater than that of their constituents, citizens should commit quite a bit of deviance, mostly of a defiant type, and rulers should do a lot of plundering. Finally, if rulers have maximum, excessive control, they should become decadent, and their subjects should become submissive.

Contingencies for the Control Balancing Process

To be effective, theories that set forth a universally operating causal process must recognize that such a process cannot work with the same degree of intensity in all circumstances. That is because the causal mechanisms the theory posits are affected by other characteristics of individuals or social situations. Theories that recognize that fact, however, and go on to identify such contingencies, and to specify how they affect the central causal process, are especially desirable. Control balance theory attempts to do just that. It identifies a number of conditions that affect its operation. They include, but are not limited to the following: (1) personal characteristics such as perceptual accuracy, the person's moral consciousness, habits, personality, intelligence, self-confidence; (2) ability to actually carry out different kinds of deviance; (3) alternative motivations for deviance that might crop up episodically; and (4) a person's history of deviance. The theory also identifies contingencies that are "outside" individuals. They include: (1) organizational influences, such as subcultural normative expectations; (2) contingencies of the situation, such as the quality of the opportunity; (3) the characteristics of risk; and (4) the intensity and/or frequency of provocations.

To illustrate how contingencies come into play, consider perceptual accuracy, only one of many potential contingencies. Perception of reality varies among those who ostensibly observe the same phenomenon, as when witnesses to an accident tell different versions of what happened. In addition, people sometimes fail to see things as they actually are. This may be because they don't have enough information, but it may also be because they misperceive or misinterpret information even when they have it. Therefore, actual control ratios are sometimes less relevant than the individuals' perceptions of their control ratios; also, individuals' perceptions of the likelihood of countercontrol is clearly more important than reality. Even when a true control imbalance portends a specific category of deviant behavior, some individuals with that control imbalance will misperceive things and act on the basis of a different control ratio. This would not mean that the theory is wrong, although its prediction in this instance would be incorrect. Instead it indicates that people's perceptual characteristics have to be accommodated in applying the theory.

Integration

This chapter has attempted to illustrate the idea of theoretical integration by describing control balance theory, which was developed to synthesize ideas and causal arguments of various extant theories into one coherent system. Up to this point, we authors have tried to help you understand the theory, but we have not shown you explicitly what theories were being integrated nor how that integration was being achieved. We will now briefly turn to that task.

The main concept of the theory is the control ratio. It, however, is not a completely original concept. Instead it is an abstraction blending several concepts associated with other theories. The first of those other theories is that developed by Gibbs (1981, 1994b) who demonstrated that control could become the key concept of most if not all sociological thinking, and who used the idea of control to create a macro-level deductive schema of relationships among variables. The set of theories built around the notion that tension from discrepancies between contending forces leads to deviance constitute a second source for the control ratio idea.

You have already been exposed to several classic theories featuring discrepancies between contending elements. They include deterrence, rational choice, and social learning approaches, all of which are rooted in utilitarian philosophy. Utilitarian theory, you will recall, maintains that the potential pain (cost) relative to the potential pleasure (reward) associated with a contemplated action determines whether the action is performed (Plamenatz, 1958). In addition, Merton's anomie formulation (1938, 1968) suggests that deviant motivation stems from one's perception of a discrepancy between personal goals, which are prescribed by the larger culture, and access to socially acceptable avenues for accomplishing those goals. Moreover, anomie theory contends that the type of deviance used as an adaptation to a goals/ means disjuncture is linked with the nature of that discrepancy.

Several other theoretical schemes also employ a relativity notion. One is Turk's conflict theory (1969). It contends that relative power among contending groups determines whether the behaviors of one group will be criminalized (made illegal) by another group. Power differences are depicted as the source of tension, leading to behaviors by superordinates and subordinates. Another equilibration theory is that of social exchange. The basic idea is that human beings strive for reciprocity in social interchanges (Blau, 1964; Homans, 1961; see also the general discussion in Alexander, 1987:Chapter 11). They want reciprocity because imbalances evoke discomforting emotions or social awkwardness (see also Tallman and Gray, 1990; Gray and Tallman, 1984).

Theories concerning the effect of power, social status, or prestige on behavior, particularly on deviant or criminal behavior, also contribute to control balance theory. The literature is replete with explanations of behavioral differences among individuals, demographic categories, and social groups—explanations that assume occupants of superior social positions will obey rules that subordinates violate (see Tittle, 1983). While this contention enjoys only weak or contradictory empirical support, it has enormous appeal. Therefore, control balance theory incorporates the idea that deprivation motivates deviance—however, the relevant deprivation is not material but rather is of a transcendent character having to do with autonomy in social relationships.

This theory, then, "integrates" other theories by developing a central concept that represents an abstraction from three sets of extant theoretical ideas: the importance of control in human affairs, the relativity of contending forces, and the centrality of autonomy for human motivation. The basic idea of control balance theory—that deviance is functional—is also adapted from other lines of theoretical work. One of them includes social bonds (or "social control") theory (Chapter 14) and self-control theory (Chapter 13). Such arguments assume self-interested pursuit of gratification so that deviance results when such impulses are not blocked. In this mode of thought, deviance and crime do something for those who commit them. Deviance is "functional" because it satisfies the urges or needs of those who commit it. Another is utilitarian/deterrence theory, which sees all human behavior as resulting from rational decision-making where the person calculates benefits and costs. Criminal or deviant behavior occurs when, on balance, it appears to be more beneficial than costly for its perpetrator. Similarly, Marxian conflict theory portrays crime as a survival tool for subordinates and a tool for competitive advantage among capitalists. The various versions of strain theory assume that crime/deviance is useful for those who commit it.

Control balance theory vaguely siphons from numerous "functional" arguments, but it explicitly draws on three theories. One of them is Katz's theory of "transcendence" (Katz, 1988), which emphasizes two latent themes. One is that deviance is motivated by an urge to escape undesirable conditions—chaos, humiliation, irrationality, or sometimes simply external control. A second theme is that deviance permits psychological or "moral" triumph. The underlying idea, and the one borrowed by control balance theory, is that deviance puts the deviator in control and is therefore attractive. All the forms of deviance that Katz describes seem to be attempts to escape control from others or circumstances, and they seem to reflect efforts to exercise control back toward the people or circumstances controlling the individual. Assertion of autonomy in Katz's formulation and in control balance theory is accomplished by triumphant redirection of control.

A second functional theory whose ideas are incorporated within the control balancing mechanism is that by Turk (1969). His theory concerns how groups negotiate their positions with strategic considerations for the power of other groups. It is built on the idea that negotiation involves efforts by subordinates to avoid control by superiors as well as efforts by superiors to expand their control. Turk's theory suggests that deviance by individuals or organized social units can be interpreted as a maneuver for managing control imbalances.

A third theory serving as a foundation for the abstract central causal process of control balance theory is psychologically oriented. According to "reactance" theory (Chapter 12), human beings are provoked to break rules or rebel whenever some freedom they perceive they have is blocked. They do this to restore, at least psychically, the lost freedom. Thus, the main idea of reactance theory that is incorporated into control balance is that behavioral constraints motivate a person to gain more control and that deviant behavior can be explained as a functional response, used to manage a control problem.

Therefore, within its central causal process, control balance theory integrates many theories that employ the notion that deviance serves its perpetrator and that this usefulness helps explain both the origin and maintenance of deviant behavior. But control balance theory goes further in integration because it makes use of several variables that are theorized to interact or converge. Each of those variables, including situational provocations, debasement, motivation for deviance, opportunity, and constraint (involving risk and seriousness), are accepted as givens; in other theories these are treated as dependent variables. Although control balance theory does not fully articulate how these theories feed in to help explain or predict the magnitude of the values that each of those variables might assume in a given case, it implicitly incorporates those causal processes.

Finally, this theory sets forth contingencies that set the parameters within which its causal effects operate and that affect the force and completeness with which effects unfold. Again, each of these contingencies is itself subject to explanation by existing theories. For instance, morality affects whether a motivated person is willing to use one or another form of deviance to overcome a control imbalance—even when the chance of countercontrol is low. And as you learned in Chapter 13, there are several theories explaining why people have the moral commitments that they have. By treating moral sentiments as a contingency, control balance theory also incorporates the theories concerning morality.

So, control balance theory implicitly brings together all the other theories we have discussed in the previous chapters. Of course, control balance theory does not explicitly demonstrate how one or another of them explains the presence of the contingencies or the values they might actually take in concrete circumstances. Thus, despite the integrative thrust of control balance theory, it does not fully articulate all the elements it integrates. Integration is never complete. To fully integrate theories, one must explicitly show how other theories explain all variables. And since there is more than one theory for each variable, such merger requires extensive ancillary integration.

Imagery for how an integrated theory should look is provided by a wagon wheel. There is a hub—for example, the control balancing process—and there are spokes and reinforcing braces connecting two or more of the spokes at different places out from the hub. These spokes and braces are represented by other theories and theory fragments that explain the variables in the theory, including the contingencies. For example, as noted, the full operation of control balancing is contingent on an individual's morality. But to explain when moral objections are likely to be high, other arguments have to be brought to bear. Perhaps the particular method of discipline used by the parents, the parents' personalities and moral beliefs, the size of the child's family, the kind of community in which the child grew up, the family's economic circumstances, role models to which the child is exposed, the individual's biological structure, as well as other things, affect moral sentiments. Since many theories pertain to how morals are developed, complete integration would have to go well beyond what is done in control balance theory.

Nevertheless, this theory "integrates" to a much greater extent than most theories. It proposes the main motivator of deviance as a perception that a given deviant act might change a control imbalance. This motivator represents an abstraction merging the motivating elements of several other theories, and is itself a product of specific activators—a convergence of predisposition toward deviance, provocations, and a feeling of having been demeaned. Furthermore, the theory explicitly acknowledges the contingencies posed by other forces, which affect how well its causal processes play themselves out. These contingencies include motivations for alternative, nondeviant behaviors. Control balancing takes place with somewhat different outcomes if, for instance, a motivated individual can prevail on the tennis court rather than having to consider slugging someone after an insult. The theory also uses constraint as an essential process, and it portrays constraint and motivation relative to each other. Constraint is portrayed as a product of other causal factors, including risk and the seriousness of the act, which are situational, and some causal forces that express themselves as contingencies. Moreover, opportunity for deviance is explicitly brought into the theory, as is the ability to perform the deviant act in question.

Summary

We began this chapter by showing that most theories for explaining deviance/crime reviewed in previous chapters are narrowly focused, in that they stress only one or two of the elements operative in behavior; for that reason they do not provide good explanation. In order to improve theories, some scholars have tried to bring the separate causal elements—motivation, opportunity, ability, absence of competing motivation, and constraint—together within one scheme by drawing on various already-formulated theories about those causal elements. A recent attempt at such so-called theoretical integration—control balance theory—was presented to illustrate this kind of theory building.

Control balance theory portrays deviance as an outcome of a number of interacting, or converging, processes that include those producing a predisposition to become motivated for deviance, situational provocations that transform the predispositions into actual motivations, opportunity that would permit motivation to be expressed in deviance, and constraint that would prevent expression of deviant motivation in actual deviance or divert it from one form to another. The key concept of control balance theory is the control ratio, which is the total amount of control a person can exercise relative to the control to which that person is subject. And the central idea is that deviance represents a device to alter a control imbalance.

According to the theory, when control is out of balance, the person is liable to become motivated for deviance. However, whether motivation is expressed in particular forms of deviance depends on the potential for countercontrolling responses. These potential counterresponses are linked to the degree of a control imbalance and the characteristics of the potential deviance as it might be expressed in particular situations that reflect different degrees of constraint. The person is always motivated to use the most effective type of deviance to alter a control imbalance, but such deviance is also most likely to stimulate countercontrol. Therefore, the chances of the most serious deviance, either predation for those with a control deficit or decadence for those with a control surplus, is greatest among those with the slightest deficits and among those with the greatest surpluses: individuals in each of these situations can most reasonably contemplate overcoming countercontrol.

Similarly, those with modestly imbalanced control ratios are most likely to engage in defiance if they have a deficit, and plunder if they have a surplus: both defiance and plunder are assumed to be less serious, and therefore less likely to bring forth countercontrol, than are predation and decadence. Finally those with the largest control deficits and those with the slightest control surpluses are likely to choose deviant forms that are appropriate to their situations. This choice implies submissiveness for those facing control deficits so overwhelming that they cannot contemplate any alternative other than complete obedience, and it implies exploitation for those with small control surpluses—because they cannot realistically contemplate more serious plunder.

An essential idea of the theory, however, is that the motivation toward deviance strongly influences the overall likelihood of some form of deviance. When people are strongly motivated but are blocked by potential countercontrol from expressing that motivation in a particular form of deviance, they will fall back to a less serious form of deviance that involves less constraint. Therefore, there is a strong relationship between motivation, which is linked to a person's control ratio, and the probability of some form of deviance, but the form of the deviance likely to be expressed depends on the interplay between motivation and constraint, assuming that opportunity exists.

This integrated theory can be applied at both the individual and macro levels to provide explanations of why individuals commit deviance and why rates of deviance vary from one social group or category to another. Further, the theory is truly integrative because it combines ideas from numerous other theories by abstractly incorporating them into the main concept, by bringing them into the causal chain or the control balancing process, or by exploiting them to provide contingencies for the theory (conditions under which it works with greater or less power).

Since narrowly focused theories are necessarily inefficient, and since existing formulations (or theory fragments) identify many factors that appear essential for understanding deviant behavior, theories integrating diverse elements of pre-existing theory fragments would appear necessary for improving the ability to explain deviance. Control balance is not the first theory based on the principle of integration, and it certainly is not the perfect theory. However, it exemplifies a style of theory building that is probably necessary for progress toward understanding crime and deviance. ◆

Chapter 16

Theories of Rate Variations

All the theories examined so far have been interpreted mainly in terms of the behavior of individual persons. The micro-, or individual-level, question has been: "Why do people like *X* or in *X's* situation do deviance or crime?" However, there are other, macro-level questions of equal or greater importance that involve another kind of explanation. Those questions are: "Why do some societies (or other social entities) exhibit higher or lower rates of deviance or crime than others?" and "Why do some societies (or other social entities) produce greater or lesser amounts of deviance at various points in time?"

Answers to these two levels of questions are not the same, although they may be related. For instance, a theory might contend that individuals in any society who commit homicide do so because of some condition, *Z*, or some combined set of circumstances, *Q*, *R*, and *Y*. Thus, if the theory is true, individual killers in the United States, England, China, or any other place in the world would operate under condition *Z* or face circumstances *Q*, *R*, and *Y*. Yet the *rates* of homicide may vary dramatically among the United States, England, China, and other countries, as indeed they do. The homicide rates in England and China, for example, are only a fraction of what they are in the United States (1.8 and 1.76 per 100,000 versus 10.1). Similarly, although the explanation for individual homicide may be the same at all points in time, the rates of homicide in a given society may go up or down during specific historical eras, as indeed they have in the United States. The U.S. homicide rate increased from 5.3 (per 100,000) in 1950 to 10.9 in 1991 and then declined to 8.2 in 1995.

The issue, then, is why, if the explanation for individual homicide is the same in the United States, England, and China, the United States has so much more of it, and if the explanation for individual homicide is the same at all points in time, why does the rate of homicide vary over time in the same society? These variations may, of course, reflect different kinds of social structures in different societies that create condition *Z*, or social circumstances *QRY*, with greater or lesser frequency, as well as temporal changes in social conditions that affect *Z* or *QRY* in specific societies. That is, some social entities may permanently or temporarily develop more of the conditions that activate the causal variables that influence individuals to kill.

The variations might also occur because different societies or social groups, or the same society or social group in different historical epochs, provide different meanings to conditions so that *Z* or *QRY* have different content from one society or social group to another or from one time period to another. For instance, if the main condition generating homicide is competitive frustration, some societies may have less homicide because their economic and cultural systems define competition as normal, and thus it is less frustrating. Alternatively, their cultural systems may provide channels by which some individuals can relieve frustration, or their cultural themes may condemn homicide of all types as unacceptable (in contrast to other societies that excuse homicide under some conditions, such as for marital infidelity or trespassing on private property). Similarly, even in a competitive society like that of the United States, frustration may vary with the health of the economy or the number of people in specific age cohorts who might serve as competitors.

A third possibility, however, is that the peculiar social environments of various societies or of the same societies at various points in time generate specific amounts of homicide through mechanisms not recognized by individual-level theories. In other words, there may be some unique group-level process that encourages homicide but that is not readily translated into micro-level application.

No matter which of these three possibilities ultimately proves correct, it is clear that explanations of individuals' behavior will not suffice as explanations for macro phenomena, at least not in a simple and straightforward manner. Therefore, some scholars have developed theories to try to answer questions about rate variations. Such theories can be divided into three types. First, some societal or group-level theories specifically deny that there is a supra-individual reality. They assume that micro-level explanatory principles can be aggregated to the ecological level (concerning large social entities such as neighborhoods, cities, or countries) to provide accounts of collections of individuals' actions. Second, some macro theories provide explanations strictly at the ecological or aggregate level, with no obvious connection to individuals' behaviors or the micro-level processes that might translate aggregate phenomena into specific acts of deviance. Third, there are theories that apply at both the individual and the ecological level, with the theorist making some effort to show how the explanatory principles apply at either level or to show how the explanatory process involves reciprocal influence.

In this chapter we will describe various theories within each of these three types. However, before those theories can be very meaningful, it is necessary to describe some of the variations that require macro-level theories.

Rate Variations

In an earlier chapter we discussed sources of information about deviant behavior and tried to show that our descriptive knowledge is weak, since systematic data are available, in any given society, for only some kinds of deviance, and even the best of those data contain much inaccuracy. For such reasons, patterns of variation in deviance among individuals are problematic. However, the facts about categorical (having to do with demographic or other divisions), societal (concerning large organized social units that are politically distinct), or ecological variations are even more problematic. Societies differ in the extent and intensity of their efforts to collect information, and for this and other reasons, the quality and availability of data about deviance in general varies from society to society. Moreover, the availability and quality of data among societies or ecological units is not equal for all kinds of deviance. Some deviance may be well documented in one society but not another, and some forms of deviance are hardly measured at all while other kinds are the focus of frequent attention. Thus, there are no systematic data among an array of countries concerning homosexual conduct, professional misbehavior, family desertion, and hundreds of other kinds of unacceptable behavior. In fact, most international data concern violations of standard criminal laws, and many of those data are unreliable. The "facts" about ecological variations that we will present, therefore, are sketchy and in any case involve only a few types of deviance among the thousands of types that actually occur.

Suicide

Some of the best cross-societal data concern suicide; such data are collected by government bureaus concerned with vital statistics—events such as births, deaths, and their causes that contribute to the growth and composition of populations—and not by agencies set up to punish wrongdoers. Nevertheless, suicide data are not necessarily reliable (see Chapter 3). Some societies have better organizations for collecting vital statistics. In addition, classifying a death as a suicide rather than as an accident or homicide is often problematic because determination of an actual cause of death is not always clearcut (see Chapter 3). The accuracy of that determination depends on the volume of resources devoted to the task, guiding ideologies, and political or social pressures. For instance, in countries where religion defines suicide as so sinful as to disqualify a soul for the afterlife, or where social sentiment defines suicide as shameful or indicative of mental illness, there is much pressure from relatives of the deceased to classify the death as something other than suicide. On the other hand, in some societies there are often pressures for certifiers of death to classify cases as suicide rather than crime in order to save the reputation of family members who might be suspected of murder.

Table 16.1 Suicide Rates (suicides per 100,000) for Various Countries, Circa 1990[a]

High		Medium		Low	
Hungary	39.9	Iceland	15.7	Uzbekistan	6.8
Sri Lanka	33.2	Norway	15.5	Liechtenstein	6.7
Finland	30.3	Yugoslavia	15.3	Argentina	6.7
CHINA	28.7	Bulgaria	14.7	Taiwan	6.7
Slovenia	27.6	Mauritius	14.2	ISRAEL	6.5
Estonia	27.1	Trinidad/Tobago	13.7	Chile	5.6
RUSSIA	26.5	New Zealand	13.5	Costa Rica	5.2
Lithuania	26.1	Singapore	13.1	Venezuela	4.8
Latvia	26.0	Poland	13.0	Barbados	4.7
Germany, East	24.4	Australia	12.9	Ecuador	4.6
Denmark	24.1	CANADA	12.7	Macao	4.4
Austria	23.6	Kyrgyzstan	12.5	Panama	3.8
Belarus	23.6	UNITED STATES	12.4	Tadjikistan	3.8
Switzerland	21.9	Hong Kong	11.7	Greece	3.5
USSR	21.1	Puerto Rico	10.5	Bahrain	3.1
Ukraine	20.7	Scotland	10.5	Colombia	3.1
Byelorussia	20.4	Uruguay	10.3	Armenia	2.8
FRANCE	20.1	Northern Ireland	9.9	Malta	2.3
Belgium	19.3	Netherlands	9.7	Mexico	2.3
Czech Republic	19.3	Ireland	9.5	St. Lucia	2.3
Kazakhstan	19.1	Romania	9.0	Albania	2.1
Czechoslovakia	17.9	Portugal	8.8	Maldives	2.0
Luxembourg	17.8	Rep. of Korea	8.0	Bahamas	1.2
GERMANY, WEST	17.5	ENGLAND/WALES	7.8	Kuwait	.8
SWEDEN	17.2	ITALY	7.6	Egypt	.04
JAPAN	16.4	Spain	7.5		
		Zimbabwe	7.4		

[a] Not all of the rates are for the exact year of 1990; some are for 1988, some 1989, some 1990, and some 1991.
Adapted from: David Lester, "Suicide in an International Perspective." *Suicide and Life-Threatening Behavior* 27, 1997b: 105–106.

Table 16.1 arrays countries with respect to suicide rates around 1990. It shows those rates varying widely from one country to another. The highest rate is close to 40 (per 100,000) while the lowest is less than 1 (.04). The challenge of macro-level theories, then, is to explain why such countries as Denmark (24.1) and China (28.7) have relatively high suicide rates while countries like Mexico (2.3) and Israel (6.5) have suicide rates that are only a fraction of those in other countries. Note in this regard that the United States (12.4) is in the middle group, with modest suicide rates. Most other major modernized nations (names capitalized) have higher suicide rates than the United States, the main exceptions being England/Wales and Israel, both of which have fairly low rates (7.8 and 6.5, respectively).

Homicide

Homicide is a second type of deviance for which international data are available. These data, however, are probably even less accurate than are the suicide data. That is because they are collected by the police. Not only are the police in various countries more or less efficient and careful in differentiating among suicide, homicide, and accidents, but the willingness of citizens to report to the police varies from society to society. Moreover, the accuracy of record keeping differs from one society to another. Finally, there are political considerations. Because of the possible impact on their tourist industry, some countries do not want to be thought of as dangerous places, so the police often use procedures that underestimate the amount of homicide. Nevertheless, differences in rates of homicide are sufficiently large to suggest real differences and to invite attempts at explanation.

Deviance in Everyday Life

Most people, both in the United States and around the world, think that America has very high crime rates and that it is one of the most unsafe countries in the world. In their recent book, *Crime Is Not the Problem*, Zimring and Hawkins (1997) put that myth to rest. After an extensive analysis of national and international crime rates, they found that while America does have a very high rate of homicide, the rates of other crimes are comparable to or lower than those of European countries. For example, the rates of robbery in the United States are comparable to those in Italy, Australia, Canada, England, the Netherlands, and Belgium. Assault rates in the United States are lower than those in Canada, New Zealand, and Australia. The problem, Zimring and Hawkins conclude, is that America has high rates of lethal assaults and violence. The reason? America has far more crimes committed with a gun than almost any other country in the world.

Table 16.2 shows that homicide rates vary dramatically from one country to another, varying from an astonishing 102 (per 100,000) in Swaziland to about 1 (per 100,000) in Madagascar. Note that the United States is included in the highest one-third in homicide rates, with a rate of about 10.1.

Although this is higher than about two-thirds of the countries for which data are available, it still is much less than the rates in several African nations and even less than Egypt and the Netherlands (14.20 and 14.81, respectively). Homicide rates in the United States, however, are greater than in most modernized countries such as Sweden (8.10) and Canada (5.74), with Germany

Table 16.2 Estimated Homicide Rates (homicides per 100,000) for Various Countries, Circa 1990[a]

High		Medium		Low	
Swaziland	102.99	Romania	8.52	Tajikistan	2.98
Sri Lanka	33.50	Latvia	8.47	Austria	2.78
Tonga	23.06	Sweden	8.10	Chile	2.69
Jamaica	21.61	Finland	8.07	Syria	2.66
Rwanda	19.43	Portugal	7.75	Greece	2.64
GERMANY	18.29	Seychelles	7.50	Norway	2.64
Lebanon	17.08	India	7.47	Qatar	2.57
Philippines	16.11	St. Kitts/Nevis	6.76	Jordan	2.48
Costa Rica	15.33	ITALY	6.50	Mauritius	2.47
Netherlands	14.81	Maldives	6.00	ISRAEL	2.43
Egypt	14.20	CANADA	5.74	Singapore	2.23
Venezuela	12.27	Ukraine	5.48	Nepal	2.16
Botswana	11.57	Denmark	5.40	Australia	2.13
Ethiopia	11.29	Lithuania	5.36	Bahrain	2.04
Thailand	10.95	Former Yugoslavia	5.18	Malta	2.02
Bermuda	10.10	Myanmar	5.05	Hong Kong	1.95
UNITED STATES	10.10	Armenia	4.45	Malaysia	1.93
RUSSIA	9.77	Bulgaria	3.92	CHINA	1.76
Kazakhstan	9.42	Peru	3.63	JAPAN	1.58
Barbados	9.04	Scotland	3.57	Cyprus	1.45
Kuwait	8.99	Hungary	3.56	Rep. of Korea	1.36
Kyrgyztan	8.82			ENGLAND/WALES	1.28
				Madagascar	1.07

[a] Average number of homicides for 1988, 1989, and 1990, divided by estimated population in 1988.

Adapted from The Fourth United Nations Survey of Crime Trends and Operations of Criminal Justice Systems, 1986–1990, United Nations Crime and Justice Information Network, and Statistical Abstract of the United States, 1988–1990, U.S. Census Bureau, Washington, D.C.

(18.29) being an exception. Explanation for this variation is not obvious, because almost any ad hoc account is contradicted by cases that don't fit the account. Take, for example, the hypothesis that homicides and poverty vary directly. While it is true that some poor countries, such as Sri Lanka and Rwanda, have high homicide rates, others, like Malaysia and Tajikistan, have low rates. It is a challenge for theorists to explain these rate variations.

Theft

The third set of international rates concerns theft (Table 16.3). These data are even less reliable than the homicide data, but the variations from country to country are large enough to require explanation beyond unreliability. The rates range from a high of 6,468 (per 100,000) in Sweden to a low of 4 in Nepal. At first glance it might be tempting to conclude that the wealthier nations have greater rates of theft, but the high rates in places like Bermuda and Barbados contradict that. Hence, it is important to apply some of the theories presented later in this chapter to try to understand these differences.

Drug Usage

It would be most helpful if there were comparable self-report surveys, or even medical/hospital data concerning drug usage for all the countries in the world. Unfortunately, such data do not exist, so we must rely on police reports. Remember that even efficient police practices and record keeping do not produce reliable data about drug use. That is because most drug use goes undetected and unreported, by both victims and observing citizens. The data, then, are based mainly on arrests, which vary with police efficiency and governmental policy about what kinds of drug use are illegal.

Table 16.3 Estimated Rates of Theft (thefts per 100,000) for Various Countries, Circa 1990[a]

High		Medium		Low	
SWEDEN	6,468	JAPAN	983	Tajikistan	179
Denmark	6,097	Botswana	884	Chile	149
UNITED STATES	5,101	St. Kitts/Nevis	861	Ukraine	139
Scotland	4,719	Maldives	846	Qatar	118
GERMANY	4,297	Mauritius	735	Lebanon	112
Norway	4,088	Venezuela	599	Romania	84
ENGLAND/WALES	4,086	Hong Kong	536	Peru	83
Bermuda	3,856	RUSSIA	484	Armenia	78
CANADA	3,737	Former Yugoslavia	480	Sri Lanka	76
Netherlands	3,035	Latvia	462	Madagascar	72
ISRAEL	2,830	Lithuania	458	Thailand	71
Australia	2,512	Egypt	458	Greece	60
ITALY	2,392	Bulgaria	411	Philippines	49
Finland	2,082	Jamaica	340	Myanmar	47
Austria	1,728	Kazakhstan	338	Jordan	41
Barbados	1,475	Costa Rica	279	CHINA	36
Malta	1,331	Malaysia	253	India	29
Seychelles	1,307	Cyprus	218	Ethiopia	24
Portugal	1,081	Kyrgyztan	202	Nepal	4
Swaziland	1,058	Rep. of Korea	190		
Singapore	1,051				
Spain	1,031				
Hungary	1,021				

[a] Average number of thefts for 1988, 1989, and 1990, divided by estimated population in 1988.
Adapted from The Fourth United Nations Crime and Justice Information Network, and Crime in the United States, 1990, Uniform Crime Reports. Federal Bureau of Investigation. U.S. Department of Justice, Washington, D.C.

Nevertheless, Table 16.4 shows that even with the tremendous errors that are likely present in drug data, variations from society to society are so large that something other than differential unreliability must be at work. The rates vary from 1,394 (per 100,000) in Bermuda to less than 1 in Armenia (.8), Madagascar (.7), Hungary (.6), Romania (.1), and China (.1). Note that, like

Table 16.4 Estimated Rates of Drug Crimes (drug crimes per 100,000) for Various Countries, Circa 1990[a]

High		Medium		Low	
Bermuda	1,394	Austria	67	Ukraine	9
UNITED STATES	379	Spain	64	Cyprus	8
SWEDEN	352	Malta	57	Costa Rica	8
Denmark	267	Portugal	54	RUSSIA	8
CANADA	241	ITALY	53	Latvia	6
Barbados	192	Finland	43	Rep. of Korea	5
Norway	186	Australia	38	Maldives	5
Jamaica	184	Netherlands	35	Syria	4
ISRAEL	166	Venezuela	32	Jordan	3
St Kitts/Nevis	164	Greece	26	Lithuania	3
GERMANY	153	JAPAN	22	India	2
Scotland	143	Kazakhstan	19	Former Yugoslavia	1.4
Thailand	88	ENGLAND/WALES	18	Nepal	1.4
Seychelles	86	Egypt	18	Tonga	1
Hong Kong	83	Kyrgyztan	18	Armenia	.8
Mauritius	83	Ethiopia	13	Madagascar	.7
Swaziland	83	Qatar	12	Hungary	.6
Botswana	73	Myanmar	10	Romania	.1
Malaysia	69			CHINA	.1

[a] Average number of drug crimes for 1988, 1989, and 1990, divided by estimated population in 1988.
Adapted from The Fourth United Nations Crime and Justice Information Network, and Crime in the United States, 1990, Uniform Crime Reports. Federal Bureau of Investigation. U.S. Department of Justice, Washington, D.C.

the data for theft, these show the United States near the highest in the world, with a rate of drug crime of 379 (per 100,000). This rate is exceeded only by Bermuda, and it is far greater than such rates in Italy (53), Japan (22), and England/Wales (18). As with the other international deviance rates, these figures pose a strong challenge for ecological-level theories.

Theories Generalizing Micro-Level Principles

Utilitarian/Deterrence

In Chapter 14 you were introduced to the utilitarian/deterrence theory, which contends that human behavior is determined by the balance of gain relative to cost inherent in potential action. According to this theory, individuals are constantly calculating the costs and benefits of various actions. They will commit deviant acts in situations that promise more gratification than cost, and they will conform where the cost exceeds the potential gain. The way in which individuals calculate costs and benefits, however, is actually quite complicated, and since it depends largely on cognitive processes linked to individual characteristics, one cannot simply assess situational or contextual costs and benefits to explain and predict individuals' behavior.

Nevertheless, many laypersons and scholars assume that the principles of rational choice can be applied to groups, categories, or societies by identifying average costs and benefits prevailing in those social units and inferring the rates of deviance expected from them. Indeed, the legal codes in most modern societies are based on that very assumption. When the legislature in a particular state enacts a law prohibiting some type of behavior and attaches a penalty to its commission, they are assuming that the result will be a lower rate of that behavior. This assumption stems from the notion that, in general, there will be a high enough probability of apprehension and punishment for violation of the law to outweigh the potential benefit of the prohibited behavior for most people. Similarly, if a given society heavily condemns suicide and it encourages informal penalties such as shame for the surviving families of persons who kill themselves, its members are assuming that the potential costs of suicide will overshadow its benefits and thereby keep the rate of occurrence low.

Following this principle of ecological aggregation, then, one would explain variations in rates of various kinds of deviance from one social context to another by reference to the distribution of relative rewards and costs associated with those forms of deviance. For instance, one would expect the rates of particular crimes to vary from one society to another in accord with the probability and severity of penalties threatened and/or imposed (Gibbs, 1975). This expectation exists because the potential benefit of criminal behavior would presumably be relatively constant across societies, leaving variation in costs as the explanatory element. And since costs involve both the chances of apprehension/punishment as well as the magnitude of penalties, one might infer that, other things being equal, crime will be lowest in those societies with the most efficient technology of crime detection, the greatest number of police officers, the fewest restrictions on activities of law enforcers and those who impose penalties (that is, the fewest guarantees of civil liberties), and the most severe penalties for crime. Crime rates, therefore, should be lowest in societies with totalitarian governments or, alternatively, in societies that are small and tightly knit, where everybody watches everybody else and responds rapidly and decisively against violators.

Similarly, variations in rates of suicide from social group to social group would be accounted for by assessing its potential social costs. Again, the benefits of suicide would be assumed to be invariant across societies. Criminal penalties obviously cannot deter suicide directly, since those who succeed in killing themselves automatically escape civil penalty. The costs must be in the form of anticipated sanctions for people and things the suicidal person values or for the person's soul in the afterlife. Thus, if a man cares about his family, the thought that they will fare badly after his death may deter suicide, just as does the expectation that the person who commits suicide will be punished in the afterlife. On a societal level, this means that in societies where there is disapproval of suicide (implying disrespect for survivors) or where it is prohibited by the dominant religion with a threat of sanctions in the afterlife, the rate of suicide should be low. And, of course, this is how most scholars explain the lower rates of suicide in countries where the Catholic religion predominates.

Application of the utilitarian/deterrence theory in its simplest form to explain rates of deviance in social units (that is, by using variations in costs as the crucial variable) usually assumes two things: (1) the average benefits of the specific deviance do not vary much from one social unit to the next, and (2) all other things that might affect the rates of deviance are similar across social units. In fact, however, neither of these two assumptions usually holds. For example, drug usage is attractive to more people in some societies than in others. Cultural prescriptions about drugs range from those in pre-modern China, where the use of opium was highly institutionalized, to the almost total denigration of any drug use in Saudi Arabia. So, regardless of penalties (although cultural proscriptions are usually accompanied by appropriate sanctions), Saudis would likely have low rates of drug use and the Chinese would have had high rates of opium use. Moreover, societies vary in their procedures for child rearing, their demographic characteristics, their religious practices, and endless other ways that could affect the level of drug use, independent of the magnitude or certainty of penalties.

Much of the early research concerning utilitarian/deterrence theory was, in fact, ecological in nature. In such a research design, a scholar will examine a number of social or political units (such as states in the United States), measuring the aggregate magnitude and certainty of penalty (such as the average sentence or the overall probability that criminal acts result in arrest or conviction) as well as the crime rates in those units (the number of crimes relative to the size of the population). Then he or she calculates the covariation between the sanction variables and the crime rate, perhaps statistically holding constant other characteristics of the political/social units. Sometimes researchers examine all these variables as they interconnect over time in order to infer whether sanction characteristics seem to affect crime or whether crime seems to bring about changes in punishment, or to assess the degree to which there is influence in either direction (examples: Chiricos and Waldo, 1970; D'Alessio and Stolzenberg, 1998; Ehrlich, 1973, 1975; Gibbs, 1968; Tittle and Rowe, 1974; see Blumstein et al., 1978; Gibbs, 1975; Tittle and Logan, 1973, for reviews).

Unfortunately, systematic data concerning sanction characteristics like certainty and severity, as well as other variables that would need to be held constant, are not available for enough of the countries listed in Tables 16.1–16.4 to determine whether deterrence operates to account for those international variations. However, it is of interest to note that some common assumptions do not appear to hold. For example, although suicide has historically not been heavily condemned in Japan, its suicide rate is less than in other countries, such as Hungary and Finland, without such a history (see Table 16.1). And despite the widespread belief that Singapore has low rates of crime due to its severe penalties (a belief fostered by publicity concerning the caning of an American youth who broke the law there), its rate of theft places it among the third of countries with the highest rates (see Table 16.3).

The results of ecological research assessing possible deterrence using states or other governmental units are mixed. While there is often evidence of deterrence, the magnitude of that effect is usually small, and sometimes the evidence suggests no effect at all, or even that sanction levels are determined by criminal behavior rather than sanctions affecting crime (the causal order is the opposite of that assumed by the deterrence notion; see Tittle, 1980a, 1985b).

A second type of research concerning effects of sanctions for aggregate populations examines changes in criminal behavior that follow discrete modifications in the conditions or probabilities of sanctions of one kind or another. This type of research follows somewhat the logic of an experiment. For instance, if a legislative body increases the penalties for homicide, or authorizes the hiring of more detectives and forensic experts to increase the chances of apprehension and conviction of murderers, a scholar can examine the homicide rate before and after the changes. If the scholar can establish that nothing else besides the sanctions changes, or can rule out the potential influence of other changes that might have occurred, and there is a decrease in crime after modifications of the sanction variables, then an inference of deterrence is justified. Several such field experiments have been conducted (Chaiken et al., 1974; Robertson et al., 1973; Ross et al., 1970; Tornudd, 1968). Their results again suggest some degree of deterrence, but such effects are usually small, highly dependent on a number of circumstances, and short-lived.

The data suggest that deterrence sometimes operates, but clearly they do not confirm the position of the theory that all crime can be explained by cost and benefit—certainly not of cost alone. Indeed, taken collectively, the ecological research on deterrence suggests (as does the micro-level research) that cost and benefit, at least as reflected in systems of criminal justice, is one factor in determining crime rates, but that it likely is a relatively minor one (for a contrary view, see Nagin, 1998). Although this conclusion may stem from the fact that the research cannot take into account the benefits of crime, such as the psychic rewards of beating somebody in a fight, or other variables that might affect crime rates, such as informal sanctions or moral training, it nevertheless calls attention to the limits of deterrence both as an explanation for deviance and as a policy tool.

Population Composition

Earlier you learned that several demographic characteristics are influential in predicting deviance. In general, younger people, males, minorities, and those without familial and institutional affiliations are more likely to commit many kinds of deviance than are others. Some, therefore, contend that the explanation for variations from society to society in rates of deviance, or temporal variations in such rates within given societies, can be found in the differing compositions of populations. Hence, if one society has a larger proportion of its population who are adolescent or young adult males than does another, one would expect higher rates of deviance in it. Similarly, a population with many recent immigrants separated from families and other conventional affiliations, or with substantial numbers of minorities, will be expected to have higher rates of deviance than other societies. And when all the demographic characteristics that place individuals at higher risk for deviance are considered simultaneously, the explanation of differing rates of deviance among societies is assumed to be even more complete.

A good illustration of the demographic argument concerns age composition of the U.S. population and changes in crime rates. Several analyses have shown that there is a good correspondence between historical trends in fertility and subsequent lagged increases or decreases in crime (Ferdinand, 1970; Sagi and Wellford, 1968; Wellford, 1973). The period following World War II was a time of increased fertility, usually called the "baby boom," which was brought about by the convergence of late child bearing by women who matured during the depression and early child bearing by women of the postwar generation. The period of high fertility lasted until the late 1960s, during which the median age of the population shifted downward and the proportion of the population in the crime-prone years increased as the first baby boomers became adolescents in the early 1960s. Since the high crime years are between approximately 15 and 24, a period of nine years, this meant that there would be an unusually large number of crime-prone people in the population until about 1991. Consistent with a demographic explanation, the crime rate began to climb in the 1960s and did not begin to fall until the 1990s.

This same kind of reasoning has led to predictions of another upsurge of crime as the children of the baby boomers reach the crime-prone years in substantial numbers (about the year 2000). Since these children are the result of normal fertility among a segment of the population that was unusually large (the baby boomers) while it was passing through the reproductive years (often called the "baby boom echo"), they will constitute an unusually large proportion of the population as well. And if the usual relationship between age and crime continues to hold, those projections of increasing crime will also prove correct.

In general, then, the demographic argument simply translates individual demographic traits into overall deviance rates. It fails, however, to take into account other conditions that have independent effects on crime and that sometimes even influence how demographics manifest themselves in deviance. For instance, some societies, such as India, with extremely high fertility and large numbers of young people, nevertheless have low rates of deviance (see Tables 16.3 and 16.4). This may be because those societies, unlike that of the United States, quickly involve youth in marital and child-rearing activities at a fairly early age so that their proneness to crime is stymied by social and familial constraints. Or it may be because some societies with a large youthful population have pervasive religious and family systems that both indoctrinate and constrain youth.

Other Micro-Level Aggregations

Almost any supposed causal influence on individuals' tendency toward deviance can be extrapolated to provide an explanation for variations over time and across societies in rates of deviance. These applications, of course, require the assumption that the particular variable or variables in question actually have a strong causal influence on deviance and that aggregate conditions do not modify how that influence might operate. In other words, it would assume that there is no "interaction" between the variables in question and other conditions in the society that might enhance, restrict, or redirect their operation. In addition, such applications always imply that "other things are equal," meaning that other things may be operative and that the variable or set of variables in question do not constitute the whole story.

For instance, much research connects individual deviant behavior to family influence (see Chapter 10; also, specifically, Canter, 1982; Cernkovich and Giordano, 1987; Loeber and Stouthamer-Loeber, 1986; Raine, 1993). On the aggregate level, this connection implies that societies with strong, intact families (whatever their form) will have lower rates of deviance than societies with structurally weaker families. Similarly, since micro-level theorizing suggests that religious participation negatively influences deviant behavior, societies or social groups with higher levels of religious participation should also have low rates of deviance. But these two articulations imply, respectively, that either family or religion is all that matters, overlooking the possibility that some societies with strong families or pervasive religions might still have high deviance as a result of other conditions, such as a competitive economy that drives people to violate rules in struggling for achievement, or heavy emphasis on violence as a means of solving problems, which results in high rates of assault and homicide.

In Chapters 11 through 15 we reviewed a number of theories to explain why individuals do deviant behavior. Almost any one of them could be "bumped up" to the aggregate level to try to account for variations in rates of deviance. We will not do that in detail. Instead, we will briefly show how the aggregation process could be done for three of the micro theories, and invite you to go through the full exercise yourself.

Psychodynamic Theory

In Chapter 12, you learned about psychoanalytic theory, which interprets deviant behavior as a product of internal conflicts or unresolved psychological problems. Many of those conflicts are theorized to stem from poor parent-child relationships, resulting in fixations, repressions, and regressions to earlier stages of development. In addition, some internal conflicts arise because of excessive societal restraints placed on innate urges (id). If this theory is correct, one would predict higher rates of deviance in societies or other social entities that have two characteristics: (1) a high proportion of parents with poor child-rearing skills, and (2) unusual constraints on natural impulses, such as denying outlets for sexual impulses.

Since there are no systematic cross-national, or even cross-city or cross-state, data concerning child-rearing skills or unusual constraints on natural impulses, it is impossible to test whether this theory, applied at the aggregate level, explains variations in rates of deviance. It is hard to imagine, however, that people in France and Denmark, where suicide rates are fairly high, have more unresolved psychodynamic conflicts than do people in Egypt and Israel, where suicide rates are much lower (see Table 16.1).

Learning Theory

Chapters 11 and 13 contain statements about how learning, especially through conditioning/reinforcement, can produce internalized psychic traits that either motivate deviant behavior or act as moral constraints to prevent the expression of natural deviogenic urges. If individuals come to reflect the reinforcements in their environments, then it follows that rates of deviance should reflect patterns of reinforcements in whole societies or other social entities. Therefore, rates of deviance should be highest in social contexts where deviant behavior is admired and rewarded more often than when it is looked down on or punished and where moral principles are neglected (see Wilson and Herrnstein, 1985).

Again, however, it is difficult to compile systematic data concerning general patterns of reinforcement for deviance in order to see if the variations in Tables 16.1–16.4 can be explained with principles of learning theory. Since the United States presumably has a "culture of violence," meaning that we probably reinforce violence more than many countries, it would follow that our homicide rates would be high, which they are. However, Australia, a country closer to the frontier than the United States and with some elements of a "culture of violence," has a very low homicide rate.

Self-Control

Chapter 13 described a formulation theorizing that people with low self-control are likely to do deviance and suggesting that low self-control stems from the failure of caregivers to follow correct procedures in dealing with young children. At the aggregate level, this theory would predict high rates of deviance in societies where the conditions for producing strong self-control are weak or lacking or, alternatively, where opportunities for deviance are great. Thus, greater numbers of people with weak self-control should emerge when one or more of the following conditions prevail: (1) many parents or other caregivers do not love their children enough to monitor their behaviors; (2) parents or caregivers cannot monitor children's behavior (because of one-parent households, working parents, illness, etc.); (3) caregivers do not recognize deviant behavior in children; or (4) caregivers do not punish misbehavior in children.

While one cannot directly measure these four conditions, it would seem logical that in modernized societies where both parents are in the labor force, the conditions for generating weak self-control would be maximized. The fact that the societies in Table 16.3 with the highest rates of theft are mostly the most modernized ones seems to support the argument. However, the rates of theft in Japan, a highly modern society, are only about one-fifth those of the countries with the highest rates. And it is hard to demonstrate that Spain, which has a theft rate of 1,031, is more modernized than Hong Kong, which has a theft rate about half that (536).

Theories Specific to Ecological Units

Social Integration/Disorganization

The General Argument

Perhaps the best-known ecological-level theory focuses on social cohesion. Various social theorists, including Durkheim (1951 [1897]), Redfield (1969 [1947]), Shaw and McKay (1969), Simmel (1971 [1903]), Toennies (1957 [1887]), and Wirth (1969 [1938]), as well as many contemporary ones (Braithwaite, 1989; Felson, 1986; Freudenburg, 1986; Friday and Hage, 1976; Tittle and Welch, 1983), have suggested that social groups with tightly knit, extensively overlapping social bonds will have low rates of deviance. Although individual "cohesion" theorists have emphasized distinct social conditions leading to integration or have stressed different mechanisms by which integration produces conformity, the following overall account can be derived by merging their various arguments.

In one conceptualization of social integration, cohesion refers to a condition characterizing an aggregate or group in which the components of that aggregate, or members of the group, are so well linked that they can act as a unit to achieve collective purposes and resist influences to separate. An appropriate comparison might be with different kinds of marbles. Some marbles are made of glass, some of plastic, and some of metal. If one places glass marbles in a press and elevates the pressure, those marbles will disintegrate into hundreds of tiny pieces. If one places plastic marbles under pressure, they will at first change shape but with more pressure they will break into several distinct pieces. But if one places steel marbles under pressure, they will resist until extremely high pressure is applied. And then instead of breaking up into parts, the steel marbles will simply change shape—become flattened. The components of steel will "hang together," though their aggregate form is altered. Thus, the metal marbles are the most cohesive, the glass ones least cohesive, and the plastic ones somewhere in between. Cohesion means "stick-together-ness" or a tendency to resist deterioration and separation. Social units can be similarly characterized by their degree of cohesion. The underlying continuum on which they can be arrayed ranges from low cohesion, sometimes called social disorganization, on one end to high social integration on the other.

When a social entity is well integrated, it means, first, that its components (residents, members, or participants) generally agree about social norms, are morally committed to upholding them, and widely participate in applying informal sanctions to those who violate them. Second, members of cohesive social units are likely to know each other or at least be interested in knowing each other as individuals, and most of their time is spent in interaction with acquaintances. Third, integrated groups have a large proportion of their members who use the group as a source of self-identity. This means that the individuals' personalities and ideas about themselves are bound up with the group as a whole. One consequence of such identity is a sense of responsibility and concern for others in the group—there is strong group identity, and any one person's injury, pain, or disappointment is felt by all. Fourth, in cohesive aggregates people evaluate each other on the basis of individual traits that are observed over long periods of time in enduring relationships rather than on the basis of symbols or indicators emerging from transitory encounters. Fifth, cohesive groups induct new members and sustain old members through shared ideologies conveyed in a consistent manner by all institutions. Finally, the members of cohesive groups are heavily dependent on that group for all of their needs; that is, they either have no alternative context in which to realize their desires or the particular group is the strongly preferred source of gratifications.

But how does cohesion produce conformity? It does so because normative consensus, personal contacts, and dependency give most people an interest (a "stake") in obeying the rules (they *want* to conform and it is advantageous for them to do so). At the same time, nonconformity subjects them to potentially devastating informal sanctions from other group members in the case of misbehavior. In addition, since status and reputation are based on individual traits like character, personality, and actions that uphold the group, conformity garners respect and prestige. Further, when participants' self-identities are linked to the group, their sense of mutual responsibility and concern makes potential deviance, especially that which might harm the group or other members, less attractive. Moreover, consistent reinforcement of shared values through education, religion, family training, and everyday communication helps guide action along conforming paths. Finally, all the features of integration noted above converge to produce a general sense of "we" among the people, enabling them to act in concert to regulate themselves, to promote conforming behavior, and to discourage deviance (Bursik and Grasmick, 1993).

An Illustration

To illustrate these features of integrated social entities, it is useful to contrast life in small towns or rural areas with life in large cities or densely populated areas—say, the whole metropolitan area of south Florida with Hope, Arkansas, a small town in a rural region well known as the birthplace and early childhood home of Bill Clinton. In south Florida few people agree about appropriate behavior, even when it is prohibited in law. For example, some people endorse "swinging" orientations to sexual conduct (in which almost any sexual activity among participants is acceptable); others support only marital sex between male and female spouses; and still others oppose any sex at all. Some people believe that any form of recreation, including drug use, is permissible; others have limited views of things that people should be allowed to do for fun; and still others do not think people should ever have any fun but instead should be dedicated to work or religion. As a result, there is no consensus about social norms; there is no widespread moral commitment to any particular set of norms; and few people can impose informal social sanctions on a large enough segment of the population to uphold any norms. Thus, many people become motivated toward deviance by the temptations of diverse norms that prescribe a plethora of behavioral possibilities. Literally one can find or do almost anything in south Florida, there will be others to do it with, and there will be plenty of people to applaud the behavior and support the perpetrator. As a result, there will be little cost in lost reputation or ability to accomplish one's general goals in life.

In Hope, Arkansas, during Clinton's childhood, by contrast, almost everybody agreed that certain things were "right" while other things were "wrong," and there was little tolerance for those who advocated behavior very far from the standard. There was general agreement that sex is appropriate for married couples—those composed of a man and a woman—when done in private and between the two of them but that it is inappropriate for almost anybody else in any other circumstances (though premarital sex was sometimes tolerated if between committed couples who intended to marry). In addition, recreation was regarded as a means to an end, not an end in itself. Everybody was expected to have some fun, but only to regenerate for important things in life. Moreover, the methods of having fun were limited; drug use was certainly not one of them. Indeed, alcohol could not even be manufactured or sold in the county where Hope is located, so drinkers had to drive thirty miles to Texarkana for alcoholic beverages. Hence, there were few alternatives to conventional behavior supported by cadres of approvers.

In south Florida, only a tiny proportion of people know each other personally. While many residents follow daily routines that bring them into contact with some of the same people at work or in their neighborhoods, almost everybody flows in and out of numerous anonymous social contexts in moving about, shopping, seeking medical care, having fun, managing children's needs, pursuing their occupations, and the like. A significant proportion of all interactions that south Floridians have is with strangers or relative strangers, not with people they know very well. Consequently, south Floridians have little in common with each other; they cannot evaluate each other on a personal basis; and they cannot identify with other people and their views or problems. Instead, much interaction is completely anonymous, oriented around formal transactions reflecting pre-designated roles and statuses. Customers and clerks enact prescribed scripts as buyers and sellers of goods; doctors and patients play out designated roles; and police and citizens confront each other as authorities and subordinates.

Under such circumstances, people can easily get away with deviance. Observers will not know the violators, or care much that they do deviance, unless it personally affects the observer. Moreover, even if someone is held accountable for deviance, it will not necessarily damage her or his reputation. Most others will not find out; if they find out, they will soon forget; and in any case future interactions will revolve around the symbols of status, not the person's history. Furthermore, because impersonality places a premium on symbols, there is an incentive to obtain such symbols by any means possible. Hence people are tempted to make false claims, to acquire material objects that invoke favorable response to status, and to pursue styles of behavior or dress that suggest things not entirely true.

In Clinton's home town, on the other hand, just about everybody knew everybody else—if not personally, at least by name recognition and reputation. Rarely were complete strangers encountered. In conducting the business of everyday living, Hope residents were not just buyers and sellers, doctors and patients, or police officers and citizens; they were individuals whose families, life histories, and foibles were known to almost all. People therefore did not want to hurt those with whom they shared a destiny, and in any case they could hardly get away with it. There were few truly anonymous situations, and knowledge of any misbehavior was quickly spread far and wide. Hence, the chances of losing respect and prestige and being shamed, ridiculed, or avoided were ever present. In addition, there was nothing to be gained by pursuing false symbols or trying to fool people because everybody would have seen right through it.

South Floridians rarely think of themselves in terms of the social context, and they are not dependent on the aggregate. South Florida is a place to live and work, desirable mainly because of amenities like warm weather and numerous restaurants, but most residents could as easily live elsewhere. And if you ask them to tell you about themselves, most will recite their occupational identities or family roles, but sense of self as a south Floridian or resident of a particular community within the metropolis would not be near the top of the list of things important to them. Hence, there is little feeling of responsibility or concern for the entity of south Florida society. And, more important, there is little dependency on that group. People perceive themselves mainly as individuals or as members of other kinds of groups (occupational, religious, demographic), so in their minds they could easily gratify all their needs in other contexts. To offend the normative code of south Florida through deviance, then, is not going to jeopardize the ability of many people to survive or to have their needs met, nor does it do violence to many people's sense of self.

Deviance in Everyday Life

In comparison with south Florida, Hope, Arkansas is reminiscent of the fictional town in the movie *Pleasantville*. In the movie, one of the main characters, David Wagner, is fascinated with the reruns of a classic television show set in the 1950s called "Pleasantville." Pleasantville is very much like the town that Beaver Cleaver lived in, or like Opie Taylor's Mayberry, North Carolina. In Pleasantville, everyone is happy, every problem is solved, and all needs are met. The problem is that David lives in the 1990s, which is inhabited by his gratingly hip sister Jennifer, with whom he constantly quarrels. After breaking the remote control to the TV while fighting, David and Jennifer are provided with a new one which magically transports them into the innocent and naive television world of Pleasantville. This black and white town is everything the myth of small-town America says it should be. Breakfast consists of plenty of eggs and bacon; there is no sex, no divorce, no adultry, no pornography; library books lack both controversy and content; and firefighters rescue cats from trees. Unlike the conflict of the 1990s, Pleasantville is a small-town, homogeneous, deviant-free utopia. That is, until Jennifer teaches the high school basketball star about the "birds and the bees." Soon thereafter, other kids join in the fun. Jennifer has become the serpent in paradise, and life in Pleasantville becomes more and more like life in south Florida.

Many residents of Hope, however, did link their sense of self with the local group, so among the main things they valued was being from Hope. To offend the moral code of that entity was to deny one's own worth because the community was largely a reflection of one's self. This convergence of self with group helped generate mutual responsibility and concern. Furthermore, it made the residents dependent on the community in a way that south Floridians could not understand. Although most long-time Hope residents, like south Floridians, could have moved elsewhere, made friends, earned a living, and gotten along fine, they did not think they could. They believed that the history and shared experience of life in the community, as well as its gratifications, could not be replaced. For Hope people, then, deviance threatened their concepts of who they were as well as their means of gratifying essential desires and needs.

Finally, the south Florida population has trouble acting in concert to achieve agreed-upon goals, and it cannot become cohesive because there are inconsistent messages from multiple sources about both the nature of the south Florida entity and appropriate behaviors. Every person that comes to south Florida, either as an immigrant or a newborn child, faces a plethora of contradictory messages about these matters. What one learns in the family may be contradicted by what is learned at school. And if family and school messages converge, they may be contradicted by mass media influences or the interpersonal communications coming from members of one or another of the many cultural enclaves in south Florida.

The story in Clinton's Hope was different. It was rare for family socialization to be inconsistent with what went on in the schools or what occurred in churches, on the job, or in recreational activities. Hence, cohesion could be regenerated continually, and as a result, when they needed to, the residents of

Hope could act together to drive out undesirable influences or solve problems.

In summary, cohesive social entities typically have lower rates of deviance mainly because their features weaken motivation for deviance among their members and increase the chances it will cost them if they deviate. But integration theorists do not simply theorize that cohesion affects deviance; they also try to specify why cohesion comes about. Some theorists contend that the convergence of three structural conditions affects the degree to which a social entity can be integrated: homogeneity, population size, and rapidity of population change. When populations are large, heterogeneous, and rapidly changing, it is physically difficult if not impossible for all members of the aggregate to interact with each other on a one-to-one basis (Mayhew and Levinger, 1976); to come to know many others personally; to impose effective informal sanctions widely (Wirth, 1969 [1938]); or to come to share common norms, culture, or values. Furthermore, rapid demographic changes, such as growth, decline, or a shift in age or gender composition will tend to threaten or undermine social cohesion because cohesion is an emergent property springing from repetitive social interaction, which requires considerable degree of stability (Freudenburg, 1986).

But according to other thinkers, such structural conditions are not all that matter. People can sometimes become dependent on a social entity or fuse their self-identities with an aggregate, despite contrary structural pressures, when (1) there is an absence of effective alternative social contexts, (2) where there is social symbiosis (where parts of a system are dependent on each other for survival or well-being, such as when plants and animals of various kinds are linked in a food chain), or (3) where there are "cohesion-generating" cultural elements such as widely shared nationalistic sentiments. Some large, heterogeneous social entities with rapid population change nevertheless remain reasonably integrated because they are dominant in their regions. That is, they offer economic and other attractions and gratifications superior to any other alternatives around, so people become committed to them as sources of need fulfillment. In addition, some social entities that otherwise might have weak integration nevertheless possess unique, long-standing cultural systems that effectively generate commitment. For example, nationalistic sentiments often bind people to their societies despite countermanding structural conditions—and sometimes these nationalistic trends seem to defy all reason.

Finally, if, as Durkheim (1951 [1897]) contends, modern economies and the societies they sustain are built on specialization with interdependency, then very large, heterogeneous, demographically unstable societies often achieve "organic" solidarity while losing "mechanical" solidarity (similar to the kind described in previous paragraphs). With modernization, each person, being able to perform but a fraction of the tasks needed for survival, depends on the entire system of interlinked roles and tasks, the parts of which are themselves also specialized but performing a different task (the division of labor). Because of such interdependency for survival most people are bound to the whole and by virtue of that are constrained in expressing their deviant impulses.

Variants

The preceding depiction of the theory of social integration draws together the diverse ideas of a number of theorists. Several sources of those ideas, however, deserve special note because their contributions may not be obvious; because they have particularly important ideas related to the general theme of social integration; or because their approaches to integration depart from the general perspective described.

Subcultural Theory. In Chapter 10, you were introduced to Claude Fischer's subcultural argument (1975, 1995) about why cities typically produce more deviance than do smaller places. His ideas are presented as an ad hoc explanation of the high rates of deviance typically found in urban areas. It is reasonable, however, to cast the subcultural contention in broader terms as a general ecological theory that might explain variations in rates of deviance among societies or other spatially bound social entities. Fischer maintains that larger population size, heterogeneity, and concentration make it possible for people with rare interests (many of which are deviant) to find and interact with each other and to form subcultures around those shared interests. At the same time, however, those demographic conditions force people to divide their social contacts into public and private realms, with the private realm including subcultural and other interpersonal alliances.

Fischer actually said little about the consequence of these trends for general social integration in larger social entities, focusing instead on whether individuals in urban places necessarily suffer a dearth of social ties and on why subcultures form in cities and help create high rates of deviance. Nevertheless, it is clear that his account has implications for cohesion. If specific structural conditions of a population produce an array of self-contained subcultures and a world of divided interpersonal relations, then one outcome is likely to be a weakened sense of integration for the population as a whole. Since the structural conditions of cities also apply to societies and other social entities, his theory can be conceived as portraying the primary causes of variation in rates of deviance in any spatially defined social entity. Those causes involve particular demographic conditions that generate subcultures of deviance and division of interpersonal relations. Those outcomes represent a form of social disorganization (of the larger entity), and they are likely to produce weak normative consensus, inconsistent socialization, and absence of self-identity/social entity linkages. All these consequences, in turn, will lead to more people having strong motivation toward deviance and to their being faced with fewer restraints.

Fischer's theory is ultimately about social integration and it is compatible with other integration theories, though even he might not readily acknowledge such. It goes beyond other integration theories, however, in pinpointing subcultures as important products of social disorganization, which then have direct effects on rates of deviance. With Fischer's formulation one would explain rate variations across social entities as the product of demographic conditions (large size, great heterogeneity, rapid population turnover) that create subcultures and other manifestations of weak social integration, which, in turn, produce deviance by providing motivation and opportunity for it, as well as weakening restraints against it.

Deindustrialization. A second argument, also developed to account for urban phenomena, can be applied to the general issue of variations in rates of deviance across social entities, and it too is based on ideas about social cohesion, although that may not be readily apparent. The urban deindustrialization hypothesis suggests that spatial redistribution of economic activities has affected specific urban subpopulations through its consequences for community organization (Anderson, 1990; W. Wilson, 1987; see Krivo and Peterson, 1996; Shihadeh and Flynn, 1996; Shihadeh and Ousey, 1996). Recent decades have witnessed the movement of industrial, manufacturing activity to the peripheries of urban locales. At first, beginning slowly in the early part of this century, but accelerating after World War II, the central city dwellers who originally came to cities seeking opportunities for a better life and who succeeded economically moved to the suburbs. As this trend increased, and for several decades, those suburbanites commuted back to the central cities to work, enjoy recreation, and shop. Meanwhile, the former central city dwellers were replaced by the continued traditional flow of migrants into downtown areas. Eventually, however, economic activities began to follow the movement of people to the suburbs, and there emerged a metropolitan network outside the boundaries of traditional cities.

This urban transformation left central cities with a dearth of well-paying jobs, indeed with a shortage of enough jobs of any kind, and it drained central city populations of people with greater education, economic success, stakes in the future, experience in community governance, and personal capabilities; these people eventually ended up in the peripheral areas (W. Wilson, 1996). Furthermore, it stifled the traditional movement of new people into central cities because opportunities came to be concentrated outside central city areas (Garreau, 1991). The net result was an increase in the homogeneity and a decline in density, size, and demographic selectivity of central city populations; that is, deindustrialization eroded the conditions that, according to most cohesion theories, ultimately produce deviance. But instead of decreasing deviance, these trends presumably enhanced alienation, led to a weakening of community bonds, contributed to the ineffectiveness of social control, and spurred deviance, particularly predatory crime, drug use, and mental illness (W. Wilson, 1996). Deindustrialization presumably produced these outcomes by undermining the bases of successful communities. Without economic resources for personal investments in neighborhoods, role models committed to conventional life styles, and prevailing attitudes of hope and optimism that render people sensitive to the opinion of others and thereby subject to social control, communities cannot achieve the cohesion to regulate themselves and counteract deviance with personal integration (Sampson et al., 1997).

Although the urban deindustrialization argument was designed to explain differences among areas or neighborhoods within cities as well as a presumed common feature of many modern cities (the decay of inner-city urban neighborhoods), it suggests that differing rates of deviance among social entities are due to weakened social cohesion. However, instead of portraying elements of social cohesion as products of population size and heterogeneity, it identifies selective change in population composition as the prime variable. Implied in the argument is the assumption that, above all, social entities must be able to provide for their residents' economic needs as well as or better than competitive social entities—in modern terms that means there must be more plentiful and better-paying employment. Otherwise, components of the population who might contribute most to cohesion will themselves be unintegrated and uncommitted. If there are alternative ways for them to meet their needs more effectively, they will leave the group. The result will be a deterioration of cohesion and a rise in deviance, even though the usual demographic conditions that presumably promote cohesion are enhanced by the flight toward greater opportunity. Thus the deindustrialization argument postulates cohesion as the cause of low rates of deviance but it conceptualizes cohesion as a product mainly of economic opportunity (an alternative context for gratifying needs, to use the previous terminology) rather than of demographic conditions.

Durkheim. Perhaps the most important, and certainly the first, scholar to call attention to social integration as a factor affecting rates of deviance was Emile Durkheim, the famous French sociologist. In a series of works, but particularly in books on suicide (Durkheim, 1951 [1897]) and on the division of labor in modern societies (Durkheim, 1933 [1893]), he presented ideas about social cohesion that have fueled thinking and research ever since. Although he contributed much to the model of social integration based on interpersonal ties and common values, embodied in what he called the "collective conscience" (mechanical solidarity), he was also intrigued with symbiotic social cohesion based on interdependency of specialized parts (organic solidarity), exemplified in contemporary economic divisions of labor. Both types of social cohesion, though quite different from each other and in some ways seemingly contradictory, were nevertheless theorized to reduce deviance. The reduction is achieved in the first instance by the bond among individuals constructed out of shared values and personal identities with the group and in the second by dependency.

In a similar counterbalancing approach, Durkheim identified opposing effects produced by social cohesion. Although he regarded social integration as the key condition affecting variations in rates of suicide (in general, he contended that greater social cohesion produced lower rates of suicide), he maintained that high degrees of social integration could also produce deviance. His prime example was altruistic suicide, which is undertaken to uphold the standards of a group. People sacrificing themselves to save drowning or endangered children; soldiers exposing themselves to certain death in combat; and sick or aged people taking their own lives to spare families or communities the burdens of their maintenance are more likely to be observed in socially integrated societies than elsewhere. Of course, such acts may not be deviant if they are honored, but Durkheim's point is that social solidarity may affect behavior in a variety of ways. Actual ethnographic evidence, in fact, shows that apparently tightly bonded social groups may not be so harmonious and may have a high rate of deviance (Edgerton, 1976, 1992). Close ties and constant interaction apparently increase the chances of disputes and conflict, often leading to misbehavior in response to hurt feelings. Thus, social cohesion is potentially a two-edged sword.

Summary

Theories of social integration postulate that rates of deviance will be products of the cohesion of social entities. The theories differ, however, in details, particularly as to the conditions that affect social integration, how social cohesion is manifest, the way that integration produces conformity, and whether the effects of integration are linear. In general, this body of theory suggests that if scholars are to understand why some societies have higher rates of deviance than others or why rates of deviance change from time to time within a given society, they must examine social cohesion and attempt to predict when cohesion will be higher or lower—because rates of deviance will correspond with variations in integration. Demographic conditions appear to be relevant, as does the presence or absence of alternative contexts for satisfying the needs and desires of group members. Tests using cities or other units have reported support for the integration argument (Chamlin and Cochran, 1997; Sampson and Groves, 1989).

However, data about differences in cohesion among societies are scarce, so it is difficult to determine if the theory accounts for the variations in suicide and crime presented earlier. And some have challenged the general formulation by noting that much deviance grows from interpersonal disputes (Edgerton, 1976) and some from acting out of altruism (Durkheim, 1951 [1897]) or the belief that they are altruistic (Katz, 1988). Since disputes are most likely among those closely bound and in constant interaction, and since the forces compelling deviance are sometimes the same ones binding people to social groups, rates of some deviance should actually vary directly with the strength of social integration—at least with the integration flowing from strong interpersonal ties.

Marxian Conflict Theories

In Chapter 11, you were introduced to Marxian Conflict Theory (Bonger, 1916), which focuses on the structural conditions of competitively based economic systems (or more specifically, capitalism) that both motivate citizens for deviance and "de-moralize" them, thereby freeing them of constraints on their deviant impulses. Even though the theory is mainly a macro-level formulation designed to explain rates of deviance among societies, it was earlier expanded to apply to the problem of individual deviance. Here, however, we return to the original intent of this type of theory.

Although there are many permutations, the basic argument is that rates of deviance will vary directly with the degree to which economic systems are capitalistic, or internally competitive. The reason is that capitalism both encourages and requires people to struggle against each other for advancement, or for survival. Capitalists (those who control means of production) must compete with other capitalists to earn a profit. To do that most effectively, they exploit their employees by paying the lowest wage possible, requiring the maximum effort from their workers, and by creating societal conditions that produce a large pool of unemployed workers. The unemployed are so deprived that they will work for minimum wages and so stand as a constant competitive threat to those holding jobs, thereby keeping wages low. Thus, capitalists are motivated toward many kinds of deviance in the struggle to best their competitors; to compete effectively, they must suppress their human sentiments toward competitors and employees, which effectively eliminates one of the most important constraints on predatory deviance. On the other hand, exploitation of employees, and the consequent competition for survival or advancement, results in workers being pitted against each other. This, in turn, motivates them toward many kinds of deviance in the struggle for survival and advancement, and at the same time encourages them to suppress human sentiments that might inhibit their competitive advantage against their peers.

In summary, then, capitalism inherently promotes selfishness and greed, which motivates people toward deviance. At the same time, it undermines moral feelings or sentiments that might inhibit deviance. The result, presumably, is a high rate of deviance in all capitalist societies, with rates of deviance among them varying by the extent to which their economies are actually capitalistic. The degree of capitalism is shown through a combination of four variables. One is the extent to which property is privately owned. Another is the degree to which economic initiatives are begun and funded by individuals or corporate entities with the objective of realizing profit. Third is the extent to which production and prices are driven solely by supply and demand. And, finally, capitalism is reflected in the extent to which buyers and sellers of products, labor, and services are free to promote their various interests exclusively in response to market conditions.

The United States, for instance, despite some assumptions to the contrary, is not an extreme capitalist society. Although much property is privately owned, every governmental unit and community holds considerable public wealth in the form of schools, hospitals, parks, roads and highways, land, prisons and jails, buildings, equipment, and such products as surplus food. In addition, many products and services are produced directly by the government or under their auspices—examples include electric power; space satellites; education, health, and child care; and public transportation systems. In addition, production and prices are not exclusively driven by market forces but often by government policy as it raises or lowers taxes, interest rates, and public expenditures for direct purposes (such as filling a societal need) or to stimulate or slow down the economy to control business cycles (booms and depressions) or inflation. Finally, economic actors are not totally free to pursue self-interest in response to market forces. Not only are there inherent restrictions, such as the tendency for individuals or groups to organize to restrain competition (reflected in business monopolies or labor unions), but the government regulates much economic activity, as when it requires sanitary conditions for the production of food products; competence in offering medical services; or full disclosure of the terms of a loan.

To our knowledge, no systematic study of variations in deviance/crime rates by degree of capitalism has been conducted, mainly because data are inadequate to measure degree of capitalism. Nevertheless, unsystematic observations and some data (Chamlin and Cochran, 1995; Messner and Rosenfeld, 1997 [1994]) suggest some support for this theory. Despite such support, however, various aberrant cases suggest that capitalism alone is not adequate to explain rates of deviance. One of the most important exceptions is Japan, a highly capitalistic society but one that has relatively low rates of many types of deviance. Various observers contend that Japan's capitalism is restrained by an overarching cultural system that emphasizes familial responsibility, which extends to the larger society and to the workplace, where employees are regarded as part of corporate families (Braithwaite, 1989). Japanese workers typically are employed for life with one company, to which they pledge loyalty and from which they receive loyalty in return.

The Japanese case, as well as others, suggests that a number of variables modify the operation of capitalism so that its effects on deviance are somewhat muted. The modulating variables include moral considerations; the emergence of organized forces like labor unions or political movements that counter the power of capitalists; and modern technology that requires highly skilled workers who are less subject to the whim of employers.

Routine Activities

❖ ❖ ❖ ❖

This theory contends that rates of predatory crime are a function of the way three specific variables are distributed in time and space. Crime occurs when motivated offenders, suitable targets, and the absence of guardianship converge. The extent to which the three come together presumably reflects the peculiar routine activities of people in a given social entity—how they conduct their lives and pursue sustenance activities. When routine activities, usually indicated by demographic and/or economic conditions, affect one or another of these variables or how they converge, then the rates of predatory crime will change. For instance, modern societies are postulated to have higher rates of burglary than less modern ones partly because much of life in modern societies takes place outside the home; partly because modernization has led to the production and distribution in most homes of objects to steal that are small enough to be portable yet valuable; partly because modern transportation, particularly in urban areas, can rapidly bring those who are motivated to commit burglary into areas where there are homes to burglarize; and partly because residences are situated favorably for undetected burglary (Cohen and Felson, 1979; Cohen et al., 1980; Felson, 1998). In other words, the circumstances of modern life bring together potential offenders and targets and lessen the chances of detection or apprehension.

Lack of guardianship is created because in modern societies both fathers and mothers often work outside the home, children attend school in institutions some distance from the home, and aged people frequently live in special institutions or communities rather than with their children and their families. As a result, houses are usually empty and unguarded for much of the day. In addition, most homes are located in areas with homogeneous make-up, so they are surrounded by other empty houses for much of the time. Not only is each house unguarded (nobody is at home, which research indicates removes a strong deterrent to burglars; see Cromwell et al., 1999), but whole neighborhoods are unguarded. Furthermore, since modern housing areas, especially those in suburban areas, are arranged in blocks so that from any one house there is a restricted view of many of the other houses. Even when some homes are occupied, others are free of surveillance by neighbors who might intervene or call the police.

Enhancement of the suitability of targets of burglary in modern society has occurred because many of the mass-produced objects in homes now can more easily be transported and sold. Consider, for example, electronic equipment. Early record players and TVs were very large and heavy, so they could not be stolen by lone burglars. Even teams of burglars had to bring trucks, which attracted attention and enhanced the chances of arrest. And since TVs and stereos were previously comparatively rare, they could more easily be traced; because of their size they could less easily be bartered without detection. Now, a burglar can steal an expensive stereo by himself, hide and transport it, and ultimately sell it without arousing much suspicion.

The third element of the theory—motivated offenders—has generally been assumed to be constant across places and times. That is, the theorists have more or less conceded that there are always potential offenders who, given the opportunity created by suitable, unguarded targets, will act. Some researchers, on the other hand, have assumed that the motivation for crime is greater among minorities, males, and youth, and so they have employed measures of those variables as proxies for criminal motivation. In addition, the theorists have not specified just what specific "routine activities" enhance the convergence of motivated offenders, suitable targets, and ineffective guardianship. Most discussions and applications of the theory have focused on demographic characteristics, such as population movements, labor force participation, and economic transactions, and on elements stemming from modern technology, such as transportation systems that permit the separation of work from home.

In essence, then, routine activities theory explains variations in predatory crime rates from society to society or from one social context by variations in the arrangement of the three conditions. For example, a modern, urbanized society would be expected to have higher rates of crime than a less modern or less urbanized one because in the less modern one, there would be fewer suitable targets that are unguarded, and perhaps relatively fewer highly motivated potential offenders.

Even though the theory was designed to explain predatory crime, it can be used to explain other deviance if one stretches the meaning of the terms in the convergence equation. For instance, rates of recreational drug use can be explained by the arrangement of activities in time and space such that potential offenders (anybody who might be interested in the pleasure of drug consumption) are presented with opportunities for drug use, which involves availability and absence of those who might disapprove or do something about it. Such convergences would presumably be greater where there are large more-or-less anonymous populations concentrated in physical surroundings containing many places for participants to meet for use or purchase of drugs and where drugs are easily imported or grown. Similarly, one might explain rates of deviant sexual activity, such as homosexual behavior and adultery, as a function of the bringing together, by the conditions of everyday life, people who might want to do those things with potential partners, in circumstances where disapproval and prevention are minimal. Ability to perform these deviant acts would imply separation from family and friends for large portions of the time and the availability of places for meeting, such as nightclubs.

Although the routine activities argument is plausible, it is difficult to assess its ability to explain cross-context rates of deviance. Much of the research has floundered because potential indicators of the concepts overlap. What is a "suitable" target is somewhat subjective, and suitability may imply absence of guardianship. Furthermore, offenders may not become motivated until there is a convergence of targets and weak guardianship, so it is hard to measure their presence without encountering tautology. And, as noted earlier, while the most modernized countries (implying deviance-favorable routine activities) generally do appear more likely to have high rates of theft, there are outstanding exceptions (Japan), while the pattern does not emerge at all for homicide (see Tables 16.2 and 16.3).

In addition, it is not at all clear just what specific aspects of "routine activities" are relevant. It is easy enough, after the fact, to note that changes in labor force participation of women may have affected rates of burglary and rape, but it is more difficult to specify ahead of time that changes in "routine activities," such as the way people do their laundry, will have some impact on crime or deviance. Furthermore, the theory overlooks other things that affect deviance, such as moral or religious restraints, cultural practices encouraging or discouraging various kinds of deviance, and a whole host of things that affect the degree to which there is strong motivation for deviance.

Deprivation of Law

A number of theorists, but most prominently Donald Black (1976, 1983), have proposed that rates of deviance vary inversely with the availability of law for resolving disputes (see Chapter 10). According to this theory, without law, inevitable human conflict will produce high rates of deviance, particularly violence and property crime as individuals and groups seek to redress their own wrongs. Law, which is tied to the development of strong political entities with power over large populations, enables—indeed requires—disputing parties to submit personal arguments to third parties for resolution. The decisions that functionaries make are supposedly impartial, which gives disputants, who nearly always assume they are right, hope for victory. Although, as Black has shown, legal decisions actually closely follow lines of status and therefore are not impartial, they are upheld by the force exercised by state authorities, who claim a virtual monopoly on its use. Because of the appeal of law as a vehicle for settling disputes once and for all (eliminating the possibility of feud) without undue cost, and because of the coercive element that requires the use of law and enforces its decisions, rates of deviance are theorized to decline as states and their accompanying legal apparatuses grow. Therefore, the greater the development of law, the lower the rates of deviance.

Although law is theorized to reduce deviance, it can never be totally effective. Lack of total effectiveness happens partly because the legal apparatus is rarely fully enough developed to reach into all situations and domains; partly because some disputes are so emotionally compelling that one or the other of the disputants will defy the mandate for legal resolution; and partly because law is not equally available to all.

Consider the limited reach of the law. Sometimes people pursuing socially unacceptable or illegal activities have disputes with others involved in the same activities, as when drug dealers and customers disagree about a deal. They cannot seek help from the law without jeopardizing themselves, so they must resort to "self-help," which sometimes produces a shoot-out. In addition, new areas of human dispute are constantly emerging, so the law is always in flux and often out of sync with other changes. The most recent examples are computer crime. Furthermore, since the law is enacted by political forces representing specialized interests, some domains in which dominant political forces prosper are simply left unregulated by law. Finally, much deviance, like unconventional sex or devil worship, may not involve disputes among social entities at all, or if they do, the disputes are among abstract ideologies embraced by differing segments of a population.

Moreover, even when law is available, not everybody will use it. The nature of disputes is such that they often bring forth anger, distress, or fear. In such highly charged situations, some people will always act irrationally, ignoring the law. They will take matters into their own hands, sometimes even resorting to physical violence, despite the possibility that they may ultimately be held accountable by the law. Then, too, some people fail to use law even when they could because they perceive that it is unjust or that their case is too weak to win, though of great importance to them.

Finally, law cannot be totally effective because there is unequal access to it. Some individuals or categories of persons are socially situated so that law is handy, while for others law is a distant reality. For instance, those without economic resources in the United States, a society with a fairly highly developed system of law, cannot count on the law to resolve their disputes. Suppose that a female of a poor inner-city area suspects that a neighborhood boy stole one of her prized possessions, a radio valued at ten dollars. Could she expect the police to conduct a thorough investigation and either recover the radio or arrest the suspect? Or alternatively, could she sue her neighbor in civil court? The answer is probably not—partly because the police are likely to regard the alleged crime as trivial; indeed, the law makes clear distinctions between offenses on the basis of economic value (misdemeanor versus felony theft).

Deviance in Everyday Life

There is empirical evidence to suggest that the police do respond differently to calls for help depending on the characteristics of the caller. In a recent study using the National Crime Victimization Survey (NCVS), Bachman (1996) found that police both responded to the crime scene quicker and did more when they got there (taking evidence, talking to witnesses) when a robbery involved a black suspect and white victim. For assault crimes involving strangers (but not non- strangers), police also were more active when the victim was white rather than a minority. For some crimes, then, being a white victim means better law enforcement.

In addition, the police are more likely to devote their time to crimes that affect those who have power and influence, the affluent members of a community. Furthermore, using the civil courts is ordinarily an expensive matter, since it involves attorney fees, time off from work to testify, and transportation costs. Therefore, if the aggrieved party is to find justice, she must do something about the presumed theft herself. What she does may itself be a crime (if, for instance, she breaks into the neighbor's house to find or recover her radio, slugs the neighbor, or steals something in retaliation), and even if it is not a crime, the dispute that develops may lead to crime by the accused party, who feels compelled to defend his person, honor, and household.

As a result, even in highly legalistic societies, there is still a lot of deviance. However, the theory does not contend that law eliminates all deviance, only that, compared with societies with less law, those with more extensive law will have lower rates of deviance and that it will be concentrated more markedly among certain categories of people (Cooney, 1997). Evidence seems to support this theory. You are accustomed to hearing that crime and deviance rates are exceptionally high in contemporary, modern societies; yet it appears that rates of violence, at least, were much higher earlier in history (Gurr, 1981). Indeed, in the United States the period from the mid-1800s to about 1930 has been called a "civilizing" era because of the apparent drop in rates of violence, especially in urban areas, which many people attribute to the development of law and enforcement agencies. And there is considerable anthropological evidence to suggest that rates of violence are often extremely high in simple, pre-modern societies (Edgerton, 1976, 1992), despite the common assumption (to some extent reflected in theories of social integration) that simple societies are harmonious and conformist.

Historical/Cultural   ❖ ❖ ❖ ❖

The final ecological-level "theory" for explaining variations from social context to social context is really not a theory; rather, it is a challenge to theories that attempt to formulate general principles with which to explain and predict variations in rates of deviance among societies. The historical/cultural perspective contends that the crime rate or deviance rate of any given society results from its unique history and culture. Hence, there can be no general theories for explaining and predicting variations in crime rates among societies. Instead, each society's crime/deviance production must be understood in terms of its own specific, peculiar characteristics.

For instance, the high rates of crime and violence in the United States are said to grow out of our frontier tradition. Much of the history of this country involved territorial expansion, with frequent claims on new land asserted by force as indigenous populations were conquered or destroyed or as countries who had previously taken the land from natives were defeated. Since coercion played such a prominent role in our history, we have presumably inherited a belief that it is acceptable to take what we want and to use violence if necessary to promote our own interests. Along with this has gone a continuing love of guns, the instruments by which the frontier was won. In addition, because the pioneers were rugged individuals who survived and prospered by their own efforts and who defended themselves without the help of others, we presumably carry over an admiration for competitive individualism that promotes selfishness and violence.

Those who embrace this historical/cultural view of the United States point to our favorite forms of entertainment as evidence of these cultural themes. Many of the most popular sports (football, boxing, hockey) involve violence; movies and TV shows frequently portray murder, mayhem, and assault; and children's toys are often oriented toward violence (such as guns, bombs, toy racks of torture, and electronic shooting games). We honor and immortalize those who embody the competitive individualistic spirit, such as John Wayne, "Rocky" (the character played by Sylvester Stallone in a series of movies), and "Dirty Harry" (the San Francisco police detective made famous by Clint Eastwood). In addition, we seem to have an unrealistic and romanticized belief in the efficacy of punishment and coercion in solving all kinds of problems from misconduct by children to workplace inefficiency. It is little wonder, then, according to this argument, that in business transactions American citizens promote their own interests above all, run roughshod over competitors in other realms of life (even in sports, which are supposedly governed by rules) and rob, steal, maul, rape, and kill at astonishing rates.

To the extent that this frontier tradition actually accounts for the high rates of deviance in the United States, and to the extent that the deviance rates of other societies can be understood as outgrowths of their natural histories and unique cultures, theories that identify general conditions of social life whose variation might account for differences among societies in rates of deviance are wrong. The obverse is true as well: to the extent that general theories can explain cross-societal variations in rates of deviance, historical/cultural accounts will fail to add anything. More than likely, we will eventually learn that general principles and cultural aspects interact in the production of deviance.

Theories That Apply to Ecological Units and to Individuals

Anomie

Anomie theory (Merton, 1938, 1968) was discussed extensively in Chapter 11, but mainly as an account of individuals' propensity toward deviance. We return to it here because it provides an explanation of variation in rates of deviance among social units. Even though Merton's account implies certain things about why individuals are likely to commit deviance, the main import of the theory is for social units, not individuals.

According to this theory, all societies (and presumably other social groups as well) can be classified by their emphases on two crucial aspects of social life—the goals their members should seek to obtain and the appropriate or acceptable means for achieving those goals. By cross-classifying societies with respect to the relative emphases they place on these two dimensions, one can identify four types of societies, one of which can be regarded as well balanced or integrated (non-anomic) and three of which are mal-integrated or unbalanced (anomic). High rates of deviance would be predicted for the anomic societies while lower rates would be expected for non-anomic societies. The high rates of deviance occur because anomic societies fail to provide the necessary normative circumstances to guide members into conformity; it places them under the stress of choosing among inconsistent or unclear alternatives.

Integrated, balanced, or non-anomic societies are those where there is more-or-less equal stress on the goals to be achieved and on the means to achieve them. That is, balanced societies not only place a lot of importance on both elements, but they try to make sure that messages about goal achievement are widely spread and that the prescribed means for appropriate goal achievement are generally available to those who might choose to use them. Such a society might, for instance, emphasize that everybody should strive for moral perfection and at the same time stress that striving for moral perfection must be done in a particular way, say by daily prayer, in order to count. This society would provide rewards for those who strive for moral perfection in the prescribed way, but would either punish or refuse to reward those who did not strive for perfection or strove for it in ways other than daily prayer. In addition, it would go to a lot of trouble to convince people that they should strive for moral perfection and use daily prayer to do so. But, equally important, the society would make sure that daily prayers were possible for all who chose to use them as a means for achieving moral perfection. Hence, if praying required special beads, particular kinds of rugs for kneeling, or private booths, that society would struggle to make sure that beads and rugs were cheap and widely available and that the private booths were plentiful and widely dispersed so as to be accessible to all. In other words, this society would intensely set forth cultural goals for everybody to try for and it would both emphasize the appropriate method for trying to reach those goals and provide the means to do so. Such procedures would be expected to produce high rates of conformity because the society's members would know how to behave and also would have realistic methods for following through on that knowledge. Using Merton's terminology, such societies would be "conformist."

Anomic societies, on the other hand, produce higher rates of deviance be-cause people either do not know what they are supposed to try to accomplish or because they do not know how to do it, or because they do not have the specified means available to them to accomplish what they do know they are expected to do. In other words the members of anomic societies are under a lot of strain. Theoretically, there are three types of such anomic societies.

One is the complete opposite of the non-anomic society described earlier; it has no widespread, intensely emphasized cultural goals for people to try to achieve, nor does it have a set of prescribed means for achieving those goals. Such a society would be almost completely normless and should have an ex-tremely high rate of deviance because there are no consistent guidelines at all for behavior. In Merton's terms, this is a "retreatist" society.

Another type of anomic society puts unequal focus on either the cultural goals or the prescribed means. There may be extreme emphasis on the means to achieve goals but much less stress on the actual goals to be obtained. For instance, a society might be devoted to the work ethic above all else. Every-body might be expected to work extremely hard simply for the sake of work it-self, not to achieve any particular goal. People would be taught to honor work, to brag about their hard work, and to believe that work per se produced all sorts of good things, such as health, personal satisfaction, God's pleasure, or the like. And in such societies individuals would be praised and enjoy pres-tige because they worked, not because their work led to wealth or to some other outcome. Such a society would be classified as "ritualistic."

The final type of anomic society overemphasizes the cultural goals rela-tive to the means. They preach the desirability of specific goals, and they re-ward those who achieve them, without much concern for how the goal achievers arrived at their destination. Because of this strain to achieve goals without guidance about how to do so, the members of such societies are pre-dicted to manifest high rates of deviance, particularly in trying to find uncon-ventional means of reaping the rewards that go with success. Hence, these are "innovative" societies. Of the four types of society, this one was of most in-terest to Merton because he thought it was best exemplified by the United States.

According to Merton's description, and much supporting evidence (Messner and Rosenfeld, 1997 [1994]), the overarching goal that is presented to all people in the United States through books, movies, folk tales, and exam-ple is that of financial success. Those who achieve that goal enjoy prestige and power; those who don't are held in much lower regard, even if they achieve other goals that people presumably value. Moreover, even though U.S. culture specifies that it is desirable to achieve financial success through conventional means—advanced education/training, clever investments, or hard work and savings—those who cut corners do not jeopardize, to any great extent, the prestige that goes with wealth. Indeed, it is said that Ameri-cans make icons of famous criminals; quickly forget the origins of ill-gotten riches obtained through business fraud, later inviting the beneficiaries to serve on advisory boards or run for political office; and admire innovative schemes that are dishonest or illegal, reserving heavy criminal penalties for minor misdeeds with poor returns while winking at monstrous white-collar crimes that enrich many well-placed individuals (Simon, 1999).

Not only does American society place relatively greater emphasis on goal achievement than on the means for such achievement, it neglects to arrange

Deviance in Everyday Life

Historically, captains of American industry often "cut corners" to ensure the profitability of their businesses. In the mid- and latter part of the nineteenth century, American businessmen who used unethical, exploitative, and downright criminal means to secure profits earned the title of "Robber Baron." The Robber Barons of that period included Cornelius Vanderbilt and Andrew Carnegie. It is argued that there are modern-day Robber Barons. For example, business opponents of Microsoft President Bill Gates swear that he uses political and economic muscle to secure a virtual market monopoly. On a smaller scale, United Airlines is acting like a Robber Baron. United increased the number of flights in and out of its hub in Denver and dramatically lowered its fares, forcing several competitors (Continental and Frontier Airlines) out of business in Denver. Having secured a dominant share of the market for itself in Denver, United Airlines increased its fares. (Dempsey, 1997)

things so that the desirable means are widely accessible to those who might choose to use them. Education, especially higher education, is not equally available to all; it is more accessible to those with the funds to pay tuition, books, and living expenses while forgoing earnings. Nor is the quality of education equal, being higher in political units (the funding unit is typically the county) with more wealth to be taxed or where public commitment to school funding is greater. And this inequality in education is true, even though there are some outstanding instances of people who grew up in poverty climbing out of destitution by taking advantage of available educational opportunities. Similarly, the possibility of becoming wealthy through clever investment is not equal for all, since investment requires capital. Those who come from wealthy families start with capital, which they can increase or lose through investment, but they most often maintain or enhance their holdings by hiring professional money managers. Those who grow up in poverty barely have enough to survive, much less invest. Again, this is generally the case despite the few well-known examples of people who started on a shoestring and obtained fabulous wealth. Finally, hard work and savings as routes to success are limited. Those who begin at the bottom often work night and day, just to earn enough to meet current expenses, particularly if there are unusual medical bills or a large number of children, so the possibility of saving or advancing to wealth is remote. U.S. society, then, is supposedly a prime example of an anomic society of the "innovative" type, and as such it is predicted by Merton's theory to have a high rate of deviance of all kinds but especially of those kinds that might facilitate the acquisition of wealth, such as theft, fraud, exploitation, or robbery.

Deviance in Everyday Life

In Vermont, a large proportion of the cost of education used to be locally funded by property taxes. School districts in wealthy residential areas thus spent far more per student than those in less affluent areas. In *Amanda Brigham et al. v. State of Vermont*, however, the Vermont Supreme Court declared that practice unconstitutional. In response to this court decision, the Vermont legislature passed Act 60, a new school financing law. Under Act 60 all school districts were put on a generally equal footing. The consequence was that 229 school districts received more state money while the 23 most wealthy school districts had to do some belt tightening. Ironically, in order to pay for the increase in school spending across the board, residents in wealthy school districts saw their property taxes rise while their educational spending per pupil declined—all in the name of equality. (Sack, 1998)

According to anomie theory, then, we can understand rates of deviance by assessing the degree of emphasis on cultural goals relative to the means of reaching those goals. The greater the mal-integration of the two, either because neither is emphasized or because one or the other is relatively overemphasized, the greater the rate of deviance. It is not clear, however, whether an overemphasis on goals to the neglect of means produces more deviance than an overemphasis on means relative to goals. Since Merton spends so much time on the "innovative" type of society, we might infer that he thought it was more productive of deviance than the "ritualistic" type. If this inference is correct, we could then expect the highest rates of deviance in retreatist societies, the second highest in innovative societies, the third highest in ritualistic societies, and the lowest rates in conformist societies.

Since it is extremely difficult to measure emphases on cultural goals and means for a large number of societies, there have been no systematic tests of anomie theory as an explanation of societal rate variations. Perhaps the best ad hoc comparison is between the United States and India, which traditionally had a tight linkage between goals appropriate to the different castes and the means for getting to the goals. As shown in Table 16.3, the United States has one of the highest theft rates in the world and India has one of the lowest. This difference is clearly consistent with Merton's argument. In addition, case history and unsystematic evidence suggest some plausibility for the argument, but some evidence also suggests that other variables come into play, so that anomie is not the whole story. Indeed, Merton admits as much in his attempt to spell out the implications of societal anomie on individual adaptations (reviewed in Chapter 11), when he notes that family training in morality is an important condition determining whether strain produces innovation or ritualism.

In Chapter 11 we reviewed a variant of anomie theory, called general strain theory. Recall that general strain theory expands the notion of strain to include the introduction of noxious stimuli and the removal of positive stimuli. Agnew originally formulated general strain theory to account for individual variation in the motivation to commit crimes. In a recent restatement and extension of the theory, however, Agnew (1999) now also casts it as a theory of variation in crime rates across communities. Agnew argues that variations in crime rates across communities are due to community differences in stress and strain. He contends (1999:126) that "high-crime communities are more likely to select and retain strained individuals, produce strain, and foster criminal responses to strain." Although his new application of strain theory explains some of the communities-and-crime literature, it has not yet been empirically tested.

Defiance

A recent theory (Sherman, 1993) was developed specifically to explain why sanctions sometimes deter, sometimes have no effect, and sometimes have the opposite effect of producing more deviance among individuals. Nevertheless, it also provides an account of rates of deviance among social units. Sherman's theory implies that all societies impose or threaten negative sanctions for misbehavior. Like those who generalize principles of individual deterrence to the ecological level, he implies that sanctioning is the key to explaining variations in rates of deviance from one social group to another.

However, he departs from the utilitarian/deterrence theorists in that he does not attribute rate variation strictly to differences in characteristics of sanctions, such as their certainty or severity. Instead, drawing on other extant theories and research, he identifies three conditions that converge to influence whether sanctions are effective producers of conformity.

In brief, the three conditions are: (1) whether sanctions are imposed with respect for the alleged offender, (2) how strongly the recipients of sanctions are bonded to the community whose representatives are attempting to impose sanctions, and (3) the degree to which offenders (or those accused) can accept shame. To the extent that (1) sanctions are typically applied legitimately (by appropriate personnel according to reasonable rules) with due regard for the dignity of the accused (and the sanctions are experienced that way by the accused), (2) offenders are tightly knit with the community or its sanctioning agents, and (3) offenders are able to accept the shame of being accused of wrongdoing and seek reintegration, then rates of deviance will be low. Rates of deviance will be high when the opposite circumstances hold, and they will be modest when these three factors are fairly evenly balanced.

The reasoning behind the three conditions is not fully developed, but it appears that the following processes are at work. First, when there is a threat of sanctions, objects of that threat are likely to become defensive because it implies a negative judgment about them, or sometimes because it is perceived as unfair. Only when accused persons perceive that their behaviors are legitimately being checked (that is, that there is a reasonable basis for the sanctioning agent to suspect them) can sanctions have a deterrent effect. If sanctions are imposed arbitrarily or in a debasing manner, implying that the process has been unfair or that the accused are unworthy persons, they provoke anger and motivate their recipients to strike back.

Second, when accused people are not bonded to the community, they will only react to sanctions in an expedient manner. That is, they will obey when there is a high probability of apprehension and costly punishment, but not otherwise. Socially bonded individuals, however, fear sanctions mainly because the sanctions imply disapproval from a group about which they care. Well-integrated persons who are sanctioned, then, learn to avoid future misbehavior in order to maintain their group memberships. Those not strongly bonded to the community issuing the sanctions, on the other hand, care little about what the members of that community might think about them. Consequently their future conduct is affected only by the direct cost implied by the sanction, not the indirect costs implied by loss of reputation associated with the sanction. Since the chances of apprehension and punishment can never be very high unless the social group is highly integrated, the direct deterrent effect of sanctions for unbonded individuals is low.

Finally, being threatened by sanctions or actually being sanctioned is to experience shame, a challenge to one's self-concept (see Scheff and Retzinger, 1991). If people can accept shame, then they are likely to want to redeem themselves by repentance and reintegration into the group that is the source of their self-concepts. Many people, however, cannot accept shame; to avoid it, they turn their emotions into rage, which leads to further deviance. Whether people can accept shame is partly dependent on their early childhood socialization; some are taught how to transform shame into redemption while others are not. A propensity to accept shame is also partly dependent on social processes. If group culture permits shamed people to repent and become reintegrated, they are far more likely to accept shame and act positively to reduce it. However, where social practice dictates stigmatization or simple punishment, then repentance implies nothing but personal suffering, and shame is less likely to be accepted by individuals in that group.

Rates of deviance, then, depend on how sanctions are used, the group standing of those receiving sanctions, and institutional and group processes. None of these variables has been measured for whole population aggregates, especially not cross-culturally, so it is not possible to assess the ability of defiance theory to explain rate variations. Moreover, to a large extent the argument relies on rates of recidivism as the key to overall rates of deviance, and these are not available for very many ecological units.

Shaming

Another important contribution to theories about social integration has been provided by Braithwaite (1989). In Chapter 14, we discussed his ideas about the importance of gossip as a process of social control that helps explain the behavior of individuals, and earlier in this chapter, we visited Braithwaite's writings in connection with the theory of social integration. His contention is that highly interdependent social groups generally have lower rates of deviance, at least partly because social integration enhances the effectiveness of informal social control, often through the mechanism of gossip. Here we return to the general theory of shaming because it suggests an additional refinement to account for variations in rates of deviance among tightly knit societies.

Although Braithwaite contends that socially integrated societies will generally have lower rates of deviance than those that are not so cohesive, he also suggests that integrated societies will differ among themselves in rates of deviance, with some having much higher rates than others. According to him, the key factor differentiating societies with high rates from those with low rates is *how* they deal with offenders. Societies may do one of three things to offenders: they can do nothing (an unlikely possibility); they can punish offenders, with the main objective being to cause pain or discomfort; or they can shame norm violators. Shaming is a process designed to produce feelings of responsibility and genuine regret in an individual for harm caused by her or his misdeed. All others things being equal, rates of deviance should be greatest where nothing is done, second greatest where offenders are punished, and least where offenders are shamed. However, not all shaming has the same effect. Indeed, when shame is long-term and stigmatizing, it often leads to further deviance, particularly if there are deviant subcultures populated by similarly stigmatized rule breakers. Only when shaming is followed by procedures and efforts to reintegrate its recipients does it produce really low rates of deviance. Thus, societies that shame violators but provide the means for their redemption will have the lowest rates of deviance.

This argument is a very powerful and plausible one, but to our knowledge no systematic attempt has been made to test this theory cross-culturally. Braithwaite makes much of United States-Japan comparisons because Japan presumably practices reintegrative shaming to a much greater extent than the United States. No doubt his argument is based partly on having observed the dramatic differences in rates of deviance, especially predatory crime, between the two countries. Tables 16.2 and 16.3 show that theft rates in Japan are only about one-fifth those in the United States, and homicide rates are only about one-seventh. This comparison, however, does not suffice as evidence of the truth of the argument. Comparing other pairs of countries might provide negative evidence for the shaming contention.

Summary and Conclusion

There are huge differences among countries in rates of deviance, as exemplified by rates of suicide, homicide, theft, and drug crimes. Patterns of variation are not the same for different kinds of deviance, however. Countries high in suicide are not necessarily high in homicide, theft, or drug crimes. And countries low in one or another of the criminal offenses, such as homicide, are not necessarily low in offenses like theft. For instance, the United States has modest suicide rates but high rates of homicide, theft, and drug crimes. Venezuela has low rates of suicide, high rates of homicide, and medium rates of drug crime and theft.

A number of theories have been proposed to account for these and other variations among social units such as cities, states, or nations. Some of the theories simply aggregate micro-level variables drawn from theories about individuals' behavior; others describe ecological-level processes that go beyond individuals; and still others propose causal mechanisms that have both individual- and ecological-level applications. While many of these formulations are plausible, few have been systematically tested with cross-context data, especially not cross-national data. One of the major challenges for students of deviance is to devise tests of the theories of rate variations and then to use the results of those tests to modify and integrate such theories for better explanation. ✦

Chapter 17

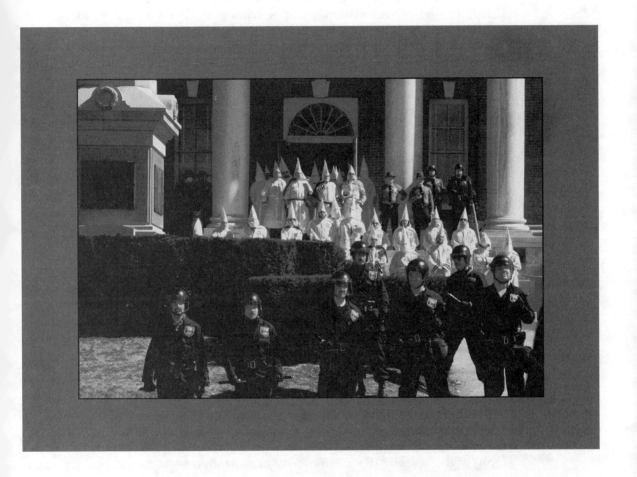

The Relevance of Practitioner Organization for Theories of Deviance

We authors have suggested that one can understand and explain particular forms of deviance or crime only by taking into account the extent to which their practitioners are organized. We argued (Chapter 2) that organization must be measured indirectly, and we presented nine indicators that collectively reflect the extent to which any given deviant or criminal activity is organized. The point was made that organization of deviance is not "all or nothing" but is a matter of degree. Specific forms of crime or deviance may be characterized by more or less of it, so various kinds of deviance can be arranged on a continuum of organization. Such a continuum conceivably extends from zero percent organized (absolutely no organization) on one end to 100 percent organized (absolute maximum organization) on the other. However, such fine-grained gradations are probably impossible to establish empirically, and in any case, their effects within specific, narrow ranges would have few practical consequences. Therefore, we divided the continuum of organization into three zones, individualized, subcultural, and fully organized. Average differences in organization among these zones are large enough to be measured—indeed, they can be readily observed without detailed quantitative measurements—and they have important implications for explaining deviance.

After having demarcated the organizational continuum, we illustrated how some forms of deviance fit into the various zones of the continuum (Chapters 3–5). Then we turned our attention to questions concerning why some behaviors are deviant and others are not (Chapters 6–7). After that we tried to establish the extent and distribution of deviance and conformity (Chapters 8–9). Eventually (in Chapters 10–16), we presented various explanations and theories that have been formulated to account for crime and deviance. Now we return to the organizational idea in order to show its implications for explanation. We will focus mainly on the general theories about individual deviance rather than the ad hoc explanations. We want to show two things: (1) that the explanatory processes highlighted in the various theories will perform more effectively if the organizational characteristics of the deviance to be explained are taken into account and (2) that in some instances the theories are severely limited because they cannot be adjusted to apply to all forms of deviance on the continuum of organization.

Practitioner Organization and External Motivation Theories

External motivation theories (Chapter 11) are those that emphasize the causal effect of forces outside individuals which either directly or indirectly impel them toward deviance. Our discussion identified three major categories of such theories—learning theories, structural inducement theories, and situational inducement theories.

Learning

Recall that learning theories emphasize processes by which individuals develop psychic traits—ideas, attitudes, values, habits, and shared understandings—that promote deviant behavior. Those theories differ, however, with respect to the sources from which such things are presumably learned.

Some emphasize general social learning from the larger culture, others place most importance on intimate reference groups, and still others focus on subcultural contexts.

Organization impinges on the causal processes that learning theory implicates in two important ways. First, those people who directly reinforce learning, or indirectly do so by their own examples (all of whom can be regarded as "teachers") can be more or less organized, and the extent to which they are organized affects the degree of learning. Sutherland recognized the potential importance of this variable when he identified "differential social organization" as a reason that rates of crime (or deviance) vary from one society to another. But he never developed the concept very well, and he did not explicitly apply it to the question of why some people experience a greater number of crime-favorable (or deviance-favorable) associations, or more effective ones, than do other people. Social learning theorists have not gone much further in that direction. As a result, standard learning theories flirt with the organizational concept but never fully develop its implications.

Similarly, the subcultural learning theories imply an organizational component in their emphasis on coherent deviogenic messages passed along from one generation to another. Intergenerational transmission assumes a certain degree of organization among people in subcultures. Yet subcultural learning theorists have not spelled out explicitly how various subcultures vary in their degree of organization, nor how such variation might impinge on the extent to which inductees acquire deviogenic characteristics. In general, then, learning-oriented scholars have given only meager attention to the organizational variable.

It is clear, however, that individuals will learn more deviogenic things the more extensively their "teachers" are organized, and, as a result, other things being equal, those exposed to deviant patterns presented by more fully organized practitioners (those who collectively score highly on the nine criteria set forth in Chapter 2) have a greater probability of doing deviance than those exposed to less organized deviant subcultures (Best and Luckenbill, 1980, 1982). Sometimes practitioners/teachers are moderately organized, as illustrated by our discussion of deviant drug use and gang delinquency. At other times they are fully organized, as were the Perfectionists and as are syndicated criminals. Practitioners of some forms of deviance, such as suicide and serial killing, are, on the other hand, hardly organized at all. It is easy enough to imagine that the probability and frequency of the deviant acts reflect, to some extent, the effectiveness of learning that individuals in these various contexts experience.

Consider what might happen if those who want to promote suicide become more organized than they are now. Isn't it likely that they will associate more readily with each other, communicate more effectively, and develop a more extensive culture that is passed on to more systematically recruited newcomers? If this were to come to pass, more people would probably regard suicide favorably, and more would be ready to use it when appropriate circumstances presented themselves. Furthermore, any given instance of suicide would probably have a greater chance of being explained by principles of learning. After all, as we noted before, learning theories currently have difficulty accounting for individualized deviance like suicide or mental illness because in our society there are few social definitions favorable to those acts or role models from whom to learn them.

Further, imagine what the consequences would be if drug users became as well organized as the Perfectionists were or as contemporary syndicated crime is. Such organized drug users would share a well-integrated philosophy justifying their activities; they would have more clearly differentiated and coordinated roles, including perhaps some designated specifically to training others in the techniques and rationales of drug use; and they would be capable of far more extensive recruitment than the haphazard enlistment that now characterizes drug use. Furthermore, they would be in a position to more effectively resist countermessages and law enforcement efforts. The net effect would probably be even more extensive drug use than there is now, and drug use would probably be more explicable by learning principles.

Because the degree of organization among practitioners is a key phenomenon affecting the extent and effectiveness with which people acquire deviogenic psychic traits, learning theories must confront it more explicitly and with greater precision if they are to improve their explanations of deviant behavior. A second way that organization (among those who practice particular forms of deviance) bears on learning explanations concerns the issue of how the things that are learned come to be expressed in behavior. Learning theories more or less assume that once criminogenic traits are incorporated into individuals' psyches, people will behave according to those traits, regardless of whether the person is acting as a lone individual or is allied with others. Thus, presumably, one who has learned that it is gratifying and appropriate to steal will do so, provided that there are things that can be stolen (and that the chances of getting caught and punished are not too great). And a person who believes that drug use is recreationally pleasing, knows how to do it, has access to drugs, and does not face too much opposition, will, according to learning theories, use drugs.

As noted before, however, this is not the whole story. Other things come into play, and one of those things is organization (or lack thereof) among people who have learned that stealing and drug use are reasonable ways to gratify their needs. Unorganized individuals probably encounter fewer cues for deviance and interpret them differently than they would in organized company with others (McCall, 1994; Warr, 1996). For example, as the research by Short and Strodtbeck (1965; Short, 1963) demonstrated, cues that might activate deviant inclinations are more likely to emerge when male youths interact regularly in groups not supervised by law-abiding adults. When continuously in interaction, youths vie for status, try to reinforce reputations, and struggle to overcome boredom. Inevitably, suggestions for criminal or deviant conduct emerge, or external cues are brought into consciousness. Those cues then are enhanced by conversation, masculinity tests, and shared histories of past misdeeds. Moreover, potential deviant opportunities are more likely to be grasped, or sought out, when group interaction activates already existing attitudes and drives. Finally, potential risk is minimized by: (1) the same masculinity tests that brought forth the cues for criminal/deviant conduct, (2) shared pluralistic ignorance, and (3) feelings of diffuse responsibility—all of which characterize subculturally organized groups of youths.

Social organization among potential offenders, therefore, interacts situationally with the products of learning in important ways to affect outcomes. And, as discussed above, organization among "teachers" affects what is learned and how well it is learned. Without taking such effects into account, learning theories cannot be efficient, even if correct. Therefore, we must recognize the extent of organization among practitioners of deviance as a contingency for the operation of learning theories—the greater the practitioner organization, the greater the power of learning to explain any given deviance. Of course, this implies that where there are low levels of organization among potential deviants, such as among those displaying bizarre behavior characteristic of mental illness, learning probably has little explanatory power. Under those circumstances, other theories must be used.

Structural Inducement

A second set of external motivation theories emphasizes characteristics of situations or structural features of societies that create problems (strain) for people, thereby motivating them to use deviant behavior as a potential solution to this strain. We described three different variants—anomie, general strain, and competitive conflict theory (Marxian)—which differ with respect to the things they identify as straining and in the specification of conditions influencing the individual's selection of one or another method of dealing with the strain. To an even greater extent than learning theories, these formulations fail to show appreciation of the importance of organization among potential deviants.

Consider how the level of organization among practitioners affects the perception of relative deprivation, which is crucial to both anomie and competitive conflict theories, and which is one of the important elements of general strain theory. Any individual may, on occasion, notice that his or her situation relative to others is deprived and become strained as a result, but interaction with others in an organized context increases the chances that somebody in the group will take note of depriving stimuli, call them to the attention of the rest, and invite commiseration about them. By this means, what might have been an infrequently experienced motivation may become a more frequent one. Therefore, to the extent that motivation stemming from strain affects the likelihood of deviance, it will have more effect in the context of socially organized deviants or potential deviants than otherwise. One can easily imagine that if suicide were a subcultural rather than an individualized form of deviance more people would stimulate each other to perceive their situations as straining. The result would probably be more suicide, and strain theory would loom larger as an explanation.

Another consideration usually overlooked by strain theories is the power of alternative motivation (see Sheley, 1983). No matter how strongly motivated toward deviance a person may be, whether that motivation gets expressed in actual deviant conduct depends to some extent on the nature and strength of competing motivations. If a potential bank robber is stimulated into action, say, by some form of strain, but at the same time is overwhelmed with hunger or learns that he has won the lottery or happens upon an especially attractive opportunity for a sexual encounter, he is less likely to act on the motivation to take down the bank. By contrast, organization among potential deviants, say shoplifters or terrorists, can ensure that criminal motivation is both frequently sparked and seldom overshadowed by competing motives. If status in such a subcultural group depends on attending to business, if there is loyalty to the group, or if physical sanctions are imminent for those who let other motives get in the way of business, and all of this is effectively communicated (all features of social organization), deviant motives will almost always prevail.

It is an implicit assumption of most theories of deviance that a person must be capable of committing a deviant act for it to occur. No matter how well motivated individuals might be for computer fraud, they simply cannot do it without computer skills or the ability to coerce a person with computer skills to do the job for them. And no matter how strong the desire to steal automobiles, those who can't drive are unlikely to commit auto theft, at least by themselves. So, even if people become motivated for various kinds of deviance by strain or the emotions stemming from strain, they may not actually commit those acts, because they lack the skill for their performance.

The effect of organization among potential violators on the ability to commit deviance is well illustrated by ethnographies of illegal drug use. As the work of numerous scholars (e.g., Agar, 1973; Beck and Rosenbaum, 1994; Goode, 1970; Inciardi et al., 1993; Johnson, 1973; Jonnes, 1996; Sterk-Elifson and Elifson, 1993; Williams, 1992) has shown (see Chapter 4), being enmeshed in an effectively organized system of crack or heroin use helps solve the problems of supply and of knowing how to consume, both of which bear on the ability to use illegal drugs. And as the work of Patricia Adler (1993) so brilliantly demonstrates, the system of organization among drug suppliers ensures that those who otherwise might not be able to smuggle drugs or maintain a cash flow can nevertheless continue to participate.

In addition, opportunity (the simple condition of a deviant act being possible) is not incorporated explicitly in most strain theories. They assume that when strain is high, the person is compelled to seek a solution. And although strain theories do specify some conditions that influence the direction the coping will take, most do not take note of the importance of social organization among practitioners in creating opportunities that would permit deviant solutions for strain or its accompanying emotions. After all, noticing, elaborating, and creating opportunities is one of the products of organized interaction. A lone individual with strain is less likely to grasp an opportunity to vandalize a school building than is a strained member of a gang. As you learned in Chapter 4, gangs often create their own opportunities for deviance. Collectively they are on the lookout for chances to do mischief—because mischief, whether stemming from strain or some other source, is part and parcel of the organizational lives of gangs. So if a school building is not handy to be vandalized, gang members may go find one, or, failing that, they may turn to other forms of deviance, which may include vandalism of private property, theft, fighting, or drug use.

Furthermore, although General Strain Theory accommodates variations in constraint that might influence whether strain leads to deviance, neither it nor the other strain theories take note of the way that practitioners, such as thieves, drug users, or corrupt police when organized among themselves, can reduce the effects of constraints by working together to spot observers or to help conceal professional misdeeds, stolen merchandise, or drug transactions. And sometimes organization, such as that among the Perfectionists, can magnify perceptions of constraint, leading to modifications in deviant behavior that otherwise might have occurred—as when Perfectionists suspended the practice of complex marriage for a time.

Finally, strain theories do not recognize that although deviance may be originally stimulated by strain, it may, because of organization among the practitioners, continue in the absence of the original straining conditions. For example, it would be difficult to attribute the behavior of the Perfectionists, as it occurred within the community itself, to strain. After all, by collective effort the Oneida group was able to overcome many of the conditions that were straining for its members prior to their joining the community. Sexual dissatisfaction, economic hardship, spiritual deprivation, and social subordination all may have played a part in stimulating people to seek fellowship within the Perfectionists. Once people were in the group, however, those problems faded into the background, at least for most members. Yet collectively they continued to do the kinds of things that the outside world regarded as unacceptable. Routinized deviance like that practiced by the Perfectionists would seem to stem from group processes themselves.

Just as learning theories appear to work poorly in explaining individualized deviance, strain theories seem deficient in explaining the forms of deviance that are partially or fully organized. However, strain theories could be modified to predict greater or lesser effects, depending on the degree to which practitioners are organized among themselves. But until they are, we must recognize how such organization: (1) impinges on perceptions of strain that might generate motivation for deviance, (2) affects alternative motivations and ability, (3) creates or stimulates perception of opportunities for deviance, (4) alters constraints or perceptions of constraints, and (5) sometimes leads to routinized deviance that operates without reference to original strains.

Situational Inducement

In Chapter 11 we presented three theories that focus on deviance arising out of situational circumstances of various kinds. They were routine activities (translated into an individual analog), rational choice, and interaction process. Routine activities theory, as applied to individuals, concerns situational activation of motivation in response to the convergence of suitable targets and the absence of guardianship, which is presumably promoted by aspects of modern life styles but which also varies among individuals. Rational choice focuses on an individual's weighing of the situational benefits relative to the costs of behavior, and acting in ways that maximize the benefits while minimizing the costs. Interaction process theory highlights acts that result from sequences of adjustment to changing circumstances, including especially the responses of other people. These external motivation theories, like the others reviewed in the preceding paragraphs, also fail to take into account the way that differential organization among deviants affects their causal processes.

Consider the importance of practitioner organization for the three elements of routine activity theory. According to the theory, whether potentially motivated people actually become motivated toward deviance depends on the arrangements in the social and physical world of suitable deviant targets and on weak guardianship of those targets. Activation of motivation is at least partly a matter of perception, in which the individual notices or interprets a favorable target-guardianship convergence. But, as we have noted before, what individuals may perceive when operating as lone individuals differs considerably from what they are likely to perceive when they are part of organized networks of people on the lookout for such convergences, or who are in the business of trying to bring about such convergences.

This difference in perception can be illustrated by imagining what would happen if serial killers, who usually operate as individualized deviants, were in fact organized as syndicated criminals are or as the Perfectionists were. We could visualize that there would be leaders planning the killings and directing their associates to seek out convergences of suitable targets that were unguarded. In addition, the serial killers would be sharing their experiences and insights with each other, thereby enhancing each other's awareness of potential convergences and leading to a culture incorporating such knowledge to be passed along from one generation of killers to the next. Furthermore, some might be pressured through the mechanism of internal group social control to act even when favorable convergences of target and guardianship were not present. In other words, the volume, pattern, and accounts for serial killing within the parameters of routine activities theory would be quite different were practitioner organization taken into account. In practice, since serial killing is individualized rather than more organized, it is probably more explicable from routine activities theory than other such forms of deviance as drug use or gang delinquency, in which organizational processes impinge more directly on perceptions of target-guardianship convergences.

To appreciate how practitioner organization bears on such convergences, consider the activities of "swingers" (married people who share sexual partners from outside the marriage). Swingers are organized into a subculture (Bartell, 1971; Breedlove and Breedlove, 1964; Walshok, 1971) within which they share information and a code of etiquette. In addition, they have systems of communication, justifying rationales, and means of informal social control. New participants are recruited systematically, and experienced veterans are brought into new contacts through deliberate means. Swinging behavior, therefore, is not simply a chance occurrence of those motivated for such sexual exchange coming into contact with suitable targets (attractive couples also willing to participate) in situations where those who might disapprove cannot do anything about it (lack of guardianship). Instead, there is much concerted effort to make sure that motivated individuals, suitable targets, and weak guardianship converge. Without this organized effort, it is unlikely that very much swinging would happen. Therefore, to attempt to explain this behavior by routine activities theory without the added organizational component would be extremely ineffective.

Rational choice theory is limited in a similar way. It zeroes in on calculations in the individual's head about the relative costs and benefits of action in specific situations. However, those calculations are heavily affected by whether the individual is part of an organized network of people who frequently contemplate particular kinds of deviant behavior. Militia groups illustrate this point (Newsweek, 1995). Perhaps some individuals weigh the costs of ignoring laws requiring payment of income taxes or legitimate debts (such as home mortgages) against the benefits to be gained, and decide to embark on a path of defiance as if they were in a social vacuum. But it is probably rare. Most of the militia members who engage in such deviance have been schooled by their association with other like-minded people to believe that it is possible, right, and sometimes even a duty to defy government-imposed taxation. They hear testimony from those who advocate defiant actions and they share thoughts with those who seemingly have gotten away with it.

Moreover, they experience a good deal of informal social pressure to defy government edicts even if they do not fully accept the rosy scenario about the financial advantages of such actions current in their groups. From an outsider's point of view, perceptions of cost and benefit become highly unrealistic among individuals in these groups, and their actions take on a surreal quality, often reflecting group influences that show little rationality. Thus, processes of choice are considerably different for those who practice individualized deviance than for those who are fully or subculturally organized, and often people's choices are far from rational.

Finally, interaction processes that, according to the theories in which they are embedded, sometimes produce deviance as a result of unique sequences of action, interpretation, and response, are no doubt contingent on organizational contexts. How a person interprets and responds to an action by another person is different depending on whether there is a reference group to judge the meaning and intent of the original action and response to it. What is regarded as an insult reflects not only the psychic organization of the individual but what observers or those who later hear about the sequence of events do or are perceived as likely to do. For instance, an actual or anticipated comment such as, "Are you going to let him get away with that?" can turn an innocent remark into an affront. Because of this, it matters a lot whether a given deviant act emanates from a more organized or less organized context. Moreover, many deviant acts become routinized so that they are not simply random occurrences stemming from unique interaction sequences (Heimer and Matsueda, 1994; Matsueda, 1992). This can be seen by considering the examples of subcultural and fully organized deviance we discussed in Chapters 4 and 5.

Some delinquency by particular gang members may result from specific, more-or-less unique interaction sequences, such as when the masculinity of a particular individual is challenged by an offhand remark (Katz, 1988; Short and Strodtbeck, 1965). But the bulk of gang activity is the result of collective patterns of misbehavior, organized and directed, or at least stimulated, by routine interaction. Outcomes of such patterns are not "unique," but instead are highly predictable. Similarly, given the cultured (shared and passed along from one generation to the next—see Chapter 2) and supervised ways that the Perfectionists repeated the activities that the outside world regarded as deviant, such as sexual exchange, female immodesty, and economic communism, there is little doubt that interaction process theory misses the explanatory mark—mainly because it does not take into account the organizational features of the deviance it is trying to explain.

Interaction process theory, therefore, seems more appropriate for explaining individualized deviance like suicide, serial killing, and lethal assault stemming from interpersonal encounters (Katz, 1988) than for subcultural or fully organized deviance. Unlike the other external motivation theories, however, it does not seem amenable to modification that would accommodate practitioner organization. Because of its focus on uniqueness of interaction sequences, the idea of routinized, group-inspired, or organizationally supported deviance seems foreign. Therefore, it should probably be regarded as a theory aimed mainly at explaining individualized deviance.

Practitioner Organization and Internal Motivation Theories

Chapter 12 discussed theories that postulate the causes of deviance to be motivators inside the psyches of individuals. Although in each of those theories the internal forces that presumably lead to deviance are interactively linked with things in the external environment that mold and shape them, the internal motivation formulations are distinct in their assumption that something inherent in human make-up impels behavior, sometimes in deviant directions. We reviewed three such theories, or sets of theories: self, reactance, and psychodynamic.

Self

Recall that these theories are rooted in a perspective called symbolic interactionism. According to that approach, people relate to their external environment mainly through chains of interaction sequences in which they anticipate how others will respond to behavior; they attach meanings to that response and adjust their behaviors continually as those external cues are encountered and interpreted. At the center of this process is an inherently driven search for a meaningful sense of self, which motivates people to act in various ways that may, depending on the reactions of others, become a more or less stable organization for behavior and thinking. Two divisions of self theory were discussed: identity/labeling and self-esteem.

Identity/labeling theory focuses on individuals' conceptions of who and what they are. Self-concepts grow from two sources. One is from trial and error, in which parents and other people in the immediate environment react in ways that solidify or undermine self-images implied by trial behavior or random actions. The other is by imposition from external sources, especially formal authorities, who may attribute particular qualities (often deviant) to an individual on the basis of specific acts. When such labels result in stigma, the social environment of a person so labeled becomes challenging and disadvantageous. The result sometimes is a crisis of self, along with diminished conventional opportunities. Under those conditions, the person may become affiliated with others similarly labeled and may undergo a transformation of self to become what she or he was labeled as.

Self-esteem theories, on the other hand, emphasize attitudes about the self—evaluative beliefs and feelings that people have about themselves. When people are not pleased with themselves, for whatever reasons, they may reject the normative system that led to those bad feelings and seek more favorable experiences in deviant behavior. Deviant behavior, then, results from self-derogation, and according to one prominent formulation, it presumably enhances self-esteem, at least under some circumstances.

These self theories pay more attention to organization among practitioners than do most other theories of deviance. Labeling theory notes the importance of organization among those who have been labeled, and self-esteem and self-derogation theories acknowledge the effect of deviant peers, who are often organized into gangs. Yet the self theories fail to follow through with full appreciation for the import of organization. Since self-concepts and self-esteem depend on reactions from others, it is clear that how those others are organized should be of prime importance. Imagine two children, a boy who is born into an ordinary middle-class family in the United States and the other, a girl born to parents active in an organized revolutionary group. The boy will try out various roles, some deviant, and probably end up evoking reactions from parents that solidify a conforming sense of self accompanied by fairly good self-attitudes. If the theory is correct, that child will not do very much deviant behavior as he proceeds through the life course. And if, perchance, he is handled by some official agency for real or suspected deviance, it is not likely to result in a label, at least partly because the individual has a strong sense of self as a conventional person, which makes him resistant to contrary attributions.

Deviance in Everyday Life

Nick Becker was a normal high school senior in rural Maryland, ready to graduate with his class in the summer of 1999 (Layton, 1999). That is, he was mildly rebellious and eager to flex his adult muscles. He had no idea what he was getting into, however, when he objected to the fact that his high school graduation included a public prayer. Nick, a lone teenager, experienced the organized force of religious conservatives in his largely rural community. Local preachers vocally denounced him, a reporter for the semi-weekly newspaper in the town wrote that he was an atheist (actually, he's agnostic), and school authorities banned him from his own graduation ceremony and a school-sponsored post-graduation party. With support from the American Civil Liberties Union and the Maryland attorney general, Nick won—the planned prayer was stricken from the official program. Nevertheless, when it came time for the scheduled "moment of silence" during the graduation ceremony, a large proportion of the crowd, and the county's highest elected official, chose to illegally recite the Lord's Prayer. Nick immediately walked out of the ceremony.

However, when the girl emits behavior indicative of an emerging anti-government orientation, it is likely the parents will respond approvingly, and they will disapprove of behaviors indicative of a conforming, conventional self-image (Newsweek, 1994a). Moreover, as the girl grows up, she is likely to be exposed mostly to other children whose parents share similar ideas, and those children in turn are likely to reinforce each others' future revolutionary selves. Even if the child encounters other potential self-definitions that provoke unpleasant personal attitudes, she may resort to direct acts of deviance to increase self-esteem. Furthermore, she is likely to suffer stigma that the outside world imposes on the revolutionary group as a whole. When she misbehaves, as most youths do, she is likely to be readily hauled into judgment by official agents like school officials, police, and juvenile courts. Attributions resulting from those contacts, in turn, limit her opportunities to become anything other than what the labeling processes have decreed. In short, the girl is much more likely to end up actually doing deviance, and the reason will only partly be because of the process of self formation—it will also depend heavily on whether that child is part of an organized group of deviance practitioners.

Second, even with deviant self-images and poor self-attitudes, deviant behavior to confirm a deviant self or to seek an enhancement of self-esteem requires opportunity; is usually stimulated by some immediate provocation; and involves overcoming fear of costly consequences. All of these conditions are enhanced by social organization among those who practice particular kinds of deviance. Consider the deviant behavior of reneging on debts, which was briefly noted in Chapter 2. It is easy enough to imagine that some people, through the processes specified by the theories, develop self-concepts built around the notion that they are sharp traders who take pride in "beating" somebody else in a business deal, or have poor self-esteem resulting from personal disgust when they contemplate themselves in debt and at the mercy of others. But such people do not always, and maybe never, renege on their debts. In other words, refusal to pay debts is not a necessary or a continuous activity. What, then, makes actual deviance happen among such people?

First, there must be opportunity. Obviously if one has no creditors, then one cannot renege on a debt. But beyond that, one has to perceive that reneging is possible. People usually find out about such possibilities from others who have simply skipped out on debts or legally took bankruptcy, or from those who talk about people who have done those things. But imagine that debt renegers were organized within a subculture (as indeed some are, like such right-wing anti-tax militia groups as the Posse Comitatas). They would share ideas about why debt rejection is not bad and why it is good, they would know how to do it because of communication among experienced renegers, and they would know the most favorable conditions for doing it. In other words, perceived opportunity is likely to be greater for some people, especially those who participate in organized practitioner groups, than for others.

In addition, debt refusal is usually preceded by provocation. Any debtor may sometimes have an urgent need to use the money for something else, or there may simply be no money available, or the individual may receive a collection notice. Those who participate in a subculture of debt renegers, however, experience constant provocation in the form of chiding about actually paying debts, and they are constantly reminded that refusal is a possibility. Finally, those who renege must imagine that there is some possibility of getting away with it; sometimes they simply have no other choice. Again, perceptions of possible escape are much more likely if one is surrounded by others who know the ropes and who are willing to help shield the individual from collectors. If nobody knows where you live, or can say when you will be home, or has even heard of you, bill collectors have a hard time serving papers or repossessing property.

As this illustration shows, the self process unfolds with greater or less force, depending on how well potential deviants are organized. In fact, one of the indicators of organization discussed in Chapter 2 is the extent to which practitioners draw their self-concepts and self-esteem from participation in the group. Consequently, to understand how those processes eventuate in deviance, one has to take organization into account. And when practitioners are hardly organized at all, the self theories appear to be particularly weak. It is hard to imagine, for instance, that people who talk nonsense (a form of behavior connected to mental illness) do so because they have self-concepts as nonsense talkers, and it is certainly difficult to conceive that anybody having been so labeled would have chosen that action to enhance self attitudes. Similarly, embezzlement is a hard case for self theories, as is suicide, although some who take their own lives no doubt do so in conformity with a self that cannot bear failure or being a burden. But if deviant behavior serves to reinforce a self-image or enhance self-esteem, it would seem that death resulting from suicide would preclude the payoff. In any case, it would appear that self theories need to take organization among practitioners more explicitly into account and perhaps treat it as a contingency for the full operation of the theories.

Reactance

According to this theory, people naturally strive to maintain their freedoms. Whenever the freedoms they think they have are threatened, or actually blocked, people feel an increase in desire for the freedom, or the things implied by the freedom so that their desire is greater than it was before the threat or blockage. As a result of reactance, people sometimes use deviant behavior to reestablish lost freedom or to gain the things jeopardized when freedom was threatened. The reactance that people feel, however, is not always attributable to psychic function alone. People can feel reactance vicariously, as the freedoms of others like them are threatened, and they can experience regained freedom by observing the adaptive behaviors of others whose freedoms are threatened. Despite this, the theory pays little attention to the possible implications of organization among those who have suffered loss of freedom or who anticipate that their freedoms might be threatened.

Consider people who defy regulations against smoking in public buildings or other prohibited places. The theory suggests something like the following scenario. An individual smoker who has been lighting up freely in public buildings one day receives a memo saying smoking will no longer be permitted there, and prohibitory signs go up. The person experiences psychological reactance; she now wants to smoke more than ever, and she wants to do it in the building. If she can, she will sneak around and continue to smoke there. If she cannot do that because the risk is too great, she will seek some other way to assert her autonomy. Perhaps she will drive to work in her friend's car, which is not registered with the building security force, and park in the boss's spot every now and again. Maybe she will take some office supplies home with her. Or she may call in sick when she is quite well. What she does, of course, depends on the magnitude of the reactance, whether she has moral feelings about the alternative modes of action, opportunities for various kinds of action, and the costs of alternative behaviors.

Imagine, however, that the employees in this particular building have organized themselves into a workers' union because they anticipate future jeopardy of their freedoms. Now directives are not likely to be issued at the boss's discretion. Instead the question is introduced for discussion by the union. Because union members are reasonably well organized (one might say, somewhere between subcultural and fully organized), they are less threatened by what the boss might do arbitrarily. Their reactance arousal is much less, so they do not develop enhanced desires to smoke in their offices. Moreover, if prohibitory signs go up, the union members have a way to regain control individually—by acting collectively, perhaps going on strike. The likelihood of deviant behavior, such as defiance of the directive or oblique violations of other rules, is much less when workers are organized. And it is not due to things going on in the heads of the individuals but instead is due to the organizational context in which freedoms are threatened.

Moreover, even lesser degrees of organization can affect outcomes. An individual smoker may react one way, but a collection of offended smokers in contact and talking about the situation will stimulate each other, both to generate more reactance and to suggest different ways of reasserting lost freedoms. Further, in concert, people will influence each other to perceive opportunities for defiance that individuals alone would not have thought about, and they will help discount risk. Thus, during a conversation among the irate smokers somebody may suggest that they boycott the company cafeteria, refuse to bus their own trays, or slow work down on their jobs. They can realistically contemplate doing these things, because as a group they have less chance of being fired or disciplined (the more organized the group is, the less is the chance of such reactions), and their actions will have a greater impact. At the very least, these actions expand the range of things to be done to overcome reactance.

Unless reactance theory takes organization into account, its explanations are largely limited to individualized deviance or to the beginnings of deviance that might result in organization. For example, one could imagine that suicide and serial killing might be ways of claiming ultimate freedom. Society and physical circumstances may seem to control everything about a person's life, but that person can assert his or her autonomy by self-destruction or outrageous murder. Reactance theory might also explain why people initially become interested in deviance that eventually involves subcultural or full organization. Maybe people do take up drugs or gang fighting to reclaim a blocked freedom, but it is a stretch to imagine that they continue using drugs or gang fighting solely because of reactance. After all, once the freedom is reasserted, reactance should dissipate. More than likely the answer to continued deviance is at least partly organization itself. Once one is in a group with its own norms, social control, status system, shared culture, and the like, to some extent behavior then becomes a product of group processes. Therefore, in answering the question, "Why do people use heroin?" reactance probably does not provide a good answer. At best, the blocked freedom-reactance-behavior process provides the initial impetus, which for most drug users probably long ago lost its motive power. Continued drug use is more likely the result of physiological addiction and involvement in subcultural organizations that provide normative expectations, opportunity, justification, and protection from the police.

Psychodynamic

Psychodynamic theory attributes deviant behavior to the operation of internal psychic mechanisms, often beyond the consciousness of the person, that represent attempts to resolve conflicts between natural urges and social demands as well as between various components of the pysche. Psychic mechanisms such as identification, displacement, ego defense, and transformation can go in deviant directions to produce socially unacceptable behavior. These psychic mechanisms are developed in social contexts, and after being routinized as part of a person's personality are often set in motion by things in the social context. However, the theory is almost exclusively concerned with processes that go on in the mind and so ignores organizational variables that might have important effects on the outcomes.

Consider the ego defense mechanism of projection in which individuals attribute to others their own undesirable traits, such as aggressiveness or hatred. Projection is regarded in psychodynamic theory as a personal characteristic leading to prejudice, hostility, and possible aggression against certain people or groups of people. However, most bigoted people get that way by deliberate training within a subcultural context where the hated group is portrayed as having the undesirable traits. And some people within such cultural contexts do not have the psychic traits supposedly at the base of projection, though they behave as if they did. Often they exhibit bigotry and discrimination out of habit, to meet normative expectations, to attain status within the subcultural group, or because they fear the controlling reactions of other members of the subculture.

Moreover, even if people have prejudices stemming from projection, their actual behaviors most often reflect their current social contexts, which can be characterized by their degree of organization for or against discriminatory behavior. Prejudiced people in academia, for example, would probably never reveal it, and they would be scrupulous to avoid any form of discrimination. That is because they would lose the respect of their peers, and they would have difficulty keeping their jobs if they were thought of as bigoted. On the other hand, some prejudiced people are recruited into affiliation with subcultural groups such as the Ku Klux Klan, which are organized specifically to promote prejudice and practice discrimination. Such people get constant support for their views, which strengthens their prejudices and their tendencies to project their own bad traits onto minorities. And they are encouraged in their practice of discrimination. As a result of this, as well as of other group processes, such as social control, status seeking within the group, and reinforcement of self-images as bigots, members of the subcultural group are far more likely to behave deviantly (from the point of view of the outside society) than are people with equivalent tendencies toward projection who are not within such groups. In other words, psychodynamic theory, even if valid, does not go very far in explaining discriminatory behavior as a product of projection. And a similar scenario could be constructed concerning reaction formation or repression.

In fact, psychoanalytic theory appears particularly weak for explaining all forms of deviance that are even reasonably well organized. At best, the theory might provide an initial impetus for deviance, but once the practitioners become organized, other processes come to the fore. Chapter 4 described two examples of subcultural deviance—drug use and juvenile gang behavior. It is easy enough to imagine that drug users and gang members might suffer psychological problems. Perhaps these individuals are expressing a form of regression to an early stage of development, the drug users by withdrawing into the warmth of a carefree existence and the gang members by affiliating within a supportive environment where they do not have to make decisions on their own. Or maybe drug users and gang members are practicing displacement to cover up homosexual tendencies, in the first instance by chemically killing the sex drive altogether or in the second instance by aggressive super-masculine activities.

Yet, whether regressors and displacers use drugs at all or have any contact with gangs depends on opportunity, which is to a large extent the product of organization among drug users and dealers and among juveniles in particular neighborhoods. Most people with the psychological tendencies at issue never have a chance to use drugs or join gangs. Among those who have such opportunities, whether they eventually become addicted or become gang members depends on the strength of subcultural organization that would encourage and reward the person for behavior connected with such organizations. And if people are in such groups, the extent of their deviant behavior reflects the peculiar characteristics of the subcultures. Some drug-using subcultures concentrate on recreational drugs used only on sociable occasions; others promote constant usage of maintenance drugs. Some juvenile gangs emphasize relatively minor misbehavior, counterbalanced with community service; others are into constant hell-raising and drug dealing. And the same holds for sectarian cults and organized crime (examples of fully organized deviance). In view of this, psychodynamic explanations of drug use and gang behavior seem far-fetched.

Psychoanalytic theory appears far more useful for explaining individualized deviance. Since this kind of misbehavior, exemplified in our earlier discussion by suicide and serial killing, is very rarely manifested in a group context, explanations that look inside the person's head make a lot more sense. It is easy to imagine that people who kill themselves suffer overwhelming depression stemming from a conflict between natural urges (id) and the ability to carry out those urges in rational (ego) or moral (superego) ways. Or perhaps some suffer overwhelming guilt as a result of some earlier misconduct and feel that they must punish themselves. They are certainly not, at least in the United States, following normative mandates, seeking status, avoiding sanctions, or any of the other factors associated with organized behavior. Similarly, serial killers may well be motivated by unconscious hatred of fathers or mothers.

Psychodynamic theory, then, must be limited to individualized deviance; alternatively, it could be modified to take into account, perhaps as contingencies, organizational features among practitioners of deviance.

Practitioner Organization and Internal Constraint Theories

Chapter 13 was devoted to some theories that generally assume deviance to be inherently attractive to almost everybody, so that motivation does not need to be explained. The theories discussed in that chapter, therefore, attempt to identify things within individuals' psyches that constrain or prevent natural impulses toward deviance from being expressed in overt deviant behavior. Two classes of such theories were described. Self-control theories focus on people's abilities to inhibit natural motivations toward deviance, assuming that conduct will necessarily be constrained if the person can foresee the consequences and is capable of managing his or her own conduct. Morality theories, on the other hand, emphasize variations in individuals' desire to control conduct, assuming that all people are capable of doing so.

Self-Control

According to self-control theory, people are born undisciplined and so must learn to contain their own impulses. They obtain such ability when early childhood caregivers are concerned enough to monitor them, actually supervise them, recognize misbehavior, and punish the misconduct. Once the ability for self-control is instilled, it remains relatively constant over the life course. With strong self-control, individuals are hypothesized to have little likelihood of committing deviance, defined as force or fraud undertaken for self-gratification. That is because they will anticipate long-range costs and exercise restraint accordingly. Those who fail to develop sufficient self-control, however, are liable for deviance, provided they encounter opportunities for it. When situations arise in which the person can gratify himself or herself easily without obvious short-range costly consequences, the person with low self-control will presumably do so because she or he is incapable of thinking beyond the moment or of deferring gratification.

Because this theory sees self-control as primary, it takes little account of organization among practitioners. Instead, it regards affiliation with organized practitioners as itself a product of weak self-control, so organization presumably contributes little more to deviance than that which would have occurred from the individual condition of self-control itself. This, however, appears to be a mistake. There are at least two crucial ways that practitioner organization intervenes in the processes featured in the theory.

First, the conduct of caregivers to a large extent reflects their organizational contexts, and if such contexts are composed of practitioners of deviance, there should be consequences for both self-control and deviance. Compare child-rearing practices among traditional Gypsies (Clebert, 1963; Kephart and Zellner, 1994; Okely, 1982; Sutherland, 1975; Yoors, 1967) and among the Amish (Ammon, 1989; Hostetler, 1980, 1989; Kephart, 1976). Gypsy children were indulged. They were not closely supervised, nor were they punished much for misdeeds, certainly not for many of the misdeeds that non-Gypsies would find unacceptable. According to the theory, then, they should all have weak self-control and they should be likely to commit much deviance, the extent of which depends on the kinds of opportunities that come along. The Amish, on the other hand, monitored their children closely and punished them for even minor misdeeds (although the children were permitted far more leeway than were Amish adults). Hence the Amish should all have strong self-control and, as a result, do little deviance regardless of opportunity.

As it turns out, most Gypsies and Amish appear to end up with good self-control that is exercised according to the norms of the respective groups. Although Gypsies are noted for irregular work habits, for various forms of fraud, and for theft, they are also known for strong loyalty to their group, for strict adherence to standards of cleanliness (as it is defined in the group), for marital fidelity, and for harmony among themselves that results in little intragroup theft and almost no violence. When Gypsies do deviance, it is mainly deviance that violates the rules of non-Gypsies. And it is not done spontaneously, with no forethought. Gypsies plan to perpetrate fraud on non-Gypsies; they don't impulsively do it. They plan to work only as long as necessary to get enough cash to do the other things that are important to them; they don't skip from job to job on whims. Moreover, with respect to the internal norms of their cultural group, they appear to be exceptionally conformist—otherwise they would not have been able to survive for centuries as outcasts, living in close quarters.

The situation is similar for the Amish, although the content of their norms are quite different. They violate many of the social rules of the non-Amish, such as dressing in unconventional ways, obstructing traffic with slow-moving vehicles, and denying their children access to higher education (not all of which, interestingly, qualify as deviance according to Gottfredson and Hirschi, 1990). With respect to their own cultural norms, they are also conformists. Almost all adhere to the religious principles of self-denial; almost all work exceptionally hard; almost nobody steals; and violence is extremely rare. Could an analyst reasonably attribute unconventional dress and denying the value of higher education (deviance, according to the non-Amish) to weak self-control?

Clearly, what the theory advances as the causes of self-control do not hold among either the Gypsies or Amish, since most of each group seem to have it. Moreover, it does not explain deviance in either group, because both do a lot of it. Perhaps it does explain those few cases among the Gypsies who violate Gypsy rules—those who steal, disrupt, and do violence against other Gypsies—as well as the few Amish who fail to follow religious rules by dressing in bright colors, buying modern appliances, or those who steal and misrepresent. But the theory does not state that normative definitions are a contingency for its applicability. Indeed, the theorists reject the idea of culturally relative norms.

Second, even if self-control determines the likelihood of affiliation in practitioner groups, which in the case of groups like the Amish and Gypsies is absurd (because people are born into those groups), the frequency and type of deviance is to a large extent a product of group processes once a person is in such groups. As noted many times before, people participating in group activities with other deviants are likely to perceive more opportunities for such deviance, to feel compelled to do it in response to group expectations (independently of motivation stemming from weak self-control), and to find justification for continuing to do it. And, of course, affiliation is itself usually a matter of opportunity, which stems from practitioners having already been organized to provide that option. It makes little sense to think that organizing among deviants can be done if they all suffer weak self-control.

Organization among practitioners may also help individuals with weak self-control exercise more control in the interest of the group. Weakly controlled people are often constrained by the presence of others who collectively stand to suffer long-range consequences. For example, even if all crooked business executives have weak self-control (which again is doubtful), collectively and in interaction with each other they may uphold and enforce the idea that impulsivity is bad for the potential success of whatever fraud they may be perpetrating. There is good reason, then, to bring organizational considerations into applications of self-control theory.

Without accommodating practitioner organization, the theory would appear limited to some forms of individualized deviance and perhaps to the act of becoming involved with practitioner groups. It could not explain deviance that results from group processes themselves, such as routine organized criminal activity, gang activities, or the practices of the Perfectionists. The theory is, of course, already hard pressed to explain many forms of unacceptable social conduct that do not involve force or fraud.

Deviance in Everyday Life

Generally, the Amish are conformists by their own standards but deviant by the standards of "normal" everyday society. However, sometimes the deviance of the Amish spreads into more general forms. In June of 1998, Pennsylvania State Police were conducting an investigation into drug selling within the Amish community. It seems that members of the Pagan motorcycle gang were selling cocaine to two young Amish men, Abner Stoltzfus and Abner King Stoltzfus (who are unrelated), who then sold the cocaine to other Amish youths. (Worden, 1998)

Morality

A second kind of internal constraint theory explains variations in deviance as reflections of differences in morality. Moral commitments by some people block their natural urges toward deviant behavior. When individuals incorporate values about right and wrong into their psyches (internalize them), they are theoretically prevented from doing deviance because anticipations of their own emotional reactions, especially guilt, serve as self-imposed sanctions. Some theorists contend that morality is a natural condition of mankind, which inevitably occurs if people are encouraged and permitted to face social challenges. Because of the absence of such challenges, some fail to fully develop higher levels of morality, so they make moral judgments in conformity with guiding principles characteristic of lower steps in an intellectual hierarchy.

A more compelling account of morality, however, is provided by social learning theory, which posits that self-standards are initially instilled by external or vicarious reinforcement (rewards and punishment). Once in place, values about right and wrong remain relatively stable because of self-reinforcement, which consists of feeling good when one acts in accord with the values and feeling bad when they are violated. The most extreme form of bad feeling is guilt, which reinforces internal moral standards and, by anticipation, prevents violation. But people may also learn ways to escape guilt, the methods for which are called "techniques of neutralization." Thus, given opportunity, variations in deviance are due mainly to differences in strength and direction of internalized moral standards, and to differences in learned methods for escaping guilt feelings.

Because social learning theory accommodates a wide span of reinforcements, considerations of organization among deviance practitioners fits nicely in the scheme (see Akers, 1985). However, the full potential effect of such organization on social learning has not been well articulated, and organization is altogether foreign to theories of moral development. The organizational context obviously affects social learning. Children growing up in satanic religious groups that sacrifice animals or perpetrate "evil" will be reinforced for different moral standards than those growing up in humanistic groups whose members believe in helping the downtrodden and oppose the killing of living creatures. And the more fully organized the practitioners, the more likely they are to be effective in presenting consistent messages embodying their values. Moreover, people may be differentially exposed to subcultural, or even fully organized, groups that teach neutralization techniques to free people from their moral constraints.

But, as we have learned already, even if morality constrains deviant impulses for many people, it does not provide the whole account for deviant conduct. For one thing, provocation and opportunity are not equal for everybody, so morality is differentially tested depending partly on whether people are involved with groups that challenge their morals or that provide opportunities for deviance that pose tests of moral commitments. In addition, practitioner organizations may be more or less strong in their internal communication and control procedures, in the effectiveness with which they perpetuate their own philosophies, and in the extent to which they satisfactorily meet the needs of individuals, including needs for self-enhancement.

Those engulfed in strongly organized groups promoting deviance may end up with moral standards consistent with the group's deviance, as did the

Perfectionists, and certainly some organizations of practitioners may facilitate deviance that is contrary to the internalized moral standards of some individuals—by helping provide justifying rationales, by rewarding behavior contrary to the individual's personal moral standards, or by punishing behavior consistent with the individual's internalized standards. Furthermore, exposure to new reinforcing contexts can lead to changes in moral standards, as so often happens to college entrants, who seem to abandon much of the morality they brought with them.

By contrast, however, new challenges posed by exposure to organized deviant groups, whether subculturally or fully organized, may lead to higher levels of moral reasoning. If morality is inherent in humans, waiting only to be brought forth through confrontation and testing, then one might expect those who navigate through heterogeneous environments, with many organized deviant groups, to move to more sophisticated levels of moral reasoning. Similarly, those with limited experience outside the deviant groups of which they are a part might be expected to remain at fairly low levels of moral sophistication. Remember, though, that higher levels of moral reasoning do not necessarily imply less deviance, so the potential connections among deviant groups, moral reasoning, and deviant behavior are complicated.

In straightforward application, theories of morality, like self-control theories, appear to be most relevant for individualized deviance or for explaining the probability of affiliation with organized deviant groups, given the opportunity for such affiliation. Since subcultural and fully organized forms of deviance involve group processes that more than likely modify and shape the moralities of their participants, moral constraint would appear less of a causal factor and more a product of group functioning. It may be reasonable to attribute interpersonal rudeness or serial killing—and perhaps first use of recreational drugs or first instance of price-fixing by business executives—to the absence or weakness of moral restraints. But it seems less reasonable to interpret patterns of recreational drug usage, delinquent gang activity, sectarian religious deviance, or terrorist activity to weak constraint. In these cases weak constraint appears to be a product of the same forces that produce deviance. Therefore, efficient explanation would seem to require that the scope of morality theories be limited, or that practitioner deviance be explicitly worked into the explanatory schemes.

Practitioner Organization and External Constraint Theories

External constraint theories focus on things in the environment that supposedly restrain the deviant impulses that everybody is assumed to have, at least sometimes. When restraining forces are weak, the individual is set free to deviate, and given that deviance is assumed to be gratifying to almost everybody, freedom produces deviance. Two versions of such theories were discussed—deterrence theory and social control theories. In general, external constraint theories pay quite a bit of attention to organization among potential deviants. At least that is true in the sense that modern versions of deterrence and social control theories recognize that fear of bad consequences is highly variable and that it is heavily influenced by the characteristics of groups with which a person is affiliated and by the degree to which an individual is bonded with such groups. These theories, however, are somewhat inconsistent in accommodating to practitioner organization, and they do not systematically and explicitly deal with it.

Deterrence

Recall that the deterrence argument is a specific application of one element of rational choice theory. Unlike its parent theory, which sees both cost and reward as variable, deterrence theory assumes that crime and deviance are rewarding for most or all people and that the extent to which they are rewarding varies little from one individual to the next. Since people are presumably motivated to maximize their rewards, the main thing determining whether people do or do not resort to deviance is the cost associated with the particular deviance in a situation where the individual happens to be. Modern formulations, though not coherently integrated, focus mainly on variations in cost as they are influenced by characteristics of the consequences (such as certainty or severity), psychic organization of the person (such as differences in what people fear), individual attributes (such as personality and demographic traits, like gender or age), and situational variations (such as the behavior of role models and the degree to which individuals are bonded to those with the power to impose sanctions).

Explicit recognition of the influence of practitioner organization on situational variables that, in turn, impinge on the deterrence process, is a prime example of how external constraint theories go further than most in accommodating practitioner organization. Contemporary formulations note that what role models do, especially proximate ones like peers in deviant groups, often influences what observers do, and it may influence what observers perceive about possible sanctions. They also recognize that strong social bonds among practitioners who defy conventional standards may make sanction considerations moot. Despite these formulations, deterrence theory has not fully incorporated the possibilities implied by practitioner organization. It does not specifically recognize that all the contingent variables, not just some of them, can be affected by the extent to which individuals are affiliated in social networks with greater or lesser organization.

Consider the potential cost of going to jail. The law assumes that all people fear incarceration, perhaps more than anything besides death. Yet among young males in delinquent gangs, incarceration is not highly feared. In fact, it often pays off in enhanced prestige among peers. Being part of an organized deviant group can also affect whether an individual thinks there is much chance of being apprehended for misbehavior. Business executives who fix prices influence each other to discount risk. Whereas one executive alone might well exaggerate in his or her mind the chances of getting caught, several executives in collusion might share experiences through which they have learned that the probabilities of bad consequences are low. Finally, through affiliation among deviant practitioners, people come to fear informal sanctions from peers more than sanctions from outsiders who disapprove of the behavior of the group's members.

While psychic organization is an individual trait, it is subject to external influence. Some potential deviants initially fear public embarrassment, but once they become embedded in deviant groups, they may change their standards of embarrassment. Public exposure is uncomfortable when behavior is contrary to one's claims about self. But if one affiliates with a group like the

Perfectionists, for example, self-images begin to undergo transformation. External claims may then be different than they would have been, for example, for individuals pursuing extramarital relationships in the outside world. In addition, perceptual ability may be more or less stable, but its effects can be altered when several people share perceptions. Although an individual may perceive large chances of costly consequences for a misdeed, others may influence his or her thinking by emphasizing the low chance of getting caught. And while specific individuals often process information inefficiently or incorrectly, groups can intensify or help correct such inefficiencies. Finally, group-reinforced commitment to certain goals, such as among revolutionaries or terrorists, may make deterrent possibilities irrelevant, except as practical considerations in strategic planning about time and place of deviant action.

Deviance in Everyday Life

The degree to which a deviant group is organized can affect the certainty with which members will be caught by authorities. For example, the U.S. State Department, the CIA, and the FBI have for years hunted members of fundamentalist Islamic groups such as the Hizballah and Islamic Jihad. These groups have been suspected of the truck-bombing of the U.S. Marine barracks in 1983 that killed several hundred soldiers, and the hijacking of a TWA plane in 1985. Despite the law enforcement resources in the hands of the United States government (not only are there numerous agents on the case, but the severity of punishment is also substantial for any terrorists who are brought to justice), it has generally been unsuccessful in apprehending many of the suspected terrorists. No small part of this is due to the substantial level of organization within these religious groups. Their organization has thwarted the effect that certainty and severity of punishment usually has.

It is very clear, then, that deterrence theory must take practitioner organization into account if its explanations and predictions are to be at all accurate. Although it requires a lot of accouterments in addition to considerations of deviant organization, it cannot hope to explain most forms of deviance without at least that consideration. Individualized, subcultural, and fully organized deviance are simply too different in crucial ways relevant to the deterrent process to permit unmitigated application of ideas about constraint based on fear of costly consequences.

Social Control

Social control theory also postulates that deviance is the result of failure of potential costs to restrain it. Here, however, the costs are not specifically intended or formally administered. Rather, they are informal ones, stemming from the person's connection with others, particularly organized groups. These informal costs can operate indirectly or directly. Indirect costs control a person's behavior because the individual anticipates consequences, particularly how others will react, without being specifically threatened or prodded. Direct control, on the other hand, stems from others' manipulations. Specific mechanisms of control involve concerns about self-image or self-esteem, social approval, investments, caring about others and what might happen to them, and beliefs.

Probably to a greater extent than any of the other theories considered, social control theories set forth explanatory processes that depend on social organization. All their theoretical mechanisms—concern for self-image and self-esteem, seeking social approval, investing in things that others regard as useful, caring about the consequences for others of one's behavior, and sharing beliefs—vary directly with the degree of organization among a person's associates. When associates are organized for conformity, those mechanisms lead toward conformity, and when associates are organized for deviance, the explanatory mechanisms lead toward deviance. In either case, the stronger the organization, the greater the chances of conformity or deviance, respectively.

The theories, however, have left the connection with organization largely implicit rather than explicit, and they have concerned themselves mainly with explaining conformity to broad-based conventional norms, not with explaining deviance generated by social control within deviant groups. This lack of explanation is partly because the theorists began with the question, "Why don't we all do deviance?" rather than the question raised by most students of deviant behavior, "Why do some people do deviance?" It is clear enough by now, however, that social control can operate to produce conformity to conventional norms as well as conformity to norms of divergent groups, which represents a form of deviance. Therefore, to use social control as an explanation, one must specify the group context and the normative content as contingencies.

The Perfectionists practiced social control, and individuals within the group were influenced toward conformity by all of the mechanisms specified by the theories—but the result was deviance from the norms of conventional society. By contrast, religious people outside the Perfectionist group, who were affiliated with more traditional religious organizations in conventional society, were influenced toward conventionality by the social control of conventional communities. Similarly, social control from their peers lead those involved in a subculture of drug use to conform—but such conformity is actually nonconformity to the normative expectations of conventional society. On the other hand, most individualized deviance, which is violation of standards of conventional society, does not seem to be linked at all with practitioner organization. Yet the absence of social control alone does not appear adequate as an explanation, because many forms of individualized deviance do not appear inherently gratifying enough to motivate violation, even without social control. Serial killing, mentally ill behavior, and suicide hardly seem things that all people would want to do. Simply positing absence of social control as the explanation for deviance will not work; to be effective the theories must use organization, particularly organization among deviance practitioners, as a contingency for some forms of deviance, and they must account for differential motivation.

Practitioner Organization and Integrated Theory

Chapter 15 described synthetic theories that pull together parts of existing theories into coherent new accounts. The purpose of integration is to overcome the limitations of extant specific theories that tend to be narrowly focused. Most specific theories of deviance dwell on either an internal or an external causal agent, and they emphasize either motivating forces or constraining factors. Some theories accommodate opportunity, ability, and alternative motivation, but many do not. Furthermore, theories differ in the extent to which they spell out the contingencies under which their causal processes operate with greater or less force. As a result, no one specific theory is adequate to explain deviance. Integrated theories are designed to incorporate more of these important elements so that they can more adequately account for deviance.

We described one of the many attempts at integration—a formulation called control balance. That theory portrays deviance as the end product of a chain of causes. Beginning with a predisposition to extend one's autonomy, the theory proposes that deviance occurs when people with a control imbalance (the amount of control they experience is not equal to the control they can exercise) are reminded of it by some provoking circumstances. When people become acutely aware that deviance can help alter a control imbalance, they are said to be motivated toward deviance. However, the kind of deviance they are likely to commit depends on opportunity and constraint. When the potential countercontrol for a particular form of deviance for a specific person is too great for that individual to realistically contemplate the action, she or he is likely to choose a less serious act. Thus, once motivated, deviance is a functional act, the expression of which represents a balancing of potential gain in control against potential countercontrol. This process unfolds with greater or less force, depending on a number of contingencies, such as moral commitments of the individual, self-control, personal psychic characteristics, and learned skills.

Since control balance theory potentially incorporates all the causal processes contained within the various theories reviewed in the preceding four chapters, practitioner organization potentially impinges on its causal processes in all the multiple ways spelled out previously in this chapter. And this integrated theory appears specifically sensitive to the import of practitioner organization, which impinges on its central variables in several ways. First, practitioner organization is a key factor affecting the individual's control ratio, which influences all the variables in the causal chain. Being part of a subculture or fully organized deviant group can sometimes raise a person's control ratio and sometimes lower it. Second, whether a person is embedded in a network of organized practitioners can affect whether, and the extent to which, various things are provoking as well as whether various kinds of deviant acts might be contemplated as ways of altering a control imbalance. An offhand remark about gang delinquents may have little impact on an individual youthful deviant, but it may be regarded as a dire insult to a member of a gang. Third, practitioner organization affects the opportunity for various kinds of deviance. When provoked, many people may contemplate homicide but end up doing nothing about it. Members of organized crime families, however, have a procedure for getting somebody efficiently eliminated. Fourth, the extent to which countercontrol is likely to be initiated and unfold with full force depends partly on a person's organizational support. In alliance with one another, Perfectionists were able to practice many forms of deviance that, as individuals, they could not have realistically contemplated for fear of the forces of informal and formal control.

Clearly, control balance would be much less compelling if it ignored the effects of practitioner organization. And this is true of other integrated theories as well. Though integration presumably makes effective explanation more likely, unless such theories explicitly make room for variations in organization among practitioners of the deviance to be explained, they will still fall short.

Practitioner Organization and Theories of Rate Variation

❖ ❖ ❖ ❖

Chapter 16 discussed theories that aim to account for differences in rates of deviance among categories of people, societies, and other social collectivities (ecological level). Some, such as utilitarian/deterrence, population composition, and psychodynamic theories simply elevate micro-level processes to the ecological level. Others, such as social integration/disorganization, Marxian conflict, deprivation of law, and historical/cultural arguments propose theoretical processes applying strictly to macro-level phenomena (although we were able to derive individual analogs for some of them). And some theories, including anomie, defiance, shaming, and routine activities, spell out distinct explanatory processes that apply in one way to the micro level and in other ways to the macro level.

Aggregated Micro-Level Theories

Without taking practitioner organization into account, one is liable to make serious errors trying to use individual theories to account for ecological phenomena. Earlier in this chapter we showed how the processes set forth by various theories to explain why individuals do deviance required accommodation to practitioner organization. It is even more important that organization among deviants be regarded as a contingency for applying those individual-level theories to explain rates of deviance among collectivities. Arguments about population composition illustrate this point.

Population Composition

As noted in Chapter 9, deviance is often, though not always, more likely in large settlements, among males, among those in the pre-adult years, among minorities, and among those socially unattached—probably because these categories of individuals are least likely to be restrained by social control. Therefore, it would appear logical to explain rates of deviance from one society or social group to another by the extent to which their populations are large, young, male, minority, and unattached. The greater the proportion of a population with those characteristics, presumably the higher the rates of deviance will be. This conclusion, however, assumes that deviance is a simple reflection of those demographic traits, and it overlooks many other considerations—including the possibility of practitioner organization.

Imagine two societies of equal size with equal proportions of their populations being male, young, minority, and socially unattached. Suppose that in one of those societies no deviants are organized into subcultural or fully organized groups so that there is no such thing as sectarian religious groups that practice deviance, no delinquent gangs, no drug subcultures, no businesses in collusion to fix prices, no system for sexual deviance by prostitutes and customers or swingers, no organized police corruption (see Newsweek, 1994b), and no organized crime. In other words, all deviance would be individualized. In the other society, however, imagine that practically every form of deviance is at least somewhat organized and that almost all of those organizations include females, people of all ages, majorities as well as minorities, and those socially attached as well as those unattached. This would mean that serial killers were organized and that they included people in all of the demographic categories. Similarly, those interested in suicide, those who wanted to use nonsense language, and those who liked to practice private behavior in public places were organized and included among themselves representatives from the various demographic categories.

It is a good bet that the second society would have much higher rates of deviance than the first one, even though the "theory" would imply no differences. The reason is clear, as we have indicated many times before. Organization around some deviant activity (1) helps intensify motivation for that behavior among the practitioners, (2) helps provide justifying rationales to overcome any moral inhibitions, (3) neutralizes conventional social control and turns the group's own social control toward generating deviance, (4) helps to create opportunities or to enhance perceptions of opportunities for deviance, (5) helps deflect alternative motivations for deviance, and (6) helps teach the abilities needed to commit deviance. Hence, in societies with many deviant organizations, the rates of deviance will go up—independent of other considerations.

Other Aggregated Micro-Level Theories

Given that practitioner organization increases the probability and frequency of deviance among a group's members, none of the individual-level theories, aggregated to the ecological level, can be very accurate without taking account of the extent to which deviants in various societies are organized. Yet few scholars who attempt to use micro theories to explain ecological phenomena appreciate practitioner organization. Even learning theories, which would seem to have the most natural connection with practitioner organization, usually neglect it. This can be illustrated by Sutherland's original statement of differential association, the root of modern learning theories of deviance. Although he tried to account for differences in crime rates from place to place and from group to group by "differential social organization," he equated that concept with "cultural or normative conflict" without recognizing the import of organization among potential deviants themselves.

Sutherland thought that normative conflict—a situation with a number of inconsistent normative messages—implied that a large proportion of people would receive an excess of crime-favorable messages and therefore learn things that enhance the probabilities of criminal behavior. Presumably, he believed that in social systems with normative conflict there are more crime-favorable messages floating around than in a social system where there is normative consistency. Hence any given individual in the system having normative conflict has a greater chance of receiving those crime-favorable messages. But does this necessarily follow? It would appear to follow only if normative conflict were also accompanied by social segregation and isolation around distinct sets of norms—that is, if there were large numbers of exclusive subcultures presenting predominantly crime-favorable messages to their participants. Sutherland never made that clear, and his later followers are similarly silent on this issue.

Ecological-Level Theories

Chapter 16 also described several theories that specifically try to account for variations in rates of deviance.

Social Integration/Disorganization

At least one theory, social integration/disorganization, has the virtue of explicitly accommodating practitioner organization. Integrated societies share common values and norms, have consistent systems of socialization of the young, feature formal and informal systems of control that reinforce each other, thrive on primary relationships of personal intimacy, and find a way for most members of the society to feel a part of the whole and to draw their identities from societal affiliation. These characteristics theoretically generate high rates of conformity, so differences in rates of deviance from society to society or social group to social group can be explained by differences in degree of social integration.

Several of the characteristics making social integration possible are undermined when a large number of deviant practitioners are allied into subcultures and fully organized groups. That is part of what the integration theorists mean by noting that heterogeneity is one of the key predisposing factors that make social disorganization likely. Societies containing many deviant practitioner groups will have diverse values and norms, inconsistent socialization of the young, contradictions between formal and informal systems of social control, and few primary relationships among large numbers of societal members, and not many individuals will have a sense of personal belonging or self-identity with the larger society. Therefore, societies with many deviant groups should have exceptionally high rates of deviance for two major reasons. First, societal integration cannot exercise its inhibiting effects on deviance, and second, each of the separate deviant groups will generate more deviance among its individual members than would have occurred if those individuals were operating outside a practitioner organization. However, to the extent that deviance is, in fact, caused by individual-level processes such as psychodynamic conflicts, psychological reactance, personal attitudes and skills, strain, or self-control, the theory of social integration will not be very effective.

Marxian Conflict

Marxian conflict theory follows most of the aggregated individual-level theories in neglecting practitioner organization in its attempts to explain rates of deviance among different societies or social groups. It is clear, however, that "de-moralizing" competition, usually associated with capitalism, does not operate in a vacuum simply to produce individualized forms of deviance. Not only do capitalists and workers organize themselves, but deviants do as well. Some affiliate to subvert the effects of competition, as illustrated by corporate price-fixing and organized criminal activities. Others organize themselves for the practice of activities that have little to do with economics, such as to promote unconventional forms of religion or to practice deviant recreation. Neither capitalism nor competitive cultural modes will provide really good explanations of variations in rates of deviance without bringing in other things, including the extent to which practitioners of deviance are organized.

Routine Activities

Rates of deviance, particularly predatory crime, are theorized to reflect the extent to which three conditions converge. Those conditions are motivated offenders, suitable targets, and lack of guardianship, and their coming together is thought to reflect the conditions of everyday life. When employment patterns, housing arrangements, and value of goods favor convergence, rates of crime will presumably be greater than when they do not. And when distributions of population, population size, and community structures permit or encourage convergence of people who want to do various kinds of deviance with the opportunity to do so without much chance of sanction, rates of other kinds of deviance will be higher than in societies in which these conditions are different. For example, one would expect greater rates of suicide when there are a large number of people who might be motivated to do it (such as larger numbers of males, older people, and social failures), where the means of doing it are easy to obtain (guns widely available, for instance), and where there are few people to prevent it (perhaps when large numbers of people are not part of integrated social networks).

Since this theory does little more than identify crucial categories of variables, it could conceivably accommodate things like practitioner organization. When potential offenders are affiliated in a subculture or a fully organized group, they are more likely to search out suitable targets that are unguarded, so organization among potential deviants could be one of the "routine activities" that affect convergence of the key variables increasing the rate of various kinds of deviance. In addition, organization of potential deviants can lead to an increase in motivation for deviance, it can help redefine for its members when targets are suitable, and it can help overcome guardianship. Indeed, many of the examples of modern routine activities that the theorists identify as affecting convergence of key causal variables may be linked to practitioner organization. For example, employment outside the household may leave houses unprotected from burglary, and organized burglars are more likely to identify such homes and be able to take advantage of that circumstance (Shover, 1996).

Although the theory could potentially take practitioner organization into account, it does not explicitly do so. In fact, theorists have not even clearly articulated the actual causal conditions they call "routine activities." Instead, they have more or less left the specification of the conditions that lead to convergence of key variables to research. Without such research, one cannot know which aspects of everyday life presumably affect deviance. For example, brushing teeth is a routine activity of people in modern societies, as is employment outside the home. However, there is nothing in the theory itself to indicate that brushing teeth is irrelevant to convergence of key causal variables while outside-the-home employment is crucial. And there is nothing in the theory to direct a researcher to those routine activities that might be connected to convergence. Since research concerning routine activities is a more-or-less random search for such conditions, scholars might well look at practitioner organization as a key condition. Better yet, the theory could be reformulated specifically to explain why some kinds of routine activities should matter, and it could thereby provide guidelines for research. When that is done, the degree of organization among various kinds of deviant practitioners might well become a key part of the theory.

Deprivation of Law

The deprivation of law argument contends that legal organization reduces deviance by providing a mode of dispute resolution that is enforced by coercive authority. Therefore, rates of deviance should vary inversely with the extent of the development of societies' systems of law. We observed in Chapter 16 that this account of intersocietal rates of deviance cannot be completely accurate because not all deviance is linked to disputes, not all people have access to law, and some things involve so much emotion that law is by-passed. Here, we add an additional reason for inaccuracy: potential practi-tioners of much deviance are organized. Because they are, legal consider-ations sometimes become less relevant. For example, the Perfectionists, syn-dicated criminals, juvenile gangs, and drug users, as well as many other devi-ants, have managed to build worlds for themselves that do not include the possibility of legal manipulations. At best, for them the law is a nuisance, of concern because it poses some degree of threat, but of little import for ongo-ing activities. For that reason, the deprivation of law theory would provide a better account of variations in rates of deviance if it specifically brought prac-titioner organization into its scheme. At present, it more or less assumes that all, or at least most, deviance is individualized, an assumption that we hope to have dispelled in this book.

Theories That Apply to Ecological Units and to Individuals

Anomie

Anomie theory explains variations in rates of deviance by the extent to which culturally defined goals match the available means for their achieve-ment. Presumably, inconsistencies in means and goals produce strong moti-vation to bring the two into alignment. This need for alignment implies that individuals will seek some form of adaptation, often deviant, when they are personally subject to a disjuncture between the goals they have adopted and the means available to achieve them. And it implies that in societies where the culturally defined goals and the means available are out of sync there will be high rates of deviant behavior. Despite the theory's reliance on social struc-ture in large-scale organizations as an explanatory tool, it ends up narrowly focused on motivations for deviance, neglecting other considerations. More-over, it ultimately emphasizes individual decision making, almost completely ignoring subcultural or deviant group organization among individuals likely to adapt in the various ways that the theory identifies. (Later, Merton did ac-knowledge that subcultures are sometimes important, though the theory it-self was not modified to incorporate this insight—see Merton, 1956, 1957.)

It is easy enough, however, to illustrate why deviant group organization is crucial. No doubt some individuals, under strain from a contradiction be-tween their own available means and culturally approved means for achiev-ing their goals, actively seek and fashion an accommodation for themselves. John Humphrey Noyes, the Perfectionist leader, was one of them. His goals, to achieve sexual freedom and religious fulfillment through communal liv-ing, flew in the face of socially approved means for sexual and religious grati-fication. He set out to do something about it by "innovating." However, most of the rest of the Perfectionists became deviants because of their exposure to Noyes or the Perfectionist community after it had been established. Perhaps they were predisposed to such influences by their own experience of strain, but it is unlikely they would have resorted to deviance, and certainly not to the extent and in the form it was practiced at Oneida, had they simply been moving around as social atoms trying to manage strain.

Once affiliated with other practitioners, of course, the group processes that we have described so often before take over, producing most of the devi-ance we associate with the Perfectionists. At that point, anomie would appear to have little influence on it. Similar arguments can be made concerning deviant drug use, delinquent gangs, organized crime, other forms of cult behavior, much homosexual conduct, bigoted antihomosexual behavior, and numerous other types of deviance. At best, anomie may predispose people to deviance, or even to affiliation with deviant practitioners, but beyond that, other forces take over. Therefore, without explicit consideration of such influences, societal anomie, even if it could be measured, is not likely to provide a very effective explanation of variations in rates of deviance. And we have already seen that strain alone does not adequately account for individuals' deviance.

Defiance

Recall that defiance theory suggests that rates of deviance in a social group depend on how sanctions are applied and received. When they are imposed by authorities whose legitimacy is recognized, when they are imposed with due regard for the dignity of the recipient, when the recipients are bonded to, and care about, the community whose agents are imposing the sanctions, and when recipients of sanctions can accept the shame implied by them, then rates of deviance are likely to be low. Rates of deviance among social groups, then, should vary inversely with the extent to which those conditions prevail.

Defiance theory to some extent recognizes the importance of organization among deviants. In its statements of conditions under which shame is acknowledged with remorse instead of being denied by rage, the theory notes that one such contingency is the group context of the sanctioned person. Clearly, if a sanctioned person is organizationally linked with others who practice the deviance for which the sanction is imposed, there is likely to be group support and denial that the behavior is shameful. In fact, the philosophy of deviant groups or subcultures usually provides rationales for why the behavior is good and why it is not wrong, along with an ingroup-outgroup orientation indicating that outsiders are out to get them. One illustration is prostitution, which is usually a subcultural phenomenon. Arresting those who offer sex for money rarely generates shame; instead, it provokes anger. Prostitutes are usually surrounded by others who long since defined the activity as nonshameful and found rationales to characterize it as an everyday, acceptable activity.

Although defiance theory is friendly to the notion, it fails to see the full import of practitioner organization. Whether agents of social control impose sanctions with dignity depends to some extent on whether those agents are themselves organized as practitioners of professional misconduct, as many

---

Deviance in Everyday Life

An organized moral entrepreneur by the name of Anita Bryant met organized deviance in 1977 when the former beauty queen led a crusade in Dade County (Miami) Florida to overturn a county ordinance that forbade discrimination on the basis of sexual preference. In 1977 Bryant, who was the official spokeswoman of the Florida orange juice industry, formed a group called "Save Our Children" that had a religiously conservative and anti-gay agenda. When Ms. Bryant tried to have the sexual equality ordinance repealed, she was met with stiff opposition from an organized gay and lesbian community in Dade County. Dade County served as a battleground over employment and housing discrimination between gay and religiously conservative groups.

police are (Newsweek, 1994b). It also depends to some extent on whether the recipients of sanctions are organized to promote perceptions of inappropriate application, to encourage behavior that invites undignified application, or to marshall political forces to make life difficult for agents of conventional society. Deviant groups and subcultures often share ideas about persecution so that almost any form of external reaction will be interpreted as a slight. Furthermore, they often promote forms of behavior that agents of conventional society will regard as rendering their members unworthy of dignified treatment. For example, defiance of the police is sometimes a route to status within delinquent gangs, among revolutionaries, and in syndicated crime groups. Finally, some deviant groups, such as corporate violators, can marshall enormous political resources against agents of conventional society so that they are handled with kid gloves.

In addition, while defiance theory notes that sanctions will have different effects on those integrated into larger communities whose agents are doing the sanctioning than on those not so integrated, it does not explicitly recognize that the degree of integration depends to some extent on the degree to which there are deviant groups and on whether the person being sanctioned is affiliated with one or more such groups. As previously indicated in this chapter, a plethora of competing groups detracts from general cohesion, and an individual's connection with a contrary subcultural group makes cohesion with the larger community less likely.

Clearly, then, defiance theory should be paired with considerations of the extent to which practitioners of deviance are organized. It may prove true that societies which generally invoke sanctions in a respectful manner and that deal with people strongly bonded to conventional societies and able to acknowledge shame have lower rates of deviance. However, a scholar can understand why that might be the case and also be able to predict rates of deviance more accurately by asking a further question about why those conditions exist in the first place. At that point, practitioner organization will loom large as a prior condition. Indeed, it might well turn out that the prevalence and strength of deviant groups will provide better prediction of rate variations than the defiance conditions themselves.

Shaming

The one theory of rate variations that most explicitly theorizes about the effects of practitioner organization is Braithwaite's shaming theory, and it is that feature that makes the theory such a powerful statement. Recall that his theory attempts to explain individuals' initial participation in deviance as a function of their integration into tight-knit groups, which makes them vulnerable to being deterred by the anticipation of shaming. The theory also tries to explain recidivism as a consequence of social reaction to their deviance, with reintegrative shaming being most effective in reducing repeat violations, and disintegrative shaming being highly productive of further violation. The reason disintegrative shaming most likely produces long-term deviance is because it leads offenders into subcultural deviant groups, if such groups are available. Group processes in such groups, as we have indicated and as Braithwaite recognizes, enhance motivation for deviance and undermine conventional constraint.

Shaming theory also explains variations in rates of deviance from society to society by use of two main conditions. One is, of course, the degree of social integration, which makes it more likely that people will be deterred by fear of shame and also more possible for reintegration to occur after shaming. Second is the prevalence of deviant subcultural groups in a society; the more such groups there are, the higher the rates of deviance. That is because such groups provide a supportive environment for those who are disintegratively shamed, as well as those who are simply punished. Affiliation with deviant subcultural groups leads to increased rates of deviance through the group processes of the deviant subcultures themselves. According to shaming theory, deviant subcultures are most likely to arise in societies that block success goals for large segments of the population, providing motivation for initial deviance, and which then stigmatize, through disintegrative shaming or punishment, those who end up breaking the rules.

It is possible that practitioner organizations are even more important than that, however. It is not clear whether social integration discourages deviant practitioner organization or whether the growth of deviant organization undermines integration. Nevertheless, the presence of deviant subcultures and fully organized deviant groups may also help generate motivation for initial deviance. Even without blocked goals, people who are exposed to practitioner groups from an early age may take on their behavioral characteristics, and, of course, they become less sensitive to shaming by conventional groups and more subject to shaming by their own deviant group. More than likely, heterogeneity itself undermines social cohesion and generates deviant groups; those deviant groups, in turn, generate motivation for deviance and undermine the potential shaming force of conventional society. Therefore, without contradicting the importance of reintegrative shaming and the social cohesion underlying it, deviant subcultures and organizations may represent key intervening variables between population composition and rates of deviant behavior that are not simply the consequence of disintegrative shaming.

Summary

It is clear that most theories of deviance are less efficient than they might otherwise be because they do not take into account the extent of organization among those who commit various deviant acts potentially explicable by these theories. Practitioner organization can enhance motivation for deviance, increase opportunities, suppress alternative motivations, provide abilities for deviance, and help discount cost. In addition, practitioner organization helps ensure continuity in deviance once it has begun (1) by reinforcing deviant behavior with peer-granted prestige and by threatening loss of membership or status for not performing the misbehaviors around which the organization has crystallized; (2) by affecting perception of opportunity; (3) by helping to overcome moral objections; and (4) by playing on self-concepts and self-esteem. Theories of deviance, therefore, probably should be applied only to the forms of misbehavior for which they are best suited, or they should be modified to treat organizational aspects as contingencies under which the theories operate with greater or less force. ✦

References

Abadinsky, Howard. 1985. Organized Crime, 2nd Ed. Chicago: Nelson Hall.

Achte, Kalle. 1988. "Suicidal tendencies in the elderly." Suicide and Life Threatening Behavior 18:55–65.

Adler, Freda. 1975. Sisters in Crime: The Rise of the New Female Criminal. New York: McGraw-Hill.

Adler, Patricia A. 1993. Wheeling and Dealing: An Ethnography of an Upper-Level Drug Dealing and Smuggling Community. New York: Columbia University Press.

Agar, Michael. 1973. Ripping and Running: A Formal Ethnography of Urban Heroin Addicts. New York: Academic Press.

Agnew, Robert. 1992. "Foundation for a general strain theory of crime and delinquency." Criminology 30:47–87.

———. 1999. "A general strain theory of community differences in crime rates." Journal of Research in Crime and Delinquency 36:123–155.

Akers, Ronald L. 1968. "Problems in the sociology of deviance: Social definitions and behavior." Social Forces 46:455–465.

———. 1985. Deviant Behavior: A Social Learning Approach, 3rd Ed. Belmont, CA: Wadsworth.

———. 1990. "Rational choice, deterrence and social learning theory in criminology: The path not taken." Journal of Criminal Law and Criminology 81:653–676.

———. 1991. "Addiction: The troublesome concept." Journal of Drug Issues 21:777–793.

———. 1992. Drugs, Alcohol, and Society: Social Structure, Process, and Policy. Belmont, CA: Wadsworth.

———. 1994. Criminological Theories: Introduction and Evaluation. Los Angeles: Roxbury Publishing.

———. 1997. Criminological Theories: Introduction and Evaluation, 2nd Ed. Los Angeles, CA: Roxbury Publishing.

Akers, Ronald L., James Massey, William Clarke, and Ronald M. Lauer. 1983. "Are self-reports of adolescent deviance valid? Biochemical measures, randomized response and the bogus pipeline in smoking behavior." Social Forces 62:234–251.

Akerstrom, Malin. 1993. Crooks and Squares: Lifestyles of Thieves and Addicts in Comparison to Conventional People. New Brunswick, NJ: Transaction Publishers.

Albini, Joseph. 1971. The American Mafia: Genesis of a Legend. New York: Appleton-Century-Crofts.

———. 1997. "Donald Cressey's contributions to the study of organized crime." Pp. 16–25 in Understanding Organized Crime in Global Perspective, edited by P. A. Ryan and G. E. Rush. Thousand Oaks, CA: Sage.

Albrecht, Stan L., Bruce A. Chadwick, and David S. Alcorn. 1977. "Religiosity and deviance: Application of an attitude-behavior contingent consistency model." Journal for the Scientific Study of Religion 16:263–274.

Alexander, Jeffrey C. 1987. Twenty Lectures: Sociological Theory Since World War II. New York: Columbia University Press.

Allen, Edward J. 1996. Merchants of Menace—The Mafia: A Study of Organized Crime. Springfield, IL: Charles C. Thomas Publishers.

Ammon, Richard. 1989. Growing Up Amish. New York: Antheneum.

Andenaes, Johannes. 1974. Punishment and Deterrence. Ann Arbor: University of Michigan Press.

Anderson, Elijah. 1978. A Place on the Corner. Chicago: University of Chicago Press.

———. 1990. Streetwise: Race, Class, and Change in an Urban Community. Chicago: University of Chicago Press.

———. 1999. Code of the Street: Decency, Violence, and the Moral Life of the Inner City. New York: W. W. Norton.

Anderson, Margaret L. 1988. Thinking About Women: Sociological Perspectives on Sex and Gender, 2nd Ed. New York: Macmillan.

Araki, Shunichi, and Katsuyuki Murata. 1987. "Suicide in Japan: Socioeconomic effects on its secular and seasonal trends." Suicide and Life Threatening Behavior 17:65–71.

Arbuthnot, Jack, Donald A. Gordon, and Gregory J. Jurkovic. 1987. "Personality." Pp. 139–183 in Handbook of Juvenile Delinquency, edited by H. C. Quay. New York: Wiley and Sons.

Archer, Dane, and Rosemary Gartner. 1984. Violence and Crime in Cross-National Perspective. New Haven: Yale University Press.

Arneklev, Bruce J., Harold G. Grasmick, Charles R. Tittle, and Robert J. Bursik, Jr. 1993. "Low self-control and imprudent behavior." Journal of Quantitative Criminology 9:225–247.

Aronson, Elliot, and Judson Mills. 1973. "The effect of severity of initiation on liking for a group." Pp. 4–10 in Interpersonal Behavior in Small Groups, edited by Richard J. Ofshe. Englewood Cliffs, NJ: Prentice-Hall.

Asch, Solomon E. 1948. "The doctrine of suggestion, prestige, and imitation in social psychology." Psychological Review 55:250-276.

——. 1956. Studies of Independence and Conformity I. A Minority of One Against a Unanimous Majority. Psychological Monographs 70(9).

Assembly Committee on Criminal Procedure (California). 1975. "Public knowledge of criminal penalties." Pp.74–90 in Perception in Criminology, edited by R. L. Henshel and R. A. Silverman. New York: Columbia University Press.

Bachman, Jerald G., Patrick O'Malley, and Jerome Johnston. 1978. Adolescence to Adulthood: Change and Stability in the Lives of Young Men. Ann Arbor, MI: Institute for Social Research.

Bachman, Ronet. 1992. Death and Violence on the Reservation. New York: Auburn House.

——. 1996. "Victim's perceptions of initial police responses to robbery and aggravated assault: Does race matter?" Journal of Quantitative Criminology 12:363–390.

Bachman, Ronet, Raymond Paternoster, and Sally Ward. 1992. "The rationality of sexual offending: Testing a deterrence/rational choice conception of sexual assault." Law and Society Review 26:343–372.

Bagley, Christopher. 1969. "Incest behavior and incest taboo." Social Forces 16:505–519.

Bailey, Kenneth D. 1987. Methods of Social Research, 3rd Ed. New York: Free Press.

Baker, Marilyn, with Sally Brompton. 1974. Exclusive: The Inside Story of Patricia Hearst and the SLA. New York: Macmillan.

Bandura, Albert. 1969. Principles of Behavior Modification. New York: Holt, Rinehart and Winston.

——. 1973. Aggression: A Social Learning Analysis. Englewood Cliffs, NJ: Prentice-Hall.

——. 1977. Social Learning Theory. New York: General Learning Press.

——. 1986. Social Foundations of Thought and Action: A Social Cognitive Theory. Englewood Cliffs, NJ: Prentice-Hall.

——. 1997. Self-Efficacy: The Exercise of Control. New York: W. H. Freeman.

Bandura, Albert, and Richard H. Walters. 1963. Social Learning and Personality. New York: Holt, Rinehart, and Winston.

Bar-Hillel, Maya. 1980. "The base-rate fallacy in probability judgments." Acta Psychologica 44:211–233.

Bar-Hillel, Maya, and Baruch Fischhoff. 1981. "When do base-rates affect predictions?" Journal of Personality and Social Psychology 4:671–680.

Barsky, Sanford H., Michael D. Roth, Eric C. Kleerup, Michael Simons, and Donald P. Tashkin. 1998. "Histopathological and molecular alterations in bronchial epitheliums in habitual smokers of marijuana, cocaine, and/or tobacco." Journal of the National Cancer Institute 90:1198–1205.

Bartell, Gilbert D. 1971. Group Sex. New York: Wyden.

Beccaria, Cesare. 1963 [1764]. On Crimes and Punishment. Indianapolis: Bobbs-Merrill.

Beck, Jerome, and Marsha Rosenbaum. 1994. Pursuit of Ecstasy: The MDMA Experience. Albany, NY: State University of New York (SUNY) Press.

Becker, Gary. 1968. "Crime and punishment: An economic approach." Journal of Political Economy 76:169–217.

Becker, Howard S. 1953. "Becoming a marijuana user." American Journal of Sociology 59:235–242.

——. 1960. "Notes on the concept of commitment." American Journal of Sociology 66:323–340.

——. 1963. Outsiders: Studies in the Sociology of Deviance. New York: Free Press.

Behan, Tom. 1996. The Camorra. London: Routledge.

Bell, Alan P., and Martin S. Weinberg. 1978. Homosexualities: A Study of Diversity Among Men and Women. New York: Simon and Schuster.

Bell, Alan P., Martin S. Weinberg, and Sue K. Hammersmith. 1981. Sexual Preference: Its Development in Men and Women. Bloomington, IN: Indiana University Press.

Bell, Daniel. 1962. "Crime as an American way of life: A queer ladder of social mobility." Pp. 127–150 in The End of Ideology, edited by D. Bell. New York: Free Press.

Bellair, Paul E. 1997. "Social interaction and community crime: Examining the importance of neighborhood networks." Criminology 35:677–703.

Benson, Donna J., and Gregg E. Thomson. 1982. "Sexual harassment on a university campus: The confluence of authority relations, sexual interest and gender stratification." Social Problems 29:236–251.

Bentham, Jeremy. 1948 [1780]. The Principles of Morals and Legislation. New York: Hefner.

Bequai, August. 1979. Organized Crime: The Fifth Estate. Lexington, MA: D. C. Heath.

Berk, Richard, and Phyllis J. Newman. 1985. "Does arrest really deter wife battery? An effort to replicate the findings of the Minneapolis spouse abuse experiment." American Sociological Review 50:253–262.

Berk, Richard, Gordon Smyth, and Lawrence Sherman. 1989. "When random assignment fails: Some lessons from the Minneapolis spouse abuse experiment." Journal of Quantitative Criminology 4:209–223.

Berkowitz, Leonard. 1969. "The frustration-aggression hypothesis revisited." Pp. 1–28 in Roots of Aggression: A Reincarnation of the Frustration-Aggression Hypothesis, edited by L. Berkowitz. New York: Atherton.

Berman, Alan L. 1996. "Dyadic death: A typology." Suicide and Life Threatening Behavior 26:342–353.

Berman, Yitzchak. 1973. "Size of population and juvenile delinquency in cities in Israel." Criminology 11:105–113.

Bernard, Thomas J. 1983. The Consensus-Conflict Debate: Form and Content in Social Theories. New York: Columbia University Press.

Bernhardt, Paul C. 1997. "Influences of serotonin and testosterone in aggression and dominance: Convergence with social psychology." Current Directions in Psychological Science 6:44–48.

Best, Joel. 1987. "Rhetoric in claims-making: Constructing the missing children problem." Social Problems 34:101–121.

——. 1990. Threatened Children: Rhetoric and Concern About Child Victims. Chicago: University of Chicago Press.

Best, Joel, and Gerald T. Horiuchi. 1985. "The razor blade in the apple: The social construction of urban legends." Social Problems 32:488–499.

Best, Joel, and David F. Luckenbill. 1980. "The social organization of deviance." Social Problems 28:14–31.

——. 1982. Organizing Deviance. Englewood Cliffs, NJ: Prentice-Hall.

——. 1996. "The social organization of deviants." Pp. 455–472 in Deviant Behavior: A Text-Reader in the Sociology of Deviance, 5th Ed., edited by D. H. Kelly. New York: St. Martin's Press.

Bieber, Irving. 1962. Homosexuality: A Psychoanalytic Study of Male Homosexuals. New York: Basic Books.

Birkbeck, Christopher, and Gary L. LaFree. 1993. "The situational analysis of crime and deviance." Annual Review of Sociology 19:113–137.

Bjerregaard, Beth, and Carolyn Smith. 1993. "Gender differences in gang participation, delinquency and substance abuse." Journal of Quantitative Criminology, 9:329–355.

Black, Albert. 1990. "Jonestown—two faces of suicide: A Durkheimian analysis." Suicide and Life Threatening Behavior 20:285–306.

Black, Donald. 1976. The Behavior of Law. New York: Academic Press.

——. 1980. Manners and Customs of the Police. New York: Academic Press.

——. 1983. "Crime as social control." American Sociological Review 48:34–45.

——. 1989. Sociological Justice. New York: Oxford University Press.

Blake, Judith, and Kingsley Davis. 1964. "Norms, values, and sanctions." Pp. 456–484 in Handbook of Modern Sociology, edited by R. E. L. Faris. Chicago: Rand McNally.

Blau, Peter. 1964. Exchange and Power in Social Life. New York: The Free Press.

Blau, Peter, and Otis Dudley Duncan. 1967. The American Occupational Structure. New York: John Wiley.

Blendon, Robert J., Ulrike S. Szalay, and Richard A. Knox. 1992. "Should physicians aid their patients in dying? The public perspective." Journal of the American Medical Association 267:2658–2662.

Block, Alan A., and Frank R. Scarpitti. 1985. Poisoning for Profit. New York: William Morrow.

Blumer, Herbert. 1969. Symbolic Interactionism: Perspective and Method. Englewood Cliffs, NJ: Prentice-Hall.

Blumstein, Alfred, Jacqueline Cohen, and David P. Farrington. 1988a. "Criminal career research: Its value for criminology." Criminology 26:1–36.

Blumstein, Alfred, Jacqueline Cohen, Somnath Das, and Soumyo D. Moitra. 1988b. "Specialization and seriousness during adult criminal careers." Journal of Quantitative Criminology 4:303–345.

Blumstein, Alfred, Jacqueline Cohen, and Daniel Nagin. 1978. Deterrence and Incapacitation. Report of the Panel on Research on Deterrent and Incapacitative Effects. Washington, DC: National Academy of Sciences.

Blumstein, Alfred, Jacqueline Cohen, Jeffrey A. Roth, and Christy A. Visher (eds.). 1986. Criminal Careers and "Career Criminals." Washington, DC: National Academy Press.

Bobrowski, Lawrence J. 1988. "Collecting, organizing, and reporting street gang crime." Special Functions Group, Chicago Police Department. Chicago: Mimeographed. As cited in Irving A. Spergel. 1990. "Youth gangs: Continuity and Change." Pp. 171–275 in Crime and Justice: An Annual Review, Vol. 12, edited by M. Tonry and N. Morris. Chicago: University of Chicago Press.

Bohm, Robert M. 1982. "Radical criminology: An explication." Criminology 19:565–589.

Bonger, William Adrian. 1916. Criminality and Economic Conditions. Translated by H. P. Horton. Boston: Little, Brown, and Company.

Bonner, Ronald L., and Alexander R. Rich. 1987. "Toward a predictive model of suicidal ideation and behavior: Some preliminary data in college students." Suicide and Life Threatening Behavior 17:50–63.

Booth, Alan, and D. Wayne Osgood. 1993. "The influence of testosterone on deviance in adulthood: Assessing and explaining the relationship." Criminology 31:93–117.

Bordua, David J. 1967. "Recent trends: Deviant behavior and social control." Annals 369:149–163.

Borg, Marian J. 1997. "The southern subculture of punitiveness? Regional variation in support for capital punishment." Journal of Research in Crime and Delinquency 34:25–45.

Bourgois, Philip. 1997. "In search of Horatio Alger: Culture and ideology in the crack economy." Pp. 57–76 in Crack in America: Demon Drugs and Social Justice, edited by C. Reinarman and H. G. Levine. Berkeley, CA: U. of California Press.

Brain, Paul F., and Elizabeth J. Susman. 1997. "Hormonal aspects of aggression and violence." Pp. 314–323 in Handbook of Antisocial Behavior, edited by D. M. Stoff, J. Breiling, and J. D. Maser. New York: Wiley.

Braithwaite, John. 1981. "The myth of social class and criminality reconsidered." American Sociological Review 46:36–57.

——. 1989. Crime, Shame, and Reintegration. New York: Cambridge University Press.

——. 1997. "Charles Tittle's Control Balance and criminological theory." Theoretical Criminology 1:77–97.

Braithwaite, Richard B. 1960. Scientific Explanation. New York: Harper and Row.

Brecher, Edward M. 1972. Licit and Illicit Drugs. Boston: Little Brown.

Breedlove, William, and Jerrye Breedlove. 1964. Swap Clubs: A Study in Contemporary Sexual Mores. Los Angeles: Sherbourne Press.

Brehm, Jack W. 1966. A Theory of Psychological Reactance. New York: Academic Press.

Brehm, Sharon S., and Jack W. Brehm. 1981. Psychological Reactance: A Theory of Freedom and Control. New York: Academic Press.

Briar, Scott, and Irving Piliavin. 1965. "Delinquency, situation inducements, and commitments to conformity." Social Problems 13:35–45.

Bridges, George S., and Martha A. Myers (eds.). 1994. Inequality, Crime, and Social Control. Boulder, CO: Westview.

Brill, A. A. 1921. Fundamental Conceptions of Psychoanalysis. New York: Harcourt, Brace.

Britt, David, and Richard Campbell. 1977. "Assessing the linkage of norms, environments, and deviance." Social Forces 56:532–550.

Broidy, Lisa M. 1995. "Direct supervision and delinquency: Assessing the adequacy of structural proxies." Journal of Criminal Justice 23:541–554.

Broverman, Donald M., Edward L. Klaiber, and William Vogel. 1980. "Gonadal hormones and cognitive functioning." Pp. 57–80 in The Psychobiology of Sex Differences and Sex Roles, edited by J. E. Parsons. New York: Hemisphere Publishing Co.

Brown, J. David. 1996. "The professional ex-: An alternative for exiting the deviant career." Pp. 633–645 in Deviant Behavior: A Text-Reader in the Sociology of Deviance, edited by D. H. Kelly. New York: St. Martin's Press.

Buckner, H. Taylor. 1971. Deviance, Reality, and Change. New York: Random House.

Bugliosi, Vincent (with Curt Gentry). 1974. Helter Skelter: The True Story of the Manson Murders. New York: Norton.

Bullough, Vern L. 1974. "Transvestites in the middle ages." American Journal of Sociology 79:1381–1394.

Burgess, Robert L., and Ronald L. Akers. 1966. "A differential association-reinforcement theory of criminal behavior." Social Problems 14:128–147.

Burkett, Steven R., and David A. Ward. 1993. "A note on perceptual deterrence, religiously based moral condemnation, and social control." Criminology 31:119–134.

Bursik, Robert J., Jr. 1980. "The dynamics of specialization in juvenile offenses." Social Forces 58:851–864.

Bursik, Robert J., Jr., and Harold G. Grasmick. 1993. Neighborhoods and Crime: The Dimensions of Effective Community Control. Lexington, MA: Lexington Books.

Bynner, John M., Patrick M. O'Malley, and Jerald G. Bachman. 1981. "Self-esteem and delinquency revisited." Journal of Youth and Adolescence 10:407–444.

Caddy, Glenn R., and Trudy Block. 1985. "Individual differences in response to treatment." Pp. 317–362 in Determinants of Substance Abuse: Biological, Psychological, and Environmental Factors, edited by M. Galizio and S. A. Maisto. New York: Plenum.

Calavita, Kitty, and Henry Pontell. 1993. "Savings and loan fraud as organized crime: Toward a conceptual typology of corporate crime." Criminology 21:519–548.

Cameron, Mary Owen. 1964. The Booster and the Snitch: Department Store Shoplifting. New York: Free Press.

Campbell, Anne. 1990. "Female participation in gangs." Pp. 163–182 in Gangs in America, edited by C. R. Huff. Newbury Park, CA: Sage.

Canter, Rachelle J. 1982. "Family correlates of male and female delinquency." Criminology 20:149–167.

Caprio, Frank S. 1955. Variations in Sexual Behavior: A Psychodynamic Study of Deviations in Various Expressions of Sexual Behavior. New York: The Citadel Press.

Carden, Maren Lockwood. 1969. Oneida: Utopian Community to Modern Corporation. Baltimore: The Johns Hopkins University Press.

Caroll, John S. 1978. "A psychological approach to deterrence: The evaluation of crime opportunities." Journal of Personality and Social Psychology 36:1512–1520.

Caspi, Avshalom, et al. 1994. "Are some people crime-prone? Replications of the personality-crime relationship across countries, genders, races, and methods." Criminology 32:163–195.

Centers for Disease Control and Prevention. 1995. Report of Final Mortality Statistics. National Center for Health Statistics.

Cernkovich, Stephen A., and Peggy C. Giordano. 1987. "Family relationships and delinquency." Criminology 25:295–321.

Chaiken, Jan M., Michael W. Lawless, and Keith A. Stevenson. 1974. The Impact of Police Activity on Crime: Robberies on the New York Subway System. Santa Monica, CA: Rand Corporation.

Chaiken, Marcia, and Jan M. Chaiken. 1984. "Offender types and public policy." Crime and Delinquency 30:195–226.

Chambliss, William J. 1973. "The saints and the roughnecks." Society 11:24–31.

———. 1975. Criminal Law in Action. Santa Barbara, CA: Hamilton.

Chambliss, William J., and Robert B. Seidman. 1971. Law, Order and Power. Reading, MA: Addison-Wesley.

Chamlin, Mitchell B., and John K. Cochran. 1995. "Assessing Messner and Rosenfeld's institutional anomie theory: A partial test." Criminology 33:411–429.

———. 1997. "Social altruism and crime." Criminology 35:203–227.

Chauncey, Robert. 1975. "Deterrence, certainty, severity, and skyjacking." Criminology 12:447–473.

Cherniak, Christopher. 1986. Minimal Rationality. Cambridge, MA: The MIT Press.

Cheung, Yuet W., Partick G. Erickson, and Tammy C. Landau. 1991. "Experience of crack use: Findings for a community-based sample in Toronto." Journal of Drug Issues 21:121–140.

Chin, Ko-lin. 1990. Chinese Subculture and Criminality. Westport, CT: Greenwood Press.

Chiricos, Theodore, and Gordon Waldo. 1970. "Punishment and crime: An examination of some empirical evidence." Social Problems 18:200–217.

Cialdini, Robert B., and Melanie R. Trost. 1998. "Social influence: Social norms, conformity, and compliance." Pp. 151–192 in The Handbook of Social Psychology, 4th Ed., Volume II, edited by D. T. Gilbert, S. T. Fiske, and G. Lindzey. Boston: McGraw-Hill.

Clark, John, and Larry Tifft. 1966. "Polygraph and interview validation of self-reported deviant behavior." American Sociological Review 31:516–523.

Claster, Daniel S. 1967. "Comparisons of risk perceptions between delinquents and non-delinquents." Journal of Criminal Law, Criminology, and Police Science 58:80–86.

Clebert, Jean-Paul. 1963. The Gypsies. London: Vista.

Cleckley, Hervey M. 1964. The Mask of Sanity. St. Louis, MO: Mosby.

Clelland, Donald, and Timothy J. Carter. 1980. "The new myth of class and crime." Criminology 18:319–336.

Clinard, Marshall B. 1957. Sociology of Deviant Behavior. New York: Harcourt Brace.

Clinard, Marshall B., and Robert F. Meier. 1992. Sociology of Deviant Behavior, 8th Ed. New York: Harcourt Brace.

Clinard, Marshall B., and Peter C. Yeager. 1980. Corporate Crime. New York: Free Press.

Cloninger, Robert C., Carmen Bayon, and Thomas R. Przbeck. 1997. "Epidemiology and axis I comorbidity of antisocial personality." Pp. 12–21 in Handbook of Antisocial Behavior, edited by D. M. Stoff, J. Breiling, and J. D. Maser. New York: Wiley.

Cloward, Richard A. 1959. "Illegitimate means, anomie, and deviant behavior." American Sociological Review 24:164–176.

Cloward, Richard A., and Lloyd E. Ohlin. 1960. Delinquency and Opportunity: A Theory of Delinquent Gangs. New York: The Free Press.

Cloyd, Jerald W. 1977. "The processing of misdemeanor drinking drivers: The bureaucratization of the arrest, prosecution, and plea bargaining situations." Social Forces 56:385–407.

Cohen, Albert K. 1955. Delinquent Boys: The Culture of the Gang. New York: The Free Press.

——. 1966. Deviance and Control. Englewood Cliffs, NJ: Prentice-Hall.

——. 1974. "The elasticity of evil: Changes in the social definition of deviance." Occasional paper #7, Oxford University Penal Research Unit. Oxford: Basil Blackwell.

Cohen, Bernard. 1969. "The delinquency of gangs and spontaneous groups." Pp. 61–111 in Delinquency: Selected Studies, edited by T. Sellin and M. E. Wolfgang. New York: Wiley.

Cohen, Lawrence E., and Marcus Felson. 1979. "Social change and crime rate trends: A routine activity approach." American Sociological Review 44:588–608.

Cohen, Lawrence E., Marcus Felson, and Kenneth Land. 1980. "Property crime rates in the United States: A macrodynamic analysis, 1947–1977, with ex-ante forecasts for the mid-1980s." American Journal of Sociology 86:90–118.

Cohen, Yinon, and Andrea Tyree. 1986. "Escape from poverty: Determinants of intergenerational mobility of sons and daughters of the poor." Social Science Quarterly 67:803–813.

Coleman, James W. 1994. The Criminal Elite: The Sociology of White Collar Crime, 3rd Ed. New York: St. Martin's Press.

Coleman, Loren. 1987. Suicide Clusters. Boston: Faber and Faber.

Collins, Randall. 1988. "Women and men in the class structure." Journal of Family Issues 9:27–50.

Colten, Craig E. 1996. The Road to Love Canal: Managing Industrial Waste Before EPA. Austin, TX: University of Texas Press.

Columbia Broadcasting System. 1969. "The business of sex." Pp. 973–985 in Delinquency, Crime and Social Process, edited by D. R. Cressey and D. A. Ward. New York: Harper and Row.

Colvin, Mark, and John Pauly. 1983. "A critique of criminology: Toward an integrated structural-Marxist theory of delinquency production." American Journal of Sociology 89:513–551.

Conger, Rand D. 1976. "Social Control and Social Learning Models of Delinquent Behavior: A Synthesis." Criminology 14:17–40.

Conger, Rand D., and Ronald L. Simons. 1997. "Life-course contingencies in the development of adolescent antisocial behavior: A matching law approach." Pp. 55–99 in Developmental Theories of Crime and Delinquency, edited by T. P. Thornberry. New Brunswick, NJ: Transaction.

Conklin, John. 1981. Criminology. New York: McMillan.

Connolly, Ceci, and John Mintz. 1998. "How big tobacco got smoked." Washington Post National Weekly Edition 15, April 6:6–9.

Consumer Reports. 1961. "The great ham robbery." Number 3 26:120–125.

——. 1963a. "The docket." Number 4 28:151.

——. 1963b. "The docket." Number 5 28:209.

——. 1968. "The docket." Number 5 33:253.

Cook, Fred J. 1966. The Secret Rulers. New York: Duell, Sloan, and Pearce.

Cook, Philip J. 1980. "Research in criminal deterrence: Laying the groundwork for the second decade." Pp. 211–268 in Crime and Justice: An Annual Review of Research, Vol. 2, edited by N. Morris and M. Tonry. Chicago: University of Chicago Press.

Cooley, Charles Horton. 1902. Human Nature and the Social Order. New York: Scribner.

Cooney, Mark. 1997. "The decline of elite homicide." Criminology 35:381–407.

Cornish, Derek B., and Ronald V. Clarke (eds.). 1986. The Reasoning Criminal. New York: Springer-Verlag.

Correctional Populations in the United States, 1996. 1997. Bureau of Justice Statistics, National Institute of Justice, U.S. Department of Justice, Washington, DC.

Counts, Dorothy Ayers. 1987. "Female suicide and wife abuse: A cross-cultural perspective." Suicide and Life Threatening Behavior 17:194–203.

——. 1990. "Abused women and revenge suicide: Anthropological contributions to understanding suicide." Pp. 95–106 in Current Concepts of Suicide, edited by D. Lester. Philadelphia: The Charles Press.

Cowgill, Donald O. 1961. "Value assumptions in recent research on migration." Sociological Quarterly 2:263–279.

Cowley, Geoffrey. 1997. "Can marijuana be medicine?" Newsweek 130: February 3, 22–27.

Cowling, Mark. 1998. Date Rape and Consent. Brookfield, MA: Ashgate.

Cox, W. Miles. 1985. "Personality correlates of substance use." Pp. 209–246 in Determinants of Substance Abuse: Biological, Psychological, and Environmental Factors, edited by M. Galizio and S. A. Maisto. New York: Plenum.

Cressey, Donald R. 1953. Other People's Money. New York: Free Press.

——. 1969. Theft of the Nation. New York: Harper and Row.

Crime in the United States. 1995–1997. Uniform Crime Reports. Federal Bureau of Investigation. U.S. Department of Justice. Washington, DC.

Crocker, Lester G. 1968. Rousseau's Social Contract: An Interpretive Essay. Cleveland, OH: Case Western Reserve University Press.

Cromwell, Paul, James N. Olson, and D'Aunn W. Avary. 1999. "Decision strategies of residential burglars." Pp. 50–56 in In Their Own Words: Criminals on Crime, 2nd Ed., edited by P. Cromwell. Los Angeles, CA: Roxbury.

Cullen, Francis T., Paul Gendreau, G. Roger Jarjoura, and John Paul Wright. 1997. "Crime and *The Bell Curve*: Lessons from intelligent criminology." Crime and Delinquency 43:387–411.

Curry, G. David, and Irving A. Spergel. 1988. "Gang homicide, delinquency, and community," Criminology 26:381–405.

D'Alessio, Stewart J., and Lisa Stolzenberg. 1998. "Crime, arrests, and pretrial jail incarceration: An examination of the deterrence thesis." Criminology 36:735–761.

Dalph, Edward W. 1979. The Silent Community: Public Homosexual Encounters. Beverly Hills, CA: Sage.

Daum, Meghan. 1996. "Safe-sex lies." New York Times Magazine, January 21:32–33.

Davis, Fred. 1961. "Deviance disavowal: The management of strained interaction by the visibly handicapped." Social Problems 9:120–132.

Davis, Kingsley. 1937. "The sociology of prostitution." American Sociological Review 2:744–755.

——. 1950. Human Society. New York: Macmillan.

Davis, Nanette J. 1971. "The prostitute: Developing a deviant identity." Pp. 297–322 in Studies in the Sociology of Sex, edited by J. M. Henslin. New York: Appleton-Century-Crofts.

Dean, Paul J., Lillian M. Range, and William C. Goggin. 1996. "The escape theory of suicide in college students: Testing a model that includes perfectionism." Suicide and Life Threatening Behavior 26:181–186.

Decker, Scott H., and Barrik Van Winkle. 1996. Life in the Gang. New York: Cambridge University Press.

Decker, Scott H., Richard Wright, and Robert Logie. 1993. "Perceptual deterrence among active residential burglars: A research note." Criminology 31:135–147.

DeFleur, Melvin L., and Richard Quinney. 1966. "A reformulation of Sutherland's differential association theory and a strategy for empirical verification." Journal of Research in Crime and Delinquency 3:1–22.

DeMaria, Richard. 1978. Communal Love at Oneida: A Perfectionist Vision of Authority, Property, and Sexual Order. New York: Edwin Mellen Press.

Demerath, Nicholas J., III. 1965. Social Class in American Protestantism. Chicago: Rand McNally.

Dempsey, Paul S. 1997. "Fighting modern-day robber barons." The Denver Business Journal, January 27, 1997.

Dentler, Robert A., and Kai T. Erikson. 1959. "The functions of deviance in groups." Social Problems 7:98–107.

Devlin, Bernie, Stephen E. Fienberg, Daniel P. Resnick, and Kathryn Roeder (eds.). 1997. Intelligence, Genes, and Success: Scientists Respond to *The Bell Curve*. New York: Springer-Verlag.

Dickson, Donald. 1968. "Bureaucracy and morality: An organizational perspective on a moral crusade." Social Problems 16:143–157.

Diekstra, Rene F. W., and Nadia Garnefski. 1995. "On the nature, magnitude, and causality of suicide behavior: An international perspective." Suicide and Life Threatening Behavior 25:36–57.

Dietz, Park E. 1986. "Mass, serial, and sensational homicides." Bulletin of the New York Academy of Medicine 62:477–491.

Dodge, Kenneth A., John E. Bates, and Gregory S. Pettit. 1990. "Mechanisms in the cycle of violence." Science 250:1678–1683.

Dorpat, Theodore L., Joan K. Jackson, and Herbert S. Ripley. 1965. "Broken homes and attempted suicide." Archives of General Psychiatry 12:213–216.

Dorr, Darwin. 1998. "Psychopathy in the pedophile." Pp. 304–320 in Psychopathy: Antisocial, Criminal, and Violent Behavior, edited by T. Millon, E. Simonsen, M. Birket-Smith, and R. D. Davis. New York: Guilford.

Dotson, James W., Deborah L. Ackerman, and Louis Jolyon West. 1995. "Ketamine abuse." The Journal of Drug Issues 25:75–157.

Douglas, Jack D. 1967. The Social Meaning of Suicide. Princeton: Princeton University Press.

Dowling, Tom. 1970. Coach: A Season with Lombardi. New York: W. W. Norton.

Downey, Kathleen, and Joel Best. 1995. "Stalking strangers and lovers: Changing media typifications of a new crime problem." Pp. 33–57 in Images and Issues: Typifying Contemporary Social Problems, edited by J. Best. New York: Adline de Gruyter.

Duberstein, P. R., et al. 1995. "Attitudes toward self-determined deaths: A survey of primary care physicians." Journal of the American Geriatric Society 43:395–400.

Dublin, Louis I. 1963. Suicide: A Sociological and Statistical Study. New York: Ronald Press.

Duff, Robert W., and Lawrence K. Hong. 1996. "Management of deviant identity among competitive women bodybuilders." Pp. 555–567 in Deviant Behavior: A Text Reader in the Sociology of Deviance, edited by D. H. Kelly. New York: St. Martin's Press.

Duncan, Otis Dudley, David L. Featherman, and Beverly Duncan. 1972. Socioeconomic Background and Achievement. New York: Seminar Press.

Duncan, Terry E., Elizabeth Tildesley, Susan C. Duncan, and Hyman Hops. 1995. "The consistency of family and peer influences on the development of substance use in adolescence." Addiction 90:1647–1660.

Dunford, Franklyn. 1992. "The measurement of recidivism in cases of spouse assault." Journal of Criminal Law and Criminology 83:120–136.

Durham, Alexis M. 1994. Crisis and Reform: Current Issues in American Punishment. Boston: Little Brown.

Durkheim, Emile. 1933 [1893]. Emile Durkheim on The Division of Labor in Society, Being a Translation of His De La Division du Travail Sociale. New York: Macmillan.

——. 1938 [1895]. The Rules of Sociological Method. New York: The Free Press.

——. 1951 [1897]. Suicide, A Study in Sociology. Translated by J. A. Spaulding and G. Simpson, edited with an introduction by G. Simpson. Reprint, Glencoe, NY: The Free Press.

——. 1961 [1903]. Moral Education: A Study in the Theory and Application of the Sociology of Education. New York: Free Press.

——. 1997. "The normal and the pathological." Pp. 15–19 in Constructions of Deviance: Social Power, Context, and Interaction, edited by P. A. Adler and P. Adler, 2nd Ed. Belmont, CA: Wadsworth.

Dusenberry, Linda, Jennifer A. Epstein, Gilbert J. Botvin, and Tracy Diaz. 1994. "Social influence predictors of alcohol use among New York Latino youth." Addictive Behavior 19:363–372.

Eagly, Alice H., and Shelly Chaiken. 1998. "Attitude structure and function." Pp. 269–322 in The Handbook of Social Psychology, edited by D. T. Gilbert, S. T. Fiske, and G. Lindzey. New York: Oxford University Press.

Edgerton, Robert B. 1976. Deviance: A Cross-Cultural Perspective. Menlo Park, CA: Cummings.

——. 1992. Sick Societies: Challenging the Myth of Primitive Harmony. New York: The Free Press.

Edmonds, Walter D. 1948. The First Hundred Years, 1848–1948. Oneida, NY: Oneida Ltd.

Egger, Steven A. 1990. Serial Murder: An Elusive Phenomenon. Westport, CT: Praeger.

——. 1998. The Killers Among Us: An Examination of Serial Murder and Its Investigation. Upper Saddle River, NJ: Prentice-Hall.

Ehrlich, Isaac. 1973. "Participation in illegitimate activities: A theoretical and empirical investigation." Journal of Political Economy 81:521–565.

——. 1975. "The deterrent effect of capital punishment: A question of life and death." American Economic Review 65:397–417.

Elifson, Kirk W., David M. Petersen, and C. Kirk Hadaway. 1983. "Religiosity and delinquency: A contextual analysis." Criminology 21:505–527.

Elliott, Delbert S. 1985. "The assumption that theories can be combined with increased explanatory power: Theoretical integrations." Pp. 123–149 in Theoretical Methods in Criminology, edited by R. F. Meier. Beverly Hills, CA: Sage.

——. 1994. "Serious violent offenders: Onset, developmental course, and termination." Criminology 32:1–21.

Elliott, Delbert S., Suzanne S. Ageton, and Rachelle J. Canter. 1979. "An integrated theoretical perspective on delinquent behavior." Criminology 16:3–27.

Elliott, Delbert S., David Huizinga, and Suzanne S. Ageton. 1985. Explaining Delinquency and Drug Use. Beverly Hills, CA: Sage.

Elliott, Delbert S., David Huizinga, and Scott Menard. 1989. Multiple Problem Youth: Delinquency, Substance Use, and Mental Health Problems. New York: Springer-Verlag.

Elliott, Delbert S., and Scott Menard. 1996. "Delinquent friends and delinquent behavior: Temporal and developmental patterns." Pp. 28–67 in Delinquency and Crime, edited by D. J. Hawkins. New York: Cambridge University Press.

Elliott, Delbert S., and Harwin L. Voss. 1974. Delinquency and Dropout. Lexington, MA: D.C. Heath.

Ellis, Lee. 1982. "Criminal behavior and r/k selection: An extension of gene-based evolutionary theory." Deviant Behavior 8:149–176.

Ellis, Lee, and Anthony Walsh. 1997. "Gene based evolutionary theories in criminology." Criminology 35:229–276.

Emerson, Robert M. 1969. Judging Delinquents: Context and Process in Juvenile Court. Chicago: Aldine.

Empey, Lamar T., and Mark C. Stafford. 1991. American Delinquency: Its Meaning and Construction, 3rd Ed. Belmont, CA: Wadsworth.

Erickson, Maynard L., and Gary F. Jensen. 1977. "Delinquency is still group behavior: Toward revitalizing the group premise in the sociology of deviance." Journal of Criminal Law and Criminology 68:262–273.

Erikson, Erik H. 1950. Childhood and Society. New York: W. W. Norton.

Erikson, Kai T. 1966. Wayward Puritans: A Study in the Sociology of Deviance. New York: Wiley.

——. 1996. "A response to Richard Leo." The American Sociologist 27:129–130.

Ermann, M. David, and Richard J. Lundman. 1996. Corporate and Governmental Deviance, 4th Ed. New York: Oxford.

Esbensen, Finn-Aang, and David Huizinga. 1993. "Gangs, drugs, and delinquency in a survey of youth." Criminology 31:565–589.

Esbensen, Finn-Aage, David Huizinga, and Anne W. Weiher. 1993. "Gang and non-gang youth: Differences in explanatory factors." Journal of Contemporary Criminal Justice 9:94–116.

Estlake, Allan. 1900. The Oneida Community: A Record of an Attempt to Carry Out the Principles of Christian Unselfishness and Scientific Race Improvement. London: George Redway.

Etzioni, Amitai. 1988. The Moral Dimension: Towards a New Economics. New York: The Free Press.

——. 1993. The Spirit of Community: Rights, Responsibilities, and the Communitarian Agenda. New York: Crown Books.

———. 1996. The New Golden Rule: Community and Morality in a Democratic Society. New York: Basic Books.

Evans, T. David, Francis T. Cullen, R. Gregory Dunaway, and Velmer S. Burton, Jr. 1995. "Religion and crime re-examined: The impact of religion, secular controls, and social ecology on adult criminality." Criminology 33:195–224.

Evans, T. David, Francis T. Cullen, Velmer S. Burton, Jr., Gregory Dunaway, and Michael L. Bensen. 1997. "The social consequences of self-control: Testing the general theory of crime." Criminology 35:475–504.

Eysenck, Hans J. 1973 [1952]. "The effects of psychotherapy: An evaluation." Pp. 365–384 in The Experimental Study of Freudian Theories, edited by H. J. Eysenck and G. D. Wilson. London, England: Methuen.

———. 1977. Crime and Personality, Revised Edition. London: Routledge and Kegan Paul.

———. 1982. "Development of a theory." Pp. 1–38 in Personality, Genetics, and Behavior, edited by C. D. Spielberger. New York: Praeger.

Eysenck, Hans, J., and Gisli H. Gudjonsson. 1989. The Causes and Cures of Criminality. New York: Plenum Press.

Eysenck, Hans, J., and Glenn D. Wilson (eds.). 1973a. The Experimental Study of Freudian Theories. London, England: Methuen.

———. 1973b. "Epilogue." Pp. 385–396 in The Experimental Study of Freudian Theories, edited by H. J. Eysenck and G. D. Wilson. London, England: Methuen.

Fagan, Jeffrey. 1989. "The social organization of drug use and drug dealing among urban gangs." Criminology 27:633–667.

Fagan, Jeffrey, Elizabeth Piper, and Melinda Moore. 1986. "Violent delinquents and urban youths." Criminology 24:439–471.

Farrington, David P. 1977. "The effects of public labeling." British Journal of Criminology 17:112–125.

———. 1986. "Age and crime." Pp. 189–250 in Crime and Justice: An Annual Review of Research, edited by M. Tonry and N. Morris. Chicago: University of Chicago Press.

Farrington, David P., Howard N. Snyder, and Terrence A. Finnegan. 1988. "Specialization in juvenile court careers." Criminology 24:461–487.

Felson, Marcus. 1986. "Linking criminal choices, routine activities, informal control, and criminal outcomes." Pp. 119–128 in The Reasoning Criminal, edited by D. B. Cornish and R. V. Clarke, New York: Springer-Verlag.

———. 1994. Crime in Everyday Life: Insights and Implications for Society. Thousand Oaks, CA: Pine Forge Press.

———. 1998. Crime in Everyday Life, 2nd Ed. Thousand Oaks, CA: Pine Forge Press.

Ferdinand, Theodore N. 1970. "Demographic shifts and criminality: An inquiry." British Journal of Criminology 10:169–175.

Ferguson, David M., L. John Horwood, and Michael T. Lynskey. 1995. "The prevalence and risk factors associated with abusive or hazardous alcohol consumption in 16-year-olds." Addiction 90:935–946.

Festinger, Leon. 1957. A Theory of Cognitive Dissonance. Stanford, CA: Stanford University Press.

Festinger, Leon, Henry W. Riecken, and Stanley Schachter. 1956. When Prophecy Fails: A Social and Psychological Study of a Modern Group That Predicted the Destruction of the World. New York: Harper and Row.

Fine, Reuben. 1962. Freud: A Critical Re-evaluation of His Theories. New York: David McKay Company.

Finestone, Harold. 1957. "Cats, kicks, and color." Social Problems 5:3–13.

Fischer, Claude S. 1975. "Toward a subcultural theory of urbanism." American Journal of Sociology 80:1319–1341.

———. 1984. The Urban Experience, 2nd Ed. New York: Harcourt Brace Jovanovich.

———. 1995. "The subcultural theory of urbanism: A twentieth-year assessment." American Journal of Sociology 101:543–577.

Fischer, Claude S., Michael Hout, Martin Sanchez Jankowski, Ann Swidler, and Kim Voss. 1996. Inequality by Design: Cracking *The Bell Curve* Myth. Princeton, NJ: Princeton University Press.

Fischhoff, Baruch, Paul Slovic, and Sarah Lichtenstein. 1977. "Knowing with certainty: The appropriateness of extreme confidence." Journal of Experimental Psychology: Human Perception and Performance 3:552–564.

Fisher, Seymour, and Roger P. Greenberg. 1977a. The Scientific Credibility of Freud's Theories and Therapy. New York: Basic Books.

———. 1977b "Overview: A total look at the findings." Pp. 392–415 in The Scientific Credibility of Freud's Theories and Therapy. New York: Basic Books.

Fogarty, Robert S. (ed.). 1994. Special Love/Special Sex: An Oneida Community Diary. Syracuse, NY: Syracuse University Press.

Foster, Lawrence. 1981. Religion and Sexuality: Three American Communal Experiments of the Nineteenth Century. New York: Oxford University Press.

Frady, Marshall. 1979. Billy Graham: A Parable of American Righteousness. Boston: Little Brown.

Fraser, Stephen (ed). 1995. *The Bell Curve* Wars. New York: Basic Books.

Freeman, Derek. 1983. Margaret Mead and Samoa, The Making and Unmaking of an Anthropological Myth. Cambridge, MA: Harvard University Press.

Freud, Sigmund. 1943 [1920]. A General Introduction to Psycho-Analysis, trans. by Joan Riviere. Garden City, NY: Garden City Publishing.

———. 1961 [1930]. Civilization and Its Discontents. New York: Norton.

Freudenburg, William R. 1986. "The density of acquaintanceship: An overlooked variable in community research?" American Journal of Sociology 92:27–63.

Friday, Paul C., and Jerald Hage. 1976. "Youth crime in postindustrial societies: An integrated perspective." Criminology 14:347–368.

Friedrichs, David O. 1996. Trusted Criminals: White-Collar Crime in Contemporary Society. Belmont, CA: Wadsworth.

Gage, Nicholas. 1971. The Mafia Is Not an Equal Opportunity Employer. New York: McGraw-Hill.

Galliher, John F., and Allynn Walker. 1977. "The puzzle of the social origins of the Marijuana Tax Act of 1937." Social Problems 24:367–376.

Gambino, Richard. 1974. Blood of My Blood: The Dilemma of the Italian American. Garden City, NY: Doubleday.

Gans, Herbert. 1962. "Urbanism and suburbanism as ways of life: A reevaluation of definitions." Pp. 625–648 in Human Behavior and Social Processes, edited by A. M. Rose. Boston: Houghton Mifflin.

Gardner, Howard. 1999. "Who owns intelligence?" The Atlantic Monthly, February:67–76.

Garfinkel, Harold. 1956. "Conditions for successful degradation ceremonies." American Journal of Sociology 61:420–424.

Garfinkel, Irwin, and Sara S. McLanahan. 1986. Single Mothers and Their Children: A New American Dilemma. Washington, DC: Urban Institute Press.

Garreau, Joel. 1991. Edge City: Life on the New Frontier. New York: Doubleday.

Gecas, Viktor. 1989. "The social psychology of self-efficacy." Pp. 291–316 in Annual Review of Sociology, edited by W. R. Scott and J. Blake. Palo Alto, CA: Annual Reviews.

Gerard, Harold B., and Grover C. Mathewson. 1973. "The effects of severity on liking for a group: A replication." Pp. 10–18 in Interpersonal Behavior in Small Groups, edited by R. J. Ofshe. Englewood Cliffs, NJ: Prentice-Hall.

Gerstein, Dean R., and Lawrence W. Green. 1993. Preventing Drug Abuse. Washington, DC: National Academy Press.

Giannangelo, Stephen J. 1996. The Psychopathology of Serial Murder. New York: Praeger.

Gibbs, Jack P. 1966. "Conceptions of deviant behavior: The old and the new." Pacific Sociological Review 9:9–14.

———. 1968. "Crime, punishment and deterrence." Southwestern Social Science Quarterly 48:515–530.

———. 1975. Crime, Punishment, and Deterrence. New York: Elsevier Scientific.

———. 1981. Norms, Deviance, and Social Control: Conceptual Matters. New York: Elsevier.

———. 1994a. "Durkheim's heavy hand in the sociological study of suicide." Pp. 30–74 in Emile Durkheim Le Suicide 100 Years Later, edited by D. Lester. Philadelphia: The Charles Press.

———. 1994b. A Theory About Control. Boulder, CO: Westview Press.

Gibbs, Jack P., and Walter T. Martin. 1964. Status Integration and Suicide. Eugene, OR: University of Oregon Press.

Ginsberg, Irving J., and James R. Greenley. 1978. "Competing theories of marijuana use." Journal of Health and Social Behavior 198:22–34.

Glueck, Sheldon, and Eleanor T. Glueck. 1950. Unraveling Juvenile Delinquency. Cambridge, MA: Harvard University Press.

Goddard, Henry H. 1914. Feeble-Mindedness. New York: Macmillan.

Goffman, Erving. 1963. Stigma: Notes On the Management of Spoiled Identity. Englewood Cliffs, NJ: Prentice-Hall/Spectrum.

Gold, Martin. 1966. "Undetected delinquent behavior." Journal of Research in Crime and Delinquency 3:27–46.

———. 1970. Delinquent Behavior in an American City. Belmont, CA: Brooks/Cole.

Goode, Erich. 1970. The Marijuana Smokers. New York: Basic Books.

———. 1993. Drugs in American Society, 4th Ed. New York: McGraw-Hill.

———. 1996. "The stigma of obesity." Pp. 332–340 in Social Deviance, edited by E. Goode. Boston: Allyn and Bacon.

Goode, Erich, and Nachman Ben-Yehuda. 1994. Moral Panics: The Social Construction of Deviance. Cambridge, MA: Blackwell.

Gorman, Tessa M. 1997. "Back on the chain gang: Why the eighth amendment and the history of slavery proscribe the resurgence of chain gangs." California Law Review 85:441–478.

Gosselin, Chris, and Glenn Wilson. 1980. Sexual Variations: Fetishism, Sadomasochism, and Transvestism. New York: Simon and Schuster.

Gottfredson, Michael R., and Travis Hirschi. 1990. A General Theory of Crime. Stanford, CA: Stanford University Press.

Gould, Stephen Jay. 1995. "Mismeasure by any measure." Pp. 3–13 in The Bell Curve Debate: History, Documents, Opinions, edited by R. Jacoby and N. Glauberman. New York: Random House.

Gouldner, Alvin W. 1970. The Coming Crisis of Western Sociology. New York: Basic Books.

Gove, Walter R. (ed.). 1975. The Labelling of Deviance: Evaluating a Perspective. New York: John Wiley.

———. 1980. The Labelling of Deviance: Evaluating a Perspective, 2nd Ed. Beverly Hills, CA: Sage.

———. 1982a. Deviance and Mental Illness. Beverly Hills, CA: Sage.

———. 1982b. "Labelling theory's explanation of mental illness: An update of recent evidence." Deviant Behavior 3:307–327.

———. 1985. "The effect of age and gender on deviant behavior: A bio-psychological perspective." Pp. 115–144, in Gender and the Life Course, edited by A. Rossi. Chicago: Aldine.

Granfield, Robert, and William Cloud. 1996. "The elephant that no one sees: Natural recovery among middle-class addicts." Journal of Drug Issues 26:45–61.

Grasmick, Harold G., and George J. Bryjak. 1980. "The deterrent effect of perceived severity of punishment." Social Forces 59:469–491.

Grasmick, Harold G., and Robert J. Bursik, Jr. 1990. "Conscience, significant others, and rational choice: Extending the deterrence model." Law and Society Review 24:837–861.

Grasmick, Harold G., and Donald E. Green. 1980. "Legal punishment, social disapproval and internalization as inhibitors of illegal behavior." Journal of Criminal Law and Criminology 71:325–335.

Grasmick, Harold G., and Herman Milligan, Jr. 1976. "Deterrence theory approach to socioeconomic/demographic correlates of crime." Social Science Quarterly 57:608–617.

Grasmick, Harold G., Karyl Kinsey, and John K. Cochran. 1991. "Denomination, religiosity, and compliance with the law: A study of adults." Journal for the Scientific Study of Religion 30:99–107.

Grasmick, Harold G., Robert J. Bursik, Jr., and Bruce J. Arneklev. 1993a. "Reduction in drunk driving as a response to increased threats of shame, embarrassment, and legal sanctions." Criminology 31:41–67.

Grasmick, Harold G., Charles R. Tittle, Robert J. Bursik, Jr., and Bruce J. Arneklev. 1993b. "Testing the core implications of Gottfredson and Hirschi's general theory of crime." Journal of Research in Crime and Delinquency 30:5–29.

Grattet, Ryken, Valerie Jenness, and Theodore R. Curry. 1998. "Homogenization and differentiation of hate crime law in the United States, 1978-1995: Innovation and diffusion in the criminalization of bigotry." American Sociological Review 63: 286–307.

Gray, Louis, and Irving Tallman. 1984. "A satisfaction balance model of decision making and choice behavior." Social Psychology Quarterly 47:146–159.

Greenberg, David F. 1981a. "Delinquency and the age structure of society." Pp. 118–139 in Crime and Capitalism, edited by D. F. Greenberg. Palo Alto, CA: Mayfield.

——. (ed.). 1981b. Crime and Capitalism: Readings in Marxist Criminology. Palo Alto, CA: Mayfield.

——. 1985. "Age, crime, and social explanation." American Journal of Sociology 91:1–21.

Greenwood, Major. 1950. "Accident proneness." Biometrika 37:24–29.

Greenwood, Major, and H. M. Wood. 1919. "A Report on the Incidence of Industrial Accidents Upon Individuals, with Special Reference to Multiple Accidents." Report 4. London: Industrial Fatigue Research Board.

Greenwood, Major, and Udny Yule. 1920. "An inquiry into the nature of frequency distributions of multiple happenings, with particular references to the occurrence of multiple attacks of disease or repeated accidents." Journal of the Royal Statistical Society, Series A, 83:255–279.

Grinnell, George Bird. 1972. The Cheyenne Indians: Their History and Ways of Life. Two Volumes. Lincoln: University of Nebraska Press.

Gross, Llewellyn (ed.). 1959. Symposium on Sociological Theory. White Plains, NY: Row-Peterson.

Grunberger, Richard. 1971. A Social History of the Third Reich. London: Weidenfeld and Nicolson.

Gurr, Ted R. 1981. "Historical trends in violent crime: A critical review of the evidence." Pp. 295–353 in Crime and Justice: An Annual Review of Research, Volume 3, edited by M. Tonry and N. Morris. Chicago: University of Chicago Press.

Gusfield, Joseph R. 1963. Symbolic Crusade. Urbana: University of Illinois Press.

——. 1967. "Moral passage: The symbolic process in public designations of deviance." Social Problems 15:175–188.

Hadaway, C. Kirk, Kirk W. Elifson, and David M. Petersen. 1984. "Religious involvement and drug use among urban adolescents." Journal for the Scientific Study of Religion 12:109–128.

Hagan, John. 1973. "Labelling and deviance: A case study in the 'sociology of the interesting.'" Social Problems 20:447–458.

——. 1989a "A power-control theory of gender and delinquency." Pp. 145–162 in Structural Criminology, edited by J. Hagan. New Brunswick, NJ: Rutgers University Press.

——. 1989b. "The class dynamics of the family and delinquency." Pp. 163–204 in Structural Criminology, edited by J. Hagan. New Brunswick, NJ: Rutgers University Press.

——. 1992. "The poverty of a classless criminology." Criminology 30:1–19.

Hagan, John, and Alberto Palloni. 1990. "The social reproduction of a criminal class in working-class London, circa 1950–1980." American Journal of Sociology 96:265–299.

Hagan, John, A. R. Gillis, and John Simpson. 1985. "The class structure of gender and delinquency: Toward a power-control theory of common delinquent behavior." American Journal of Sociology 90:1151–1178.

Hagan, John, John Simpson, and A. R. Gillis. 1987. "Class in the household: A power-control theory of gender and delinquency." American Journal of Sociology 92:788–816.

Hagedorn, John. 1988. People and Folks: Gangs, Crime and the Underclass in a Rust Belt City. Chicago: Lake View Press.

——. 1990. "How do gangs get organized?" Pp.150–167 in Juvenile Delinquency: A Justice Perspective, edited by R. A. Weisheit and R. G. Culbertsen. Prospect Heights, IL: Waveland Press.

Hall, Calvin S. 1954. A Primer of Freudian Psychology. New York: World Publishing.

——. 1973 [1963]. "Strangers in dreams: An empirical confirmation of the Oedipus complex." Pp. 113–122 in The Experimental Study of Freudian Theories, edited by H. J. Eysenck and G. D. Wilson. London, England: Methuen.

Hall, G. Stanley. 1904. Adolescence: Its Psychology and Its Relation to Physiology, Anthropology, Sociology, Sex, Crime, Religion, and Education. New York: Appleton.

Hall, Jerome. 1947. General Principles of Criminal Law. Indianapolis, IN: Bobbs-Merrill.

Hall, John R. 1987. Gone from the Promised Land: Jonestown in American Cultural History. New Burnswick, NJ: Transaction Publishers.

Hall, Susan. 1972. Gentleman of Leisure: A Year in the Life of a Pimp. New York: New American Library.

Haller, Mark H. 1997. "Bureaucracy and the Mafia: An attractive view." Pp. 52–58 in Understanding Organized Crime in Global Perspective, edited by P. J. Ryan and G. E. Rush. Thousand Oaks, CA: Sage.

Hamm, Mark S. 1993. American Skinheads: The Criminology and Control of Hate Crime. Westport, CT: Praeger.

Hammurabi, King of Babylon. 1904. The Code of Hammurabi, King of Babylon, About 2250 B.C., translated by R. F. Harper. Chicago: University of Chicago Press.

Hanson, Bill, George Beschner, James M. Walters, and Elliott Bovelle. 1985. Life With Heroin: Voices From the Inner City. Lexington, MA: Lexington Books.

Harrison, Maureen, and Steve Gilbert (eds.). 1996. The Rape Reference. San Diego, CA: Excellent Books.

Hart, Stephen D., and Robert D. Hare. 1997. "Psychopathy: Assessment and association with criminal conduct." Pp. 22–35 in Handbook of Antisocial Behavior, edited by D. M. Stoff, J. Breiling, and J. D. Maser. New York: John Wiley.

Harvey, Dale G., and Gerald T. Slatin. 1975. "The relationship between child's SES and teacher expectations: A test of the middle-class bias hypothesis." Social Forces 54:140–159.

Hawkins, Gordon. 1973. "God and the Mafia." Pp. 43–72 in The Crime Establishment, edited by J. E. Conklin. Englewood Cliffs, NJ: Prentice-Hall.

Hazelwood, Robert D., and John W. Douglas. 1980. The Lust Murderer. Federal Bureau of Investigation Law Enforcement Bulletin 49:18–22. Washington, DC: U.S. Government Printing Office.

Healy, William. 1915. The Individual Delinquent. Boston: Little Brown.

Hearst, Patricia Campbell (with Alvin Moscow). 1982. Every Secret Thing. Garden City, NY: Doubleday.

Heiden, Konrad. 1944. Der Fuehrer: Hitler's Rise to Power (trans. by Ralph Manheim). Boston: Houghton Mifflin.

Heimer, Karen, and Ross L. Matsueda. 1994. "Role-taking, role commitment, and delinquency: A theory of differential social control." American Sociological Review 59:365–390.

Hendin, Herbert. 1987. "Youth suicide: A psychosocial perspective." Suicide and Life Threatening Behavior 17:151–165.

Henry, Andrew F., and James F. Short, Jr. 1954. Suicide and Homicide: Some Economic, Sociological, and Psychological Aspects of Aggression. New York: The Free Press.

Henry, Bill, and Terrie E. Moffitt. 1997. "Neuropsychological and neuroimaging studies of juvenile delinquency and adult criminality." Pp. 280–288 in Handbook of Antisocial Behavior, edited by D. M. Stoff, J. Breiling, and J. D. Maser. New York: Wiley and Sons.

Herman, Nancy J. 1997. "Return to sender: Reintegrative stigma-management strategies of ex-psychiatric patients." Pp. 304–323 in Construction of Deviance: Social Power, Context, and Interaction, edited by P. A. Adler and P. Adler. Belmont, CA: Wadsworth.

Herrnstein, Richard J., and Charles Murray. 1994. The Bell Curve: Intelligence and Class Structure in American Life. New York: Free Press Paperbacks.

Hickey, Eric W. 1991. Serial Murderers and Their Victims. Pacific Grove, CA: Brooks/ Cole.

Hindelang, Michael J., Travis Hirschi, and Joseph Weis. 1981. Measuring Delinquency. Beverly Hills, CA: Sage.

Hirschel, J. David, and Ira Hutchinson. 1992. "Female spouse abuse and the police response: The Charlotte, North Carolina experiment." Journal of Criminal Law and Criminology 83:73–119.

Hirschel, J. David, Ira Hutchinson, and Charles Dean. 1992. "The failure of arrest to deter spouse abuse." Journal of Research in Crime and Delinquency 29:7–33.

Hirschi, Travis. 1969. Causes of Delinquency. Berkeley, CA: University of California.

Hirschi, Travis, and Michael Gottfredson. 1983. "Age and the explanation of crime." American Journal of Sociology 89:552–584.

Hirschi, Travis, and Michael J. Hindelang. 1977. "Intelligence and delinquency: A revisionist review." American Sociological Review 42:571–587.

Hobbes, Thomas. 1957 [1651]. Leviathan, edited by M. Oakeshott. Oxford: Basil Blackwell.

Hoebel, E. Adamson. 1960. The Cheyennes: Indians of the Great Plains. New York: Holt, Rinehart and Winston.

——. 1968. The Law of Primitive Man. New York: Atheneum.

Holmes, Ronald M., and J. DeBurger. 1985. "Profiles in terror: The serial murderer." Federal Probation 39:29–34.

——. 1988. Serial Murder. Newbury Park, CA: Sage.

Holmes, Ronald M., and Stephen T. Holmes. 1998. Serial Murder, 2nd Ed. Thousand Oaks, CA: Sage.

Homans, George C. 1961. Social Behavior: Its Elementary Forms. New York: Harcourt, Brace, and World.

Hooker, Evelyn. 1957. "The adjustment of the male overt homosexual." Journal of Projective Techniques 21:18–31.

Hooton, Ernest A. 1939. The American Criminal. Cambridge, MA: Harvard University Press.

Horney, Julie, D. Wayne Osgood, and Ineke H. Marshall. 1995. "Criminal careers in the short-term: Intra-individual variability in crime and its relation to local life circumstances." American Sociological Review 60:655–673.

Horowitz, Ruth. 1995. Teen Mothers: Citizens or Dependents? Chicago: University of Chicago Press.

Horwitz, Allan V. 1990. The Logic of Social Control. New York: Plenum Press.

Hostetler, John A. 1980. Amish Society. Baltimore: Johns Hopkins University Press.

——. 1989. Amish Roots: A Treasury of History, Wisdom, and Lore. Baltimore: Johns Hopkins University Press.

Howitt, Dennis. 1995. Pedophiles and Sexual Offenses Against Children. New York: Wiley.

Hoyert, Donna L., Kenneth D. Kochanek, and Sherry Murphy. 1997. Death: Final Data for 1997. National Center for Health Statistics. National Vita Statistics Reports, Vol. 47, number 19. Rockville, MD: Public Health Service.

Huba, G. J., J. A. Wingard, and P. M. Bentler. 1981. "A comparison of two latent causal variable models for adolescent drug use." Journal of Personality and Social Psychology 40:180–193.

Huesman, L. Rowell, Jessica F. Moise, and Cheryl-Lynn Podolski. 1997. "The effects of media violence on the development of anti-social behavior." Pp. 171–180 in Handbook of Antisocial Behavior, edited by D. M. Stoff, J. Breiling, and J. D. Maser. New York: John Wiley.

Huff, C. Ronald, (ed.). 1990. Gangs in America. Newbury Park, CA: Sage.

Hughes, Steven L., and Robert A. Neimeyer. 1990. "A cognitive model of suicidal behavior." Pp. 1–28 in Current Concepts of Suicide, edited by D. Lester. Philadelphia: The Charles Press.

Huizinga, David, and Delbert Elliott. 1990. "The role of arrest in domestic assault: The Omaha experiment." Criminology 28:183–206.

Humphrey, Derek. 1991. Final Exit. New York: Carol Press.

Humphreys, Laud. 1970. Tearoom Trade: Impersonal Sex in Public Places. New York: Aldine.

Hyman, Irwin A. 1984. Testimony before the Subcommittee of Elementary, Secondary, and Vocational Education of the Committee on Education and Labor, U.S. House of Representatives.

Ianni, Francis A. J., and Elizabeth Reuss-Ianni. 1972. A Family Business: Kinship and Social Control in Organized Crime. New York: New American Library.

Inciardi, James A., Dorothy Lockwood, and Anne E. Pottieger. 1993. Women and Crack Cocaine. New York: Macmillan.

Jacobs, Bruce A. 1993. "Undercover deception clues: A case of restrictive deterrence." Criminology 31:281–299.

——. 1996. "Crack dealers and restrictive deterrence: Identifying narcs." Criminology 34:409–431.

Jacobs, Jerry. 1971. Adolescent Suicide. New York: Wiley.

Jacoby, Joseph E. 1994. Classics of Criminology, 2nd Ed. Prospect Heights, IL: Waveland Press.

Jacoby, Russell, and Naomi Glauberman (eds.). 1995. The Bell Curve Debate: History, Documents, Opinions. New York: Random House.

Jang, Sung Joon, and Terence P. Thornberry. 1998. "Self-esteem, delinquent peers, and delinquency: A test of the self-enhancement thesis." American Sociological Review 63:586–598.

Jankowski, Martin Sanchez. 1991. Islands in the Street: Gangs and American Urban Society. Berkeley: University of California Press.

Janus, Samuel S., and Cynthia L. Janus. 1993. The Janus Report on Sexual Behavior. New York: John Wiley and Sons.

Jarjoura, G. Roger. 1993. "Does dropping out of school enhance delinquent involvement? Results from a large scale national probability sample." Criminology 31:149–171.

Jencks, Christopher, et al. 1972. Inequality: A Reassessment of the Effect of Family and Schooling in America. New York: Basic Books.

——. 1979. Who Gets Ahead? The Determinants of Economic Success in America. New York: Basic Books.

Jenkins, Phillip. 1988. "Serial murder in England, 1940–1985." Journal of Criminal Justice 16:1–15.

Jenness, Valerie. 1993. Making It Work: The Prostitutes' Rights Movement in Perspective. New York: Aldine De Gruyter.

——. 1995. "Social movement growth, domain expansion, and framing processes: The gay/lesbian movement and violence against gays and lesbians as a social problem." Social Problems 42:145–170.

Jenness, Valerie, and Kendal Broad. 1997. Hate Crimes: New Social Movements and the Politics of Violence. New York: Aldine De Gruyter.

Jensen, Gary F., and Kevin Thompson. 1990. "What's class got to do with it? A further examination of power-control theory." American Journal of Sociology 95:1009–1023.

Jensen, Gordon D., and Luh Ketut Suryani. 1992. The Balinese People: A Reinvestigation of Character. New York: Oxford University Press.

Jesilow, Paul, Henry Pontell, and Gilbert Geis. 1993. Prescription for Profit: How Doctors Defraud Medicaid. Berkeley: University of California Press.

Jessor, Richard, and Shirley L. Jessor. 1977. Problem Behavior and Psychosocial Development: A Longitudinal Study of Youth. New York: Academic Press.

Jessor, Richard, John Donovan, and Francis Costa. 1991. Beyond Adolescence: Problem Behavior and Young Adult Development. New York: Cambridge University Press.

Jobes, David A., Alan L. Berman, and Arnold R. Josselson. 1987. "Improving the validity and reliability of medical-legal certifications of suicide." Suicide and Life Threatening Behavior 17:310–325.

Johnson, Bruce D. 1973. Marijuana Users and Drug Subcultures. New York: Wiley-Interscience.

——. 1978. "Once an addict, seldom an addict." Contemporary Drug Problems 7:35–53.

Johnston, Lloyd, Patrick O'Malley, and Jerald Bachman. 1991. Monitoring the Future, 1990. Ann Arbor, MI: Institute for Social Research.

——. 1998. National Survey Results on Drug Use. Monitoring the Future Study, 1975–1997. Rockville, MD: National Institute on Drug Abuse.

Johnstone, John W. C. 1981. "Youth gangs and black suburbs." Pacific Sociological Review 24:355–373.

Jones, Robert Alun. 1986. Emile Durkheim: An Introduction to Four Major Works. Beverly Hills, CA: Sage.

Jonnes, Jill. 1996. Hep-Cats, Narcs, and Pipe Dreams. New York: Scribner.

Jungermann, Helmut. 1983. "The two camps on rationality." Pp. 63–86 in Decision Making Under Uncertainty: Cognitive Decision Research, Social Interaction, Development, and Epistemology, edited by R. W. Scholz. Amsterdam: North-Holland.

Kahneman, Daniel, and Amos Tversky. 1973. "On the psychology of prediction." Psychological Review 80:237–251.

Kahneman, Daniel, Paul Slovic, and Amos Tversky. 1982. Judgment Under Uncertainty: Heuristics and Biases. Cambridge: Cambridge University Press.

Kallick, M., D. Suits, T. Dielman, and J. Hybels. 1976. Survey of American Gambling Attitudes and Behavior. Gambling in America, Appendix 2. Washington, DC: U.S. Government Printing Office.

Kamin, Leon J. 1995. "Lies, damned lies, and statistics." Pp. 81–105 in *The Bell Curve* Debate: History, Documents, Opinions, edited by R. Jacoby and N. Glauberman. New York: Random House.

Kandel, Denise B. 1978. Longitudinal Research on Drug Use. New York: John Wiley.

——. 1980. "Drug and drinking behavior among youth." Annual Review of Sociology 6:235–285.

Kandel, Denise B., Ronald C. Kessler, and Rebecca Z. Margulies. 1978. "Antecedents of adolescent initiation into states of drug use: A developmental analysis." Pp. 73–99 in Longitudinal Research on Drug Use, edited by D. Kandel. Washington, DC: Hemisphere.

Kanter, Rosabeth Moss. 1973. Commitment and Community: Communes and Utopias in Sociological Perspective. Cambridge, MA: Harvard University Press.

Kaplan, David E., and Alec Dubro. 1986. Yakuza: The Explosive Account of Japan's Criminal Underworld. Reading, MA: Addison-Wesley.

Kaplan, Howard B. 1975. Self-Attitudes and Deviant Behavior. Pacific Palisades, CA: Goodyear.

——. 1980. Deviant Behavior in Defense of Self. New York: Academic Press.

——. 1995. "Drugs, crime, and other deviant adaptations." Pp. 3–46 in Drugs, Crime and Other Deviant Adaptations: Longitudinal Studies, edited by H. B. Kaplan. New York: Plenum.

Kaplan, Howard B., Robert J. Johnson, and Carol A. Bailey. 1987. "Deviant peers and deviant behavior: Further elaboration of a model." Social Psychology Quarterly 50:277–284.

Kaplan, Howard B., Steven S. Martin, and Cynthia A. Robbins. 1982. "Application of a general theory of deviant behavior: Self-derogation and adolescent drug use." Journal of Health and Social Behavior 23:274–294.

Kaplan, Howard B., Steven S. Martin, Robert J. Johnson, and Cynthia A. Robbins. 1986. "Escalation of marijuana use: Application of a general theory of deviant behavior." Journal of Health and Social Behavior 27:44–61.

Katz, Jack. 1988. Seductions of Crime: Moral and Sensual Attractions in Doing Evil. New York: Basic Books.

Keane, Carl, Paul S. Maxim, and James J. Teevan. 1993. "Drinking and driving, self-control, and gender: Testing a general theory of crime." Journal of Research in Crime and Delinquency 30:30–46.

Kelly, Robert J. 1997. "Trapped in the folds of disclosure." Pp. 39–51 in Understanding Organized Crime in Global Perspective, edited by P. A. Ryan and G. E. Rush. Thousand Oaks, CA: Sage.

Kempf, Kimberly. 1993. "The empirical status of Hirschi's control theory." Pp. 143–185 in Advances in Criminological Theory, Vol. 4, edited by W. S. Laufer and F. Adler. New Brunswick, NJ: Transaction.

Kephart, William M. 1976. Extraordinary Groups: An Examination of Unconventional Life-Styles. New York: St. Martin's Press.

Kephart, William M., and William W. Zellner. 1994. Extraordinary Groups: An Examination of Unconventional Life-Styles, 5th Ed. New York: St. Martin's Press.

Kercher, Kyle. 1987. "Explaining the relationship between age and crime: The biological vs sociological model." Presented at the annual meeting of the American Society of Criminology, Montreal.

Kiesler, Charles A., and Sara B. Kiesler. 1969. Conformity. Reading, MA: Addison-Wesley.

Kiger, Kenna. 1990. "The darker figure of crime: The serial murder enigma." Pp. 35–52 in Serial Murder: An Elusive Phenomenon, edited by S. A. Egger. New York: Praeger.

King, Harry, and William Chambliss. 1972. Box Man: A Professional Thief's Journal. New York: Harper and Row.

Kinsey, Alfred C., Wardell B. Pomeroy, and Clyde E. Martin. 1948. Sexual Behavior in the Human Male. Philadelphia: Saunders.

Kitagawa, Evelyn M., and Philip M. Hauser. 1973. Differential Mortality in the United States: A Study in Socioeconomic Epidemiology. Cambridge, MA: Harvard University.

Kitsuse, John I. 1962. "Societal reactions to deviant behavior: Problems of theory and method." Social Problems 9:247–257.

Kitzman, Harriet, et al. 1997. "Effect of prenatal and infancy home visitation by nurses on pregnancy outcomes, childhood injuries, and repeated child-bearing: A randomized controlled trial." Journal of the American Medical Association 278:644–652.

Kleck, Gary. 1982. "On the use of self-report data to determine the class distribution of criminal and delinquent behavior." American Sociological Review 47:427–433.

Klein, George S. 1976. Psychoanalytic Theory: An Exploration of Essentials. New York: International Universities Press.

Klein, Malcolm W. 1971. Street Gangs and Street Workers. Englewood Cliffs, NJ: Prentice-Hall.

——. 1995. The American Street Gang. New York: Oxford University Press.

Klein, Malcolm W., and Lois Y. Crawford. 1967. "Groups, gangs and cohesiveness." Journal of Research in Crime and Delinquency 4:63–75.

Klein, Malcolm W., and Cheryl L. Maxson. 1989. "Street gang violence." Pp. 198–234 in Violent Crime and Violent Criminals, edited by N. A. Weiner and M. E. Wolfgang. Newbury Park, CA: Sage.

Kleinknecht, William. 1996. The New Ethnic Mobs: The Changing Face of Organized Crime in America. New York: Free Press.

Kline, Paul. 1981. Fact and Fantasy in Freudian Theory, 2nd Ed. New York: Methuen.

Klockars, Carl B. 1974. The Professional Fence. New York: The Free Press.

——. 1979. "The contemporary crises of Marxist criminology." Criminology 16:477–491.

Kluegel, James R., and Eliot R. Smith. 1986. Beliefs about Inequality: American Views of What Is and What Ought to Be. New York: Aldine De Gruyter.

Knapp Commission. 1973. The Knapp Commission Report on Police Corruption. New York: George Brasiller.

Knox, George W. 1994. An Introduction to Gangs. Bristol, IN: Wyndham Hall Press.

Knutson, Jeanne N. 1981. "Social and pyschodynamic pressures toward a negative identity: The case of an American revolutionary terrorist." Pp. 105–150 in Behavioral and Quantitative Perspectives on Terrorism, edited by Y. Alexander and J. M. Gleason. New York: Pergamon.

Koehler, Jonathan. 1996. "The base rate fallacy reconsidered: Descriptive, normative, and methodological challenges." Behavioral and Brain Sciences 19:1–53.

Kohlberg, Lawrence. 1963. "The development of children's orientations toward a moral order: I. Sequence in the development of moral thought." Vita Humana 6:11–33.

——. 1984. Essays in Moral Development. Volume II: The Psychology of Moral Development. San Francisco, CA: Harper and Row.

Kornhauser, Ruth Rosner. 1978. Social Sources of Delinquency: An Appraisal of Analytic Models. Chicago: University of Chicago Press.

Kressel, Neil J. 1996. Mass Hate: The Global Rise of Genocide and Terror. New York: Plenum.

Krivo, Lauren J., and Ruth D. Peterson. 1996. "Extremely disadvantaged neighborhoods and urban crime." Social Forces 75:619–650.

Krohn, Marvin D., Lonn Lanza-Kaduce, and Ronald L. Akers. 1984. "Community context and theories of deviant behavior: An examination of social learning and social bond theories." The Sociological Quarterly 25:353–371.

La Barre, Weston. 1969. They Shall Take Up Serpents: Psychology of the Southern Snake-Handling Cult. New York: Schocken.

Labovitz, Sanford, and Robert Hagedorn. 1971. "An analysis of suicide rates among occupational categories." Sociological Inquiry 41:68–72.

LaFave, Wayne R. 1965. Arrest: The Decision to Take a Suspect Into Custody. Chicago: Little Brown.

Lang, Alan R. 1983. "Addictive personality: A viable construct?" Pp. 157–235 in Commonalities in Substance Abuse and Habitual Behavior, edited by P. K. Levison, D. R. Gerstein, and D. R. Maloff. Lexington, MA: DC Heath.

Langbein, Laura I., and Allan J. Lichtman. 1978. Ecological Inferences. Beverly Hills, CA: Sage.

Langevin, R., D. Paitich, R. Freeman, K. Mann, and L. Hardy. 1978. "Personality characteristics and sexual anomalies in males." Canadian Journal of Behavioural Science 10:222–238.

Lanza-Kaduce, Lonn. 1988. "Perceptual deterrence and drinking and driving among college students." Criminology 26:321–341.

Larzelere, Robert E., and Gerald E. Patterson. 1990. "Parental management: Mediator of the effect of socioeconomic status on early delinquency." Criminology 28:301–323.

Latane, Bibb, and Sharon Wolf. 1981. "The social impact of majorities and minorities." Psychological Review 88:438–453.

Lattimore, Pamela, and Ann Witte. 1986. "Models of decision making under uncertainty: The criminal choice." Pp. 129–155 in The Reasoning Criminal: Rational Choice Perspectives on Offending, edited by D. B. Cornish and R. V. Clarke. New York: Springer-Verlag.

Laub, John, and Robert Sampson. 1988. "Unraveling families and delinquency: A reanalysis of the Gluecks' data." Criminology 26:355–380.

Lauer, Robert H. 1974. "Rate of change and stress: A test of the 'future shock' thesis." Social Forces 52:510–516.

Laumann, Edward O., John H. Gagnon, Robert T. Michael, and Stuart Michaels. 1994. The Social Organization of Sexuality: Sexual Practices in the United States. Chicago: The University of Chicago Press.

Layton, Deborah. 1998. Seductive Poison: A Jonestown Survivor's Story of Life and Death in the People's Temple. New York: Anchor Doubleday.

Layton, Lyndsey. 1999. "The grad who got religion." Washington Post, June 22, 1999.

Leacock, Eleanor (ed.). 1971. The Culture of Poverty: A Critique. New York: Simon and Schuster.

Leibman, Faith H. 1989. "Serial murderers." Federal Probation 53:41–45.

Lemert, Edwin M. 1951. Social Pathology. New York: McGraw-Hill.

——. 1967. Human Deviance, Social Problems, and Social Control. Englewood Cliffs, NJ: Prentice-Hall.

Leo, Richard A. 1995. "Ethnography, and the need for an evidentiary privilege for academic researchers." The American Sociologist 26:113–134.

Lester, David. 1983. Why People Kill Themselves, 2nd Ed. Springfield, IL: Charles C. Thomas Publishers.

——. 1987. Suicide as a Learned Behavior. Springfield, IL: Charles C. Thomas Publishers.

——. 1992. Why People Kill Themselves, 3rd Ed. Springfield, IL: Charles C. Thomas Publishers.

——. 1995. Serial Killers: The Insatiable Passion. Philadelphia: The Charles Press.

——. 1996. Patterns of Suicide and Homicide in the World. Nova Science Publishers: New York.

——. 1997a. Making Sense of Suicide. Philadelphia: Charles Publishers.

——. 1997b. "Suicide in an international perspective." Suicide and Life Threatening Behavior 27:104–111.

Levin, Jack, and James Alan Fox. 1985. Mass Murder: America's Growing Menace. New York: Plenum Press.

Levine, Murray, and Barbara Benedict Bunker. 1975. Mutual Criticism. Syracuse, NY: Syracuse University Press.

Levitin, Teresa E. 1975. "Deviants as active participants in the labeling process: The visibly handicapped." Social Problems 22:548–557.

Lewis, Oscar. 1961. The Children of Sanchez: Autobiography of a Mexican Family. New York: Random House.

——. 1966. "The culture of poverty." Scientific American 215:19–25.

Leyton, Elliott. 1986. Compulsive Killers: The Story of Modern Multiple Murders. New York: New York University Press.

Liebow, Elliot. 1967. Tally's Corner: A Study of Negro Streetcorner Men. Boston: Little Brown.

Lindesmith, Alfred R. 1947. Opiate Addiction. Bloomington, IN: Principia Press.

——. 1965. The Addict and the Law. Bloomington: Indiana University Press.

——. 1968. Addiction and Opiates. Chicago: Aldine.

Link, Bruce G. 1987. "Understanding labeling effects in the area of mental disorders: An assessment of the effects of expectations of rejection." American Sociological Review 52:96–112.

Link, Bruce G., Francis T. Cullen, Elmer Struening, Patrick Shrout, and Bruce P. Dohrenwood. 1989. "A modified labeling theory approach to mental disorders: An empirical assessment." American Sociological Review 54:400–423.

Lipset, Seymour, and Reinhard Bendix. 1959. Social Mobility in Industrial Society. Berkeley: University of California Press.

Liska, Allen E. 1994. "Modeling the conflict perspective of social control." Pp. 53–71 in Inequality, Crime, and Social Control, edited by G. S. Bridges and M. A. Myers. Boulder, CO: Westview.

Llewellyn, Karl N., and E. Adamson Hoebel. 1941. The Cheyenne Way. Norman: University of Oklahoma Press.

Lodhi, Abdul, and Charles Tilly. 1973. "Urbanization, crime, and collective violence in 19th century France." American Journal of Sociology 79:296–318.

Loeber, Rolf, and Magda Stouthamer-Loeber. 1986. "Family factors as correlates and predictors of juvenile conduct problems and delinquency." Pp. 29–151 in Crime and Justice, Vol. 7, edited by M. Tonry and N. Morris. Chicago: University of Chicago Press.

Loeber, Rolf, Magda Stouthamer-Loeber, Welmoet Van Kammen, and David P. Farrington. 1991. "Initiation, escalation and desistance in juvenile offending and their correlates." Journal of Criminal Law and Criminology 82:36–82.

Lofland, John. 1967. Doomsday Cult: A Study of Conversion, Proselytization, and Maintenance of Faith. Englewood Cliffs, NJ: Prentice-Hall.

——. 1969. Deviance and Identity. Englewood Cliffs, NJ: Prentice-Hall.

Lofland, John, and Rodney Stark. 1965. "Becoming a world-saver: A theory of conversion to a deviant perspective." American Sociological Review 30:862–874.

Loftin, Colin, and Robert H. Hill. 1974. "Regional subculture and homicide: An examination of the Gastil-Hackney thesis." American Sociological Review 39:714–724.

Logan, Charles H. 1972. "General deterrent effects of imprisonment." Social Forces 51:64–73.

Lombroso, Cesare. 1876. The Criminal Man (L'uomo Delinquente). First Edition. Milan: Hoepli. Second Edition (1878) through Fifth Edition (1896) Turin: Bocca.

Longshore, Douglas. 1998. "Self-control and criminal opportunity: A prospective test of the general theory of crime." Social Problems 45:102–113.

Longshore, Douglas, Susan Turner, and Judith A. Stein. 1996. "Self-control in a criminal sample: An examination of construct validity." Criminology 34:209–238.

Lorber, Judith. 1994. Paradoxes of Gender. New Haven, CT: Yale University Press.

Luckenbill, David F. 1977. "Criminal homicide as a situated transaction." Social Problems 25:176–186.

Lunde, Donald T. 1976. Murder and Madness. Stanford, CA: Stanford Alumni Association.

Lutzker, John R. 1998. Handbook of Child Abuse Research and Treatment. New York: Plenum.

Lynam, Donald R., Terrie Moffitt, and Madga Stouthamer-Loeber. 1993. "Explaining the relationship between IQ and delinquency: Class, race, test motivation, school failure, or self-control?" Journal of Abnormal Psychology 102:187–196.

Lyon, Don, and Paul Slovic. 1975. "Dominance of accuracy information and neglect of base rates in probability estimation." Acta Psychologica 40:287–298.

Maas, Peter. 1968. The Valachi Papers. New York: Putnam.

——. 1997. Underboss: Sammy The Bull Gravano's Story of Life in The Mafia. New York: Harper-Collins.

MacAndrew, Craig, and Robert B. Edgerton. 1969. Drunken Comportment: A Social Explanation. Chicago: Aldine.

Maguire, Kathleen, and Ann L. Pastore. 1995. Sourcebook of Criminal Justice Statistics, 1994. U.S. Department of Justice, Bureau of Justice Statistics. Washington, DC: U.S. Government Printing Office.

Maher, Lisa. 1996. "Hidden in the light: Occupational norms among crack-using street-level sex workers." Journal of Drug Issues 26:143–176.

Males, Mike. 1994. "California: Suicide decline, 1970–1990." Suicide and Life Threatening Behavior 24:24–33.

Malinosky-Rummell, Robin, and David J. Hansen. 1993. "Long-term consequences of childhood physical abuse." Psychological Bulletin 114:68–79.

Malinowski, Bronislaw. 1926. Crime and Custom in Savage Society. London: Routledge and Kegan Paul.

——. 1985 [1927]. Sex and Repression in Savage Society. Chicago: University of Chicago Press.

Maltz, Michael D., and Marianne W. Zawitz. 1998. "Displaying violent crime trends using estimates from the National Crime Victimization Survey." Bureau of Justice Statistics, Technical Report, NCJ 167881, U.S. Department of Justice, Washington, DC.

Mankoff, Milton. 1971. "Societal reaction and career deviance: A critical analysis." The Sociological Quarterly 12:204–218.

Maris, Ronald W. 1969. Social Forces in Urban Suicide. Homewood, IL: Dorsey Press.

——. 1981. Pathways to Suicide. Baltimore: Johns Hopkins University Press.

——. 1997. "Social suicide." Suicide and Life Threatening Behavior 27:41–49.

Markle, Gerald E., and Ronald J. Troyer. 1979. "Smoke gets in your eyes: Cigarette smoking as deviant behavior." Social Problems 26:611–625.

Marx, Gary T. 1981. "Ironies of social control: Authorities as contributors to deviance through escalation, nonenforcement, and covert facilitation." Social Problems 28:221–246.

Matsueda, Ross. 1988. "The current state of differential association theory." Crime and Delinquency 34:277–306.

——. 1992. "Reflected appraisals, parental labeling, and delinquency: Specifying a symbolic interactionist theory." American Journal of Sociology 97:1577–1611.

Matsueda, Ross, and Karen Heimer. 1987. "Race, family structure, and delinquency: A test of differential association and social control theories." American Sociological Review 52:826–840.

——. 1997. "A symbolic interactionist theory of role-transitions, role-commitments, and delinquency." Pp. 163–213 in Developmental Theories of Crime and Delinquency, edited by T. P. Thornberry. New Brunswick, NJ: Transaction.

Matza, David. 1964. Delinquency and Drift. New York: John Wiley.

Mauss, Armand. 1975. Social Problems as Social Movements. New York: J. B. Lippincott.

——. 1994. The Angel and the Beehive: The Mormon Struggle for Assimilation. Urbana: University of Illinois Press.

Maxfield, Michael G., and Cathy S. Widom. 1996. "The cycle of violence revisited 6 years later." Archives of Pediatrics and Adolescent Medicine 150:390–395.

Maxson, Cheryl L. 1990. "Street gang violence: twice as great or half as great." Pp. 71–100 in Gangs in America, edited by C. R. Huff. Newbury Park, CA: Sage.

——. 1995. "Research in brief: Street gangs and drug sales in two suburban cities." Pp. 228–235 in The Modern Gang Reader, edited by M. W. Klein and C. L. Maxon. Los Angeles: Roxbury Publishing.

Mayhew, Bruce H., and Roger L. Levinger. 1976. "Size and density of interaction in human aggregates." American Journal of Sociology 82:86–110.

McAuliffe, William E., and Robert A. Gordon. 1974. "A test of Lindesmith's theory of addiction: The frequency of euphoria among long-term addicts." American Journal of Sociology 79:795–840.

McCaghy, Charles H. 1976. Deviant Behavior: Crime, Conflict, and Interest Groups. New York: Macmillan.

McCall, Nathan. 1994. Makes Me Wanna Holler: A Young Black Man in America. New York: Random House.

McCarthy, John D., and Dean R. Hoge. 1984. "The dynamics of self-esteem and delinquency." American Journal of Sociology 90:396–410.

McCleary, Richard, Barbara C. Nienstadt, and James M. Erven. 1982. "Uniform Crime Reports as organizational outcomes: Three time series experiments." Social Problems 29:361–372.

McClosky, Herbert, and John Zaller. 1984. The American Ethos: Public Attitudes toward Capitalism and Democracy. Cambridge, MA: Harvard University Press.

McCord, Joan. 1982. "A longitudinal view of the relationship between parental absence and crime." Pp. 113–128 in Abnormal Offenders, Delinquency, and the Criminal Justice System, edited by J. Gunn and D. P. Farrington. Chichester: Wiley.

——. 1991. "Family relationships, juvenile delinquency, and adult criminality." Criminology 29:397–417.

McCord, William, Joan McCord, and A. Howard. 1961. "Familial correlates of aggression in nondelinquent male children." Journal of Abnormal and Social Psychology 1:79–93.

McHugh, Peter. 1966. "Social disintegration as a requisite of resocialization." Social Forces 44:355–363.

Mead, George Herbert. 1934. Mind, Self, and Society. Chicago: University of Chicago Press.

Meerloo, Joost A. M. 1962. Suicide and Mass Suicide. New York: Grune and Stratton.

Megargee, Edwin I., and Martin J. Bohn. 1979. Classifying Criminal Offenders: A New System Based on the MMPI. Beverly Hills, CA: Sage.

Meier, Robert F. (Ed). 1985. Theoretical Methods in Criminology. Beverly Hills, CA: Sage.

Meier, Robert F., and Gilbert Geis. 1997. Victimless Crimes? Prostitution, Drugs, Homosexuality, Abortion. Los Angeles: Roxbury Publishing.

Meier, Robert, F., and Weldon T. Johnson. 1977. "Deterrence as social control: The legal and extralegal production of conformity." American Sociological Review 42:292–304.

Meier, Steven E., Thomas A. Brigham, David A. Ward, Faith Meyers, and Lovenia Warren. 1996. "Effects of blood alcohol concentrations on negative punishment: Implications for decision making." Journal of Studies on Alcohol 57:85–96.

Menard, Scott, and Barbara J. Morse. 1984. "A structuralist critique of the IQ-delinquency hypothesis: Theory and evidence." American Journal of Sociology 89:1347–1378.

——. 1986. "IQ and delinquency: A response to Harry and Minor." American Journal of Sociology 91:962–968.

Mercandante, Linda A. 1990. Gender, Doctrine, and God: The Shakers and Contemporary Theology. Nashville, TN: Abingdon Press.

Merlo, Alida V. 1995. "Female criminality in the 1990s." Pp. 119–134 in Women, Law, and Social Control, edited by A. V. Merlo and J. M. Pollock. Boston: Allyn and Bacon.

Merton, Robert K. 1938. "Social structure and anomie." American Sociological Review 3:672–682.

——. 1949. "Social structure and anomie: Revisions and extensions." Pp. 226–257 in The Family: Its Function and Destiny, edited by R. Anshen. New York: Harper and Row.

——. 1956. "The socio-cultural environment and anomie." Pp. 24–50 in New Perspectives for Research on Juvenile Delinquency, edited by H. L. Witmer and K. Kotinsky. Washington, DC: U.S. Government Printing Office.

——. 1957. "Social structure and anomie." Pp. 131–160 in Social Theory and Social Structure. Glencoe, IL: The Free Press.

——. 1968. "Social structure and anomie." Pp. 185–214 in Social Theory and Social Structure. Glencoe, IL: The Free Press.

Messerschmidt, James W. 1986. Capitalism, Patriarchy, and Crime. Totowa, NJ: Rowman and Littlefield.

Messner, Steven F., and Richard Rosenfeld. 1997 [1994]. Crime and the American Dream, 2nd Ed. Belmont, CA: Wadsworth.

Messner, Steven F., Marvin D. Krohn, and Allen E. Liska (eds.). 1989. Theoretical Integration in the Study of Deviance and Crime: Problems and Prospects. Albany: State University of New York Press.

Miethe, Terance D., and Robert F. Meier. 1994. Crime and Its Social Context. Albany: State University of New York Press.

Milgram, Stanley. 1974. Obedience to Authority: An Experimental View. New York: Harper and Row.

Miller, Eleanor M. 1986. Street Women. Philadelphia: Temple University Press.

Miller, Leonard, Dorothy Rice, Thomas Novotny, Xiulan Zhang, and Wendy Max. 1998. Health Care Costs of Smoking. Public Health Reports. Office of Smoking and Health. Centers for Disease Control and Prevention. Atlanta, GA.

Miller, Walter B. 1958. "Lower class culture as a generating milieu of gang delinquency." Journal of Social Issues 14:5–19.

——. 1975. Violence by Youth Gangs and Youth Gangs as a Crime Problem in Major American Cities. National Institute for Juvenile Justice and Delinquency Prevention, U.S. Department of Justice. Washington, DC: U.S. Government Printing Office.

——. 1980. "Gangs, groups, and serious youth crime." Pp. 115–138 in Critical Issues in Juvenile Delinquency, edited by D. Schicor and D. Kelly. Lexington, MA: Lexington Books.

——. 1982. "Crimes by youth gangs and groups in the United States." A report prepared for the National Institute of Juvenile Justice and Delinquency Prevention of the U.S. Department of Justice, Washington, DC.

Minor, W. William. 1980. "The neutralization of criminal offense." Criminology 18:103–120.

——. 1981. "Techniques of neutralization: A reconceptualization and empirical examination." Journal of Research in Crime and Delinquency 18:295–318.

Minor, W. William, and Joseph Harry. 1982. "Deterrent and experiential effects in perceptual deterrence research: A replication and extension." Journal of Research in Crime and Delinquency 19:190–203.

Moffitt, Terrie E. 1990. "The neuropsychology of delinquency: A critical review of theory and research." Pp. 99–169 in Crime and Justice, Volume 12, edited by N. Morris and M. Tonry. Chicago: University of Chicago Press.

——. 1993. "Adolescence-limited and life-course-persistent antisocial behavior: A developmental taxonomy." Psychological Review 100:674–701.

——. 1997. "Adolescence-limited and life-course-persistent offending: A complementary pair of developmental theories." Pp. 11–54 in Developmental Theories of Crime and Delinquency, edited by T. P. Thornberry. New Brunswick, NJ: Transaction Publishers.

Moffitt, Terrie E., Donald R. Lynam, and Phil A. Silva. 1994. "Neuropsychological tests predicting persistent male delinquency." Criminology 32:277–300.

Moffitt, Terrie E., Avshalom Caspi, Phil A. Silva, and Magda Stouthamer-Loeber. 1995. "Individual differences in personality and intelligence are linked to crime: Cross-context evidence from nations, neighborhoods, genders, races and age-cohorts." Current Perspectives on Aging and the Life Cycle: 3:1–34.

Moffitt, Terrie E., et al. 1998. "Whole blood serotonin relates to violence in an epidemological study." Biological Psychiatry 43:446–457.

Moore, Joan W. 1978. Homeboys: Gangs, Drugs, and Prison in the Barrios of Los Angeles. Philadelphia: Temple University Press.

——. 1991. Going Down to the Barrio: Homeboys and Homegirls in Change. Philadelphia: Temple University Press.

Moore, Mark H., and Steward Wakeling. 1997. "Juvenile justice: Shoring up the foundation." Pp. 253–301 in Crime and Justice: An Annual Review, Vol. 22, edited by M. Tonry. Chicago: University of Chicago Press.

Morash, Merry. 1983. "Gangs, groups, and delinquency." British Journal of Criminology 23:309–335.

Morganthau, Tom. 1997a. "The war over weed." Newsweek 130: February 3, 20–22.

——. 1997b. "The Next Level." Newsweek 130: April 7.

Moscicki, Eve K. 1995. "Epidemiology of suicidal behavior." Suicide and Life Threatening Behavior 25:22–35.

Mullen, Robert. 1966. The Latter-Day Saints: The Mormons Yesterday and Today. Garden City, NY: Doubleday.

Murphy, Robert F. 1980. The Dialectics of Social Life: Alarms and Excursions in Anthropological Theory. New York: Columbia University Press.

Nagel, Ilene H., and John Hagan. 1983. "Gender and crime: Offense patterns and criminal court sanctions." Pp. 91–144 in Crime and Justice: An Annual Review of Research, Vol. 4, edited by M. Tonry and N. Morris. Chicago: University of Chicago Press.

Nagin, Daniel S. 1998. "Criminal deterrence research at the outset of the twenty-first century." Pp. 1–42 in Crime and Justice: A Review of Research, edited by M. Tonry and N. Morris. Chicago: University of Chicago Press.

Nagin, Daniel S., and David P. Farrington. 1992a. "The stability of criminal potential from childhood to adulthood." Criminology 30:235–260.

——. 1992b. "The onset and persistence of offending." Criminology 30:501–523.

Nagin, Daniel S., and Raymond Paternoster. 1991a. "On the relationship of past to future participation in delinquency." Criminology 29:163–189.

——. 1991b. "The preventive effects of the perceived risk of arrest: Testing an expanded conception of deterrence." Criminology 29:561–588.

——. 1994. "Personal capital and social control: The deterrence implications of a theory of individual differences in criminal offending." Criminology 32:581–606.

Nash, Roy. 1976. Teacher Expectations and Pupil Learning. London: Routledge and Kegan Paul.

Nathan, Debbie, and Michael Snendeker. 1995. Satan's Silence. New York: Basic Books.

National Center for Health Statistics. 1995. Advance Data from Vital and Health Statistics, No. 231. Atlanta: Centers for Disease Control and Prevention.

National Highway Traffic Safety Administration. 1997. Traffic Safety Facts. Washington, DC: U.S. Government Printing Office.

National Institute on Drug Abuse. 1994. National Household Survey on Drug Abuse: Main Findings, 1993. Rockville, MD: NIDA.

——. 1997. National Household Survey on Drug Abuse: Main Findings, 1996. Rockville, MD: NIDA.

Neisser, Ulrich, et al. 1996. "Intelligence: Knowns and Unknowns." American Psychologist 51:77–103.

Nettler, Gwynn. 1978. "Social status and self-reported criminality." Social Forces 57:304–305.

——. 1985. "Social class and crime, one more time." Social Forces 63:1076–1077.

Newsweek. 1983. "Burying Crime in Chicago." May 16:63.

——. 1984. "The random killers." 86, November 26:100–106.

——. 1994a. "Inside the anti-abortion underground." 124, Aug. 29:28.

——. 1994b. "Why good cops go bad." 124, Dec. 19:30–33.

——. 1995. "The view from the far right." 125, May 1:36–39.

——. 1997a. "The next level." 129, April 7:28–36.

——. 1997b. "Far from home." 129, April 17:37–39.

——. 1997c. "Christ and comets." 129, April 7:40–43.

Nisbett, Richard E., and Dov Cohen. 1996. Culture of Honor: The Psychology of Violence in the South. Boulder, CO: Westview.

Nisbett, Richard E., and Eugene Borgida. 1975. "Attribution and the psychology of prediction." Journal of Personality and Social Psychology 32:932–943.

Nisbett, Richard E., and Lee Ross. 1980. Human Inference: Strategies and Shortcomings of Social Judgment. Englewood Cliffs, NJ: Prentice-Hall.

Norris, Joel. 1989. Serial Killers. New York: Anchor Books.

Nye, F. Ivan. 1958. Family Relationships and Delinquent Behavior. New York: John Wiley.

O'Brien, Michael. 1987. Vince: A Personal Biography. New York: William Morrow.

O'Carroll, Patrick. 1989. "A consideration of the validity and reliability of suicide mortality data." Suicide and Life Threatening Behavior 19:1–16.

O'Donnell, John A. 1964. "A follow-up of narcotic addicts: mortality, relapse, and abstinence." American Journal of Orthopsychiatry 34:948–954.

Ofshe, Richard, and Ethan Watters. 1994. Making Monsters: False Memories, Psychotherapy, and Sexual Hysteria. Berkeley, CA: University of California Press.

Ogle, Robbin, Daniel Maier-Katkin, and Thomas S. Bernard. 1995. "A theory of homicidal behavior among women." Criminology 33:173–193.

Okely, Judith. 1982. The Traveler Gypsies. New York: Cambridge University Press.

Olds, David L., et al. 1997. "Long-term effects of home visitation on maternal life course and child abuse and neglect: Fifteen-year follow-up of a randomized trial." Journal of the American Medical Association 278:637–643.

——. 1998. "Long-term effects of nurse home visitation on children's criminal and antisocial behavior: Fifteen-year follow-up of a randomized controlled trial." Journal of the American Medical Association 280:1238–1244.

Oliver, Bernard J., Jr. 1967. Sexual Deviation in American Society. New Haven, CT: College and University Press.

Olweus, Dan. 1979. "Stability of aggressive reaction patterns in males: A review." Psychological Bulletin 86:852–875.

Olweus, Dan, Ake Mattsson, Daisy Schalling, and Hans Low. 1980. "Testosterone, aggression, physical and personality dimensions in normal adolescent males." Psychosomatic Medicine 42:253–269.

——. 1988. "Circulating testosterone levels and aggression in adolescent males: A causal analysis." Psychosomatic Medicine 50:261–272.

Orbach, Israel, Yiegal Gross, and Hananya Glaubman. 1981. "Some common characteristics of latency-age suicidal children." Suicide and Life Threatening Behavior 11:180–190.

Orne, Martin T. 1962. "On the social psychology of the psychological experiment: With particular reference to demand characteristics and their implications." American Psychologist 17:776–784.

Oschlies, W. 1979. Juvenile Delinquency in Eastern Europe: Interpretations, Dynamics, Facts. Cologne: Boehlau Verlag.

Osgood, D. Wayne, Lloyd D. Johnston, Patrick M. O'Malley, and Jerald G. Bachman. 1988. "The generality of deviance in late adolescence and early adulthood." American Sociological Review 53:81–93.

Packer, Herbert L. 1968. Limits of the Criminal Sanction. Stanford, CA: Stanford University Press.

Padilla, Felix M. 1992. The Gang as an American Enterprise. New Brunswick, NJ: Rutgers University Press.

Palamara, Frances, Francis T. Cullen, and Joanne C. Gersten. 1986. "The effects of police and mental health intervention on juvenile deviance: Specifying contingencies in the impact of formal sanction." Journal of Health and Social Behavior 27:90–106.

Parker, Jerry, and Harold G. Grasmick. 1979. "Linking actual and perceived certainty of punishment: An exploratory study of an untested proposition in deterrence theory." Criminology 17:366–379.

Parker, Robert Allerton. 1973 [1935]. A Yankee Saint: John Humphrey Noyes and the Oneida Community. Hamden, CT: The Shoestring Press.

Parsons, Talcott. 1937. The Structure of Social Action. New York: Free Press.

——. 1951. The Social System. New York: Free Press.

Pate, Anthony, and Edwin Hamilton. 1992. "Formal and informal deterrents to domestic violence: The Dade county spouse assault experiment." American Sociological Review 57:691–697.

Paternoster, Raymond. 1986. "The use of composite scales in perceptual deterrence research: A cautionary note." Journal of Research in Crime and Delinquency 23:128–168.

——. 1987. "The deterrent effect of the perceived certainty and severity of punishment: A review of the evidence and issues." Justice Quarterly 4:173–218.

——. 1989a. "Absolute and restrictive deterrence in a panel of youth: Explaining the onset, persistence/desistance, and frequency of delinquent offending." Social Problems 36:389–309.

——. 1989b. "Decisions to participate in and desist from four types of common delinquency: Deterrence and the rational choice perspective." Law and Society Review 23:7–40.

Paternoster, Raymond, and Robert Brame. 1998. "The structural similarity of processes generating criminal and analogous behaviors." Criminology 36:633–669.

Paternoster, Raymond, and Lee Ann Iovanni. 1989. "The labeling perspective and delinquency: An elaboration of the theory and an assessment of the evidence." Justice Quarterly 6:379–394.

Paternoster, Raymond, and Alex Piquero. 1995. "Reconceptualizing deterrence: An empirical test of personal and vicarious experiences." Journal of Research in Crime and Delinquency 35:251–286.

Paternoster, Raymond, and Sally S. Simpson. 1996. "Sanction threats and appeals to morality: Testing a rational choice model of corporate crime." Law and Society Review 30:549–583.

Paternoster, Raymond, Charles W. Dean, Alex Piquero, Paul Mazerolle, and Robert Brame. 1997. "Generality, continuity, and change in offending." Journal of Quantitative Criminology 13:231–266.

Paternoster, Raymond, Linda Saltzman, Gordon Waldo, and Theodore G. Chiricos. 1983a. "Estimating perceptual stability and deterrent effects: The role of perceived legal punishment in the inhibition of criminal involvement." Journal of Criminal Law and Criminology 74:270–297.

——. 1983b. "Perceived risk and social control: Do sanctions really deter?" Law and Society Review 17:457–479.

——. 1985. "Assessments of risk and behavioral experience: An exploratory study of change." Criminology 23:417–433.

Patterson, Gerald R. 1980. "Children who steal." Pp. 73–90 in Understanding Crime, edited by T. Hirschi and M. Gottfredson. Beverly Hills, CA: Sage.

——. 1982. Coercive Family Process. Eugene, OR: Castalia.

Patterson, Gerald R., and Magda Stouthamer-Loeber. 1984. "The correlation of family management practices and delinquency." Child Development 55:1299–1307.

Patterson, Gerald R., Patricia Chamberlain, and John B. Reid. 1982. "A comparative evaluation of a parent-training program." Behavior Therapy 13:638–650.

Payne, William D. 1973. "Negative labels: Passageways and prisons." Crime and Delinquency 19:33–40.

Pearson, Frank S., and Neil Alan Weiner. 1985. "Toward an integration of criminological theories." Journal of Criminal Law and Criminology 76:116–150.

Pearson, Geoffrey. 1983. Hooligan: A History of Reportable Fears. New York: Schocken.

Petee, Thomas A., Trudie F. Milner, and Michael R. Welch. 1994. "Levels of social integration in group contexts and the effects of informal sanction threat on deviance." Criminology 32:85–106.

Petersilia, Joan. 1978. "The validity of criminality data derived from personal interviews." Pp. 30–47 in Quantitative Studies in Criminology, edited by C. Wellford. Beverly Hills, CA: Sage.

Peterson, William. 1969. Population, 2nd Ed. London: Macmillan.

Petrunik, Michael, and Clifford D. Shearing. 1983. "Fragile facades: Stuttering and the strategic manipulation of awareness." Social Problems 31:125–138.

Pfohl, Stephen J. 1977. "The 'discovery' of child abuse." Social Problems 24:310–323.

Pfuhl, Erdwin H., Jr. 1986. The Deviance Process, 2nd Ed. Belmont, CA: Wadsworth.

Phillips, David P. 1974. "The influence of suggestion on suicide: Substantive and theoretical implications of the Werther effect." American Sociological Review 39:340–354.

——. 1977. "Motor vehicle fatalities increase just after publicized suicide stories." Science 196:1464–1465.

——. 1979. "Suicide, motor vehicle fatalities, and the mass media: Evidence toward a theory of suggestion." American Journal of Sociology 84:1150–1174.

Phillips, David P., and Lundie L. Carstensen. 1988. "The effect of suicide stories on various demographic groups, 1968–1985." Suicide and Life Threatening Behavior 18:100–114.

Phillips, David P., and Todd E. Ruth. 1993. "Adequacy of official suicide statistics for scientific research and public policy." Suicide and Life Threatening Behavior 23:309–319.

Phillips, David P., Todd E. Ruth, and Sean McNamara. 1994. "There are more things in heaven and earth: Missing features in Durkheim's theory of suicide." Pp. 90–100 in Emile Durkheim Le Suicide One Hundred Years Later, edited by D. Lester. Philadelphia: Charles Press.

Piaget, Jean. 1926. The Language and Thought of the Child. New York: Harcourt, Brace.

———. 1952. The Origins of Intelligence in Children. New York: International Universities Press.

Piattelli-Palmarini, Massimo. 1994. Inevitable Illusions: How Mistakes of Reason Rule Our Minds. New York: Wiley.

Pineo, Peter C. 1976. "Social mobility in Canada: The current picture." Sociological Focus 9:1091–1123.

Piquero, Alex, and Raymond Paternoster 1998. "An application of Stafford and Warr's reconceptualization of deterrence to drinking and driving." Journal of Research in Crime and Delinquency 35:3–39.

Piquero, Alex, and Andre Rosey. 1998. "The reliability and validity of Grasmick et al.'s self-control scale: A comment on Longshore et al." Criminology 36:157–173.

Plamenatz, John. 1958. The English Utilitarians. Oxford: Basil Blackwell.

Platt, Anthony. 1994. "Thinking and unthinking 'social control.'" Pp. 72–79 in Inequality, Crime, and Social Control, edited by G. S. Bridges and M. A. Myers. Boulder, CO: Westview.

Platt, S. D. 1984. "Unemployment and suicidal behavior." Social Science and Medicine 19:93–115.

———. 1986. "Parasuicide and unemployment." British Journal of Psychiatry. 149:401–405.

Plous, Scott. 1993. The Psychology of Judgment and Decision Making. New York: McGraw-Hill.

Plutchik, Robert, and Herman M. Van Praag. 1995. "The nature of impulsivity: Definitions, ontology, genetics, and relations to aggression." Pp. 7–24 in Impulsivity and Aggression, edited by F. Hollander and D. J. Stein. New York: Wiley.

———. 1997. "Suicide, impulsivity, and antisocial behavior." Pp. 101–108 in Handbook of Antisocial Behavior, edited by D. M. Stoff, J. Breiling, and J. D. Maser. New York: John Wiley.

Polakowski, Michael. 1994. "Linking self-control with deviance: Illuminating the structure underlying a general theory of crime and its relation to deviant activity." Journal of Quantitative Criminology 10:41–78.

Pollock, John. 1979. Billy Graham: Evangelist to the World. New York: Harper and Row.

Polsky, Ned. 1967. Hustlers, Beats, and Others. Chicago: Aldine.

President's Commission on Law Enforcement and Administration of Justice. 1967 Task Force Report: Juvenile Delinquency and Youth Crime. Washington, DC: U.S. Government Printing Office.

Pressley, Sue Anne. 1997. "Tough lessons in an Alabama town." Washington Post, September 2:A3.

Quay, Herbert C. 1987. "Intelligence." Pp. 106–117 in Handbook of Juvenile Delinquency, edited by H. C. Quay. New York: Wiley and Sons.

Quinney, Richard. 1970. The Social Reality of Crime. Boston: Little Brown.

———. 1979. Criminology, 2nd Ed. Boston: Little Brown.

———. 1980. Class, State, and Crime, 2nd Ed. New York: Longman.

Rachman, Stanley. 1971. The Effects of Psychotherapy. Oxford: Pergamon Press.

———. 1974. The Meaning of Fear. Baltimore: Penquin Books.

Raine, Adrian. 1993. The Psychopathology of Crime. New York: Academic Press.

———. 1997. "Antisocial behavior and psychophysiology: A biosocial perspective and a prefrontal dysfunction hypothesis." Pp. 289–304 in Handbook of Antisocial Behavior, edited by D. M. Stoff, J. Breiling, and J. D. Maser. New York: John Wiley.

Rankin, Joseph, and L. Edward Wells. 1990. "The effect of parental attachments and direct controls on delinquency." Journal of Research in Crime and Delinquency 27:140–165.

Rapp, Rayna. 1982. "Family and class in contemporary America." Pp. 168–187 in Rethinking the Family: Some Feminist Questions, edited by B. Thorne and M. Yalom. New York: Longman.

Reckless, Walter C. 1967. The Crime Problem, 4th Ed. New York: Appleton-Century-Crofts.

Reckless, Walter C., Simon Dinitz, and Barbara Kay. 1957. "The self-component in potential delinquency and potential non-delinquency." American Sociological Review 25:566–570.

Redfield, Robert. 1969 [1947]. "The folk society." Pp. 180–205 in Classic Essays on the Culture of Cities, edited by R. Sennett. New York: Appleton-Century-Crofts.

Regulus, Thomas A. 1995. "Race, class, and sociobiological perspectives on crime." Pp. 46–65 in Ethnicity, Race, and Crime: Perspectives Across Time and Place, edited by D. F. Hawkins. Albany: State University of New York Press.

Reich, Charles A. 1970. The Greening of America: How the Youth Revolution Is Trying to Make America Livable. New York: Random House.

Reinarman, Craig. 1987. American States of Mind: Political Beliefs and Behavior Among Private and Public Workers. New Haven, CT: Yale University Press.

Reinarman, Craig, Dan Waldorf, Sheigla B. Murphy, and Harry G. Levine. 1997. "The contingent call of the pipe: Bingeing and addiction among heavy cocaine smokers." Pp. 77–97 in Crack in America: Demon Drugs and Social Justice, edited by C. Reinarman and H. G. Levine. Berkeley: University of California Press.

Reiss, Albert J., Jr. 1951. "Delinquency as the failure of personal and social controls." American Sociological Review 16:196–207.

———. 1986. "Co-offending influences on criminal careers." Pp. 121–160 in Criminal Careers and Career Criminals, Vol. 2, edited by A. Blumstein, J. Cohen, J. A. Roth, and C. A. Visher. Washington, DC: National Academy Press.

———. 1988. "Co-offending and criminal careers." Pp. 117–170 in Crime and Justice: A Review of Research, Volume 10, edited by M. Tonry and N. Morris. Chicago: University of Chicago Press.

Report of Final Mortality Statistics. 1995. National Center for Health Statistics, Centers for Disease Control and Prevention. Hyattsville, MD: U.S. Department of Health and Human Services.

Ressler, Robert K. (with Tom Shachtman). 1997. I Have Lived in the Monster. New York: St. Martin's Press.

Reuter, Peter. 1983. Disorganized Crime: The Economics of the Visible Hand. Cambridge, MA: MIT Press.

Reuter, Peter, and Jonathan Rubinstein. 1978. "Fact, fancy and organized crime." The Public Interest 53:45–67.

Richards, Pamela, and Charles R. Tittle. 1981. "Gender and perceived chances of arrest." Social Forces 59:1182–1199.

Roberts, Robert E., Y. Richard Chen, and Catherine R. Roberts. 1997. "Ethnocultural differences in prevalence of adolescent suicidal behavior." Suicide and Life Threatening Behavior 27:208–217.

Robertson, Constance Noyes. 1970. Oneida Community: An Autobiography, 1851–1876. Syracuse, NY: Syracuse University Press.

———. 1972. Oneida Community: The Breakup, 1876–1881. Syracuse, NY: Syracuse University Press.

Robertson, Leon S., Robert F. Rich, and H. Laurence Ross. 1973. "Jail sentences for driving while intoxicated in Chicago: A judicial policy that failed." Law and Society Review 7:55–67.

Robins, Lee N. 1966. Deviant Children Grown Up. Baltimore: Williams and Wilkins.

———. 1978. "Sturdy childhood predictors of adult antisocial behavior: Replications from longitudinal studies." Psychological Medicine 8:611–622.

Roethlisberger, Fritz, and William J. Dickson. 1964 [1939]. Management and the Worker. New York: John Wiley and Sons.

Rogers, Joseph W., and M. D. Buffalo. 1974. "Fighting back: Nine modes of adaptation to a deviant label." Social Problems 22:101–118.

Rogovin, Charles H., and Frederick T. Martens. 1997. "The evil that men do." Pp. 26–38 in Understanding Organized Crime in Global Perspective, edited by P. J. Ryan and G. E. Rush. Thousand Oaks, CA: Sage.

Rose, Nancy Ellen. 1995. Workfare or Fair Work: Women, Welfare, and Government Work Programs. New Brunswick, NJ: Rutgers University Press.

Rosen, Lawrence. 1985. "Family and delinquency: Structure or function?" Criminology 23:553–573.

Rosen, Lawrence, and Kathleen Neilson. 1982. "Broken homes." Pp. 126–135 in Contemporary Criminology, edited by L. Savitz and N. Johnston. New York: Wiley.

Rosenberg, Florence R., and Morris Rosenberg. 1978. "Self-esteem and delinquency." Journal of Youth and Adolescence 7:279–291.

Rosenberg, Morris. 1979. Conceiving the Self. New York: Basic Books.

Rosenberg, Morris, Carmi Schooler, and Carrie Schoenbach. 1989. "Self-esteem and adolescent problems: Modeling reciprocal effects." American Sociological Review 54:1004–1018.

Rosenhan, David L. 1973. "On being sane in insane places." Science 179, Jan 19:250–258.

Rosenthal, Robert, and Lenore Jacobson. 1969. Pygmalion in the Classroom. New York: Harper and Row.

Rosoff, Stephen M., Henry N. Pontell, and Robert Tillman. 1998. Profit Without Honor: White-Collar Crime and the Looting of America. Upper Saddle River, NJ: Prentice-Hall.

Ross, H. Lawrence. 1982. Deterring the Drinking Driver: Legal Policy and Social Control. Lexington, MA: DC Heath, Lexington Books.

———. 1986. "Implications of drinking-and-driving law studies for deterrence research. Pp. 159–171 in Critique and Explanation, Essays in Honor of Gwynn Nettler, edited by T. Hartnagel and R. Silverman. New Brunswick, NJ: Transaction Books.

———. 1993. Confronting Drunk Driving. New Haven: CT: Yale University Press.

Ross, H. Lawrence, Donald T. Campbell, and Gene V. Glass. 1970. "Determining the social effects of a legal reform: The British 'breathalyser' crackdown of 1967." American Behavioral Scientist 13:493–509.

Ross, H. Lawrence, Richard McCleary, and Gary LaFree. 1990. "Can mandatory jail laws deter drunk driving? The Arizona Case." Journal of Criminal Law and Criminology 81:156–167.

Rossi, Peter H., Emily Waite, Christine E. Bose, and Richard E. Berk. 1974. "The seriousness of crimes: Normative structure and individual differences." American Sociological Review 39:224–237.

Rousseau, Jean-Jacques. 1968 [1743]. The Social Contract, translated by M. Cranston. Harmondsworth, England: Penquin Books.

Rowe, Alan R., and Charles R. Tittle. 1977. "Life cycle changes and criminal propensity." Sociological Quarterly 18:223–236.

Rowe, David C., D. Wayne Osgood, and W. Alan Nicewander. 1990. "A latent trait approach to unifying criminal careers." Criminology 28:232–270.

Rubenstein, Jonathan. 1973. City Police. New York: Farrar, Straus, and Giroux.

Rutter, Michael, and Marjorie Rutter. 1993. Developing Minds: Challenge and Continuity Across the Life Span. New York: Basic Books.

Ryan, William. 1971. Blaming the Victim. New York: Random House.

Sachs, Steven L. 1997. Street Gang Awareness. Minneapolis, MN: Fairview Press.

Sack, Joetta L. 1998. "In Vermont's funding shakeup, a bitter pill for the 'gold towns.' " Education Week on the Web. October 28, 1998.

Sagi, Philip C., and Charles F. Wellford. 1968. "Age composition and patterns of change in criminal statistics." Journal of Criminal Law, Criminology, and Police Science 59:29–36.

Sakinofsky, Issac, and Antoon A. Leenears. 1997. "Suicide in Canada with special reference to the difference between Canada and the United States." Suicide and Life Threatening Behavior 27:112–126.

Saltzman, Linda, Raymond Paternoster, Gordon P. Waldo, and Theodore G. Chiricos. 1982. "Deterrent and experiential effects: The problem of causal order in perceptual deterrence research." Journal of Research in Crime and Delinquency 19:172–189.

Sampson, Robert J. 1991. "Linking the micro- and macrolevel dimensions of community social organization." Social Forces 70:43–64.

Sampson,Robert J., and W. Byron Groves. 1989. "Community structure and crime: Testing social disorganization theory." American Journal of Sociology 94:774–802.

Sampson, Robert J., and John H. Laub. 1993. Crime in the Making: Pathways and Turning Points Through Life. Cambridge, MA: Harvard University Press.

——. 1997. "A life-course theory of cumulative disadvantage and the stability of delinquency." Pp. 133–161 in Developmental Theories of Crime and Delinquency, edited by T. P. Thornberry. New Brunswick, NJ: Transaction.

Sampson, Robert J., and William J. Wilson. 1995. "Toward a theory of race, crime, and urban inequality." Pp. 37–54 in Crime and Inequality, edited by J. Hagan and R. D. Peterson. Stanford, CA: Stanford University Press.

Sampson, Robert J., Stephen W. Raudenbush, and Felton Earls. 1997. "Neighborhoods and violent crime: A multilevel study of collective efficacy." Science 277:918–924.

Sanday, Peggy Reeves. 1990. Fraternity Gang Rapes: Sex, Brotherhood and Privilege on College Campus. New York: NYU Press.

Scarce, Rik. 1994. "(No) trial (but) tribulations: When courts and ethnography conflict." Journal of Contemporary Ethnography 23:123–149.

Scheff, Thomas J., and Suzanne M. Retzinger. 1991. Emotions and Violence: Shame and Rage in Destructive Conflicts. Lexington, MA: Lexington Books.

Schlegel, Alice, and Herbert Barry III. 1991. Adolescence: An Anthropological Inquiry. New York: The Free Press.

Schlegel, Kip, and David Weisburd. 1992. White-Collar Crime Reconsidered. Boston: Northeastern University Press.

Schneider, Joseph W. 1978. "Deviant drinking as disease: Alcoholism as a social accomplishment." Social Problems 25:361–384.

Schuessler, Karl F., and Donald R. Cressey. 1950. "Personality characteristics of criminals." American Journal of Sociology 55:476–484.

Schur, Edwin M. 1971. Labeling Deviant Behavior: Its Sociological Implications. New York: Harper and Row.

——. 1973. Radical Non-intervention: Rethinking the Delinquency Problem. Englewood Cliffs, NJ: Prentice-Hall.

Schwendinger, Herman, and Julia Schwendinger. 1974. The Sociologists of the Chair. New York: Basic Books.

——. 1983. Rape and Inequality. Beverly Hills, CA: Sage Publications.

Scott, John Finley. 1971. Internalization of Norms: A Sociological Theory of Moral Commitment. Englewood Cliffs, NJ: Prentice-Hall.

Scott, Robert A. 1969. The Making of Blind Men: A Study of Adult Socialization. New York: Russell Sage.

Scruton, David L. 1986. Sociophobics: The Anthropology of Fear. Boulder, CO: Westview.

Scully, Diana, and Joseph Marolla. 1984. "Convicted rapists' vocabulary of motive: Excuses and justification." Social Problems 31:530–544.

Sears, Donald T. 1991. To Kill Again. Wilmington, DE: Scholarly Resources.

Sebald, Hans. 1992. Adolescence: A Social Psychological Analysis, 4th Ed. Englewood Cliffs, NJ: Prentice-Hall.

Sellin, Thorsten. 1938. Culture Conflict and Crime. New York: Social Science Research Council.

Servadio, Gaia. 1976. Mafioso: A History of the Mafia From Its Origins to the Present Day. New York: Stein and Day.

Shaffer, David. 1974. "Suicide in childhood and early adolescence." Journal of Child Psychology and Psychiatry and Applied Disciplines 15:275–291.

Shavit, Yossi, and Arye Rattner. 1988. "Age, crime and the early life course." American Journal of Sociology 93:1457–1470.

Shaw, Clifford R., and Henry D. McKay. 1969. Juvenile Delinquency and Urban Areas, Revised Edition. Chicago: University of Chicago Press.

Sheehy, Gail. 1973. Hustling: Prostitution in Our Wide-Open Society. New York: Delacorte Press.

Sheley, Joseph F. 1983. "Critical elements of criminal behavior explanations." Sociological Quarterly 24:509–523.

Sherif, Muzifer. 1936. The Psychology of Social Norms. New York: Harper.

Sherman, Lawrence W. 1993. "Defiance, deterrence, and irrelevance: A theory of the criminal sanction." Journal of Research in Crime and Delinquency 30:445–473.

Sherman, Lawrence W., and Richard Berk. 1984. "The specific deterrent effects of arrest for domestic assault." American Sociological Review 49:261–272.

Sherman, Lawrence W., and Barry Glick. 1984. "The quality of arrest statistics." Police Foundation Reports 2:1–8.

Shihadeh, Edward S., and Nicole Flynn. 1996. "Segregation and crime: The effect of black social isolation on the rates of black urban violence." Social Forces 74:1325–1352.

Shihadeh, Edward S., and Graham C. Ousey. 1996. "Metropolitan expansion and Black social dislocation: The link between suburbanization and center-city crime." Social Forces 75:649–666.

Shneidman, Edwin. 1985. Definition of Suicide. New York: John Wiley and Sons.

Shoemaker, Donald J. 1996. Theories of Delinquency: An Explanation of Delinquent Behavior. New York: Oxford University Press.

Short, James F., Jr. 1963. "The responses of gang leaders to status threats: An observation on group process and delinquent behavior." American Journal of Sociology 68:571–579.

Short, James F., Jr., and Fred L. Strodtbeck. 1965. Group Process and Gang Delinquency. Chicago: University of Chicago Press.

——. 1974. Group Process and Gang Delinquency. Chicago: University of Chicago Press.

Shover, Neal. 1996. Great Pretenders: Pursuits and Careers of Persistent Thieves. Boulder, CO: Westview.

Shover, Neal, Stephen Norland, Jennifer James, and William E. Thornton. 1979. "Gender roles and delinquency." Social Forces 58:162–175.

Shragge, Eric. 1997. Workfare: Ideology for a New Underclass. Toronto: Garamond Press.

Shumaker, Sally Ann, and Daniel Stokels. 1982. "Residential mobility as a social issue and research topic." Journal of Social Issues 38:1–19.

Sigelman, Carol K., and Lee Sigelman. 1976. "Authority and conformity: Violation of a traffic regulation." Journal of Social Psychology 100:35–43.

Silberman, Matthew. 1976. "Toward a theory of criminal deterrence." American Sociological Review 41:442–461.

Simmel, Georg. 1971 [1903]. "The metropolis and mental life." Pp. 324–339 in On Individuality and Social Forms, edited by D. N. Levine. Chicago: University of Chicago Press.

Simon, David R. 1999. Elite Deviance, 6th Ed. Boston: Allyn and Bacon.

Simon, David R., and D. Stanley Eitzen. 1993. Elite Deviance, 4th Ed. Boston: Allyn and Bacon.

Simon, Herbert A. 1957. Models of Man. New York: Wiley.

Simon, Rita J. 1975. Women and Crime. Lexington, MA: DC Heath.

Simons, Ronald C., Martin G. Miller, and Stephen M. Aigner. 1980. "Contemporary theories of deviance and female delinquency: An empirical test." Journal of Research in Crime and Delinquency 17:42–53.

Singer, Simon I. 1996. Recriminalizing Delinquency: Violent Juvenile Crime and Juvenile Justice Reform. New York: Cambridge University Press.

Skolnick, Jerome. 1966. Justice Without Trial. New York: Wiley.

Slovic, Paul, Baruch Fischhoff, and Sarah Lichtenstein. 1982. "Facts versus fears: Understanding perceived risk." Pp. 463–489 in Judgment Under Uncertainty: Heuristics and Biases, edited by D. Kahneman, P. Slovic, and A. Tversky. New York: Cambridge University Press.

Smart, Carol. 1979. "The new female criminal: Reality or myth?" British Journal of Criminology 19:50–59.

Smith, Carolyn, and Terrence P. Thornberry. 1995. "The relationship between childhood maltreatment and adolescent involvement in delinquency." Criminology 33:451–481.

Smith, Douglas A., and Robert Brame. 1994. "On the initiation and continuation of delinquency." Criminology 32:607–629.

Smith, Douglas A., and Raymond Paternoster. 1990. "Formal processing and future delinquency: Deviance amplification as selection artifact." Law and Society Review 24:1109–1131.

Smith, Douglas A., and Christy Visher. 1980. "Sex and involvement in deviance/crime: A quantitative review of the empirical literature." American Sociological Review 45:691–701.

Smith, Dwight C., Jr. 1971. "Some things that may be more important to understand about organized crime than Cosa Nostra." University of Florida Law Review 24:1–30.

Smith, Gene M., and Charles P. Fogg. 1978. "Psychological predictors of early use, late use, and nonuse of marijuana among teenage students." Pp. 101–113 in Longitudinal Research on Drug Use, edited by D. B. Kandel. Washington, DC: Hemisphere Publishing.

Snow, David A., and Cynthia L. Phillips. 1980. "The Lofland-Stark conversion model: A critical reassessment." Social Problems 27:430–447.

Sowell, Thomas. 1995. "Ethnicity and IQ." Pp. 70–79 in The Bell Curve Wars: Race, Intelligence, and the Future of America, edited by S. Fraser. New York: Basic Books.

Spector, Malcolm, and John I. Kitsuse. 1977. Constructing Social Problems. Menlo Park, CA: Cummings.

Spergel, Irving A. 1964. Slumtown, Racketville, Haulberg. Chicago: University of Chicago Press.

——. 1983. "Violent gangs in Chicago: segmentation and integration." Chicago: University of Chicago School of Social Service Administration.

——. 1984. "Violent gangs in Chicago: In search of social policy." Social Service Review 58:199–226.

——. 1986. "The violent gang in Chicago: A local community approach." Social Service Review, 60:94–131.

——. 1990. "Youth gangs: Continuity and change." Pp. 171–276 in Crime and Justice: A Review of Research, Volume 12, edited by M. Tonry and N. Morris. Chicago: University of Chicago Press.

Stack, Steven. 1980. "Interstate migration and the rate of suicide." International Journal of Social Psychiatry 26:17–26.

——. 1982. "Suicide: A decade review of the sociological literature." Deviant Behavior 4:41–66.

——. 1990. "Media impacts on suicide." Pp. 107–120 in Current Concepts of Suicide, edited by D. Lester. Philadelphia: The Charles Press.

Stafford, Mark, and Mark Warr. 1993. "A reconceptualization of general and specific deterrence." Journal of Research on Crime and Delinquency 30:123–135.

Stander, Julian, David P. Farrington, Gillian Hill, and Patricia M. E. Altham. 1989. "Markov chain analysis and specialization in criminal careers." British Journal of Criminology 29:317–335.

Stark, Rodney. 1979. "Whose status counts?" American Sociological Review 44:668–669.

Stark, Rodney, and James McEvoy III. 1970. "Middle-class violence." Psychology Today 4:52–54.

Statistical Abstract of the United States. 1997. Washington, DC: U.S. Government Printing Office.

——. 1998. U.S. Department of Commerce, Bureau of the Census. Washington, DC: U.S. Government Printing Office.

Steffensmeier, Darrell J. 1978. "Crime and the contemporary woman: An analysis of changing levels of female property crime, 1960–1975." Social Forces 57:566–584.

——. 1986. The Fence. Totowa, NJ: Rowman and Littlefield.

Steffensmeier, Darrell J., and Emilie A. Allan. 1995. "Age-inequality and property crime: The effects of age-linked stratification and status-attainment processes on patterns of criminality across the life course." Pp. 95–115 in Crime and Inequality, edited by J. Hagan and R. D. Peterson. Stanford, CA: Stanford University Press.

Steffensmeier, Darrell J., and Michael J. Cobb. 1981. "Sex differences in urban arrest patterns, 1934–1979." Social Problems 29:37–50.

Steffensmeier, Darrell J., and Renee Hoffman Steffensmeier. 1980. "Trends in female delinquency." Criminology 18:62–85.

Steffensmeier, Darrell J., and Cathy Streifel. 1991. "Age, gender, and crime across three historical periods: 1935, 1960, 1985." Social Forces 69:869–894.

Steffensmeier, Darrell J., Emilie Allen, and Cathy Streifel. 1989a. "Development and female crime: A cross-national test of alternative explanations." Social forces 68: 262–283.

Steffensmeier, Darrell J., Emilie Andersen Allen, Miles D. Harer, and Cathy Streifel. 1989b. "Age and the distribution of crime." American Journal of Sociology 94:803–831.

Stephens, Richard C. 1987. Mind-Altering Drugs: Use, Abuse, and Treatment. Beverly Hills, CA: Sage.

——. 1991. The Street Addict Role: A Theory of Heroin Addiction. Albany: State University of New York Press.

Sterk-Elifson, Claire. 1996. "Just for fun? Cocaine use among middle-class women." Journal of Drug Issues 26:63–76.

Sterk-Elifson, Claire, and Kirk W. Elifson. 1993. "The social organization of crack cocaine use: The cycle in one type of base house." The Journal of Drug Issues 23:429–441.

Stillion, Judith M., and Eugene E. McDowell. 1996. Suicide Across the Life Span, 2nd Ed. Washington, DC: Taylor and Francis.

Stillion, Judith M., Eugene E. McDowell, and J. B. Shamblin. 1984. "The suicide attitude vignette experience: A method for measuring adolescent attitudes toward suicide." Death Education 8:65–80.

Stone, Michael H. 1993. Abnormalities of Personality. New York: Norton.

Storr, Anthony. 1972. Human Destructiveness. New York: Basic Books.

Stryker, Sheldon. 1980. Symbolic Interactionism. Menlo Park, CA: Benjamin/ Cummins.

Sudnow, David. 1965. "Normal crimes: Sociological features of the penal code in a public defender's office." Social Problems 12:255–275.

——. 1967. Passing On: The Social Organization of Dying. Englewood Cliffs, NJ: Prentice-Hall.

Susman, Elizabeth J., Lorah D. Dorn, and George P. Chrousos. 1991. "Negative affect and hormone levels in young adolescents: Concurrent and longitudinal perspectives." Journal of Youth and Adolescence 20:167–190.

Susman, Elizabeth J., et al. 1989. "Hormones, emotional dispositions, and aggressive attributes in young adolescents." Child Development 58:1114–1134.

Sutherland, Anne. 1975. Gypsies: The Hidden Americans. New York: Free Press.

Sutherland, Edwin H. 1937. The Professional Thief. Chicago: University of Chicago Press.

——. 1939. Principles of Criminology, 3rd Ed. Philadelphia: Lippincott.

——. 1949. White-Collar Crime. New York: Dryden.

——. 1950a. "The diffusion of sexual-psychopath laws." American Journal of Sociology 56:142–148.

——. 1950b. "The sexual psychopath laws." Journal of Criminal Law and Criminology 40:543–554.

Sutherland, Edwin H., Donald R. Cressey, and David F. Luckenbill. 1992. Principles of Criminology, 11th Ed. Dix Hills, NY: General Hall.

Svare, Bruce, and Craig H. Kinsley. 1987. "Hormones and sex-related behavior: A comparative analysis." Pp. 13–58 in Females, Males and Sexuality: Theories and Research, edited by K. Kelley. Albany: State University of New York Press.

Sweet, James A., and Larry L. Bumpass. 1987. American Families and Households. New York: Russell Sage Foundation.

Sykes, Gresham, and David Matza. 1957. "Techniques of neutralization: A theory of delinquency." American Sociological Review 22:664–670.

Symonds, Carolyn. 1971. "Sexual mate-swapping: Violation of norms and reconciliation of guilt." Pp. 81–109 in Studies in the Sociology of Sex, edited by J. M. Henslin. New York: Appleton-Century-Crofts.

Tabor, James D. 1995. Why Waco? Cults and Battles for Religious Freedom in America. Berkeley: University of California Press.

Takahashi, Yoshitomo. 1989. "Mass suicide by members of the Japanese Friends of the Truth Church." Suicide and Life Threatening Behavior 19:289–296.

Talese, Gay. 1971. Honor Thy Father. New York: World Books.

Tallman, Irving, and Louis N. Gray. 1990. "Choices, decisions, and problem-solving." Annual Review of Sociology 16:405–433.

Tannenbaum, Frank. 1938. Crime and the Community. Boston: Ginn.

Tavris, Carol, and Carole Offir. 1977. The Longest War. New York: Harcourt, Brace, and Jovanovich.

Taylor, Ian, Paul Walton, and Jock Young. 1973. The New Criminology. London: Routledge and Kegan Paul.

Teevan, James J. 1976. "Subjective perception of deterrence (continued)." Journal of Research in Crime and Delinquency 13:155–164.

Tennenbaum, David J. 1977. "Personality and criminality: A summary and implications of the literature." Journal of Criminal Justice 5:225–235.

Thomas, Charles W., and David M. Peterson. 1977. Prison Organization and Inmate Subcultures. Indianapolis: Bobbs-Merrill.

Thomas, Robert David. 1977. The Man Who Would Be Perfect: John Humphrey Noyes and the Utopian Impulse. Philadelphia: University of Pennsylvania Press.

Thomlinson, Ralph. 1965. Population Dynamics: Causes and Consequences of World Demographic Change. New York: Random House.

Thornbery, Terence P. 1987. "Toward an interactional theory of delinquency." Criminology 25:863–892.

Thornbery, Terence P., and Margaret Farnworth. 1982. "Social correlates of criminal involvement: Further evidence of the relationship between social status and criminal behavior." American Sociological Review 47:505–518.

Thornbery, Terence P., Marvin D. Krohn, Alan J. Lizotte, and Deborah Chard-Wierschem. 1993. "The role of juvenile gangs in facilitating delinquent behavior." Journal of Research in Crime and Delinquency 30:55–87.

Thrasher, Frederick. 1927. The Gang. Chicago: University of Chicago Press.

Tierney, Kathleen J. 1982. "The battered women movement and the creation of the wife beating problem." Social Problems 29:207–220.

Tithecott, Richard. 1997. Of Men and Monsters. Madison: University of Wisconsin Press.

Tittle, Charles R. 1972. Society of Subordinates: Inmate Organization in a Narcotic Hospital. Bloomington: Indiana University Press.

——. 1975. "Deterrents or labeling." Social Forces 53:399–410.

——. 1977. "Sanction fear and the maintenance of social order." Social Forces 55:579–596.

——. 1978. "Response to Gwynn Nettler." Social Forces 57:306–307.

——. 1980a. "Evaluating the deterrent effects of criminal sanctions." Pp. 381–402 in Handbook of Criminal Justice Evaluation, edited by M. Klein and K. Teilmann. Beverly Hills, CA: Sage.

——. 1980b. Sanctions and Social Deviance: The Question of Deterrence. New York: Praeger.

——. 1983. "Social class and criminal behavior: A critique of the theoretical foundation." Social Forces 61:334–358.

——. 1985a. "A plea for open minds, one more time: Response to Nettler." Social Forces 63:1078–1080.

——. 1985b. "Can social science answer questions about deterrence for policy use?" Pp. 265–294 in Social Science and Social Policy, edited by L. Shotland and M. M. Mark. Beverly Hills, CA: Sage.

——. 1988. "Two empirical regularities (maybe) in search of an explanation." Criminology 26:75–85.

——. 1989a. "Influences on urbanism: A test of predictions from three perspectives." Social Problems 36:270–288.

——. 1989b. "Prospects for synthetic theory: A consideration of macro-level criminological activity." Pp. 161–178 in Theoretical Integration in the Study of Deviance and Crime: Problems and Prospects, edited by S. F. Messner, M. D. Krohn, and A. E. Liska. Albany: State University of New York Press.

——. 1989c. "Urbanness and unconventional behavior: A partial test of Claude Fischer's subcultural theory." Criminology 27:273–306.

——. 1994. "The theoretical bases for inequality in formal social control." Pp. 221–252 in Inequality, Crime, and Social Control, edited by G. S. Bridges and M. A. Myers. Boulder, CO: Westview.

——. 1995. Control Balance: Toward a General Theory of Deviance. Boulder, CO: Westview Press.

Tittle, Charles R., and Debra A. Curran. 1988. "Contingencies for dispositional disparities in juvenile justice." Social Forces 67:23–58.

Tittle, Charles R., and Harold G. Grasmick. 1997. "Criminal behavior and age: A test of three provocative hypotheses." The Journal of Criminal Law and Criminology 88:309–342.

Tittle, Charles R., and Charles H. Logan. 1973. "Sanctions and deviance: Evidence and remaining questions." Law and Society Review 7:371–392.

Tittle, Charles R., and Robert F. Meier. 1990. "Specifying the SES/delinquency relationship." Criminology 28:271–299.

Tittle, Charles R., and Raymond Paternoster. 1988. "Geographic mobility and criminal behavior." Journal of Research in Crime and Delinquency 25:301–343.

Tittle, Charles R., and Alan R. Rowe. 1973. "Moral appeal, sanction threat, and deviance: An experimental test." Social Problems 20:488–498.

——. 1974. "Certainty of arrest and crime rates: A further test of the deterrence hypothesis." Social Forces 52:455–462.

Tittle, Charles R., and Wayne J. Villemez. 1977. "Social class and criminality." Social Forces 56:475–502.

Tittle, Charles R., and David A. Ward. 1993. "The interaction of age with the correlates and causes of crime." Journal of Quantitative Criminology 9:3–53.

Tittle, Charles R., and Michael R. Welch. 1983. "Religiosity and deviance: Toward a contingency theory of constraining effects." Social Forces 61:653–682.

Tittle, Charles R., Wayne J. Villemez, and Douglas A. Smith. 1978. "The myth of social class and criminality: An empirical assessment of the empirical evidence." American Sociological Review 43:643–656.

——. 1979. "Reply to Stark." American Sociological Review 44:669–670.

——. 1982. "One step forward, two steps back: More on the class criminality controversy." American Sociological Review 47:435–438.

Toby, Jackson. 1957. "Social disorganization and stake in conformity: Complementary factors in the predatory behavior of hoodlums." Journal of Criminal Law, Criminology, and Police Science 48:12–17.

——. 1981. "Deterrence without punishment." Criminology 19:195–209.

Toennies, Ferdinand. 1957 [1887]. Community and Society (Gemeinschaft and Gesellschaft), translated and edited by C. P. Loomis. East Lansing: Michigan State University Press.

Toffler, Alvin. 1970. Future Shock. New York: Bantam.

Tonry, Michael, and Kathleen Hatlestad. 1997. Sentencing Reform in Overcrowded Times: A Comparative Perspective. New York: Oxford University Press.

Tornudd, Patrik. 1968. "The preventive effect of fines for drunkenness." Pp. 109–124 in Scandinavian Studies in Criminology, Vol. 2. Oslo: Universitetsforiaget.

Trice, Harrison M., and Paul Michael Roman. 1970. "Delabeling, relabeling, and alcoholics anonymous." Social Problems 27:538–546.

Triplett, Ruth A., and G. Roger Jarjoura. 1994. "Theoretical and empirical specification of a model of informal labeling." Journal of Quantitative Criminology 10:241–276.

Tuan, Yi-Fu. 1979. Landscapes of Fear. New York: Pantheon.

Tuck, Mary, and David Riley. 1986. "The theory of reasoned action: A decision theory of crime." Pp. 156–169 in The Reasoning Criminal: Rational Choice Perspectives on Offending, edited by D. B. Cornish and R. V. Clarke. New York: Springer-Verlag.

Tunnell, Kenneth. 1993. Political Crime in Contemporary America: A Critical Approach. New York: Garland Publishing.

Turk, Austin T. 1969. Criminality and Legal Order. Chicago: Rand McNally.

——. 1982. Political Criminality: The Defiance and Defense of Authority. Beverly Hills, CA: Sage.

Turkus, Burton B., and Sid Feder. 1952. Murder, Inc.: The Story of "The Syndicate." New York: Permbooks.

Tygart, C. E. 1991. "Juvenile delinquency and number of children in a family: Some empirical and theoretical updates." Youth and Society 22:525–536.

Tyler, Gus. 1962. Organized Crime in America: A Book of Readings. Ann Arbor: University of Michigan Press.

Unnithan, N. Prabha, Lin Huff-Corzine, Jay Corzine, and Hugh P. Whitt. 1994. The Currents of Lethal Violence: An Integrated Model of Suicide and Homicide. Albany: State University of New York Press.

U.S. Census Bureau. 1990. Census of Population, General Population Characteristics, U.S. Washington, DC.

Vandiver, Kermit. 1996. "Why should my conscience bother me? Hiding aircraft brake hazards." Pp. 118–138 in Corporate and Governmental Deviance, edited by M. D. Ermann and R. J. Lundman. New York: Oxford.

Vanneman, Reeve, and Lynn Weber Cannon. 1987. The American Perception of Class. Philadelphia: Temple University Press.

Van Voorhis, Patricia, Francis T. Cullen, Richard A. Mathers, and Connie Chenoweth Garner. 1988. "The impact of family structure and quality on delinquency: A comparative assessment of structural and functional factors." Criminology 26:235–261.

Vaughn, Diane. 1983. Controlling Unlawful Organizational Behavior. Chicago: University of Chicago Press.

Vigil, James Diego. 1988. Barrio Gang: Street Life and Identity in Southern California. Austin: University of Texas Press.

——. 1993. "The Established Gangs." Pp. 95–112 in Gangs: The Origins and Impact of Contemporary Youth Gangs in the United States, edited by S. Cummings and D. J. Monti. Albany: State University of New York Press.

Vigil, James Diego, and J. M. Long. 1990. "Emic and Etic Perspectives on Gang Culture: The Chicano Case." Pp. 55–68 in Gangs in America, edited by C. R. Huff. Newbury Park, CA: Sage.

Von Krafft-Ebing, Richard. 1965. Psychopathia Sexualis: A Medico-Forensic Study, translated by H. E. Wedeck. New York: G. P. Putnam's Sons.

Wahlsten, Douglas. 1997. "The malleability of intelligence is not constrained by heritability." Pp. 71–87 in Intelligence, Genes, and Success: Scientists Respond to The Bell Curve, edited by B. Devlin, S. E. Fienberg, D. P. Resnick, and K. Roeder. New York: Springer-Verlag.

Waldo, Gordon P., and Simon Dinitz. 1967. "Personality attributes of the criminal: An analysis of research studies, 1950–65." Journal of Research in Crime and Delinquency 4:185–201.

Waldorf, Dan. 1973. Careers in Dope. Englewood Cliffs, NJ: Prentice-Hall.

Walsh, Marilyn. 1977. The Fence. Westport, CT: Greenwood Press.

Walshok, Mary Lindenstein. 1971. "The emergence of middle-class deviant subcultures: The case of swingers." Social Problems 18:488–495.

Walters, Glenn. 1992. "A meta-analysis of the gene-crime relationship." Criminology 30:595–613.

Walters, Glenn D., and Thomas White. 1989. "Heredity and crime: Bad genes or bad research." Criminology 27:455–486.

Ward, David A., and Charles R. Tittle. 1994. "IQ and delinquency: A test of two competing explanations." Journal of Quantitative Criminology 10:189–212.

Warr, Mark. 1989. "What is the perceived seriousness of crimes?" Criminology 27:795–821.

——. 1993. "Age, peers, and delinquency." Criminology 31:17–40.

——. 1996. "Organization and instigation in delinquent groups." Criminology 34:111–138.

Warr, Mark, and Mark Stafford. 1991. "The influence of delinquent peers: What they think or what they do?" Criminology 29: 851–866.

Warren, Carol A. B. 1974. Identity and Community in the Gay World. New York: Wiley.

Warren, Marguerite. 1991. Comparing Male and Female Offenders. Newbury Park, CA: Sage.

Weber, Max. 1961. "Legitimate order and types of authority." Pp. 229–235 in Theories of Society, Vol. 1, edited by T. Parsons, E. Shils, K. D. Naegele, and J. R. Pitts. Glencoe, IL: The Free Press.

Weeks, John R. 1981. Population: An Introduction to Concepts and Issues, 2nd Ed. Belmont, CA: Wadsworth.

Weil, Andrew T., Norman E. Zinberg, and Judith M. Nelsen. 1968. "Clinical and psychological effects of marijuana in man." Science 162:1234–1242.

Weinberg, Martin S. 1999. "The nudist management of respectability." Pp. 301–310 in Deviance: The Interactionist Perspective, 7th Ed., edited by E. Rubington and M. S. Weinberg. Boston: Allyn and Bacon.

Wellford, Charles F. 1973. "Age composition and the increase in recorded crime." Criminology 2:61–70.

——. 1975. "Labeling theory and criminology: An assessment." Social Problems 22:335–347.

Wells, Gary L., and John H. Harvey. 1977. "Do people use consensus information in making causal attributions?" Journal of Personality and Social Psychology 35:279–293.

Wells, L. Edward. 1989. "Self enhancement through delinquency: A conditional test of self-derogation theory." Journal of Research in Crime and Delinquency 26:226–252.

Wells, L. Edward, and Joseph H. Rankin. 1983. "Self-concept as a mediating factor in delinquency." Social Psychology Quarterly 46:11–22.

——. 1986. "The broken homes model of delinquency: Analytic Issues." Journal of Research in Crime and Delinquency 23:68–93.

——. 1988. "Direct parental controls and delinquency." Criminology 26:263–285.

——. 1991. "Families and delinquency: A meta-analysis of the impact of broken homes." Social Problems 38:71–90.

Werth, James L. 1996. "Can Shneidman's 'ten commonalities of suicide' accommodate rational suicide?" Suicide and Life Threatening Behavior 26:292–299.

West, Donald J. 1982. Delinquency. Cambridge, MA: Harvard University Press.

West, Donald J., and David P. Farrington. 1973. Who Becomes Delinquent. London: Heinemann Educational Books.

——. 1977. The Delinquent Way of Life. New York: Crane Russak.

Westermarck, Edward. 1922. The History of Human Marriage. London: Macmillan.

Westley, William. 1970. Violence and the Police. Cambridge, MA: MIT Press.

Weston, Jim. 1993. "Community policing: An approach to youth gangs in a medium-sized city." Police Chief 60:80–84.

Wharton Econometrics Forecasting Associates. 1986. "The income of organized crime." Pp. 423–425 in Report to the President and Attorney General: The Impact of Organized Crime Today. Washington, DC: U.S. Government Printing Office.

White, H. 1974. "Self-poisoning in adolescents." British Journal of Psychiatry 124:24–35.

White, Jennifer, et al. 1994. "Measuring impulsivity and examining its relationship to delinquency." Journal of Abnormal Psychology 103:192–205.

Whyte, William F. 1955. Street Corner Society. Chicago: University of Chicago Press.

Widom, Cathy S. 1989. "The cycle of violence." Science 244:160–166.

——. 1997. "Child abuse, neglect, and witnessing violence." Pp. 159–170 in Handbook of Antisocial Behavior, edited by D. M. Stoff, J. Breiling, and J. D. Maser. New York: John Wiley.

Wilkins, Leslie T. 1964. Social Deviance, Social Policy, Action, and Research. Englewood Cliffs, NJ: Prentice-Hall.

——. 1965. Social Deviance. Englewood Cliffs, NJ: Prentice-Hall.

Wilkinson, Karen. 1974. "The broken family and juvenile delinquency: Scientific explanation or ideology?" Social Problems 21:726–739.

Williams, Kirk, and Richard Hawkins. 1986. "Perceptual research on general deterrence: A critical review." Law and Society Review 20:545–572.

Williams, Terry. 1992. Crackhouse: Notes from the End of the Line. Reading, MA: Addison-Wesley.

Wilson, Edward O. 1978. On Human Nature. Cambridge, MA: Harvard University Press.

Wilson, Glenn D., and David N. Cox. 1983. The Child-Lovers: A Study of Paedophiles in Society. London: Peter Owen.

Wilson, Harriett. 1987. "Parental supervision re-examined." British Journal of Criminology 27:275–301.

Wilson, James Q. 1968. Varieties of Police Behavior. Cambridge, MA: Harvard University Press.

——. 1993. The Moral Sense. New York: Free Press.

Wilson, James Q., and Richard J. Herrnstein. 1985. Crime and Human Nature. New York: Simon and Schuster.

Wilson, William Julius. 1987. The Truly Disadvantaged: The Inner City, the Underclass, and Public Policy. Chicago: University of Chicago Press.

——. 1993. The Ghetto Underclass. Newbury Park, CA: Sage.

——. 1996. When Work Disappears. New York: Knopf.

Winick, Charles. 1964. "Physician narcotic addicts." Pp. 261–280 in The Other Side, edited by H. S. Becker. New York: Free Press.

Winship, Christopher, and Sanders Korenman. 1997. "Does staying in school make you smarter? The effect of education on IQ in The Bell Curve." Pp. 215–234 in Intelligence, Genes, and Success: Scientists Respond to The Bell Curve, edited by B. Devlin, S. E. Feinberg, D. P. Resnick, and K. Roeder. New York: Springer-Verlag.

Winslow, Robert W. 1969. Crime in a Free Society: Selections from the President's Commission on Law Enforcement and Administration of Justice. Belmont, CA: Dickenson Publishing Company.

Wirth, Louis. 1969 [1938]. "Urbanism as a way of life." Pp. 143–164 in Classic Essays on the Culture of Cities, edited by R. Sennett. New York: Appleton-Century-Crofts.

Wolfgang, Marvin E., and Franco Ferracuti. 1967. The Subculture of Violence. London: Social Science Paperbacks.

Wolfgang, Marvin E., Robert M. Figlio, and Thorsten Sellin. 1972. Delinquency in a Birth Cohort. Chicago: University of Chicago Press.

Wolfgang, Marvin E., Terence P. Thornberry, and Robert M. Figlio. 1987. From Boy to Man, From Delinquency to Crime. Chicago: University of Chicago Press.

Won, Shirley. 1991. "2000 Dutch patients choose euthanasia annually, forum told." Canadian Medical Association Journal 145:1341–1342.

Wood, Peter B., Betty Pfefferbaum, and Bruce J. Arneklev. 1993. "Risk-taking and self-control: Social psychological correlates of delinquency." Journal of Crime and Justice 16:111–130.

Worden, Amy. 1998. "Bikes and buggies." Associated Press Report.

Wright, Bradley R. Entner, Avshalom Caspi, Terrie E. Moffitt, Richard A. Miech, and Phil A. Silva. 1999. "Reconsidering the relationship between SES and delinquency: Causation but not correlation." Criminology 37:175–194.

Wright, Loyd. 1985. "Suicidal thoughts and their relationship to family stress and personal problems among high school seniors and college undergraduates." Adolescence 20:575–580.

Wright, Richard T., Scott H. Decker, Allison K. Redfern, and Dietrich L. Smith. 1992. "A snowball's chance in hell: Doing field research with residential burglars." Journal of Research in Crime and Delinquency 29:148–161.

Wrong, Dennis H. 1994. The Problem of Order: What Unites and Divides Society. New York: Free Press.

Yablonsky, Lewis. 1959. "The delinquent gang as a near-group." Social Problems 7:108–117.

——. 1962. The Violent Gang. New York: Macmillan.

Yoors, Jan. 1967. The Gypsies. New York: Simon and Schuster.

Zilboorg, Gregory. 1937. "Considerations on suicide, with particular reference to that of the young." American Journal of Orthopsychiatry 7:15–31.

Zimring, Franklin E. 1981. "Kids, groups, and crime: Some implications of a well-known secret." Journal of Criminal Law and Criminology 72:867–885.

Zimring, Franklin E., and Gordon Hawkins. 1973. Deterrence: The Legal Threat in Crime Control. Chicago: University of Chicago Press.

——. 1997. Crime Is Not the Problem: Lethal Violence in America. New York: Oxford University Press.

Zuckerman, Marvin. 1979. Sensation Seeking: Beyond the Optimal Level of Arousal. Hillsdale, NJ: Erlbaum.

——. 1994. Behavioral Expressions and Biosocial Bases of Sensation Seeking. New York: Cambridge University Press. ✦

Subject Index

A

Name Index